The Encyclopedia of
Careers and Vocational Guidance

EIGHTH EDITION

123014

The Encyclopedia of Careers and Vocational Guidance

WILLIAM E. HOPKE

Editor-in-Chief

VOLUME 2

Professional Careers

J.G. FERGUSON PUBLISHING COMPANY

Chicago, Illinois

123014

Library of Congress Cataloging-in-Publication Data

The Encyclopedia of careers and vocational guidance/ William E. Hopke, editor-in-chief. 8th ed.
 p. cm.
 Contents: v.1 Industry profiles — v.2. Professional careers — v.3. General and special careers —v.4. Technicians' careers. Includes indexes.
 ISBN 0-89434-117-0 (set). —ISBN 0-89434-113-8 (v.1). —ISBN 0-89434-114-6 (v.2). —ISBN 0-89434-115-4 (V.3).
— ISBN 0-89434-116-2 (v.4)
 1. Vocational guidance—Handbooks, manuals, etc. 2. Occupations—Handbooks, manuals, etc. I. Hopke, William E.
HF5381.E52 1990
331.7'02—dc20
                                                                                              90-3743
                                                                                              CIP

ISBN 0-89434-117-0 (set)
     0-89434-113-8 (volume 1)
     0-89434-114-6 (volume 2)
     0-89434-115-4 (volume 3)
     0-89434-116-2 (volume 4)

Copyright © 1990, 1987, 1984, 1981, 1975, 1972, 1967, by J.G. Ferguson Publishing Company

Printed in the United States of America
N-8

Editorial Staff

Editorial Director: C.J. Summerfield

Assistant Editor: Amy I. Brown

Contributing Editors: Susan Ashby, John Morse, Nancy Parsegian, Mark Toch, James Unland

Writers: Pamela Dell, Lillian Flowers, Jim Garner, Phyllis Miller, Jeanne Rattenbury, Fran Sherman

Photo Editor: Carol Parden

Indexer: Carol Nielson

Designer: Shawn M. Biner, Biner Design

Copyeditors and Proofreaders: Wordsmiths

Production Manager: Tom Myles

Contents

Volume 2: Professional, Administrative, and Managerial Careers

KEY TO OCCUPATIONAL CATEGORIES

 Industry Profiles. This represents the articles that outline descriptions of industries in Volume 1.

 Professional, Administrative, and Managerial Occupations. Covering careers that involve extensive academic training or practical training, these occupations include many of the jobs that require undergraduate or graduate school education. Volume 2

 Clerical Occupations. Clerical occupations are those involved with handling the records, communications, and general office duties required in every business. Volume 3

 Sales Occupations. This section includes sales careers for goods, services, and property, and careers for sales-related business. Volume 3

 Service Occupations. Careers in service comprise occupations that assist people in various aspects of life, from protection by law enforcement to physical care. Volume 3

 Agriculture, Forestry, and Conservation Occupations. Encompassing the occupations that work with various elements of nature, this category includes skilled and technicians' work related to farm production, mining, animal care, and wildlife services. Volume 3 and 4

 Processing Occupations. These are occupations that involve the mixing, treating, and recomposition of materials, chemicals, and products, normally through the use of machinery or tools. Volume 3

 Machine Trades Occupations. Careers in machine trades are those that work with machine assembly, maintenance, and repair. They work with metals, plastics, wood, paper, and stone in construction and repair. Volume 3

 Bench Work Occupations. With an emphasis on hand tools and dexterity skills, bench workers make and repair products that require manual deftness, such as jewelry or optical equipment. Volume 3

Structural Work Occupations. This category details the occupations involved in construction and repair of all large structures from bridges to homes. Volume 3

 Emerging Technician Occupations. Falling mainly into the fields of science and technology, these technicians occupations are either not yet catalogued into one of the sections following or will not be catalogued into an existing field. Volume 4

 Engineering and Science Technician Occupations. These technicians work with scientists and engineers as part of a team trained in the technical aspects of the work performed. Volume 4

 Broadcast, Media, and Arts Technicians Occupations. The technicians who operate, maintain, and repair the equipment involved in broadcasting and the arts are trained to run electronic, electrical, and mechanical equipment. Volume 4

 Medical and Health Technician Occupations. Responsible for the technical equipment used in medical fields, these technicians run the sophisticated machinery used by medical specialists. Volume 4

 Miscellaneous Occupations. In this section are the occupations that require skilled or semi-skilled levels of training. This includes a diverse range of job categories, including graphics arts, transportation and technicians in information services as well as other fields. Volume 3 and 4

Professional, Administrative, and Managerial Occupations

It is often difficult to determine the category into which a given job falls: professional, administrative, or managerial. Conceivably a job could fall into two or even three of these classifications, being professional in social recognition, administrative in training, and managerial in nature. As a rule, vocations described as professional require a high degree of mental activity on the part of the worker and are concerned with theoretical or practical aspects of complex and detailed fields. Administrative persons may be concerned with the broad application of administrative theories and techniques and the direction at high levels of large private or public organizations. Managerial persons are usually responsible for supervisory tasks and the direction of personnel assigned to specific jobs and goals within the establishment or organization.

Preparation for professional work is usually of two types, the highly formalized extensive academic training or the practical experience that develops into training that is equivalent to the more formalized education. Often professions require a combination of the two.

Many of the professions require some type of licensing before beginning practice. Examples of such professions are medicine, dentistry, law, pharmaceutics, and, in most cases, teaching. These licensing requirements indicate only that a person has met some minimum requirements in training and education; licensing does not rate one professional over another.

People such as musicians or actors are indicative of those occupations that demand extensive acquired abilities with relatively little formal education and yet are properly termed "professional." On the other hand, the occupations of engineering, architecture, astronomy, medicine, and teaching are primarily concerned with the application of a formal and well-organized body of knowledge acquired through extensive training of a more formalized nature and are termed "professional" mainly because

of this training and the use to which it is placed.

Managerial and official occupations differ in the traits required to perform the varied types of supervisory responsibilities. Many require the knowledge and skills that one learns in a college program with a major in management.

These occupations vary in the length of preparation required. More education is being required as a basic entry factor in many occupations. Demand for college graduates is increasing because of the complexity and the rising level of required skills.

Because of the continuing growth in the number of people employed in the professions, the emphasis will continue to be on acquiring a college education. This theme will be repeated during the coming years. The professions often require long periods of academic preparation, and with the promise and security they offer college training will be in great demand.

The number of students going on to graduate work will also increase proportionately on both the master's degree and doctorate levels. (The master of arts or science degree normally takes one to two years beyond the bachelor's degree, while the doctorate or Ph.D. degree takes three or more years of formal training beyond the bachelor's degree.)

These increases, of course, indicate that the competition among professionally trained personnel for entry and advancement in the professions will increase considerably, especially in the jobs offering the greatest social recognition and the highest financial recompense.

At the beginning of managerial and official positions are traineeships. Trainees are often placed in a variety of the company's jobs to learn the many varied activities. Assistants' jobs are a training ground for advancement into more responsible positions. In addition, many trainees go through managerial and official training programs. Such programs serve as another entry point for more advanced positions.

Accountants and auditors

Definition

Accountants compile, analyze, verify, and prepare such business and financial records as profit and loss statements, balance sheets, cost studies, and tax reports. Within this broad sphere, accountants may specialize in areas such as auditing, tax work, cost accounting, budgeting and control, or systems and procedures. Accountants may also specialize in a particular business or field; for example, *agricultural accountants* specialize in drawing up and analyzing financial statements for farmers and for farm equipment companies.

History

Accounting records and bookkeeping methods have been used from early periods of history down to the present time. Records found in Babylonia date back to 3600 B.C., and accounts were kept by the Greeks and the Romans.

Modern accounting began with the technique of double-entry bookkeeping, which was developed in the fifteenth and sixteenth centuries. Generally credited with developing double-entry bookkeeping, Luca Pacioli, an Italian mathematician, printed his treatise on accounting and bookkeeping in 1494.

After the Industrial Revolution, business became more complex, and the need for accounting methods grew. With the development of governmental and industrial institutions in the nineteenth and twentieth centuries, accurate information and records to aid in making decisions on economic and management policies and procedures, as well as periodic reports for both public and private use, became necessary.

The accounting profession in the United States dates back only to 1880, when English and Scottish investors began buying stock in American companies. To keep an eye on their investments, they sent over British accountants, many of whom realized the great potential that existed and stayed to establish their own businesses.

Federal legislation, such as the income tax in 1913 and the excess profits tax in 1917, helped bring about an accounting boom that has made the profession one of the largest in business today.

Nature of the work

Accountants' duties depend upon the size and nature of the firm or institution in which they are employed. The major fields of employment are public, private, and government accounting.

Public accountants work independently on a fee basis or as a member of an accounting firm and perform a variety of tasks for any business or individual wishing to make use of their services. Among the services performed are auditing bookkeeping accounts and records, preparing and certifying financial statements, conducting financial investigations and furnishing testimony in legal matters, and assisting in formulating certain budget policies and procedures.

Private accountants, sometimes called *industrial* or *management accountants*, handle financial records of the firm at which they are salaried employees.

Government accountants work on the financial records of government agencies or, when necessary, audit the records of private companies. In the federal government, many accountants are employed as *bank examiners, Internal Revenue agents*, and *investigators*, as well as in regular accounting positions.

Each of these areas employs accountants specializing in a particular aspect of accounting.

General accountants supervise, install, and devise general accounting, budget, and cost systems. They are responsible for maintaining records, balancing the books, and preparing and analyzing statements on all financial aspects of business for administrative officers, who can then make sound business decisions.

Budget accountants review expenditures of departments within a firm to make sure expenses allotted are not exceeded. They also aid in drafting new budgets and may devise and install budget control systems.

Cost accountants are responsible for determining unit costs of products or services by analyzing records and depreciation data. They classify and record all operating costs, including manufacture and distribution, for use by management in controlling expenditures.

Property accountants keep records of equipment, buildings, and other property either owned or leased by a company. They prepare amortization schedules and statements showing appreciation or depreciation in value, which are used for income tax purposes.

Systems accountants design and set up special accounting systems for organizations whose needs cannot be handled by a standardized system. This may involve installation of machine accounting processes and includes instructing relevant personnel in the new methods.

Tax accountants prepare federal, state, or local tax returns of an individual, business, or corporation according to prescribed rates, laws, and regulations. They may also conduct research on the effects of taxes on firm operations and recommend changes to reduce taxes. This is one of the most involved of all fields of accounting, and many specialize in one particular phase of tax accounting such as individual income, property, or corporation.

Auditors examine and vouch for the accuracy and completeness of accounting records of an establishment by inspecting items in books of original entry, such as daybooks or journals, to ensure proper transaction records. They may also prepare financial statements for clients.

Internal auditors conduct the same kind of examination and evaluation for one particular company. Because they are salaried employees of that company, their financial audits then must be certified by a qualified independent auditor. Internal auditors also review procedures and controls and appraise the efficiency and effectiveness of operations and make sure their companies are complying with corporate policies and government regulations.

Tax auditors review financial records and other information provided by taxpayers to determine the appropriate tax liability. State and federal tax auditors usually work in government offices but may perform a field audit in a taxpayer's home or office.

Revenue agents are employed by the federal government to examine selected income tax returns and, where it seems necessary, to conduct field audits and investigations to verify the information reported and adjust the tax liability accordingly.

Chief bank examiners enforce good banking practices throughout a state. They schedule bank examinations to ensure that the financial institutions are complying with state laws, and, in certain cases, take steps to protect a bank's solvency and the interests of its depositors and shareholders.

Requirements

An accountant must be able to work independently and also supervise the work of others who perform the more routine phases of oper-

The accountant reviews on-line data before posting it to the general ledger.

ations. Personal qualities necessary to the study of accountancy are: facility in working with figures and ability to think logically; clarity of both oral and written expression; neat, accurate, and orderly habits of work; and sound judgment and the ability to make one's decisions based on such judgments.

High-school students preparing for an accounting career should be proficient in arithmetical and numerical concepts, speaking, and writing. Familiarity with computers is also increasingly a requirement as the accounting field becomes more dependent upon these tools. Achievement in high-school subjects such as general business training, bookkeeping, and mathematics may indicate potential success in accounting.

Post–high-school training in accounting may be obtained in a wide variety of institutions such as private business schools, junior colleges, universities, and correspondence schools. A bachelor's degree with a major in accounting is generally recommended by professional associations for persons entering the field. It is possible, however, to become a successful accountant by completing the program of any of the above-mentioned institutions. A four-year college curriculum usually includes about two years of liberal arts courses, a year of general business subjects, and a year of specific accounting work.

Better positions, particularly in public accounting, often require a bachelor's degree

Accountants and auditors
Professional, Administrative, and Managerial Occupations

with a major in accounting. Large public accounting firms prefer persons with a master's degree in accounting. For beginning positions in accounting, the federal government requires four years of college (including twenty-four semester hours in accounting or auditing) or an equivalent combination of education and experience.

Special requirements

Certified public accountants (CPAs) must pass a special qualifying examination and hold a certificate issued by the state in which they wish to practice. In most states, a college degree is required for admission to the CPA examinations. More than half of the states require certification or registration to practice as a public accountant, and the requirements vary considerably in these states. The remaining states have no regulations concerning practice in accountancy except for the CPA. Interested students may obtain information about regulations from the board of accountancy in the state in which they plan to practice.

The CPA examination of the American Institute of Certified Public Accountants is used by all states. Nearly all states require at least two years of public accounting experience or its equivalent before a CPA certificate can be earned. More than nine out of ten successful CPA candidates in recent years have been graduates of four-year college or university programs.

Recent reports by the American Institute of Certified Public Accountants indicate that a few states already require CPA candidates to have a graduate degree and other states may soon follow suit.

To become a Certified Internal Auditor (CIA), college graduates with two years' experience in internal auditing must pass a four-part examination given by the Institute of Internal Auditors.

Accountants who meet the required educational and professional standards set by the National Association of Accountants may earn a Certificate in Management Accounting by passing a series of exams.

Opportunities for experience and exploration

One may explore the accounting field while in high school by visiting offices where the prac-

tice of accounting may be observed. Part-time employment during the school year or summer also provides an opportunity to gain some knowledge about the type of work involved. It may also be possible to gain some experience in school and community organizations and through service in the armed forces. The work-study and internship programs found in the curricula of some colleges offer an opportunity to obtain experience in public accounting or in business firms. Previous work experience is very helpful in qualifying for positions upon completion of training.

Related occupations

Training in accounting is also of value in other occupations that call for an ability to analyze financial data and design internal control systems. Workers in related occupations include actuaries, appraisers, bank officers, budget officers, FBI special agents, financial analysts, loan officers, purchasing agents, securities sales workers, tax collectors and revenue agents, and underwriters.

Methods of entering

Junior public accountants usually start in jobs involving fairly routine duties such as counting cash, verifying additions, and other detailed work. In private accounting, beginners are likely to start in clerical positions such as cost clerk, ledger clerk, and timekeeper. They may also enter as junior internal auditors, and as trainees in technical or junior executive positions. In the federal government, most beginners are hired as trainees.

Advancement

Junior public accountants usually advance to semi–senior positions within two or three years and to senior positions within another several years. Those successful in dealing with top-level management may eventually become supervisors, managers, and partners in larger firms or go into independent practice. Private accountants in firms may become chief plant accountant, senior internal auditor, or manager of internal auditing, depending on their specialty. Some rise to become controllers, treasurers, and even corporation presidents. Federal

4

government trainees are usually promoted within a year or so.

Although advancement may be rapid for able accountants, especially in public accounting, those with inadequate academic preparation are often assigned to routine jobs and find themselves handicapped in obtaining promotions. Accountants who want to get to the top of their profession and remain there usually find it necessary to continue their study of accounting and related problems in their spare time. Even those who may have already obtained college degrees, gained experience, and earned a CPA certificate may spend many hours in study and research to keep up with business and legal developments in their work. Thousands of practicing accountants have enrolled in formal courses offered by universities and professional associations to specialize in certain areas of accounting, broaden or update their professional skills, and become eligible for advancement and promotion.

Employment outlook

Accountants are employed wherever business, industrial, or government organizations are located. Most of them, however, work in large urban areas.

In the early 1990s, almost one million persons were employed as accountants, making the field one of the largest professional employment fields in business. By far the largest number of accountants were found in private business and industry, but approximately 10 percent worked in federal, state, and local government agencies. About one-third were certified public accountants (CPAs), and almost 2.5 percent were licensed public accountants. About 10 percent of all accountants were self-employed.

It is expected that employment opportunities for accountants will grow much faster than the average for all occupations through the 1990s because these workers are essential to management of all kinds of businesses. The increasing complexity of accounting should create a greater demand for college-trained accountants. Applicants who gained actual experience in part-time jobs while still in school will have an advantage when applying even for entry-level positions. For certified accountants, such as CPAs, the range of job opportunities should be greater than for other accountants. Major industrial centers will continue to be the best source of jobs; however, there will also be many openings in small industrial communities. Accountants without college degrees may

find more opportunities among small businesses and in accounting and tax preparation firms, especially in less populated areas.

Accounting employment throughout this decade and perhaps beyond should expand rapidly because of the complex and changing systems of taxation, growth in both the size and the number of business corporations that have to make financial reports to stockholders, a more general use of accounting in the management of business, and more use of accounting services by small business firms. The increased use of new types of record-keeping systems and of computers will create a demand for well-trained accountants to serve as consultants to managers of various business and industrial organizations.

Accounting jobs are more secure than most during economic downswings. Despite fluctuations in the national economy, there is a continuing need for financial data and tax reports.

Earnings

Beginning salaries of accountants in private industry averaged $21,000 a year in the early 1990s. Experienced accountants earned between $31,800 and $65,000, depending on the demands of their work. Accountants who were in charge of all accounting for large firms had annual salaries ranging from $40,000 to more than $80,000. Auditors' salaries averaged $21,500 for beginners and ranged from $30,300 to more than $40,000 for experienced professionals. Government salaries for accountants and auditors were from about $14,800 for starting junior accountants and auditors to an average of about $35,000 for those with experience. In public accounting firms, beginning accountants averaged $20,500 a year. Junior public accountants averaged $24,100, with some of them earning more than $35,000 annually. Experienced accountants, particularly those who were owners and partners, often earned considerably more.

Conditions of work

Accountants ordinarily work between thirty-five and forty hours a week and, in general, work under the same conditions as most office workers. Public accountants are subject to considerable pressure during the busy tax period, which runs from November to April. During this time, and often at other times as well, they may find it necessary to work long hours and more than five days a week. Most of the public accountant's work is performed in the client's office, and sometimes a considerable amount of traveling is necessary to serve clients whose offices are not located nearby. Private and governmental accountants are also sometimes involved in much travel. Most, however, work in the same place daily and have more regular working hours.

Social and psychological factors

Accountants must work well on their own and with others, as they may often supervise and instruct people with whom they are associated. High ethical standards and a pleasing personality are essential for success in the field in general. These qualities are almost indispensable in public accounting, because clients must be found and retained to remain in business. The accountant who is able to concentrate for hours at a time and has an aptitude for problem solving usually finds the work challenging, interesting, and satisfying.

GOE: 11.06.01; SIC: Any industry; SOC: 1412

◇ **SOURCES OF ADDITIONAL INFORMATION**

American Accounting Association
5717 Bessie Drive
Sarasota, FL 33583

American Institute of Certified Public Accountants
1211 Avenue of the Americas
New York, NY 10036

American Society of Women Accountants
35 East Wacker Drive, Suite 2250
Chicago, IL 60601

American Woman's Society of Certified Public Accountants
111 East Wacker Drive, Suite 600
Chicago, IL 60601

EDP Auditors Association
455 East Kehoe Boulevard
Suite 106
PO Box 88180
Carol Stream, IL 60188

Financial Executives Institute
PO Box 1938
10 Madison Avenue
Morristown, NJ 07960

Foundation for Accounting Education
200 Park Avenue
New York, NY 10166

National Association of Accountants
10 Paragon Drive
Montvale, NJ 07645

National Society of Public Accountants
1010 North Fairfax Street
Alexandria, VA 22314

For information on accreditation and testing, please contact:

Accreditation Council for Accountancy
National Society of Public Accountants
1010 North Fairfax Street
Alexandria, VA 22314

Institute of Internal Auditors
249 Maitland Avenue
Altamonte Springs, FL 32701

◇ **RELATED ARTICLES**

Volume 1: Accounting; Banking and Financial Services; Business Administration
Volume 2: Actuaries; Financial institution officers and managers; General managers and top executives; Management trainees; Statisticians
Volume 3: Bookkeeping and accounting clerks; Cashiers; Financial institution clerks and related workers; Financial institution tellers; Tax preparers

Actors

Definition

Actors play parts or roles in dramatic productions on the stage, in motion pictures, or on television or radio. They impersonate or portray characters, either serious or comic, by speech and gesture and, possibly, song and dance.

History

The earliest example of a human acting performance is found in dance. Disguised with a mask depicting the subject to be portrayed, the dancer told the action of the story. Often such ceremonies were of a religious nature and were an important part in the society's culture.

Among the ancient Greeks, who used the stage as a forum for topical themes and stories, drama began to assume a more controlled and recognizable form. They placed a greater premium on the actors and began to depict a particular setting through the use of scenery. Playgoing was often a great celebration and was very important to the Greek people.

During the Renaissance the formal settings for plays developed. The Italians developed pictorial sets and found the methods for creating them.

The first English theater was established in 1576 by James Burbage, and the first in the United States in 1716 at Williamsburg, Virginia. Various forms of traveling shows became popular following the Civil War, and, by 1900, stock companies were extremely popular. These companies presented a standard repertoire of plays, and facilities were developed for them in hundreds of towns. They moved from town to town as demand warranted.

As might have been anticipated, the public began to prefer certain actors. It was this expressed preference that resulted in what today is termed the "star system," with each play starring one or more performers who has gained prominence through their acting.

Prohibitive transportation costs and the popularity of motion pictures led to the decline of the traveling stock system by 1915. New York gradually became the center of the legitimate theater and remains so despite the ever-increasing number of local theater companies springing up throughout the country. Hollywood is the recognized center of the motion picture industry and filmed television. Other major production centers are Miami and Central Florida, Chicago, San Francisco, Dallas, and Houston. Today, paid employment in motion pictures greatly exceeds paid employment in the theater. The greatest source of employment for actors is television commercials, which account for about 50 percent of all actors' earnings.

Nature of the work

The imitation or basic development of a character for presentation to an audience often seems like a glamorous and fairly easy job. In reality, it is demanding, tiring work requiring a special talent.

The actor must first find a part available in some upcoming production. This may be in a comedy, drama, musical, or opera. Then, having read and studied the part, the actor must audition before the director and other people having control of the production. This requirement is often waived for established artists.

If selected for the part, the actor must spend hundreds of hours in rehearsal and must memorize many lines and cues. In addition to such mechanical duties, the actor must determine the essence of the character being portrayed and the relation of that character in the overall scheme of the play. Radio actors must be especially skilled in expressing character and emotion through the voice.

While waiting to be discovered, or while studying and perfecting their craft, many actors and actresses work as *extras*, the nonspeaking characters that people the background on screen or stage.

The actor is not, of course, the only person responsible for the success of any production. Playwright, producer, director, scenery or set designer, and a score of others are all integral parts of any production.

Like actors and actresses, numerous other performers have occupations that make similar demands. They include *narrators*, *magicians*, *puppeteers*, *ventriloquists*, *clowns*, *comedians*, *impersonators*, *mimes*, and *stunt performers*.

Some actors eventually go into other, related occupations and become *dramatic coaches*, *drama teachers* (see also the article titled "Adult and vocational education teachers" elsewhere in this volume), *producers*, *stage directors*, *motion*

These actors and actresses are performing a scene from William Shakespeare's play *Henry IV, Part 1.*

picture directors, television directors, radio directors (*see also* the article titled "Radio and television program directors" elsewhere in this volume), *stage managers, casting directors,* or *artist and repertoire managers* (*see also* the article titled "Literary agents and artists' managers" elsewhere in this volume).

Requirements

As acting becomes more and more involved with the various facets of our society, a college degree will become more important to those who hope to have an acting career. It is felt that the actor who has completed a liberal arts program is more capable of understanding the wide variety of roles that are available. In addition, graduate degrees in the fine arts or in drama are nearly always required should the individual decide to teach dramatic arts in a college rather than to perform as a professional.

College can also serve to provide acting experience for the hopeful actor. Approximately 534 colleges and universities throughout the nation offer dramatic arts programs and present theatrical performances. Actors and directors recommend that those interested in acting gain as much experience as possible through acting in plays in high school and college or in those offered by community groups.

Formal training may also be obtained at special dramatic arts schools. Most are found in New York and Los Angeles. New York also has a public school especially conceived for hopeful performers. The High School of Performing Arts, a part of the New York public school system, offers selected students work in regular high-school courses plus a great deal of work in dramatic arts.

Prospective actors will be required not only to have a great talent for acting but also a great determination to succeed in the theater and motion pictures. They must be able to memorize hundreds of lines and should have a good speaking voice. The ability to sing and dance is also gaining increasing significance for the young actor.

Special requirements

The primary special requirement for an actor is outstanding talent and the ability and patience required to learn the craft.

Performers on the Broadway stages must be members of Actors' Equity Association before being cast. While union membership may not always be a requirement, many actors find it advantageous to belong to a union that covers their particular field of performing arts. These organizations include the Actors' Equity Association (stage), Screen Actors Guild or Screen Extras Guild (motion pictures and television films), or American Federation of Television and Radio Artists (TV, recording, and radio). In addition, some actors may benefit from membership in the American Guild of Variety Artists (nightclubs, and so on), American Guild of Musical Artists (opera and ballet), or organizations such as the Hebrew Actors Union or Italian Actors Union for productions in those languages.

Opportunities for experience and exploration

The best way to explore this career is to attempt a bit part in a local production or to assume a major role in a school production. Even working on the props or lighting will provide insight into the field.

Also, attend as many dramatic productions as possible and try to talk with people who either are currently in the theater or have been at one time. They can offer much advice to individuals interested in a career in the theater.

Many books have been written about acting, not only concerning how to perform but also about the nature of the work, its offerings, advantages, and disadvantages. Those interested in acting can speak with those employed in the dramatic arts departments at various colleges and universities.

Related occupations

Numerous occupations call for acting skills or are related to acting. Acting ability is required by choreographers, dancers, disc jockeys, drama teachers or coaches, and radio and television announcers. Workers in fields related to acting include playwrights, script writers, set designers, and stage managers. Persons interested in acting also may choose occupations involved in the business aspects of theater and film production, such as agents for actors, directors, and playwrights; booking managers; and company managers.

Methods of entering

Probably the best way to enter acting is to start with the local, hometown, or college productions and to gain as much experience as possible on that level. Very rarely is an inexperienced actor or actress given an opportunity to perform in New York or Hollywood. The field is extremely difficult to enter; the more experience and ability beginners have, however, the greater the possibilities for entrance.

Those venturing to New York or Hollywood are encouraged first to have enough money to support themselves during the long waiting and searching period normally required before a job is found. Most will list themselves with a casting agency that will help them find a part as an extra or a bit player. These agencies keep names on file along with a description of the individual's features and experience, and if a part comes along that may be suitable, they contact that person. Very often, however, names are added to their lists only when the number of people in a particular physical category is low. For instance, the agency may not have enough athletic young women on their roster, and if the applicant happens to fit this description, her name is added.

Advancement

New actors or actresses will normally start in bit parts and will have only a few lines to speak, if any. The normal procession of advancement would then lead to larger supporting roles and then possibly to a role as understudy for one of the main actors or actresses. The understudy usually has an opportunity to fill in should the main actor or actress be unable to give a performance. Stardom is the next step, but only a very small number of actors and actresses ever reach that pinnacle.

Employment outlook

Motion pictures, television, and the stage are the largest fields of employment for actors, and most of the opportunities for employment in these fields are either in Hollywood or in New York. On stage, even the road shows often have their beginning in New York, with the selection of actors and actresses conducted there along with rehearsals.

Faster than average growth in opportunities is expected through the 1990s because of the increase in theatrical and motion picture productions. Also contributing to this favorable outlook are the development of permanent acting companies in urban centers and the growing number of dinner theaters and summer and winter stock companies. It is anticipated that other opportunities will open up in the expansion of public TV broadcasting and cable television. In addition, virtually every major U.S. city now has very active local production of TV commercials, creating important income for regional actors. Finally, many openings will occur as actors leave the field for other professions.

The field is overcrowded now and is expected to be so for years to come. This is true in all phases of the art, including radio, television, motion pictures, and the theater, and even those who are employed are normally employed during only a small portion of the year. Many actors must supplement their income by working in other areas, as secretaries, waiters, taxi drivers, for example. Almost all performers are members of more than one union to take advantage of various opportunities as they become available.

It should be recognized that of the 100,000 or so actors and actresses in the United States today, an average of only about 20,000 are employed at any one time. Of these, very few have ever achieved stardom. A somewhat larger number are well-known, experienced performers who are frequently cast in supporting roles. The great majority are still looking for the right break. There are many more applicants in all areas than there are positions.

Earnings

The wage scale for actors and actresses is largely controlled through bargaining agreements reached by various unions in negotiations with producers. These agreements normally control the minimum salaries, hours of work permitted per week, and other conditions of employment. Actors' Equity Association represents actors and actresses who work in the legitimate theater; the Screen Actors Guild and the Screen Extras Guild represent those who work in motion pictures or film television and TV commercials; and the American Federation of Television and Radio Artists represents those who work in television or radio. In addition, each artist enters into a separate contract that may provide for higher salaries.

In the early 1990s, actors in Broadway productions made a minimum weekly salary of about $700. Those in smaller productions "off-Broadway" received minimums that ranged from $240 to $465 a week depending on the size of the theater. The rate for touring shows was an additional $70 a day.

Motion picture and television minimum rates were $398 daily or $1385 for a five-day week. Extras earned a minimum of $91 a day. Motion picture actors also receive additional payments known as "residuals" as part of their guaranteed salary. All motion picture actors receive residuals whenever films, TV shows, and TV commercials in which they appear are re-run, sold for TV exhibition, or put on videocassette. Residuals often exceed the actors' original salary and account for about one-third of all actors' income.

The annual earnings of persons in television and movies are affected by frequent periods of unemployment. Actors' Equity Association and the Screen Actors Guild reported that in the early 1990s more than 80 percent of their members earned $5,000 or less annually and less than 5 percent earned more than $25,000 from acting.

In all fields, well-known actors have salary rates above the minimums, and the salaries of the few top stars are many times higher. The average annual earnings, however, are usually low (only $10,400 for screen actors in the early 1990s) for all but the best-known performers because of the periods of unemployment.

Conditions of work

Actors work under varying conditions. Those employed in motion pictures may work in air-conditioned studios one week and be on location in a hot desert the next.

Those in stage productions perform under all types of conditions. The number of hours employed per day or week vary, as do the number of weeks employed per year. Stage ac-

tors normally perform eight shows per week with any additional performances paid for as overtime. The basic workweek after the show opens is about thirty-six hours unless major changes in the play are needed. The number of hours worked per week is considerably more before the opening, because of rehearsals. Evening work is a natural part of a stage actor's life. Rehearsals often are held at night and over holidays and weekends. If the play goes on the road, much traveling will be involved.

A number of actors cannot receive unemployment compensation when they are waiting for their next part, primarily because they have not worked enough to meet the minimum eligibility requirements for compensation. Sick leaves and paid vacations are not usually available to the actor. However, union actors who earn the minimum qualifications now receive full medical and health insurance under all the actors' unions. Those who earn health plan benefits for ten years become eligible for a pension upon retirement.

Social and psychological factors

There are many social and psychological factors involved, including the acclaim that a star performer receives. There is an opportunity of performing before an audience and receiving recognition. There is change, travel, excitement, and much hard work.

On the other hand, the field is very uncertain. Aspirants never know whether they will be able to get into the profession and, once in, there are uncertainties as to whether the show will be well received and, if not, whether the actors' talent can survive a bad show. The work is difficult and demanding, and only those with talent, a strong desire, determination, and hope will succeed.

GOE: 01.03.02; SIC: 7929; SOC: 324

◇ **SOURCES OF ADDITIONAL INFORMATION**

Actors' Equity Association
165 West 46th Street
New York, NY 10036

American Federation of Television and Radio Artists
260 Madison Avenue
New York, NY 10016

American Guild of Musical Artists
1727 Broadway
New York, NY 10019

American Guild of Variety Artists
184 Fifth Avenue
New York, NY 10019

Associated Actors and Artistes of America (AFL-CIO)
165 West 46th Street
New York, NY 10036

National Endowment for the Arts
Information Office
1100 Pennsylvania Avenue, NW
Washington, DC 20506

Screen Actors Guild
7065 Hollywood Boulevard
Hollywood, CA 90028

Theatre Communications Group
355 Lexington Avenue
New York, NY 10017

◇ **RELATED ARTICLES**

Volume 1: Broadcasting; Motion Pictures; Performing Arts
Volume 2: Adult and vocational education teachers; Dancers and choreographers; Literary agents and artists' managers; Musical occupations; Radio and television announcers and newscasters; Radio and television program directors
Volume 3: Models; Stage production workers

Actuaries

Definition

Actuaries deal with statistical, mathematical, and financial calculations involving probability of future payments or contingencies in pension and insurance plans, such as insurance against losses arising from death, disability, sickness, and unemployment. They determine the proper basis and methods for valuing liabilities and maintaining permanent financial stability of insurance and pension organizations.

Actuaries set formulas that try to predict the number of policies that will incur losses and how much money the company will pay in claims. This determines the overall cost of insuring a group, company, or individual. Increase in risk increases potential cost to the company and the company increases their rates to cover this.

Casualty actuaries specialize in property and liability insurance, life actuaries in health and life insurance. An increasing number of actuaries deal only with pension plans.

Although many actuaries are employed in insurance companies, the federal and state governments, as well as private business and industry, make up a good portion of employers for actuaries. Consulting practices are also important areas in which actuarial work may be found.

History

The term *actuary* was used for the first time in 1762 when the charter for the first life insurance company to use scientific data in figuring premiums, the Equitable Society of London, was written. The basis of actuarial work was laid in the early eighteenth century when Blaise Pascal and Pierre de Fermat derived an important method of calculating actuarial probabilities, resulting in what is now termed "the science of probability."

The first mortality table was produced in the late seventeenth century when Edmund Halley's attention was called to the regularity of various social phenomena, including the excess of male over female births. Halley, an English astronomer, is known as the father of life insurance.

The post of actuary created in 1821 by the British government for the Commissioner for the Reduction of the National Debt resulted in the first official recognition of the profession. As more complex forms of insurance were de-

Nature of the work

Actuaries are basically mathematicians who aim to design and maintain insurance and pension programs on a sound financial basis. They may be employed by a number of different types of insurance companies, including life, health, accident, automobile, fire, or workers' compensation organizations. They may deal in pension programs sponsored and administered by various levels of government, private business, or fraternal or benevolent associations. Whatever the nature of the employer's product, actuaries are key to the sound financial management of the various insurance plans involved.

Using a knowledge of mathematics, probability, statistics, and principles of finance and business, actuaries determine premium rates and the various benefits of insurance plans. To do this, they must first assemble and analyze statistics, data, and other pertinent information. Based on this information, they are able to develop mathematical models of rates of death, accident, sickness, disability, or retirement and construct tables regarding the probability of such things occurring as unemployment or property loss from fire, theft, accident, or natural disaster. After calculating all probabilities and the resulting costs to the company, the actuaries can determine the premium rates for insurance to cover the expected losses from such circumstances.

As an example of how this works: based on their analyses, actuaries are able to determine how many of each 1,000 people twenty-one years old today are expected to survive to age sixty-five. They can calculate how many of them are expected to die this year or how many are expected to live until age eighty-five. The probability that such an insured person may die during the period before reaching sixty-five is a risk to the company. The actuaries must figure a price for the premium that will cover all claims and expenses as they occur and still be profitable for the company assuming the risk. At the same time, the price must be competitive with what other insurance companies are charging. In the same way, actuaries calculate premium rates and determine policy provisions for each type of insurance coverage. Most actuaries specialize as casualty actuaries, dealing with property and liability insurance, or as life actuaries, working with life and health insurance. In addition, those who concentrate on pension plans form a third, and growing, group of specialists.

Actuaries work in many departments in insurance companies, including underwriting, group insurance, investment, pension, sales, and service. In addition to their own company's

Two actuaries are discussing data from a computer printout.

veloped in the nineteenth century, the need for actuaries grew.

The need for organization was felt in 1889, and a small group of qualified actuaries formed the Actuarial Society of America. Two classes of members, fellows and associates, were created seven years later, and special examinations were developed for use in determining eligibility for membership. Forms of these examinations are still in use today.

By 1909, the American Institute of Actuaries was created, and these two groups consolidated in 1949 into the present Society of Actuaries.

In 1911, the Casualty Actuary Society was formed as a result of the development of workers' compensation laws. The compensation laws opened many new fields of insurance, and the Casualty Actuarial Society has since moved into all the many aspects of property and liability insurance.

The first actuaries were concerned primarily with statistical, mathematical, and financial calculations needed in the rapidly growing field. Today they deal with problems of investment, selection of risk factors for insurance, agents' compensation, social insurance, taxation, development of policy forms, and many other aspects of insurance.

business, they analyze characteristics of the insurance business as a whole. They study general economic and social trends, as well as legislative, health, and other developments, all of which may affect insurance practices. With this broad knowledge, some actuaries reach executive positions where they can influence and help determine company policy. Actuary executives may communicate with government officials, company executives, policyholders, or the public to explain complex technical matters. They may testify before public agencies regarding proposed legislation that has a bearing on the insurance business, for example, or explain proposed changes in premium rates or contract provisions.

Actuaries employed by the federal government will likely work with a particular type of governmental insurance or pension program, such as veterans' insurance or social security. Those who work for state governments are concerned with the supervision and regulation of insurance companies, the operations of state retirement or pension systems, and problems related to unemployment insurance and workers' compensation. Others may be employed as consulting actuaries, working on a fee basis, to set up pension and welfare plans for various unions or governmental agencies or private enterprise. They calculate the amount of future benefits to be paid to the workers and determine how much the employer will contribute to the plans. These pension plans are evaluated by actuaries enrolled under the provisions of the Employee Retirement Income Security Act of 1974 (ERISA), who prepare reports on their financial soundness.

Requirements

A bachelor's degree with a major in mathematics or statistics is usually required for entry into actuarial work. A degree in actuarial science is even more advantageous. Employers in search of actuaries are interested both in ability and achievement in mathematics as well as in an applicant's personal characteristics. The abilities to assume positions of leadership and to deal and work with people are prime requisites. Prospective actuaries should have a talent for detail work. At the same time, a broad outlook will be needed if they are to understand overall business and economic problems and trends. The ability to think along far-reaching outlines of policy planning is also necessary.

High-school students interested in being actuaries should take as much mathematics as possible. They should continue this training on through the bachelor's degree, taking courses in elementary and advanced algebra, differential and integral calculus, descriptive and analytical statistics, principles of mathematical statistics, probability, and numerical analysis. Because mathematics and statistics are essential requirements for actuaries, some companies may hire applicants with degrees in engineering, economics, or business administration, provided their background in the essentials is strong enough. Computer science is vital to actuarial training. Courses in accounting and insurance also are useful. Although only about thirty colleges and universities offer a degree in actuarial science, degrees in mathematics and statistics are available at several hundred schools.

Special requirements

Full professional status in an actuarial specialty is based not only on previous training, both formal and on-the-job, but also on the successful completion of a series of examinations. The actuary may become an "associate" in the Society of Actuaries after the successful completion of five examinations out of a total of ten for the life and health insurance and pension fields, and in the Casualty Actuarial Society after successfully completing seven out of ten in the property and liability field. Persons who successfully complete the entire series of exams for either organization are granted full membership and the title "fellow." The American Society of Pension Actuaries gives seven examinations in the pension field. It awards membership after the successful completion of two actuarial examinations and confers fellowship status on those who pass three actuarial and two advanced consulting exams.

Because the first parts of the examination series of each society cover similar materials, students need not commit themselves to a specialty until they have taken three examinations. These three test competence in subjects such as linear algebra, numerical methods, operations research, probability, calculus, and statistics. Completion of the entire series may require from five to ten years.

Preference in employment is usually given to those people who have completed at least the first two examinations and to those with experience. Students proposing to become actuaries should complete at least two of the preliminary examinations while still in college, as these examinations cover subjects usually taught in colleges and universities, whereas the more advanced examinations cover aspects of the profession itself. These preliminary examinations may also help students in determining prior to graduation whether or not they will enter the actuarial profession.

Consulting pension actuaries who service private pension plans and certify their solvency must be enrolled by the Joint Board for the Enrollment of Actuaries, a U.S. government agency. To be accepted, applicants must meet certain experience and educational requirements as stipulated by the Joint Board.

Opportunities for experience and exploration

Exploration of the work of the actuary may be initiated in a number of different ways. Inquiries sent to the organizations listed at the end of this article will result in basic information. Visits to insurance companies for talks with actuaries or insurance employees in general are another possibility. Summer employment is offered by a number of insurance companies that are willing to hire and train college undergraduates during summer months. Beginning actuaries often rotate among jobs to learn various actuarial operations and different phases of insurance work. At first they may prepare tabulations for actuarial tables or perform other simple tasks. With experience, they may prepare correspondence, reports, and research. Because of the need for additional trained actuaries, insurance companies are encouraging young people to talk with their employees and representatives regarding the possibility of careers in actuarial science.

Related occupations

Actuaries assemble and analyze statistics. The work calls for an interest in solving problems, conducting research, and interpreting numerical data. Skills in these areas are also needed by such workers as economists, engineering analysts, financial analysts, mathematicians, and statisticians.

Methods of entering

The best way to enter this occupation is by taking the necessary beginning examinations already mentioned while still in college. Once students have graduated and passed these exams successfully, they are in a very good position to apply for beginning jobs in the field and can command higher starting salaries. After a position is secured and some time has been spent in on-the-job training, newcomers in the field will be ready to take the more advanced examinations that will qualify them as a fellow in the particular society applied for. These examinations are usually taken by those in junior actuarial positions because they require extensive home study and experience in insurance work.

Advancement

Advancement within the profession to assistant, associate, or chief actuary is dependent to a great degree upon the individual's on-the-job performance, competence on the actuarial examinations, and the display of leadership capabilities.

Some actuaries qualify for administrative positions in underwriting, accounting, or investment because of their broad general knowledge and their knowledge of the insurance field. Many advance to administrative or executive positions, such as head of a department, vice-president or president of a company, manager of an insurance rating bureau, partner in a consulting firm, or, possibly, state insurance commissioner. Advancement is open to actuaries in many areas.

Employment outlook

The prospects for entry into the field are now excellent and are expected to remain so through the late 1990s, especially for applicants who have passed at least two professional exams while at college and who have a good background in statistics and mathematics. Currently a shortage of fully qualified actuaries exists, and even more will be needed as the number and type of insurance and pension programs grow.

Actuaries will be in particular demand in the insurance field to establish rates in the several new areas of coverage that are growing, such as prepaid legal, dental, and kidnap insurance. As more people are living longer, the insurance industry must meet the need for improved and extended health care and retirement benefits, and actuaries must determine rates based on probabilities of such factors as retirement, sickness, and death. In many cases, actuarial data that have been supplied by rating bureaus are now being developed in new actuarial departments created in companies affected by new competitive rating laws that are being passed in many states. Other new areas of insurance coverage that will involve actuaries include product and pollution liability insurance, as well as greater workers' compensation and medical malpractice coverage.

About 9,400 actuaries were employed in the United States in the early 1990s. More than half of these worked for private insurance companies, the majority in life insurance, the rest in property and casualty insurance. Perhaps one-third of all actuaries were employed by independent consulting firms. Some actuaries worked for rating bureaus (associations that supply actuarial data to member companies), and others were in business for themselves or were employed by private organizations to administer independent pension and welfare plans. Still others were employed by federal or state government agencies or taught in colleges and universities. Many actuaries work in five cities that are major insurance company headquarters: New York, Hartford, Chicago, Philadelphia, and Boston.

Because of new state and federal legislation in areas relating to pension reform, no-fault automobile insurance, competitive rating, and other new proposals, a real need will exist in the field of actuarial studies. This trend will continue throughout the 1990s. In addition, the need for actuaries is not likely to be affected by economic recession, especially in the field of insurance, which is considered a priority by most individuals and businesses.

Earnings

The average starting salary in the life insurance field was $19,000 to $24,000 a year in the early 1990s. This was for new college graduates who had not passed any actuarial examinations. Starting salaries for new graduates who had passed one exam were between $21,000 and $25,000; those who had passed two exams averaged between $23,000 and $26,000. In some cases, college graduates were able to command up to $30,000 a year for entry-level jobs. Salary ranges depend on the part of the country in which an actuary wishes to work.

Although data is not available for casualty companies and consulting firms, actuaries in those fields earn similar salaries to those in the insurance field. Most companies give merit increases to actuaries as they gain experience and pass examinations. In the insurance field, actuaries who became associates in the early 1990s earned salaries in the $32,000 to $45,000 range; those who became fellows were paid from $44,000 to $55,000. Top executive salaries for actuaries in the life insurance field were $60,000 a year and more.

Conditions of work

Actuaries can normally expect to work in quiet, pleasant, well-ventilated, and well-lighted facilities. They usually work at a desk or table, where they spend most of the day. Many, however, find it necessary to travel to various units of the organization or to other businesses. This is especially true of the consulting actuary.

Actuaries usually work thirty-five to forty hours per week, receive vacation with pay, and are covered by sickness, accident, and hospitalization insurance as well as pension plans.

Social and psychological factors

Actuaries must be able to work either by themselves or with others and be able to express themselves clearly both in speech and in writing. It is absolutely necessary that they maintain high ethical standards if they expect to make progress within the field and if they expect to represent their company as the company wishes to be represented. There is a great amount of detail work requiring much concentration and mental effort, and the stress level among actuaries is relatively high. If properly oriented to the work, however, the actuary will usually find it satisfying, rewarding, and interesting.

GOE: 11.01.02; SIC: 63; SOC: 1732

◇ SOURCES OF ADDITIONAL INFORMATION

American Academy of Actuaries
1720 I Street, NW, 7th Floor
Washington, DC 20006

American Council of Life Insurance
1001 Pennsylvania Avenue, NW
Washington, DC 20004

American Society of Pension Actuaries
2029 K Street, NW, 4th Floor
Washington, DC 20006

Casualty Actuarial Society
One Penn Plaza
250 West 34th Street, 51st Floor
New York, NY 10019

Society of Actuaries
Committee on Education and Examination
475 North Martingale Road
Schaumburg, IL 60143

Adult and vocational education teachers

Definition

Adult and vocational education teachers teach courses that help prepare post–high-school students and other adults for specific occupations or that provide personal enrichment. *Adult education teachers* offer basic education courses, such as reading and writing, or continuing education courses, such as literature and music. *Vocational education teachers* offer courses designed to prepare adults for specific occupations, such as computer programmer or automobile mechanic.

History

Organized education for adults has existed in America since early colonial times, when courses were started to help people make up for schooling they might have missed as children or to help them prepare for jobs. Apprenticeships were an early form of vocational education in the American colonies as individuals were taught a craft by working with a skilled person in a particular field. For example, a young boy might agree to work for a printer for five to ten years and at the end of that time would have the ability and opportunity to open up his own printing business. Training programs continued to develop as carpenters, bricklayers, and other craftspeople learned their skills through vocational training courses.

Peak periods in adult education typically occurred during times of large waves of immigration. Evening schools filled with foreign-born persons eager to learn the language and culture of their new home and to prepare for the tests necessary of citizenship. Following the Civil War, the United States witnessed an educational renaissance characterized by the emergence of hundreds of literary societies and reading circles.

But it has been the twentieth century that has culminated these sporadic efforts into a real movement. In the aftermath of the Industrial Revolution, the impact of science and technology on patterns of living has become so great that people need continuing education to adapt their lifestyles. Also, the rise in educational levels with each generation has spawned a new appreciation for education: the more people learn, the more they want to learn.

In 1911, Wisconsin established the first State Board of Vocational and Adult Education in the country, and in 1917 the federal government threw its support behind the continuing education movement by funding vocational training in public schools for individuals over the age of fourteen. Immediately after World War II, the U.S. federal government took another large stride in financial support of adult and vocational education by creating the G.I. Bill of Rights, which provided money for veterans to pursue further job training.

Today colleges and universities, vocational high schools, private trade schools, private businesses, and other organizations offer adults the opportunity to prepare for a specific occupation or pursue personal enrichment. More than twenty million people in the United States take advantage of this opportunity each year, creating many jobs for teachers in this field.

Nature of the work

Adult and vocational education courses take place in a variety of settings, such as high schools, universities, religious institutions, and businesses. Job responsibilities entail many of the same skills as that of a full-time teacher, including planning and conducting lectures, supervising the use of equipment, grading homework, evaluating students, writing and preparing reports, and counseling students.

Adult education teachers are concerned with either basic education or continuing education. Basic education includes reading, writing, and mathematics courses and is designed for students who have not finished high school yet who are too old to attend a regular high school courses. Many of these student return to school to earn the equivalent of a high-school diploma (GED).

Basic education teachers should be able to deal with students at different skill levels, including some who might not have learned proper study habits. These teachers should be able to clearly explain information that is often complex and unfamiliar. Patience and good communications skills are important.

Adult education teachers who focus on continuing education ordinarily instruct students who have finished high school or college and are taking courses for personal enrichment. Class topics might include history, art appreciation, photography, and a host of other subjects. Teachers should be well versed in their field and be able to communicate knowledge and enthusiasm. Adult education teachers must also be able to teach students who are at different levels of ability and be able to demonstrate techniques if a particular skill, such as painting, is being taught.

Vocational education teachers generally prepare students for specific careers that do not require a college degree, such as cosmetologist, chef, or automobile repair. Teaching methods usually include demonstrating techniques and having the students observe and then emulate these techniques. For example, an instructor teaching computer maintenance will show students the tools and techniques necessary to repair a computer.

A vocational education teacher will also need to present effectively appropriate material in lectures and discussion groups.

Teachers who specialize in service-industry areas include *psychiatric aide instructors*, who provide clinical and academic training in psychiatric nursing; *business education instructors*, who provide instruction in secretarial procedures, office equipment use, and other commercial subjects; *flying instructors*, who may teach Federal Aviation Administration regulations in addition to flight procedures; *ground services instructors*, who teach airport personnel air-transportation policies, regulations, and procedures, such as load planning, reservations, and ticketing; *training representatives*, who provide instruction for employees of business and governmental organizations; *customer-service-representative instructors*, who teach employees company policies, systems, and routines for handling customers' requests; *police-academy instructors*, who teach investigative methods, law, marksmanship, and self-defense; *field-service representatives*, who train persons to recognize and repair aircraft malfunctions; and *bus, trolley, and taxi instructors*, who teach students how to drive vehicles, repair minor malfunctions, keep records, and file accident reports.

Teachers specializing in goods-producing areas include *vocational training instructors*, who teach specific trades in schools or in industrial plants; *weaving instructors*, who teach workers how to operate looms among other weaving techniques; *textile instructors*, who teach workers how to operate machinery, examine cloth for defects, and grade cloth according to quality standards; *watch assembly instructors*, who teach workers how to use precision procedures and tools to make wristwatches; *pottery and porcelain decorating instructors*, who provide training in painting decorations on plates, bowls, and other dinnerware; *apparel manufacture instructors*, who provide training in maintaining knitting, looping, and sewing machines; *rocket-motor case assembly instructors*, who teach workers how to assemble, inspect, and repair rocket-motor cases;

Teachers who specialize in areas of personal, individual interest include *driving instructors*, who lecture on traffic laws and teach skills using actual vehicles and driving simulators; *correspondence school instructors*, who provide and grade material on various subjects via the mail; *modeling instructors*, who demonstrate self-improvement techniques including good posture, wardrobe coordination, and cosmetic application; *art teachers*, who instruct pupils in painting, sketching, designing, sculpting, and other art techniques; *drama teachers*, who teach

17

A teacher is instructing new American citizens the English language. English is just one of many subjects available for adult education.

tification that that field requires. Teacher certification and coursework covering techniques in teaching vocational subjects may also be required to teach in high schools and technical and community colleges.

Many adult education teachers must also have prior experience in their chosen field as well as teacher certification. Specific skills, however, are often enough to secure a continuing education teaching position. For example, a person well trained in painting may be able to teach a course on painting even without a college degree or teaching certificate.

Special requirements

Many states require teacher certification for both adult and vocational education teachers. For information on certification requirements contact the department of education of the individual states.

Opportunities for experience and exploration

High-school students have many opportunities to see adult or vocational education teachers at work. Often high schools will be the site of an adult or vocational education class and students may discuss career questions with teachers before or after an actual class. Some high-school instructors may teach adult or vocational education courses part-time, and these instructors may be another good source for career information. Registering for a continuing education or vocational education course is another way of discovering the skills and disciplines needed to succeed in this field.

Students who think they may be interested in becoming adult education instructors might consider volunteering to tutor their peers in high school and college. Also, those with special skills or hobbies might offer to share their knowledge at local community centers or retirement homes.

diction, dialects, and body expression, as well as other elements of stagecraft, play writing, and play direction; *music teachers*, who instruct individuals and groups in instrumental or vocal music, and may also teach music appreciation, theory, sight-reading, and composition; *physical-education instructors*, who provide training in calisthenics, gymnastics, and other health-related activities; and *bridge instructors*, who teach the card game's suits and values, methods of scoring, and playing of hands.

Requirements

Most adult and vocational education teachers have professional experience in their area of teaching. Requirements vary according to the subject and level being taught, and the state in which the instruction takes place. Many states now require a teacher to have a bachelor's or graduate degree in the subject being taught. To teach vocational education courses, an instructor usually needs several years experience in a particular field as well as any professional cer-

Related occupations

Adult and vocational education teachers possess many of the same organizational, communications, and administrative skills as other teachers, school administrators, and social workers.

Methods of entering

The primary means of entry is to have several years of professional experience in a particular field, a desire to share that knowledge with other adults, and often, a teaching certificate or academic degree. People with these qualifications should contact college, private trade schools, vocational high schools, or other appropriate institutions to receive additional information about employment opportunities.

Advancement

A skilled adult or vocational education teacher may become a full-time teacher, a school administrator, or a director of a vocational guidance program. To be an administrator, a master's degree or a doctorate may be required. Advancement may also take the form of higher pay and additional teaching assignments. For example, a person may get a reputation as a skilled ceramics teacher and be employed by other adult education organization as an instructor.

Employment outlook

Employment opportunities are expected to grow about as fast as the average for all occupations during the early 1990s. The biggest growth areas are projected to be in computer technology, automotive mechanics, and medical technology. As demand for adult and vocational education teachers continues to grow, major employers will be vocational high schools, private trade schools, community colleges, and private adult education enterprises. The federal government will also offer opportunities such as the Department of Agriculture's programs to teach farming skills. Labor unions also will have a need for teachers, as they offer continuing education opportunities to their members.

About half of all employment opportunities are part-time, so many adult and vocational education teachers also have other jobs, often in unrelated areas.

Earnings

Because many adult and vocational education teachers are employed part-time, they are often paid by the hour, with no health insurance or other benefits. Hourly rates range from $6 to $50 an hour and depend heavily on the subject being taught, the training and education of the instructor, and the geographic region of the institution.

Full-time adult and vocational education teachers can expect to earn between $14,500 and $24,000 a year to start, with yearly earnings being greatly influenced by the same variables that affect part-time work. Experienced instructors can earn between $25,000 and $35,000 a year, with some highly skilled teachers earning even more.

Conditions of work

Working conditions vary according to the type of class being taught and the number of students participating. Courses are usually taught in a classroom setting, but may also occur in a technical shop, laboratory, art studio, music room, or other location depending on the subject matter. Average class size is usually between ten and thirty students, but may vary, ranging from one-on-one instruction to large lectures attended by sixty to seventy students.

Like many other types of teachers, adult and vocational education teachers may only work nine or ten months a year, with summers off. About half of the adult and vocational education teachers work part-time, averaging anywhere from two to twenty hours of work per week. For those employed full-time, the average work week is between thirty-five and forty hours. Much of the work is in the evening or on weekends, as many adult students work on weekdays.

Social and psychological factors

An adult or vocational teacher should feel comfortable teaching a wide variety of students. Some of these students may have had behavioral patterns that kept them from completing a comprehensive high school. Patience, energy, and good communications skills are vital. A teacher should be able to explain sometimes complex information in a variety of ways and with patience and compassion. Many hours of out-of-class preparation may be required, especially when a teacher is just beginning.

Leadership skills are important as a teacher directs and influences a large number of students and may also work with a teacher's assistant. A teacher should be comfortable talking in front of a group and also be able to counsel students one-on-one. A teacher must be able to work effectively with students in the classroom and also work with administrative officials, such as a principal, in the development of course material.

Although there is sometimes the need to work under pressure, the rewards that come from helping people in an educational framework can be great.

GOE: 11.02.01, 11.02.02; SIC: 82; SOC: 239

◇ **SOURCES OF ADDITIONAL INFORMATION**

American Vocational Association
1410 King Street
Alexandria, VA 22314

National Community Education Association
119 North Payne Street
Alexandria, VA 22314

American Association for Adult and Continuing Education
1112 16th Street, NW, Suite 420
Washington, DC 20036

◇ **RELATED ARTICLES**

Volume 1: Education
Volume 2: College and university faculty; School administrators; Teachers, kindergarten and elementary school; Teachers, preschool; Teachers, secondary school

Advertising workers

Definition

The purpose of advertising is to attract buyers. *Advertising workers* plan, research, create, produce, and place ads for clients who make or have products or services to sell. They appeal to the public through newspaper and magazine ads, radio and television commercials, and outdoor displays.

History

The merchant who 7,000 years ago stood in an Egyptian marketplace and called to the crowd to come see the quality of some new wares was advertising. The minstrel who traveled across ancient Europe singing and playing along the way was also advertising. Advertising by word of mouth was popular for many centuries because few people could read or write. Yet, during the same period of time, enterprising merchants used objects and signs to advertise. In Shakespeare's England, for example, a green bush hanging over the entrance to a shop meant that it was a wineshop. The sign of a spinning wheel identified the weaver's shop.

Two jars of colored water, seen even today in many drugstores, were the symbol of the apothecary.

As cities grew and more people learned to read, advertising increased in complexity. Following the invention of the printing press, merchants advertised their services by posting handbills anywhere that crowds might gather. In the eighteenth century, when newspapers gained popularity, they carried advertisements for everything from tea to wigs and medicines to take away warts. One of the problems confronting merchants in those days was where to place their advertisements so they would do the merchant the most good. Many of those merchants discovered that an agent who specialized in accepting advertisements and posting them conspicuously could be hired. These agents undoubtedly were the first advertising workers. As competition grew, many of these agents offered to compose as well as post the advertisements for their clients.

In more recent times, advertising has become very important to businesses. With increased competition among new business establishments, advertising has become vital. The advertising worker's job also has grown more complex as the means of advertising become more numerous newspapers, magazines, posters, billboards, radio, and television. Today, advertising is a necessity in the marketing of mass-produced goods. Advertising informs many people of what is for sale, where, at what price, and why they should buy it.

Nature of the work

There are a number of major categories of advertising workers. Job descriptions may differ for each worker, although they do have a correlation in their work. Large advertising agencies may employ hundreds of people to work in a dozen different departments, while small agencies may have a handful of employees whose responsibilities cover more than one aspect of the work. Most agencies, however, have at least five departments: contact, planning, and marketing; research and development; media; creative; and production. (*See also* Volume 1: Advertising.)

Advertising agency managers are concerned with the overall activities of the agency. They formulate plans to generate more business by soliciting new accounts or additional business from established accounts. They meet with department heads to coordinate their operations and to set up policies and procedures. (*See also* the article titled "Marketing, advertising, and public relations managers" elsewhere in this volume.)

Account executives are responsible for maintaining good relations between the agency and specific clients assigned to the executives. After studying a client's advertising problems, account executives develop an advertising campaign or strategy, including a budget. With the client's approval, then, they work with all the departments of the agency (research, media, creative, production) to complete the campaign. As a necessary part of the job, account executives must be able to sell ideas and have some knowledge of overall marketing strategies.

In some agencies, an account supervisor directs the work of several account executives and may be directly responsible to the head of the agency. (For more information on account executives *see also* the article titled "Marketing, advertising, and public relations managers" elsewhere in this volume.)

Research and development directors gather and analyze information needed to make a client's advertising campaign successful. They try to find out who the buyers will be and what theme will have the most impact, what kind of

packaging and price will have the most appeal, and which media will be most effective.

Research and development directors conduct local, regional, or national surveys to determine potential sales for the product or service offered and gather information about competitors' products, prices, sales, and methods of advertising. They use this information to study the client's product and to determine how it may be used to best advantage. To find the advantages and disadvantages of a client's product in relation to competing products, samples are often distributed to a segment of the public. Later, the users of these samples are asked their opinion of the product. This information may be used immediately to find the most convincing selling theme or later as testimonials for the product. With the available information on purchasing power, buying habits, and preferences of people, research directors can help determine how, when, and where the client's product might be introduced to the public.

Media planners are specialists employed by agencies because of their ability to determine which print or broadcast media will be most effective. They choose the medium that will reach the greatest number of potential buyers with minimal cost to the client. Media planners must know and be able to judge what kinds and how many people in what parts of the nation can be reached through various publications, radio and television broadcasts, and other media. (For more information about media planners *see also* the article titled "Marketing, advertising, and public relations managers" elsewhere in this volume.)

Media buyers, often referred to as *space buyers* or *time buyers* (space referring to newspapers and magazines, and time referring to radio and television), do the actual purchasing of time and space, under a general plan laid down by the media director, who supervises the work of planners and buyers. Buyers maintain heavy telephone contact and keep up extensive correspondence with people from the media.

Media assistants are responsible for the detail work involved in planning and buying space and time. They keep detailed records of when an ad appeared, for which client, and at what cost. They also help planners research and analyze the numbers and percentages of consumers using media.

Creative directors develop the creative concept for advertising materials and direct the activities of artists and writers involved in carrying out the plans. They confer with the client and with agency department heads to determine the approach to be taken and to set up budgets and schedules. When layouts are com-

This artist is using a blade to carefully cut and paste artwork for a new advertisement that he is designing.

pleted, the creative director presents them to the client for approval.

Art directors plan the visual presentation of the client's message. Just as copywriters create a message with words, art directors create a message with pictures and designs that reinforces the advertising strategy and copy. Art directors who work on filmed commercials combine film techniques, music and sound, and actors to influence the viewers.

Art directors need to have a basic knowledge of graphics and design, printing, photography, and filmmaking. With the help of layout artists, they decide on placement of pictures and text, choose typefaces for the printed matter, and make sketches of the ads. Generally several layouts are submitted to the client, who chooses one. The art director then selects an illustrator or photographer, or a TV producer, and the project goes to the production department of the agency.

Copywriters take the ideas submitted by account executives and creative directors and write descriptive copy in the form of headlines, jingles, slogans, and other techniques designed to attract the attention of potential buyers. Some products appeal to special groups of people, such as business executives or sports enthusiasts; the media these people read or watch would be used to sell products to them. In addition to being able to write, copywriters must know something about people and what makes them buy; they must also know the product and be familiar with the various advertising media.

Copywriters work closely with art directors to make sure that type and artwork together form a unified, eye-catching arrangement. In large agencies, copywriters may work under the supervision of a copy chief.

Production departments in large ad agencies may be divided into print production and radio and TV production departments, each with its own managers and staff.

Production managers and their assistants convert and reproduce written copy and artwork into printed, filmed, or tape-recorded form so it can be presented to the public. They work closely with printing, engraving, and other firms concerned with the reproduction of advertisements and must be familiar with various printing processes, papers, inks, typography, still and motion picture photography, and other processes and materials.

Many advertising workers are not necessarily found working in an advertising agency. In the advertising field, talent can be utilized in positions such as artists and writers, researchers and statisticians, media specialists and administrators, accountants, secretaries, clerks, photographers, and printers. Advertising workers are employed in many kinds of business organizations. The greater number are, however, employed by advertising agencies that plan and prepare advertising material for their clients on a commission or service fee basis.

Some large industries, however, and nearly all department stores prefer to handle their own advertising. Advertising workers in such organizations prepare ads especially for their employers. They may also be involved in the planning, preparation, and publication of special promotional materials such as sales brochures or articles describing the activities of the organization.

Some advertising workers are employed by owners of advertising media such as newspapers, magazines, radio and television networks, and outdoor advertisers. Workers employed in these media are mainly *sales representatives* who sell advertising space or broadcast time to advertising agencies or companies that maintain their own advertising departments.

Advertising services and supply houses employ photographers, photoengravers, typographers, printers, marketing research specialists, product and package designers, producers of display materials, and others who assist in the preparation of various advertising materials.

Requirements

So many different kinds of work are done by advertising workers that it would be impossible to write a single set of qualifications for all of them. As far as educational requirements are concerned, no one pattern of education or background preparation for success as an advertising worker can be found. The American Association of Advertising Agencies notes that most agencies employing beginners today prefer college graduates. While art directors, TV producers, and production department workers are less likely to need a college degree, for copywriters and for media and research workers, it is almost mandatory. Copywriters should have a bachelor's degree. Media directors and research directors with a master's degree have a distinct advantage over those with only an undergraduate degree. And some research department heads even have doctorates. Most account executives have a degree in business administration.

While the requirements of agencies may vary somewhat, graduates of liberal arts colleges or graduates with majors in such fields as journalism, business administration, or marketing research are preferred. A good knowledge of English is a necessity for advertising workers, but their education should also include a variety of literature courses and social studies courses such as sociology, psychology, and economics. Other courses useful to various advertising workers include writing, math and statistics, advertising and marketing, art, philosophy, and languages. Some 900 degree-granting institutions throughout the United States offer specialized majors in advertising as a part of their curriculum.

Special requirements

Emphasis is placed on one's ability to use language, both spoken and written, and visual communication. Working with ideas is essential because the purpose of the advertising worker is to sway the public to the point of buying. New and imaginative approaches toward this goal are the responsibility of the advertising worker.

Opportunities for experience and exploration

Some experience can be gained by taking writing and art courses in school. Summer vacation jobs in advertising or sales provide good background. Part- or full-time work in a local department store or newspaper office is also helpful. Some advertising or research organizations employ students to interview people or do other types of work connected with marketing research. In some cases it may be possible to obtain work in an advertising agency as a clerk or messenger who picks up or distributes to various departments within an agency or to service houses associated with an agency.

Internships in an advertising agency or department store that does its own advertising are a way of exploring and determining where an individual's personal characteristics and qualifications can best be used in advertising work. Work in marketing departments of large companies that do a lot of advertising is also valuable experience.

Related occupations

The marketing and public relations fields also are involved in communicating information about a firms' products, services, or activities. Occupations in these areas include art directors, commercial and graphic artists, copy chiefs, copywriters, editors, lobbyists, market research analysts, public relations specialists, sales promotion specialists, sales representatives, and technical writers.

Methods of entering

Some of the larger advertising agencies recruit college graduates and place them in training programs designed to acquaint the beginner with all aspects of advertising work, but these opportunities are limited and highly competitive. Many graduates, however, enter by applying to business establishments that have a need for beginners in advertising work. Newspapers, radio and television stations, printers, photographers, as well as advertising agencies, are but a few examples of businesses employing advertising workers. Persons who have had work experience in sales positions often enter the advertising field. High-school graduates employed in advertising may find it necessary to begin as clerks or assistants to research and production staff members or to copywriters. The *Standard Directory of Advertising Agencies* lists the names and addresses of ad agencies. Persons interested in applying for employment with any of these companies can find the directory in almost any public library.

Advancement

The path of advancement in an advertising agency generally leads from trainee to skilled worker to division head and then to department head. It may also lead from department to department as an employee gains responsibility with each move. Opportunities are limitless for those with talent, leadership capability, and ambition. Many of the top advertising executives reached that position before the age of forty.

Management positions require experience in all aspects of advertising, including work experience in an agency, with advertisers, and in various advertising media. If copywriters, account executives, and other workers employed by advertising agencies demonstrate outstanding ability to deal with clients and supervise co-workers, they usually have a good opportunity to advance to management positions. Other workers, however, prefer to acquire specialized skills, and for them advancement may mean more responsible work and increased pay.

Advertising workers in department stores, mail order houses, and other large firms that have their own advertising departments also can earn promotion. Advancement in any phase of advertising work is usually dependent on experience, training, and past work effectiveness. Some qualified copywriters and account executives set up their own agencies.

Employment outlook

In the early 1990s more than 250,000 persons worked in jobs that required knowledge of advertising skills and techniques. Advertising agency workers were concentrated in Chicago, New York, and Los Angeles, but retail and small advertising firms existed throughout the country.

Employment opportunities in the advertising field are expected to increase rapidly through the late 1990s. A demand should arise for additional workers to create and carry out advertising plans so that advertisers can effectively compete in a market overflowing with domestic and foreign products and services being offered to consumers.

It is projected that advertising agencies will enjoy much faster than average employment growth, as will industries that service the agencies and other businesses in the advertising field, such as establishments that offer commercial photography, art, graphics services, and direct mail. Opportunities for advertising workers look very favorable in the radio and television industry as well, as this medium is increasingly used for commercial messages.

In addition to the new jobs, many openings will become available to replace workers who change positions, retire, or leave the field for other reasons. Competition for these jobs will be keen, however, because of the large number of qualified professionals in this traditionally desirable field. Opportunities will be best for the well-qualified and well-trained applicant. Employers favor those who are college graduates and who have experience and can demonstrate a high level of creativity and strong communications skills. Persons who are not well qualified or prepared for agency work will find the advertising field increasingly difficult to enter. This will also be true for those who seek work outside of agencies.

Earnings

Salaries of advertising workers vary depending on the type of work, the size of the agency, its geographical location, the kind of accounts handled, and the agency's gross earnings. Salaries are also affected by amount of education, aptitude, and experience.

In the early 1990s, earnings for experienced workers in advertising agencies averaged $71,200 a year for the chief executives, $59,700 for account supervisors, and $31,400 for account executives. Research directors made $61,000 a year. In the creative departments, the directors earned $59,000, the copywriters $35,900, and the art directors $34,000. Salaries for media workers averaged $46,000 for media directors, $25,600 for media planners, and $23,500 for media buyers. Production managers were paid about $31,000 a year.

In other businesses and industries, heads of advertising departments had annual earnings of about $57,000, and advertising managers made $38,000. Media managers were paid $38,500, whereas media planners and media buyers averaged $26,400 a year. Salaries of advertising workers are generally higher in consumer product firms than in industrial product firms because of the competition in consumer product sales.

The wide range of jobs in advertising makes it difficult to estimate average salaries for all of them. Entry-level jobs, of course, may pay considerably less than the figures given in the preceding paragraphs. The young person interested in advertising should realize that salaries are dependent on such factors as experience, the quality of work produced, size and location of the advertising agency, and its accounts.

Conditions of work

Persons interested in advertising work will find that the best opportunities for employment are found in large cities, especially in New York, Chicago, Detroit, and Los Angeles. The same is true for those interested in entering the field through advertising service and media. Some major agencies, however, do operate branches in various smaller cities throughout the nation, and a number of independent agencies also exist in and around large metropolitan areas. Conditions in most agencies are similar to those found in other offices throughout the country, except that workers must frequently work under great pressure to meet deadlines. A normal forty-hour week can be expected but may include evening and weekend work when necessary. Bonus checks and time off during slack periods sometimes are means of compensation for unusual workload and hours. Usually advertising workers find their jobs a constant challenge to their initiative, imagination, and creative abilities.

Social and psychological factors

A variety of educational and work experiences are necessary for those interested in advertising. Personal characteristics are also important. Advertising workers must like and be able to get along well with people. Workers must be able to function independently but must also be able to cooperate with others in the joint effort needed to plan and carry off an advertising program. Advertising workers also are involved with numerous clients whose products or services differ. Advertising is not, therefore, a job that involves routine, and workers must be able

to meet and adjust to the challenge presented by each new product or service advertised. The ability to think clearly and logically is important, because commonsense approaches rather than gimmicks convince people that something is worth buying. Imagination is also necessary, not only to create effective advertising, but also to keep up with consumer demand and, if possible, to anticipate it. In general, advertising workers should be imaginative, flexible, creative, and interested in people and have the ability to sell ideas, products, and services of their clients.

GOE: 01.02.03, 01.06.01, 11.09.01; SIC: 7311, 8999; SOC: 125, 322, 3313, 4153, 71

◇ SOURCES OF ADDITIONAL INFORMATION

American Advertising Federation
1400 K Street, NW, Suite 1000
Washington, DC 20005

American Association of Advertising Agencies
666 Third Avenue, 13th Floor
New York, NY 10017

Association of National Advertisers
155 East 44th Street
New York, NY 10017

Business/Professional Advertising Association
100 Metropolex Drive
Edison, NJ 08817

◇ RELATED ARTICLES

Volume 1: Advertising; Marketing; Packaging; Public Relations
Volume 2: Commercial artists; Designers; Marketing, advertising, and public relations managers; Marketing research personnel; Media specialists; Photographers and camera operators; Public relations specialists; Writers and editors
Volume 3: Display workers; Radio, television, and print advertising sales workers
Volume 4: Museum technicians; Packaging and paper products technicians

Air traffic controllers

Definition

Air traffic controllers organize and direct the movement of aircraft into and out of the airport. They issue control instructions and advisories by radio to the pilots to provide for the safe, orderly, and expeditious flow of air traffic both in the air and on the ground.

History

The history of air traffic controllers follows very closely the development of air travel in general. It is difficult to determine when air traffic controllers began their work, but as daily flights increased, some method of control became necessary. Added to these passenger-carrying flights were thousands of cargo or air-freight flights, all of which placed a tremendous traffic burden on the existing airport facilities.

Also, it was necessary that pilots receive in-flight information on weather, other air traffic in their area, and flight conditions in general. Thus, air traffic controllers were employed to assist in carrying out these control functions. The use of *Instrument Landing System* (ILS) allowed the number of planes being tracked to increase dramatically. *Airport Surveillance Radar* allows controllers to survey air activity in a 50 mile radius.

Nature of the work

Almost all air traffic controllers are employees of the Federal Aviation Administration (FAA), which is responsible for ensuring the safe, orderly, and expeditious flow of air traffic. Controllers work in one of three different areas: airport traffic control towers, air route traffic control centers, or flight service stations.

Tower air traffic control specialists supervise flight operations within a specific area surrounding an airport. These employees are stationed in about 328 airport control towers to issue clearances or authorization to the pilots of planes ready for takeoff, those preparing to land, and those flying within the area. They coordinate the altitudes at which planes within the area will fly and advise the pilots regarding weather, wind direction, and the relative position of other aircraft. Their advice is based on their own observations, information received from the National Weather Service, air route traffic control en route centers, flight service stations, aircraft pilots, and other sources.

Controllers maintain separation between landing and departing aircraft, transfer control of planes on instrument flights leaving their airspace to the en route controllers, and receive control of planes on instrument flights coming into their airspace from controllers at adjacent facilities.

Air traffic control specialists control the movements of a number of aircraft within the area, and these vehicles usually appear as tiny bars, or "blips," on a radar screen. Because of this, they must be able to recall quickly the registration number of each plane under their control, its type and speed, and its position in the air and must take these facts into consideration as they give instructions and information to other aircraft. They must also remain in contact with the air traffic control centers so as to more efficiently control traffic and prevent congestion in the area.

Air traffic coordinators, or *en route controllers*, work at one of twenty-four regional centers in the United States. They coordinate the movements of en route aircraft between airports but out of range of the airport traffic controllers. Through radar and electronic equipment, they maintain contact with planes within their area, giving instructions, air traffic clearances, and advice about flight conditions. They keep track of all flights within the center's airspace and transfer control of the aircraft to controllers in the adjacent center or to the approach control or terminal when the craft enters that facility's airspace. En route controllers work in teams of two or three, depending on how heavy the traffic is in their area.

Station air traffic control specialists make up the third group of controllers. They provide preflight or in-flight assistance to pilots from more than 300 flight service stations linked by a broad communications system. These controllers give pilots information about the station's particular area, including terrain, weather, and anything else necessary to guarantee a safe flight. They may suggest alternate routes or different altitudes, alert pilots to military operations taking place along certain routes, inform them about landing at airports that have no towers, assist pilots in emergency situations, and participate in searches for missing or overdue aircraft.

Requirements

Trainees for air traffic control positions are selected from applicants who receive a high score on a federal civil service examination. The written test measures aptitudes for arithmetic, abstract reasoning, three-dimensional spatial visualization, and other indicators of an ability to learn the controller's duties.

Applicants for airport tower or en route traffic control jobs must be less than thirty-one years of age, pass physical and psychological examinations, and have vision that is or can be corrected to 20/20.

They must also have completed a four-year degree program in a recognized college or have three years of responsible experience in administrative, professional, investigative, technical, or other types of work that would prepare the applicant to take on a position of great responsibility. Equivalent combinations of the previously mentioned requirements are also considered.

All applicants are interviewed in an effort to determine if the candidates have the required alertness, decisiveness, motivation, the necessary poise, and the ability to work under extreme pressure.

Those accepted into the training program receive eleven to seventeen weeks of intensive instruction at the FAA Academy in Oklahoma City. There they receive training in the fundamentals of the airway systems, civil air regulations, radar, and aircraft performance characteristics. They practice on machines designed to simulate emergency situations to determine their emotional stability under pressure, stress, and strain. The standards for those who successfully complete this program are very high; about 50 percent of the trainees are dropped during this period.

After completing the program, it takes several years of experience, rigorous on-the-job training, and further study to become a fully qualified controller.

New controllers at airport towers usually begin as ground controllers. As they become progressively more competent, they move up to local controllers, departure controllers, and finally arrival controllers. New en route controllers begin by delivering printed flight plans to teams, before advancing to radar associate controllers and then radar controllers.

Special requirements

Persons hoping to enter the field must be articulate, have a good memory, and self-control.

The air traffic controller monitors the flow of airplanes in and out of an airport. Such a task involves intense concentration.

It is imperative that they be able to express themselves clearly, remember rapidly changing data that affects their decisions, and be able to operate calmly under very difficult situations involving a great deal of strain. They must also be able to make good, sound, and quickly derived decisions. A poor decision may mean the loss of a large number of lives.

Air traffic controllers are required to take a physical examination every year and a performance exam twice a year.

The only license they hold is the air traffic control certificate. Failure to become certified within a specific time is cause for dismissal.

Opportunities for experience and exploration

Those persons interested in this occupation and who live near an airfield may be able to arrange a visit for on-site observations of the work carried on by these people. Talks with those employed in the field would be helpful.

A number of opportunities exist in the military service for people to gain experience in these and related jobs, which may provide an excellent opportunity for exploration while the individual is gaining necessary experience.

Other possibilities include talking with pilots, who see air traffic controllers from a different viewpoint.

Most airlines will supply those interested with all the information available in either of these two areas, and many will be helpful in arranging interviews either with those employed as traffic controllers or with pilots.

Related occupations

Other workers who are involved in the direction and control of air traffic include airline radio operators and airplane dispatchers.

Methods of entering

As might be expected, experience in related fields, including those of pilots, air dispatch operators, navigators, or other positions in the military service, or in actual air control work is a necessity for the person who does not have a college degree, and it is desirable even for those with the degree. Thus, one of the better methods of entering would be to start in one of the related fields, either with a civilian airline or in the military service.

The field is entered through the federal civil service system, which requires passing the written examination, the physical examination, and the interview. Placement is on a competitive basis.

Advancement

After becoming a controller, those who do particularly well may reach the level of supervisor or manager. Many others advance to even more responsible positions in air control, and others might work into some of the top administrative jobs with the FAA. Competitive civil service status can be earned at the end of one year on the job, and career status after the satisfactory completion of three years of work in the area.

In the case of both airport control operators and en route control operators, the responsibilities become more complex with each successive promotion.

Employees in the higher grades may be responsible for a number of different areas, including the coordination of the traffic control activities within the control area; the supervision and training of en route traffic controllers or airport traffic controllers in lower positions; and maintaining good relationships with various aeronautical agencies.

Employment outlook

The demand for people in this field is expected to grow slowly through the late 1990s because of the expected introduction of new, automated control equipment. There will be some increase in opportunities because of recent congressional actions and greater demand for air travel, but most of the job openings will occur when older, more experienced controllers change employment, retire, or otherwise leave the field. Competition for these jobs will be stiff, however, because the relatively high pay and liberal retirement program of this occupation attract many more qualified applicants than are needed to fill the openings.

Of the nearly 23,500 air traffic controllers employed in the early 1990s, almost half were airport traffic controllers working in control towers at key airfields. The rest were employed at air route traffic control centers and flight service stations throughout the United States, Guam, and Puerto Rico. The vast majority of all air traffic controllers worked for the Federal Aviation Administration, some worked for the Department of Defense, and others were employed by private air traffic control companies to provide service to non FAA towers.

In this relatively small field, employment opportunities will be best for college graduates and individuals with civil or military experience as controllers, pilots, or navigators. Those who are hired will enjoy more job security than workers in most other occupations. Air traffic controllers may face a decline in their workload during recessions, when there is less demand for air travel, but they are seldom laid off.

Earnings

The pay scale for air traffic controllers varies from year to year, depending on increases approved by Congress. In the early 1990s, trainees started at about $18,400 a year, while controllers at the top levels earned approximately $47,000 to $59,000. The average salary for all controllers was about $37,400 per year. Some workers with a great deal of seniority earned in excess of $63,000. Because of the complexity of their job duties and the tension involved in their work, air traffic controllers are offered special dispensation or compensation, including a more liberal retirement program, than other federal employees.

Conditions of work

Depending on length of service air traffic controllers receive thirteen to twenty-six days of paid vacation and thirteen days of paid sick leave per year, plus life insurance and health benefits. In addition, they are permitted to retire earlier and with fewer years of service than other federal employees.

Controllers are employed on a basic forty-hour week, If they work additional hours, they receive overtime pay or equivalent time off. They may be required to work nights and weekends on a rotation basis, because most control towers and centers must be operated twenty-four hours a day, seven days per week. Usually a higher salary is paid those who work between 6:00 P.M. and 6:00 A.M. This may amount to about ten percent above the regular base pay.

The working facilities are usually clean, well lighted, and ventilated.

Social and psychological factors

The work pace may change from one moment to the next as airplanes enter or leave the area. There is a continuous pressure, however, and the constant feeling that a number of pilots are relying upon the controller for correct, accurate information and advice. The strain becomes even more severe as emergencies develop. It is not an easy job, and only those people who are emotionally stable should enter the field. There is, however, a feeling of accomplishment in knowing that the job is a highly important one and that the responsibilities, when properly carried out, mean much safer air transportation for everyone.

GOE: 05.03.03; SIC: 4581, 9621; SOC: 392

◇ **SOURCES OF ADDITIONAL INFORMATION**

Air Traffic Control Association
2020 North 14th Street, Suite 410
Arlington, VA 22201

Federal Aviation Administration
Office of Personnel and Training
800 Independence Avenue, SW
Washington, DC 20591

National Association of Air Traffic Specialists
4780 Corridor Place, #B
Beltsville, MD 20705

◇ **RELATED ARTICLES**

Volume 1: Aviation and Aerospace; Military Service; Transportation
Volume 2: Pilots; Radio and telegraph operators
Volume 3: Airplane dispatchers; Flight engineers
Volume 4: Aeronautical and aerospace technicians; Avionics technicians

Animal trainers

Definition

Animal trainers teach animals, including aquatic mammals and birds, to obey commands, to compete in shows or races, or to perform tricks to entertain audiences. They also may teach dogs to protect property or to act as guides for the visually impaired. Animal trainers may specialize with one type of animal or with several types. Elephant trainers, for example, require years of practice and training before they are able to train an elephant alone.

History

Animals have long been trained for pure entertainment. Generations of children have felt the thrill of placing a penny in the tiny paw of the organ-grinder's monkey. Crowds have watched as the snake charmer mesmerized his deadly companion. There have been dancing bears and prancing horses, dogs who turned somersaults, performing chimps and elephants, and parrots who recited rhymes. Circuses used trained animals long before zoos were common.

The training of animals, however, actually began thousands of years ago for very practical purposes. Evidence found in archaeological digs indicates that dogs may have been the first animals to be domesticated. They were used by Stone Age Europeans to help hunt down wild game for food. Then, when tribes banded together in agricultural communities, dogs were trained to herd other domesticated animals, such as goats and sheep, and to stand guard at campsites and outside of dwellings. The ancient Egyptians are known to have bred special qualities into dogs intended for specific purposes.

Early humans quickly saw the advantages of training larger animals to do much of the heavy labor involved in farming and building. Horses, water buffalo, elephants, and camels are among the animals used by various cultures to pull wagons and plows and to carry heavy loads. They also served as the sole means of transportation, carrying passengers on their backs or drawing wheeled carts and carriages, until animals were replaced by engine-driven vehicles.

Animal training today is still an important activity. Some animals are trained simply to be well-behaved pets, others for sports or entertainment. Still others are taught to do useful work. Humankind's first animal friend, the dog, for example, can be found doing police work, guiding the blind, guarding valuable property, and working with farm animals.

Nature of the work

Many different animals are capable of being trained, from dogs and horses to lions, bears, and elephants; from parakeets and cockatoos to whales, porpoises, and seals. The techniques used to train them, however, are basically the same, regardless of the type of animal.

Animal trainers conduct a program consisting primarily of repetition and reward to teach animals to behave in a particular manner and to do it consistently. First the trainers evaluate an animal's temperament, ability, and aptitude to determine whether it is trainable and which methods would be most effect. Then, by painstakingly repeating routines many times, rewarding the animal with a treat whenever it does what is expected, they train it to obey or perform on command. In addition, animal trainers generally are responsible for the feeding, exercising, grooming, and general care of the animals, either handling the duties themselves or supervising other workers.

Trainers usually specialize and are identified by the animal they work with. Some of them organize or direct animal shows and sometimes take part in an act; they may also rehearse animals for specific motion pictures, television films, stage productions, or circus programs, and sometimes cue the animals during a performance.

Not all trainers prepare animals for the entertainment field, however. *Dog trainers*, for example, may work with dogs to be used in police work to search for drugs or missing persons. Some train guard dogs to protect private property; others train guide dogs for the blind and may help dog and master function as a team.

Horse trainers specialize in training horses for riding or for harness. They talk to and handle the horse gently to accustom them to human contact, then gradually get them to accept harnesses, bridles, saddles, and other riding gear. Following the general methods previously described, the trainers teach the horses to respond to commands that are either spoken or given by use of the reins, and in some cases the spurs. Draft horses are then ready for further conditioning so they can be relied on to draw equipment either alone or as part of a team. Show horses are given special training to qualify them to perform in competitions. Horse trainers sometimes have to retrain animals that have developed bad habits, such as bucking or biting. Besides feeding, exercising, and grooming, these trainers sometimes make arrangements for breeding the horses and may help mares deliver their foals.

A highly specialized occupation in the horse-training field is that of *racehorse trainers*, who must create a training plan for each horse individually. By studying the animal's performance record and becoming familiar with its behavior during workouts, they can adapt their training methods to take advantage of its peculiarities. Like other animal trainers, racehorse trainers oversee the exercising, grooming, and feeding of their charges. They also clock the running time during workouts to determine when a horse is ready for competitive racing. Racehorse trainers coach jockeys on how best to handle a particular horse during a race and may give owners advice on purchasing horses.

Requirements

Above all, persons wanting to be animal trainers should like animals and have a genuine interest in working with them. Animals can't be fooled; they will respond more favorably to someone who is sensitive to their nature.

Establishments that hire trainers often require previous experience as an animal keeper or aquarist, because proper care and feeding of the animals is an essential part of a trainer's responsibilities. Racehorse trainers often begin as jockeys or grooms in training stables.

Although there are no formal education requirements to enter this field, animal trainers in zoos, circuses, and the entertainment field are sometimes required to have some education in animal psychology in addition to their caretaking experience. Trainers of guide dogs for the blind prepare for their work in a three-year course of study at a school that trains the dogs and instructs their blind owners.

Most trainers begin their careers as keepers and gain on-the-job experience in evaluating the disposition, intelligence, and trainability of the animals they look after. At the same time, they learn to make friends with their charges, develop a rapport with them, and gain their confidence. The caretaking experience is an important building block in the education and success of an animal trainer. Although previous training experience may give job applicants an advantage in being hired, they still will be expected to spend time caring for the animals before advancing to the position of trainer.

Special requirements

Racehorse trainers must be licensed by the state in which they work. Otherwise, there are no special requirements for this occupation. Animal trainers who are themselves part of an entertainment act, however, should have good stage presence and a pleasing voice and be able to speak well before an audience.

Opportunities for experience and exploration

Students wishing to enter this field would do well to learn as much as they can about animals, especially animal psychology, either through coursework or library study. Interviews with animal trainers and tours of their workplaces might be arranged to learn first-hand about the practical aspects of the occupation.

Part-time or volunteer work in animal shelters, pet shops, or veterinary offices offers would-be trainers a chance to become accustomed to working with animals and to discover whether they have the aptitude for it. Experience can be acquired, too, in summer jobs as animal caretakers at zoos, aquariums, museums that feature live animal shows, amusement parks, and for those with a special interest in horses racing stables or riding stables.

Related occupations

Other occupations that involve close contact with animals include veterinarians, dairy farmers, animal production technicians, various biological scientists, and farriers.

Methods of entering

Persons who want to become animal trainers generally start out as animal keepers or caretakers and rise to the position of trainer only after acquiring experience within the ranks of an organization. They enter the field by applying directly for a job as animal keeper, letting the employer or their supervisor know of their ambition so they will eventually be considered for promotion.

Students with some background in animal psychology and previous experience caring for a specific animal may find summer jobs as trainers at large amusement or theme parks, but these jobs are not plentiful, and application should be made early in the year.

Advancement

Most establishments have very small staffs of animal trainers, which means that the opportunities for advancement are limited. The progression is from animal keeper to animal trainer. A trainer who directs or supervises others may be designated head animal trainer or senior animal trainer.

Some animal trainers go into business for themselves and, if successful, hire other trainers to work for them. Others become agents for animal acts.

Employment outlook

The demand for animal trainers is not great, because most employers have no need for a large staff and tend to promote from within. Applicants must be well qualified to overcome the heavy competition for the jobs that are available. The field is expected to remain limited into the mid-1990s even though some openings may be created as zoos and aquariums expand or provide more animal shows in an effort to increase revenue.

Employers of animal trainers are located throughout the country. The best prospects are those that have large numbers of elephants, apes, lions, dolphins, porpoises, seals, and birds, as these are among the species most often trained to perform.

Earnings

Animal trainers can earn widely varying amounts depending on their specialty and place of employment. Because of this diversity, formal salary ranges are not available for most of these occupations. In the field of racehorse training, however, trainers are paid an average fee of from $35 to $50 a day for each horse, plus ten percent of any money their horses win in races. Show horse trainers may earn as much as $30,000 to $35,000 a year. Trainers in business for themselves set their own fees for teaching both horses and owners.

Conditions of work

The working hours for animal trainers vary considerably, depending on type of animal, performance schedule, and whether travel is involved. For some trainers, such as those who work with show horses, the hours can be long and quite irregular.

Except in warm climates, animal shows are seasonal, running from April or May through mid-autumn. During this time, much of the work is conducted outdoors. In winter, trainers work indoors, preparing for the warm-weather shows. Trainers of aquatic mammals, such as dolphins and seals, must feel at ease working around, in, and under water.

The physical strength required depends on the animal involved. Pushing or pulling an elephant into position, for example, is quite different from manipulating a dog. All animal trainers, however, need greater than average agility.

Trainers who work with wild animals need to exercise particular caution, as there is always the danger of a previously docile animal becoming temperamental.

Social and psychological factors

Trainers must be perceptive enough about animals to recognize those that are trainable and those that are not. They must also be able to relate to animals on an individual basis because not all animals will respond the same way to a particular stimulus.

In addition, this occupation calls for an infinite amount of patience. Trainers must spend long hours repeating routines, rewarding their pupils for performing well, while never getting angry with them or punishing them when they fail to do what is expected. Trainers must be able to exhibit the authority to keep the animals under control without raising their voices or using physical force. Calmness under stress is particularly important when dealing with wild animals.

GOE: 03.03.01; SIC: 0752, 7948; SOC: 328, 5617

SOURCES OF ADDITIONAL INFORMATION

American Association of Zoological Parks and Aquariums
Route 88, Oglebay Park
Wheeling, WV 26003

National Congress of Animal Trainers and Breeders
Route 1, Box 32H
23675 West Chardon Road
Grayslake, IL 60030

RELATED ARTICLES

Volume 1: Biological Sciences
Volume 2: Museum occupations; Veterinarians
Volume 3: Agricultural scientists; Beekeepers; Dairy farmers; Dog groomers; Farriers; Fishers, commercial
Volume 4: Animal health technicians; Animal production technicians; Fish-production technicians

Anthropologists and archaeologists

Definition

Anthropologists and *archaeologists* trace the origin and evolutionary development of the human race through the study of changing physical characteristics and cultural and social institutions.

History

Although anthropology dates back to Aristotle in a technical sense, it became an established science during the Victorian era or the era of exploration. It accompanied such developments as the Industrial Revolution, the birth of geology, and Darwin's theory of evolution. Archaeology also began to develop during the Victorian era, primarily because of the emphasis placed upon exploration.

Anthropology developed rather slowly with little real growth until the 1930s, when governments began to stress the use of applied anthropological research.

Prior to the nineteenth century, anthropologists relied primarily on facts gathered from travelers' reports and documents received from nonprofessional observers. In the twentieth century, however, much stress has been placed on actual exploration by trained anthropologists and archaeologists.

Nature of the work

Anthropology, in which archaeology plays an important part in the gathering, analyzing, and reporting of data, is concerned with the study and comparison of people in all parts of the world, their physical characteristics, customs, languages, traditions, material possessions, and social and religious beliefs and practices. Anthropologists constitute the smallest group of social scientists, yet they cover the widest range of subject matter.

Anthropological data, including that acquired by archaeological techniques, may be applied to solving problems in human relations in fields such as industrial relations, race and ethnic relations, social work, political administration, education, public health, and programs involving transcultural or foreign relations.

Cultural anthropology, the area in which the greatest number of anthropologists specialize, deals with human behavior and studies aspects of both extinct and current societies, including religion, language, politics, social structure and traditions, mythology, art, and intellectual life. *Cultural anthropologists*, also called *ethnologists*, classify and compare cultures according to general laws of historical, cultural, and social development. To do this effectively, they often work with smaller, less complex, and perhaps more easily understood societies, including the tribal societies of Asia.

Archaeologists have a particularly important role in the areas of cultural anthropology. They apply painstaking specialized techniques to reconstruct a record of past cultures by studying, classifying, and interpreting artifacts such as pottery, clothing, tools, weapons, and ornaments, to determine cultural identity. They obtain these artifacts through excavation of sites including buildings and cities, and establish the chronological sequence of the development of each culture from simpler to more advanced levels. *Prehistoric archaeologists* study cultures that existed prior to the period of recorded history, while historical archaeologists study more recent societies. The historic period spans several thousand years in some parts of the world and sometimes only a few hundred years in parts of the Western hemisphere. *Classical archaeologists* concentrate on ancient Mediterranean and Eastern cultures. An *artifacts conservator* or preservationist restores and preserves artifacts found at archaeological sites. Through the study of the history of specific groups of peoples, whose society may be extinct, cultural anthropologists and archaeologists are able to reconstruct their cultures including the pattern of daily life and the areas in which the members of that society expressed the greatest interest.

Anthropologists may also be involved in the application of anthropological concepts to current problems, using their research to find solutions. *Anthropological linguists* study the ways in which people use language and how this affects and is affected by their behavior. *Anthropological psychologists* study the effect of culture on the individual's personality. One of the most relevant specializations to modern life is urban anthropology in which the effect of current social and cultural trends is projected and necessary changes proposed. *Urban anthropologists* work with architects, designers, and

Two anthropologists study stone tools from Zaire that are believed to be among the oldest known utensils fashioned by prehistoric man.

Some anthropologists will use archaeological data to study the daily life, routine, and interests of peoples who lived many years ago. Those studying ethnology are interested in living people, usually simple societies, and their customs and beliefs. Linguistics is the scientific study of languages, which leads to a more thorough understanding of the people who spoke those languages. Other anthropologists specialize in cultural theory, or the study of contacts between various cultures, including the characteristics of cultural change.

Archaeologists often must travel extensively to perform field work on the site where a culture once flourished. Site work is often slow and laborious. Conducting digs to uncover artifacts may take years to produce valuable information.

Another important aspect of archaeology is the cleaning, restoration, and preservation of artifacts. This work may take place on the site of discovery to minimize deterioration of textiles and mummified remains. Careful recording of the exact location and condition of artifacts is essential for further study.

Many anthropologists work for the federal and state governments, teach in colleges and universities, and work in museums. Those employed by the government serve as consultants to save or restore valuable cultural resources. They may survey a site and assess its value before the start of a construction project such as a hydroelectric power plant or highway.

Teachers may lecture to groups on various subjects related to anthropology including sociology or geography. In addition to correcting papers, holding conferences with students and colleagues, and preparing lectures, they may also engage in research and the writing of papers or articles prepared for public presentation or publication in professional journals.

Those employed in museums will often find themselves combining both their management and administrative duties with their training in anthropology in carrying out various field work projects, including excavations and research on various anthropological collections already gathered.

An important part of museum work performed by artifact conservators is the cleaning, repairing, and reinforcing of specimens such as weapons, tools, and pottery using chemical and skilled mechanical techniques. Artifacts may be restored by polishing, joining together broken fragments, or other procedures. These techniques have also been applied to halt deterioration of buildings and monuments that suffer the effects of twentieth-century pollution.

city planners on housing projects. Some assist social services to provide better health care and education to immigrant groups.

Physical anthropologists are concerned primarily with the biology of human groups. They study the differences between the members of past and present human societies and are particularly interested in the geographical distribution of human physical characteristics. Some physical anthropologists concentrate on the human and primate skeletal remains from various areas of the world and, through the study of these remains, learn more about the people and their society. They apply their intensive training in human anatomy to the study of human evolution and to establish differences between races and groups of people. Physical anthropologists may also apply their knowledge of human anatomy to modern problems such as designing furniture and special equipment and sizing clothing. Their work on the effect of heredity and environment on cultural attitudes towards health and nutrition enables medical anthropologists to help develop urban health programs. *Anthropometrists* research growth and development by measuring the human body and skeleton.

Requirements

High-school students planning to enter anthropology should study English composition and literature, mathematics (preferably beyond algebra), history, geography, natural science, computer science, and foreign languages. Typing, sketching, simple surveying, and photography may also be helpful.

The high-school graduate should be prepared for a long training period beyond high school. Most of the better positions in anthropology and archaeology will require a doctorate, which entails about four to six years of work beyond the bachelor's degree. Before starting graduate work, however, the undergraduate will probably study such basic courses as psychology, sociology, history, geography, mathematics, logic, English composition, and literature, as well as modern and ancient languages.

The final two years of the undergraduate program will provide an opportunity for specialization not only in anthropology but in some specific phase of the discipline.

Students planning to become physical anthropologists should concentrate on the biological sciences. The physical sciences and oral history/folklore studies are an important supplement to archaeological studies, as is field training arranged through the university. A wide range of interdisciplinary study in languages, history, and the social sciences, as well as the humanities, is particularly important in cultural anthropology, including the area of linguistics and ethnology. Independent field study is also done in these areas.

In starting graduate training, students should select an institution that has a good program in the area in which they hope to specialize. This is important, not only because the training should be of a high quality, but because most graduates in anthropology and archaeology will receive their first jobs through their graduate universities. Employers often look first to the graduates of the institutions offering the strongest programs in anthropology and archaeology.

Special requirements

Although some beginning jobs in anthropology may be open to applicants who have master's degrees, those promoted to the top positions will have doctorates. Assistantships and temporary positions may be available to holders of bachelor's or master's degrees but are usually

An urban archaeology team examines artifacts that will provide clues to the living patterns of early nineteenth-century city dwellers in Philadelphia.

available only to those working toward a doctorate.

Opportunities for experience and exploration

Anthropology and archaeology may be explored in a number of ways. Very often Boy Scout and Girl Scout troops will participate in camping expeditions for exploration purposes. Local amateur anthropological or archaeological societies may have weekly or monthly meetings and guest speakers, carry on study of developments in the field, and engage in exploration on the local level.

Trips to museums will also introduce students to the world of anthropology and archaeology. Both high-school and college students may work in museums on a part-time basis during the school year or during summer vacations. Voluntary archaeological work is available, also. This experience can be of great value to those considering the field.

Related occupations

Anthropologists and archaeologists are interested in how social institutions work. This is also true of a number of other occupations, including economists, geographers, historians, market researchers, political scientists, psychologists, sociologists, and urban planners. Other workers who require a knowledge of physical, environmental, and biological science include astronomers, biochemists, chemists, geologists, geophysicists, life scientists, meteorologists, oceanographers, physicists, and soil scientists.

Methods of entering

The most popular way of entering these occupations is through graduate schools. Graduates in anthropology or archaeology will normally be approached prior to graduation by prospective employers. Often, professors will provide the student with introductions as well as recommendations.

Students often have an opportunity to work as a research assistant or a teaching fellow while in graduate school, and frequently this experience is of tremendous help in qualifying for a job in another institution. Also, graduates may be able to remain at the institution from which they received their degrees to teach or engage in research.

Advancement

Because of the relatively small size of this field, advancement is not likely to be fast and the opportunities for advancement may be somewhat limited. Most people beginning their teaching careers in colleges or universities will start as instructors and eventually advance to assistant professor, associate professor, and possibly full professor. Researchers on the college level have an opportunity to head research areas and to gain recognition among colleagues as an expert in many areas of study.

Anthropologists and archaeologists employed in museums also have an opportunity to advance, possibly becoming head of the museum.

Employment outlook

About 7,000 anthropologists and archaeologists were employed in the United States in the early 1990s. It is anticipated that most new jobs arising through the rest of the 1990s will be nonteaching positions in consulting firms, research institutes, corporations, and federal, state, and local government agencies. Among the factors contributing to this growth is environmental, historic, and cultural preservation legislation. There is a particular demand for persons with the ability to write environmental impact statements.

Archaeologists with a master's degree may be supervisors in charge of digging or collecting specimens. These people may be hired on a full-time or on a temporary contract basis for consulting firms, government agencies, academic institutions, and museums. The fields of environmental protection and historic preservation are growing, and interest in ethnic studies may spur demand for anthropological research in that area as well.

Although college and university teaching has been the largest area of employment for anthropologists, the demand is expected to decline through the 1990s in this area as a result of the steady decrease in student enrollment. Overall, the number of job applicants will be greater than the number of openings available. Competition will be great even for those with doctorates who are seeking faculty positions, and many will find only temporary or nontenured jobs. Junior college and high-school teaching jobs will be very limited, and those holding a bachelor's or master's degree will have few opportunities. Other areas of potential employment include foreign jobs. Museums and local governments conduct archeological studies and may require outside expertise. Strong language skills and extensive work in the field are normal prerequisites.

Earnings

In the early 1990s, the federal government recognized education and experience in certifying applicants for entry level positions with starting salaries for anthropologists with bachelor's degrees ranging from approximately $14,800 to $18,400 a year. Anthropologists with master's degrees received a starting salary of about $22,500, and those with doctorates generally started at around $27,200. The average annual salary for all anthropologists and archaeologists in the federal government was around $38,800 in the early 1990s.

Beginning salaries for anthropology faculty in colleges and universities ranged from approximately $14,000 to more than $20,000 a year for persons with doctorates. Salaries vary depending on the institution, with the lower range in those schools that grant only undergraduate degrees in anthropology. Salaries for associate professors averaged about $25,300 annually, and full professors were earning $32,000 or more per year.

Many anthropologists and archaeologists earn additional income through writing for publication or through summer jobs.

Conditions of work

The majority of anthropologists and archaeologists are employed by college and universities and, as such, have good working conditions, although field work may require extensive travel and difficult living conditions. They are normally under regular academic vacation and sick leave plans, and most colleges and universities having programs in anthropology and archaeology will have good retirement plans. The physical facilities are normally clean, well lighted, and ventilated.

Anthropologists and archaeologists work about forty hours per week although the hours may be irregular. Physical strength and stamina is necessary for field work of all types. Those working on excavations, for instance, may work during most of the daylight hours and spend the evening planning the next day's activities. Those engaged in teaching may spend many hours in laboratory research or in preparing lessons to be taught. The work is interesting, however, and those employed in the field are usually highly motivated and unconcerned about long, irregular hours or primitive living conditions.

Social and psychological factors

Anthropologists and especially archaeologists should have great interest in natural and cultural history and enjoy reading, research, and writing. All of these may be solitary activities.

The rewards inherent in the work include job security and the major satisfaction gained from working in an area one truly enjoys. There is also the satisfaction of knowing that the work is helping to create a better life for everyone through a better understanding of humanity, past and present.

GOE: 11.03.03; SIC: 822; SOC: 1919

◇ **SOURCES OF ADDITIONAL INFORMATION**

American Anthropological Association
1703 New Hampshire Avenue, NW
Washington, DC 20009

Archaeological Institute of America
675 Commonwealth Avenue
Boston, MA 02215

Society for American Archaeology
808 17th Street, NW, Suite 200
Washington, DC 20006

Society for Historical Archaeology
PO Box 231033
Pleasant Hill, CA 94523

U.S. Department of the Interior
Washington, DC 20240

Wenner-Gren Foundation for Anthropological Research
1865 Broadway, 11th Floor
New York, NY 10023

◇ **RELATED ARTICLES**

Volume 1: Education; Social Sciences
Volume 2: College and university faculty; Geographers; Geologists; Historians; Linguists; Museum occupations; Sociologists
Volume 4: Biological specimen technicians

Architects

Definition

Architects are responsible for the planning, design, and supervision of construction of all types of facilities. To obtain this end, they consult with clients, plan layouts of structures, prepare sketches of proposed buildings, write specifications, and prepare scale and full-sized drawings.

Architects may also help clients to obtain bids, select a contractor, and negotiate the construction contract, and they sometimes visit

Architects work in large, spacious offices so that drafters have the room and light needed to design structures. These particular architects are using a computer system to calculate certain design specifications.

construction sites to ensure that the work is going according to specification.

History

Although more interested in functional cover than aesthetic value, the first architects appeared when people found themselves in need of something more than natural shelter. Outstanding examples of architecture have been found in many ancient cultures, but the Greeks are considered the first to have beautified architectural harmony. The most famous of their structures, the Parthenon designed by Ictinus, was the apex of simplicity and subtle beauty and a major influence on the Byzantine architects.

The principle of the dome was refined, culminating in the Cathedral of Florence designed by Brunelleschi. Another famous architect of the Renaissance was Michelangelo, designer of the famous St. Peter's basilica in Rome.

The architectural center moved then from Italy to France and then to England where Sir Christopher Wren became the most dominant influence. Architecture then seems to have entered into a dormant period. Architectural principles were widely known and enabled fairly functional homes to be built for people of modest means. When major structures were commissioned, however, the architects turned to a presentation of Gothic ostentation. This state of affairs dominated architecture until it was finally broken by Louis Sullivan, an American, and his most famous pupil, Frank Lloyd Wright.

Perhaps no architect will ever again so completely dominate a profession as Wright has.

After his dictum of "form follows function" and his successful application of this idea to his buildings, all molds were broken. Architects now give full rein to their creative instincts and talents.

Nature of the work

The architect normally has one goal: to design, in compliance with existing laws and regulations, a building that will satisfy the client. To obtain this goal, the architect must wear many hats. The job begins with consultations with a client. After learning what the client wants, the architect takes into consideration local and state building and design regulations, climate, soil on which the building is to be constructed, water tables, zoning laws, fire regulations, the client's financial limitations, and numerous other requirements and regulations. The architect then prepares a set of plans which, upon the client's approval, will be developed into final design and working drawings.

The final design will show the exact dimensions of every portion of the building, including the location of electrical outlets and fixtures, plumbing, heating and air-conditioning facilities, windows, doors, and all other features of the building.

The architect works closely with engineers to determine the type of materials to be used in the construction and usually works with a consulting engineer on the plumbing, heating, and electrical work to be done.

The architect will then assist the client in the letting of bids to general contractors, one of which will be selected to construct the building to the specifications. The architect will assist the client through the completion of the job, making certain the correct materials are used and that the specifications are faithfully followed.

Throughout the process the architect works closely with the crew. The crew might well consist of an architectural designer, who specializes in design drawings; a structural designer, who designs the frame of the building in accordance with the work of the architectural designer; the project manager or job superintendent, who sees that the full detail drawings are completed to the satisfaction of the architect; and the specification writer and estimator, who will convert the drawings into terminology and instructions that can be understood by the contractor and all the subcontractors.

The architect's job is very complex. He or she is expected to know construction methods, engineering principles and practices, and materials. The architect must also be up-to-date on new design and construction techniques and procedures. Although architects once spent most of their time designing buildings for the wealthy, they are now more often involved in the design of small or large housing developments, individual dwellings, supermarkets, industrial plants, office buildings, shopping centers, air terminals, schools, banks, and dozens of other types of buildings. They may specialize in any one of a number of fields including building appraisal, city planning, teaching, architectural journalism, furniture design, lighting, or heating.

Regardless of the area of specialization, the architect's major task is that of understanding the clients' needs and then reconciling them into a meaningful whole.

Requirements

Persons interested in architecture should be well-prepared academically and be intelligent, observant, responsible, and self-disciplined. They should have a concern for detail and accuracy, be able to communicate effectively both orally and in writing, and be able to accept criticism constructively. Although great artistic ability is not necessary, architectural aspirants should be able to visualize spatial relationships and have the capacity to solve technical problems. Mathematical ability is also important. In addition, architects should possess organizational skills and leadership qualities and be able to work well with others.

High-school students hoping to enter the field should take a college preparatory program that includes courses in English, mathematics, physics, art (especially free-hand drawing), social studies, history, and foreign languages. Courses in business and computer science will also be useful.

Because most state architecture licensing boards require a professional degree, high-school students are advised, early in their senior year, to apply for admission to one of the ninety-three schools of architecture that are accredited by the National Architectural Accrediting Board (NAAB). Competition to enter these schools is highly competitive. Grades, class rank, and aptitude and achievement scores count heavily in determining who will be accepted.

Most schools of architecture offer a five-year program leading to a bachelor of architecture degree or a six-year master of architecture program. In the six-year program, a pre-professional degree is awarded after four years,

and the graduate degree after a two-year program to satisfy licensing requirements. Many students prepare for an architecture career by first earning a liberal arts degree, then completing a three- to four-year master of architecture program.

A typical college architecture program includes courses in architectural history and theory, building design, including its technical and legal aspects, and science and liberal arts.

Special requirements

All states and the District of Columbia require that individuals be licensed before calling themselves architects or contracting to provide architectural services in that particular state. The requirements for licensure generally include graduation from an accredited school of architecture and three years of practical experience in a licensed architect's office before the individual is eligible to take the rigorous four-day architect registration examination.

Opportunities for experience and exploration

Most architects will welcome the opportunity to talk with young men and women interested in entering architecture and may be willing to have them visit their offices where they can gain a firsthand knowledge of the type of work done by architects.

Other opportunities may include visiting the design studios of a school of architecture or working for an architect or building contractor during summer vacations. Also, many architecture schools offer summer programs for high-school students. Books and magazines on architecture provide a broad understanding of the nature of the work and the values of the profession. So, too, do the many pamphlets published by various architectural associations. Libraries will usually have a supply of information available, such as copies of catalogs from schools that offer a program in architecture. These catalogs will normally outline the program the student would follow at the respective institution and will present descriptions of all courses included in the program.

Guidance counselors in schools usually have access to various interest inventories or aptitude tests that may also be of some assistance to the individual faced with making vocational decisions.

Related occupations

The skills that an architect relies on to design buildings and related structures also apply to workers in other occupations, such as building contractors, civil engineers, designers, drafters, industrial designers, interior designers, landscape architects, surveyors, and urban planners.

Methods of entering

Those entering architecture following graduation usually start as intern-architects in an architectural office, where they assist in preparing architectural plans. They also may handle related details, such as administering contracts, researching building codes and construction materials, and writing specifications. Some architecture graduates go into allied fields such as construction, engineering, landscape architecture, or real estate development. Others may develop graphic, interior design, or product specialties. Still others put their training to work in the theater, film, or television fields or in museums, display firms, and architectural product and materials manufacturing companies.

Advancement

Architects in large firms are given progressively more complex jobs and may advance to supervisory or managerial positions. Some become partners in established firms, but the eventual goal of many architects is to establish their own practice.

Employment outlook

Approximately 84,000 licensed architects were employed in the United States in the early 1990s. Most of them worked in architectural firms. About one-third were self-employed. Others worked for builders, real estate developers, or other businesses with large construction programs. A smaller but growing number were employed in government agencies such as the Departments of Defense, Interior, Housing and Urban Development, and the General Services Administration.

Although faster than average growth in the field is expected through the rest of the decade, it may not be as rapid as in recent years. The number of architects needed will depend on the volume of construction. Rapid growth is predicted in the area of nonresidential structures such as office buildings and shopping centers. The construction industry, however, is extremely sensitive to fluctuations in the overall economy, and a recession could result in layoffs. On the positive side, employment of architects is not likely to be affected by the growing use of computer technologies. Rather than replacing architects, computers are being used to make more and better designs.

Competition for employment will continue to be strong, particularly in prestigious architectural firms that offer potential for advancement. Most job openings will not be newly created positions but will become available as architects transfer to other occupations or leave the field.

Earnings

Recent graduates of a school or college of architecture started between $18,000 and $22,000 a year in the early 1990s. Newly licensed architects earned an average of $26,000, and those with several years of experience were able to command salaries of $40,000 or more.

Well-established architects who are partners in an architectural firm or who have their own businesses generally earn much more than do the salaried employees. Those who are partners in very large firms can earn more than $100,000 a year.

The average salary for architects working in the federal government in the early 1990s was about $36,500.

Conditions of work

Architects normally work a forty-hour week with their working hours falling between 8:00 A.M. and 6:00 P.M. There may be a number of times when they will have to work overtime especially when under pressure to complete an assignment. Self-employed architects may be required to work more irregular hours and often will meet with clients in their homes or offices during the evening.

Architects usually work in ventilated, well-lighted offices. They may, however, spend a considerable amount of time outside of the office visiting clients or viewing the progress of a particular job in the field. There is usually a considerable variation in the routine, supplied by visits with clients, contractors, and salespeople. Some architects are required to travel extensively, which also provides a break in the routine.

Most architects will have at least two weeks of vacation with pay and will be covered by hospital insurance and retirement plans.

Social and psychological factors

A great deal of personal gratification is available to the successful architect, not the least of which is viewing the completed product. The buildings can be seen, felt, used, and admired not only by those residing or working in them, but by the general public as well. The product will be seen for years to come.

If the project is successful, architects have the satisfaction of knowing that they have succeeded in meeting the needs of the client and have, hopefully, added to the beauty of the city, town, or area in which the building was constructed.

A certain feeling of adventure is also inherent in the architect's work because he or she never really knows what the next job will entail.

GOE: 05.01.07; **SIC:** 8712; **SOC:** 161

◇ **SOURCES OF ADDITIONAL INFORMATION**

American Institute of Architects
1735 New York Avenue, NW
Washington, DC 20006

Association of Collegiate Schools of Architecture
1735 New York Avenue, NW
Washington, DC 20006

Association of Women in Architecture
7440 University Drive
St. Louis, MO 63130

National Council of Architectural Registration Boards
1735 New York Avenue, NW, Suite 700
Washington, DC 20006

National Organization of Minority Architects
c/o Earl Kai Chan
Earl Kai Chan and Associates
5232 East Pima Street, Suite A
Tucson, AZ 85712

Society of American Registered Architects
1245 South Highland Avenue
Lombard, IL 60148

◇ **RELATED ARTICLES**

Volume 1: Construction; Engineering
Volume 2: Drafters; Engineers; Landscape architects; Urban and regional planners
Volume 4: Architectural and building construction technicians; Civil engineering technicians

Archivists and curators

Definition

Archivists and *curators* contribute to the study of the arts and sciences by analyzing objects from historical documents and ancient artifacts to living plants and animals, and determining which are significant enough to be preserved for posterity. Archivists keep track of records such as letters, contracts, photographs, and blueprints; curators manage collections in museums and other exhibiting institutions.

History

Although people collect documents and objects for centuries, archivists and curators have es-

The museum curator is examining the collection of primitive art to ensure that the pieces are displayed correctly.

tablished themselves as professionals only in last hundred years or so. The first museum was built in Egypt in the fourth century B.C., and ever since then societies have attempted to understand their own and other cultures by assembling objects of aesthetic, historical, or scientific value. Museums accumulated objects rapidly and sometimes indiscriminately, accepting items regardless of their actual merit. By the eighteenth century, museums were holding so many items that they had to formulate acquisition policies to keep from becoming community attics full of possibly useless articles. The idea of arranging collections in a systematic order was pioneered by the renowned Louvre museum in France when it opened in 1793.

Each year, as new scientific discoveries are made and new works are published, the need for sifting through and classifying items grows greater. Archivists and curators have emerged as the individuals who, because of their education, can best determine the value of collections and best help the general public understand and appreciate them. Like librarians, they know exactly where items are kept, whether within their own collections or in those of others. And like historians, they can explain the significance of such items in the development of civilization.

Nature of the work

Archivists analyze documents, such as government records, minutes of corporate board meetings, letters from famous persons, and charters of nonprofit foundations. To determine which ones should be saved, they consider such factors as when each was written, who wrote it, and for whom it was written. Then, archivists appraise documents based on their knowledge

of political, economic, military, and social history. Archives are kept by various organizations, including government agencies, corporations, universities, and museums, and the value of documents is dictated by whoever owns them. For example, the U.S. Army may not be interested in General Motors' corporate charter, and General Motors may not be interested in a Civil War battle plan. Archivists understand and serve the needs of their employers.

After selecting appropriate documents, archivists help make them accessible to others by preparing reference aids such as indexes, guides, bibliographies, descriptions, and microfilmed copies of documents. For easy retrieval, they file and cross-index selected documents in alphabetical and chronological order. Archivists may also preserve and repair historical documents.

Many archivists conduct research using the archival materials at their disposal, and they may publish articles detailing their findings. They may advise government agencies, scholars, journalists, and others conducting research by supplying available materials and information.

Curators supervise collections in exhibiting institutions such as museums, zoos, aquariums, botanic gardens, and historic sites. To improve their employers' educational and research facilities, curators sift through items acquired through donations and bequests and select those of value to the institution. They may obtain and develop new collections by negotiating loans, purchases, and exchanges, and sometimes by gathering in the field. They maintain inventories of possessions and may design exhibits.

Depending on the size of their employing organization, curators may perform many or few administrative duties. Such duties may include preparing budgets, representing their institutions at scientific or association conferences, soliciting support for institutions, and interviewing and hiring personnel. Some curators help formulate and interpret institutional policy. They may plan or participate in special research projects and write articles for scientific journals.

Requirements

Archivists usually must have at least a master's degree in history or a related field. For some positions, a second master's degree in library science or a doctorate degree is prerequisite. Candidates with bachelor's degrees may serve as assistants while they complete their formal training. Curators must have at the very minimum a bachelor's degree accompanied by museum experience. The bachelor's degree should be in a discipline related to the museum's specialty. Many museums also require a master's degree and most prefer a doctorate. Curators often need to be knowledgeable in a number of fields because so many sciences overlap. More than seventy colleges offer undergraduate courses in archival science or museum science.

Special requirements

Those archivists and curators employed by the federal government may have to take a civil service examination. Those working for smaller institutions should have good people skills because they often have administrative duties in addition to their scholarly activities.

Opportunities for experience and exploration

Students interested in archival work should study history and literature and might try to get part-time jobs in libraries. A fun extra-credit project could be to construct a "family archive," consisting of letters, birth and marriage certificates, special awards, and any other documents that would help someone understand a family's history. Many museums and cultural organizations train volunteer guides called "docents" to give tours of their institutions; college students can work as docents over the summer or even part-time during the school year.

Related occupations

Other occupations that employ skills such as those necessary to the work of archivists and curators include librarians, computer programmers, exhibit designers, anthropologists, and zoologists.

Methods of entering

Candidates for positions as archivists or curators should apply to institutions for entry-level positions only after completing their undergraduate degrees. Many would-be archivists

and curators choose to work part-time, or even without pay, as research assistants, interns, volunteers, to gain the experience that will help them secure permanent positions.

Advancement

Archivists usually work in small sections, units, or departments, so internal promotion opportunities are limited. Promising archivists advance by transferring to larger units with supervisory positions.

Because the best jobs as archivists and curators are contingent upon education, the surest path to the top is to pursue one or more doctorates. Ambitious archivists and curators should also attend conferences and workshops to stay current with developments in their fields. Curators can enhance their status by conducting independent research and publishing their findings.

Employment outlook

Job opportunities for archivists and curators are expected to increase about as fast as the average for all occupations through the year 2000. Competition for jobs as archivists and curators, however, is keen. Curators will probably enjoy more opportunities than archivists because museums are expected to proliferate as public interest in art, history, technology, and culture increases.

Earnings

Salaries for archivists and curators vary considerably from institution to institution and may depend upon education and experience. Persons employed by the federal government or by prestigious museums generally earn far more than those working for small organizations. In the early 1990s, starting salaries for archivists and curators with bachelor's degrees averaged approximately $15,000 a year; salaries for those with experience averaged $19,000. Professionals with master's degrees started at $23,000; those with doctorates, $28,000 and up. Archivists and curators employed by the federal government earned more than $35,000 a year.

Conditions of work

Archivists and curators usually work in offices Both occupations are fairly sedentary. Archivists have less opportunity for physical activity than curators, who occasionally install exhibits and who may walk a fair deal if they are employed by zoos and arboreta. Archivists may suffer from eyestrain.

Social and psychological factors

Archivists and curators tend to work either alone or with very few coworkers. But because they are usually passionate about their work, most do not mind the solitude of their environments. Also, they do not operate under as much stress as many other professionals do.

GOE: 11.03.03, 11.07.04; SIC: 8231, 8412; SOC: 2520

◇ **SOURCES OF ADDITIONAL INFORMATION**

Society of American Archivists
600 South Federal Street
Chicago, IL 60605

American Association of Museums
1225 I Street, NW
Suite 200
Washington, DC 20005

American Association of Botanical Gardens and Arboreta
PO Box 206
Swarthmore, PA 19081

American Institute for Conservation of Historic and Artistic Works
1400 16th Street, NW
Suite 340
Washington, DC 20036

◇ **RELATED ARTICLES**

Volume 2: Anthropologists and archaeologists; Designers; Genealogists; Historians; Librarians
Volume 3: Display workers
Volume 4: Library technicians; Museum technicians; Planetarium technicians

Assessors and appraisers

Definition

Assessors and *appraisers* collect and interpret data to make judgments about the value, quality, and use of property. Assessors are government officials who evaluate property for the express purpose of determining how much the real estate owner should pay the city or county government in property taxes. Appraisers evaluate property to help persons make decisions about purchases, sales, investments, mortgages, or loans.

Assessors are public servants who are either elected or appointed to office, while appraisers are employed by private businesses such as accounting firms, real estate companies, and savings institutions, and by larger assessors' offices.

History

Persons have served as assessors since colonial times. Until the 1930s most assessors were lay people, and unscientific methods were used to estimate the value of property. With the advent of computers, assessing has become much more scientific. Today, assessments are based on a combination of economic and statistical analysis and common sense.

Appraising, too, was informal until the early part of the twentieth century. In 1922 the National Association of Real Estate Boards (NAREB) defined specializations of its real-estate functions to encourage professionalism in the industry. An independent appraisal division was not organized because appraisers were few and the importance of sound appraisals was not then appreciated.

At that time, appraisal work was largely performed as a part-time adjunct to a general real-estate business, by persons who were not specifically trained in the field. As a result, the "boom" period of the 1920s saw many abuses of appraisals, such as making of loans in excess of the real value of the property based on inaccurate estimates. The events of the Great Depression in the 1930s further highlighted the need for professionalism in appraising. Real-estate owners defaulted on their mortgages, real-estate bond issues stopped paying interest, and real-estate corporations went into receivership. The NAREB eventually recognized appraising as a significant branch of specialization in 1928, but clearly defined appraisal standards and appraisal treatises were not formulated until the 1930s.

Since then, appraising has emerged as a complex profession offering many responsibilities and opportunities. Reliable appraisals are required when real estate is sold, mortgaged, taxed, insured, or developed. Buyers and sellers of property want to know market value as a guide in their negotiations, and may need economic feasibility studies or advice about other investment considerations for a proposed or existing development. Mortgage lenders require appraisals before issuing loans, and insurance companies often need an estimate of value before underwriting a property.

Nature of the work

Property is divided into two distinct types: real property and personal property. Real property is land and the structures built upon the land, while personal property includes all other types of possessions. Appraisers answer questions about the value, quality, and use of real property and personal property based on selective research into market areas, the application of analytical techniques, and professional judgment derived from experience. In evaluating real property they try to analyze the supply and demand for different types of property, such as residential dwellings, office buildings, shopping centers, industrial sites, and farms to estimate their values. Appraisers analyze con-

struction, condition, and functional design. They review public records of sales, leases, previous assessments, and other transactions pertaining to land and buildings so as to determine the market values, rents, and construction costs of similar properties. Appraisers collect information about neighborhoods such as availability of gas, electricity, power lines, and transportation. They may also interview persons familiar with the property, and they take into account the amount of money it would take to make needed improvements on the property.

Appraisers also must consider such factors as location and changes that could influence the future value of the property. A residence worth $200,000 in the suburbs may be worth only a fraction of that in the inner city or in a remote rural area. But that same suburban residence may depreciate in value if an airport is scheduled to be built nearby. After conducting a thorough investigation, appraisers usually prepare a written report that documents their findings and conclusions.

Assessors (also called *valuer-generals* and *assessment commissioners*) perform all these appraising duties, and then go one step further to compute the amount of tax to be levied on property, using applicable tax tables. The primary responsibility of the assessor is to prepare an annual assessment roll, which lists all properties in a district and their assessed values. To prepare the assessment roll, assessors and their staffs must first locate and identify all taxable property in the district. To do so, they prepare and maintain complete and accurate maps, which show the size, shape, location, and legal description of each parcel of land. Next, they collect information about other features of parcels, such as zoning, soil characteristics, and availability of water, electricity, sewers, gas, and telephones. They describe any building and how land and buildings are used. This information is put in a parcel record. They analyze relationships between property characteristics and sales prices, rents, and construction costs to produce valuation "models" or formulas that are used to estimate the value of every property as of the legally required assessment date. For example, assessors try to estimate how much an additional bedroom adds to the value of a residence, how much an additional acre of land adds to the value of a farm, or how much competition from a new shopping center detracts from a downtown department store. Finally, assessors prepare and certify an assessment roll listing all properties, owners, and assessed values and notify owners of the assessed value of their properties. Because taxpayers have the right to contest their assessments, assessors must be prepared to defend their estimates and methods.

Most appraisers deal with land and buildings, but some evaluate other items of value. *Personal property assessors* in some areas help the government levy taxes on owners of taxable personal property by preparing lists of personal property owned by businesses and, in a few areas, householders. In addition to listing the number of items, these assessors also estimate the value of taxable items.

Art appraisers determine the authenticity and value of works of art, including paintings, sculptures, and antiques. They examine works for color values, style of brushstroke, and other characteristics to establish their age or to identify artist. Art appraisers are well versed in art history, art materials, techniques of individual artists, and contemporary art markets, and they use that knowledge to assign values. Art appraisers may use complex methods such as X rays and chemical tests to detect frauds.

Requirements

Good appraisers are good investigators. They must be familiar with sources of information on such diverse topics as public records, construction materials, building trends, economic trends, and governmental regulations affecting use of property. They should know how to read survey drawings and blueprints, and be able to identify features of building construction.

Appraisers must understand equity and mortgage finance, architectural function, demographic statistics, and business trends. Many of these skills are learned on the job, but because appraising is a complex profession, candidates should have some college education, and, preferably, a college degree.

High-school students who are interested in this field should take courses in mathematics, civics, English, and, if available, accounting and computer science. In addition to these, college students should enroll in mathematics, engineering, economics, business administration, architecture, and urban studies classes. A degree in finance, economics, statistics, mathematics, urban studies, computer science, public administration, business administration, or real estate and urban land economics is desirable. Art appraisers should hold at least a bachelor's degree in art history.

Basic training in assessment and appraisal is offered by professional associations such as the International Association of Assessing Officers, the American Institute of Real Estate

Appraisers, and the Society of Real Estate Appraisers.

Special requirements

In addition to technical skills, appraisers need good communication skills because they deal with a variety of people and write many reports. Some states have certification standards for appraisers; interested students may contact the local real estate board to learn more about these. Also, some states may require assessors who are government employees to pass civil service or other examinations before they can start work. But even when appraisers are not required to pass tests, they must exercise judgment, ethical integrity, and unbiased objectivity.

Opportunities for experience and exploration

To learn the particulars of building construction that appraisers need to know, able-bodied students might consider applying to construction companies for summer jobs. To practice the methods used by appraisers, students may want to write detailed analyses of assets and shortcomings when choosing a college or buying a car.

Related occupations

Appraisers and assessors need a strong background in mathematics and a firm understanding of real estate and construction. Other occupations that require similar skills include real estate agents and brokers, real estate and property managers, construction trades, architects, and surveyors.

Methods of entering

After acquiring mathematical and technical knowledge in the classroom, persons interested in appraising should apply to local assessors, real estate brokers, or large accounting firms, among others. Because assessing jobs are often civil service jobs, they may be listed with government employment agencies.

Advancement

Appraising is a dynamic field, affected yearly by new legislation and technology. To distinguish themselves in the business, top appraisers continue their education and pursue certification through the various national appraising organizations, such as the American Institute of Real Estate Appraisers, the Society of Real Estate Appraisers, and the American Society of Appraisers, and the International Association of Assessing Officers. Certified appraisers are entrusted with the most prestigious projects and can command the highest fees. Assessors can advance by moving to areas of broader jurisdiction, as from town to county.

Employment outlook

Appraisers and assessors need never fear that their occupations will become obsolete. As long as governments levy property taxes and as long as persons buy and sell property, they will need appraisers to help them make decisions. The real estate industry, however, is influenced dramatically by the overall health of the economy, and so appraisers can expect to benefit more than average during periods of growth, and suffer more than average during recessions and depressions.

Earnings

Many variables affect the earnings of assessors and appraisers, but generally speaking, salaries range from $20,000 for beginners to $60,000 and above for professionals with thirty years' experience and additional credentials. Appraisers employed in the private sector tend to earn higher incomes than those in the public sector. Assessors' salaries generally increase as the population of the jurisdiction increases. Earnings at any level are enhanced by higher education and professional designations.

Conditions of work

Appraisers and assessors enjoy a variety of working conditions, from the comfortable offices where they do their paperwork to outdoor construction sites, which they visit in both the heat of summer and the bitter cold of winter. Many appraisers spend mornings at their desks and afternoons in the field. Experienced appraisers may frequently have the opportunity to travel out of state.

Assessors' offices might employ administrators, property appraisers, mappers, systems analysts, computer technicians, public relations specialists, typists, and clerical workers. In small offices, one or two people might handle most tasks; in large offices, some with hundreds of employees, specialists are more common.

Social and psychological factors

Appraising is a very people-oriented occupation, both in the office and out. Appraisers must be unfailingly cordial, and they have to deal calmly and tactfully with people who challenge. Appraising can be a high-stress occupation. Appraisers feel great pressure to appraise accurately because a lot of money rides on their calculations.

GOE: 11.06.03; SIC: 9311; SOC: 1135

◇ SOURCES OF ADDITIONAL INFORMATION

American Association of Certified Appraisers
800 Compton Road
Suite 10
Cincinnati, OH 45231

American Institute of Real Estate Appraisers
430 North Michigan Avenue
Chicago, IL 60611

American Society of Appraisers
PO Box 17265
Washington, DC 20041

American Society of Farm Managers and Rural Appraisers
950 South Cherry Street, Suite 106
Denver, CO 80222

International Association of Assessing Officers
1313 East 60th Street
Chicago, IL 60637

International Society of Appraisers
PO Box 726
Hoffman Estates, IL 60195

National Association of Independent Fee Appraisers
7501 Murdoch Avenue
St. Louis, MO 63119

Society of Real Estate Appraisers
225 North Michigan Avenue
Suite 724
Chicago, IL 60601

◇ **RELATED ARTICLES**

Volume 1: Construction; Real Estate
Volume 2: Architects; Property and real estate managers; Real estate agents and brokers
Volume 3: Construction workers
Volume 4: Architectural and building construction technicians

Association executives

Definition

Association executives coordinate the day-to-day operations of membership institutions such as trade associations, professional societies, and service organizations.

History

Since the establishment of the first trade unions in the Middle Ages people have been coming together in groups for their mutual benefit. Whether their purpose is to share knowledge, leverage power, acquire benefits, or just socialize with others of like interests, individuals know that they can usually achieve goals more readily when they join forces. These include professional societies such as the American Medical Association and labor unions such as the United Auto Workers among thousands of groups promoting common interests such as stamp collecting. For these organizations to serve their members efficiently, they must have staffs that carry out their programs. These staffs are led by association executives.

Nature of the work

Association executives perform a variety of duties, depending upon their positions within their organizations. These positions can include *executive director, associate director, business manager,* and *department heads* responsible for marketing, public relations, publications, educa-

tion, research, membership, and fund development. In a small association, all of these responsibilities may rest with one or two persons. Associations with staffs of more than one hundred may employ separate individuals to head these and other departments.

Association executives carry out the objectives of their organizations as defined by the board of directors. These objectives generally include the professional betterment and improved welfare of their members, as well as influencing policy, both public and internal, on behalf of their members. To help members develop their professional skills, associations prepare education materials, plan workshops and seminars, and provide technical assistance. They often maintain professional libraries, and they may also sponsor yearly conventions where new products and services are introduced, and where members can share problems and solutions with their peers.

To determine the well-being of their members, associations conduct surveys of salaries, benefits, and other concerns. They analyze survey results, and when they find unsatisfactory conditions, they organize committees enact solutions. Associations publish their survey conclusions, as well as other information of interest to members, such as relevant research findings, policy changes, or government legislation in journals and newsletters.

Association executives help create an optimum working environment by representing their constituencies in negotiations with government, labor, and business leaders.

Finally, to ensure the integrity of their institutions, associations may investigate the activities of their members and dismiss any that do not maintain their standards and thereby reflect poorly on the institution.

Requirements

Because association executives have many responsibilities, they must master a wide variety of skills. They must be good planners, coordinators, communicators, and people managers. They must have expertise in public relations, marketing, and financial management. Executives are often called upon to speak in public, so they should be articulate, personable, and persuasive. A college education is usually expected if not required of association executives. General studies in the humanities and business administration are most valuable.

This association executive is reading over financial statements to ensure that the association remains solvent.

Special requirements

Most associations are not-for-profit organizations and therefore cannot provide their executives with the same salaries and benefits as they might earn at for-profit corporations. Association executives, however, can expect to work at least as hard as their private-sector counterparts. Therefore, association executives be very committed and loyal to their employers, and must be able to derive satisfaction from knowing that they are helping hundreds, thousands, or even hundreds of thousands of other people lead better lives.

Opportunities for experience and exploration

Students interested in association management should join school organizations such as student council, ethnic clubs, and debate teams, and should seek positions of responsibility within those organizations. Students might also consider joining the newspaper or yearbook staff to learn the publication process.

Related occupations

Association executives need to possess all of the skills and talents that there counterparts in industry have. In fact, many move into the not-for-profit sector after years of working for for-profit companies. Other occupations that are similar include top executives and general managers, management trainees, retail managers, and any other position in business management.

Methods of entering

Most associations are structured such that they have entry-level positions, such as administrative assistant and marketing assistant. Recent college graduates might consider finding the *Encyclopedia of Associations* in the library and sending cover letters and resumes to the organizations representing interests similar to their own.

Advancement

A talented worker can rise through the ranks, from assistant to associate, manager, and director positions. Ambitious association executives can hasten their advancement by taking continuing education courses and attending seminars and workshops. A master's degree in business administration and certification from the American Society of Association Executives or its local chapters are helpful in achieving top positions.

Employment outlook

Job opportunities for association executives are plentiful. Although some organizations disband after achieving their objectives, there are always others to take their places, and most established groups grow larger each year, necessitating more and better trained staff persons.

Earnings

Budgets and membership rolls vary widely from association to association, and so do the salaries of their workers. A middle-manager at a large association can earn more than the chief executive of a small association. In the early 1990s, salaries generally ranged from $35,000 to $75,000. Almost all association executive enjoy generous benefits, including comprehensive health insurance and pension plans.

Conditions of work

Most association executives work in comfortable, modern offices, though some may be required to travel a fair deal to coordinate affairs with affiliate offices. The majority of association headquarters are located in big cities such as New York, Chicago, and Washington, D.C. A forty-hour work week is standard, but many association executives work additional hours, especially prior to major events such as conventions or seminars.

Social and psychological factors

Association management is challenging, creative work, and, as such, it can also be stress-

ful. The satisfaction of mastering difficult work, however, generally outweighs minor anxieties along the way. Association work provides many opportunities for socializing both in and out of the office. National associations may employ many persons while local associations may have small staffs. Association executives interact with many people because association activities tend to be people-oriented and their day-to-day operations require constant communication with members and affiliate offices.

SOC: 1354; SIC: 86; GOE: 11.05.01

◇ **SOURCES OF ADDITIONAL INFORMATION**

American Society of Association Executives
1575 I Street, NW
Washington, DC 20005

Institute of Association Management Companies
1133 15th Street, NW, Suite 1000
Washington, DC 20005

◇ **RELATED ARTICLES**

Astronauts

Definition

Astronauts attempt to extend our knowledge of both outer space and our physiological and psychological adaptation to that environment.

To this end they conduct experiments and gather information while in space flight and on the moon. They also conduct experiments with the spacecraft itself to develop new concepts in design, engineering, and the navigation of a vehicle outside the earth's atmosphere. Most of this article concerns pilot astronauts, although some information is included on scientist astronauts.

History

The idea of flying into space and to the moon is not a new one. The first science fiction story, for instance, was published in A.D. 160, and indicates that humans, even then, had begun to think about moving beyond earth to other planets. In 1638, an Englishman by the name of Francis Godwin wrote about journey to the moon in a vehicle utilizing birdlike propulsion.

In 1865 the idea of jet power first was introduced. At that time Achille Eyraud of France wrote about a trip to Venus in a vehicle using this mode of force. In 1903, Konstantin E. Tsiolkovsky, a Russian schoolteacher, published the first scientific paper on the use of rockets for space travel.

Robert H. Goddard of the United States and Hermann Oberth of Germany, however, are recognized as the fathers of space flight. It was Goddard who designed and built a number of rocket motors and ground tested the liquid fuel rocket. His experiments were carried on as early as 1923, and in March 1926 he launched the first successful liquid fuel rocket. Oberth published *The Rocket into Interplanetary Space* in 1923, which discussed technical problems of space and described what a spaceship would be like.

Although there were few significant advances beyond this initial firing until after World War II, the Russians and Germans did carry on experiments in the 1930s, and it was quite evident in the 1940s that space flights were to become a reality. The Germans were at that time carrying on extensive experiments with their famed V-2 rockets, and test pilots were being employed to fly rocket-powered aircraft of various types. After the war, Werner von Braun and other German rocket experts came to the United States to work on NASA's space program.

In 1948, the U.S. government's School of Aviation Medicine began carrying out a number of experiments concerned with weightlessness, and the school's Department of Space Medicine was organized in February 1949. A wide variety of studies were carried on by this department including investigations of isolation in space flight, the amount of oxygen needed in flight, and the types of food, clothing, and temperature controls to be used. They also began

One of the first roles of astronauts was lunar exploration; one of the future expeditions may be voyages to Mars.

developing emergency procedures for the maintenance of life in case of cabin failure.

The actual space age began, however, on October 4, 1957, when Sputnik I was launched by the U.S.S.R. The second major success came with the launching of Soviet cosmonaut Yuri A. Gagarin on April 21, 1961. He was followed by American astronaut Alan B. Shephard, Jr., who was propelled 117 miles above the earth on a suborbital fight. And in 1962 John Glenn circled the earth three times in less than five hours in a space capsule traveling at a speed of about 17,545 miles an hour. He became the first American to orbit the earth.

American astronaut Neil Armstrong became the first man to set foot on the moon in July 1969.

In the mid-1970s, astronauts carried out the first repair work in space and proved humans could live and work for months in a state of weightlessness.

In April 1981, the United States launched the first orbiting space shuttle, designed for repeated flights into space. Today, space shuttles are used almost routinely for scientific missions and to launch satellites farther into space.

Nature of the work

Crew-carrying space shuttles such as *Atlantis*, *Columbia*, and *Discovery* are launched into space where they orbit the earth on missions lasting up to thirty days. Then they return to earth and are made ready for their next trip.

Although the nature of the work carried on by astronauts varies from flight to flight and is expected to change radically from year to year, their major concern today is one of carrying out experiments and research. Satellites released from a shuttle can be propelled into much higher orbits than the spacecraft itself is capable of reaching, thus permitting a much wider range of observation.

While on their missions, astronauts may deploy and retrieve satellites or service them. They also may operate laboratories related to astronomy, earth sciences, materials processing, or manufacturing and engage in other activities. One of the goals for the near future is the development of a permanent U.S. space station. Astronauts will be involved in setting up and servicing such projects.

The basic crew of a space shuttle is made up of five persons: the commander, the pilot, and three mission specialists, all of whom are NASA astronauts. Some flights also call for a payload specialist, who becomes the sixth member of the crew. From time to time, other experts will be on board. Depending on the purpose of the mission, they may be engineers, technicians, physicians, or scientists such as astronomers, meteorologists, or biologists. The orbiter can carry a total of seven persons.

The commander and the pilot of a space shuttle are both *pilot astronauts* who know how to fly aircraft and spacecraft. Commanders are in charge of the overall mission. They maneuver the orbiter, supervise the crew and the operation of the vehicle, and are responsible for the success and safety of the flight. Pilots help the commanders control and operate the orbiter and may help manipulate satellites by using a remote control system. Like other crew members, they sometimes do work outside the craft or look after the payload.

The three mission specialists are also trained astronauts. They work along with the commander and the pilot. Mission specialists work on specific experiments, perform tasks outside the orbiter, use remote manipulator systems to deploy payloads, and handle the many details necessary to carry out the mission. One or more payload specialists may be included on flights. A payload specialist may not be a NASA astronaut but is an expert about the cargo being carried into space.

Although their actual work is conducted in space, astronauts are involved in extensive groundwork before and during launchings. Just prior to lift-off, they take their positions quickly and go through checklists to be sure nothing has been forgotten. Computers on board the space shuttle perform the countdown automatically and send the vehicle into space. When the rocket boosters are used up and the external fuel tank becomes empty, they separate from the orbiter. Once in orbit, the astronauts take control of the craft and are able to change its position or course or to maneuver into position with other vehicles.

Astronauts are part of a complex system. Throughout the flight, they remain in nearly constant contact with Mission Control and various tracking stations around the globe. Space technology experts on the ground monitor each flight closely, even checking the crew members' health via electrodes fitted to their bodies. Flight directors provide important information to the astronauts and help them solve any problems that may arise.

Astronauts perform many kinds of experiments in space. They test themselves, animals, plants, and minerals to see how they are affected by an environment in which there is no gravitational pull.

An important part of their work is the deployment of satellites. Communications satellites transmit telephone calls, television programs, educational and medical information, emergency instructions, and so on. Other satellites are used to observe and predict weather, to chart ocean currents and tides, and to measure the earth's various surfaces and check its natural resources. Space telescopes taken above the earth's atmosphere allow astronomers to study the solar and other star systems more thoroughly than is possible from the ground.

In conducting tests, astronauts use or operate a number of special cameras, sensors, meters, and other highly technical equipment.

Between flights, as part of their general duties, astronauts may travel to companies that manufacture and test spacecraft components, where they talk about the spacecraft and its mission.

Requirements

There are actually three major requirements for selection as a pilot astronaut candidate. The candidate must be a jet pilot with many hours of experience in the flying of high-performance, jet-propelled aircraft; the candidate must be a college graduate with a minimum of a bachelor's degree in engineering, the physical or biological sciences, or mathematics; and he or she must be between five feet four inches and six feet four inches tall. (Mission specialists may be as little as five feet tall.)

Pilot candidates must have acquired 1,000 hours jet pilot time. Graduation from an armed forces test pilot school is desirable. Pilot candidates are normally selected on the basis of superior academic achievement, extensive flying skills, physical condition, and an insatiable intellectual curiosity. As individuals they must be able to respond intelligently to strange and different conditions and circumstances.

Actual training as astronauts includes instruction in all aspects of space flight and consists of classroom instruction in astronomy, astrophysics, meteorology, star navigation, communications, computer theory, rocket engines and fuels, orbital mechanics, heat transfer, and space medicine. Much of their training involves field work and practical application of the classroom theory. Their laboratory work, for instance, will include work in space flight simulators during which many of the actual characteristics of space flight will be simulated along with some of the emergencies that may occur in flight.

To insure their safety while in flight, astronauts also learn to adjust to changes in air pressure and extreme heat and observe their physical and psychological reactions to these changes. They need to be prepared to respond to various possible circumstances.

Their training includes trips to the factories in which the various vehicles, including the spacecraft and rocket boosters, are built. The astronauts must gain a complete understanding of their craft and such trips assist them in gaining this understanding. They also develop new breathing habits to maintain calm in stressful situations and provide control over physical responses. The are also required to study survival techniques to be employed should they come down in a remote or uninhabited area.

Those who are accepted into the training program are not promised space flight at the time of acceptance. Their suitability for the job is continuously measured during one year of training at the Johnson Space Center in Houston, Texas. Those not qualifying for space flights are utilized in the various ground procedures involved in the preparation and execution of space flights.

High-school students looking forward to a career as an astronaut should follow a regular college preparatory curriculum in high school but should endeavor to take as much work as possible in mathematics and science.

Astronauts must be highly trained, skilled pilots with a tremendous desire to learn about outer space and to participate in the highly dangerous exploration of it. They must have a deep curiosity with extremely fine and quick reactions. They may have to react in emergency conditions that may never before have been experienced, and to do so they must be able to remain calm and to think quickly and logically.

Special requirements

Astronauts must pass specific tests devised by the space program, including physical exams with exceptionally high standards for vision, hearing, and blood pressure. The test for pilot astronauts is even stricter than that for mission specialists.

Although not a requirement, astronauts may be members of technical and professional societies such as the American Institute of Aeronautics and Astronautics (AIAA), the American Astronautical Society, and the Society of Experimental Test Pilots.

Opportunities for experience and exploration

Students who wish to become astronauts may find it helpful to write to various organizations concerned with space flights or to talk with people employed as pilots or test pilots if there is the opportunity. It may also help to speak with individuals in colleges and universities who are involved in various aspects of space investigation including astronomers, meteorologists, or others engaged in the sciences.

Talks with engineers who are engaged on space projects may also be of some assistance. It is primarily a task of drawing together bits of information until a fairly accurate picture of the job of the astronaut is formed. Even then, the classified details will be known only to the astronauts or those very closely allied to their training.

Related occupations

Not everyone with a strong desire to fly and to explore outer space can become an astronaut. These same interests, however, can be satisfied in such other occupations as aerospace engineers, aircraft pilots and flight engineers, astronomers, and, to a certain extent, meteorologists. In addition, there are numerous technical, administrative, and clerical occupations in organizations that use, manufacture, or service aircraft or are related in some way to aerospace technology.

Methods of entering

Entrance into the profession involves, as previously stated, much experience as a pilot or extensive scientific experience. Those hoping to qualify as pilot astronauts are encouraged to gain experience in all kinds of flying, perhaps through the military service, as well as experience as a test pilot. Persons interested in becoming mission specialist astronauts should earn at least one advanced degree and gain experience in one or more fields. Applications may be made when vacancies for astronauts and openings of new programs are announced.

Advancement

Advancement is not a formal procedure. Those who gain experience as astronauts will likely work into positions of management as they retire from actual flight status. Some astronauts may direct future space programs, head space laboratories or factories, or even become leaders of space colonies. Beyond this, advancement possibilities are unknown.

Employment outlook

Because of the nature of the program at the current time, including the great expense involved in each flight and the consequential limited number of flights, there is no need for a large number of astronauts.

Much of the demand will depend upon the success of the programs and the relative rapidity with which the programs develop. Plans for future expansion include a space station where private firms will manufacture substances and items that can be made more perfectly in space —such things as vaccines, enzymes, crystals, metal alloys, and ball bearings. The satellite communications business is expected to grow as private industry becomes more involved in producing satellites for commercial use. But these projects are not likely to change significantly the employment picture for astronauts before the year 2000.

Earnings

Salaries for astronauts who are members of the armed forces consist of base pay, an allowance for housing and subsistence, and flight pay. In the early 1990s, the total was more than $44,000 a year for a major, $54,000 for a full colonel.

The rate of pay for civilians is different. During the same period, a civil service rating of GS-15 was worth between $52,000 and $66,000 a year. Astronauts who were neither military nor civil service employees received similar compensation.

In addition, astronauts get the usual benefits, including vacations, sick leave, health insurance, retirement pensions, and bonuses for superior performance. They work a normal forty-hour week when preparing and testing for a spaceflight, but, as countdown approaches and activity is stepped up, they may work long hours, seven days a week. While on a mission, of course, they work as many hours as necessary to accomplish their objectives.

Conditions of work

Astronauts do work that is difficult, challenging, and potentially dangerous. They work closely as a team because their safety depends on their being able to rely on one another.

The training period is rigorous, and conditions in the simulators and trainers can be restrictive and uncomfortable. Exercises to produce the effect of weightlessness may cause air sickness in new trainees.

Astronauts on a spaceflight have to become accustomed to floating around in cramped quarters. Because of the absence of gravity, they must eat and drink either through a straw or very carefully with fork and spoon. Bathing is accomplished with a washcloth, as there are no showers in the spacecraft. Astronauts buckle and zip themselves into sleep bunks to keep from drifting around the cabin. Sleeping is generally done in shifts, which means that lights, noises, and activity are a constant factor.

During the launch and when working outside the spacecraft, astronauts wear specially designed spacesuits to protect them against various facets of the new environment. Once in orbit, they may wear comfortable work clothes.

While not in flight, astronauts' working conditions are good. The astronauts are respected by others and have an opportunity to work with intelligent, interesting, and motivated people.

Even as space flights become more frequent with the space shuttles, it should always be understood that the work is done with the forefront of knowledge about space travel. The true test of the equipment is in flight, which means that safety may be at risk. The job has risks and will continue to have for some time.

Social and psychological factors

The work in which astronauts are involved is hazardous even though most of the anticipated dangers have been protected against. There is a great deal of psychological pressure, however, in that they must deal with unknown dangers and are involved in such complex operations that even a minor defect could spell the end for both the astronaut and the ship.

The work is challenging, however, and the astronauts have the satisfaction of knowing that they are venturing into an area never before inhabited by humans. They have the satisfaction of providing answers to phenomena that have been the interest and concern of scientists for hundreds of years.

GOE: none; SIC: 9661; SOC: none

◇ SOURCES OF ADDITIONAL INFORMATION

American Institute of Aeronautics and Astronautics
370 L'Enfant Promenade, SW
Washington, DC 20024

Astronaut Candidate Program
Mail Code AHX
NASA-Johnson Space Center
Houston, TX 77058

National Aeronautics and Space Administration
Office of Educational Programs and Services
400 Maryland Avenue
Washington, DC 20025

◇ RELATED ARTICLES

Volume 1: Aviation and Aerospace; Military Service; Physical Sciences; Transportation
Volume 2: Air traffic controllers; Astronomers; Engineers; Pilots
Volume 3: Aircraft mechanics and engine specialists; Airline dispatchers; Flight engineers
Volume 4: Aeronautical and aerospace technicians; Avionics technicians

Astronomers

Definition

Astronomers study the universe and its celestial bodies by collecting and analyzing data. They also compute positions of stars and planets; calculate orbits of comets, asteroids, and artificial satellites; make statistical studies of stars and galaxies; and prepare mathematical tables giving positions of the sun, moon, planets, and stars at a given time. Astronomers also study the size and shape of the earth and the properties of its upper atmosphere through observation and through information obtained by means of spacecraft and earth satellites.

Astronomers use ground-based telescopes for night observation of the skies. They have also launched orbiting telescopes that will magnify the stars at a much greater percentage than land based capability allows.

History

The term *astronomy* is derived from two Greek words, *astron*, meaning star, and *nemein*, meaning to arrange or distribute. The ancient Egyptians first used astronomy after they observed that the Nile River overflowed when the star Sirius reached a specific position in the sky. After a great deal of study, the Egyptians established a calendar, the first in history to be based on the cycles of the sun and the moon.

The Babylonians made the first scientific use of astronomy, employing their knowledge of mathematics to assist them in the study of the heavens. The Greeks carried on this study, and in 150 B.C., Hipparchus developed a comprehensive catalog of the positions of various stars and studied the eclipses of the sun and moon. Hipparchus' studies were published 300

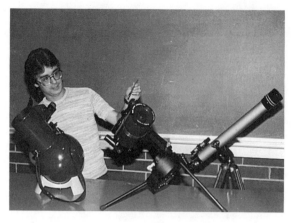

This astronomer is demonstrating how to use three different types of telescopes. The telescopes vary in capacity and complexity.

Nature of the work

The astronomer's work is perhaps the most theoretical of all the sciences. But more than that, it provides a laboratory and a proving ground for theories of time, space, and the observation of matter and energy.

Astronomers are primarily concerned with the universe and all of its celestial bodies. They are responsible for the collection, selection, and analysis of information concerning the moon, planets, sun, and stars and are concerned with the determination of their shapes, sizes, brightness, and motions.

They are interested in the orbits of comets, asteroids, and even artificial satellites. Information on the size and shape, the luminosity and position, the composition, characteristics, and structure as well as temperature, distance, motion, and orbit of all celestial bodies is of great relevancy to their work.

The launching of space vehicles and satellites has increased the importance of factual material concerning the makeup of heavenly bodies and their particular environments. This information has a direct relationship to the maintenance of astronauts in space.

Although the telescope is the major instrument used in observation, many other complex devices are also used by astronomers in carrying out these studies, including spectrometers for the measurement of wavelengths of radiant energy, photometers for the measurement of light intensity, balloons for carrying various measuring devices, and electronic computers for processing and analyzing all the information gathered.

Astronomers are usually expected to specialize in some particular branch of astronomy.

The *astrophysicist* is concerned with applying the concepts of physics to stellar atmospheres and interiors.

Specialists in celestial mechanics are concerned in part with the motions and positions of objects in the solar system. They would thus have a particular interest in the calculation of orbits of earth-launched objects.

Radio astronomers study, with extremely sensitive radio telescopes, the source and nature of celestial radio waves.

Many fields are available for specialization and, as more information becomes available through research and study, even greater specialization is expected to develop.

The great majority of astronomers either teach or do research or a combination of both. Astronomers in many colleges and universities are expected to teach such subjects as physics and mathematics in addition to astronomy. Other astronomers are engaged in such activi-

years later by Claudius Ptolemy, a Greek astronomer. These publications gained notice in about A.D. 808 and aroused much interest during the next several hundred years. The great intellectual awakening of the Renaissance was taking place during this period, thus assisting to a great extent the entire growth of astronomy as a science.

Nicolaus Copernicus, early in the sixteenth century, proved with the use of mathematics that the earth moves around the sun. This theory was voiced earlier by Aristarchus of Samos, but it had received little credence, primarily because of the strong belief that the earth was the center of the universe.

In the early seventeenth century, observations were being made by the naked eye and without the use of optical aids. Galileo, around 1609, heard of the invention of the telescope and constructed one of his own. Using this instrument, he made a series of important discoveries about the heavenly bodies, including the fact that Venus had phases comparable to those of the moon.

Perhaps the greatest of the early astronomers was Sir Isaac Newton, who did much to elaborate upon and clarify the work of Galileo. He also defined the law of universal gravitation. Then, in the nineteenth century, more improvements in optical aids and various other instruments came about, new discoveries were made, and women began to enter the field. In the twentieth century much headway has been made. The use of observational techniques has come to include observations from balloons, and the launching of man-made satellites equipped with various types of observational equipment has aided in the gathering of pertinent information.

ties as the development and design of astronomical instruments, administration, technical writing, and consulting.

Requirements

The very nature of the work of astronomers calls for individuals with a strong but controlled imagination. They must be able to see relationships between what may appear to be on the surface unrelated facts, and they must be able to form various hypotheses regarding these relationships. Their thinking must be precise and logical, and they must be able to concentrate over long periods of time. They should also express themselves well both in writing and speaking.

Formal training should begin in high school, where prospective astronomers should take mathematics up to and including analytical geometry and trigonometry, science courses including chemistry and physics, English, foreign languages, and courses in the humanities and social sciences.

Students should then select a college program with wide offerings in physics, mathematics, and astronomy. They should take as many of these courses as feasible. Those people hoping to attain a high level of professional achievement will find a doctorate a necessity. Although it is possible to begin work in the field with a lesser degree of preparation, advancement is much more probable for those with such training. This formal training will normally take about three years beyond the bachelor's degree.

Graduate school entrance requirements include an undergraduate major in physics or astronomy/physics, a B average or better, and satisfactory performance on the Graduate Record Exam (GRE). Bachelor's degrees in astronomy were offered by some sixty-one institutions in the United States in the early 1990s. Some sixty-seven institutions offer doctorates in the field.

Special requirements

As previously mentioned, the doctorate is a special requirement of all young people seeking high-level teaching or research positions in astronomy. A few of the astronomy courses typically offered in graduate school are celestial mechanics, galactic structure, radio astronomy, stellar atmospheres and interiors, theoretical astrophysics, and binary and variable stars.

Some graduate schools require that an applicant for a doctorate spend several months in residence at an observatory. In most institutions the graduate student is allowed the flexibility to take courses that will be of the most value in the chosen astronomical specialty or particular field of interest.

Opportunities for experience and exploration

A number of summer or part-time jobs are usually available in observatories. The latter may be either on a summer basis or year-round. These jobs not only offer experience in astronomy but often act as stepping stones to good jobs upon graduation. Students employed in observatories might work as guides or as assistants to astronomers.

Students may also test their interest in this field by working part-time, either as an employee or as a volunteer, in planetariums or science museums.

A number of articles have been written about the work of astronomers, and a letter to the organizations listed at the end of this article may well result in material that would be of assistance to the person interested in a career in astronomy.

Related occupations

Astronomy is sometimes considered a subfield of physics, which in turn is closely related to other scientific occupations in chemistry, geology, and geophysics. The attitudes and aptitudes that make a person suitable for astronomy also may be applied to occupations in industrial research. In addition, training in this field is excellent preparation for science teachers, science writers, laboratory technicians, and computer programmers.

Methods of entering

A chief method of entry for astronomers with a doctorate is to register with the college's placement bureau and to wait to be contacted by one of the agencies looking for astronomers.

Graduates with bachelor's or master's degrees could normally obtain semiprofessional positions in observatories, planetariums, or in some of the larger colleges and universities offering training in astronomy. Their work assignment might be as research assistants, optical workers, observers, or technical assistants. Those employed by colleges or universities might well begin as instructors. Federal government positions in astronomy are usually earned on the basis of competitive examinations given periodically by the Board of U.S. Civil Service Examiners for Scientific and Technical Personnel. Jobs with some municipal organizations employing astronomers are often based on competitive examinations. The examinations are usually open to those with bachelor's degrees.

Advancement

Because of the relatively small size of the field, advancement may be somewhat limited. A professional position in a large university or governmental agency is often considered the most desirable post available to an astronomer because of the opportunities it offers for additional study and research. Those employed in a college may well advance from instructor to assistant professor to associate professor and then to professor. There is also the possibility of eventually becoming a department head.

Opportunities also exist for advancement in observatories or industries employing people in astronomy. In these employment situations, as in those in colleges and universities, advancement depends to a great extent on the astronomer's ability, education, and experience.

Employment outlook

Astronomy is one of the smallest science fields, employing only about 3,500 people in the early 1990s. Approximately 60 percent of professional astronomers are faculty members at colleges and universities or are affiliated with those institutions through observatories and laboratories. About 30 percent are employed by the federal government directly or by federally supported national observatories and laboratories. Fewer than 10 percent work in business and private industry, although the number of these jobs available is growing rapidly. The rest work in planetariums, science museums, or other public service positions involved in presenting astronomy to the general public; teach physics or earth sciences in secondary schools; or are science journalists and writers.

Currently, there are about 150 openings each year for professional astronomers. These

result from the normal turnover when workers retire or leave the field for other reasons. Competition for these jobs, particularly among new people entering the profession, will continue to be strong. It is anticipated, however, that the employment outlook for astronomers will become more favorable by the late 1990s. At that time, many of those who entered the field of astronomy during its tremendous growth period in the 1960s will be reaching retirement age, providing an increase in opportunities.

The greatest growth in employment of astronomers is expected to occur in business and industry. Companies in the aerospace field will need more astronomers to do research that can affect their competitive position. Astronomers will be hired by consulting firms that supply astronomical talent to the government for specific tasks. In addition, a number of companies will hire astronomers to work in related areas where they can use their background and talents in instrumentation, remote sensing, spectral observations, and computer applications to unusual problems.

The federal government is also expected to provide a greater number of employment possibilities for astronomers. Several agencies, including the National Aeronautics and Space Administration (NASA), the U.S Naval Observatory, the Army Map Service, and the Naval Research Laboratory, currently employ, and are expected to continue to employ, trained astronomers.

Few new observatories will be constructed, and those currently in existence are not expected to greatly increase the size of their staffs. It is possible, however, that many smaller colleges and universities will begin developing research programs in astronomy, and thus new positions might be available in the future.

Earnings

In educational institutions salaries are normally regulated by the salary schedule prevailing in that particular institution. Starting salaries for assistant professors in the early 1990s averaged about $20,000 for nine months. As the astronomer advances to higher-level teaching positions, the salary increases significantly. Full professors and department heads can make $50,000 or more per academic year. Many faculty members augment their salaries with summer work at their universities or with summer research support.

Average salaries for astronomers employed in government are comparable to those in the larger universities, but the freedom to pursue independent research is not available to government and industry astronomers.

Well-trained and experienced astronomers will often find their services in demand as consultants. Fees for this type of work may run as high as $200 per day in some of the more specialized fields of astronomy.

Conditions of work

Astronomers' activities may center around the optical telescope. For viewing purposes, most telescopes are located high on a hill or mountain and normally in a fairly remote area where the air is clean and the view is not affected by lights from unrelated sources. There are some 300 of these observatories in the United States. Some of the more famous include Mt. Palomar, Mt. Wilson, Lick, Yerkes, and McDonald.

Astronomers working in these observatories usually are assigned to observation from three to six nights per month and spend the remainder of their time in an office or laboratory where they study and analyze their data. They must also prepare reports. They may well work with others on one segment of their research or writing and then work entirely alone on the next. Their work is normally carried on in clean, quiet, well-ventilated, and well-lighted facilities.

Those astronomers in administrative positions, such as director of an observatory or planetarium, will maintain fairly steady office hours but may also work during the evening and night. They usually are more involved in administrative details, however, and not so much in observation and research.

Those employed as teachers will usually have good facilities available to them, and their hours will vary according to class hours assigned. Work for those employed by colleges and universities may often be more than forty hours per week if the amount of work they must do at home developing lessons and correcting papers and doing all that is necessary to stay current with their field is included.

Social and psychological factors

Astronomers usually find a great deal of satisfaction in their work. They gain this satisfaction from knowing that they are adding to the supply of information already gathered about the universe and that the data they are gathering and analyzing will assist others in learning the truths about our universe. The opportunity for scientific observation and research is unlimited in astronomy. Astronomers gain satisfaction from knowing that their findings and research are important to the entire world.

Teachers in colleges or universities gain the satisfaction of helping others learn about our universe. They have the pleasure of encouraging the interest of others in astronomy by their teachings, an area they greatly enjoy themselves.

The job enables astronomers to work alone or with others, and it offers much satisfaction and pleasant working conditions. Astronomers have the opportunity of dedicating their working lives to their chief scientific interest. They also have the satisfaction of knowing that the job offers a great deal of personal freedom as well as the respect of the community.

There are drawbacks, of course. Night work is often required, and much of the work is tedious, tiresome, and routine. This work requires a person of dedication and purpose to tolerate the watching, waiting, observing, and recording that is often necessary for progress. Then, too, astronomers often have to go where the job is and where the equipment is available.

GOE: 02.01.01; SIC: 8412; SOC: 1842

 SOURCES OF ADDITIONAL INFORMATION

Amatuer Astronomers Association
1010 Park Avenue
New York, NY 10028

American Astronomical Society
2000 Florida Avenue, NW, #300
Washington, DC 20009

American Institute of Physics
335 East 45th Street
New York, NY 10017

Harvard-Smithsonian Center for Astrophysics and Space Sciences
60 Garden Street
Cambridge, MA 02138

Interagency Board of Civil Service Examiners
1900 E Street, NW
Washington, DC 20415

International Planetarium Society
Hansen Planetarium
15 South State Street
Salt Lake City, UT 84111

Scientists Institute for Public Information
355 Lexington Avenue
16th floor
New York, NY 10017

◇ **RELATED ARTICLES**

Volume 1: Biological Sciences; Chemistry; Education; Nuclear Sciences; Physical Sciences
Volume 2: Astronauts; College and university faculty; Geologists; Geophysicists; Meteorologists; Museum occupations; Physicists
Volume 4: Planetarium technicians

Biochemists

Definition

A *biochemist* studies the chemical composition of living organisms. This scientist identifies and analyzes the chemical processes related to biological functions such as reproduction and metabolism. The biochemist also studies the effect of environment on living tissue.

History

When farmers in biblical times fermented grain to produce alcohol, they undertook the first biochemical investigations. The earliest forays into biochemistry in the modern era were conducted by Antoine-Laurent Lavoisier and Pierre-Simon Laplace more than 200 years ago. They proved that the law of conservation of matter applied to living as well as nonliving systems.

By the early nineteenth century, pioneer biochemists had begun the identification of the materials found in living cells. Baron Justus von Liebig recognized the presence of nitrogen in compounds that were later named proteins. The German chemist, Emil Fischer, traced the chemical structure of carbohydrates, which appear in nearly all plants and animals.

Other biochemists discovered and named the "enzyme," a catalyst that appears naturally in yeast. A tremendous impetus to biochemistry was the mechanics of the fermentation process that had been practiced for some 2,000 years. Biochemists have widened their searches in recent years to include the composition of protein molecules and chromosomes that make

up human life itself. They are on the threshold of synthesizing these elemental substances.

Nature of the work

Most biochemists employed in the United States work in the fields of medicine, biomedicine, nutrition, and agriculture. In medicine, they investigate the causes and cures of disease and methods of diagnosis; in biomedicine, they delve into genetics, brain function, and physiological adaption; in nutrition, they examine the effects of food deficiencies on human performance, including the ability to learn; in agriculture, they undertake studies to discover more efficient methods of crop cultivation and storage and ways to control pests.

Biochemists' principal tool in recent years has been the electron microscope, which permits them to examine molecular structures, but they also devise new instruments and analytical techniques as needed.

About seven out of ten biochemists are engaged in pure research, often for a university medical school or nonprofit organization such as a foundation or research institute. The remaining 30 percent do applied research, using the discoveries of basic research to solve practical problems or develop products. For example, the discovery of how a living organism forms hormones led to hormone synthesis in the laboratory and production on a mass scale. The distinction between basic and applied research is one of degree, however; biochemists often engage in both types of work.

Requirements

At the very least, beginning biochemists require a bachelor's degree in biochemistry or in chemistry, genetics, microbiology, or biology to qualify for jobs as research aides or technicians. Graduate training in biochemistry is a necessity, however, for positions in research and teaching and for advancement in all types of work.

Some schools award a bachelor's degree in biochemistry, and all colleges and universities offer a major in biology or chemistry. Undergraduate courses include chemistry, biology, biochemistry, mathematics, physics, statistics, and computer science. Graduate study in biochemistry is intensive. To earn a master's degree requires about two years of coursework and seminars, as well as an original laboratory research project. Candidates for a doctorate must engage in original research leading to new scientific findings and must write a formal thesis. Study for a doctorate generally takes about four years.

Special requirements

Biochemists who wish to work in a hospital may need certification by a national certifying board such as the American Board of Clinical Chemistry.

The biochemist conducts research on the effects of radiation and other pollutants on living matter. These experiments require concentration and precision.

Opportunities for experience and exploration

The analytical, specialized nature of most biochemistry makes it unlikely that a student interested in the profession will gain much exposure to it before college. Many high-school chemistry and biology courses, however, allow students to work with laboratory tools and techniques, and many of the recent discoveries in genetics and molecular structures have been described in book form for aspiring biochemists.

Related occupations

Biochemists are classified with other workers in the biological sciences. This group of occupations includes animal breeders, aquatic biologists, biophysicists, food technologists, geneti-

cists, pharmacologists, plant breeders, and plant pathologists.

Methods of entering

Biochemists fresh from a college undergraduate program usually begin work in industry or government as research assistants doing testing and analysis. In the drug industry, for example, they may analyze the ingredients of a product to verify and maintain its quality. Biochemists with a master's degree may enter the field in positions in management, marketing, or sales, whereas those with a doctorate often go into basic or applied research.

Advancement

Biochemists with a graduate degree have more opportunities for advancement than do those with only an undergraduate degree. Some graduate students become research or teaching assistants in colleges and universities, qualifying for professorships when they receive their advanced degrees. Experienced biochemists who have doctorates can move up to high-level administrative positions and supervise research programs. Other highly qualified biochemists, who prefer to devote themselves to research, often become leaders in a particular aspect of their profession.

Employment outlook

The prospects through the 1990s are excellent. Employment will increase in health-related fields, where the emphasis is on finding cures for such diseases as cancer, muscular dystrophy, AIDS, and mental illness. Additional jobs will be created to produce genetically engineered drugs and other products in the new and rapidly expanding field of genetic engineering. In this area, the outlook is best for biochemists with advanced degrees who can conduct genetic and cellular research.

In addition to the opportunities resulting from growth in the field, some new biochemists will be needed each year to replace those who retire, die, or change jobs. Biochemists with bachelor's degrees who have difficulty entering their chosen career may find openings as technicians or technologists or may choose to transfer their skills to work in the other biological sciences.

Earnings

Starting salaries paid to biochemists employed by colleges and universities are comparable to those for other professional faculty members. In the early 1990s, assistant professors earned an average of about $24,800 per year; associate professors, about $30,000; and full professors, about $38,200. In industry, the average income for all biochemists with a bachelor's degree was approximately $21,000 per year; for those with a master's, $27,000; and for those with a doctorate, $36,200. Starting salaries for biochemists in the federal government in the early 1990s ranged from about $14,800 to $18,400 a year for those with a bachelor's degree, from about $18,400 to $22,500 for persons with a master's degree, and from about $27,200 to $33,600 for biochemists with a doctorate.

Conditions of work

Biochemists work generally in clean, quiet, and well-lighted laboratories where physical labor is at a minimum. They must, however, take the proper precautions in handling chemicals and organic substances that could be damaging.

Biochemists in industry generally work a forty-hour week, although they, like their counterparts in research, often put in many extra hours. Much personal time must be devoted to keeping up with the literature in their field. Many biochemists travel occasionally to attend meetings or conferences. Those in research write papers for presentation at meetings or for publication in scientific journals.

Social and psychological factors

Individuals interested in biochemistry must have the patience to work for long periods of time on a project without positive results. They also must be able to recognize when a particular endeavor has reached a dead end and, regardless of the investment of time and energy, should be dropped. Biochemistry is often a team affair, and the individual should be able to function in a situation where blame may be personal but credit is shared by all. Successful biochemists are continually learning and increasing their skills. By keeping informed of new discoveries and mastering new techniques, they are able to maintain stimulating and exciting careers.

GOE: 02.02.03; SIC: 2836, 8071, 8221; SOC: 1854

◇ **SOURCES OF ADDITIONAL INFORMATION**

American Association for Clinical Chemistry
2029 K Street, NW, 7th Floor
Washington, DC 20006

American Association of Pathologists
9650 Rockville Pike
Bethesda, MD 20814

American Institute of Biological Sciences
730 11th Street
Washington, DC 20001

American Society for Biochemistry and
Molecular Biology
Education Information
9650 Rockville Pike
Bethesda, MD 20814

Directory of Graduate Research
American Chemical Society
1155 16th Street, NW
Washington, DC 20036

◇ RELATED ARTICLES

Volume 1: Biological Sciences; Chemicals
and Drugs; Chemistry
Volume 2: Biologists; Biomedical engineers;
Chemists
Volume 4: Biological technicians; Biomedical
technicians; Chemical technicians; Laboratory
technicians; Medical laboratory technicians

Biologists

Definition

Biologists study the origin, development, anatomy, function, distribution, and other basic principles of living organisms. They are concerned with the nature of life itself; with humans, microorganisms, plants, and animals; and with the relationship of each organism to its environment. Biologists do research in many specialties that advance the fields of medicine, agriculture, and industry.

History

From earliest times, humans have observed and studied all living things around them. Often early theories regarding life were incorrect. Around 600 B.C. a Greek philosopher, Anaximander, developed the theory that all living things originally came from water. In the 11th century A.D., Avicenna wrote *Canon of Medicine*. His publication became the most important book of medical treatment for 700 years.

As Europe emerged from the Middle Ages, early scientists from many countries contributed to the development of biology. In 1514, Vesalius, a Belgian, became the first to dissect human bodies and founded anatomy. In the seventeenth century, an Englishman, William Harvey, discovered circulation of blood and contributed to the development of physiology. Scientific techniques were improved when Anton van Leeuwenhoek, a Dutchman, developed the microscope. In the eighteenth century, a Swedish naturalist, Carolus Linnaeus, developed a classification system for scientifically categorizing plants and animals.

The term "biology" was coined by Jean-Baptiste Lamarck, a distinguished French naturalist. During the nineteenth century, Charles Darwin developed a theory of evolution of all biological life. Matthias Schleiden and Theodor Schwann discovered the cellular makeup of all living organisms. An Austrian monk by the name of Gregor Johann Mendel used generations of garden peas to test his theories that provided the foundation for the science of genetics. Louis Pasteur of France and Robert Koch of Germany helped found bacteriology.

It was only natural that the rich flora and fauna of the United States encouraged the development of American biologists. John James Audubon and Louis Agassiz were among the pioneers in zoology. Asa Gray in botany and Luther Burbank in plant breeding also made distinguished contributions to biology. The whole field was aided by the establishment in 1887 of what is now known as the National Institutes of Health.

In recent years, biologists have made spectacular contributions in many fields. In agriculture, for example, the development of hybrid corn led to a 20 to 30 percent increase in bushels grown per acre. Penicillin, discovered by Sir Alexander Fleming on the eve of World War II, saved countless thousands of lives during that conflict and is still one of our leading medicines. Because of the work of biologists, organ transplants have become commonplace; the terms *DNA, genes,* and *cloning* have become familiar to the average person; and the public has an interest in ecology and the environment.

This biology student gains practical work experience in a corporate co-op program where he can prepare for a career in health and environmental research.

Nature of the work

Because of the breadth of the field the nature of the work performed by individual biologists varies widely.

Biology can be divided into many specialties. The most important is the distinction between the botanist and the zoologist. The *botanist* is concerned with plants and their environment, structure, heredity, and economic value in such fields as agronomy, horticulture, and medicine. The *zoologist* studies all types of animals to learn their origin, interrelationships, classification, life histories, habits, diseases, relation to environment, growth, genetics, and distribution. Another major division is that of microbiology. The *microbiologist* studies bacteria, viruses, molds, algae, yeasts, and other organisms of microscopic or submicroscopic size.

The interests of the biologist differ from those of the chemist, physicist, and geologist, who are concerned with nonliving matter.

The biologist may also be called a *biological scientist*, or *life scientist*. Biologists may be identified by their specialties. For example, *anatomists* study animal bodies from basic cell structure to complex tissues and organs. They determine the ability of body parts to regenerate and investigate the possibility of transplanting organs and skin. Their research is applied to human medicine. *Physiologists* are biologists who specialize in studying all the life stages of plants or animals. Some specialize in a particular body system or a particular function such as respiration. *Entomologists* study insects and their relation to other life forms. *Histopathologists* investigate diseased tissue in humans and animals. *Parasitologists* study animal parasites and their effects on humans and other animals.

A *pharmacologist* may be employed as a researcher by a pharmaceutical company spending most of the time working in the laboratory. This may be experimenting on the effects of various drugs and medical compounds on mice or rabbits. Working within a controlled environment, pharmacologists precisely note the type, quantity, and timing of medicines administered as a part of their experiments. Periodically, they make blood smears or perform autopsies to study different reactions. They usually work with a team of researchers, headed by one with a doctorate and consisting of several biologists with master's and bachelor's degrees and some laboratory technicians.

Biologists may also work for government agencies concerned with public health. *Staff toxicologists*, for example, study the effects of toxic substances on humans, animals, and plants. The data they gather is used in consumer protection and industrial safety programs to reduce the hazards of accidental exposure or ingestion. *Public-health microbiologists* conduct experiments on water, foods, and the general environment of a community to detect the presence of harmful bacteria so that pollution and contagious diseases can be controlled or eliminated.

Animal breeders specializing in improving the quality of farm animals may work for a state agricultural department, agricultural extension station, or university. Some of their work is done in a laboratory, but much of it is done outdoors working directly on animals. Biologists known as *plant breeders* may discover and develop strains of wild and cultivated plants that may prove of economic value.

Other specialists in the field of biology include the following:

Apiculturists study and do research with bees. They investigate causes of and ways of controlling disease in bees, study the phases and effects of pollination, and experiment in breeding improved bee strains.

Aquatic biologists study animals and plants that live in water and how they are affected by their environmental conditions, such as the salt, acid, and oxygen content of the water, temperature, light, and other factors.

Biophysicists apply physical principles to biological problems. They study the mechanics, heat, light, radiation, sound, electricity, and energetics of living cells and organisms and do research in the areas of vision, hearing, brain function, nerve conduction, muscle reflex, and damaged cells and tissues.

Cytologists examine the cells of plants and animals, including those cells involved in reproduction. They use microscopes and other instruments to observe the growth and division of cells and to study the influences of physical and chemical factors on both normal and malignant cells.

Ecologists study the distribution and abundance of organisms and their relation to their environment.

Geneticists study heredity in various forms of life. They are concerned with how biological traits such as color, size, and resistance to disease originate and are transmitted from one generation to another. They also try to develop ways to alter or produce new traits, using chemicals, heat, light, or other means.

Mycologists study edible, poisonous, and parasitic fungi, such as mushrooms, molds, yeasts, and mildews, to find those useful to medicine, agriculture, and industry. Their research results in benefits such as the development of antibiotics, the propagation of mushrooms, and methods of retarding fabric deterioration.

Nematologists study nematodes (roundworms) that are parasitic to plants, transmit diseases, attack insects, or attack other nematodes that exist in soil or fresh- or saltwater. They investigate and develop methods of control.

Plant pathologists research plant diseases and the decay of plant products to identify symptoms, determine causes, and develop control measures. They attempt to predict outbreaks by studying how different soils, climates, and geography affect the spread and intensity of plant disease.

Requirements

By nature, the biologist is curious and early in life this curiosity may have been reflected in

A biologist from the Environmental Protection Agency inspects a filter that tests water for the presence of parasites.

rock collections, stamp collections, or samples of mounted butterflies.

Professional biologists must be systematic in their approach to solving the problems that they face. They should have a probing, inquisitive mind, and an aptitude for biology, chemistry, and mathematics. Patience is required. Consider, for example, the hundreds of biologists who will spend much of their research life seeking the cause of and cure for cancer.

Useful high-school courses include English, biology, physics, chemistry, Latin, geometry, algebra, and typing. Prospective biological scientists also should obtain a broad undergraduate college training. In addition to courses in all phases of biology, useful related courses include organic and inorganic chemistry, physics, and mathematics. Modern languages, English, biometrics (the use of mathematics in biological measurements), and statistics are also useful. In view of the growing use of computers to help solve the problems of science, coursework or computer experience would be valuable. Undergraduate programs include laboratory practice and may involve field or collecting work.

Nearly all institutions offer undergraduate training in one or more biological science. These vary from liberal arts schools offering basic majors in botany and zoology to large universities that permit specialization (entomology, bacteriology, physiology, and so on) at the undergraduate level.

For the highest professional status, a doctorate is required. This is particularly true of top research positions and most higher level college teaching openings. A large number of colleges and universities offer courses leading to a master's degree and a doctorate. A study made by the National Science Foundation showed that among a group of biological scientists listed on the National Scientific Manpower Register, 10 percent held a bachelor's degree, 33 percent held a master's or professional medical degree, and the remaining 57 percent had earned a doctorate.

Candidates for a doctorate specialize in one of the subdivisions of biology. A number of sources of financial assistance are available to help finance graduate work. Most major universities have a highly developed fellowship (scholarship) or assistantship (part-time teaching or research) program.

Outside organizations, such as the U.S. Public Health Service and the National Science Foundation, make awards to support graduate students. In a recent year, for example, the Public Health Service made 8,000 fellowship and training grants. In addition, major universities often hold research contracts or have their own projects that provide part-time and summer employment for undergraduate and graduate students.

Special requirements

The chief requirement for employment as a biologist is suitable educational background. In general, this is a bachelor's or master's degree for a junior-level position and a doctorate for top professional status.

A state license may be required for biologists who are employed as technicians in general service health organizations (such as hospitals or clinics). To qualify for this license, proof of suitable educational background is necessary.

Biologists seeking public school teaching positions must, in addition to coursework in their major field, have completed state requirements for a teacher's certificate. These requirements vary between states.

In general, the prospective teacher must have six to eight hours of student or practice teaching and eight to twelve hours of related education courses. Some states now require the equivalent of a master's degree for full certification.

Opportunities for experience and exploration

Students may measure their aptitude and interest in the work of the biologist by taking courses in this area. Laboratory assignments, for example, provide actual information on techniques used by the working biologist. Many schools hire students as laboratory assistants to work directly under a teacher and help administer the laboratory sections of courses.

School assemblies, field trips to federal and private laboratories and research centers, and career conferences provide additional insight into career opportunities. Advanced students often are able to attend professional meetings and seminars.

Part-time and summer positions in biology or related areas are particularly helpful. Students with some college courses in biology may find summer positions as laboratory assistants. Graduate students may find work on research projects being conducted by their institution. Beginning college and advanced high-school students may find employment as laboratory aides or hospital orderlies or attendants. Despite the menial nature of these positions, they afford a useful insight into careers in biology. High-school students often have the opportunity to join volunteer service groups at local hospitals.

Student science training programs (SSTPs) allow qualified high-school students to spend a summer doing research under the supervision of a scientist.

Related occupations

The list of other occupations that deal with living organisms is long and diverse. Such occupations include agricultural scientists, life science technicians, oceanographers, and soil scientists, as well as such conservation occupations as forester, forestry technician, range manager, and soil conservationist. Persons with an interest in biology may find a wide choice of compatible jobs in the health field. Occupations involving the raising of plants and animals also share a relationship with the field of biology. These occupations include animal breeders, farmers and farm managers, florists, greenskeepers, landscape contractors, and nursery managers. (See volume 1: Biological Science for an overview of occupations related to this field)

Methods of entering

Biologists seeking employment as teachers usually will find their college placement office the best source of assistance. Public and private high schools and an increasing number of colleges hire teachers through the college at which they studied. Most placement offices assemble credentials (copies of letters of recommendation, information on academic and work experience, and so on) to provide useful background on teaching candidates. Private employment agencies also place a significant number of teachers. Some teaching positions are filled through direct application. Some superintendents of schools like to hire teachers who have demonstrated their initiative and interest by writing to file for a position.

Biologists interested in private industry and nonprofit organizations also may apply directly for employment. College seniors often participate in campus interviews conducted by representatives of employing organizations. Private and public employment offices frequently have listings from these employers. Experienced biologists often change positions on the basis of meeting people at professional seminars and national conventions.

Special application procedures are required for positions with governmental agencies. Civil service applications for federal, state, and municipal positions may be obtained by writing to the agency involved and from high-school and college guidance and placement bureaus, public employment agencies, and (for federal positions) at post offices. Many positions require a written test. Others are filled on the basis of an evaluation of the candidate's background.

Advancement

In a field as broad and as deep as biology, numerous opportunities for advancement exist. To a great extent, however, advancement depends on the individual's level of education. A doctorate is generally required for college teaching, independent research, and top-level administrative and management jobs. A master's degree is sufficient for some jobs in applied research, and a bachelor's degree may qualify for entry-level jobs.

With the right qualifications, the biologist may advance to the position of project chief and direct a team of other biologists. Many biologists use their knowledge and experience as background for administrative and management positions. Often, as they develop professional knowledge, biologists move increasingly from strictly technical assignments into positions in which they interpret biological knowledge.

The usual path of advancement in biology, as in other sciences, comes from specialization and the development of the status of an expert in a given field. Biology offers an unusually large number of specialties and subspecialties. Biological science may also be coupled with other major fields to explore problems that require an interdisciplinary approach: biochemistry, biophysics, biostatistics (or biometrics). Biochemistry, for example, utilizes the methods of chemistry to study the composition of biological materials and the molecular mechanisms of biological processes. Similarly, biophysics uses such tools of physics as heat, light, radiation, sound, and electricity to study the response of living organisms to physical forces.

Employment outlook

An average increase in the employment of biologists is predicted through the 1990s, although competition will be stiff for the high-paying jobs and government jobs will be less plentiful.

Advances in genetic research leading to new drugs, improved plants, and medical discoveries should open up some opportunities. Private industry should also need more biologists to keep up with the advances in biotechnology. Products now made by chemical or other means will soon be produced by biological methods. Efforts to preserve the environment may also result in an increased number of jobs.

Biologists with advanced degrees will have the advantage in finding positions, although this varies by specialty, with genetic, cellular, and biochemical research showing the most promise. Scientists with only a bachelor's degree may find openings as science or engineering technicians or health technologists and technicians. Many colleges and universities are cutting back on their faculties, but high schools and two-year colleges may have teaching positions available. High-school biology teachers are considered to be teachers rather than biologists, however.

Because biological scientists are usually employed on long-term research projects or in agriculture, which are not greatly affected by economic fluctuations, they rarely lose their jobs during recessions. In the early 1990s, approximately 61,000 biologists were employed in the United States (not counting an almost equal number on the faculties of colleges and universities). More than one-third worked in research and development laboratories for private industry, mainly in pharmaceutical, chemical, and food companies. About one-fifth were employed by the federal government, and one-sixth by state and local governments. About one-fifth held nonteaching positions at colleges or universities, and the rest worked for non-profit research organizations or hospitals or were self-employed.

Earnings

In the early 1990s, the federal government paid biologists with bachelor's degrees starting salaries of approximately $14,800 to $18,400 a year, depending on their college records. Those with master's degrees started at about $18,400 to $22,500, and those with doctorates, at $27,200 to $32,600. Biologists in the federal government averaged $37,200 annually in the early 1990s.

Beginning salaries in private industry averaged $19,000 a year for persons with bachelor's degrees. In general, the highest salaries are earned by biologists in business and industry, followed in turn by those who are self-employed, working for nonprofit organizations, in military service, and working for the U.S. Public Health Service or other positions in the federal government. The lowest salaries are earned by teachers and by those working for various state and local governments.

Conditions of work

The actual work environment of the biologist varies greatly depending upon his position and type of employer. One biologist may work outdoors or travel much of the time. Another wears a white smock and spends years working in a laboratory.

Biologists frequently work under some pressure. For example, those employed by pharmaceutical houses work in an atmosphere of keen competition for sales that encourages the development of new drug products and, as they are identified, the rapid testing and early marketing of these products. The work is very exacting, however, and the pharmaceutical biologists must exercise great care to ensure that adequate testing of products has been properly conducted.

Social and psychological factors

Significantly, the biological sciences are called the "life sciences." The purity of the water we drink, the food we eat, and the medicines we take are all the result of modern biological science.

Many industries and fields (medicine, pharmacy, agriculture, forestry, wildlife management, pest control, and so on) depend upon the biologist for basic scientific knowledge. In large part, as a result of the work of the biologist, the life expectancy of a newborn infant has grown in the last century from thirty-eight to more than seventy years.

The ultimate significance of the biologist is seen in the fact that more than 1.5 million different species of life inhabit the earth. Biologists are needed to help preserve this biological diversity into the next century.

GOE: 02.02.03; SIC: 2836, 8071, 8221, 8731, 8733; SOC: 1854

◇ SOURCES OF ADDITIONAL INFORMATION

American Association of Immunologists
9650 Rockville Pike
Bethesda, MD 20814

American Association of Pathologists
9650 Rockville Pike
Bethesda, MD 20814

American Genetic Association
PO Box 39
Buckeystown, MD 21717

American Institute of Biological Sciences
730 11th Street, NW
Washington, DC 20001

American Institute of Nutrition
9650 Rockville Pike
Bethesda, MD 20814

American Physiological Society
9650 Rockville Pike
Bethesda, MD 20814

American Society for Cell Biology
9650 Rockville Pike
Bethesda, MD 20814

American Society for Microbiology
1913 I Street, NW
Washington, DC 20006

**American Society for Biochemistry and
Molecular Biology**
9650 Rockville Pike
Bethesda, MD 20814

American Society of Parasitologists
Department of Biological Sciences
University of Texas
500 West University Avenue
El Paso, TX 79968

American Society of Plant Physiologists
15501 Monona Drive
Rockville, MD 20855

American Society of Zoologists
104 Sirius Circle
Thousand Oaks, CA 91360

Botanical Society of America
Ecology and Evolutionary Biology
75 North Eagleville Road
U-43 University of Connecticut
Storrs, CT 06268

Ecological Society of America
Center for Environmental Studies
Arizona State University
Tempe, AZ 85287

Entomological Society of America
9301 Annapolis Road
Lanham, MD 20706

**Federation of American Societies for
Experimental Biology**
9650 Rockville Pike
Bethesda, MD 20814

Genetics Society of America
9650 Rockville Pike
Bethesda, MD 20814

Mycological Society of America
Harvard University Herbaria
22 Divinity Avenue
Cambridge, MA 02138

National Institutes of Health
Bethesda, MD 20014

Society of Nematologists
Department of Nematology
University of California
Riverside, CA 92521

Society of Protozoologists
American Type Culture Collections
12301 Parklawn Drive
Rockville, MD 20852

**U.S. Department of Health and Human
Services**
Washington, DC 20201

◇ **RELATED ARTICLES**

Volume 1: Biological Sciences; Chemicals
and Drugs; Chemistry; Health Care
Volume 2: Biochemists; Chemists; Food tech-
nologists
Volume 3: Agricultural scientists
Volume 4: Biological specimen technicians;
Biological technicians; Chemical technicians;
Medical laboratory technicians

Biomedical engineers

Definition

Biomedical engineers are highly trained scientists
who employ engineering and life science principles in research conducted on the biological
aspects of animal and human life. They either
develop new theories, or they modify, test, and
prove existing theories on life systems. They
design health-care instruments and devices or
apply engineering principles to human systems. The artificial heart is a product of biomedical engineering.

Biomedical engineers are employed in industry, in hospitals, in research facilities of ed-

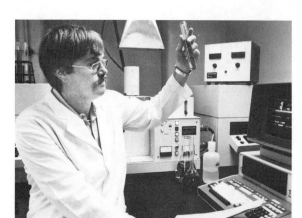

This biomedical engineer examines the contents of a test-tube, comparing his observations with a computer readout.

Nature of the work

In using engineering principles to solve medical and health-related problems, the biomedical engineer works closely with life scientists, members of the medical profession, and chemists. Most of the work revolves around the laboratory. There are three interrelated work areas: research, design, and teaching.

Biomedical research is multifaceted and broad in scope. It calls upon engineers to apply their knowledge of mechanical, chemical, and electrical engineering as well as anatomy and physiology in the study of living systems. Using computers, they employ their knowledge of graphic and related technologies to develop mathematical models that simulate physiological systems.

In biomedical engineering design, medical instruments and devices are developed. Engineers work on artificial organs, ultrasonic imagery devices, cardiac pacemakers, and surgical lasers. They may also design and build systems that will update hospital, laboratory, and clinical procedures. A final design implication is the assisting of health-care personnel in observing and treating physical handicaps and ailments.

The teaching aspect of biomedical engineering is on the university level. Teachers may conduct classes, advise students, serve on academic committees, and supervise or conduct research.

Within the field of biomedical engineering, an individual may concentrate on a particular specialty area. Some of the well-established ones are bioinstrumentation, biomechanics, biomaterials, systems physiology, clinical engineering, and rehabilitation engineering. These specialty areas frequently depend on one another.

Bioinstrumentation is the application of electronics and measurement principles and techniques to develop devices used in diagnosis and treatment of disease. Computers are becoming increasingly important in this specialty.

Biomechanics is mechanics applied to biological or medical problems. Efforts in this area have developed, among other things, the artificial heart, the artificial kidney, and the artificial hip.

Biomaterials are both living tissue and man-made materials used for implantation. The selection of an appropriate material to place in the human body may be one of the most difficult tasks faced by the biomedical engineer.

Systems physiology involves using engineering strategies, techniques, and tools to gain a comprehensive and integrated understanding of living organisms ranging from bacteria to hu-

ucational and medical institutions, in teaching, and in government regulatory agencies.

History

The advancement of human knowledge along with the achievements made in technology have created many new professions. Biomedical engineering is one of these. It is an interdisciplinary field that brings together two time-honored professions—biology and engineering.

Biology is the study of life. The term was coined by French naturalist Jean-Baptiste Lamarck early in the nineteenth century. More than the last 200 years, many advances have been made in this science. The theory of evolution was developed by Charles Darwin; Matthias Schleiden and Theodor Schwann discovered the cellular makeup of living organisms; and Gregor Johann Mendel pioneered in genetics. Other similarly striking developments also have been made.

Engineering is one of the world's oldest professions. It is concerned with using sources of energy in nature and the properties of matter in a manner that is useful to humans, particularly in machines, products, and structures. Engineering is a broad field encompassing many disciplines, including civil, material, chemical, and industrial engineering, among others. In total professional employment, it is second only to teaching.

Biomedical engineering arose primarily after 1945 in response to the need to apply engineering principles to biology.

mans. Biomedical engineers in this specialty examine such things as the biochemistry of metabolism and the control of limb movements.

Clinical engineering is the application of technology for health care in hospitals. The clinical engineer is a member of the health-care team along with physicians, nurses, and other hospital staff.

Rehabilitation engineering is a new and growing specialty area of biomedical engineering. Its goal is to expand the capabilities and improve the quality of life for individuals with physical impairments. Rehabilitation engineers often work directly with the disabled individual.

Requirements

Biomedical engineers should have a strong willingness to learn. They should be scientifically inclined and be able to apply their knowledge in problem solving. This is a far-ranging, interdisciplinary profession that requires long years of schooling so that a broad background in both engineering and biology can be gained. In particular, biomedical engineers have to be familiar with chemical, material, and electrical engineering as well as physiology and computers.

Most engineers possess an undergraduate degree in a major field of engineering and an advanced degree (preferably a Ph.D.) in some facet of biomedical engineering. Recently, some universities have instituted bachelor of science programs in biomedical engineering within a traditional engineering major.

Special requirements

The only special requirement for this profession is a willingness to gain a multidisciplinary scientific education in a university setting. To teach, biomedical engineers usually need a doctorate.

Opportunities for experience and exploration

Several ways exist to explore the opportunities available in this occupation. Undergraduate and graduate courses offer a great deal of exposure. Securing employment in a hospital or other facility where biomedical engineers are employed can also provide insight into the field, as can interviews with qualified personnel.

Related occupations

Biomedical engineers apply the principles of both engineering and life science in their work. Related occupations may fall into either of these two categories. They include engineers of all types, such as chemical engineers, electrical engineers, and industrial engineers; life scientists such as biologists, physiologists, and zoologists; engineering and science technicians; and specialists such as ergonomists and prosthetists and orthotists.

Methods of entering

A variety of routes may be taken to gain employment as a biomedical engineer. Recent graduates may use college placement services. They may apply directly to employers, often to personnel offices in hospitals and industry. A job may be secured by answering an advertisement in the employment want-ad section of a newspaper. Information on job openings also is available at the local office of the U.S. Employment Service.

Advancement

Advancement opportunities are tied directly to one's educational and research background. In a nonteaching capacity, a biomedical engineer with an advanced degree can rise to a supervisory position.

In teaching, a doctorate in biomedical engineering follows the usual academic career ladder. By demonstrating excellence in research, teaching, and departmental committee involvement, one can become a full professor, department chair, or dean.

The ability to receive research grant funding also can be a means of advancing in both nonteaching and teaching sectors.

Employment outlook

In the early 1990s, there were more than 4,000 biomedical engineers in the United States. They were employed in all parts of the country in hospitals, colleges and universities, medical and engineering schools, federal and state agencies, and private industry.

It is expected that there will be a greater need for skilled biomedical engineers through the 1990s. Prospects look particularly good in the large health care industry, which will continue to grow rapidly, primarily because people are living longer. New jobs will become available in biomedical research in prosthetics, artificial internal organs, computer applications, and instrumentation and other medical systems. In addition, a demand will exist for teachers to train the biomedical engineers needed to fill these positions.

Earnings

How much a biomedical engineer earns is dependent upon the amount of education and experience he or she possesses. In the early 1990s, the federal government pay scale for holders of a bachelor's degree ranged from approximately $19,000 to $24,000 a year. Biomedical engineers with a master's degree could start at about $26,000; and those with a doctorate, at around $28,000. The average salary for all engineers in the federal government was $38,000 a year.

In colleges and universities in the early 1990s, salaries for full-time faculty members on nine-month contracts ranged from about $21,300 for instructors to $45,500 for professors, with the average being about $35,500 per year. In addition, university professors can supplement their income significantly by writing and consulting.

Earnings in the private sector generally run higher than those in government or education.

Conditions of work

This is a highly demanding job intellectually. Relatively little physical labor is required but long hours are frequently spent in the laboratory. The work involves much use of sophisticated machinery and cooperation with other qualified personnel.

Those engaged in university teaching will have heavy student contact in the classroom, the laboratory, and the office. They will also be expected to serve on relevant committees while carrying their teaching, research, and writing loads. As competition for teaching positions increases, the requirement of professors to publish papers will also incrase, thus increasing faculty involvement in research. Professors

may be responsible for obtaining government or private research grants for the school.

Social and psychological factors

Biomedical engineering is a time-consuming, detail-oriented profession that is both challenging and rewarding. The work is directly related to improving the human condition, sometimes producing dramatic and swift results. The fruits of research and development, however, may take years to achieve, and government approval of products may add even more years to the fruition of a project.

In research and in design, the biomedical engineer is a crucial part of a project team, working with other highly-skilled individuals. In teaching, the biomedical engineer can experience strong satisfaction from interesting students in the field, though to do so requires demonstrating equally strong enthusiasm for the subject. Teaching, particularly on the graduate level, also requires research and lab work.

GOE: 02.02.01; SIC: 8711; SOC: 1639

◇ **SOURCES OF ADDITIONAL INFORMATION**

Accreditation Board for Engineering and Technology (ABET)
345 East 47th Street
New York, NY 10017

Alliance for Engineering in Medicine and Biology
1101 Connecticut Avenue, NW, Suite 700
Washington, DC 20036

Biomedical Engineering Society
PO Box 2399
Culver City, CA 90231

◇ **RELATED ARTICLES**

Volume 1: Biological Sciences; Engineering
Volume 2: Biologists; Engineers; Ergonomists; Prosthetists and orthotists
Volume 4: Biomedical engineering technicians; Instrumentation technicians; Orthotic and prosthetic technicians

---

Buyers, wholesale and retail

Definition

The *buyer* purchases merchandise from manufacturers and wholesalers at an appropriate price, in sufficient quantity, and with sufficient customer appeal to warrant its rapid and profitable resale to the public by the department store or chain store for which the retail buyer works or, in the case of the wholesale buyer, resale to retail firms, commercial establishments, and other institutions. Sometimes a buyer is referred to by the type of goods purchased, for example, jewelry buyer or toy buyer.

History

As civilization developed, humans increased their dependence upon goods provided through retail establishments. One of the first buyers was Marco Polo, whose travels to the Far East were designed to purchase spices, silks, and drugs for wealthy customers in Venice, Italy. Christopher Columbus was motivated in large part by the desire to develop a shorter trade route to India. Many of the early roads and shipping routes through Europe and Asia were developed specifically for the movement of foreign goods by wholesalers to the local markets.

As the early American retail stores became more specialized and grew in size, a functional division occurred in store operations. To replace the owner operator, who performed almost all of the store's tasks, there emerged sales clerks, receiving and shipping clerks, advertising managers, personnel officers, and buyers.

A wider range of available merchandise called for more astute selection and purchasing techniques. The development, in turn, of railroads, automobiles, and airplanes permitted buyers to travel to metropolitan areas where goods were available for firsthand examination.

The buyer is now a key part of the retail and wholesale industry, which has annual sales in the billions of dollars and employs millions of workers. (In 1956, for the first time, more people in the United States were engaged in the distribution of goods than in their manufacture.)

Nature of the work

Wholesale and retail buyers are part of a complex system of production, distribution, and merchandising. They both are concerned with recognizing and satisfying the huge variety of consumer needs and desires. Both wholesale and retail buyers usually specialize in acquiring one or two lines of merchandise.

Wholesale buyers purchase goods from manufacturers or from other wholesalers and sell it to retailers. They must be familiar with the products and capabilities both domestic and foreign manufacturers and be able to anticipate their customers' requirements. Wholesale buyers service retail outlets of all sizes throughout the country and must be able to satisfy their diverse needs in a timely and cost-effective manner. They consult catalogs and computerized directories to learn about the products that are available, and they often consult with retail buyers to keep abreast of consumer preferences.

Retail buyers work under one of two organizational patterns. In the first, working directly under a merchandise manager, the buyer combines purchasing activities with direct supervision of salespeople in the department involved. Thus, one person purchases the goods and then takes responsibility for their successful marketing. In the second pattern, merchandising and buying are separated. Buyers serve as specialists and have no supervisory responsibilities. In this case, however, buyers cooperate with the sales staff to promote maximum sales.

Assistant buyers work directly with experienced buyers. They also spend much of their time maintaining sales and inventory records. In addition, they may accompany buyers on purchasing trips or act for buyers who are away.

Regardless of the method of organization, all retail buyers perform many functions in common. The size of the store that employs them, the types of goods that they purchase, and their own personal philosophy of the role of the buyer directly affect the nature of their work. All buyers must know three things: their employer, their goods, and their customers.

Retail buyers must first understand the basic merchandising policies of their store. Does their employer seek volume sales of relatively low-quality goods or a more limited sale of high-quality goods? What is the usual cost of

73

The buyer often meets with sales representatives to examine and discuss merchandise. If the buyer is impressed with the product, she will consider purchasing quantities of it.

selling and rate of profit? How much discretion is allowed each buyer in the type and the quantity of purchases? The amount of purchases will be affected by the size of the buyer's annual budget, the timing in each buying season, and trends in the market. Retail buyers readily adopt a proprietary interest in their work. Success in buying is directly related to the clearly labeled profit or loss shown by particular departments.

All buyers are experts in the merchandise with which they deal. They order goods months ahead of their expected sale. They must be able to predetermine salability based upon cost, style, and competitive items. Buyers must be able to ascertain directly such product elements as purpose, construction, durability, quality, and style. Additionally, buyers must be well acquainted with the best sources of supply for each type of goods they purchase.

In keeping with an assignment to provide the store with goods that customers will buy at a price permitting a profit for the store, the retail buyer must be aware of customer tastes, style preferences, and price quality relationships. Buyers must also know the sizes, colors, and other features that will most satisfy customer needs.

Depending upon the location, size, and type of store, a retail buyer may deal directly with traveling salespeople (ordering from samples or catalogs); may order by mail or by telephone directly from the manufacturer or wholesaler (based largely upon past selling experience); may travel to key cities to visit mer-

chandise showrooms and manufacturing establishments; or (more likely) may use a combination of these approaches.

Buying trips to such cities as New York, Chicago, San Francisco, and Philadelphia are an important part of the work of the buyer for a larger store. Buyers of such specialized products as glassware, china, liquors, and gloves may make yearly trips to major European production centers. Sometimes manufacturers of similar items organize trade shows to attract a number of buyers. Buying trips are difficult; six to eight suppliers may be visited in a single day. The buyer must be able to estimate quickly the opportunity for profitable sale of the merchandise while examining it. The important element is not how much the buyer personally likes the merchandise but how much the customers will buy. Most buyers operate under an annual purchasing budget for the departments that they represent. All commitments to purchase merchandise are made against the background of available funds remaining. Buying trips also provide a useful fund of background knowledge on the status of merchandise that is available in each field.

As new merchandise appears on the shelves of their stores, buyers often work with salespeople to point out its distinctive features and elements of style.

Mergers between stores and expansion of single department stores into chains of stores have created central buying positions. These buyers order in unusually large quantities. As a result, they may develop a set of specifications for goods desired and ask manufacturers to bid on the right to provide these goods, rather than merely selecting products from those that are already available. Goods purchased by central buyers may be marketed under either the manufacturer's label (as is normally done) or ordered with the store's label or a chain brand.

To meet this competition, independent stores often retain the services of resident buyers who operate in major manufacturing or wholesaling areas. Often these resident buyers are not employed exclusively by one store, but they may buy for many stores located in different cities. The resident buying operation permits group-buying of salable goods at the most advantageous price.

Requirements

A college degree is not required for the job of the buyer, but is becoming increasingly more significant. Retailing experience is also a distinct advantage.

High-school courses that are helpful include business mathematics, English, speech, economics, home economics, and merchandising.

Prospective buyers may take collegiate training in one of the specialized retailing institutions. They may also attend a general college or university. Useful courses include business administration, marketing, retailing, buying, and economics. The wide variety of college backgrounds among successful buyers suggests that employers are flexible in terms of preferred major. Newly hired graduates may have a major in merchandising, marketing, fashion, fashion design, or advertising.

Personal qualifications are particularly important. The buyer must be intelligent (to quickly weigh alternative purchases), enthusiastic (to share an appreciation for merchandise with the salespeople who will handle it), energetic (to stand the grueling pace of buying trips and the many physical and emotional pressures inherent in the job), analytical (to recognize the marketing opportunities for merchandise), and venturesome (to take the occasional gamble that marks inspired buying). Buyers must also be able to work well with all kinds of people.

Special requirements

There are generally no special requirements for buying other than the hiring standards imposed by individual employers.

In some areas of buying, such as purchasing technical equipment, buyers may need to have technical training and belong to professional groups in the appropriate field.

Opportunities for experience and exploration

The best method of exploring interest and aptitude in retailing and buying is through part-time or summer experience in a store. This position, of course, would not be at the level of a buyer. Any position in a retail establishment, however, provides helpful insight into merchandising careers. One of the best times to obtain store experience is during the Christmas holiday season.

Some high schools and high-school clubs offer distributive education work that provides actual experience in a retail store.

Door-to-door selling experience also provides a measure of aptitude for retailing.

Most high-school and college career conferences include speakers speaking on retailing in general or on buying in particular.

Related occupations

Buyers must have a knowledge of marketing and be able to assess consumer demand. Other occupations with similar requirements include comparison shoppers, insurance sales agents, manufacturers' sales representatives, purchasing agents, retail sales workers, sales managers, travel agents, and wholesale trade sales representatives.

Methods of entering

Most prospective buyers secure their first position by direct application to the personnel office of a particular retail establishment. College seniors may participate in campus interviews conducted by merchandising employers. Public and private employment services frequently refer applicants to suitable entry positions.

Because of the knowledge of retailing required, preliminary work experience in a store is often necessary before promotion to the level of buyer. In fact, most buyers begin their careers as retail salesclerks. The next step up the ladder is usually the job of head of stock. The head of stock maintains stock inventory records and keeps the merchandise itself in a neat and well-organized fashion to both protect its value and permit easy accessibility. The head of stock usually supervises the work of several employees. This person also works in an intermediate position between the salespeople on the floor and the buyer who provides the merchandise.

The next step to becoming a full-fledged buyer may be that of assistant buyer. For many department stores, promotion to full buyer requires this experience.

Large department stores or chains operate executive training programs for college graduates seeking buying and other retail executive positions. A typical program consists of sixteen weeks of successive work experience in a variety of departments. This is supplemented by formal classroom work conducted by senior executives and training department personnel. Following this orientation, trainees are placed in junior management positions for an additional period of supervised experience and training.

Advancement

The position of buyer offers an opportunity for a substantial career in itself. Buyers are key employees of the stores or companies that employ them. As they serve on their jobs, buyers are given increased responsibility that takes the form of greater independence in activity, more authority to make commitments for merchandise, and transfer to the most difficult buying assignments.

Buyers may be promoted to merchandise manager and supervise other buyers, help develop the store's merchandising policies, and coordinate buying and selling activities with related departments.

If buyers find no opportunity for top buying positions with their employer or seek advancement beyond the buyer level, they may secure a more promising position with one of the many other retail stores in this country. Experience in one store is highly applicable to the work of other establishments in the same line.

Because of their grasp of retailing fundamentals and the fact that the quality of their performance is clearly demonstrated, many top executive positions in the retail industry are filled by persons from the ranks of buyers. Some buyers become merchandise managers, vice-presidents in charge of merchandising, or even store presidents.

Many buyers use their knowledge of the retail business and contacts developed with potential suppliers to provide background to help in setting up their own business.

Employment outlook

Of the 192,000 wholesale and retail buyers employed throughout the country in the early 1990s, most worked for department stores, clothing stores, grocery stores, machinery wholesalers, electrical goods distributors, and grocery wholesalers. About two-thirds of these jobs were in retail establishments.

Prospects for buyers are expected to increase through the 1990s, but at a slower than average rate. The growth of branch stores is expected to create a demand for buyers, but this will be offset by other factors. Centralization of buying, as stores consolidate or participate in joint purchasing activities, may reduce the number of buyers needed, as will the increased use of the tools of automation. Computers, as an illustration, help control inventory, maintain records, reorder merchandise, analyze purchasing preferences and trends, and perform related tasks.

Most job openings that occur will be the result of having to replace experienced workers who transfer to other occupations or are promoted to managerial positions. Competition to fill the vacancies will be keen because the field of merchandising is attractive to many college graduates, and jobseekers can be expected to outnumber the opportunities available. Qualified applicants will most likely be given preference over newcomers to the field.

Earnings

How much a buyer earns depends on the quantity and type of product purchased, as well as on the employer's sales volume. Mass merchandisers such as discount or chain department stores pay among the highest salaries.

In the early 1990s, most buyers made between $14,600 and $29,000 a year. Buyers who prove that they can operate in the competitive conditions that mark their field may earn more than $40,000 a year.

In addition to basic salary, buyers often receive cash bonuses based on their performance and may be offered incentive plans such as profit sharing and stock options. Benefits usually include an employee's discount of 10 to 20 percent on merchandise purchased for personal use.

Conditions of work

Buyers work in a dynamic atmosphere. They must make important decisions on an hourly basis. The results of their work—both successes and failures—show up quickly on the profit and loss statement. As stores must hire buyers who can produce the greatest margin of profit, buyers work under conditions of constant pressure.

Buyers frequently work long or irregular hours. Prior to purchasing expeditions, extra hours may be required to bring records up-to-date, review stocks, know the store's overall marketing design for the coming season, and plan most effectively for the time spent on travel. While their trips are stimulating, buying expeditions are physically and mentally demanding. Upon the return from buying trips, the buyers must help organize selling efforts for the new merchandise and also catch up with the backlog of work accumulated in their absence.

If they combine buying with sales supervision, buyers must spend long hours standing.

They also must adjust to the fact that their store may be open evenings and weekends. Buyers must be prepared to handle cases of customer complaints. Despite the unreasonableness of some criticisms, the buyer must begin with the assumption that "the customer is always right."

An important advantage of buying is the varied nature of the work and the fact that no two days are ever alike. As they note the results of one season's activities, buyers anticipate with advanced planning how to improve upon past results.

Seniority is less vital in buying than in most areas of the business world. A high percentage of positions are filled by men and women in the twenty-five-to-thirty-five age bracket.

Many stores recognize the pressures on the buyer and grant more liberal vacation allowances than provided for other employees.

Social and psychological factors

Buyers play an important role in our largest national industry. The skill with which they order merchandise directly affects the sales volume of their store and its share of the total retail market.

Another measure of the economic impact of the buyer may be indicated by the large number of out-of-town buyers visiting major metropolitan areas.

Because they possess so much power to order goods, buyers are often entertained or given favors by manufacturers. Care should be exercised not to let this hospitality influence judgment in ordering.

Finally, buyers both predict and establish standards of fashion and style.

GOE: 08.01.03; SIC: Any industry; SOC: 1442

◇ **SOURCES OF ADDITIONAL INFORMATION**

International Mass Retail Association
570 Seventh Avenue, Suite 900
New York, NY 10018

National Retail Merchants Association
100 West 31st Street
New York, NY 10001

◇ **RELATED ARTICLES**

Volume 1: Marketing; Retailing; Wholesaling
Volume 2: Export-import specialists; Purchasing agents; Retail business owners; Retail managers
Volume 3: Counter and retail clerks; Manufacturers' sales workers; Retail sales workers; Wholesale trade sales workers

Career counselors

Definition

Career counseling, or career/vocational counseling, consists of those activities performed or coordinated by individuals that have the professional credentials to work with and counsel other individuals or groups of individuals about occupations, careers, career decision making, career planning, and other career development related questions or conflicts. To work as a professional engaged in career/vocational counseling, the individual must demonstrate minimum competencies in six designated areas. These six areas are general counseling, information, individual and group assessment, management and administration, implementation, and consultation. Professional career counselors work in both private and public settings and are authorized to do so by the National Board for Certified Counselors (NBCC).

History

Though the history of career counseling in the United States dates back to the turn of the cen-

A career counselor leads a conference to discuss the prospects of self-employment.

tury and the founding of the National Career Development Association (formerly NVGA) in 1913, it is recent history that has given formal standards to the profession of career counseling. In 1980 the National Career Development Association established a committee for the pre-service and in-service training of vocational guidance personnel. Based on several professional studies the training committee developed a list of competencies necessary for persons who planned to perform career/vocational counseling. The NCDA in 1984 established its national credentialing process. At the same time, negotiations were entered with the National Board for Certified Counselors to assume responsibility for the credentialing of professional career counselors. The National Board for Certified Counselors now certifies professional career counselors to work in both public agencies and in the private sector.

Nature of the work

A professionally or nationally certified career counselor helps people make decisions and plans life/career directions. Strategies and techniques are tailored to the specific need of the person seeking help. It is likely that the career counselor will do one or more of the following: conduct individual and group personal counseling sessions to help qualify life/career goals; administer and interpret tests and inventories to assess abilities and interests, and identify career options; utilize career planning and occupational information to help individuals better understand the world of work; assist in developing individualized career plans; teach job hunting strategies and skills and assist in the development of resumes; help resolve personal conflicts on the job; assist in understanding the integration of work and other life roles; provide support for persons experiencing job stress, job loss, and career transition.

Requirements

To perform effectively career counselors must be competent in general counseling. They must have skills in building good relationships and the ability to use counseling techniques in assisting individuals with career choice and life career plans. Career counselors must have knowledge of education, training, employment trends, labor market, and career resources that provide information about job tasks, functions, salaries, requirements, and future outlooks related to broad occupational fields.

In addition, counselors must have information related to career development and decision making, and a knowledge of the changing roles of men and women and the linkage of work, family, and leisure. Competencies in individual and group assessment skills are essential. Knowledge of testing techniques and measures of aptitude, achievement, interests, values, and personality is required. The ability to evaluate job performance and individual effectiveness is helpful. The career counselor must also have management and administrative skills. Lastly, career counselors must have the ability to provide effective career consultation to influential individuals, such as parents, teachers, employers, community groups, and the general public.

The minimum educational program in career/vocational counseling is an earned graduate degree in counseling or a related professional field from a regionally accredited higher education institution and a completed supervised counseling experience, which includes career counseling. A growing number of institutions offer post-master's degree training in career development and career counseling. Such programs are highly recommended for persons with a master's degree in counseling who wish to specialize in vocational/career counseling. These programs are frequently called "Advanced Graduate Specialist Programs" or "Certificates of Advanced Study Program."

Special requirements

Those who wish to become a national certified career counselor must be a nationally certified counselor in addition to holding an earned graduate degree in counseling or a related professional field. Additionally, candidates for certification must have supervised counseling experience, which includes career counseling. Such counselors must also acquire a minimum of three years of full-time career development work experience. Further, one must obtain written endorsements of competence in career counseling from a work supervisor or a professional colleague and successfully complete a knowledge-based certification examination.

Opportunities for experience and exploration

Persons interested in becoming career counselors should seek out professional career counselors and discuss the field with them. They might also contact the National Board for Certified Counselors (NBCC) for certification information. Additionally, they may consult the National Career Development Association for competency statements and consumer guidelines. Undergraduate students interested in career counseling as a profession should take courses in counseling, psychology, sociology, and business management and administration.

Methods of entering

Journals specializing in information for career counselors frequently have job listings or information on job hotlines and services. School placement centers also are a good source of information, both because of their standard practice of listing job openings from participationg firms and because schools are a likely source of jobs for career counselors. Placement officers should be aware of which schools are looking for applicants. Standard sources of job listings, such as newspapers, should also be inspected regularly.

Related occupations

Career counselors utilize similar counseling skills to general counselors, mental health counselors, and family and group counselors. Their expertise, however, is related to career and leisure counseling and to the information necessary to conduct career-related activities. Career counselors have, in addition to general counseling skills, specific knowledge related to the world of work and to decision making that involves occupational information.

Related occupations using occupational information are vocational educators who teach employable skills and disseminate information about current trends in practices in specific careers, job placement counselors who assist clients in securing meaningful employment, and career development specialists who coordinate career development activities from initial selection to retirement planning.

Advancement

New employees in agencies are frequently considered trainees for the first six months to a year of their employment. During the training period, they acquire the specific skills that will be required of them during their tenure with the agency. Frequently, the first year of employment is probationary. After several years' experience on the job, supervisory or administrative positions may be obtained by some career counselors.

In the private practice of counseling, one may advance by expanding one's practice and hiring other career counselors as employees or by expanding one's knowledge base and venturing out into related fields, such as consultation with business and industry. The opportunities for advancing in private practice are excellent. However, in both the private and public sector, a doctorate is generally recommended.

Employment outlook

Employment opportunities for career counselors are expected to show an average increase through the end of the 1990s. As a result of technological, social, and economic factors, many employees presently in the labor force will be displaced. These workers will have to be counseled and trained for other occupations, creating a demand for career counselors. There are also career counseling specialties developing in markets such as placement of the disabled or the learning impaired. In addition, the private practice of counseling, and career counseling in particular, is on the increase throughout the nation. However, most job openings will result from the need to replace counselors who transfer to another field or who leave the work force altogether.

79

Earnings

Salaries vary greatly within the career/vocational counseling field. Salaries of those employed in schools, colleges, and mental health settings are commensurate with salaries of general or mental health counselors. As such, average entry salaries range from $22,000 to $25,000 per year for providers of service to $30,000 to $35,000 per year for directors of career counseling centers.

Salaries in business and industry are somewhat higher than salaries in educational or mental health agencies. Direct providers of service average from $27,000 to $32,000 per year and directors of career development or career counseling projects or programs receive salaries between $35,000 and $45,000 per year.

In private practice, the range is yet wider. Some practitioners earn as little as $15,000 per year and others earn in excess of $100,000 per year.

Often, persons who work in agencies have part-time practices of career counseling. This is frequently the way that people start out in private practice, where average earnings, depending on the section of the country in which one lives, range from $28,000 to $45,000 per year. To succeed in private practice, the practitioner should have entrepreneurial skills, as well as counseling skills.

Conditions of work

Most career counselors work in generally pleasant conditions. For the most part, the work is accomplished in an office. All career counseling positions require contact with people and many require contact with people of diverse ages, backgrounds, and sexes. Regular hours are typical for persons working in agencies.

Private practice, however, may require extremely long hours. Flexible schedules to provide services in the evenings and on weekends are sometimes required.

Depending on the type of counseling done, group lectures may be part of the counselor's job. Addressing classes, or groups of clients, or establishing target jobs, developing resumes, or handling interviews, may be part of the counselor's role.

Social and psychological factors

The professional career vocational counselor is sometimes under a great deal of stress because he or she frequently works with persons who are making major life decisions. Frequently, decisions made within the office of the career counselor profoundly affect relationships within families, organizations and communities at large.

Nationally certified career counselors not only have the choice to continue their own education, but the obligation to do so if they wish to renew their certification.

There is ample opportunity to meet a wide variety of publics, ranging in age from school age to retirement. There is constant stimulation as new information enters the career counseling field itself. Working in an area where the need for services has expanded enormously in recent times is extremely satisfying to persons who enjoy helping others.

GOE: 10.01.02; SIC: 8211; SOC: 24

◇ **SOURCES OF ADDITIONAL INFORMATION**

American Association for Counseling and Development
5999 Stevenson Avenue
Alexandria, VA 22304

Career Planning and Adult Development Network
4965 Sierra Road
San Jose, CA 95132

National Association of Career Development Consultants
145 Oak Hill Plaza
King of Prussia, PA 19406

The National Career Development Association
5999 Stevenson Avenue
Alexandria, VA 22304

◇ **RELATED ARTICLES**

Volume 1: Human Resources; Social Services
Volume 2: College career planning and placement counselors; Employment counselors; Guidance counselors; Personnel and labor relations specialists

Cartographers

Definition

Cartographers prepare maps, charts, and drawings from aerial photographs and survey data. They also conduct map research, investigating topics such as how people use maps.

History

Maps have been prepared and used ever since people started investigating the earth's surface. Explorers, warriors, and traders have all used maps as a way of navigating around the world or establishing property rights. The earliest surviving maps were designed on clay tablets more than 3,000 years ago. Early civilizations, such as the Egyptians and the Greeks, used maps drawn on papyrus to show a specific trade route or to trace the conquests of an army. These maps were often not detailed in terms of geographic features but nevertheless provided important records of land use. During this early period, advances such as the establishment of a system of measuring longitude and latitude helped create more uniform and accurate mapping procedures.

In the fourteenth and fifteenth centuries, mapmaking began to change because of the impact of world travel. Explorers such as Christopher Columbus began to observe and collect geographic information from around the world and use this information to make maps. Specific geographic features, such as the location of a natural harbor or a dangerous coastline, were documented and then used to chart courses of safe navigation.

Mapmaking continued to develop as surveying and other means of mathematical measurements evolved. Today, the most sophisticated computer and satellite technology is used in compiling geographic information and planning and drafting maps.

Nature of the work

Cartographers utilize manual and computerized drafting instruments, standard mathematical formulas, photogrammetric techniques, and precision stereoplotting apparatus. They work along with other mapping scientists to plan and draft maps and charts. For example, a cartographer may work with a land surveyor to interpret geographic information and transfer that information into a series of symbols that are plotted onto a map. Cartographers must therefore be skilled in reading and understanding detailed photographs or drawings and must be able to use drafting tools to create an accurate representation of these data. They must also be able to plot the names of places onto overlays from which a final map is made. Cartographers often work with old maps, using updated information to keep these maps current. Research may also be a part of the job, with much time being devoted to applying computers to mapmaking.

Technological advances have significantly changed the cartographer's job. In the last few years, computer and satellite technology has been applied with great success to the field. For example, video signals from a satellite detector are digitized and transmitted to earth where a computer process is used to read the data and create a map with enhanced geographic patterns, such as vegetation and soils. With the addition of computer mapping software and data merging software, this technology allows mapping exercises to be done in a fraction of the time that it once took. It also permits far larger amounts of data to be collected with just the flip of a switch. Clearly computer-driven display devices will be the primary mapmaking tools of the future. Therefore, cartographers must be trained in computer science.

Several areas of specialization within the field of cartography exist. *Cartography supervisors* design maps and as well as coordinate and oversee the activities of all those involved in the mapmaking process. Supervisors are often employed in larger mapmaking operations.

Cartographic drafters prepare the maps by detailing natural and constructed features, political boundaries, and other features. Most drafters now prepare maps through a hand technique called "scribing," a process by which a sharp tool is used to scratch line impressions on a coated plastic sheet. This process has replaced the traditional ink drawings that were used for generations.

Mosaicists lay out photographic prints on tables according to the sequence in which photographs were taken to form a photographic mosaic of the geographic area. These mosaics are subsequently use in photogrammetric activities such as topographic mapping. Mosaicists

Cartographers spend much of their time working over large light tables.

rapher, many people entering the field join the American Congress on Surveying and Mapping. It and its affiliate, the American Cartographic Association, are actively involved in professional training programs and other aspects of career development.

Opportunities for experience and exploration

One of the best opportunities for experience is a summer job or internship with a construction firm or other company that prepares maps. The federal government may also have some summer or part-time opportunities for cartographic assistants.

Related occupations

Cartographers are related in work to geologists and geophysicists. Other jobs of possible interest include geographer, oceanographer, and surveyor. A cartographer may also be able to transfer his or her knowledge of the earth's surface into the areas of transportation, land use planning, or weather research. Other related fields include drafting and design.

also examine aerial photographs to verify location of established landmarks.

Photogrammetrists prepare original maps or charts from aerial photographs and survey data and apply mathematical formulas to identify the scale of cartographic features.

Stereo-plotter operators prepare maps from aerial photographs, using instruments that produce simultaneous projections of two photographs taken of the same area.

Topographical drafters prepare and correct maps from original sources, such as other maps, survey notes, and aerial photographs.

Requirements

High-school students should take courses in geography, mathematics (including algebra and trigonometry), mechanical drawing, and computer science. A bachelor's degree in engineering or a physical science, such as geography or geodesy, is the best method of becoming a professional cartographer. A college program should include courses in technical mathematics, surveying and measurements, drafting, and photogrammetry and mapping. Field work may also be required.

Special requirements

Although no additional training programs or special licenses are needed to become a cartog-

Methods of entering

Most cartographers are hired upon completion of a bachelor's degree in engineering or geography. People who are interested in becoming involved as a technician may be able to secure an entry level position after completing a specialized training program, which takes about two years. A portfolio of completed maps may be required by employers during the interviewing process.

Advancement

As is the case in most professions, advancement is linked to the quality of work performed, training, and experience. A cartographer who proves adept at drafting and designing maps and understands the other steps in the mapmaking process stands a good chance of becoming a supervisor. A cartographer, however, should expect to work directly on maps throughout his or her career.

Employment outlook

In the early 1990s, some growth in employment of cartographers and other mapping scientists may occur in the private sector. The increasing demand for sophisticated land and sea maps will require specialized mapping. Little or no growth is expected in employment by departments and agencies of the federal government. The greatest growth in employment will be in Geographic Information Systems (GIS), which in large part are sophisticated mapping systems.

Earnings

Most of the approximately 5,000 cartographers in the federal government earn between $16,000 and $50,000 annually, with the average wage about $28,000 per year. Those in the private sector also have a wide salary range. An entry level cartographer may earn $13,000 per year, while a highly trained cartographer could easily earn $42,000 annually.

Conditions of work

Cartographers mainly work in a typical office setting with easy access to drafting tables and computer mapping systems. Most cartographers never actually visit the locations that they are mapping. The average work week is between thirty-five to forty hours, although occasionally longer hours are required if a mapping project is on a deadline.

Cartographers may choose to work on a freelance basis. Project hires allow companies to bring in cartographers for a short-term basis to accomplish mapping needs, without hiring a permanent staff. For large map-producing companies, project cartographers may be brought in to help during heavy deadline work. Because of the cost of mapping, most small companies buy rights to maps produced by large firms.

Social and psychological factors

Cartographers must pay close attention to detail and be patient, systematic, and accurate in their work. They should be able to work cooperatively and take direction from a supervisor.

Cartography supervisors should have leadership abilities. At times, the ability to work long hours under pressure may be needed.

GOE: 05.03.02; SIC: 7399; SOC: 3734

◇ **SOURCES OF ADDITIONAL INFORMATION**

General information about career opportunities in cartography and two free pamphlets ("Cartography: A Career Guide" and "Careers in Cartography, Geodesy, and Surveying") is available from:

American Congress on Surveying and Mapping
210 Little Falls Street
Falls Church, VA 22046

American Society of Cartographers
PO Box 1493
Louisville, KY 40202

General information on careers in photogrammetry and a pamphlet titled "Careers in Photogrammetry" is available from:

American Society of Photogrammetry and Remote Sensing
210 Little Falls Street
Falls Church, VA 22046

North American Cartographic Information Society
6010 Executive Boulevard
Suite 100
Rockville, MD 20852

◇ **RELATED ARTICLES**

Volume 1: Book Publishing; Engineering; Magazine Publishing
Volume 2: Engineers; Geographers; Graphics programmers; Surveyors
Volume 4: Surveying and mapping technicians

Cartoonists and animators

Definition

Cartoonists and animators are illustrators who draw simple pictures to amuse, educate, and persuade people.

History

The first cartoons appeared hundreds of years ago, but it has only been in the twentieth century that they have become an everyday phenomenon. Today, we see cartoons in the editorial and funny pages of daily newspapers, in comic books, textbooks, and magazines, in movie theaters, children's television, and commercials (*Charlie the Tuna* is an example of a commercial animation). Many cartoon characters have become household words, such as *Little Orphan Annie, Superman*, and *Charlie Brown* to name just a few. Some comic strips create fantasy worlds for their readers to escape to; others, such as Walt Kelly's *Pogo* and Garry Trudeau's *Doonesbury*, are so relevant to the real world that their readers may often refer to them rather than the evening news to learn about current events.

Animation, a specialization of cartooning, has emerged more recently and suddenly than its parent art, due largely to the efforts of one man, Walt Disney. A current trend in animated movies is live-action features in which human actors interact with cartoon characters to stunning effect. Because of the many applications of their work, cartoonists and animators have become some of the busiest and most popular artists of the modern age.

Nature of the work

Cartoonists draw illustrations for newspapers, books, magazines, greeting cards, movies, television shows, civic organizations, private businesses, or just about anybody, themselves included, with a message to convey. Cartoons are most often associated with newspaper comics or with children's television, but they are also used to highlight and interpret information in publications as well as in advertising.

Whatever their individual specialty, cartoonists translate ideas onto paper or film in order to communicate these ideas to an audience. Sometimes the ideas are original; other times they are directly related to the news of the day, to the content of a magazine article, or to a new product. After cartoonists come up with ideas, they discuss them with their employers, whether they be editors, producers, creative directors at advertising agencies, or others. Next, they sketch drawings and submit these for approval. Their employers may suggest changes, which cartoonists then make. Cartoonists use a variety of art materials including pens, pencils, markers, crayons, paints, transparent washes, and shading sheets. They may draw on paper, acetate, or bristol board.

Comic-strip artists tell jokes or short stories with a series of pictures. Each picture is called a frame, or a panel, and each frame usually includes words as well as drawings. *Comic book artists* also tell stories with their drawings, but their stories are longer, and they are not necessarily meant to be funny.

Motion-cartoonists, or *animators*, draw a great number of pictures, each of which varies only a little from the ones before and after it in a series. When these drawings are photographed in sequence and then projected at high speeds, they appear to be moving. You can achieve a similar effect by drawing stick figures on the pages of a note pad, and then flipping through the pages very quickly.

Editorial cartoonists comment on society by drawing pictures with messages that are usually funny, but which often have a satirical edge. Their drawings often depict famous politicians. *Portraitists* are cartoonists who specialize in drawing caricatures. Caricatures are pictures that highlight someone's prominent features, such as a large nose, to make them recognizable to the public. Most editorial cartoonists are also talented portraitists.

Storyboard artists at advertising agencies may draw cartoons that give a client an idea of what a television commercial will look like before it is produced. If the client likes the idea, the actions represented by cartoons in the storyboard will be reproduced by actors on film.

Requirements

Cartoonists must be creative. In addition to having artistic talent, they must generate ideas, although it is not unusual for cartoonists to collaborate with writers on ideas as well. Whether they create cartoon strips or advertising campaigns, they must be able to come up with concepts and images that the public will respond to. They must have a good sense of humor and an observant eye, to detect people's distinguishing characteristics and society's incongruities.

Cartoonists need not have a college degree, but some art training is usually expected by employers. To comment insightfully on contemporary life, it is also useful to study political science, history, and social studies. Animators must attend art school to learn specific technical skills.

Cartoonists have an ability to emphasize distinctive features of nearly all types of people, animals, and even objects.

Special requirements

Cartoonists need to be flexible people. Because their art is much more commercial than painting and sculpting, they must be willing to accommodate their employers' desires if they are to build a broad clientele and earn a decent living. They must be able to take suggestions and rejections gracefully.

Opportunities for experience and exploration

High-school students who are interested in becoming cartoonists should submit their drawings to their school paper. They might also want to draw posters to publicize activities, such as sporting events, dances, and meetings.

Related occupations

The work of cartoonists and animators requires a highly developed sense of design, shape, color, and the full range of artist skill. These talents are employed by other workers such as cartographers, painters and sculptors, graphic artists, drafters, and packaging professionals.

Methods of entering

Formal entry-level positions for cartoonists are rare, but there are several ways for artists to enter the cartooning field. Most cartoonists begin piecemeal, selling cartoons to small publications, like community newspapers, that buy free-lance cartoons. Another way is to assemble a portfolio of their best work and apply to publishers or the art departments of advertising agencies, among others. Cartoonists may have to be willing to work for what equals less than minimum wage to get established.

Advancement

Like that of all artists, cartoonists' success depends upon how much the public likes their work. Cartoonists have "made it" when they work for the most prestigious clients at the best wages.

Employment outlook

Job opportunities for visual artists are expected to grow faster than average through the year 2000, but competition for both salaried and free-lance cartooning jobs is keen. Almost two thirds of all visual artists are self-employed, but free-lance work can be hard to come by and many free lancers earn little until they acquire experience and establish a good reputation.

Earnings

Free-lance cartoonists may earn anywhere from $50 to $1,000 or more per drawing, but top dollar generally goes only for big, full-color projects such as magazine cover illustrations. Comic strip cartoonists are usually paid according to the number of publications that carry their strip, with some syndicated cartoonists earning hundreds of thousands of dollars a year. Self-employed artists do not receive fringe benefits such as paid vacations, sick leave, health insurance, or pension benefits.

Conditions of work

Most cartoonists work in big cities where employers such as television studios, magazine publishers, and advertising agencies are located. Cartoonists generally work in comfortable environments, at drafting tables or drawing boards with plentiful light. Some may develop backaches or eyestrain, however, from working continuously on projects. Staff cartoonists work a regular forty-hour workweek, but may occasionally be expected to work evenings and weekends to meet deadlines. Freelance cartoonists have erratic schedules, and the number of hours they work may depend simply on how much money they want to earn. They may often work evenings and weekends, but are not required to be at work from nine to five, Monday through Friday.

Social and psychological factors

Cartoonists must often follow instructions that are contrary to what they would most like to do, which can be frustrating. Many free-lance cartoonists spend a lot of time working alone at home, but cartoonists have more opportunities to interact with other people than most working artists.

GOE: 01.02.03; SIC: 27, 7351; SOC: 324

◇ **SOURCES OF ADDITIONAL INFORMATION**

National Cartoonists Society
Nine Ebony Court
Brooklyn, NY 11229

Cartoonists Guild of New York
11 West 20th Street, 8th Floor
New York, NY 10011

Caricaturists Society of America
224 Highland Boulevard
Brooklyn, NY 14043

Society of Illustrators
128 East 63rd Street
New York, NY 10021

◇ **RELATED ARTICLES**

Volume 1: Book Publishing; Broadcasting; Design; Magazine Publishing; Motion Pictures; Newspaper Publishing
Volume 2: Advertising workers; Commercial artists; Designers; Graphics programmers; Painters and sculptors
Volume 4: Film laboratory technicians; Graphic arts technicians

Caterers

Definition

Caterers plan, coordinate, and supervise food service at parties and other social functions. Working along with their clients, they purchase appropriate supplies, plan the menu, supervise the food preparation, direct the serving of the food and refreshments, and ensure the overall smooth functioning of the event. As entrepre-

neurs, they are also responsible for budgeting, bookkeeping, and other administrative tasks.

History

Even though food preparation has been practiced in some form or another since humans began to eat, it has only been the last several hundred years that has seen the development of the art of making large meals attractive and appetizing.

Not surprisingly, the first people to engage in this activity were royalty and other wealthy individuals who would have their chef serve up a variety of entrees at a banquet or other large function. The chef might also have been responsible for making sure that none of the servants missed their serving cues and that the entertainment went off without a hitch.

During the late 1700s and early 1800s in the United States, land owners and other wealthy individuals began holding large, lavish parties that required hiring special cooks or chefs for the occasion. Special recipes were often created, and chefs who could continually make tasty dishes were called on again and again to cater these parties.

Today, entertaining is no longer reserved just for wealthy individuals, and caterers continue to find work planning and making meals for wedding receptions, graduation parties, and a host of other social and business functions.

These caterers are serving food at a large banquet. They are also capable of serving for small parties.

Nature of the work

A caterer is a combination chef, purchasing agent, personnel director, and accountant. Often a caterer will also play the role of host, allowing the client to enjoy his or her own party. A caterer's responsibilities will vary according to the size of the catering firm and the specific needs of individual clients. While preparing quality food is a concern no matter what the size of the party, larger events require far more planning and coordination. For example, a large catering firm may organize and plan a formal event for a thousand people, including planning and preparing a seven-course meal, lavishly decorating the hall with flowers and wall-hangings, employing twenty or more wait staff to serve the food in an elegant manner, and arranging the entertainment. The catering firm will also set up the tables and chairs and provide the necessary linen, silverware, and dishes. A catering company may organize fifty or so such events a month or only several a year. A smaller catering organization may concentrate on simpler events, such as preparing food for an informal buffet for fifteen people.

Caterers not only service individual clients, but also industrial clients as well. A caterer may be called on to supervise a company cafeteria or plan food service for an airline or a cruise ship. Often these caterers may take over full-time su-

pervision of these food operations, including ordering the food and other supplies, supervision of personnel and food preparation, and overseeing the maintenance of equipment.

A caterer needs to be flexible in food-preparation approaches, able to prepare food on- or off-premises depending on logistical considerations and the wishes of the client. If the caterer is handling a large banquet in a hotel or other location, the caterer will usually prepare the food on-premises, using kitchen and storage facilities as needed. The caterer might also work in a client's kitchen for an affair in a private home, as having cooking and storage facilities on-premises often eases food preparation and transportation concerns. In both these cases, the caterer must visit the site of the function well before the actual event to determine how and where the food will be prepared. Frequent phone contact may also be necessary to coordinate events. Caterers may also prepare the food off-premises, working either in their own kitchens or in a mobile kitchen. Frequent contact with the client is important in off-premises food preparation as well.

Working with the client is obviously a very important aspect of the caterer's job. Clients always want their affairs to be a little special, and the caterer's ability to present such items as a uniquely shaped wedding cake or provide beautiful decorations will enhance the atmosphere and usually lead to customer satisfaction. The client may have his or her own desires that the caterer implements, or as is more likely, the caterer and client will work together (within a budget) to develop a menu and atmosphere the client can enjoy. A large part of ensuring client satisfaction is for the caterer to present the food in a pleasant fashion. Many caterers have their own special recipes and they are always on the lookout for quality fruits, vegetables, and meats. The caterer should have an eye for detail and be able to make fancy hors d'oeuvres and eye-catching fruit and vegetable displays.

Although caterers can usually prepare a variety of dishes, they may have a special dish (Cajun or Italian cuisine, for example) that the client is especially interested in. The caterer may also have a special serving style (such as serving food in Renaissance period dress) that sets them apart from other caterers. Developing a reputation in a certain area may be an effective marketing technique.

The caterer is a coordinator, working with suppliers, food servers, and the client to ensure an event comes off as planned. The caterer must be in frequent contact with all concerned making sure, for example, that the food is delivered on time and the entertainment performs as promised.

Good management skills are extremely important. The caterer must not only be able to supervise the preparation and serving of food, but also know how much food and other supplies to order, what equipment will be needed, and be able to coordinate the various activities so as to ensure a smooth-running event. Purchasing the proper supplies entails knowledge of a variety of food products, their suppliers, and the contacts needed to get the right product at the best possible price.

If the caterer has a large operation, he or she may appoint a manager to oversee an event. The manager will take care of the ordering, planning, and supervising responsibilities, and may even work with the client. But, the caterer is still finally responsible for the success of the event.

As entrepreneurs, caterers have important administrative responsibilities, such as overseeing the budgeting and bookkeeping of the operation. The caterer must make sure that the business continues to make a profit while keeping its prices competitive. Caterers must know how to figure costs and other budget considerations, plan inventories, buy food, and ensure compliance with health regulations.

Caterer helpers prepare and serve hor d'oeuvres and other food and refreshments at social functions, under the supervision of the head caterer. They help arrange tables and decorations, and then assist in the cleanup.

Requirements

Although there are no specific educational or professional requirements, a caterer should combined the ability to understand proper food preparation with the ability to manage a food service operation. Many people develop these skills through on-the-job training, beginning as a caterer's helper or as a worker in a restaurant.

As the catering business has grown more competitive, many successful caterers are choosing to get a college degree in business administration, home economics, nutrition, or a related field. Others get their training through the various vocational schools and community colleges that have begun to offer apprenticeships and other forms of professional training.

High-school students should take courses in mathematics, business administration, and home economics. They should also take courses in English and other communications courses. A college program should include coursework in nutrition, health, and business management.

Special requirements

Most states require caterers to be licensed, and inspectors may make periodic visits to ensure that local health and safety regulations are being maintained in the food preparation process.

As a measure of professional status, many caterers become certified through the National Association of Catering Executives (NACE). To qualify for certification, caterers must meet educational and professional requirements and pass a written examination. Further information on the certification process is available from the NACE at the address given at the end of this article.

Opportunities for experience and exploration

The food industry is one of the best in terms of offering opportunities for experience and exploration. An aspiring caterer can get part-time work in a restaurant or as an assistant banquet manager at a hotel. With some experience and training, it might even be possible to work as a manager with a large catering company. High-school students may work in the school cafeteria or even set up their own small catering service by working at parties for friends and relatives.

Related occupations

Food service directors, hotel managers, residence supervisors, supermarket administrators, and managers of restaurants and coffeeshops all plan and coordinate operations that entail food ordering and food preparation.

Methods of entering

Some caterers get into the profession as a matter of chance after helping a friend or relative prepare a large banquet or volunteering to coordinate a group function. Most caterers, however, begin their careers after graduating from college with a degree in a program such as home economics, or finishing a culinary training program at a vocational school or community college.

Qualified individuals may begin work as a manager for a large catering firm or as a manager for a hotel banquet service. An individual will most likely start a catering business only with a large amount of experience, and plenty of money to cover the purchase of equipment and other start-up costs.

Advancement

As with most service oriented businesses, the success of a caterer depends on the quality of his or her work and the reputation that the person develops. Well-known caterers can expand their business, often growing from a small business to a larger operation. This may mean hiring assistants and buying more equipment to be able to serve a larger variety of clientele. Caterers who initially worked out of their own home kitchen may get an office or even relocate to another area in order to take better opportunity of catering opportunities. Sometimes successful caterers will use their skill and reputation to secure a full-time position in a large hotel or restaurant planning and coordinating banquets. They may also work full-time for an industrial client, such as a company cafeteria or airline.

Employment outlook

With the food service industry going strong in the United States, employment opportunities in catering figure to continue to grow through the early 1990s. Opportunities will be bright for firms that can handle weddings, bar and bat mitzvahs, business functions, and other celebrations.

Although the opportunities are bright, competition is keen as many hotels and restaurants are branching out to offer catering services. Like all service industries, catering is sensitive to the economy, and a downturn in the economy may limit catering opportunities. Despite the competition and possible economic considerations, highly skilled and motivated caterers should be in demand throughout the country, especially in and around large metropolitan areas.

Earnings

Earnings vary widely depending on the size and location of the catering operation and the skill and motivation of the individual entrepreneur. Many caterers charge according to the number of guests attending a function. In many cases therefore, the larger the event, the larger the profit. Earnings are also influenced by whether a caterer works full- or part-time. Even very successful caterers often remain at it part-time, either because they enjoy their other job or to protect themselves against a downturn in the economy.

The general salary range for a full-time caterer might be anywhere between $10,000 and $30,000 per year, depending on skill, reputation, and experience. An extremely successful caterer can easily earn more than $50,000 annually. A part-time caterer may earn $5,000 to $11,000 per year, subject to the same variables as the full-time caterer. Because a caterer is an independent business person, vacation and other benefits are usually not part of the salary structure.

A caterer who works as a manager for a company cafeteria or other industrial client may earn between $13,000 and $23,000 per year, with vacation, health insurance, and other benefits usually included.

Conditions of work

Caterers may either work on-premises at a social function or prepare the food off-premises in their own kitchen or a mobile kitchen. In all cases, these should be modern, well-furnished kitchens with large ovens, refrigerators, and plenty of counter and storage space. A caterer often works long hours planning and preparing for an event, and the day of the event might easily be a fourteen-hour workday from setup to cleanup.

There is a lot of variety in the type of work a caterer does. A caterer may plan a 500-person sit-down dinner with lavish decorations and entertainment, or a small brunch for twenty people. The caterer must always work closely with all types of clients and be able to adapt to last minute changes.

Caterers often spend long hours on their feet, and although the work can be physically and mentally demanding, caterers usually have a great deal of work flexibility. As entrepreneurs, they can usually take time off when necessary. Caterers often work more than sixty hours a week when busy, with most of the work on weekends and evenings, when events tend to be scheduled.

Social and psychological factors

Caterers must be able to plan ahead, work gracefully under pressure, and have an ability to adapt to last minute mishaps. Attention to detail is critical, as is the ability to work long hours under demanding situations. A caterer must be able to direct a large staff of workers in the kitchen and be able to interact with clients and guests in a lavish ballroom.

Communications skills are vital. As an entrepreneur, a caterer must be responsible for the various aspects of running a business, from keeping accurate bookkeeping records to complying with health and safety regulations.

Although the work is often demanding, the rewards of coordinating a successful event for a client can be very rewarding.

GOE: 11.11.04; SIC: 5812; SOC: 1351

◇ SOURCES OF ADDITIONAL INFORMATION

Information on certification and other career information is available from:

National Association of Catering Executives
2500 Wilshire Boulevard, #603
Los Angeles, CA 90057

Career information is available from:

Mobile Industrial Caterers Association
7300 Artesia Boulevard
Buena Park, CA 90621

International Food Service Executives Association
3017 West Charleston Boulevard, Suite 50
Las Vegas, NV 89102

◇ RELATED ARTICLES

Volume 1: Baking; Food Processing; Food Service
Volume 2: Dietitians; Food technologists; Health and regulatory inspectors; Home economists; Restaurant and food service managers
Volume 3: Cooks, chefs, and bakers; Fast food workers; Food service workers
Volume 4: Dietetic technicians

Chemists

Definition

The *chemist* performs analytical and research work in the field of chemistry, and may make

quantitative and qualitative analyses to determine chemical and physical properties of many substances. Chemists are also trained to make a variety of chemicals and perform tests on manufactured goods, such as foods, drugs, plastics, dyes, paints, and petroleum products. They may also supervise research activities in industry and prepare reports about research projects.

History

Chemistry was first studied and applied more than 5,000 years ago. Originally chemistry was the art of extracting medicinal materials from plants. In the Middle Ages chemistry (or alchemy as it was then called) concerned itself with the study of metals and the search for a universal cure for disease. Today, with the increasing speed of scientific and material progress, chemistry is concerned with a great deal more than medicines and precious metals. Chemists contribute to advances not only in medicine, space science, and other similar frontier areas, but also in a wide range of manufactured goods and consumer products.

Nature of the work

About one-half of today's chemists are engaged in research and development. The majority of these chemists work on applied research projects in which they apply their knowledge to the improvement and creation of new products. Wonder drugs for use in medicine, synthetic materials to replace the demand on dwindling natural material supplies, and fuels that can meet the demand of space travel are only a few examples of the products that chemists have helped develop.

The remainder of research chemists work on basic research projects. The main purpose of basic research is to extend scientific knowledge rather than to solve immediate practical problems. Many important practical applications, however, have resulted from basic research. Chemists also work in analysis and testing because various tests must be made at practically every stage in the manufacture of a product.

Some chemists are employed in college teaching and administrative work, while still others are employed in production, patent work, technical sales, technical writing, technical library work, materials purchasing, and market research.

Within the various branches of chemistry there are many fields from which to choose. Agricultural chemists, adhesives chemists, paint chemists, nutritional chemists, petroleum chemists, leather chemists, and pharmaceutical

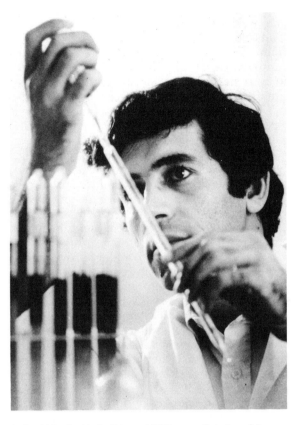

A chemist involved in the Enhanced Oil Recovery Project carefully mixes injection fluids with crude oil.

chemists are examples of specialized chemists. Following are several other specializations.

Water-purification chemists analyze the filtered water in purification plants and test samples from various points along the distribution system to make sure it meets prescribed standards. They determine and monitor the kinds and amounts of chemicals needed to purify and soften the water to make it suitable for drinking.

Wastewater-treatment plant chemists investigate the efficiency of wastewater treatment processes to ensure that water pollution control requirements are met. They test samples of streams, raw and treated wastewater, sludge, and other by-products for various solids, acids, alkalinity, and other substances and devise ways to improve the treatment processes.

Instrumentation chemists examine the wastewater discharged by industries using a municipal wastewater treatment plant to see if it meets pollution control requirements. Any variation that shows up in the analysis is used to determine surcharge assessments to be levied against the company that is at fault.

Each field is further divided into subfields and more specialized occupations. *Chemical lab-*

91

oratory chiefs head up chemical labs and are responsible for planning and carrying out programs for research, product development, improvement of manufacturing processes, and analysis and testing of substances, compounds, liquids, and gases. As chief chemists, they direct the laboratory staff, review and interpret reports, and keep management advised of activities under their control.

Laboratory supervisors train, assign, and oversee workers who perform chemical and physical tests to ensure the quality of products. They help develop tests, solve testing problems, and compile test information related to the operating efficiency of the equipment or processes.

Food chemists develop and improve foods and beverages. They analyze methods of cooking, canning, freezing, and packaging and study their effects on the appearance, taste, aroma, freshness, and vitamin content of various products; test samples of cereal, dairy products, meats, vegetables, beer, and other goods to make sure they meet with food laws; and experiment with new foods, additives, and preservatives.

Colorists develop color formulas to match customer specifications for printing textile and plastic materials. They also coordinate color shop activities with the production schedule of the printing department.

Perfumers devise formulas for perfumes and other aromatic products and set production standards for the compounding and distillation departments. They test fragrances by smelling samples in an air-filtered room. Characteristics they check include odor, body, harmony, strength, and permanence.

Assayers determine the value and properties of ores and minerals. They separate metals from the impurities and conduct tests involving spectrographic analysis, chemical solutions, and a variety of chemical and laboratory equipment.

This list is by no means complete. It illustrates, however, the variety of jobs available within chemistry, and helps to give an idea of the rapidly changing nature of the chemical industry.

Though chemists may specialize in one of the particular industrial fields mentioned above, their training and interest usually transcend the academic limitation inherent in specialization. While completing their training in college or in graduate work, chemists usually concentrate their work in one of the five main branches of chemistry: organic, inorganic, physical, analytical, or biochemistry.

The organic chemist specializes in the chemistry of carbon and its compounds, most of which are substances originally derived from animal and vegetable matter. The main job is to determine structure, composition, and other physical and chemical properties.

The inorganic chemist is concerned with compounds of noncarbon structure, including most of the metals and minerals.

The physical chemist is interested in the study of the quantitative relationships between the chemical and physical properties of organic and inorganic substances, for example, how a substance designed for use in a space capsule is affected by heat of reentry.

The analytical chemist, as the term implies, analyzes the exact chemical composition of substances and tests them to determine quality, purity, and other characteristics.

The biochemist is concerned with chemical reactions of living organisms and the effect of chemicals on life processes.

Requirements

A bachelor's degree in chemistry is usually regarded as the minimum educational requirement for the beginning chemist. Persons hoping to obtain better, more responsible jobs should plan on extensive graduate work. Chemists employed in supervisory positions in industry, in teaching, or in research positions in industry or universities usually have their doctorates.

People with superior intelligence and with a marked proficiency in mathematics and the natural sciences, combined with an ability to express themselves easily in the company of others, should examine chemistry as a possible career. An imaginative and orderly mind, one that combines the exactness required of mathematics with the experimentation employed in science, is an important personal asset of the prospective chemist. A preoccupation with the "why" of things as well as a keen interest in the "how" is also important.

Being able to communicate and get along with others is a significant personal quality needed especially in today's chemical laboratories, where teams of specialists work together on problems requiring close cooperation. A chemist must also be endowed with more than average patience and a capacity to stick with the job despite the many delays and pitfalls to which experimentation is subject.

High-school students with an interest in chemistry should have three to four years of English; four years of mathematics, including algebra, geometry, and trigonometry; three to four years of science, including biology, chemistry, and physics; two years of social studies; and at least two years of a foreign language (preferably German, French, or Russian) prior to entering college. Computer experience is also helpful. The college training leading to a bachelor of science degree in chemistry includes required courses in analytical, inorganic, organic, and physical chemistry supplemented by courses in mathematics, physics, biology, and liberal arts. College students should also try to take additional courses in German, French, and/or Russian, because many technical papers valuable for research are written in these languages, and a reading knowledge of at least one of them may be required to earn an advanced degree. College students are also urged to study a programming language.

Because graduate training is essential for most responsible positions, particularly in research and teaching, many students go on to obtain either a master's degree or a doctorate in chemistry after completing their undergraduate work. In graduate school a chemistry student is required to have courses in a specialty or field of interest, plus a great deal of laboratory research.

The preparation of a substance through extraction involves complex and delicate laboratory procedures.

Special requirements

Other than the customary evidence of professional competency, no special requirements such as licenses or certificates are necessary for most jobs in this field. However, because their work is directly related to the health, safety, and welfare of the public, clinical chemists dealing with information on samples from the human body may need to be certified by the American Board for Clinical Chemistry or the National Registry in Clinical Chemistry.

Opportunities for experience and exploration

The high-school student who has enjoyed science as a hobby has had experience with chemistry and an opportunity to test any interest in this field. Some students are fortunate enough to obtain part-time jobs in chemical labs as assistants and thereby observe the chemical field firsthand. While the number of such opportunities is not small, knowledge about their availability is limited. There are also science fairs and clubs that provide resources to interested students.

Related occupations

Persons with an aptitude for chemistry may also find some of the following occupations to be compatible with their interests: agricultural scientists, biochemists, biological scientists, chemical engineers, chemical laboratory technicians, environmental researchers, metallurgists, occupational safety and health workers, physicists, and pollution control specialists.

Methods of entering

College graduates can seek assistance from their college or university placement office. Professors who have worked closely with chemistry students throughout their college careers are often able to guide students into branches of chemistry best suited to their individual interests and abilities. In many cases companies send recruiters to interview graduating chemists.

Many first jobs for industrial chemists are especially well adapted to supplementing theoretical college training with valuable on-the-job experience. Some schools offer cooperative education programs wherein a student can work for a bachelor's degree in chemistry and at the same time gain related work experience. Upon graduation such students are usually selected for more responsible jobs. Beginning chemists with a bachelor's degree usually start out as trainees in laboratory research and development or in analysis and testing, quality control, technical service, production, or sales.

Advancement

Most graduates with a bachelor's degree in chemistry begin work in company-sponsored training programs. Most recent graduates are likely to find employment in manufacturing industries, particularly industrial chemicals. Some advance into high-level research and management positions. With experience and the benefit of additional industrial training, many chemists advance to more responsible positions.

Chemists with a master's degree can usually qualify for applied research positions in government and private industry, and for teaching positions in colleges and universities. A doctorate offers the chemist the best possibility for advancement, however, because it is required for basic research work, higher-level college or university teaching, and for many top-level positions in various other areas of employment.

Employment outlook

More than 86,000 chemists were employed in the early 1990s. Of the almost 60 percent who worked for manufacturing companies, more than half were with chemical manufacturers. Chemists were also employed by federal agencies (primarily the Departments of Defense, the Interior, Health and Human Services, and Agriculture); state and local governments (mostly in health and agriculture); nonprofit research organizations; and colleges and universities.

The employment outlook in all these areas through the 1990s is only fair. Although the output of the chemical industry, where most of the jobs are, is expected to increase, it will not result in many new opportunities for chemists. This is because of improvements in productivity and because a greater amount of the chemists' work will be contracted out. Most of the job openings will be to replace chemists who transfer to other occupations or leave the field for other reasons.

The most promising areas should be in pharmaceuticals and biotechnology. Dependent on new development in research and technology, career fields should expand for pharmaceuticals as new discoveries are found. On the other hand, the petroleum refining and most other manufacturing industries that use

chemists are expected to show very little growth, if any.

Some chemistry graduates may choose to teach high-school chemistry; others may qualify as engineers, particularly if they have taken engineering courses. Those with a doctorate may be employed as college or university faculty.

Earnings

A chemist's earning power is determined by a combination of several factors: ability, education, experience, initiative. The importance of graduate training is pointed out by the following statistic: in the early 1990s, the average starting salaries per year in private industry for well-qualified, inexperienced chemists with these various college degrees were as follows: bachelor's, $23,400; master's, $28,000; doctorate, $36,400. Earnings increase markedly with experience. During the same period, experienced chemists in private industry had median salaries of $33,000 with a bachelor's degree, $37,900 with a master's, and $47,800 with a doctorate.

Federal government starting salaries in the early 1990s were approximately as follows: an inexperienced chemist with a bachelor's degree, $14,800 to $18,400, depending on college record; with two full years of graduate study, $22,500; with a doctorate, $27,200 to $32,600. The average for all chemists in the federal government was $38,600 a year.

In addition to salary, industry offers a number of fringe benefits. The industrial chemist is usually qualified to obtain group insurance plans, retirement programs, bonuses, hospitalization plans, and others. University teachers often have the advantage of similar fringe benefits, as do chemists employed in the federal government.

Conditions of work

The chemist usually works a thirty-five-to-forty-hour week. Typically this work week would be from Monday through Friday. It is not uncommon, however, because research and experimentation do not respect the limitations of time, to work on Saturdays and Sundays.

Laboratories are well equipped and well lighted. The work is typically indoor and characterized by a close working relationship with other members of the "chemical team."

Social and psychological factors

The chemist deals with other people in an often close, professional, and satisfying relationship. Observing the scientific contribution of each member of the chemical team, the beginning chemist soon learns to respect the special abilities and talents of each person. Along with the satisfaction gained from close interpersonal relationships, chemists find reward in the realization that their work is geared to create and improve quality of consumer products. They very often have the opportunity to publish the results of this work in technical journals and to present talks on the research to local and national groups of chemists. Chemists are usually not subject to close supervision.

GOE: 02.02.01, 02.02.02. 02.02.03; SIC: 2819, 2833, 3559, 8221, 8731; SOC: 1845

◇ SOURCES OF ADDITIONAL INFORMATION

American Association for Clinical Chemistry
2029 K Street, NW, 7th Floor
Washington, DC 20006

American Chemical Society
1155 16th Street, NW
Washington, DC 20036

American Institute of Chemists
7315 Wisconsin Avenue, NW
Bethesda, MD 20814

Association of Official Analytical Chemists
1111 North 19th Street, Suite 210
Arlington, VA 22209

Chemical Manufacturers Association
2501 M Street, NW
Washington, DC 20037

International Chemical Workers Union
1655 West Market Street
Akron, OH 44313

◇ RELATED ARTICLES

Volume 1: Biological Sciences; Chemicals and Drugs; Chemistry; Plastics
Volume 2: Biochemists; Engineers; Food technologists; Pharmacists; Pharmacologists; Toxicologists
Volume 3: Industrial chemical workers; Pharmaceutical industry workers; Soil scientists
Volume 4: Chemical-radiation technicians; Chemical technicians; Drug technicians; Laboratory technicians; Medical laboratory technicians

Chiropractors

Definition

Chiropractors are health practitioners who treat patients primarily by manual manipulation (adjustments) of parts of the body, especially the spinal column. This approach to health care is based upon the principle that interference with the nervous system impairs normal functions and lowers resistance to disease. Chiropractic manipulation, particularly of the spinal column, is intended to assist the nervous system to function properly.

History

The relief of painful symptoms in the bones has been avidly sought since time began. Where there is no pathological condition or disease and distress is alleviated, a person experiences a sense of well-being, strength, and health. Chiropractic is a system of treatment based on the principle that a person's health is determined largely by the nervous system, the network of the body by which the sensation of pain and pleasure, heat and cold, touch, and all the

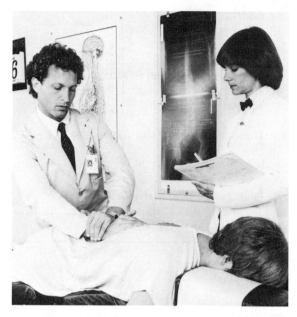

A chiropractor administers treatment to a patient as his assistant takes notes.

senses are transmitted to the brain. The core of the central nervous system is the spinal cord, which is protected by the bones of the vertebrae that make up the backbone or spinal column. Many believe that moving the bones of the back by gentle manipulation can relieve pressure on the nerves that emerge between the vertebrae and thus ease any pain or discomfort caused by such pinching. The relief of interference in the nervous system by chiropractic is intended to restore normal functions of the body and increase resistance to disease. In the twentieth century the practice of such manipulation developed as a branch of health care as the science of medicine grew. It has its greatest popularity in the United States, and chiropractic is practiced widely here and in Canada.

Nature of the work

Chiropractors do not use prescription drugs or surgery. Most chiropractors use X rays to help locate the source of patients' difficulties in the spine and other joints. In addition to manipulation or adjustment, chiropractors may use light, water, electric, massage, heat, and ultrasound therapy, as well as biofeedback to aid the relief of symptoms. They also prescribe diet, rest, exercise, and support of the afflicted part of the body.

Chiropractors are not medical doctors, although general hospitals began accepting chi-

ropractors as staff members in 1983. Most chiropractors, however, maintain offices in a professional building with other specialists or at their clinics. In addition, they may serve on the staff of a hospital that specializes in chiropractic treatment or in alternative health care centers and clinics.

Many people consult a chiropractor because they know another person who has been successfully treated or because they do not wish to use drugs or to have surgery if they can avoid it. Chiropractic treatment involves practitioners' using their hands to move and manipulate joints while the patient is relaxed. Knowledge of anatomy, skillful positioning, firm movement, and sometimes great control of strength are needed to achieve the desired effect. Often the treatment must be repeated through a series of visits by the patient, and the chiropractor may prescribe things for the patient to do at home to maintain and improve the results of the manipulation. Most chiropractors will take a general history of the patient's health that can help in both diagnosis and treatment. Chiropractors do not merely relieve symptoms but practice with an overall intention to promote good health and well-being in their patients.

Requirements

The most important requirement in any health care profession is the desire to help people in need and to promote wholeness and good health. A high-school student needs to begin to acquire the knowledge of the human body by taking as many courses in biology, zoology, organic, and inorganic chemistry as possible. Math and physics are important to the understanding of movement and stress. Chiropractic requires a scientific aptitude, a good business sense, and the ability to put patients at ease.

All chiropractic colleges require a minimum of two years of undergraduate study, including courses in English, the social sciences, biology, chemistry, physics, and mathematics. The course in a chiropractic college is generally an additional four years and emphasizes classes in manipulation and spinal adjustments. Most offer a broad curriculum, including subjects such as physiotherapy and nutrition. In most chiropractic colleges the first two years consist of classroom and laboratory work in subjects such as anatomy, physiology, and biochemistry, while the last two years stress clinical work with patients. The degree awarded upon completion of chiropractic training is Doctor of Chiropractic (D.C.).

Special requirements

All fifty states and the District of Columbia regulate the practice of chiropractic by certain educational requirements including specific courses such as English, chemistry, biology, or physics to be taken during the two years of undergraduate work. In addition, chiropractors must pass a state board exam to obtain a license to practice. The type of practice and the educational requirements for which a chiropractor may be licensed varies from state to state. In general a four-year course following two years of undergraduate work is needed and most state boards recognize only academic training in chiropractic colleges accredited by the Council on Chiropractic Education. In the early 1990s, fourteen of the fifteen chiropractic colleges in the United States were fully accredited, with the other school working toward accreditation.

Several states require that chiropractors pass a basic science examination, and all state boards accept the National Board of Chiropractic Examiners' test given to fourth-year chiropractic students in place of a state examination.

Opportunities for experience and exploration

Students may obtain a part-time or summer job in a clinic area specializing in chiropractic. Other health-care work in nursing homes or hospitals is also of value.

Related occupations

Chiropractors diagnose, treat, and help prevent diseases, disorders, and injuries. Professions that require similar skills include dentists, naturopathic doctors, optometrists, osteopathic physicians, physicians, podiatrists, and veterinarians.

Methods of entering

A newly licensed chiropractor might begin working in a clinic or in an established practice with another chiropractor. Most chiropractors work in cities with a population of less than 50,000.

Advancement

Most chiropractors set up a new practice or purchase an established one. A chiropractor may start as a salaried employee in a large practice and a successful practitioner may establish a group practice or set up a clinic with associated health care practitioners.

Employment outlook

Of the nearly 40,000 chiropractors in the early 1990s, about 96 percent were in private practice, and the great majority practiced alone, without partners. Some chiropractors worked in clinics or were employed as assistants to other practitioners, and a few had faculty or research positions at chiropractic colleges.

Demand for chiropractic is increasing with the growth of public acceptance of the profession as well as the broader coverage of chiropractic services by public and private health insurance. Employment of chiropractors is expected to grow faster than the rate for all professions. College enrollments are also increasing, however, and new chiropractors may find it increasingly difficult to establish a practice in those areas where other practitioners already are located. Also the cost of equipment such as X ray and other diagnostic tools is very high for a private practitioner, and group practices with other chiropractors or related health-care professionals are likely to provide more opportunity for employment or for purchasing a share of a practice.

Earnings

Chiropractors in well-established practices in the early 1990s had incomes comparable to other professionals with an average of about $75,000 a year after expenses. New graduates found earnings relatively low in the beginning, around $20,000, whereas working with an established practitioner as an associate brought around $25,000 a year.

Conditions of work

Chiropractors may take an office in a professional building or in their home. They can usually set their own hours, but the work week is generally thirty-five to forty hours per week.

Social and psychological factors

Chiropractic requires a keen sense of observation to diagnose a condition and determine the appropriate treatment. Considerable hand dexterity is needed at all times but exceptional strength is not necessary. More important is sureness of movement and a genuine desire to help patients. Chiropractors should be able to work independently and handle responsibility and be painstaking with detail. Sympathy and understanding are desirable for dealing effectively with patients.

GOE: 02.03.04; SIC: 8041; SOC: 289

◇ **SOURCES OF ADDITIONAL INFORMATION**

American Chiropractic Association
1701 Clarendon Boulevard
Arlington, VA 22209

Council on Chiropractic Education
4401 Westown Parkway, Suite 120
West Des Moines, IA 50265

International Chiropractors Association
1110 North Glebe Road, Suite 1000
Arlington, VA 22201

◇ **RELATED ARTICLES**

Volume 1: Biological Sciences; Chemistry; Health Care
Volume 2: Ergonomists; Kinesiotherapists; Licensed practical nurses; Physical therapists; Physicians; Registered nurses
Volume 3: Medical assistants; Nursing and psychiatric aides
Volume 4: Physical therapist assistants

City managers

Definition

A *city manager* is an administrator who coordinates the day-to-day running of a local government. Appointed by a community's elected officials, the manager directs the administration of city or county government in accordance with the policies determined by the city council or other elected authority.

Also called a *town manager* or a *county manager*, the duties will vary from place to place. In general, the manager ensures the smooth continuity of local government by creating departments and appointing heads and supervisors as provided by state or local law. The manager also does long-range planning for the area of responsibility, to prepare for population growth and the need for increased services. Sometimes the city manager is an urban planner and only involved in the development of the area or community. City managers may also be responsible for preparing the detailed annual budget. Detailing would include specific estimates on all budget items.

History

For centuries the administration of government has been carried out by persons appointed to perform specific services such as collecting taxes, planning streets and water supply, and law enforcement. These civil servants have been assigned their responsibilities by kings and dictators, by local rulers, and in democratic societies by elected officials, mayors, or local councils. Because the term of office to which officials may be elected may be only a few years, it has always been necessary to have persons with special skills to maintain the continuity of running a government.

It is no longer possible for towns and cities to develop at random. Long-term plans and people to carry them out are needed in every town or city of any size. Many aspects of city life such as building public works, including health and sanitation provision, and collecting the revenues needed to construct and maintain them must go on irrespective of the government or party in power.

Population growth and industrial expansion place increasing pressure on housing, transportation, recreation, and other facilities of cities. Problems associated with the growth of modern cities and towns, such as air and water pollution and rising crime rates must be dealt with. To effectively deal with problems, as well as with the overall running of the town or city, many communities are hiring specialists in urban management techniques: city managers.

Nature of the work

A city manager is usually appointed by the community's elected officials and is responsible to them, directing and coordinating the administration of local government policy. The city manager may in turn appoint department heads and staff needed under state or local ordinances. An important part of the city manager's work is supervising the activities of these departments that collect and disburse taxes, enforce the law, maintain public health, construct public works, and purchase supplies and equipment. The city manager must prepare annual budgets of the costs of these services and submit estimates to the elected officials for approval. In addition the city manager must provide reports of ongoing and completed work to the representatives of the people that live in the city.

The city manager must also plan for future growth and expansion of population and the need for public services. This may require preparing and writing proposals and recommending zoning regulations controlling the location and development of residential and commercial areas. It may be necessary to present these proposals at meetings of the elected authority as well as at public meetings of citizens.

City managers work closely with *urban planners* to coordinate new and existing programs. (*See also* the article titled "Urban and regional planners" elsewhere in this volume.) In smaller cities that have no planning staff that work may be done entirely by the manager. Additional staff may be provided for the city manager, including an *assistant city manager, department head assistants, administrative assistants*, and *management analysts*. (*See also* the article titled "Management analysts" elsewhere in this volume.)

The staff of a city manager have a variety of titles and responsibilities. Changes in administration are studied and recommended by management analysts. Administrative and staff work such as compiling statistics and planning work procedures is done by *administrative assistants*, also called *assistants to the city manager* or

The responsibilities of a city manager involves attendance at civic hearings and discussions with elected officials.

executive assistants. Department head assistants may work in several areas, such as law enforcement, finance, or law, but are generally responsible for just one area. Responsibility for specific projects such as developing the annual budget, as well as organizing and coordinating programs, belongs to assistant city managers who may also supervise city employees and act for the city manager in the manager's absence. In addition, management assistants work under the city manager's direction, answering correspondence, receiving visitors, preparing reports, and administering programs.

Requirements

A college education and preferably a graduate degree in public or business administration are the minimum requirements for those seeking a career in city management. In some cases a graduate degree in a field related to public administration, such as urban planning, political science, or law, may be accepted.

In high school the student should pursue a broad college preparatory program that includes mathematics and statistics as well as social studies. Computer science is an important tool in any administrative preparation. About 350 colleges and universities offer bachelor's and master's degrees in public administration. Degree requirements in some schools include completion of an internship program in a city manager's office that may last from six months to a year, during which time the degree candidate observes local government operations and does research under the direct supervision of the city manager.

Special requirements

Persons planning to enter city management positions frequently must pass civil service examinations. This is one basis for becoming eligible for appointments to local government. Notice of these examinations is publicized nationally. Other requirements will vary from place to place and will be stated in positions advertised.

Opportunities for experience and exploration

The high-school and college student may find opportunities for becoming involved in student government. In addition, vacation jobs in their local government offices can provide experience and some understanding of areas in city management in which they may be interested.

Related occupations

Because city managers are responsible for the smooth running and operation of the daily business of local government their jobs are very similar to those performed by top executives and general mangers in private business.

Methods of entering

Nearly all city managers begin as management assistants. Most new graduates work as management analysts or administrative assistants to city managers for several years to gain experience in solving urban problems, coordinating public services, and applying management

techniques. Others work in a specific department such as finance, public works, or planning. They may acquire supervisory skills and also work as assistant city manager or department head assistant.

Advancement

Advancement takes place as the beginning assistant moves to more inclusive and responsible jobs within local government. At least five years of experience are generally necessary to compete for the position of city manager. City managers are often employed in small cities at first and during their careers may seek and obtain appointments in cities of increasingly larger size.

Employment outlook

In the early 1990s more than 5,000 city managers were employed, more than half of them in the eastern half of the United States. Most city managers work in a council manager form of government, where an elected council appoints the city manager as the chief administrative officer. Many other city managers work for municipalities that have a mayor-council form of government and the mayor appoints the city manager. A few city managers work for county governments, metropolitan or regional planning organizations, councils of governments, and even large corporations that must maintain a large work force overseas.

Although city management is a growing profession, the field is still relatively small. Few job openings are predicted each year through the mid-1990s, and applicants with only a bachelor's degree will have difficulty finding employment. Even an entry-level job often requires an advanced degree.

In greatest demand are those persons who can use the more sophisticated management techniques, including computerized tax and utility billing, electronic traffic control, and applications of systems analysis to urban problems. The demand for city managers will increase as more cities convert to the council manager form of government, the fastest growing form of city government.

In the meantime keen competition exists as the number of applicants exceeds demands for city managers as well as for administrative assistants, and assistant city managers. Those persons with the best qualifications and education can be considered.

Earnings

The average salary for all city managers in the early 1990s was more than $45,000 a year. Individual earnings, of course, vary depending on the person's education and experience, as well as on the size of the city employing him or her. In a very large city, an experienced city manager may earn more than $100,000 a year.

Salaries are set by the city council, and good city managers are sometimes given higher than average pay as an incentive to keep them from seeking more lucrative opportunities. Benefits for city managers include paid vacations, health insurance, sick leave, and retirement plans. Cities may also pay travel and moving expenses and provide a city car or a car allowance.

Conditions of work

City managers generally work in well-lighted and well-ventilated offices. They often work overtime at night and on weekends reading and writing reports or finishing paperwork. To provide information to citizens of current government operations or to advocate certain programs, city managers frequently appear at public meetings and other civic functions. When a problem arises or a crisis occurs, they may be called to work at any hour.

Social and psychological factors

Persons who plan a career in city management should like to work with others as part of a team and also be able to lead. They often need to work under stress and should be able to still pay attention to details. In emergencies, they must be able to quickly isolate the problem and provide a number of possible solutions. City managers also must be dedicated to public service because they have the interests of many persons under their control. They must also be willing to put in long hard hours in times of crisis.

GOE: 11.05.03; SIC: 9111; SOC: 112

◇ **SOURCES OF ADDITIONAL INFORMATION**

The personnel offices of the local government in your area can provide information about positions. Information on academic programs in public management careers can be obtained by writing to:

National Association of Schools of Public Affairs and Administration
1120 G Street, NW, Suite 520
Washington, DC 20005

◇ **RELATED ARTICLES**

Volume 1: Politics and Public Service
Volume 2: General managers and top executives; Management analysts; Political scientists; Urban and regional planners

College admissions directors

Definition

College admissions directors coordinate and oversee the admissions programs of public and private colleges and universities. They supervise the work of *college admissions counselors* who review records, interview prospective students, and process applications for admission. Admissions directors are closely involved in the recruiting of new students and are responsible for carrying out administrative policies that have been established by an academic governing board.

Admissions directors frequently work with a team of counselors. Reviewing students applications may be done individually or by group decision. Directors decide on borderline and disputed applications.

Colleges admissions officers spend much of their time meeting candidates. In this instance, the officer greets a prospective student before conducting an interview.

History

Before the Civil War, most U.S. colleges and universities managed their administration with a president, a treasurer, and a part-time librarian. Members of the faculty were often responsible for the administrative tasks of the day, and there was no uniformity whatsoever in regard to college admissions requirements.

By 1860 the average number of administrative officers in U.S. colleges was still only four, but as the job of running an institution expanded in scope and function, the responsibilities of administration began to splinter. After creating positions for *registrar*, *secretary of faculty*, *chief business officer*, and a number of departmental deans, most schools next hired a director of admissions to oversee the application and acceptance of students.

The growth in administration was a response not only to ever-increasing student enrollment and to the demands for new services, but also to the need of faculty to be free of the details of administration.

As the nineteenth century moved into its second half, it became clear to many in the field of education that nowhere was organization more obviously and urgently necessary than in the area of admissions. There were at that time no uniform standards for making admissions decisions.

This frustrating lack of uniformity led several eastern schools and a few prominent college presidents, President Eliot of Harvard and President Butler of Columbia among them, to establish organizations whose purpose would be to put an end to the chaos. In the last years of the nineteenth century, these organizations were joined in the cause by the National Education Association and its celebrated "Committee of Ten."

The attention given by concerned university administrators to the issue of standardizing college entrance requirements ultimately led to the formation of the College Entrance Examination Board and, despite some early clashes, its purpose and goals were soon well accepted. The first College Board examinations were held in June 1901, and by 1910 twenty-five leading eastern colleges were making use of the Board's standard exams.

These early agencies of standardization in admissions gave rise to a whole range of national organizations that recognized the common problems and accepted the necessity of achieving some common standards. Such organizations, still vital and active today, were instrumental in developing the basic fabric of American college and university accreditation and led to the establishment of college admissions departments as essential to the successful operation of any institution of higher learning.

Nature of the work

The job of college admissions director is demanding and diverse. Those in this position are responsible for a wide range of important tasks and for the many employees who work in the admissions office. They review cases of general and special admission and coordinate recruitment activities. They confer with the staff of other schools to explain admission requirements and policies of student credit transfer. They also evaluate course offerings from other schools to determine their equivalency to courses offered on their own campus.

Admissions directors are responsible for planning and producing application and admissions materials to be disseminated to prospective students and to other schools. They often are required to develop the school's recruiting program as well.

There is usually a high volume of paperwork to be done in this job. Admissions directors are in charge of maintaining important student files and so will often oversee computerized record keeping. They may make recommendations on improving the admissions procedures and may serve on a policy-making admissions committee. In many cases the admissions director is also involved in administering the school's financial aid programs.

Aside from admissions directors in charge of the admissions departments of two-year and four-year colleges and universities, there are those who work in professional colleges such as schools of business, law, and medicine.

Requirements

Those who wish to become college admissions directors must usually obtain at least a master's degree in a field such as student counseling and personnel services or in higher education administration. It may also be an asset to have training in computer science and data processing.

This job requires that a person show an aptitude for organizing and coordinating work in an efficient manner. Those interested in work as the director of an admissions department must have confidence, motivation, and determination, as well as an ability to work well with and motivate others. As a manager, the college admissions director must be decisive and have a sound understanding of managerial principles and practices, which may be achieved both on the job and by taking college courses.

High-school and college students interested in this field would do well to have courses in written and spoken English, foreign languages, social sciences, and mathematics. A bachelor's degree in any field is usually acceptable but most students major in student personnel or in subjects such as economics, psychology, or sociology. Other important studies may include education, counseling, information processing, business, and finance.

Special requirements

Although there is no license or special certification necessary to become a college admissions director, there are several professional groups that set standards for those in this position. Such organizations include the American Association of Collegiate Registrars and Admissions Officers; the National Association of College Deans, Registrars, and Admissions Officers; and the National Association of College Admission Counselors.

Opportunities for experience and exploration

To learn something about what the job of admissions director entails, high-school and college students may first wish to talk to the ad-

missions personnel in their own school or in the admissions offices of any nearby colleges, universities, or private schools. Another possibility would be to talk to college recruiters on high-school campuses, as they are usually employed by the admissions offices of the schools they represent.

College admissions offices frequently hire college students for part-time jobs or internships in their department and this is an excellent opportunity to gain firsthand experience. Because admissions counselors and directors must be skilled in working with students, it may also be helpful for college students interested in this field to work as dorm counselors or to participate in extracurricular activities that involve interacting closely with others.

Related occupations

Universities and colleges have become complex organizations that need skilled administrators with various and diverse talents. Related occupations within the academic community include college admissions counselors, evaluators, and recruiters; financial aid officers and directors; college and university registrars; school principals; foreign student advisors; academic deans; alumni directors; athletic directors; department heads of colleges and universities; and presidents of educational institutions. The skills needed to administer a department in a university are the same as those sought in the business world.

Methods of entering

There are several different types of entry level positions available in the typical admissions office. College students who are able to get part-time work or an internship at the admissions office where they attend school will find that this is a great advantage when seeking work in this field after graduation. Any other experience working with people or with computerized data may also be helpful.

Advancement

Entry level positions, which usually require only a bachelor's degree, include admissions counselors, who advise students regarding admissions requirements and decisions; evaluators, who check high-school transcripts and college transfer records to determine whether applying students may be admitted; and recruiters, who visit high-school campuses to provide information about their school and to interest students in applying for admission.

Advancement from any of these positions will depend on the way in which an admissions office is organized as well as how large it is. One may move up to assistant director or associate director, or, in a larger office, into any of many specialized divisions of admissions that may exist, such as freshman or graduate admissions, minority admissions, transfer admissions, or foreign student admissions. Advancement may also come through transferring to larger schools or systems.

Workshops and seminars are available through professional admissions directors associations for those interested in staying informed and becoming more knowledgeable in their field, but it is highly unlikely that an admissions office employee may gain the top administrative level without a graduate degree.

Employment outlook

The number of admissions directors employed at any time is determined by college and university enrollment and by state and local expenditures for education.

Employment in the field of education administration is expected to grow more slowly than the average for all occupations through the early 1990s, and declining college enrollments and leaner budgets will most likely make the job market very competitive through the 1990s. Admissions offices, however, are expected to remain relatively unaffected by this trend.

Although the competition for jobs in this field will continue to be strong, it is predicted that the next ten years will see a large number of openings as older directors retire and others leave the profession or find work elsewhere.

Earnings

Salaries for admissions directors vary widely among two-year and four-year colleges and among public and private institutions, but are generally comparable to those of college faculty.

In the early 1990s the median yearly pay was $43,000 for a director of admissions. Earnings may range from an annual $21,000 for those just beginning in the field and go up to approximately $70,000 or more for an admissions department head.

Conditions of work

The college or university environment is usually an extremely pleasant place in which to be employed. Offices are often spacious and comfortable and the campus may be a scenic, relaxing work setting.

Employment as a director of admissions is usually on a twelve-month basis. The position requires much direct contact with students and so working hours may vary according to student needs. It is not unusual to work long hours during peak enrollment periods, such as the beginning of each quarter or semester. Directors are sometimes required to work evenings and weekends to provide wider student access to the admissions services.

Beside a great deal of office and telephone work, admissions directors may frequently travel to other colleges and to career fairs, high schools, and professional conferences to interview and provide information about the school for which they work. This travel may be especially extensive in the spring when new students are being recruited.

Admissions personnel are usually provided with health and life insurance, sabbaticals, and reduced tuition or other fringe benefits.

Social and psychological factors

College admissions directors must be very organized and have great skill in leading and dealing with others, both staff and students. It is important that they have the patience and tact to handle a wide range of personalities as well as an emotional steadiness when confronted with unusual and unexpected situations. They should be able to function well under the pressures of deadlines and student, staff, and public demands. The need to travel may be an asset for the single person but a drawback for someone with a family.

Admissions directors must be dedicated to the institution for which they work as they are important representatives of their school and are always being looked to for advice and guidance. This may be rewarding but it is also a responsibility that demands a dedicated, loyal character.

The admissions director is continually meeting a wide range of new people, including students, staff, faculty, and others, which serves to add interest and diversity to the job. Working in the academic atmosphere, one may also be motivated to further his or her own education.

GOE: 11.07.03; SIC: 8221; SOC: 1281

College and university faculty

Definition

College or university faculty members instruct students in specific subjects. They are responsible for oral lectures and the giving and grading of exams. They may also carry on research, write for publication, and aid in administration. They may also serve as consultants to various educational or scientific organizations.

History

Historians believe that the idea of a college or university goes back many centuries. It is thought that the Arabs developed institutions resembling universities long before such schools were developed in Europe. The European universities were begun during the Middle Ages. No one can set the exact date on which any one of them was founded, as each evolved slowly from monastery schools, and each was initiated primarily to train a select few for the professions, notably the profession of theology.

Two of the most notable of the early European universities were the University of Bologna in Italy, thought to have been established in the twelfth century, and the University of Paris, which was chartered in 1201, but had actually been started earlier. These universities were considered to be models after which other European universities were patterned.

Oxford University in England was probably established during the twelfth century, but the first records of university organization that have come down to us are dated 1214. Oxford University served as a model for early American colleges and universities, and today is still considered one of the world's leading institutions.

Harvard, the first U.S. college, was established in 1636. Its stated purpose was to train

University faculty spend much of their time conducting research with the assistance of graduate students.

men for the ministry. The second U.S. college, William and Mary College, was established 57 years after Harvard first opened its doors. It was also established for religious training. During the years between 1636 and 1769, nine colleges were founded in the colonies. All except one were founded by religious sects for the purpose of perpetuating their own ministry.

Not until 1795 was a state university founded; it was the University of North Carolina. The University of Georgia was established in 1801. These two state-supported institutions introduced a new concept in higher education and initiated the process of freeing the curriculum from ties with the church.

The first liberal arts curriculum was introduced with the establishment of the University of Virginia in 1825. The innovations made in higher education by this college were to be adopted later by other colleges and universities.

Although the original colleges in the United States were patterned after Oxford University, they later came under the influence of German universities. During the nineteenth century, more than 9,000 Americans went to Germany to attend the universities that had been established there. The emphasis in German universities was on scientific method. Most of the people who had studied in Germany returned to the United States to teach in universities. They brought with them the objective, factual approach to education and to other fields of learning in which they had studied.

Colleges for women developed more slowly than those for men. The first Wesleyan Female College in Macon, Georgia, was established exactly 200 years after the founding of Harvard College.

The junior college movement in the United States has been one of the most rapidly growing educational developments of all time. Junior colleges first came into being just after the turn of the twentieth century.

Nature of the work

College and university faculty members have three main functions to perform. Their first and most important job is the teaching responsibility. Most college and university teachers are in class approximately nine to twelve hours each week. However, they may put in two hours of preparation for every hour spent in class so the actual time devoted to teaching responsibilities may be approximately thirty-six hours each week. Associate professors and full professors may spend only six to eight hours a week in actual classroom work.

The standard teaching technique for college and university faculty members is the lecture method. Many other methods are also used, however. In some courses, teachers rely heavily on laboratories to transmit course material. Some faculty members employ the discussion method as a teaching device. Others use visual aids to instruct students. Many combine all methods or go from one to the other.

Another important responsibility of the college and university faculty member is the advising of students. Not all serve as faculty advisers, but those who do must set aside a large block of time to see the students for whose program they are responsible. Faculty advisers may have any number of students assigned to them, from fewer than ten to more than one hundred, depending on the amount of responsibility that the adviser is expected to assume and the administrative policies of the college in which they work. Their responsibility for the student may involve only looking over the student's planned program of studies to make sure that he or she meets requirements for graduation, or it may involve working intensively with each student on many aspects of college life. The faculty advisers may see the students for whom they are responsible only once during a semester, or they may see them several times each week.

A third responsibility that the college and university faculty member is expected to assume is for research and for publication. Faculty members who are heavily involved in research programs sometimes are assigned to a smaller teaching load than those who are not so involved. Most faculty members who do research publish their findings in various scholarly journals. They also write books that may be based on research findings or on their own knowledge and experience in their field. Most textbooks are written by college and university teachers.

Some faculty members eventually rise to the position of *department head* and have charge of the affairs of an entire department, such as English, mathematics, or biological sciences.

Department heads, faculty, and other professional staff members are aided in their myriad duties by *graduate assistants*, who may help develop teaching materials, conduct research, give examinations, teach lower-level courses, or carry out a variety of other activities.

Some college and university faculty members are *extension work instructors*. This means that they conduct classes at times and places other than the normal ones for the benefit of persons who otherwise would not be able to take advantage of the institution's resources. They may teach courses in the evenings or on weekends. They may travel away from the campus and meet with a group of students at another location. The teacher may work in the extension division entirely and meet all classes off campus, or may divide the time between on-campus and off-campus teaching. It is not usually possible to spend fifteen hours in class each week if the teacher also must allow for many hours of travel time.

An extension work instructor may give instruction by correspondence to certain students who are not able to come to the campus at that time. Correspondence courses usually are available only to undergraduate students. There may be a standard course of study for the subject, and the teacher's responsibility may be primarily to grade the papers that the student sends in at periodic intervals and to advise the student of his or her progress. The teacher may perform this service in addition to other duties or may be assigned to correspondence work as a major teaching responsibility.

The teacher in the junior college has many of the same kinds of responsibilities as does the teacher in the four-year college or university. One will spend approximately the same number of hours each week teaching classes and will also spend about the same amount of time in preparation. Because the junior college is comprised only of the freshman and sophomore years in college, the faculty member will teach only undergraduates and will not be concerned with tutorial methods that must be employed when working with advanced graduate students. He or she may be assigned to student advising and may help students plan their academic programs. The teacher may also engage

in research and may publish the findings if desired.

Another type of faculty member is the *business education instructor*, who teaches commercial subjects such as shorthand, typing, filing, use of office machines, secretarial procedures, business mathematics, and personality development in business schools and community colleges. (*See also* the article titled "Adult and vocational education teachers" elsewhere in this volume.)

Requirements

At least one advanced degree is required to be employed as a teacher in a college or university. The master's degree is considered the minimum standard, however, and graduate work beyond the master's is usually desirable. A doctorate is required to advance in academic rank above instructor in most institutions.

The faculty member in a junior college may be employed with only a master's degree. Advancement in responsibility and in salary, however, are more likely to come to those who have earned a doctorate. A number of states that maintain public junior colleges require state certification for teaching in these two-year schools. A faculty member must have completed the master's degree and certain courses in education to qualify.

The high-school student who is interested in college teaching should enroll in a college preparatory course. The student will want to take subjects that will give a wide background of information upon which to base a later specialty.

Special requirements

A number of states require state certification to teach in public two-year colleges.

Opportunities for experience and exploration

The high-school student has probably seen or read many works of fiction that supposedly depict the life of the college teacher. Few fictionalized accounts, however, give an accurate picture either of the customary life of the college teacher or of the kind of work that is done.

High-school students may visit the campuses of colleges when they can make an appointment; they should seek permission to visit classes or to talk with some of the college faculty members. The may ask a high-school counselor to provide them with occupational materials that will discuss the vocation of college teaching.

Related occupations

Teaching at any level requires many of the same aptitudes, but not necessarily the extensive education and training, as does teaching in colleges and universities. In addition to teaching occupations in elementary schools and high schools, there are those in vocational and trade schools. Other occupations that involve teaching, communicating information and ideas, and/or research include consultants, librarians, lobbyists, policy analysts, and trainers and employee development specialists. Related occupations in a college or university setting include academic deans, advisers to foreign students, alumni secretaries, athletic directors, and registrars.

Methods of entering

The placement office in the college or university from which the prospective teacher receives a degree will have a list of teaching vacancies in the student's field. The student may choose from among the positions available and apply to one or to several colleges.

The graduate student's major professor will often know of vacancies on the faculties of other colleges and universities. Many graduate students find positions because of the professional relationships of the faculty members under whom they have studied.

Some professional associations maintain lists of teaching opportunities in their areas. They may also keep lists of applicants for positions to put college administrators in touch with persons who might like to become applicants.

Advancement

The usual advancement pattern for the college teacher is from instructor, through assistant professor, to associate professor, to full professor. All four academic ranks are concerned pri-

marily with teaching and research. College faculty members who have an interest in and a talent for administration may be advanced to head of department, or to dean of their college. Some few become college or university presidents.

The instructor is usually an inexperienced college teacher. He or she may hold a doctorate or may have completed all the requirements for one except for the dissertation. Most colleges look upon the rank of instructor as the period spent during which the college is trying the teacher out. If the instructor has the potentiality to become a good college teacher and has completed the doctorate, he or she is usually advanced to the position of assistant professor within three to four years. Those who cannot be advanced at the time are often released to find other employment.

A college faculty member may be initially employed by an institution at the rank of assistant professor or may be promoted to that rank from instructor. If one comes to the faculty at the assistant professor rank, it is usually because one has had college teaching experience elsewhere.

Most colleges have clearly understood promotion policies from rank to rank for faculty members and many have written statements about the number of years in which instructors and assistant professors may remain in grade. Administrators in many colleges hope to encourage younger faculty members to increase their skills and competencies and thus to qualify for the more responsible positions of associate professor and full professor.

Employment outlook

There were approximately 754,000 faculty members employed in colleges and universities in the early 1990s. About 70 percent of them taught in public institutions. Approximately 30 percent of the full-time faculty members teach in universities, almost 50 percent in four-year colleges, and more than 20 percent in two-year colleges.

The demand for faculty members in universities and colleges will depend on the size of the college-age population and the proportion who attend college. Despite earlier predictions, enrollments did not decline when the number of college-age persons became smaller; instead, a larger percentage of this group entered college. If this trend continues, the outlook for college and university faculty members should be moderately favorable through the 1990s. By the end of the decade, enrollments are expected to increase as the baby-boom generation reaches college age. Also, it is anticipated that there will be a larger number of faculty retirements. These two factors should create an even greater demand for faculty.

In the meantime, there will continue to be keen competition for the openings that become available. Many applicants may have to accept part-time or short-term positions. Nonacademic jobs in government or industry may be available to these persons.

The brightest opportunities for college and university faculty members are in engineering, computer science, the physical sciences, and mathematics. These college departments are experiencing some faculty shortages because many teachers have left for more attractive jobs in nonacademic fields. Better prospects may exist also in community colleges that emphasize adult education.

Earnings

The average college or university faculty member is employed for a period of nine or ten months, and the stated salary is for that period. One may earn additional salary by teaching in summer school or by spending the summer in writing for publication, working as a consultant, conducting certain research projects, or performing other income-producing work.

The salaries vary widely according to faculty rank and type of institution. Faculty members in public colleges and universities generally have higher salaries than those in private schools. In the early 1990s, salaries for full-time faculty on nine-month contracts averaged around $37,000. In general, faculty members in four-year schools average higher salaries than those in two-year institutions. Professors averaged about $47,400; associate professors, $35,300; assistant professors, $29,200; and instructors, $22,090.

Most colleges and universities offer other benefits in addition to salary. Benefits often include retirement plans, insurance plans, leave policies, and other benefits. Some colleges offer faculty housing. Occasionally, this housing is without cost, but usually there is a modest rental.

Conditions of work

A college or university is usually a very pleasant place in which to work. There is an atmosphere of purposefulness and of alertness that usually provides a stimulating environment in which to work.

On some campuses, the buildings are old and not always well lighted or air-conditioned. The college or university faculty member will often have to share an office with one or more colleagues. One seldom will have a private secretary, but will share secretarial service with one or several fellow faculty members.

Except for their time in class, the announced office hours when they meet with students, and the time needed for their academic meetings, college faculty members' time may be arranged as they see fit. They may spend time in study, in research, or in the laboratory. College faculty members establish their own patterns of work, according to their own special needs and interests. Most college teachers work more than forty hours each week. Although the time spent in class may require only a fraction of the normal working week, the college teacher's many additional duties and interests will keep one on the job a great many hours beyond what is generally considered to be an average working period.

Social and psychological factors

Most college and university faculty members are very happy with the work that they are doing. They enjoy the association with their fellow faculty members and the opportunity to work with students. The college community offers many satisfying social opportunities both for the college teacher and for his family. There is often intellectual stimulation to be found in the programs provided by the college or university for its faculty and students. There are lectures, debates, plays, concerts, and many other interesting programs.

GOE: 11.02.01; SIC: 8221; SOC: 22

◇ SOURCES OF ADDITIONAL INFORMATION

American Association of University Professors
1012 14th Street, NW, Suite 500
Washington, DC 20005

American Council on Education
One Dupont Circle, NW, Suite 800
Washington, DC 20036

National Education Association
1201 16th Street, NW
Washington, DC 20036

Fulbright Scholar Awards
Council for International Exchange of Scholars
(CIEA)
11 Dupont Circle, NW
Suite 300
Washington, DC 20036

College career planning and placement counselors

Definition

Career planning and placement counselors are college personnel workers who assist students to determine a field of work appropriate to their academic background, to seek out prospective employers in that field, and to prepare for interviewing and other job search techniques. The counselor helps students and alumni to examine their interests and skills, to determine a goal, to seek out career opportunities, and to look for appropriate employment.

History

The concept of central meeting places where laborer and job meet to satisfy mutual needs is an ancient one. Its beginnings, in fact, can be traced back to the old and barbaric custom of slave markets. In contemporary times, however, the system has evolved into the civilized exchange of payment for services.

In the United States, the first funded employment office was established in San Francisco in 1886. There, employers would gather with men seeking jobs, and agreements were reached on the basis of capability and demand. Today the system is a highly evolved one, and public and private placement services perform the essential task of matching skills and jobs in a society as technological and complex as ours.

Nature of the work

The college career planning and placement counselors may specialize in some specific area appropriate to the students and graduates of the school, such as law and education, part-time and summer work, and internships as well as field placements. In a liberal arts college, the students may need more assistance in identifying an appropriate career. To do this the counselor may have interest and aptitude tests administered and interview the student to determine career goals.

The counselor may work with currently enrolled students who are seeking internships and other work programs while still at school. Alumni who wish to make a career change may also seek the services of the career counseling and placement office at their former school. Once the student, new graduate, or alumnus has determined the career goal with the counselor, he or she begins the search for actual employment.

College placement counselors also gather complete job information from prospective employers, and make the information available to interested students and alumni. Just as counselors try to find an applicant for a particular job listing, they also must seek out jobs for specific applicants. To do this, they will call employers who might be interested and try to encourage them to hire the individual they think is qualified for their business.

College placement and career planning counselors are responsible for the arrangements and details of on-campus interviews by large corporations and maintain an up-to-date library of vocational guidance material and recruitment literature.

Counselors may also give assistance in preparing the actual job search by working with the applicant writing resumes and letters of application, as well as practicing interview skills through role-playing and other techniques. They may also give the applicant additional information on business procedure and personnel requirements in the chosen field. Arranging the interview with the prospective employer, including corporate recruiters is also a part of the career and placement counselor's responsibility.

Some career and placement counselors work with secondary school authorities, advising them on the needs of local industry and specific preparation requirements for both employment and for further education. In two-year colleges the counselor may participate in the course content planning, and in some smaller schools the counselor may also teach.

Counselors often serve as liaisons between students and prospective employers.

Requirements

Although there is no educational program in career and placement counseling offered at colleges and universities, a graduate degree in some related field is required. Graduate work would include courses in vocational and aptitude testing, counseling techniques, personnel management and occupational research, industrial relations, and group dynamics and organizational behavior. A master's degree in counseling, college student personnel work, or a behavioral science is a usual minimum.

Special requirements

There are no special requirements other than those mentioned.

Opportunities for experience and exploration

Students interested in this career should seek out professional placement people and discuss the field with them. In addition they should take courses in psychology, sociology, counseling, personnel administration, and business subjects.

Related occupations

Other occupations concerned with education and career counseling include college and student personnel workers, employment counselors, equal employment opportunity/affirmative action specialists, personnel workers and managers, teachers, and training and employee development specialists.

Methods of entering

Sometimes alumni who have demonstrated deep interest in their alma mater plus ability in working with people may find employment as an assistant in the college placement office. Other occupational areas also provide an excellent background for college placement work, such as teaching, business, previous placement training, experience in employment agencies, or work as an assistant in the placement office.

Advancement

Opportunity for advancement to assistant and associate placement director, director of student personnel services, or similar administrative positions depends largely upon the type of college or university and the size of the staff. In general, a doctorate is preferred and may be necessary for advancement.

111

Employment outlook

Nearly all four-year colleges and universities and many two-year community colleges provide career planning and placement to their students and alumni, including special groups—adults planning a career change, as well as minority, low-income, and handicapped students. In many schools, however, career planning and placement is the responsibility of just one person who may have some clerical assistance.

Approximately 5,000 persons worked as college career and placement counselors in the early 1990s. Job opportunities in college placement may show slow growth, however, through the late 1990s because of an anticipated leveling off in the enrollment of students. If this situation arises, competition in this field will be stiff. Graduates with master's degrees in counseling or a related field with a business or industry background may have the advantage in finding employment among the openings that occur as older, experienced counselors transfer to other fields or leave for other reasons.

Earnings

Annual earnings of career planning and placement counselors in the early 1990s varied greatly among educational institutions. The average salary was about $31,200. Earnings were lowest in the Southeast and highest in the Far West. Larger institutions generally paid the highest salaries. Benefits included holidays and vacations, pension and retirement plans, and in some institutions, reduced tuition.

Although college placement and career planning counselors normally work a forty-hour week, irregular hours and overtime are frequently required during the peak recruiting period. Counselors receive the same employment benefits as other professional personnel employed by colleges and universities, and generally work on a twelve-month basis.

Social and psychological factors

Career and placement counseling involves a great deal of contact with people, not only the students, graduates, and alumni one works with, but also prospective employers. Because the work involves major life decisions for the student, the care and attention required of the counselors is vital and may be stressful. It carries a degree of responsibility for the counselor that may be greater than simply finding a person a job. Sometimes the counselor must help applicants to be more realistic in their job goals, which requires tact and consideration. There is also a great deal of additional pressure at times when recruiting is heavy, particularly near graduation. For persons who enjoy working with young people in a university environment, however, college placement and career counseling work can be challenging, rewarding, and pleasant.

GOE: 10.01.02; SIC: 8221; SOC: 24

◇ **SOURCES OF ADDITIONAL INFORMATION**

American Association for Counseling and Development
5999 Stevenson Avenue
Alexandria, VA 22304

College Placement Council
62 Highland Avenue
Bethlehem, PA 18017

For information on colleges and universities that offer training in guidance and counseling as well as on state certification and licensure requirements, contact your state department of education.

For information about job opportunities and entrance requirements, contact your state employment service office.

◇ **RELATED ARTICLES**

Volume 1: Education; Social Sciences
Volume 2: Career counselors; College admissions directors; College student personnel workers; Employment counselors; Employment firm workers; Guidance counselors; Personnel and labor relations specialists; Psychologists

College financial aid administrators

Definition

College financial aid administrators direct the scholarship, grant-in-aid, and loan programs that provide financial assistance to students at a college or university.

History

The first college established in the United States was Harvard College in 1636. It was founded by a grant from the Massachusetts Bay Colony, and in the years since, it has grown to one of the world's great places of learning, mainly through the gifts of many benefactors. Universities and colleges today still depend on grants for many things, including financial assistance for students who would otherwise have trouble meeting the costs of their college education.

After World War II, returning veterans took advantage of readily available government scholarships and entered America's colleges and universities by the thousands. This great influx of scholarship students caused financial aid administration to become a major program. Today, as the costs of a college education continue to rise dramatically, many students are relying on financial assistance in the form of student loans, grants, scholarships, and work-study programs.

Nature of the work

Almost every college and university in the country has a program that offers financial aid to help students meet the costs of tuition, fees, books, and other living expenses. The job of the college financial aid administrator is to keep students informed of the financial assistance available to them and to be sure that the students applying for assistance receive the amounts they are entitled to. At smaller colleges, this work might be done by a single person, the *financial aid officer*. At larger colleges and universities, the staff might be much larger, with the financial aid officer heading a department and directing the activities of *financial aid counselors*, who handle most of the personal contact with students.

Financial aid administrators must have a thorough knowledge of the types of aid and the programs for which students can qualify. Financial assistance can come from the federal and state governments, private foundations, local banks, community groups such as the Jaycees, and the college's own endowment fund. Students and their families are likely to be unaware of all of the many options available, and they count on financial aid administrators to explain the complex requirements of the aid in more easily understandable terms.

When students apply for financial aid that is awarded on the basis of need, they must submit a form showing their families' financial status or, if the students are putting themselves through school, their own income and expenses. This form is available from the College Scholarship Service or the American College Testing Program. These agencies have developed methods to estimate the contribution to a student's college costs that a family should be able to make, given its financial situation and income. This figure, plus whatever funds a student can supply from savings and employment, is subtracted from the cost of attending the college. This estimate can be used to determine how much aid a student is entitled to. The financial aid administrator then does everything possible to see that the student receives as much financial help as he or she is entitled to, and solves any problems or hitches that arise.

Financial problems are only one worry that students face when entering college. Many personal and academic pressures can threaten a student's career. The financial aid administrator may be expected to spot these problems, counseling students when appropriate or referring them to any department or campus service that can give more effective help. The administrator should be concerned that students have every fair chance to graduate.

In addition to working with students and their parents, financial aid administrators also interact a great deal with the various departments and committees of the university. Financial aid administrators stay in contact with the counseling services, admissions office, alumni office, and business offices. The efforts of all these departments must be coordinated so that financial aid available does the greatest amount of good for the greatest number of students. Currently enrolled students should also be kept informed of new developments in aid, so financial aid administrators may have to work with student government and activities committees.

College financial aid administrators must analyze each applicant's monetary situation before granting tuition aid.

Most colleges and universities have a standing committee on student aid made up of faculty and staff members. At their regular meetings, financial assistance policies are reviewed for fairness, effectiveness at meeting prescribed goals and the needs of students, and consistency with federal and state regulations. Financial aid administrators attend these meetings to keep everyone informed of current aid policies, submit reports, and give their advice when new programs are being considered. Often the committee will hear the grievances of students who feel they were wrongly denied financial aid. The decisions of this policy-making group are then formalized and sent to the higher university officials for approval.

In some small colleges, the financial aid administrator reports to the college president directly. In larger colleges and universities, the administrator may report to the dean of student affairs or academic affairs, the director of student services, the director of admissions, or the school's chief business officer. This keeps the college administration informed of department procedures and the activities of the faculty-staff committee. Because of the large number of students being considered for financial aid, policies must be detailed and explicit in covering who is granted aid. Administrators at small colleges may also be called on to perform other functions, acting as admissions officers, course registrars, or counseling and placement officers.

Community contact is an important part of the responsibilities of the financial aid administrator. They may meet with alumni and other possible donors to promote an endowment fund drive, or consult with civic groups that are interested in setting up financial aid programs. They communicate with public and private grantor agencies to stay informed of policy changes and the availability of funds. Financial aid administrators also keep in touch with high-school students and counselors, promoting the opportunities for financial aid through seminars, presentations, and literature.

Requirements

Whether they work in colleges or universities, most financial aid advisors have earned their bachelor's degree, and many have gone on to master's and doctoral degrees. Fields of study include educational administration, student personnel, business, and public administration, but any discipline is usually acceptable for beginning counselors.

Currently, ninety-two doctorate programs in higher education administration are offered at universities around the country, while there are about 500 graduate programs in student counseling and personnel services. To pursue the field of financial aid administration, students in high school should follow a general college preparatory curriculum, including English, mathematics, sociology, and history.

Special requirements

Financial aid administrators meet with their peers through a number of professional associations. These groups exist in every state, and there are also many regional groups. National organizations include the National Association of Student Financial Aid Administrators and the National Association of Student Personnel Administrators.

These various groups meet often with the U.S. Department of Education, state higher education agencies, the College Scholarship Service, and the American College Testing Program. The purpose of these meetings is to ensure that scholarships and other financial aid is distributed properly and fairly. Guidelines for administering financial aid are sometimes debated and adopted at these meetings so that colleges will not unfairly use need-based financial aid as a way of recruiting students. Administrators commit to these policies so that students will be able to choose their college based on the quality of the education offered, not on the availability of needed financial aid.

Opportunities for experience and exploration

There are many ways for undergraduate and graduate students to gain experience as an assistant while continuing with their studies. Students are often hired as residence hall directors and advisors, student union officers, student housing aides, activities advisors, and assistants to various faculty and staff members. After gaining experience in campus administration in this way, they are usually well prepared to work as assistants in the financial aid office. Financial aid offices may also hire students without previous experience as peer counselors.

Related occupations

College financial aid administrators have the same abilities and skills that managers and executives need to work in private industry. Financial skills are also necessary for work in the banking and financial services industries.

Methods of entering

If a student is attending a larger college or university with a large financial aid office, he or she may be able to turn part-time work into a full-time position upon graduation. If the institution is small, or there are no foreseeable job openings, the school's financial aid administrator may know of another school in the state that is hiring. Because financial aid administrators are usually familiar with one another, the good opinion and recommendation of one might open doors to jobs at other schools.

Advancement

Experience and education are the keys to advancement for financial aid administrators. At colleges with small staffs, an administrator usually advances by raises in pay. After a time, administrators may find it necessary to transfer to larger schools with opportunities for advancement and higher pay.

Advancement at larger colleges and universities depends on the size of the financial aid department and the work it does. Persons could move through the ranks from financial aid counselor to administrator to director of fi-

nancial aid. Highest paid of these is the director of financial aid. Directors often have gone further educationally than others on staff. About half of the directors of financial aid across the nation have earned their master's degrees, while about 5 percent have earned doctoral degrees.

Employment outlook

Employment of education administrators in general is expected to grow more slowly than average for all occupations in the next decade. Enrollments are a major factor in the demand for campus administrators, and college enrollments are expected to decline through the mid-1990s, then increase slightly. However, some authorities on college employment consider job prospects good for financial aid administrators. As college becomes more and more expensive, the demand for student financial aid is increasing. While employment at some colleges may be affected by lower enrollments, it is unlikely that cuts would be made in financial aid departments.

Earnings

Salaries for financial aid administrators depends on experience, responsibility, level of advanced education, and the particular college or university where they are employed. In the early 1990s salaries can range from $14,000 to $50,000 a year, while directors can earn up to $60,000.

Financial aid administrators also receive paid vacations, health insurance, pension plans, and other benefits. While some institutions offer tenure to financial aid administrators after a certain length of service, most do not have their contracts renewed automatically like tenured professors.

Conditions

Financial aid administrators work in bright, well-equipped offices. The atmosphere can become hectic at crucial times such as the beginning of the academic year. Administrators, however, usually have their own offices, or at least enough privacy, in which to conduct confidential interviews with students and their parents.

A forty-hour week is usually standard for financial aid administrators, but this can increase at peak work times. Salaried workers may be ineligible for overtime pay, but some schools may allow administrators to take reciprocal time off. Because of the nature of the work and the fact that most colleges offer summer terms, financial aid offices operate year round. Administrators may travel on the job, as they attend seminars and conventions and visit high schools and other universities.

Social and psychological factors

A desire to help other people and skills in communicating are essential to the job of a financial aid administrator. A great deal of tact and patience is needed when discussing delicate financial matters with students and their families. Financial aid administrators should be able to relate to students and be aware of the many pressures—financial and otherwise—that exist in college life. A calm and understanding voice may be enough to keep a student from giving up and dropping out of college.

On the job, financial aid administrators should be very detail-oriented and organized, but they also need to be flexible in their procedures. Government assistance programs and regulations change very often, and administrators need to be able to respond quickly and effectively. Administrators also have to communicate well with the representatives of private sources of aid and the other departments in the college. Leadership is also an important quality, so that department staff can be inspired to do their best work. Sound fiscal management skills are an absolute necessity.

A financial aid administrator's job is not an easy one, but there can be many personal rewards. People attracted to this job enjoy the atmosphere on a college campus, working with intelligent and dedicated people. Most of all, they gain a certain feeling of accomplishment in helping make it possible for young people to attend and stay in college, working toward their dreams.

GOE: 11.07.03; SIC: 8221; SOC: 1281

◇ **SOURCES OF ADDITIONAL INFORMATION**

American Association of University Administrators
PO Box 870122
Tuscaloosa, AL 35487

National Association of Student Financial Aid Administrators
1900 L Street, NW, Suite 200
Washington, DC 20036

The College Board
45 Columbus Avenue
New York, NY 10023

◇ **RELATED ARTICLES**

Volume 1: Education; Social Services
Volume 2: College admissions directors; College and university faculty; College career planning and placement counselors; College student personnel workers; Fundraisers; Guidance counselors; School administrators

College student personnel workers

Definition

College student personnel workers develop and administer services for students in institutions of higher education. Some of the services provided for students that are the responsibility of college student personnel workers are housing and social, cultural, and recreational activities. They usually supervise such programs as the resident advisor programs in dormitories. Job titles vary but the more common titles are *dean, director, officer, associate dean, assistant director,* and *advisor*. Department titles are usually "student affairs" or "student relations."

History

The ideal of a liberal education is as old as the classical Greek concept of *paidaiea*, the education of the whole person, body, mind, and spirit. At first undertaken on a one-to-one relationship between student and *mentor*, learning began to involve groups of students seeking out a particular teacher.

In the Middle Ages, the great universities developed not so much for students, but as places where scholars could gather to share knowledge with one another. As they did this in public, students would gather to listen and this method of sharing knowledge through lecture has continued to the present day. In addition, those students who were interested in learning more from a scholar might engage him on a private tutorial basis, or get together with other students to be led by the scholar in a seminar. With the tremendous growth in literacy and the need to provide facilities for studying the sciences in particular, colleges and universities in the twentieth century developed an administrative structure to meet the expanded size and needs of the faculty and student body.

Nature of the work

Student personnel workers are responsible for student housing, religious life, counseling, health, athletics, financial aid, on-campus and summer employment, career counseling and placement, learning assistance, skills development, and cultural activities. On many campuses they provide special services for veterans and for women, minority, handicapped, and foreign students. They may administer the student union, bookstore, and campus security.

The *registrar* prepares class schedules, makes classroom and student assignments, provides transcripts, and assembles enrollment and other statistical data for government and educational agencies.

The *director of admissions* supervises the work of admissions counselors who interview prospective students and process applications. Recruiting students and adult learners is an important part of the admissions office's responsibility. This may involve travel to various schools including the metropolitan areas from which many of the students at the institution are drawn. Special programs to seek and recruit students may be designed and implemented by the admissions office, which will coordinate efforts with the public relations office, the faculty, and other administrative areas in planning policies and search activities.

A college student personnel worker guides a student through the various extracurricular opportunities available on campus.

The *director of placement* is responsible for assisting students in career planning and job placement. (*See also* the article titled "College career planning and placement counselors" elsewhere in this volume.)

Admissions and records are closely related in student personnel administration, although admissions officers and registrars normally report to the dean of academic affairs, not to the dean of students.

The *dean of students* heads the entire student personnel program. Associate or assistant deans may be in charge of specific programs such as student life or housing. An important part of the dean of students' job is evaluating the changing needs of students and helping develop institutional policies. For example, an increase in handicapped students requires provision for housing, financial aid, and counseling to meet special needs. Older students have different needs and the dean of students must plan for things such as a greater proportion of part-time students who have full-time jobs and can only attend classes in the evenings and at weekends.

The *director of student affairs* assists student groups in planning and arranging social, cultural, and recreational events. Student activities staff may manage the student union, assist in the orientation of new students, promote student participation in cultural and recreational events. The student affairs office usually publishes a calendar of events and a student handbook.

The director of residence life and housing is responsible for operational matters such as room assignment, damage control, residence hall supply and maintenance, and the fiscal,

College student personnel workers
Professional, Administrative, and Managerial Occupations

food, and housekeeping arrangements for student residences.

Residence counselors live in the residence halls and, in general, try to help the students live in harmony. They may provide help and advice to students with personal problems. They may also manage the food and housekeeping services of the residence in which they live.

The *director of religious activities* coordinates the activities of the various denominational groups. Sometimes called the *dean of chapel*, the position may also involve acting as liaison between the administration and the chaplains of various faiths in organizing religious activities on campus. The office of religious activities may also provide marital and other counseling services.

Most colleges and universities provide assistance to students with personal problems through a counseling service staffed with professionals and graduate students in the field of psychology. Students may come to the counseling center on their own or may be referred by a residence hall counselor, a faculty member, or a friend. *Counselors* and *counseling psychologists* are supervised by the *director of counseling*. (*See also* the article titled "Psychologists" elsewhere in this volume.)

Counseling needs may arise for many reasons. A student may lack self-confidence in academic work or in personal life. Students may suffer from loneliness, drug abuse, or marital problems. On many campuses, counselors try to reach students by establishing telephone hotlines and by organizing group sensitivity sessions. Counseling center staff may administer aptitude and interest tests and assist with admissions and orientation.

Foreign students may need special help with admissions, orientation, housing, financial aid, English as a foreign language, academic and personal counseling. *Foreign-student advisers* administer and coordinate many of the services that students from other countries might need. They might also work as advisers to international associations and nationality groups as well as to U.S. students who wish to study abroad.

Veterans' coordinators provide information and services to veterans and potential military enlistees. They advise students on their eligibility for benefits or other forms of assistance, interpret laws and regulations to students, and supervise the processing of applications for benefits.

The planning and administration of the college or university student health program is the responsibility of the student health service officers and staff who are generally qualified

health care practitioners, nurses, physicians, and paramedics.

The director of the service may hire staff, arrange for facilities and equipment, and organize the processing of new students. In addition they prepare budgets, authorize expenditures, and develop programs and services to meet the students' health care needs.

Intercollegiate athletic activities are administered by *athletic directors* who hire and discharge coaches, schedule sports events, and direct publicity efforts, as well as prepare the budget and authorize expenditures by the athletic department.

Financial aid counselors advise students about their eligibility for various forms of financial aid such as scholarships, loans, grants, fellowships, work-study programs, teaching or research assistantships, and campus jobs. They may maintain and keep up-to-date job listings for students who need to be employed. Often, the financial aid office contacts alumni to find job possibilities for students. The staff of the financial aid office is directed by a *financial aid officer*. (*See also* the article titled "College financial aid administrators" elsewhere in this volume.)

Requirements

A bachelor's degree is the minimum requirement for college student personnel workers. Because of the diversity in duties the education and background required varies considerably. In filling entry-level jobs, schools often prefer persons who have a bachelor's degree in a social science, such as economics or history.

High-school students interested in a career in working with students should elect a broad college preparatory program. Computer science is always a useful adjunct for anyone wishing to be employed in an organization that deals with a sizable group of people, as does a college or university.

A graduate degree in student personnel administration is available at about 500 universities and is required for higher-level student personnel positions.

Special requirements

Some student personnel positions require specialized training. A master's degree in counseling or in clinical or counseling psychology usually is required for work as a college counselor. Counseling psychologists need a doctorate. Directors of religious life usually are members of the clergy. Familiarity with computers and information systems is an asset for work in admissions, records, or financial aid.

Some of the more responsible positions are filled by individuals who have developed organizational and interpersonal skills in other areas and fields such as business, social service, philanthropy, or the ministry.

Opportunities for experience and exploration

Many graduate students obtain experience by working in the residence halls or the financial aid or admissions office. Part-time employment is often available to undergraduates as part of a financial aid or work-study program. Participation in student government in high school may provide useful experience of the variety of administrative needs of a student body.

Related occupations

College student personnel workers are education administrators and, as such, use their organizational and leadership skills to provide services to individuals. Similar qualifications are required in such other occupations as health services administrators, library directors, museum directors, professional and membership organization directors, recreation and park managers, and social service agency administrators.

Methods of entering

The best training in college administration is on the job. Therefore a student who has the opportunity to work in the administrative offices of their college or university will have the best experience to seek a position after graduation. If the alma mater does not have a position available, the new graduate will find that similar positions exist at most colleges and universities.

Advancement

Entry-level positions include student activities advisers, student union staff, admissions counselors, and financial aid counselors. In all of these positions opportunities exist for advancement and promotion with experience. The position of director of most of these administrative areas will require at least a master's degree in student personnel administration or a related field.

Residence hall counselors and counseling service staff require the appropriate training in psychology; at least a master's and preferably a doctorate. Experience as a resident hall advisor is helpful as well. In other areas such as student health and campus ministry, the appropriate professional degree and qualifications would be needed for advancement to more responsible administrative positions.

Employment outlook

Declining or static enrollments in four-year colleges and universities are likely to make the employment situation highly competitive in college student personnel positions until the late 1990s. Those least likely to be affected are in admissions and financial aid, while student life services will be cut back or the positions will be filled in many cases by graduate students.

Two-year colleges will continue to have higher enrollments, but, as these institutions tend to rely on a commuting student body and put less emphasis on student life on campus, employment opportunities are still limited.

Most openings will result from the need to replace personnel who transfer to other positions, retire, or leave the field for other reasons.

Earnings

Salaries vary greatly in college student personnel work, depending to a great extent on the part of the country and the size of the institution. In the early 1990s, approximate average annual salaries included $38,900 for admissions directors and registrars, $38,700 for directors of development and alumni affairs, $30,900 for financial aid directors, and $27,200 for directors of student activities. Salaries for entry-level positions are somewhat lower, particularly because colleges and universities have a number of part-time workers available in the student body.

Conditions of work

Most student personnel workers have pleasant surrounding in which to work. All of the positions require contact with students and so the hours may vary to meet the students' needs. Long hours are not unusual at peak times such as fall registration and orientation. Flexible schedules to provide services to students in the evenings and at the weekends may also be required. In the early spring admissions counselors will be particularly busy recruiting new students and this may require some travel, and the same is true for athletic staff. Counseling, health, and religious activity staff must also have flexible hours to be available to students and must also cope with emergency situations.

Employment in schools and colleges is usually on a twelve-month basis. In most schools, college student personnel workers are entitled to pensions, life and health insurance, sabbaticals, and other fringe benefits such as reduced tuition.

Social and psychological factors

Student personnel administration requires leadership and organizational skills, commitment to the purpose of the institution, and a desire to serve. College student personnel workers must be especially good at working with people. Individuals in this field need the patience to cope with a variety of persons in need and the emotional stability to deal with the unusual and unexpected. The ability to function under stress is important.

Working in a college or university atmosphere can be very rewarding. Opportunity exists to meet a wide range of people, students, staff, and faculty. Interest and inclination may also be generated in such an atmosphere for workers to pursue their own academic career at a higher level or to explore a new field. Meeting the needs of students, a group of persons assembled in similar situations with similar goals, can be very rewarding.

GOE: 11.07.03; SIC: 1281; SOC: 1281

◇ SOURCES OF ADDITIONAL INFORMATION

American Association for Counseling and Development
5999 Stevenson Avenue
Alexandria, VA 22304

American Association of University Administrators
PO Box 870122
Tuscaloosa, AL 35487

National Association of Student Personnel Administrators
1700 18th Street, NW
Washington, DC 20009

◇ RELATED ARTICLES

Volume 1: Education; Social Sciences
Volume 2: College admissions directors; College career planning and placement officers; College financial aid administrators; Guidance counselors; School administrators

Commercial artists

Definition

Commercial artists create artwork that is designed to attract the attention of readers or viewers and to stimulate their interest in particular products or ideas found in publications, packaging, television, or advertising. Commercial artists specialize in various types of art or in one communications media.

Commercial art differs from fine art in that it is normally done to enhance or promote a product. Some commercial art however, may cross over as fine art if it is executed well. Fine art is art admired on its own merit.

History

Art has long been used as a means of communication. The sketches and scribblings of the cave dweller mark the earliest attempt to communicate ideas and feelings. Although we have developed language to communicate knowledge and ideas to live more effectively and productively, art has remained a means for communicating some of the more intense emotional aspects of life. Historically, art has been considered, along with literature, a chief source of knowledge about other people and other cultures. Commercial art might be considered that pictorial part of a civilization that is devoted to communicating the various ways in which the products of its businesses and industries can be useful.

With the growth of American business and industry and the competition for markets, the work of the commercial artist has assumed considerable importance. Producers of similar products are competing for customers. Producers of different products, although not in direct competition, must attract the potential buyer by indicating the significance of their own product. The necessity to advertise has long been recognized, but the emphasis on the communicative aspects of art, as a result of newspapers, magazines, and television, has grown rapidly. Thus, commercial art is a relatively new field.

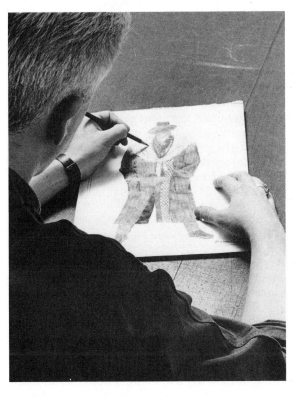

A textile designer puts the finishing touches on a sketch of menswear.

Nature of the work

Commercial artists prepare illustrations and designs for advertisements and displays such as those in newspapers, magazines, and television commercials; food store displays; packaging for various merchandise; wallpaper and gift wrapping designs; greeting card illustrations; and roadside billboards. They may also illustrate magazine articles or books or deal with the production of spot illustrations or cartoons.

The work involves drawing, sketching, painting, lettering, retouching photographs, making charts, maps, cartoons, or designing to communicate an idea.

Most commercial artists begin their careers as paste-up and mechanical artists, letterers, or assistant package designers. They may advance to various positions depending upon their qualifications and interests.

Graphic designers, or *layout artists*, plan the style and arrangement of photographs, artwork, and type for communications media such as books, magazines, newspapers, television, and print or TV advertising. They prepare sample layouts and supervise the work of others who execute the ideas. Book designers are graphic artists who specialize in books, including the design of book jackets, selection of type, and illustrations for the text.

Illustrators prepare drawings for consumer advertisements and illustrations for magazine articles and books. *Medical and scientific illustrators* have training in biology and the physical sciences so they can draw accurate illustrations of parts of the human body or animals and plants. Their work is in demand for use in textbooks, medical journals, lecture presentations, and medical advertising. *Fashion illustrators* specialize in distinctive illustrations of the latest women's and men's fashions.

Two other specialties among commercial artists are *cartoonists* and *animators*. Cartoonists draw newspaper comic strips, political cartoons, or comic books and must have the creative ability to generate ideas or work with a partner who thinks up the ideas. Animators draw a series of many pictures that are put onto film to make an animated cartoon. Most animators are employed in the motion picture industry. (*See also* the article titled "Cartoonists and animators" elsewhere in this volume.)

Art director is a position of high advancement for the commercial artist. For a description of this occupation, see "Designers" elsewhere in this volume.

The commercial artist gets a starting idea from the producers of goods, who describe the idea they want to convey and the various media and materials which might be used. Preliminary sketches or designs are prepared to show the general arrangement of the illustration and the amount of space to be used. Layout work, beyond the preliminary or draft stage, focuses on the size, color, and arrangement of pictured and lettered material.

Requirements

An artistic ability is the most important requirement for this career. The ability to draw, to sketch, or to letter is basic and, in addition, one needs to know how to deal with color and composition. Certain personal characteristics are also important. One of the most important of these is originality—an ability to come up with new ideas, to be imaginative and creative, to think of new ways to express both old and new ideas.

Persistence is also essential. Commercial artists must be able to stick with a project not only until they are satisfied but until they satisfy others. Thus, they must be able to take correction and be able to work with others on special group assignments.

Although natural ability and certain personal qualifications are a basic consideration, training in the techniques of applied art is an essential part of the preparation of the commercial artist. High-school art courses offer an opportunity to study the fundamentals of design and color, and the basic lettering and drawing techniques. Because the commercial artist is required to work on projects dealing with all phases of society and life, a general academic education and extensive educational training in the fine arts of painting, sculpture, and architecture are also important parts of the preparation.

Preparation beyond high school can be secured at four-year colleges or universities, junior colleges, or specialized art schools. The college and university generally offer four-year programs leading to a bachelor's degree. In addition to a major in art, students are required to pursue courses of a general educational nature.

A growing number of art schools, particularly those connected with a university, require four or more years of study and offer a bachelor or bachelor of fine arts degree. In this course of study, the student gets a liberal arts education, plus work in perspective, design, color harmony, composition, use of pencil, pen, and other art media. Subsequent study includes drawing from real life, advertising layout, lettering, typography, and illustration.

Experience in photography is sometimes useful as is some background in business practices. Free-lance commercial artists must have the ability to sell themselves and their work. Students interested in medical or scientific illustrating should obtain education in the area of interest. College courses in science, as well as in the arts, are essential.

Special requirements

No specific license or related requirement is necessary to gain admission to the field. Membership in professional associations is voluntary; however, many commercial artists are members of professional associations, such as the Society of Illustrators or the American Artists' Professional League.

The commercial artist usually maintains a portfolio containing examples of his or her best work. Although this is not a specific requirement, the portfolio is essential in seeking employment, particularly initial employment, and in obtaining free-lance assignments.

Opportunities for experience and exploration

Most elementary, junior high, and senior high school programs provide opportunities for students to explore their interest in art and to identify their strengths and weaknesses. In many schools, students have formal art courses in which they are exposed to a variety of art media. Special projects as part of other courses or as part of in-school or out-of-school activities (posters for various events, holiday and extracurricular organization decorations, school bulletin boards) also can be used to explore one's interest and ability in activities similar in nature to the duties of a commercial artist.

At the senior high-school or higher education level, part-time and summer work possibilities offer a chance to observe actual working conditions. Many talented individuals will find their services in demand in connection with local fundraising drives or community events. Some students, to gain experience, have offered their services to local merchants.

Related occupations

Many occupations are related to that of the commercial artist. They include art directors, commercial designers, fashion artists, graphic designers, illustrators, and set illustrators. Medical illustrators might also explore the work of cartographers, drafters, industrial designers, and technical illustrators.

Commercial and graphic design knowledge or capabilities may be applied to many occupations in advertising, such as account executive or creative director. Other occupations that rely on visual art skills include architects, display workers, floral designers, industrial designers, interior designers, landscape architects, and photographers. Jobs in the printing industry often are related to graphic art. Training in commercial art may also be applied to teaching art and design.

Methods of entering

Graduates of the commercial schools of art and of college or university programs will find the placement services of their institutions helpful in locating positions. Each year a number of openings become available in the advertising departments of business and industrial firms, advertising agencies, and commercial art studios. Many firms and business organizations, such as greeting card companies, television studios, motion picture studios, department stores, sign shops, publishing firms, and printing houses, employ a number of staff artists.

Many initial jobs in commercial art are routine, and beginning commercial artists are apt to be assigned to assist the more experienced artists. Thus, they may perform routine color or layout jobs, make corrections, or paste and assemble model advertisements. On-the-job training, however, is a vital part of one's program of preparation and serves as a means of getting started in the field. Some apprenticeship opportunities, for those who are unable to finance training in art beyond high school, are available in printing, display, and outdoor advertising.

Advancement

Young artists who show ability in beginning jobs can look forward to advancement as layout artists, illustrators, letterers, or to other specialized functions within the field. Some become art directors and assume major executive posi-

tions; others move to free-lance work after having established a good reputation. From on-the-job apprentice or helper levels of employment, one becomes more involved with the creative and challenging aspects of technical and managerial problems.

Employment outlook

Commercial artists and graphic designers held about 176,000 jobs in the early 1990s. Almost 60 percent of these workers were self-employed. Employment in this field is expected to grow rapidly through the 1990s. Increased emphasis on visual appeal in communications, products, and services will result in the creation of new jobs in advertising agencies and graphic arts studios. Many at least partially qualified people are attracted to what they consider a glamorous field, however, making the competition heavy for salaried and free-lance jobs. Nevertheless, artists with exceptional talent are always in great demand; those with outstanding portfolios will be shown preference by employers.

The majority of commercial artists work in large cities such as New York, Boston, Chicago, Los Angeles, and San Francisco, where the largest users of commercial art are located. Employers of commercial artists include, besides advertising agencies and graphic arts studios, publishers of books, magazines, newspapers, catalogs, and calendars; companies that publish house journals; and organizations that handle their own advertising, such as retail stores, motion picture and television companies, government agencies, and firms that manufacture appliances, home furnishings, and other durable goods. In addition, commercial artists work for public relations and publicity firms, commercial printers, display companies, and mail order houses.

Earnings

Earnings, as in most positions, depend upon the experience and background of the artist. In the early 1990s, the median income for all full-time salaried commercial artists was about $20,000 a year, with the middle 50 percent receiving between $15,200 and $26,000. An experienced specialist can earn as much as $100,000 a year.

It is most difficult to establish the earnings of the free-lance commercial artist for a number of reasons: the income is dependent upon the amount of artwork sold; the fee for various artists is related in part to their reputation and the demand for their work; and the nature of the work—lettering, sketches, color or black and white—pays differently. Because of the many variables, it can be speculated that the income of the free-lance commercial artist could range from as little as $7,000 a year to as much as $75,000 or $100,000 or more.

Conditions of work

The workweek of the commercial artist is generally thirty-five to forty hours the year round. Occasionally, the production or seasonal demands of the employer necessitate work under pressure with strict time deadlines and, sometimes, budget limitations. The tensions of rush work, particularly if the project involves a considerable amount of creativity, are further complicated when the job requires the cooperation of a number of individuals. The commercial artist works usually in well-lighted, ventilated studios or offices. The free-lance artist usually works irregular hours.

Social and psychological factors

The student who is interested and has ability in art will find opportunities for artistic expression ranging from the routine copy to the highly creative job. The commercial artist has a chance to fulfill the needs for creation and self-expression, both of which might be considered important psychological needs for those who are artistically inclined. Some will find satisfaction in carrying out the creative ideas of others, some will engage in the continuous process of searching for perfection and will find endless enjoyment with the "never quite satisfied" state of mind. Although it is often said that artists live relatively in a world of their own, the world of commercial artists is very real. Their work necessitates being in constant touch with the pulse of society. They must be up-to-date with the current trends and thinking of the times. Their day-to-day work is far from solitary. They will be receiving ideas or instructions from colleagues and superiors necessitating constant contacts with others at work and extending into their personal life.

Unlike the fine artist who may spend a lifetime searching for the gratifications of high achievement or self-expression, the commercial artist may be able to achieve a measure of success, prestige, recognition, and self-expression in the performance of daily assignments.

GOE: 01.02.03; SIC: 7336; SOC: 322

◇ **SOURCES OF ADDITIONAL INFORMATION**

American Advertising Federation
Educational Services
1400 K Street, NW, Suite 1000
Washington, DC 20005

American Institute of Graphic Arts
1059 Third Avenue
New York, NY 10021

Association of Medical Illustrators
2692 Huguenot Springs Road
Midlothian, VA 23113

Graphic Artists Guild
11 West 20th Street, 8th Floor
New York, NY 10011

National Art Education Association
1916 Association Drive
Reston, VA 22091

National Association of Schools of Art and Design
11250 Roger Bacon Drive, Number 5
Reston, VA 22090

National Cartoonists Society
Nine Ebony Court
Brooklyn, NY 11229

Society of Illustrators
128 East 63rd Street
New York, NY 10021

◇ **RELATED ARTICLES**

Volume 1: Advertising; Book Publishing; Design; Magazine Publishing; Newspaper Publishing; Packaging; Textiles
Volume 2: Advertising workers; Cartoonists and animators; Designers; Fashion designers; Industrial designers; Interior designers and decorators; Painters and sculptors
Volume 3: Lithographic occupations; Photoengravers
Volume 4: Drafting and design technicians

Computer programmers

Definition

Computer programmers work in the field of electronic data processing. It is their job to write and to code the instructions that control the work of a computer, which can only follow carefully prepared instructions as to what to do on each assignment. Systems programmers specialize in maintaining the general instructions that control an entire computer system; this includes giving instructions to the system on how to allocate time to the jobs fed into it.

History

Data-processing systems and their supporting personnel are a product of World War II. During this war, pieces of information that had to be compiled and organized for responsible persons to be able to make appropriate decisions became so numerous that it was not possible for human beings to collect and put them in order in time for the necessary decisions to be made. It was obvious that a quicker way had to be devised to gather and organize information if decisions based on logic and not on guesses were to be made. Physicists who were working in the defense effort combined their skills with those of engineers and technologists and produced the computers.

Data-processing systems are a logical outgrowth of the tools that have helped people handle the informational aspects of our environment for many centuries. One of the first of these tools was the abacus, which is still used in certain Eastern countries. In some respects, it may be said that the telegraph, typewriter, adding machines and calculators were produced to help us gather and organize information. The computer is actually an extension of these devices.

The first computer to be put to use to work out civilian problems was installed by the Bureau of the Census in 1951 to help compile the data from the 1950 census. This machine was large and complicated, and seemed impractical to design, install, and use for problems of less scope than analysis of the entire population. However, three years later the first computer was installed by a business firm. Since 1954, many thousands of data-processing systems have been installed in government agencies, industrial firms, banks, insurance agencies, educational systems, publishing houses, colleges and universities, and scientific laboratories.

Because the machines are useless until there is someone to implement them, personnel to program and operate the computers have evolved along with the data systems themselves.

Nature of the work

Broadly speaking, there are two types of computer programmers: systems programmers and applications programmers. Systems programmers maintain the instructions (called programs or software) that control the entire computer system, including both the central processing unit and the equipment with which it communicates, such as terminals, printers, and disk drives. Applications programmers write the software to handle specific jobs and may specialize as *engineering and scientific programmers* or as *business programmers*. Some of the latter specialists may be designated *chief business programmers* and supervise the work of other business programmers.

Programmers often work from descriptions prepared by systems analysts (*see also* the separate article titled "System analysts" elsewhere in this volume), listing in detail the steps the computer must follow to complete a task. In smaller companies, analysis and programming may be handled by the same person, called a programmer-analyst.

A programmer analyzes the request that is being made of the instrument, obtains from the persons who make the request information about the kinds of results that they want, discovers the kinds of data that will be needed to attack the problem, and plans the way in which the machine will have to respond to produce the information required. The programmer prepares a flow chart to show the steps in sequence that the machine must make. He or she must pay attention to minute detail and instruct the machine in each step of the process. These instructions are then coded in a programming language, such as BASIC, COBOL, FORTRAN, PASCAL, or RPG. When the program is completed, the programmer tests its working practicality by having it perform on simulated data. If the machine responds according to expectations, actual data will be fed into it and the program will be activated. If the computer does not

Computer programmers must understand exactly how a computer thinks. Only then can he design and install a program that runs smoothly.

respond as anticipated, the program will have to be "debugged," or examined for errors that must be eliminated. Finally, the programmer prepares an instruction sheet for the computer operator who will run the program.

The programmer's job, then, is concerned with both an overall picture and with minute details. One works from two points of view: from that of the persons who want certain information produced and from that of technological problem-solving. The work is equally divided between meeting the needs of other people and comprehending the capabilities of the machines.

Electronic data systems do not involve just one machine; depending upon the kind of system being used, the operation may require other machines such as printers. In addition, the introduction of newer computers often requires the rewriting of entire programs.

The visible results of the work of the programmer may be in one of several forms, such as magnetic tape or disks, that can be stored easily and fed back into the machine at any future time for further study. The computer will print the results of the program at a high rate of speed in a way that is comprehensible to the specific machine language being used.

Programmers may specialize in certain types of work depending on the kind of problem to be solved and the place of work. Making a program involved with a payroll is, for example, very different from programming the study of structures of chemical compounds. *Information system programmers* specialize in programs for storing and retrieving physical science, engineering, or medical information; text analysis; and language, law, military, or library science data. *Process control programmers* develop programs for systems that control automatic operations for commercial and industrial enterprises, such as steel making, sanitation plants, combustion systems, computerized production testing, or automatic truck loading. *Numerical control tool programmers*, program the tape that controls the machining of automatic machine tools. (*See also* the separate article titled "Numerical control tool programmers" elsewhere in this volume.)

Requirements

Most employers of programmers specify that they prefer college graduates. Employers, however, have been known to take persons as programmers who have attended college but who have not graduated. Personal qualifications such as a high degree of reasoning ability, patience, and persistence and an aptitude for mathematics are often as influential as formal training in obtaining entry positions with data systems. Many personnel officers administer aptitude tests to determine potential for the work of a programmer. Employers usually send the new employee to a computer school before the person will be qualified to assume programming responsibilities. One is usually sent to school at company expense; the training period may last as long as five weeks. It generally takes a year or more before a programmer can master all aspects of the job.

A few high schools in large urban areas have courses to train students in using data processing equipment. Many junior and community colleges have also begun two-year programs in data-processing, which create opportunities for graduates to seek employment in technical jobs with computer systems. Many colleges and universities now offer courses and degree programs in computer sciences.

Some employers whose work is highly technical require that programmers be qualified in the area in which the firm or agency operates to be considered for a position. Engineering firms, for example, prefer to employ young persons with an engineering background and then provide them with training in the acquisition of data-processing skills.

Those employers who specify a college degree do not always state the major field in which the degree is to be obtained, although mathematics is highly favored. Other majors may be business administration, accounting, engineering, or physics. Entrance requirements for jobs with the federal government are much the same as those in private industry.

Special requirements

Ability to solve difficult problems in a logical and objective manner is the programmer's special requirement. There are no special licenses for programmers. Experienced programmers may earn a Certificate in Computer Programming (CPP) by passing exams given by the Institute for Certification of Computer Professionals.

Opportunities for experience and exploration

A high-school student who has high interest and good grades in mathematics and science and who is interested in possibly entering the data-processing field as a programmer, might visit a large bank or insurance company in the community and seek an appointment to talk with one of the programmers on the staff. Future programmers may be able to visit the data-processing center and see the machines in operation. They might talk with a sales representative from one of the large manufacturers of data-processing equipment and request whatever brochures or pamphlets the company publishes to inform the public of machine functions. Interested students should talk with their high-school guidance counselor to seek help in securing information about the field.

It is a good idea to start early and get some hands-on experience operating a computer. If your high-school computer courses are not available, classes may be available evenings, weekends, or during the summer at a nearby junior college or vocational school. Joining a computer club and reading professional magazines are other ways to become more familiar with this career field.

High-school and college students who can operate a computer may be able to obtain part-time jobs in business computer centers or in some larger companies.

Related occupations

Computer programmers share many characteristics with other workers in mathematics, business, and science who solve detailed problems. These occupations include actuaries, computer applications engineers, engineering analysts, financial analysts, mathematicians, operations research analysts, statisticians, and systems analysts.

Methods of entering

There is no standard way to secure an entry position as a programmer. A person interested in this kind of work, with the necessary qualifications, should apply for a position with the particular industry or agency desired. In some instances, an applicant for a job may express an interest in data processing to the personnel officer. There may be an opportunity for direct placement in the data system department of the firm, or to accept placement in another department of the firm, and to request transfer should a vacancy occur in data processing.

Application for a job may also be made to the manufacturers of data-processing equipment. If employed, a would-be programmer would have an opportunity to learn a great deal about all aspects of computer operations.

School placement offices may help their graduates find employment. Many companies send recruiters to college campuses to interview candidates. Other sources for jobs include newspaper want ads and employment agencies.

Advancement

The programmer who is more interested in the analysis aspect of his job than in the actual charting and coding of the program may want to consider acquiring additional training and experience to become a systems programmer or systems analyst. One may be interested in administration and may wish to become head of the programming department. One may wish to take on additional responsibility for the total computer operation and be placed in charge of the data systems center.

As programmers acquire experience, their salaries are increased. This may represent adequate advancement for programmers who enjoy the kind of work they do and have no wish to change jobs.

Employment outlook

Since 1954, the number of computer programmers has grown from none to approximately 479,000 in the early 1990s. They work for manufacturing companies, data-processing service firms (including those that write and sell software), banks, insurance companies, government agencies, and colleges and universities throughout the country.

Employment opportunities for computer programmers should be excellent through the 1990s as the increasingly complex demands of our economy expand the usage of computers. Businesses, scientific organizations, government agencies, and schools continue to look for new applications for computers and to make improvements in software already in use. Also, there is a need to develop complex operating programs that can use higher-level computer languages and can network with other computer equipment and systems.

As a result of the rapid growth in this field, more and more schools are offering programming courses and turning out greater numbers of qualified programmers. Employers have raised their hiring standards accordingly. Job applicants with the best chances of employment will be college graduates with a knowledge of several programming languages—especially the new ones that apply to computer networking and data-base management—and those who have participated in work-study programs or have had training in an applied field such as accounting, science, engineering, or management. Competition for jobs will be heavier among graduates of two-year data-processing programs and among people with equivalent experience or with less training.

Earnings

Most full-time programmers in the early 1990s earned between $20,700 and $33,900 per year, with a median of about $27,000. The top ten percent make more than $43,000 a year.

In the early 1990s, the federal government paid programmers with a college degree a beginning salary of approximately $14,800.

Programmers in the West and the North are generally paid more than those in the South. Also, the pay for programmers is higher in public utilities and data-processing service firms than in banks and schools.

Conditions of work

Most programmers work under pleasant conditions. The machines require an atmosphere that is dust free and in which the temperature is constant both in summer and in winter. Those who work with the machines benefit from such requirements.

Because machine operations are often fairly new in most agencies and firms, the offices in which they are housed are usually newly designed and decorated. Although most of the facilities are not luxurious, they are clean, modern, and well equipped.

The workweek for the average programmer is between thirty-five to forty hours. The circumstances surrounding each job, however, make for variations in the specified pattern. In some job situations, the programmer may have to work some nights or weekends on short notice when the program is going through its trial runs, or when there are many demands for additional services.

Most programmers receive the customary vacation and sick leave, and are included in such company benefits as group insurance and retirement benefit plans.

Social and psychological factors

Because the occupation is relatively young, many programmers are also young. They are engaged in an exploratory operation to determine the best ways in which to accomplish a job for which large organizations feel a great need. Some of the excitement of pioneering work still exists in this occupation.

Some computer programmers work on different locations as they are needed. They may be required to stay in one place for months or only a few days. Travel may be frequent for programmers in companies with many branch offices.

GOE: 11.01.01; SIC: Any industry; SOC: 3971, 3972, 3974

◇ **SOURCES OF ADDITIONAL INFORMATION**

American Federation of Information Processing Societies
1899 Preston White Drive
Reston, VA 22091

Association for Computing Machinery
11 West 42nd Street, 3rd Floor
New York, NY 10036

Data Processing Management Association
505 Busse Highway
Park Ridge, IL 60068

◇ **RELATED ARTICLES**

Volume 1: Computer Hardware; Computer Software; Electronics; See also specific industries
Volume 2: Data base managers; Graphics programmers; Numerical control tool programmers; Systems analysts
Volume 3: Computer and peripheral equipment operators; Data entry clerks
Volume 4: Computer-service engineering technicians; Scientific and business data-processing technicians

Conductors, railroad

Definition

Railroad conductors supervise trains and train crews either on passenger trains, freight trains, or in the railroad yard. They are responsible for seeing that train orders are carried out, and for the safety of their passengers and cargoes during travel time.

History

On many of today's passenger trains, the conductor's most important task is to see to the comfort and safety of the passengers. For the first conductors this was no simple task. The earliest trains had seats bolted to the platforms that looked much like today's flat cars. There were no roofs over those cars and consequently passengers were exposed to the elements and flying sparks from the tender boxes of locomotives. More often than not, the conductor had to extinguish fires started by flying sparks on the train and in passengers' clothing. By the late 1830s as trains crossed our western territories, the conductor's job became far more difficult and dangerous. Indians and outlaws frequently attacked trains or tore up tracks and damaged bridges. As the nation became more settled, and railroads increased, the conductor came to assume many of the duties that we see performed today.

Because railroads carry freight from state to state, the federal government passed many laws concerning them. Accordingly, this increased the importance of the conductors' jobs. For many years railroads have been important to the economy and survival of our nation. This was especially true during the world wars. Though decreasing somewhat in volume of activity, railroads are still an important means of transportation. The conductor is a key worker in this field.

Nature of the work

The conductor is the "captain" of the train. It is the conductor's responsibility to see that railroad trains are moved according to orders and instructions issued by a railroad dispatcher. Railroad conductors fall into three basic categories: *passenger car conductors, pullman (sleeping car) conductors,* and *road freight conductors.*

Before a freight or passenger train departs from the terminal, the conductor receives orders from the dispatcher. He or she then confers with other members of the train crew such as the engineer, firer, brakers, porters, and dining room employees to see that they understand the orders. Prior to, as well as during, the trip the conductor inspects the cars and arranges for repairs whenever necessary. The conductor sees to it that passenger cars are

An Amtrak conductor checks the departure time of the Superliner, a luxury passenger train for long-distance travelers.

On freight trains the conductor primarily supervises the activities of the crew. Before the start of the trip he or she obtains bills of lading and written orders from the station agent. The conductor also supervises the make-up of trains before departure, and throughout the course of the trip periodically he or she checks the condition of the train's cargo. The conductor also supervises the removal of freight at its proper destination.

Yard conductors seldom travel great distances on trains. They are usually stationed at a switching point or terminal where they signal the engineer and direct the work of switching crews who make up or withdraw cars from a train. Based on a knowledge of train schedules, the yard conductor or yard foreman is responsible for seeing that cars destined to arrive at various points along one of many routes are put together and ready to leave on time. Today many yards are mechanized. In this case, yard conductors supervise the movement of cars through electronic devices.

Requirements

Many conductors acquire the knowledge to assume their positions through years of practical experience gained as brakers. Although some high-school education is required, a college education is not a necessity. Conductors are usually brakers who have had several years of experience and have passed examinations testing their knowledge of signals, timetables, air brakes, operating rules, and related subjects.

The financial costs of becoming a conductor are small. No special tools or equipment are needed. Conductors are only required to buy the uniforms they wear. The high-school student interested in becoming a conductor will do well to take as many manual arts and electrical courses as possible. Academic subjects such as English and speech are also important because conductors are required to write some reports and speak to fellow workers and passengers.

Special requirements

Perhaps, the one special requirement to become a conductor is seniority. This is achieved through work with the railroad company. Usually, one does this in the job of the braker. Most freight, passenger, and yard conductors belong to the United Transportation Union.

clean or that freight cars are properly sealed and that passengers are seated and comfortable. During the trip the conductor collects tickets and cash fares from passengers. When passengers or freight arrives at a designated destination, it is the conductor's responsibility to supervise debarking or unloading. If a freight car is to be set out or added to the train along its route, the conductor sees that it is done. The conductor signals the engineer at the proper time for departure from stops along the run. At the conclusion of the trip he or she is responsible for reporting to company officials about relevant events of the trip. Reports include information about the number of passengers carried, the condition of freight upon its arrival, and the time the train arrived and departed from various stations along the route. In the event of an emergency during the trip, the conductor is responsible for whatever course of action is taken. The conductor should be well-versed on the procedures in many different types of emergencies, including evacuating the train. All persons employed on the train are subject to the conductor's authority.

Opportunities for experience and exploration

It has already been indicated that a conductor assumes a position as a result of experience and, because this is true, there is little opportunity to experience the work of a conductor except through observation. Otherwise, high-school students interested in a career as a railroad conductor can sometimes obtain experience through part-time work during holiday seasons or during the summer. A student with some interest and experience in mechanics and electrical work will also have some advantage over others who lack such experience.

Related occupations

Persons interested in railroading as a career might also consider these occupations: brake couplers or brakers, engine dispatchers, engine supervisors, engineers or assistant engineers, station managers, switch tenders, terminal superintendents, or yard managers. Managerial positions in other transportation industries also offer the opportunity to supervise work crews and the transport of people and commodities. Examples of these positions include managers of air cargo and ramp services, air station managers, managers of automatic services, bus transportation managers, operations managers, traffic managers, and managers of truck terminals.

Methods of entering

The average age of railroad conductors is slightly over fifty years. Often, experience as a braker numbers ten to twelve years. This is in addition to other years of experience acquired in various aspects of railroading. Because most railroads have separate seniority lists for yard or road service employees, most conductors usually remain in one of these two types of railroad service throughout their career. Some conductors, however, start on yard assignments and move up to freight service and finally to passenger service. The method of becoming a conductor differs somewhat and is usually determined by a particular railroad company. Thus, the person interested in becoming a conductor must expect to spend many years in related work gaining experience, and awaiting a turn for promotion as vacancies occur on the seniority list. Direct contact with unions and railroad companies is recommended for those interested in obtaining more information about entering this occupation.

Advancement

People become conductors through experience gained on other railroading jobs. After passing the required examinations those who qualify for promotion sometimes are temporarily assigned as conductors whenever the opportunity arises while they are still working as brakers. On other railroads, conductors are assigned to "extra board" which means that they are assigned to temporary positions wherever they are needed. In any event those promoted receive regular assignments as vacancies occur and seniority permits. As mentioned above, people become yard, passenger, or freight conductors according to which senior list they are on. There are exceptions to these rules in some cases depending on the policies of the railroad company and union officials. Conductors who show promise and ability may eventually be promoted to managerial positions such as trainmaster.

Employment outlook

Conductors will continue to be needed during the coming years. Job openings are expected to be created as the need exists to replace conductors who transfer to other kinds of work or who retire or die. Future job opportunities are, however, not promising. Since 1945 railroads have been steadily losing passengers to airplanes, automobiles, and other means of transportation. Rail passenger services to many points have been discontinued. Although the volume of railroad freight business has increased since 1945, this was accomplished through mechanization, automation, and longer but fewer trains. The number of conductors employed by large railroads in 1955 was 45,200 but by the early 1990s, the number had fallen to around 24,000.

Earnings

Like most occupations the daily wage or hourly rate varies with the size of the railroad. Other factors that affect wages are the type of service, number of cars on the train, and the location of the train's run. For example, conductors receive extra pay on trains passing through mountain regions. Usually basic wages for conductors are guaranteed by union contract. Yard conductors employed by Class 1 line-haul railroads earned an average of $24,000 a year in the early 1990s. Other figures indicated that conductors in road service were paid approximately $25,000 per year, while conductors on through freight trains averaged $24,500. Passenger train conductors averaged $24,000, and for assistant passenger conductors and ticket collectors the average annual wage was $20,000. The families of conductors can usually travel on trains at a reduced rate or free of charge. In addition to retirement plans sponsored by unions and railroads, conductors are eligible for social security and other government benefits.

Conditions of work

Except for the case of the yard conductor, railroad conductors are traveling much of the time. Although the basic work day is eight hours and a five-day week, days and nights are not considered different, and Sunday is treated as a work day. The same basic pay rate prevails on each case. For work beyond these hours, yard conductors receive one and one-half times their basic wage rate. Depending on miles traveled and hours worked, passenger and freight conductors may receive additional pay. Along with other members of the train's crew, conductors work nights, weekends, and during holidays when travel is especially heavy. If as a conductor you are required to "lay over" while awaiting a train to return to the home terminal, you pay for your own meals and other living expenses. Conductors on temporary assignments or on extra board work usually have irregular hours. Once you receive a regular assignment, however, you can expect to maintain a regular schedule and remain on a run for years.

Conductors on all major railroads are covered by union contracts negotiated by the United Transportation Union.

Social and psychological factors

In addition to being a leader among other members of the train crew, the conductor also has the most direct and frequent contact with the public. He or she, therefore, must be capable of assuming responsibility, directing the work activities of others, and acting as the railroad's

representative to passengers. A conductor must have a good working knowledge about the operation of the train and of its mechanical details. Because working hours can be irregular, the conductor must be in good health. In addition he or she must be self-sufficient and capable of occupying free hours because much of the time is spent away from home.

GOE: 11.11.03; SIC: 4011; SOC: 8113

◇ **SOURCES OF ADDITIONAL INFORMATION**

American Railway and Airline Supervisors Association
Three Research Plaza
Rockville, MD 20850

American Council of Railroad Women
CSX Transportation
Resource Department
500 Water Street
Jacksonville, FL 32202

Association of American Railroads
American Railroads Building
50 F Street, NW
Washington, DC 20001

International Brotherhood of Locomotive Engineers
1370 Ontario Street
Mezzanine
Cleveland, OH 44114

Transportation Communication International Union
Three Research Plaza
Rockville, MD 20850

United Transportation Union
14600 Detroit Avenue
Lakewood, OH 44107

◇ **RELATED ARTICLES**

Volume 1: Aviation and Aerospace; Civil Service; Transportation
Volume 3: Brake operators, brakers; Locomotive engineers

Construction inspectors, government

Definition

Construction inspectors for federal, state, and local governments examine the construction, alteration, or repair of highways, streets, sewer and water systems, dams, bridges, buildings, and other structures to be sure they comply with the building codes and ordinances, zoning regulations, and contract specifications.

History

Building is one of the oldest technologies known to humankind. Once primitive man moved from caves, earliest man-made shelters were built from hay, mud, or skins. As construction skills and needs progressed, so did the complexity of the buildings and structures. As long as there has been civilization, governments have been involved in construction. As evidence, we still have with us today the ancient Egyptian pyramids, Greek harbors and waterworks, and Roman bridges and highways.

Construction is one of the major industries of the modern world, one that offers many opportunities for advancement. Public construction, performed for the federal, state, and local governments, includes such structures as public housing projects, schools, hospitals, administrative and service buildings, industrial and military facilities, highways, and sewer and water systems.

Because public construction is paid for out of tax money, bonds, or other public funds, the government has an obligation to the people to see that the work is carried out legally, properly, safely, and economically. To ensure this, the federal, state, and local governments employ construction inspectors.

Nature of the work

This occupation is made up of four broad categories of specialization: building, electrical, mechanical, and public works.

Building inspectors examine the structural quality of buildings. They check the plans before construction, visit the worksite a number of times during construction, and make a final inspection when the project is completed. Some building inspectors specialize, for example, in structural steel or reinforced concrete buildings.

Electrical inspectors visit worksites to inspect the installation of electrical systems and equipment. They check wiring, lighting, generators, and sound and security systems. They may also inspect the wiring for elevators, heating and air-conditioning systems, kitchen appliances, and other electrical installations.

Mechanical inspectors inspect plumbing systems and the mechanical components of heating and air-conditioning equipment and kitchen appliances. They also examine gas tanks, piping, and gas-fired appliances. Some mechanical inspectors specialize in elevators, plumbing, or boilers.

Elevator inspectors inspect both the mechanical and the electrical features of lifting and conveying devices, such as elevators, escalators, and moving sidewalks; they also test their speed, load allowances, brakes, and safety devices.

Plumbing inspectors inspect plumbing installations, water supply systems, drainage and sewer systems, water heater installations, fire sprinkler systems, and air and gas piping systems; they also examine building sites for soil type to determine water table level, seepage rate, and other conditions.

Heating and refrigeration inspectors examine heating, ventilating, air-conditioning, and refrigeration installations in new buildings and approve alteration plans for those elements in existing buildings.

Public works inspectors make sure that government construction of water and sewer systems, highways, streets, bridges, and dams conforms to contract specifications. They visit worksites to inspect such things as excavations, mixing and pouring concrete, and asphalt paving. They also keep records of the amount of work performed and the materials used so that proper payment can be made. These inspectors may specialize in highways, reinforced concrete, or ditches.

Construction inspectors often use measuring devices and other test equipment, take photographs, keep a daily log of their work, and write reports. If any detail of a project does not comply with the various codes, ordinances, or contract specifications, or if construction is being done without proper permits, the inspectors have the authority to issue a stop-work order.

This construction inspector is examining the width and evenness of a vertical steel beam. Uniformity is essential in the construction of skyscrapers.

Requirements

Persons interested in becoming government construction inspectors must be high-school graduates who have taken courses in drafting, algebra, geometry, and English. Preferred are graduates of an apprentice program, persons with at least two years toward an engineering or architectural degree, or graduates of a community or junior college. Required courses are usually in construction technology, blueprint reading, technical math, English, and building inspection.

To become a construction inspector, several years' experience is usually required as a construction contractor or supervisor or as a craft or trade worker, such as carpenter, electrician, plumber, or pipefitter. This experience is to demonstrate a thorough knowledge of construction materials and practices either in general or as related to a specialty.

Construction inspectors receive most of their training on the job. The first two weeks or so are spent under the supervision of an experienced inspector, learning about inspection techniques; codes, ordinances, and regulations; contract specifications, and how to keep records and prepare reports. Then the new inspector is put to work on a simple project, such as a residence, and is gradually advanced to more complex types of construction.

Special requirements

Some states require certification for employment. Inspectors can earn a certificate by passing examinations on construction techniques, materials, and code requirements. The exams are offered by three model code organizations: the International Conference of Building Officials; Building Officials and Code Administrators International, Inc.; and Southern Building Code Congress International, Inc.

Government construction inspectors are expected to have a valid driver's license, because they must be able to travel to and from the construction sites. They must also be able to pass a civil service exam.

Inspectors should be in good physical condition to withstand the rigors of walking, climbing, and crawling all over a worksite.

Opportunities for experience and exploration

Students who think they may wish to pursue a career in construction can test their interest and aptitude by taking manual training and shop courses. Vocational high schools offer a variety of such courses, with classes scheduled during the day or evening.

Field trips to construction sites and interviews with contractors or building trade union officials are a good way to gain practical information about what it is like to work in the industry and how best to prepare for it.

Summer jobs at a construction site provide an overview of the work involved in a building project. Students may also seek part-time jobs with a general contracting company or with a specialized contractor such as plumbing or electrical, or as a carpenter's helper. Jobs in certain supply houses will help students become familiar with the materials used in construction.

Related occupations

Construction and building inspectors must have a knowledge of construction principles and law and be able to coordinate data, diagnose problems, and communicate with people. Similar skills are also required by occupations such as drafters, estimators, industrial engineering technicians, and surveyors.

Methods of entering

Persons right out of high school usually enter the construction industry as a trainee or apprentice. Information about these programs may be obtained from local contractors, building trade unions, or school vocational counselors. Graduates of technical schools or colleges of construction and engineering may expect to start work, for example, as an engineering aide, drafter, estimator, or assistant engineer.

Those who wish to become construction inspectors for the government may have to gain their initial experience in private industry. Jobs may be found through school placement offices, employment agencies, unions, or by applying directly to contracting company personnel offices. Application may also be made directly to the employment offices of the federal, state, or local government.

Advancement

An engineering degree is usually required to become a supervisory inspector.

The federal, state, and large city governments provide formal training programs for their construction inspectors to keep them abreast of new building code developments and to broaden their knowledge of construction materials, practices, and inspection techniques. Inspectors for small agencies can upgrade their skills by attending state-conducted training programs or taking college or correspondence courses.

Employment outlook

In the early 1990s, federal, state, and local governments employed about 50,000 construction and building inspectors, more than half of whom worked in municipal and county building departments. Large inspection staffs are employed by the cities and suburbs that are experiencing rapid growth. Federal inspectors may work for such agencies as the Department of Defense, the Tennessee Valley Authority, or the Departments of Housing and Urban Development, Agriculture, and Interior.

The need for government construction inspectors through the 1990s is expected to grow at a slower rate than the national occupational average. There will be a demand for qualified inspectors to keep up with increased construction activity and a rising concern for public safety and improved quality of construction, but some of the inspection functions will be assumed by engineers, construction managers, and maintenance supervisors. As technology becomes more complex and state governments begin to establish professional standards for inspectors, the outlook will be more favorable for those who have some college, are certified inspectors, or who are currently employed as carpenters, electricians, or plumbers.

The level of new construction fluctuates with the economy, but maintenance and renovation continue during the downswings, so inspectors are rarely laid off. The usual job openings occur as older, experienced inspectors die, retire, or leave for another occupation.

Earnings

In the early 1990s, construction inspectors were paid a median salary of about $27,100 a year. Earnings are slightly higher in the North and West than in the South and are considerably higher in large metropolitan areas.

Construction inspectors who worked for the federal government in the early 1990s earned an average annual salary of approximately $26,100.

Conditions of work

Construction inspectors work both indoors and out, dividing their time between their offices and the worksites. They generally travel to and from the sites in a government car.

Inspection sites are dirty and cluttered with tools, machinery, and debris. Although the work is not considered hazardous, inspectors must climb ladders and stairs and crawl under buildings.

The hours are regular except in case of an accident at the site, in which case the inspector has to remain on the job until the reports have been completed. The work is steady year-round, not seasonal as are some other construction occupations. In times when there is a slowdown of new construction, the inspectors are kept busy examining the renovation of older buildings.

Social and psychological factors

This occupation will appeal to active, creative persons who enjoy working with tools and equipment. Flexibility is an asset to be able to work comfortably both in an office setting and on a construction site, to spend time traveling frequently between the two, and to work extra hours during an emergency. The work calls for an ability to coordinate data, diagnose problems, and communicate with people at different levels. The job requires great attention to detail and involves ongoing learning.

GOE: 05.03.06; SIC: Any industry; SOC: 1472

◇ SOURCES OF ADDITIONAL INFORMATION

Building Officials and Code Administrators International
4051 West Flossmoor Road
Country Club Hills, IL 60477

International Conference of Building Officials
5360 South Workman Mill Road
Whittier, CA 90601

Southern Building Code Congress International
900 Montclair Road
Birmingham, AL 35213

Information about employment in this field by the federal government may be obtained from:

U.S. Office of Personnel Management
1900 E Street, NW
Washington, DC 20415

Department of Housing and Urban Development
Administrative Officer
451 7th Street, SW
Washington, DC 20410

Additional information on a career as a state or local government construction inspector may be obtained from the state or local employment service.

◇ RELATED ARTICLES

Volume 1: Construction
Volume 2: Engineers
Volume 4: Architectural and building construction technicians; Civil engineering technicians

Cost estimators

Definition

Cost estimators compile and analyze economic data to prepare estimates of the cost of construction or manufacturing projects. They conduct studies and utilize data, such as labor and material costs, to help contractors or other project planners determine how much a project will cost, and if in fact a project should be done.

History

Business people need to be able to predict how much a future project will cost so as to determine what they can get or charge in re-

turn. No effective business project can be undertaken without a thorough assessment of the costs. This information has become more important as mass production techniques have made business decisions more expensive and long-term commitment vital to economic success.

As production techniques become more and more specialized, it has become necessary to have one individual responsible for collecting and analyzing cost information on the many facets of production. Costs of labor, materials, transportation, equipment, and many other factors all must be collected and interpreted before a construction or manufacturing decision can be made. The cost estimator fulfills this function and is the vital link between a product idea and its implementation.

As long as there are buildings to be constructed or new products to be manufactured, there will be a need for experts who can establish how much the project will cost so that the people paying for the project will be able to make wise business decisions.

Nature of the work

Cost estimators collect and analyze information on the various factors influencing costs, such as the labor, materials, and machinery needed for a particular project. The scope of the work is largely determined by the type and size of the project being estimated. On a large building project, for example, the estimator reviews architectural drawings and other bidding documents before any construction begins. Then the estimator visits the potential construction site to collect site development costs, such as the costs involved for electricity and other services.

After compiling a thorough understanding of the construction process and the people and machinery involved, the estimator writes a quantity survey, or "takeoff," by completing standard estimating forms that provide spaces for the entry of dimensions of the project, number of units, and other information.

Sometimes more than one estimator is used on a project. Estimators may specialize in one area. For example, one estimator may assess the electrical costs of a project while another concentrates on the transportation or insurance costs of that same projects. It is then the responsibility of a chief estimator to combine the reports and submit one development proposal.

The cost estimator's role is to bring together complex data in assessing costs. In the manufacturing process, for example, an estimator may work with engineers to develop charts showing that labor costs should go down as the project progresses because the workers will learn the manufacturing process, become more efficient, and thereby increase productivity. Charts may also be used to measure how prices for a particular part compare with prices paid in the past and what can be expected to be paid in the future.

To be effective, an estimator must keep up-to-date on the prices for labor, materials, and all the other factors that influence costs. This requires the ability to collect and interpret data. An estimator should also be able to compute and understand accounting and mathematical formulas and be able to make sound decisions based on these computations. More and more, computers are being used to do the routine calculations, leaving the estimator more time to

A group of administrators attend a presentation given by a cost estimator. The cost estimator must be prepared to answer the challenging questions of his clients.

analyze data and evaluate effective production techniques.

Particular areas of specialization within the field of cost estimating include the following.

Paperboard box estimators, estimate the cost of manufacturing paperboard boxes based on material costs and quality, quantity, and packaging considerations. They work with production personnel to develop procedures to minimize waste and thereby reduce costs.

Printing estimators, estimate the labor and material costs of printing and binding books, pamphlets, and other printed matter. They work with customers to analyze production costs, using such factors as size and number of pages, paper stock requirements, and binding operations.

Requirements

Construction and manufacturing firms usually prefer estimators to have experience with their procedures and a thorough knowledge of the costs involved in production. This makes on-the-job training vital. To prepare for this on-the-job training, a high-school student should take courses in accounting and mathematics. An English course and a course in writing are also recommended. Postsecondary two-year training programs, such as those offered at community colleges or technical school, are also helpful. Coursework should include physics and technical drawing, as well as specific courses covering manufacturing and construction processes.

Some employers request that an entry level estimator have a bachelor's degree in civil engineering or mathematics. The federal government, for example, will only accept entry level applicants with a college degree.

Special requirements

Although there are no licencing requirements, many cost estimators find it helpful to become certified. To become certified, an estimator must have between three and seven years experience in the field and pass a written and oral test. Information on certification procedures and other professional training is available from organizations such as the American Society of Professional Estimators and the National Estimating Society.

Opportunities for experience and exploration

Experience is especially important in a field such as this, with so much emphasis on on-the-job training. Part-time work with a construction crew or manufacturing firm, especially during the busy summer months, should be beneficial. Talking with those in the field is another way of finding out about career opportunities.

Related occupations

Accountants, engineers, mathematicians, and actuaries all utilize many of the same mathematical and analytical skills needed by a cost estimator.

Methods of entering

Many cost estimators are trades people who display a particular aptitude or interest for cost analysis. For example, an experience plumber may become an estimator on the contracting

projects done by his or her company. Other people complete a two- year training program or bachelor's degree and then enter the work force.

Advancement

As in many professions, promotions for cost estimators are dependent on skill and experience. Advancement usually comes in the way of more responsibility and higher wages. A skilled cost estimator at a large construction company may become a chief estimator. Some experienced cost estimators also go into consulting work.

Employment outlook

Employment for cost estimators is expected to increase about as fast as the average through the early 1990s. Many cost estimators work in the construction field and therefore employment is tied to a large extent to the amount of construction work that takes place. Residential construction is expected to slow over the next decade, but commercial and industrial buildings should pick up the slack.

As always, experienced cost estimators and highly trained college graduates have the best job prospects.

Earnings

Salaries vary according to the size of the construction or manufacturing firm and the type of work done. Average starting salaries range between $15,000 and $25,000 per year, with experienced cost estimators averaging about $30,000 annually. Those with certification should earn between $30,000 and $50,000 per year, with some specialists making even more.

Conditions of work

Much of the work takes place in a typical office setting, with accounting records and other information close by. However, it is not unusual for an estimator to visit a construction site or a manufacturing facility to inspect production procedures. Often the work entails consulting with engineers, work supervisors, and other professionals involved in the production or manufacturing process. Estimators usually work a forty-hour week, although longer hours may be required if a project is on deadline. Overtime hours almost always occur in the summer when construction projects are in full force.

Social and psychological factors

An estimator should be able to work long hours collecting and analyzing complex economic data. The person should be well organized and be able to work under deadline pressure. An estimator should be able to work as part of a team but be able to make independent judgments after consultation with other professionals and an analysis of cost information. An estimator must be able to handle the pressure that comes from developing and submitting a cost assessment totaling millions of dollars. An estimators effectiveness in gauging costs is often a determining factor in whether a contracting company or other business succeeds or fails.

GOE: 05.03.02; SIC: Any industry; SOC: 149

◇ **SOURCES OF ADDITIONAL INFORMATION**

Information about career opportunities and professional training is available from:

American Society of Civil Engineers
345 East 47th Street
New York, NY 10017

American Society of Professional Estimators
6911 Richmond Highway
Suite 230
Alexandria, VA 22306

National Association of Women in Construction
327 South Adams Street
Fort Worth, TX 76104

National Estimating Society
101 South Whiting Street, Suite 313
Alexandria, VA 22304

For information on government programs, write for the booklet called:

Educating Scientists and Engineers: Grade School to Grad School
Superintendent of Documents
US Government Printing Office
Washington, DC 20402

◇ **RELATED ARTICLES**

Volume 1: Construction; Design; Engineering; See also specific industries
Volume 2: Engineers
Volume 3: See specific Processing or Structural work occupations
Volume 4: See specific Scientific and engineering technicians occupations

Credit analysts, banking

Definition

Credit analysts in banking analyze financial information to determine the amount of risk involved in lending money to businesses or individuals. They contact banks, credit associations, and others to obtain credit information and then prepare a written report of findings in which customer credit limits are suggested.

Credit analysts normally concentrate on one of two different areas. Commercial and business analysts evaluate risks in business loans; consumer credit analysts evaluate personal loan risks.

Credit analysts rely heavily on computers to calculate complex formulas and organize data. They must be proficient in spreadsheet software, word processing, and often statistical software as well.

History

Extending financial credit to help someone along is an age old tradition, practiced by friends and businesses to help people through hard times. As the use of credit cards and other forms of borrowing has skyrocketed in the last several years, however, lending money has become a large, sophisticated enterprise.

As late as fifty to seventy-five years ago, lending money was largely based on a person's reputation. Money was lent after talking with a potential borrower's friends and business acquaintances. Now, of course, much more financial background information is demanded and only accepted forms of accounting are used to determine if a loan applicant is a good risk.

As business has expanded and more money is needed to keep the economic engines going, a need has been created for a group of professionals who are experts in the field of credit analysis.

Nature of the work

Credit analysts work in two spheres— commercial loans used by businesses and consumer loans used by individuals. In both cases an analyst studies financial documents, such as a statement of assets and liabilities, submitted by the person or company seeking the loan and consults with banks and other financial institutions who have previously loaned money to the applicant.

The scope of work used in a credit check depends in large part on the size and type of loan being requested. A background check on a $3,000 car loan, for example, is much less detailed than a $400,000 commercial improvement loan for an expanding business. In both cases financial statements and references will be checked by the credit analyst, but the larger loan will entail a much closer look at economic trends to determine if there is a market for the product being produced and the likelihood of the business failing. Because of these increased responsibilities, many credit analysts work solely with commercial loans.

In studying a commercial loan application, a credit analyst is interested in determining if the business or corporation is well managed and financially secure, and if the existing economic climate is favorable for the success of such an operation. To do this, a credit analyst examines balance sheets and operating statements to determine the assets and liabilities of a company, its net sales, and its profits or losses. An analyst must be familiar with accounting and bookkeeping methods to ensure that the applicant company is operating under accepted principles. A background check of the leading officials of the applicant company is also done to determine if they personally have any loans outstanding. An on-site visit to the company by the analyst may also be necessary to compare how its operations stack up against similar companies.

Analyzing economic trends to determine market conditions is another responsibility of the credit analyst. To do this, the analyst computes dozens of ratios to show how successful the company is in relationship to other similar businesses. Profit-and-loss statements, collection procedures, and a host of other factors are all analyzed. This ratio analysis can also be used to measure how successful a particular industry is likely to be given existing market considerations. Economic indicators are collected and mathematical formulas are applied. As in many other professions, the use of computers is revolutionizing the collection and analysis of information. Now, many computer programs are available to highlight economic trends and interpret other important data.

The credit analyst always provides a report on findings to bank executives. This report will include a complete financial history of the applicant, and usually conclude with a recommendation on the amount of loan, if any, that should be advanced. Bank executives use this report extensively in making final loan decisions.

Requirements

Credit analysts should have an aptitude for mathematics and be able to make sound decisions after analyzing detailed financial information. They should be able to work with both customers and coworkers and be able to communicate effectively, in written and verbal form.

A high-school student should take courses in mathematics, accounting, and bookkeeping. An English course, especially one that stresses good writing skills, would also be beneficial. Most credit analysts have a bachelor's degree in accounting, finance, or business administration. Coursework should include business management, economics, statistics, and accounting. Some credit analysts go on to receive a master's of business administration (MBA) or a master's in some other related field.

Special requirements

There are no licenses needed to become a credit analyst. Upon being hired, however, most entry level analysts spend about a year in a trainee program in which they are introduced to the various banking procedures utilized at their specific financial institution.

Opportunities for experience and exploration

A part-time job as a bank clerk or teller will help familiarize a person with banking procedures. Additionally, this is a good way of making contact with banking officials. Various clubs and organizations may have opportunities for volunteers to develop experience working with budgets and other financial statements.

Related occupations

Business managers, real estate appraisers, art appraisers, pawnbrokers, and claim agents all deal with financial information and utilize many of the same analytical and mathematical skills needed by a credit analyst. Business owners and real estate investors also need many of the same evaluative skills.

Methods of entering

Most entry level positions go to college graduates with degrees in fields such as accounting, economics, and business administration.

Advancement

There are many good advancement possibilities for a skilled credit analyst. Promotions may include a job with more responsibility, such as a middle management position at a bank, with a corresponding increase in salary. Those in a smaller bank may be promoted within or may chose to move to a larger financial institution.

Employment outlook

With the field of cash management growing, banks and other financial institutions need credit analysts. Job prospects are expected to grow faster than average through the early 1990s. There may be some competition for highly desired positions. Banks hire about half of the credit analysts, so opportunities should be best in areas with a great number of banks.

Earnings

As always, wages depend on experience and education. The size of the financial institution is also a determining factor, with large banks tending to pay more than smaller facilities. Starting salaries for those with a bachelor's degree range between $14,000 and $20,000 per year. Those entering with an MBA or other master's degree can expect to earn $20,000 to $32,000 a year, perhaps more.

Conditions of work

The cost estimator's work setting is somewhat dependent on the size of the bank, but in most cases a credit analyst works in a typical modern office setting. A commercial credit analyst may visit a business or corporation seeking a loan. An analyst can expect to work a forty-hour week, but overtime may be necessary if a project is on deadline.

Social and psychological factors

A credit analyst should be able to spend long hours reading and analyzing financial reports. Attention to detail is critical. The analyst should be able to understand the economic and other factors that determine why some businesses succeed and others do not. An analyst should be patient and work well alone and with other people. Finally, a credit analyst should be able to work in pressurized situations, with loans of millions of dollars possibly dependent on his or her analysis.

GOE: 11.06.03; SIC: 61; SOC: 1419

◇ **SOURCES OF ADDITIONAL INFORMATION**

For general information about careers in banking contact:

American Bankers Association
1120 Connecticut Avenue, NW
Washington, DC 20036

General information about the area of consumer credit is available from:

National Foundation for Consumer Credit
8701 Georgia Avenue
Suite 507
Silver Spring, MD 20910

◇ **RELATED ARTICLES**

Volume 1: Banking; Insurance
Volume 2: Accountants and auditors; Financial institution officers and managers; Economists; Insurance claim representatives
Volume 3: Bookkeeping and accounting clerks; Collections workers; Financial institution clerks and related workers; Financial institution tellers; Securities and financial services sales representatives

Crime laboratory technologists

Definition

Crime laboratory technologists apply scientific principles and methods to the analysis, identification, and classification of physical evidence relating to criminal, or suspected criminal, cases. Technologists may also be called upon to testify as expert witnesses and to present scientific findings in court.

History

In Scotland during the late 1780s a man was convicted of murder when the soles of his boots matched a plaster cast of footprints taken from the scene of the crime. This is one of the earliest recorded cases of the use of physical evidence to link a suspected criminal with the crime.

In the late nineteenth century scientists learned to analyze and classify poisons so their presence could be traced in a body. At about the same time a controversy arose over the different methods of identifying individuals. As a result, fingerprinting emerged in the early twentieth century as the most reliable method of identifying someone.

Forensic pathology (medical examination of suspicious or unexplained deaths) also came into prominence at this time, as did ballistics, aided by the invention of the comparison microscope—a microscope that enabled the investigator to look at two bullets side by side and compare their individual markings. Similar markings found on different bullets may prove that they were fired from the same weapon. Gun barrels "scar" the bullet in a unique pattern.

These investigations by pioneer forensic scientists led to the acceptance by the courts and the police of the value of scientifically examined physical evidence in establishing guilt or innocence, confirming identity, proving authenticity of documents, and establishing cause of death. As the result of this acceptance, crime laboratories were established. One of the first established and one of the largest and most complete is the Federal Bureau of Investigation laboratory, founded in 1932. Today, the FBI laboratory examines many thousands of pieces of evidence each year, and FBI technicians and scientists present their findings in trials all over the United States and around the world.

As the forensic sciences proved their worth, crime laboratories were established in larger cities and by state police departments. These laboratories are used in turn by many communities too small to support a lab of their own. The scientific analysis of evidence has become an accepted part of police procedure.

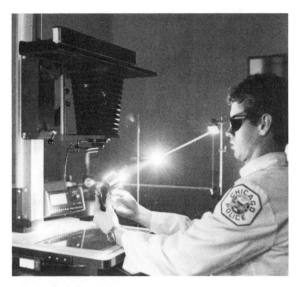

A crime laboratory technologist uses a laser beam to detect fingerprints on a gun.

Nature of the work

Crime laboratory technologists use the instruments of science and engineering to examine physical evidence. They use spectroscopes, microscopes, gas chromatographs, infrared and ultraviolet light, microphotography, and other laboratory measuring and testing equipment to analyze fabric, dust, dirt, paint, paper and ink to identify their composition and origin. They analyze poisons, drugs, and any substances found in bodies by examining tissue samples, stomach contents, and blood samples. They analyze and classify blood, hair, fingernails, human and animal bones and tissue, and other biological specimens. They also examine firearms, bullets, and explosives.

At the scene of a crime or suspected crime, technologists collect and label evidence. This may involve searching for spent bullets or bits of an exploded bomb and other objects scattered by an explosion, footprints, fingerprints, and tire tracks that must be preserved by plaster casting before they are wiped out. Crime laboratory technologists take notes and photograph crime scenes to preserve the arrangement of objects and bodies that must be moved. They are sometimes called on to reconstruct the scene of a crime by making a floor plan or map that shows accurately the location of bodies, weapons, and furniture.

Technologists do not interpret their findings relative to the criminal investigation in which they are involved; that is the work of police investigators. The purpose of crime laboratory work is to provide reliable scientific analysis of evidence that can then be used in criminal investigations and, if needed later, in court proceedings.

Crime laboratory technologists work with physical evidence. They seldom have direct contact with persons involved in crimes or suspected crimes, or with police investigators except when collecting evidence and reporting findings. The bulk of their time is spent in the laboratory.

Requirements

Persons interested in careers as crime laboratory technologists should have an aptitude for scientific investigation, an inquiring attitude of mind, and the ability to make precise measurements and observations. Patience and persistence will also be helpful qualities. Technologists must bear in mind that the accuracy of their laboratory investigations has great consequences for others.

Almost all jobs in this field require at least a bachelor's degree. A number of colleges and community colleges in the United States offer programs in forensic pathology and various other aspects of crime laboratory work. These courses are often spread throughout the school, in the anatomy, physiology, chemistry, or biology departments, or they may be grouped together as part of the criminal justice department.

Persons interested in this field should begin their preparation by taking a heavy concentration of science courses in high school, including especially chemistry, biology, physiology, and

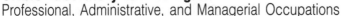

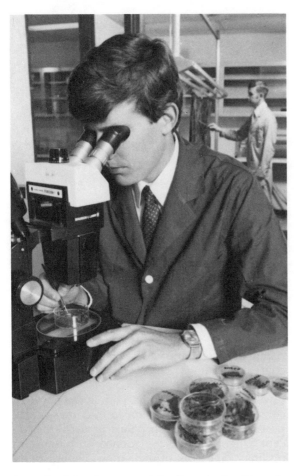

An examiner in the microscope analysis unit searches for evidence of hairs and fibers on a pillbox. In the background, a technologist removes debris from a garment.

physics. A basic grounding in spoken and written communication will also be useful because technologists must write very detailed reports of their findings and are sometimes called on to present findings in court.

Special requirements

There are no special requirements for a career as a crime laboratory technologist. However, certification may be desirable for persons who work in toxicology and document examination. Specialists in these and other areas may also be required to have undergraduate and graduate course work in their area. In a field such as toxicology, advanced chemistry work is important. The certificate programs are available through the Forensic Sciences Foundation (a branch of the American Academy of Forensic Sciences).

Opportunities for experience and exploration

A large community police department may have a crime laboratory of its own whose technologists can give specific information about their work and the preparation that helped them most. Smaller communities often use the facilities of a larger city nearby or the state police laboratory. In such a case, a school counselor or a representative of the local police may be able to arrange a tour of the laboratory for interested students.

Many schools have chemistry and other science clubs where interested persons can discuss all aspects of scientific investigation and attend lectures and demonstrations on scientific subjects. Such a club may be able to arrange a tour of a large laboratory facility.

Related occupations

Other workers in related areas of law enforcement include customs officers, FBI agents, fingerprint classifiers, and police officers. Persons interested in laboratory work might also consider such occupations as chemists, food technologists, medical technologists, microbiologists, soil scientists, or toxicologists.

Methods of entering

Crime laboratories are maintained by the federal government, the states, and many local governments. Applications should be made directly to the personnel department of the government agency supporting the laboratory. Civil service appointments usually require an examination. Such appointments are usually widely advertised well in advance of the examination date.

Advancement

Advancement in a large crime laboratory is usually from an assisting position to working independently at one or more special types of analysis. From there technologists may advance to project leader, or being in charge of all aspects of one investigation. In smaller laboratories, one technician may fill many roles and there may be no advancement in title, but a progression to more responsibility comes with experience.

Employment outlook

The employment outlook for crime laboratory technologists in the early 1990s appears stable. This is a small career group, numbering only a few thousand (not including the many scientific experts who are called in as consultants only when their expertise is needed). Population increases, a rising crime rate, and the greater emphasis on scientific methodology in crime investigation indicate an increased need for trained technologists, although pressure to reduce government spending tends to hold down hiring. Nevertheless, the number of technologists is expected to show some growth throughout the 1990s.

Earnings

Earnings for crime laboratory technologists in local and regional laboratories in the early 1990s ranged from about $15,000 a year for new employees to about $30,000 for experienced technicians. These salaries varied with the size of the laboratory and with the geographic location.

In the early 1990s, on the federal level, FBI crime laboratory technicians without a college degree earned approximately between $25,200 and $32,800 per year in journeyman-level positions, depending on their length of service with the FBI.

Conditions of work

Crime laboratory technologists work under clean, quiet, air-conditioned conditions. The work is varied and interesting. Eye strain and contact with strong chemicals, however, are possible. Little heavy physical work is involved.

Social and psychological factors

In gathering evidence and in analyzing it crime laboratory technologists need to be able to con-

centrate, sometimes in a crowded, noisy situation. They also need to be able to arrive at and present their findings impartially. In larger laboratories they often work in teams under the direction of a senior technologist and need to be able to work as part of a team.

GOE: 02.04.01; SIC: 9221; SOC: 389

◇ **SOURCES OF ADDITIONAL INFORMATION**

American Academy of Forensic Sciences
218 East Cache La Poudre
Colorado Springs, CO 80903

American Society of Questioned Document Examiners
1432 Esperson Building
Houston, TX 77002

Federal Bureau of Investigation
U.S. Department of Justice
Washington, DC 20535

National Bureau of Document Examiners
250 West 57th Street
Suite 2032
New York, NY 10107

Society of Forensic Toxicologists
1013 Three Mile Drive
Grosse Pointe Park, MI 48230

◇ **RELATED ARTICLES**

Volume 1: Biological Sciences; Chemistry
Volume 2: Biochemists; Biologists; Chemists; Toxicologists
Volume 3: FBI agents; Fingerprint classifiers; Private investigators
Volume 4: Biological specimen technicians; Biological technicians; Chemical technicians; Laboratory technicians; Medical laboratory technicians

Dancers and choreographers

Definition

Dancers perform dances alone or with other persons. Through dancing, they attempt to tell a story, interpret an idea, or simply express rhythm and sound by supplying preconceived physical movements to music. *Choreographers* create or develop dance patterns and teach them to performers. They sometimes direct and stage presentations of their work.

History

Dancing is one of the oldest of the arts. Just as humans learned to express ideas and feelings in word and picture, the dance became another way of expressing emotions. The first formal dances were the ritualistic, symbolic dances of early tribal societies: the dance designed to excite the emotions, such as the war dance; the dance purporting to communicate with the gods, such as the rain dance. Dances gradually become a traditional part of the culture. In the United States, the square dance became a part of our folkways. People have learned to dance for self-expression, and dancing has become a popular leisure-time activity. Dancing has also become a popular form of entertainment and, for those who provide the entertainment, a career.

Nature of the work

Dancers usually dance together as a chorus. As they advance in their profession, dancers may do special numbers with other selected dancers and, when a reputation is attained, the dancer may do solo work. This process holds true regardless of the type of dancing. There are four basic types of dancing and although some dancers become proficient in all four, most dancers attempt to specialize in one specific area.

The *acrobatic dancer* performs a style of dancing characterized by difficult gymnastic feats.

The *ballet dancer* performs artistic dances suggesting a theme or story. The ballet is perhaps one of the most exacting and demanding forms of the dance. Most other types of dancers need some type of ballet training.

The *interpretive* or *modern dancer* (sometimes referred to as a *classical dancer*) performs dances that interpret moods or characterizations. Facial expression and the body are utilized to express the theme of the dance.

The *tap dancer* performs a style of dancing that is distinguished by rhythm tapped by the feet in time with the music.

In all dancing, grace and execution are basic. Some dances require specific traditional movements and precise positions. Others provide for planned movement but permit sufficient variation in execution. The dancer thus is able to include a spin, a dip, a pause, or some other effect that provides a certain amount of individuality and flair to the performance.

Dancing is one of the professions that permits the performers to make the most of their physical features and personality. Part of the success of dancers depends on the ability to utilize their assets in ways that will permit their full expression.

Dancers may perform in classical ballet or modern dance, in dance adaptations for musical shows, in folk dances, or in tap and other types of popular dancing productions.

A few dancers have become choreographers, who create new ballets or dance routines and must know not only dancing and music, but costume, lighting, and dramatics, as well. Others are dance directors and train the dancers in new productions. Many dancers combine teaching with their stage work or are full-time *dance instructors* in schools of the ballet or in colleges and universities. (*See also* the article titled "Adult and vocational education teachers" elsewhere in this volume). Some open their own dancing schools.

Requirements

There are no formal educational requirements, but an early start (around eight for ballet) and years of practice are basic to a successful career. The preparation for a professional dancing career is as much a test of one's personal characteristics as it is of one's talent. The aspirant needs, first and foremost, to be enthusiastic about dancing, for the basic desire to achieve success is an ingredient that will help to overcome some of the disappointment and despair that seem to be hurdles normally encountered.

The physical demands of daily practice as well as the demands of the dance routine necessitate good health and a strong body. A dancer must also have a feeling for music, a sense of rhythm, and grace and agility. Good feet with normal arches are required. Persistence and sensitivity, as they apply to the day-to-day preparation of the dancer, are also important personal characteristics.

While in high school, and a good high-school education is highly recommended, students should elect courses in speech, music, and dramatics, and engage in extracurricular activities that will enhance their knowledge of these areas. High-school students may also continue their dance studies during the summer. Some summer camps feature dance training, and special summer classes are available in some large cities.

After high school a number of avenues of advanced training are available. About 240 colleges and universities offer programs leading to a bachelor's or higher degree in dance, generally through the departments of physical education, music, theater, or fine arts. These programs provide an opportunity for a college education and advanced preparation and training. Other possibilities include study with professional dancing teachers or attendance at a professional dance school. There are a number of such schools in the country; most of them are located in large cities.

Experience as a performer is usually required for teaching in professional schools, and graduate degrees are generally required by colleges and conservatories.

Alvin Ailey stars in his production *Revelations*, a black ethnic ballet.

there is the real opportunity to assess one's qualifications, both personal and physical. It is not difficult to accept the acclaim of an audience or to identify one's strengths as a dancer, but these experiences should also be used to identify weaknesses. Constant and realistic appraisal of one's progress can be extremely helpful in developing plans for additional experience. Most dancers continue with classes in dance throughout their professional careers.

Special requirements

No special licensure is required for dancing. Professional dancers, however, are usually members of one of the appropriate unions covering their dancing specialties.

Opportunities for experience and exploration

Plans to enter the highly competitive profession of dancing necessitate that one take advantage of every opportunity to gain experience and to explore the chances for success in achieving the goal. It is not too difficult to locate opportunities to perform in one's own community, and it is wise to dance publicly early and often. In addition to the experience that can be gained,

Related occupations

There are many occupations in the entertainment and recreation fields that may satisfy the need to express concepts and emotions through body movements or to perform before an audience.

Any of the following occupations may be considered in place of or in addition to dancing: acrobats, actors and actresses, animal trainers, aquatic performers, athletes, bareback riders, dance critics, dance instructors, dance notators (who write down the movements, music, costumes, background, and other details of a dance performance), dance therapists, drama teachers, ice skaters, models, music teachers, musicians, physical education instructors, recreation workers, singers, sports instructors, stage directors, stage managers, and talent agents who work with dancers and other entertainers.

Methods of entering

The only way to get started in dancing is to dance, to take advantage of every performance opportunity possible. Local groups are usually in the market for entertainment at their meetings or social affairs. These appearances provide the opportunity to polish routines and develop the professional air that distinguishes the professional from the amateur performer. Breaking the professional barrier by achieving one's first paid performance can be accomplished in several ways. Take advantage of every audition. Follow the announcements in the trade magazines. Circulate among other dancers. Attend shows and get to know everyone who may be in a position to help with a job. Another possibility that should be considered is to register with recognized booking agents.

Advancement

As in all performing arts, the star on the dressing room door is the dream of all dancing aspirants. Yet top billing, the name in lights, the program headliner are positions of accomplishment reserved for a very small number. Most dancers will find that the opportunities for advancement to stardom are numerous and varied even though few will eventually achieve stardom. The aspiring dancer, even with the dream of stardom, may find a large measure of success in the successful pursuit of many of the beginning and intermediate employment opportunities. Many dancers start by earning a spot in the dancing chorus of a Broadway musical, in the line at a supper club, or in a dancing group on a television variety show or spectacular. Such opportunities permit further study and lessons, yet enable one to work with experienced choreographers and producers. Earning a spot as a chorus dancer in television on a regular weekly show could provide as many as thirteen, twenty-six, or thirty-nine performances with the same group.

In recent years, a number of musical stock companies have originated throughout the United States, thus providing another avenue for employment. Although many of these operate only in summer, they provide experience of a Broadway nature. Outdoor spectaculars— exhibitions, parades, fairs, festivals—often use dance acts.

Working on the road can be an exciting, yet tiring, opportunity. Chorus groups with traveling musicals and cafe shows provide regular employment for a season. The numbers are rehearsed before the tour and very little adapta-

tion or change is possible. One does get a chance to perform in a variety of situations and with different bands or orchestras because accompaniments are different in each club or community performance. Dancers may also advance, if their interests lie in that direction, to choreographing, one of the most creative and responsible jobs in dancing. Other dancers find positions as teachers and some eventually open their own school.

Employment outlook

Employment of dancers is expected to increase faster than the national occupational average through the early 1990s, but those seeking a career in dancing will find the field highly competitive and uncertain. For performers, there are limited opportunities because there are more trained dancers than needed. Television has provided added openings but, on the other hand, the number of stage and screen productions is declining. The best opportunities may exist in regional ballet companies, opera companies, and dance groups affiliated with colleges and universities. The turnover rate in dancing is rather high so there are always openings for the newcomer. Although generalization is difficult, the average chorus dancer can expect a career of five to ten years at best. Most ballet dancers stop dancing for an audience before they are forty years of age.

The dancer who can move from performing to teaching will find other employment possibilities in colleges, universities, and schools of dance; with civic and community groups; and in the operation of dance studios.

Dancing as a performing career is characterized by irregular employment. There is often a long span of time between engagements. For that reason, it is difficult to calculate the exact number of persons employed in this field. In the early 1990s, it is estimated that professional dancers held about 10,000 stage, screen, and TV jobs at any one time, and several times that number were employed as dance instructors in schools, colleges, universities, and dance studios. In addition, some persons trained in dance therapy were employed by hospitals to work in this relatively new field to treat patients with physical disabilities or certain kinds of mental disorders.

Dancers may find work throughout the United States, but about half of the major dance companies are located in New York. Other cities that have full-time dance companies are San Francisco, Seattle, Chicago, Dallas, Houston, Salt Lake City, Cincinnati, Cleveland, Milwaukee, Boston, Philadelphia, Pittsburgh, Atlanta, Miami, and Washington, D.C.

Earnings

For the performing dancer, the conditions of employment, the hours of work, and salaries are established in agreements between the unions and the producers. Union contracts set only minimums, however, and a dancer's contract with the employer may actually contain more favorable terms.

Dancers may join various unions depending on the type of dance they perform. The American Guild of Musical Artists is the union to which dancers belong who perform in opera ballets, classical ballet, and modern dance. Those on live or taped television join the American Federation of Television and Radio Artists. Dancers in films have the Screen Actors Guild or the Screen Extras Guild. Those who appear on stage in musical comedies join Actors' Equity Association. And those who dance in nightclubs and variety shows belong to the American Guild of Variety Artists.

The minimum salary for dancers engaged in opera and other stage productions was about $72 per performance in the early 1990s. The single performance rate for ballet dancers was $183. Dancers on tour were paid an additional $52 to $62 a day to help cover room and board. Minimum performance rates for dancers on television ranged from $520 to $573 for a one-hour show. A dancer's performance rate also covers eighteen hours of rehearsal over a three-day period. With rehearsals and performances, a normal workweek runs thirty hours (six hours a day maximum). Extra pay is earned for any additional hours worked.

Many performing dancers must supplement their income with other work. This is difficult in some ways because they must always be prepared to accept a new contract or engagement.

Union contracts provide for various health and welfare benefits.

Conditions of work

The irregularity of employment is the most difficult aspect of the profession. Dancers are never certain where they will be employed or under what conditions. One may wait weeks for a contract. An offer may involve travel, night hours, or weekend rehearsals. If it is a Broadway stage show, one may work twenty weeks, forty weeks, three years, or possibly the show will fold after the third performance.

Social and psychological factors

Dancing requires considerable sacrifices of both a personal and social nature. Dancing is the performing dancer's life. The demands of practice and the need to continue lessons and to learn new routines and variations leave little time for recreational or social activities. As a career, dancing necessitates greater emphasis on self than on others, for the intensive competition and the need to project oneself to get ahead leave little time for other pursuits.

In dancing, performers exact from themselves all that is possible to express the feelings and the emotions of the dance. As a person, the dancer must be able to deal with a variety of emotions, for as his or her career is developed, a variety of feelings and emotions will be encountered. Among these are: the fulfillment of basking in the applause of the audience; the disappointment of being turned away from an audition; the fear while waiting for the next contract; the disillusionment of being squeezed out of the market; the happiness of being complimented on a performance; the awe in sensing a spellbound audience watching every movement of the dance. Unlike many jobs, these feelings assume a greater importance to dancers, for their entire way of life, in fact their very life, is centered on their reactions, and the reaction of others, to their work.

GOE: 01.05.01, 01.05.02; SIC: 7911, 7929; SOC: 327

◇ SOURCES OF ADDITIONAL INFORMATION

American Dance Guild
31 West 21st Street, 3rd Floor
New York, NY 10010

American Dance Therapy Association
2000 Century Plaza, Suite 108
Columbia, MD 21044

American Guild of Musical Artists
1727 Broadway
New York, NY 10019

Dance Educators of America
85 Rockaway Avenue
Rockville Center, NY 11570

National Dance Association
1900 Association Drive
Reston, VA 22091

◇ **RELATED ARTICLES**

Volume 1: Performing Arts; Recreation
Volume 2: Actors and actresses; Recreation workers

Data base managers

Definition

Data base managers are responsible for implementing and coordinating data processing systems that collect, analyze, store, and transmit computer information. They consult with other upper management officials to discuss computer equipment purchases, determine requirements for various computer programs, and allocate access to the computer system. They direct training of data base personnel and set work standards for these personnel.

History

Computers are playing a larger and larger role in all aspects of our lives. Nowhere is this more apparent than in the private and governmental sectors as computers are being applied to a rapidly growing range of business, military, and educational situations. Recent developments in electronics have made it possible to build miniature digital computers, minicomputers, and microprocessors. Integrated circuits have made low-cost, high-speed computer systems available to many businesses and other organizations that previously could not afford them.

As more and more businesses acquire computer systems, other companies are scrambling to keep up, either to compete with these companies in information retrieval capabilities or cooperate with them in the rapidly developing area of linking up computers to exchange information. Exchanging of computer information through telephone lines is going on at all levels of business and governmental activity. This explosion is growth in the computer field has led to increasingly large and complex data bases. (A data base is a collection of information stored in a computer.) Correspondingly, the need for trained professionals to manage these data bases has also grown.

Nature of the work

Data base managers are the professionals trained to develop, implement, and coordinate computer-driven information systems. They ensure the smooth flow of information throughout organizations that are rapidly incorporating the latest technological developments into their operations.

Data base managers are responsible for the flow of computer information within an organization and therefore combine general management ability with a detailed knowledge of computer programming and systems analysis. Specific responsibilities are determined by the size and type of organization. For example, a data base manager for a telephone company may develop a system for billing customers while a data base manager for a large store may develop a system for keeping track of merchandise in stock. In all cases, a data base manager must have a thorough knowledge and understanding of the company's computer operations.

A data base manager's responsibilities can be grouped into three main areas: planning what type of computer system a company needs; implementing and managing this system; and supervising computer-room personnel.

To adequately plan a computer system, a data base manager must have extensive knowledge of the latest computer technology and the specific needs of a company. The data base manager meets with other high ranking company officials, such as the president or vice president, and together they decide on how to apply the available technology to their company's needs. Decisions include what type of hardware and software equipment to order and how the data should be stored—in the computer's memory, on disk, or on tape. A data base manager must be aware of the cost of the proposed computer system as well as the budget within which the company is operating. Long-term planning is also important. The manager must ensure that the computer system can process the existing level of computer information the company receives as well as the anticipated load and type of information the company could receive five or ten years down the line. For large companies, this could mean purchasing several computers that have integrated systems with a large memory capability. Whatever the size of the operation, a data base manager is responsible for writing a proposal that summarizes the company's needs and includes specific computer equipment to meet these needs. The data base manager must be familiar with accounting principles and mathematical formulas in developing the proposal. It is not usual for a manager to modify an existing computer system or develop a whole new system based on a company's needs and resources.

Implementing and managing a computer system entails a variety of administrative tasks. The manager must decide how to organize and store the information (data) files so that the appropriate people get access to the right material. Program files must be coded for efficient retrieval. Scheduling access to the computer is another vital administrative function. The data base manager works with representatives from all the departments and works out a schedule so that each department can use the computer when it needs to. This can be a tricky proposition, as often departments will want the computer at the same time. The data base manager must prioritize needs and monitor usage so that each department can do its work. All computer usage must be documented and filed away for future reference.

Safeguarding the computer operations is another important responsibility of the data base manager. The manager must make plans in case a computer system fails or malfunctions so that the information stored in the computer is not lost. A duplication of computer files may be a part of this emergency planning. A backup system must also be employed so that the company can continue to process information. Increasingly, a data base manager must also safeguard a system so that only authorized personnel have access to certain information. Computerized information may be of vital im-

The responsibility of a data base manager includes verifying data over the phone with his clients.

portance to a company, and the data base manager must ensure that it does not fall into the wrong hands.

Implementation of a computer operation often involves coordinating the integration of many complex computers into a single system. As an operation grows this may require the modification of the system. For example, a large company may have separate data bases at different locations around the company. The data base manager will coordinate access, often by having the computers "talk" or exchange information over the telephone.

Like any type of manager, a data base manager must be able to supervise and motivate others. They must be able to train personnel and plan and coordinate all of their activities. Interpersonal skills are very important as computer programmers, systems analysts, and others must all be supervised in a firm, yet fair manner. Communications skills are vital, as is the ability to problem solve touchy personnel issues. Sometimes travel is involved as the manager supervises workers at different locations.

A data base manager must be able to analyze a computer operation and decide if it is operating at top efficiency. The manager must be able to recognize equipment or personnel problems and adjust the system accordingly. The manager is often working with an operation that processes millions of bits of information at a huge cost. This demands accurateness and efficiency in decision-making and problem-solving abilities.

Requirements

Prior experience with computers is vital. Students in high school should take computer programming courses and any electronics or other technical courses that provide understanding of how a computer operates. Mathematics and accounting courses are also desirable. As always, courses in English will enhance communications abilities and are therefore helpful. Computer courses, if not offered at school, are frequently offered in community education centers or at large computer retail stores.

A bachelor's degree in computer science or business administration is usually the minimum education needed for an entry position. Courses should include data processing, systems analysis methods, software and hardware concepts, management principles, and information systems planning. More and more businesses, especially larger companies, want data base managers to have a master's degree in computer science or business administration. Experience as a computer programmer or systems analyst is also desirable.

Individuals interested in working for a particular type of company, for example an electronics firm should acquire as much knowledge as possible about that specific field.

Special requirements

No license or certificate is needed. Some data base managers, however, do become certified for jobs in the computer field by passing an examination given by the Institute for Certification of Computer Professionals. The institute is sponsored by the Data Processing Management Association. The examination is offered in selected cities throughout the United States every year. For further information on certification, contact either of the above organizations at the addresses given at the end of this article.

Opportunities for experience and exploration

High-school computer clubs offer a good forum for learning about computers and meeting others interested in the field. Some businesses offer part-time work or summer internships in their computer departments for students with some background in computers. In addition, there are training programs, such as those offered at summer camps, that use an intensive three to six week period to teach computer literacy.

Related occupations

Arbitrators, office managers, and employment claim officials all utilize many of the same management skills as a data base manager. Similar computer aptitude is needed by computer programmers, system analysts, and computer sales consultants.

Methods of entering

A bachelor's or master's degree in computer science or business administration is usually required for entry level positions. Some applicants with extensive on-the-job computer training may be promoted to this position without a degree, but as the field gets more and more sophisticated a college degree will continue to be the most dependable means of entering the profession.

Advancement

Skilled data base managers have excellent advancement opportunities. As a manager gets experience in developing and integrating computer systems, advancement will take the form of more responsibilities and higher wages. A person at a small company may move to an upper level position such as vice-president of the firm or may move to a better paying, more challenging data base manager position at a larger company. A skilled data base manager at a larger company may also be promoted to an executive position, such as vice-president or president.

Some successful data base managers become consultants or start their own businesses. There are also opportunities in teaching.

It may be necessary to relocate to another part of the United States to take full advantage of advancement opportunities, but the rapidly growing field is sure to offer advancement opportunities at all levels in a variety of settings.

Employment outlook

The use of computers and data processing systems in almost all businesses creates tremendous opportunities for well-qualified personnel. Employment is expected to increase faster than the average through the early 1990s. As always, those with the best education and the most experience in computer systems and personnel management will enjoy the best job prospects.

Data base managers may work for investment companies, telecommunications firms, banks, insurance companies, publishing houses and a host of other large and middle-sized businesses. There are also many opportunities with the federal government and city and state governments. Additionally, opportunities to teach, either as a consultant or at a university or community college, may also exist.

Employment opportunities should to be best in large urban areas because of the multitudes of businesses that have computer systems. Smaller communities, however, are also rapidly developing significant job opportunities, so skilled workers should be able to pick from a wide range of jobs throughout the country.

Earnings

Earnings vary greatly according to the size and type of organization and an individual's experience, education, and job responsibilities. A person with a bachelor's degree at a medium-sized company can expect to earn between $22,000 and $28,000 per year to start. Those at a large company and those with a master's degree can expect to earn between $28,000 and $39,000 per year to start, perhaps more if the responsibilities are great.

Conditions of work

The work environment is a typical modern office, usually located next to the computer room. Most of the manager's planning and analysis activities are done in the office, with supervisory work and equipment monitoring taking place in the computer room. Occasionally, travel is required for conferences and visits to affiliated data base locations.

Data base managers average about fifty hours of work a week, but overtime is not unusual. Emergencies may require a manager to work long hours without a break, sometimes through the night.

Social and psychological factors

A data base manager should be able to take charge of a specific area and should be able to direct and motivate others. The manager should be able to spend long hours working alone analyzing complex information, such as mathematical formulas. A manager must be able to make decisions in a firm way and also have the interpersonal skills to work well with others. The manager should be able to communicate well with executives as well as computer-room personnel. Attention to detail is critical as is the ability to work under pressure. Time demands of work can be extraordinary, with long hours needed in emergency situations, such as when the computer system malfunctions.

A data base manager must remain calm and be able to analyze data, sometimes in a short time span. The manager should be able to take the pressure of working with sensitive material and take precautions to safeguard security of the system. Sometimes this involves limiting access to computer information.

GOE: 11.05; SIC: Any industry; SOC: 137

◇ **SOURCES OF ADDITIONAL INFORMATION**

Information of certification is available from:

Institute for Certification of Computer Professionals
2200 East Devon Avenue, Suite 268
Des Plaines, IL 60018

General information on career opportunities is available from:

Data Processing Management Association
505 Busse Highway
Park Ridge, IL 60068

For a list of publications and seminars for continued education in systems management, please write to:

Association for Systems Management
24587 Bagley Road
Cleveland, OH 44138

Associated Information Managers
3821-F South George Mason Drive
Falls Church, VA 22041

◇ **RELATED ARTICLES**

Volume 1: Computer Hardware; Computer Software
Volume 2: Computer programmers; Graphics programmers; Systems analysts
Volume 3: Computer and peripheral equipment operators
Volume 4: Scientific and business data-processing technicians

Demographers

Definition

Demographers are population specialists who collect and analyze vital statistics related to human population changes, such as births, marriages, and deaths. They plan and conduct research and surveys to study population trends and assess the effects of population movements.

History

Population studies of one kind or another have been going on since the dawn of civilization. Early cave dwellers often used symbols marked on walls to represent the number of people in a group or the number of domesticated animals the group had.

These recording techniques were refined and expanded most extensively by the Roman Empire as it spread throughout the world 2,000 years ago. As the Empire grew, government representatives collected information on a conquered territory, such as its population and the extent of its property holdings. In the mid-1600s, the English became the first country to systematically record and register all births and deaths.

In recent years, as census taking has become more comprehensive and the scientific methods of collecting and interpreting demographic information have improved, demographers have taken a leading role in developing detailed population studies that reveal the essential characteristics of a society, such as the availability of health care and the income level of it constituents.

Nature of the work

Demography is a science that organizes many population facts into a systematized picture of the data. A demographer works to establish ways in which numbers, sets of numbers, or groups of numbers may be organized to produce new and useful information. For example, demographers may study data collected on the frequency of disease in a certain area and use this in the development of graphs and charts to plot the spread of that disease and also forecast the probability that the medical problem may spread.

Many demographers work on the basis of a "sampling" technique in which the characteristics of the whole population are judged by taking a sample of a part of it. For example, demographers may collect data on the educational level of residents living in various locations throughout a community and then use this information to make a projection of the average educational level of the community as a whole. In this way, demographers can conduct research and forecast trends on various social and economic patterns throughout an area.

Demographers not only conduct their own surveys but also often work with statistics gathered from governmental sources, private surveys, and public opinion polls. For example, demographers may compare different statistical information such as an area's average income level and its population and use it to make forecasts of the future educational and medical needs of the community. They may also tabulate the average age, income, and educational levels of a farming community and compare it with the same statistics of an urban environment.

Statistics often give the user an incomplete or confusing picture so it is through mathematical and computer processes that the demographer helps reveal comprehensive information about a specific area. Computers have radically changed the role of the demographer. Now, much greater amounts of data can be collected and analyzed. In the Bureau of Census, for example, demographers work with material that has been compiled as a result of the nationwide census that is conducted every ten years. Millions of pieces of demographic information, such as age, gender, occupation, educational level, and country of origin are collected from people around the country. A demographer may take this statistical information, analyze it, and then use it to forecast population growth or economic trends.

Governmental organizations of all types use the services of a demographer to investigate and analyze a variety of social science questions, such as rates of illness, availability of health and police services, and other issues that define a community. Private companies may also use the information to help make marketing decisions, such as where to open a new store and how to best reach possible customers. Sometimes, a demographer's analysis will be published and utilized by the community as a whole.

Demographers may work on long-range planning for governmental or private agencies. Population trends are especially important in such areas as educational and economic planning, and a demographers analysis is often used to help set policy on health care issues and a host of other social science concerns. Local, state, and national governmental agencies all utilize the demographer's statistical forecasts in an attempt to accurately provide transportation, education, and other services.

Demographers may conduct research for colleges and universities. Part of their job responsibility may include teaching demographic research techniques to students. They may also work as consultants to private businesses. Much of their time is spent in library research, analyzing demographic information of various population groups.

Applied statisticians use accepted theories and known statistical formulas to collect and analyze data in a specific area, such as the availability of health care in a specified location.

Demographers conduct to extensive research. They transfer their work onto computers to calculate and organize vast amounts of data.

Requirements

A college degree in sociology with an emphasis in demography or a related field is usually required to work as a demographer. In addition, a person should enjoy employing logic to solve problems and have an aptitude for mathematics. Aspiring demographers must also enjoy detailed work and must like to study and to learn. Research experience is also helpful.

A high-school student interested in pursuing a career as a demographer should take college-preparatory courses, such as social studies, English, and mathematics (algebra and geometry). College coursework is often within the sociology department and should include classes in social research methods, public policy, statistics, and computer applications.

As the field gets more competitive, many demographers get a master's degree or a doctorate in sociology.

Special requirements

No licenses or certificates are necessary. Demographers who work for the federal government may need to pass a civil service examination, and those who teach in the schools below

155

the college level usually must be certified as teachers. Attaining a position with the federal government has become especially competitive, and successful applicants usually require a master's degree or a doctorate in sociology.

Many demographers belong to organizations that encourage continuing education and other forms of professional enrichment. These organizations include: the American Statistical Association and the Society for Industrial and Applied Mathematics. Addresses for these and other organizations are listed at the end of this article.

Opportunities for experience and exploration

A part-time of summer job at a company that has a statistical research department is a good way of gaining insight into the career of demographer. Discussions with professional demographers are another way of learning about the rewards and responsibilities in this field. Often, high-school students may ask their mathematics teachers to give them some simple statistical problems related to population changes and then practice the kinds of statistical techniques that demographers use.

Related occupations

Actuaries, statisticians, economic analysts, and mathematicians, all are involved in collecting and interpreting large quantities of data. They, along with demographers, must establish trends after analyzing this information.

Methods of entering

The usual method of entering the profession is through completion of an undergraduate or graduate degree in sociology with an emphasis in demographic methods. Qualified applicants should apply directly to private research firms or other companies that do population studies. College placement offices may be helpful in supplying possible leads in this regard. For those interested in working for a government agency, jobs are listed with the Civil Service Commission. Most teaching jobs at the college level require a master's or other graduate degree.

Advancement

After having gained experience on the job, a demographer may become head of a research department, with an accompanying increase in salary and responsibility. Those with the most training and the highest degree of education are most likely to be promoted.

Employment outlook

Although economic variables impact the need for demographers, the tremendous amount of social science research going on in the United States and elsewhere should increase the need for trained professionals to analyze and interpret population data. This trend is expected to continue through the early 1990s. Employment opportunities should be greatest in and around large metropolitan areas, where many colleges, universities, and other research facilities are located. As always, those with the most training and greatest amount of education should enjoy the best job prospects.

Earnings

Earnings vary widely according to education, training, and place of employment. A demographer with a bachelor's degree can expect to earn between $19,000 to $23,000 a year to start. Those beginning work with a graduate degree should earn between $26,000 to $30,000 per year. Experienced demographers should average between $34,000 and $40,000 per year, with very skilled workers earning even more.

Starting salaries may be somewhat higher in governmental agencies than private industry, although private industry may offer greater earning potential. Those working in teaching should expect to earn somewhat less than other demographers.

Conditions of work

Most demographers work in well-lighted offices or classrooms. Those engaged in research may work with other demographers assembling related information. Most of the work revolves around analyzing population data or interpreting computer information. A demographer is also usually responsible for writing a report detailing his or her findings.

There may be some travel to attend a conference or do limited field research. A demographer should expect to work a forty-hour week and have an annual vacation and other benefits, such as sick leave and group insurance. Overtime may be required if a project is on deadline.

Social and psychological factors

Demographers should be able to spend long hours working alone analyzing complex population statistics. They should be able to apply detailed mathematical formulas and draw conclusions from different types of data. Patience and persistence are important character traits. The ability to work within a group is necessary, as is the ability to communicate findings in a clear and coherent fashion.

Demographers must be willing to pursue many years of education in order to advance. Not every demographer will need to get a doctorate, but each person must consider the possibility of advanced study, whether they decide to pursue it or not.

GOE: 11.03.02; SIC: 7392, 96; SOC: 1733, 1916

American Statistical Association
1429 Duke Street
Alexandria, VA 22314

Population Association of America
1429 Duke Street
Alexandra, VA 22314

Population Reference Bureau
777 14th Street, NW, Suite 800
Washington, DC 20005

Society for Industrial and Applied Mathematics
1400 Architects Building
117 South 17th Street
Philadelphia, PA 19103

For information on demographers for the U.S. government, contact regional offices of the Department of Commerce, or the national office at:

Bureau of the Census
Public Information Office
Department of Commerce
14th Street and Constitution, NW
Washington, DC 20230

◇ **SOURCES OF ADDITIONAL INFORMATION**

American Sociological Association
1722 N Street, NW
Washington, DC 20036

◇ **RELATED ARTICLES**

Volume 1: Social Science
Volume 2: Mathematicians; Sociologists; Statisticians

Dental hygienists

Definition

A *dental hygienist* administers preventive dental treatment, gives instructions on teeth care, may take X rays, and in general, assists the dentist in routine tasks.

The most common routine for the dental hygienist is the administration of a semi-annual cleaning. This involves removing tartar, stains, and plaque from teeth.

History

The work of the dental hygienist has developed from the modern dentist's need for assistance in carrying out routine tasks of dental care. The dental hygienist has been able to supplement the dentist, freeing the latter for skilled work.

The first dental hygienists were trained by dentists themselves. The first school for dental hygiene was organized early in the twentieth century, and in 1915 the first state legalized the practice of dental hygiene. The profession has since expanded and gained stature.

Nature of the work

The dental hygienist's task is to help prevent tooth decay and to maintain a healthy condition in the mouth. This is done mainly through cleaning teeth by removing stains and calcium deposits, polishing teeth, and massaging gums, a process called "oral prophylaxis." The dental hygienist also instructs the patient on the proper way to maintain dental health and to guard against oral disease.

Other responsibilities depend on the employer, whether it is a private dentist, a school system, or a public health agency. The private dentist might require that the dental hygienist take and develop X rays, mix compounds for filling cavities, sterilize instruments, assist in surgical work, or even carry out clerical tasks such as making appointments and filling in insurance forms.

Although some of these tasks might also be done by a dental assistant, only the dental hygienist is licensed by the state to clean teeth. Also, the licensed hygienist submits a chart of each patient's teeth, noting possible decay or disease. The dentist studies this in making further diagnoses. The hygienist might well fill the duties of receptionist or office manager, functioning in many ways to assist the dentist in carrying out the schedule.

The school hygienist, too, has a busy program: that of cleaning and examining the teeth of students in a number of schools. The hygienist also gives classroom instruction on correct brushing and flossing of teeth, the importance of good dental care, and the effect of good nutrition. Dental records of the students are kept, and parents must be notified of any need for further treatment. The work of the school hygienist is typical of the dental hygienist's primary functions—education and prevention of dental decay and disease.

The dental hygienist may also be employed by a local, state, or federal public health agency. Again the hygienist will be called upon to carry out an educational program for adults and children, as well as oral prophylaxis, in public health clinics, schools, and other public facilities. A few dental hygienists may assist in research projects. For those with further education, teaching in a dental hygiene school may be possible.

Requirements

Two types of training are available to the prospective dental hygienist. One is a four-year college program offering a bachelor's degree; the other, more widely offered, is a two-year program leading to a dental hygiene certification. The bachelor's degree is often preferred by employers, and more schools are likely to require completion of such a degree program in the future. In the early 1990s, there were more than 200 accredited schools in the United States that offered one or both of these courses.

The minimum requirement for admission to a dental hygiene school is graduation from high school. Aptitude tests sponsored by the American Dental Hygienists' Association are frequently required by dental hygiene schools to help the applicants determine whether they will succeed in this field. Skill in handling delicate instruments, a sensitive touch, and depth perception are important attributes. The hygienist should be personally clean and healthy.

Classroom work emphasizes basic and dental sciences and liberal arts. Lectures are usually combined with laboratory work and clinical experience.

Special requirements

Dental hygienists, after graduation from accredited schools, must pass state licensing examinations, both written and clinical. In the early 1990s, candidates in forty-nine states and the District of Columbia could complete part of their state licensing requirements by passing the National Board of Dental Examiners' written examination. Upon passing the exam, wherever it may be taken, a dental hygienist becomes an R.D.H., registered dental hygienist, but to practice in another state must pass that state's exam even though a temporary license may be given.

Opportunities for experience and exploration

Work as a dental assistant might be a stepping-stone to a dental hygienist's career. As a dental assistant, one could closely observe the work of a dental hygienist. The individual could then assess personal aptitude for this work, discuss any questions with other hygienists, and enroll in a dental hygiene school where experience as a dental assistant would certainly be helpful. A high-school student might be able to find such work on a part-time or summer basis. A prospective dental hygiene student also might arrange to observe a dental hygienist working in a school or a dentist's office, or to visit an accredited dental hygiene school where clinics are often functioning. The aptitude testing program required by most dental hygiene schools helps students assess their future abilities as a dental hygienist.

Related occupations

Other occupations that involve supporting a health practitioner in an office setting include dental assistants, medical assistants, office nurses, ophthalmic medical assistants, physician assistants, and podiatric assistants. Workers who apply technical knowledge to examine and treat patients or to perform research in offices, hospitals, or laboratories also include dialysis technicians, electroencephalographic technicians, medical laboratory assistants and technicians, medical technologists, nuclear medical technologists, and ultrasound technicians.

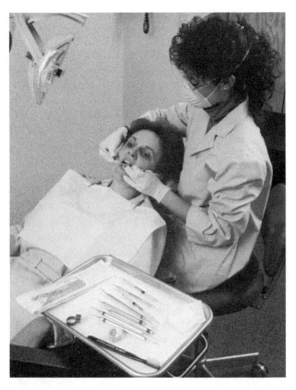

A dental hygienist cleans the teeth of a woman. In accordance with current practices, it is common for hygienists to wear mouth guards and gloves during an examination.

Methods of entering

Once dental hygienists have passed the National Board exams and/or a licensing exam in a particular state, they must decide on an area of work, such as a private dentist's office, school system, or public health agency. Hospitals, industrial plants, and the armed forces employ a small number of dental hygienists. Most dental hygiene schools maintain placement services, and little difficulty arises in finding a satisfactory position.

Advancement

Opportunities for advancement, other than increases in salary and benefits that accompany experience in the field, usually require postgraduate study and training. Educational advancement may lead to a position as administrator, teacher or director in a dental health program or to a more advanced field of practice. The dental hygienist should bear in mind that postgraduate study often places one in competition with dentists generally working in these areas.

Employment outlook

Accurate figures are not available for the number of dental hygienists employed in the United States because dentists frequently hire them to work only two or three days a week and many hygienists hold more than one part-time job. Therefore, although dental hygienists held about 87,000 jobs in the early 1990s, the number of workers may have been considerably smaller.

The demand for dental care is expected to increase rapidly through the 1990s. Population growth, rising personal incomes, public awareness of the importance of oral health, and the availability of dental insurance should result in more jobs for dental hygienists. In addition, there will be the need to replace workers who leave the field. Job growth also depends on practice patterns in dentistry. The use of dental hygienists is more prevalent in some areas than in others. Young dentists are more inclined to hire hygienists because they have been taught in dental school how to make effective use of a support staff. Opportunities are greater, too, because of the trend toward group dental practice. One factor might slow this upswing. If current competition among dentists becomes sufficiently strong and patient loads decline,

159

dentists may be forced to perform the functions of the dental hygienist themselves.

Earnings

The dental hygienist's income is influenced by such factors as education, experience, locale, and type of employer. Most dental hygienists who work in private dental offices are salaried employees, though some are paid a commission for work performed or a combination of salary and commission. In the early 1990s, the average earnings of most hygienists, a majority of whom worked only part-time, ranged between $12,500 and $22,500 a year. Experienced dental hygienists earned from about $14 to $18 per hour, which for full-time work would translate to approximately $24,500 to $31,500 annually. Salaries in large metropolitan areas are generally higher than in small cities and towns. Dental hygienists in research, education, or administration may earn higher salaries. The beginning salary under federal government employment in the early 1990s was approximately $12,900 to $14,400 a year.

Conditions of work

Work conditions for the dental hygienist in a private office, school, or government facility are generally pleasant, with well-lighted, modern, and adequately equipped facilities. The hygienist, however, must do most of the work standing, and should be in good physical condition to do so on a day-to-day routine. Full-time hygienists in a private office work a thirty-five to forty-hours per week; some work part-time at two jobs. Many private offices are open one-half day on Saturday. Government employees work hours regulated by the particular agency. For a salaried dental hygienist in a private office, a paid two- or three-week vacation is common. In a school system or college, the summer months may be considered an extended vacation, possibly with salary on a ten- to twelve-month basis, unless some type of summer clinic is to be carried on. Additional benefits are usually extended to all employees of the school system. Part-time or commissioned dental hygienists in private offices usually have no paid vacation. Benefits will vary, however, according to the hygienist's agreement with the employer.

Social and psychological factors

The dental hygienist has an opportunity to work with people to improve and protect their health. There is satisfaction in knowing that the preventive and educative work of the dental hygienist shows significant results. The dental hygienist is the dentist's only aide licensed to work directly in the mouth of the patient; this provides a higher professional status and an indication that the dental hygienist is giving valuable service to public health.

GOE: 10.02.02; SIC: 8021; SOC: 363

◇ **SOURCES OF ADDITIONAL INFORMATION**

American Association of Dental Examiners
211 East Chicago Avenue, Suite 1812
Chicago, IL 60611

American Dental Hygienists' Association
444 North Michigan Avenue, Suite 3400
Chicago, IL 60611

American Dental Association
211 East Chicago Avenue
Chicago, IL 60611

Division of Dental Health
Public Heath Service
U.S. Dept. of Health and Human Services
Washington, DC 20201

◇ **RELATED ARTICLES**

Volume 1: Health Care
Volume 2: Dentists
Volume 3: Dental assistants
Volume 4: Dental laboratory technicians

Dentists

Definition

Dentists attempt to maintain healthy teeth through such preventive and reparative practices as extracting, filling, cleaning, or replacing teeth; performing corrective work, such as straightening teeth; treating diseased tissue of the gums; performing surgical operations on jaw or mouth; and making and fitting false teeth.

History

Dentistry was in earliest times a primitive, yet necessary practice, for health problems in the mouth and teeth have long existed. For centuries, the practice of dentistry consisted largely of curing toothaches by extraction or the use of herbs and similar methods to alleviate pain. These home practices were employed only in emergencies; dental care and correction as they now exist in the modern profession were not conceived of. We no longer see a well-meaning father, barber, or blacksmith preparing to extract a tooth to relieve a toothache. Dentistry, today, is a professional field of great significance to the health of the public.

Nature of the work

A dentist may be a general practitioner or may specialize. Most dentists are general practitioners, with only 20 percent practicing as specialists. The largest number of these specialists are orthodontists, followed by oral surgeons, pedodontists, periodontists, prosthodontists, endodontists, oral pathologists, and public health dentists.

General practitioners must be proficient in many areas of dentistry. They must be on the alert for any condition in the mouth requiring special treatment, such as crooked teeth, diseased gums, oral cancer (for they may have to treat such special conditions), as well as clean teeth, fill cavities, and extract teeth. General practitioners must be able to use and understand X rays as well as be well acquainted with laboratory work.

The specialists referred to above devote their time and skills to specific dental problems:

Orthodontists correct irregularities in the development of teeth and jaws by the use of braces and similar devices.

Oral surgeons perform difficult tooth extractions, remove tumors from the gums or jaw, and set jaw fractures.

Periodontists treat diseased gums and other tissues that support the teeth.

Prosthodontists specialize in making artificial teeth or dentures to precise specifications and measurements.

Pedodontists specialize in children's dental problems.

Oral pathologists examine and diagnose tumors and lesions of the mouth.

Endodontists treat diseased inner tooth structures, such as the nerve, pulp, and root canal.

Public-health dentists deal with treatment and education of the public to the importance of dental health and care through public health agencies.

In charge of dental programs in hospitals are *dental service directors*. These administrators help set policies and procedures, establish training programs for students and interns, and supervise the hiring, promotion, duty assignments, and work schedules of staff members.

Requirements

The dental profession is selective, and standards are high. College grades and the amount of college education are carefully considered. All dental schools approved by the American Dental Association require applicants to pass the Dental Admissions Test, which tests a student's ability to succeed or fail in dental school. Information on tests and testing centers may be obtained from the Council on Dental Education of the American Dental Association.

A prospective dental student should plan an academic program of study in high school with an emphasis on science and math. Liberal arts courses are also significant for meeting college entrance requirements. Participation in extracurricular activities is also important. Experience in getting along with others is important in a profession so closely associated with people. The student should also note the importance of manual dexterity and scientific ability. Skilled, steady hands are necessary, as well as good space and shape judgment, and some ar-

161

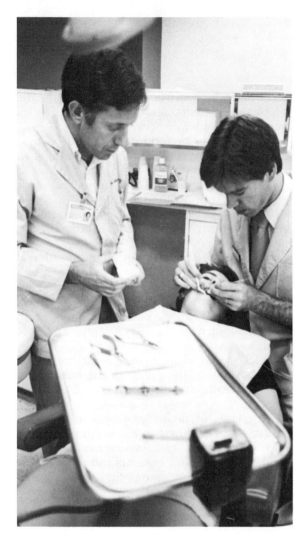

A student of dentistry cleans a person's teeth as his instructor looks on.

schools give the degree of doctor of dental medicine (D.D.M. or D.M.D.).

Dental students who wish to enter a specialized field should plan on postgraduate study ranging from two to four years. A specialist can only become certified by passing specialty board exams. Further training may be obtained as a dental intern or resident in an approved hospital. Of course, a dentist must continually keep abreast of developments in the profession through reading professional magazines and journals, short-term graduate courses, and frequent seminars.

Special requirements

Dentists are required to qualify for a license in all states by graduating from an approved dental school and passing a state board examination or, in some states, the National Board of Dental Examiner's exam. In sixteen states and the District of Columbia, a specialist must pass a special state exam to be licensed. Generally, dentists licensed in one state are required to take another exam to practice in another state. However, twenty states grant licenses to dentists from other states based on their credentials.

Opportunities for experience and exploration

A high-school student might be able to gain an awareness of the demands of dentistry by observing a dentist at work. Perhaps work as a dental hygienist, assistant, or laboratory technician might stimulate one to continue study in dentistry. Because of the nature of dentistry, however, actual practical experience would be impossible. A careful study of personal traits and aptitudes would be good preparation.

The high-school student might want to talk to and observe several dentists, obtain pertinent information from dental schools, discuss the matter with parents and school counselor, and finally, arrange to take the Dental Admission Test at the end of the first year, or during the second year, of college study.

Related occupations

Persons who are interested in dentistry but who may not be able to make such a long-term

tistic ability. Good vision is required because of the detailed work.

Dental schools require at least three to four years of college-level predental education. About 80 percent of the students entering dental schools have already earned a bachelor's or master's degree. Professional training in a dental school generally requires four academic years. Many dental schools are working on an interdisciplinary curriculum in which the dental student studies basic science with medical, pharmacy, and other health profession students. Clinical training is frequently begun in the second year. Most all schools now feature a Department of Community Dentistry, which involves a study of communities, urban ghetto problems, sociology, and includes treatment of patients from the community. Generally the degree of doctor of dental surgery (D.D.S.) is granted upon graduation, although some

commitment to prepare for that occupation might consider work as dental assistants or dental hygienists. Other professionals who examine, diagnose, and treat patients, and whose scientific training is long and rigorous, include optometrists, physicians, podiatrists, psychologists, and veterinarians.

Methods of entering

Once a dentist has graduated from an approved dental school and passed a state licensing examination, there are three avenues of entry into private practice. A new dentist may open a new office; purchase an established practice; or join another dentist or group of dentists to gain further experience. There are, however, other choices for licensed dentists. They may enter the armed forces as a commissioned officer, or through civil service procedures may become eligible for work in the U.S. Public Health Service. They may choose to work in a hospital, clinic, or school, and for some the dental laboratory or teaching of dentistry will provide satisfying careers.

Advancement

Advancement for the newly licensed dentist in private practice depends on personal skill in handling patients as well as dental work. Through the years the successful dentist builds a reputation and thus advances with the confidence of the patients. The quality of the work depends in part on an ability to remain in close contact with developments in the field. For salaried dentists in the various areas of employment, advancement will also depend on the quality and skill of their work as well as on suitable personal characteristics. Advancement may take the form of a step from general practitioner to specialist, a step requiring further study and generally providing higher income. Teachers may look forward to administrative positions or to appointments as professors.

Advancement or success of dentists at least from a financial viewpoint, may depend on the location of practice; people in higher income areas are more likely to request dental care. In small towns and sparsely populated areas a great need exists for dentists and competition is slight. In cities it may be more difficult to become known and competition is stiffer despite the larger pool of possible patients.

Employment outlook

Opportunities for dentists are anticipated to be very good through the 1990s. People are more concerned about dental health and can better afford dental care, especially because dental insurance is becoming more readily available. The growing population of elderly and of middle-aged persons born before the advances in dental health that took place in the 1950s will require increased services in terms of restorative dentistry. At present, the majority of dentists are located in large cities; thus, small communities and less populated areas are prime locations for establishing a dental practice.

Also, the scientific advances in the field of dentistry offer a promising future for specialists. The work, for example, of the oral pathologist or orthodontist becomes invaluable as people become increasingly aware of the need for such care. Public health programs, too, can be expected to expand. Dentistry today is becoming more a preventative than reparative practice.

Interestingly, the number of applicants to dental schools is decreasing, yet standards remain high and admission is competitive. High-school students must be aware of the importance of maintaining high grades if they wish to meet this competition. Despite diminishing enrollments, the number of new graduates entering the field each year is larger than the number of openings that arise from replacement needs. Dentists rarely leave the profession except to retire, and many continue to work beyond retirement age, simply reducing the number of hours they put in.

In the early 1990s, about 143,000 dentists held about 151,000 jobs. Almost nine out of ten were in private practice. Of the remainder, about half worked in research or teaching or held administrative positions in dental schools. Some practiced in hospitals and clinics. About 2,000 civilian dentists were employed in federal government agencies such as the Veterans Administration and the U.S. Public Health Service.

Earnings

Beginning dentists, faced with the expense of purchasing equipment and the problem of establishing a practice, generally earn enough to cover expenses and little more. But income rises rapidly as the dentist's practice becomes established. In the early 1990s, the average income of the self-employed general practitioner after expenses was about $59,000 a year, with the specialist earning an average of $100,000.

The area in which a dentist practices also has an effect on his or her income. In any high-income urban area, dental services are in great demand, but there is an advantage to setting up practice in a small town, where there is likely to be less competition from established practitioners and where the cost of living may be lower than in large cities.

Dentists' earnings are lower during economic downturns when people tend to postpone dental treatment except for emergencies.

Conditions of work

Because most dentists are in private practice, they are free to set their own hours and establish offices and atmospheres suitable to their individual tastes. No doubt, the beginning dentist must set aside expensive decorating plans in favor of suitable equipment, but most dentists' offices are designed to be pleasant and comfortable. Dentists may have a dental assistant, hygienist, or laboratory technician, or they may carry out the special duties of each themselves. The dentist in private practice sets individual hours and practices after office hours only in emergencies. Salaried dentists working for a clinic, hospital, or the Public Health Service are subject to conditions set by their employers.

Another qualification worth considering is the expense of education for a degree in dentistry as well as the initial expense of setting up a practice. The prospective dental student must be reasonably sure of meeting both of these financial demands.

Social and psychological factors

The dentist is very much involved with other people; confidence and skill are essential for putting a patient at ease. High academic standards are demanded by dental schools, but of equal importance are personality traits: a liking for people, calmness, and the ability to act in difficult situations. Personal neatness is also essential.

A dentist may find satisfaction in the artistry of the work, in the ability to halt or prevent some disease of the mouth, and to set aside for some individual the many personal problems caused by improperly formed teeth.

Although dentists work with people, private practitioners also have the satisfaction of being on their own and of running their own business. The success of this career depends largely on their own skill as dentists and an ability to communicate this to the patients.

GOE: 02.03.02; SIC: 8021; SOC: 262

◇ **SOURCES OF ADDITIONAL INFORMATION**

American Association of Dental Schools
1625 Massachusetts Avenue, NW
Washington, DC 20036

American Dental Association
211 East Chicago Avenue
Chicago, IL 60611

For a list of accredited schools for post-graduate and post-doctoral work, write to:

Accredited Dental School Educational Programs
American Dental Association
211 East Chicago Avenue
Chicago, IL 60611

Admission Requirements of US and Canadian Dental Schools
American Association of Dental Schools
1625 Massachusetts Avenue, NW
Washington, DC 20036

For information on financial aid for dental studies, write to:

Directory of Grants, Awards, and Loans
Bureau of Health Professionals
Health Resources and Services
US Department of Health and Human Services
Rockville, MD 20857

◇ **RELATED ARTICLES**

Designers

Definition

Designers arrange or design elements or details to create objects, products, materials, or displays that are pleasing to the eye and serve the purpose for which they were intended.

History

The history of design as an applied art parallels that of fine art. In every age, examples of practical art can be found alongside paintings and sculpture. Many of today's designers can find their counterparts in antiquity.

The prehistoric cave dwellers who devised a plan for sewing fur garments had no idea they were doing anything other than protecting themselves against the elements. Nor did the Stone Age textile designers who invented the weaving of cloth and went on to use berries, leaves, animal matter, and other natural dyes to produce appealing patterns on the cloth. Also among the world's earliest designers were the metalworkers who put their creative touch on tools, weapons, and jewelry.

Although the field of package design did not emerge formally until the middle of the twentieth century as an outgrowth of advertising, ancient artisans led the way, designing "packaging" in the form of urns, jars, phials, chests, and baskets for the many products used in everyday living, such as oils, grains and other foodstuffs, perfumes, and ointments.

Stone reliefs from Assyrian palaces depict ornate thrones, chairs, and tables, while Egyptian tombs give evidence of elaborately carved, vividly painted couches, chairs, and chests—all created by forerunners of today's furniture designers.

Floral designers, too, can find their beginnings thousands of years ago, in the custom of using flowers to decorate homes, churches, and other public places and giving bouquets to express love, sympathy, or congratulations.

Societies throughout history have erected monuments and statues to commemorate events or to honor special persons. Designers have been responsible for huge arches and fountains to celebrate a nation's accomplishments and for smaller granite or marble memorials to mark the burial places of loved and respected individuals.

Some design occupations had more recent origins. Stained glass was developed in Europe in the Middle Ages, introducing a new medium for artists. Banknote designers can trace their craft to the fifteenth century when the first printed impressions were made from engraved designs. The artful placement of objects for sale has been a means of attracting customers for as long as people have been providing merchandise to one another, but it was the development of general retailing in the seventeenth century that led to the need for professional merchandise display designers. And the work of theater set designers became more complex with the introduction of realistic theater around the end of the nineteenth century.

The problem of combining beauty and function has preoccupied artisans in all periods of history, and utilitarian art has been used to promote commerce for as long as civilized humans have been employing symbols, characters, or letters of an alphabet. Only the formal aspect of design occupations is relatively modern.

Nature of the work

Designers are practical artists whose creations are intended to be functional as well as attractive. There are many kinds of designers. Some specialize in a type of product, such as furniture, textiles, or packaging; others work with a particular kind of material, such as metal, glass, or stone. Some specialize in floral arrangements, museum exhibits, or settings for movies and plays.

Whatever the specialty, all designers take a similar approach to a project, whether it is for a brand-new design or for a variation on an existing one. They begin by determining the needs and preferences of the clients and the potential users, buyers, or viewers. In the case of consumer products, for example, designers have to consider a number of factors. Decisions have to be made about the shape, size, and weight of the item and the colors and materials to be used. The way a product works will influence its design. It must be easy for the customer to use and to maintain or store, and it must meet safety standards. Designers may compare their product with similar ones on the market and analyze the success or failure of a competitive product to design one that is easily

A woman generates ideas for textile design by sketching patterns on various types of paper. These papers simulate fabric surfaces, providing the appearance of certain textiles.

identified and has more sales appeal. Another factor in certain design decisions is cost. Economy of production is especially important for mass-produced articles if they are to compete for their share of the market.

After a plan has been conceived and the details worked out, the designer makes sketches to present for approval. Depending on what is being designed and for whom, the sketches may go to an art or design director, a product development team, a film or play producer, or directly to the client.

Once a sketch has been approved, the designer constructs a model or sample or prepares detailed plans drawn to scale. Designers, especially those who have their own businesses, may then supervise the craft workers who actually carry out the design.

Designers who are self-employed must also make presentations from time to time in the hope of attracting new clients or soliciting additional business from former clients. In addition, they must handle the paperwork and other details involved in running a business.

Specialized occupations in the design field include the following:

Package designers design boxes, cans, wrappings, and other containers for foods, beverages, toiletries, cosmetics, medicines, housewares, and other consumer products.

Furniture designers design furniture for homes, offices, hotels, stores, and other uses.

Cloth designers, sometimes known as *textile designers,* design prints woven into or printed on fabrics for clothing or furnishings.

Fur designers design new or restyled fur coats and other fur garments.

Stained-glass artists design stained-glass windows, art objects, and decorative articles.

Ornamental-metalwork designers, also called *art-metal designers,* design ornamental metal items such as railings, lattice work, grills, statues, plaques, and light fixtures.

Memorial designers design stone memorials such as monuments, statues, and mausoleums.

Floral designers, often called *florists,* design arrangements of live, cut, dried, and artificial flowers and foliage.

Banknote designers design engraving plates for government bonds and other securities, currency, and stamps.

Art directors, set designers, and *set decorators* design sets and scenic effects for motion picture, television, and stage productions.

Display managers design merchandise displays for retail store windows and interiors, and sometimes special exhibits such as trade shows.

Display designers, sometimes called *display and banner designers* or *flag decorators and designers,* design decorative displays for streets, buildings, fairgrounds, and other locations where celebrations and special events are held.

Exhibit designers, also known as *museum exhibition chiefs* or *curators of exhibits,* design permanent and temporary exhibits and displays for museums. (*See also* the article titled "Archivists and curators" elsewhere in this volume.)

Requirements

As with all artists, designers need artistic talent, creativity, and imagination. They must be sensitive to beauty and have an eye for detail and a strong sense of color, balance, and proportion. To a great extent, these qualities are inborn, but they can be developed through training, both on the job as well as in professional schools, colleges, and universities.

Certain designers need specialized knowledge. For example: Furniture designers must be able to read manufacturing specifications and prepare blueprints. Stained-glass artists must understand stresses and be familiar with glass-cutting techniques. Ornamental-metalwork designers must have a knowledge of the properties of metal and fabrication techniques. Memorial designers have to be able to carve and form plaster models. Banknote designers need to know about engraving and printing; set designers, drafting; display managers, merchandising, and so on. The best way to acquire specialized skills and knowledge is often through formal coursework.

More and more designers are recognizing the value of formal training, and at least two out of three persons entering the field today have a college degree or some college education. In the early 1990s, 143 colleges and art schools offered design programs that were accredited by the National Association of Schools of Art and Design. At many schools, design students must take a year of basic art and design courses before being accepted into the bachelor's degree program. In addition, applicants may be asked to submit samples of their work to prove artistic ability.

Professional schools award a certificate or an associate degree in design to students who successfully complete a two- or three-year course of study.

A bachelor of fine arts (BFA) program at a four-year college or university may include courses such as principles of design, art and art history, painting, sculpture, mechanical and architectural drawing, architecture, computerized design, basic engineering, fashion designing and sketching, garment construction, and textiles.

Many junior colleges, adult education programs, and correspondence schools offer courses in design. Floral designers may learn their craft in commercial floral design schools or at a few colleges and universities that offer degrees in floriculture and floristry and whose programs also include business-oriented courses such as flower marketing and shop management.

With or without specialized education, designers seeking employment should have a good portfolio containing samples of their best work. This is extremely important and can make a difference when an employer must choose between two otherwise equally qualified candidates.

A period of on-the-job training is expected for all beginning designers. The length of time it takes to become fully qualified may run from one to three years, depending on prior education and experience as well as innate talent.

A graphics designer prepares the layout of a weather forecast backdrop that will appear on television.

Special requirements

The importance of a higher education for museum exhibit designers must be emphasized. Many museums require not only a bachelor's degree but often a master's, usually in art, with emphasis on design, museography, or graphics. Some museums require a degree in architecture, engineering, or museum studies; others will accept such a degree in lieu of a preferred one.

There are no special requirements, such as licensing or union membership, for the designers described in this article.

Opportunities for experience and exploration

High-school students who think they might want to pursue a career in design have a number of ways to find out whether they have the talent, ambition, and perseverance to succeed in the field. Those who are already certain of their goals may use these opportunities to begin creating a portfolio for use when they are ready to begin interviewing for jobs or to satisfy college or art school requirements.

Whether they intend to enter the job market immediately upon graduation or go on to college or a specialized school, students should take as many art and design courses as possible while still in high school. Also, to get an insider's view of various design occupations, they could enlist the help of art teachers or school guidance counselors to make arrangements to tour design centers and interview designers.

167

While studying, students can get practical experience by participating in school and community projects that call for design talents. These might include such activities as building sets for plays, setting up exhibits, planning seasonal and holiday displays, and preparing programs and other printed materials.

Part-time and summer jobs offer would-be designers an excellent way to become familiar with the day-to-day requirements of a particular design occupation and to gain some basic related experience. Possible places of employment include design studios, design departments in advertising agencies and manufacturing companies, department and furniture stores, flower shops, fur salons, workshops that produce ornamental items, and museums. Museums also use a number of volunteer workers. Inexperienced persons are often employed as sales, clerical, or general helpers; those with a little more education and experience may qualify for jobs in which they have a chance to develop actual design skills.

Related occupations

Other workers who use the principles of design to make objects, materials, or interiors visually pleasing and suitable for their intended purpose include architects, artists, engineers, landscape architects, merchandise display workers, and photographers.

Methods of entering

The strongest recommendation a designer can have is a good portfolio, because employers depend on samples to evaluate design ability. Beginning designers should have a portfolio of their best work from school or part-time jobs. The portfolio should continually be updated to reflect the designer's growing skills, so it will always be ready for possible job changes.

Job interviews may be obtained by applying directly to companies that employ designers. Many colleges and professional schools have placement services to help their graduates find positions, and sometimes it is possible to get a referral from a previous part-time employer.

Advancement

As part of their on-the-job training, beginning designers generally are given the simpler tasks to perform under direct supervision. As they gain experience, they move up to more complex work with increasingly less supervision.

Experienced designers, especially those with leadership capabilities, may be promoted to chief designer, design department head, or other supervisory position. Some experienced designers eventually go into business for themselves.

Employment outlook

Chances for employment look very good for qualified designers through the 1990s. The design field in general is expected to grow at a faster than average rate. In particular, there will be a demand for industrial designers to design products to meet new safety requirements and to satisfy quality-conscious consumers. The proliferation of high-technology products in medicine and transportation, as well as for business and offices, should also create more jobs for industrial designers. In addition, an increasing population with more money to spend should result in more opportunities for fashion, floral, and set designers.

Because the design field is a popular one, appealing to many talented individuals, competition is expected to be strong in all areas, with the possible exception of floral design. Beginners and designers with only average talent or without formal education and technical skills may encounter some difficulty in securing employment.

About 259,000 persons held design jobs in the early 1990s. About 40 percent were self-employed, a higher proportion than is found in most occupations. Salaried designers work in many different industries, including the wholesale and retail trade (department stores, furniture and home furnishings stores, apparel stores, florist shops); manufacturing industries (machinery, motor vehicles and aircraft, metal products, instruments, apparel, textiles, printing and publishing); service industries (business services, engineering, architecture); construction firms; and government agencies.

Earnings

The range of salaries for designers is quite broad. In the early 1990s, about half of all experienced full-time designers had approximate annual earnings of between $16,800 and $34,400. However, a group of about ten percent were paid less than $15,200, while another group of ten percent received more than $46,500. The median pay for designers was about $25,500, except for floral designers, who earned less. Average annual earnings for floral designers ranged from approximately $8,700 for beginners to $13,000 for those with experience. Some floral designers, however, earned more than $25,000.

Earnings of self-employed designers depend on individual talent and business ability but, in general, are higher than those of salaried designers.

Salaried designers who advanced to the position of design manager or design director earned about $55,000 a year; and, at the level of corporate vice-president, made between $65,000 and $75,000. The owner of a consulting firm can make $85,000 and upwards.

Conditions of work

Most designers work regular hours in clean comfortable, pleasant offices or studios. Conditions vary depending on the design specialty.

Designers who supervise craft workers or who construct their own models may also spend some time in workshops and handle special tools. Memorial designers may visit outdoor sites to plan placement of monuments. Set designers, especially for television, often put in long, irregular hours and work under pressure in a fast-paced, rapidly changing environment. Florists are on their feet for much of the day and usually have to work overtime during holidays.

Some designers work in small establishments with few employees; others, in large organizations with large design departments. Some deal mostly with their coworkers; others may have a lot of public contact. Free-lance designers are paid by the assignment. To maintain a steady income, they must constantly strive to please their clients and to find new ones.

Social and psychological factors

Designers must first be receptive to new influences, willing to explore and adapt new ideas to bring freshness and originality to their own work. Then they need persistence in developing their creative ideas and applying their skills to solving design problems. Finally, they must be able to communicate their ideas both verbally and visually.

Creative ideas originate in the mind of the individual person. Designers need the ability to work independently when devising their concepts but must be able to cooperate with others to execute the designs. It takes self-discipline to plan and begin projects on one's own and to adhere to schedules to meet deadlines. And it takes tact and sensitivity to supervise artisans effectively.

Designers who are self-employed should also have sound business sense and enough sales ability to present themselves and their services in a persuasive manner.

GOE: 05; SIC: Any industry; SOC: 6859

◇ **SOURCES OF ADDITIONAL INFORMATION**

American Association of Museums
1225 I Street, NW
Washington, DC 20005

American Floral Art School
539 South Wabash Avenue
Chicago, IL 60605

American Horticultural Society
PO Box 0105
Mt. Vernon, VA 22121

American Institute of Commemorative Art
2446 Sutter Court, NE
Grand Rapids, MI 49505

American Monument Association
933 High Street, Suite 220
Worthington, OH 43085

American Society of Furniture Designers
PO Box 2688
High Point, NC 27261

Design International
3748 22nd Street
San Francisco, CA 94114

Industrial Designers Society of America
1142-E Walker Road
Great Falls, VA 22066

Monument Builders of North America
1612 Central Street
Evanston, IL 60201

Dispensing opticians
Professional, Administrative, and Managerial Occupations

National Association of Schools of Art and Design
11250 Roger Bacon Drive
Number 5
Reston, VA 22090

Package Designers Council International
PO Box 3753
Grand Central Station
New York, NY 10017

Society of American Florists
1601 Duke Street
Alexandria, VA 22314

Society of Publication Designers
60 East 42nd Street
Suite 1416
New York, NY 10165

Textile Designers Guild
11 West 20th Street, 8th Floor
New York, NY 10011

◇ **RELATED ARTICLES**

Volume 1: Apparel; Design; Packaging; Textiles
Volume 2: Commercial artists; Industrial designers; Interior designers and decorators; Landscape architects
Volume 3: Display workers
Volume 4: Drafting and design technicians; Exhibit technicians; Graphic arts technicians

---

Dispensing opticians

Definition

Dispensing opticians measure and fit clients with prescription eyeglasses and contact lenses. They help clients with the selection of appropriate frames and order all necessary ophthalmic laboratory work.

History

The Chinese are thought to have invented glasses as a means of improving vision as early as 500 B.C. glasses began to be widely used in Europe for reading during the 1500s, when printed matter first became widely available. The craft of grinding lenses to correct visual problems continued to spread throughout Europe over the next several hundred years.

Further development of eyeglasses was made by Benjamin Franklin, who invented the bifocal lens in the eighteenth century. Bifocals have a two-part lens—one part is used to aid reading and the other part is used to aid distance vision. By the late nineteenth century, a Swiss physician, A.E. Frick, had made the first

contact lens. These first contact lenses were made of heavy glass and were rather uncomfortable to wear. By using lighter, more flexible material, later developers were able to create contact lenses that today only cover the cornea (a portion of the eyeball).

With more than 50 percent of the people in the United States now wearing prescription glasses or contact lenses, dispensing opticians and others involved with eye care figure to continue to develop ways of making corrective lenses more comfortable and easier to wear.

Nature of the work

Dispensing opticians must be familiar with the methods, materials, and operations employed in the optical industry. The tasks performed include making certain that the eyeglasses are made according to the optometrist's prescription specifications, determining exactly where the lenses should be placed in relation to the pupils of the eyes, assisting the customer in selecting appropriate frames, preparing work or-

170

ders for the optical laboratory mechanic, and sometimes selling optical goods.

The dispensing optician should be good both at working with people and with administrative tasks. The ability to do mechanical tasks, such as adjusting frames so that they fit a customer's face, is also important.

Interpersonal skills are important because the dispensing optician works with the customer in determining which type of frames is best suited to the person's needs. Considerations include the customer's habits, facial characteristics, and the thickness of the corrective lenses.

The dispensing optician prepares work orders for the ophthalmic laboratory so that the factory can grind the lenses and insert them in the frames. Information that the optician is responsible for recording on the work order includes lens prescriptions, the lens size, and the style and color of the frames.

After the lenses return from the lab, the dispensing optician is responsible for making sure the glasses fit the customers face. The optician will use small handtools and precision instruments to make minor adjustments to the frames. This requires steady hands and good hand-eye coordination.

Most dispensing opticians work with prescription eyeglasses, but some work with contact lenses. Dispensing opticians must exercise great precision, skill, and patience in fitting contact lenses. They must measure the curvature of the cornea, and then, following the optometrist's prescription, prepare complete specifications to be followed by the optical mechanic that will manufacture the lens. They must teach the customer how to remove, adjust to, and care for the lenses, a process that can take several weeks.

The dispensing optician offers a variety of eye wear to her customer.

Requirements

Although many dispensing opticians learn their skills on the job, in recent years there has been a trend toward a technical training program to provide the background necessary to be successful in this field. Employers prefer to hire graduates of two-year college programs in opticianry. These associated degree holders are able to advance more rapidly than those who simply complete an apprenticeship program. Two-year optician programs are offered at community colleges and trade schools, and include courses on mechanical optics, geometric optics, ophthalmic dispensing procedures, contact lens practice, and business concepts. The two-year program also includes courses in communications, mathematics, and laboratory work in grinding and polishing procedures.

Some dispensing opticians complete an apprenticeship program offered by optical dispensing companies. The program may be formal, such as in a large company, or informal, as is usually the case in smaller operations. These on-the-job programs include some of the same subjects as those covered in the two-year associate degree program, and may take two to four years to complete. Some specialized training programs may be offered by contact lens manufacturers and professional societies: These are generally shorter and usually cover a particular area of technical training, such as contact lens fitting.

A high-school degree is generally necessary to enter an apprenticeship or other training program. High-school courses should include algebra, geometry, and physics. In addition, mechanical drawing coursework is also helpful.

Persons interested in becoming a dispensing optician should have good finger dexterity and good eye-hand coordination.

Special requirements

More than twenty states currently require licensing of dispensing opticians. Licensing usually requires meeting certain educational standards and the ability to pass an oral and written examination. For more specific information on the licensing procedure, the licensing boards of the individual states should be consulted.

Professional credentials may also include voluntary certification. Certification is offered by the American Board of Opticianry and the National Contact Lens Examiners. Addresses for these two organizations can be found at the end of this article.

Some states may permit dispensing opticians to fit contact lenses, providing they have additional training.

Opportunities for experience and exploration

Part-time or summer employment in an optical shop is an excellent method of gaining an insight into the skills and temperament needed to excel in this field. A high-school student can also explore opportunities in the field through discussions with professionals already working as dispensing opticians.

Related occupations

Jewelers, tailors, watch repairers, and orthodontic technicians all perform work requiring good hand-eye coordination and finger dexterity. All these occupations also involve customer service as well.

Methods of entering

The usual ways of entry are either through completion of a two-year associate degree or though completion of an apprenticeship program.

Advancement

As dispensing opticians become more skilled, they usually advance to supervisory or managerial positions in a retail optical store or become sales representatives for manufacturers of eyeglasses or lenses. Some open their own stores. A few dispensing opticians, with additional college training, become optometrists. The amount of additional training a dispensing optician needs to become an optometrist depends on the individual's educational background.

Employment outlook

The increased demand for dispensing opticians began several years ago and is expected to continue into the future, with employment expected to grow much faster than the average through the early 1990s. The reasons for this increased demand include an increasingly aging population with a corresponding increase in the number of people who need corrective eyeglasses. (Middle age is a time that many people start using glasses for the first time.) The fact that good vision is being emphasized in the home, school, and work environments also has led to greater use of corrective lenses. Educational programs, such as vision screening programs, also have expanded the awareness of the general population to eye problems and thereby expanded the market for eyeglasses. Also, insurance programs are increasingly covering optical needs, meaning more clients can afford optical care.

Employment opportunities should be especially good in larger urban areas because of the greater number of retail optical stores. Those with an associate degree in opticianry should be most successful in their job search.

Earnings

Beginning salaries average between $15,000 and $20,000 per year for dispensing opticians just entering the field. Experienced workers can expect to make between $21,000 and $30,000, with the average about $24,500 per year. Supervisors earn about 20 percent more than skilled workers, depending on experience, skill, and responsibility. Dispensing opticians who own their own stores can expect to make considerable more. Apprentices usually start at about 60 percent of the skilled worker's rate.

Conditions of work

The majority of dispensing opticians work in retail shops or department showrooms. The work requires little physical exertion and is usually performed in a well-lighted, quiet environment. Customer contact is a big portion of the job. Some laboratory work may be required, especially if a dispensing optician works with a larger outfit that makes eyeglasses on the premises. The wearing of safety goggles and other precautions are necessary in a laboratory environment. Dispensing opticians should expect to work forty hours a week, although overtime is not unusual. They should be prepare to work evenings and weekends, especially if employed by a large retail establishment.

Social and psychological factors

Because the majority of the work entails customer service, a dispensing optician should be able to interact with a variety of people. Patience is important, as is the ability to advise people on decisions concerning eyewear. Dispensing opticians should be careful and accurate when adjusting frames and filling out work orders. They should be able to follow instructions and also display leadership abilities if they are left to manage the store, as sometimes occurs.

GOE: 05.05.11, 05.10.01; SIC: 5995; SOC: 449, 6864

National Academy of Opticianry
10111 Martin Luther King, Jr., Highway
Suite 112
Bowie, MD 20715

National Association of Optometrists and Opticians
18903 South Miles Road
Cleveland, OH 44128

Information on certification training programs, and financial aid is available from:

US Department of Health and Human Services
Public Health Service
Health Resources and Services
Bureau of Health Professions
Division of Student Assistance
Rockville, MD 20857

◇ **SOURCES OF ADDITIONAL INFORMATION**

General information about career opportunities is available from:

American Board of Opticianry
10341 Democracy Lane
Fairfax, VA 22030

◇ **RELATED ARTICLES**

Volume 1: Health Care
Volume 3: Optometrists; Opticians and optical mechanics
Volume 4: Ophthalmic laboratory technicians; Optics technicians; Optometric technicians

Dietitians

Definition

A *dietitian* assures the proper feeding of individuals and groups by planning meals with proper nutritional value for hospitals, institutions, schools, restaurants, or hotels and providing individuals with diet instructions. A dietitian also purchases food, equipment, and supplies. They may also be responsible for food preparation directly. This would require supervising chefs and other food service employees; and preparing various kinds of educational nutrition materials.

History

For most of history, little information has been available on how to prepare nutritionally sound meals. Families planned their meals on the basis of what they could afford and the need to introduce some variety in the diet occasionally. In the last fifty years, however, scientists have learned more about nutrition and its influence on health. Nutritional information has been disseminated widely, and food planning has become important in the home and in institutional life. Hospitals, schools, industrial plants,

Dieticians often inspect institutional food to ensure that the nutritional value meets government standards.

and other institutions turned to the new dietetics profession for aid.

In the late nineteenth century, hospital workers were employed to teach ways of preparing food for patients, and the field of dietetics actually came into existence as an outgrowth of this early hospital work. Although the medical profession had been aware of the value of nutrition in developing and maintaining good health, the dietitian's profession was slow to develop. The professional status of the dietitian has risen considerably during this century. The modern dietitian is trained to function in a number of specialized areas—hospital dietetics, research, teaching, writing, commercial food service, and school and college food service. In many ways the dietitian helps to promote health through nutrition.

Nature of the work

The dietitian's work may vary according to the chosen area of specialization. The dietitian, in general, is trained in the science of foods and nutrition and in food service management. Various careers branch out from this basic foundation. One of the best known is the field of hospital dietetics. Here the dietitian works as part of the hospital's professional staff, dedicated to promoting the health of patients. In large hospitals there are opportunities for further specialization: food administration, therapeutics, outpatient clinic work, teaching, and research.

The *administrative dietitian,* specifically trained in food administration or management, is responsible for the training and work of food service supervisors and other assistants as they prepare meals. This person, also known as the *chief dietitian,* helps to formulate policies of the department, enforces sanitary and safety regulations, prepares departmental budgets, and is in charge of buying food, equipment, and other supplies. This requires a sound understanding of purchasing techniques; menus must be planned on a large scale and with a view toward economy. The administrative dietitian tries to coordinate the work of the dietetic department with that of other departments in the hospital so that they may function effectively for the patient's welfare.

The *clinical dietitian,* sometimes called a *therapeutic dietitian,* plans and supervises the preparation of diets to meet the individual needs of patients for whom physicians have prescribed dietary requirements. This dietitian discusses each patient's needs not only with the physician and other members of the health-care team, but also with the patient and other family members, explaining the purpose of the diet, discussing likes and dislikes, and preparing the patient for carrying on the diet at home. The therapeutic dietitian works with the hospital administration concerning policies in planning diets.

The *community dietitian* is usually associated with a community health program sponsored by a public or private health or social service agency. The dietitian counsels individuals and groups on proper nutrition to maintain health and prevent diseases. Special diets are planned for expectant mothers, diabetics, persons who are overweight or recovering from an illness, the elderly, and others with special nutritional problems. Families are taught how to plan and prepare meals and how to shop for food wisely and economically.

Most dietitians do some teaching to explain their particular area of work to dietetic interns, nurses, and medical and dental students. Others teach on a full-time basis, usually in hospitals affiliated with medical centers. The *teaching dietitian* plans and teaches courses for the department of dietetics and supervises dietetic interns.

The *research dietitian* studies the nutritional needs of healthy and sick people. Research dietitians may specialize in how the body uses food, nutritional education, or food management. These specialists usually work in a hospital or university, and they need advanced training or education.

The dietitian in a small hospital may well function in all of the above-mentioned areas. Each may have one professional assistant, but must delegate much responsibility to food service supervisors and others with some training and experience in dietetics.

In a college with a home economics department, the dietitian may be a teacher as well as a food service manager. In the public schools, the dietitian must plan and supervise the preparation of food that is attractive to young people yet economical and nutritious. These school and college dietitians may also be asked to perform catering services for school functions.

Many dietitians work as *consultant dietitians* to food companies, schools, hospitals, restaurants, and other public and private establishments. Some business organizations may conduct research in nutrition; a dietitian may work in the home economics division of food, equipment, and utility companies. This work may consist of promoting a product—developing recipes, giving information on nutrition that is related to the company's product, maintaining experimental kitchens, and presenting radio and television programs. Administrative dietitians also work in commercial food service, restaurant management, and in industrial food service where plants maintain cafeterias for their employees.

As a college or university teacher the dietitian with advanced degrees has much to offer. Such a position may also provide an opportunity for research in foods and nutrition. With advanced training, a dietitian may specialize in foods and nutrition. Such dietitians often work for public health services or participate in nutrition research, which is considered increasingly important in new public health programs.

The armed forces and the U.S. Public Health Service offer many career opportunities for trained dietitians in administrative, therapeutic, teaching, and research areas. Many dietitians are employed by public schools, colleges, and universities. Their responsibilities are much like those of the hospital administrative dietitian.

Requirements

For those interested in dietetics as a career, a bachelor's degree, with a major in foods and nutrition or food service management, is necessary. Certain required courses have been recommended by the American Dietetic Association; usually undergraduate courses are required in foods and nutrition, food service management, chemistry, bacteriology, physiology, mathematics, psychology, sociology, and economics. The American Dietetic Association also recommends satisfactory completion of one year of dietetic internship in a program approved by the Association. (A dietetic internship is required for active membership in the

organization and for registration with the Commission on Dietetic Registration.) Students may enter hospital food service administration or a clinical internship and gain practical experience based on what has been learned during college. Special projects are also conducted. Many employers prefer to hire dietitians who have had this particular kind of internship experience.

Graduate work is necessary to teach in colleges and universities. There are about 270 colleges or universities offering master's degrees in nutrition. Some junior colleges and vocational schools offer training in dietetics, but this does not qualify one professionally. Usually such graduates can find positions as food service supervisors or other jobs requiring a certain amount of training.

The dietitian as a person must be able to get along with all types of people—physicians, administrators, patients, kitchen employees. One must have a good sense of business and an ability to work with details. The administrative dietitian must supervise employees and will need teaching ability and patience in instructing interns and informing patients of their dietetic needs. A person in this career should have an interest in science because all aspects of dietetics and nutrition are related to science. The dietitian, too, should like good food and have a knack for making it attractive and tasty. The dietitian's work is demanding and requires good health and emotional stability.

Special requirements

Most dietitians seeking success in the profession will gain greater professional status by meeting all requirements for membership in the American Dietetic Association and earning the credential Registered Dietitian (R.D.).

Opportunities for experience and exploration

If possible, the high-school student interested in dietetics should find part-time or summer employment in hospital kitchens, restaurants, or other food-related institutions. Here you can see dietitians in action, talk with them and learn as much as possible about the demands of the profession. Such a student should also undergo self-evaluation. A high-school homemaking course might help with this process, or even practice in running the kitchen at home. An interest in science is a must because many college courses in science are required of the dietetic major. The student can also take vocational interest tests to help measure interests and abilities and their relationship to a career in dietetics.

Related Occupations

Persons interested in nutrition and food service are also found in such occupations as consumer safety officers, food and home economists, food purchasing agents, food service managers, food technologists, health educators, hospital administrators, and public health biologists.

Methods of entering

Generally, the dietitian completes all educational requirements before looking for a job. This educational program includes a nine- to twelve-month dietetic internship where one can gain valuable on-the-job experience.

Most colleges and universities offer placement services for graduate dietitians. In some cases, the dietitian in charge of the internship may be able to assist in finding positions. A graduate dietitian might apply to the personnel departments of business organizations that hire dietitians.

Advancement

Once dietitians have gained experience they may be promoted to assistant or chief director of a dietary department, or manager of a restaurant. Dietitians employed through the government's civil service program advance on the basis of seniority and performance.

Dietitians interested in teaching or research generally must have graduate education to get high-level positions. A master's degree or doctorate will also hold more weight with employers in business, as will previous hospital or institutional experience.

Employment outlook

In the early 1990s, there were about 46,000 registered dietitians working in the United States. Approximately 60 percent of those employed worked in hospitals and other health care institutions, including the Department of Veter-

ans Affairs and the U.S. Public Health Service. Local government programs and school systems, colleges, and universities accounted for about 15 percent of the jobs. Other employers of dietitians included prison systems, hotels and restaurants, and companies that provided food service for their employees. Many dietitians worked as consultants, either full or part time.

A career in dietetics is expected to offer excellent employment opportunities throughout the 1990s. While hospitals, nursing homes, retirement communities, and social service programs have an expanding need for qualified dietitians, the number of dietitians completing internship is not sufficient even at the present time to meet this need. Research programs in food and nutrition will also require more experienced, qualified dietitians. Many vacancies will occur when experienced workers either stop working or transfer to other fields. Also, a number of dietitians are moving into management positions in private industry. Opportunities are expected to increase in colleges and universities, restaurant chains, catering companies, medical supply houses, and other businesses and industries.

Earnings

In the early 1990s, hospitals started recent graduates of approved internship programs at an annual salary of about $20,600. Graduates without internship training generally received lower starting salaries. Many dietitians with experience working in hospitals were paid more than $28,000 per year.

In the federal government, dietitians who had a bachelor's degree and had completed the internship started at approximately $18,700. Experienced dietitians working for the federal government in the early 1990s made an average of about $29,300.

In addition to salary, dietitians usually receive the customary benefits, such as paid vacations and holidays, sick leave, health insurance, and retirement plans.

Conditions of work

Variations exist in work conditions depending on where the dietitian works—large or small hospital, restaurant, school cafeteria—and depending also on the kind of dietetic work that is done—administrative, therapeutic, clinic. Work may be done in offices or kitchens and may include consulting with patients and hospital personnel. Generally, the dietitian works in pleasant surroundings—sanitary, well equipped, and ventilated.

Some hospitals provide accommodations for living in, offering room, board, and laundry service for a small fee. Such living conditions are optional. Most college dietitians no longer live in; one who is in charge of a residence hall food service is usually provided with an apartment. In other areas of dietetics, dietitians provide their own living quarters.

Dietitians commonly work a forty-hour week, although some hospital and restaurant dietitians have to work weekends and irregular hours. Staff dietitians usually take turns supervising on weekends and holidays. Dietitians usually have from two to four weeks of vacation each year after one year of service.

Social and psychological factors

The dietitian works closely with members of the medical team in a hospital, and has a great responsibility in promoting good health in patients. He or she can have a sense of achievement and of providing valuable information and care. Personal relationships are varied; the dietitian works with all types of people and must inspire their confidence and cooperation. The dietitian must also be able to communicate with the medical professionals and be responsible for personal work and that of the kitchen help. Disadvantages to be considered are the lengthy preparation required, the sometimes irregular hours, and a salary that is not always considered adequate in relation to the amount of educational and professional preparation and responsibility required. The dietitian working in a small hospital with little or no assistance may be under considerable pressure. Students who study the profession and who have examined their own interests and abilities, however, are prepared for any disadvantages and appreciate the personal rewards of the career.

GOE: 05.05.17, 02.02.04, 11.02.02, 11.05.02; SIC: 5812, 8049; SOC: 302

◇ **SOURCES OF ADDITIONAL INFORMATION**

The American Dietetic Association
216 West Jackson Boulevard, Suite 800
Chicago, IL 60606

American Institute of Nutrition
9650 Rockville Pike
Bethesda, Md 20814

◇ **RELATED ARTICLES**

Volume 1: Food Processing; Food Service; Health Care
Volume 2: Caterers; Chemists; Food technologists; Home economists; Restaurant and food service managers
Volume 4: Dietetic technicians

Drafters

Definition

The *drafter* prepares clear, complete, and accurate working plans and detail drawings from rough sketches, specifications, and calculations of engineers, architects, and designers to be used for engineering or manufacturing purposes according to the specified dimensions. The drafter utilizes knowledge of various machines, engineering practices, mathematics, building materials, and other physical sciences to complete the drawings.

History

Since ancient times, people have relied on drawings to communicate ideas. In fact, many times humans have been able to communicate

A drafter translates an engineer's rough sketches into working blueprints. The task requires concentration and precision.

their thoughts more adequately through drawings than through language. Even today many people find it much easier to give directions by drawing than by telling or writing. Many find it easier to assemble new equipment if the instructions include diagrams and drawings. In industry, drafting is the conversion of ideas from people's minds to precise working specifications from which products can be made.

The industrial world has come to rely on drafters to develop the working specifications from the new ideas and findings of those in the laboratories, shops, and factories of America.

Nature of the work

The drafter prepares detailed plans and specification drawings from the ideas, notes, or rough sketches of scientists, engineers, architects, and designers. Sometimes drawings are developed after visiting a project in the field or as the result of a discussion with one or more persons involved in the job. The drawings, which usually provide a number of different views of the object, must be exact and accurate. They vary greatly in size depending on the type of drawing. Some layout or assembly drawings are twenty-five to thirty feet long, while others are very small. They must contain enough detail, whatever their size, so that the part, object, or building can be constructed from it. Such drawings usually include information concern-

ing the quality of materials to be used, their cost, and the processes to be followed in carrying out the job. In developing their drawings made to scale of the object to be built (often called "layouts"), drafters, at their large, tilted drawing tables, use a variety of instruments, such as protractors, compasses, triangles, squares, drawing pens, and pencils.

Drafters are often classified according to the type of work they do or the level of responsibility. *Senior drafters* use the preliminary information and ideas provided by engineers and architects to make design layouts. They may have the title of *chief drafter* and assign work to other drafters and supervise their activities. *Detailers* make complete drawings, giving dimensions, material, and any other necessary information of each part shown on the layout. *Checkers* carefully examine drawings to check for errors in computing or in recording dimensions and specifications. *Tracers*, who are usually assistant drafters, make corrections and prepare drawings for reproduction by tracing them on transparent cloth, paper, or plastic film.

Drafters may also specialize in a particular field of work, such as mechanical, electrical, electronic, aeronautical, structural, or architectural drafting.

Although the nature of the work of drafters is not too different from one specialization to another, there is a considerable variation in the type of object with which they deal. Thus, within this career field workers may focus on and apply some of their own special interests. For example:

Commercial drafters do all-around drafting, such as plans for building sites, layouts of offices and factories, and drawings of charts, forms, and records. *Computer-assisted drafters* use computers to make drawings and layouts for such fields as aeronautics, architecture, or electronics.

Civil drafters make construction drawings for roads and highways, river and harbor improvements, flood control, drainage, and other civil engineering projects. *Structural drafters* draw plans for bridge trusses, plate girders, roof trusses, trestle bridges, and other structures that use structural reinforcing steel, concrete, masonry, and other structural materials.

Cartographic drafters prepare maps of geographical areas to show natural and constructed features, political boundaries, and other features. *Topographical drafters* draft and correct maps from original sources, such as other maps, surveying notes, and aerial photographs. (*See also* the article titled "Cartographers" elsewhere in this volume.)

Architectural drafters draw plans of buildings, including artistic and structural features. *Landscape drafters* make detailed drawings from sketches furnished by landscape architects.

Heating and ventilating drafters draft plans for heating, air-conditioning, ventilating, and sometimes refrigeration equipment. *Plumbing drafters* draw diagrams for the installation of plumbing equipment.

Mechanical drafters make working drawings of machinery, automobiles, power plants, or any mechanical device. *Castings drafters* prepare detailed drawings of castings, which are objects formed in a mold. *Tool design drafters* draft manufacturing plans for all kinds of tools. *Patent drafters* make drawings of mechanical devices for use by lawyers to obtain patent rights for their clients.

Electrical drafters make schematics and wiring diagrams to be used by construction crews working on equipment and wiring in power plants, communications centers, buildings, or electrical distribution systems.

Electronics drafters draw schematics and wiring diagrams for television cameras and TV sets, radio transmitters and receivers, computers, radiation detectors, and other electronic equipment.

Electromechanisms design drafters draft designs of electromechanical equipment such as aircraft engines, data processing systems, gyroscopes, automatic materials handling and processing machinery, or biomedical equipment. *Electromechanical drafters* draw wiring diagrams, layouts, and mechanical details for the electrical components and systems of a mechanical process or device.

Aeronautical drafters prepare engineering drawings for planes, missiles, and spacecraft. *Automotive design drafters* and *automotive design layout drafters* both turn out working layouts and master drawings of components, assemblies, and systems of automobiles and other vehicles, but automotive design drafters make original designs from specifications, whereas automotive design layout drafters make drawings based on prior layouts or sketches.

Marine drafters draft the structural and mechanical features of ships, docks, and marine buildings and equipment. Projects range from petroleum drilling platforms to nuclear submarines.

Geological drafters make diagrams and maps of geological formations and locations of mineral, oil, gas deposits. *Geophysical drafters* draw maps and diagrams based on data from petroleum prospecting instruments such as seismographs, gravity meters, and magnetometers. *Directional survey drafters* plot boreholes for oil and gas wells. *Oil and gas drafters* draft plans for the construction and operation of oil fields, refineries, and pipeline systems.

A design team working on electrical or gas power plants and substations may be headed up by a *chief design drafter*, who oversees architectural, electrical, mechanical, and structural drafters. *Estimators and drafters* draw specifications and instructions for installing voltage transformers, cables, and other electrical equipment that delivers electric power to consumers.

Requirements

Drafting is a career that relies heavily on one's education. In high school it is especially important to elect science and mathematics courses, mechanical drawing (minimum of one to two years) and wood, metal, or electric shop. If they are not offered at school, a community college or training college may offer non-degree classes as well as college level courses. Most high-school students will find it possible to take English, social studies, science, mathematics, and one or more of these specialized courses each year.

Training beyond high school is possible through apprenticeship, junior college, or technical institute programs. Apprenticeship programs usually run three to four years. During this period, the apprentice works on the job and is required to take related classroom work in theory and practice. Information about apprenticeship programs can be obtained from a school counselor, a mechanical drawing or shop instructor, or from the local, state, or national apprenticeship training representatives.

A number of two year colleges and technical institutes offer drafting programs. Preparation beyond high school in the physical sciences, mathematics, drawing, sketching and drafting techniques, and in other technical or applied subject areas, is essential for certain types of beginning positions and for advancement to positions of greater salary and more responsibility.

Students interested in drafting should have a good sense of space perception (ability to visualize objects in two or three dimensions); form perception (ability to compare and to discriminate between shapes, lines, and forms and shadings); and coordinated eye-finger-hand movements.

They should also appraise their preference for situations dealing with things or objects; their interest in things scientific, technical, or mechanical in nature; and their preference for activities of an abstract or creative nature.

Special requirements

No specific licensure or related requirements are necessary to work in this field.

Opportunities for experience and exploration

The high-school program provides several opportunities for experiences in which one can explore an interest in and abilities for a career in drafting. Mechanical drawing is a good course to elect if one wants to explore some of the possibilities in this field and actually engage in some typical work routines and assignments. Many of the abilities and personal characteristics that are considered important in drafting can be tested here in the day-to-day performance of class and outside preparations.

Certain hobby or leisure time activities that require the preparation of drawings or use of blueprints (woodworking, building models, repairing or remodeling projects) and school or community organizations that offer experiences in different situations and tasks can be meaningful avenues of exploration. After the completion of one or two courses in mechanical drawing it may be possible to locate a part-time or summer job with the opportunity to work with or near drafters. Opportunities to observe drafters at work, to talk with them about their responsibilities, and to listen as they discuss various aspects of their work can be arranged.

Related occupations

Drafters must be able to understand and prepare detailed drawings and to make accurate and precise calculations and measurements. Other workers who require similar skills include architects, engineering technicians, engineers, landscape architects, photogrammetrists, and surveyors.

Methods of entering

Those who prepare for drafting by pursuing a post–high-school program in a technical institute or junior college can receive assistance in securing positions upon graduation through the placement office or by personal recommendation of the faculty. Applicants for government positions may need to take a civil service

examination. If one is planning to enter drafting in an apprenticeship program, it is helpful to seek additional information and assistance through local or regional apprenticeship council offices, employers, or union officials.

Advancement

Beginning or inexperienced drafters often start as tracers. Students with some formal post–high-school technical training often qualify for positions as junior drafters who revise detail drawings and gradually assume assignments of a more complex drawing nature. With additional experience and skill, advancement may follow to positions as checkers, detailers, or senior drafters. The design drafter has perhaps the most creative of all possible positions in drafting. Practically all of the work of the designer results from close working relationships with engineers and scientists, either in the development of an idea or in the preparation of preliminary "on the board" layout designs. Movement from one to another of these job classifications is not necessarily restricted because each business must modify its work assignments to the skills and experience of those in its employ. In general, however, these levels of responsibility and skill are the guidelines to progress and promotion.

Drafters often move into related positions. Some typical positions include those of technical report writers, sales engineers, engineering assistants, production foremen, and installation technicians.

Employment outlook

In the early 1990s, more than 348,000 drafters were employed in business, industry, and government positions. About one-third worked for engineering and architectural companies, and another third worked for manufacturers of machinery, electrical equipment, fabricated metals, and other durable goods. Other industries that employed drafters included construction, communications, transportation, and utilities. More than 13,000 drafters worked for government agencies, most of them at the state and local level. The majority of the federal government drafters worked for the Department of Defense.

Little or no growth is anticipated in the employment of drafters through the end of the 1990s, despite the anticipated expansion of technological and scientific processes. New products and processes of more complex design will call for more drafting services, as will the general growth of industry. However, the increased use of computer-aided design (CAD) systems is expected to offset some of the demand, particularly for lower-level drafters who do routine work. On the other hand, CAD equipment can produce more and better variations of a design, which could stimulate additional activity in the field and create opportunities for drafters who are willing to switch to the new techniques. In addition, vacancies will have to be filled as older, experienced drafters retire or change occupations.

Employment trends for drafters fluctuate with the economy. In the event of a recession, fewer buildings and manufactured products are designed, which could reduce the need for drafters in architectural, engineering, and manufacturing firms.

Earnings

In private industry, the general salary average for beginning drafters was about $18,000 a year in the early 1990s. Experienced drafters earned from $22,000 to $29,000 per year, depending upon the nature of their position and the responsibility involved. Those whose preparation qualified them for positions as senior drafters had salaries averaging $32,000.

Conditions of work

The drafter usually works in a well-lighted, air-conditioned, quiet room. This may be a central drafting room where drafters work side by side. Some drafters are attached to an individual department (engineering, research, development) where they work alone or more closely with one or two other drafters and with engineers, designers or scientists. Occasionally, depending upon the nature of the current assignment, drafters may need to visit other departments or construction sites to consult with engineers or to gain first-hand information. Because the work is generally not seasonal or subject to particular busy periods, most drafters work a forty-hour week with little overtime required. Drafters work at drawing tables for long periods of time at arrangements that require undivided concentration, close eyework, and very precise and accurate computations and drawings. There is generally little pressure, but occasionally last-minute design changes, or a rush order, may necessitate a deadline.

Social and psychological factors

Although drafters may be very busy with their own drawings, they are always part of a team in that their efforts are coordinated with those of other drafters, scientists and engineers. In this sense, then, drafters can find some satisfactions, both in the preciseness and accuracy of the work and in the completion of the total project to which they have contributed. The prospective drafter must be alert to the routine, demanding, and sometimes lonely aspects of the work, yet willing to accept a share of the responsibility through the constructive suggestions offered by colleagues and superiors.

Although the beginning years of copy drawing, revising, and other more or less routine tasks, may tend to become monotonous or cause a certain amount of unrest or dissatisfaction, the person who can use these years to establish a reputation in the field can look forward to additional creative outlets and greater responsibilities for these specialized talents.

GOE: 05.03.02; SIC: 871; SOC: 372

◇ SOURCES OF ADDITIONAL INFORMATION

American Institute for Design and Drafting
966 Hungerford Drive, Suite 10-B
Rockville, MD 20854

International Federation of Professional and Technical Engineers
8701 Georgia Avenue, Suite 701
Silver Spring, MD 20910

National Association of Trade and Technical Schools
2251 Wisconisn Avenue, NW
Washington, DC 20007

◇ RELATED ARTICLES

Volume 1: Automotives; Aviation and Aerospace; Construction; Design; Electronics; Engineering; Plastics; Rubber
Volume 2: Architects; Cartographers; Engineers; Industrial designers
Volume 4: CAD/CAM technicians; Drafting and design technicians

Economists

Definition

An *economist* is concerned with the solution of economic problems arising from the production and distribution of goods and services in such areas as the utilization of natural resources, manpower, and manufactured products. The economist compiles, processes, and interprets economic and statistical data.

History

Economics, as a career field, is relatively new although people have always been concerned with the economic aspects of our existence. Each civilization has had to deal with problems concerning the production and distribution of its goods. In fact, civil wars and international wars have been waged as a result of issues relative to trade and commerce, taxation, and the need for use of natural resources. As humans have become more interdependent and as nations have become more complex in their structure, the need to collect, analyze, and report on information that might be helpful in working toward solutions to these problems has been emphasized. In the United States, we have always had economists, and the study of economics has long been recognized. The need for these specialists in business and industry, and in greater numbers in government, to study more intensively and scientifically the problems of the nation's economy is, however, primarily a development of the twentieth century.

Nature of the work

The economist is concerned with a variety of problems, most of which, in one way or another, are related to the supply and demand for goods and services and the means by which these goods are produced, traded, and consumed.

Economists are employed in a variety of work settings, but the majority are engaged in college and university teaching and research or as researchers in government agencies. College professors teach courses in economics, such as principles of economics, business cycles, history of economic thought, and labor economics. In addition to their classroom teaching, they also engage in writing, research, speaking, and consulting activities. They contribute to the formulation of new ideas and economic theory and research the theoretical and practical economic problems of the times. Government economists deal with the development and conduct of studies that collect information on various problem areas. Their data is used to study further possible changes in the economic policies of the government and to assess the economic conditions of the country. This data is generally published in government bulletins and reports. Some economists are also employed in nonprofit research organizations.

Economists are also employed by business and industrial firms. In such positions they concentrate on studying company policy in relation to general business conditions, national and international trade policies, and governmental regulations and policies. The results of their information are used by company management in making decisions about company policies and concerns and for planning the future activities of the business.

Because of the ever-expanding fund of economic knowledge, economists tend to specialize in one specific area. Examples of such specialization are noted below.

Agricultural economists study economic aspects of agricultural problems pertaining to exploitation of rural resources and production and marketing of farm products. Their study leads to increased efficiency of farm management, improved farm income, and favorable agricultural legislation. They forecast production and consumption of agricultural products; locate optimum markets; and recommend improvements in agricultural financing.

Financial economists study the nature of and the relationships between the quantity of money, credit, and purchasing power to develop monetary policies and to forecast financial activity. They investigate credit structures and collection methods to improve them. They examine banking methods and procedures to devise techniques for regulation of lending and fixing interest and discount rates, and they may recommend or establish domestic and international monetary policies.

International economists collect and analyze statistical data and other information on foreign trade to effect favorable trade balances and to establish acceptable international trade policies. They are deeply concerned with the underlying reasons for trade controls and barriers such as tariffs and cartels. They also study exchange controls and the operation of foreign exchanges to formulate policies on investments and transfer of capital.

Labor economists attempt to forecast labor trends and recommend or establish labor policies on such subjects as labor legislation, social insurance, industrial accident provisions, and similar regulations. They study the operation of labor unions and industrial policies of management and may be called upon to devise techniques for settling labor disputes. They may also act as an adviser or consultant to government agencies, business, or industrial organizations.

Industrial economists study the organizational structures of business concerns in relation to production and marketing of goods and services to make maximum use of assets and to develop desirable markets. They investigate methods of financing; production costs and techniques; and marketing policies to discover possible improvements. They analyze market trends to relate production to future consumption and interpret effects of government regulations and legal restrictions on industrial policies.

Requirements

A bachelor's degree with a major in economics is considered the minimum preparation for a beginning or entry job as an economist. Such positions usually involve research activity with an emphasis on the collection and treatment of study data. In beginning government positions, the candidate must have completed at least twenty-one semester hours in economics (economic theory, history, methods, and analysis) and three hours of statistics, accounting, or calculus. A master's degree or doctorate in economics is required for teaching positions in colleges and universities. Those who wish to advance to positions in government or industry involving more research opportunity and greater responsibility should plan additional graduate study beyond the bachelor's degree.

The high-school student should plan to take a college preparatory program, being certain to include as much mathematics as possible, as well as any elective or advanced placement courses in the social sciences.

Among the personal attributes that are desirable for success in the field are dependability, accuracy, patience, and objectivity. An applicant should also have above-average ability, a real desire to learn, a willingness to study, and an interest in activities of a scientific or

Many economists teach at universities on the graduate and undergraduate level. In addition to teaching, they often working as consultants on a free-lance basis.

technical nature and in activities of an abstract and creative nature. An economist must be able to analyze and interpret data, reason abstractly and solve problems, and express ideas in speech and in writing.

Special requirements

No specific licensure or related requirements are necessary to gain admission to the field or to obtain the right to be an economist. Membership in professional associations is voluntary, and most economists choose to join one or more of these associations as a means of keeping abreast of changes and trends in the field.

Opportunities for experience and exploration

High-school students can explore their interests and abilities in economics by studying topics in social studies related to economics and mathematics. The college student will find a number of extracurricular activities available that might be useful for exploratory purposes. Actual work opportunities in economics are limited; however, students should be alert to summer and part-time employment opportunities with business or industrial firms and in the field of agriculture.

Related occupations

The ability to understand and interpret financial matters may be applied to the work of accountants and auditors, actuaries, budget officers, credit analysts, financial analysts, financial managers, loan officers, securities and financial services sales workers, and underwriters.

Methods of entering

The college graduate may find the college placement office and professors of great help in contacting potential employers. The bulletins of the various professional associations in economics are sources of job opportunities for the beginning economist. Those electing to pursue graduate study can secure assistance from their college adviser or in the college counseling center.

Each year the federal government has a number of beginning positions for economists. Applicants who can meet the stated qualifications, such as age, training, and experience, can arrange to take the civil service examination that is usually required. The person seeking a job should watch for federal and state government announcements concerning open positions.

Advancement

An economist's advancement is dependent on such factors as amount and type of training, experience, personal interest, and drive. Promotion to jobs requiring more skill and competency is available in all specialized areas. Such jobs are characterized by more administrative, research, or advisory responsibilities and, consequently, promotions are governed to a great extent by personal evaluation of job performance in the beginning or primary fields of work.

Employment outlook

In the early 1990s, about 37,000 economists were employed in private industry and government, and another 22,000 held faculty positions in economics or marketing at colleges and universities. Most of those in private industry worked in economic and market research, management consulting, banking, securities and investments, advertising, and insurance. Most of the economists in government were employed at the federal level, primarily in the Departments of Agriculture, Labor, and State. In addition, about 20 percent of all economists owned their own consulting firms.

The overall demand for economists is expected to increase rapidly through the end of the 1990s. The greatest growth will be evident in business, with little or no change in federal, state and local government and a decline in the employment of economists in colleges and universities.

Private industry will employ more economists as businesses become more accustomed to relying on scientific methods of analyzing business trends, forecasting sales, and planning purchases and production schedules. The best opportunities appear to be in manufacturing, financial services, advertising, research, and consulting. A number of jobs will be created to satisfy the continued need for economic analyses by lawyers, accountants, engineers, health service administrators, urban and regional planners, environmental scientists, and others.

Because of declining college enrollments, economists with master's degrees and doctorates will face strong competition in the academic field but may find good jobs in business, especially if they are skilled in quantitative techniques and their application to economic modeling and forecasting and market research, including the use of computers. Persons having only a bachelor's degree may experience great difficulty finding employment as economists but may obtain jobs as management or sales trainees or as research or administrative assistants.

The largest concentration of jobs for economists can be found in large cities, especially in New York and Washington, D.C. American economists are also employed in foreign countries by international companies and organizations and by U.S. government agencies.

Earnings

In the early 1990s, the average starting salary for economists with a bachelor's degree was about $22,400 a year. The median annual earnings for all full-time economists was $36,600. Salaries were highest for economists in general administration and international economics, and lowest for those in market research and econometrics.

During the same period, business economists had a median base salary of $54,000 a year. The highest-paying businesses were securities and investment, retail and wholesale trade, and insurance; the lowest-paying were education, nonprofit research, and real estate.

Federal government positions for beginning economists with a bachelor's degree started at approximately $14,800 to $18,400, depending upon their academic records. Candidates with a master's degree started at approximately $22,500; with a doctorate, at $27,200 to $32,600, depending on their qualifications. The average salary of experienced economists in federal government positions was about $40,700.

Conditions of work

The economist generally has pleasant working conditions. The work, for the most part, is accomplished in an office or classroom.

The average workweek of most economists is forty hours, particularly for those employed in governmental or business positions. The number of hours per day, holiday and vacation leave, health and pension benefits are similar to those of workers in other organizations.

Social and psychological factors

Careers in economics offer many opportunities and are sufficiently varied to enable the potential employee to locate positions that will provide the work environment and work tasks necessary to the individual's feeling of satisfaction and accomplishment.

Basic to all positions is an understanding of and an ability to work with other people. Yet, in research one can find opportunities where this contact is minimal. Many positions provide an opportunity for the economist to achieve the

prestige and esteem of fellow employees, because he or she may be responsible for the collection, analysis, and interpretation of data upon which future administrative policy and action may be based. Economists must be ready to assume this responsibility; senior staff economists must be able to engender this sense of responsibility in the staff.

GOE: 11.03.05; SIC: 8732, 8733, 8748; SOC: 1912

 ◇ **SOURCES OF ADDITIONAL INFORMATION**

American Economic Association
1313 21st Avenue, South
Nashville, TN 37212

Joint Council on Economic Education
432 Park Avenue South
New York, NY 10016

National Association of Business Economists
28790 Chagrin Boulevard, Suite 300
Cleveland, OH 44122

◇ **RELATED ARTICLES**

Volume 1: Automotives; Banking and Financial Services; Civil Service; Education; Foreign Service; Foreign Trade; Law; Marketing
Volume 2: College and university faculty

Employment counselors

Definition

Employment counselors, also known as *vocational counselors*, provide educational and vocational guidance services to both individuals and groups. They assess their clients' interests and skills and help them obtain suitable employ-

ment. Employment counselors may advise clients about study and training programs. Clients may be recent graduates, professionals wishing to change jobs or careers, or displaced executives looking to continue their career path, or some other person wishing to enter or re-enter the job market.

History

At one time people could live their whole lives never venturing more than a few miles from where they were born. Parents, grandparents, generations of the same families would be born, live, and die in the same locality. People made their livelihood off the land on which they lived and often pooled their labor and shared their skills with one another. For some, this way of life was not enough. They wanted a better life or a different one. The land might no longer be able to support the number of people living on it. A specialized skill might not be in great enough demand to support the number of persons able to provide it.

The history of emigration to America is the story of millions of people seeking a new life and a place to use their skills. For many the skills needed in the growing industrialized society had to be learned and specialization of skills increased as new needs of a growing population had to be met. New jobs and occupations came into being. Not only did workers have to learn how to perform these and to train others to perform them, but also individuals to find those workers were needed.

Around the turn of the twentieth century, public interest in changing and improving social and educational conditions began to develop. Probably the single most influential undertaking was Hull House in Chicago, founded by Jane Addams to improve the living conditions of the people in the surrounding slum area. Similar settlement houses followed in other large cities.

One such center, the Civic Service House in Boston, began the United States' first program of vocational guidance. A Vocational Bureau, advocated by Frank Parsons, was established there in 1908, to help young people choose, train for, and enter appropriate careers.

The idea of vocational counseling had become so appealing that by 1910 enough people were interested in it that a national conference on vocational guidance could be held in Boston. Three years later, the National Guidance Association was organized, and in 1915, the journal that would become the *Vocational Guidance Quarterly* was started.

The federal government gave support to vocational counseling by initiating a program to assist veterans of World War I in readjusting to civilian life.

During the depression years, agencies such as the Civilian Conservation Corps and the National Youth Administration made an attempt at vocational counseling. The N.Y.A. formulated policies that were designed to guide its personnel in their efforts to assist young people in making suitable career choices. Nevertheless, lack of trained personnel and of leadership in organizing guidance services curtailed the effectiveness of this attempt.

On June 6, 1933, the Wagner-Pyser Act established the United States Employment Service. Adequate provisions were made for training and staffing the program, and it has proven to be a highly effective one. The Act provided for the states to come into the program, each on a voluntary basis. States came into the Service one by one, each state developing its own plan under the prescribed limits of the Act.

The Department of Veterans Affairs, too, has provided employment counseling programs for former service personnel. Vocational guidance was initiated in 1943. By the end of World War II, the Veterans Administration was counseling more than 50,000 veterans each month. Other state and federal government agencies involved with vocational guidance services are: the Bureau of Indian Affairs, the Bureau of Apprenticeship and Training, the Office of Manpower Development, and the Department of Education.

The profession of employment counseling has become important to the welfare of society as well as the individuals within it. Each year thousands of people need help to acquire the kinds of information that make it possible for them to avoid career pitfalls and take advantage of career opportunities.

Nature of the work

The employment counselor works with people of all ages and of all educational backgrounds—school dropouts, high-school and college graduates, and professional people. Every day the counselor deals with persons from all socioeconomic levels, of all races, both sexes, and of many different political and religious beliefs. In the case of *vocational-rehabilitation counselors*, who work with handicapped individuals, they must additionally take into account their clients' physical limitations. (*See also* the article titled "Rehabilitation counselors" elsewhere in this volume.)

In their work, educational counselors perform many services. They establish a friendly relationship with the people whom they are advising. The counselor tries to discover just what kind of help the counselee expects to receive, and helps the counselee to understand just what the counselor is prepared and able to do for the counselee. The counselor will talk to counselees in an attempt to gain some insights into their personality and into the way they approach and try to solve the problems that face them, and endeavors to learn something of counselees' interests. Counselors also try to discover what skills the counselees believe they have, and what skills they think may need strengthening. A counselor may help the counselee to complete a form that sets forth such vital data as name, place of residence, age, educational background, work history, and other information that the counselor must have to help these people deal with their problems.

The counselor may also administer some tests, such as standardized achievement and aptitude tests, which help to understand the counselee.

Vocational counselors must have several kinds of competency and must recognize the fact that they carry many serious responsibilities. One of the responsibilities is to the counselees themselves. Most important in the relationship between counselor and counselees is the counselor's competence in helping the counselees come to understand themselves. Counselees must see themselves as potential employees and know what skills they have to offer to an employer, or what skills they may have the potentiality for developing. Because some persons have unrealistic ideas of what they may be able to do to earn a living, helping counselees to see themselves clearly is a crucial part of the counselor's responsibility.

Another of the competencies that the counselor must have is a thorough knowledge and understanding of the world of work. The counselor must know the "job families" and must have a sure knowledge of the ways in which one can obtain detailed information about the specific jobs in those "families." To assist a counselee with career decisions, the counselor must know about the availability of jobs, the probable future of certain jobs, the education or training necessary to enter them, the kinds of salary or other benefits that certain jobs offer, the conditions that certain jobs impose on employees (night work, travel, work outdoors), and the satisfactions that certain jobs provide their employees.

Vocational and educational counselors must also be competent to work with employers. Employers will come to trust their judgment about the choice of applicants whom they refer. Counselors should know the job well enough and the counselee well enough to be reasonably sure that the right recommendation is being made.

Counselors must also recognize their responsibility to society as they attempt to help persons choose, train for, and enter into appro-

Personnel workers spend much of their time interviewing prospective employees.

priate vocations. Dissatisfaction and disappointment in a career can lead to absenteeism, job-hopping, low-level performance, or even to alcoholism. The "right person in the right job" contributes to stable employment and to stable family and community life.

The vocational counselor may work with the counselee for a brief period of time or for many months or years. The time factor depends upon the nature of the problem and the personality of the person.

Counselors never attempt to tell counselees what they must do. Their function is to help counselees decide for themselves the wisest course of action.

An extremely important part of employment counseling and placement is meticulous record keeping. The follow-up of successfully placed applicants and satisfied employers is one aspect of the need for detailed records. The records should convey to a new counselor an exact profile of the work that has been undertaken with a particular client. High ethical standards of strictest confidentiality between the client and all staff involved in counseling and placement must be kept at all times.

Requirements

Entry requirements for employment and placement counselors are far from uniform. Some states require a master's degree in counseling or a related field. The majority of counselors in state agencies, however, have a bachelor's degree plus additional courses in guidance and counseling. Experience in counseling, interviewing, and job placement also may be required, particularly in the case of those without advanced degrees.

Most private agencies prefer, and some require, a master's degree in vocational counseling or in a related field such as psychology, personnel administration, counseling, guidance education, or public administration. Many private agencies prefer to have at least one staff member who has a doctorate in counseling psychology or another advanced degree. For those lacking an advanced degree, employers usually emphasize experience in closely related work such as rehabilitation counseling, employment interviewing, school or college counseling, teaching, social work, or psychology.

There is usually an initial period of training for newly hired counselors or counselor trainees. In addition, both new and experienced counselors often enroll for training at colleges and universities during the regular school year or at institutes or summer sessions. Private and community agencies often provide in-service training opportunities.

Individuals interested in this field should include broad college preparatory work in their high-school program. Computer science would be a valuable tool because much record keeping is computerized. Coursework in college should emphasize psychology and sociology. Graduate level courses include techniques of counseling, psychology of careers, assessment and appraisal, cultures and environment, and occupational information. Counselor education programs at the graduate level are available in nearly 500 colleges and universities, mainly in departments of education and psychology. To obtain a master's degree, students must complete one to two years of graduate study including actual supervised experience in counseling.

Special requirements

The requirements of private and community agencies vary greatly with regard to education and experience. The federal and state employment services require in addition to educational minimums that counselors in public employ-

ment offices meet civil service or merit system requirements.

Opportunities for experience and exploration

Summer employment in an employment agency would be a good way to explore the field of employment counseling. Interviewing the director of a public or private agency would give an understanding of what the work involves and the qualifications such an organization requires of its counselors.

The high-school student who enjoys working with others will find helpful experiences in working in the dean's or counselor's office. A student's own experience in seeking summer and part-time work is also valuable in learning what the job seeker must confront in business or industry.

Related occupations

Various types of counselors and other workers help people evaluate their interests, abilities, and disabilities and offer them guidance in dealing with career, academic, and social problems. They include college and student personnel workers, equal employment opportunity/ affirmative action specialists, members of the clergy, occupational and physical therapists, personnel workers and managers, psychiatrists, psychologists, social workers, teachers, and training and employee development specialists.

Methods of entering

Academic qualifications are very important for entering employment counseling. The testing procedures and interviewing skills can only be acquired through training. Qualified college graduates who wish to become vocational counselors should seek information about the necessary examinations. If one wishes to enter a public vocational or employment service, one should write to the director of that service to learn what sort of qualifying examination is given, and when and where it is administered. If the position requires the taking of a civil service examination, one may learn from the local postmaster the name and address of the nearest civil service examiner or one may write to the

Office of Personnel Management in Washington, D.C.

If prospective vocational counselors wish to be employed in a private agency, industry, or labor union, they should get in touch with the personnel officer in the concern in which they hope to work.

The placement office of the graduate's own college or university may have lists of vacancies for vocational counselors. The director of this office will know how one can apply for vacant positions.

The American Association for Counseling and Development regularly issues a Placement Service Bulletin for its members.

Advancement

New employees in federal–state employment services, or other publicly supported vocational counseling agencies or departments, are usually considered trainees for the first six months of their employment. During this time, they learn the specific skills that will be expected of them during their career with the agency. The first year of employment is probationary.

Positions of responsibility may be attained by counselors after several years of experience on the job, if they have an interest in and talent for supervisory or administrative work. Advancement to administrative positions often means giving up the actual counseling work, which may not be a pleasing prospect to those who enjoy working with counselees.

Experienced counselors may advance to supervisory or administrative positions as directors of agencies or supervisors of guidance. Some move into research, consulting work, or college teaching. Others go into private practice and set up their own counseling agencies.

Employment outlook

There should be average growth in employment in this field through the 1990s, although most job openings will result from having to replace counselors who retire, change occupations, or leave the field for other reasons. Although only moderate opportunities are anticipated for employment and rehabilitation counselors in state and local governments, rapid growth is expected in the development of human resource and employment assistance programs in private business and industry, which should produce more jobs.

In the early 1990s, some 4,000 persons held positions in public employment offices as employment counselors or counseling supervisors. Several hundred other workers, although not classified as employment counselors, were engaged in counseling activities in these offices. In addition, several thousand placement and employment counselors worked for various private or community agencies, primarily in large cities. Some worked in institutions such as prisons, training schools for delinquent youths, and mental hospitals.

Earnings

Salaries of employment counselors in state employment offices vary considerably from state to state. The average minimum salary in the early 1990s was about $15,700 and the average maximum salary was about $21,400 a year. Earnings in private industry are generally higher. Counselors generally receive benefits such as vacations, sick leave, pension plans, and insurance coverage.

Conditions of work

Employment counselors usually work about forty hours a week, but in some agencies this is done on a flexible schedule with evening appointments made with clients who work during the day.

Counseling is done in offices and though working space is often limited, privacy has been recognized as a critical factor in the counseling process. Most offices are designed to be free from noise and distractions to allow confidential discussions with clients.

Social and psychological factors

Employment counselors help people evaluate their interests, abilities, and attitudes toward work and assist them in finding the job that best suits them. A person's work occupies the greatest part of his or her waking life and counselors need to be respectfully aware of the importance of their work in the life of other people. The counselor must also have fair judgment of the potential of clients to guide them realistically. The counselor's own ego strength is important during those times when they can not succeed in helping a client.

Persons aspiring to be employment counselors should have a strong interest in helping others make and carry out vocational decisions. They should be able to work independently, keep detailed records, and maintain a high standard of ethics and confidentiality.

GOE: 10.01.02; SIC: 8299; SOC: 24

National Council on Rehabilitation Education
1200 Commercial
Emporia State University
VH 336
Emporia, KS 66801

◇ **SOURCES OF ADDITIONAL INFORMATION**

American Association for Counseling and Development
5999 Stevenson Avenue
Alexandria, VA 22304

National Career Development Association
5999 Stevenson Avenue
Alexandria, VA 22304

◇ **RELATED ARTICLES**

Volume 1: Education; Human Resources; Social Sciences; Teaching
Volume 2: Career counselors; College career planning and placement officers; Employment firm workers; Guidance counselors; Human services workers
Volume 3: Correction officers

Employment firm workers

Definition

Employment firm workers act as intermediaries in the employment process by helping people find jobs and helping employers fill vacancies. They assist job seekers by assessing their interests and skills and helping them obtain suitable employment. They assist employers by recruiting qualified personnel for existing positions.

History

The success of any business depends on the quality of its employees, and, therefore, the matching of job seekers with appropriate jobs is an important function in our economy. This "matchmaking" process has been going on a long time, with both governmental agencies and private firms trying to place qualified people in jobs that match their interests and abilities.

The first employment firms in the United States were private establishments, but state governments were quick to join in the effort in the mid-1800s with agencies in New York, Massachusetts, and several other states. The federal government became involved in helping job seekers find work in the early 1900s and increased its efforts dramatically in the 1930s as a result of the millions of workers left jobless because of the Great Depression. The U.S. Employment Service was established in 1933 and agencies like the Civilian Conservation Corps and the National Youth Administration also made an effort in job placement and vocational counseling.

As the economy has continued to expand each year, thousands of workers have turned to employment firms to help them find appropriate jobs. Large and small businesses have also turned to employment firms for assistance in finding qualified applicants. This has led to a demand for skilled employment firm workers.

Nature of the work

Specific job responsibilities depend on the job title within the employment firm worker field.

Personnel recruiters seek out and recruit qualified applicants for existing job openings with companies. They maintain contacts within the local business community and may travel extensively to seek out qualified applicants. After interviewing applicants, recruiters recommend those most qualified to fill positions with the appropriate company. To aid in the analysis of the applicants, recruiters may arrange skills tests, evaluate the applicant's work history, and check personal references. Much of this work is done by phone or through computer matching services.

Recruiters not only seek out qualified applicants, they also must be able to present these applicants with an accurate picture of the company or companies seeking employees. They must be able to answer applicant questions about the company that is hiring, and they need to know about the company's personnel policy in regard to wages and promotional possibilities. They must also be familiar with equal employment opportunity and affirmative action guidelines.

Employment interviewers often have many of the same responsibilities as personnel recruiters, but may also do administrative tasks, such as administering applicant skills tests or completing a background check on the applicant.

Employment consultants help job seekers find employment and help businesses find workers for existing positions. They interview job seekers and utilize tests to evaluate the skills and abilities of applicants. They discuss job openings with applicants, including such issues as job responsibilities and benefits. The employment consultant then attempts to find job openings that match the skills and interests of individual applicants. They often put an applicant directly in touch with a potential employer. If a specific opening does not exist, they may contact various firms to see if they need an applicant or suggest that the applicant take additional skills training to qualify for existing positions.

Consultants may also offer suggestions on resume writing, interviewing techniques, and personal appearance to help applicants secure a position. Often, a consultant will have an expertise in a particular area, such as accounting or law, and work with applicants interested in jobs in that field.

Employment clerks function as intake workers and interview job seekers to get pertinent information, such as work history, education, and occupational interests. They then refer the applicant to an employment consultant or counselor. Employment clerks also have administrative duties, such as checking appli-

Employment firm workers evaluate a person's credentials, provide advice concerning future employment, and match a person's abilities with current jobs that are available.

cant references, filing applications, and compiling personnel records.

Employment agency managers supervise the business operations of an employment agency. They establish agency rules and regulations, prepare agency budgets, purchase appropriate equipment and supplies, resolve client complaints, and in general are responsible for the day-to-day operations of the agency. They are also responsible for hiring and evaluating staff workers, and overseeing their training.

Government personnel specialists do essentially the same work as their counterparts in private companies, except they deal with openings that are subject to civil service regulations. Much of government personnel work concentrates on job analysis because civil service jobs are strictly classified according to entry requirements, duties, and wages.

Requirements

Although there are no specific educational requirements for work in this field, most employers mow demand a college education for all employment firm workers. High-school graduates may start out as employment clerks and advance with experience to the position of employment consultants, but such a situation is becoming rare. Some employers favor college graduates who have majored in personnel administration while others prefer individuals with a general business background. Persons interested in personnel work with a government agency may find it an asset to have a degree in personnel administration or public administration.

High-school students interested in pursuing a career in the employment firm field should take college-preparatory courses, such as social studies, English, mathematics, and speech arts. Business courses are also valuable. In college, a combination of courses in the social sciences, behavioral sciences, business, and economics is recommended. Other relevant courses might include principles of management, business administration, psychology, and statistics.

Special requirements

Although most employment firms must be licensed, the workers themselves do not normally need any special license or certificate. Those who work for the government usually must pass a civil service examination.

As a way of attaining increased professional standing, employment workers may become certified by the National Association of Personnel Consultants (NAPC). Employment workers who have at least two years work experience may receive the title of Certified Personnel Consultant after passing an examination. Further information on the certification process is available from the NAPC at the address given at the end of this article.

Opportunities for experience and exploration

Part-time work as a clerk or a personnel assistant are good ways of exploring this field. Large department stores and other large firms usually have personnel departments and are good places to begin looking for part-time or temporary work. High-school students may also find part-time work in their school's counseling department. Discussions with employment firm workers are another good way of learning about the rewards and responsibilities in this field. Some temporary agencies hire from the pool of people they send out on assignments, after they are shown the person has good management and clerical skills.

Related occupations

Other occupations that require interviewing skills and interpersonal relations include customer service managers, career consultants, rehabilitation counselors, and psychologists.

Methods of entering

Those with a bachelor's degree in personnel administration or related field should apply directly to employment firms for a job opening. Colleges and universities have placement offices that can be helpful in supplying possible leads in this regard. Those interested in working for a government agency must pass a civil service test. Openings in the government are usually listed with the Office of Personnel Management. High-school graduates may apply for entry-level jobs as an employment clerk or personnel assistant, but these positions are increasingly going to those with a college degree.

Entry-level workers are usually trained on-the-job or in formal training programs, where they learn how to classify jobs and interview applicants.

Advancement

After trainees have mastered the basic personnel tasks, they are assigned to specific areas, such as personnel recruitment. This increase in responsibility is usually matched with an increase in salary and prestige. In time, skilled workers may become department heads or office managers. A few highly skilled employees may become top executives with employment firms. Advancement may also be achieved by moving into a higher position in another firm.

Employment outlook

Employment opportunities are expected to grow about as fast as the average for all occupations through the early 1990s. The demand will be greatest in private industry as employers become more aware of the benefits of utilizing employment firms to find part-time and temporary help. Opportunities in government work will result primarily from the need to replace workers rather than to fill new positions. In addition, there will be the normal vacancies created when experienced workers retire or change occupations.

Jobs in the employment field are protected somewhat against changes in the economy. If the economy is growing and businesses are expanding, companies will utilize employment firms to fill existing positions. On the other hand, if there is a downturn in the economy, more job seekers will utilize these firms in an attempt to improve their job prospects. Job opportunities will be greatest in large urban areas, where there are more jobs, and a higher degree of job turnover.

Although opportunities in this field will continue to grow, the competition for each job will be keen. There is expected to be an abundance of college graduates and experienced workers for each opening.

Earnings

Employment firm fees are usually paid by the company that hires an applicant, but occasionally the applicant will pay the fee. Earnings vary widely and depend on job responsibilities and the size of the firm. Employment clerks usually start at between $13,500 and $15,000 per year, with experienced clerks earning between $18,000 and $21,000 per year. Beginning employment consultants earn between $19,000 and $23,000 per year, with experienced consultants earning $25,000 and up depending on success in placing workers. In most private companies, employment consultants are paid a basic salary and they earn a commission for each job opening that they fill. Federal employees are usually paid according to civil service grade level, with merit increases. Employment agency managers usually start at between $29,000 and $32,000 per year, with experienced managers earning $50,000 and up depending on specific job responsibilities and the size of the firm. Some managers are also paid a commission on each job opening they help fill. Full-time employment firm workers receive health insurance, vacation, and other benefits.

Conditions of work

Employment firm workers almost always work under pleasant conditions. Their offices are designed to make a good impression on outside visitors and prospective employees and are therefore modern, attractive, and nicely furnished. Employees in this field are seldom required to work more than a forty-hour week, although they may do so if they are working on a special project. There may be some clerical work, such as typing and filing. Many agencies are small (under ten employees), but others can be quite large, employing over fifty employees. Employment consultants may face some pressure to fill existing job openings.

Some personnel recruiters travel extensively. Recruiters attend professional conferences and visit college campuses to interview prospective employees.

Social and psychological factors

Workers in this field should have a pleasant outgoing personality and enjoy working with people of different levels of education and experience. Much of the workday is spent talking to job seekers or prospective employers, either on the phone or in person. Employment firm workers must exercise sensitivity and tact when interviewing potential customers or clients. Good writing and speaking skills are vital. Attention to detail is another valued characteristic. Objectivity and fairmindedness are required to consider matters from both the employee's and employer's point of view. Employment firm workers cooperate as part of a team but at the same time must be able to handle individual responsibility. Decision-making ability is especially important for employment agency managers.

Occupations in the employment firm field offer the possibility for much personal satisfaction, such as the gratification that comes from helping job seekers find fulfilling careers.

GOE: 11.03.04; SIC: 7361; SOC: 143

◇ **SOURCES OF ADDITIONAL INFORMATION**

Information on certification is available from:

National Association of Personnel Consultants
1432 Duke Street
Alexandria, VA 22314

General career information is available from:

American Society for Personnel Administration
606 North Washington Street
Alexandria, VA 22314

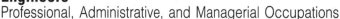

International Personnel Management
Association
1617 Duke Street
Alexandria, VA 22314

**National Employment Counselors
Association**
Education Office
5999 Stevenson Avenue
Alexandria, VA 22304

◇ **RELATED ARTICLES**

Volume 1: Business Administration
Volume 2: Career counselors; Employment
counselors; Human services workers; Management trainees; Personnel and labor relations
specialists
Volume 3: Clerical supervisors and managers
Volume 4: Career guidance technicians

Engineers

Definition

Engineers apply the theories and principles of
science and mathematics to practical technical
problems for the benefit of humanity. In addition to the conception, design, and development of new machinery, products, systems,
and processes, they may be involved in such
varied activities as planning, testing, construction or production, operation, maintenance,
and management of engineering projects.

History

Engineering in one form or another is among
the oldest of professions. The Egyptian pyramids are examples of ancient engineering feats,
and many of the bridges, roads, and aqueducts
constructed by the ancient Romans are still in
use today.

Engineers were originally simply builders
who worked with stone and other basic materials. They were either self-taught or learned
their craft from more experienced workers.

The military operations of the early nations
of the world created a demand for engineers
capable of planning fortifications and the machines and means necessary to destroy or overcome such fortifications.

Engineering seems to have developed
along two lines. First, with an expanding population and the advance of civilization, it became necessary to develop roads, harbors,
buildings, bridges, and canals. The second development came with the increased application

of power to mechanical operations that called
for people capable of designing and constructing such machinery.

From these beginnings, engineering has
grown until it is now the second largest profession in the United States, exceeded only
by teaching. The engineering profession today
recognizes more than twenty-five major
specialties.

Nature of the work

The engineer, regardless of the area of specialization, is basically concerned with the application of scientific principles to practical, everyday problems. Such application has several
aspects and in general these aspects can be classified as research and development, construction, production, sales, administration, consultation, and teaching.

Usually engineers whose duties are essentially in research conduct experiments using
known scientific principles. They hope to apply
this scientific knowledge to the development of
new machines, products, or processes and
much of the work involves planning, conducting, and reporting laboratory and field experiments. They make observations of tests and experiments and report findings. They may work
a long time on just one phase of a development
problem, and usually they have many of these
to solve before they can improve the model or
process to the point where it may be considered
worthy of production or construction. They
draw plans, list specifications, and suggest new

and improved designs. About one-third of all professional engineers are employed in research, development, and design activities.

The engineers who work in construction are concerned with the conversion of designs or plans to reality whether it is a dam to be constructed, a skyscraper to be erected, a machine to be built, or a communications system to be installed. They deal with the purchase of materials, the equipment to be used, the assignment of work crews, and the scheduling of work activities. They must consider cost and time factors in handling various phases of the construction project, and they will consult with additional engineers, suppliers, and others regarding progress and problems. About ten out of every one hundred engineers are involved in construction activities.

Production engineers plan, supervise, and evaluate production activities in whatever work setting they may be employed. They may be involved in the production of goods or in situations where services such as power or communication is the main production concern. They deal with many technical phases of operation and test manufactured products to ensure that standards or specifications are maintained. They suggest ways for improving the manufacturing or service processes. Between five and ten percent of the professional engineers are engaged in production engineering.

Sales engineers are employed to assist in the sale of specialized equipment. They aid potential customers by helping them assess their equipment needs, by recommending new and more efficient processes employing old equipment, and by helping in the solution of plant problems. In extremely difficult production problems, they may assist in the development of a custom-made machine that their firm would manufacture. Less than five percent of all engineers are engaged in sales activities. It is an aspect of engineering, however, that appeals to those who enjoy meeting and working with a variety of people.

Approximately one-third of all engineers are employed in administrative or management positions. In these positions, they deal with people and policy more than with the technical problems of production. They usually have had a number of years of experience in one or more kinds of engineering and have proved themselves as highly competent individuals capable of assuming management responsibilities. This involves working with others in the determination and interpretation of company policy.

Consulting engineers help others solve their technical or scientific problems. Approximately five percent of the professional engineers work as consultants to business, indus-

An engineer explains the new refining unit she designed that uses a catalyst to reduce wax content in diesel fuels.

try, and government. Engineering consultants usually have had a number of years of work experience in research, construction, production, or sales. They obtain information about the project under discussion and offer suggestions relative to the planning or conduct of the project. In the process, they may need to study research findings, make field visits to the proposed work site or plant, or develop specific proposals, plans, or designs. Their work is varied because the nature of a client's need for a consultant is dependent on the specifics of the project.

Most professors in colleges of engineering have been trained as engineers or have had very similar preparation and experience. Some young engineers, usually those with outstanding academic records and considerable experience in research, are selected for teaching immediately upon completion of their program. Others enter teaching after a number of successful years as practicing engineers. Employment as a member of the faculty in a college of engineering usually requires a doctorate. Thus, the engineer who plans to enter this dimension of engineering should recognize the additional preparation necessary, as well as the need for scholarly achievement. Engineering professors, in addition to their instructional responsibilities, usually engage in research and consulting activities. Much of their research is conducted in the college laboratories or in field experiments. They are often employed by business, industry, or the government in a consulting capacity.

Most initial positions in engineering will be found in the research, construction, production, and sales dimensions. Administrative, consulting, and teaching positions are areas into which one may move after some years of experience. While engineering may seem wide-ranging, it also provides broad opportunities for specialization.

The engineering profession recognizes more than twenty-five major specialties. Although all branches of engineering are covered in this occupational description, thirteen will be discussed in some detail—aerospace, agricultural, ceramic, chemical, civil, electrical, industrial, marine, mechanical, metallurgical, mining, nuclear, and petroleum engineering—and twelve others are described briefly following the *Related Articles* section.

Requirements

The preparation for an engineering career, both in high school and in college, is extremely important. In high school, one should take as much mathematics as possible, especially algebra and geometry. Physics and chemistry are the most helpful science subjects, although earth science and biology are valuable background courses. Because engineers must communicate with others both in speech and in writing, and because they should understand and appreciate the relationship of their work to the economy of the country, English and social studies are important areas of study. Any of the following courses are recommended electives: a foreign language (three to four years), metal or electric shop, mechanical drawing, and speech.

Most positions require a bachelor's degree in engineering. Graduate study for the master's degree or doctorate is becoming increasingly important for advancement to positions in the teaching, research, and administrative aspects of engineering. Also, some engineering specializations are only available at the graduate level.

Nearly 260 colleges, universities, and engineering schools offer education leading to a bachelor's or higher degree in engineering. Ad-

missions requirements vary considerably; however, engineering schools usually require a strong background in mathematics and the physical sciences, and place great emphasis on the general quality of an applicant's high-school work. College preparatory courses are a requirement at most universities.

Admission requirements and curricula may vary considerably among colleges and universities. High-school students are advised to look for engineering schools that are accredited by the Accreditation Board for Engineering and Technology (ABET). Not only will they be guaranteed a quality education, but they will need a bachelor's degree from an approved school if they plan to go on to graduate study. It is wise to start early to investigate the various schools, both directly and through school counselors, to avoid being disappointed later by being turned down for not having adequately prepared for the school of one's choice.

In a typical four-year engineering curriculum, the first two years are spent in studying basic science courses—mathematics, physics, and chemistry—and the humanities, social sciences, and English. During the last two years, the emphasis is on engineering and advanced mathematics and science courses.

Some engineering curricula require more than four years to complete. A number of institutions offer five-year programs leading to the master's degree. About fifty engineering schools have arrangements with liberal arts colleges whereby a student may spend three years in the college and two years in the engineering school, receiving a bachelor's degree from each. This type of program usually offers an opportunity for greater diversification in one's studies.

A five- or six-year cooperative program, whereby a student can spend alternate periods in engineering school and in employment in industry or government, is offered in some institutions. Through this type of program, students are provided the opportunity to finance part of their education and can gain practical experience coordinated with classroom study.

Like the other professions, engineering requires certain basic personal characteristics: an understanding of the importance of accuracy; good judgment; honesty with one's self and with others; perseverance; and the ability to work with others as part of a team. In addition, engineering requires considerable ability to work with mathematics; an understanding of abstract concepts; the capability to handle such concepts in terms of technical problem solving; and the ability to visualize structures or mechanical operations in three dimensions. Much engineering work also requires the making of clear sketches (not finished artwork) of complex things or operations and the verbal explaining of ideas and devices to others in precise and understandable language.

Further, an engineer's education does not end with graduation. Professional engineers should be prepared to continue their education throughout their careers if they expect to keep up with the rapid advances in technology.

Special requirements

All fifty states and the District of Columbia require the licensing or registration of professional engineers whose work may affect the public welfare or the personal life, health, or property of its inhabitants. Although varying from state to state, the usual requirements for licensure are graduation from an approved engineering program, four years of experience, and the passing of a state examination in engineering. Information on specific licensing or registration requirements can be obtained by writing to the state licensure or examining board in the capital of the state in which the individual desires to practice.

Opportunities for experience and exploration

The engineering profession is represented by a number of professional organizations whose objectives focus on the many experiences available through curricular activities and through clubs and organizations. For high-school students to understand how engineers actually apply science to solve human problems and to satisfy human needs, they should take part in such extracurricular activities as JETS (Junior Engineering Technical Society) and other engineering groups. There is also the possibility of summer or part-time work in construction projects, research laboratories, or manufacturing plants.

Related occupations

Engineering involves the application of scientific and mathematical principles. Persons interested in this field may also want to explore the occupations of architects, engineering and science technicians, life scientists, mathematicians, and physical scientists.

Methods of entering

Most engineers secure their first positions as a result of contacts made through the college placement office or as a result of a recommendation of one of their professors. Some get their first position through friends or relatives, while others take positions with firms where they have been employed perhaps during the summer or in connection with work-study or field experiences.

Advancement

Initial positions with many firms are usually structured so that the new graduate can spend some time in working as an assistant to an experienced engineer or in special training programs designed to orient the engineer to company processes, procedures, policy, and products. Beginning positions with other firms, usually the smaller ones, are more specific, and new graduates must fit into the particular slot or niche for which they are employed.

Engineers are promoted to positions involving administrative and supervisory responsibility or to jobs requiring higher-level skills and understanding. Some try to improve their chances for promotion by obtaining an advanced degree in business administration. Others eventually leave for nontechnical managerial, administrative, or sales jobs. A few engineers become patent attorneys after obtaining a law degree. Top-level executives in government and industry are often drawn from the engineering field.

Earnings

Average salaries for engineers can be examined by studying the employment setting and the amount of education required. Average salaries for beginning engineers having a bachelor's degree were about $27,900 a year in private industry in the early 1990s. Graduates with a master's degree and no experience started at about $33,100, and those having the doctor's degree averaged about $42,200 to start.

Beginning positions in the federal government with a bachelor's degree were about $18,700 or $23,200 a year, depending on college records. Beginning engineers with the master's degree could start at about $26,000. Those with the doctorate could begin at about $28,000. The average salary for all engineers in the federal government in the early 1990s was about $38,000 a year.

Engineers can expect increased earnings as they gain experience. For example, in private industry in the early 1990s, junior-level engineers received an average of $27,900 per year, mid-level engineers with no supervisory responsibilities earned $42,700, and senior-level managerial engineers were paid an average of $79,000 a year.

Social and psychological factors

Engineers are surely on the frontiers of America: in research, production, and construction, and in all areas of endeavor from the atmosphere, the astronaut, and aerospace to the ocean floor, the aquanaut, and oceanography. The very best of an individual is demanded, both physically and mentally, but for the young person who wants to find a worthwhile career and who is willing to work at building a future the opportunities exist in engineering.

The possibilities for opportunity to advance, to build a rewarding and satisfying future are limitless. The work is challenging and varied, depending on the dimension of engineering activity and the specialization one eventually selects. One can find a means of self-expression in the creative aspects of some positions or the satisfaction of a job well done in some of the production or construction activities. These personal satisfactions may, in the long run, be as important as the financial rewards. You must identify what you hope to obtain from the work. Somewhere in engineering you may find an opportunity to achieve these goals.

GOE: 05.01; SIC: Any industry; SOC: 8244

◇ SOURCES OF ADDITIONAL INFORMATION

The following organizations provide information about the engineering field in general. For specific information about the engineering specialties, see the sources listed in the appropriate sections of this article.

Accreditation Board for Engineering and Technology
345 East 47th Street
New York, NY 10017

American Association of Engineering Societies
415 Second Street, NE
Suite 200
Washington, DC 20002

Engineering Manpower Commission
415 Second Street, NE
Washington, DC 20002

International Federation of Professional and Technical Engineers
8701 Georgia Avenue
Suite 701
Silver Springs, MD 20910

National Action Council for Minorities in Engineering
3 West 35th Street
New York, NY 10001

National Society of Professional Engineers
1420 King Street
Alexandria, VA 22314

Society of Women Engineers
345 East 47th Street
Room 305
New York, NY 10017

For information on the projected demand for specific types of engineers, and on federal programs for eductional assistance, write to:

Educating Scientists and Engineers: Grade School to Grad School
Superintendent of Documents
US Government Printing Office
Washington, DC 20402

◇ RELATED ARTICLES

Volume 1: Automotives; Aviation and Aerospace; Ceramics; Construction; Energy; Engineering; Machining and Machinery; Metals; Mining; Nuclear Sciences; Plastics; Public Utilities
Volume 2: Biomedical engineers; Packaging engineers
Volume 4: Biomedical equipment technicians; Civil engineering technicians; Industrial engineering technicians; Parking engineering technicians

Aerospace engineers

Nature of the work

Aerospace engineers specialize in the design, construction, or testing of aircraft. They have been involved in many aerospace developments, particularly missiles and space capsules, and have been responsible for many of the advances in air transportation. They design all types of aircraft and test models to determine their maneuverability, structural stability, and other characteristics under flight conditions. They supervise the assembly of the plane and the installation of the engines, instruments, and other equipment. They engage in research involving the design and development of airplane, missile, and space structures, engines, parts, and other equipment.

Many aerospace engineers specialize in a particular type of aircraft, such as jet-propelled, missile, or spacecraft. Specialists among aerospace engineers include *aerodynamists*, who analyze the forces that affect the flight of aircraft; engineers employed in *research, design, testing, product sales, cost-analysis,* and *field-service*; as well as *project engineers*, who direct and coordinate the activities of design personnel.

Employment outlook

Aerospace engineers, numbering approximately 53,000 in the early 1990s, were employed mainly by the aircraft manufacturing and aerospace industries. The remainder worked for agencies in the federal government (such as the National Aeronautics and Space Administration [NASA] or the Department of Defense), commercial airlines, business and engineering consulting firms, and communications equipment manufacturing companies.

Employment opportunities for aerospace engineers are expected to decrease, along with federal spending for military aircraft, missiles, and other aerospace systems, through the end of the 1990s. In the civilian sector, however, rapid growth is anticipated. More jobs should be created to design and produce quieter, more fuel-efficient commercial aircraft and to fill the demand for business aircraft and helicopters.

The majority of jobs for aerospace engineers are found in California, Washington, and Texas, where the largest aerospace manufacturers are located. One factor that may limit the employment of aerospace engineers in the fu-

Aerospace engineers work on a full-scale model of a newly designed Air Force missile.

ture is that a higher proportion of job openings in aerospace manufacturing may be for materials, mechanical, or electrical engineers. It should be remembered, too, that defense-related jobs are dependent on how much money is allocated for defense spending. Any cutbacks in this budget can result in layoffs of aerospace engineers.

Conditions of work

Most aerospace engineers work indoors in offices or plants, others work outdoors at testing sites or launching pads, and a few travel extensively to plants and construction sites. Those in engineering departments or research laboratories usually work in modern, clean, well-lighted, temperature-controlled buildings. Depending on their activities, they may work at desks, drafting tables, or computer terminals or with research and testing equipment. Production engineers direct assembly work in plants or factories.

◇ **SOURCES OF ADDITIONAL INFORMATION**

For information on the engineering field in general, see the sources listed in the introductory section of this article.

American Institute of Aeronautics and Astronautics
370 L'Enfant Promenade, SW
Washington, DC 20024

Agricultural engineers

Nature of the work

Agricultural engineers apply engineering principles to problems in the food and agriculture industries. They design or develop agricultural equipment and machines, supervise their production, and conduct tests on new designs and machine parts. They develop plans and specifications for agricultural structures and utilities and for drainage and irrigation systems. These engineers work on flood control, soil erosion, and land reclamation projects. They design food processing systems and equipment to convert farm products to consumer foods. Agricultural engineers contribute to making farming easier and more profitable through the introduction of new farm machinery and through advancements in soil and water conservation.

Agricultural engineers in industry may be engaged in *research* or in the *design, testing,* or *sales* of equipment.

Employment outlook

Agricultural engineers are employed by producers and distributors of agricultural equipment, power and light companies, and food processing firms. In the federal government, agricultural engineers find positions with such agencies as the Soil Conservation Service and the Agricultural Research Service of the Department of Agriculture. Some find employment on the faculties of colleges and universities; others are employed by state and local governments; and a few are self-employed as agricultural contractors, equipment retailers, or consultants.

Because of farm automation, more complex food processing systems, and increased awareness of the importance of saving our natural resources, the demand for agricultural engineers is expected to grow rapidly through the end of the 1990s. The use of farm waste as raw material for industry is also expected to provide additional opportunities for employment. These specialists will also be required to develop more efficient farm methods as well as techniques for increasing crop yields to meet the needs of a growing population.

Conditions of work

Agricultural engineers usually work in offices or laboratories, except for work outdoors to field-test equipment and processes. Some agricultural engineers travel a great deal, to food processing plants, for example. There is rarely any need for hard physical labor, however.

◇ **SOURCES OF ADDITIONAL INFORMATION**

For information on the engineering field in general, see the sources listed in the introductory section of this article.

American Society of Agricultural Engineers
2950 Niles Road
St. Joseph, MI 49085

Ceramic engineers

Nature of the work

Ceramic engineers direct the processing of nonmetallic minerals, clay, or silicates into many ceramic products, such as pottery, bricks, glassware, coatings for spacecraft parts, or porcelain-enameled stoves. Ceramic materials require high temperatures to process. It is in the kiln firing that ceramics take on their durable quality.

Ceramic engineers work with known nonmetallic materials. They also develop new materials—materials which have specific qualities such as heat resistance or durability. As part of their research and development work, they study the chemical and physical properties of materials that can be used. They also design and supervise the construction of ceramic manufacturing plants and equipment. It is convenient to associate the specializations in ceramic engineering with the product—whitewares (porcelain and china dinnerware, high-voltage electrical insulators); refractories (fire- and heat-resistant materials); glass (windows, light bulbs, tableware, electronic equipment parts); abrasives; cements; porcelain enamels; structural clay materials (sewer pipe, roofing tile, brick); and coatings (high-temperature coatings for jet engines, missiles, and spacecraft).

Specialists in ceramic engineering include *design, research, test,* and *product sales* engineers.

Employment outlook

Ceramic engineers are employed mostly in plants that manufacture ceramic and glass products. Other industries that employed ceramic engineers included iron and steel, electrical and electronic, chemical, mining, computer, and semiconductor. The aerospace industry is a major employer. As in the other engineering specializations, some ceramic engineers work in colleges and universities.

The field of ceramic engineering is growing much faster than the supply of engineers. It is predicted that, through the end of the 1990s, there will be many openings for ceramic engineers in medicine, electronics, nuclear energy, and defense programs. Numerous job opportunities should be arise from the need to develop improved materials and products, such as ceramic automobile engines, which are more fuel efficient than other engines. Ceramic engineers will be needed, too, in research to find ceramic substitutes for minerals that are in rapidly dwindling supply.

Some of the newest fields that will directly affect ceramics are semiconductors and superconductors. Also, other advanced ceramics are denser than the older ceramics, thus allowing a sturdier, less corrosive, less vulnerable base for product development.

Conditions of work

Some ceramic engineers work in an office, others in a plant or factory. The offices are generally modern, clean, and well lighted and ventilated, but the factories can be noisy and hot. Intense heat is used in the manufacture of ceramic materials, but the furnace controls are often located in a separate, air-conditioned instrument room.

◇ **SOURCES OF ADDITIONAL INFORMATION**

For information on the engineering field in general, see the sources listed in the introductory section of this article.

American Ceramic Society
757 Brooks Edge Plaza Drive
Westerville, OH 43081

National Institute of Ceramic Engineers
757 Brooks Edge Plaza Drive
Westerville, OH 43081

Chemical engineers

Nature of the work

Chemical engineers are involved in every dimension of engineering activity. They plan, design, and construct chemical plants and equipment. In production activities, they are concerned with research to develop and improve the processes for producing large quantities of chemicals on a commercial scale. Synthetic rubbers and textile fibers, antibiotics, plastics, and detergents are products that the chemical engineer has helped to develop or improve.

Like the other engineering specialties, chemical engineering has its *research, test,* and *equipment sales engineers.* In addition, there are *absorption-and-adsorption engineers,* who design equipment and chemical processes that are used to remove and separate gas or liquid components; and *chemical design engineers, processes,* who design equipment and processes intended to produce chemical changes in elements and compounds.

Employment outlook

More than two-thirds of the 52,000 chemical engineers employed in the United States in the early 1990s worked in manufacturing industries, primarily in the chemical, petroleum, and related industries. About one-fifth were employed by engineering services or consulting firms, designing chemical plants and doing other work on a contract basis. A small number worked for institutions of higher education and agencies of the federal government or were independent consultants.

Opportunities for employment are expected to increase at an average rate through the 1990s. Although the chemical industries will continue to expand, the number of jobs for chemical engineers will not keep pace because of anticipated productivity improvements and because companies will contract out more of the work. Chemical engineers may find the better opportunities in the fields of pharmaceuticals and biotechnology or in nonmanufacturing industries, especially the service industries.

Conditions of work

Chemical engineers work with processes, equipment, products, and people. They may work in offices, laboratories, or plants, where conditions may vary depending on the job or the company. Their work sometimes involves travel to new or existing plant sites.

◇ **SOURCES OF ADDITIONAL INFORMATION**

For information on the engineering field in general, see the sources listed in the introductory section of this article.

American Chemical Society
1155 16th Street, NW
Washington, DC 20036

American Institute of Chemical Engineers
345 East 47th Street
New York, NY 10017

Civil engineers

Nature of the work

Civil engineers design and supervise the construction of highways, airstrips, bridges, dams, buildings, water-supply and sewage systems, and many other types of structures. Many opportunities exist for specialization within this area. Civil engineers may choose to concentrate on *airports, hydraulics, irrigation, railroads, radioactive materials waste management, sanitation or public health, structural engineering, transportation, waterworks, forests,* or *highways.* The hydroelectric projects, thruways, cloverleafs, air terminals, canals, and skyscrapers—some of which are world renowned for their beauty or grandeur—are typical projects on which civil engineers have worked.

Employment outlook

Civil engineering is one of the oldest and largest fields of specialization, employing about 199,000 engineers in the early 1990s. Almost 40 percent of the civil engineers are employed by government agencies—federal, state, county, and city. More than one-third work in firms that provide engineering consulting services, primarily developing designs for new construction projects. Most of the rest worked for construction companies, public utilities, railroads, and manufacturing establishments.

The employment picture for civil engineers looks very good through the rest of the 1990s: Population growth and an expanding economy call for more or new transportation systems, water resource and disposal systems, manufacturing plants, office buildings, and other structures. Civil engineers will also be in demand to repair or replace existing roads, bridges, and public buildings. Job opportunities exist throughout the country but are more plentiful in major industrial and commercial centers. Civil engineers working in construction and related industries can be adversely affected in the event of an economic downturn, when many construction projects are cut back.

Conditions of work

Civil engineers may work in offices, laboratories, or factories, or they may work outdoors, depending on their specialty. Some highway engineers, for example, work in field trailers at construction sites; transportation engineers may have to do outdoor research on street use, traffic flow, and pedestrian traffic. Others may

City governments often employ transportation engineers to design and restructure mass transit systems.

work outdoors on projects such as pipelines and airports.

Many civil engineers travel extensively or are required to work in inaccessible areas where the weather may be extremely hot or cold. Then, when the project is completed, they move on to the next one, staying only two or three years in each place.

◇ SOURCES OF ADDITIONAL INFORMATION

For information on the engineering field in general, see the sources listed in the introductory section of this article.

American Society of Civil Engineers
345 East 47th Street
New York, NY 10017

Institute of Transportation Engineers
525 School Street, SW, Suite 410
Washington, DC 20024

Electrical and electronics engineers

This systems engineer operates a software program in search of design flaws.

Nature of the work

Electrical engineers are concerned with the design, development, and production of electrical and electronic equipment and its use in the generation, transmission, and distribution of electricity. In the past, electrical engineers have worked on the development and improvement of electrical appliances for home and business. Although electrical equipment manufacturing is an important field for electrical engineers, many are working currently in the development and construction of electric motors and power generating and transmission equipment. Electrical engineers who concentrate on problems in power generation are involved from time to time in the planning and construction of large electric power plants and stations. With rapid industrial growth, electrical engineers are being consulted relative to problems with and designs for electronic or electrical circuits on which automated or complex industrial machines can operate.

Electronics engineers are electrical engineers who specialize in the planning, testing, and production of electronic instruments and equipment. They may specialize in computers, acoustic products such as stereo phonographs, industrial controls, aerospace and missile systems, and medical equipment and devices.

As in other branches of engineering, electrical engineers may be designated *research, design, test,* and *product sales* engineers. Electronics engineers also may specialize in *research, design, testing,* or *product and system sales.* Other electrical engineers choose to become *petroleum prospecting engineers* or *illuminating engineers* or to concentrate on *central office facilities planning, electrolysis-and-corrosion control,* or *electronic data-processing systems.*

In a field as large as electrical engineering, there are many narrower specialties as well, such as *outside-plant cable engineers,* whose work is concerned with submarine telecommunications cables. In the area of communications, there are also *outside-plant engineers,* who work with the overhead or underground lines, cables, and conduits used for telephones and other communications; *transmission-and-protection engineers; central-office equipment engineers;* and *customer-equipment engineers.*

Engineers whose activities affect the supply of electrical power include *distribution-field engineers, power system engineers,* and *protection engineers;* also *engineers of system development, induction coordination,* and *power-distribution* and *power-transmission.*

Radio and television transmission also requires the services of a number of electrical engineers. Engineers in charge of *studio operations* and *transmitters* work with the broadcasting equipment at radio and TV studios and transmitter stations, whereas *commercial engineers* are concerned with the wire facilities that connect the network of radio and TV stations.

Employment outlook

Electrical engineering is the largest branch of the engineering specializations. Approximately 401,000 electrical engineers were employed in the early 1990s, chiefly for manufacturers of electrical and electronic equipment, aerospace instruments and aircraft, professional and scientific equipment, and electronic computers and business machines. Service or utility suppliers hiring a good number of electrical engineers include light and power companies and the telephone and telegraph industry. Engineering and business consultants, educational institutions, and government agencies—federal, state, and local—employ the remaining engineers.

Through the end of the 1990s, the supply of new jobs for electrical and electronics engineers is expected to be much greater than the number of graduates entering this employment market. Growth in this field has been so rapid that engineering schools are experiencing a shortage of faculty and laboratory equipment and may have to restrict the enrollment of students. The increased demand for electrical and electronics engineers has been brought about primarily by business and government needs for computers, communications equipment, and military electronics. Other factors contributing to the excellent employment outlook are greater consumer demand for electrical and electronic goods and increased research and development on robots and other types of automation.

Job security and opportunities for advancement will be best for electrical and electronics engineers who keep up with the rapid changes in technology. Because much of the electrical and electronics engineering work is related to defense, cuts in the defense budget could mean a reduction of jobs in that area.

Conditions of work

Electrical engineers generally work in offices, laboratories, or production departments that are modern and comfortable. On occasion, they may have to inspect a building site before formulating their plans. Some engineers travel a great deal, especially those in sales or marketing.

Engineers in this field work mostly with others, although on small projects they may work alone or with only one or two other persons.

◇ **SOURCES OF ADDITIONAL INFORMATION**

For information on the engineering field in general, see the sources listed in the introductory section of this article.

Institute of Electrical and Electronics Engineers (IEEE)
345 East 47th Street
New York, NY 10017

Eta Kappa Nu
PO Box 2982
Station A
Champaign, IL 61801

Industrial engineers

Nature of the work

Industrial engineers are concerned with production processes and seek the most efficient and effective utilization of personnel, materials, and machines. They are responsible for the plant layout—the arrangement of the machinery and apparatus or other equipment used in production operations. They also plan the work flow and work areas to keep health and accident hazards at a minimum. The selection of tools, machines, and other equipment, as well as the manufacturing processes and procedures to be employed, are part of their supervisory functions. They analyze the various production jobs, conduct time and motion studies, and deal with other aspects of plant standards and performance. They devise systems for controlling the accounting and inventory of materials and for studying the quality and cost of materials.

Specific occupation titles for specialists within the industrial engineering field include *product-safety, safety, standards, factory lay-out, fire-prevention research, fire-protection, industrial-health, manufacturing, production, quality-control,* and *time-study engineers.*

Employment outlook

There were approximately 117,000 industrial engineers employed in the early 1990s, more than 80 percent in manufacturing industries. The remaining engineers worked for a variety of other organizations, including insurance companies, public utilities, banks, hospitals, retail businesses, government agencies, and consulting firms. Their work opportunities are numerous both in manufacturing and non-manufacturing settings. Wherever a need exists for the efficiency of production or business processes, industrial engineers will find employment opportunities.

Employment opportunities for industrial engineers are expected to grow at a faster than average rate through the 1990s. The general expansion of industry, with increased use of automation and more complex business operations, will require the services of more engineers. In addition, companies wanting to reduce costs and increase productivity through scientific management and safety engineering will create a number of openings.

Conditions of work

Industrial engineers work for many kinds of businesses, so their working conditions vary depending on who is employing them. Most industrial engineers work in pleasant offices that are clean, comfortable, well lighted, and well ventilated. Because their research involves on-site observation of workers and processes, however, they may spend a great deal of time in factories and other facilities. This work is generally not considered dangerous.

◇ **SOURCES OF ADDITIONAL INFORMATION**

For information on the engineering field in general, see the sources listed in the introductory section of this article.

Institute of Industrial Engineers
25 Technology Park/Atlanta
Norcross, GA 30092

Marine engineers

Nature of the work

Marine engineers work closely with naval architects to design and build ships and other maritime vessels. The naval architects plan the frame and hull; the marine engineers design the ship's machinery. Together, they try to produce lighter vessels that use less fuel and require less maintenance, thus saving millions of dollars a year for their employers or clients.

Ships and other craft are designed for many different uses. Some must be equipped with special piping to carry oil and liquefied natural gas. Newsprint ships are built with several hatches so they can take on four 1,750-pound rolls of paper at once. Some ships carry loaded barges to a specified destination, where they are put into the water and hitched to tugboats for final delivery. Others carry vehicles that are driven on board by longshore workers, fastened down for the trip, then driven off by other longshore workers at the point of disembarkation.

The concerns of the naval architect include size, weight, speed, water displacement, draft (how deep in the water the ship will lie when loaded), and interior design (cargo holds, passenger berths, elevators, ladder walls). The purpose of a vessel determines whether it will be diesel-, steam-, or gas-powered. Elements, such as cargo, determine structural needs. Oil ships travelling in rocky shoreline may need double hulls. Marine engineers design and build the engines that power the ships. They plan and direct the placement of the power plants, propulsion systems, navigation equipment, radio and radar gear, fire control and electric power systems, and the systems for heating, air-conditioning, and refrigeration. Engineers also test equipment, repair ships, and design equipment used on docks and in marine structures.

Marine engineers may specialize in *equipment design, research, testing,* or *sales.* Those responsible for repair and maintenance are called *port engineers.*

Employment outlook

Marine engineers are employed by private shipbuilding establishments, naval architecture and marine engineering design firms, and the American Bureau of Shipping. They also work for the Naval Sea Systems Command, the Maritime Administration, and the U.S. Coast Guard, either in Washington, D.C., or in shipyards, laboratories, and field offices located elsewhere. Some marine engineers work for aerospace firms that do research in oceanography, others plan offshore platforms for oil drilling, and still others teach or conduct research at colleges and universities.

Because the number of marine engineers is small, government and industry often hire mechanical and civil engineers with the understanding that they will take graduate studies to adapt their skills to marine engineering. Employment opportunities for engineers with these skills are very good. Although the United States has only some 850 ships in the merchant fleet, it ranks eighth in the world for tonnage. The current trend is to increase the size rather than the number of vessels. Marine engineers will be needed to create new designs for larger oil tankers (already some are four and a half times the length of a football field), ships that carry containers and barges, Arctic tankers, submarines, and oil drilling platforms. Marine engineers are also in demand to design ships for the U.S. Navy, including destroyers, hydrofoil and air-cushion vehicles, and patrol and escort craft. Commercial fishing and pleasure boating are two other areas that contribute to the favorable employment outlook for marine engineers.

Conditions of work

Most marine engineers work for engineering design firms in offices often employing no more than a dozen workers. Conditions are similar to executive offices in many other fields. Engineers at large shipyards or naval bases may spend time aboard ship, directing the placement or hookup of engines and other equipment. Marine engineers work with shipowners, naval architects, other engineers, and naval officers.

◇ **SOURCES OF ADDITIONAL INFORMATION**

For information on the engineering field in general, see the sources listed in the introductory section of this article.

Society of Naval Architects and Marine Engineers
601 Pavonia Avenue
Jersey City, NY 07306

Mechanical engineers

Nature of the work

Mechanical engineers specialize in the design and manufacture of motors and machines for producing, transmitting, or using power. They design and develop machines that generate power, such as internal combustion engines, jet and rocket engines, gas and steam turbines, and nuclear reactors. Machines that use power, such as the automobile, heating, refrigerating, and air-conditioning units, lathes and other machine tools, fans, and presses, are designed and developed by mechanical engineers. Mechanical engineering provides for a number of specialized branches of work—heating, refrigerating, and air-conditioning; aviation (jet and rocket powered engines); instrumentation (gauges, thermometers, and measuring instruments); hydraulics or fluid mechanics; machines for special industries, such as petroleum, rubber, plastic, and construction; automotive (cars, trucks, buses); marine equipment; steam power (boilers, steam engines, turbines); and railroad equipment.

Mechanical engineers are employed in a large variety of work settings and are involved in all aspects of engineering—research and development, production, sales, administrative, and consulting activities. Among the specialists are *automotive engineers; mechanical design engi-*

An engineer examines a custom-made computer graphics program. He is hired to analyze the design and suggest changes to the system.

neers of facilities (plant systems) and of products; and utilization engineers, who are concerned with the use of gas as a source of power. This field also has engineers who specialize in mechanical research, mechanical equipment testing, and mechanical equipment sales. Plant engineers are factory engineers who design, construct, and maintain the machinery in an industrial plant.

Employment outlook

About 233,000 mechanical engineers were employed in the early 1990s in what is the second largest engineering specialization. More than 60 percent worked in manufacturing, primarily in the machinery, transportation equipment, electrical equipment, and fabricated metal products industries. The remainder had jobs in consulting firms, government agencies, and institutions of higher education.

The growing demand for machinery and machine tools and the increasing complexity of industrial machinery and processes are ex-

pected to maintain a favorable employment climate throughout the 1990s in a field that is growing faster than the average.

Job opportunities will be available in fields such as transportation systems, environmental controls, bioengineering, propulsion systems, robotics, and energy conversion. Mechanical engineers will also be needed to fill the usual vacancies left by workers who retire or change occupations.

Conditions of work

Most mechanical engineers work indoors in offices, research laboratories, or production departments of factories. Some work outdoors at construction projects or mine sites. Those who work in offices often use them as a base for projects located elsewhere.

Mechanical engineers do most of the creative work at drafting boards or on computers. With the increasing sophistication of computer software, engineers are creating more designs with computer assistance.

Engineers in manufacturing will spend a good deal of time working in production areas where the equipment is assembled and tested. Depending on the type of equipment tested, the work site can be noisy.

◇ **SOURCES OF ADDITIONAL INFORMATION**

For information on the engineering field in general, see the sources listed in the introductory section of this article.

American Institute of Plant Engineers
3975 Erie Avenue
Cincinnati, OH 45208

American Society of Mechanical Engineers
345 East 47th Street
New York, NY 10017

National Association of Power Engineers
235 East 24th Street
Terre Haute, IN 47803

Metallurgical engineers

Nature of the work

Metallurgy consists of two main branches, extractive and physical. *Extractive metallurgists* are concerned with the extraction, removal, or separation of metal from its ore. Because metals in their natural state are found in rocks or in combination with other chemical elements, it is usually necessary to process them to free them from other metallic or nonmetallic materials. Extractive metallurgy deals with the further refinement of the isolated metal to ensure the complete removal of all unwanted substances, making it as pure as possible. Physical metallurgy involves the study of the structure and properties of metal. *Physical metallurgists* study the physical characteristics of metals and their alloys and work with methods of effectively converting refined metals into useful final products. Persons working in the field of metallurgy may be referred to as metallurgists or metallurgical engineers. Metallurgists, however, are generally engaged in such activities as research and development or analysis and testing, whereas the metallurgical engineer is usually more involved in the processing of ores or in the converting of refined metals to new products or goods.

Foundry metallurgists are specialists in methods of making castings; *metallographers* in improving grades and types of metals; and *welding engineers* in the fabrication of metals.

Employment outlook

Metallurgical engineering involves a smaller number of engineers than some of the other specializations. There were an estimated 18,000 metallurgical engineers employed in the United States in the early 1990s. About one-fifth of them worked in the metal-producing industries—iron and steel, copper, aluminum, and others. Others were employed in aeronautics and aerospace, machinery, electrical equipment, and other industrial firms that use metals. Some metallurgical engineers work for business and engineering consulting firms and government agencies.

The employment rate for metallurgical engineers is predicted to rise at a rapid rate through the end of the 1990s. They will be needed to develop new metals and alloys and to adapt current ones to new uses, as well as to develop ways to recycle solid waste materials and process the low-grade ores that at this time are not profitable to mine.

Conditions of work

Metallurgical engineers work in laboratories or plants, or both. Extractive metallurgists generally work at mills, smelters, or mines, but they spend most of their time in labs testing and controlling procedures. Physical metallurgists work in plants, where they coordinate the laboratory work with the work in production. Physical metallurgists who do only research usually spend all their time in the lab, rarely in the plant. Modern plants as a rule are well lighted, clean, safe, and often air-conditioned.

◇ **SOURCES OF ADDITIONAL INFORMATION**

For information on the engineering field in general, see the sources listed in the introductory section of this article.

American Institute of Mining, Metallurgical, and Petroleum Engineers
345 East 47th Street
New York, NY 10017

American Society for Metals
Metals Park, OH 44073

The Iron and Steel Society of AIME
420 Commonwealth Drive
Warrendale, PA 15086

For information on scholarships and awards and competitions, write to:

Minerals, Metals, and Materials Society
420 Commonwealth Drive
Warrendale, PA 15086

Mining engineers

Nature of the work

Mining engineers deal with the location and removal of minerals and mineral deposits from the earth. These may be metals (iron, copper), nonmetallic minerals (limestone, gypsum), or coal. Mining engineers conduct preliminary surveys of mineral deposits and examine them to ascertain whether they can be extracted effectively without excessive costs, using either underground or surface mining methods. They plan and design the development of mine shafts and tunnels, devise means of extracting minerals, and select the methods to be used in transporting the minerals to the surface. They supervise all mining operations and are responsible for mine safety. Mining engineers normally specialize in design, research and development, or production.

Mining equipment engineers may specialize in *design, research, testing,* or *sales of equipment and services*. Mines also have their *safety engineers*.

Employment outlook

In the early 1990s, there were approximately 5,200 mining engineers employed in the United States.

More than 60 percent of the mining engineers had jobs in the mining industry itself, while others worked for government agencies, manufacturing companies, or consulting firms. Engineers in the mining industry generally work in small communities where the mineral deposits are situated, but those who specialize in research, management consulting, or sales often are located in metropolitan areas.

The demand for mining engineers is not expected to be strong throughout the 1990s and will continue to experience slow growth as long as other energy sources—petroleum, natural gas, and nuclear energy—are readily available at more reasonable prices. The employment rate for mining engineers in the United States also depends on the price of coal from other countries. A certain number of mining engineers, however, will always be needed. As mineral deposits are depleted, engineers will have to devise ways of mining less accessible low-grade ores to meet the demand for new alloys and new uses for metals. More technologically advanced mining systems and more

firmly enforced health and safety regulations will also have a positive effect on the employment of mining engineers, as will the need to replace the many engineers who transfer to other occupations.

Conditions of work

Mining engineers who are designers, researchers, consultants, administrators, or teachers work in offices, laboratories, or classrooms. Others work at the mine sites, where conditions vary depending on the location of the mine, what kind of mine it is, and what the engineer does. Underground mines are a maze of tunnels, whereas surface mines are open pits the size of a football stadium. Some mines, such as the salt mines under Detroit, Michigan, are located in or near densely populated regions; others are in remote areas such as Alaska or Greenland.

Living at most mine sites is similar to living in a small town, and the engineers share the same conditions as the miners. Workers in foreign or remote locations are provided low-cost housing, schools, and hospitals by the mining companies. Modern techniques and strictly enforced safety measures make mining easier and safer than it used to be.

◇ **SOURCES OF ADDITIONAL INFORMATION**

For information on the engineering field in general, see the sources listed in the introductory section of this article.

American Institute of Mining, Metallurgical, and Petroleum Engineers
345 East 47th Street
New York, NY 10017

National Coal Association
1130 17th Street, NW
Washington, DC 20036

Society of Mining Engineers of AIME
PO Box 625005
Littleton, CO 80127

Nuclear engineers

Nature of the work

Nuclear engineering is a relatively new field. It came into existence around the middle of this century, after scientists discovered a way to split the center (nucleus) of the atom, thus releasing neutrons and energy. When atomic fission (splitting) results in an uncontrolled chain reaction, in which released neutrons split other atoms and release still more energy, an explosion occurs. Nuclear weapons are designed to make use of this effect. But the splitting process can be slowed down and controlled by a nuclear reactor. In this way, nuclear energy—also called "atomic energy"—is used today to produce heat and electricity. It is also used to help detect the age of objects or measure their size, to trace the movement of blood through the body, recover natural resources, promote the healthy growth of plants, and to see inside metal objects. The possibilities for new applications are seemingly limitless. Nuclear engineers and scientists are continually looking for additional ways to produce and use nuclear energy.

Nuclear engineers plan, design, and develop nuclear equipment such as reactor vessels and cores, radiation shields, and the instruments and controls that produce nuclear energy. They direct and monitor the operation of nuclear power plants to ensure they function efficiently and conform to safety standards. Some nuclear engineers engage in research and conduct tests relating to the release, control, and utilization of nuclear energy. Based on their findings, they prove or modify theories about nuclear energy, develop new concepts of nuclear energy systems, and find new uses for radioactive materials, in industry or medicine for example. Nuclear engineers may study the nuclear fuel cycle to find more economical ways to make and use nuclear material and safer ways to dispose of nuclear waste. And some may work on the development of nuclear weapons.

Nuclear equipment engineers may choose to specialize in *design, research, testing,* or *sales.* Other specialists in the field of nuclear engineering include the following. *Nuclear-fuels reclamation engineers* design systems whereby nuclear fuels are reprocessed. *Nuclear-fuels research engineers* test various fuels to find the safest and most efficient ways to use them. *Nuclear-criticality safety engineers* analyze methods of transporting, handling, and storing nuclear fuels and recommend measures to prevent an accidental nuclear reaction. *Radiation protection en-* *gineers* monitor the radiation levels in water and check for corrosion of equipment used in nuclear power plants.

Employment outlook

Of the almost 14,000 nuclear engineers in the early 1990s, almost one-fifth were employed by the federal government. Nearly half of these were civilian employees of the Navy, about a third worked for the Nuclear Regulatory Commission, and the rest had jobs with the Department of Energy or the Tennessee Valley Authority. Nuclear engineers in nongovernment positions worked mostly for public utilities or consulting companies. Some were employed by manufacturers of nuclear equipment.

Jobs for nuclear engineers will not be very plentiful throughout the 1990s because energy conservation and concern about the safety of nuclear power plants have brought about a reduction in the demand for electric power. Nevertheless, as the number of new graduates in this field is small and has been declining in recent years, employment opportunities should be good for nuclear engineers. It is unlikely that many new nuclear plants will be started before the end of the decade, but nuclear engineers will be needed to operate plants already in existence or presently under construction. Also, some will be required to elevate safety standards and to work in areas related to defense.

Conditions of work

Most nuclear engineers work in clean, modern, well-equipped offices or laboratories. A large number work outdoors, however, at job sites where they may be installing, testing, or starting up new equipment. Some nuclear engineers, especially those in sales, may do some traveling.

Although radioactive materials can be dangerous and require careful handling, strict safety laws have kept the injury rate for nuclear engineers lower than that for industry in general. Work done with radioactive substances is conducted with robotic equipment. Testing of radiation exposure is done on all workers entering and exiting the nuclear power plants. Because of the nature of the facility, identification tags and door codes or passes are required for all employees.

For information on the engineering field in general, see the sources listed in the introductory section of this article.

American Nuclear Society
555 North Kensington Avenue
LaGrange Park, IL 60525

U.S. Council for Energy Awareness
1776 I Street, NW
Suite 400
Washington, DC 20006

Petroleum engineers

Nature of the work

Petroleum engineers begin work after an exploration team finds a possible oil or gas field. They decide which drilling methods will extract the maximum amount of oil or gas from the site, then supervise the operation and the shipment from field to refinery. Petroleum engineers work constantly to increase the proportion of oil recovered from each natural reservoir and to develop new sources for oil and gas. They conduct research on drilling methods and ways to recover oil and gas in such previously inaccessible areas as the Arctic and the ocean floor. Petroleum engineers also may help appraise oil field properties and act as consultants to oil firms.

Oilfield equipment engineers may specialize in *design, research, testing,* or *sales of equipment and services.* In petroleum production, *chief engineers for research* develop and improve methods of drilling wells and producing oil or gas; *chief petroleum engineers* are involved with the development of oil fields; *chief engineers* direct the activities of workers in engineering departments of petroleum production or pipeline companies; and *specialist field engineers* collect and analyze fluid samples from oil- or gas-producing formations.

Employment outlook

In the early 1990s, there were approximately 22,000 petroleum engineers employed in the United States.

Most of the petroleum engineers were employed by major oil companies; smaller, independent oil exploration, production, and service companies; and organizations in fields closely related to the oil industry. Others worked for government agencies, consulting firms, and equipment suppliers. Some were independent consultants. Petroleum engineers are employed in oil-producing states such as Texas, Oklahoma, Louisiana, and California, as well as overseas in oil-producing countries.

The employment of petroleum engineers is expected to show only slow growth through the end of the 1990s. Domestic petroleum companies have reduced their exploration and production activities because of the drop in oil prices. As a result, new graduates will be faced with strong competition for the few job opportunities that will be available. It is anticipated that the price of oil will eventually rise enough to stimulate activity once again in exploration and production, but most job openings in the meantime will be to replace petroleum engineers who transfer to other occupations or leave the work force altogether.

Conditions of work

Most petroleum engineers work in offices located in cities of varying size and make occasional visits to an oil field. Those who work full-time in the fields have to contend with all kinds of weather. Overseas oil companies arrange housing typical of the country or build special communities for their employees to live in.

◇ SOURCES OF ADDITIONAL INFORMATION

For information on the engineering field in general, see the sources listed in the introductory section of this article.

American Petroleum Institute
1220 L Street, NW
Washington, DC 20005

American Institute of Mining, Metallurgical, and Petroleum Engineers
345 East 47th Street
New York, NY 10017

Society of Petroleum Engineers
PO Box 833836
Richardson, TX 75083

Miscellaneous engineers

Nature of the work

The field of engineering is so diversified that anyone going into it is sure to find a specialty to suit his or her own interests and aptitudes. Besides the engineering occupations in the broader areas already described, there are others that are less easily classified, either because the occupation is unique in itself or because it interacts with a number of other categories. Some of these engineering occupations are described in the paragraphs that follow.

Fire-protection engineers devise ways to prevent and control fires in structures such as factories, office and government buildings, stores, high-rise apartments, and houses, as well as in vehicles such as automobiles, buses, trains, planes, and spacecraft. These engineers may function as designers, inspectors, or investigators. Their recommendations for fire-protection mechanisms in buildings may include wall panels, fire doors, heat and smoke detectors, sprinkler systems, or fire escapes, as well as fire-resistant paints, fabrics, and furnishings. For a plant that uses chemicals, they consider not only prevention of fire and explosion while the chemicals are in use, but safe means of disposing of the chemicals afterward. Fire-protection engineers inspect structures, investigate causes of fire, and sometimes redesign structures based on their findings. Those who work for the government or for insurance companies also may ensure that owners and workers obey safety laws. In their plans for vehicles, fire-protection engineers recommend fire-protection materials, devise procedures for and means of escape in case fire breaks out, and design safe methods for using fuels and diffusing exhaust fumes. Fire-protection engineers may work on a variety of projects or may specialize.

Materials engineers study plans for a new product and recommend which materials, such as metals, ceramics, polymers, fibers, or paper, would be best for its manufacture. The choice of materials is based on consideration of such factors as strength, weight, and cost, as well as how the product is intended to be used. Materials engineers may suggest already existing materials or may improve or develop new ones for specific products. They also test failed products to see what the problem may have been. Before making their recommendations, these engineers take into account government safety and environmental standards. Equipment used in this occupation may include microscopes, X rays, ultrasound devices and other test apparatus, and computers or calculators.

Optical engineers design optical systems for specific optical instruments, such as cameras, telescopes, and viewing and display devices. For these instruments to work effectively, their optical systems must be built with precision, with their components mounted in exact relation to one another and to the instruments. Optical engineers are extremely careful in drawing up plans and in repeated inspection and testing of the systems until they are accurate. They also design testing equipment to detect any deviations. Work in this occupation may require collaboration with electrical and mechanical engineers.

Ordnance engineers design, test, and develop explosive materials and ammunition for military use. Relying on a knowledge of explosives and plastics chemistry, ballistics theory, fuse technology, metallurgy, electronics, and fluidics (which refers to the pressures and flows of a channeled fluid), they prepare designs to meet the specifications of military authorities. In addition, they may negotiate production contracts with procurement personnel. Ordnance specifications are based on desired characteristics, the nature of the target objective, and the type of delivery system used. Ordnance engineers may also help develop such delivery systems, as well as fire-control components and nonexplosive material.

Maintainability engineers are concerned with the maintenance requirements of products being designed, and they look for ways to keep breakdowns to a minimum and to reduce the time necessary to restore mechanisms to working condition. They study designs of products such as aircraft, ships, or electronic control or navigation systems in advance of production and suggest refinements to improve their maintainability. These engineers devise tests to demonstrate how easy it is to keep the equipment working properly, recommend a program of maintenance procedures, and offer advice on the makeup of the crew and training requirements.

Photographic engineers design and construct photographic equipment for scientific and industrial purposes. They are also involved in setting up the equipment, planning procedures, and determining which materials are needed to achieve desired objectives. The occupation combines a knowledge of engineering, chemistry, and photographic techniques. Photographic engineers may be sought out to give advice on matters such as high-speed photography, radiography, graphic arts, and aerial and space photography.

Pollution-control engineers seek to prevent pollution of the environment by designing systems for air and water quality control, noise abatement, and solid waste disposal. They study the problem, devise methods of identifying and measuring pollutants, and design and build systems to reduce their concentration. Pollution-control engineers set policies and standards. They determine whether industries are complying with pollution control laws and, depending on their findings, recommend that the companies be issued or denied a permit to construct or operate facilities that contribute to generating pollution.

Reliability engineers try to prevent or reduce the chance of failure of major products such as aircraft, ships and submarines, or electronic communication or control systems. They begin by analyzing the preliminary design concepts. They consider how the equipment is intended to be used, identify potential trouble spots, and suggest revisions in the design that will make the product more reliable for the customer. Reliability engineers evaluate the dependability of a product by conducting tests and analyzing information from customers about the number of unit failures and their causes.

Logistics engineers coordinate the personnel, materiel, and facilities involved in manufacturing or servicing products, systems, or equipment. The logistics programs they develop ensure the efficiency and economy of a product from its conception on the drawing board through production, distribution, and its usable life. Logistics engineers prepare handbooks, bulletins, and information systems; encourage the use of standardized, interchangeable parts; and make recommendations on such matters as timing, location of areas of operation, and environmental and human factors that affect workers. Their efforts are intended to benefit management, subcontractors, and customers alike.

Project engineers have charge of specific engineering projects. It is their responsibility to see that the programs are completed satisfactorily, on time, and within the established budget. To accomplish this, project engineers plan, organize, and control all aspects of a project. They set up and monitor schedules, assign personnel to particular tasks or phases of work, and keep a rein on expenditures. These engineers make sure a product design complies not only with engineering principles, but with company standards and customer specifications. They also resolve design and test problems as they arise and must approve any changes in the original plans.

Resource-recovery engineers are concerned with recovering solid wastes and converting them into marketable products. They study chemical and mechanical ways to process such wastes to determine whether recycling can be accomplished efficiently and economically. They inspect solid-waste resource recovery facilities to see that their construction and use comply with government regulations, and they provide technical advice to design engineers and others concerned. Resource recovery engineers help find or develop markets for materials that have been reclaimed and give public lectures to promote interest in the practice of recovering solid-waste resources.

Soils engineers analyze the soils on land being considered for construction or development to determine whether it is suitable for the proposed project and what kinds of problems may be encountered. They study soil and rock samples from both above and below the surface of the ground for evidence of its characteristics and stability. Then they figure what weights the soil can bear and prepare maps, charts, and

reports of their test results. The reports and recommendations of soils engineers affect decisions concerning slope angles and trading of the property and foundation design and height of the structures to be erected. Soils engineers may take part in studies regarding the impact of certain factors on the environment.

Employment outlook

Any discussion of job outlook for such a diverse group of engineering occupations must be fairly general. It is safe to say, however, that employment prospects for those with engineering degrees are expected to be good through the end of the 1990s. Much of the growth in this field will result from increased investment in industrial plants and equipment to produce more goods and services. The need for defense-related products and improved transportation facilities will also create a demand for more engineers.

Job security for engineers is higher than for most other workers because many engineers are employed on long-term projects that continue even during economic recessions. A possible exception would be in industries such as aerospace and electronics in the event of large cutbacks in spending for defense or research and development.

Conditions of work

The working conditions for the engineers in this group vary depending on the nature of their duties. Some spend most of their time at a desk or in a laboratory; others may work outdoors, in plants, or at test sites. Some engineers travel extensively.

◇ **SOURCES OF ADDITIONAL INFORMATION**

For information on the engineering field in general, see the sources listed in the introductory section of this article.

Air and Waste Management Association
PO Box 2861
Pittsburgh, PA 15230

American Academy of Environmental Engineers
PO Box 269
132 Holiday Court, Suite #206
Annapolis, MD 21401

National Institute of Packaging, Handling and Logistic Engineers
6902 Lyle Street
Lanham, MD 20706

Society of Packaging Professionals
Reston International Center, Suite 212
11800 Sunrise Valley Drive
Reston, VA 22091

Society of Plastics Engineers
14 Fairfield Drive
Brookfield Center, CT 06805

Water Pollution Control Federation
601 Wythe Street
Alexandria, VA 22314

Enologists (wine makers)

Definition

Enologists direct and manage all activities of a winery, including the planting of the grapes and the producing, storing, and shipping of the wine. They utilize knowledge of the wine growing industry to select the type of grapes grown and then set standards for and supervise the workers in the production process from harvesting to fermenting.

Enologist work with different varieties of grapes in a type or species to develop the strongest, most resistant to disease, most flavorful line of grape for wine production.

The staff members of a wine-making company gather at a laboratory to sample wine. They must ensure a consistent taste and quality in the wine they produce.

History

Wine making has been practiced for more than 5,000 years, having been part of different cultures all over the world. The ancient Egyptians had hieroglyphics (picture writings) representing wine making, and it was an important commodity in Palestine during the time of Jesus. The Chinese made wine more than 4,000 years ago and the Greeks and Romans also used wine extensively.

Throughout history, wine's distinctive flavor has been used as a drink to accompany a meal, or as part of the religious practices of many religions. In fact, it was its use in religious services that spread the use of wine in Europe, as the Roman Catholic Church used it in its Mass. Wine also has had medicinal (curative) purposes, such as its use as a relaxant.

Wine has been cultivated in the United States since the late 1700s. It is a major industry now, with growth primarily in the eastern part of the country and California. More than 80 percent of the domestic wine is cultivated in California. Enologists have played an instrumental role in the growth of the wine industry, experimenting with different types of grapes and growing conditions.

Nature of the work

Enologists are involved in all aspects of wine production and therefore must have a thorough knowledge of the wine making business. They should be able to analyze the ripeness and sugar content of grapes, decide what vines are best to grow, determine when vines are ripe enough to be picked, and coordinate the pro-

duction of the wine making process. Production decisions include how much additives, such as yeast or bacteria, to use and at what temperature fermentation should occur.

Selection of the proper grapes is a vital part of an enologist's planning responsibilities. This selection process includes analyzing the various varieties of European and native American grapes to determine which are best suited to grow in a specific area given existing soil and climate conditions. For example, an enologist in California must ensure that grapes chosen to grow in that climate can withstand the heat of the summers, while an enologist in New York must ensure that grapes chosen to grow in that climate can withstand the lower temperatures present there. Other factors determining which type of grapes to grow include the species ability to withstand disease.

The type of grape or grapes chosen to cultivate determines the time of planting and specific pruning methods. Grapes producing red wine are processed in a different fashion than grapes producing white wine. Production methods also vary according to the size of the winery and the type of containers and stainless steel tanks used in the crushing and fermentation processes. The enologist has the final word in all production decisions. He or she will consult with other winery staff and then decide issues involving the testing and crushing of grapes, the cooling, filtering, and bottling of the wine, and the type of storage casks in which to place the wine. The enologist is also responsible for researching and implementing appropriate modifications in the growing and production techniques to ensure the best quality product at the lowest possible cost. This involves keeping up with technological improvements in production methods and an ability to read and analyze a profit-and-loss statement and other parts of a balance sheet.

As a manager, the enologist is responsible for overseeing all personnel matters. Enologists may hire and fire employees, coordinate work schedules, and develop a salary structure. Interpersonal skills are utilized in establishing rapport with the workers in the vineyard and production areas and communications skills are needed to present written and oral reports, and, when necessary, to train workers for a particular job.

Although bookkeeping and other administrative tasks are often delegated to an assistant, enologists must have an understanding of accounting and mathematical formulas utilized in business transactions. Production costs and other expenses must be carefully recorded. The increased use of data-processing equipment for analyzing and recording business information means that the enologist should have some training in computer science.

An enologist is also involved with decisions regarding the marketing of the finished product. Transportation and other distribution costs must be known, and the potential markets on the national and international level must be analyzed. Labor, machinery, and other production costs, such as any money spent on insecticides, must all be analyzed and recorded in the effort to determine the price of the finished wine and where the wine will be sold. In the final analysis, the enologist is largely responsible for the economic success of a winery.

Requirements

Although some wineries offer on-the-job training in the form of apprenticeships to high-school graduates, the majority of entry level positions go to college graduates, so a college degree is the recommended first step on the career path for those looking to enter the field. High-school students should take courses in mathematics, biology, chemistry, and physics. English and other courses that enhance communications skills should also be taken. Foreign languages, particularly French and German, may enhance opportunities for study or research abroad.

A college degree in enology or viticulture (the cultivation of grapes) is preferred, but a person who graduates with a degree in horticulture or another subject concerning the science of growing will also have many of the skills needed to be successful. Coursework should include biology, soil science, chemistry, and botany. Specific courses related to winery management should include wine analysis, winery practices, and the marketing of wine. General business courses and computer classes should also be part of the degree program.

As competition in the field increases, many enologists are choosing to pursue a master's degree.

Special requirements

Although no licenses or certificates are necessary to work in the field, many enologists chose to continue professional enrichment programs through affiliation with organizations such as the American Society for Enology and Viticulture. The address for several professional organizations can be found at the end of this article.

Opportunities for experience and exploration

Part-time or summer employment at a winery is an excellent method of gaining an insight into the skills and temperament needed for this profession. A high-school student can also explore opportunities in the field through discussions with professionals already working as enologists. Because many technical colleges offer evening courses, it may be possible for a high-school student to audit a course or take a course for future college credit.

Related occupations

A production superintendent in a factory or mill, a manager of a food processing plant, and a brewing director of malt liquors all are involved with working with organic material (living matter, such as grapes and other plants) and assembling that substance into a manufactured product (such as wine or beer). Horticulturists work with the growth and production of plants for seed and consumption.

Methods of entering

The usual method of entry is to be hired by a winery after completing an undergraduate or graduate degree in enology or viticulture. Sometimes, summer or part-time employment can lead to an offer of a permanent job and an apprenticeship program at the winery provides the necessary training.

Advancement

As in most professions, advancement depends on skill, experience, and education. Enologists at small wineries may become managers at larger facilities. Those at larger facilities may move on to direct a number of wineries as part of a nationwide organization. A relatively small number of enologists may start their own wineries.

Because of the relatively small number of wineries in the country, and the fact that enologists have high-level management positions from the start, advancement opportunities are somewhat limited.

217

Employment outlook

Job growth is tied somewhat to a rise in population, as a greater number of people in the United States will lead to a demand for more wine. Technological advances in wine production may also open up job opportunities. Employment is expected to grow a little faster than average into the early 1990s. Obviously, job opportunities will be best in California, where 80 percent of the U.S. wineries are located. Most of the California wine is cultivated in the San Joaquin, Napa, and Sonoma valleys.

Earnings

Beginning salaries average between $18,000 to $28,000 per year, depending on experience, education, and the size of the winery. (Larger wineries tend to pay more than smaller operations.) Experienced enologists can make anywhere from $30,000 to $85,000 per year, with some highly skilled enologists making even more.

Conditions of work

An enologist can expect to work both indoors in a winery and outdoors in a vineyard. Indoor work will be split between planning and administrative tasks that may take place in an office setting and supervisory tasks that take place along the assembly line.

Enologists have a good deal of variety in their jobs as they constantly alternate between analyzing the grapes in the field, assessing current production techniques, planning marketing strategies for the upcoming harvest, and other responsibilities. Physical labor, such as lifting a forty-pound wine case or pruning a vineyard may be required, but as a rule the job is not that physically demanding.

During most of the year an enologist works forty hours a week, but during the late summer and early fall when the grape harvest occurs, an enologist should expect to work long hours six or seven days a week.

Social and psychological factors

As a manager, an enologist should be able to communicate and work well with people. The enologist should be clear and concise in giving directions. An enologist should have leadership abilities and also be able to follow instructions at times. The ability to interpret data is vital as much of the enologist's planning responsibilities involve working with crop and market forecasts. Attention to detail is critical. An enologist should be able to spend long hours analyzing information, and also be able to make and implement decisions concerning this information. At times, the ability to work long hours under pressure will be required. Some travel may be necessary for conferences or other professional obligations.

GOE: 05.02.03; SIC: 2084; SOC: 132

◇ **SOURCES OF ADDITIONAL INFORMATION**

General information about career opportunities is available from:

American Society for Enology and Viticulture
PO Box 1855
Davis, CA 95617

Association of American Vintners
Box 307
East Rochester, NY 14445

American Wine Society
3006 Latta Road
Rochester, NY 14612

◇ **RELATED ARTICLES**

Volume 1: Agriculture; Biological Sciences; Chemistry
Volume 2: Biologists; Chemists
Volume 3: Agricultural scientists; Beekeepers; Dairy farmers; Farmers; Farm operatives and managers
Volume 4: Agribusiness technicians; Agricultural equipment technicians; Biological technicians; Farm crop production technicians; Ornamental horticulture technicians

Ergonomists

Definition

Ergonomists study the workplace to determine the effects of the work environment on the activities of individuals and groups. They conduct research and analyze data concerning the physical factors of the workplace (noise, temperature, and so on) and evaluate the design of machines to see that they are safe, usable, and conducive to productive work. Ergonomists are frequently called on to advise factory owners, managers, or other top business officials on how to best plan and implement design proposals that integrate human factors into the work environment.

History

Although work has played an important and enduring role in our society, it is only recently that people have begun to research actively the work environment. The study of people at work began about one hundred years ago as employers and employees alike began to realize that job productivity was tied to job satisfaction and the nature of the work environment.

The concerns of many of the early ergonomists centered around increasing industrial production while maintaining safety on the job. They began to design machines and other equipment that not only improved production but also reduced the number of job-related accidents. As it became clear that improved working conditions not only increased productivity and safety but also improved the workers' morale, ergonomists began investigating other physical and psychological factors that influenced humans at work.

Today, with the world of work constantly changing and workplaces utilizing computers and other forms of automation, there is a need for professionals to help adapt the workplace to reflect these changes. The adaptations involve physical and psychological needs. This is where the ergonomist can play a vital role. The ergonomist can help develop methods to more humanely adapt the workplace to technological changes and also prepare the workplace for the different types of jobs and other changes that are sure to follow. (*See also* "Human Factors Specialists" elsewhere in this volume.)

Nature of the work

Ergonomists are concerned with the relationship between people and work. They deal with organizational structure, worker productivity, and job satisfaction. A major portion of their work concerns designing machines and other equipment that is both usable and comfortable to the user. For example, ergonomists may study assembly line procedures and suggest changes so as to reduce the monotony and make it easier to unload and thereby obtain optimum efficiency in terms of human capabilities. They may also investigate environmental factors, such as lighting and room temperature that influence the workers' behavior and productivity.

Ergonomists usually work as part of a team, with different specialists focusing on a particular aspect of the work environment. For example, one ergonomist may focus on the safety aspects of the machinery, and another ergonomist may focus on environmental issues, such as the volume of noise and the layout of the surroundings.

After analyzing relevant data and observing how workers interact in the work environment, ergonomists submit a written report of their findings and then make recommendations to company executives with suggestions for changes or adaptations in the workplace. They may make proposals for new machinery or suggest a revised design for machinery already in place. They may also suggest environmental changes, such as the painting of the walls so that employees can better enjoy the work environment.

With backgrounds in psychology or industrial design, ergonomists are interested in designing or redesigning workplaces that are productive yet comfortable. They may focus on something as large as redesigning the computer terminals for a large multinational corporation, or they may focus on designing more comfortable chairs or easier-to-use telephones at a local family-owned business. Ergonomists may work as consultants for governmental agencies and manufacturing companies, or engage in research at colleges or universities. Often, an ergonomist will specialize in one particular area of work analysis.

Ergonomists are concerned with both the social and physical work environments. They are involved with personnel training and development, and the interaction between hu-

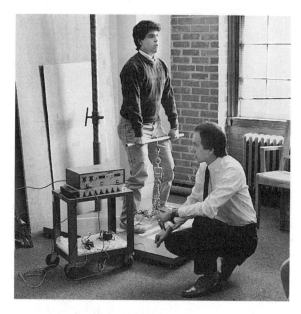

An ergonomist conducts a test to measure human static strength. He is applying the concept of fitting a task to a worker.

mans and machines. They may plan various kinds of tests that will help screen applicants for employment with the firms. They also help engineers and technicians to design systems that require people and machines to interact. They may also develop aids for training people to use those systems.

Ergonomists write reports, speeches, and occasionally may write manuals of instructions for machine operations and other purposes.

Requirements

The ergonomist must bring together a variety of business administration and interpersonal relationship skills. Most ergonomists have their undergraduate degrees in either psychology or industrial engineering. These undergraduate degrees are usually not enough to prepare a person for an entry-level position, but rather serve as the best preparation for graduate work in the same areas. Courses should include industrial engineering, psychology, statistics, computer applications, and health sciences. Research techniques should also be studied as part of the degree program. In general, a master's degree is required for most positions, and a doctorate is a big plus, especially for those who want to work as an instructor or in upper management.

High-school students should take college-preparatory courses, such as mathematics, physical sciences, English, psychology, and statis-

tics, if possible. Students should take all the science courses that can fit into their schedule to prepare for later work with scientific methods. They should also take modern foreign languages, especially French or German, because reading comprehension of these languages is often a requirements for completing a doctoral thesis. Mathematics is valuable for graduate work in statistics.

Special requirements

There are no special licenses or certificates needed to work as a ergonomist. Those who work for the federal government may need to pass a civil service test. The American Board of Examiners in Professional Psychology offers diplomas in industrial-organizational psychology to those persons with a doctorate and experience who can pass the required psychology examinations. Because this is a new and growing field, it is especially important to keep up-to-date on the latest developments. Belonging to a professional organization, such as the American Psychological Association or the Human Factors Society, is a good way of doing this. Addresses for several organizations are listed at the end of this article.

Opportunities for experience and exploration

Only those with the required educational credentials can get hands-on experience, so the most practical way to explore career opportunities is to talk with those already working in the field. A great deal of career information can also be found in professional journals or other similar publications.

Related occupations

Other occupations concerned with evaluating human behavior in regards to the work environment include, school psychologists, directors of counseling, and vocational-rehabilitation counselors. Social workers and job analysts also utilize many of the same skills as ergonomists. Human factors specialists also do work that is similar. Consulting work is common. (For more information on consulting, *see* Volume 1: Personal and Consulting Services.)

Methods of entering

Those with the proper credentials should contact large industrial companies or manufacturing firms to apply for a position. Governmental agencies, consulting firms, and college and university research departments all also hire qualified ergonomists. College placement offices may be helpful in providing job leads in this regard. Public and private employment services may also refer qualified applicants to suitable entry positions.

Persons with a post-graduate degree in psychology or industrial engineering should have the best employment opportunities.

Advancement

Because ergonomics is still a relatively new field, advancement opportunities are considered good for the foreseeable future. There are not that many people involved in the field, and therefore there are many opportunities for qualified individuals, especially those who have a special area of expertise. Many ergonomists develop skills at a first job and then either use that experience to find higher paid work at a different company or use it to get increased responsibility at their initial firm.

Qualified ergonomists often are promoted to management positions, with an accompanying increase in earnings and responsibility. They can also start their own consulting firms or branch off into teaching or research. Those in government work may choose to move to the private sector, where higher salaries are the norm. But others may opt for the security and job responsibilities of a government position.

Employment outlook

As the work environment has become more complex and workers are expecting more from their jobs, the opportunities for ergonomists has continued to grow. This trend is expected to continue through the early 1990s. The occupation should be somewhat insulated from changes in the economy. If the economy grows, more companies will need to adapt workplaces to increase production capabilities. If the economy slows down, many companies will need to cut costs and improve productivity. The skilled ergonomist can facilitate both situations.

The majority of ergonomists now work for large manufacturing firms and this should continue into the future. Smaller firms will also continue to utilize ergonomists. Computer companies and others that utilize automated systems will need ergonomists to help them develop effective and stimulating work environments. The government will also be looking to hire experts who can design safe and productive work environments. Colleges, universities, and other research facilities will also look to ergonomists to interpret data and supply new ideas for productive work environments. Some ergonomists will specialize in being free-lance consultants and witnesses in legal proceedings.

Earnings

Although exact earnings obviously depend on the individual's education and experience and the type of work sought, in general the earning potential of ergonomists reflect the many years of study and experience needed to become proficient in the field. Beginning ergonomists may earn anywhere from $26,000 to $55,000 per year, with those with a doctorate the upper end of the salary spectrum. Experienced ergonomists often earn more than $60,000 per year, especially those who work in private industry. Again, those with a doctorate tend to earn more than those with a master's degree. Full-time employees usually receive health insurance, vacation, and other benefits.

Ergonomists who work as consultants usually get paid a negotiated fee, with rates ranging from $60 to $180 per hour, depending on the individual's skill and reputation. These consultants have more control over their working hours, but usually do not receive health insurance or other benefits. Many ergonomists may hold a full-time positions and then consult or teach part-time.

Conditions of work

Ergonomists encounter various working conditions depending on specific duties and responsibilities. An ergonomist may work in a typical office environment, with computer and data processing equipment close at hand, or the ergonomist may work in a factory, investigating production problems. Usually, the ergonomist will combined the two, working in an office setting and making frequent visits to a factory or other location to work out particular production issues. Although the majority of work is not strenuous, ergonomists may occasionally assemble or revamp machines.

Ergonomists often work as part of a team, but they may also work on an individual research project, spending much time alone. They usually work a forty-hour week, although overtime is not uncommon, especially if a particular project is on deadline. There may be occasion weekend and evening work. Those involved with research or teaching may only work ten months a year, although many of these ergonomists work as consultants when not working full-time.

Social and psychological factors

Ergonomists should be able to conduct research or develop project proposals while working as part of a team or while working alone. They must be able to spend long periods analyzing complex data and should be able to come up with creative solutions to sometimes difficult production questions. Good oral and written communications skills are vital, as an ergonomist must be persuasive in discussing production alternatives with company executives.

An ergonomist should have good decision-making ability and be able to handle the pressure that may come when suggesting production changes that may have a long-term economic impact on the company instituting those changes. Confidence and strength of character are therefore important characteristics. Ergonomists should have leadership skills and be able to motivate others. They should also be able to work with other professionals who might not always agree with their analysis.

GOE: 11.03.01; SIC: Any industry; SOC: 1915

◇ **SOURCES OF ADDITIONAL INFORMATION**

Career information is available from:

American Psychological Association
1200 17th Street, NW
Washington, DC 20036

Human Factors Society
PO Box 1369
Santa Monica, CA 90406

Industrial Designers Society of America
1142-E Walker Road
Great Falls, VA 22066

◇ **RELATED ARTICLES**

Volume 1: Social Sciences
Volume 2: Psychologists; Sociologists

Export-import specialists

Definition

Export-import specialists plan and coordinate business transactions involving the importing or exporting of goods from one or more foreign countries. They may work for the government, an international company, or as a representative of an individual client. Depending on their specific job responsibilities, export-import specialists may be involved in various aspects of foreign trade, from negotiating trade agreements to planning and supervising the actual delivery of goods. Most specialists work with exportation or importation; they rarely do both.

History

Trade between countries has historically been tied to the conquering of one nation by another. During the expansion of the Roman Empire, for example, there was much trade between the Far East and Europe. Exotic clothes and spices from the Orient made their way into the eager hands of wealthy Europeans. Shipping routes and roads were built for trade. When the Roman Empire fell about 1,600 years ago, international trade slowed until the Crusades 600 years later again increased contact among nations.

In the fifteenth and sixteenth centuries, explorers such as Christopher Columbus and Ferdinand Magellan undertook long voyages to open new trade routes. In fact, the voyage by Columbus that led to the discovery of the New World was undertaken with the idea of finding a shorter sea route from Europe to the Indies.

In North America, the early colonists traded products or raw materials from this country, such as tobacco and furs, and received clothes and other manufactured goods from England in return.

Now, the importing and exporting of goods in the United States accounts for almost $900 billion in sales each year. The growth of foreign business and its importance to the national economy has created a need for specialists who can handle the complex problems of international business.

An export-import specialist leads a group of retailers through an overseas production facility. He can advise them on legal means of importing the goods.

Nature of the work

There are a variety of professionals involved in the export-import industry. Some may be involved only with the importing of raw materials or finished goods, while others may only be involved with the exporting or these items. Many specialists, however, are involved in both the importing and exporting of foreign trade. All specialists must understand international law and be aware of export-import regulations, such as duty fees, but specific responsibilities vary according to the area of specialization.

Export managers direct foreign sales activities, including negotiating sales and distribution contracts and arranging payment for exported goods. They handle details involved in the transportation of goods, including licensing agreements, customs declarations, and packing and shipping. Export managers work with foreign buyers, federal agents, and company executives to coordinate shipping, air freight, and other transportation methods. They also supervise clerical staff in preparing foreign correspondence and in the preparation of foreign language material, such as sales literature and bid requests, meant to expedite foreign trade.

Customs-house brokers act as intermediaries between importers and the customs service through the preparation of entry papers for goods arriving from abroad. They file appropriate documents to allow delivery of foreign goods and assess import duties and taxes. Custom-house brokers act as trouble-shooters between importers and the federal government, counseling importers on relevant rules and regulations, working out any last minute problems, and arranging for storage of goods in warehouses, if necessary.

Wholesalers buy imported goods for sale on domestic markets or buy domestic products for sale abroad. Some may buy both imported and exported material for later sale. Often, wholesalers specialize in buying or selling a specific good or raw material from a foreign country, such as clothes or jewelry. Wholesalers often arrange for the packing and shipping of goods, and work with U.S. and foreign customs officials to ensure timely and accurate delivery.

Import-export agents manage activities of import-export firms, coordinating settlements between foreign and domestic buyers and sellers. They plan delivery of goods and supervise workers in the shipping and receiving departments. Import-export agents act as trade representatives throughout the freight handling process, overseeing the assessment of import and export taxes, the granting of entry permits, and resolving any questions or concerns on the part of customs officials or foreign or domestic business people.

Requirements

While not required for some positions within the export-import field, a college degree is becoming increasingly more important. Specific degree programs will depend on the type of job desired, but in general undergraduate degrees in business management, political science, or economics are helpful. Coursework should include classes in international trade, marketing, business administration, communications, computer applications, and statistics. Many people who want management positions in the

223

export-import field are now deciding to get a master's in business administration (MBA), with an emphasis in international trade.

High-school students interested in a career as an export-import specialist should take college-preparatory classes, such as English, social studies, geography, and mathematics. Developing a fluency in a foreign language, especially one that is widely used in international trade, such as Japanese, Russian, or German, is very important.

Special requirements

There are generally no special requirements for export managers, wholesalers, or import-export agents, but customs-house brokers must be licensed by the U.S. Customs Service. The licensing process requires passing a written examination covering export-import rules and regulations. Specifics on the licensing procedures are available from the U.S. Customs Service at the address given at the end of this article.

In some areas of wholesaling, such as the buying or selling of technical equipment, wholesalers may need to have technical training and belong to appropriate professional groups. Companies that export sensitive material, such as military hardware, must get an export license from the U.S. Department of Commerce.

As a means of enhancing professional standing, many export-import specialists belong to professional organizations, such as the American Association of Exporters and Importers, and the National Foreign Trade Council.

Opportunities for experience and exploration

High-school students can seek part-time or summer employment in a large store or other retail establishment, as it may provide helpful insight into a merchandising career. After graduation from high school, an internship with an international company would be very valuable in ascertaining the rewards and responsibilities of a career as a export-import specialist. In addition, discussions with professionals already working in the field are an excellent way of learning about career opportunities. For more information, see Volume 1: Foreign Trade.

Related occupations

Occupations that share the sales and supervisory responsibilities of an export manager include service representatives, advertising managers, and sales managers.

Custom-house brokers share a variety of job responsibilities with professionals involved in coordinating financial arrangements, such as real-estate agents, credit negotiators, and brokerage house managers.

Wholesalers are related in job function with others involved with buying and selling merchandise, such as sales supervisors, commissary managers, and retail store managers.

Import-export agents manage transportation of goods and services, much like an airport manager, a harbor manager, or a transportation director.

Methods of entering

Those without a college degree may begin as a clerk or assistant in a warehouse and work their way up by learning shipping and receiving procedures. The vast majority of entry-level positions, however, are now reserved for college graduates. Most college graduates secure their first position by applying directly to the U.S. Customs Service, individual seaports and airports, international trading companies, and other organizations that hired export-import specialists. College placement offices may be helpful in providing job leads in this regard. Public and private employment services may also refer qualified applicants to suitable entry positions.

Persons with a master's in business administration, and a fluency in one or more foreign languages will have the best opportunities in this field.

Advancement

Those in the export-import field usually have constant contact with other international firms, and therefore have frequent opportunities to switch employers. Specific advancement opportunities depend to some extent on the specialty within the field, and vary greatly depending on the skill and drive of the individual.

Experienced export managers may become the marketing manager or vice president in charge of coordinating overseas distribution. Customs-house brokers may become export managers or be promoted to another position within the export-import department of a company. After developing contacts and sales expertise, wholesalers may also become management consultants or start their own export-import firm. Import-export agents may become sales representatives for other export-import firms, or also go into business for themselves.

Employment outlook

If the world economy continues to grow, opportunities in the export-import field should grow at a faster than average rate through the early 1990s. The overall stability of employment in this field, however, is largely dependent on the general condition of the economy. To some extent, job prospects will vary from industry to industry and firm to firm. For example, it may be harder to find work as a textile wholesaler representing a U.S. firm than as a computer wholesaler.

Job prospects should be best in major trade cities, such as New York, Chicago, Los Angeles, and New Orleans. Other large metropolitan areas should also offer good employment opportunities. Major employers will include the U.S. government, airlines, shipping firms, international manufacturing companies, and oil companies. Many people will find work overseas, either with a foreign company, or as a representative of a U.S. company.

Those with the most experience and education will have the best job possibilities, particularly in a competitive or desirable job market.

Earnings

Earnings vary widely depending on specific job responsibilities, and the size of the export-import firm. Export managers may earn anywhere from $20,000 to $25,000 a year to start, with experienced managers earning more than $37,000 per year.

Custom-house brokers may be paid according to the amount of foreign trade they handle. Beginning brokers can expect to earn $19,000 to 24,000 per year, with experienced brokers earning over $35,000 per year.

The salaries of wholesalers are directly related to the amount of goods they buy and sell. Earnings can range from $23,000 to $90,000 per year, with highly skilled wholesalers earning over $150,000 annually. Some companies adjust salaries to reflect total volume of sales. Other companies pay straight commission (usually about 10 percent of total sales), while others pay a combination of salary, commission, and

benefits. While wholesalers can make huge amounts of money, a slow period could adversely effect their earning potential.

Import-export agents may also earn a bonus if they buy or sell merchandise. Beginning agents earn between $16,000 and $20,000 per year, with experienced agents earning between $23,000 and $35,000 per year.

Conditions of work

Export-import specialists usually work in comfortable offices or customs buildings. They usually work a forty-hour week, although long hours may be required to negotiate a trade agreement or plan and coordinate delivery of goods. Evening and weekend work may be needed so as to be on hand to meet scheduled shipments.

There may be a lot of travel, especially for wholesalers and those stationed overseas. These employees must adapt to the living and working conditions of the host country, and should be aware of, and sensitive to, cultural differences in these countries.

Social and psychological factors

Export-import professionals should have a variety of personal characteristics, such as the ability to quickly analyze purchasing decisions and evaluate products being shipped in. They should have good verbal and written communication skills and be able to work well with other people. Those who speak one or more foreign languages will be able to communicate far more effectively with trading partners and other foreign representatives.

Export-import specialists should be able to handle detailed work, such as writing trade agreements and dealing with customs rules and regulations. They must be able to work long hours, occasionally under pressure. In addition, they should be able to handle the type of emergencies and misunderstandings that may arise as a result of a trade agreement involving representatives from many nations sending large shipments of goods around the world. Export-import specialists should be disciplined enough to negotiate contracts representing huge sums of money and be energetic enough to withstand extended buying and selling trips. They should be able to exhibit leadership skills but also be able to work as part of a team. Often this team will be made up of people from widely different ethnic and cultural backgrounds. Living overseas, export-import specialists should recognize that political crises or other emergencies may arise that could threaten business dealings and sometimes physical safety. Despite the occasional pressures, careers in this field offer challenge and excitement.

GOE: 11.05; SIC: 2371; SOC: 125, 1342

◇ SOURCES OF ADDITIONAL INFORMATION

American Association of Exporters and Importers
11 West 42nd Street
New York, NY 10036

National Association of Export Companies
17 Battery Place, Suite 1425
New York, NY 10004

National Customs Brokers & Forwarders Association of America
One World Trade Center
Suite 1153
New York, NY 10048

National Federation of Export Associations
1511 K Street
Suite 825
Washington, DC 20005

National Foreign Trade Council
100 East 42nd Street
New York, NY 10017

Sales and Marketing Executives International
Statler Office Tower
Suite #458
Cleveland, OH 44115

◇ RELATED ARTICLES

Volume 1: Foreign Trade; Retailing
Volume 2: Buyers, wholesale and retail; Economists; Interpreters; Marketing research personnel; Retail business owners
Volume 3: Retail sales workers; Shipping and receiving clerks; Traffic agents and clerks; Wholesale trade sales workers

---

Fashion designers

Definition

Fashion designers create original designs for the new types and styles of apparel.

History

Before the invention of the sewing machine by Elias Howe, in 1846, all garments were made by hand. In the earliest days of civilization, after people began to dress in garments that were made from materials other than animal skins, thread was spun by hand and material was woven by hand from the spun thread.

Styles changed slowly. Often, people wore garments of approximately the same style all their lives. Their concern was not so much for

changing or unusual styles as it was for garments that would help them maintain body temperature. Minor variations in decoration were sometimes introduced to lend a little interest to clothing.

The wealthy, who had leisure time, were greatly concerned with fashion and had complex garments designed and made by individual dressmakers and tailors. The French courts were particularly well known for their display of lavish styles. Rose Bertin, who designed for the French royalty of the eighteenth century, was one of the first and most famous of the fashion designers. Her male counterpart is still a legend—Beau Brummell.

About 1764, James Hargreaves of England invented a spinning jenny that made it possible to spin thread by a crude machine. Approximately twenty years after the invention of the spinning machine, a loom powered by steam was invented by Edmund Cartwright. This invention opened the way to rapid production of fabrics.

By the early 1800s, housewives were accustomed to making clothing, although they could by that time purchase materials from dry goods stores. Ready-made dresses were still a development of the future. People who could afford to do so employed dressmakers to make clothing for the family.

Frederick Worth opened the first exclusive dress salon in Paris in 1854. To this day, French fashions are imitated in the United States, even though the American garment industry has assumed a position of leadership in clothing production throughout the world.

In 1863, the first mass-produced paper patterns were introduced by Ebenezer Butterick, and even today, home sewing is still an important part of the American fashion scene.

After the invention of the sewing machine in 1846, ways were devised by which clothing could be produced in quantities through mass production. Just before the turn of the twentieth century, the cutting machine was invented. Other factory methods began to be devised to make it possible to turn out more garments in one week than had previously been possible in a year's work. In 1980, more than 275 million dresses were manufactured in the United States.

This fashion designer examines photo spreads of clothing that she and her colleagues designed.

Nature of the work

Fashion designers create designs for almost anything that is a part of the costume of men, women, or children. They may design both outer and inner garments, or hats, purses, shoes, gloves, costume jewelry, scarves, or beachwear.

The designer's original idea for a garment is usually sketched. After the first rough sketch has been prepared, the designer begins to shape the pattern pieces that make the garment. The pieces are then drawn to actual size on paper, and cut out on a rough material, often muslin. The muslin pieces are sewn together and fitted on a model.

The designer makes modifications in the pattern pieces or other features of the rough mock-up and thus completes the design. From the rough model, sample garments are made in the fabric that the designer intended to use. Sample garments are displayed at a "showing" to which press representatives and buyers are invited and which designers supervise.

In some companies, designers are involved in every step of the production of the line, from the original idea to the completed garments. Many designers prefer to supervise workrooms. Others work along with workroom supervisors and solve problems that arise in the production of the garments.

Most manufacturers produce new styles four times each year: spring and summer; fall and winter; "cruise" (clothing designed for those who plan winter vacations); and, "holiday" (special styles for the winter holiday season). Designers may be expected to create between 50 to 150 styles for each showing. Their calendar of work differs from that of the rest of the world. They must be working on spring and summer designs during fall and winter months, on fall and winter clothing during the warm seasons of the year.

Designers work cooperatively with the head of the manufacturing firm by which they are employed. They design a "line" that is consistent with the ideas of their employers. They also must work cooperatively with those who do the actual production of the garments and must be able to estimate the cost of a garment.

Designers must spend time in exploration and research, visiting textile manufacturing and sales establishments to learn of the latest fabrics and their uses and capabilities. They must know about fabric, weave, draping qualities, and strength of materials. A good understanding of textiles and their potentialities underlies

227

much of designers' work. They must "shop" through stores and shops to see which things are being bought by the public and which are passed by. They must visit museums and art galleries to get ideas about color and design. They must go to places where people congregate—to the theater, sports events, business and professional meetings, and resorts—to discover what people are wearing.

Designers must keep abreast of changing styles. If the styles are too far ahead of public taste, they will find that purchasers reject the designs. If, however, they cling to styles that have been successful in the past, they may find that the taste of buyers has surged ahead. Either way it may be equally disastrous for the employers.

There are many opportunities for specialization in fashion designing. The most common of the specialties is that of a particular type of garment such as, for instance, resort wear or sports fashionwear.

One of the interesting specialties in fashion designing is theatrical design, a relatively limited field but challenging to those who are interested in combining a liking for the theater with a talent for clothing design.

Requirements

Fashion designing is a highly competitive business. The better an aspiring designer is prepared, the broader the opportunities will be. A college degree is recommended, though not required. Graduation from a special school for fashion design is considered highly desirable. Employers are seeking designers who have had courses in mathematics, business, design, sketching, art history, costume history, literature, patternmaking, clothing construction, and textiles.

Some colleges offer a four-year degree in fine arts with a major in fashion design. Many reputable schools of fashion design in the United States offer a two- or three-year program that does not lead to a degree but instead offers a diploma or certificate.

The high-school student who is interested in fashion designing should take as many courses as possible in art, in clothing construction, and in textiles.

Prospective fashion designers must be artistically creative, with an unusual ability in garment construction. They should also be imaginative and able to work well with their hands.

Special requirements

No special requirements exist for designers. Those working in theatrical designing, however, must hold union membership.

Opportunities for experience and exploration

The young person who enjoys sewing and who sews well may have taken the first step toward exploring a career in the fashion world. If the skills in garment construction are adequate, the next step may be an attempt at designing and making clothing. Courses in art and design will help assess any talent and ability as a creative artist.

Students who are able to obtain a summer job in a department or specialty store can observe retailing practices and gain some practical insights into the merchandising aspects of the fashion world. They should visit a garment manufacturer to see fashion employees at work.

Those who are interested in fashion design should take every opportunity to attend style shows, visit art galleries, observe clothing worn by fashion leaders, and "shop" through all kinds of stores in which garments are sold. They should read widely in the many books and magazines that are published about fashion, particularly *Women's Wear Daily*, which is the best known periodical of the garment industry.

Related occupations

Persons interested in fashion design may also find an outlet for their talents in other art and design fields, as fashion illustrators, fashion photographers, fur designers, interior designers, jewelry designers, or textile designers, for example. Individuals who enjoy fashion but who may not be able to fulfill that interest in design can consider such occupations as fashion consultants, fashion writers, merchandise displayers, retail buyers, retail sales workers, or tailors.

Methods of entering

Few persons ever begin their careers as fashion designers. Frequently, well-trained college graduates begin in positions as assistant designers and prove that they have ability before they are entrusted with the responsible job of the designer. Many young persons find that assistant designer jobs are difficult to locate, so they accept beginning jobs in the workroom, cutting or constructing garments.

Advancement

Advancement in fashion designing varies a great deal. There is much moving around from firm to firm, and vacancies occur rather regularly. The aspiring designers should continue to create their own designs and should look for opportunities to show their work to employers. They should collect a portfolio of work as fast as possible.

Employment outlook

The designer is the key person in the garment industry, yet relatively few of them are needed to make employment possible for thousands of persons. It is estimated that there are more than 30,000 designers and assistant designers in the United States and that they represent less than one percent of the garment industry employees. Some designers work only for the high-priced custom trade, some for the mass market, some work on "exclusive" designs, which will be made for only one person. Many designers are employed by manufacturers of paper patterns.

Good designers will always be needed. They will not, however, be needed in great numbers. Fashion designers enjoy high pay and prestige, and those at the top of their profession rarely leave their positions. Therefore, opportunities for newcomers are limited. There are always more people hoping to break into the field than there are jobs available. It takes a great deal of talent and perseverance to achieve success as a high-fashion designer. The employment outlook may be better in other fields, such as children's clothing. In addition, openings are more readily available for assistant designers.

Earnings

Fashion designers are to be found in almost every income bracket. Income depends in part upon the size of the firm for which the designer works and the volume of business that it does. Income also depends upon the kind of fashion designing in which the designer is engaged.

Salaries for entry positions may average approximately $12,000 to $14,000 per year. For experienced designers, salaries may range between $19,000 and $40,000 a year. A few highly skilled and well-known designers have annual incomes of better than $62,000. As designers become well known, they are usually offered a share of the ownership of the company for which they design. Their percentage of ownership increases with their reputation.

Theatrical designers usually work on a contract basis. Although the remuneration for the total contract is usually good, there may be long periods of idleness between contracts. The annual income for theatrical designers may not exceed that of designers on regular salary, though while they are working they may be making more than $1,000 per week.

Conditions of work

Many designers work in cluttered and noisy surroundings. Their work space may consist of a large room that has long tables for cutting out patterns or garments. There may be only one or two other persons working in the room, or there may be many others. The designer may have a small office adjacent to the working space.

Some designers have spacious, well-lighted, and well-ventilated work spaces that are arranged neatly and are free from undue disturbance.

Many designers travel a great deal, either to other cities or to other locations in the same city for showings or conferences. They may spend time in stores or shops looking at clothing that has been manufactured by competitors.

Although some designers may observe traditional work hours during many weeks of the year, they may have to work many more than forty hours each week during rush periods. Styles previewed in spring and fall require a great amount of work during the weeks and months preceding.

Social and psychological factors

The garment industry is important to the economy of the country. The fact that changing styles create a demand for new clothing long before serviceable garments are worn out makes a real difference to the prosperity level of society. The fashion designer holds an important place in the nation's standard of living.

GOE: 01.02.03; SIC: 513; SOC: 6859

National Association of Schools of Art and Design
11250 Roger Bacon Drive, Suite 21
Reston, VA 22090

◇ **SOURCES OF ADDITIONAL INFORMATION**

International Fashion Group
9 Rockefeller Plaza
New York, NY 10020

International Association of Clothing Designers
240 Madison Avenue
12th Floor
New York, NY 10016

◇ **RELATED ARTICLES**

Volume 1: Apparel; Design; Performing Arts; Textiles
Volume 2: Buyers, wholesale and retail; Designers
Volume 3: Jewelers and jewelry repairers; Models
Volume 4: CAD/CAM technicians; Textile technicians

Financial institution officers and managers

Definition

Financial institution officers and managers oversee the activities of banks, savings and loan associations, and personal credit institutions such as credit unions and finance companies. These establishments serve business, government, and individuals. Among the many services they perform, they lend money, keep savings, enable people and businesses to write checks for goods and services, rent safe-deposit boxes for storing valuables, manage trust funds, advise clients on investments and business affairs, issue credit cards and traveler's checks, and take payments for gas and electric bills.

History

Archaeology shows that banking is an ancient and long-practiced profession. Clay tablets have been discovered indicating the Greeks, Romans, and Egyptians made and recorded financial business. With the coming of the Middle Ages, the already historically old practice of banking suffered a setback. Bartering or exchanging goods became the accepted practice. But bartering was complicated and time-consuming. For example, a pig farmer who wanted lumber not only had to find a trader with lumber but also one with lumber who wanted a pig. In the seventeenth century, the modern concept of bank notes (currency) gained popularity, and bartering became mainly an activity of the past. At this time goldsmiths in London began to issue paper receipts for gold and other valuables that were deposited in their warehouses. The paper money we use today is a modern version of these seventeenth-century receipts.

The first bank in the United States opened its doors during the term of George Washington. The number and structure of banks was often reflected in the sometimes turbulent but continuous growth of the nation. By 1913, however, banks had become so numerous that federal control of banks was needed. The Federal Deposit System, as we know it today, is the result of the efforts to coordinate the activities of the many banks throughout the nation. As banks have grown in numbers, so have their services. They have even changed some of our concepts of money. For example, banks have simplified the problem of carrying around and exchanging large sums of money. Today we use checks. More than 90 percent of all business today is conducted by the use of checks. The number of banks and other financial institutions has grown by leaps and bounds within the past twenty-five years. The economic health of the nation is reflected by the business that banks do.

Savings and loan associations are specialized thrift institutions that invest the money deposited in their savings accounts primarily in mortgage loans.

The officers of financial institutions often gather to discuss analyses and reports executed by the younger members of the firm.

Nature of the work

Financial institutions may be commercial banks, which provide full banking service for business, government, and individuals; investment banks, which offer their clients financial counseling and brokering; Federal Reserve Banks, whose customers are affiliated banks in their districts; savings and loan associations, which provide many of the usual banking services but specialize in home mortgages; or other organizations such as credit unions and finance companies.

These institutions employ many officers and managers whose duties vary depending on the type and size of the firm as well as on their own level or area of responsibility within it. All financial institutions operate under the direction of a president, who is guided by policies set by the board of directors. Vice-presidents are department heads or may be responsible for certain key clients. Controllers handle bank funds, properties, and equipment. Large institutions may also have treasurers, loan officers, and officers in charge of departments such as trust, credit, and investment. A number of these positions are described in more detail below.

The *financial institution president* directs the overall activities of the bank, savings and loan association, or consumer credit organization, making sure that its objectives are achieved without violating government regulations or overlooking any legal requirements. This officer is responsible for earning as much of a return as possible on the institution's investments within the restrictions demanded by government and sound business practices. He or she helps set policies pertaining to investments, loans, interest, and reserves; coordinates the activities of the various divisions, departments,

and branch offices; and delegates authority to subordinate officers, who administer the operation of their own areas of responsibility. Financial institution presidents study financial reports and other data to keep up with changes in the economy that may affect their firm's policies.

The *vice-president* coordinates many of the operations of the institution. This person is responsible for the activities of a regional bank office, branch bank, and often an administrative bank division or department. As designated by the board of directors, he or she also supervises programs such as installment loan, foreign trade, customer service, trust, and investment. The vice-president prepares studies important to management and planning, such as workload and budget estimates and activity and analysis reports.

The *administrative secretary* usually writes directions for supervisory workers that outline and explain policy. The administrative secretary acts, in effect, as an intermediary between minor supervisory workers and the executive officers.

The *financial institution treasurer* directs the bank's monetary programs, transactions, and security measures in accordance with banking principles and legislation. Treasurers coordinate program activity and evaluate operating practices to ensure efficient operations. They oversee receipt, disbursement, and expenditure of money, and sign documents approving or effecting monetary transactions. They direct the safekeeping and control of assets and securities and maintain specified legal cash reserve. They review financial and operating statements and present reports and recommendations to bank officials or board committees.

The *controller* authorizes and controls the use of funds kept by the treasurer. This person also supervises the maintenance of accounts

231

and records. He or she analyzes these records so that the directors or other bank officials may know how much the bank is spending for salaries, operating expenses, and other expenses. Controllers often formulate financial policies.

The *financial institution manager* establishes and maintains relationships with the community. This person's responsibility is to supervise accounting and reporting functions and establish operating policies and procedures. He or she directs several activities within the bank. The assets, records, collateral, and securities held by the financial institution are in the manager's custody. He or she approves credit and commercial, real estate, and consumer loans, and directs personnel in trust activities.

The *loan officer* and the credit and collection manager both deal with customers who are seeking or have obtained loans or credit. The loan officer specializes in examining and evaluating applications for lines of credit, installment credit, or commercial, real estate, and consumer loans, and has the authority to approve them within a specified limit or recommend their approval to the loan committee. To determine the feasibility of granting a loan request, the officer analyzes the applicant's financial status, credit, and property evaluation. The job may also include handling foreclosure proceedings. Depending on training and experience, the officer may analyze potential loan markets to develop prospects for loans. He or she negotiates the terms of transaction and draws up the requisite documents to buy and sell contracts, loans, or real estate. Credit and collection managers make up collection notices for customers who already have credit. When the bank has difficulty collecting accounts or receives a worthless check, credit and collection managers take steps to correct the situation. Finally, this manager's responsibility is to keep records of all credit and collection transactions.

The *loan counselor* studies the records of the account when payments on a loan are overdue and contacts the borrower to discuss payment of the loan. This person may analyze the borrower's financial problems and make new arrangements for repayment of the loan. If a loan account is uncollectable, he or she prepares a report for the bank or thrift institution's files.

The *credit card operations manager* is responsible for the overall credit card policies and operations of a bank, commercial establishment, or credit card company. He or she establishes procedures for verifying the information on application forms, determines applicants' creditworthiness, approves the issuance of credit cards, and sets a credit limit on each account. This manager coordinates activities involved with reviewing unpaid balances, collecting de-

linquent accounts, investigating and preventing fraud, voiding lost or stolen credit cards, keeping records, and exchanging information with the company's branches and other credit card companies.

The *letter of credit negotiator* works with clients who hold letters of credit used in international banking. This person contacts foreign banks, suppliers, and other sources to obtain documents needed to authorize the requested loan, then checks the documents to see if they have been completed correctly so that the conditions set forth in the letter of credit meet with policy and code requirements. Before authorizing payment, the negotiator verifies the client's credit rating and may request increasing the collateral or reducing the amount of purchases, amending the contract accordingly. The letter of credit negotiator specifies the method of payment and informs the foreign bank when a loan has gone unpaid for a certain length of time.

The *trust officer* directs operations concerning the administration of private, corporate, and probate trusts. Officers examine or draft trust agreements to ensure compliance with legal requirements and terms creating trusts. They locate, inventory, and evaluate assets of probated accounts. They also direct realization of assets, liquidation of liabilities, payment of bills, preparation of federal and state tax returns on trust income, and collection of earnings. They represent the institution in trust fund negotiations.

The *reserve officer* maintains the institution's reserve funds according to policy and as required by law. He or she regulates the flow of money through branches, correspondent banks, and the Federal Reserve Bank. He or she also consolidates financial statements and calculates the legal reserve, and, in addition, compiles statistical and analytical reports of the reserves.

The *foreign-exchange trader* maintains the balance that the institution has on deposit in foreign banks to ensure its foreign exchange position and determines the prices at which that exchange will be purchased and sold. This officer's conclusions are based on an analysis of demand, supply, and the stability of the currency. He or she establishes local rates of exchange based upon money market quotations or the customer's financial standing. He or she also buys and sells foreign exchange drafts and computes the proceeds.

The *securities trader* performs securities investment and counseling service for the bank and its customers. This person studies financial background and future trends and advises financial institution officers and customers regarding investments in stocks and bonds. He or she transmits buy-and-sell orders to a trading desk or broker as directed, and recommends purchase, retention, or sale of issues, then notifies the customer or the bank of the execution of trading orders. He or she computes extensions, commissions, and other charges for billing customers and making payments for securities.

The *operations officer* is in charge of the internal operations in a department or branch office of a financial institution. This person is responsible for the smooth and efficient operation of a particular area. Duties include interviewing, hiring, and directing the training of employees, as well as supervising their activities, evaluating their performance, and making certain that they comply with established procedures. The operations officer audits accounts, records, and certifications and verifies the count of incoming cash. He or she prepares reports on the activities of the department or branch, controls the supply of money for its needs, and performs other managerial tasks of a general nature.

The *credit union manager* directs the operations of credit unions, which are chartered by the state or federal government to provide savings and loan services to their members. This manager reviews loan applications, arranges automatic payroll deductions for credit union members wishing to make regular savings deposits or loan payments, and assists in collecting delinquent accounts. He or she prepares financial statements, helps the government audit credit union records, and supervises bookkeeping and clerical activities. Acting as management representative of the credit union, the credit union manager has the power to sign legal documents and checks on behalf of the board of directors. This person also oversees control of the credit union's assets and advises the board on how to invest its funds.

Requirements

The young person who wishes to be a financial institution officer should have a college education. Many bank officials have followed a liberal arts or general course of study; others have obtained a business administration background with a major in banking. The variety of services offered by bank and thrift institutions gives the student flexibility in choosing a major.

In some cases high-school graduates who exhibit executive ability in clerical, supervisory, and administrative work are considered for officer positions as they occur. Many organizations have their own educational programs in

which employees, on a voluntary basis, may participate. Most costs are usually borne by the bank.

In the banking business the ability to get along well with others is essential. Financial institution officers should show tact and should convey a feeling of understanding and confidence in their employees and customers. Honesty is perhaps the most important qualification in financial institution officers. They handle large sums of money. They have access to confidential financial information about the individuals and business concerns associated with their institutions. They, therefore, must have a high degree of personal integrity.

Special requirements

Financial institution officers do not need special licenses to perform their duties, nor must they join special organizations before they can accept a position. Officers may, however, join such organizations as the American Bankers Association.

Opportunities for experience and exploration

Except for high-school courses that are business oriented, the average high-school student will find few opportunities for experience and exploration during the school year. Teachers may be able, however, to arrange for a class tour through a financial institution so that some knowledge about banking services can be gained. For the high-school student, some part-time, after-school work may be available. More than likely, the most valuable experience will be gained through a part-time or a summer job in banks or other institutions. They sometimes hire qualified high-school students with the hope that they will continue their careers after graduation. Those interested in part-time or summer work should contact any institutions near them.

Related occupations

Financial institution officers and managers prepare through education and experience to work in various areas of finance, such as asset management, lending, credit operations, securities investment, or insurance risk and loss control.

Workers with similar training and ability include accountants and auditors, budget officers, credit analysts, loan officers, insurance consultants, pension consultants, real estate advisors, securities consultants, and underwriters.

Methods of entering

One way of entering banking as a regular employee is through part-time or summer employment. Anyone can apply for a position by writing to a financial institution officer in charge of personnel or by arranging for an interview appointment. Many institutions advertise in the classified section of local newspapers. The larger banks recruit on college campuses. An officer will visit a campus and conduct interviews at that time. Student placement offices can also arrange for interviews.

Advancement

There is no "set position" or "schedule" for advancement among financial institution officers. Advancement depends on the size of the institution, the services it offers, and your personal qualifications. Usually, the smaller the employer the slower the advancements. Larger city financial institutions, and smaller ones as well, often offer special training programs that take place at night, during the summer, and in some special instances, during scheduled working hours. Persons who take advantage of these opportunities usually find that advancement comes more quickly. The American Banking Institute, for example, offers training in every phase of banking through its own facilities or the facilities of the local universities and banking organizations. The length of this training may vary from six months to two years. Years of service and experience are required for a top level financial institution officer to become acquainted with policy, operations, customers, and the community. Similarly, the National Institute of Credit offers training and instruction through its parent entity, the National Association of Credit Management.

Employment outlook

Approximately 200,000 officers and managers were employed in banks and other financial institutions in the early 1990s, and the number is expected to increase at an average rate during the next decade. New jobs will be created by a general expansion of financial services, and the more extensive use of electronic computer equipment will make financial managers more productive. However, the need for skilled professionals in this field will increase primarily as a result of greater domestic and foreign competition, changing laws affecting taxes and other financial matters, and a growing emphasis on accurate reporting of financial data for both financial institutions and other corporations.

Competition for these jobs will be strong, however, for several reasons. Financial institution officers and managers are often promoted from within the ranks of the organization, and, once established in their jobs, they tend to stay in them for many years. Also, more qualified applicants are becoming available each year to fill the vacancies that do arise when older, more experienced workers retire, die, or leave the field for other reasons. Chances for employment will be best for persons familiar with a range of financial services, such as banking, insurance, real estate, and securities, and for those experienced in computers and data-processing systems.

Financial institution officers and managers enjoy job security even during economic downswings, which seem to have little immediate effect on banking activities. The only area with chance of fluctuation is in savings and loan institutions.

Earnings

Those who enter banking in the next few years will find the earnings to be dependent on their experience, the size of the institution, and its location. In general, starting salaries in financial institutions are not usually the highest, although among larger financial institutions in big cities, starting salaries often compare favorably with salaries in large corporations. After five to ten years' experience, the salaries of officers usually are slightly higher than those in large corporations for persons of comparable experience.

In the early 1990s, financial managers earned a median annual salary of $30,400. The lowest ten percent, which included those in entry-level and trainee positions, were paid $17,100 or less, while the top ten percent received more than $52,000 a year. Group life insurance, paid vacations, profit sharing plans, and hospitalization and retirement plans are some of the benefits offered.

Conditions of work

Working conditions in financial institutions are very pleasant. They are usually clean, well maintained, well lighted, and often air-conditioned. They are generally located throughout cities for convenience of their customers and thus for employees also. For financial institution officers, hours may be somewhat irregular as many organizations have expanded their hours.

Social and psychological factors

Banks have been described as "department stores of finance." The complicated financial transactions of our present-day business world could not be carried on without the services of banks. From savings accounts for small children to loans to large industries, banks have helped communities grow and prosper. Bank officials who make decisions have the satisfaction of knowing they have helped hundreds of individuals.

GOE: 11.05.02; SIC: 602, 603; SOC: 122

◇ **SOURCES OF ADDITIONAL INFORMATION**

American Bankers Association
1120 Connecticut Avenue, NW
Washington, DC 20036

Bank Administration Institute
60 Gould Center
Rolling Meadows, IL 60008

Federal Reserve System
Board of Governors
Personnel Division
Washington, DC 20551

Institute of Financial Education
111 East Wacker Drive
Chicago, IL 60601

National Association of Bank Women
500 North Michigan Avenue, Suite 1400
Chicago, IL 60611

National Association of Credit Management
520 8th Avenue
New York, NY 10018

◇ **RELATED ARTICLES**

Volume 1: Banking and Financial Services
Volume 2: Accountants and auditors; Credit analysts, banking; Economists; General managers and top executives
Volume 3: Financial institution clerks and related workers; Financial institution tellers

Food technologists

Definition

Food technologists study the physical, chemical, and biological composition of food; develop methods for safely processing, preserving, packaging, distributing, and storing it; and search for ways to improve its flavor, appearance, nutritional value, and convenience. Food technologists conduct tests to ensure that products meet industry and government standards, from fresh produce to packaged meals.

History

Primitive humans were governed by their food supplies. They could not settle in areas unless most of their needs could be satisfied there, and they were often forced to move with the seasons. Until they learned to preserve certain foods, they alternated between feast and famine. One of the earliest methods of food preservation was drying. Grains were sun- and air-dried to prevent molding and insect dam-

A food technologist inspects eggs before they are shipped to a pasteurizing plant. At the plant, they will be processed to make bottled salad dressing.

age. Fruits and vegetables dried in the sun and meats dried and smoked over a fire were stored for use during times of need. Fruits were preserved by fermenting them into wines and vinegars, and fermented milk became curds, cheeses, and yogurts. With more certain food supplies, humans were free to move into areas once considered uninhabitable. Food storage also protected them from crop loss in natural disasters and drought. Winter storage was practiced.

Methods of food preservation improved over the centuries, but they had severe limitations until the evolution of the scientific method made it possible to understand the reasons certain preservations were successful and to devise technological methods to accomplish what had previously been impossible. By creating conditions unfavorable to the growth or survival of spoilage microorganisms and preventing deterioration by enzymes, scientists were able to extend the storage life of foods well beyond the normal period.

Beginning with the canning industry in the early 1800s, what was once the task of the individual household has become a major industry. Foods processed in a variety of ways are readily available to the consumer and have become such an accepted part of modern life that one rarely gives a thought to the complexities involved. The safety of the process; the taste, appearance, and nutrition of the food; the development of new products and production methods; the packaging and distribution of the products—all these and more are the responsibility of food technologists.

Nature of the work

Households that still preserve some of their own food by freezing, canning, jellying, or other methods may take pride in their art but rarely do it out of necessity. Most of the food processing done today is the result of mass production.

Technologists usually specialize in one phase of food technology. About one-third of them are involved in research and development. A large number are employed in quality-control laboratories or in the production or processing areas of food plants. Some teach or perform basic research in colleges and universities, work in sales or management positions, or are employed as technical writers or consultants. The branches of food technology in which these workers may specialize are numerous and include cereal grains, meat and poultry, fats and oils, seafood, animal foods, beverages, dairy products, flavors, sugar and starches, stabilizers, preservatives, colors, and nutritional additives.

Food technologists in basic research study the structure and composition of food and observe the changes that take place during storage or processing. The knowledge they gain may enable them to develop new sources of proteins, determine the effects of processing on microorganisms, or isolate the factors that affect the flavor, appearance, or texture of foods. Technologists engaged in applied research and development have the more practical task of creating new food products and developing new processing methods. They also continue to work with existing foods to make them more nutritious and flavorful and to improve their color and texture.

A rapidly growing area of food technology is biotechnology. Food technologists in this area work with plant breeding, gene splicing, microbial fermentation, and plant cell tissue cultures to produce enhanced raw products for processing.

Foods may lose their characteristics and nutritive value during processing and storage. Food technologists seek ways to prevent this by developing new and improved methods for processing, production, quality control, packaging, and distribution. They conduct chemical and microbiological tests on products to be sure they conform to standards set by the government and by the food industry. They also determine the nutritive content—that is, the amounts of sugar, starch, protein, fat, vitamins, minerals—that federal regulations say must be printed on the labels.

Food technologists in quality-control laboratories concentrate on ensuring that foods in every stage of processing meet industry and government standards. They check to see that raw ingredients are fresh, sufficiently ripe, and suitable for processing; conduct periodic inspections of processing line operations; and test after processing to be sure that various enzymes are not active and that bacteria levels are low enough so the food will not spoil or be unsafe to eat.

Some technologists test new products in test kitchens or develop new processing methods in laboratory pilot plants. Others devise new and improved methods for packaging and storing foods. To solve problems, they may confer with processing engineers, flavor experts, or packaging and marketing specialists.

In processing plants, food technologists are responsible for preparing production specifications and scheduling processing operations. They see that proper temperature and humidity levels are maintained in storage areas and that wastes are disposed of properly and other sanitary regulations are observed throughout the plant. They also make recommendations to management in matters relating to efficiency or economy, such as new equipment or suppliers.

Some food technologists have positions in other fields where they can apply their specialized knowledge to such areas as advertising, market research, or technical sales.

Requirements

Educational requirements for this field are high. Beginners need at least a bachelor's degree in food technology. Some technologists hold degrees in other areas, such as chemistry, biology, engineering, agriculture, or business, and nearly half have advanced degrees. Master's degrees and doctorates are mandatory for college teaching and are usually necessary for management and research positions.

Undergraduate programs in food technology are offered by approximately fifty colleges and universities. Courses include physics, biochemistry, mathematics, microbiology, the social sciences and humanities, and business administration, in addition to food technology courses such as food preservation, processing, sanitation, and marketing. Most of these schools also offer advanced degrees, usually in specialized areas of food technology. To successfully complete their program, candidates for a master's degree or a doctorate must perform extensive research and write a thesis reporting their original findings. Specialists in administrative, managerial, or regulatory areas

may earn advanced degrees in business administration or law rather than in food technology.

Food technologists should have analytical minds and enjoy technical work. In addition, they must be able to express themselves clearly and be detail oriented.

Special requirements

There are no additional requirements for the occupation of food technologist.

Opportunities for experience and exploration

Students in high school can test their technical and analytical interests and aptitudes by taking courses in biology, chemistry, physics, and mathematics, along with other college preparatory courses. School guidance counselors and science teachers are a good source of advice in planning programs aimed toward a career in food technology. They may also be able to arrange field trips to local food processing plants and plan interviews with or lectures by experts in the field.

Because of the educational requirements for food technologists, it is not likely that students will be able to acquire actual experience while still in high school. Part-time and summer employment as workers in food processing plants, however, would provide an excellent overview of the industry. More advanced college students may have opportunities for jobs helping out in research laboratories.

Related occupations

The work of food technologists is closely related to that of agricultural scientists. The field of agricultural science includes such occupations as agronomists, animal breeders, animal scientists, apiculturists, dairy scientists, entomologists, horticulturists, plant breeders, poultry scientists, and soil scientists. On a broader level, food technology is related to biology and other natural sciences, such as chemistry and physics. Prospective food technologists might also find the following occupations of interest: dieticians or dietetic technicians, food service workers, or home economists.

Methods of entering

Graduates in food technology may avail themselves of the services of college placement offices, or they may obtain jobs as a result of summer employment. Also, recruiters from private industry frequently conduct interviews on campus. Faculty members may be willing to grant referrals to exceptional students. Another method is to make direct application to individual companies.

Advancement

For food technologists with a bachelor's degree, there are two general paths to advancement depending on whether they work in production or in research. They may begin as quality-assurance chemists or assistant production managers and, with experience, move up to more responsible management positions. Or they may start as junior food chemists in the research and development laboratory of a food company and advance to section head or another research management position.

Technologists who hold master's degrees may start out as food chemists in a research and development laboratory. Those with doctorates usually begin their careers in basic research or teaching.

Employment outlook

In the early 1990s, approximately 148,000 food technologists and engineers were employed in food-related activities. About 8,000 of them worked in research and development in the food processing industry. Others worked for federal agencies such as the Food and Drug Administration and the Departments of Agriculture and Defense or for state regulatory agencies. Some were employed by private counseling firms or the United Nations and other international organizations. Many food technologists teach and do basic research at colleges and universities.

The food processing industry is one of the twenty major industry groups that form the manufacturing sector of the United States and is the third largest employer. Because it serves a basic need, its growth is generally steady and is not greatly affected by economic fluctuations.

The growth in this field through the end of the 1990s will result from several factors that will encourage the food industry to create more jobs for food technologists. Consumer prefer-ences are changing rapidly. A larger and more varied supply of wholesome and economical food is needed to satisfy current tastes. The food industry will have to produce convenience foods of greater quality not only for use in private homes but for the food service institutions that supply airlines, restaurants, and other major customers. More technologists may be hired to research and produce new foods from modifications of wheat, corn, rice, and soybeans, such as the "meat" products made from vegetable proteins. The food industry has increased its spending in recent years for this kind of research and development and is likely to continue to do so. Finally, as products and processes become more complex and as higher standards are applied by industry and government, more food technologists will be required in quality control and production.

Despite the additional need for food technologists, however, most job openings will occur as older, experienced workers retire, die, or transfer to other fields. Opportunities are equally distributed throughout the states, although the products worked on vary by locality. For example, potatoes are processed in Maine and Idaho, cereal and meat products in the Midwest, and citrus fruits and vegetables in Florida and California.

Earnings

The median salary for all food technologists was around $34,000 a year in the early 1990s. Beginners with bachelor's or master's degrees received approximate annual salaries between $21,000 and $24,000. With eleven to fifteen years' work experience, technologists with bachelor's or master's degrees earned about $37,000; those with doctorates earned about $42,000. Experienced food technologists in the federal government were paid an average salary of $35,000 a year.

Conditions of work

Most food technologists work regular hours in clean, well-lighted, temperature-controlled offices, laboratories, or classrooms. Technologists in production and quality-control work in plants where food is processed and may be subject to machine noise and hot or cold conditions.

Social and psychological factors

Individuals suited to this challenging occupation will have analytical minds and an interest in technical subjects. Much of the work is painstaking, requiring strict attention to detail. With today's life-styles, millions of people rely on processed, packaged convenience foods to satisfy their appetites and their nutritional needs. These people's health and safety depend on the care and concern of food technologists. One careless step could result in an epidemic of food poisoning.

To offset this grave responsibility is the satisfaction of fulfilling a basic need for the entire population, perhaps even creating a new food that will bring pleasure to everyone's tastebuds.

GOE: 02.02.04; SIC: 873; SOC: 1853

◇ **SOURCES OF ADDITIONAL INFORMATION**

For information on research and inspection offices for food, write to:

The Department of Agriculture
Information Staff
Agriculture Marketing Service
Washington, DC 20250

Institute of Food Technologists
221 North LaSalle Street
Chicago, IL 60601

National Food Processors Association
1401 New York Avenue, NW
Washington, DC 20005

◇ **RELATED ARTICLES**

Volume 1: Agriculture; Food Processing
Volume 2: Biochemists; Chemists; Dietitians; Home economists
Volume 3: Agricultural scientists; Bakery products workers; Canning and preserving industry workers; Confectionery industry workers; Dairy products manufacturing workers; Macaroni and related products industry workers
Volume 4: Chemical technicians; Dietetic technicians

Foreign Service officers

Definition

Foreign Service officers represent the government and the people of the United States by conducting relations with foreign countries and international organizations. They promote and protect America's political, economic, and commercial interests overseas; observe and analyze conditions and developments in foreign countries and report to the State Department and other agencies; guard the welfare of Americans abroad; and help foreign nationals traveling to the United States.

Foreign Service officers are normally employees in embassies in countries abroad. Given diplomat status in the foreign country, the officers serve as a direct link between the host country and the government of the country they represent.

History

The Foreign Service is a branch of the U.S. Department of State, which plans and carries out U.S. foreign policy under the authority of the president. Established in 1789, the State Department was placed under the direction of Thomas Jefferson, the first U.S. secretary of state and the senior officer in President Washington's cabinet. It was his responsibility to initiate foreign policy on behalf of the U.S. government, advise the president on matters related to foreign policy, and administer the foreign affairs of the United States with the help of employees both at home and abroad.

As the technological advances in transportation and communication made it easier and faster for people to travel and for countries to engage in mutual trade, the State Department's

An American foreign service officer stationed in Brazil discusses international affairs to officials of Haiti's Ministry of Foreign Affairs.

assignments became more complex and far ranging. Today, its domestic organization is made up of many bureaus and offices. There are bureaus for Inter-American, European, Far Eastern, Near Eastern, South Asian, and African affairs, each headed by an assistant secretary of state. The regional bureaus are further divided into offices or "desks" for each country within the geographical area. Workers in charge of the offices or desks carry on an extensive correspondence with American officials abroad and handle the other day-to-day details of international relations, keeping the secretary and undersecretaries of state advised on matters in their regions.

The Foreign Service consists of three groups located in approximately 300 posts throughout the world. Members of the Foreign Service Officer Corps are the principal representatives of the U.S. government in foreign countries. Officers of the U.S. Information Agency (USIA) specialize in public affairs, information, and cultural affairs. The third group is the Foreign Service staff, which includes the many secretarial, clerical, and technical employees and other specialists needed to carry out the activities of the Foreign Service.

Nature of the work

Foreign Service officers (FSOs) work in embassies and consulates throughout the world. Between foreign assignments, they may have duties in the Department of State in Washington, D.C., or they may be temporarily detailed to the Department of Defense, the Department of Commerce, or other government departments and agencies. Similarly, Foreign Service Infor-

mation officers (FSIOs) serve abroad or may work in USIA headquarters in Washington.

The work of Foreign Service officers is divided into four broad areas: administration, consular affairs, economic and commercial affairs, and political affairs.

Administrative officers who work in embassies and consulates manage and administer the day-to-day operations of their posts. Some handle financial matters such as planning budgets and controlling expenditures. Others work in general services; they purchase and look after government property and supplies, negotiate leases and contracts for office space and housing, and make arrangements for travel and shipping. Personnel officers deal with assignments, promotions, and personnel relations affecting both U.S. and local workers. This includes the hiring of the local workers and arranging labor and management agreements.

Administrative officers based in Washington do similar work and act as liaison between the Department of State and their colleagues overseas.

Consular officers help and advise U.S. citizens abroad as well as foreigners wishing to enter the United States as visitors or residents. They provide medical, legal, personal, and travel assistance to U.S. citizens in cases of accidents or emergencies, such as helping those without money to return home, finding lost relatives, visiting and advising those in foreign jails, and distributing social security checks and other federal benefits to eligible persons. They issue passports, register births and deaths and other information, serve as notaries public, and take testimony needed by courts in the United States. In addition, these officers issue visas to foreign nationals who want to enter the United States and decide which of them are eligible for citizenship.

Consular officers located in the Bureau of Consular Affairs in Washington provide support and help for their fellow officers abroad.

Economic and commercial affairs may be handled by one officer at a small post or divided between two full-time officers at a large post.

Economic officers study the structure of a country's economy and the way it functions and try to determine how the United States might be affected by trends, trade patterns, and methods of setting prices. Their analysis of the economic data, based on a thorough understanding of the international monetary system, is passed along to their counterparts in Washington. Economic officers in Washington write position papers for the State Department and the White House, suggesting U.S. policies to help improve economic conditions in foreign nations.

Commercial officers concern themselves with building U.S. trade overseas. They carry out marketing and promotion campaigns to encourage foreign countries to do business with the United States. When they learn of potential trade and investment opportunities abroad, they inform U.S. companies that might be interested. Then they help the firms find local agents and advise them about local business practices. Most commercial officers are members of the Foreign Commercial Service of the U.S. Department of Commerce.

Political officers overseas convey the views and position of the United States to government officials of the countries where they are based, keep the United States informed about any political developments that may affect U.S. interests, and may negotiate agreements between the two governments. Political officers are alert to local developments and reactions to American policy. They maintain close contact with foreign officials and political and labor leaders and try to predict changes in local attitudes or leadership that might have an effect on American policies. They report their observations to Washington and interpret what is happening.

Political officers in Washington study and evaluate the information submitted by their counterparts abroad. They keep the State Department and White House officials informed of developments overseas and the possible effects on the United States. They suggest revisions in U.S. policy and see that their fellow officers abroad carry out approved changes.

The U.S. Information Service assigns information and cultural officers to serve at diplomatic missions in foreign countries. Information officers prepare and disseminate information designed to help other countries understand the United States and its policies. They distribute press releases and background articles and meet with members of the local press, radio, television, and film companies to give them information about the United States. Cultural officers engage in activities that promote an understanding and appreciation of American culture and traditions. These activities may involve educational and cultural exchanges between the countries, exhibits, lectures, performing arts events, libraries, book translations, English teaching programs, and youth groups. Cultural officers deal with universities and cultural and intellectual leaders. Many officers work on both information and cultural programs.

Requirements

The Foreign Service is open to any United States citizen who is at least twenty years old and who passes the written, oral, and physical examinations. Applicants should be unusually skilled in the English language so as to be able to express clearly the policies and proposals of the United States. In addition, it would be to their advantage to be fluent in at least one foreign language. Foreign Service officers also need the ability to analyze tabular and quantitative data and to promote ideas and concepts basic to the development of the United States and other countries.

Although a college diploma is not a requirement, most candidates for foreign service have at least a bachelor's degree. More than half of those selected have a master's degree, a law degree, or a doctorate. Regardless of the level of education, candidates are expected to have a broad knowledge of foreign and domestic affairs and to be well informed on U.S. history, government, economics, culture, literature, and business administration. The fields of study most often chosen by those with a higher education include history, international relations, political science, economics, law, English-American literature, and foreign languages.

Previous professional experience is also an asset, especially if it entailed management work for federal, state, local, or international governments. The written exam given to Foreign Service applicants covers skills and aptitudes in a number of areas. One section tests their understanding of government institutions, international relations, history, geography, philosophy, literature, the arts, science, and current events. Another tests their knowledge and skills as related to the functions of the departments of State and Commerce and the United States Information Agency. And, finally, there is a written essay that measures the applicants' basic English writing ability.

Oral exams are conducted by a panel of Foreign Service examiners as part of the evaluation and selection process. Only those candidates who have passed the written exam undergo this further assessment. In this phase, timed exercises are given to applicants to measure their ability to discuss current political, cultural and economic issues; to solve problems; to summarize information; to interact with a group; and to manage effectively.

Physical examinations are strict. Foreign Service officers must have exceptionally good health because medical and sanitation facilities at certain foreign posts may be minimal or not up to U.S. standards, and climates vary considerably. Candidates will be rejected if they have a physical condition that requires frequent or prolonged treatment, worsens in some climates, or is likely to cause much time lost from work.

Certain personal qualifications are important, too. To be a successful Foreign Service officer requires a strong desire for public service and a willingness to commit and dedicate oneself to such a career. Persons wanting to enter this field should have above average intelligence coupled with a sensitivity to the needs of others. Language and cultural differences can create obstacles in dealing with foreigners. Foreign Service officers must remain flexible and exercise great tact in such situations.

Special requirements

Other than the requirements described above, which in themselves are high, there are no special requirements to enter this field.

Opportunities for experience and exploration

It may be difficult finding part-time or summer jobs that are directly related to foreign service. Students may have to exercise some ingenuity to obtain relevant work experience. Places to inquire include federal, state, and local government agencies, foreign consulates and trade centers, community organizations involved in relocating and training newcomers from foreign countries, import/export companies, and large manufacturing companies, banks, and other establishments that have an international or foreign trade department. Students who are able to get part-time, temporary, or volunteer work with these or similar organizations will undoubtedly be employed to do simple clerical work—typing, filing, messenger, or mail room tasks, for example—but will benefit from exposure to business on an international level and perhaps an opportunity to develop their foreign-language skills.

Foreign Service officers need a broad foundation of knowledge in a variety of areas. High–school students wanting to explore the field can begin to acquire relevant learning by taking as many courses as possible in subjects such as English and foreign languages, literature, history, geography, economics, political science, and the areas of international relations, business administration, and law. College juniors, seniors, and graduate students may qual-

ify for internships offered by the U.S. Department of State. One type of internship is a paid summer position, and the other is a year-round work-study program without pay.

Involvement and holding office in school and community clubs, associations, and other groups offer excellent training in the techniques of management and organization. Proficiency in these areas is also important in foreign service.

Related occupations

On the domestic front, persons interested in the work of Foreign Service officers are likely to find the following occupations of similar interest: city managers, consumer affairs directors, customs agents, park superintendents, police commissioners, postmasters, or public works commissioners. Individuals with a facility for foreign languages might consider becoming interpreters or translators. Others could exercise their aptitudes and skills in the import-export or travel fields.

Methods of entering

Foreign Service exams are given each year on the first Saturday in December throughout the United States and at all Foreign Service posts. Applications must be received by mid-October. Interested persons may request an application from the Foreign Service Officer Recruitment Branch, Box 9317, Rosslyn Station, Arlington, VA 22209.

Advancement

New recruits are given a temporary appointment as career candidates. This probationary period lasts no longer than four years. During this time all Foreign Service officers must learn a foreign language. Candidates who do well may be recommended by the selection board to receive a commission before the end of the four-year period. Those who fail to show potential as career officers are dropped from the program.

Commissioned Foreign Service officers are rated by their supervisors once a year. A promotion board decides who is eligible for advancement. Promotions are based on merit. Officers who do good work can expect to advance from Class 6 through Class 1 by the time they complete their careers. Class 1 officers generally direct programs and work in management.

Those who do exceptionally well may eventually serve as ambassadors. The highest levels that Foreign Service officers can attain are career minister and career minister for information.

Employment outlook

The need for Foreign Service officers throughout the 1990s is not expected to change significantly. Openings occur when older, more experienced officers retire, die, or transfer to another field, but competition for these vacancies is strong.

Out of approximately 15,000 applicants who take the written exams each year, only about 250 FSOs and FSIOs are appointed. Altogether there are about 10,300 persons working for the Foreign Service in Washington and overseas. Of these, approximately 4,400 are Foreign Service officers, 900 are Foreign Service information officers, and 5,000 work as staff specialists.

Earnings

Foreign Service officers are paid on a sliding scale. The exact figures depend on their qualifications and experience. In the early 1990s, the range for new appointees with a bachelor's degree was approximately $18,000 to $26,000 a year. Appointees with a graduate degree and appropriate experience started at $20,000 to $29,000. Senior officers may earn about $53,000 to $69,000 a year.

Benefits are usually generous, although they may vary from post to post. Officers are housed free of charge or are given a housing allowance. They receive a cost-of-living allowance, higher pay if they work in an area that imposes undue hardship on them, medical and retirement benefits, and an education allowance for their children.

Most officers overseas work regular hours as in any office. They may work more than thirty to forty hours a week, though, because they are theoretically on call around the clock, seven days a week. Foreign Service officers receive paid vacation of anywhere from thirteen to twenty-six days a year, depending on their length of service. They get three weeks of home leave for each year of duty overseas.

Conditions of work

Foreign Service officers may be assigned to work in Washington or in any embassy or consulate in the world. They generally spend about 60 percent of their time abroad and are transferred every two to four years.

FSOs may serve tours of duty in such major world cities as London, Paris, Moscow, Singapore, or Peking or in the less familiar locales of Iceland, Madagascar, Nepal, or the Fiji Islands. Environments range from elegant and glamorous to remote and primitive.

Most offices overseas are clean, pleasant, and well equipped, much like those at home. But Foreign Service officers sometimes have to travel into areas that may present health hazards or cause environmental stress. Customs may differ considerably, medical care may be substandard or nonexistent, the climate may be extreme, or other hardships may exist. In some countries there is the danger of earthquakes, typhoons, or floods; in others, the danger of political upheaval.

Although embassy hours are normally the usual office hours of the host country, other tasks of the job may involve outside activities, such as attending or hosting dinners, lectures, public functions or other necessary social engagements.

Social and psychological factors

A career in the Foreign Service can be a demanding one, but it is also an interesting one that can be extremely gratifying. To those who welcome a challenge, it offers variety and adventure and the satisfaction of doing important work. Foreign Service officers can take pride in knowing that they are helping the president and the secretary of state carry out the foreign policy of the United States. They are protecting the interests of U.S. citizens abroad and helping people in foreign countries.

FSOs overseas may find conditions quite different from what they are accustomed to. They must be flexible and able to take occasional hardships. Dealing with people whose language, customs, and culture are different calls for great tact and special care to avoid misunderstandings. As representatives of the U.S. government, Foreign Service officers are expected to conduct themselves at all times in a manner that is above reproach.

GOE: 11.09.03; SIC: 9721; SOC: 1139

Fundraisers

Definition

Fundraisers develop and coordinate the plans by which charity organizations raise funds, generate publicity, and fulfill the organizations' fiscal objectives.

History

Although philanthropy may be as old as mankind itself, organized fundraising is a relatively modern refinement of the old notions of charity. It may surprise you to learn that some people make a living organizing charity appeals and fund drives, but philanthropy ranks among the ten largest industries in the United States. In 1988 alone, Americans donated more than $100 billion to various religions, charities, research centers, schools, hospitals, libraries, and special social programs. Because of government policies in the 1980s that cut federal money available to these causes, the burden to raise necessary funds from private citizens, foundations, and corporations is heavier than ever before. The most familiar forms of fundraising are the much publicized and visible types, such as telethons, direct mail campaigns, and canned food drives. Successful fundraising does not depend on a high profile, however; often it requires marketing the appeal for funds to the people most likely to donate. Successful fundraising requires careful planning, staffing, and execution. An experienced fundraiser can make all the difference between a successful revenue campaign and a disappointing one.

Nature of the work

Fundraising combines many different skills and directs them toward one effort. These skills include financial management and accounting; public relations; marketing; human resources management; and media communications. To be successful, the appeal for funds has to address the people most likely to donate, and they have to be convinced of the good work being done by the cause they are supporting. Strong media support and savvy public relations are key to this. Fundraisers also have to bring together people—including volunteers, paid staff, board members, and other community contacts—and direct them toward the common goal of enriching the charity.

Fundraisers are usually employed in one of three different ways. They may be members of the staff of the organization or charity in question; for example, many colleges and hospitals maintain fundraisers on staff, who may be referred to as *solicitors,* and who report to the *development director* or *outreach coordinator.* They may also be employed by fundraising counseling firms, which for a fee will help nonprofit organizations manage their campaigns, budget their money and resources, determine the feasibility of different revenue programs, and counsel them in other ways. Many for-profit companies also have fundraisers on staff to plan and conduct charity social events, such as fundraising balls, formal dinners, telethons, walk-a-thons, parties, or carnivals. Corporations perform these philanthropic functions both to help the charity and the community to generate favorable publicity.

To illustrate how a revenue-raising campaign might be conducted, consider a private high school (Branton Academy) that is trying to raise money to build a new facility. The principal of Branton approaches a fundraising counseling firm to study the possible approaches that could be taken in this effort. It is estimated that building a new facility and acquiring the land would cost the academy $800,000. The fundraising firm's first job is to ask difficult questions about the realism of the academy's goal. What were the results of the academy's last fundraising effort? Do the local alumni tend to respond to solicitations for revenue? Are the alumni active leaders in the community, and can their support be counted on? Are there enough potential givers besides alumni in the area to reach the goal? Are there enough volunteers on hand to launch a revenue campaign? What kind of publicity—good and bad—has the academy recently generated? What other charities, especially private schools, are trying to raise money in the area at that time?

Once the fundraising consulting firm has a solid understanding of what the academy is trying to accomplish, it conducts a feasibility study to see if there is community support for such a project. If community support exists—that is, if it appears that the fundraising drive could be a success—the consulting firm consults with officials at Branton to draft a fundraising plan. The plan will describe in detail the goals of the fundraising appeal, the steps to be taken to meet those goals, the responsibilities of the paid staff and volunteers, budget projections for the campaign, and other important policies. For the Branton Academy, the fundraising consultant might suggest a three-tiered strategy for the campaign: a bicycle marathon by the students to generate interest and initiate the publicity campaign, followed by a month-long phone drive to people in the area, and ending with a formal dinner dance that charges $50 a plate to attendees.

Once the plan is agreed to, the fundraising consultants make sure that all the pieces are in place. They organize training for the volunteers, especially those involved in phone solicitation, and give them tips on how to present the facts of the campaign to contributors and how to get them to support Branton's efforts. The fundraisers make arrangements for publicity and press coverage, sometimes employing a

A fund raiser spends much of his time soliciting money from business executives. Such a task involves casual presentations over lunch and more formal gatherings in the evenings.

professional publicist, so that people will have heard about the campaign before they are approached for donations. During the campaign, the consultants and the staff of Branton will research possible large contributors, such as corporations, philanthropic foundations, and wealthy individuals. These potential sources of revenue will receive special attention and personal appeals from the fundraising professionals and the principal and trustees of Branton. If the fundraising effort is a success, Branton Academy will have both the funds it needs to expand and a higher profile in the community.

This example is fairly clear and straightforward, but the financial needs of most charities are so complex that a single, month-long campaign would be only part of their fundraising plans. The American Cancer Society, for instance, holds many charity events in an area every year, in addition to occasional phone drives, marathons, year-round magazine and television advertising, and special appeals to large individual donors. Fundraisers who work on the staff of charities and nonprofit organizations may need to push several fund drives at the same time, balancing their efforts between long-range endowment funds and special projects. Every nonprofit organization has its own unique goals and financial needs; therefore, fundraisers have to tailor their efforts to the characteristics of the charity or organization involved. This requires imagination, versatility, and resourcefulness on the fundraiser's part. The proper allocation of funds is also a weighty responsibility. Fundraisers must also be strong in "people" skills—especially communications—because their personal contact with volunteers, donors, board members, community groups, local leaders, and members of the press may be an important factor in the success of any revenue appeal.

Requirements

Fundraising is not a curriculum taught in any school, either high school or university. More and more, however, colleges now offer courses in the broader field of philanthropy of which fundraising is one part. Most fundraisers have earned a university degree. A broad liberal arts background, with special attention to the social sciences, is a great benefit to fundraisers because of the nature of most fundraising work. Special degrees and training which could benefit fundraisers include psychology, social work, sociology, public relations, business administration, education, and journalism. This type of education will give fundraisers an insight into the concerns and efforts of most nonprofit organizations and how to bring their worthwhile efforts to the public's attention. Courses in economics, accounting, and mathematics are also very useful.

To pursue a career in fundraising, high-school students are advised to follow a college preparatory curriculum. In addition to the subjects mentioned above, English, speech, and history classes are recommended, as well as a foreign language, bookkeeping, and computer training. Extracurricular activities such as student council and community outreach programs can cultivate important leadership qualities and give students a taste of what fundraising work requires.

Special requirements

There are no licensing or certification requirements for fundraisers. However, numerous professional organizations exist, including the National Society of Fund Raising Executives, the American Association of Fund-Raising Counsel, and the Direct Mail Fundraisers Association.

Opportunities for experience and exploration

The best way for students to gauge their interest in a fundraising career is to volunteer their help to churches, social agencies, health charities, schools, and other organizations for their revenue drives. All of these groups are looking for volunteers and gladly welcome any help they can get. Students will be able to see the various efforts that go into a successful fundraising drive and the work and dedication of professional fundraisers. In this way, students can judge whether they enjoy this type of work. Interested students may want to interview the fundraisers they meet, for their advice in ways to gain more experience and find employment.

Related occupations

Fundraisers must have excellent communications and personal skills. These types of abilities are also required of association executives, psychologists, employment counselors, sociologists, and social workers.

Fundraisers are also responsible for promoting organizations. Marketing and public relations workers do the same type of work.

Methods of entering

The key to a job in fundraising is experience. Both private consultants and nonprofit staffs prefer to hire fundraisers who already have worked on other revenue drives. Because their budgets are always tight, nonprofit organizations are especially reluctant to hire people who need to be trained from scratch on the job. For some small organizations, fund raising staff may be volunteers.

Colleges offer many opportunities for experience, because nearly every college has at least one staff member—and often have whole offices—in charge of generating donations from alumni and other sources. These staff members will have useful advice to give on their profession, including private consulting firms that hire fundraisers. A student may have to serve as a volunteer for such a firm first to get to know the people involved and be considered for a permanent position.

Another way to gain experience is to work for the United Way of America, which offers a one-year internship program for college graduates interested in a career in fundraising. The United Way is composed of more than 2,300 community coalitions nationwide that conduct fundraising drives for more than 38,000 health and social programs. The 6,000 people who work for local United Way groups would be able to teach interns about every facet of successful fundraising, from marketing to community planning.

Professional fundraisers and volunteers can also gain useful knowledge from the National Academy for Voluntarism, which conducts ongoing training and seminars.

Advancement

Once working for a private consulting firm, fundraisers can advance to higher-paying jobs by gaining experience and developing skills. As responsibilities increase, fundraisers may be put in charge of certain aspects of a campaign, such as the direct mail or corporate appeal, or may even direct an entire campaign. Those who work for a large social or nonprofit agency will also find that promotions are determined by skill and creativity in handling difficult assignments. After gaining experience with several nonprofit agencies, some fundraisers move on and start counseling businesses of their own.

Employment outlook

The job prospects of people who wish to become fundraisers is good. As federal funding of nonprofit organizations continues to decrease, these groups are having to raise their operating revenue themselves. They are discovering that hiring full-time fundraisers is a smart investment. Private fundraising counseling firms have also reported their needs for skilled employees. These firms usually require some experience before hiring, but since there are so many fundraising causes that will eagerly welcome volunteers, people should have no problem gaining this needed experience. Both public agencies and private consulting firms keep a full-time staff of fundraisers, while part-time workers may be taken on during special periods and campaigns.

Earnings

While beginning fundraisers do not earn much, their salaries will increase as they gain experience or head successful revenue efforts. Experienced fundraisers can be very highly paid, while some of the best can earn more than $150,000 a year. To attract and retain experienced fundraisers, private agencies and nonprofit organizations will also offer competitive salaries and good benefits. While some nonprofit organizations may offer performance bonuses, they are not usually tied directly to the amounts raised.

Salaries for beginning fundraisers in nonprofit organizations may be between $15,000 and $20,000 a year, although some organizations have a higher starting salary bracket.

Conditions of work

The working conditions for professional fundraisers can sometimes be less than ideal. During revenue campaigns, they may have to work in temporary facilities. Their working hours can be very irregular, because they have to meet and work with volunteers, potential donors, and other people whenever those people are available. When campaigns become intense, fundraisers may have to work very long hours, seven days a week. With all the activity that goes on during a campaign, the atmosphere may become stressful, especially as deadlines draw near. So many demands are put on fundraisers during a campaign—to arrange work schedules, meet with community groups, track finances, and so on—that they must be very organized, flexible, and committed to the overall strategy for the appeal.

Social and psychological factors

While the atmosphere during a revenue campaign can be very hectic, fundraisers can get a very rewarding sense of accomplishment when the drive is over and the financial goals have been met. Fundraisers also receive a good deal of satisfaction from the idea that their efforts at raising revenue will benefit worthy social causes and that they were able to help these charities and nonprofit organizations make the most out of their resources and manpower.

Because they need to be able to talk and work with all kinds of people, fundraisers need to be outgoing and friendly. Leadership is also an important quality, because they need to gain the respect of volunteers and inspire them to do their best. Their enthusiasm for a campaign can be a major factor in other people's commitment to the cause. Through their creativity, responsibility, and resourcefulness, fundraisers can create a career that is both personally exciting and socially beneficial.

GOE: 08.02.08, 11.09.02; SIC: 7389, 8399; SOC: 4366

◇ **SOURCES OF ADDITIONAL INFORMATION**

American Association of Fund-Raising Counsel
25 West 43rd Street
New York, NY 10036

Direct Mail Fundraisers Association
445 West 45th Street
New York, NY 10036

National Association of Hospital Development
112-B East Broad Street
Falls Church, VA 22046

National Easter Seal Society
70 East Lake Street
Chicago, IL 60601

National Network of Grantmakers
2000 P Street, NW, Suite 412
Washington, DC 20036

National Society of Fund Raising Executives
1101 King Street, Suite 3000
Alexandria, VA 22314

United Way of America
701 North Fairfax Street
Arlington, VA 22314

◇ **RELATED ARTICLES**

Volume 1: Marketing; Politics and Public Service; Public Relations
Volume 2: Association executives; Health services administrators; Marketing, advertising, and public relations managers; Marketing research personnel; Public relations specialists
Volume 3: Public opinion researchers; Telemarketers

Funeral directors and embalmers

Definition

The *funeral director*, also called a *mortician* or *undertaker*, makes arrangements with families of the deceased for burial, plans funeral services, and supervises personnel who prepare bodies for burial. An *embalmer* uses chemical solutions to disinfect, preserve, and restore the body and employs cosmetic aids to simulate a lifelike appearance.

History

Since prehistoric times people have tried to deal with the awesome and inevitable mystery of death by means of rituals and ceremonies. Primitive peoples often buried weapons and utensils with their dead, as if to aid the dead person in an afterlife.

Embalming was practiced by the Egyptians as early as 4000 B.C. Bodies were covered with dry powdered natron and soaked in a soda solution, rubbed with oil and spices (and sometimes tar and pitch), and carefully wrapped in linen. Mummies preserved in this manner have

remained intact until their discovery by archaeologists in this century.

Modern methods of embalming began to be developed in the eighteenth century in Europe. Precise anatomical knowledge and the development of standardized chemical preparations and new synthetic materials enable the embalmer to restore the appearance of the deceased to a condition approximating life.

Nature of the work

Funeral directors are responsible for all the details surrounding the ceremony of burial. They arrange for the body to be transported to the funeral home and assist the family of the deceased in the choice of casket and type of funeral service. They supply the newspapers with an obituary notice, and contact the appropriate clergy if there is to be a religious service. They direct the placement of the casket and floral displays in the viewing parlor or chapel. If a service is held in the funeral home, the director arranges seating for guests and engages an organist or provides recorded music. After the service, they and their assistants place the casket in the hearse and organize the procession of cars to the cemetery, where arrangements have been made for the burial. Often, the funeral director is called upon to make arrangements for transporting a body to another state for burial.

The great majority of embalmers are employed in funeral homes. When an unautopsied body is brought to a funeral home, the body and hair are cleansed, and the beard shaved or trimmed as requested. The body is positioned in a comfortable-appearing manner, and an incision is made either at the base of the neck or in the groin to secure access to a major artery and vein. Tubes are inserted into the artery and vein. The tube in the artery is attached to a mechanical pump that introduces a preservative and disinfectant solution into the blood vascular system. Circulation of the chemical solution into the arterial network eventually forces the blood out of the drainage tube in the vein. The treatment is concluded by another procedure that removes gases and liquids from the trunk organs and introduces an additional disinfectant chemical into the area. The preparation of an autopsied body is much more complex, depending on the extent of the postmortem examination and the skills of the pathologist. The embalmer may repair disfigured parts of the body and improve the facial appearance, using wax, cotton, plaster of Paris, and cosmetics. When the embalming process is complete, the body is dressed and casketed.

Embalmers employed by hospitals and medical schools prepare bodies for autopsies and dissection classes, assist hospital pathologists during autopsies, and maintain records.

Requirements

Tact, understanding, and a genuine desire to help people at a time of great stress are essential qualities for anyone wishing to enter the funeral service field. Good physical health and emotional stability are also very important.

Almost all the states require funeral service practitioners to have completed a post–high-school course in mortuary science varying from nine months to three years, plus an apprenticeship varying from one to three years. Some schools of mortuary science have arrangements with local area funeral homes to provide students with either a work/study program or a brief familiarization period of school-supervised funeral service work (residency or apprenticeship).

High-school students planning a career in funeral service should take as many basic sci-

ence courses as possible, especially in biology and chemistry. A typical two-year curriculum at a school of mortuary science would include courses in anatomy, embalming practices, funeral customs, psychology, accounting, and public health laws. Some colleges and universities now offer four-year programs in funeral service.

Special requirements

All states require embalmers to be licensed, and most states require licenses for funeral directors as well. Some states grant a combination single license covering the activity of both embalmer and funeral director.

After successfully completing their formal education, including an internship or apprenticeship of one to three years (one year is the norm), prospective funeral service practitioners must pass a state board examination that may consist of written and oral tests and demonstration of skills to receive a license to practice in the state. If they wish to practice in another state, they may have to pass that state's examination as well, although some states have reciprocal courtesy arrangements to waive this requirement.

Opportunities for experience and exploration

High-school and college-age young people may work part-time in clerical or custodial jobs in local funeral homes, although state licensing requirements prohibit them from performing more specialized duties.

Related occupations

Although the field of funeral service is unique, a variety of occupations share some of the interests, aptitudes, and skills of funeral directors and embalmers. These may include, for example, biological specimen technicians, biologists, clergy and religious workers, emergency medical technicians, grief counselors, medical assistants, medical-laboratory technicians, nursing aides, perfusionists, physicians (including pathologists and surgeons) and physician assistants, registered nurses, surgical technicians, taxidermists, and veterinarians.

Methods of entering

Most funeral service licensees begin their careers in funeral homes, working with experienced licensed funeral directors and embalmers. Almost all schools of mortuary science maintain close contact with funeral homes in the area and notify students of job openings.

Advancement

For many years, most funeral homes were family businesses. Younger members of the family or their husbands or wives were expected to move up into managerial positions when the older members died or retired. That is changing. Some funeral family members choose careers in other fields. Then, too, firms are being acquired or consolidated with other firms. While there still are family businesses that will continue as such, they are not as prevalent as they once were. A growing number of firms conduct a greater number of funerals each year. These firms employ people in specialized positions and provide more opportunities for advancement.

With sufficient finances or financial backing, funeral service practitioners may establish their own business or purchase a portion or all of an existing one. Some licensees choose to work for manufacturers or suppliers of funeral merchandise. There are embalmers who make an independent career of doing embalming and restorative art for area funeral homes. And an increasing number of licensees specialize in selling funeral and disposition arrangements in advance of need.

Employment outlook

There are approximately 22,000 funeral homes in the United States. In the early 1990s, they employed most of the 45,000 licensed funeral directors and embalmers who held jobs.

The demand for funeral directors and embalmers is expected to be strong through the rest of the decade. As a rule, there are more job openings in this field than there are qualified applicants to fill them. In addition, new personnel are always needed to replace funeral-home employees who retire, die, or otherwise leave the profession. One factor may temper this favorable outlook in some areas, however, where mergers, acquisitions, and consolidations could cut out some positions because of the "pooling" of licensees and other employees in multi-unit funeral-home enterprises.

Job security in this field is relatively unaffected by economic downswings. Further, despite the flux and movement in the population, funeral homes are a stable institution. The average firm has been in the community for more than forty years, and homes with a history of more than one hundred years are not exceptional.

Earnings

The average starting salary for entry-level funeral directors and embalmers in the early 1990s was between $16,000 and $18,000 a year, plus benefits. Many owners of funeral homes earned more than $45,000 annually. Apprentice positions may be salaried. General apprenticeships pay between $12,000 and $14,000, with an increase with experience.

In some metropolitan areas, many funeral-home employees are unionized; in these cases, salaries are determined by union contracts and are generally higher.

Conditions of work

In firms employing two or more licensees, funeral directors and embalmers generally work an eight-hour day, five or six days a week; however, because their services may be needed at any hour of the day or night, shifts are usually arranged so that someone is always available at night and on weekends. In businesses with smaller volume, there is more flexibility in work scheduling. Licensed employees of these firms, as well as some in firms with greater volume, are occasionally involved in tasks related to the operation of the funeral home in addition to caring for the dead and serving the living.

Employees who transport bodies and accompany the funeral procession to the cemetery are frequently required to lift heavy weights and to be outdoors for a considerable time in inclement weather. Robust health and stamina are important in these positions. Sometimes funeral directors and embalmers may handle the remains of those who have died of contagious diseases, but the risk of infection, given the strict sanitary conditions required in all funeral homes, is less than it would be for a physician or nurse.

Social and psychological factors

Funeral directors, as stated above, must be tactful, discreet, and compassionate in dealing with people at a time of great emotional stress. They must be able to provide firm guidance to those who may be confused and upset, while at the same time respecting their wishes and, often, their financial limitations. They must be especially tolerant toward a diversity of religious and philosophical beliefs.

Funeral directors, especially in smaller communities, are looked upon as respected professionals who provide an essential service. They have the satisfaction of helping people through a time of crisis and enabling them to express their grief over the loss of a loved one.

GOE: 11.11.04; SIC: 7261; SOC: 1359

◇ **SOURCES OF ADDITIONAL INFORMATION**

American Board of Funeral Service Education
14 Crestwood Road
Cumberland, ME 04021

National Foundation of Funeral Service
1614 Central Street
Evanston, IL 60201

National Funeral Directors Association
11121 West Oklahoma Avenue
Milwaukee, WI 53227

National Funeral Directors and Morticians Association
PO Box 377993
Chicago, IL 60637

National Selected Morticians
1616 Central Street
Evanston, IL 60201

◇ **RELATED ARTICLES**

Volume 1: Biological Sciences
Volume 2: Biologists; Psychiatrists; Psychologists
Volume 4: Mortuary science technicians

Genealogists

Definition

Genealogists conduct research into the ancestral background of individuals or families to discover and identify the personal history of those people or families.

History

In a rapidly changing world, people sometimes find comfort and stability in learning about their family tree, or "genealogy." The current resurgence in genealogy's popularity can be traced to "Roots," the television series in the 1970s about the history of a single black family. This is not a new phenomenon, however. People from the dawn of time have defined themselves by their ancestors. The books of the Old Testament contain numerous passages outlining the family histories of the biblical patriarchs. Many religions in parts of Africa, China, and Japan have ancestor worship as one of their main tenets. Evidence of the importance of family lines can be seen even today; for example, certain surnames such as "Johnson" and "Peterson" remind us of how important it has been for people to recognize their lineage and be known as "John's son" and "Peter's son."

Genealogy can also have useful applications. Often the line of family descent must be known before a person can inherit title to land and property or be eligible for certain college scholarships. Membership in certain societies, such as the Daughters of the American Revolution and the Hereditary Order of the Descendants of Colonial Governors, depends on a proper and verifiable family history. Most people, however, trace their genealogies merely for the sake of information and enjoyment. In fact, genealogy has become the third most popular hobby in America, second only to coin and stamp collecting.

Nature of the work

Genealogists trace family histories by examining historical documents and answering questions about how and where people were born, were married, lived, and died. It is like historical detective work, in which the genealogist fills in the missing facts through research and deduction.

A genealogist usually needs to advertise in some way for people to know of his or her services. Customers come to genealogists to have questions answered. These questions vary: customers may want to know the lineage of their family since coming to America, or even further back into their country of heritage, or they may wish to find out how they became related to a single ancestor and some facts about his or her life. The customer will also tell the genealogist all the known information about the family tree, and back it up with documents such as birth certificates, family bibles, wedding licenses, and old letters when necessary.

From this starting point, the genealogist begins working on a complex puzzle, not knowing where his or her efforts will lead. Sometimes tracing a person's family history can be fairly straightforward, and the genealogist's research will yield impressive results. At other times, the genealogist may be thwarted by incomplete records, dead ends, and conflicting information. It is very difficult, when accepting an assignment, for a genealogist to know how long it will take to complete the work or how successfully the customers questions can be answered.

Nothing prevents someone from looking up his or her own family history, but genealogists are much more familiar with sources of information and more likely to do the right historical detective work. Genealogists will often start their search in the public library, searching for names and dates in telephone directories, census records, military service records, newspaper clippings, letters files, diaries, and other sources. They may also contact local genealogical groups and historical societies to check any relevant information that may be on hand. Visits to the county courthouse can reveal a wealth of important data, including records of births,

marriages, divorces, deaths, wills, tax records, and property deeds. A truly resourceful genealogist will look for information in places other people might not think of, including the local newspaper's records, school board records, clubs, houses of worship, immigration bureaus, funeral homes and cemeteries. A genealogist can never have too many possible sources of information, because each fact about a historical person's life and death should be authenticated in at least two different places if the research is to be considered valid. Often two pieces of information will conflict, and a third source of validation must be found.

If possible, a genealogist will also seek out and interview relatives and other persons who may know something about the family being researched. These people may have information that is not available anywhere else, including personal stories, photographs, family bibles, and letters. The recollections of these people may also provide clues about where to look for information in other parts of the country or other countries. For example, if an old neighbor reminisces about a deceased family member making frequent visits to Boston, the genealogist might look into the possibility that a branch of the family settled there.

Once the local sources of family information have been explored, the genealogist considers other long-distance sources to contact by mail and telephone. One of these might be the Genealogical Department of the National Archives and Records Service in Washington, D.C., from which the genealogist can find out about immigration records, passport applications, pension claims, and other data. The genealogist might also contact the Genealogical Department of the Church of Jesus Christ of Latter-Day Saints (the Mormon Church) in Salt Lake City, Utah. The church has the world's largest collection of genealogical information, and its library contains more than eight million individual family records, as well as one and a half million reels of original records from all parts of the world. It might also be necessary to gather information from records in other countries by contacting the genealogical societies and government agencies there. Proficiency in a foreign language such as French or German can prove very valuable when the customer would like research to continue this far.

For these national and international inquiries, the genealogist find the work of other professional family historians invaluable. Networking among genealogists has been going on for quite a long time, longer than in most other professions. In exchange for information from a distant city, the genealogist will offer his or her services to that colleague if research ever needs to be done in his or her local area. Networking also benefits genealogists who specialize in certain topics or regions, so that their colleagues can learn of their specializations and steer potential customers to them.

Once the research has been completed, the genealogist organizes the pertinent family information in the manner requested by the customer. From the raw information, the genealogist could prepare a basic family tree, showing births, marriages, and deaths. From this starting point, genealogical reports can grow more detailed and informative. Some customers even hire the genealogist to write a complete family history, which describe the life stories of ancestors; pictures of them, their homes, and their neighborhoods; maps; stories and anecdotes; and whatever else might have turned up in the research that would interest family members. Some people go so far as to have many copies of their family history printed and bound, to be given as gifts to other family members, friends, libraries, and historical and genealogical societies.

Genealogists carefully record the sources of all their information, including the time spent gathering each piece of data. It is important to have available the exact title and page of each reference volume or record book, and the names and addresses of people interviewed in the course of research. Genealogists will take photos of any tombstones, monuments, or markers that give relevant data and will make photocopies of official records, letters, and other printed matter when possible. All this extra information is important in showing the accuracy of the research done, and may also help any genealogical work that someone might undertake in the future.

Working with historical records can be very difficult. Records can exist on yellow, crumbling paper and be handwritten in very hard-to-read script. Often historical records are incomplete or, worse to the genealogist, misleading. A genealogist can follow an investigative trail for months, only to hit a dead end. With experience, genealogists learn to spot irregularities and questionable sources, thus saving themselves and their customers time and expense. In the United States, for example, immigration officials in the past had trouble pronouncing or spelling the ethnic names that new immigrants brought with them; often, an ethnic name was "Americanized" and simplified, or simply was misspelled. Genealogists have to be aware of these inconsistencies. Even though some historical question can never be answered, the genealogist finds a challenge in the historical mysteries they unravel.

Almost all genealogists are self-employed, although in some large cities service firms have sprung up employing several genealogists of different specialties and qualifications. Many genealogists do family history work only part-time while holding other jobs such as librarians, writers, teachers, and college faculty members.

Requirements

There are no formal requirements for becoming a genealogist. Many competent genealogists are self-taught or have learned the trade from another genealogist. A college degree in genealogy, however, can be a distinct advantage because it demonstrates to customers the capacity for research and dedication to the profession. While less than a dozen universities across the country offer bachelor's degree programs in family history, more than fifty offer advanced degrees. In addition, many adult education programs and extension courses can be taken to bolster one's skills in genealogy. A week-long seminar is offered by the National Institute on Genealogical Research in Washington, D.C., with lectures by staff members of the National Archives.

High-school students interested in a career in genealogy should study history, English literature and composition, geography, sociology, and psychology. Foreign languages can also be a plus. Students should endeavor to gain as much skill in research methods and library use as possible. Knowledge of computer use is also important; many libraries and document archives now have computerized catalogs and research systems, and software has been developed for genealogists to use on their personal computers. Because they may eventually do genealogical work only on a part-time basis, students may wish to look into related fields, such as librarians, historians, and free-lance writers, that will offer the free time to conduct genealogical research. Of course, students may enter any field they wish and still be able to make the time to do genealogical work.

Special requirements

Several professional organizations exist for genealogists, with the stated purpose of furthering the profession and offering benefits to members. There are many advantages to membership, including newsletters, publications, seminars, conferences, and the opportunity to build a network of colleagues and friends. Some of these organizations also offer educational sessions and certification or accreditation programs. Customers will often ask for any professional certifications that testify to a person's qualifications and show that work is done according to a code of ethics. The Board for Certification of Genealogists publishes a list of the genealogists it has tested and certified under six different categories. The Genealogical Department of the Church of Jesus Christ of Latter-Day Saints also has a world-wide accreditation program with similar requirements.

Opportunities for experience and exploration

One of the best ways to explore the subject of genealogy is to discuss it with the staff of your local library. They will be able to recommend many good books on the subject and put you in touch with any local genealogical societies, which often meet in the public library. These societies are open to anyone interested in the subject and always welcome new members, even people still in high school. Members will be glad to talk about their profession and can point out magazines and other resources. They may even give students some tips on preparing their own family tree, along with blank forms on which to work.

Students may also find it useful to talk about the profession of genealogy with practitioners in their offices. They will be listed in the local telephone directory, and librarians may also have their business cards on file. These people may be able to give advice on good schools or training programs, opportunities for jobs, and some of the pitfalls of doing genealogical work for a full-time job.

In some communities, short educational courses are offered in genealogy. This provides an opportunity to discover what resources and facilities are available locally for genealogical study, as well as providing beginning skills in the field.

Related occupations

The work of the genealogist requires good reading and writing skills as well as an inquisitive and organized nature. Other jobs that require the same skills include historians, librarians, information scientists, teachers, and private detectives.

Methods of entering

For students earning a degree in genealogy, their teachers and faculty advisers might hear of job openings and keep students informed of them. New graduates can send out letters and resumes to practicing genealogists, in hopes of getting a job, an internship, or customer referrals. More likely, however, a new genealogist is going to have to work on his or her own to drum up business. This may require advertising in the Yellow Pages, local newspapers, and genealogical magazines. The genealogist might also leave his or her business card with the local public or university library and historical society. As with any self-employed profession, steady work is never guaranteed, and the new genealogist may have to supplement his or her income when first starting out.

Advancement

If a genealogist is self-employed, professional advancement will depend on his or her professional skills, dedication to quality work, cleverness, and efforts to find new clients. Professional certification can help, because professional societies publish lists of accredited members and distribute them to the public upon request. Genealogists can also advance by diversifying their skills, either by gaining more accreditation or by expanding their services into related work such as writing family histories and designing family crests and coats of arms. As a person does more genealogical work, the more proficient he or she becomes, and the more likely that satisfied customers will tell their friends and neighbors about the skillful work.

Employment outlook

Despite the recent resurgence in popularity, genealogy holds limited prospects for growth in the future. Interest in the profession will likely stay at current levels, and it may improve slightly. The majority of genealogical work is done by people researching their own families. These people consult genealogists about how to get started, and they may seek professional help when they run into a problem they can't figure out or wish to uncover information in other parts of the country or the world.

Lawyers and people with legal claims sometimes employ genealogists to determine a person's right to a legacy, title, or family name.

Societies whose members are required to prove a certain heritage, such as the Daughters of the American Revolution, employ genealogists to verify the ancestral claims made by prospective members. Physicians and medical researchers are beginning to trace these family histories of people with certain diseases, genetic weaknesses, and other hereditary maladies in hopes of finding a cure. These and other sources of income are available to the enterprising genealogist.

Earnings

Most genealogists, whether self-employed or working for a genealogy service company, charge for their services by the hour. Depending on the complexity of the assignment, fees range from about $10 an hour up to $50 an hour plus expenses. An experienced genealogist is usually able to command a higher fee because he or she is more likely to conduct productive research and not meet so many dead ends. For a larger project like researching and writing an entire family history, a genealogist may charge a single fee. This can be a bad idea, however, if research takes longer than anticipated. In addition, this type of assignment is quite rare.

Genealogists will probably find it is a good idea to develop ways to supplement their income. They might write articles for magazines and journals, but it may not pay much, if anything. They might also write a book on how to trace family history, but many good books on the subject have already been written and remain in print. Qualified persons might be able to teach courses in family history at community colleges, public libraries, or other adult education venues.

Conditions of work

Because most of them are self-employed, genealogists generally set their own working hours and manage their own time. The profession is usually a solitary one, as genealogists spend much of their time looking through old records and searching library files, or working in their homes organizing data and updating their records. Their search for information can take them into stuffy, badly lit archive vaults and basements, where they spend hours sifting through hundreds of documents looking for a single, vital piece of information. These documents can be crumbling and yellow, written in ink that is fading and hard to read. Hours or days of effort can produce nothing, or the genealogist can discover rich treasures of previously undocumented and unused information.

Genealogy can require a good bit of legwork as well. Trips to schools, cemeteries, churches, and homes for personal interviews can be enjoyable as well as interesting. A genealogist might even be called on to travel to a distant city or even abroad to complete his or her research, take pictures of old family homes, locate and interview distant relatives, and so on.

Social and psychological factors

Genealogists are the sort of people who love puzzles and mysteries. Indeed, solving historical mysteries, by examining and weighing evidence and questioning the proper people, is what their job is all about. Genealogists need to be inquisitive, patient, honest, and thorough. They should be willing to check out any possible source of useful information, and not become discouraged when possible leads on data fall through. They should be well organized and thorough in their documentation and record-keeping. They should also be greatly interested in history and be able to work well on their own for extended periods while conducting their research.

Genealogists find their historical detective work very fulfilling and often fascinating. They enjoy filling the gaps in understanding, preserving history in a useful and interesting way, and answering people questions about where they've come from. They also meet interesting people—both customers, historians, and other genealogists—and gain some personal satisfaction of bringing family members in touch with one another.

GOE: 11.03.03; SIC: 7299; SOC: 1913

◇ **SOURCES OF ADDITIONAL INFORMATION**

American Society of Genealogists
PO Box 4970
Washington, DC 20008

Association of Professional Genealogists
PO Box 11601
Salt Lake City, UT 84147

255

Federation of Genealogical Societies
Information Office
PO Box 220
Davenport, IA 52805

The Genealogical Institute
Education Department
PO Box 2045
Salt Lake City, UT 84122

General managers and top executives

Definition

General managers and *top executives* plan, organize, direct, and coordinate the operations of organizations in business and industry, government, and education.

History

Management plays an important part in any enterprise in which one person directs another person or group of people. Thus, management in its simplest and earliest form began with the need for survival: in the tribe or village where activities such as food production or defense strategies had to be coordinated and directed. In fact, civilization could not have grown to its present level of complexity without the planning and organizing involved in effective management. The growth from village to city and from city-state to nation was brought about by leaders managing agricultural, trade, religious, military, government, and educational activities.

Some of the earliest examples of written documents had to do with the management of business and commerce. Accumulation of vast amounts of wealth necessitated effective record-keeping of taxes, trade agreements, laws, and rights of ownership. As interpreters and administrators of religious and secular law, priests became the first managers and executives in business and religious matters; usually, too, they were very influential as advisors to the rulers of a country.

The technological advances created by the Industrial Revolution brought about the need for a distinct class of managers. The management movement came out of the need for skilled, trained managers to organize and operate complex factory systems. Also, the divided efforts of specialized workers in factories had to be managed and coordinated.

As businesses began to diversify their product production, industries became so complex that the administration of production had to be decentralized. The authoritarian type of manager faded with the expanded scope of managers and the transition to the emerging professional manager took place. In the 1920s large corporations began organizing their growth around decentralized administration with centralized policy control. Individual and group dynamics were incorporated into management practices as human relations studies showed the importance of employee attitudes and behavior for the overall productivity of a company.

Much of the progress and success of the scientific management movement in the twentieth century can be attributed to the programs of professional management associations and educational institutions. They provided a forum for the exchange and evaluation of creative management ideas and technical innovations. Eventually these management concepts spread from manufacturing and production to office, personnel, marketing, and financial functions; and from private industry to government, education, and health services.

In recent decades management philosophy has incorporated even more humanistic attitudes toward personnel—the underlying assumption is that employees control their own activities because of a commitment to the goals of the company. Today management is more oriented toward results than toward activities, a philosophy that recognizes individual differences in styles of working and functioning.

Nature of the work

Corporate president or chief executive officer, executive vice president for sales and marketing, department store manager, college president, school superintendent, and city manager—these are examples of general managers and top executives who formulate the policies and direct the operations of private firms and government agencies, schools, and hospitals.

The *president* establishes an organization's goals and policies along with other top executives, usually the *chief executive officer, executive vice-presidents,* and the *board of directors.* Top executives plan business objectives and develop policies to coordinate operations between divisions and departments and establish procedures for attaining objectives. Activity reports and financial statements are reviewed to determine progress and revise operations as needed. The president also directs and formulates funding for new and existing programs within the organization. Public relations plays a big part in the lives of top executives as they deal with executives and leaders from other countries or organizations, and with customers, employees, and various special interest groups. Although the president or chief executive officer retains ultimate authority and responsibility, the chief operating officer may be the one to oversee the day-to-day operations of the company. Other duties may include serving as chairman of committees, such as management, executive, engineering, or sales.

The *executive vice president* directs and coordinates the activities of one or more departments, depending on the size of the organization. In very large organizations, the duties of executive vice president may be highly specialized; for example, they may oversee the activities of general managers of marketing, sales promotion, purchasing, finance, personnel training, industrial relations, administrative services, data processing, property management, transportation, or legal services. In smaller organizations, an executive vice president might be responsible for a number of these departments. Executive vice presidents also assist the chief executive officer in formulating and administering the organization's policies and developing its long-range goals. Also, executive vice presidents may serve as mem-

While traveling to an airport, a business executive reviews reports and catches up on his daily responsibilities.

bers of management committees on special studies.

General managers direct their department's activities within the context of the organization's overall plan. With the help of supervisory managers and their staffs, general managers implement organizational policies and goals. This may involve developing sales or promotional materials; analyzing the department's budgetary requirements; hiring, training, and supervising staff; or coordinating their department's activities with other departments.

Requirements

The educational background of general managers and top executives varies as widely as does the nature of their diverse responsibilities. Most general managers have a bachelor's degree in liberal arts or business administration. In college, their major is often, though not always, related to the department they direct or the organization they administer; for example, accounting for a general manager of finance, computer science for a general manager of data processing, education for a school principal, engineering or science for director of research and development.

Graduate and professional degrees are common. Many managers and top executives in administrative, marketing, financial, and manufacturing activities have a master's degree in business administration (MBA) or management science. Managers in highly technical manufacturing and research activities often have a master's degree or doctorate in a technical or scientific discipline. A law degree is mandatory for general managers of corporate legal departments, and hospital administrators generally have a master's degree in health ser-

257

vices administration or business administration. College presidents and school superintendents generally have a doctorate, often in education administration. In some industries, such as retail trade or the food and beverage industry, competent individuals without a college degree may become general managers.

Most general managers in government have a degree in public administration or in fields such as economics, psychology, sociology, or urban studies. City managers usually have a degree in liberal arts or a master's degree in public administration. Police and fire chiefs are graduates of police or fire academies, often with a degree in police or fire science or a related field.

Special requirements

Management recruiters generally look for people who hold master's degrees in business administration, management science, or public administration. Advanced professional certificates or doctoral programs for training top management in business and government are also offered by some graduate business schools. The Certified Administrative Manager Program administered by the Administrative Management Society certifies managers twice yearly. Managers also join professional or trade groups to keep up with advances in their field. Often an organization will send its managers and executives to seminars and educational programs for further training.

Opportunities for experience and exploration

To get experience as a manager, start with your own interests. Whether you're involved in drama, sports, school publications, or a part-time job, there are various managerial duties associated with any organized activity. These can involve planning; scheduling; managing players, employees, and volunteers; fundraising; or budgeting. Goals have to be set, decisions made, activities and people coordinated, and responsibilities delegated to get a project completed.

Local business will have job opportunities through which you can get first-hand knowledge and experience of management structure. Generally, a retail store or food establishment will have a general manager who oversees other managers or supervisors; they, in turn,

oversee employees. If the business is privately owned, the owner may be the manager. In a large corporation, there will be an entire management structure above the general manager.

Related occupations

General managers and top executives plan, organize, direct, control, and coordinate the activities, programs, and departments of an organization. The members of the board of directors, the chief executive officer and chief operations officer, administrators, directors, supervisors, and superintendents are also involved in these activities. Occupations in government with similar functions are governor, mayor, postmaster, commissioner, director, and office chief. In education, related occupations include college president, admissions director, financial aid director, student activities director, school principal, or superintendent. Other related positions are association executive, director of research and development, project director, budget director, program manager, personnel manager, financial manager, public relations manager, management consultant, health services managers, hotel and restaurant managers, property managers, and department store managers.

Methods of entering

Generally, those interested in management will have a college degree, although management positions in retail stores, grocery stores, and eating and drinking establishments will usually be filled by promising employees who have a high-school diploma. In government, industry, education, and the medical field, aspiring managers will have at least a bachelor's degree in the field they want to go into or in business administration; often they will have a graduate degree in a specialized field or in business. Degrees in computer science are also in great demand in business and government.

Many organizations have management trainee programs that college graduates can enter. Such programs are advertised at college career fairs or through college job placement services. Often, however, these management trainee positions in business and government are filled by employees who are already working for the organization and who demonstrate management potential.

Executives and managers who wish to move up into top executive or higher management positions can do so within their existing organization or with another one. Managers change organizations for a variety of reasons. They may desire better working conditions or a higher salary, or they may wish to relocate geographically. Often those in management choose to move from government to private industry or vice versa, or they may desire a more challenging or creative position. Executive search companies are in the business of recruiting executives for their client firms from another company. Major newspapers such as the *Wall Street Journal* or the *New York Times* advertise such positions nationally, and the library will have numerous other publications that specialize in various fields such as industry, government, education, or health care.

Advancement

Most general management and top executive positions are filled by experienced lower level managers and executives who display traits such as leadership, self-confidence, creativity, motivation, decisiveness, and flexibility. In small firms, where the number of jobs is limited, advancement to a higher management position may come slowly. In large firms, promotions may occur more quickly.

Advancement may be accelerated by participating in different kinds of educational programs available for managers. These are often paid for by the organization. Company training programs broaden knowledge of company policy and operations. Training programs sponsored by numerous industry and trade associations and continuing education courses in colleges and universities can familiarize managers with the latest developments in management techniques. Participation in interdisciplinary conferences and seminars can expand knowledge of national and international issues influencing the manager's firm.

Other more personal factors may influence one's ability to advance to higher management positions. Top managers must have well-developed personal relations skills and be able to communicate effectively, both orally and in writing. Other traits considered important for top executives are intelligence, decisiveness, intuition, creativity, honesty, loyalty, a sense of responsibility, and planning and organizing abilities.

General managers may advance to top executive positions, such as executive or administrative vice-president, in their own firm or they may move to a corresponding position in a larger firm. Similarly, vice-presidents may ad-

vance to peak corporate positions—president or chief executive officer. Presidents and chief executive officers, upon retirement, may become members of the board of directors of one or more firms. Sometimes general managers and top executives establish their own firms.

Employment outlook

General managers and top executives hold more than two and a half million jobs. Management is found in every industry, with employment more concentrated in the largest industries, such as food, clothing, banking, education, health care, and business services.

Employment of general managers and top executives is expected to increase about as fast as the average for all occupations. In addition to openings arising from increased demand, many management openings will occur each year to replace those who transfer to other positions, start their own businesses, or retire. The large supply of competent lower-level managers seeking top management positions, however, should result in substantial job competition. Individuals whose accomplishments reflect strong leadership qualities and improved productivity will have the best job opportunities.

Projected employment growth varies by industry. Employment of management in the computer and data processing fields is expected to double. Firms supplying management, consulting, public relations, and other business services will probably experience very rapid growth. Management needs in engineering, architectural, and surveying services firms are expected to grow rapidly, and the demand for management is also expected to increase greatly in some health care industries, such as out patient clinics and social services facilities. Much faster than average employment growth is projected for management in the hotel, restaurant, and travel industries, whereas employment of general managers and top executives in education and in hospitals is expected to increase only about as fast as the average for all occupations. Some manufacturing industries are expected to have very little change in their management needs.

Earnings

Salary levels for general managers and top executives vary substantially, depending upon the level of responsibility, length of service, and type, size, and location of the organization. Top-level managers in large firms can earn ten times as much as their counterparts in small firms. Also, salaries in large metropolitan areas such as New York City are higher than those in smaller cities. Generally, too, salaries in manufacturing and finance are higher than salaries in state and local governments.

General managers and top executives in the private sector receive additional compensation in the form of bonuses, stock awards, company-paid insurance premiums, use of company cars, paid country club memberships, expense accounts, and generous retirement benefits.

In the early 1990s, the estimated median annual salary for general managers and top executives was around $50,000. Top executives of large corporations are the most highly paid management personnel. Their base salary may exceed $1 million, and additional compensation, in the form of stocks and other fringe benefits, may be as much as their base salary.

Although it is very difficult to find work at an equivalent level, top executives are often provided with a good compensation package if they are laid-off or dismissed by the board of directors.

Conditions of work

General managers are provided with comfortable offices near the departments they direct. Top executives may be provided with spacious, lavish offices, and may enjoy such privileges as executive dining rooms, company cars, country club memberships, and liberal expense accounts. Such conditions are commonly used to facilitate meetings and negotiations with top executives from other corporations, government, or other nations. Long hours, including evenings and weekends, are common, and business discussions often occur during social engagements.

Substantial travel is often required. General managers often travel between national, regional, and local offices. Top executives may travel to meet with executives in other corporations, both here and abroad. Reimbursement of an accompanying spouse's travel expenses helps executives cope with frequent periods away from home. Meetings and conferences sponsored by industries and associations occur regularly and provide invaluable opportunities to meet with peers and keep up with the latest developments. In large corporations, job transfers between the parent company and its local offices or subsidiaries are common.

Social and psychological factors

General managers and top executives often work long hours under intense pressure to attain, for example, production and marketing goals. The long hours—an eighty-hour workweek is not uncommon—limit time available for family and leisure activities. Physical stamina and a deep commitment to the organization are required to keep up this pace week after week, especially when extensive travel is involved. In smaller organizations the skill of the director or top executive may directly determine the continued success of the company.

Often executives are involved in intense negotiations; for example, when meeting with government officials, private interest groups, or competitors, or with foreign governments or organizations. Flexibility and the ability to get along with widely diverse groups of people are essential assets for the top executive and general manager. In such situations it is important to have the resourcefulness, creativity, and self-assurance to make on-the-spot decisions and command the respect and cooperation of one's peers.

In situations within the organization, considerable skill in managing people is required. The executive or manager needs to delegate authority and assign responsibility, motivate and develop employees, and handle complaints and problems. Integrity and honesty are highly desirable qualities, for these enhance the respect that subordinates will have for their managers.

The changing face of our economy and society has influenced the management movement with newer ways of thinking. Older management techniques developed in an economic society that emphasized efficiency, productivity, and profits, whereas newer techniques emphasize human and social concerns as well, such as personal job satisfaction, interpersonal relations, or environmental protection.

The trend toward a merging of these economic and social values has made modern management practices more responsive to the needs of society and the individual. The modern manager not only recognizes the need for the organization to provide goods, services, and programs efficiently and effectively, but also recognizes that the organization is a structure through which the individual finds contribution and achievement for the benefit of society as a whole.

GOE: 11; SIC: Any industry; SOC: Any industry

◇ **SOURCES OF ADDITIONAL INFORMATION**

Administrative Management Society
4622 Street Road
Trevose, PA 19047

AMA International
American Management Association
135 West 50th Street
New York, NY 10020

National Management Association
2210 Arbor Boulevard
Dayton, OH 45439

Women in Management
2 North Riverside Plaza, Suite 2400
Chicago, IL 60611

Information about general managers and top executives in specific industries may be obtained from organizations listed in encyclopedias or directories of associations in libraries.

◇ **RELATED ARTICLES**

Geographers

Definition

Geographers study, analyze, and record knowledge about the significant patterns of people and natural phenomena throughout the world and relate these characteristics to human activities as they vary from place to place.

History

The recording of travel routes and reports on new lands visited, as well as on the people, characterized the early efforts of the geographer. In time, people improved the ability to report their findings so that others might profit from their explorations. Through the years, the work of the geographer has expanded from the study of the earth's surface (that is, the character, structure, and plant and animal life of an area) to include studies dealing with the economic, political, and cultural life of an area. Thus, the field of geography has come to be concerned with the human and cultural activities of a region as they relate to world trade, international relations, and international events.

Nature of the work

A great deal of the work of the geographer is dependent upon the setting of the work and the specific area of specialization. Many geographers find employment in colleges and universities and governmental agencies, while some are employed by business and industrial firms. Most of these positions involve teaching or research responsibilities.

A small but growing number of geographers work for map companies, textbook publishers, travel agencies, manufacturing firms, chain stores, and market research organizations.

Geographers involved in the research areas of their field usually study and analyze distri-

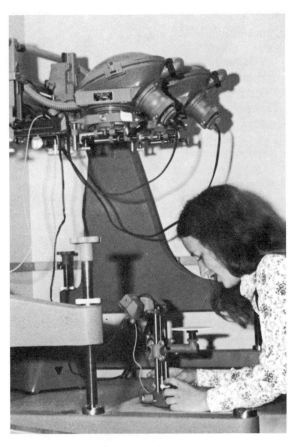

A cartographer uses a plotter to produce detailed contour maps for several government agencies.

bution of soils, vegetation, land forms, climate, and mineral and water resources. In this work they often utilize surveying and meteorological instruments. Geographers also analyze political organizations, transportation systems, and a wide variety of other activities. Some geographers spend much of their time in the field, preparing and interpreting statistics and analyzing aerial photographs and other data that they have collected. Many construct and interpret maps, graphs, and diagrams.

The majority of geographers specialize in one of the main branches of geography. Some of the responsibilities of various geography specialists are the following:

Cartographers are concerned with the design and construction of maps, as well as the compilation of necessary data for them.

The work of *economic geographers* entails analyzing the geographic distribution of economic activities, including manufacturing, mining, farming, trade, and communications.

Regional geographers study all the geographic aspects of a particular area, such as a river basin, an island, a nation, or even an entire continent. They are concerned with the physical,

economic, political, and cultural characteristics of the area, and often may be called upon to advise on special problems of the region.

Urban geographers study and analyze metropolitan problems of a geographic nature; assist in planning and developing such urban and suburban projects as residential developments, traffic control, shopping centers, and parking areas; and advise business and industry on plant locations and other related problems.

Political geographers study such factors as natural resources, national boundaries, physical features of land and their relation to local, state, national, and international affairs. They also consult and advise on problems of a political, ethnic, or economic nature.

Physical geographers study the processes that create the earth's physical characteristics, such as land forms, oceans, climate, or weather, and the significance of these patterns over time. Physical geographers may specialize, too. A *climatologic geographer* analyzes climate and weather and how and why they change.

Medical geographers study how health is affected by our physical setting, including environmental quality. They study and analyze health effects of vegetation, minerals in the water supply, climate, and air pollution. They may also analyze access to health care by geographic region or setting.

In a relatively new but rapidly growing field known as Geographic Information Systems (GIS), geographers combine computer graphics, artificial intelligence, and high-speed communications in the mapping, manipulation, storage, and selective retrieval of geographic data sets. In this way, they are able to display and analyze a wide variety of natural, cultural, and economic information in applications as diverse as worldwide weather forecasting, emergency management, crime prevention, and the monitoring of metropolitan land use.

Requirements

The bachelor's degree with a major in geography is generally considered the basic education required for most positions as a professional geographer. Advanced university degrees, the master's or the doctor's degree, are usually required for most college teaching positions and for those employment opportunities involving a considerable amount of research activity.

Many colleges and universities offer undergraduate programs in geography. A good number of these institutions also have a curriculum leading to the master's degree or doctorate.

Courses taken by students majoring in geography include weather and climate; political, physical, human, urban, and regional geography; meteorology; and cartography. Undergraduate study usually includes formal classroom instruction as well as some field study.

Among the personal attributes that are desirable for success in this field are better than average scholastic ability, particularly for those specialties that may require advanced study; interest and ability to concentrate on scholarly materials for long periods of time; strong interest in one or more of the related social or physical sciences; and a preference for activities dealing with people and ideas.

A prospective geographer will require some basic and advanced statistical and mathematical skills and should be able to interpret maps and graphs; express ideas in speech and in writing; and analyze, solve problems, and make sound judgments.

Special requirements

No specific license or related requirement is necessary to gain admission to the field or to obtain the right to practice this profession. Membership in professional associations is voluntary; however, most professional geographers choose to join one or more of these associations as a means of keeping abreast of changes and trends in the field.

Opportunities for experience and exploration

There are increasing opportunities to apply direct learning in actual work situations through college internship programs. A few summer and part-time employment opportunities are available in business or industrial firms. Information about these openings is available through the college summer placement office. Field experiences, offered as part of the college program, can provide opportunity for potential geographers to test their knowledge and personal qualifications in a very real and practical way. Students who have doubts about their interests or abilities will find it helpful to investigate the possibilities for trial exploratory experience in conjunction with the programs that they are considering at specific colleges or universities.

Related occupations

Geographers are classified with workers in mathematics and the physical sciences, such as criminalists, environmental analysts, materials scientists, and pollution control technicians. Anyone interested in geography might also want to look into the following occupations: anthropologists, cartographers, economists, marketing researchers, meteorologists, political scientists, surveyors, or urban planners.

Methods of entering

Some beginning jobs are available in the teaching of geography. Generally, these positions are available in the public schools; however, quite often high-school teaching jobs require study in other related fields so that the applicant can qualify as a teacher of social studies, history, or science. Many beginning geographers find positions connected with mapmaking either in government or private industry. Some obtain positions as research or teaching assistants while working for advanced degrees. Others enter the planning field. Those geographers with advanced degrees can qualify for teaching and research positions on the college level. Many consulting jobs also are available.

Each year the federal government has beginning positions in one or more of the geography specialties. Applicants who can meet the stated qualifications, such as age or training, can arrange to take the civil service examination that is usually required. The person seeking a job should watch the federal and state government announcements concerning open positions.

In general, college graduates will find their college placement office and their major professors of great help in contacting potential employers. The bulletins of the various professional associations are sources of job opportunities for the beginning geographer.

Advancement

Like many professional lines of endeavor, advancement is dependent on such factors as amount and type of training, experience, and personal interest and drive. Promotion to jobs requiring more skill and competency are available in all specialty areas. Such jobs are characterized by more administrative, research, or advisory responsibilities and, consequently,

Geographers
Professional, Administrative, and Managerial Occupations

promotions are governed, to a great extent, by personal evaluation of job performance in the beginning or primary fields of work.

Employment outlook

Geography is generally considered a very small profession. With the increased emphasis on planning and research in U.S. business and government, however, the number of geographers in business has doubled in recent years. In the early 1990s, more than 15,000 geographers were employed. Employment opportunities for these professionals are expected to be good through the rest of the decade. Geographers will be needed to analyze or select sites for retail stores and shopping centers, banks, supermarkets, and industrial parks. There will also be a demand for them in urban renewal, highway programs, and environmental planning.

Competition for college and university teaching jobs will be strong. Many geographers with graduate degrees will seek research and management jobs in government and industry and in research and consulting firms. Others will fill nonacademic positions in cartography, health services, climatology, flood management, conservation, and environmental planning.

Earnings

Earnings and other benefits depend a great deal on the amount of training, the nature of the employment situation, and the personal interests and attributes of the individual employee.

Geographers with bachelor's degrees and no experience had a starting salary of between $16,000 and $18,000 a year in the early 1990s. With an additional year of graduate study (a master's degree), geographers could expect a salary range of $20,000 to $22,000 a year, and those with doctorates started with salaries around $24,000. Initial starting salaries are dependent on the college record of the particular individual.

In the early 1990s, the average salaries of persons with doctorates employed in colleges and universities were about $24,000 per year for an unranked instructor, $28,250 for an assistant professor, $34,000 for an associate professor, and $44,500 for a full professor. The beginning salaries of geographers in the federal government were about $14,800 or $18,400 for those

with a bachelor's degree, $22,500 with a master's degree, and $27,200 with a doctorate.

In addition to salaried income, the geographer should consider the opportunities for supplemental earnings through consulting, research, and writing activities. These opportunities are generally available to experienced geographers and provide the professional geographer with an opportunity to add to his or her net income as personal interests and abilities permit. For example, the geographer who enjoys writing has the opportunity to prepare and publish articles, pamphlets, and travel or college textbooks.

Conditions of work

The geographer generally has very pleasant working conditions. The work, for the most part, is accomplished in an office or classroom under the typical working conditions of a business, school, or federal agency.

The average workweek of most geographers is forty hours, particularly for those employed in government or business positions. Thus, the number of hours per day, holiday and vacation leave, health and pension benefits, and so on, are similar to those of other workers employed by the particular company or agency.

In some types of positions, however, there are some unusual work situations. One of the most common demands is the necessity for travel away from home. These periods of time can extend from a few days to a few years depending on the nature of the assignment. Sometimes these assignments are located in the less developed regions of the world, which may require living under somewhat adverse conditions. Often these opportunities are challenging for the person who enjoys the adventure of new places and people.

Social and psychological factors

Geography as a career is very similar to many other professional occupations. One can seek and find employment in situations that are more or less routine and scheduled, or one can find opportunity for positions that demand change and flexibility both in approach to day-to-day tasks and in the work environment.

One has an opportunity to become intimately involved in many aspects of world living, and can be an active participant in the day-

264

to-day problems and issues of national and international concern.

Because of the varied opportunities for specialization within the profession, young career aspirants can usually find an employment outlet for their own particular abilities and interests. Thus, the person with a strong interest in anthropology can concentrate on the human or ethnic aspects of the field, while another with an interest in economics can develop particular competencies dealing with marketing or natural resources. Many other individual interests and needs can be accommodated within the broad employment spectrum. This permits more occupational exploration than may be generally possible in the career development patterns of other fields.

GOE: 02.01.01; SIC: 8211; SOC: 1849

◇ **SOURCES OF ADDITIONAL INFORMATION**

American Geographical Society
156 Fifth Avenue, Suite 600
New York, NY 10010

Association of American Geographers
1710 16th Street, NW
Washington, DC 20009

Society of Women Geographers
1619 New Hampshire Avenue, NW
Washington, DC 20009

◇ **RELATED ARTICLES**

Volume 1: Book Publishing; Civil Service; Construction; Education; Magazine Publishing; Military Services; Real Estate
Volume 2: Anthropologists and archaeologists; Cartographers; College and university faculty; Economists; Geologists; Meteorologists; Urban and regional planners
Volume 4: Surveying and mapping technicians

Geologists

Definition

Geologists study all aspects of the earth, including its origin, history, composition, and structure. Along more practical lines, geologists may, through the use of theoretical knowledge and research data, locate ground water, oil, minerals, and other natural resources; advise construction companies and government agencies on the suitability of locations being considered for buildings, highways, dams, tunnels, and other structures; and prepare geologic reports, maps, and diagrams.

History

Geology is a comparatively young science that may be said to have been started about 1795 by James Hutton, a retired British physician. Hutton noticed one day, on a walk along the shore of his seacoast farm, the constant erosion of the land by the ocean. As he watched, he realized that the whole continent must have been formed in this way, and it was Hutton's musings on this idea that led to the first principles of geology. In 1799, William Smith published his division of the geological record into ages and, in 1830, Sir Charles Lyell published *Principles of Geology*, which put the earlier thoughts of Smith and Hutton into an orderly system.

From these beginnings, geology has made rapid advances, both in scope and knowledge. With the development of more intricate instruments, such as the X-ray diffractometer, which determines mineral structure, and the petrographic microscope, which permits study of how rocks have been formed and modified by

A geologist tests soil from a mining operation in New Mexico where uranium deposits are being explored.

earth processes, geologists are able to study areas they were previously unable to reach.

Nature of the work

The geologist's work may be said to be divided into three phases. The first phase is locating and obtaining physical data and material. This phase may necessitate the drilling of deep holes to obtain samples, the collection and examination of the materials found on or near the surface, and possibly the preparation of geological maps. The geologist may spend three to six months of each year in field work.

The second phase involves laboratory work. Here the geologists carry out studies for which they may have had neither time nor equipment while in the field. Under controlled temperatures and pressures, geological specimens may be thoroughly analyzed.

In the third phase of the geologist's work, the information gained from the first two phases is compiled and assembled into reports that may be used by future geologists.

This, basically, is what a geologist's work entails. There is, however, opportunity for a wide variety of specializations. Following are examples of such specializations:

Marine geologists specialize in the study of the oceans, including the seabed.

Paleontologists specialize in the study of the earth's rock formations, including remains of plant and animal life, to estimate the age of the earth.

Geochronologists are geoscientists who use radioactive dating and other techniques to estimate the age of rock and other samples from an exploration site.

Petroleum geologists, who comprise the majority of geologists, attempt to locate natural gas and oil deposits through exploration and study of the data obtained. They are expected to recommend the acquisition, retention, or release of company owned or leased properties. They also estimate oil reserves and assist petroleum engineers in determining exact production procedure.

Closely related to petroleum geologists are the *economic geologists,* who search for new resources of minerals and fuels.

Engineering geologists are responsible for the application of geological knowledge to problems arising in construction of roads, buildings, bridges, and other structures.

Mineralogists are interested in classification of and the physical chemical properties of minerals composing rocks and mineral deposits. To this end they examine, analyze, and classify minerals and precious stones to develop data and theories on their origin, occurrence, and possible uses in industry and commerce.

Petrologists study the arrangement of minerals within rocks for the purpose of classifying and determining their origin and cause of metamorphosis. (*See also* the article titled "Petrologists" elsewhere in this volume.)

Stratigraphers study distribution and relative arrangement of sedimentary rock layers. This enables them to study evolutionary changes, as in fossils and plants, and successive changes in distribution of land and sea, as interpreted from the character of fossil content.

Closely related to stratigraphers are *sedimentologists,* who determine processes and products involved in sedimentary rock formations and paleontologists, who identify and classify fossils found within the sediments. Geochronologists determine the approximate age of rock formations.

Geohydrologists study the nature and distribution of water within the earth.

Geomorphologists study the form of the earth's surface and the processes, such as erosion and glaciation, that bring about changes.

In addition to such specializations as above, an increasing number of people combine detailed knowledge of geology with equally detailed knowledge in another field. *Geochemists*, for example, are concerned with chemical composition of, and changes in, minerals and rocks, while *planetary geologists* must apply their knowledge of geology to interpretations of data that has been gathered concerning surface conditions on the moon and other planets.

Obviously the geologist is far from limited in a choice of work, although a basic knowledge of all sciences is essential in each broad area of specialization.

Requirements

For employment as a geologist, a bachelor's degree is a minimum necessity. To persons with these credentials, only a few jobs are available, and these are usually closely supervised, routine jobs. A master's degree is required for beginning positions in research, teaching, or exploration. For those wishing to make significant advancements in research and college-level teaching, a doctorate is required. The geologist who works in the field or in administration must have skills in business administration and in working with other people.

A number of colleges, universities, and institutions of technology offer education in geology. Students in undergraduate work usually spend about a fourth of their time studying geology courses, such as physical geology, historical geology, mineralogy, and invertebrate paleontology. About a third of their study time is spent in related natural sciences and in mathematics, with the rest in such subjects as English composition, economics, and foreign languages.

Students seeking graduate degrees in geology concentrate on advanced courses in geology, placing major emphasis on their particular fields.

Persons interested in the geological profession should have an aptitude not only for geology, but also for physics, chemistry, and mathematics. Personal qualifications such as a liking for outdoor activities and physical stamina are requisites for the kind of working conditions involved.

Special requirements

The major requirements are those discussed above: sufficient education and certain personal requirements. No licenses are necessary, but a thorough knowledge of the profession is essential.

Opportunities for experience and exploration

Students interested in a career in geology should attempt to read as much as possible about geology and geologists. It would also be helpful to take a college course in field geology to get an idea of the applications of geology.

Possibly the student's best chance for association with geologists and geological work would be to join the clubs or organizations concerned with such things as rock collecting, or amateur geological groups, in your area or through local museums.

Related occupations

Other workers concerned with the physical environment include environmental engineers, geophysicists, meteorologists, and oceanographers. The petroleum and natural gas industry, which employs many geologists, also employs many other scientific and technical workers in occupations related to exploration and extraction. These include drafters, engineering technicians, petroleum engineers, science technicians, and surveyors. Persons interested in geology will find similar aspects in the work of cartographers and of some chemists, computer scientists, mathematicians, and physicists.

Methods of entering

After completing sufficient educational requirements, preferably a master's degree or doctorate, the geologist may look for work in various areas. The school placement bureau and the head of the department are usually prepared to give advice and assistance in finding a satisfactory job. For those interested in teaching, a number of positions are available, but it is best to hold a doctorate. College graduates may also take government civil service examinations, or possibly find work on state geological surveys, which are sometimes based on civil service competition. Representatives from companies seeking geologists will also come to the college placement office to interview.

Advancement

The geologist with a bachelor's degree has little chance of advancing to a high-level position. Just as in many other fields, the more education and experience, the easier it is to advance. The person with a doctorate will be most likely to receive the college professorship, the important administrative and research positions. In a few areas, such as administration, the individual's personality and ability in working with people will also influence his or her advancement.

Employment outlook

The majority of all geologists are employed in private industry. Most of them work for oil and gas companies, primarily in oil and gas exploration; the rest work for business service and consulting firms or are self-employed. The federal government employs geologists in the Department of the Interior (in the U.S. Geological Survey, the Bureau of Mines, or the Bureau of Reclamation) and in the Departments of Defense, Agriculture, and Commerce. Geologists also work for state agencies, nonprofit research organizations, and museums.

Employment of geologists is expected to grow more slowly than the average for all occupations throughout the 1990s. The drop in the price of oil has caused a reduction in exploration activities by the petroleum industry. Because most jobs for geologists are in or related to that industry, competition for employment is expected to be heavy until oil prices increase enough to make more exploration worthwhile. New sources of gas and oil will have to be found eventually, however, which should improve the outlook. In the meantime, most jobs that open up each year will be to replace geologists who change occupations or leave the field for other reasons.

The best opportunities for knowledgeable, experienced geologists—especially those with advanced degrees—will be in environmentally related research.

There is some public pressure for large industries, particularly for petroleum and gas producers, to have board members with conservation backgrounds to assist on environmental impact evaluations of all projects.

Earnings

Salaries for geologists rank in the same bracket as those for engineers and other scientists, and often at the top of that bracket.

In the early 1990s, beginning geologists with bachelor's degrees earned about $19,200 per year in industry. In the federal government, beginning geologists with bachelor's degrees earned about $14,800 or $18,400, depending on college records; with master's degrees, salaries started at approximately $18,400 or $22,500; and, with a doctorate, salaries started at about $27,200 or $32,600. The average salary for all geologists in the federal government was $37,500 a year.

Industrial companies generally offer the highest salaries; colleges and universities offer the lowest salaries, but often college teachers can earn additional income through research, writing, and consulting. Also salaries for foreign assignments may range much higher than those in the United States.

Conditions of work

Some geologists' work may be physically demanding. They may commonly spend considerable time in the field living a camper's life, often primitive and rugged. A geologist may be sent to remote, unpopulated places where the members of the geological team will be the only companions.

Hours are also spent working in the laboratory and in preparing reports. The work is time-consuming and strenuous, but enjoyable to the geologist.

Social and psychological factors

The person who chooses geology as a profession must be thoroughly interested in the work to weather the physical hardships connected with it. One would also have to consider the problems of family life in the field work aspect of this profession. A geologist, however, can find great satisfaction in working effectively with other members of a team, in contributing to our knowledge of the world, in having the opportunity to travel and to enjoy both outdoor life and detailed laboratory work. Salaries for qualified geologists rank high among the scientific field.

GOE: 02.01.01; SIC: 1382, 1899; SOC: 1847

◇ **SOURCES OF ADDITIONAL INFORMATION**

American Geological Institute
4220 King Street
Alexandria, VA 22302

Association of Engineering Geologists
323 Boston Post Road
Sudbury, MA 01776

Geological Society of America
PO Box 9140
Boulder, CO 80301

◇ **RELATED ARTICLES**

Volume 1: Agriculture; Biological Sciences; Chemistry; Energy; Engineering; Metals; Physical Sciences; Rubber
Volume 2: Astronomers; Biochemists; Biologists; Chemists; College and university faculty; Engineers; Geographers; Geophysicists; Oceanographers; Petrologists
Volume 3: Agricultural scientists; Petroleum drilling occupations
Volume 4: Chemical technicians; Engineering technicians; Geological technicians

Geophysicists

Definition

Geophysicists are concerned with matter and energy and how they interact. They study the physical properties and structure of the earth, from its interior to its upper atmosphere and including land surfaces, subsurfaces, and bodies of water. Geophysicists may apply their knowledge to practical problems such as predicting earthquakes, locating raw materials and sources of power, and evaluating sites for power plants.

History

Geophysics is another new, promising twentieth-century career field. Geology is concerned with the study of the history and composition of the earth as recorded by rock formations and vegetable fossils. Physics is concerned with all forms of energy, the properties of matter, and the relationship between energy and matter. Geophysics is the study of the physics of the earth and, therefore, you might say that the geophysicist is an "earth physicist," one who is concerned with the physical aspects of the earth from its inner core to outer space.

The combination of geology and physics—an alliance between the earth and physical sciences—is part of the progress that humanity has made in searching for new understandings of the world. We read about biochemistry, biomathematics, space medicine, nuclear physics, bioastrophysics, and medical electronics. These are simply labels for specialties. But they represent far more; they represent the combining of fields of knowledge, the attack on frontiers of the unknown, and perhaps most important of all—change and challenge.

The importance of geophysics today goes well beyond abstract knowlege. Our expanding population—in fact, the growth in population throughout the world—and increased technology are placing heavier demands on our natural mineral and petroleum resources. We are accelerating our search for these deposits and our explorations are taking us to the bowels of the earth, to the deepest points in the ocean, and to faraway points in space.

Nature of the work

Geophysicists use the principles and techniques of geology, physics, chemistry, mathematics, and engineering in their work. They apply the knowledge of these basic sciences in studying the surface, atmosphere, waters, and solid bodies of the earth.

In general, all geophysicists study seismic, gravitational, electrical, thermal, and magnetic phenomena to determine structure and composition of the earth, and the forces causing movement and warping of the surface. Many of

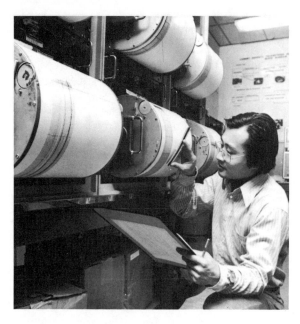

A seismologist records data to determine the location of earth tremors and predict the possibility of earthquakes.

their instruments are highly complex and designed to make very precise measurements.

The duties of the geophysicist cover a wide variety of activities. Many are involved in field work where they engage in exploration and prospecting. Others work in laboratories where research activities are the center of attention. In general, the work of the geophysicist is concerned with service (the field geophysicist), research (the laboratory geophysicist), and college or graduate-level teaching.

The nature of work of geophysicists in specialized fields is as follows:

Geodesists measure the shape and size of the earth to determine fixed points, positions, and elevations, on or near the earth's surface. They perform surveys, using the gravimeter, to measure minute variations in the earth's gravitational field. They also collect data that is useful in learning more about the weight, size, and mass of the earth. Geodesists are active in tracking satellites orbiting in outer space.

Geomagneticians, using the magnetometer, measure variations in the earth's magnetic field from magnetic observatories and stations. They are also concerned with conditions affecting radio signals, solar phenomena, and many other aspects of space exploration. The data gathered can be most helpful in working with problems in radio and television transmittal, telegraphy, navigation, mapping, and space exploration and space science.

Applied geophysicists use data gathered from the air and the ground, as well as computers, to analyze the earth's crust. They look for oil and mineral deposits and try to find places where hazardous wastes can be safely disposed of.

Exploration geophysicists, sometimes called *geophysical prospectors,* use seismic techniques to look for possible oil and gas deposits. They may use sonar equipment to send sound waves deep into the earth and record the resulting echo to estimate if an oil deposit lies hidden in an area.

Hydrologists are concerned with the surface and underground waters in the land areas of the earth. They map and chart the flow and the disposition of sediments; measure changes in water volume; and collect data on the form and intensity of precipitation, and the disposition of water through evaporation and ground absorption. The information that the hydrologist collects is applied to problems in flood control, crop production, soil and water conservation, irrigation and inland water projects. Some hydrologists study glaciers and their sedimentation.

Seismologists are specialists in the study of earthquakes. With the aid of the seismograph and other instruments that record the location of earthquakes and the vibrations of the earth which they cause, they examine active fault lines and areas of the earth where earthquakes have occurred. Seismologists are often members of field teams whose purpose is to examine and evaluate possible building or construction sites. They also may explore for oil and minerals. In recent years, seismologists have contributed to the selection of missile launching sites.

Tectonophysicists study the structure of mountains and ocean basins, the properties of the earth's crust, and the physical forces and processes that cause movements and changes in the structure of the earth. A great deal of the work is research and the findings are helpful in locating oil and mineral deposits.

Volcanologists study volcanoes, their location, and their activity. They are concerned with their origin and the phenomena of their processes.

Planetologists use the data from artificial satellites and astronauts' equipment to study the makeup and atmosphere of the planets, the moon, and other bodies in our solar system. Recent advances in this field have greatly increased our knowledge of Jupiter, Saturn, and their satellites.

Meteorologists and *oceanographers,* often classified as *geophysicists,* are discussed in separate articles in this volume.

Briefly, meteorologists study the atmosphere and its fluctuations. This includes weather study and forecasting. Oceanographers study various aspects of the oceans.

Requirements

A strong interest in the physical and earth sciences is essential for this field. In high school, basic courses in earth science, physics, and chemistry and four years of mathematics are necessary. Advanced placement work in any of the mathematics or science areas would add to preparation for the necessary college courses. Other recommended courses include mechanical drawing and electric shop. Social studies and English courses, beyond those usually required, should be elected if possible.

Four years of college, with a bachelor's degree in geophysics, is usually required for most positions. Physics, mathematics, and chemistry majors can locate positions in geophysics, but some work in geology is highly desirable and often required (particularly for certain government positions).

Graduate work at the master's or doctoral level is generally required for research and college teaching positions and for positions of leadership and responsibility in government work. Advanced graduate study is usually required to qualify for positions of a policy-making or policy-interpreting nature in private or government employment.

Many colleges and universities offer a bachelor's degree in geophysics, and a growing number of them award advanced degrees. An undergraduate major in geophysics is not usually required for graduate entrance. Information about schools, the programs they offer, and opportunities for scholarship assistance can be obtained by writing to the sources of additional information listed. Some important personal characteristics for a geophysicist are a strong interest in mathematics and science, particularly the physical and earth sciences; an interest in situations involving activities of an abstract and creative nature (observing nature, performing experiments, exploring new areas, and studying the physical environment); an interest in outdoor activities such as hiking and camping; and above-average general scholastic ability, including above-average verbal, numerical, and spatial aptitudes.

The outdoor aspects of the work of the geophysicist require good physical health. In the field the geophysicist must have good physical coordination and excellent stamina.

Special requirements

There are no special requirements for licensure or admission to the profession. Those who seek employment in the federal government will have to take a civil service examination and be able to meet the educational, experience, and other specified requirements for the type and level of position in which they are interested in applying.

One may wish to join and participate in the activities of the organizations that represent the profession. Membership in these associations is voluntary but many geophysicists find that this is a way to keep abreast of developments in their field.

Opportunities for experience and exploration

A student in high school can begin to explore various aspects of this field in science classes, particularly in earth and physical science courses. Some of the activities that may offer an opportunity for exploration are units of study dealing with electricity, rocks and minerals, metals and metallurgy, the universe and space, and weather and climate. Of course, there are many other chances, too, to find out more about this field of work and to engage in classroom experiences similar to the types of work a geophysicist performs.

Personal hobby interests can provide many exploratory possibilities. Leisure-time activities dealing with electricity or electronics, radio, rock and mineral collections, and maps or mapping are typical of the many hobby opportunities possible for tryout.

The college that one attends may have a chapter of the Society of Exploration Geophysicists. Participation in chapter activities would give the student a chance to learn more about the field and to engage in experiences that would help in planning more wisely for a future in geophysics. During the summers, employment as an aide or helper with a geophysical field party may be available.

Related occupations

Individuals with a leaning toward the physical sciences might also want to explore the work of astronomers, chemists, environmental researchers, geographers, geologists, groundwater professionals, hydrologists, mathematicians and mathematical technicians, meteorologists, mineralogists, oceanographers, paleontologists, petrologists, physicists, pollution control engineers and technicians, prospectors, soils engineers, and weather observers.

Methods of entering

Most college placement offices are prepared to help students locate positions in business, industry, or government agencies. Other job contacts can be made through major professors, friends, or relatives. Some companies visit the college campuses in the spring of each year to interview candidates who are interested in positions as geophysicists. The college placement office can usually provide helpful information relative to the number of requests they have handled and the firms that have listed through them.

Advancement

If employed by a private firm, a new employee with only a bachelor's degree will probably have an on-the-job training period. As a company trainee, you will be assigned to a number of different jobs in different aspects of the company operations. This will aid in learning about the different methods in the company operations and in becoming familiar with their routine. If assigned to a field party, the employee will probably work with a junior geophysicist, which in many companies is the level of assignment received after the training has ended.

Advancement with an employer will depend on the competency, initiative, and willingness of the employee to assume responsibility. From a junior geophysicist advancement is usually to intermediate geophysicist, and eventually to geophysicist. From this point, one can transfer to research positions or, if the geophysicist remains in field work, to party chief. The party chief's job is to coordinate the work of people in a crew—trainee, junior, intermediate, and full geophysicists, surveyors, observers, drillers, shooters, and helpers—and to complete the purpose of a mission. Advancement with the company may eventually lead to supervisory and management positions.

Geophysicists can often transfer to other jobs in the fields of geology, physics, and engineering, depending on the nature of their qualifications and experience.

Employment outlook

Geophysicists are employed primarily by the petroleum industry or by mining companies, exploration and consulting firms, and research institutions. A few offer their services on a fee or contract basis. Many work for the federal government, mainly the Coast and Geodetic Survey, the U.S. Geological Survey, the Army Map Service, and the Naval Oceanographic Office. Many geophysicists go into teaching.

The demand for geophysicists is expected to increase slowly throughout the 1990s. The best opportunities will be available to those with advanced degrees.

Some of the developments that may affect supply and demand are: a decrease in the number of students majoring in geophysics may result in fewer employment possibilities in college and university teaching; the total number of graduates with degrees in geophysical sciences is expected to remain small and insufficient to meet the moderate increase in job openings in industry for any one year; and the federal government will need more geophysicists to study its water, conservation, flood control, and other problems and to assist in space science projects. The petroleum industry, the largest employer of geophysicists, has cut back on its exploration activities because of the recent drop in the price of oil. More geophysicists will be needed by petroleum and mining companies, however, to locate fuel and mineral deposits that are less accessible and to do research on such problems as radioactivity, cosmic and solar radiation, and the use of geothermal energy to generate electricity. The growing need to find new sources of energy will undoubtedly make the work of geophysicists more important.

Transfers, retirements, and deaths will add to the need for geophysicists each year.

Earnings

The salaries of geophysicists are comparable to the earnings of those in other scientific professions. The general salary range for beginning geophysicists can be examined by studying the employment setting and the amount of education required. Federal government salaries for the early 1990s ranged as follows: beginning positions with a bachelor's degree averaged about $14,800 or $18,400 per year; with a master's degree, $18,400 or $22,500 per year; with a doctorate, $27,200 or $32,600 per year. Additional compensation is awarded to those who are required to live outside the United States. In private industry in the early 1990s, beginning positions with a bachelor's degree averaged about $19,200 per year.

Both the federal government and private industry provide additional benefits, including vacations, retirement pensions, health and life insurance, and sick benefits.

Positions in colleges and universities paid average salaries ranging from about $21,300 to $35,500, depending upon experience, education, and the professional rank. These, however, are academic year salaries, meaning that their amount represents nine to ten months of service. Faculty members may teach in summer school for additional compensation and also engage in writing, consulting, and research work for government, industry, or business.

cient employment possibilities, travel preferences may be only matters of individual concern. However, the young person who is attracted to the field aspects of geophysics, yet does not wish to travel extensively or to be away from home for any length of time, may need to compromise in establishing his or her career plans.

GOE: 02.01.01; SIC: 1081, 1481; SOC: 1847

Conditions of work

The geophysicist in the field works under a variety of conditions and very often the hours are irregular. He or she is outdoors most of the time in all kinds of weather. The work requires lifting and carrying small tools and equipment and occasionally might require some heavy lifting. Generally there is considerable walking and standing and use of the arms and hands. The field geophysicist is often required to travel and very often field parties work in isolated areas. Volcanologists visit and observe erupting volcanoes whenever possible, so they face danger and possible disaster conditions.

The geophysicist who is employed in a laboratory or office generally works a regular forty-hour week under conditions that are typical for these types of positions.

Social and psychological factors

Geophysicists often work as a team and must be able to get along with other workers. As a member of a field party, or of a laboratory research team, each member makes an important contribution to the success of the venture. The satisfaction in the work may result from the individual's feeling of being a part of the team through the ideas and suggestions one may offer and the activities one may carry on as a team member.

The opportunities for travel, both within and outside the country, offer challenging and interesting possibilities to those who are interested in new faces and places. The young, single person particularly, may wish to do this before establishing a home and family. On the other hand, those whose family ties are strong may not wish to engage in travel. With suffi-

◇ SOURCES OF ADDITIONAL INFORMATION

American Geological Institute
4220 King Street
Alexandria, VA 22302

American Geophysical Union
2000 Florida Avenue, NW
Washington, DC 20009

Marine Technology Society
1825 K Street, NW
Suite 203
Washington D.C. 20006

National Academy of Sciences
2101 Constitution Avenue, NW
Washington, D.C. 20418

Society of Exploration Geophysicists
PO Box 702740
Tulsa, OK 74170

◇ RELATED ARTICLES

Volume 1: Aviation and Aerospace; Biological Sciences; Education; Energy; Engineering; Metals; Military Services; Nuclear Sciences; Physical Sciences
Volume 2: Chemists; College and university faculty; Engineers; Geologists; Oceanographers; Physicists
Volume 3: Petroleum drilling occupations
Volume 4: Chemical technicians; Engineering technicians; Geological technicians

Graphics programmers

Definition

Graphics programmers design the software necessary that allow computers to generate graphic designs, charts, and illustrations for manufacturing, communications, entertainment and other industries.

History

The first machines that could be considered modern computers were used in 1951 to organize the population data compiled in the 1950 U.S. Census. At that time, computers were considered nothing more than electronic systems for storing and retrieving information. Because of their immense size and development costs, plus the difficulty of installing and programming them, it was thought that computers would only be useful for huge projects such as a nationwide census. But private companies were quick to explore ways to harness the power of the computer to gain an edge over their competitors. Today, nearly forty years later, computer technology has been adapted for use in practically every field and industry, from manufacturing to medicine, from telephones to space exploration, from engineering to entertainment.

Computers are used not only to store and organize data; they also communicate data to an increasingly important degree. The old saying goes, "A picture is worth a thousand words," and so computer scientists have made great efforts to adapt computer technology for visual presentation. Graphics are an important communications tool: They can be used to illustrate difficult or abstract concepts, show ratios and proportions, or demonstrate how forces such as the weather change over time. As graphics in computer use have expanded, so has the need for programmers who can adapt graphics to computers.

Nature of the work

The graphics programmer's job is the same as those of other types of computer programmers; they determine what the computer will be expected to do, and to write instructions for the computer that will allow it to carry out these functions. In spite of its many capabilities, computers are not able to think for themselves. For a computer to perform any operation at all, detailed instructions must be written into the its memory in a computer language such as BASIC, COBOL, or PASCAL. It is the programmer's job to tell the computer how to do what it is expected to do.

As an example of what a graphics programmer does on the job, let's consider how a graphic computer program could be developed to monitor the operations of a chemical plant. Working with a computer systems analyst, the graphics programmer's first step is to ask the managers and personnel of the plant what they would like the computer to do—show where the work for each chemical product starts, how one stage of operations affects others, where problems in automated sections are occurring, and so on. Then the programmer finds out where the "input," or incoming information, for the computer will come from; the current work at a certain filtration station, for example, could be sent to the computer by an employee using a standard keyboard, while automatic sensors could alert the computer that a dangerous amount of pressure is building up in a processing tank.

Once the expectations of the program and the sources of input are identified, the programmer usually prepares a flow chart, which illustrates on paper how the computer will process the incoming information and carry out its operations. The programmer then begins to write the instructions for the computer in a language such as BASIC or COBOL. The coded instructions will also contain comments so other programmers can understand the program. Once the program is written, it is tested thoroughly using sample data to be sure it is operating as intended. The programmer reviews the results of the test to see if any errors were made. If any problems or "glitches" exist, the program must be altered and retested until it produces the correct results. This is known as "debugging" the program. Once the program is ready to be put into operation, the programmer prepares the written instructions for the people who will be operating and consulting the graphics program in their daily work.

Many diverse industries now use computer graphics in one form or another. In medicine, physicians, nurses, and technicians can view the internal organs of humans with computer graphics; scanners feed vital information about a patient's body to a computer, which interprets the input and displays a graphic representation of his or her internal conditions. Computer graphics are used in flight simulators by airlines and NASA to train pilots and astronauts. Weather forecasters use computer graphics to show changes in weather patterns, and television newscasters use them to explain statistical information and stock market reports in more meaningful ways. Business people insert computer-generated graphs and charts to make their reports more interesting and informative. Engineers use computer graphics to test the wear and stress of building materials and machine parts. Even the movie industry has found ingenious ways to use computer graphics for special effects in films such as "Star Wars," and television is also using computer graphics for enhancing news stories and presentations. Professional artists have explored computer graphics for creating works of art.

Current computer technology offers two different ways to produce graphics electronically. The first, called "vector display," draws lines on a screen or automatically on paper. The second method, called "raster graphics" or "pixel graphics," is more sophisticated, and creates images by controlling the individual dots on the video screen. By maneuvering the pixels (short for "picture elements") to create an image, the programmer can use this method to create graphics with much more flexibility. The placement and movement of the dots is specifically described in the programming language. If the programmer writes instructions for the image to move, the result is computer animation, which is used in video games and television commercials.

Graphics programmers can be employed either by software manufacturing companies or by the companies that buy and use the software, known as the "end user." The programmer who works for a software manufacturer will work on programs designed to fit the needs of prospective customers. For example, the programmer might work on a report-writing program for businesses, and so develop simple ways for people to display and print statistical data in the form of diagrams, pie charts, and bar graphs. Programmers, working alone or as part of a team, must make the product "user friendly." On the other hand, programmers who work for the end user have to tailor commercial software to fit their company's individual needs. If a company has limited computer needs or cannot afford to keep a programmer on payroll, it can call an independent consulting firm that has graphics programmers on staff.

Graphics programmers must be aware of their clients' needs in order to design software that will be useful.

Requirements

A bachelor's degree in computer science or a related field is essential for anyone wishing to enter the field of computer graphics programming. It is not a good idea, however, to major in graphics programming exclusively, unless students plan to go on to earn a master's degree or doctorate in the field. It is better for students to complete a general computer science curriculum, choosing electives such as graphics or business programming if they are available. In some universities that do not have computer science departments, computer graphics courses are available through the engineering department. Because there are many specialties within the field of computer graphics—such as art, mapmaking, animation, and computer-aided design/computer-aided manufacturing (CAD/CAM)—students should examine the courses of study offered in several schools before choosing the one they wish to attend. An associate's degree or a certificate from a technical school may enable students to get a job as a keyboard operator or other paraprofessional position with some firms, but future advancement is unlikely. Competition for all types of programming jobs is increasing and will limit the opportunities of those people with less than a bachelor's degree.

While in high school, students should take classes that satisfy the admission requirements of the college or university they plan to attend. Most major universities have requirements for English, mathematics, science, and foreign languages. Other classes that are useful include physics, statistics, logic, and perhaps drafting.

Special requirements

Currently there are no certification or licensing requirements for graphics programmers. But because computer technology advances so rapidly, programmers who do not keep up with the field through additional college course work and attendance at seminars may find themselves blocked from advancement or even out of a job. Graphics programmers can benefit from membership in professional societies by attending conferences and seminars that these groups sponsor. These societies include the National Computer Graphics Association and SIGGRAPH, the Special Interest Group on Computer Graphics of the Association for Computer Machinery.

Opportunities for experience and exploration

Students interested in a career in computer graphics programming should contact the computer sciences department of a local university. It may be possible to speak with a faculty members whose specialty is computer graphics or sit in on a computer graphics class. Students might also find out if there are any big manufacturers or computer software firms in their area. By contacting the public relations department of the company, students might be able to speak with someone who works with or designs computer graphics systems or who can demonstrate how one works. Another method for exploring the computer graphics field is to attend computer expositions and the regional conferences held by the National Computer Graphics Association and SIGGRAPH, which should provide many opportunities to speak with professional graphics programmers.

Related occupations

Because the computer field is so complex and the industries related to computers are growing so dramatically, many different types of jobs are available. Some of these include systems analysts, computer operators, peripheral equipment operators, systems programs, and data base managers.

Methods of entering

While an undergraduate, the best method for students for finding out about job opportunities is to contact the guidance department at their college or university. Counselors will be able to keep students informed of companies hiring for computer programmers, including graphics programmers. Many big employers will send recruiters to universities with computer science departments, usually working cooperatively with the guidance department. The guidance department can also tell students about any firms offering work-study programs, which are an excellent way to gain training and experience. As employers become increasingly selective about new hiring and seek to hold down the costs of in-house training, work-study jobs are a great opportunity not only for on-the-job experience but also for a possible position after graduation from college.

Another possible source of entry-level jobs is the numerous placement agencies that specialize in recruiting professional staff, including computer programmers. These agencies often advertise in major newspapers, technical journals, and computer magazines. They can also help match programmers to temporary jobs, as more firms try to lower their personnel costs and hire free-lance programmers as the need arises. Programmers can also find out about new job opportunities by attending computer graphics conferences and seminars and "networking" with their professional peers.

While most technical schools offer placement services for new graduates, there is no guarantee that job seekers will find work.

Advancement

The computer industry experiences a high rate of turnover, as large numbers of programmers and other employees move from company to company and from specialty to specialty. Some programmers leave their positions to accept higher paying jobs with other firms, while others leave to start their own companies or computer consulting firms. These extremely mobile conditions offer many opportunities both for job seekers and those people looking for career advancement. In most companies, especially larger firms, advancement will depend on an employee's experience and length of service. In most firms, programmers need to serve as junior staff before they are promoted. Employees who exhibit skill and innovation, however, can quickly rise within the company and, depending on the company's structure, be promoted to staff programmers, systems analysts, and project managers.

Employment outlook

The demand for all types of computer programmers is strong, and employment is expected to grow much faster than the average for all occupations through the early 1990s. This is especially true for graphics programmers because it is such a new field. Currently some 479,000 computer programmers are employed across the country in numerous fields, including computer graphics. The number of job opportunities currently outstrips the number of qualified graphics programmers, mainly because of a lack of qualified teachers, who often leave college faculties to take more lucrative jobs with private firms. As more applications for computer graphics are explored in every field and occupation, the demand for graphics programmers will grow even more. One specialty expected to grow is CAD/CAM, which will need twice the number of programmers it now employs by the middle of the 1990s. However, because more and more people are entering the computer field, employers are becoming more selective in their hiring. Competition is fierce for entry-level jobs, even for people holding bachelor's degrees.

Earnings

The median earnings of full-time computer programmers in early 1990s were about $27,000 a year, according to U.S. government figures. The middle half of these people earned between $20,700 and $33,900 annually. Industry offers graphics programmers the highest earnings, as opportunities expand in aerospace, electronics, electrical machinery, and public utilities. Programmers who work as independent consultants and contractors may earn even more money, but their income is rarely constant or assured.

Conditions of work

Most programmers work in clean, modern offices with state-of-the-art equipment. They usually put in eight to twelve hours a day and work a forty to fifty-hour week. They may have to work at odd hours, depending on the availability of the computers they are working with.

To meet deadlines or finish rush projects, they may be forced to work evenings and weekends. Programmers work alone or as part of a team of programmers, and often consult with the end users of the graphics program, as well as engineers and other specialists.

Programmers sometimes travel in their work, to attend seminars, conferences, and trade shows. Graphics programmers who work for software manufacturers may need to travel to assist current clients in their work, or to solicit new customers for the software.

Graphics programmers in visual illustration departments of motion pictures or television production may spend months designing graphics for a clip that lasts minutes. The labor involved may be time pressured.

Social and psychological factors

Graphics programmers must be intelligent, imaginative, and logical thinkers. Their work requires them to understand abstract concepts and to be creative in their problem solving but also analytical, precise, and detail-oriented. While some simple programs can be written and put into operation in a few hours, more complex programs requiring a great deal of calculation and data input may take a year or more to complete. Programmers should have the perceptive skills and perseverance to tackle complex problems and think them through from beginning to end. Because they often work under a deadline, graphics programmers should be able to work under pressure while not sacrificing the absolute accuracy their work requires.

Computer programming is often a solitary job, as programmers work long hours independently on projects. They often have to work as part of a team of programmers, however, so the ability to work well with others is also important.

Graphics programming is often considered the most glamorous division of the computer industry. The work of graphics programmers can end up in television programs, commercials, big-budget movies, and video arcades. Graphics programmers enjoy prestige and admiration from coworkers and even people outside the computer industry. Many programmers gain a great deal of satisfaction working in the unexplored areas where art and technology meet.

GOE: 11.01.01; SIC: 737; SOC: 397

◇ **SOURCES OF ADDITIONAL INFORMATION**

National Computer Graphics Association
2722 Merrilee Drive, Suite 200
Fairfax, VA 22031

Special Interest Group on Computer Graphics
Computer Graphics Lab
Department of Computer Sciences
University of Waterloo
Waterloo, Ontario
Canada, N2L 2G1

◇ **RELATED ARTICLES**

Volume 1: Computer Hardware; Computer Software; Electronics
Volume 2: Cartographers; Computer programmers; Drafters; Industrial designers; Mathematicians; Numerical control tool operators; Statisticians; Systems analysts
Volume 3: Computer and peripheral equipment operators; Data entry clerks
Volume 4: CAD/CAM technicians; Robotics technicians

Groundwater professionals

Definition

Groundwater professionals analyze the supply, characteristics, and condition of water supplies beneath the earth and society's most responsible way to use these resources.

History

While geology is a science that has existed for years, hydrogeology, or the study of groundwater supplies, is relatively new. For many centuries, people have relied on water from wells, underground springs, and aquifers for everything from drinking water to irrigation. This use of groundwater is bound to continue: Estimates are that groundwater use in the United States has doubled in the past thirty years. In 1980, 111 million Americans, or about 40 percent of the nation's population, got their water from private wells or from wells owned by public utilities.

Hydrogeology is expected to be a booming field in the next decade for a number of reasons. For the people who rely on surface water, most of the sites best suited for building water reservoirs have already been developed. These sites are holding less water than in the past because of sedimentation. Additionally, reservoirs are becoming much more expensive to build, and public concerns about the environ-ment have restricted the number of new reservoirs under development.

Another factor is the growing public concern over the contamination of groundwater supplies. Safe drinking water is an important issue in virtually every community, and thousands of groundwater wells across the country have been permanently closed because they had become too polluted to be reclaimed. This situation has prompted legislation from both local and state lawmakers and Congress. Congressional legislation such as the Superfund and the Safe Water Drinking Act have mandated millions of dollars for the cleanup, monitoring, and protection of the nation's groundwater supplies, creating a huge demand for professional hydrogeologists. The Congressional Research Service of the Library of Congress estimates that 10,000 groundwater professionals will be needed in the next decade to deal with the problems of contaminated groundwater. This figure is more than double the number of trained hydrogeologists currently working.

Employment in the field of geology used to depend on oil companies and their search for new supplies of crude oil. Since the 1970s, however, economic fluctuations have led to instability in this type of career. Jobs in geology are becoming much more specialized than in the past, especially in groundwater research. The future needs of a growing and environmentally safe United States have made hydrogeology an exciting and important career.

Nature of the work

The work of the groundwater specialist combines the skills of many different disciplines, including biology, chemistry, geology, mathematics, physics, and engineering. In the course of their work, groundwater specialists draw on all of these occupations to explore, survey water resources, and advise policy makers on the most beneficial and responsible use of groundwater supplies.

Groundwater professionals are often enlisted to discover new sources of safe water for municipalities and industrial areas. This is done through surveying the geophysical characteristics of an area, drilling for core samples, measuring the capacity of any liquid reserves found, and finding the geologic and hydrologic boundaries of the source of water. If possible, the source of the groundwater is determined, as well as its ability to replenish itself if tapped for use. The hydrogeologist then determines how the water would be best used and makes recommendations to the government or private authority for its use. The groundwater professional often designs new well systems and oversees the drilling of wells. In their work, groundwater professionals may design and use computer systems that allow them to create models of groundwater flow.

A major environmental concern that many hydrogeologists will face in their work is groundwater contamination. Already more than 2,800 public and private wells have been closed because of pollution, and federal, state, and private sector sources will be spending millions of dollars in the coming years to clean up existing waste problems and to limit future contamination. In response to these situations, the groundwater specialist collects samples and tests the water to gauge the level of the pollution. The nature and extent of contamination, combined with the geologic and hydrologic characteristics of the surrounding land, determine whether the water supply is permanently tainted or can be made usable again in the future. Groundwater professionals are often called on to find remedies for the sources of pollution. For example, if a landfill is leaking waste into a source of groundwater, the groundwater specialist may be asked to devise solutions, such as digging new drainage systems for the landfill or building new containment facilities.

Among those responding to a recent survey by the Association of Ground Water Scientists and Engineers (AGWSE), nearly half of groundwater specialists work for private consulting firms. Around 24 percent work for regional, state, county, or municipal govern-

Two groundwater professional test a plot of land for pollutants.

ments, while nearly eight percent are employed by the federal government. Around 6.5 percent either teach or work for research institutions.

Requirements

An advanced degree is practically a necessity for groundwater professionals; almost two-thirds of the people responding to the AGWSE survey had earned master's degrees, while 11 percent had earned a doctorate. While employers may hire graduates who have studied a hydrologic curricula, they often take new employees with related specialties, such as petroleum geology and mining engineering. Government agencies are particularly likely to hire groundwater professionals who have a less specialized academic background.

In addition to a degree in hydrogeology, other college majors that can lead to a career in groundwater science include geology, petroleum geology, engineering geology, civil engineering, chemistry, and microbiology. Specific courses that could prove useful include groundwater engineering, organic and inorganic chemistry, engineering hydrology, stratigraphy, calculus, cartography, and computer science. Both the National Water Well Association and the American Institute of Hydrology publish information on the various college programs in groundwater science, which prospective students should consider carefully before choosing a school. Groundwater science is a rapidly developing field, and enterprising young graduates may be able to fill interesting and important niches in their careers if they are qualified.

If a career in groundwater science is of interest, high school students should follow a college preparatory curriculum, with heavy emphasis on mathematics and science. Because groundwater specialists often have to write proposals and deliver reports and scientific papers, both in college and afterward, good verbal and composition skills are also important.

Special requirements

Many professional groups have been organized for groundwater scientists of all types. These include the National Water Well Association and the American Institute of Hydrology. Related industry groups are the American Institute of Professional Geologists, the Association of Engineering Geologists, the American Geophysical Union, and the American Society of Civil Engineers.

Because groundwater science is a relatively new field, practitioners must keep up with the latest developments in research and techniques. To meet this need, seminars, workshops, and courses are offered by some of the above groups. Some certification programs have also been developed to measure experience and knowledge of groundwater science. Both the American Institute of Hydrology and the Association of Ground Water Scientists and Engineers, which is a division of the National Water Well Association, offer certification programs.

Opportunities for experience and exploration

The best opportunities for gain experience in the groundwater sciences occur during the college years. Many professors employ students in their research at the university, sometimes for a small salary. This gives students the chance to gain experience both in fieldwork and in the compilation and interpretation of collected data and computer modeling. Students may also be able to find a part-time or summer job with a private consulting firm. Experience is an important factor in the hiring decisions of employers, so students are best advised to consider all possible methods of training and learning skills that would be useful on the job.

Related occupations

The work of groundwater professionals involves many of the same skills and interests as the work of biologists, chemists, geologists, and physicists.

Methods of entering

Upon graduation, there are many ways to learn about the openings in the industry. Groundwater professionals are so in demand that it shouldn't be difficult to learn about the entry-level positions available. One obvious place to start is the want ads, both in the daily newspaper and in the various professional journals that exist. In fact, the number of want ads looking for hydrogeologists in 1987 was ten times the number of ads five years earlier. Nearly 75 percent of these ads, according to a recent study, are placed by private consulting firms.

Local chapters of groundwater and geological societies sometimes have lists of job opportunities or bulletin boards with important notices. New graduates can also look for work at state employment offices or the local branches of federal agencies. Because most employers are looking for people who are already experienced in groundwater science, new jobseekers may have to temper their desire for the job they ultimately want with the need to gain experience with a government agency or educational institution.

Advancement

For groundwater professionals, getting ahead depends on their experience and level of education. However, there are good opportunities for advancement in the field. In private firms, hydrogeologists usually begin by doing the majority of the field work. As time goes on, they may be promoted to administrative or management positions, spending more time in the office, dealing with clients, and directing the activities of other groundwater specialists and office staff.

The same circumstances are true for those professionals working for government agencies. Experience is usually the key to upward mobility. Instead of clients, administrators for governments and public agencies may meet with planning commissions, public interest groups, legislative bodies, and industry groups.

Groundwater science is a young field. The AGWSE survey mentioned earlier found that 75 percent of currently employed groundwater professionals have less than ten years of experience. This situation in the industry offers plenty of opportunities for advancement to skilled young hydrogeologists. With some experience, ambitious professionals might wish to start their own firm. For adventurous types, many countries overseas have a desperate need for skilled hydrogeologists.

Employment outlook

The field of groundwater science is expected to grow in the upcoming decade and job prospects are strong. The number of groundwater specialists employed in the 1990s is projected by some experts to be six to seven times greater than the number employed during the 1980s. The protection of the nation's groundwater is not an issue that is likely to fade away. The actions of conservation groups, waste handlers, local governments, state departments of resources, Congress, and the Environmental Protection Agency will ensure that safe groundwater remains an important concern in America. The annual budget for Superfund alone is estimated to be $20 billion, a figure many people in government and environmental groups consider too low. One expert expects that the job market in all the geosciences for the next decade will be dominated by waste-related concerns.

Earnings

The AGWSE survey found that the average salary for groundwater professionals was $38,250. More than three quarters of the respondents to the survey were earning between $25,000 and $50,000 annually. Salaries and benefits depend in part on the employer. Those working for private consulting firms earned more than those employed by government bodies or educational institutions. Salaries also increase for those professionals who have earned advanced degrees in the field. The increasing demand for groundwater scientists, moreover, is bound to push salaries upward in all areas.

Conditions of work

Groundwater scientists generally split their time between field work and office work. While conducting tests and monitoring the digging of wells in the field, working conditions can test a person's endurance and stamina, but many geoscience professionals look forward to outdoor work. Conditions in offices vary from employer to employer, but generally the facilities are comfortable and equipped with state-of-the-art technical facilities. Most groundwater professionals work a forty-hour week, but this may change because of project deadlines or unexpected developments in the field.

Social and psychological factors

While conducting research and analyzing data, groundwater professionals generally work alone or in very small groups. However, it is not a solitary profession. Strong professional friendships can develop among colleagues in a firm or an agency, and many societies exist that afford educational and networking opportunities. Groundwater scientists also work with other groups of people, such as conservation groups and legislative bodies, for the common purpose of protecting and managing the environment.

Besides their relatively good salaries, groundwater professionals can gain a great deal of personal satisfaction from their work. Groundwater science is one of the key disciplines in the fight to protect the earth and its resources, a social concern that will be with us for decades. Because hydrogeology is a young science, there is still a lot to be learned about the movement and qualities of groundwater and how it can be used most effectively. Groundwater professionals can justiafably feel that their work is important, as they improve the quality of life of people living today and of the generations yet to come.

GOE: 02.01.01; SIC: 8999; SOC: 1847

◇ **SOURCES OF ADDITIONAL INFORMATION**

American Association of Petroleum Geologists
Box 979
Tulsa, OK 74101

American Geological Institute
4220 King Street
Alexandria, VA 22302

American Geophysical Union
2000 Florida Avenue, NW
Washington, DC 20009

American Institute of Hydrology
3416 University Avenue, SE
Suite 200
St. Paul, MN 55114

American Institute of Professional Geologists
7828 Vance Drive
Suite 103
Arvada, CO 80003

Association of Engineering Geologists
323 Boston Post Road
Suite 2D
Sudbury, MA 01776

Association for Women Geoscientists
10200 West 44th Avenue
Suite 304
Wheat Ridge, CO 80033

Geological Society of America
PO Box 9140
3300 Penrose Place
Boulder, CO 80301

National Water Well Association
6375 Riverside Drive
Dublin, OH 43017

Society of Independent Professional Earth Scientists
4925 Greenville
Suite 170
Dallas, TX 75206

U.S. Geological Survey
907 National Center
Reston, VA 22902

The Universities Council on Water Resources
4543 Faner Hall
Southern Illinois University
Carbondale, IL 62901

◇ **RELATED ARTICLES**

Volume 1: Biological Sciences; Chemistry; Engineering; Mining; Physical Sciences; Waste Management
Volume 2: Biochemists; Biologists; Chemists; Engineers; Geographers; Geologists; Geophysicists; Health and regulatory inspectors; Petrologists; Surveyors
Volume 3: Soil scientists; Wastewater treatment plant operators
Volume 4: Biological technicians; Chemical technicians; Civil engineering technicians; Coal mining technicians; Fluid-power technicians; Geological technicians; Hydrological technicians; Industrial safety and health technicians; Petroleum technicians; Pollution-control technicians; Water and wastewater treatment technicians

Guidance counselors

Definition

The *guidance counselor* provides a planned program of guidance services for all students, principally in junior and senior high schools. He or she helps students choose and prepare for vocations and careers, but in addition, is prepared to counsel students with educational, social, and personal problems.

Guidance Counselors are specifically school-related positions. *Career counselors* have a broader range of possible assignments and are covered in a separate article.

History

Counseling in secondary schools, as a comprehensive guidance service, is an outgrowth of the earlier program of vocational guidance in schools. Such programs were slowly adopted by school systems through the 1920s—Boston and New York were among the first—but with the Depression years, school budgets were at a low point and the vocational guidance movement came to a standstill.

Not until after World War II, when the many and swift changes of a society in transition began to be felt, did guidance services begin to show signs of growth. Many factors contributed to the sudden spurt. There was a great migration from rural to urban living, and city as well as urban area schools became overcrowded. Students lost their individual identity in the crowds of fellow students. More courses were being offered in more schools, and choices among them became ever more difficult to make. More mothers began to take jobs outside of the home when it became necessary for families to have two sources of income because of the rising cost of living. Fewer young people, therefore, were enjoying the advantages of adult association and counseling in their own homes.

The changes brought about by technological developments made it difficult for parents to help their children with wise career choices. Old familiar jobs were disappearing from society and strange new ones were developing. As living standards improved, more parents, who themselves had not gone to college, planned a college education for their children. The lack of experience with college admissions procedures made parents hesitate to try to help their children with college choices.

During the years following World War II, school guidance programs gradually evolved the philosophy heretofore outlined. They grew slowly but steadily, both in numbers and in expanded programs. Services supportive or supplemental to the guidance programs in the school were also developing slowly at the same time. Many colleges and universities initiated training programs for guidance counselors during this period. Certification standards for counselors were established or upgraded. State departments of education inaugurated or expanded guidance departments. The U.S. Office of Education embarked upon an ambitious leadership program for guidance services. The National Defense Education Act of 1958 made provisions for federal support of guidance programs in secondary schools.

Nature of the work

The guidance counselor is an educational specialist who works in a school setting to provide a planned program of guidance services for the benefit of all students who are enrolled in the school. The guidance program is not one single plan, but is the combination of many related activities. It has several aims, but its most important one is to help each student in the process of growth toward maturity. The guidance program is designed to help students learn to

A guidance counselor advises a student on educational options, showing a list of colleges and universities that may interest him.

help themselves—to achieve the independence of a contributing member of society.

All guidance programs are unique. Each one is built especially for the school in which it functions. With varying emphases, depending upon the needs of the students in the school and the community in which the school is located, the counselors may plan for a variety of guidance services. They may conduct an orientation program for all students who are new to the school; organize, administer, score, and interpret a standardized testing program; assist students in choosing their course of studies, planning for the wise use of their time, developing more effective study habits, and making tentative choices of goals for their life work; or counsel with students in matters involving educational, vocational, or personal social problems.

The counselor may collect and organize materials for students to read about such topics as occupations, personal or social matters (such as etiquette or proper dress), and post–high-school educational opportunities or may conduct group guidance meetings in which topics of special concern or interest to the age-group involved are discussed.

Counselors may confer with parents, with such professional personnel as school psychologists, social workers, and health officers, and with other faculty and staff members to assure a totally effective school program. They may assist students in selecting the post–high-school training that will best meet their educational and vocational needs and in applying for admission to the school of their choice, help those who need scholarships, and write reference letters to college admissions officers or prospective employers.

283

Guidance counselors may participate in employment surveys of the community and assist students to find part-time jobs. They may plan, organize, and conduct both Career Days and College Days or conduct follow-up studies of students who have left school or graduated, requesting their help in evaluating the curriculum in the light of their post–high-school work experiences.

Counselors may conduct in-service education courses for other faculty members or speak at meetings of interested members of the community. The counselor will refer students who have problems that are beyond the competency of anyone in the school to meet to such community resources as social welfare agencies, child guidance clinics, health departments, or other services.

Requirements

The basic requirement for a school counselor in many states is a bachelor's degree plus certain stipulated courses at the graduate level. More than half of the states are now requiring master's degrees in counseling and guidance for certification as a school counselor. Requirements vary among states as to the amount and kind of training and work experience.

The high-school student who is interested in becoming a school counselor should enroll in a college preparatory course. He or she should take courses in humanities, social studies, psychology (if offered), and speech. Courses in mathematics are important, since mathematical and statistical theory underlie much of the standardized testing program. Those considering a future in this career should be especially interested in English courses because both written and spoken communication with others is vital to be effective with students.

The prospective counselor's most important asset is an ability to relate easily and well to others. To achieve a sound relationship with other adults and with children, the prospective counselor must have a sincere interest in them and in their welfare. Guidance counselors must be able to relate to all kinds of persons, whether or not they share a similar background.

The counselor must be a mature and stable person. He or she must be able to remain calm in the face of emergencies and be patient and resourceful. A sense of humor, a sense of proportion, high moral values, and an objective point of view are all essential. Although the counselor is not an administrator, he or she should be able to provide leadership to the guidance program.

Special requirements

Most state certification standards require that counselors have teaching experience. Undergraduate students who hope to become guidance counselors should take courses that will permit them to be certified to teach. The teaching experience requirement may be as short as one year or as long as two to three. Some states also require that counselors have work experience outside of the teaching field, in addition to teaching.

Opportunities for experience and exploration

The high-school student who is interested in finding out about the job of guidance counselor should volunteer to work in the counselor's office. This first-hand opportunity to observe the work of the counselor will help students decide if guidance is an appropriate career choice.

Related occupations

People who go into counseling enjoy helping others analyze themselves and learn how to deal with various problems of a personal, social, academic, or career nature. These workers may be clergy and religious workers, college and student personnel workers, employment counselors, equal employment opportunity/ affirmative action specialists, mental health counselors, occupational therapists, personnel workers and managers, physical therapists, psychiatrists, psychologists, rehabilitation counselors, social workers, teachers, or training and employee development specialists. Although each of these occupations may have a different emphasis, they are all worth exploring by persons considering guidance counseling as a career.

Methods of entering

The graduate's college or university placement office will most likely have a list of vacancies for counseling positions. Professors may have firsthand knowledge of available jobs. The American Association for Counseling and Development provides a placement service bulletin for its members. This bulletin may be obtained on a subscription basis. It provides lists of vacancies, with accompanying position descriptions for various school counseling positions.

Advancement

Some schools have more than one counselor on the staff. One of the staff members who is both experienced and qualified may be asked to assume the responsibilities of school guidance director. The title may be misleading, however, as one does not usually "direct" the program; rather, one coordinates it. The school principal is the actual director of the program.

Some counselors with many years of experience may be appointed as guidance coordinator or director for a city or county school system. Their duties usually include program development.

For the most part, when counselors are advanced, they are promoted to positions outside of counseling itself, such as to principalships or supervisory jobs. Some counselors obtain advanced degrees and become college or university teachers.

Employment outlook

Guidance counselors held almost 100,000 jobs in education services in the early 1990s, most of them in secondary schools, the rest in elementary schools and colleges and universities. Employment of school counselors is expected to experience slow growth through the end of the 1990s. Although enrollment in elementary schools will increase substantially, this rise will not be reflected in either secondary schools or colleges and universities. In fact, college enrollment is on the decline.

Most of the employment opportunities for guidance counselors will arise from the need to replace workers who retire, transfer to other fields, or leave for other reasons.

Earnings

The average annual salary of school counselors was reported to be around $31,200 in the early 1990s, depending on size, grade level, and location of the school. Salaries were generally lower in the Southeast and higher in the Far West. Some school counselors augment their income by working summers in the school system or in other jobs.

Conditions of work

Most counselors have a private office in which they may talk with students, parents, and faculty members. The counselor works both in that private office and in other parts of the school. He or she must mingle with students, faculty, and staff members to be available to help them with their various concerns.

The counselor will spend a part of each day in conferences and meetings. Many of these meetings will be held after school hours. Some will be held in the evenings.

The guidance counselors usually work more than forty hours a week. They often arrive at school earlier than do many other staff members. Counselors seldom leave the school when the final bell has sounded for the day. They may return to the school in the evening to talk with parents who are unable to come to the school during working hours. The counselor may also take paperwork home to do in the evenings.

Social and psychological factors

Counselors usually find their work to be personally satisfying and rewarding. They can see the results in the many students to whom their guidance services have made a real and important difference.

Difficulties may arise with students who have emotional problems or problems that extend beyond the scope and capabilities of the counselor. The counselor may be in a position to recommend other help for the student, such as psychological or drug counseling, but the choice normally rests with the student to follow up.

GOE: 10.01.02; SIC: 8211; SOC: 24

◇ **SOURCES OF ADDITIONAL INFORMATION**

For information concerning guidance counseling in a given state, contact the State Department of Education

American Association for Counseling and Development
5999 Stevenson Avenue
Alexandria, VA 22304

National Council of Accreditation of Teacher Education
2029 K Street, NW
Suite 500
Washington, DC 20006

U.S. Department of Education
Information Office
Washington, DC 20202

◇ **RELATED ARTICLES**

Volume 1: Education; Social Sciences
Volume 2: Career counselors; College career planning and placement counselors; College student personnel workers; Employment counselors; Employment firm workers; Human services workers; School administrators; Social workers; Teachers, secondary school

Health and regulatory inspectors

Definition

Health and regulatory inspectors are employed by the federal, state, or local governments to enforce those laws that protect the public health and safety, as well as certain regulatory laws that govern, for example, labor standards, immigration, and transportation.

History

In the United States, as in many other nations, federal, state, and local laws provide services and protection to citizens in many areas of daily life. An important aspect of the enforcement of law involves setting acceptable standards and then providing ways and means of ensuring that these standards are met.

Common law (unwritten but adhered to by most persons) in England has long been that certain roads and footpaths be open to the general public. The major roads, however, were essential to the kingdom for carrying on trade and other commerce within the nation, and for access to seaports for both military and commercial ventures. In the twelfth century these important roads were designated the "King's highways," that is, roads that were to be maintained passable and safe. Letting a "highway" fall into disrepair or charging a toll to use it was forbidden. Inspectors were appointed by "the Crown" (the ruler and the council of state) to ensure that these highways met certain standards.

Even today inspectors are appointed in Great Britain by the Crown (not the government) to ensure standards in other areas such as school curriculum and quality of teaching.

Generally, written law only states that something must or must not be done. Rather than wait until the law is actually "broken," governments have found it more efficient to provide the service of inspectors to maintain a continuous watch on the way in which the requirements of law are carried out. If a law requires that food be stored at a certain temperature to prevent the growth of microorganisms, regular inspections of the place where the food is stored to make sure the law is kept are better than waiting until disease or illness occurs. Food quality standards are also enforced. In the same way, the government takes responsibility for public safety in transportation and other industries, labor standards and immigration, and preservation of the environment through a system of regular inspection and reporting.

Nature of the work

Specialists in the health field such as chemists, microbiologists, engineers, and other health workers work with health inspectors in the areas of food, drugs, cosmetics, and other consumer products to ensure that government standards are met. Health inspectors must ensure compliance with health and safety laws and regulations while the specialists in the various areas determine how such compliance can best be met.

Food and drug inspectors have the responsibility to check firms that produce, store, handle, and market food, drugs, and cosmetics.

Packaging must be accurately labeled showing the contents, and the inspectors perform spot checks to confirm this. The weight or measurement of a product must also be accurate. The inspectors use different equipment for testing, including scales, thermometers, chemical testing kits, container sampling devices, ultraviolet lights, and cameras. They look for evidence of bacteriological or chemical contamination and assemble evidence that a product is harmful to the public health or does not meet other standards.

Food inspectors are empowered by state and federal law to inspect meat, poultry, and their by-products to ensure these are safe for public consumption. In a slaughterhouse the inspection team leader is always a veterinarian who can ensure that the animals and birds are healthy. Proper sanitation, processing, packaging, and labeling is inspected constantly. Inspection specialists concerned with raising animals for consumption and with processing meat and meat products include *veterinary livestock inspectors, veterinary virus-serum inspectors,* and *veterinary meat-inspectors.*

Agricultural inspectors include commodity graders who may specialize in dairy products, eggs and egg products, processed or fresh fruit or vegetables, or grains. Their job is to ensure that retailers and consumers will get reliable and safe commodities. Eggs must meet size and weight standards, dairy products must meet the standards set for butterfat content, and other products must meet standards of cleanliness and quality. The inspectors check product standards and issue official grading certificates. They also ensure sanitation standards by regular inspection of plant and equipment.

Agricultural quarantine inspectors work to protect crops, forests, gardens, and livestock from the introduction and spread of plant pests and animal diseases. They inspect aircraft, ships, railway cars, and other transportation entering the United States for restricted or prohibited plant or animal materials. They also work to prevent the spread of agricultural disease from one state or one part of the country to another.

Agricultural-chemical registration specialists review and evaluate information on pesticides, fertilizers, and other products containing dangerous chemicals. If the manufacturers or distributors of the products have complied with government regulations, their applications for registration are approved.

Environmental health inspectors are also called *sanitarians.* They work primarily for state and local governments to ensure that standards of cleanliness are met in food processing plants, restaurants, hospitals, and other institutions.

Government inspectors check poultry before the meat is packaged and shipped to wholesale distributors.

This involves the inspection of handling, processing, and serving of food; of the treatment and disposal of garbage, sewage, and refuse; and determining if water and air meet government standards.

Finding the nature and cause of pollution means inspecting those places where pollution might occur, testing for pollutants, and collecting samples for analysis. The environmental health inspector initiates action to stop pollution and is vigilant to ensure that offenses are not repeated.

In urban situations the environmental health inspector may specialize in just one area such as *industrial waste inspection, water-pollution control,* or *pesticide control. Sanitation inspectors* investigate complaints of property neglect or illegal dumping within a community.

The category of health and safety inspectors also includes *health care facilities inspectors, building code inspectors, boiler inspectors, furniture and bedding inspectors, marine-cargo surveyors,* and *mortician investigators.*

Health inspectors may travel to a variety of sites in their work such as restaurants, hospitals, or other institutions. The health inspectors in a processing plant generally work on that site all the time, and the same may be true of dairy product inspectors and sewage processing plant inspectors. The work involves making reports to the government regulatory agency for which the inspector works, as well as to the management of the institution or company being inspected.

Regulatory inspectors do similar work to health inspectors because both occupations involve protecting the public by enforcing laws and regulations relating to public health and safety.

Customs and immigration inspectors enforce the laws that regulate persons and goods entering and leaving the country. *Immigration inspectors* prepare reports, process applications, and maintain records of persons seeking to enter the United States. They interview and inspect the passports of persons to determine whether they are legally eligible to enter and live in the country. *Passport-application examiners* review and approve applications for U.S. passports.

Customs inspectors enforce the laws that regulate imports and exports. They inspect cargo at all points of entry and exit to the United States to determine the amount of tax that must be paid and to ensure that no prohibited goods enter or leave. Merchandise for delivery to commercial importers is examined by *customs import specialists,* who consider, in addition to legal restrictions the amount of duty to be levied, such things as import quotas and observation of trademark laws. Customs inspectors also inspect the baggage of persons entering or leaving the country to ensure that proper taxes have been paid and all goods have been declared. *Customs patrol officers* conduct surveillance at points of entry into the United States to prohibit smuggling and to detect customs violations.

Transportation inspectors not only ensure that vehicles meet safety requirements, but that the personnel who operate the equipment are properly trained to meet the standards regulated by law.

The regulations of the Federal Aviation Administration (FAA) are ensured by *air safety inspectors,* who usually specialize in general aviation or commercial aircraft. They inspect maintenance, manufacturing, repair, and operations procedures and also certify pilots, instructors, and schools. They are generally responsible for the quality and safety of aircraft equipment and personnel. State and local *motor vehicle inspectors* perform similar functions to ensure safety and trained personnel in motor transportation, while *automobile testers* check the safety of cars and trucks at state-operated inspection stations. *Railroad inspectors* have the same responsibility in their field. In the maritime field, *admeasurers* take physical measurements of a ship and compute its capacity to determine the type of license, safety equipment, and fees required.

Occupational-safety-and-health inspectors enforce the regulations of the Occupational Safety and Health Administration (OSHA), and of state and local governments. Safety and health workers are also employed in the private sector where they have similar responsibilities. This involves inspecting machinery, working conditions, and equipment to ensure that proper safety precautions are used that meet government standards and regulations. Safety health inspectors make regular visits and also respond to accident reports or complaints about a plant, factory, or other workplace. They write reports on safety standards that have been violated and describe conditions to be corrected. They may also discuss their findings with management to ensure standards will be met.

Mine inspectors enforce the laws and regulations that protect the health and safety of miners. They visit mines and related facilities and discuss with the miners and with management their findings. They write reports describing violations and other findings and decisions. They ensure that hazards and violations are corrected. Should a mine accident occur, the inspector may direct rescue operations, and also investigate and report on conditions and causes.

Wage-hour compliance inspectors ensure that equal opportunity regulations, minimum wage and overtime laws, and the employment of minors conditions are all met. They inspect personnel records and may also interview employees to verify time and payroll information. Compliance inspectors may respond to complaints or may perform regular spot checks of a variety of employers.

Alcohol, tobacco, and firearms inspectors ensure compliance with laws governing taxes, competition, trade practices, and operating procedures. They inspect wineries, breweries, and distilleries; cigar and cigarette factories; explosives and firearms dealers, manufacturers, and users; and wholesale liquor dealers and importers. These inspectors work for the Treasury Department of the federal government and their main concern is that all revenue on these various commodities be collected.

Chief bank examiners investigate banking practices throughout a state to ensure that banks comply with laws established by the government to protect against mismanagement and bank failure.

Logging-operations inspectors see that contract provisions and safety laws are adhered to and that no loss of timber is caused by damage to trees left standing.

Attendance officers, also known as *truant officers,* enforce the laws pertaining to compulsory education by investigating the continued absence of pupils from school.

Government property inspectors prevent the waste, damage, or theft of government-owned equipment and materials handled by private contractors.

Quality assurance inspectors check products produced for the government by private companies to see that they meet order specifications and legal requirements.

Investigators investigate possible violations of federal, state, and municipal laws related to such activities as revenue collection, employment practices, or fraudulent benefit claims. They interview witnesses, gather facts, and observe conditions, and may serve legal papers or testify in court. They also look into the character of persons applying for a license or permit. Investigators may have occupational titles derived from their function or the agency where they are employed, such as weights and measures inspector, internal revenue investigator, welfare investigator, postal inspector, or claims investigator.

License inspectors make sure that valid licenses and permits are displayed by establishments to which they were granted and that licensing standards are maintained. These workers may inspect one class of business such as rooming houses or taverns.

Requirements

There is such a variety of skills involved in these inspection jobs that the qualifications and education required depend on the area of work. Inspectors in the federal government must pass the Professional and Administrative Career Examination (PACE) to work in consumer safety; alcohol, tobacco, and firearms; wage-hour compliance; occupational safety and health; and customs and immigration. A bachelor's degree and three years' work experience are required to take this examination. Coursework and other preparation must be related to the job. For example, applicants for food inspector positions must pass an examination based on specialized knowledge.

Mine safety inspectors may have to take a general aptitude test in addition to having mining experience. They also need to possess some specific skills such as electrical engineering qualifications for mine electrical inspectors.

Air safety inspectors often have completed considerable training in the armed forces. They generally have pilot certificates as well as experience in aviation maintenance. No written examination is required but air safety inspectors must have an FAA Air Frame and Power Plant certificate.

No written examination is required for agricultural commodity graders and quarantine inspectors but they need experience and education in agricultural science.

A bachelor's degree in the physical or biological sciences or in environmental health is required for sanitarians or environmental health inspectors. Thirty-five states require licensing.

A combination of classroom and on-the-job training in inspection procedure and applicable law is the usual preparation for inspection positions at the state and local as well as the federal level. High-school students should be prepared with a good general educational background to pursue degree work in the specialized area in which they are most interested.

Special requirements

The specific degree and training qualifications vary for each position and area in which inspection is done. For federal positions, a civil service examination is generally required. Education and experience in the specific field is usually necessary.

Opportunities for experience and exploration

High-school students interested in work as a health or regulatory inspector may explore their interest in the work by talking with persons who are employed as inspectors and by talking with their high-school counselors. Employment in a specific field during vacations could be valuable preparation and an opportunity to determine if the general field, such as food preparation, is of interest. The armed forces can be valuable training and preparation in such areas as transportation.

Related occupations

Other workers who, like health and regulatory inspectors, are responsible for enforcing laws and regulations include construction and building inspectors, customs patrol officers, customs special agents, fire marshals, fish and game wardens, revenue agents, and state and local police officers.

Methods of entering

Applicants may enter the occupations by applying to take the appropriate civil service examinations. Education in specific areas may be required. Some positions require a degree or other form of training. Others need considerable on-the-job experience in the field.

Advancement

Health and regulatory inspectors in the federal government are promoted on the civil service "career ladder." Advancement is automatic, usually at one-year intervals for those persons whose work is satisfactory. Additional education may also contribute to advancement to supervisory positions. (*See* Volume 1: Civil Service, for complete details of promotion and salary structure of civil service employment, as well as an overview of government structure.)

Employment outlook

Approximately 125,000 persons worked as health and regulatory inspectors in the early 1990s. About 31 percent worked for state governments, 28 percent for the federal government, and 20 percent for local governments. The remaining 21 percent were employed by the U.S. Postal Service and by private industry, mainly in insurance companies, hospitals, and manufacturing firms.

Most environmental health inspectors work for state and local governments. The federal government employed the majority of inspectors in certain areas, such as food and agriculture, which come under the U.S. Public Health Service or the U.S. Department of Agriculture. Consumer safety is evenly divided between local government and the U.S. Food and Drug Administration.

Regulatory inspectors work for the Federal Aviation Administration, Treasury Department, Department of Labor, and the Department of Justice.

Government workers are generally less affected than many other workers by economic changes. The employment of health and regulatory inspectors, however, is likely to grow more slowly than other professions through the end of the 1990s. Slow growth in government spending and in government regulatory programs is the cause of this. Enforcement of regulatory compliance is necessary, but job openings are likely to occur mainly to replace persons who transfer to other occupations, retire, or die.

Earnings

Most federally employed health and regulatory inspectors received average starting salaries around $14,800 a year in the early 1990s. Some, such as air safety inspectors and postal inspectors, started at a higher level. The median annual salary for all inspectors, except those in construction, was $25,200; and ten percent earned more than $46,000.

Examples of annual salaries paid by the federal government to experienced health and regulatory inspectors in the early 1990s include the following: Postal and transportation inspectors received from about $42,900 to $46,800; inspectors for consumer safety, coal mines, wage and hour compliance, equal opportunity compliance, and agriculture, tobacco, and firearms earned between $31,800 and $38,500; and internal revenue, customs and immigration, and food and agricultural commodity inspectors ranged from $26,100 to $38,500.

Health and regulatory inspectors for state and local governments generally earn salaries lower than those paid by the federal government.

Conditions of work

Health and regulatory inspection involves considerable field work in most areas and some inspectors travel frequently. Mine inspection can be dangerous, and agricultural and food inspection may bring contact with unpleasant odors and other difficult working conditions. Many inspectors work long and irregular hours.

The work is important to public health and safety and can be rewarding. Compensation and job security are generally good and travel and automobile expenses are reimbursed when necessary. Many jobs are done during regular office hours though some may involve shift work in the thirty-five to forty-hour workweek.

Social and psychological factors

Most health and regulatory inspectors live a busy life. They meet many people and work in different environments. In general, persons wanting to enter this area of work should be able to work well with people. They should also be able to accept responsibility and do detailed work. They should be able to express themselves well in speech and in writing. Some of the work may be performed under stress and a good sense of one's own competence and skill is important.

GOE: 06; SIC: Any industry; SOC: Any industry

Public Health Service
Department of Health and Human Services
200 Independence Avenue, SW
Washington, DC 20201

◇ **SOURCES OF ADDITIONAL INFORMATION**

The civil service commissions for state and local employment will provide information on health and regulatory inspection positions under their jurisdiction. The federal government provides information on available jobs from local offices of the employment service, the U.S. Office of Personnel Management, and at Federal Job Information Centers. The specific agency concerned with a job area can also be contacted.

◇ **RELATED ARTICLES**

Volume 1: Civil Service
Volume 2: Construction inspectors, government
Volume 3: Occupational safety and health workers
Volume 4: Fire safety technicians; Nuclear power plant radiation control technicians; Pollution-control technicians

Health services administrators

Definition

Health services administrators direct the operation of hospitals and other health care organizations. They are responsible for facilities, services, programs, staff, budgets, and relations with other organizations.

History

Health care institutions have changed much since the Pennsylvania Hospital was established in Philadelphia in 1752 by Benjamin Franklin and Dr. Thomas Bond. The rapid advance of medical science and the high degree of specialization by physicians, the increasing need for technical assistants, the requirement of expensive and elaborate equipment—all depend on effective organization to assure efficient use. This growing complexity has brought about the comparatively new professional occupational area of hospital or health services administration. In the past, physicians, nurses, or workers in other fields were appointed to the position of hospital administrator with little or no training. The earliest recognition of hospital administration as a separate profession came in 1898 when the Association of Hospital Superintendents was organized. This group, whose membership includes nearly all of the hospitals in the United States, today is known as the American Hospital Association. The medical profession recognized it in 1919, and the hospital standards were established by the American College of Surgeons in 1918. By then the profession had a foundation, and hospitals began their development toward the complex institutions they are today. It was not until 1933, however, that any real action was taken for the training of hospital administrators. In that year, a group of leading administrators in the United States and Canada met to found the American College of Hospital Administrators (now the American College of Healthcare Executives) with the purpose of increasing general effectiveness of hospital administration and raising the standards of the field.

The broad range of today's health care institutions includes, in addition to general hospitals, extended care facilities, nursing homes, rehabilitation institutions, psychiatric hospitals, health maintenance organizations (HMOs), and outpatient clinics.

A hospital administrator consults with a doctor concerning hospital expenses and patient care.

Nature of the work

The day-to-day work of the health services or hospital administrator involves the organizing and management of many and varied activities. Usually aided by a staff, the administrator makes available to the physicians and nurses the necessary personnel, equipment, and auxiliary services. This person is responsible for hiring and supervising personnel; handling the budget, including setting the fee schedule to be charged patients; and establishing billing procedures. He or she assists in planning current and future space needs; purchasing supplies and equipment; adopting measures to ensure the maintenance of buildings and equipment; and providing for mail, phones, laundry, information, and other services for patients and staff. In some health care institutions many of these duties are delegated to assistants or to various department heads.

The administrator works closely with the institution's governing board in the development of plans and policies. Following the board's directions, the administrator may carry out large projects concerned with expanding and developing the hospital's services. These services include organizing fund-raising campaigns and planning new research projects.

Health services administrators meet regularly with their staff to discuss progress and solve the facility's problems. Administrators may develop training programs for nurses, interns, and other members, in cooperation with the medical staff and department heads. Ad-ministrators may also represent the health care facility at community or professional meetings.

Requirements

The training needed to qualify for this work depends, to a large extent, on the qualifications established by the individual employer or a facility's governing board. Most prefer persons with a graduate degree in hospital or health services administration. A few require that their administrators be physicians or registered nurses, while others look for people who have formal training in law or business administration and also experience in the health field. Specialized training in hospital or health services administration is taken at the graduate level. The future administrator may have a liberal arts foundation with a strong background in the social sciences and in the theories of business economics. The graduate program then is generally a two-year course in which one year is spent in academic work and the other as an administrative resident, a full-time on-the-job training position in a facility approved by the university the candidate is attending. Successful completion of the course work, the residency, and perhaps a thesis is required to earn the master's degree.

Many universities offer doctorates in hospital or health services administration. The American College of Healthcare Executives provides financial assistance to a limited number of students for graduate work in this field. The U.S. Public Health Service offers awards for this type of graduate study.

Much of this job consists of dealing with people; with the hospital's governing board, the medical staff, the department heads and other employees; the patients and their families, and perhaps the community-at-large. Therefore, health services administrators must be successful in human relationships. Tact, sympathy, and self-control are important assets in this profession. Administrators must deal often with people who are undergoing severe stress.

Administrators also must be able to coordinate the facility's many related but independent professional levels. They need to understand financial processes, purchasing operations, organizational development, and public relations. They also must have the ability to make decisions with speed or with studied care, depending on the demands of each situation. They must be able to function under heavy responsibility. And, of course, health services administrators should have a deep interest in health care and the problems of the sick and injured patients.

Special kinds of hospitals such as mental hospitals often employ administrators who are physicians in the specialty of the hospital. Usually religious groups employ administrators of the same faith in the hospitals operated by religious groups.

Special requirements

In Minnesota administrators of state-licensed hospitals are required to register with the State Board of Health. Those who register must have at least two years of experience or one year of formal training in hospital administration.

Some universities granting graduate-level degrees in health services administration require a period of on-campus course work followed by residency in a hospital. During this time the individual works in various departments of a hospital as an assistant to the supervisors of those departments.

Opportunities for experience and exploration

Young persons considering a career as a health services administrator will find opportunities in high school to develop some of the skills needed by people in this occupation. Administrators need to be leaders and talented speakers. Experience in club work as a leader or membership in debate and speech clubs is helpful. Working in a school's health center will also be useful. In large cities or community hospitals, part-time work after school and during the summer is available. Health services administrators are usually available to speak with individuals interested in the work but arrangements for an appointment should be made in advance of the visit. Courses in chemistry, biology, and other sciences will also be helpful in evaluating interest in hospital or health services administration.

Related occupations

Like health services administrators, many other managers have similar responsibilities in setting policies, planning programs, creating marketing plans, and coordinating the activities and use of resources of a facility, organization, or department. These other workers are employed in health care and other fields and include college or university department heads, community organization directors, comptrollers, data-processing directors, department store managers, emergency medical services coordinators, public health directors, recreation superintendents, and social welfare administrators.

Methods of entering

The health services administrator in training as an administrative resident is sometimes offered a job by the hospital where the residency is served. You may be offered a job to remain there as an administrative assistant or a department head. Too, the hospital's administrator at the place of training may assist you in locating a job.

You may also find assistance in obtaining a job at your university's placement bureau or through the bulletins of state and national associations, which often list information about persons seeking employment with the suggestion that a health care facility contact the applicant directly.

In the larger cities, there are employment agencies that specialize in hospital positions and medical workers. These agencies advertise positions available, or the applicant may advertise in the "situations wanted" column in hospital and medical journals.

Positions in federal and state-owned health care institutions are filled by the civil service or by political appointment. Appointment to armed forces hospitals are handled by the services in the various branches.

Although the four-year college program and then graduate work is becoming the accepted method of entry, it is still possible to gain experience and training in subordinate positions and work up into health services administration.

Advancement

It is difficult to graduate from college and step into a position as health services administrator. Persons usually gain experience that qualifies for advancement by working in one or more specialized administrative areas found in a hospital. Experience gained in administration of hospital personnel, records, budget, and finance is valuable and necessary. Adequate experience and graduate work usually lead to

293

promotion as a department head in one of these areas. Assistant to the administrator is the next promotion and may eventually lead to appointment as hospital administrator.

Employment outlook

Every large hospital and most small ones employ an administrator. Health services administrators also run clinics, nursing homes, mental health facilities, centers for mental retardation and developmental disabilities, psychiatric hospitals, veterans hospitals, and other health services institutions. In addition, they are also employed by planning agencies and government bureaus.

Employment opportunities in the health care field will be excellent through the 1990s as the industry continues to diversify and take on a profit-making posture. Not all areas will grow at the same rate, however. Changes are taking place in the health care system because of the need to control rising costs. This will have the greatest effect on hospitals, traditionally the largest employer of health services administrators. The number of hospitals may decline as separate companies are set up to provide services such as ambulatory surgery, alcohol and drug rehabilitation, or home health care. So, while hospitals themselves may offer fewer jobs, many new openings will be available in the subsidiaries.

The trend toward outpatient care, which is a result of cost containment practices, has created a favorable employment outlook in facilities such as HMOs and group medical practices, surgicenters, and centers for urgent care, cardiac rehabilitation, diagnostic imaging, and so forth. Also, with Americans living longer than ever before, opportunities should be plentiful in long-term care facilities, such as nursing homes, home health agencies, adult day care programs, life care communities, and other residential facilities.

Colleges and universities are graduating more health services administrators than hospitals can employ. As a result, competition for top administrative jobs will be stiff. Many administrators will work in health care settings other than hospitals, or they may be offered jobs at the department head or staff level.

As hospitals continue to shift toward a business orientation, the demand for MBA graduates should remain steady. Persons with strong business or management skills will also find excellent opportunities as administrators in nursing homes and other long-term facilities,

where a graduate degree in health services administration is not ordinarily a requirement.

Earnings

Salaries of health services administrators depend on the type of health care institution, the size of the administrative staff, the budget, and the policy of the governing board. There is only slight variance in the different sections of the country. In the early 1990s, administrators earned an average annual salary of $51,000 in hospitals with fewer than 100 beds. In hospitals of 100 to 349 beds, administrators earned an average of $81,000. And in the largest hospitals, with at least 1,000 beds, administrators averaged almost $132,000 a year. The salary range for associate administrators was from $37,500 to $76,000 annually, depending on size of the hospital.

Chief administrators of nursing homes usually earn less than administrators of similar-sized hospitals. In the early 1990s, these executives had average salaries ranging from about $36,000 to $46,200, depending on experience.

In HMOs, the average annual salary for the chief executive administrator was $94,000; and for an associate administrator, about $63,000.

New graduates with master's degrees started at about $22,500 a year in Veterans Administration hospitals. The beginning salary of recent graduates in the private sector was $30,000.

Many administrators receive free meals and sometimes housing and laundry service. They usually receive paid vacations and holidays, sick leave, hospitalization and insurance benefits, and pension programs. The executive compensation package nowadays often includes management incentive bonuses based on job performance.

Conditions of work

To perform efficiently in the many and varied functions, the health services administrator usually has a large, centrally located office. He or she needs to maintain good communication with the staff and thus engages in frequent personal contact with members of various departments. Administrators must also monitor patient care.

Most administrators work five and one-half days each week. The number of hours varies considerably, however, depending on the demands for service. Administrators are on call twenty-four hours a day because any emergency may require their direction. Board members are business or community leaders, and therefore, the administrator can expect evening meetings with them. Some administrators work sixty hours a week.

Social and psychological factors

Because the nonprofit hospital sometimes lags behind industry in adopting new methods and in reacting to the effects of automation, many opportunities and challenges exist in hospital administration for competent, far-sighted leadership. With little routine work and much diversity, boredom is seldom a problem.

The health services administrator is often under pressure from many sides and under a heavy load of responsibility, but this is true for most any executive position. The demands on time and personal life may be particularly disadvantageous to family members. Another often serious disadvantage may be the lack of clear-cut authority and organizational structure, which causes conflicts among the administrative staff, the trustees, and the medical staff. It is probable that large medical facilities will be restructured for efficiency in the future. In addition you must be able to deal with government regulations and government officials.

Turnover is greater in small health care facilities where few opportunities for salary increments and advancements exist. Where there are more social pressures because of small-town living, where the interpersonal relations are closer, and where the administrators tend to be less adequately prepared, there are more rapid personnel changes than in the larger institutions.

GOE: 11.07.02; SIC: 806; SOC: 121

◇ SOURCES OF ADDITIONAL INFORMATION

American College of Health Care Administrators
325 South Patrick Street
Alexandria, VA 22314

American College of Healthcare Executives
840 North Lake Shore Drive
Suite 1103 W
Chicago, IL 60611

Association of University Programs in Health Administration
1911 North Fort Myer Drive
Suite 503
Arlington, VA 22209

Healthcare Financial Management Association
2 Westbrook Corporate Center, Suite 700
Westchester, IL 60154

National Health Council
350 Fifth Avenue, Suite 1118
New York, NY 10118

◇ RELATED ARTICLES

Volume 1: Business Administration; Health Care
Volume 2: General managers and top executives; Licensed practical nurses; Physicians; Registered nurses

Historians

Definition

Historians prepare in narrative, brief, or outline form a chronological account or record of past or current events. They study, assess, and interpret the activities and conduct of individuals or of social, ethnic, political, or geographic groups.

By using written records, documentation, or even verbal recounting of events, historians piece together the known elements of a period of time to form a written account of history.

History

The work of the historian dates back as far as history itself. In each civilization certain individuals have taken it upon themselves to record significant events in some way—by pictures, writing, or the spoken word. Cave dwellers left pictures, for example, on cave walls in France that reveal a world of history to the modern observer. Men in ancient Egypt, Greece, and Rome wrote accounts of the life and events of those great civilizations, with the Greek, Herodotus, generally considered the first historian. Archaeologists could probably learn some of this information by digging into the ruins of old civilizations, but the ancient historians' written descriptions and stories can tell us much more. Their writings can help us to know the people and leaders who lived centuries ago. We also learn about wars, battles, and military leaders, and how their actions may have influenced the development of our modern civilization. Often we can understand our world more clearly if we are able to know the events and influences of the past. One of the purposes of the historian has always been to present us with the facts of history necessary to reach this understanding.

Much of our knowledge of history has been gleaned by modern professional historians who have studied manuscripts, documents, ruins, and other traces of earlier periods. Some of the manuscripts or writings they study were written as actual historical accounts; others may be letters, diaries, or fiction with some historical basis.

Nature of the work

Modern historians are trained to gather, interpret, and evaluate the records of the past to describe and analyze past events, institutions, ideas, and people. Literary skill is essential to their work, but scientific methods are also invaluable.

Most historians are college teachers, although some do writing, research, and lecturing.

Historians who are called *archivists* are responsible for identifying, preserving, and cataloging historical documents of any value to the writing, researching, or teaching historian. They are really history librarians who have learned the technique of selectivity: they have learned to recognize historical materials that are worth preserving. The archivist knows it would be impossible to save all the material that comes into his hands. Such historians may work in museums, libraries, historical societies, and also the U.S. government, where they may collect materials, write about the activities of various departments, and prepare pamphlets, exhibits, and lectures. Mainly, government historians do research and administrative work. (*See also* the article "Archivists and curators" elsewhere in this volume.)

Genealogists specialize in family histories, using public records such as birth and death certificates, military records, and real estate deeds to trace connections between individuals. They are like detectives in a sense, but their work is far from glamorous and they must have the patience to continue following up leads in one historical record after another. (*See also* the article "Genealogists" elsewhere in this volume.)

Biographers specialize in writing about the life of an individual, usually a famous one. Research in library sources and through personal interviews is an important first step in the work. They must have a knowledge not only of their subject's life in depth, but also of the particular era or field in which the person was important. The biographer must write with careful attention to detail but must also have a creative flair for making an event seem interesting to the reader.

Dramatic arts historians research the accuracy of historical details in stage, motion picture, television, and radio presentations. They authenticate such things as customs, speech, costumes, architectural styles, modes of transportation, and other items peculiar to a particular period of history. The research department of a motion picture or television production company may be headed up by a *research director*.

Curators work for a museum, special library, or historical society. They identify and preserve historical documents and other artifacts of the past. Often curators help scholars with research in the institution's collection. *State-historical society directors* are curators who coordinate the activities of a state historical society. They direct the research staff, review publications and exhibits, speak before various groups and organizations, and perform the many administrative duties involved in running a historical institution. Curators need writing skills, the patience to search for connections among papers or objects, and the ability to work with other people in their institution as well as visiting scholars and researchers.

Another modern trend for professional historians is specialization in the history of a specific country or region, or a specific period: ancient, medieval, or modern, or even the history of a particular industry, war, or social movement.

Requirements

The main educational requirement for a historian is graduate study. A master's degree in history is the minimum requirement for a college instructor's position, but the doctorate is much more desirable, and required in many colleges and universities. To make any advancement, to become a professor or administrator, or to reach any other high level of employment, a doctorate is essential. Historians working for museums, historical societies, research councils, or the federal government generally have doctorates or the equivalent in training and experience. A person is rarely considered a professional historian without this educational background.

Some jobs for beginners with a bachelor's degree in history are available, usually with federal, state, or local governments. These jobs usually require a knowledge of the archivist's work, but advancement without further education is not likely. A number of high-school teaching positions are also available, provided the applicant meets state requirements for certification.

The high-school student interested in some type of career as a historian should lay the foundations for further education with a strong college preparatory course, majoring in history and other social science courses. A college degree in history will be the next layer of the foundation. A knowledge of foreign languages, at least two, is also important for the student planning to earn a doctorate. This background should be begun in high school and carried on throughout college. A broad education in the liberal arts and sciences is most important in understanding history.

Certain personal requirements are also important. A real liking for history and a sense of the spirit of the past are essential, especially as one works long hours in research and writing. The historian needs an analytical mind capable of sifting facts scientifically, and at the same time he or she needs a literary mind and a writer's skill to effectively spark the imagination of the reader. The historian who is also a teacher must be able to express his or her thoughts in speech, enjoy working with students, and be prepared to work fairly long hours.

Special requirements

The only special requirements, as mentioned above, are educational ones. A doctorate is very important for those who want to succeed as

Historians spend a great deal of time conducting research in libraries. They use their findings to deliver lectures and to write scholarly books and articles.

historians. No special licensing requirements exist for historians.

Opportunities for experience and exploration

High-school students can learn much about a possible career as a historian by analyzing the degree of their interest in history. High-school students must also investigate the requirements of graduate schools. This may seem remote, but they will have to gauge their own ability to meet the demands of graduate school. The quality of marks, especially in history, will help to indicate how well one can succeed in the historian's field.

There is little opportunity to experiment with actual teaching, but students could experiment with research and writing, seeking the advice of their history teacher.

The college graduate with a bachelor's degree in history might experiment with high-school teaching or beginning jobs in federal, state, or local governments. This would provide time and experience for the person not sure of the desire to continue in graduate work.

Related occupations

The work of historians is similar to that of anthropologists and archaeologists. Other occupations that require an interest in history and research include librarians, political scientists, research directors (television, radio, and motion pictures), sociologists, and writers and journalists. Teaching in any of these specialties is another option for persons with the right qualifications.

Methods of entering

Usually historians make no effort to enter the field until completing the educational requirements. Once they have acquired a master's degree in history, they may apply for an instructor's position at a college or university, but chances of employment are much greater once a doctorate is earned. The demand for college teachers is decreasing, especially in this field, so graduate preparation is necessary before applying for a position. The same method would apply to those seeking government employment or work in some library, museum, or other organization.

Advancement

The historian will advance in proportion to his or her education, experience, and personal qualities as a writer, researcher, or teacher. University teachers usually begin as instructors. The next step is assistant professor, then associate professor, and finally full rank as a professor.

Historians in other areas of employment will advance as they gain experience and contribute to their work. Historians who begin with the doctorate have already achieved a relatively high level of importance. Historical writers may find their achievement based on their writing skill and accuracy of research, and its success with the reader.

Employment outlook

Approximately 20,000 historians were employed full-time in the early 1990s, most of whom worked in colleges and universities. This figure does not include high-school history teachers who are usually classified as teachers. Many historians were employed in archives, historical societies, libraries, and museums or worked for the federal government in the National Archives and the Departments of Defense, Interior, and State; others were employed by other government organizations, nonprofit foundations, research councils, and large corporations. Some historians worked in politics or journalism or served as consultants to radio, TV, or film producers.

Overall, the employment of historians will experience little, if any, growth through the end of the 1990s, although specialists in archival work may find an expanding job market. Historians with a knowledge of computer software and how to build a data base will also have an increasing advantage. Historians to teach in high schools and at various college levels will be needed in only slightly larger numbers than it takes to replace those who leave the profession.

Historians with doctorates and those who have completed all requirements for the degree except the dissertation will have the greatest opportunities for jobs. Competition, however, is so keen in this field that many historians with doctorates will have to accept part-time positions or find work in other occupations. Historians holding only master's degrees will also face much competition. Few openings will be available for high-school teachers. Some history majors will be able to work as trainees in administrative and management positions in government agencies, nonprofit foundations, civic organizations, and rarely, in private industry.

Earnings

In the federal government in the early 1990s, beginning salaries for historians with a bachelor's degree averaged $14,800 or $18,400 a year, depending on the individual's academic record. A master's degree made the beginning employee eligible for a salary of about $22,500. Additional education and training brought even higher starting salaries. With a doctorate, historians could start at $27,200 a year, and those who were unusually qualified started at $32,600.

College and university instructors in the early 1990s earned around $21,300 a year, while professors' salaries ranged from $27,900 to $45,500. In larger universities, some professors were paid as much as $100,000 per year. In addition, there are ways for historians in colleges and universities to supplement salaries—research and travel grants, fees for lectures, and book royalties (usually small except in the case of textbooks). A successful writer may have a very high income.

Conditions of work

College history teachers and government employees enjoy a pleasant atmosphere for their work. The archivist might spend long hours in library stacks going over dusty materials, but such work is interesting to him or her and could not be considered disagreeable. Most colleges and universities offer benefits such as retirement, life, and health insurance programs.

Social and psychological factors

Historians find their work satisfying for they are doing what they want to do. They enjoy the reading, writing, researching, and teaching involved in their profession. To go through the lengthy preparation of a professional historian if one did not enjoy the subject matter would be unusual. For the history teacher the many satisfactions of the teacher in communicating knowledge to students may be very rewarding. The researcher finds pleasure in various discoveries, and the skilled writer can enjoy injecting a sense of history into a book and hoping it will arouse this sense in the reader.

GOE: 11.03.03; SIC: 8221; SOC: 1913

◇ **SOURCES OF ADDITIONAL INFORMATION**

American Association for State and Local History
172 Second Avenue North
Nashville, TN 37201

American Historical Association
400 A Street, SE
Washington, DC 20003

Canadian Historical Association
395 Wellington Street
Ottawa, Ontario
Canada K1A ON3

Organization of American Historians
112 North Bryan Street
Bloomington, IN 47401

For information on publications and awards for historical research in material sciences, industry, and commerce, write to:

Newcomen Society of the United States
412 Newcomen Road
Exton, PA 19341

◇ **RELATED ARTICLES**

Volume 1: Civil Service; Education; Library and Information Science; Social Sciences
Volume 2: Archivists and curators; College and university faculty; Economists; Genealogists; Geographers; Librarians; Museum occupations; Political scientists; Teachers, secondary school; Writers and editors

Home economists

Definition

Home economists improve and help others to improve products, services, and practices that affect the comfort and well-being of the home and family.

Home economics covers a range of subjects from nutrition, food preparation, and meal planning to economics and the psychology of family relations. All the aspects of household and home management are involved in this broad field.

History

Home economics made its debut in the late 1800s. At this time there was a large growth in the idea of education for women, and "domestic science," as home economics was then known, seemed a suitable subject of the young women of the day. Domestic science spread slowly, but by 1890 it was taught in most public schools across the nation. During the same period, colleges and universities also began offering the subject. The most important step in the establishment of home economics was the Morrill Act of 1862, which made possible the land-grant colleges, where home economics has achieved much of its growth and stature through research, teaching, and the extension service.

During this period, the family was undergoing deep-seated transitions. Traditionally, all needs of the American home had been met within the home by the family members. The Industrial Revolution changed this, for family members were drawn out of the home to work in factories, and many of the family's needs were necessarily met from outside. Enlightened people saw a need for the home economist to help the family adjust to change and to apply new scientific discoveries and products to the betterment of the home.

One of the earliest home economics activities was the establishment of the "New England Kitchen," which provided nutritious meals for workers to carry home as a means of improving diet. Soon families began to feel more and more need for professional advice and help; this led to the growth of the broad field known as home economics.

In modern times, the home economist has branched out into every segment of family life both in the United States and abroad. Homemakers look to the home economist for expert advice through consumer magazines, radio and television programs, home bureaus, university extension centers, and adult education courses. Behind the scientific knowledge and organization of modern homemaking information, behind the manufacture of the many consumer products for today's family and the home, works the home economist.

Nature of the work

Today, the home economist works in education, institution management, dietetics, research, social welfare, extension service, and business.

The junior and senior high-school home economics teacher instructs students on subjects such as foods, nutrition, textiles, clothing, child development, family relations, home furnishings and equipment, household economics, and home management. Many metropolitan areas also offer adult education classes in skills such as tailoring, gourmet cookery, and budgeting.

College teachers educate home economics majors for professional careers and have a responsibility to be leaders in the field by writing articles and textbooks, doing independent research, making speeches, and taking an active part in professional organizations.

The business world holds an especially wide range of opportunities for the professional home economist. In general, most business home economists interpret consumers' needs to manufacturers, test and improve products and recipes, prepare booklets on product uses, plan educational programs and materials, and serve as a communications link between the consumer and the manufacturer. However, there are many other home economics careers that may appeal to a variety of personalities and interests.

Public utility companies hire home economists to assist homemakers with kitchen and laundry planning, conduct cooking schools, and present related demonstrations.

Home economists are employed by newspapers, magazines, radio and television stations, and with publishing companies and advertising agencies to write copy on subjects such as food, budgets, fashions, home decoration, and home management.

Retail stores offer many jobs for the trained home economist to help customers select home furnishings and equipment or to work in advertising, buying, fashion coordinating, and display.

Financial institutions hire a small but growing number of home economists to advise consumers on budgeting, spending, and saving.

The extension service home economists are part of an educational system supported by the federal government, states, and counties to educate and advise families, both rural and urban, on family life, nutrition, child care, and other aspects of homemaking.

Home economists specializing in dietetics or institution management work in hospitals, hotels, restaurants, clubs, and schools, planning nutritious, attractive meals for large numbers; ordering food and supervising its care, storage, and preparation; directing employees; handling budgets; planning special diets for patients; and so on. The dietitian also may teach nutrition to student nurses, medical students, or dietetic interns. Community dietitians counsel groups or individuals on nutritional eating habits, nutrition on a budget, prevention of disease, and nutrition for older people and convalescents. (*See also* the article "Dietitians" elsewhere in this volume.)

Home economists in research create products, develop procedures, and establish facts that make life easier and better for families. Researchers are employed by colleges and universities, government agencies, agricultural experiment stations, industrial and commercial companies, and private agencies.

Health and welfare agencies hire home economists to collaborate with social workers, nurses, and physicians; to consult with low-income families needing help with management problems; and to develop community programs in health and nutrition, money management, and child care. For home economists with wanderlust, there are jobs all over the world. Their services are in demand especially in the developing countries, where home economics knowledge is in demand for advising ministries of education, agriculture, and health; conducting research; setting up schools of home economics; assisting in the development of community projects; and working directly with people to help them solve problems of living. The Peace Corps has a great need for home economists, as do many other agencies.

A home economics advisor introduces a homemaker to publications concerning house management.

Requirements

The minimum requirement for work as a home economist is a bachelor's degree in home economics. College teaching, research, and nutrition require master's or doctor's degrees in most cases. Many colleges and universities offer degrees in general home economics, as well as specialization in subject areas of home economics, including home economics education, child development, foods and nutrition, dietetics, institution management, textiles and clothing, family economics and home management, household equipment and furnishings, and applied art. College work usually includes a core curriculum that gives the student an overview of the subject areas so that he or she can choose intelligently from an area of specialization. In addition to home economics subjects, the home economics major receives a broad background in liberal arts and sciences. High-school students should prepare for college with the usual basic academic course, including science, mathematics, English, social studies, and a foreign language. Home economics courses are not required for college admission, but may be useful in judging aptitude and interest.

Those who plan to enter teaching fields must also complete state requirements for teacher certification. These requirements vary.

Special requirements

As mentioned previously, graduate work is important in many areas of specialization within home economics. Other than that, there are no special requirements for home economists.

Opportunities for experience and exploration

While it would seem that high-school home economics courses would be the best opportunity to find out about home economics as a profession, this is not always true. Many high-school home economics courses are concerned with teaching homemaking skills and knowledge to those whose education will end with high school. The high-school home economics teacher, who is a professional home economist, can, however, provide useful information. The 4-H club in the student's community offers a look at extension work in action. One might find a summer job in a home economics-related activity, such as child care, clerking in a shop, hospital kitchen work, and so on. College bulletins and information services also yield valuable information on home economics.

Related occupations

The interests and aptitudes required by home economists can apply as well to occupations in other fields. These occupations include association managers, fashion coordinators, librarians, market research, merchandise displayers, museum curators, school social workers, urban planners, and vocational instructors.

Methods of entering

The graduate home economist has no trouble entering the field. Most colleges and universities have placement centers to assist students and bring employers and graduates together. Many large firms go from campus to campus interviewing prospective employees. Those interested in teaching apply to boards of education in the same manner as other would-be teachers.

Advancement

Advancement depends on the particular area of home economics in which an individual is employed. In teaching and government work, there is usually a set pattern of advancement based on training and experience. The individual who adds to these qualifications and experience acquires salary increases and better positions. In business the individual can strive for success. Additional training and experience must be combined with ambition, suitable personality, and an ability to get along with people. Positions of responsibility are available in every area of home economics for those who are career-minded enough to work for them.

Employment outlook

Home economists are employed throughout the country in business, teaching, research, and social welfare. A small number are self-employed consultants.

Opportunities for employment are expected to be excellent throughout the 1990s. The demand for home economists will be highest for specialists in marketing, merchandising, family and consumer resource management, food service and institutional management, food science and human nutrition, environment and shelter, and textiles and clothing. Job openings will be numerous for home economists with bachelor's and advanced degrees alike. In college teaching, however, because of declining enrollments, most job openings will occur to replace workers who change occupations, retire, or leave the field for other reasons.

Earnings

Earnings for home economists depend on education, experience, specialty, and where employed. Annual salaries in the early 1990s ranged from $12,000 to $85,000.

Public school home economics teachers usually earn the same salaries as other teachers. These salaries vary among different school systems, and increase with experience and additional education. In the early 1990s, the average annual salary for high-school teachers was about $27,000. The average salary for college and university teachers was about $35,500.

Home economists in the federal government started in the early 1990s at about $18,400 with a bachelor's degree and no experience. With additional education and experience, salaries ranged from $22,500 to $32,600 and more.

Conditions of work

Home economists generally work under pleasant conditions in any area of employment. Teachers often work extra hours assisting students and sponsoring home economics clubs, as well as teaching adult education classes, for which they are often paid extra. Extension workers, too, work longer hours. Teachers, however, enjoy the usual fringe benefits of the profession, including paid sick leave, group insurance, retirement plans, as well as having two to three months free each year for travel, further study, or other professional enrichment.

Those in business and other areas generally work a forty-hour week, and receive fringe benefits, paid vacations, retirement, sick leave, and so on.

Social and psychological factors

The home economist's work is interesting and worthwhile. Home economists can feel they are making a real contribution to the world by strengthening family life.

An essential quality for the successful home economist is the ability to be at ease in front of a group, and in turn to make the group feel at ease. Both for home economists working in education or public programs and for the homemaker, the importance of quality home life is becoming more appreciated. The value of that contribution has become more apparent as fewer families can afford to have one parent at home.

GOE: 11.02.03; SIC: 8211, 8731; SOC: 239

◇ **SOURCES OF ADDITIONAL INFORMATION**

American Home Economics Association
2010 Massachusetts Avenue, NW
Washington, DC 20036

American Vocational Association
1410 King Street
Alexandria, VA 22314

Home Economics Education Association
1201 16th Street, NW
Washington, DC 20036

For information on awards, competitions, and foreign exchange programs, write to:

Future Homemakers of America
Student Information
1910 Association Drive
Reston, VA 22091

◇ **RELATED ARTICLES**

Volume 1: Apparel; Baking; Education; Food Service; Health Care; Military Services; Personal Services; Social Sciences; Social Services; Travel and Tourism
Volume 2: Adult and vocational education teachers; College and university faculty; Dietitians; Economists; Food technologists; Social workers; Teachers, secondary school
Volume 3: Homemaker-home health aides
Volume 4: Dietetic technicians; Home health technicians

Hotel and motel management

Definition

A *hotel or motel manager* is in charge of personnel, the money for operating the hotel, and promotion of the hotel. Managers are responsible for operating matters such as rates of the rooms, use of guests' credit, and the assignment of personnel. They have overall responsibility for operating hotels profitably and providing the best possible services for guests.

History

Inns for the lodging of guests have been in existence for a long time. Biblical stories recount people staying at inns. In England some inns of the fifteenth and sixteenth centuries were noted for their special features of luxury. Other inns, however, were notorious for crowding and lack of clean facilities. Inns in the early days of the United States were for sleeping and had few of the luxuries and services found in hotels today. Early hotels in this country were usually for providing meals and overnight rest for travelers. This is still their basic function; however, many of the hotels today, with their pools, nightclubs, fine restaurants, and other facilities have become the destination, rather than a stopover, for travelers. Modern hotels offer such services as laundering, cleaning, tailoring, baby-sitters, and barber service. In the twentieth century the need to coordinate the complex aspects of running a hotel created the job of hotel manager.

Nature of the work

The manager's concerns include housing, feeding, and entertaining the traveling public. In small hotels, the manager may also be the owner. In such cases, the responsibilities may include the operation of the front office and overseeing all other functions of the hotel. For example, the manager may personally greet guests, assign the rooms, handle their mail, and perform many other duties. Small hotel managers usually spend a good deal of time performing clerical tasks and bookkeeping.

There are differences in the size of hotels and the services provided by them. Large establishments are highly specialized and have a wide variety of facilities for their guests. Larger hotels and motels are sometimes owned and operated by hotel chains and are controlled by a board of directors that establish the general policy and hire the manager. Chains employ *branch operation evaluation managers* to travel to various branches periodically and examine the facility to make sure it is being operated and maintained according to company standards. Nevertheless, the hotel manager has complete charge of the hotel, is responsible for the operation of the hotel, and sees to the administration of policy. Because of this the manager of

A hotel manager consults with a staff member about the day's schedule of events.

a very large hotel with many employees must delegate responsibilities to department heads who supervise the workers who carry out the orders. Department managers may include the following:

Promotion managers publicize the establishment and plan sales and marketing programs to solicit business from conventions, social and business functions, and travel bureaus.

Convention managers direct the actual arrangements for conventions and group meetings scheduled to be held in the hotel.

Food service managers coordinate the planning, purchase, preparation, and serving of food and beverages in the hotel dining rooms and coffee shops, as well as for room service and banquets.

Liquor establishment managers run the cocktail lounges, nightclubs, or other rooms in a hotel where alcoholic beverages are sold.

Front office managers are concerned with room reservations and assignments, greeting guests, answering their inquiries, and handling their requests and complaints.

Hotel recreational facilities managers are in charge of making available for guests such activities as swimming, boating, skating, and other sports. Particularly for hotels accomadating corporate clientele, on-premises workout rooms, swimming pools, and other athletic facilities are becoming more prominent.

Executive housekeepers are responsible for keeping the establishment clean, orderly, and attractive and for maintaining an inventory of housekeeping supplies and equipment.

Routine work does not require much supervision, but the hotel manager must be available at any time to deal with emergencies or problems that might arise. A major responsibility of the manager is community relations and marketing. Conventions, training seminars, and workshops are all held at hotels and motels. In addition, hotels often are used as campaign headquarters and for union negotiations. The manager must carefully select the people who meet the general public in an effort to present the hotel's services in a favorable way.

Requirements

Successful hotel managers must have the ability to handle many business matters. They should have the ability to get along with guests as well as hotel employees. The more comfortable they are with people, the more likely their success. The ability to make quick decisions of a business and social nature while maintaining composure under stress is vital. A great deal of patience and tact as well as a sense of humor are extremely necessary in dealing with all types of personalities.

As administrators, they must have the ability to make quick decisions and devise procedures that will help to improve services. In large establishments, the ability to coordinate the operations of various departments with a minimum of friction among staff members is a most important requirement. Under all circumstances they must be able to control their tempers in settling problems with guests or staff members. A considerable knowledge of all phases of hotel business gained by experience and training is needed. A great deal of physical endurance is a necessity, and small details and big decisions must leave the manager unruffled. The ability to remember names and make people feel at home is a unique asset that provides a most favorable impression. In constantly dealing with and directing people, the manager must be able to act fairly but firmly. A hotel manager must have a real interest in people and the ability to be diplomatic in any and all situations.

Hotel executives have tended to favor promotion of capable employees from the ranks of their staffs and may continue to favor this policy. A high-school education, however, is essential and most serious candidates have found that business college or specialized training increases the opportunities for advancement even in small establishments or resorts.

Special requirements

Many large hotel chains believe the best managers are those who have been prepared for their career by such well-established schools as the Cornell School of Hotel Administration in New York State. More than one hundred colleges in the nation offer specialized four-year curriculum in hotel administration and food management. Several junior colleges offer specialized courses in hotel work, and the Educational Institute of the American Hotel and Motel Association offers home study courses in this field.

In any case the hotel manager must understand hotel administration, hotel accounting, the economics of food service, and general hotel engineering. A strong cultural background in history, psychology, literature, and languages are also helpful. Even with specialized requirements, college-trained people will usually be required to start in the front office as desk clerks, registration clerks, or department heads.

Opportunities for experience and exploration

The high rate of turnover in various hotel jobs such as bellhops, kitchen helpers, and maintenance workers makes it relatively easy to obtain experience in hotel work. Most resort hotels prefer to hire students as seasonal workers and commercial establishments usually have part-time openings available for ambitious persons in search of experience. Usually the pay in these jobs is not high enough to keep people for long periods, but many who prove their ability are moved up to more responsible positions.

Thus, these entry jobs give the person interested in management an opportunity to deal with the hotel public and to see the operation of the house from all perspectives. As a part of the service department one may work as a bellhop, baggage porter, elevator operator, doorkeeper, or even house detective. In other departments, a person may learn what the manager expects from waiters, waiters' or waitresses' assistants, bartenders, and cooks. This will also give one an opportunity to learn and more deeply understand the problems peculiar to maintenance of the vast variety of equipment in operation in the hotel complex. Work in the housekeeping department will aid one in understanding the problems and procedures in keeping the hotel clean and attractive.

In some smaller hotels where work is less specialized, the personnel may perform a number of duties that overlap into several departments. Most hotels and summer resorts offer many opportunities for enjoyment, at the same time providing valuable opportunities for experience and exploration.

Certain large hotels in major cities offer paid work-study programs to high-school students. The goal of the program is to expose students to hotel management positions that they may not have considered for their careers. Working afternoons during the school year and full-time during the summer, the students have an opportunity to work in different departments and to discuss in weekly classes the skills required for the various jobs.

Related occupations

Hotel and motel managers organize and direct a business dealing with the public. Many other managers in a variety of fields have similar responsibilities. These workers include airport managers, building superintendents, city managers, camp managers, club managers, department store managers, executive chefs, funeral directors, hospital administrators, mobile home park managers, motion picture producers, office managers, park superintendents, recreation supervisors, restaurant managers, supermarket managers, and travel agency managers.

Methods of entering

The most direct method of entering the hotel business is by taking a job as a bellhop, waiter's assistant, doorkeeper, desk clerk, or any of a vast number of other positions that may be available. Most hotel managers are eager to identify alert, hardworking employees who will assist in making their tasks less demanding. Because most hotels promote capable employees from their own staffs to management positions, ambitious employees apply themselves to their jobs, regardless of how insignificant they may seem. Effective hotel staffs function as a team and have a great deal of respect and consideration for the services performed by one another. The effective manager attempts to foster this team spirit as an important morale factor.

Graduates of colleges who have majored in hotel administration have the best opportunity for advancement if they possess all the other personality characteristics necessary for a top management position. Yet, even these college

Hotel and motel management
Professional, Administrative, and Managerial Occupations

grads are required in their college training to spend summers employed in service positions in hotels or restaurants. Not only does this provide them with on-the-job training and an understanding of various departments, it also affords many contacts for future employment. A degree in hotel management is becoming more essential as this field grows.

Advancement

After a trainee has proven successful in an on-the-job assignment, he or she is often moved to another interdepartmental job for the broadest possible experiences. These new assignments are usually in the nature of an advancement. Thus, the bellhop may be promoted to bell captain or service manager. The waiter may be promoted to headwaiter or maitre d'hotel. The desk clerk may be put in charge of the front office. On occasion a trainee may be rotated to other departments for more varied experience. Many large hotels have established special programs for management trainees and both college and noncollege people find themselves in competition for assignments to more responsible posts. College training helps the employee but does not assure advancement until you have proven your worth in a lesser task. Usually the college graduate will advance more rapidly than the person without such training, but even here several years' experience is usually necessary before advancement into top management is made. The manager of a large hotel has worked in a great variety of departments and, having done so, has developed a more complete view of the operation of the business. A basic consideration for advancement seems to be proof of successful hotel experience.

Employment outlook

Many new hotels and motels are being built in both urban and resort areas to accommodate an increase in domestic and foreign tourism. In addition, existing hotels are expanding their services to meet the needs of conventions and greater numbers of business and personal travelers. As a result, employment of hotel managers is expected to grow rapidly throughout the 1990s, and the demand for assistant managers to take the place of those who are promoted will increase as managers retire or transfer into other areas.

Opportunities for employment and advancement will be decidedly better for persons who have a college degree in hotel administration.

In the early 1990s, about 78,000 managers were working in hotels and motels throughout the country. An additional number were self-employed owners of smaller establishments.

Earnings

The size and location of a hotel are major factors in determining the earnings of an owner manager. The profits will depend greatly upon the size of the building, the investment, the services rendered, the length of the season, the wages paid the staff, and a great variety of miscellaneous charges and general maintenance expenses.

In the early 1990s, average annual earnings of general managers ranged from about $38,400 in hotels and motels with fewer than 200 rooms to more than $87,000 in large hotels with 600 rooms or more. The average for all hotel and motel managers was $63,900 per year. Assistant managers earned an average of $21,100 in small hotels with fewer than 200 rooms up to an estimated average of $45,500 in hotels with 600 rooms or more. The overall average for assistant hotel and motel managers was $34,500 a year.

Salaries of assistant managers varied greatly depending on their level of experience and the scope of their responsibilities. For example, front office managers had average salaries of about $24,700, whereas food and beverage managers averaged around $42,000 a year.

Many hotels provide managers and their families with living quarters, meals, and use of the hotel facilities as part of their remuneration. In some cases managers also share in profits or receive a yearly bonus of up to 20 percent of their annual salary, depending upon the successful operation of the establishment. Other benefits such as paid vacations, insurance, and hospitalization are usually supplied, also.

Conditions of work

The working conditions in hotels are as varied as are hotels themselves. Because professional managers usually live in the hotel, they enjoy the same facilities as do the guests. Thus, the conditions existing are largely of their own choosing. If managers demand efficient operation and are able to deal well with guests and staff, the environment can be most pleasant. The manager who trains a staff well will be able to enjoy leisure time without being called upon to make petty decisions. Though the job will be physically and mentally demanding, the general atmosphere and decor of the surroundings are just as restful or exciting as managers wish to make them. Hotel managers usually work a regular workweek but because they live in the hotel they must be on call twenty-four hours a day, seven days a week.

Management of a small or residential hotel is usually found less physically demanding than the same position in a large commercial hotel. Managers of large chains are at times required to travel from one assignment to another, while those employed in nonchain establishments usually spend most of their time in one office or in general observation of various departments within their establishment.

The manager of the hotel occupies a position of prestige in a quality hotel and works in surroundings that are usually comfortable.

Social and psychological factors

New hotels require the mobility of their managers to move from one section of the country to another. Hotel managers have to be experts in human relations and must deal with many kinds of persons who come to the hotel for varied reasons.

The very high rate of turnover in the relatively unskilled hotel occupations constantly forces the manager to recruit new and competent help. More technological developments continue to displace workers such as elevator operators, dishwashers, and clerical workers. The hotel manager must constantly deal with difficult situations and sometimes unreasonable or troublesome guests. Thus, a great deal of tension is common in this job.

GOE: 11.11.01; SIC: 7011; SOC: 1351

◇ SOURCES OF ADDITIONAL INFORMATION

American Hotel and Motel Association
1201 New York, Avenue, NW
Washington, DC 20005

American Youth Hostels
PO Box 37613
Washington, DC 20013

Club Managers Association of America
7615 Winterberry Place
Bethesda, MD 20817

Council on Hotel, Restaurant and Institutional Education
1200 17th Street, NW
Washington, DC 20036

Hotel Employees and Restaurant Employees International Union
1219 28th Street, NW
Washington, DC 20007

Hotel Sales and Marketing Association International
1300 L Street, NW
Suite 800
Washington, DC 20005

National Executive Housekeepers Association
1001 Eastwood Drive
Suite 301
Westerville, OH 43081

For information on scholarships, certification, and job placements and opportunities, contact:

Educational Foundation of the National Restaurant Association
250 South Wacker Drive
14th Floor
Chicago, IL 60606

International Association of Hospitality Accountants
Box 27649
Austin, TX 78755

◇ RELATED ARTICLES

Volume 1: Business Administration; Food Service; Hospitality; Travel and Tourism
Volume 2: Caterers; General managers and top executives; Public relations specialists; Restauranht and food service managers
Volume 3: Hotel and motel industry workers; Hotel clerks; Hotel housekeepers and assistants; Receptionists

Human factors specialists

Definition

Human factors specialists are concerned with the way people function and interact with technological products and processes to preform tasks and jobs. They are concerned about the design of facilities, equipment, tools, tasks, and environments to make them compatible with anatomical, physiological, biomechanical, perceptual, cognitive, and behavioral characteristics of human beings. Their goal is to establish a balance among personnel selection, training, and engineering and design of tools and procedures for safety, comfort, satisfaction, and efficiency (such as, for user-friendliness).

History

The basic concepts of human factors and ergonomics are as old as mankind. Humans quickly discovered that tool make work easier and safer and make play more enjoyable. As a profession, however, the origins of ergonomics can be traced to the 1930s and 1940s when teams of engineers and psychologists were assembled to figure out why so many accidents, mishaps, and close-calls seemed to result from human error. These accidents continued to occur despite the employment of well-trained, motivated people who had been assigned to operate and maintain the wide variety of new and complex equipment.

Industrial engineers brought their methods-time-measurement (MTM) techniques and other skills to the problem. Psychologists, physiologists, anthropologists, and other professionals brought their knowledge and skills to determine human capabilities and limitations. Together they worked out what has been called the "systems engineering" approach. Studies were made of human performance, analyzing problems with information presentation and related control actions, work space arrangement, and operator skills. Designers began to recognize the importance of reflecting the characteristics of the user in the equipments they designed, and incorporated it into new designs.

Since the 1960s, human factors activities have broadened to include space systems, industrial and office settings, consumers products, and computer and information systems.

Nature of the work

Human factors and ergonomics professionals apply their skills to a limitless variety of products, jobs, and systems. Many practitioners develop principles for designing computer hardware and software, while others focus on aerospace, communication, training, transportation, or military systems. Some ergonomists develop knowledge about human functioning in systems while others apply it. Some professionals train others in the principles of human factors at universities or as independent consultants.

Physical ergonomists focus on people as physical engines in manual and mechanical systems that require mainly human strength and motor skills. *Information ergonomists* focus on people as information processors in manual, mechanical, and automatic systems that require mainly perceptual and interpretive skills. Often the two concerns are combined because the human has to be considered as a whole. Thus, these professionals integrate human factors with technological factors through research, design, testing, and evaluation in industry, academia, and government. In the United States and Canada, they are often better known as *human factors specialists/engineers*.

Ergonomists can be found working in industry, business, government, and academia. Their common objective is to improve the usability of equipment and products and the quality of working and living environments. Data and methods developed by the human factors profession have been used to design and evaluate office equipment and facilities, power-plant control rooms, agricultural equipment, industrial work stations, airplanes and spacecrafts, training materials, medical devices, and all sorts of vehicle controls and displays.

For example, how safely people get from place to place in their cars is an indicator of how comprehensively human factors have been considered in the design and evaluation of driving. Some of this depends on driver skill but much more depends on system design. When an automobile driver wants to go somewhere, he or she has a fairly complex task to perform that can be made simpler, safer, more comfortable, and convenient depending on how well human factors technology and engineering technology are combined to make drivers, vehicles, roadways, and environment function properly. The driver has to monitor a continual stream of information from inside and outside of the car and must react to that information by navigation, guidance, and control of vehicle speed and position. Many tasks are performed in a limited amount of time to arrive safely at the desired destination.

Driver training and selection by state licensing are only part of the human factors equation for an effective traffic system. Vehicle design (displays, controls, seating, spaciousness, restraints, and external lighting as aids to the driver and other road users) and roadway/ environmental design (traffic signs, signals striping, road surface, width, curvature, illumination) also form parts of the human factors equation.

Because human factors specialists have to work with people of varied backgrounds and experiences, good communication skills are vital, as is an interest in people and technology for the benefit of society. Reports and persuasive presentations of the ergonomic viewpoint to decision makers are often important aspects of the human factors specialists. Economics and engineering compromises can easily erode the influence of ergonomics in system development. Unfortunately, the argument that people are flexible and can adapt to poor designs too often prevails.

Requirements

Since human factors specialists deal principally with the human factors aspects of technology, a solid academic foundation in the human sciences is needed. Mathematics and physical sciences form the basis of technology, so they are also very important. High-school students interested in ergonomics, or other aspects of humanizing technology by design, should take the same college-preparatory courses that they would take for further studies in science and engineering: English, mathematics, statistics, biology, behavioral science, industrial arts, and a foreign language (preferably German) if the student's aspirations included obtaining a doctorate. Consequently, undergraduate education for a human factors specialist tends to be concentrated in psychology or industrial engineering.

Some universities will advise students to take an interdisciplinary program from a variety of academic departments. A review of academic specialties of the Human Factors Society (HFS) membership shows the dominance in study of life sciences, which is why many human factors specialists prefer to call themselves engineering psychologists, especially if they

have advanced degrees and are engaged primarily in research and teaching.

Because human factors specialists are likely to be involved with the development of new or advanced systems, products, and procedures, the human role relative to such developments may have to be experimentally determined. Therefore, students need a good foundation in research methods and techniques (experiment design, statistical inferences, and interpretation of human performance and systems performance data).

While entry into the field of ergonomics with a bachelor's degree is possible, 73 percent of HFS members have advanced degrees. If the career goal is a university appointment, a doctorate is generally required.

Special requirements

Special licensing or certification to work as a human factors specialist generally is not required. Various employers, however, may set some specific professional standards and testing procedures, depending on their specific job requirements. Some may prefer to hire people with engineering backgrounds, others may prefer life sciences backgrounds.

Because the human factors profession is expanding so rapidly into new areas (design for the aged and physically impaired, technology transfer to development countries, to name a few) it helps to join a professional organization to remain abreast of recent developments and professional opportunities. Student chapters exist at several universities.

Opportunities for experience and exploration

Because ergonomists comprise only 0.2 percent of all engineering and technology professionals, it may be difficult to find someone in the profession to talk to. Exploration of the profession is possible by contacting the Human Factors Society. Attending a local chapter or national meeting can also be a valuable experience.

Related occupations

The multidisciplinary nature of the human factors profession and its approach to problem solving relate ergonomics to several other occupations. Among them are safety engineering, industrial engineering, industrial hygiene, industrial or organizational psychology, industrial design, vocational counseling, product development and marketing, personnel training, personnel selection, and most engineering professions. What makes human factors technology unique is its emphasis on the proper integration of people with technological products, facilities, and environments, by exchanging information in results of design, training, and personnel selection.

Methods of entering

Those with proper credentials should decided whether they want to start their career in human factors performing research. Research opportunities exist mainly in U.S. governmental agencies, universities, and large industrial and manufacturing companies. Consulting firms, small businesses, and some industrial firms tend to hire people who can make a direct contribution to the development of a product or process through design, testing, and evaluation. There are also some research and consulting firms who specialize in providing human factors services to clients.

The *Bulletin* of the Human Factors Society frequently lists available jobs. The Society also conducts a job placement service at its annual meeting. College placement offices, as well as public and private employment agencies, may also be helpful in matching job leads and qualified applicants.

Persons with postgraduate degrees in experimental engineering, industrial psychology, industrial engineering (with human factors emphasis), or with a second degree in industrial design have the best employment opportunities.

Advancement

As technology has become more complex, both workers and consumers expect more safety, convenience, and satisfaction in their working and leisure activities. Because the human factors specialist addresses these expectations in his or her work directly, the trend to increased emphasis on ergonomic issues should remain a part of all engineering efforts in the future.

Ergonomics is increasingly recognized as a vital component of technological advancements. Because both ergonomics and human

factors are still relatively new fields, opportunities are considered good for the foreseeable future. As skills are gained beyond academic education, specialized expertise may develop that can enhance advancement opportunities. Experience with system development teams in problem solving and good communication skills are also often considered solid credentials for higher management positions. People with good business skills and advanced knowledge in ergonomics can also enhance their income by becoming independent consultants.

The occupation is somewhat insulated from changes in the economy. In good times, the new products and services are in demand. In a slowing economy, productivity issues and cost-effectiveness of products and procedures become more important. Both concerns provide opportunities for ergonomic efforts.

Earnings

Earnings for human factors specialists depend on the individual's education, work experience, and type of work sought. Entry-level specialists may earn anywhere from $26,000 to $40,000 per year. Those with doctorates earn salaries at the upper end of the spectrum. Experienced professionals often earn more than $60,000 per year, especially those who work in private industries. Full-time employees usually receive health insurance, vacation, and other benefits.

Independent ergonomic consultants usually get paid a negotiated fee, with rates ranging form $60 to $180 per hour, depending on the individual's skill and reputation. As with most freelancers, these consultants have more control over their working hours, but usually do not receive health insurance or other benefits. Many may hold full-time positions and then consult or teach part-time.

Conditions of work

Human factors specialists encounter various working conditions, depending on specific duties and responsibilities. They may work in a typical office environment, with computer and data-processing equipment close at hand, or they may work in a factory, investigating production problems. Usually, they will combine the two, working in an office setting and making frequent visits to a factory or laboratory location to work out particular system development issues. Most of the work is not physically strenuous.

Specialists often work as part of a product or systems design team. They may, however, also work on individual research projects. They usually work a standard forty-hour week, although overtime is not uncommon, especially if a particular project is on deadline. There may be occasional work on weekends and evenings. Those involved with research or teaching may work only ten months a year, although many of them work as consultants when not working full-time.

Social and psychological factors

Human factors professionals should be capable of conducting research and developing project proposals while working as part of a team or while working alone. They must be able to spend long periods analyzing complex data and should be able to come up with creative solutions to difficult sociotechnical questions. Good oral and written communications skill are vital. He or she must be persuasive in discussing system design alternatives with company executives, engineers, and marketing strategists. Human factors specialists should also have good decision-making abilities to handle the pressure that may come when suggesting ergonomic changes with long-term economic impacts. They should also be able to work with other professionals who might not always agree with their analysis or recommendations.

GOE: 11.03.01; SIC: Any industry; SOC: 1915

◇ **SOURCES OF ADDITIONAL INFORMATION**

Human Factors Society
PO Box 1369
Santa Monica, CA 90406

American Psychological Association
Division 21
1200 17th Street, NW
Washington, DC 20036

Industrial Designers Society of America
1142-E Walker Road
Great Falls, VA 22066

Institute of Industrial Engineers
25 Technology Park/Atlanta
Norcross, GA 30092

◇ **RELATED ARTICLES**

Volume 1: Human Resources; Engineering
Volume 2: Engineers; Ergonomists

Human services workers

Definition

Human services workers assist people seeking help from public aid, health and mental health agencies and services, and work under the direction of certified social workers and other professional staff members.

History

Charity and philanthropy have existed in society for centuries. Before the twentieth century, however, they consisted mainly of donations from the affluent that were distributed by church groups to the needy. No efforts were made to improve the lot of the poor except to those in emergency situations, and no systematic methods were established to follow up on charity cases or improve the conditions of the poor in any permanent way.

This frame of mind began to erode after the Industrial Revolution, when public opinion about the inequities of wealth began to change. In 1889, Jane Addams founded Hull House in Chicago, an act that is usually considered the birth of formal social work. The daughter of a banker, Addams' philosophy of helping the underprivileged gain a better, more permanent

A human services worker assists an elderly woman in a nursing home.

standard of living inspired many others to launch similar programs in other parts of the world. After World War I, social work began to be recognized as a true occupation. The Great Depression of the 1930s provided further impetus to the growth of social work, as the federal government joined with state, municipal and private efforts to ease the pain of poverty. The social disruptions of the years following World War II contributed to further growth in social work.

Nature of the work

Human services workers are employed in a variety of institutional and community settings, administering help and support to the poor, the aged, the handicapped and mentally ill, substance abusers, parolees and others having trouble with adjustments in life. The job of the human services worker is primarily one of supporting the work of the social workers, psychologists, and other professional staff of agency or program, and carrying out the directives and the duties of the agencies by which they are employed. Like social workers, their work can be any of three types: casework, group work and community organization work.

Casework involves direct, face-to-face interaction between the clients needing help and the workers providing it. When most people think of social work, they probably think of casework. The *case aide* assists the regular social worker on the simpler aspects of these cases, under close and regular supervision.

In a way, all human services workers are involved in casework, but their duties can vary a great deal because of the agency they work for, their experience, and the severity and com-

plexity of the social problems they will be addressing. It can occur in offices, hospitals, homes, community centers, schools, and numerous other settings. Casework could involve helping a single mother get the government benefits she deserves, assisting old persons get to and from hospitals and community centers, or helping the physically and mentally handicapped become more self-sufficient in the daily living. They may transport or accompany clients to group meal sites, adult day care programs, or doctors' offices. They stay in touch with clients through home visits and telephone calls, checking to be sure that needed services are being received. *Management aides* serve tenants in public housing projects. They are employed by housing agencies or other groups to help tenants relocate, inform tenants of the use of facilities and the location of community services such as recreation centers and clinics, explain the management's rules about sanitation and maintenance, and advise homemakers needing assistance in child care, money management, and housekeeping problems. They may at times help resolve disagreements between tenants and landlords.

Group work takes place in a more or less regular setting, such as community centers, homes for the aged or developmentally disabled, hospitals, halfway houses, settlement houses, and correctional facilities. Programs in these settings can be directed to help old people stay active and alert, provide support for children and adults with serious illnesses, help prison inmates and parolees learn new skills, or helps groups such as migrant workers and recent immigrants find answers to their problems of economic and social adjustment. One type of human services worker involved in group social work is the *human relations or drug and alcohol counselor*, who assists in developing, organizing, and conducting programs dealing with the causes of and remedies for substance abuse and human conflict situations.

The last type of social work—community organization work—examines and tries to alleviate the problems that can affect an entire community, such as juvenile delinquency. After social workers and other professionals devise a plan of action for addressing these problems, they work together with human services workers to reach out to the people affected, coordinate the efforts of different social agencies and groups, and improve the master plan through review and revision.

One of the first steps of effective social work is letting the people in the community know what kinds of services are being offered to them. This type of community outreach can be performed by a *community worker* or *social-*

services aide. These people visit individuals and families and address neighborhood groups to publicize supportive services available to the unemployed, the homeless, single parents, parolees, school dropouts, families with problems, and others needing special assistance. The community worker can also help in community-wide planning by interviewing residents of specific neighborhoods and investigating the needs and opinions of the residents who are currently disadvantaged.

After a client contacts the social service agency with a request for more help, he or she is interviewed by a human services worker, to identify the services he or she needs and possibly to determine the eligibility for benefits. This can be a complex job, because the worker needs to examine financial documents such as rent receipts and tax returns to determine whether the client is eligible for food stamps, Medicaid, or other welfare program. At this time, the worker may be able to suggest ways that the client can cut or avoid the red tape that surrounds many entitlement programs. If the client is entitled to the benefits of the program, the human services worker may be called on by his or her superior to do many things. These could include anything from caring for the client's children during a client's job or medical appointments to offering the client emotional support. In some food stamp programs, *food-management aides* advise low-income family members how to plan, budget, shop for, and prepare balanced meals, often accompanying or driving the client to the store and offering suggestions on the most nutritious and economical food to purchase with the food stamps.

The same kind of personal interaction is required of human service workers employed in group work at nursing homes, institutions, hospitals, and so on. The search for alternatives to institutional care has brought forth a variety of community-based facilities and programs, such as neighborhood clinics, mental health centers, emergency shelters, drop-in centers for drug abusers and the mentally ill, group homes, and halfway houses. Because of the wide range of services available in these settings, the responsibilities of human service workers varies a great deal. In a community mental health center, for example, workers may help individuals trying to overcome drug or alcohol addiction master the practical aspects of everyday living such as cooking and laundry, and teach them ways to communicate more effectively with others. Workers may also assist the professional staff in the different treatments offered, including group activities; music, art, and dance therapies; and individual and group counseling. Halfway houses and

group homes also serve adults such as the elderly and retarded who need some supervision or assistance on a day-to-day basis. Their purpose is to give people with mental and physical impairments the chance to live in a warm, community setting instead of an institution. In these types of homes, human services workers might have to drive residents to daytime community centers, doctors' appointments, or shopping centers. They may have to organize recreational activities, help clients plan and prepare meals, or call employers who are interested in hiring the handicapped.

In every situation, human services workers operate under the direction of the professional staff and monitor and record the steps and progress involved in the rendering of services. Record keeping is an important part of the duties of human services workers. They must prepare and maintain the records and case files of every person they work with and their response to the various programs and treatment. They must also track costs in group homes in order to stay within budget. Accurate record keeping is important because it may have an impact on the client's eligibility for future benefits, the proper assessment of a program's success, and the determination of future funding.

Requirements

Human services workers have a wide range of educational backgrounds. However, a person's level of education will usually determine the kind of work he or she does and the amount of responsibility he or she will be entrusted to. Some employers will hire people with a high school education, but these people might find it hard to rise beyond clerical and other mundane duties. Because higher education is the key to advancement in this field, high school students should pursue a college preparatory curriculum, with classes in English, mathematics, political science, psychology and sociology.

At the college level, people interested in careers in human services have many options for study. Approximately 300 certificate and associate degree programs in human services or mental health were offered at community and junior colleges, vocational-technical institutes, and other postsecondary institutions. In addition, about 150 programs offered a bachelor's degree in human services, and a small number of these have programs leading to a master's degree. Academic programs such as these generally prepare students for definite occupations; for example, a student could earn an associate's degree for working with developmentally disabled adults. Because the educators at these colleges and universities stay in regular contact with the social work employers in their area, the programs are continually revised to meet the changing needs of the area. Students are exposed early and often to the kinds of situations they may encounter on the job.

Undergraduate and graduate programs typically include courses in psychology, sociology, crisis intervention, family dynamics, therapeutic interviewing, rehabilitation, and gerontology. Through classroom simulation and mandatory internships, students develop skills in interviewing, observing, and recording behavior; learn techniques of individual and group counseling; and are introduced to program planning. As stated earlier, career advancement almost always depends on formal education, such as a bachelor's or master's degree in social work, counseling, rehabilitation, or some other related field. Many employers encourage their workers to further their education, and some may even reimburse part of the costs of school. In addition, many employers provide in-service training such as seminars and workshops.

Special requirements

Human service workers need to be compassionate and patient, with a strong desire to help others. Employers look for caring, responsible individuals. Employers, especially those in group homes, must screen employees very carefully and are selective in their hiring, because they have been entrusted with the well-being of vulnerable people. Human service workers must also be able to manage their time effectively and have a high degree of maturity and stability to work with other people's problems without becoming overwhelmed or discouraged.

Opportunities for experience and exploration

Students interested in a career as a human services worker should first get a taste of what the occupation requires. Students may be able to find a summer job working with a local human services agency or institution. If paying jobs are not available, students should look into volunteer work, which could be done either in the summer or after school. Volunteer work could include reading to blind or elderly persons, vis-

iting nursing homes, organizing group recreation programs at the YMCA, or performing light clerical duties. By getting to know the administrators and supervisors at these agencies, students will improve their chances of staying informed when full-time jobs become available.

Related occupations

The work done by human services workers requires the same aptitudes as those needed by social workers, personnel workers, employment firm workers, teachers, psychologists, and psychiatrists.

Methods of entering

By talking with their high-school counselor and contacting local and state human services agencies, students will gain a good idea of where jobs are available. Sometimes summer jobs and volunteer work can develop into full-time employment upon graduation. In any case, such work and experience is noticed by the people hiring human services workers. Employers try to be selective in their hiring, because so many human services jobs involve direct contact with people who are impaired and therefore vulnerable to exploitation. Evidence of helping others can be a definite plus.

Advancement

Job performance has a bearing on pay raises and some advancement for human services workers. However, further study in higher education determines whether a worker will be promoted into positions with more responsibility and decision-making capacity.

Employment outlook

About 88,000 people were employed as human services workers in early 1990s. Of these, approximately one-third were employed by state and local governments, primarily in mental health centers, public welfare agencies, and facilities and programs for the mentally retarded and developmentally disabled. Another 25 percent worked in agencies offering adult day care, group meals, crisis intervention, counseling, and other social services. Some human services workers supervised the residents of group homes and halfway houses, while others held jobs in clinics, community mental health centers, and psychiatric hospitals.

The U.S. Department of Labor anticipates that employment for human services workers will grow much faster than the average for all occupations through the early 1990s. Much of this growth is expected to occur in homes for the elderly, mentally impaired, and developmentally disabled. Growing numbers of people in the United States are living longer, and the need for workers to make their stays in groups homes more comfortable and stimulating is growing with it. Mental health professionals are also starting to learn of the value that day programs and communal living has for the elderly and the disabled, so the relatively new concept of adult day care is rapidly gaining endorsement.

While the growing population of elderly persons is the dominant factor in the expected rise in adult day care, new ideas in treating handicapped or mentally ill persons also underlies the anticipated employment growth in group homes and residential care facilities. Public concern for the homeless, many of whom are former mental patients who were left to their own devices during the deinstitutionalization programs of a few years ago, will likely bring about new community-based programs and group residences. Additional pressure will push for more group homes as more developmentally disabled people reach the age of twenty-one and no longer qualify for programs and services offered by public schools.

Job prospects in public agencies are not as bright as they once were, because of fiscal policies that tighten the eligibility requirements for federal welfare and other payments. State and local governments are expected to remain major employers, however, as the burden of providing social services such as welfare, child support, and nutrition programs is shifted from the federal government to the state and local level.

One major reason that qualified applicants should have little trouble in finding a job as a human services worker is the high turnover rate for people in the profession. Because the work is emotionally draining and carries a great deal of responsibility for relatively little pay, employers are always needing to replace their staff. Turnover is especially high for persons working as counselors in group homes and those persons without formal academic training. It is for this reason that summer, volunteer, or part time work experience is recommended for interested students.

Earnings

The amount a person can earn as a human services worker depends in part on his or her employer and amount of experience. According to the limited amount of data available, starting salaries for human services workers range from $10,000 to $14,000 a year. Experienced workers can earn up to $20,000 annually.

Conditions of work

Working conditions for human services workers vary, depending on their employer and the type of work they are engaged in. People employed by government agencies work a standard forty-hour week, spending some of their time in the office and the rest in the field interviewing clients and performing other support services. Some weekend and evening work may be required, but compensatory time off is usually granted. Human services workers in community-based settings work in roughly the same conditions. Workers in residential settings generally work in shifts. Because of the twenty-four-hour staffing needs of group homes, workers usually work some evenings and weekends.

Depending on where they are employed, human service workers operate in a variety of settings. Offices and facilities may be clean and cheerful, or they may be dismal, cramped, and inadequately equipped. While out in the field with clients, workers may also find themselves in dangerous, squalid areas.

Social and psychological factors

Human services workers can get a great deal of emotional satisfaction from their work. Helping parolees and people on welfare to find jobs, providing people with information on benefit programs to which they are entitled, helping the elderly and disabled to live comfortable, fulfilling lives, offering inner city kids alternatives to gangs and delinquency—these are the intangible benefits that attract most people to this field.

This can be a stressful and emotionally draining occupation, however. Daily contact with people in dire straits, whose lives border on the edge of hopelessness, surrounded by squalor and difficulties, can weaken the spirit of many people in human services. Even people with a great and burning desire to help others can find the job overwhelming after a time.

GOE: 10.01.02; SIC: 8322; SOC: 2032

National Staff Development and Training Association
810 First Street, NE, Suite 500
Washington, DC 20002

◇ **SOURCES OF ADDITIONAL INFORMATION**

College for Human Services
345 Hudson Street
New York, NY 10014

National Organization for Human Service Education
Executive Offices Building 6
National College of Education
2840 Sheridan Road
Evanston, IL 60201

◇ **RELATED ARTICLES**

Volume 1: Civil Service; Health Care; Human Resources; Social Services
Volume 2: Career counselors; Employment counselors; Occupational therapists; Physical therapists; Recreational therapists; Recreation workers; Rehabilitation counselors; Social workers; Therapists, miscellaneous

Industrial designers

Definition

Industrial designers combine technical knowledge of materials, machines, and production with artistic talent to improve the appearance and function of machine-made products. Some designers are self-employed and specialize in one particular product. Corporate designers work for a company and design many different products for that company's needs; corporate designers may also work with the company's engineers on long-range planning.

History

The Industrial Revolution influenced many aspects of our life. Such inventions as the steam engine, the power loom, and the sewing machine took people off the farms and into the factory. Never before had it been possible to produce textiles, clothing, and other materials rapidly and at lower costs. Another significant step was the introduction of mass production. Eli Whitney worked out his ideas of making many interchangeable gun parts; Henry Ford established and refined the process with the standardization of auto parts.

In this century, industry has become a mainstay of our economy. Rarely do families today produce their own food or build a house from materials found on their property. Today's consumer has become extremely dependent on the variety of manufactured goods. We buy cars, washing machines, food, clothing, and books. We also buy little things: paper clips, tiepins, shoelaces, and ballpoint pens. All these things are available to us because of modern industry.

These changes in production of material goods have made possible the work of the industrial designer. As earlier manufacturers raced to meet demands for their goods and to fight competition, the industrial designer's job came into being.

Nature of the work

Industrial designers are part engineer, part artist, part merchandiser. They may design anything from cars to vacuum cleaners. They are the people behind the "new, improved" items that are widely advertised.

Much thought and preparation go into the products being designed. First, the designer delves into the background of a product or others similar to it. The purpose may be to find ways of improving an old product or to design an entirely new product. The designer has to consult other experts to determine how successful an idea will be commercially. Will it sell? Can it be produced economically? Whether one is working on a new radio or a submarine, one may design various improvements or changes, or may design an entirely new product. All the designer's sketches and suggestions must be submitted to company officials who study the proposals and select the one they feel will be most successful. The designer may then make a model of the new design. Often it is made of clay first so that it may be changed easily. The final model is carefully made by skilled workers and is a guide used in production.

The designer must strive to make each product functional and easy to use, attractive in appearance, and as economical as possible in terms of production costs. The designer needs to understand the consumer, sales principles, and engineering principles and problems.

Because these products must ultimately be sold to the public, designers should be very much aware of consumer psychology and its relation to the consumer. For example, they may design the package in which the product is contained or displays with which it is connected. This facet of design has become increasingly important. The consumer may be influenced by the appearance of the package—its shape, color, or some other appeal. Also, the package must fit the product, protect it in shipping, perhaps be used for display purposes. Great competition exists among manufacturers to catch the consumer's eye.

Industrial designers may also design the layout of gas stations, grocery stores, offices, trucks, and other company facilities so that they present a coordinated image to the public. Selling the public is a key function of the industrial designer.

Most designers work on only a few products; they are experts in a particular area of manufacturing. Companies with an eye to the future, however, may have their senior designers working on long-range plans, which result in such examples as sketches of cars of the future.

Requirements

The most important requirement for the person interested in this career is completion of a course of study in industrial design. Some students of architecture, science, and engineering have entered this field, but specialized training including art and business is considered almost essential. Art schools, art departments of universities, and technical colleges usually offer

This industrial designer draws sketches of a new hair dryer for the home.

courses in industrial design. Most college or university courses take four years, but in some schools a five-year course is required. Each leads to a bachelor's degree in industrial design or fine arts. Some schools also offer a master's degree. Often art schools grant a diploma for three years of study in industrial design. Programs in industrial design at least eighteen colleges and art schools were accredited by the National Association of Schools of Art or recognized by the Industrial Designers Society of America.

Of course, graduation from high school is necessary to enter any college or university. Also, art schools and colleges may require students to present a portfolio of artwork. Once enrolled, some schools require students to complete their freshman or sophomore year before majoring in industrial design.

School programs vary; some emphasize engineering and technical work, others emphasize art background. But certain basic courses are common to every school: two-dimensional design (color theory, spatial organization), and general three-dimensional design (abstract sculpture, art structures). Students also have a great deal of studio practice, learning to make models of clay, plaster, wood, and other easily worked materials. Some schools even use metalworking machinery. Technically oriented schools generally require a course in basic engineering. Schools offering degree programs also require courses in English, history, science, and other basic subjects. Such courses as merchandising and business are also important for anyone working in a field so closely connected with the consumer.

As for the personal qualifications the most important is a creative and artistic ability. Mechanical and business interests are also assets for the industrial designer. One should be able to get along well with others—often designers work with other staff members in developing their designs. The industrial designer has to know the consumer's needs, likes, and dislikes to create products that will sell as well as function. One must also be able to create ideas and carry them out all the way to the assembly line.

Special requirements

No licensing is required, but generally, employers want to hire someone holding a college degree or diploma from an art or technical school. The person with engineering, architectural, or other scientific background will have a good chance at beginning jobs provided he or she can also give evidence of artistic and creative talent.

Opportunities for experience and exploration

An excellent opportunity to explore this field would be part-time or summer employment in an office where industrial design is being carried out. In fact, any job that would help the student learn about the consumer would be valuable experience. Students might also be able to take some high-school industrial arts and creative arts courses that would help them determine their interest and ability, as well as offer experience and practice.

They might also learn something about the industrial designer's work through artistic hobbies—ceramics, woodworking, sketching, and others, or by reading magazines related to the field. If part-time work is impossible, they might be able to visit a factory to see the design process in action.

Related occupations

Possessing both technical and artistic interests and aptitudes, industrial designers have much in common with such other workers as architects, engineers (especially packaging engineers), and other designers (especially package designers and furniture designers). Prospective industrial designers may also want to examine the work and requirements of interior designers, landscape architects, merchandise displayers, photographers, and visual artists.

Methods of entering

Once the educational background in industrial design or perhaps in some related field is completed designers can start looking for a job. Usually they can apply directly to companies that hire industrial designers or they make application through newspaper want ads. The majority of manufacturing companies are located in New York, Massachusetts, California, Ohio, Illinois, Michigan, and Texas. Colleges, universities, and other schools may offer placement services to help their graduates find jobs. A designer applying for a job is generally expected to present a portfolio of work that will give an idea of the person's artistic and creative ability. A qualified industrial designer might also get help in finding a job through the Industrial Designers Society of America.

Advancement

Beginning industrial designers usually start as assistants to other designers. They will do routine work and hold little responsibility for design changes. With experience and the necessary personal qualifications, the designer may be promoted to supervisory positions with major responsibility for design. Some senior designers, as mentioned before, may be given a free hand in designing the products of the future. With experience, established reputation, and financial backing, the industrial designer may be able to establish a consulting firm.

Employment outlook

In the early 1990s, more than 5,000 persons were working in this field. About half of them were employed by manufacturing companies. Many worked for consulting firms, and some had jobs in architectural or interior design firms. A few were free lancers.

Employment of industrial designers is expected to show faster than average growth through the end of the 1990s. This favorable outlook is based on the need to improve product quality and safety, to design new products for businesses and offices, and to design high-technology products in medicine and transportation. In addition, as the population increases, so will the demand for new products or for modernizing old products for personal use. This is a job, however, that is somewhat controlled by the economic picture. It thrives in times of prosperity but is cut back in periods of recession.

The best prospects for industrial designers appear to exist in companies that manufacture business and office machines, biomedical equipment, environmental protection devices and systems, and industrial ceramics.

Earnings

In the early 1990s, the beginning industrial designer with no experience earned about $20,000 to $23,000 a year when employed by a manufacturing firm; in consulting firms, salaries were usually lower. Salaries for experienced designers depend on ability and the employer of each individual. The figures available indicate that senior designers earned from $29,500 to $34,700 while design project directors received between $34,000 and $42,000 per year. Managers who direct design departments in large companies had annual salaries ranging from $39,000 to $51,500. Owners or partners of consulting firms had fluctuating incomes, depending on business for the year. Most consultants earned from $50,000 or more per year; a few of the most outstanding and talented designers earned as much as $225,000 per year.

Conditions of work

Working conditions for the industrial designer are generally pleasant. Good lighting is very important for one who spends long hours at the drawing board. The designer may consult with engineers, other designers, and company officials. He or she may also spend time in the factory supervising the production of his design.

Most industrial designers work a forty-hour week, but there are exceptions. A designer working hard to meet a deadline may work more hours, or if business is slow, fewer hours.

Social and psychological factors

The industrial designer's work is usually interesting and satisfying. For the artist there is great pleasure in seeing ideas come into reality, in creating a product that functions effectively and appears attractive to the consumer. There is the challenge of always improving a product, or of developing an entirely new idea. Competition is always forcing the designer to move ahead.

One should not consider becoming an industrial designer, however, unless he or she has the artistic ability, business talent, and sincere interest required. Competition is keen, and those with outstanding ability and personal qualifications are the ones that get the top jobs and high salaries. Another problem to be considered is the general economic picture; if business is good, employment prospects are good; if business is slow, jobs are scarce. Long-range planning is important when deciding to become an industrial designer. There are financial rewards and a sense of artistic accomplishment for the qualified industrial designer.

GOE: 01.02.03; SIC: Any industry; SOC: 322

◇ **SOURCES OF ADDITIONAL INFORMATION**

Industrial Designers Society of America
1142-E Walker Road
Great Falls, VA 22066

National Association of Schools of Art and Design
11250 Roger Bacon Drive, No. 21
Reston, VA 22090

◇ **RELATED ARTICLES**

Industrial traffic managers

Definition

Industrial traffic managers arrange for transportation of raw materials, equipment, and finished products to and from industrial and business firms.

History

Traffic managers were first employed by railroads. In the early part of the nineteenth century, businesses that used railroads to ship their products had to bargain with the rail freight operators for this service. Competition among rail freight operators was keen. Owners of railroads needed individuals who could not only persuade businesses to ship by rail but who knew how to ship goods at a profit for the railroad. A good traffic manager became a valuable employee. In 1887 the federal government passed legislation that regulated freight rates. Many railroads no longer employed traffic managers, and those who were retained became shipping clerks.

The talents of a good traffic manager were once again needed as trucks and airplanes began competing with railroads for freight. Since World War II, traffic management has become a well-developed area of work. The importance attached to this job resulted from the great growth in industrial plants; the need for more raw materials; and the need to ship more goods, more often. Traffic managers employed by transportation companies are not discussed in this article.

Nature of the work

Traffic managers are in charge of the activities of personnel in shipping and receiving. They are responsible for the distribution of goods within their own company as well as outgoing goods. They must first consider the type and quantity of goods to be shipped—is it liquid, bulky, light or heavy, or fragile. They must have a knowledge of physics regarding the distribution of weight to lower per-inch stress. They need to know scientific theories regarding combustibles, inflammables, and other chemical and corrosive problems.

Then, they must determine which is the most economical and quickest means of shipping these goods—water, rail, pipeline, highway. When goods are delayed en route to a destination, industrial traffic managers must determine why the delay occurred. They make arrangements with owners of transportation companies to speed up transportation. When goods are damaged in shipment, traffic managers make adjustments with a transportation company or the customer. Traffic managers occasionally design or select shipping containers that best meet the needs of the firm for which they are employed. Some are responsible for the actual packing of goods and also for their companies' warehouse and transportation facilities.

Because many aspects of transportation are subject to federal, state, and local regulations, traffic managers must be very familiar with these and all legal matters that concern shipping in their company. This includes reviewing restrictions on items that may not be allowed to be shipped on interstate highways, through tunnels, or in airplanes.

In most companies, traffic managers are responsible for the personnel of their department. Payroll and other related problems may be directed to them for solution. They may be required at times to handle insurance questions or they may plead a case before the Interstate Commerce Commission or other federal boards. In a small firm, the traffic manager may have to produce claims, approve routine bills, trace lost shipments, lease port and terminal facilities, or clear goods through customs.

The manager works closely with the purchasing, shipping, advertising, production control, and legal departments.

The purchasing department staff may seek the manager's advice on the cheapest way to transport incoming raw material. The production department staff may consult with the manager on the desirability of buying a new warehouse or plant site. They would need his or her viewpoint on the advantages and disadvantages for transportation in the move. The manager may have to decide if it is feasible for the company to operate its own fleet of trucks or other transportation. The traffic manager is a link between the senior company officials and the traffic department. This is important in developing transportation management policy with a minimum of cost.

Requirements

Industrial traffic managers must have graduated from high school or have equivalent education. The subjects with the greatest value are English, mathematics, chemistry, physics, geography, bookkeeping, typing, and business practice. In addition, a good understanding and use of English and two years of science are necessary.

Education beyond high school is becoming increasingly important to those interested in higher-level positions in traffic management. A bachelor's degree with courses in transportation, management, economics, statistics, marketing, and commercial law is preferred by some firms. Others seek those with a business administration degree and a major in transportation. Some law training is valuable.

Those with exceptional drive can reach the top without a college degree. Some kind of special study, however, is essential—night courses, correspondence, college extension, traffic institute courses. These last courses are conducted by those with transportation management experience. On-the-job experience may sometimes be used as a substitute.

Advanced training is valuable because the traffic manager must deal with a system of many variable rate schedules, regulations, routes, and schedules. Managers should have efficiency, economy, and safety in mind. They must be able to express themselves in speech and in writing. They must be able to read and understand complex transportation language.

A basic interest in geography is needed, also, because the traffic manager should come to know the nation's maps most thoroughly.

Basic leadership qualities such as enthusiasm, initiative, tact, honesty, and thoroughness are essential. In addition, the traffic manager must be able to accept responsibility and give orders effectively. This person should be at ease when meeting and talking with all kinds of people.

The traffic manager should learn new developments in industry and in the United States economy which will affect the work.

A large chalkboard helps this traffic manager chart and guide the movement of a company's numerous riverboats.

Special requirements

The traffic manager may be called on periodically to argue a case for the company before the Interstate Commerce Commission, the Federal Maritime Commission, or Civil Aeronautics Board. Because of this, the manager needs some training in legal knowledge to pass the Interstate Commerce Commission examination for licensing people to argue cases.

For status in the profession, those in traffic management will seek "certified" membership in the American Society of Transportation and Logistics. The organization requires passing of a rigid examination and certain work experience for membership.

Opportunities for experience and exploration

Opportunities to gain experience in high school are somewhat limited. Students can, however, obtain part-time work after school or during the summer in the shipping department of many business organizations. Experience can also be gained in less direct ways. Industrial firms frequently advertise or publish articles in professional journals that discuss new innovations in packaging and shipping. By reading such articles, those interested in traffic management can become acquainted with and keep abreast of developments in the field.

Related occupations

In dealing with transportation and products, industrial traffic managers must be able to analyze, make decisions, plan, and direct others. These same abilities are required by managers

321

and administrators in many fields. Some of these workers include crating-and-moving estimators, import-export agents, passenger traffic agents and managers, purchasing agents, shipping services sales representatives, and warehouse managers.

Methods of entering

Those interested in traffic management might take a summer job with the traffic department of a large plant. Anyone interested, with appropriate high-school background, can grow with an industry in the traffic or related department. College graduates, graduates of transportation courses at special schools, and experienced people will be more favored than high-school graduates for first employment and promotion. Those with more education and experience will spend less time at beginning jobs. They may also be considered earlier for advancement.

Advancement

New employees often work in the shipping room. They route shipments, write bills of lading, and process other shipping forms. They also may start in the general traffic offices doing clerical work such as filing freight rate schedules or figuring freight charges. They may then be promoted to rate analyst and review freight rates and prepare special rate studies. The next step up may be called rate supervisor. These people keep traffic files and arrange miscellaneous transportation services. Then senior rate clerks figure rate statements and give rate and route information. Well on the way toward the management level is the position of freight claim supervisor, who files damage loss claims, processes payment checks, and aids in the development of efficient packaging materials.

The individual on the way up may have to give extra hours to learn all phases of the traffic manager's position. Experience and demonstrated ability are considered to be the most important factors in promotion to the higher-level jobs.

Employment outlook

In the early 1990s, more than 18,000 persons were employed as industrial traffic managers. The majority worked for manufacturing or freight transportation companies, and some were employed by chain stores and other establishments that ship a large volume of goods. A few experts served as consultants on transportation problems.

Employment opportunities for industrial traffic managers look good through the early 1990s. The demand for these workers is growing steadily. As industry decentralizes in an effort to overcome competition and reduce costs, there will be greater need to move goods among the various branches. Because of rising shipping expenses, industry will require experts who can manage traffic efficiently at reasonable costs. In addition, new freight transportation regulations have created a need for more managers skilled in buying and selling freight transportation services. Traffic managers who can work with computers will have the least difficulty finding employment.

Earnings

The earnings for the traffic manager are dependent on many conditions pertinent to a particular firm. Salary may be affected by location and size of firm, transportation costs and sales volume, number of subordinates, employer's gross business per year, personal experience, and education. Most traffic managers in the early 1990s had salaries of $25,000 to $40,000 a year. Top-level managers were making at least $50,000, and some earned upwards of $100,000.

Other traffic department positions are on lower-graded scales. Beginners with a college degree may earn around $17,000 to $25,000, depending on their degree; those with a high-school diploma, beginning training as traffic clerks, shipping clerks, or dispatchers, may start at $10,400 to $14,300 a year.

Conditions of work

The traffic manager works mostly in comfortable offices, but often consults in the factory. At times this person may travel to other branches of the company and to court hearings to represent the company's transportation interests.

The traffic manager ordinarily works standard office hours, thirty-five to forty hours per week. He or she may be required to spend extra hours preparing reports and attending meetings.

Beginners and lower echelon positions in traffic departments may involve a routine of repetitious detail. Conditions, though sanitary, may be moderately dirty, noisy, and uncomfortable, depending on the particular job and place of employment.

Social and psychological factors

There are some indications of the type of person who will make a good traffic manager. Interest in the different means of transportation is helpful. A willingness to study is desirable in light of the increasing stress on college training and earning of a degree.

Traffic managers need sound business judgment based on cost consciousness, a good memory for detail, and should be able to make prudent decisions under pressure.

They should look on problems of transportation as challenges if they are to cope with the maze of rates, regulations, routes, and schedules encountered in this work.

GOE: 11.11.03; SIC: Any industry; SOC: 1341, 1342

⬦ **SOURCES OF ADDITIONAL INFORMATION**

American Society of Transportation and Logistics
PO Box 33095
Louisville, KY 40232

Transportation Clubs International
303 East 3rd Street, Suite 201
Sanford, FL 32771

⬦ **RELATED ARTICLES**

Volume 1: Packaging; Transportation; See also specific industries
Volume 3: Shipping and receiving clerks; Traffic agents and clerks

Insurance claims representatives

Definition

Insurance claims representatives, or *claims adjusters,* investigate claims for personal, casualty, or property loss or damages; determine the extent of the insurance company's liability; and try to negotiate an out-of-court settlement with the claimant.

History

Insurance is an action or process that insures a party against loss or damage by a contingent event, such as fire, accident, illness, or death.

In modern times, organized insurance first developed in the maritime industry. It began in the 1600s at Lloyd's Coffee House as a means of sharing the risks of commercial voyages. Underwriters received a fee for the portion of the financial responsibility they shouldered.

As the need for protection developed, other types of insurance arose. After the London Fire of 1666, fire insurance became available in the United States. Accident insurance appeared in the United States in 1863; automobile in 1898.

Life insurance was designed originally to minimize the loss from death by pooling the risk with others. It first appeared in Philadelphia in 1759. Today, companies are selling life insurance policies worth one trillion dollars in protection.

As the insurance business grew and became more complex, the need for specialized personnel, like claims representatives, developed.

Nature of the work

An insurance company's reputation and success is dependent upon its ability to quickly and effectively investigate claims, negotiate eq-

Insurance claims representatives spend much of their time sifting through financial statements, claims forms, and individual insurance policies.

uitable settlements, and authorize prompt payments to policy holders. Claims representatives perform these duties.

Claims clerks review insurance forms for accuracy and completeness. Frequently, this involves calling or writing the insured party or other people involved to secure missing information. After placing this data in a claim file, the clerk reviews the insurance policy to determine coverage. Routine claims are transmitted for payment; if further investigation is needed, the clerk informs the claims supervisor.

In companies specializing in property-liability insurance, *claims adjusters* may perform some or all of the duties of claims clerks. They can determine whether the policy covers the loss and the amount claimed. Through investigation of physical evidence, the securing of testimony from relevant parties—including the claimant, witnesses, police, and, if necessary, hospital personnel—and the examination of reports, they promptly negotiate a settlement. In this, adjusters make sure that the settlement reflects the actual claimant losses while making certain the insurer is protected from invalid claims.

Adjusters may issue payment checks or submit their findings to claims examiners for payment. If litigation is necessary, adjusters recommend this action to legal counsel and they may attend court hearings.

Some claims adjusters do not specialize in one type of insurance, but most do. They act exclusively in one field, whether it be fire, marine, automobile, or product liability. A special classification is the *claims agent for petroleum*, who handles activities connected with the locating, drilling, and producing of oil or gas on private property. In states with "no fault" insurance, adjusters are not concerned with responsibilities, but they still must determine the

amount of payment. To help settle automobile insurance claims, an *automobile damage appraiser* examines damaged cars and other vehicles, estimates the cost of labor and parts, and determines whether it is more practical to make the repairs or to pay the claimant the pre-accident market value of the vehicle.

The trend among casualty insurers is to employ telephone or inside adjusters. They use the phone and the mail to gather information—including loss estimates—from the claimant.

Drive-in claim centers also have been developed to provide on-the-spot settlement. After determining the loss, the adjuster issues a check immediately.

In life and health insurance companies, *claims examiners* perform all the functions of claims adjusters. Examiners in these companies, and in others where adjusters also are employed, review settled claims to make sure the settlements and the payments adhere to company procedures and policies. They report on any irregularities. In cases involving litigation, they confer with attorneys. Where large claims are involved, a senior examiner frequently handles the case.

Requirements

Claims representatives are in a people-oriented job. They must be able to communicate effectively so as to gain the respect and confidence of the parties concerned. They should be mathematically adept and have a good memory. Knowledge of legal and medical terms and practice, as well as state and federal insurance laws and regulations, is required.

College graduates are preferred for insurance claims jobs. If the individual possesses special experience—like auto repair specialists as auto adjusters—a degree is not required. No college major is preferred but certain ones may indicate a possible specialty. An engineering degree would be valuable in industrial claims, and a legal background would be helpful in ones involving workers' compensation and product liability. In any case, on-the-job training is usually provided.

Supplementary professional education is encouraged by insurance companies. A number of options are available. A six-semester program in claims adjusting is offered by the Insurance Institute of America. Following passage of six examinations, an Associate in Claims (AIC) designation is awarded to participants. The College of Insurance in New York City offers a program leading to a professional certificate in insurance adjusting. In addition, life and health claims examining programs are offered by both the Life Office Management Association (LOMA) and the International Claim Association (ICA), both of which lead to a professional designation.

Special requirements

Most states require licensing of claims representatives. The requirements can include: being twenty or twenty-one years of age, state residency, the filing of a surety bond, the completion of an approved course in loss adjusting or insurance, and the passing of a written exam.

Opportunities for experience and exploration

Wide opportunities exist for career exploration, ranging from getting a job with an insurance company, to taking relevant coursework and interviewing people in the field.

Related occupations

Other workers who negotiate contracts and investigate claims for companies and individuals include automobile damage appraisers, contract administrators, contractors, and lease buyers, among others.

Methods of entering

One can enter this occupation through direct application to an employer, by answering a newspaper "help wanted" ad, or by using the local office of the U.S. Employment Service Office.

Advancement

Depending upon the individual, advancement prospects are good. As they demonstrate competence and advance in coursework, trainees are assigned higher and more difficult claims. Promotions are possible to department supervisor in a field office or a managerial position in the home office. Sometimes claims workers

transfer to underwriting and sales departments.

Employment outlook

Growth among claims representatives is expected to be higher than the national average for all occupations through the 1990s. This will be a result of increased insurance sales, resulting in a larger number of insurance claims, as well as of changes in the population, economics, trends in insurance settlement procedures, and opportunities arising from death, retirement, and job changing.

The predominance of that group most in need of protection, those from twenty-five to fifty-four, indicates the need for more claims jobs. Also, as the number of working women rises, so will their demand for increased insurance coverage. In addition, new and expanding businesses will require insurance for plants and equipment, as well as employees.

Employment opportunities are expected to be particularly favorable for claims representatives who specialize in complex business insurance such as marine cargo, workers' compensation, and product and pollution liability insurance.

Earnings

In the early 1990s, inside adjusters earned a median annual salary of approximately $19,200; for senior inside adjusters, the median was $21,500. During the same period, outside adjusters received a median of $22,500 per year, with senior outside adjusters getting $29,000. Adjusters are also furnished a company car or reimbursed for business travel.

Claims examiners made a median salary of $29,100 a year in the early 1990s; claims supervisors, $32,300; and claims managers, $41,300. In addition, insurance companies have liberal vacation policies and employee-financed life and retirement programs.

Conditions of work

Presently, claims adjusting is primarily an outside job involving physical exercise and, perhaps, extensive travel. It usually entails evening and weekend work so that claimants can be contacted. An adjuster may be on call twenty-four hours a day.

Inside adjusters work in offices, as do clerks and examiners. They work thirty-five to forty hours a week and occasionally travel. They may work longer during peak claim loads or when quarterly or annual reports are due.

Social and psychological factors

This job can be emotionally taxing as well as trying. It involves heavy contact with people and requires an attention to detail. One must be a sympathetic and empathetic listener. Frequently, a claims representative must deal with draining, difficult, and tragic situations. Decisions have to be made swiftly, even under the above circumstances.

GOE: 07.04.02, 07.05.02; SIC: 63; SOC: 4782, 4783

◇ SOURCES OF ADDITIONAL INFORMATION

Alliance of American Insurers
1501 Woodfield Road, Suite 400 West
Schaumburg, IL 60173

Insurance Information Institute
110 William Street
New York, NY 10038

National Association of Independent Insurance Adjusters
222 West Adams Street
Chicago, IL 60606

National Association of Independent Insurers
2600 River Road
Suite 845
Des Plaines, IL 60018

General information about claims representative careers also is available from many insurance companies.

Information on public insurance adjusting can be obtained from:

National Association of Public Insurance Adjusters
300 Water Street
Suite 400
Baltimore, MD 21202

To find out about life insurance contact:

American Council of Life Insurance
1001 Pennsylvania Avenue, NW
Washington, DC 20004

◇ RELATED ARTICLES

Volume 1: Insurance
Volume 2: Financial institution officers and managers; Underwriters
Volume 3: Insurance agents and brokers, life; Insurance agents and brokers, property and casualty; Insurance policy processing occupations

Interior designers and decorators

Definition

Interior designers and *decorators* evaluate, plan, and design the interior areas of residential, commercial, and industrial structures. They may confer and advise clients on architectural requirements, space planning, and the function and purpose of the environment. They help the client select equipment, fixtures, and they supervise the coordination of color and materials. The designer obtains estimates and costs consistent with the client's budget and supervises the execution and installation of the project. Some designers specialize in a particular aspect of interior design such as furniture, carpeting, or art works. Others specialize in particular environments such as homes, offices, or transportation, including ships, aircraft, and trains.

History

A love for beauty has been associated with much of the world's history. This appreciation has been expressed in many art forms—music, painting, sculpture, and poetry—but one way to bring it into the pattern of everyday life has been through some kind of decoration of the interiors of buildings. The Egyptians decorated their temples and palaces; the Greeks and Romans created their own styles of architecture and interior design. Individuals throughout history have added personal touches of decoration to their homes, but until recently major decorating projects have been the privilege of the wealthy. Artists such as Michelangelo were employed to design and beautify palaces and other buildings, making use of sculpture, paintings, and other wall coverings. Kings sometimes made names for themselves by the decorating trends started in their palaces. Such trends came to include furniture, draperies, and sometimes clothing. Home designs and furniture may have been largely functional as in the early American tradition or extremely ornate as in the style of Louis XIV of France.

As our country has become more prosperous, the profession of interior design has found a place for its services, in planning the interiors of homes, restaurants, hotels, theaters, stores, offices, and other buildings. Another influence in the development of the interior designer's profession has been the growth of modern industry, including large-scale production of furniture, fabrics, carpeting, and other decorating materials.

Nature of the work

The terms "interior designer" and "interior decorator" are sometimes used interchangeably. However, there is an important distinction to be made between the two. Whereas interior designers plan and create the overall design for interior spaces, interior decorators focus on the decorative aspects of the design and furnishing of interiors. In other words, interior design includes interior decoration, but interior decoration does not encompass interior design.

Interior designers perform many different services, depending on type of project and the client's requirements. They may design interiors for residences, hotels, restaurants, schools and universities, office buildings, factories, or clubs. In addition to planning the interiors of new buildings, they may also redesign existing interiors. A job may range from accomplishing a single detail in a private residence to designing and coordinating the entire interior arrangement of a huge building complex.

Interior designers begin by evaluating a project. They must consider the use to which the space will be put as well as the needs, desires, and tastes of the client. Their designs must suit both the project's functional requirements and the client's preferences. Often the designer works closely with the architect in planning the complete layout of rooms and use of space; the designer's plans must fit in with the architect's blueprints and other building requirements. This type of work is usually done in connection with the building or renovation of large buildings. Interior designers may design the furniture and accessories to be used on a project, or they may plan from materials already available. They select and plan the arrangement of furniture, draperies, floor coverings, wallpaper and paint, and other decorations. The designer must consult and respect the tastes of clients and the amount of money they wish to spend. When the designer is working on a private home, the work becomes even more personal. The personalities, way of life, needs, and financial situation of the family must be considered in planning the decoration of the home.

Interior designers make a presentation to their clients that usually includes scaled floor plans, color charts, photographs of furnishings, samples of materials for upholstery, draperies, and wall coverings, and often also includes color renderings or sketches. They will probably also be asked to make a cost estimate of furnishings, materials, labor, transportation, and incidentals required to complete the installation.

Once plans are approved by the client, the interior designer assembles materials—drapery fabrics, upholstery fabrics, new furniture, paint and wallpaper—and supervises the work done with these materials, often acting as agent for the client in contracting the services of craftworkers and specifying custom-made merchandise. The interior designer must be concerned with every item involved in the design. Designers must be familiar with many materials used in interior furnishing. They must know when certain materials are suitable, how these will blend with other materials, how they will wear. They must also be familiar with historical periods influencing design and have a knack for using and combining the best contributions of these designs of the past. Because designers supervise the work done from their plans, they also must know something about the work of painters, carpet layers, carpenters, cabinetmakers, and other craft workers. They must also be able to buy materials and services at reasonable

An interior designer must consider color, fabric, and texture when selecting carpet samples to show a client.

prices, and still produce quality work. A reputation as an interior designer depends on all these things.

Other jobs are also available for the interior designer. Many work in large department and furniture stores, advising customers on plans for decoration and suggesting purchases. Their major task is to sell the store's merchandise through the decorating service. Such interior designers, too, must be familiar with the materials they sell, the trends in decorating, and a knowledge of historical periods in decorating.

Some interior designers are in advertising or journalism related to their special area. Others may find the design of theater, motion picture, and television settings an interesting outlet for their talent and training. A few designers may become teachers or lecturers.

Many designers are fortunate enough to establish their own businesses. For a few this is a consulting service, but most designers sell all or some of the materials used in their work; for example, drapery fabrics, furniture, carpeting, and other accessories. Whether such designers work alone or with assistants depends on the

financial success and workload of the individual business.

Some designers are involved in the renovation of old buildings and research the styles in which the rooms were originally decorated and furnished. This may involve supervising the manufacture of furniture and accessories to be used. The design of interiors of ships and aircraft may also require supervising manufacture.

A great deal of paperwork is involved in interior design, much of it to do with budgets and costs. The designer must figure quantities and obtain estimates, as well as make them. Orders must be placed and deliveries carefully checked. All of this requires an ability to attend to detail in the business aspect of interior design.

Requirements

Although formal training may not always be necessary to find employment in the field of interior design, it is becoming increasingly important and is probably essential for advancement. Most architectural firms, department stores, and design firms accept only professionally trained persons for beginning positions.

Professional schools offer three-year certificates or diplomas in interior design. Colleges and universities award undergraduate degrees in four-year programs and graduate study may also be available. Studies include art history, architectural drawing and drafting, fine arts, furniture design, and the types of materials used such as fibers, wood, metals, and plastics. Knowledge of lighting and electrical equipment, as well as furnishings, art pieces, and antiques is important. Courses in business and management are useful and research methods to keep up with government regulations and safety standards are necessary. In addition, keeping up with product performance and new developments in materials and manufacture is part of the ongoing education of the interior designer.

Individuals with background in architecture or environmental planning may also qualify for employment in interior design as may art historians, and others with qualifications in commercial or industrial design.

With experience, department store designers may advance to department head. Persons who work with furnishings in architectural firms often become more involved in product design and sales with manufacturers. If a designer can build on work done to acquire potential customers and can find the necessary capital, he or she may start a business.

Interior designers need to be able to sense people's needs that may not always be clear. At the same time an integrity of artistic taste and also of current and enduring fashion trends is essential. Artistic talent involves an eye for color, proportion, balance, and detail, and the ability to visualize. Then the designer must be able to render the image clearly to the client and finally carry it out consistently. The designer must also be able to work well with suppliers, craft workers, and others to ensure that the work is done to specifications and to the clients' expectations.

Special requirements

In addition to formal education and on-the-job experience, membership in a professional society is an important achievement that may enhance job opportunities. Membership in the American Society of Interior Design (ASID) or the Institute of Business Designers generally requires at least two years of practical experience after finishing three or four years of formal education and the successful completion of a written and a design-problem examination. The design-problem test takes ten hours and includes lighting and electrical plans as well as space allocation and furnishing arrangement.

Opportunities for experience and exploration

One might first become interested in interior decoration through a high-school course in home economics or possibly because of a talent for art. Certain aptitude tests might help students determine whether their ability is sufficient for success as an interior designer.

The person interested in interior design might also be able to find a part-time or summer job in a department or furniture store in a position where one could learn more about the materials used in interior decorating and perhaps see the store's interior design service in action. Even general selling experience would be valuable.

Related occupations

Individuals drawn to the field of interior design may also find compatible careers as architects, curators, furniture designers, interior decora-

tors, merchandise displayers, set designers and decorators, or space analysts (office planners). Interior designers also are generally related to other workers in commercial art, such as fashion designers, floral designers, illustrators, jewelry designers, memorial designers, photographers, and visual artists. In addition, similar talents are required of automotive designers, drafters, and industrial designers.

Methods of entering

Most of the large department stores and design firms with established reputations hire only trained interior designers. Many schools, however, offer apprenticeship or internship programs in cooperation with professional studios or offices of interior design. These programs make it possible for students to apply their academic training in an actual work environment prior to graduation. After graduating from a two- or three-year training program, the beginning designer must be prepared to spend one to three years as an apprentice or assistant to an experienced interior designer before achieving full professional status. This is the usual method of entering the field of interior design and achieving membership in either of the professional organizations. Sometimes placement in an apprenticeship job can be difficult; if so, experience may be gained as a salesclerk for interior furnishings, as a shopper for matching accessories or fabrics, or even as a receptionist or stockroom assistant. Any job offering practical experience is valuable and may serve as a good stepping-stone to an entry-level designer's job.

Advancement

Once one has entered the profession through an apprenticeship of basic experience, the even longer climb to success begins. As designers gain experience, they may move up into positions of greater responsibility and eventually be promoted to heads of design departments, interior furnishings coordinators, or supervisors of other departments. Others may open their own decorating firms. Consulting is another common area of work for the established designer. (*See* Volume 1: Personal and Consulting Services.) In any case, success in this field depends not only on experience but on talent, personality, and other personal qualifications.

Employment outlook

In the early 1990s, approximately 41,000 people worked as interior designers, primarily in large cities and their suburbs. About 59 percent of the designers were self-employed. Of the balance, 12 percent worked for interior design firms, 10 percent for retail stores, and 7 percent for architectural firms. The rest were employed by large corporations as facilities managers.

Employment opportunities are expected to be very good through the 1990s for designers with formal training and talent. It will be difficult, however, for those lacking this to get ahead in the profession. The service offered by the interior designer is, of course, in many ways a luxury. Thus, in times of prosperity, there is a steady increase in jobs for interior designers; when the economy slows down, however, job opportunities in this field decrease markedly.

Competition is strong in this field, especially in large cities,both for the new jobs and for those created through death, retirement, or other factors. At present, there is a need for industrial interior designers in housing developments, hospital complexes, hotels, and other large building projects. Also, as the building of houses increases, more work will be available for residential designers.

Earnings

In the early 1990s, beginning salaries for graduates of interior design schools ranged from about $12,000 to $18,000 a year. The median salary for experienced designers was around $25,500. The middle 50 percent earned between $16,800 and $34,400 a year, with the top 10 percent making more than $46,500. Interior designers well established in their own localities earn considerably more. Nationally recognized designers may earn $60,000 or more annually.

A wide range of earnings exists among designers in business for themselves. Income depends on such factors as amount of business, reputation, economic level of their clients, and the designer's own knack for running a successful business. Even the earnings of designers employed by firms or stores vary because some receive salaries plus a commission while some receive a commission only. The general practice of interior design firms is to charge fees for advisory services. Although department and furniture stores sometimes charge such fees, they usually rely on profit from sales of materials for their income.

Conditions of work

Working conditions for interior designers are different depending on where they are employed. They may spend the day in a department store office or working with the decorating materials sold by the firm and the clients who purchase them; they might be in a workroom supervising the making of draperies, or consulting with other craftworkers who help them carry out decorating plans.

Whether designers are employed by a firm or operate their own business, a good deal of their time will be spent in the client's home. While more and more offices are using the services of the interior designer, the larger part of the business still lies in the field of home decoration. There the designer works intimately with the customer, planning, selecting, receiving instructions, and sometimes subtly guiding the customer's tastes and choices in order to achieve an atmosphere that is both aesthetic and warm.

Hours for the interior designer can often be irregular, patterned to suit the client. Often deadlines must be met, and if there have been problems and delays on the job, the designer must work feverishly to complete the work on schedule. The more successful a designer becomes, the longer and more irregular are the hours. The beginner works fairly regular hours. The main objective of all the pressure endured by the designer is to please the customer and thus help establish a reputation. Customers are sometimes difficult, too. They may change their minds several times, forcing the designer to revise plans. But the work is interesting and provides a variety of activities.

Social and psychological factors

The person who wishes to be a successful interior designer must expect a long, hard struggle. Competition is keen, and the individual must possess a combination of talent, personality, and business sense to reach the top. Long years of training and experience are necessary before one can expect to make any real advancement, and income is only moderate—even for many experienced interior designers. A beginning designer must take a long-range career view, accept jobs that offer much practical experience, and put up with long hours and difficult clients. There may be many discouragements in trying to please the clients and in bidding for contracts. There are pressures in meeting deadlines and in gaining cooperation from the workers who help to realize the designer's plans. This is why an understanding of people and an ability to work with others is so important to the designer.

There are many satisfactions, too, in this profession. The interior designer has a chance for artistic expression and for the interpretation of the client's tastes. There is the pleasure of working with beautiful things and of seeing the material results of plans and ideas. The work is interesting and stimulates the ambitious designers to do their creative best. Also, once designers have gained experience, they may open their own business and enjoy the independence of being self-employed. If, through one's own talent and personal qualifications, one can establish a reputation, the financial rewards will be good. This is where business experience can be very helpful. The interior designer has to be an artist, a craftworker, a sales person, and often a business administrator. Successful interior designers have to put much hard work and patience into their careers. Anyone considering a career in interior design should be aware of the demands that will be made, should study personal qualifications and artistic talent, and measure the extent of desire for success before entering this competitive field.

GOE: 01.02.03; SIC: 7389; SOC: 322

◇ **SOURCES OF ADDITIONAL INFORMATION**

American Society of Interior Designers
1430 Broadway
New York, NY 10018

Foundation for Interior Design Education Research
60 Monroe Center, NW
Grand Rapids, MI 49503

Institute of Business Designers
341 Merchandise Mart
Chicago, IL 60654

Interior Design Educators Council
14252 Culver Drive
Suite A-311
Irvine, CA 92714

International Society of Interior Designers
433 South Spring Street
10th Floor
Los Angeles, CA 90013

National Council for Interior Design Qualification
118 East 25th Street
New York, NY 10010

◇ **RELATED ARTICLES**

Volume 1: Advertising; Design; Furniture; Textiles
Volume 2: Architects; Commercial artists; Designers
Volume 3: Display workers
Volume 4: Drafting and design technicians

Interpreters

Definition

The *interpreter* translates the spoken passages of a foreign language into another specified language. The job may be designated according to the language interpreted, such as French interpreter or Spanish interpreter. Simultaneous interpreters translate as the speaker continues speaking. Consecutive interpreters follow after the speaker pauses.

History

From the time when people who spoke different languages first wanted to communicate with each other, interpreters have been needed. Until relatively recently, however, those who were able to speak two languages well enough to interpret them did so as a favor or sideline in connection with some other occupation. Interpreting as a profession has arisen only recently with modern high-speed communication and high-level diplomacy.

Many diplomats and high-level government officials have always employed persons who might serve as interpreters should the need arise. For a long time, however, the need for an interpreter was not so sufficiently pressing that such persons were required to spend many of their working hours performing this service. The ability to speak more than one language became an asset when the person was applying for a position as embassy attache or secretary. It was not, however, the only talent to be considered by the employing officer. It was, in effect, only an additional reason why this person's qualifications might be reviewed for an occupation.

For many years, diplomacy was practiced largely between two nations at any one time. It was comparatively rare that more than two languages should be spoken at the conference table. The League of Nations was established by the Treaty of Versailles in 1919 and came into being on January 10, 1920. This international agency established a new pattern of communication. For the first time, diplomatic discussions began to be carried out in many different languages, though the "language of diplomacy" was then considered to be French.

Since the early 1920s, multinational conferences of all kinds have become more frequently the established pattern. Trade and educational conferences are now held with participants of many nations in attendance. The United Nations, which took over international diplomacy when the League of Nations was dissolved, has established such a demand for full-time interpreters that the occupation now provides career opportunities for many well-qualified persons. In addition, the European Common Market with headquarters in Brussels, Belgium, provides regular employment for a large number of interpreters.

Nature of the work

There are two systems of interpretation—simultaneous and consecutive. Simultaneous interpretation has been developed since the charter of the United Nations. In part, the invention and development of electronic sound equipment has made it possible. The simultaneous interpreter is able to convert to a second language a spoken sentence that still is being completed in the first language. The simultaneous interpreter may be so skillful that in many cases he or she is able to complete a sentence in the second language at almost the pre-

cise moment that the speaker is finishing the same sentence in the original language. The interpreter is able to comprehend the speaker's intention for the conclusion of the sentence from the way in which it is phrased, and from the context in which it is placed. The interpreter knows, too, something of the speaking habits of the person whose speech is being interpreted and thus is able to anticipate the way in which the sentence will be completed. The interpreter may also make judgments about the intent of the sentence or phrase from the speaker's gestures, facial expressions, and inflections. At the same time, the interpreter must be careful not to summarize, edit, or change what is being said.

All international conference interpreters are simultaneous interpreters. Although this is a difficult skill to master, it is now expected of these responsible language experts. In simultaneous interpretation, the interpreter must listen, comprehend, convert to a second language, and speak within a matter of seconds.

Consecutive interpretation, which is traditional, is now considered too slow a method for the hurried pace of modern diplomacy. The consecutive interpreter waits until the speaker has paused and then converts to the second language what the speaker has said to that point. The speaker must then wait until the interpreter has finished to start the next sentence. Because in consecutive interpretation every sentence is repeated, this method takes twice as long as does simultaneous interpretation.

Interpreters are placed in a position to see and hear clearly all that is going on. In formal situations, such as those at the United Nations and other international conferences, interpreters are often assigned to a glass-enclosed booth. As speakers talk into a microphone, sound is transmitted to the interpreter's booth. Interpreters usually wear headphones that relay the speaker's voice, and interpreters in turn speak into a microphone. Interpreters observe speakers closely, so as to note not only their words but also their gestures and expressions.

Each delegate is seated behind a small electronic panel that contains buttons or dials. Simply by manipulating the controls, the delegate can tune in the voice of the interpreter who is speaking in the most familiar language.

Because of the difficulty of the job and the nervous tension which it produces, interpreters usually work in pairs. Two will be assigned to each booth and alternate in thirty-minute shifts.

Many interpreters work in situations other than formal diplomatic meetings. Some serve "on call" to travel with visitors from foreign countries who are touring this country. Usually, they employ consecutive interpretation. Their job is to make sure that the visitors are understood wherever they go, and to be sure that the visitors understand what is said to them. Such interpreters may be scheduled to travel to any place in this country with such groups.

Other interpreters may be asked to accompany a group of United States citizens on official tours abroad. On such assignments, they may be sent to any foreign country and may be away from the United States for long periods of time.

Still another assignment for interpreters is with embassies and consulates abroad. As in previous years, however, the interpreter may also be given other responsibilities to carry out in addition to his or her work with languages.

Interpreters also work on short-term assignments. Foreign visitors do not always tour. Services of an interpreter may be required for only brief intervals such as a single interview with representatives of the press or for an exchange of ideas with persons whose opinions may be of interest to the visitors.

Although most interpreters work either for a governmental agency or for an international agency, some are employed by private firms. Large import-export companies often have interpreters on their payrolls, though the interpreters may also perform other duties for the firm. Large banks, companies that have overseas branches, organizations and associations that have international affiliates, and large communications and transportation firms often employ both interpreters and translators, with a *translator director* to direct and coordinate their activities.

Translators work with written language in the same way that interpreters deal with the spoken word. They read and translate into another language such things as novels, plays, essays, nonfiction and technical works, legal documents, records and reports, speeches, and other written material. Translators generally follow a certain set of procedures in their work. They begin by reading the text and making notes on what they do not understand. Then they look up words and terms in specialized dictionaries and glossaries to clarify the meaning of questionable passages. They may also do additional reading on the subject to arrive at a better understanding of it. Next they write a rough draft and then a final draft in the target language.

Another type of interpreter is one who provides communication between persons who cannot hear and those who can. *Deaf interpreters* translate spoken material into a language that can be understood by the deaf. This may be

Delegates at a United Nations conference on the Peaceful Uses of Outer Space listen to interpreters translate speeches into one of six official languages.

done in either of two ways. *Sign language interpreters* translate a speaker's words into American Sign Language (ASL), using their hands and fingers, and then repeat aloud the deaf person's signed response to the speaker. *Oral interpreters* carefully mouth words without voicing them aloud for the benefit of deaf persons who can speech-read. Sign language interpreters usually combine their hand finger gestures with such clearly defined lip movements.

Requirements

Because interpreting is a new professional field, no formal requirements for education or training have been drawn up, though preferences have been stated by employers. Prospective employers are as much concerned with the general cultural background of the interpreter as they are with comprehension of the required languages. Because of the necessity for the interpreter to be proficient in grammar, to have an excellent vocabulary in all of the languages spoken, and to have sound knowledge in a wide variety of subjects, most employers require college degrees. In Europe there are academic programs for the training of interpreters. Although some of these programs are as long as the traditional college preparation, not all of the training institutions grant degrees. The University of Geneva's School of Interpreters (Ecole d'Interpretes) is an example of this kind

333

of program. A diploma from this institution is greatly treasured by prospective interpreters.

Scientific and professional interpreters are thought to be best qualified if they have achieved college and graduate degrees in the field in which they are to interpret. Many scientific disciplines employ such highly technical language that it would be difficult for someone who is not an expert in the field to comprehend the meaning of the terminology well enough to be able to convert it to another language. Scientific interpretation is a high-level specialty.

Interpreters for the U.S. Department of State do have test requirements for their translators and interpreters. Three exams are offered: the non-professional escort interpreter; lower level professional; and higher level professional interpreter. The exams are pass/fail. The requirements for application are several years of foreign language practice, advanced education in the language (preferably abroad), and fluency in vocabulary for a very broad range of subjects. It is extremely difficult to pass the exam with only an undergraduate degree and a year abroad for the study of the foreign language. Applications for testing may be requested from the Department of State address at the end of this article.

Interpreters should be able to speak at least two languages fluently. They should speak without accent in each language, and should know the languages so well that they do not need to consult dictionaries to find the particular meaning of an unusual word in the other language. Most authorities advise that the prospective interpreter read daily newspapers in the languages in which they work to keep current both in developments and in usage. Men and women whose parents were born in another country and who spoke a language other than English in their homes are often well qualified to become interpreters.

In addition to language skills, interpreters should acquire effective techniques in public speaking. They should pay special attention to diction and should work on the quality of their voice to assure that it is pleasant.

High-school students interested in a career as an interpreter should enroll in a college preparatory course. They should be especially interested in English courses, because they likely will be translating another language into English. A thorough knowledge of one's own language is a good basis for building an understanding of another language. If students are interested in becoming proficient in one or more of the Romance languages, they would do well to take basic courses in Latin. They should devote as much time as possible to the study of one modern foreign language, but should not neglect such studies as geography, economics, world history, and political science.

Many hundreds of colleges and universities in the United States offer bachelor's degrees in languages. In addition, the Georgetown University School of Languages and Linguistics offers a one- or two-year program of study in interpretation and translation. Graduate degrees in interpretation and translation may be earned at the University of California at Santa Barbara, the University of Puerto Rico, and the Monterey Institute of International Studies.

Special requirements

One of the unique requirements for prospective interpreters is the experience of having traveled or lived in foreign countries. Students who may have an opportunity to attend school or college abroad should take the opportunity if they hope to become interpreters.

Anyone who contemplates a career as an interpreter should evaluate his or her personal assets. An individual should be poised, calm, and may possess the temperament that is necessary for a job as an interpreter. The student who enjoys reading and studying and who looks forward to spending life learning as much as possible in a wide cultural background will probably be a good candidate for a career in languages. Above all, the linguist must love languages and have a talent for them. He or she must enjoy exploring the meanings of words, word history, and the complexities of sentence structure. He or she must also think of language as the expression of a people, or a nation, or region, and find keys to understanding national and individual personality in the ways in which language is formed and expressed.

Although interpreters need not be certified to obtain a job, employers often show preference to certified applicants. Court interpreters who successfully pass a very strict written test may earn certification from the Administrative Office of the U.S. Courts, Washington, DC 20544. (As of 1990, these tests were being given only for Spanish-language interpreters.) Deaf interpreters who pass an examination may qualify for either comprehensive or legal certification by the Registry of Interpreters for the Deaf (RID). Certain translators of foreign languages may be granted accreditation by the American Translators Association upon successful completion of that organization's required exams.

Opportunities for experience and exploration

High-school students who have an opportunity to visit the United Nations to watch the proceedings may be able to gain some idea of the techniques and responsibilities of the job of the interpreter. Occasionally, an international conference session is televised, and the work of the interpreters may be observed by the viewing public. The student must recognize the fact that interpreters who work in these important conferences are in the top positions of the vocation. Not everyone may aspire to such responsible jobs. The work of most interpreters is far less spectacular, but not necessarily less interesting.

A young person who feels that his or her language skills are adequate for the job of interpreter should try to find an opportunity to travel in the country in which the second language is spoken. If he or she can converse easily and without accent in that language, and can interpret to others in the party who may not understand the language well, the young person may be encouraged to consider entering the occupation of interpreter.

Related occupations

Persons with a facility for languages and the proper credentials may also consider other occupations in fields where such knowledge is considered an asset. These occupations include hotel workers, import-export workers, information clerks, librarians, museum guides, receptionists, sales clerks or sales representatives, teachers or tutors, tour guides, or travel agents.

Methods of entering

Those who consider themselves to be qualified for the responsible job of interpreter may apply directly to the firm, agency, or organization for which they may wish to work. Even though the vocation of interpreting is growing and the need for qualified interpreters is increasing steadily, top jobs are still hard to obtain and competition for them is keen. The prospective interpreter may be wise to develop supplemental skills that can be used while perfecting interpreting techniques and waiting for an opportunity to demonstrate competency in this area. Such organizations as the United Nations employ secretaries who know two or more languages and who can take shorthand and transcribe notes in each of them. The United Nations also has a need for tour guides who speak more than one language well. Although secretarial and tour guide jobs may seem to have less prestige than the job of conference interpreter, such positions may constitute initial steps toward a worthwhile career goal.

Advancement

Competency in language determines the speed of advancement for interpreters. Job opportunities and promotions into positions of responsibility are plentiful for those who have acquired great proficiency in languages. However, an interpreter can never feel that his or her skills are adequate. This is a career that takes constant work and study. Persons who are successful recognize this fact and maintain an interest in keeping abreast of current happenings in the countries in which their languages are spoken. Although many persons do not realize it, language changes constantly. Names for new inventions, machines, or processes are constantly being added to a language. Those who do not keep up with language changes will find that their communication skills have become outdated and they will sound stilted and old-fashioned.

Employment outlook

Employment opportunities for interpreters and translators are scarce and likely to remain so. In the early 1990s, for example, it was estimated that no more than 400 simultaneous interpreters were employed in the three main markets (the federal government, international organizations, and organizations that work internationally, such as the Rotary Club). For the rest of the decade, most job openings that occur will probably be to replace personnel who transfer to other work, retire, or otherwise leave the field. However, these vacancies will quickly be filled by competent, experienced workers. In addition, the large proportion of interpreters who work on a free-lance basis may face a continuing struggle to find work. In view of this outlook, beginning interpreters and translators can expect to face considerable difficulty finding jobs, whether full-time or free-lance.

Interpreters are employed by the United Nations, the World Bank, the Organization of American States, the Inter-American Development Bank, and the U.S. Departments of State,

Labor, and Agriculture. They also work for agencies such as the Agency for International Development and organizers of international, scientific, medical, and social congresses. In private industry, they are employed by business firms, shipping companies, airlines, and banks.

Translators work for many of the same organizations. In addition, they are employed by the Bureau of Census, the Central Intelligence Agency, the Defense Intelligence Agency, the Library of Congress, and the armed forces. In private industry, employers also include publishing houses, commercial translation firms, law offices, travel agencies, hotels, newspapers, radio and TV networks, import-export companies, and manufacturers. Foundations such as the Red Cross, the YMCA, and the Ford Foundation also hire some translators.

The employment outlook for deaf interpreters is good because of increased efforts on the part of government and private agencies to provide education and employment for persons with disabilities. There is a demand for deaf interpreters in many fields. Possible employers include public health agencies, employment agencies, hearing and speech clinics, hospitals, rehabilitation centers, public schools, trade and technical schools, colleges and universities, business and industry, government agencies, theaters, television stations, churches and religious agencies, law enforcement agencies, and the courts.

Earnings

Top-ranking conference interpreters can have an average annual income of more than $55,000 a year. In the early 1990s, senior interpreters working for the federal government had starting salaries of about $38,000 a year. Free-lance conference interpreters were paid from $280 (State Department) to $330 (private sector) a day; and State Department escort interpreters, from $90 to $115 a day. Federally certified court interpreters (as well as qualified court interpreters in languages other than Spanish) were paid $210 per day, $110 for half days. Rates paid by state courts vary widely but are generally much lower. Interpreters who free lance cannot expect to work regularly. To earn top salaries, interpreters must be employed by an agency, association, or firm on a regular basis.

Earnings are generally lower in private industry than in government, whereas the United Nations and other international agencies pay higher rates than the U.S. government.

The earnings of full-time deaf interpreters are dependent on education, experience, and qualifications. Salaries may range from $8,000 to $15,000 or more per year. In the early 1990s, free-lance interpreters were paid from $10 to $25 an hour, depending on their skills and the demands of the job. The pay was generally higher for certified individuals.

Conditions of work

Interpreters work under a wide variety of circumstances and conditions. Conference interpreters probably have the most adequate physical facilities in which to work. Their glass-enclosed booths are well lighted and temperature controlled. They often are provided with lounges to which they may go when not actively engaged in their work. Buildings in which international conferences are held are usually attractive and comfortable.

Interpreters who work in escort service are often required to travel for long periods of time. Their day begins and ends with that of the group or person for whom they are interpreting. They will follow the schedule of their group, and will attend the same meetings, eat at the same places, and travel through the same factories or farms as do the persons with whom they are working. A free-lance interpreter may work out of one city or may sign up for travel assignments and may be assigned anywhere in the world as needed.

Interpreters who work with international banking firms or with international courts may also undergo considerable nervous strain and fatigue. The knowledge that a great deal depends upon their absolute accuracy in interpretation is in itself tension-producing.

Social and psychological factors

The ethical code of interpreters is a rigid one. They must hold private proceedings in strict confidence. If the session in which they are interpreting is a secret one, they must give no hint of its content to anyone. Upon occasion, they may be subject to pressures to reveal the nature of decisions reached. Such pressures could possibly pose psychological problems.

The ethics of interpreting also demand that interpreters shall not distort the meaning of the sentences that are spoken by the conference participants. No matter how much they may agree or disagree with the speaker, they must be objective in the way in which they interpret what has been said. The interpreter should be as unobtrusive as possible in any proceedings he or she attends.

GOE: 01.03.02, 11.08.04; SIC: 7389; SOC: 329

◇ **SOURCES OF ADDITIONAL INFORMATION**

American Association of Language Specialists
1000 Connecticut Avenue, NW, Suite 9
Washington, DC 20036

American Society of Interpreters
PO Box 9603
Washington, DC 20016

American Translators Association
109 Croton Avenue
Ossining, NY 10562

Georgetown University
School of Languages and Linguistics
Division of Interpretation and Translation
Washington, DC 20057

Office of Language Services
Interpreting Division
Room 2212
U.S. Department of State
Washington, DC 20520–2204

Monterey Institute of International Studies
PO Box 1978
Monterey, CA 93940

Secretariat Recruitment Service
United Nations
New York, NY 10017

Persons interested in a career as deaf interpreter may request information from the following:

Alexander Graham Bell Association for the Deaf
3417 Volta Place, NW
Washington, DC 20007

Gallaudet University
Department of Linguistics and Interpreting
800 Florida Avenue, NE
Washington, DC 20002

The Registry of Interpreters for the Deaf
51 Monroe Street, Suite 1107
Rockville, MD 20850

◇ **RELATED ARTICLES**

Volume 1: Civil Service; Foreign Service; Foreign Trade
Volume 2: Foreign Service officers; Linguists

Kinesiotherapists

Definition

Kinesiotherapists are health care workers who plan and conduct exercise programs to help their patients develop or maintain endurance, strength, mobility, and coordination. Many of their clients are people who have disabilities. But they also work with patients who are recovering from injuries or illness and need help to keep their muscle tone during long periods of inactivity. The word kinesio is derived from the Greek work *kinesis*, meaning motion. Kinesiotherapy literally means motion therapy.

History

Kinesiology is a study that looks at the way the principles of mechanics and anatomy affect human movement. The practice of kinesiotherapy developed during World War II, when physicians in military hospitals saw that appropriate exercise could help wounded patients heal faster and with better results, particularly for injuries to the limbs.

By 1946 Veterans Administration hospitals were using prescribed exercise programs in rehabilitation treatment. Before long other hospitals and clinics recognized the benefits of kinesiotherapy and instituted similar programs.

Within a few years the new therapy was an important part of many treatment programs, including programs for chronically disabled patients.

Nature of the work

Kinesiotherapists work with a wide range of people, both individually and in groups. Their patients may be disabled children or adults, geriatric patients, psychiatric patients, the developmentally disabled, or amputees. Some may have had heart attacks, strokes, or spinal injuries. Others may be affected by such conditions as arthritis, impaired circulation, or cerebral palsy.

These professionals work to help their clients be more self-reliant, enjoy leisure activities, and even adapt to new ways of working. Giving their patients constant encouragement and support is an important part of their work.

Kinesiotherapists' responsibilities may include teaching patients to use artificial limbs or walk with canes, crutches, or braces. They may help visually impaired people learn how to move around without help or teach patients who cannot walk how to drive cars with hand controls. For mentally ill people, therapists may develop activities that help them release tension or teach them how to cooperate with others.

The work is physically demanding. Therapists work with such equipment as weights, pulleys, bikes, and rowing machines. They demonstrate exercises so their patients can learn to do them and also may teach members of their patients' families to help the patients exercise. When patients are very weak or have limited mobility, therapists may help them exercise by lifting them or moving their limbs.

Kinesiotherapists work as members of medical teams. Physicians give them prescriptions that describe the kind of exercise their patients should have, and then the therapists develop programs to meet the needs of specific patients. Other members of the medical team may include nurses, psychologists, social workers, and vocational counselors.

Kinesiotherapists write reports on their clients' progress to provide necessary information for other members of the medical team. These reports, which describe the results of the exercises used in the patients' treatment, may also provide useful information for researchers.

These therapists do not do the same work as physical therapists, orthotists, or prosthetists. Physical therapists test and measure the functions of the musculoskeletal, neurological, pulmonary, and cardiovascular systems and treat the problems that occur in these systems. Orthotists are concerned with supporting and bracing weak or ineffective joints and muscles, and prosthetists are concerned with replacing missing body parts with artificial devices.

Requirements

High-school students interested in this field should prepare for their college studies by taking courses in biology, mathematics, physics, health, and social science. College students must earn bachelor's degrees in four-year, approved programs at accredited schools. They major in physical education and have kinesiotherapy as a specialty. Their programs include education, clinical studies, biological sciences, and behavioral sciences. In the early 1990s, fifteen colleges and universities offered the necessary programs.

After graduation, the students go on to a clinical internship, which consists of 1,000 hours of training at an approved health facility under the supervision of certified kinesiotherapists.

Kinesiotherapists must have maturity and objectivity, and should be able to work well with patients and with other staff members. They must have good communication skills to explain the exercises so that patients can understand their instructions.

Therapists need stamina to demonstrate the exercises and help patients do them. They need patience because exercise programs are repetitive and are carried out over long periods. And a good sense of humor can help keep up their patients' morale.

These professionals also must know how to plan and carry out their programs, and they must stay current on new developments in their field.

Special requirements

Although certification is not mandatory for every job, it is desirable. Certification requires a bachelor's degree in the specified accredited courses, 1,000 hours of clinical practice, and successful completion of an examination administered by the American Kinesiotherapy Board. To take the examination, applicants must be members of the American Kinesiotherapy Association.

After meeting all these requirements, candidates become nationally certified kinesiotherapists. And because they have earned undergraduate degrees in physical education, they also may become state-certified physical education teachers.

Opportunities for experience and exploration

High-school students who are interested in this work can get experience in several ways. They can take courses in physical exercise and in planning and carrying out exercise programs, such as classes offered in scouting and by such organizations as the YMCA and YWCA.

Opportunities for volunteer, part-time, or summer work may be available at facilities that have kinesiotherapy programs, such as hospitals, clinics, nursing homes, and summer camps for disabled children. Health and exercise clubs also may have summer work or part-time jobs. In addition, students may be able to visit kinesiotherapy departments at health-care centers to talk with staff members and see how they work.

Related occupations

Students interested in kinesiotherapy also may wish to consider related work. For example, other therapy workers include physical therapists, occupational therapists, recreational therapists, art therapists, and music therapists.

They also may wish to consider work as psychiatric aides, nurses, orthotists, prosthetists, special education teachers, physical education teachers, athletic trainers, or team physicians. (*See also* Volume 1: Health Care.)

Methods of entering

The American Kinesiotherapy Association maintains an employment service for certified kinesiotherapists, and most colleges offer their graduates placement assistance. Therapists also may apply at health facilities that have kinesiotherapy programs, including private and state hospitals, Department of Veterans Affairs hospitals, clinics, and rehabilitation centers.

A kinesiotherapist conducts an exercise class for patients who have suffered from back strain. The exercises are designed to stretch muscles and instill balance coordination.

Advancement

Kinesiotherapists usually start as staff therapists at health care facilities. After several years of work they may become supervisors or department heads. Some set up their own businesses as consultants. With advanced training, experienced kinesiotherapists may go on to executive positions at health care centers, clinics, colleges, and related facilities.

Employment outlook

The employment outlook for kinesiotherapists is expected to be good through the early 1990s. The demand for their services is growing because of the increasing emphasis on services for disabled and retarded persons, patients with specific disorders, and the growing number of older adults. Some medical workers also handle patients with chronic pain by using physical rehabilitation and retraining.

The importance of outpatient care is expected to increase. More opportunities for part-time workers also are expected. In addition, job openings are expected to occur as many of the early kinesiotherapists reach retirement age and other workers change jobs or leave for other reasons.

Earnings

Salary levels depend on the location, the employer, and the therapist's experience. Starting salaries are about $16,000 to $18,000 a year. Experienced staff members earn up to $30,000, and therapists in administrative positions make about $22,000 to $35,000.

Benefits vary, but they often include paid vacations, health insurance, and pension plans.

Conditions of work

Kinesiotherapists who work in such facilities as hospitals and clinics usually work a forty-hour week. Health care facilities must meet health codes; therefore, they are usually clean and bright. Most private and federal institutions are in modern buildings.

The number of patients the therapist works with, both individually and in groups, usually depends on the size of the facility. Therapists may see their patients in hospitals and other health centers, or they may visit patients in their own homes. Their clients may be confined to beds, chairs, or wheelchairs. Exercises are often performed in pools or on ramps, stairways, or exercise tables.

Social and psychological factors

Because they are medical professionals, kinesiotherapists usually can expect recognition and respect. However, they must be prepared to meet the physical and emotional demands of their work.

Therapists may feel discouraged when their patients make little progress or have severe limitations. To counteract this tendency, they must learn to be objective. The real satisfaction of this occupation comes from seeing their patients improve and lead fuller lives.

GOE: 10.02.02; SIC: 8069; SOC: 289

◇ **SOURCES OF ADDITIONAL INFORMATION**

American Medical Association
535 North Dearborn Street
Chicago, IL 60610

American Kinesiotherapy Association
259-08 148th Road
Rosedale, NY 11422

American Physical Therapy Association
1111 North Fairfax Street
Alexandria, VA 22314

American Society of Allied Health Professionals
1101 Connecticut Avenue, NW, Suite 700
Washington, DC 20036

Health Occupation Students of America
4108 Amon Carter Boulevard, Suite 202
Fort Worth, TX 76115

National Rehabilitation Association
633 South Washington Street
Alexandria, VA 22314

◇ **RELATED ARTICLES**

Volume I: Education; Health Care; Social Services
Volume 2: Medical technologists; Occupational therapists; Physical therapists; Physicians; Physician assistants; Prosthetists and orthotists; Recreational therapists; Registered nurses; Rehabilitation counselors; Teachers, kindergarten and elementary school; Teachers, secondary school; Therapists, miscellaneous
Volume 3: Homemaker-home health aides; Medical assistants; Nursing and psychiatric aides
Volume 4: Home health technicians; Orthotic and prosthetic technicians; Physical therapist assistants; Psychiatric technicians

Labor union business agents

Definition

Labor union business representatives or *agents* manage the daily business matters of labor unions and act as liaisons between the union and management during contract negotiations.

History

The idea of workers or craftworkers banding together for their mutual benefit has existed for centuries. In the Middle Ages, groups such as blacksmiths and carpenters organized themselves into guilds, which established product and wage standards, set requirements for entering the trade, and erected barriers to outside competition. The first guilds in the United States were organized around the time of the Revolutionary War.

Unions were first organized, both in England and the United States, by workers in response to the Industrial Revolution of the nineteenth century. In 1886, the group that was to become one of the nation's most powerful unions—the American Federation of Labor and Congress of Industrial Organizations (AFL-CIO)—was founded. Through collective bargaining tactics, the AFL was able to get higher wages, shorter hours, workers' compensation and child labor laws. The beginning of this century saw huge growth in union membership, which jumped from less than 800,000 in 1900 to more than 5 million by 1920. Unionism got a further boost from such New Deal federal legislation as the Wagner Act in 1935, which established the National Labor Relations Board.

There are essentially two types of unions: the craft union, whose members are all skilled in a certain craft such as carpentry or electrical work; and the industrial union, whose members work in the various jobs of a certain industry such as automobiles or steel manufacturing. A company that hires only union members is called a "closed shop," while a union shop is one that requires newly hired workers to join a union after a certain time period. In the 1970s some twenty states eliminated the closed shop by passing "right to work" laws. The economic recession in the early 1980s caused a weakening of many unions' power, as employers in financially troubled industries asked unions for contract concessions in order to save the jobs of existing

employees. Today, approximately 200 unions across the country can boast a collective membership of more than 25 million workers.

Nature of the work

Union business agents act as representatives for the working members of the union, who are often called the "rank and file." Agents are usually elected by those members in a democratic fashion, although sometimes they are appointed by the union's elected officers or executive board. A union agent normally represents a certain number of workers. In an industrial union, an agent could speak for workers in several small plants or a single large plant. In a craft union, an agent will represent a single trade or group of craftworkers.

Unions are structured in many ways like corporations and government groups. In the same way that a company will follow the procedures described in its articles of constitution to conduct meetings and elect its board of directors, a union follows the rules set down by its own constitution and democratically elects its leaders and representatives. Union leaders must be responsive to the wills of their union members, or they may be overruled in union meetings or defeated in their next bid for re-election. In industrial unions, the local unions are directed by a central union, which is led by a regional director and is part of a larger national or international union. Craft unions are organized somewhat differently. Each craft is represented by a different business agent, and several of these agents work on the staff of a district council. These district councils are like an organization of unions, each governed independently of the others and banding together for bargaining strength.

One of the most important aspects of a union business agent's job is his or her role as a liaison, or "go-between," for workers and employers. This role becomes most apparent at the times when the union and its employers need to negotiate a new contract. The business agent needs to know what the members of the union want while talking with management about wages, benefits, pensions, working conditions, layoffs, worker's compensation, and other issues. The agent will explain the union's position to management during pre-bargaining talks. During negotiations, the agent will keep

A labor union business agent represents the labor force during contract negotiations with a company's upper management.

the rank and file informed of the progress of contract talks, advising them of management's position. The business agent needs to be able to drive a hard bargain with employers yet, at the same time, be aware of the realities of the employers' position so that a contract that everyone agrees to can be written. If a contract agreement cannot be reached, the business agent may have to help organize a general strike, which can hurt both labor and management.

At other times, the business agent has many responsibilities to make certain that the union is serving its members properly. The agent often handles grievances expressed by union members, and, if necessary, will work with people in the company to solve them. It is also the agent's job to make sure that the terms of the union's contract are carried out by the employers. The agent is in constant contact with the union membership through the shop steward, who can be elected by the membership or appointed by the business agent. The public image of the union is also an important concern for the business agent. This involves everything from contacting newspaper reporters and other members of the media to organizing charity drives. The business agent is often in charge of recruiting new members for the union, finding jobs for those members who are out of work, conducting union meetings, and renting meeting halls.

Requirements

To succeed as a union business agent, a person needs to have both relevant job skills and leadership qualities. Agents should have first-hand experience in the trade, industry or profession whose unions they represent, so that they can appreciate the problems and concerns of the

workers. Most business agents join a profession or apprentice a trade, after which they get involved with the union as members and move up through the ranks of leadership. If no union exists at their company, they may organize one.

On a personal level, agents must also possess leadership skills. They must be committed to the cause of the union and to the rights and concerns of the workers. Their role in negotiations requires intelligence, persuasiveness, self-discipline, and patience. They must be able to command the respect of both the employer and the rank and file. A good command of the English language, both written and oral, is essential if an agent is to vocalize the concerns of the workers, understand the terms of union contracts, and persuade the representatives of the company and the union members to accept an agreement. If the union leadership has reached a decision that may be unpopular, the agent will have to explain the reasoning behind it to the rank and file. A high-school diploma is important to a union business agent. Coursework should include English, mathematics, and public speaking. History, political science, and economics are also useful, as are technical courses such as shop and electronics. To gain experience in policy-making and to nurture leadership qualities, students should get involved with the student council, debate society and other clubs in high school.

Special requirements

A college degree can also be very valuable for union business agents. Many colleges now offer curricula in labor and industrial relations. Additional courses that union business agents would find useful include psychology, collective bargaining, labor law, occupational safety and health, economics, and political science. Some unions may offer to reimburse some of the costs of higher education for those people interested in ascending to union leadership. In most cases, business agents will receive less formal training, often on-the-job with more experienced union leaders.

Opportunities for experience and exploration

Students who are interested in becoming business agents should first identify the industry in which they would like to work, whether it is a blue-collar or white-collar industry. After graduation from high school, they should seek an entry-level job in that industry to see whether they enjoy the work and to observe union activity up close. Attending union meetings and talking with stewards and business agents will lend insight into the daily responsibilities of union leadership.

Related occupations

Labor union business agents must be skilled in interpersonal relations and communications. They will often find themselves in complex situations that involve the livelihoods of many workers and their families. Additionally they must constantly consider the positions of both parties in a negotiation. Other occupations that require these skills include top executives and general managers, personnel and labor relations specialists, psychologists, therapists, and management trainees.

Methods of entering

Almost all union business agents first work for a number of years in their respective industry and work their way up from the inside. Each type of industry has its own requirements for joining, such as previous experience, training and apprenticeships. Once in the union, there are usually opportunities to become involved in union matters, serve on committees, and so on. These efforts and dedication to the union may attract the attention of union leadership, who will encourage a person to run for a local union job in the next election. People are usually elected or appointed to the job of shop steward initially. If they prove to be popular and effective in that position, they may be elected to union business agent. The process of electing or selecting representatives varies from union to union, but a union business agent usually serves a term of about three years.

Advancement

A union business agent is in many ways like a politician. In the same ways that a local politician can work his or her way from local to state government and possibly Washington, D.C., a union business agent can move upward in the ranks of union leadership. If a business agent does his or her job well, gains popularity and keeps a high profile, he or she might move up

the ladder and serve as business agents at the council headquarters or regional union offices. An agent might even become an officer in an international union.

Employment outlook

The success of union business agents depends to a great extent on the strength and growth prospects of their particular union and their industry in general. The best opportunities for employment and advancement exist in those industries expected to grow in years to come.

Recent years have seen a shift in the U.S. economy away from manufacturing toward service industries. The U.S. Bureau of Labor Statistics predicts that by the year 2000, nearly four out of five jobs will be in industries that produce or render services. These industries include insurance, banking, legal services, health care, accounting, retailing, data processing, and education. The growth of these industries and the industries that support them will provide the greatest growth in jobs in the upcoming decades, and so may provide the greatest opportunities for unionization and union business agents. Unions already exist for public workers, such as teachers, police and fire fighters. Opportunities for unionization will arise in the field of health care, for workers such as nurses, nursing and medical assistants, technicians, and custodians. Secretaries, salespersons, and data processors may also begin to organize unions.

The manufacturing sector of the economy, which traditionally has been very highly unionized, is expected to lose jobs, because of increasingly efficient technologies and competition from overseas. However, certain areas of opportunity will exist. Increases are expected in certain durable goods industries such as electronic computing equipment, medical supplies, plastics and commercial printing. Construction is the only goods-producing sector of the economy that is expected to show a steady increase in employment in the next decade.

Earnings

The earnings of business agents vary from union to union. Their pay is usually prescribed in the union's bylaws or constitution. Normally agents' wages conform closely to the wages of the other members of the union. Most union business agents earn somewhere between $17,500 and $28,300 a year, although some may earn more. In addition, agents get the same benefits as other union members, such as paid holidays, health insurance and pension plans. Some agents may drive a car owned by the union and have their expenses paid while they travel on union business.

Conditions of work

An agent's dedication to the union often dictates the amount of hours worked every week. Most agents work a forty-hour week, but they may work much longer hours during contract bargaining talks and membership organizing drives. They are also expected to be available twenty-four hours a day to handle emergencies.

Agents generally split their time between office work at council or local headquarters and field work. They spend many hours visiting factories and construction sites, meeting with stewards and listening to the opinions of the rank-and-file members. In these visits, they have to deal with the working conditions of their industry. Agents also travel a great deal, and can be on the road for long periods of time.

Social and psychological factors

Union business agents must be ambitious, compassionate, intelligent, and hard-working. They must be committed to the goals of the union and the best interest of the workers. At the same time, they need to understand the realities of the industry they are in and anticipate the concerns of employers. Because of their roles as liaison between the workers and management and between the workers and the union hierarchy, they can experience a great deal of emotional stress as they listen to the concerns and demands of each side. Negotiation requires a great deal of judgment, persuasive ability, and mental and emotional strength.

To reach an agreement, business agents may have to convince both workers and management to give up some of their demands and agree to others. If an agreement can't be reached, the agent may have to help arrange a strike, a drastic step that may or may not be successful. The job of a union business agent is not easy, but it can be personally rewarding to work for the interests of the union and improve the lives of the union membership.

GOE: None; SIC: Any industry; SOC: None

◇ SOURCES OF ADDITIONAL INFORMATION

American Federation of Labor and Congress of Industrial Organizations (AFL-CIO)
815 Sixteenth Street, NW
Washington, DC 20006

American Federation of Teachers (AFT)
555 New Jersey Avenue, NW
Washington, DC 20001

International Brotherhood of Teamsters, Chauffeurs, Warehousemen and Helpers of America
25 Louisiana Avenue, NW
Washington, DC 20001

International Union, United Automobile, Aerospace and Agricultural Implement Workers of America (UAW)
8000 East Jefferson Avenue
Detroit, MI 48214

United Steelworkers of America
Five Gateway Center
Pittsburgh, PA 15222

U.S. Department of Labor
200 Constitution Avenue, NW
Washington, DC 20210

◇ RELATED ARTICLES

Volume 1: Apparel; Automotives; Baking; Business Administration; Chemicals and Drugs; Civil Service; Construction; Education; Food Processing; Food Service; Health Care; Letter and Package Delivery; Machining and Machinery; Metals; Plastics; Printing; Pulp and Paper; Retailing; Rubber; Textiles; Transportation; Trade Unions
Volume 2: Employment counselors; Personnel and labor relations specialists; Occupational safety and health workers;
Volume 3: Blue-collar worker supervisors

Landscape architects

Definition

Landscape architects plan the arrangement of outdoor areas for people to use, with a special emphasis toward protecting the natural environment. They make design and planning recommendations for new housing communities, commercial centers, parks and plazas, recreation facilities, parkways and highways, and on nature conservation areas.

History

As a profession, landscape architecture has been practiced in the United States for the last one hundred years. The most dramatic growth in this profession, however, has occurred following the environmental movement of the 1960s, when the public respect for protecting our valuable natural resources reached an all-time high. Landscape architects have played a key role in the wise use of our natural resources while providing for the increasing housing and recreation needs of the American public.

In the early part of the twentieth century, landscape architects were employed mainly by the wealthy or by the government on public-works projects. In 1918, an interest in the development of playground facilities originated and at about the same time the idea of the subdivision of large land holdings into lots for sale to individuals or companies was born. These two phases of growth, plus the addition of the automobile to the American scene, opened many new opportunities for landscape architects. The development of recreational areas has become more important as has the development of streets, bypasses, and parkways. Landscape architects are needed in most projects of this nature. Both public and private building has flourished since the end of World War II. Both developers and community planners have tended to draw upon the services of landscape architects more than ever.

Nature of the work

The primary function of landscape architects is to plan and design outdoor spaces that make the best use of the land and at the same time respect the special needs of the natural environment. To do this, they must have the combined talents of the scientist, architect, and the engineer. They concern themselves with the arrangement of and along with the objects included on it, such as land forms, buildings, shrubbery, plants or trees, and open spaces.

They may be involved in a number of different types of projects, including parks or gardens, scenic roads, housing projects, college or high-school campuses, country clubs, cemeteries, or golf courses, and all of these in existence today in some way reflect the skill and talent of landscape architects. They may serve the members of a school board in planning a new elementary or high school, the manufacturer who wishes to develop a factory in a particular suburban location, homeowners hoping to improve the land surrounding their home, a governmental agency developing a master plan for a new military installation, or a city governmental agency planning a new suburban development or an urban renewal project.

Whether or not landscape architects perform all or only a portion of the required services will depend upon the size of their office, as well as the client's wishes and the funds available with which to carry out the project. They normally will begin the project by reviewing carefully the client's desires in regard to ultimate purpose, type of structures needed, and funds available. They will then study the site itself, observing and mapping such features as the slope of the land, existing structures, plants, and trees. They will also consider different views of the site, shady and sunny areas, structure of the soil, and existing utilities. Other special features will also be noted.

The landscape architect will consult with a number of different people, including engineers, architects, city officials, zoning experts, real estate agents and brokers, landscape nursery workers, or others who may be involved in the project, so as to develop a complete understanding of the job. He or she will then develop drawings which will be presented to the client for approval. Some projects will take many months before these drawings are ready to be presented to the client for review.

Upon receiving the approval of the client, the landscape architect will develop working drawings and will outline in detail such things as the method of construction of walks, terraces, or steps. One will also draw up lists of materials to be used in completing the project. After developing the final plans and the mate-

Landscape architects put the finishing touches on the final stages of a neighborhood redevelopment project. Such work requires large open spaces where there is room and sufficient light to draw.

rials list, the landscape architect invites construction companies to submit bids for the job. Depending upon the nature of the project and the contractual agreement, landscape architects may remain on the job and supervise the grading, construction, and planting or they may leave the project once work has begun. If they remain on the job, they will be the clients' representative until such time as the job is completed and clients have approved and accepted it as meeting their specifications. Some landscape architects specialize in such projects as parks and playgrounds, waterfronts, campuses, hotels and resorts, shopping centers, roads, or public housing.

Requirements

An accredited bachelor's or master's degree in landscape architecture is usually the minimum requirement for entry into the field. A number of programs are offered through nonaccredited institutions, but they are normally acceptable only when an individual is unable to attend an accredited institution.

The high-school student preparing to enter a college program in landscape architecture should take courses in English composition and literature; social sciences, including history, government, and sociology or psychology; natural sciences, including biology and possibly chemistry or physics; and mathematics.

Undergraduate and graduate programs in landscape architecture are offered in about forty-five colleges and universities, and some fifty-six of these programs are accredited by the American Society of Landscape Architects, the official accrediting agency for programs in landscape architecture. Requirements for admission to the programs will usually be the same as admission to a liberal arts program, although some may require more high-school mathematics than others and some may ask for a course in mechanical drawing on the high-school level. The college program will normally require from four to five years for completion and will offer a broad training in areas dealing with the social, political, and economic features of our society, as well as specific work in landscape architecture. Work will usually be taken in six basic areas of the profession, including landscape design, landscape construction, plants, architecture, graphic expression (mechanical and freehand drawings), and verbal expression. Work in these areas will usually constitute more than one-half of the curriculum. Work will also be taken in natural sciences, civil engineering, English, social sciences, and mathematics.

The basic intent of landscape architecture programs is to train those entering the profession to apply their knowledge and their appreciation of the various facets of land, water, and plants to the skillful development of the land for its efficient, safe, and pleasant use.

Aspirants to landscape architecture should demonstrate an interest in art and nature and must have a good sense of business, especially if they hope to organize an independent business. Interest in environmental protection, community improvements, and landscape design is crucial to one entering this profession.

Special requirements

In thirty-nine states, there are licensing requirements that must be met by those hoping to practice independently as landscape architects in those states. To qualify for the examination, landscape architects usually must have a degree from an accredited program and two to three years of experience in the field. They must also pass an exam. Most states use the

Uniform National Examination (UNE). Prepared by the Council of Landscape Architectural Registration Boards, this is a nationally recognized exam that tests design, environmental, and business skills required to practice.

Opportunities for experience and exploration

Those interested in learning more about the field can gather information and experience in a number of ways. Some may work for landscape architectural firms during the summer months through an internship program. The more experience an individual can gain prior to graduation from college, the greater will be the opportunities for a better than average job and salary upon entering the field.

Although summer employment is not always feasible, it is usually possible to at least talk with someone engaged in landscape architecture. Information as to the type of work done, the advantages and disadvantages, salary, and recommended landscape architecture programs would all be of help to the individual considering entering the field.

Related occupations

Landscape architects appreciate the environment and enjoy working outdoors. Other occupations that may suit persons with similar interests include arborists, civil engineers, conservation officers, foresters and forestry technicians, geographers, landscape gardeners, nursery managers, ornamental horticulturists, park superintendents, and urban planners.

Methods of entering

Students graduating from landscape architecture programs will usually have a placement service available to them. Although these placement services do not normally, even in accredited institutions, guarantee a position, they can be of great help in making initial contacts. They will also make available to the employer a complete set of the applicant's credentials, including a transcript of college work and any recommendations that may be available. These credentials would normally be released only upon the applicant's approval.

Available positions are posted by the American Society of Landscape Architects and published in the *Landscape Architectural News Digest* and *Landscape Architecture*, the society's journals. Students majoring in landscape architecture are eligible to join the organization prior to graduation from college, and the services of the organization may be of assistance in finding a position. Positions are also advertised in major metropolitan newspapers.

Governmental positions are normally filled through civil service competitive examinations. Information regarding vacancies may be obtained through the local, state, or federal civil service commissions.

Advancement

Those just entering the field will normally begin as junior drafters and will be assigned rather minor jobs, including the tracing of drawings, lettering, and simple drafting work. After two or three years, they may be assigned the responsibilities of a senior drafter and thus become qualified to carry a drawing through all of the stages involved in its completion. Those who demonstrate ability in all phases of work will usually advance to more responsible positions, and may become associates of the firm and develop some specialty within landscape architecture.

The ultimate objective of most landscape architects, however, is to gain the experience necessary to organize and develop their own landscape architectural firm or to work in a senior position within a major practice.

Employment outlook

About 18,000 landscape architects were employed in the United States in the early 1990s, and the outlook for those hoping to enter the field is expected to be very good in the coming years.

The increase in the demand for landscape architects is a result of several major factors, including the growth in new construction, the need to refurbish existing sites, and the increase in city and environmental planning and historic preservation. Nevertheless, most job openings are expected to result from the need to replace experienced workers who transfer to other occupations or leave the field for other reasons.

The need for landscape architecture depends to a great extent on the construction industry. In the event of an economic downturn, when the construction business can be expected to drop off, opportunities for landscape architects will also dwindle. On the other hand, the growing use of computer-aided design is not a cause for concern. This new technology will be used to create more and better designs rather than to reduce the number of landscape architecture jobs.

Earnings

Most recent graduates in this field start work as an assistant or junior landscape architect. In private industry, their starting salaries ranged from $18,000 to $22,000 a year in the early 1990s. With about five years' experience, landscape architects ranged between $25,000 and $50,000 per year, and senior partners in a design firm had annual earnings between $60,000 and $100,000 and more.

Landscape architects in independent practice normally earn higher wages than their salaried counterparts, but their earnings will, of course, vary widely depending upon their success. The average income for all landscape architects tends to be highest in the Pacific states and lowest in the Midwest.

Federal civil service annual starting salaries in the early 1990s were $14,800 to $18,400 a year for graduates with a bachelor's degree and $18,400 to $22,500 a year for those with a master's degree. Experienced landscape architects were paid between $27,700 and $36,000, and those at the top grade level were able to earn more than $60,700 a year. The average annual salary for all landscape architects in the federal government was about $36,600.

Conditions of work

Landscape architects are found in every state in the United States and in small towns and cities as well as heavily populated areas. The majority of them, however, are employed in the more highly populated states.

The majority of practicing landscape architects are in business for themselves or work for other landscape architects or in practice with other architects, engineers, and planners. Others are employed by government agencies concerned with public housing, city planning, or parks and recreational areas, while still others teach in the colleges and universities in which programs in landscape architecture are offered.

Practice conditions will vary. As previously indicated, the landscape architect may spend several days in the field without returning to the office, while at other times, one will spend most of the week or month in the office.

The work is often stimulating and satisfying and is usually varied once the apprenticeship has been completed. Those employed on a salary basis, both in government and for private firms, usually work regular hours. They may also look forward to the possibility of being able to develop and operate their own landscape architecture business at some point in the future.

Practice opportunities often begin with routine drafting and office work related to landscape architectural projects. Later, one becomes more involved with actual project design and development. These responsibilities often require extensive time in the office and meeting with project owners and local planning officials. Professional employment security is often a function of the health of the nation's construction economy; however, those in senior positions are less affected by changes in the economy than those who have had only a few years of experience.

Social and psychological factors

The work of a landscape architect is challenging and there is a feeling of satisfaction in creating better surroundings for people while protecting the natural environment. The work is congenial, and the finished product is something that may be admired by people for years. It is a means of earning a livelihood in a pleasant, enjoyable manner; great satisfaction can be derived in knowing that one's efforts have resulted in a better environment for everyone.

GOE: 05.01.07; SIC: 0781; SOC: 161

◇ SOURCES OF ADDITIONAL INFORMATION

General information and two pamphlets, "Guide to Educational Programs in Landscape Architecture" and "Landscape Architecture Accredited Programs" are available by writing to:

American Society of Landscape Architects
1733 Connecticut Avenue, NW
Washington DC 20009

Associated Landscape Contractors of America
405 North Washington Street
Falls Church, VA 22046

U.S. Department of Agriculture
Forest Service
Washington, DC 20250

U.S. Department of Interior
National Park Service
Washington, DC 20240

◇ **RELATED ARTICLES**

Volume 1: Design; Construction
Volume 2: Architects; Designers; Drafters; Urban and regional planners
Volume 3: Landscapers and grounds managers
Volume 4: Drafting and design technicians; Ornamental horticulture technicians; Park technicians

Lawyers and judges

Definition

Lawyers, also called *attorneys*, are trained professionally to represent the state or a client in the working out of the laws that govern society. *Judges* are public officials who administer the law. They preside over courts, arbitrate disputes, and advise lawyers, juries, parties engaged in lawsuits, and court personnel.

History

The tradition of governing people by laws has been established over centuries. Societies throughout history have built up systems of law that have been studied and drawn upon by later governments. The earliest known law is the Code of Hammurabi, developed about 1900 B.C. by the ruler of the Sumerians. Another early law was the law of Moses, known as the Ten Commandments.

The great orators of ancient Greece and Rome set up schools for young boys to learn by apprenticeship the many skills involved in pleading a law case. To be an eloquent speaker was the greatest advantage. The legal profession has matured since those earlier times; a great deal of training and a thorough knowledge of legal matters are required of the modern lawyer and judge.

Much modern European law was organized and refined by legal experts assembled by Napoleon; their body of law was known as the Code Napoleon. English colonists coming to America brought English common law from which American laws have grown. In areas of the United States that were heavily settled by Spanish colonists, there are traces of Spanish law. But in all cases, the laws of other countries and other times were adapted by lawyers and courts to fit the needs and customs of the American society.

Throughout history lawyers and judges have always been prominent and respected individuals, active in public affairs.

Nature of the work

All lawyers may give legal advice and represent clients in court when necessary. No matter what area they may specialize in, their job is to help clients know their rights under the law and then help them achieve these rights before a judge, jury, government agency, or other legal forum, such as an arbitration panel. The availability of such legal advice is important to everyday citizens, for lawyers are not just involved in murder or robbery cases. Lawyers may represent businesses and individuals. For businesses they handle tax matters, arrange for issuance of stock, handle claims cases, represent the firm in real estate dealings, and in general, advise on all legal matters. For individuals they may be trustees, guardians, or executors; they may draw up wills, advise on income taxes, or on buying and selling a home. Some work solely in the courts; others carry on all business outside of court, such as drawing up

349

A lawyer reviews current bankruptcy laws for a company that is experiencing financial troubles.

wills, mortgages, deeds, contracts, and other legal documents, and handle the background work necessary for court cases, for example, doing research in a law library or at the courthouse to study law and precedent. A number of lawyers work to establish and enforce laws for the federal and state governments, drafting legislation, representing the government in court, or serving as judges.

There are also positions for professors in law schools. Administrators, research workers, and writers are also important to the profession. Administrative positions in business or government may be of a nonlegal nature, but the qualities, background, and experience of a lawyer are often helpful in such positions.

Other individuals with law training may choose not to practice, but follow careers in which their background and knowledge of law is important, for example, tax collectors, credit investigators, FBI agents, insurance adjusters, and probation officers.

Some of the specialized fields for lawyers are as follows:

Maritime lawyers, sometimes referred to as *admiralty lawyers,* specialize in laws regulating commerce and navigation on the high seas and any navigable waters, including inland lakes and rivers. Although there is a general maritime law, it operates in each country according to that country's courts, laws, and customs. Maritime law covers contracts, insurance, property damage, and personal injuries.

Civil lawyers work in a field also known as private law. They handle damage suits and breach-of-contract suits; prepare and draw up deeds, leases, wills, mortgages, and contracts;

and can act as trustee, guardian, or executor of an estate when necessary.

Probate lawyers specialize in planning and settling estates. They draw up wills, deeds of trust, and similar documents for clients who want to plan for the eventual disposition of their assets to designated heirs. Upon a client's death, then, probate lawyers vouch for the validity of the will and represent the executors and administrators of the estate.

Corporation lawyers advise corporations concerning their legal rights, obligations, or privileges. They study constitutions, statutes, previous decisions, ordinances, and decisions of quasi-judicial bodies that are applicable to corporations. They advise corporations as to the advisability of prosecuting or defending a law suit. They act as agent of the corporation in various transactions and seek to keep clients from expensive litigations.

Criminal lawyers specialize in law cases dealing with offenses against society or the state such as theft, murder, or arson. They interview clients and witnesses to ascertain facts in a case, correlate their findings with known cases, and prepare a case to defend a client against the charges made. They conduct a defense at the trial, examining witnesses and summarizing the case with a closing speech to a jury.

District attorneys, also known as *prosecuting attorneys,* represent the city, county, state, or federal government in court proceedings. They gather and analyze evidence and review legal material relevant to a lawsuit. Then they present their case to the grand jury, which decides whether the evidence is sufficient for an indictment. If it is not, the suit is dismissed and there is no trial. If the grand jury decides to indict the accused, however, the case goes to court, where the district attorney appears before the judge and jury to present evidence against the defendant.

Patent lawyers specialize in securing patents for inventors from the U.S. Patent Office and prosecuting or defending suits of patent infringements. They prepare detailed specifications for the patent and may organize a corporation or advise a corporation to commercialize on a patent.

Tax attorneys handle cases resulting from problems of inheritance, income tax, estate tax, franchises, and real estate tax, among other things.

Insurance attorneys advise insurance companies about legal matters pertaining to insurance transactions. They approve the wording of insurance policies, review the legality of claims against the company, and draw up legal documents.

An *international lawyer* specializes in the body of rules that are observed by nations in their relations with one another. Some of these laws have been agreed to in treaties, some have evolved from customs and traditions.

Real estate lawyers handle the conveyance of property, perform such duties as searching into records and deeds to establish titles of property, holding funds for investment, and acting as trustees of property. They draw up legal documents and act as agents in various real estate transactions.

Title attorneys deal with titles, leases, contracts, and other legal documents pertaining to the ownership of land and gas, oil, and mineral rights. They prepare documents to cover the purchase or sale of such property and rights, examine documents to determine ownership, advise organizations about legal requirements in regard to titles, and participate in the trial of lawsuits in connection with titles.

It is important to note that once one is licensed to practice law, one is legally qualified to practice any one or more of these and many other specialties. Some general practitioners handle both criminal and civil matters of all sorts. To become licensed, graduates must be admitted to the bar of that state. *Bar examiners* test the qualifications of applicants. They prepare and administer written exams covering legal subjects, examine candidates orally, and recommend admission of those who meet the prescribed standards.

Lawyers who become judges are either elected or appointed to preside over federal, state, county, or municipal courts. Judges administer court procedures during trials and hearings and establish new rules on questions where standard procedures have not previously been set. They read or listen to claims made by parties involved in civil suits and make decisions based on facts, applicable statutes, and prior court decisions. They examine evidence in criminal cases to see if it will support the charges. Judges listen to the presentation of cases, rule on the admission of evidence and testimony, and settle disputes between attorneys. They instruct juries on their duties and advise them of laws that apply to the case. They sentence defendants found guilty of criminal charges and decide who is responsible in noninjury civil cases. Besides their work in the courtroom, judges also research legal matters, study prior rulings, write opinions, and keep abreast a legislation that may affect their own rulings.

Some judges have other titles such as *magistrate* or justice and are not subject to constitutional and state regulations. Magistrates hear civil cases in which damages do not exceed a prescribed maximum and minor misdemeanor cases that do not involve penitentiary sentences or fines that exceed a certain amount.

Requirements

A high-school diploma, a college degree, and three years of law school are minimum requirements for a law degree. To enter any law school approved by the American Bar Association, a student must satisfactorily complete at least three years and usually four years of college work.

Most law schools do not specify any particular courses for prelaw education. Usually a liberal arts course is most advisable, with courses in English, history, economics, social sciences, logic, and public speaking. The same general requirements would apply to the high-school student considering a career in law. Such a student should plan on a strong college preparatory course; specialized training will come later, while high-school and college education should be devoted to an understanding of society and the way it functions. A college student planning on specialization in a particular area of law, however, might also take courses significantly related to that area. Those interested should write to several law schools to find out any requirements and to see if they will accept credits from the college the student is planning to attend.

In the early 1990s, about 176 law schools in the United States were approved by the American Bar Association; others, many of them night schools, were approved by state authorities only. Most of the approved law schools, however, do have night sessions to accommodate part-time students. Such a course usually takes four years.

Law school training itself consists of required courses such as contracts, criminal law, and property. The second and third years may be devoted to specialized courses of interest to the student. The study of cases and decisions is of basic importance to the law student, who will be required to read and study thousands of these cases. A degree of juris doctor (J.D.) or bachelor of laws (LL.B.) is usually granted upon graduation. Some law students considering specialization, research, or teaching may go on for advanced study. All lawyers will continue studying throughout their careers—the law always changes.

Certain personal characteristics are important too; these include high moral character and indefatigability. A good intellect is required to complete the intensive education program pro-

Lawyers must conduct extensive research in preparation for legal briefs. In large law firms, this task is delegated to the younger lawyers.

or she intends to practice. In a few states, graduates of law schools within the state are excused from these written examinations. Once lawyers have been admitted to the bar in one state, they can practice in another state without taking a written examination if the states have "reciprocity"; however, they will be required to meet certain state standards of good character and legal experience. Federal courts and agencies have their own rules regulating admission to practice. Other requirements vary among the states. For example, a few states will allow a person who has spent several years reading law in a law office, but has no college training or who has a combination of reading and law school experience, to take the state bar examination. Few people now enter law practice in this manner. Two states will accept the study of law by correspondence. Some states require that a newly graduated lawyer serve a period of clerkship in an established law firm before he or she is eligible to take the bar examination.

Almost all judges appointed or elected to any court must be lawyers and members of the bar, usually with years of experience.

Opportunities for experience and exploration

A high-school student can select several ways to learn about the law profession, although he or she may not actively participate in the field until licensed to do so. Students may find it helpful to talk to lawyers about their profession and its demands, observe the lawyer working, attend court sessions. The prospective lawyer can also learn a great deal by reading, and possibly obtaining a summer or part-time job in a law office. The high-school guidance counselor may be able to help students assess their interests and abilities in relation to a law career. The aptitude tests required by law schools will also help the prospective lawyer make a decision. Usually a student with an interest in abstract subjects in school is more likely to find a lawyer's work satisfying.

vided by college and law school. Most law schools require that applicants take the Law School Admission Test. It is important to be able to read intelligently and critically, to be able to express oneself adequately, both in writing and speaking, and to be able to reason logically. These are skills that can be developed effectively, provided one has the fundamental capacity.

The prospective lawyer should also have an understanding of people because much time will be spent in consulting with all kinds of persons. The lawyer's work also requires an ability to work with details.

Related occupations

Legal training is of value to workers in a number of other occupations; for example: arbitrators, corporate executives, credit investigators, FBI agents, hearing examiners, insurance adjusters, journalists, legal assistants, legislative assistants, lobbyists, patent agents, political of-

Special requirements

Every state requires that lawyers be admitted to the bar of that state before they can practice. They require that the applicant graduate from an approved law school and that he or she pass a written examination in the state in which he

fice holders, probation officers, tax collectors, and title examiners.

Methods of entering

As discussed above, the first steps in entering the law profession are graduation from an approved law school and passing a state bar examination. Usually beginning lawyers do not go into solo practice right away. It is often difficult to become established, and additional experience is helpful to the beginning lawyer. Also, most lawyers do not specialize in a particular branch of law without first gaining experience. Beginning lawyers, then, usually work as assistants to experienced lawyers. At first they do mainly research and routine work. After a few years of successful experience, the lawyer may be ready to go out on his or her own. Another choice open to the beginning lawyer is to join an established law firm. Or one may enter into partnership with another lawyer. There are also positions with banks, business corporations, insurance companies, private utilities, and with a number of government agencies.

Advancement

Lawyers with outstanding ability may expect to go a long way in their profession. As we have seen, beginning lawyers generally start as law clerks, but as they prove themselves and develop their abilities many opportunities for advancement will arise. They may be promoted to junior partner in a law firm or establish their own practice. As their number of clients grows, lawyers begin to feel that their practice is established. The lawyer may enter politics and become a judge, mayor, congressman, or other governmental leader. Top positions are available in business, too, for the qualified lawyer. Lawyers working for the federal government advance according to the civil service system.

Employment outlook

About 60 percent of approximately 527,000 practicing lawyers in the United States in the early 1990s were in private practice, either in law firms or alone. Most the rest were employed in government, mostly at the local level. The majority of the lawyers working for the federal government held positions in the Departments of Justice, Treasury, and Defense. Lawyers also held positions as house counsel for public utilities, transportation companies, banks, insurance companies, real estate agencies, manufacturing firms, welfare and religious organizations, and other businesses and nonprofit organizations.

The demand for lawyers is expected to continue growing rapidly through the 1990s, but record numbers of law school graduates have created strong competition for jobs. This competition is predicted to remain keen even though the number of graduates has begun to level off.

The outstanding graduates, especially of the country's best law schools, will have no trouble finding jobs during the next few decades. These graduates, the top ten percent of their classes, will be able to find salaried positions in well-known law firms, on legal staffs of corporations, in government agencies, and in law schools. Lawyers in solo practice will find it hard to earn a living until their practice is fully established. The best opportunities for those wishing to set up private practice exist in small towns or suburbs of large cities, where there is little competition from large law firms, it is easier to obtain clients from among the local people, and the cost of office space is less.

Graduates with lower class standings and from lesser known schools may have difficulty in obtaining the most desirable positions. But other opportunities are available; for example, salaried positions where a knowledge of law is an asset if not a requirement. Banks, insurance companies, real estate firms, government agencies, and other organizations often hire law graduates for administrative, managerial, and business work. Legal positions in the armed forces are also available.

In the long run the need for lawyers is expected to increase. Our society becomes increasingly complex, businesses are expanding, and thus the need for lawyers, particularly specialists, may never be outgrown. At present, openings come from deaths, retirements, and other departures from the field, as well as from economic growth. Salaried positions are found mainly in large cities where most law firms, government agencies, and corporations are established. In the legal profession, as in many other fields, the individual who is well qualified in training, ability, and personality has the best chance of obtaining the most desirable jobs.

The number of judges employed is not likely to change much in the next several years. Judges who retire, leave office, or die will need to be replaced. There may be an increase in judges in cities with large population growth.

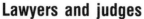

Earnings

Not all lawyers earn extremely high salaries. Incomes generally increase as the lawyer gains experience and becomes known in the field as a capable individual. The beginning lawyer in solo practice may barely make ends meet for the first few years.

In the early 1990s, the starting salary for federal government lawyers was approximately $22,500 to $27,200 per year, depending on qualifications. Average starting salaries for lawyers in business were nearly $31,000.

Experienced lawyers earn salaries that vary widely depending on the type, size, and location of the employers. The average for most experienced lawyers in private industry in the early 1990s was more than $101,000 a year, whereas general attorneys in the federal government received an average of about $46,000. Patent attorneys in the federal government averaged around $55,400.

Judges generally earn less than lawyers, although their incomes overall are good. In the early 1990s, associate judges of the highest state courts had annual salaries ranging from $44,400 to $81,900. Appellate court judges earned from $47,200 to $76,700. General trial court judges averaged from $39,900 to $74,600.

Conditions of work

Offices and courtrooms are usually pleasant surroundings for the lawyer. The lawyer will also spend time in law libraries or record rooms, in the homes and offices of clients, and sometimes in jail cells.

Many lawyers never work in a courtroom. Unless they are directly involved in litigation, they may never perform at a trial.

Judges and lawyers may have evening hours assigned for court appearance. Some courts, such as small claims, family, or surrogate, may have evening hours to provide flexibility to the community. Criminal arraignments may be held at any time of the day or night. Court hours are usually 9:00 to 5:00 with a one hour lunch break, for most lawyers and judges.

There are certain disadvantages to the lawyer's work. Often one has to work long hours, spending evenings and weekends preparing cases and materials, working with clients. In addition to the work, the lawyer must always keep up with the latest developments in the profession. Also, it takes a long time to become a qualified lawyer, and it may be difficult to earn an adequate living until one becomes established if one becomes a solo practitioner.

Social and psychological factors

Lawyers occasionally suffer from the stress of their adversarial role in trials, their dealings with threatening or disturbed individuals and the long hours of preparation. In spite of these disadvantages, the lawyer's career can be extremely satisfying. An attorney is a respected member of the community and often a political leader. The lawyer is responsible for the effective functioning of law in our country's government; it is rewarding to carry out these laws for the sake of clients. Lawyers are professional people, and to the extent that they use their training, skills, and knowledge, they become established as successful lawyers. This establishment brings many personal as well as financial rewards.

GOE: 11.04.02; SIC: 8111; SOC: 211

Legal assistants

Definition

A *paralegal assistant* researches laws, investigates facts, prepares documents, and, in general, does background work for the lawyer. A *legal investigator* helps research and prepare cases relating to the administrative appeals of civil service members.

History

The U.S. legal system has undergone many changes over the past few decades as more and more people are turning to lawyers for help in settling disputes. This increase in litigation has placed greater demands on members of the legal profession. To help meet these demands and to help provide legal services to more people at a lower cost, lawyers have increasingly used paralegals, or legal assistants.

The first legal assistants were given a limited number of routine duties; many started as legal secretaries who were gradually given more responsibilities. Today, however, the work of the legal assistant has grown and expanded, and formal training programs have been established.

Paralegals have taken on much of the routine work that lawyers once did themselves, allowing lawyers to concentrate on the more skilled aspects of providing legal services. The paralegal profession is continuing to grow, and legal assistants are gaining wider acceptance as professionals.

Nature of the work

Legal assistants perform a variety of functions to assist lawyers in preparing cases. Although the lawyer assumes responsibility for the paralegal's work, the paralegal may take on all the duties of the lawyer except for setting fees, appearing in court, accepting cases, and giving legal advice.

Legal assistants spend much of their time in libraries, researching laws and compiling facts to help lawyers prepare cases for trial. After analyzing the laws and facts that have been compiled for a particular client, the legal assistant often writes a report that the lawyer may use to determine how to proceed with the case.

If a case is brought to trial, the paralegal may help prepare legal arguments and draft pleadings to be filed in court. Legal assistants also keep files and correspondence relating to cases.

Not all paralegal work centers around trials. Legal assistants also draft contracts, mortgages, and other documents. They may help with corporate matters, such as shareholder agreements, contracts, and employee benefit plans. In addition, legal assistants may review financial reports.

Some paralegals work for the government. Legal assistants who work for the government may be involved in a number of projects. They may prepare complaints or talk to employers to find out why health or safety standards are not being met. They often analyze legal documents, collect evidence for hearings, and prepare explanatory material on various laws for use by the public.

Other paralegals are involved in community or public work. They may help specific groups, such as poor or elderly members of the community. They may file forms, research laws, and prepare documents. They may represent clients at hearings, although they may not appear in court on behalf of a client.

Many legal assistants work for large law firms, agencies, and corporations and specialize in a particular area of law. Other legal assistants work for smaller firms and have a general knowledge of many areas of law. Most legal assistants have varied duties, and an increasing number are using computers in their work.

Requirements

The requirements for paralegals vary from one employer to another. Some law firms and corporations promote legal secretaries and other clerical workers, gradually training them to become legal assistants over a period of time. Most employers today, however, prefer to hire paralegals who have completed formal training and education programs. These formal programs usually range from one to three years and are offered in a variety of educational settings: four-year colleges and universities, law schools, community and junior colleges, business schools, proprietary schools, and legal assistant associations. The programs have varying admission requirements, but good grades in high school and college are always an asset.

355

This paralegal is taking notes from various law-related publications. The notes will be used to help lawyers prepare for a case.

There are several hundred paralegal programs, about one hundred of which have been approved by the American Bar Association.

Some paralegal programs require a bachelor's degree for admission; others do not require any college. In either case, however, persons with a college degree often have an edge over those who do not have one. High-school students should take a broad range of subjects, including English, social studies, and languages; Spanish may be particularly helpful. Typing may also be helpful but is not necessary. Good communication and research skills are extremely important.

Special requirements

At the present time, paralegals are not required to be licensed or certified. Instead, lawyers often follow guidelines for employing paralegals; these guidelines are designed to protect the public from the practice of law by unqualified persons.

Paralegals may, however, opt to be certified. To do so, they must pass an extensive two-day test conducted by the National Association of Legal Assistants Certifying Board. Paralegals who pass the test may use the title CLA (Certified Legal Assistant) after their names. The exam has been offered since 1976; to date, approximately 2,300 legal assistants have achieved this certification.

Opportunities for experience and exploration

There are several ways a person can explore the possibility of a career as a legal assistant. A person may work part-time as a secretary or in the mailroom of a law firm to get an idea of the nature of the work. Students may join an organization that is affiliated with the legal profession or talk directly with lawyers and paralegals. And persons interested in a career as a legal assistant can write to schools with paralegal programs or to the organizations listed at the end of this article for general information.

Related occupations

Many individuals have an interest in the law and the legal system but are unwilling or unable to undertake the extensive training to become a lawyer. With proper training, some of these persons become paralegals. Others may fulfill their career needs in related fields as, for example, abstractors, claim examiners, compliance and enforcement inspectors, court reporters, law librarians, legal secretaries, occupational safety and health workers, patent agents, police officers, and title examiners.

Methods of entering

Although some law firms promote legal secretaries to paralegal status, most employers prefer to hire individuals who have completed paralegal programs. Those interested in becoming legal assistants should seriously consider attending paralegal school. In addition to providing a solid background in paralegal studies, most schools help graduates find jobs. Even though the job market for paralegals is expected to grow very rapidly over the next ten years, those with the best credentials will get the best jobs.

The American Association for Paralegal Education (AAfPE) is a national organization established in 1981 to promote high standards for paralegal education and, in association with the American Bar Association, to develop an approval process for paralegal education programs. A complete list of member institutions is available from AAfPE headquarters at the address listed at the end of this article.

Advancement

There are no formal paths of advancement for legal assistants; paralegals do not usually become lawyers or judges. There are, however, some possibilities for advancement as large law firms are beginning to establish career programs for legal assistants.

For example, a person may be promoted from a legal assistant to a head legal assistant who supervises others. In addition, a paralegal may specialize in one area of law, such as environmental law, real estate, or patents and trademarks. Many legal assistants also advance their careers by moving from a small law firm to a larger one.

Expert paralegals who specialize in one area of law may go into business for themselves. Rather than work for one law firm, these paralegals often contract their services to many lawyers. Some paralegals with bachelor's degrees may decide to attend law school.

Employment outlook

Employment of legal assistants has grown tremendously since this occupation emerged in the late 1960s. In the early 1990s, there were about 61,000 legal assistants in the United States, most of whom were employed by private law firms.

The employment outlook for these professionals is excellent. Paralegals will represent the fastest-growing profession in the country through the end of the decade, according to a U.S. Department of Labor study, with the number of paralegals expected to more than double.

One reason for the expected growth in the profession is the financial benefits of employing paralegals. The legal assistant, whose duties fall between those of the legal secretary and those of the attorney, helps make the delivery of legal services more cost-effective to clients. With the growing need for legal services among the general population and the increased popularity of prepaid legal plans, there will be a tremendous demand for legal assistants in private law firms. There are also many new areas in which paralegals can work. In the private sector, many will be employed by banks, insurance companies, real estate firms, and corporate legal departments. In the public sector, legal assistants will be needed for community legal service programs, government agencies, consumer organizations, and the courts.

Earnings

The salaries of legal assistants vary. The size of the employing firm, the education and experience of the employee, and the city in which the employee works are some of the factors that determine the annual earnings of the legal assistant. Paralegals who are employed by large law firms generally earn more than those who work for small ones, and legal assistants usually earn more in large metropolitan cities.

In the early 1990s, the annual salary of the beginning paralegal averaged about $17,200. With three to five years' experience, the pay averaged $21,400, and salaries averaging $25,200 were not uncommon for legal assistants who had more than ten years' experience. Top-flight paralegals in really busy offices can earn as much as $40,000 a year; and paralegal supervisors, from $40,000 to $50,000.

The federal government hired beginning legal assistants in the early 1990s at a starting salary of $14,800 or $18,400 a year, depending on their training and other qualifications. The average annual salary of legal assistants in government was about $28,600.

Conditions of work

Legal assistants often work in offices that are pleasant and comfortable. Much of the work is performed in a library and at desks. Most paralegals work a forty-hour week, although long hours are not uncommon when there is pressure to meet a deadline.

Many of the paralegal's duties involve routine tasks. The legal assistant, however, may be given increasingly difficult assignments over time. The legal assistant often works alone, compiling facts and drafting reports for the lawyer.

Paralegals work in a variety of settings. In addition to law firms, legal assistants also work for banks, accounting firms, and government agencies. Some work for groups interested in specific issues, such as ecology and consumer protection.

Social and psychological factors

The legal assistant has an opportunity to help ensure that our country's laws are carried out fairly and effectively; the job demands a person of high morals and ethics. The paralegal is part of a profession that carries a substantial amount of power and prestige.

Because much of the paralegal's work involves researching facts in the legal library, the person must be able to work independently and must have good writing and communication skills. Because much of the work is routine, the paralegal must also have a great deal of patience.

Legal assistants perform a very important service. Their work is of tremendous help to lawyers, and their contributions are recognized by members of the legal profession, adding to the satisfaction gained from this career.

GOE: 11.04.02; SIC: 8111; SOC: 211

◇ SOURCES OF ADDITIONAL INFORMATION

American Bar Association
750 North Lake Shore Drive
Chicago, IL 60611

American Association for Paralegal Education
PO Box 40244
Overland Park, KS 66204

Legal Assistant Management Association
PO Box 40129
Overland Park, KS 66204

National Association of Legal Assistants
1601 South Main Street, Suite 300
Tulsa, OK 74119

National Federation of Paralegal Associations
104 Wilmot Road, Suite 201
Deerfield, IL 60015

National Paralegal Association
10 South Pine Street
PO Box 629
Doylestown, PA 18901

◇ RELATED ARTICLES

Volume 1: Law
Volume 2: Lawyers and judges; Librarians
Volume 3: Court reporters; Secretaries; Stenographers

Librarians

Definition

The *librarian* is one who works in public, academic, or special libraries, where books, magazines, audiovisual materials, and a variety of other informational materials are cataloged and kept for the purpose of study and reference and for loan to patrons. Librarians help people select the materials and find information best suited for their use and are responsible for the selection and purchase of books and other materials that will be added to the library. They may engage in research to aid in special programs for communities, schools, industries, and other organizations. Librarians are responsible for ordering, cataloguing and classifying all the materials to be held by the library. They may specialize in one field of research and study, such as children's books, or they may be generalists.

History

It may be that we take books for granted. A relatively small amount of money will buy a classic in a paperback edition, but for centuries only wealthy people or institutions such as monasteries could obtain books. Until the invention of the printing press, books had to be copied by hand and were rare and very expensive; also, few people, other than the clergy and royalty, knew how to read. The history of libraries dates back to the private collections of such individuals. Later, the printing press made books available to a larger number of people due to increased quantity and decreased price, and a whole new world of communications was gradually opened up to the public.

In 1638, John Harvard left his private collection of books to the Massachusetts Bay Colony's new college, which was later named for him; this collection became the foundation for the first library in the United States. In the eighteenth century, the versatile Benjamin Franklin initiated the idea of a library where books could be borrowed. From this basic idea have grown the thousands of public, private, and special libraries.

In recent years libraries have expanded services and now distribute films, records and compact discs, audio- and videotapes, braille books, and talking books. The federal government gives financial aid for the improvement of school libraries.

University and college libraries support the academic programs of their institutions, but many of the large ones are mostly research libraries. The last fifty or so years, however, have seen the emergence of research libraries not directly connected with educational institutions. Early printed books and manuscripts are the specialty of the Morgan Library in New York. The Library of Congress is an important research center and the Dag Hammarskjold Library at the United Nations is a research center of world affairs. The New York Public Library and the Boston Public Library are outstanding examples of public research libraries.

Nature of the work

The librarian has a number of jobs—some technical, others interpersonal. The professional librarian must select and order all books, periodicals, audiovisual material, and other items for the library; this entails evaluating newly published materials as well as seeking out older ones. Many libraries now have added records, audio- and videotapes, compact discs, films, film strips, slides, maps, art pieces, and photographs to their loan services. The selection and purchase of these is also a responsibility of the librarian. The quality and extent of a library collection, therefore, are considerably influenced by the librarian. To organize and maintain such a program requires skilled business sense, efficiency, and an ability to determine which materials are necessary.

Librarians must also know the community and people that their libraries serve; this is best accomplished by learning the public's reading interests and resource needs. The librarian must be prepared to help readers find materials and help them use resources effectively. The librarian, then, is expected to be thoroughly acquainted with all materials in the library from card and online catalogs to reference books. Librarians may be called upon to review books; prepare bibliographies; give advice to students,

schools, or other organizations on sources of information; organize a children's story hour and summer reading programs; or arrange an exhibit. Librarians serve all kinds of people—young, old, those using the library for pleasure, and those using it for research; they serve community groups and business.

Often librarians may choose to work with a special age group, for example, children, or to work in a particular kind of community, large or small. The librarian in a small library may hold a considerable responsibility to the community. In a large library, the librarian may have only one special function, perhaps in a particular department, such as children's literature, the arts, science, or history.

The technical tasks of the librarian may include ordering, cataloging, and classifying materials according to the Dewey Decimal, Library of Congress, or other system. All new additions to the library must be cataloged by title, author, and subject in either card or computerized catalog files. Labels and card pockets must be placed on the items and they must then be properly shelved. Books and other materials must be kept in good condition or, if necessary, repaired or replaced. Purchasing, maintenance, and evaluation of circulation systems is another technical task of the librarian. Considerable technical knowledge of computer systems may be necessary in deciding upon the extent and scope of the proper circulation for the library. The actual process of circulating books, such as stamping due dates, collecting fines, and tracking down overdue materials, however, is usually handled by nonprofessional library staff such as work study students, part-time employes, library technicians, or others.

There are different types of libraries and specialists in the profession. Some librarians may be entirely devoted to public services while others are concerned with technical matters. The librarian may be employed by a public library; school, college, or university library; or special library. Some librarians work as independent information consultants.

Public library work is probably the best known classification. At the head of a public library system is the *library director*, who sets library policies and plans and administers programs of library services, usually under the guidance of a governing body, such as a board of directors or board of trustees. Library directors have overall responsibility for the operation of a library system. Among their many duties, they coordinate the activities of the *chief librarians*, who supervise branch libraries or individual departments, such as the circulation, general reference, or music department; periodical reading room; or readers' advisory service.

A reference librarian assists a caller who has a question. She can direct the caller to the proper sources of information.

In a large public library a chief librarian would supervise a staff of assistant librarians and division heads, and would administer and coordinate the functions of the library. The work of the library staff would entail all the responsibilities previously discussed. Some librarians who specialize in a single area or type of library are as follows.

Acquisitions librarians choose and buy books and other media for the library. They do not work with the public, but deal with publishers and wholesalers of new books, booksellers of out-of-print books, and distributors of audiovisual materials.

Catalog librarians, with the aid of *classifiers,* classify books and other materials by subject matter, assign classification numbers, and prepare cards to help users find what they are looking for. Many libraries have computerized the acquisitions and cataloging functions, making it possible for the user to retrieve materials faster. Automated libraries no longer have bulky card catalogs, but provide small computer terminals instead.

Reference librarians advise users and help them find information they are seeking in encyclopedias, almanacs, and other reference books. They also have access to special materials that may be filed in areas not open to the public or kept in other libraries but are available on request to those who need the information for research.

Children's librarians help children select books, teach them about the library, and conduct story hours. *Young-adult librarians* perform similar services for junior and senior high-school students. Instead of story hours, however, they plan programs of interest to young adults, such as creative writing workshops, film discussion groups, music concerts, or photography classes. *Adult services librarians* work with the adult age group regardless of reading interest or request. They may help conduct education programs such as community development, creative arts, public affairs, problems of the aging, and home and family.

Community outreach librarians or *bookmobile librarians* bring library services to outlying or to special communities such as nursing homes or inner-city housing projects.

School librarians, also known as *school library media specialists,* are also certified to teach. They work with young people in the school setting, selecting materials useful to students in their classwork, teaching them to use the library effectively, helping them with assignments, and working with teachers on research. School librarians or (in some large schools) specialists known as *audiovisual librarians* select and maintain films, videotapes, slides, prints, records, cassettes, and other nonbook materials and supervise the purchase and maintenance of the equipment needed to use the materials.

College and university librarians serve students, faculty members, and research workers, especially in reference work. They may be called upon to teach the use of the library. Some librarians may be specialists in any of the various subject areas.

Special collections librarians must be experts on the literature in their particular fields. The responsibility of these librarians is to acquire and organize materials in a special field; for example, the *medical librarian* maintains materials of particular interest to physicians and others associated with medicine.

Special library librarians develop and manage libraries or information centers for business and industrial firms, nonprofit corporations, and government agencies. The materials collected usually pertain to subjects of particular interest to the organization. Special librarians also develop services unique to the user group. They often work with a client to narrow and define the search for information and in many cases will anticipate the needs of the parent organization.

Institution librarians plan and direct the library programs for residents and staff of institutions such as hospitals, prisons, and other extended-care facilities. The special needs of the residents may include reading aids such as prism glasses, page turners, or talking books.

Bibliographers usually work in research libraries, compiling lists of books, periodicals, articles, and audiovisual materials on selected topics. They also recommend purchase of new materials in their special fields.

Information scientists, or *technical librarians,* are specialists trained in computer sciences. More and more libraries today are tied into remote computer data bases through their computer terminals, making it unnecessary for a library to have on hand all the materials users may request. Information scientists design systems for storing and retrieving information. They also develop procedures for collecting, organizing, interpreting, and classifying information. (*See also* the article title "Information scientists" elsewhere in this volume.)

Library technicians, also called *library assistants,* assist readers in the library or on the telephone. They provide information on library services, facilities, and rules. They also do cataloging, prepare orders of materials and books, maintain files, work on checkouts, and many other varieties of jobs within specialized areas such as audiovisual or data processing. (*See also* the article title "Library technicians" in Volume 4.)

Requirements

Any student planning a career in library work must be prepared to graduate from high school and college and take a fifth year of specialized study to earn a master's degree in library science (MLS). Usually it is a good idea to enroll in a liberal arts college to get a broad educational background because the librarian should be familiar with numerous subject areas. The next step is enrollment in a graduate school of library science, of which sixty were accredited by the American Library Association in the early 1990s. To be accepted into graduate school, the student must have graduated from an accredited four-year college or university, must have had a good academic record while in college, and must often be able to read at least one foreign language. More than half of the accredited library schools do not require any introductory courses in library science while in college. It would be wise, though, to check graduate school catalogs for specific requirements.

Special library librarians must have a very strong background in the subject in which they wish to work, for example, law librarians or medical librarians. Professional training in library science must also be obtained. Most special librarians have a degree in their subject specialization in addition to their MLS. For work in research libraries, university libraries, or special collections, a doctorate may be required. It is commonly required for the top administrative posts of these types of libraries.

Graduate library schools offer a master's degree in library science. During the graduate year, the student takes courses in reference work, cataloging, classification, library organizations, and administration. Many library schools have work-study programs where students take coursework along with practical experience in a library. Scholarships may be available from state and federal educational funds and from library schools, libraries, and library associations.

Information scientists need education in computer sciences or education in mathematics, computers, and systems analysis.

Personal qualifications are also important. A librarian should have above-average intelligence, be in good health, and, of course, have a special interest in books and an ability to work with details as well as people. The librarian is often expected to take part in community affairs, cooperating in the preparation of exhibits, presenting book reviews, and explaining library use to community organizations. The librarian should be a leader in developing the cultural tastes of the library patrons. An imaginative, resourceful, tactful, patient person is needed. In administrative work, the librarian should have a good sense of business. Library specialists, too, must have particular personal qualifications; for example, the young-adult librarian must have a real liking for teenagers. (For more information *see* Volume 1: Library and Information Science.)

Special requirements

As we have seen, the master's degree in library science is essential. Librarians in special areas must meet other special requirements, such as post-graduate work in a specific field for special collections. The school librarian is required to earn teacher's certification in addition to preparation as a librarian. Public librarians must be certified in most states. Certain other requirements for education and experience have been set up by various state, county, and local governments. The federal government requires completion of a four-year college course, including at least twenty-four hours a week of library science or experience for beginning jobs. Appointment to a higher level on the civil service scale may be obtained by librarians with a year of graduate work.

Opportunities for experience and exploration

There are several ways for a high-school student to explore the field of librarianship. First of all, students will have their own personal experience with the library: reading, doing research for class projects, or just browsing. This experience might arouse an interest in library work, a desire to find out what goes on behind the scenes. Once interested in library work, a student might be able to work as an assistant in the school library or find part-time work in a public library. Some schools may have library clubs to learn about library work.

Related occupations

Persons attracted to the work of the librarian generally have a strong desire to acquire and to share information, knowledge, and ideas. Other workers with similar interests include archivists, encyclopedia researchers, information brokers, information scientists, museum curators, publishers' representatives, records managers, writers, editors, proofreaders, indexers, and teachers.

Methods of entering

Generally, a librarian must complete all educational requirements before applying for a job. Schools of library science may be able to find satisfactory jobs for their graduates. School librarians must apply directly to school boards. Individuals interested in working for the federal government may take a civil service examination. Often public libraries, too, are under a civil service system of appointment.

Advancement

The beginning librarian should gain experience by taking a job as an assistant. There is much to learn from practical experience before attempting to take complete charge of a library. One may also get initial experience in a small library and then advance by transferring to a larger library. Within a large library, promotions to higher positions are possible, for example, to the supervision of a department. Experienced librarians with the necessary qualifications may advance to positions in library administration.

A doctorate would be desirable for reaching top administrative levels. Experienced librarians may also go into specialized areas of library work, becoming increasingly valuable to business and industry, as well as other fields.

Employment outlook

In the early 1990s, an estimated 136,000 people were employed as full-time professional librarians. About half of them worked in school libraries; the rest held jobs in college and university, public, and special libraries. In addition, about 7,800 audiovisual specialists were employed in library/media centers.

The employment of trained librarians is expected grow slightly faster than average growth through the 1990s. Although library school enrollments have declined dramatically, the number of positions that will open because of retirement, death, and workers leaving the field will exceed the number of available librarians. Public libraries will be faced with escalating materials costs, tighter budgets, and increased circulation while having to rely more heavily on volunteers and support staff.

Opportunities will be best in special and research libraries, especially for those librarians with technical and scientific backgrounds, including medicine, law, business, engineering, and the physical and life sciences. The outlook is good also for those skilled in developing computerized library systems as well as for those with a command of foreign languages. The expanding use of computers to store and retrieve information and to handle routine operations will require that librarians have computer skills. The automation of libraries will in no way replace librarians, however; personal judgment and knowledge will still be needed in libraries.

Employment opportunities will also arise for librarians with a background in information science and library automation. The rapidly expanding field of information management has created a demand for qualified people to set up and maintain information systems for private industry and consulting firms. Individuals with a knowledge of libraries and computers may apply their skills in such nontraditional library settings as bibliographic cooperatives, regional information networks, and information search services. Many companies are establishing in-house reference libraries to assist in research work. Some have developed full lending library systems for employees.

Earnings

In the early 1990s, the average starting salary for a graduate with a master's degree from an accredited library school was about $20,900 per year. Salaries, however, are dependent on such factors as the location, size, and type of library, amount of experience, and responsibility of the position.

In public libraries, starting salaries for graduates with master's degrees were about $19,300. In school libraries, starting salaries were about $23,400. Special libraries paid an average starting salary of $22,000 a year.

Experienced librarians in the early 1990s received average earnings of $28,400 in school libraries and $30,200 to $38,400 in special libraries. The median salary for librarians in colleges and universities was $29,000 per year.

In the federal government, the average salary for all librarians was about $35,000.

Conditions of work

Most libraries are pleasant and comfortable places in which to assist those doing research, studying, or reading for pleasure. Great care is usually taken with the lighting conditions in most study areas. The librarian deals with all types of people. The librarian who does not have an assistant must also do a great deal of physical activity, such as walking, reaching, bending, and climbing ladders. The librarian must do a considerable amount of reading to keep informed and better serve library patrons.

On the average, librarians work from thirty-five to forty hours per week, although some of this time may be put in on evenings or weekends. School librarians usually work the same hours as teachers in a particular school system. Librarians working for the government or as special librarians usually work a forty-hour week. Paid vacations, sick leaves, and various insurance and pension plans are available to many librarians.

Social and psychological factors

The librarian finds a career that is interesting, intellectually stimulating, and satisfying in its personal relationships. The field demands considerable professional training and special personal qualifications, including a love for books, an interest in people, accuracy, poise, an inquiring mind, initiative, and above-average intelligence.

The librarian can foster certain special interests by becoming a special librarian. Perhaps one has a great interest in science or medicine, and yet does not have the qualifications required of a physician or physicist. To become a special librarian in one of these areas might be a fulfillment of interest and ability.

There is, of course, some routine in library work, but the trend is to place clerical duties in the hands of assistants, freeing the professional librarian for administrative, research, personal, and community services. One disadvantage may be irregularity in work hours, for example, working evenings and weekends.

The good librarian enjoys the work and the people being served. Probably a real interest in reading and working with written materials contributes most to the enjoyment of library work.

GOE: 11.02.04; SIC: 8231; SOC: 251

◇ **SOURCES OF ADDITIONAL INFORMATION**

General information and the pamphlets "Graduate Library Education Programs" and "Undergraduate Programs in Library Education" are available by writing to:

American Library Association
50 East Huron Street
Chicago, IL 60611

Association for Library and Information Science Education
5623 Palm Aire Drive
Sarasota, FL 34243

American Society for Information Science
1424 16th Street, NW, Suite 404
Washington, DC 20036

Medical Library Association
6 North Michigan Avenue
Suite 300
Chicago, IL 60602

Music Library Association
PO Box 487
Canton, MA 02021

Special Libraries Association
1700 18th Street, NW
Washington, DC 20009

For information on scholarships, program information, and education, request the *Library Career Training Programs* booklet from:

U.S. Department of Education
Office of Educational Research and Improvement
Library Programs
555 New Jersey Avenue, NW, Room 402
Washington, DC 20208

◇ **RELATED ARTICLES**

Volume 1: Library and Information Science
Volume 2: Archivists and curators; Computer programmers; Data base managers; Medical record administrators; Museum occupations; Systems analysts
Volume 4: Library technicians; Medical record technicians

Licensed practical nurses

Definition

Licensed practical nurses, sometimes called *licensed vocational nurses*, are trained to assist in the care, treatment, and convalescence of physically and mentally ill persons. Their work may be in assisting registered nurses and physicians or working under various other kinds of circumstances. Whatever the job duty, however, they always work under the direct supervision of professionally trained health care personnel.

History

In 1938, New York State passed the first state law to require that practical nurses be licensed. Even though the first school for the training of practical nurses was started almost seventy years ago, and the establishment of other schools followed, the programs of training lacked standardization in their preparation and requirements. After the 1938 law was passed, a movement began to have organized training programs that would assure new standards in the field.

The role and training of the practical nurse has undergone drastic changes since the first school was opened. The Ballard School, located in New York City, was begun by the Young Women's Christian Association, Central Branch. The program was an eight-week training course. Now extended programs of training are offered throughout the country, and all states have laws to assure training standards and to assure qualification for licensure. The

field of practical nursing now serves an important role as a part of the health care team.

Nature of the work

The job duties of licensed practical nurses are diverse. They may be employed for the nursing care of newborn babies, the aged, the handicapped, the mentally ill, or for nursing individuals with other types of needs or illnesses.

In their work, these nurses carry out prescribed medical treatments, keep checks on temperature and blood pressure readings, administer drugs and medications as they are instructed, and care for the comfort, personal cleanliness, and hygiene of the patient.

The duties of the licensed practical nurses are often determined by their place of employment, but in every instance the major concern is always the care and welfare of the patient. In physicians' offices and hospital settings, practical nurses may assist in the preparation of patients for examinations and operations, perform simple routine laboratory tests, and in some cases, be responsible for clerical duties. If employment is in a private home, the duties may be more varied. Although some minor domestic duties may be assumed in direct relation to the welfare of the patients, practical nurses are not trained to assume maid or cleaning duties.

In some instances, licensed practical nurses are employed by public health agencies. In these roles they make home visits to patients and take an active part in community health projects. If employment is in a public health agency, the work of the practical nurse is supervised by a community health staff nurse.

The skills needed to perform these duties are learned and practiced in approved schools offering programs of study in practical nursing.

Requirements

All states, as well as the District of Columbia, require that applicants pass an examination to become licensed. Applicants must have graduated from an approved school of practical nursing before taking this examination. State boards of nursing determine whether or not a school will be rated as an approved school of practical nursing. The standards may also be set by state boards of vocational education for schools offering training under their direction. Licensed practical nurses, or licensed vocational nurses, as they are called in Texas and California, may identify themselves by using the initials "LPN" or "LVN" after their names.

A high-school education is almost always demanded for entrance into practical nurse training. Practical nursing training can be obtained through adult education programs, vocational schools, and in private schools. Many community and junior colleges also offer this curriculum.

Programs of training for practical nurses usually include the academic and the practical. Classroom instruction in basic nursing education includes information on nutritional practices, community health, body structure and organ function, types and symptoms of disease and illness, medicines and the administration of medication, and the hygienic procedures of patient care. Students practice nursing techniques on mannequins and, as they progress, are allowed to work with real patients.

Students should be cautious in enrolling in correspondence schools for practical nursing. These credits are usually not acceptable for licensure because they do not include practical or clinical supervision. Applicants for training are usually required to have a health examination, personal interview, previous records of educational training, and references of character, personality traits, and ability. Many schools now require applicants to take one or more psychological tests.

There were about 1,128 state-approved practical nurse training programs offered in the early 1990s, and more than half of these were trade, technical, or vocational school programs.

Licensed practical nurses can pursue postgraduate training that allows them to specialize in certain areas such as operating room tech-

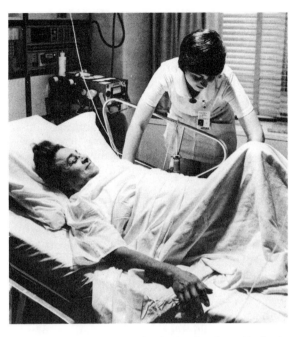

Licensed practical nurses are equipped to handle patients with all sorts of ailments. They are trained to treat each patient with great care and tenderness.

nique, emergency ward care, premature nursery, or psychiatric nursing. This training is sometimes available through hospital on-the-job training programs.

Individuals who are interested in becoming licensed practical nurses need a desire to be of service to others and the emotional stability to care for patients while working in hospital or home settings where illness may prevail.

Important personal traits are an even temperament, great patience, understanding, tact, dependability, maturity, and sound judgment. Licensed practical nurses must often deal with difficult or emergency situations and with many kinds of people under varied circumstances.

Special requirements

Graduation from an approved school of practical nurse training and state licensure are the special requirements of this occupational field. Exceptionally good emotional, mental, and physical stamina are almost to be considered as prerequisites to success in these jobs. Different titles require different levels of education and training. For an overview, see Volume 1: Health Care, and check the "Related Articles" section at the end of this article.

Opportunities for experience and exploration

Students may explore their interest in this field in a number of ways. They may read books on careers in the nursing field, talk with their high-school guidance counselors, the school nurse, local public health nurses and with those already employed as licensed practical nurses. Visits to hospitals to observe the work and to talk with hospital personnel may also be valuable.

Students may sometimes wish to take interest and aptitude tests to explore how compatible their interests are to those employed in this work and to help determine their strengths and weaknesses for the occupation.

Some hospitals now have volunteer service programs in which high-school students may work, and in doing so they both render a valuable service and are able to explore their interests. Other volunteer work experiences may be obtained through the Red Cross or in community and public health services. Camp counseling jobs sometimes offer related experiences that students can draw upon as background knowledge. Some schools offer participation in Future Nurses Clubs.

Related occupations

Individuals drawn to the field of licensed practical nursing are likely also to be interested in other occupations in or related to health care. They may find it worthwhile to explore the occupations of child care workers in institutions, dental assistants, emergency medical technicians, homemaker-home health aides, industrial hygienists, medical assistants, medical record administrators, nursing assistants, occupational therapists, physical therapists, psychiatric aides and technicians, public health educators, recreational therapists, respiratory therapists, sanitarians, or surgical technicians.

Methods of entering

Licensed practical nurses may enter this field by locating job openings through local employment agencies, newspaper advertisements, or by applying directly to hospital employment offices and personnel divisions. Direct applications may also be made to public health centers, to physicians' offices and clinics, and to homes for the aged. Sometimes positions are open in business and industry and job applications in these instances are processed through the personnel department.

Individuals who are interested in private nursing duty can sometimes list their availability on hospital registers or with physicians' offices.

Practical nurses who are graduates of approved schools of nursing that meet the requirements of the U.S. Office of Personnel Management and who are able to pass the written civil service examinations may find employment in federal government positions. Information on these positions and the examinations required is usually obtained through the postings in the United States Postal Service stations.

Advancement

Opportunities for advancement in this occupation are primarily limited to salary increases granted on the basis of length of service and good job performance. Increases are usually given periodically.

Some individuals may obtain higher pay by completing postgraduate training courses that prepare them for more specialized work or by continuing their education until they satisfy the formal requirements for registered nurses. Other opportunities may come through changes in places of employment that may offer more favorable and pleasant working conditions as well as pay increases.

Employment outlook

About 631,000 jobs were held by licensed practical nurses in the early 1990s. Approximately 50 percent of the jobs were in hospitals, 20 percent in nursing homes, and the rest in doctors' offices, clinics, and a number of other health care settings. Private-duty LPN jobs are held by licensed practical nurses who are either self-employed or are employees of a nurses' registry or temporary help agency.

The outlook for employment of LPNs through the 1990s is predicted as much better than average, although there will be a shift in places of employment. Fewer LPN jobs will be available in hospitals, where the emphasis on acute care and high technology requires more highly trained medical professionals, whereas more openings will exist in nursing and personal care homes, psychiatric institutions, private-duty nursing, and home-care settings where care and treatment is less technologically oriented.

The trend toward outpatient care will not provide as many jobs as one might expect, because HMOs, clinics, urgent care centers, and other outpatient facilities generally prefer to hire registered nurses. The same is true of home health agencies because increasingly complex treatments are now available for home care.

The best opportunities for LPNs will be in long-term care for elderly and disabled patients, an area that is experiencing rapid growth. Jobs for LPNs will be plentiful in nursing homes and in nonlicensed personal care homes. Also, private duty may be obtained through nursing registries or temporary help agencies, or direct contact with patients and their families.

Earnings

Average salaries of licensed practical nurses during the early 1990s ranged from about $13,000 to $18,000 a year. The median salary for all full-time LPNs was about $15,600 a year, with the top ten percent earning more than $21,000.

Beginning salaries for licensed practical nurses in hospitals, medical schools, and medical centers in the early 1990s were approximately $14,700. The federal government paid annual starting salaries of about $11,800 for LPNs with no experience, $13,300 for those with six months' experience, and $14,800 for one year's experience.

In hospitals and other health care institutions, licensed practical nurses can expect to receive paid vacations, hospitalization and health insurance, and retirement plans.

Conditions of work

Practical nurses must be adaptable and flexible. They usually work regularly assigned eight-hour work schedules; however, they may be subject to twenty-four-hour duty call and have to work night shifts, Sundays, and holidays.

Working conditions in hospitals are usually in clean, neat, and pleasant physical surroundings; however, the observation and care of persons in pain and illness may be factors to be considered in this type of work. As a service rendered, the work can be most rewarding, but it can also be depressing and discouraging in that pain, discomfort, and death are a part of

this professional health care environment. The work can be physically and mentally strenuous and exposure to contagious disease is always possible. However, adequate precautions minimize this hazard.

The work demands that practical nurses be on their feet many hours at a time. Bending, stretching, stooping, lifting, and walking is required in this work.

These individuals must deal with many difficult situations and sometimes very upsetting emotional experiences with their patients and the families of patients.

In some jobs, where licensed practical nurses are involved in private duty, they may frequently move from home to home to work with different cases. In every situation the practical nurse will face making new adjustments in working with patients, families, physicians, and other nurses.

Social and psychological factors

Licensed practical nurses are part of a health care team. They must be willing to work in teamwork cooperation, which may often mean accepting with a willing attitude the orders and instructions of more highly skilled personnel, such as physicians and registered nurses. The work of licensed practical nurses is always under the direct and close supervision of other health care professionals.

Licensed practical nurses have a professional code of ethics that they are honor bound to observe. The National Federation of Licensed Practical Nurses and state associations for licensed nurses have worked to promote the dignity and status of the field. Many LPNs are members of such organizations.

Individuals who find their interests and qualifications are compatible and who are motivated to be of service to others may find the field of practical nursing to offer satisfying, challenging, and rewarding experiences.

GOE: 10.02.01; SIC: 80; SOC: 366

◇ **SOURCES OF ADDITIONAL INFORMATION**

American Health Care Association
1201 L Street, NW
Washington, DC 20005

American Assembly for Men in Nursing
Rush University/College of Nursing
600 South Paulina, 474-H
Chicago, IL 60612

American Hospital Association
840 North Lake Shore Drive
Chicago, IL 60611

National Association for Practical Nurse Education and Service
1400 Spring Street, Suite 310
Silver Spring, MD 20910

National Federation of Licensed Practical Nurses
PO Box 18088
Durham, NC 27703

Department of Veterans Affairs
Recruitment and Placement Service
810 Vermont Avenue, NW
Washington, DC 20420

For information on accredited schools and programs, write:

National League for Nursing
Ten Columbus Circle
New York, NY 10019

◇ **RELATED ARTICLES**

Volume 1: Health Care
Volume 2: Physician assistants; Registered nurses
Volume 3: Homemaker-home health aides; Medical assistants; Nursing and psychiatric aides
Volume 4: See Medical and health technician occupations

Linguists

Definition

Linguists study the components and structure of the world's various languages, the relationships among them, and their effect on the societies that speak them.

History

Language is a universal characteristic of the human species. Of all the creatures on earth, mankind is the only one that communicates with a true language. Every known group or society of people throughout history has had its own language, but even the earliest languages we know of were complex systems of words and meanings. They certainly weren't "primitive" in the ways we might think, and were no less precise than the languages people use today.

Language determines, to some extent, the way we think and how society operates. Around the world, there are between 3,000 and 4,000 different speech communities, or groups of people using a specific, unique language. These speech communities are divided still further by dialects. In America, people from various regions may speak with an accent, but many languages contain dialects that are so different from each other that it is often very difficult for one group of speakers to understand another.

The comparative study of languages began in the late eighteenth century, when scholars first began to study the similarities that existed between the ancient languages of Greek, Sanskrit, and Persian. In the nineteenth century, much work was accomplished in identifying and classifying languages into families, or groups of related languages. At that time, the Indo-European family of languages was first classified and studied.

In the twentieth century, linguists have begun to study the structures on which languages are built. While this structure includes grammar and semantics, it also involves the way words change, compound, and sound to carry different meanings. In certain ways, a language reflects the beliefs, values, and social interactions of the societies that speak it. Many linguists today are examining exactly how this works.

In the past forty years or so, however, linguistics has ceased to be a strictly academic pursuit. The study of language has been put to many practical uses outside of the university setting. These uses include speech therapy, improvements in the way we teach language, and the development of special computer languages. When mankind finally develops computers that can operate from verbal commands and answer in spoken words, you can be certain that linguists were involved in the project.

Nature of the work

Linguists study and explore every aspect of spoken and written language: the sound, meaning and origin of words; systems of grammar; semantics, or the way words combine to mean what they mean; the evolution of both individual languages and families of languages; and the sounds that are used in a language's vocabulary. Linguists study both dead languages, such as Latin and Classical Greek, and modern languages. *Philologists* examine the structure, origin and development of languages and language groups by comparing ancient and modern tongues. *Etymologists* specialize in the history and evolution of words themselves. Contrary to what you might think, linguists don't yet know all there is to know about the world's languages. Some languages in remote parts of the world, such as the Pacific Islands, South America, and Africa, have existed for centuries and have yet to be studied closely by linguists.

While some linguists are employed by private companies or the federal government, most linguists conduct their work at a college or university. In fact, colleges and universities employ more linguists than all other employers combined. Like other college faculty members, linguists will usually teach a few classes a week while conducting their own research, applying for grants, and writing scholarly articles. The *scientific linguist* studies the components of language to understand its social functioning and apply linguistic theory to practical concerns and problems.

Many linguists carry on their research from a entirely theoretical point of view, that is, the work doesn't have any intended applications or practical value outside itself. Of course, this doesn't mean that their work is unimportant: Many times, purely theoretical work can lead to unexpected practical applications or can build a foundation for work by later scholars. Also,

Linguists use computer software to study the world's languages. Such software offers an extensive data base, allowing linguists to compare and examine several languages in a short period of time.

these linguists may believe that their work is important entirely because it adds to our knowledge of history and civilization and gives us insight into various world cultures. In fact, the first people who studied linguistics did so as a purely academic exercise. They created the study methods, such as the phonetic alphabet, that make modern linguistic study possible. Without their pioneering work, we would know much less about humans and their language systems, and some things we take for granted, like personal computers, might not have been possible.

Some linguists study ancient languages from archaeological evidence such as the paintings and hieroglyphics inside the pyramids of Egypt. Because this evidence is sometimes incomplete, linguists may need to reconstruct parts of the language and make assumptions based on accepted linguistic theory. Still, their work adds greatly to our knowledge of what daily life was like in these ancient cultures.

Other linguists choose to study languages being spoken today. Many of these languages are spoken by people in remote parts of the

369

world, but they can also be close to home, such as the languages of Native American tribes. Because some of these languages have never been written down, a linguist may need to spend years talking to native speakers, living with them to gain a complete knowledge of their culture. Such work is valuable because many of these ancient languages, with their rich oral histories and traditions, are in danger of extinction, because of electronic communications and the encroachment of modern civilizations.

Other work by linguists may have more immediate applications. For example, a linguist may study the physiology of language, that is, the ways in which the lips, tongue, teeth, and throat combine to make the sounds of language. This knowledge can have many applications. For example, knowledge of physiology can make it easier to teach foreign languages that contain unfamiliar sounds. The Japanese language, for example, does not contain a clear "l" sound, but linguists can develop methods of teaching English to native Japanese speakers that will overcome this. Knowledge of language physiology can also aid in the treatment of speech and reading deficiencies of children, handicapped persons, stroke victims, or people who have suffered brain damage.

Linguistic theory itself can have many practical applications. These include the development of improved methods of translation, such as computer-enhanced translation. Linguistic theory can help in the preparation of language-teaching handbooks, dictionaries, and audio-tapes. Literacy programs, at home and abroad, also depend on the work of linguists. In other countries, these programs are often run by anthropologists and missionaries.

Linguists are not only concerned with existing languages. They also develop artificial languages, such as Esperanto and Interlingua, which simplify the spelling and grammar rules of other languages in order to create a "universal" language people can understand easily. Linguists also study sign language, such as AMESLAN, or American Sign Language. In some very interesting experiments, linguists and other scientists have taught simplified sign language to gorillas. Future experiments in communication with other species, such as dolphins, whales and dogs, will also depend on the expertise of skilled linguists.

Outside the academic world, linguists are finding more and more applications for their talents. Computer experts and linguists work together in the development of new computer languages, based on the rules of human language, that will be more user-friendly. The development of voice-activated computers will also capitalize on the skill and efforts of lin-

guists. In the future, this field, known as *computational linguistics*, may offer many opportunities.

Publishers sometimes have linguists on staff, especially dictionary publishers who rely on the work of etymologists. Using their knowledge of language, some linguists find work in simplifying the wording of complicated documents, such as treaties, trade agreements, and tax and insurance forms. If they are skilled speakers of one or more foreign languages, linguists may find work with the U.S. State Department. They may find work as *interpreters* or *translators* of novels, textbooks, machinery manuals and other materials. (*See also* the article titled "Interpreters" elsewhere in this volume.) Many linguists work as translators or interpreters in their spare time for extra money.

Requirements

Employers require at least a bachelor's degree in linguistics, English or a foreign language, though some will accept degrees in history, science, mathematics or engineering. Advanced degrees with some independent study in languages could be very helpful. To teach and work at a university level, doctoral degrees are essential. In the United States, more than 150 universities and colleges offer degrees in linguistics, and more than 50 offer doctoral programs.

Linguistic work calls for people who are inquisitive, patient and precise in nature, and have a strong affinity for working with words, language and sound. Strong research, reading, and writing skills are also important. Over time, linguists can develop a discerning ear that can identify the sounds of speech in any language. Linguists should also have an interest in people of other cultures and be able to relate to them well.

A broadly based, college prep curriculum is important to high school students interested in linguistics. Classes in English, literature, speech, foreign language, and Latin are essential, along with history, psychology, sociology, and the other social sciences. Students may also find mathematics, philosophy, logic, computer courses and voice training helpful.

Special requirements

Linguists do not need to be licensed or registered, but they may find useful opportunities through membership in various professional organizations, including the Linguistic Society of America, the American Society for Applied Linguistics, and the Association for Computational Linguistics.

Opportunities for experience and exploration

High-school students interested in a possible career in linguistics should expose themselves to languages other than their own. Language clubs are a good way to do this. Students should also take advantage of opportunities to travel to other countries and communicate with people of different language backgrounds to gain insight into how important language is to culture.

If a university is located nearby, a student may wish to call and arrange an appointment with a member of the Linguistics Department. This could offer insights into what a career in a university setting is like.

Related articles

Linguists are comfortable with intense study and close attention to detail. Their inquisitiveness and learn to know the unknown. These same qualities are necessary for work as computer programmers, editors, university faculty, and writers.

Methods of entering

The start of a linguistics career begins on the college campus, where students meet the professional linguists who can guide them through their studies. The professional grapevine can keep students aware of openings for graduate teaching assistants and of campus recruiting visits by potential employers. In graduate school, students can find work tutoring undergraduate linguistics classes or assisting professors in their research or classroom work. Such experience is very important when it comes time to look for employment.

Linguists interested in working for the federal government should watch for civil service announcements and apply to the federal agency for which they want to work. The Armed Forces also sponsor the Defense Language Institute, for military personnel. Admittance is based on scores from The Defense Language Aptitude Battery Test. Linguists who are attracted to the prospect of missionary work should contact the representatives of the mission branch of their church or denomination.

Advancement

Those linguists working in a university setting will likely find advancement through promotions to associate and full professorships and, possibly, to department head. Advancement may also come in the form of grants that allow a linguist to establish a clinic, research program or other special project.

Linguists working in the private sector may advance through promotion to an administrative job in publishing or the chance to write and market computer software. Then again, depending on individual goals, a linguist working for a private firm may pursue a teaching position at a university, or a linguistics professor may leave to take a job with a firm.

Employment outlook

While the employment outlook for linguists has improved over the past decade, it is still not good. There are more qualified linguists than there are jobs for them, and most openings will occur as other linguists die, retire or leave the field.

However, the efforts of professional associations such as the Linguistic Society of America have succeeded in opening up more jobs for linguists in the private sector. The communications revolution has also expanded opportunities. Computers have made the work of academic linguists easier and have created opportunities for linguists in developing computer languages and software that are more like human language. Literacy programs both in the United States and in other countries may also offer opportunities for linguistic work.

As private companies expand and business becomes more international in scope, a knowledge of foreign language and culture may prove very beneficial to those linguists who develop additional business skills. Those people who do not limit themselves to strictly linguistic work and instead market their skills in areas where they can be useful should be able to carve out their own employment niche.

Earnings

Salaries for linguists who work on university staffs as instructors, assistant professors or full professors can range from $14,000 a year to $50,000 a year or more. They may also earn extra money from sales of their writings, monetary grants, or free-lance work as translators or interpreters. Beginning salaries for linguists in private businesses and scientific or government agencies range from $12,000 to $14,000 a year, while experienced linguists, depending upon their position, can earn from $30,000 to $60,000 a year or more. Linguists who work part-time or free lance can arrange contracts to be paid by the hour or by the project. Their earnings start at $7.50 to $10.00 an hour and can go as high as $50.00 an hour for specialized or technical work.

Conditions of work

For linguists working in colleges or universities, the working conditions are usually very good. College campuses are generally pleasant and peaceful, with a rich cultural life and stimulating, intelligent coworkers and students. Faculty members are usually accorded respect by both their peers and students. While junior faculty members may have to share their offices, the availability of secretaries and other support staff is usually good. Linguistics professors usually share a linguistics lab that has the sound spectrographs, tape recorders, computers, and other equipment they will need for their work. Linguistics professors commonly spend between three and twelve hours a week in the classroom, and divide the rest of their work week between student office hours, research, preparation of class materials and writing. They often put in more than a thirty-five or forty-hour week, but they are able to structure their time to suit their interests and working habits. They also receive ample vacation time, which they often use for study, research and travel.

Linguists in the private sector generally also work thirty-five to forty-hour weeks, while they may have to work overtime to meet certain deadlines. Publishing firms and government agencies employing linguists generally have pleasant atmospheres and good equipment. Linguists involved in missionary work or overseas literacy programs generally live among the native people and adjust to their standard of living. Missionaries generally work long hours and receive no more than subsistence wages; however, their devotion to a higher cause enables them to adapt to uncomfortable surroundings.

Social and psychological factors

The work of a linguist requires patience, persistence, an inquiring mind and the ability to work independently in very exacting detail. At the same time, linguists who work with living languages and speech therapy need to be able to work well with people and relate to their culture and background. They should enjoy reading, writing, and research.

Professionally, linguists at universities must get used to working in small departments; most linguistics departments have no more than five or six members. However, because the field is relatively small, they generally enjoy the support and respect of their coworkers and peers in the field. With the various applications of linguistic theory—helping disabled people speak and read better, improving literacy at home and abroad, helping develop computer programs on the cutting edge of technology, increasing the store of knowledge of the world's cultures—linguists can usually find some facet of their work that is fulfilling and personally rewarding.

GOE: 11.03.02; SIC: 8221; SOC: None

◇ **SOURCES OF ADDITIONAL INFORMATION**

American Association for Applied Linguistics
1325 18th Street, NW, Suite 211
Washington, DC 20036

Association for Computational Linguistics
Bellecore, MRE ZA379
445 South Street
Box 1910
Morristown, NJ 07960

Linguistic Society of America
1325 18th Street, NW, Suite 211
Washington, DC 20036

Modern Language Association of America
10 Astor Place, 5th Floor
New York, NY 10003

U.S. Department of State
Language Services Division
Department of Admissions
Washington, DC 20520

Defense Language Institute
Foreign Language Center
Presidio of Monterey, CA 93944

Literary agents and artists' managers

Definition

Literary agents and *artists' managers* serve as intermediaries between artists such as writers, actors, and musicians and potential employers such as publishers, television producers, and nightclub owners. In essence, agents and managers sell a product—their clients' creative talent. In addition to finding work for their clients, agents and managers may also negotiate contracts, pursue publicity, and advise clients in their careers.

History

Writers and performers have been present in cultures since the beginning of recorded history, but the business of promoting writers and performers is a product of the twentieth century. Modern mass publishing and distribution systems, as well as the advent of the radio, television, and motion picture industries, have created a market for the writer's art that never existed before. Movie studios used to have staff writers. Today, independent writers create novels, magazine articles, screenplays, and scripts for voracious readers and videophiles. Similarly, Broadway, Hollywood, and new music forms such as jazz, the blues, and rock 'n' roll—all of which emerged in this century— have broadened the scope of the performing arts, providing countless new opportunities for actors, dancers, and musicians. It was perhaps only appropriate that "brokers" should emerge to bring people who need each other together: creators and producers. These brokers are literary agents and artists managers.

Nature of the work

Most agents, both literary and performing arts, can be broken down into two broad groups: those who represent clients on a case-by-case basis, and those who have intensive, ongoing partnerships with clients. Literary agents do not typically have long-term relationships with clients except for established authors. They may represent writers just one time, electing to represent them only after reading manuscripts and determining their viability. Literary agents market their clients' manuscripts to editors, publishers, television and movie producers, among other buyers. Many of the most prestigious magazines and newspapers will not consider material unless it is submitted by an agent; busy editors rely on agents to screen manuscripts so that only the best, most professional product reaches them. Sometimes, editors go directly to agents with editorial assignments, knowing that the agents will be able to find the best writer for the job.

After taking on a project, such as a book proposal, a play, a magazine article, or screenplay, agents approach publishers and producers in writing, by phone, or in person and try to convince these decision-makers to use their clients' work. When a proposal is accepted by a publisher or other, agents may negotiate contracts and rights, such as translation and excerpt rights, on behalf of their clients. Rather than pay authors directly, publishers pay their agents, who deduct their commission from the total and return the rest to the author.

Agents who represent established writers perform additional duties for their clients, such as directing them to useful resources, evaluating drafts and offering guidance, speaking for

Agents spend much of their work day on the phone, coordinating schedules with clients and discussing contracts.

them in matters that must be decided in their absence, and in some instances, serving as arbiters between coauthors. Also, to ensure that writers devote as much time as possible to their creative work, agents take care of such business as bookkeeping, processing income checks, and preparing tax forms.

Those artists' managers who handle hundreds of clients at a time are usually known as *talent agents*. After reviewing actors, dancers, and musicians, talent agents form contracts with a select group and then send them on auditions for plays, movies, commercials, industrial films, trade shows, among others. If, for example, a motion picture production company needs a short, freckle-faced woman to fill a role, talent agents may send all of their actresses who fit that description to audition, in the hopes that one of them will be whom the director wants.

The term "artists managers" is usually reserved for those agents who work very closely with performers to help them build their careers. In addition to sending their clients on auditions, artists managers may coach actors on monologues or help musicians choose their repertoire. They may schedule tours and nightclub engagements for their clients and negotiate contracts and promotional details, such as what size typography must be used when printing clients' names in advertisements and playbills. Artists managers for singers are more involved in the business side of the industry. Agents handle the schedule. Like literary agents, talent agents and artists' managers work for a percentage of their clients' earnings.

Requirements

Agents and managers need not have any specific education or technical skills, but they must have a knack for recognizing marketable talent and they must know how to promote that talent successfully. They must be familiar with the needs of publishers and producers so as not to approach anyone inappropriately. Agents must be persistent without crossing over the line to harassment, for they must not alienate any of the publishers and producers they will want to contact in the future. A college degree is not necessary, but would-be agents with a college degree are more likely to be hired before those without. High-school students who are interested in becoming agents should take classes in literature, composition, theater, and music. Desireable areas of study on the undergraduate level include liberal arts, performing arts, and business administration. It is also helpful to study the law, although agents need not be lawyers. Some colleges offer programs in arts management, but these teach students how to run cultural institutions like theatres and museums, not how to become agents.

Special requirements

Because agents' continued success depends on their ability to maintain good relationships with clients and potential employers for their clients, they must have "good people" skills; they must be able to interact tactfully and amicably with a wide variety of people, from demanding clients to busy editors. Moreover, because artists' careers have their ups and downs, and production and publishing are fields with high turnover rates, agents can never become complacent. They must be flexible, adaptive people, able to establish new relationships quickly and with finesse.

Opportunities for experience and exploration

Students interested in literary management can acquaint themselves with current trends in book publishing and with the kinds of books that particular publishing houses issue by working part-time at bookstores and libraries. Those living in big cities may even be able to get jobs with book and magazine publishers. Students interested in artist management should get involved with dramatic and musical productions at their schools, either on stage or behind the scenes, to begin learning show business. They might also look for part-time jobs or volunteer to usher at local entertainment centers, such as theaters and concert halls. Some literary and talent agents also sponsor internships.

Methods of entering

Just as journalism is good training for public relations work, employment within a production facility, publishing house, or entertainment center is a good beginning for agents because it provides an insiders' knowledge of agents' target markets. The other optimum approach is to send resumes to any and all agencies and to be willing to start at the bottom, probably as office workers, to learn the field.

Some talent agents start by moonlighting, booking engagements for up-and-coming acts that are not yet well enough established to warrant the attention of full-time professional agents.

Advancement

How far agents advance depends almost entirely on their entrepreneurial skills. Native ability alone isn't enough; successful agents must be persistent and ambitious. In addition to proving themselves to their agency superiors and clients, they must earn the trust and respect of decision-makers in the arts marketplace. Once agents earn the confidence of a number of successful artists, they can strike out on their own and perhaps even establish their own agencies.

Employment outlook

Agents work in an extremely competitive field. Most individuals who attempt to go into business for themselves as agents fail within one year. There were only approximately one thousand independent agents working in the United States in the early 1990s; only thirty-five to fifty of these were full-fledged artists' managers who had managed to stay in business for more than five years. Most job openings within agencies are the result of turn-over, rather than the development of new positions.

Earnings

In the early 1990s, agents generally earned between $16,000 and $60,000 annually year, with a rare few making hundreds of thousands of dollars a year. Because independent agents take a percentage of their clients' earnings, their livelihoods are contingent upon the success of their clients, which is in turn contingent on the agents' ability to promote talent. Some beginning agents can go as long as a year without making any money at all, but, if at the end of that time, their clients are beginning to gain notice, the agents' investment of time may well pay off.

Agency staff workers typically earn beginning salaries equivalent to that of general office workers and are paid more generously only as they prove their worth to their employers. Sometimes agency staffers working on commission can actually earn more money than their bosses.

Conditions of work

Agents' hours are often uncertain, for in addition to fairly regular office hours, they often must meet on weekends and evenings with clients, as well as those producers and editors with whom they are trying to build relationships. Talent agents may also spend many evenings at theaters and nightclubs, looking for new artists to represent. The majority of their time, however, is spent in the office on the phone. Novices can expect no more than a cubicle whereas established agents may enjoy luxurious office suites.

Los Angeles and New York are the country's leading entertainment centers, and so most agents work in either of those two cities. Some agencies have branch offices in other large U.S. cities and affiliate offices overseas, especially in London. Established agents may travel internationally frequently, both to meet with clients and to scout out new talent and new opportunities for their talent.

Social and psychological factors

Typically, agencies do not employ large numbers of persons, and so socializing in the workplace may well be limited almost entirely phone conversations with entertainment or publishing industry personnel. As a rule, talent agencies tend to employ more persons than literary agencies. Agents work in high-stress conditions, but many find the excitement of the work more than compensates for the stress.

GOE: 11.12.03; SIC: None; SOC: 145, 7922

◇ **SOURCES OF ADDITIONAL INFORMATION**

Independent Literary Agents Association
432 Park Avenue South, Suite 1205
New York, NY 10016

Society of Author's Representatives
10 Astor Place, 3rd Floor
New York, NY 100003

Association of Talent Agents
9255 Sunset Boulevard, Suite 318
Los Angeles, CA 90069

National Association of Performing Arts Managers and Agents
c/o Pentacle
104 Franklin Street
New York, NY 10013

◇ **RELATED ARTICLES**

Volume 1: Book Publishing; Broadcasting; Magazine Publishing; Newspaper Publishing; Performing Arts; Recording
Volume 2: Actors and actresses; Writers and editors
Volume 3: Models

Management analysts and consultants

Definition

Management analysts and consultants analyze business or operating procedures to devise the most efficient methods of accomplishing work. They gather and organize information about present operating problems and procedures and prepare recommendations for implementing new systems or changes. They may update manuals outlining established methods of performing work and train personnel in new applications.

History

Within the great burst of energy of the English Industrial Revolution, there arose an urgent need for solving the chronic problems on crude production lines. Thus management experimentation was born.

Josiah Wedgwood (1730–1795) applied new labor- and work-saving methods to his pottery business and was the first to formulate the concept of mass-producing articles of uniform quality. He believed the manufacturing process

could be organized into a system that would use, and not abuse, the people harnessed to it. He organized the interrelationships between people, material, and events in his factory, and took the time to reflect upon them. He updated, scrutinized, studied, and diagnosed. In short, he did in the eighteenth century what management analysts and consultants do today. The message conveyed by his enormous financial success traveled far.

By 1820, American mills were producing huge quantities of cheap, well-made goods that found ready markets around the world. But the next real advance in the practice of management came in 1860, when railroad man Daniel McCallum published his organizational chart for the Erie Railroad.

Andrew Carnegie was a nineteenth-century American business leader with an exceptionally clear understanding that intelligent management translated into usable power. He said, "Take from me all the ore mines, railroads, and manufacturing plants and leave me my organization, and in a few years I promise to duplicate the Carnegie Company."

In 1870, Charles T. Sampson solved a critical management problem by being one of the first to experiment with the use of Chinese labor in the United States, a dubious ethical decision but a dramatically successful financial one. The increase in productivity and profit at his shoe factory led other businesses to call him in for consultation about their own management problems. Using Sampson's techniques, they duplicated his success.

Next, Frederick W. Taylor, born in 1878, became creator of the "efficiency cult" in American business. Taylor invented the world-famous "differential piecework" plan, in which a productive worker could significantly increase his take-home pay by stepping up the pace of his work.

Taylor's well-publicized study of the Midvale Steel plant in Pennsylvania was the first true time-and-motion study. It broke down elements of each part of each job and timed it, and was therefore able to quantify maximum efficiency. He earned many assignments and inspired James O. McKinsey, in 1910, to found a firm dealing with management and accounting problems.

In 1912, Frank Gilbreth, a former bricklayer turned independent contractor, left his building business to become a full-time management consultant. He built a reputation for expertise in the elimination of duplication of effort and the expurgation of delays by more orderly arrangements of workers and their access to materials, and he became a major challenger to Taylor. Gilbreth descended from the Wedgwood tradition of adapting the environment to stimulate worker satisfaction and efficiency. To Taylor, on the other hand, the worker was in a sense an extension of the machine itself, so the two men inevitably clashed. But out of the controversy of both bodies of work emerged the "efficiency experts" of the twentieth century.

In that same year, Emerson wrote *The Twelve Principles of Efficiency*. The third principle instructed the reader to "take competent counsel" because no single person could master all functions in an organization. This further encouraged professional fees for management analysts and consultants.

Consulting firms continued to develop through the 1920s and 1930s. Then management analysts got a better name during World War II, when the country, in its hour of peril, turned to the leaders of industry, who understood the large-scale organization of resources and knew how to make bureaucracies respond on a massive scale. In this case, the consultancy definitely added to the success of the task at hand. During the Vietnam War, however, incorrect information and a failure to translate management theory into practical, realistic terms, led to a failure in this area. The reputa-

tion of management analysis and consulting suffered.

Today, however, management analysts and consultants are thriving. As the stakes become higher in the business world and technological advances lead to the heightened possibility of dramatic loss or gain, many executives feel more secure relying on all the specialized expertise they can find.

Nature of the work

Management analysts and consultants are called in to solve any of a vast array of organizational problems. They are often needed when a rapidly growing small company needs a better system of control over inventories and expenses.

The role of the consultant is to come into a situation in which a client is unsure or inexpert and recommend actions or provide assessments. Therefore there are many different types of management analysts and consultants. In general, they all require knowledge of general management; operations; marketing; logistics, materials management, and physical distribution; finance and accounting; human resources; electronic data processing and systems; and management science.

They may be called in when a major manufacturer must reorganize its corporate structure when acquiring a new division. They are there when a company relocates to another state and needs assistance coordinating the move, planning the new facility, and training new workers. Management analysts are enlisted when a division chief of a government agency wants to know why the division's contracts are always going over budget.

The work of management analysts and consultants is quite flexible—it varies from job to job. In general, management analysts and consultants collect, review, and analyze data; make recommendations; and assist in the implementation of their proposals. Some projects require several consultants to work together, each specializing in a different area. Other jobs require the analysts to work independently.

Public and private organizations use management analysts for a variety of reasons. Some don't have adequate resources to handle a project. Others, before they pursue a particular course of action, will consult an analyst to determine what resources will be required or what problems will be encountered. Some organizations are seeking outside advice on how to resolve organizational problems that have al-

Management analysts and consultants
Professional, Administrative, and Managerial Occupations

Hired to locate manufacturing problems in a steel company, a management consultant discusses the result of his research and analysis with the officers of the company.

ready been identified or to avoid troublesome problems that could arise.

Firms providing consulting practitioners range in size from solo practitioners to large international organizations employing hundreds of people. The services are generally provided on a contract basis. A company will choose a consulting firm that specializes in the area that needs assistance, and then the two firms negotiate the conditions of the contract. Contract variables include the proposed cost of the project, staffing requirements, and deadline.

After getting a contract, the analyst's first job is to define the nature and extent of the project. It is at this point that they analyze statistics and other types of data, such as annual revenues, employment, or expenditures. They may also interview employees and observe the operations of the organization on a day-to-day basis.

The next step for the analysts is to use their knowledge of management systems to develop solutions. While preparing recommendations, they must take into account the general nature of the business, the relationship of the firm to others in its industry, the firm's internal organization, and the information gained through their data collection and analysis.

Once they have decided on a course of action, management analysts and consultants usually write reports of their findings and recommendations and present them to the client. They often make formal oral presentations about their findings as well. Some projects require only reports; others require assistance in implementing the suggestions.

In government agencies, management analysts use similar skills to those required in the private sector. For example, if an agency is planning to purchase several personal computers, analysts determine which type to buy, considering the agency budget and data processing needs. They would assess the various machines available and determine which best meets the department's needs.

Requirements

Employers generally prefer to hire management analysts and consultants with a master's degree in business or public administration, or at least a bachelor's degree and several years of appropriate work experience. Most government agencies offer entry level analyst and consultant positions to people with bachelor's degrees and no work experience. Many entrants are also career changers who were formerly mid- and upper-level managers. With half the practicing management consultants self-employed, career changing is a common route into the field.

Many fields of study provide a suitable formal educational background for this occupation because of the diversity of problem areas addressed by management analysts and consultants. These include many areas in the computer and information sciences, engineering, business and management, education, communications, marketing and distribution, and architecture and environmental design.

Special requirements

There are no special licenses or certificates required to be a management analyst or consultant. When hired directly from school, management analysts and consultants are often required to participate in formal company training programs. These programs may include instruction on policies and procedures, computer systems and software, and management practices and principles. Because of their previous industry experience, most of those who enter at midlevel are not required to participate in these programs. Regardless of background, most management analysts and consultants routinely attend conferences to keep abreast of current developments in the field.

Opportunities for experience and exploration

The reference departments of most libraries include business areas that will have valuable research tools such as encyclopedias of business consultants and who's who of business consultants. These books should list all management analysis and consulting firms in the country, describing their annual sales and areas of specialization (industrial, high-tech, small business, retail, and so on). Interested students can call or write to these firms and ask for more information.

Related occupations

Management analysts and consultants collect, review, and analyze data, make recommendations, and assist in the implementation of their ideas. Others who utilize similar skills are financial analysts, financial planners, managers, computer systems analysts, operations research analysts, systems and methods experts, efficiency experts, top executives, staff specialists, and economists.

Methods of entering

In practice, anyone with some degree of business expertise or an expert field can begin to work as a consultant. The number of one- and two-person consulting firms in this country is well over 100,000. Establishing a wide range of appropriate personal contacts is by far the most effective way to get started in this field. Consultants have to sell themselves and their expertise, a task far tougher than selling a tangible product the customer can see and handle. Many consultants get their first clients by advertising in newspapers, magazines, and trade or professional periodicals. After some time in the field, "word-of-mouth" advertising is often the primary force.

Thousands of business-school professors work part-time as management analysts or consultants, entering on the basis of their academic achievement.

Others enter the field through CPA accounting firms. These are called Management Advisory Services. Others begin as in-house consultants, working for organizations that have their own management consulting operations.

Advancement

A brand new consultant in a large firm may be referred to as an *associate* for the first couple of years. The next progression is to *senior associate*, a title that indicates three to five years experience and the ability to supervise others and do more complex and independent work. After about five years, the analyst who is progressing well may become an *engagement manager* with the responsibility to lead a consulting team on a particular client project. The best then become senior engagement managers, leading several study teams or a very large project team. Around the seven-year mark, those who excel the most will be considered for appointment as *junior partners* or *principals*. Partnership involves responsibility for marketing the firm and leading client projects. Some time later, the final step is to *senior partnership* or *director*, but few are expected to successfully run this full course. Management analysts and consultants with entrepreneurial ambition may open their own firms.

Employment outlook

Management analysts and consultants held more than 126,000 jobs in the early 1990s. About half of these people were self-employed. Federal, state, and local governments employed many of the others. The Department of Defense employed the majority of those working for the federal government. The remainder worked in the private sector for companies providing consulting services.

Although management analysts and consultants are found throughout the country, the majority are concentrated in the metropolitan areas.

Through the early 1990s, employment of management analysts is expected to grow faster than the average for all occupations. Industry and government agencies are expected to rely more and more on the expertise of these professionals to improve and streamline the performance of their organizations. Many job openings will result from the need to replace personnel who transfer to other fields or leave the labor force.

The job growth will be the strongest for specialists who have previous work experience in the field they are consulting for, and for consultants with graduate degrees.

Earnings

Salaries and hourly rates for management analysts and consultants vary widely, according to experience, specialization, education, and employer. In the early 1990s, those who were wage and salary workers had median annual earnings of about $35,400. The middle 50 percent earned between $26,520 and $48,600. Ten percent earned less than $19,800, while ten percent earned more than $62,040.

In the federal government, management analysts with a bachelor's degree had a starting salary of $17,280 in the early 1990s. Entrants with a superior academic record could begin at $21,360. The average salary for management analysts working in the federal government in the early 1990s was $38,520.

Typical benefits for salaried analysts and consultants include health and life insurance, retirement plans, vacation and sick leave, profit sharing, and bonuses for outstanding work. All travel expenses are generally reimbursed by the employer.

Self-employed management consultants receive none of these benefits and generally have to maintain their own office, but their pay is usually much higher than salaried consultants. The sky is the limit in terms of the fees a highly respected consultant can charge. Even ten years ago, it was not unheard of for a management analyst to make more than $2,000 per day or $250,000 in one year from consulting just two days per week.

Many consultants can demand between $400 and $1000 per day. Their fees are often well over $40 per hour.

Conditions of work

Management analysts and consultants generally divide their time between their own offices and the client's office. Much of their time is spent indoors in these fairly pleasant surroundings, but they may also have to spend time at a client's production facility where conditions are not so favorable. Here they must follow established safety procedures as they encounter potentially hazardous operations.

Management analysts and consultants often work fourteen to sixteen hour days; six or seven day workweeks can be fairly common, especially when there are deadlines to meet. They also spend a great deal of time on the road. While self-employed consultants may enjoy the luxury of setting their own hours and workload and doing much of their work at home, they sacrifice the benefits provided by the large firms, so their fees are not free and clear. They also must face the anxiety caused by knowing that their livelihood depends on their ability to maintain and expand their clientele, which can be difficult.

Although those in this career usually avoid much of the potential tedium of working for one company from nine to five, they face many stressful pressures resulting from deadlines and client expectations. Because the clients are generally paying generous fees, they want to see dramatic results, and the management analyst can feel the weight of this.

Management analysts and consultants are often responsible for recommending layoffs of staff, so they may face hostility from employees of the clients' organizations. It's important that they learn to deal with people diplomatically.

Social and psychological factors

Management analysts and consultants must be excellent at handling people. They require a great deal of tact, enlisting cooperation while exerting leadership, debating their points, and often having to point out people's errors to them. Consultants must be quick on their feet, able to refute objections with finality. They must be able to make excellent presentations.

A management analyst must be unbiased and analytical, with a disposition toward the intellectual side of business and a natural curiosity about the way things work best.

Management analysts must be discreet, as they will have to preserve confidential material. They must be independent self-starters, as they'll rarely have someone standing over them, telling them what to do. To be successful, they must have a sense of relevance, fact consciousness, precision and persuasivness of speech, comprehensiveness, self-discipline, and thoroughness.

GOE: 05.01.06; SIC: 874; SOC: 142

◇ **SOURCES OF ADDITIONAL INFORMATION**

ACME, Inc.—Association of Management Consulting Firms
230 Park Avenue
New York, NY 10017

Association of Managing Consultants
19 West 44th Street
Suite 810
New York, NY 10036

Institute of Management Consultants
19 West 44th Street
Suite 810-811
New York, NY 10036

American Institute of Certified Public Accountant
Management Advisory Services Division
1211 Avenue of the Americas
New York, NY 10036

Academy of Management
PO Drawer KZ
Mississippi State University
Mississippi State, MS 39762

Association of Internal Management Consultants
Box 304
East Bloomfield, NY 14443

◇ **RELATED ARTICLES**

Volume 1: Business Administration; Personal and Consulting Services
Volume 2: Economists; General managers and top executives; Management trainees

Management trainees

Definition

The position of *management trainee* is an important stepping stone to being an actual manager of any firm or business. In special programs, some quite short in length but some lasting one to two years or more, management trainees learn on the job what it takes to plan and run a business operation. Under close supervision by experienced personnel they receive training and perform tasks in any of a number of different departments to become familiar with the work performed by other employees and to acquire managerial techniques and skills necessary for promotion to management positions.

A trainee position differs from an assistant position in that the trainee is designated to move into management automatically, after fulfilling the requirements of the training program. The assistant's move up is done through promotion.

History

The training of human beings to perform specific skills and to use precise knowledge to their benefit has been going on ever since our earliest ancestors first began to communicate practical pieces of information to one another for practical tasks such as hunting and gathering.

It is generally believed that humans began amassing knowledge at the beginning of the Stone Age, when the invention of tools, language, and various types of man-made shelters and clothing, for instance, made it necessary for the unskilled to learn from the skilled. At that point training took one small formal step forward. As the skills of one craftsman were developed, an apprentice would commonly be used so that the skills and techniques would be passed on from generation to generation. This was common practice for medicine men as well as tool makers. Well-trained laborers and craftspeople began to oversee the work of those just beginning.

The earliest management training, although not formally set up as such, seems to have occurred in the guilds of eleventh and twelfth century England. These guilds, which were associations of workers pursuing the same or similar occupations, had three levels of membership. The master workers trained and oversaw the work of apprentices and journeymen and for the most part prepared the skilled journeymen to take on the responsibility of managing the work of apprentices.

Not until the industrial revolution, however, did the need for formalized training became apparent. As business and industry grew in complexity and sophistication, the hierarchy of management began to take form, and there came to be an interest in job training.

Because the U.S. system of public education did not provide such job training in the early days of the industrial revolution, training was first provided by businesses themselves or by trade groups. Training for managers was pursued "in-house" and very early on included the "case method" developed by a professor at Harvard Law School in the 1880s. This nondirective training technique allowed trainees to learn about their jobs through studying the case histories of others. Another training technique, psychodrama, or role playing, was added to many management training programs in the first decades of this century and is still widely used today.

By the end of the First World War, there were many factors compelling businesses to provide a stable source of competent management training. The losses in manpower that the war had caused as well as the failure of job apprenticeship to provide skilled management candidates motivated many industries to develop training programs that could quickly replenish the managerial ranks. In addition, many colleges and universities responded to the need of industry for management personnel by developing full business education programs.

The first formal U.S. organization for managers, the National Association of Foremen, was founded in 1925 and was comprised of business and industrial managers, from supervisory level to middle and executive management. This organization, which is now known as the National Management Association, was also very active in the development of training programs, for both workers and managers, from its inception through World War II.

In the years following the Great Depression, management training programs, like general job training, were drastically cut back because of the large numbers of skilled managers who had lost jobs elsewhere and were eager to be hired wherever possible. But as the 1930s came to a close, the United States was bolstering its armaments for the possibility of war and management realized it was unable to produce adequately without competent managers at every level. As the need for skilled management dramatically increased, industry began once again to recruit management trainees.

Training programs for both management and the trades proliferated and training directors were kept busy sending qualified trainees quickly on to the work force. By 1945, nearly two million supervisory trainees had received certificates from government-provided training programs.

Since the 1960s the need for management training has been universally recognized and numerous theories and techniques of management are now in practice. Under government pressure, most businesses began in the 1970s to pay serious attention to upgrading the positions of women and racial minorities to supervisory levels and to giving them greater responsibility. Today there is much emphasis on involving women and minorities in management training programs all over the country and big business is offering abundant managerial opportunities to men and women alike.

Nature of the work

Management trainees perform work specific to the business or agency that employs them, often getting a chance to work in many different areas. A trainee in restaurant management may get experience in food preparation, cooking, waiting on tables, and in acting as host or hostess before actually learning management functions such as bookkeeping, food and beverage ordering, or hiring and firing staff. In a bank, a management trainee may work as a teller or a loan desk assistant while acquiring management skills.

In large firms with more than one site, a trainee may be transferred from one location to the next during the training period, often relocating to different cities throughout the country. Many large businesses offer management training programs in many different departments. A field management trainee would learn to perform managerial duties that take place outside the offices or headquarters. Such a training program often involves special courses relating to the particular requirements of management in the field.

Administrative trainees, on the other hand, will learn functions of office management such as scheduling and budget preparation. Trainees in both types of programs will often make visits to plants or field locations to increase their knowledge of the business.

In many fields, the duties of trainees are broad and varied. Often the program may involve special instruction or home study and include learning the background or history of the business. Trainees may be taught to function as managers at various levels, such as in-house, district, and senior management.

Many trainees work directly under an experienced manager or a special mentor on the job. In such a situation, the trainee may be asked to perform important learning tasks, such as creating a plan for an ad or sales campaign or to provide ideas for solving particular problems within the firm. In such a program, the trainee often follows the overseeing manager in all of his or her daily duties.

Two management trainees attend a demonstration of their company's mainframe computer.

Requirements

Management trainees with at least a bachelor's degree will find easiest entry into management training programs, both at large and small private firms as well as at government agencies. A graduate or postgraduate degree in business administration is an excellent credential, although majors in engineering or in science are a plus in many businesses. A strong liberal arts background is often more than acceptable. Also, because computers are so much a part of business today, it is important for almost any management trainee to be familiar with computer operations.

Some companies make a point of looking for management trainees who have acquired a master's degree or a doctorate, in a field relating to the work the firm is involved in. A business in the computer industry, for example, may prefer a candidate whose degree is in computer science or information processing. Trainees at any level may be sent by their firm to receive additional schooling in fields they have not already studied, such as economics or finance.

In any case, all companies are interested in applicants who have a record of good grades and often consider grade point average when deciding between acceptance or rejection of a potential trainee. Students who have proved to be active in clubs, sports, or other group events are often considered desirable by employers, as these activities indicate social skills or the desire to work in cooperation with others.

Although research shows that nearly half of all salaried managers have a bachelor's degree or higher and that this figure is always growing larger, there is still room for those who may not yet be college graduates. Persons with a good deal of experience in a particular field may be accepted into management programs and work toward their college diploma while learning on the job. In addition, many firms whose structure are less complex or which include numerous small outlets may have different standards of hiring than larger firms. Such companies will often accept into their management programs ambitious high-school graduates with good academic records.

Special requirements

Aside from receiving a diploma or an academic degree, there are no special requirements for a management trainee. Neither managers nor trainees are required to join unions or to have special licenses or other credentials.

There are a number of professional organizations open to those in managerial positions and though not usually required by employers, these groups provide an opportunity for professionals to come together and to stay informed of advancements in their fields. Such organizations also frequently offer their members special programs and events designed to increase knowledge or skills in management. Membership in a professional group is often encouraged by employers in both government and the private sector.

Opportunities for experience and exploration

In nearly any community one will be able to find companies that offer management training programs. Contact the personnel departments of any business you may be interested in and ask if they offer management training. You may also wish to inquire about the possibility of speaking to any managers or training directors who are employed. If you have neighbors or friends in business or industry managerial positions, they can often answer questions about the opportunities at their own places of work or may give you some insight into any training programs that they know of.

One good source of information is always the library. The reference librarian should be able to direct you to sources of information about specific businesses and to material published by national management associations. Always keep informed, through your college or university placement department, of business recruiters who visit on campus to talk with students about the career opportunities provided by their particular companies.

Related occupations

Work as a management trainee is directly related to management positions in any field. Other occupations related to management trainee are gathered by the U.S. Department of Labor under the classification of miscellaneous managers and officials not else where classified. These include managers of industrial organizations, department and program managers, superintendents of plant protection, customer and technical service managers, directors of research and development, presidents, vice presidents, project directors, service directors, and membership directors. Other related occupations also include consultants, maintenance superintendents, field representatives, and security officers.

Methods of entering

Generally, those seeking entry into management training make getting a college degree their first priority. College and universities often have job placement services that help students find work after graduation and through which companies may recruit trainees. On-campus career fairs may also put students in touch with personnel recruiters from large firms with established management training programs.

Graduates may wish to contact directly the personnel departments of firms they are interested in, sending a letter and resume. They may then be requested to come in for an interview. If the interview involves traveling to another city, the company will ordinarily pay travel expenses.

A training program in a large firm may include both new employees and trainees brought in from other departments of the company. Many managers have had a great deal of experience in the work force before entering training programs. Government agencies in particular tend to cull trainees from their own ranks of employees.

Because the search for management trainees is a continuous business for most firms, those interested in such programs will do well to watch for career days at school, to keep informed of possible opportunities listed by the college personnel services, and to regularly check the classified ads placed by businesses searching for new management candidates.

Advancement

The ability of any management trainee to advance is dependent upon how many management positions are available in the firm. A small company may have only two or three managerial positions, whereas a large company will have more staff and greater opportunities to advance quickly.

Management trainees will often train for upper or middle management positions rather than having to begin as an entry level manager. Such trainees are often selected because they have advanced degrees. Many trainees find that, after a few years of management with one firm, they can advance by moving to positions of greater responsibility and income at another firm.

Employment outlook

There are currently thousands of management training programs throughout the country, training anywhere from a few management candidates concurrently to many more than that in bigger firms. There are now more than 8 million managers working in business and government, half of whom work in the clothing, banking, or real estate industries.

Although the demand for management trainees varies from one firm to another and from one year to the next, the need for such trainees is constant and growing, and is now surpassing the need for most other workers.

Large companies tend to hire about the same number of trainees each year, whereas smaller firms may recruit trainees according to demand. When business is slow, fewer applicants will receive management training. Sometimes firms will cut back if the work load lessens, but for the most part management trainees have good job security.

Earnings

Earnings in any management program vary widely from one firm to the next. Pay rates may be determined by the earnings of others in the field, by the size of the firm, and often by the trainee's own background or experience. It is not unusual for management trainees to start at a salary 10 to 20 percent higher than that offered in other similar types of positions.

Conditions of work

Management trainees, for the most part, do not perform difficult, dirty work or manual labor, although they work under varied kinds of conditions and in many different types of environments. Firms with several offices or branches throughout the country may have central training locations to which they send all their management trainees. Such centers may be part of the company headquarters or in a separate location of their own and are ordinarily equipped with up-to-date training materials and equipment. Trainees are often sent to live at the center for extended periods of time during the training period. In some cases, this will require travel to a distant location, which may be disruptive to the trainee's normal home life.

Some management trainees rotate from one job to another, others remain at one station, usually in an office, a store, or a plant or building site. Managerial candidates with special training may be assigned to unusual locations, such as a nuclear power plant or an oilfield. Because most managers have an office, no matter what environment they work in, their train-

ees will usually be involved in some desk work. Management offices may be part of a broad complex of suites in a large building, such as is the case of many government job sites, or the office may be as simple as a tiny room in a shed at a building site.

Management training often requires a great deal of adapt ability. To learn all the skills in their particular business, trainees may have to wear work clothing, safety glasses, or hard hats while performing certain jobs.

Although the working hours for most management trainees may be officially set at forty hours per week, trainees often end up working many extra hours. Such time may be spent not only in long hours on the job but also at home studying and doing paper work. Most employers expect the dedicated trainee to devote additional time and thought to their work, and the willingness to do so is often a criterion for qualifying for a managerial position.

Management trainees ordinarily receive benefits comparable to those of other employees and are often provided with tuition aid programs by their employers for additional study related to their work.

Social and psychological factors

Flexibility is the key to success in any management training program. Although trainees may rotate every few months, or even every few weeks, from one position to the next, they may find it difficult when the time comes to move to a new location or department. It is best to try to remain completely adaptable to the changes in duties and responsibilities.

Gaining a managerial position depends on doing well in the management training program and the resultant competitiveness may be anxiety-producing for some management trainees. The job may also seem stressful because there is so much to learn and the trainee is under pressure to excel.

Although management styles differ from one manager to the next, most companies look for trainees who display good social skills and who seem to have some ability to gain the trust and loyalty of others. Trainees must prove that they are good team players and that they have a talent for shrewd decisions, fair play, and diplomacy. Management candidates who have well-developed self confidence and a clear understanding of their role within the firm or department have the best chance of doing well when promoted to the position of manager.

GOE: 11.05.02; SIC: Any industry; SOC: 139

◇ **SOURCES OF ADDITIONAL INFORMATION**

A pamphlet titled "Sources of Information About Careers" is available by writing to:

American Management Association
135 West 50th Street
New York, NY 10020

Further career information may be obtained from:

Academy of Management
PO Drawer KZ
Mississippi State University
Mississippi State, MS 39762

Administrative Management Society
4622 Street Road
Trevose, PA 19047

Employment Management Association
5 West Hargett Street
Suite 1100
Raleigh, NC 27601

National Management Association
2210 Arbor Boulevard
Dayton, OH 45439

Women in Management
2 North Riverside Plaza, Suite 2400
Chicago, IL 60606

◇ **RELATED ARTICLES**

Volume 1: Business Administration
Volume 2: City managers; College admissions directors; College financial aid administrators; Data base managers; Financial institution officers and managers; General managers and top executives; Hotel and motel managers; Industrial traffic managers; Literary agents and artists' managers; Management analysts and consultants; Marketing, advertising, and public relations managers; Property and real estate managers; Restaurant and food service managers; Retail business owners; Retail managers; School administrators
Volume 3: Clerical supervisors and managers; Farm operatives and managers; Landscapers and grounds managers; Range managers

---

Marketing, advertising, and public relations managers

Definition

A *marketing, advertising, or public relations manager* directs the activities of an agency, executes the advertising, marketing, or public relations policies of an organization, and plans and conducts public relations programs to create and maintain a favorable public image for an employer or client.

History

Advertising dates back to ancient times. Babylonian tradesman hired barkers to shout the praises of their wares on the street. Adver-

tising signboards were seen outside shops from the earliest days of written language. The walls themselves were advertising media.

Organized marketing had its start as early as the thirteenth century, when businessmen in different cities formed a league to promote trade and commerce. In 1681, early catalogs for books and other goods appeared.

American advertising dates back to colonial times, when handbills publicized everything from land sales to print shops. Mass advertising first became prominent in the 1800s, as industrialization produced unprecedented quantities of consumer merchandise.

The mid-nineteenth century was the Age of Invention—it saw the birth of the sewing machine, phonograph, icebox, washing machine, and more. All of these were advertised in the news papers. Suddenly Americans believed they "needed" products that hadn't even been available to "want" before. In 1860, $22 million was spent on advertising. By 1867, the yearly figure was up to $50 million.

In 1867, the first advertising agency was formed. It was called George P. Powell & Co., and was based in New York. Its primary function was the buying and selling of advertising space.

In-house advertising departments became popular in U.S. companies in the 1940s and 1960s. After that time, companies began to depend more on outside agencies for their major promotions.

In the mid-1980s, corporate belt-tightening caused many companies to cut back their public relations operations. Around that same time, the advertising, marketing and public relations fields became the primary targets of "merger mania." As agencies merged with or were bought by other agencies, jobs were duplicated, and many people were laid off. In the late 1980s, several large U.S. advertising agencies were acquired by foreign investors.

Although the effects of these shifts continue to be felt, advertising, marketing, and public relations are an extremely important aspect of the business world today. Herein lie many of the creative or "glamor" jobs so largely sought in the overall marketplace. In a market of many virtually identical products, it's the promoters that influence consumer decisions.

Nature of the work

The primary objective of any firm is to market its products or services profitably. In small firms, all marketing responsibili- ties may be assumed by the owner or chief executive officer. In a large firm offering numerous products and services nationally or worldwide, experienced marketing, advertising, and public relations managers coordinate these activities. In large firms, the executive vice-president for marketing directs the overall marketing policy, including sales, marketing strategy, advertising, sales promotion, and public relations activities. Middle and supervisory managers generally oversee staffs of professionals and technicians who do this work.

Marketing managers or product group managers develop the firm's detailed marketing strategy. With the help of product managers and *market research managers*, they determine the demand for the company's products and services and identify potential consumers such

A marketing manager discusses a draft of a new marketing proposal with her supervisor.

as businesses, wholesalers, retailers, government agencies, or the general public. Marketing managers develop pricing strategy to maximize the firm's profits and share of the market. Along with sales, product, and other managers, they monitor trends that indicate the need for new products and services and oversee product development. Marketing managers work with *advertising and sales promotion managers* to best describe the firm's products and services and sway potential users.

In industry, *advertising managers* confer with department heads to discuss possible new accounts and to outline new policies or sales promotion campaigns. They confer with officials of newspapers, radio, and television stations, billboard advertisers, and advertising agencies to negotiate advertising contracts. Advertising managers allocate advertising space to departments or products. They review and approve television and radio advertisements before release. They review rates and give authorization to projects. *Advertising managers* involved in print and publicity direct staff engaged in developing advertisements and direct research for advertising campaigns. They authorize information for publication, such as interviews with reporters or articles about the company.

An *advertising manager* in an agency formulates plans to extend business with established accounts and to solicit new accounts. They coordinate the activities of various departments, such as sales, graphic arts, media, and research. They inspect layouts and advertising copy and edit radio and television scripts. Advertising managers conduct meetings with department supervisors to outline and initiate new advertising policies and procedures. They also may confer with clients to provide marketing or technical advice.

Public relations managers generally supervise staffs of *public relations specialists*. They direct

387

publicity programs to promote the image of the firm to consumers, stockholders, or the general public. Using any necessary communication media, public relations managers may be called upon to clarify or justify the firm's philosophy and actions regarding health or environmental issues. Presentations may be made to special-interest groups. In large, product-oriented firms, they may be responsible for evaluating ads and sales promotion programs in terms of compatibility with public relations efforts. In service-oriented firms, they may actually supervise advertising and promotional efforts. Public relations managers may produce internal company communications, conferring with labor relations managers and financial managers. They may assist company executives in drafting speeches, and may oversee various forms of public contact. They often respond to outside requests for information.

Requirements

Most employers prefer that marketing, advertising, and public relations managers have a broad liberal arts background. A bachelor's degree in sociology, psychology, literature, or philosophy is often acceptable. Requirements will vary according to the individual job.

For marketing and sales management positions, some employers prefer a bachelor's or master's degree in business administration with an emphasis on marketing. Courses in business law, economics, accounting, finance, mathematics, and statistics are highly recommended. In highly technical industries, such as aircraft and guided missile manufacturing, a bachelor's degree in engineering or science combined with a master's degree in business administration is desirable.

Some employers want their advertising managers to have bachelor's degrees in advertising. The curriculum should include courses in marketing, consumer behavior, communications methods and technology, and visual arts courses.

For public relations management positions, some employers look for people with bachelor's or master's degrees in public relations or journalism. The curriculum should include courses in advertising, business administration, public affairs, political science, and creative and technical writing. Familiarity with computerized word-processing applications is important for many marketing, advertising, and public relations management positions.

Special requirements

Marketing, advertising, and public relations specialists do not need to obtain a license or special certification or join a union to get a job. Membership in a professional group is not required, but such a membership will help managers to keep abreast of current developments in the field.

Opportunities for experience and exploration

At least eighty-seven American universities offer undergraduate courses in advertising, and some offer degrees in it. Many also offer courses in marketing as well. High-school guidance counselors can help students to determine which colleges offer such programs.

It may be possible to find a summer job or apprenticeship at an advertising agency or marketing or public relations firm. The marketing, advertising, and public relations departments of local corporations or department stores may provide these opportunities as well. When students are first exploring these fields, what they learn is more important than what they earn. Even if an apprenticeship pays nothing but allows them to gather some of the experience or portfolio pieces they need, their time could be well rewarded.

The magazines and trade journals related to these fields make for valuable reading. You may find them more interesting than most such publications. It's also a good idea to pay close attention to any particularly well done advertisements found in magazines, newspaper, or on television or radio. You can then study the whole advertising campaign for that product. Think about whether these ads would influence consumers to buy the product, and why. Then consider the kinds of ads you would produce if you were promoting that product. Another good learning experience is to draw up some sample ads for those products.

Related occupations

Other personnel involved with marketing, advertising, and public relations include art directors, commercial and graphic artists, copy chiefs, copywriters, editors, lobbyists, market research analysts, public relations specialists, sales representatives, technical writers, account executives, brand managers, publicists, media directors, and market researchers.

Methods of entering

Many jobs in this field are gained through personal contacts with friends, relatives, and teachers. Newspaper classified ads can be a source of employment as well, as can employment agencies. There are certain employment agencies that specialize in the advertising, marketing, and public relations fields, but these are rare.

When one is first starting out, it is often easier to find entry-level "in-house" jobs in the advertising, public relations, or marketing departments of companies or department stores than it is to try to find work in a much sought after agency. Much specialized experience can be gained in this way. Entry level market research jobs are not difficult to get. Even if hopefuls start as production assistants or glorified go-fers, if they work diligently and pay close attention to what is going on around them, they will find opportunities to advance.

Advancement

Most marketing, advertising, and public relations management positions are filled by promoting experienced staff or related professional or technical personnel, such as sales representatives, purchasing agents, buyers, advertising workers, and public relations specialists. Promotions may occur more quickly in large firms than in small firms, as there are more positions to fill.

Demonstrated experience, ability, and leadership will lead to promotion. Participating in management training programs can accelerate this advancement. Many firms provide their employees with continuing education opportunities, either in-house or at local colleges or universities. Many encourage employee participation in seminars or conferences. Numerous marketing and related associations sponsor national or local training programs that deal with different phases of management activities, often in collaboration with colleges. There are opportunities to learn about brand and product management, international marketing, sales management evaluation, telemarketing and direct sales, marketing communication, organizational communication, and data-processing procedures and management. Many firms will pay all or part of the cost of these courses for their employees.

One good strategy for advancement is to become the best-informed person in the agency on a particular account. For a gasoline account, for example, it would be a good idea to read books on oil geology and the production of petroleum products, and trade journals in the field. Visiting the client's refineries and research laboratories, and even talking to motorists at service stations can pay off. Knowing more about the business at hand than the superiors do puts a person in a good position to get ahead.

Because of the importance and high visibility of their jobs, marketing, advertising, and public relations managers are often prime candidates for advancement. Successful managers are often promoted to higher positions in their own or other firms. Some become top executives, or, if they have sufficient capital, they may open their own management or consulting firms.

Employment outlook

By the early 1990s, marketing, advertising, and public relations managers held about 400,000 jobs in this country. Approximately one third of that number were employed by motor vehicle dealers; advertising agencies; management, consulting, and public relations firms; department stores; computer and data processing services firms; and radio and television broadcasting stations.

The employment of marketing, advertising, and public relations managers is expected to increase faster than the average for all occupations through the year 2000. This is related to increasingly intense domestic and foreign competition in the field of consumer products and services, which creates a greater demand for marketing and promotional efforts. Also, many job openings occur each year to replace managers who move into higher positions or leave the labor force. Still, the ample supply of experienced professional and technical personnel and recent college graduates seeking these management positions may result in significant job competition. The best opportunities will go to college graduates with extensive experience who possess a high level of creativity and strong communication skills.

Because of the increasing use of computers, employment of marketing, advertising, and public relations managers is expected to grow most rapidly in the data processing services industry. Other business services industries should show faster than average growth as well, as businesses find it increasingly cost-effective to contract out these services rather than try to handle them in-house. Examples of firms that offer these services are advertising agencies, public relations firms, and establishments offering direct mail, commercial photography, art, and graphics services. Extremely rapid growth is also expected in the radio and television broadcasting industry, and in travel, hotel, restaurant, and amusement and recreation services industries, as personal incomes and leisure time increase.

Opportunities for marketing, advertising, and public relations managers are expected to decrease in some manufacturing industries. Opportunities for these jobs will grow no faster than the average for all occupations in the educational services industry and hospitals.

Earnings

The median annual salary of marketing, advertising, and public relations managers was $42,480 in the early 1990s. The lowest ten percent earned $21,240 or less, while the top ten percent earned well over $63,000. But salaries between $90,000 and $120,000 are not uncommon for these positions. Many of these managers earn bonuses equal to ten percent or more of their salaries. Salary levels vary substantially depending upon the level of managerial responsibility length of service, extent of sales territory, and size and location of the firm.

Conditions of work

Working under pressure is unavoidable for marketing, advertising, and public relations managers. Schedules change, problems arise, and deadlines and sales goals must be met. They generally are given offices close to top executives or managers and to the departments they direct. While this is convenient, it can actually increase the pressure. Long hours, including evenings and weekends, are usual.

Substantial travel is often involved in these positions, and job transfers between headquarters and regional offices are common, which could be disruptive to family life. Attendance at meetings sponsored by associations or industries is often mandatory. Advertising managers may have to travel to meet with clients or media representatives. Public relations managers

may travel to meet with special-interest groups or government officials. Depending on the specific job, marketers can be traveling twenty days out of thirty.

Social and psychological factors

People interested in becoming marketing, advertising, and public relations managers should be mature, creative, highly motivated, resistant to stress, flexible, and decisive. They will need the ability to communicate persuasively, both in speaking and writing. They need tact, good judgment, and an exceptional ability to establish and maintain effective relationships with supervisory and professional staff members and clients.

In these positions it helps to be an efficient administrator, willing and able to set high standards, capable of strategic thinking, research-minded, and prepared to share credit for good work and accept blame for bad work. It helps to have a clear understanding of how to budget and control expenditures and how promotions work: in other words, how to convert a favorable consumer attitude toward your product into increased sales.

GOE: 11.09.01; SIC: 7311, 8732, 8743; SOC: 125

◇ SOURCES OF ADDITIONAL INFORMATION

American Advertising Federation
1400 K Street, NW
Suite 1000
Washington, DC 20005

American Association of Advertising Agencies
666 Third Avenue
13th Floor
New York, NY 10017

American Marketing Association
250 South Wacker Drive
Suite 200
Chicago, IL 60606

Council of Sales Promotion Agencies
176 Madison Avenue
5th Floor
New York, NY 10016

Promotion Marketing Association of America
322 Eighth Avenue
Suite 1201
New York, NY 10001

Public Relations Society of America
33 Irving Place
New York, NY 10003

Women in Advertising and Marketing
4200 Wisconsin Avenue, NW
Suite 106-238
Washington, DC 20016

◇ **RELATED ARTICLES**

Volume 1: Advertising Business; Broadcasting; Business Administration; Magazine Publishing; Newspaper Publishing
Volume 2: Advertising workers; Management analysts and consultants; Management trainees; Marketing research personnel; Media specialists; Public relations specialists; Writers and editors
Volume 3: Public opinion researchers; Radio, television, and print advertising sales workers; Telemarketers

Marketing research personnel

Definition

The *marketing research personnel* collect, analyze, and interpret data to determine potential sales of a product or service. To this end they prepare reports and make recommendations on subjects ranging from preferences of prospective customers to methods and costs of distribution and advertising. They research available printed data and accumulate new data through personal interviews and questionnaires. Some marketing workers specialize in one industry or area. For example, agricultural marketing specialists prepare sales forecasts for food businesses, which use the information in their advertising and sales programs.

History

Knowing what customers want, why they want it, and what price they are willing to pay for it have been concerns of manufacturers and producers of goods and services for some time. The sampling of public opinion to determine how many people would react in any given situation is not new. On July 24, 1824, the *Harrisburg Pennsylvanian* printed the results of a straw vote on the upcoming presidential election taken in Wilmington, Delaware. In 1916, the *Literary Digest* began its now historic poll. It mailed out millions of ballots to people selected from telephone directories and other lists.

With the increase in business and the trend toward better distribution of manufactured products, businesses saw in market research a way to maintain contact with what the people wanted. Market research began in an effort to serve these business interests. The application of research methods to other fields followed and, in the 1930s and 1940s, the statistical needs of the government gave new impetus to the increase of knowledge in the field.

Emphasis on market research did not really occur until after World War II. From this point, however, new knowledge of techniques and increased uses of the findings have developed at a rapid pace.

Through the many aspects of marketing research, the preferences of people are noted in the type of goods and services provided by business. The marketing of goods, from the identification of customer likes and dislikes to the distribution of company products, is the concern of the marketing research worker.

Nature of the work

The marketing research worker collects, analyzes, and interprets all kinds of information that would help a company improve its product, arrange sales and distribution policies, and make decisions regarding its future plans and direction.

One area of market research is company services and products. Here studies are made

391

Much marketing research is conducted in retail outlets, where consumers of a particular product are easily selected for questioning.

on current products or those in an experimental stage. Information on the brand name or trademark and product design or packaging are illustrative of the data collected. Also included in this aspect of market research would be studies of the services and products of competitors.

Another area of market research is sales methods and policies. Here, the marketing research worker is concerned with detailed studies of the firm's sales records. Information on sales in various geographical areas is analyzed and compared in relation to previous sales records, to changes in population, and to total and seasonal sales volume. In this way, peak sales periods and sales trends in various sections may be noted. Such information helps plan future sales campaigns, sales quotas, and commissions.

Advertising research is closely related to sales research. Studies on the effectiveness of advertising in different sections of the country and of the advertising media used are conducted and compared with sales records. These data are helpful in planning advertising campaigns and in selecting the media to be used in different regions of the country.

Market research on consumer demand and opinion usually reflects the opinions of the men and women who use the goods or services. Questionnaires and interviews are usually used to gather information on consumer reaction to the style, design, price, use, and need for the product. The purpose of these studies is to attempt to find out who uses the product, or to ascertain potential users of the product or services. In addition, consumer opinion about the product or services is sought as well as suggestions for its improvement. Information of this type is helpful, for example, in forecasting sales, in planning modifications in design, or in determining color changes or options.

There are four basic market research jobs. One is the statistician who develops samples and weighs questionnaire returns. Another, the project supervisor, plans a study from the beginning. In conjunction with statisticians and other specialists he or she may design the questionnaire, determine the number and location of the interviews to be conducted, then analyze the returns and make the final report and recommendations. The heavy office work, such as examining the questionnaires when they come in from the field, counting the answers, fitting noncategorical answers into codes, and making up the primary count for the reports, is done by tabulators and coders. The final type of market research worker is the field interviewer who must meet all kinds of people and obtain from them the various kinds of information that have been set out in the questionnaire.

Obviously the marketing research worker must be thoroughly familiar with research techniques and procedures. Sometimes the problem is clearly defined and information can be gathered readily. Other times, the company executives may know only that a problem exists as evidenced by a decline in sales. The research worker is expected to collect the facts that will aid in dealing with this problem.

After the information has been collected, it is tabulated and analyzed. The results and recommendations are reported to company executives and to the interested departments.

Marketing research workers are employed mainly by business and industrial firms and by private research organizations that handle local surveys for companies on a contract basis. Advertising agencies also employ a number of market research analysts. Most of these organizations and agencies are located in larger cities with several having branch offices in smaller urban areas.

Requirements

In high school, courses in English and social studies are most important. Students should plan to take mathematics and to elect any courses in speech, journalism, psychology, or sociology that may be available.

A college degree is generally required for careers in market research. Majors in economics, business administration, or marketing provide a good background for most types of market research positions. Work in sociology and psychology is very helpful for those who lean toward consumer demand and opinion research, whereas work in statistics or engineering might be helpful for those who lean toward certain types of industrial or analytical research. A master's or MBA degree is frequently expected for special work in market research, statistics, economics, or computer science.

Graduate work at the doctorate level is not necessary for most positions but highly desirable for those who plan to become involved with complex research studies.

In general, the marketing research analyst should be intelligent, facile with words and numbers, and particularly interested in dealing with problem-solving situations involving data-collection and data-analysis processes.

Special requirements

There are no special requirements for licensure or admission to the profession. Marketing research workers will find it necessary to keep abreast of modern advances in research techniques and processes. Data-processing equipment and procedures and new advances in statistical treatment of data will require that researchers participate continually in professional activities designed to keep them informed of new processes and trends in the field.

Opportunities for experience and exploration

The high-school program may offer some opportunities for one to test abilities and interests as they relate generally to the field. Experiments in science, problems in student government, committee work, and other school activities provide a host of situations requiring mental processes similar to those of the marketing research worker. Part-time job opportunities may exist in one's area for employment as a survey interviewer. Participation in the training and field phases of several consumer surveys would offer actual contact with market

research supervisors, and at the same time provide experience in a real project.

Other work opportunities may be available where one can work on the coding and tabulation of survey data. Notices of such opportunities usually appear in the local newspapers or one may apply directly to research organizations in his or her area. These part-time positions are temporary and sporadic but usually the telephone or personal contacts can be made at the worker's convenience within a given period of time.

Related occupations

Other workers who possess many of the same talents as the marketing researcher include advertising agency workers, economists, public relations specialists, sales managers and sales representatives, sales promotion specialists, and statisticians.

Methods of entering

College placement offices are prepared to help students locate positions in marketing research. Contacts can be made with potential employers usually through professors, friends, relatives, and often as a result of summer employment during the college years.

Advancement

Most marketing research workers begin as junior analysts or research assistants. In these positions they will assist in training survey interviewers, in preparing survey questionnaires and related materials, and in tabulating and coding survey results. After sufficient experience in these and other aspects of research project development and conduct, the worker can move to positions involving supervisory and planning responsibilities. One might become an assistant manager, or manager of a city branch office of a large private research organization, or one might become a marketing research director for an industrial or business firm.

Some related positions to which one might transfer include various opportunities in advertising and sales. Such opportunities as regional sales manager or advertising manager are examples of closely allied fields of endeavor. Employment possibilities exist in other fields, such as data processing, university teaching, statistics, and industrial research and development. These opportunities are dependent on one's interest, experience, and preparation. Advancement and transfer to these related areas is sometimes possible because the market research analyst works closely with various other departments in a company. This provides one with an opportunity to learn more about their operation and to get to know, and to be known by, key executives in management positions.

Employment outlook

An estimated 29,000 full-time marketing research workers were employed in the early 1990s. This is a relatively small field, but is expected to grow rapidly through the rest of the decade. It is anticipated that there will be ample job opportunities for those trained in marketing research.

Increasing competition among producers of consumer goods and services and industrial products, combined with a growing awareness of the value of market research data, will contribute to the expansion of opportunities in the field. In addition, there will be new jobs opening up in nonmanufacturing settings such as banks, local government, and health care systems. For example, a city may employ marketing researchers to conduct a survey to find out the best place to build a school or hospital.

Many new graduates are attracted to this field, creating a competitive situation. The best jobs and the highest pay will go to those individuals who hold a master's degree or doctorate in marketing research, statistics, economics, or computer science.

Earnings

Beginning salaries in marketing research depend a great deal on the qualifications of the applicant, the nature of the position, and the size of the firm. In the early 1990s, a market research trainee with one or more college degrees could expect a beginning salary of $18,000 to $30,000 a year, depending upon the area of the country in which the firm was located. Some major package product firms paid outstanding beginners $35,000 to $45,000 a year.

Experienced market research workers in positions involving supervisory or planning responsibilities may earn as much as $69,000 per year, and in some of the top positions, such as marketing research director for a large firm, the salary earned could range from $100,000 to $150,000 annually.

Because most marketing research workers are employed by business or industrial firms, the usual medical, pension, vacation, and other benefits are available.

Conditions of work

Market research workers usually work a normal forty-hour week. Occasionally, they have to work overtime to meet a project deadline or to obtain data immediately for some other company emergency. Field and phone research may require evening and weekend hours in order to reach people who work during the day. Telemarketers regularly have evening assignments. They work in comfortable offices usually located in the firm's main headquarters. Some positions require traveling to various regions of the country, but these are generally short assignments. The market analyst is not required to be away from home for long periods of time.

Social and psychological factors

Persons who enjoy variety and change will find the "new problems and new faces" aspects of market research work most satisfying. In a large firm, the marketing research worker may be called in on a company problem at any time. New problems of research often seem insurmountable and, for many workers, this constitutes the real challenge of the work. Tackling such a problem and eventually solving it, of course, can provide considerable satisfaction to a person who accepts this kind of a challenge. Working under the pressure of deadlines is one of the unattractive features for certain people. Others find that they work particularly well when forced to complete a project or solve a problem within a specified period of time.

The traveling required in some positions appeals to those who find pleasure in visiting strange places and meeting new people. Traveling, however, is not essential in all positions and those who do not find this aspect of the work satisfying can avoid, for the most part, accepting such positions without endangering their career plans.

GOE: 11.06.03; SIC: 8742; SOC: 1912

◇ **SOURCES OF ADDITIONAL INFORMATION**

American Marketing Association
250 South Wacker Drive, Suite 200
Chicago, IL 60606

American Statistical Association
1429 Duke Street
Alexandria, VA 22314

Marketing Research Association
111 East Wacker Drive, Suite 600
Chicago, IL 60601

◇ **RELATED ARTICLES**

Volume 1: Advertising; Computer Software; Marketing; Public Relations; Social Sciences
Volume 2: Advertising workers; Marketing, advertising, and public relations managers; Public relations specialists; Statisticians
Volume 3: Public opinion researchers; Statistical clerks; Telemarketers

Mathematicians

Definition

A *mathematician* solves or directs the solution of problems in higher mathematics, including algebra, geometry, number theory, logic, and topology. The application of this work may be in scientific fields such as engineering, physics, and astronomy, or in business as management tools for the problems of production, logistics, and development. Theoretical mathematicians are concerned with the development of relationships among mathematical forms and the underlying principles that can be applied to a variety of problems including electronic data processing and military planning. Applied mathematicians develop the actual techniques and approaches to problem solving in the physical, biological, and social sciences. A mathematician may act as a consultant to industry to assist research personnel to set up the application of a problem-solving method.

History

People have been concerned with mathematics since earliest times and each civilization has contributed significant advances. Euclid, the geometrician, Eratosthenes, the astronomer, and Archimedes, the physicist, are examples of men who contributed new knowledge to their fields or who extended knowledge in their fields through the application of mathematics.

In the twentieth century alone, we have come to recognize the contribution of mathematics not only in reference to such important technological advances as the automobile, television, nuclear energy, and our space exploration, but as it can be applied to the research and experimental efforts in such fields as sociology, psychology, and education. Space vehicles and electronic computers are but two developments that characterize the dynamic nature and increasing importance of mathematics in the future. Mathematics may be one of the oldest and most basic of sciences, yet it is always contributing to the new.

Although mathematics may be considered a "pure" science, that is one which may be studied for its own sake, this abstract knowledge has often been applied to produce engineering and other scientific achievements. The non-Euclidean geometry developed by Bernard Riemann in 1854 seemed quite impractical at the time, yet some years later, Albert Einstein used it as part of his work in the development of his theory of relativity. This theory in turn appeared to have no practical application at the time, but later became the basis for work in nuclear energy.

Nature of the work

There are two broad areas of opportunity in mathematics—theoretical and applied. The du-

Mathematicians use complex computer systems to generate and test new theories.

ties performed, the processes involved, the work situations, and the equipment used vary considerably in both areas depending upon the institutional or organizational setting. The nature of the work and the work expectations, however, follow the general pattern that is described for each of these areas.

Theoretical mathematicians deal with pure and abstract mathematical concepts without concern for the practical application of their work to everyday problems. They are concerned with the advancement of mathematical knowledge, the logical development of mathematical systems, and the study and analysis of relationships among mathematical forms. Pure mathematicians focus their efforts mainly on problems dealing with the investigative and developmental aspects of principles of mathematics and mathematical reasoning.

Applied mathematicians are concerned with the development and application of mathematical knowledge to practical and research problems in the social, physical, life, and earth sciences. Business, industry, and government rely heavily on the mathematician, particularly in their research and development programs. Therefore, it is necessary for mathematicians to have some knowledge of their employer's operations and products as well as competence in their own field. Applied mathematicians work on problems ranging from stability of rockets to effects of new drugs on disease.

The applied and theoretical aspects of the mathematician's work are not always clearly delineated and in many positions, usually those dealing with the application of mathematics, the worker may become involved in

both. The rapidly expanding reliance on electronic computers demands that, in addition to a fundamental knowledge about general modern computing equipment, the mathematician should have some basic experience in computer programming and operation.

Specialists in the field of applied mathematics include the following:

Computer-applications engineers formulate mathematical models and develop computer systems to solve scientific and engineering problems.

Engineering analysts apply logical analysis to scientific, engineering, and other technical problems and convert them to mathematical terms to be solved by digital computers.

Operations-research analysts employ the same method to solve management and operational problems.

Financial analysts analyze from a statistical standpoint information concerning the investment programs of public, industrial, and financial institutions, such as banks, insurance companies, and brokerage and investment houses. They interpret data, construct charts and graphs, and summarize their findings in terms of investment trends, risks, and economic influences.

Weight analysts are concerned with weight, balance, loading, and operational functions of ships, aircraft, space vehicles, missiles, research instrumentation, and commercial and industrial products and systems. They use computers to analyze the weight factors of structural assemblies, components, and loads and work with design engineering personnel to coordinate these specifications with other phases of product development.

Requirements

The basic educational requirement for this profession is a bachelor's degree with a major in mathematics. The undergraduate program includes work in algebra, geometry, numerical analysis, topology, and statistics. Typical courses include differential equations, linear algebra, advanced calculus, number theory, and theory and application of digital computers. In addition to these and other courses from which the mathematics major may select, students should sample broadly in the humanities and the social, physical, and life sciences.

For work in research and an ever-increasing number of jobs in industry, government, and research, an advanced degree is required. A doctorate is necessary for college-level teaching and for more advanced research work.

Training in the field to which the mathematics will be applied is important. This could include physics, engineering, business and industrial management, economics, statistics, chemistry, and biology.

Other qualifications that should be considered and assessed are interests in mathematics in relation to basic arithmetic processes, graphs and statistics, basic algebraic and geometric concepts and ideas, abilities in abstract reasoning, analyzing and interpreting mathematical ideas, speed and accuracy with numbers, and spatial visualization.

Personal characteristics such as intellectual curiosity and imagination are also necessary qualifications for this field.

Special requirements

Generally, there are no special licenses or certificates required for employment as a mathematician. Government positions usually require that the applicant take a civil service examination, in addition to meeting certain specified requirements that vary according to the type and level of position. To qualify for certification as a high-school mathematics teacher, one must meet specific requirements established by each state education department.

Opportunities for experience and exploration

High-school students who are interested in mathematics may wish to accelerate their studies by enrolling in summer session programs offering regular or elective mathematics courses. Some schools have specialized mathematics honors or advanced placement courses as part of their regular summer or evening school programs. There are also mathematics competitions for high-school students. These competitions may include college scholarship awards. These opportunities should be investigated so that students can assess their potential for further experience and exploration in mathematics.

Summer and part-time employment in government agencies and industrial firms provide valuable experiences and offer students opportunities to test their knowledge, interests, abilities, and personal characteristics in practical work settings.

Related occupations

With a degree in mathematics, interested persons could enter such other occupations as actuaries, computer programmers, operations research analysts, statisticians, or systems analysts. A strong background in mathematics may qualify others for work in such fields as economics, engineering, finance, or genetics.

Methods of entering

Most college placement offices help students find positions in business and industry upon graduation. Teaching positions in high schools are usually obtained by personal contacts through friends, relatives, or college professors, or through the college placement office by application and interview. College and university assistantships, instructorships, and professorships are obtained often by recommendation of one's professor or department chairperson.

Positions in federal, state, and local governments are usually announced well in advance of the civil service examination and students can check for such notices on bulletin boards in their college placement offices or other locations such as post offices and government buildings.

Advancement

Numerous opportunities for advancement to higher-level positions or into related areas of employment are available to the mathematician. Promotions of mathematicians are generally made on the basis of advanced preparation, individual appraisal by one's superior officers, or by competitive examination.

Opportunity in closely allied fields, such as statistics, accountancy, actuarial work, and computers permit the professional mathematician to change employment, to relocate geographically, or to advance to better positions with higher salaries with a minimum of inconvenience.

Employment outlook

Approximately 20,000 mathematicians were employed in the early 1990s, most of them in government and in service and manufacturing industries. An additional 19,000 held faculty positions in colleges and universities. The majority of government mathematicians were located in the federal government, mainly in the Defense Department and, in smaller numbers, in the National Aeronautics and Space Administration and Commerce Department. Those in the private sector worked primarily for business services, including research and development laboratories, educational services, computer and data-processing services, noncommercial educational and research organizations, and engineering, architectural, and surveying services; for manufacturers of guided missiles, space vehicles, and aircraft; and for manufacturers of office, computing, and accounting machines. Mathematicians also worked for banks, insurance companies, and public utilities.

Overall employment of mathematicians is expected to show modest gains through the end of the 1990s.

A continuing shortage of mathematicians with a doctorate will create favorable opportunities in both the applied and theoretical areas. Applied mathematicians with a doctorate will be favored in industry, while theoretical mathematicians will fare better in teaching and research positions in colleges and universities.

Industry and government will need mathematicians to work in operations research, mathematical modeling, aerodynamics, numerical analysis, computer systems design and programming, information and data processing, applied mathematical physics, robotics, market research, and commercial surveys, and as consultants in industrial laboratories.

For mathematicians with a master's degree, jobs in college teaching or theoretical research may be rare, but openings should be plentiful in applied areas such as computer science and data processing. The best opportunities for mathematicians with only a bachelor's degree will exist for those with a strong background— or, even better, a double major—in computer science. Holders of bachelor's or master's degrees in mathematics who also meet state certification requirements are in demand as high-school mathematics teachers.

Earnings

The income of the mathematician varies with the level of training and the work setting. In the early 1990s, beginning positions ranged as follows: with a bachelor's degree, approximately $24,400 a year; with a master's degree, $30,600; with a doctorate, about $39,500. Starting salaries paid in industry were higher than those in government or educational institutions.

In the early 1990s in the federal government the mathematician with a bachelor's degree and no experience could expect a starting salary ranging from $14,800 to $18,400 a year. Those with a master's degree could begin at $22,500 to $27,200. Positions requiring the doctorate offered starting salaries of $27,200 to $32,600. The average for all mathematicians working in government was $38,100 per year.

In the early 1990s, the median annual earnings for all mathematicians with a doctorate was as follows: in business and industry, $51,200; in educational institutions, $40,200; and in the federal government, $48,300.

Conditions of work

The mathematician in industrial and government positions usually has regular hours and works a forty-hour week. The work environment is generally pleasant, well lighted, and typical of the modern, well-equipped office. The work is not considered hazardous, but may require long periods of close concentration and eye or nerve strain. Professional mathematicians who work with or near computers will probably work in air-conditioned buildings because these machines are extremely sensitive to temperature changes.

Social and psychological factors

The young man or woman considering a career in mathematics should recognize the increased emphasis being placed on the study of mathematics in our society. Other fields of study, such as the biological, physical, and social sciences, are demanding more preparation in mathematics from their students. Nonetheless, the future development of our nation is dependent on a continued supply of well-qualified theoretical and applied mathematicians who can assume responsible positions in government, industry, and educational institutions. In these positions they will need to communicate with other scientists and technicians as well as management personnel. Therefore, mathematicians, in addition to their own specialized competencies, will need to be conversant with basic concepts and ideas in other areas, such as psychology, economics, and engineering.

GOE: 02.01.01; SIC: 8221; SOC: 1739

◇ **SOURCES OF ADDITIONAL INFORMATION**

American Mathematical Society
PO Box 6248
Providence, RI 02940

Association for Women in Mathematics
Box 178
Wellesley College
Wellesley, MA 02181

Institute of Mathematical Statistics
3401 Investment Boulevard, Suite 7
Hayward, CA 94545

Mathematical Association of America
1529 18th Street, NW
Washington, DC 20036

National Council of Teachers of Mathematics
1906 Association Drive
Reston, VA 22091

Society for Industrial and Applied Mathematics
1400 Architects Building
117 South 17th Street
Philadelphia, PA 19103

◇ **RELATED ARTICLES**

Volume 1: Engineering; Mathematics; Physical Sciences
Volume 2: Accountants and auditors; Actuaries; Astronomers; College and university faculty; Computer programmers; Engineers; Operations-research analysts; Statisticians; Systems analysts
Volume 4: Engineering technicians; Mathematical technicians; Scientific and business data-processing technicians

Media specialists

Definition

Media specialists are school staff members who help teachers find and use the audiovisual aids they need for their classes. They are responsible for acquiring and maintaining their schools' audiovisual equipment, which includes cameras, slide and film projectors, overhead and opaque projectors, television equipment, recording equipment, and microcomputers. They also are responsible for acquiring and maintaining the software used with the equipment, such as records, audiotapes, films, and filmstrips.

Media specialists are sometimes called *library media specialists, audiovisual specialists,* or *school media center directors.*

History

Audiovisuals are teaching materials that make use of both sight and hearing. The develop-

ment of these materials has had a strong impact on teaching methods, and almost every school now has its own audiovisual equipment.

Nature of the work

Media specialists help teachers select appropriate media, order materials that teachers request, and show teachers and students how to work with audiovisual equipment. They must be familiar with media methods and materials, and they must know the subjects that each grade studies, how children learn, and what training aids are best for specific age levels and topics.

Because they are responsible for acquiring audiovisual products, media specialists keep up-to-date by studying manufacturers' literature, talking with salespeople, inspecting new products, and attending professional conferences and conventions. They also use cameras,

A media specialist discusses the procedures and responsibilities of handling media equipment with his student-assistants.

film, and art supplies to make their own audiovisual materials and may help teachers produce special materials for class projects.

Media specialists usually work in media centers in their schools or school districts. To keep track of all the audiovisual aids stored in their media centers, they assign each item a number, maintain catalogs of software, and keep schedules showing when teachers plan to use specific materials. They perform such simple maintenance work as cleaning lenses and changing light bulbs, and they call in skilled technicians for more complicated maintenance or repairs.

Requirements

High-school students should take courses in communications, graphic arts, television, photography, psychology, and sociology, and college students should earn their undergraduate degrees in educational media or instructional technology. Large school systems often require a master's degree in educational media, instructional technology, communications, education, library science, or library media.

Requirements vary throughout the United States. Some school systems allow teachers to become media specialists by taking twelve semester hours in media, and other schools require both the additional training and media experience.

Media specialists must be creative, inventive, and adaptable. They must have good manual skills and the ability to work with machines. They also must be able to handle responsibility and work under pressure. They need to have the skills to operate different types of audiovisual equipment, and to be able to teach others how to operate equipment.

Special requirements

In some states, media specialists employed in the public school systems must have state certification, and in other states they must be certified teachers. Media specialists who work for private schools and in industry or business, however, rarely need certification.

Media specialists may belong to the School Media Specialists division of the Association for Educational Communications and Technology (ACET).

Opportunities for experience and exploration

Students who are interested in becoming media specialists should volunteer to work in their schools' media programs. They also should read books and periodicals that deal with visual aids and education, and they should try to find summer or part-time employment with stores that sell audiovisual aids or companies that produce audiovisual equipment or software.

Related occupations

Media specialists are in the group of workers who are concerned with administering libraries and performing related library services. Other workers in this group include library directors, library branch or department heads, audiovisual librarians, bookmobile librarians, children's and young adult's librarians, institutional librarians, special collections librarians, catalog librarians, music librarians, bibliographers, classifiers, and library technical assistants.

Methods of entering

Many media specialists are teachers who take additional training to qualify for this work. In addition, qualified graduates usually obtain help from their schools' placement services.

Advancement

Media specialists who work in school systems may become media program coordinators for school districts and eventually advance to become curriculum development superintendents. Some media specialists advance by taking jobs with companies that develop or sell teaching aids, and some even start their own media product companies.

Employment outlook

There are increasing opportunities for media specialists in business, industrial, medical, and government organizations that use media materials to train workers and get their messages to the public. And media specialists who have worked in the schools may find jobs with educational product companies as software producers or as researchers who help their firms determine the materials that schools need.

Openings are also expected in library media centers, and some media specialists will work with health and welfare services to develop materials that teach people how to maintain their health and spend money wisely. In addition, media specialists who have earned doctorates may find work as college instructors or directors of college media programs.

Earnings

Media specialists' salaries are determined by their experience and where they work, and their pay scales and benefits equal those of teachers. In the early 1990s, beginning salaries ranged from $12,000 to $18,000, and salaries for media directors in large school systems ranged from $20,000 to $40,000.

Conditions of work

Most media specialists work in grade schools or high schools, and they usually work in media centers that have facilities for previewing software, making audiovisual aids, and storing equipment. Teachers often visit them to discuss materials they need for their classes, to look through catalogs, to see slides and films, and to make their own audiovisual aids for classroom projects. Media specialists sometimes go out to visit other media centers, libraries, radio and television stations, and film studios.

They frequently work late, take work home, and go to night and weekend meetings. Although many have long summer vacations, they use much of that time to organize materials, order supplies, preview films, see new products, and attend classes to improve their skills.

Social and psychological factors

New developments in media approaches to learning keep media specialists' work interesting. They are constantly busy checking orders in and out, inspecting new products, and working with teachers, and they are often responsible for large budgets. Although their work can be stressful, most media specialists enjoy their jobs.

GOE: 11.07.03; SIC: 8231; SOC: 251

◇ **SOURCES OF ADDITIONAL INFORMATION**

Association for Educational Communications and Technology
1126 16th Street, NW
Washington, DC 20036

American Association of School Librarians
50 East Huron Street
Chicago, IL 60611

◇ **RELATED ARTICLES**

Volume 1: Education; Library and Information Science
Volume 2: Librarians; Teachers, kindergarten and elementary school; Teachers, secondary school
Volume 3: Teachers aides
Volume 4: Audiovisual technicians; Library technicians

Medical record administrators

Definition

Medical record administrators design and develop systems for documenting, storing, and retrieving medical information. They train and supervise medical record department personnel, compile statistics required by government agencies, help the medical staff evaluate patient care or carry out research studies, and may testify in court actions involving medical records.

History

Medical practitioners have written down information about their patients' illnesses and treatments for hundreds of years. Before the twentieth century, such information was kept mostly to help practitioners learn as much as possible from their own experience. There was little centralization or standardization of this information, so it was difficult to organize it and share the knowledge that can result from studying many instances of similar successes and failures.

By the early 1900s, medical record keeping was changing, along with many other aspects of medicine. Medicine was more sophisticated, more scientific, and more successful in helping patients. Hospitals were increasingly accepted as the conventional place for middle-class patients to go for care. As a consequence, hospitals became more numerous and better organized. With medical record keeping becoming more important and time-consuming, it seemed natural and more efficient to centralize it in the hospital. Recommendations by distinguished committees representing the medical profession helped to encourage standardized record-keeping procedures.

By the 1920s, there were many hospitals in the United States with central libraries of patient records, and there were employees specifically charged with responsibility for keeping those records in good order. As time passed, this task became more complicated. The personnel primarily responsible for maintaining patient records, who were initially called medical record librarians, eventually became differentiated into two basic professional categories. These two professional categories are now designated medical record administrator and medical record technician.

A national professional organization for medical record professionals, the American Medical Record Association (AMRA), was founded in the United States in 1928. Formal educational programs to train medical record administrators (MRAs) were initiated in 1935. In October 1971, AMRA's House of Delegates took action to officially change the professional designation Registered Record Librarian (RRL) to Registered Record Administrator (RRA).

In recent years, a trend toward the computerization of medical records, the growing importance of privacy and freedom of information issues, and the changing requirements of third-party reimbursement organizations all have had a major impact on the field of medical records and can be expected to continue to reshape this area of health care in future years.

Nature of the work

For each patient in a hospital, clinic, or other medical institution, a record must be kept. This report contains all information pertinent to the patient's illness or injury, from medical history to daily temperature, results of laboratory tests, surgery, medications, and treatments, and physician's notations concerning the case. After the patient leaves the hospital, this information is kept in a permanent central file.

Medical records are important for research, insurance claims, legal actions, administrative reports, and evaluation of treatment and medications. They may also be referred to in the training of medical personnel or in the planning of community health care programs.

The task of maintaining an information system that meets medical, administrative, ethical, and legal requirements involves a team of workers headed by a medical record administrator.

Medical record administrators plan systems for documenting, storing, and retrieving medical records, using methods that meet standards set by accrediting and regulatory agencies. Administrators are also responsible for maintaining the records and for releasing the information contained in them.

These professionals process medical-legal documents for insurance claims and legal actions and may be required to produce records and testify in court about their record-keeping procedures. They also compile information about births, deaths, and other statistics for federal and state agencies.

Administrators train and supervise assistants, medical record technicians, medical secretaries, and other medical record staff. Some of these professionals teach college students in clinical training in hospitals.

Medical record administrators take part in basic and applied research in the health care field. They collect and analyze patient and institutional data from medical records. With their staff, they prepare indexes; classify and code diseases, operations, and treatments; and cross-reference data on the records. As head of the medical department, they also prepare budgets, order office equipment and supplies, design forms and other materials, and look after many other administrative details.

Medical record administrators are key members of the management team. They serve on committees and work closely with all departments of the hospital and with physicians to improve efficiency while, at the same time, providing quality patient care.

Medical record administrators must be able to keep track of an abundance of important paperwork. Such organizational skills are valued in the health care industry.

Requirements

It is possible to meet requirements for work as a medical record technician with two years of college in a program accredited by the Committee on Allied Health Education and Accreditation (CAHEA) of the American Medical Association in collaboration with the American Medical Record Association (AMRA). However, to become a medical record administrator it is necessary to enroll in a four-year college course leading to a bachelor's degree in medical record science or to earn a bachelor's degree supplemented by a one-year course in medical record science.

These training requirements are necessary to be eligible to take the registration examination of the American Medical Record Association. In the past it was possible to find a job on an apprenticeship basis, but today formal training and college background are considered essential. A list of schools approved for teaching medical record librarians can be obtained from the American Medical Record Association.

The course of study includes anatomy, physiology, fundamentals of medical science, medical terminology, medical record science, organization and administration, legal aspects of medical records, and ethics. Practical training consists of experience in hospital admitting and discharging procedures, standard indexing and coding practices, compiling statistical reports, analyzing and abstracting information from medical records, and becoming acquainted with the work and record systems of related departments, such as X-ray, pathology, medical library, and outpatient.

The medical record administrator should have a definite interest in working with details and must be well organized and accurate and dedicated to obtaining all necessary data. Often this detailed work must be done in the presence of frequent interruptions. Because the information handled by the medical record administrator is generally confidential, one must exercise good judgment in making such information available to various sources. The medical record administrator must be able to get along with others and inspire their cooperation, for much of the work consists of gathering data from physicians and hospital departments, or in dispensing information.

Special requirements

After graduating from an approved school of medical record science, the administrator is eligible to take the registration examination of the American Medical Record Association. To take and pass this examination is wise professionally. Having passed this examination, the medical record administrator becomes an RRA (Registered Record Administrator). As the requirements of medical insurers puts pressure on facilities to supply specific detailed reports, certified administrators will be preferred in hiring.

Opportunities for experience and exploration

A high-school student interested in work as a medical record administrator might be fortunate enough to find summer or part-time clerical or typing work in a medical record department or in some related department of a hospital or other institution. This would give the student a chance to observe the administrator's work and measure his or her own interest and aptitude in relation to this experience. Interested individuals could also learn much by talking to a medical record administrator and reading available literature on the profession. Prospective medical record administrators should also have a good idea of their own personal qualifications and how they fit in with the demands of the profession.

Related occupations

Persons interested in this field must be good organizers, communicators, planners, and administrators. These qualities are also important in such occupations as hospital administrators, medical librarians, and information scientists. Individuals who may not be able or willing to complete the educational requirement to become a medical record administrator may consider working as medical record technicians or medical record clerks. In addition, there are many record-keeping jobs in other fields that may appeal to someone who is detail-oriented.

Methods of entering

Although it has been possible in the past to enter the medical record field on an apprenticeship basis, most medical record professionals, today, find it necessary to graduate from an approved school of medical record science, ideally with a bachelor's degree. It would also be an advantage to take the registration examination before applying for a job. However, because of the great need for medical record administrators, this registration procedure is not essential and may also be taken after employment, if desired. Help in finding work is available through the American Medical Record Association and school placement offices and through professional journals and local newspaper ads. An individual may also apply directly to institutions or take a civil service examination if interested in working for the federal government.

Advancement

The well-qualified medical record professional has good hopes of advancing in the profession. Because of the shortage of medical record personnel at the present time, it is not difficult to find a good position as a beginning job. Many jobs for medical record technicians are available in large hospitals, and a newly graduated administrator from an approved school might even find a position as the head of a record department in a small hospital. Those who pass the registration examination have additional professional status and often better chances for advancement.

A medical record administrator with the proper qualifications may advance from assistant to associate to chief medical record administrator in a large hospital or by moving into other administrative or supervisory positions, such as coordinator of medical record departments of several hospitals. Also, as the profession develops, there will be a greater need for qualified teachers in medical record programs as the enrollment increases.

Employment outlook

In the early 1990s, there were about 33,000 medical record professionals. Most of them worked in hospitals; others held positions in nursing homes, clinics, medical group practices, HMOs, and other health care facilities. They are also employed by insurance, accounting, and law firms that specialize in health matters; by public health departments; and by manufacturers of medical record systems, services, and equipment. Some self-employed medical records specialists act as consultants.

Employment opportunities for qualified medical record personnel through the end of the 1990s are expected to be excellent. More jobs will be created as the number of hospitals and other health care facilities continues to grow and as records become more numerous and complex. Those in the medical field are becoming increasingly aware of the significance of medical records and the value of handling them efficiently. Researchers find such records invaluable. Hospital insurance programs present increasing amounts of paper work. Legal requirements must be met. For example, the federal government introduced in 1983 a new payment system for Medicare that was expected to expand the opportunities for medical records personnel, because of its detailed record-keeping requirements.

Earnings

The medical record administrator's salary is determined in part by the location, size, and type of employing agency. Also taken into consideration is the individual's skill, experience, and willingness to take on challenging and demanding responsibilities.

Entry-level medical record administrators in the early 1990s earned an average starting salary that ranged from about $17,000 to $21,000 a year. Beginning medical record administrators who worked for the federal government were paid between $14,400 and $18,700. With additional education and at least five years' experience, administrators typically earned in the range of $25,000 to $31,000. Those with advanced degrees earned an average of about $31,000 to $40,000 a year.

Medical record administrators usually work forty hours or less a week. They receive the usual fringe benefits.

Conditions of work

The medical record administrator usually works under pleasant conditions although surrounded by the instruments of the work—file cabinets, computer terminals, and general office equipment. Most health care institutions have well-lighted offices and modern equipment.

The medical record administrator may do considerable walking to gather data and consult individuals throughout the institution. If it is a large hospital, there will be clerks, typists, and assistants to carry out routine tasks, but in a small facility this person may well be involved in a number of clerical activities including lifting and carrying reports and medical record files.

Social and psychological factors

This is a demanding profession, one requiring skills in organization, personal relationships, and a great deal of responsibility. The contributions of the medical record administrator, a young and growing profession, have already been recognized by those in the medical field. The information compiled, organized, and maintained can be of significant benefit to the medical researcher who studies new cures and aspects of disease. The medical record worker, then, can feel personal satisfaction in knowing that this work is contributing to the advancement of medical science. The fulfillment of the numerous responsibilities presents many pressures, especially to the administrator with little clerical assistance. Frequent interruptions and the many requests for information may make it difficult to carry out all the required work. Depending on the size of the medical facility, and the size of the record keeping staff, the quantity of work may be large.

GOE: 07.05.03; SIC: 806; SOC: 131

◇ SOURCES OF ADDITIONAL INFORMATION

For information on certification, education, and employment, contact:

American Medical Record Association
875 North Michigan Avenue
Suite 1850
Chicago, IL 60611

Medical Records Institute
PO Box 289
Newton, MA 02160

◇ RELATED ARTICLES

Volume 1: Health Care; Library and Information Science
Volume 2: Health services administrators; Librarians; Systems analysts
Volume 4: Library technicians; Medical record technicians; Scientific and business data processing technicians

Medical technologists

Definition

Medical technologists, also called *clinical laboratory technologists* are health professionals whose jobs include many health care roles. They perform laboratory tests essential to the detection, diagnosis, and treatment of disease. They work under the direction of specialists in the biological sciences.

Clinical laboratory technologists are integral to the health care system. The specific responsibilities of technologists are determined by the extent and nature of their education and training and, in some cases, by the kind of setting in which they work. Some, such as *clinical chemists, hematologists*, and *microbiologists*, specialize in a specific subdiscipline. Others, called *clinical laboratory technologists* and *medical technologists*, are generalists, whose education qualifies them to perform testing and related roles in the major clinical laboratory subdisciplines.

Technologists in clinical practice ensure the quality of laboratory tests done for diagnosis. They may be responsible for interpreting the data and results and reporting their findings to the attending physicians. Many also assist attending physicians in correlating test results with clinical data, and recommend tests and test sequences in light of clinical considerations. Medical technologists may also discharge management and supervisory tasks, including serving as laboratory directors, managers of lab sections, and staff supervisor over other technologists and laboratory practitioners.

Other medical technologists are employed in research, education, health policy development (particularly in government organizations), veterinary science, public health and epidemiology study and application, diagnostic equipment research and development, and other related fields to the theoretical and the practical applications of medical technology.

History

Technological developments and medical breakthroughs of the latter part of the twentieth century have greatly facilitated reliable analysis of human blood, tissue, and fluids. Physicians depend upon laboratory tests in routine checkups, diagnosis, and treatment of disease.

The history of clinical laboratory work is in-tertwined with the development of medicine itself. In the fourth century B.C. the Greek physician Hippocrates established that disease had natural causes. He is credited with establishing medicine as a separate and important study.

Another Greek physician, Galen, developed experimental research on animals for medical investigation. In A.D. 100, Galen began formulating theories from scientific experiments.

Other milestones in medicine were the discovery of the system of blood circulation (1616) by one of the early leaders in medical science, William Harvey; observation of microorganisms through the microscope by Antonie van Leeuwenhoek in 1683; Jan Swammerdam's study and discovery of red blood cells (1658); and the work of Robert Koch and Louis Pasteur in bacteriology in the late 1800s. At the close of the nineteenth century, bacteriology and other medical specialties developed rapidly, creating demand for full-time laboratory personnel.

In the early part of the twentieth century, many physicians taught some of their assistants how to perform some of the laboratory procedures that were frequently utilized in their practice. The quality of the work done by these assistants varied greatly, and many physicians and medical educators concerned themselves with this problem.

In 1932, an attempt was made to standardize the training programs that were then available for the preparation of medical technologists. The formation of the first independent professional society of clinical laboratory technologists was established in Chicago. The following year, the predecessor for the American Society for Medical Technology (ASMA) was established. The Board of Registry of Medical Technology of the American Society of Clinical Pathology and the ASMA, in association with the Council on Medical Education and Hospitals of the American Medical Association, instituted standards of education and practice for medical technologists. These standards have been revised periodically.

Nature of the work

Medical technologists perform laboratory tests to help physicians detect, diagnose, and treat diseases. The work of medical technologists is generally done under the supervision of a senior medical technologist, a clinical laboratory supervisor, or a physician who has specialized in diagnosing the causes and nature of disease.

The specific tasks performed by medical technologists are determined by the kind of setting in which they work. Technologists employed by small laboratories conduct many kinds of tests, such as blood counts, urinalyses, and skin tests. They use microscopes to examine body fluids and tissue samples to determine the presence of bacteria, fungi, or other organisms. They sometimes prepare slides from sample tissues and body cells to ascertain, for example, whether an individual has developed cancer. Depending on the laboratory facilities and needs, they may be responsible for operating highly sophisticated medical instruments and machines. They conduct research and maintain and repair the instruments and equipment used in testing. Medical technologists employed in large laboratories generally specialize.

Medical technology specialists normally have advanced degrees in their area of expertise. They are capable of handling more sophisticated equipment and testings because of their education and training. They may be responsible for ordering, purchasing, maintaining, and repairing the specialized equipment and instruments required for the laboratory tests. They design new laboratory procedures, and establish or continue training and education of other employees in laboratory procedures and skills.

Clinical laboratory directors oversee the laboratory or the laboratory department. They are responsible for the supervision of the technologists on the staff and for the maintenance of the quality of the work done. They may be in charge of sustaining the budget and determining the financial needs and responsibilities of the lab. They will assign duties, hire and fire staff, and establish work rules and standards.

Clinical laboratory supervisors, or *medical technologist supervisors*, are the managers of the staff on a day to day basis. The supervisor assigns work schedules and assignments, reviews work and lab results, and may assist in training and continued education of the staff. The supervisor may also continue in the role of medical technologist by performing tests and functions that other techs in the office also do. The *chief medical technologist* supervises the work of the entire laboratory operations, assigns duties, and reviews the reports and analyses.

A *chemistry* or *biochemistry technologist* tests specimens of blood, urine, gastric juices, and spinal fluid to detect the presence of chemicals, drugs, and poisons, as well as levels of sub-

A medical laboratory technician uses a specialized computer to analyze specimens.

stances made by the body, such as sugar, albumin, and acetone. This information may be used in the diagnosis of metabolic disease such as diabetes. Precise measurements are made with equipment maintained by the technologist.

A *microbiology* or *bacteriology technologist* examines specimens for microorganisms, including viruses, fungi, parasites, and bacteria. It may be necessary to isolate and grow a specific organism to make a better identification for diagnosis. Treatment of a condition may depend on the results of testing various ways of dealing with the organism itself, before the patient can be treated. Work in microbiology isolated the germs that cause tuberculosis and developed the drugs that would destroy those organisms.

Cytotechnologists stain and mount slides with specimens and examine them under a microscope to detect and diagnose disease or damage to the cells.

Histotechnologists, or *tissue technologists*, prepare specimens of tissue and bone for examination by pathologists. The specimens are preserved in a variety of ways, including freezing. Many times tumors are submitted for biopsy while a patient is on the operating table. These specimens are prepared by the histopathology technologist and results of the technologists testing help the surgeon to make a more exact diagnosis. These technologists may also assist pathologists at autopsies and preserve organs for later examination and reference.

Immunohematologists type blood and cross-match donor and recipient for compatibility. They perform other blood tests and maintain the equipment and supplies of blood in several different forms to be used for transfusion.

Phlebotomists are probably the most familiar medical technologist because they draw blood during physical examinations. Responsible for obtaining blood samples for whatever testing is required, the phlebotomist draws the quantity of blood specified for the testing procedure, labels the vials, and transports them to the testing facility without damage or heating of the samples. Phlebotomists normally have a year of training or practice before applying for certification.

Cardiopulmonary technologists perform diagnostic tests on a patient's heart and blood vessels or lungs, using laboratory equipment such as electrocardiograph and phonocardiograph machines, stethoscopes, catheters, or respiratory equipment.

Medical-laboratory assistants are assistants to medical technologists and technicians. They run routine tests and perform related work that can be learned in a relatively short period of time. They may specialize in one area of work in a laboratory, such as identifying different types of blood on slides. Assistants may also clean and sterilize laboratory equipment, glassware, and instruments; keep records of tests; identify specimens; and prepare solutions following standard laboratory formulas.

Requirements

For medical technologists, a baccalaureate degree is usually required, consisting of at least three years of college studies, including work in chemistry, the biological sciences, and mathematics, in addition to a twelve-month program in a school of medical technology. Most of these approved schools are associated with colleges and universities, and have affiliations with hospitals. Upon completing programs in these approved schools, students are awarded a bachelor's degree. A few of these schools, however, have higher requirements than the minimal requirements listed above. Advanced work in medical technology leading to graduate degrees and subsequent employment in teaching and research positions is available at an increasing number of universities.

High-school students interested in a career in medical technology should take as many courses in the biological and physical sciences as possible. The work of the medical technologist is very important to the health and welfare of many individuals. Because of the nature of the work, students interested in careers in medical technology should possess the following

characteristics: accuracy, patience, and the ability to work under pressure. Other essential characteristics are manual dexterity and good eyesight (with or without glasses). Because the medical technologist must survive a rigorous training program, above-average scholastic aptitude is also necessary.

Medical laboratory assistants are usually trained on the job. Recently, increasing numbers of assistants have completed one-year training programs in vocational schools, community and junior colleges, and in hospitals. The Committee on Allied Health Education and Accreditation of the American Medical Association has approved approximately one hundred programs for assistants. The Accrediting Bureau of Health Education Schools accredits programs in the propriety schools.

Special requirements

Certification of medical technologists verifies that people in the profession have met the educational standards recognized by the certifying body. After passing appropriate examinations, candidates may be certified as medical technologists, MT(ASCP), by the Board of Registry of the American Medical Technologists; as Registered Medical Technologists, RMT, by the International Society for Clinical Laboratory Technology; or as Clinical Laboratory Scientists, CLS, by the National Certification Agency for Medical Laboratory Personnel. For the CLS, a bachelor's degree in medical technology, or a bachelor's degree in biology or physical science plus additional training and/or education in medical technology, are the minimum requirements for someone applying to take the examination.

Medical technologists need to secure a license in some states, including California, Florida, Georgia, Hawaii, Nevada, and Tennessee. Licenses will be required with more regularity in all the states, as the insurance companies involve the evaluation of laboratory certification (which affects the diagnoses of patients) in the cost of insurance to doctors and clinics.

Opportunities for experience and exploration

High-school students may do volunteer work in hospitals or medical facilities. Sometimes these workers are known as candy stripers. Interested students will have difficulty gaining any direct experience on a part-time basis in medical technology. The first experiential opportunities afforded students generally come in the clinical and laboratory phases of their training program. Those interested can explore a career in medical technology in several ways. They can write to the sources listed at the end of this article for more reading material on medical technology, or they can visit a medical technologist to watch and learn about the work. A visit to an AMA approved school of medical technology to discuss career plans with the admissions counselor would also be valuable.

Methods of entering

Graduates of schools of medical technology may receive assistance from placement services at the schools in securing the first jobs. Hospitals, laboratories, and other companies employing medical technologists often get in touch with these placement offices and notify them of job openings. Positions may also be secured with the assistance of various registries of medical technologists. Newspaper advertisements and commercial placement agencies are other sources of initial employment.

Advancement

Advancement can be relatively rapid in the field of medical technology. With satisfactory experience and perhaps more training, a medical technologist can advance to supervisory positions or specialist fields in clinical laboratory work. Considerable experience is required for advancement to a position as chief medical technologist in a large hospital. Graduate training in necessary for advancement to positions in research and teaching. Assistants can become technicians with further education and experience.

Employment outlook

Employment growth in this field is expected to maintain the level it has held, with a slight chance of increase in the number of positions. However, because of the relatively small number of people applying for licenses for medical technology positions, the number of openings for employment ius quite large. Because of the shortage in staff, the employee salaries are ris-

ing, the benefits can be good, and the promotion possibilities are also good.

Earnings

Medical technologists earn an average starting salary of about $19,600 in the early 1990s in hospitals, medical schools and medical centers, while experienced technologists averaged $26,100. Specialists' starting salaries vary between about $15,000 and $19,000. Experienced specialists make between $20,000 and $26,000.

Beginning medical technologists working for the federal government received annual salaries of about $15,500, with the salary determined by their academic records, education, and experience. The average for all medical technologists in the federal government is $25,000 in the early 1990s.

Conditions of work

Most medical laboratory workers are employed in hospitals. Some work in clinics, physicians' offices, pharmaceutical labs, public health agencies, and research institutions. Others work in Veterans Administration hospitals and laboratories as well as in the armed forces and the U.S. public health service.

Medical laboratory personnel usually work a thirty-five to forty hour week, with night or weekend duty often required in hospitals. However, with the current staff shortage, overtime in some facilities has become common, with required amounts of overtime hours assigned to staff.

Benefits generally include paid vacations and sick leave, and in some cases, retirement plans. Laboratories are clean and well lighted. Medical technologists must exercise meticulous care in their work to avoid risk of exposure to diseases, or contamination of a testing sample, requiring the retesting of the patient. As medical technology improves the equipment, and as experiments become more precise, exact work is required. Plastics have replaced glass so risk of cuts from broken equipment is greatly reduced. Chemicals and their containers and usage have also improved with the advancement of technology so chemical burns are rare. Technologists must often stand on their feet for long periods of time and usually are required to do much bending and lifting of supplies and packages.

Social and psychological factors

Medical assistants may find the work repetitive and eventually boring, but have chance for advancement with further education. All lab workers must often work under pressure at painstaking tasks. Work loads can be heavy because of staff shortage in the workplace, and frequently one person must fill the role of more than one title.

◇ **SOURCES OF ADDITIONAL INFORMATION**

Accrediting Bureau of Health Education Schools
Oak Manor Offices
29089 US 20 West
Elkhart, IN 46514

American Association For Clinical Chemistry
2029 K Street, NW, 7th Floor
Washington, DC 20006

American Society of Blood Banks
1117 North 19th Street, Suite 600
Arlington, VA 22209

American Society for Clinical Pathologists
2100 West Harrison
Chicago, IL 60612

American Society of Cytology
1015 Chestnut Street, Suite 1518
Philadelphia, PA 19107

American Society for Medical Technology
2021 L Street, NW, Suite 400
Washington, DC 20036

Committee on Allied Health Education and Accreditation
535 North Dearborn Avenue
Chicago, IL 60610

International Society for Clinical Laboratory Technology
818 Olive, Suite 918
St. Louis, MO 63101

National Certification Agency for Medical Laboratory Personnel
1101 Connecticut Avenue, NW, Suite 700
Washington, DC 20036

National Institutes of Health
Warren Grant Magnuson Clinical Center
Bethesda, MD 20982

Department of Veterans Affairs
Office of Personnel
Washington, DC 20420

◇ **RELATED ARTICLES**

Volume 1: Biological Sciences; Health Care
Volume 2: Biochemists; biomedical engineers
Volume 3: Medical assistants
Volume 4: Pharmaceutical technicians; Medical and Health Technician Occupations

Merchant marine occupations

Definition

Merchant marine occupations are concerned with managing and operating vessels that carry cargo and passengers on the world's waterways. Officers are licensed by the U.S. Coast Guard; unlicensed crew members must be certified by the Coast Guard for specific skills needed for their particular role on board the ship. Merchant Marines include the ship captain and crew.

History

Shipbuilding was an important industry in the early days of the American colonies. There was ample timber, enough craft workers had emigrated to begin the trade in America, and deepwater rivers and channels provided perfect launching sites. The *Blessing of the Bay* was the first ship built in America, launched from Mystic Seaport in Connecticut in 1620. Great Britain lacked the ready timber to build her own fleet and commissioned the building of many ships. Trade increased and so did the number of proud and hardy workers of the merchant fleet.

Congress appointed a Marine Committee in 1776, at the beginning of the American Revolution, and the Constitutional Navy was formed.

From 1812 to 1840, the American merchant marine flourished. Boys from the wealthiest families went to sea, international trade increased, and the most beautiful ship ever produced in America came into its own: the clipper ship.

But the majesty of the clipper was short-lived, as iron and steam began to replace the sleek wooden vessels. Great Britain, always short of timber for its own shipbuilding, suddenly swept the industry, for it had the iron and the skilled workers who only had to adapt their talents to a new product.

Before the Civil War, immigrants began leaving Europe at an enormous rate. The need for a regular passenger run was developing as was the need for a means of carrying the mails. In 1840, Samuel Cunard, a Canadian, began the first regularly scheduled steamers from Boston, to Halifax, and then to Liverpool.

The Civil War saw the merchant marine blockading the Atlantic and Gulf ports for four years. The end of the war left the fleet depleted, ships tied up, and depression settled over the country.

Efforts were made to stimulate a revival of the merchant marine. Theodore Roosevelt attempted to stimulate intercoastal and overseas trade by establishing the Canal Zone in Panama. A Federal Maritime Commission was appointed in 1905, recommending government subsidies and new mail lines. The recommendations were not accepted by Congress, and American trade continued to be carried by foreign ships.

Working conditions for seamen were bad. Andrew Furuseth, president of the International Seaman's Union, fought for recognition and improved conditions for his members. He finally won his point when the Seaman's Act was passed in 1915.

The merchant marine again proved its importance in wartime during World War I. In 1916, President Wilson signed an act establishing the Shipping Board and the government was thus empowered to build, buy, and charter ships. When war was declared, the Shipping Board was responsible for providing seamen and ships. The end of the war caused another depression in American merchant shipping that lasted until World War II. The bombing of Pearl Harbor caused the greatest shipbuilding in American merchant marine history. The Liberty

The first woman towboat master on the Panama Canal radios her position. Today, civilian clothing is commonly worn in many merchant marine occupations.

ship was selected for mass production and, in all, more than 6,000 Liberty and Victory ships were built between 1941 and 1945. By the end of the war, 733 ships were lost.

World War II showed the need for well-trained officers on merchant vessels, and in 1943, the United States Merchant Marine Academy at Kings Point, New York, was dedicated. In 1974, the academy admitted its first women.

Today, merchant shipping in the United States continues to lag behind other nations. Both shipbuilding costs and operating costs for a ship afloat run much higher than elsewhere.

Nature of the work

The number of workers on a cargo ship or tanker ranges from twenty to forty, and on passenger ships may be 680.

The *captain* or *master*, who is in command of the ship, is responsible for navigation, discipline, safety of ship, passengers, crew, and cargo. The captain is also the sole representative of the ship's owner and arranges organizational assignments of duties for ship's operation, navigation, and maintenance with the chief mate.

The deck department consists of the following personnel:

The *chief mate*, also known as *first mate* or *chief officer*, acts as the master's first assistant. He or she is in charge of all cargo planning, deck work, and assists with navigation, discipline, and helps maintain order.

The *second mate* is in charge of mails, and the care and maintenance of all navigating equipment and charts.

The *third mate* is responsible for maintenance of lifeboats and fire-fighting equipment; acts as signal officer in charge of all signaling equipment; and assists with cargo work.

One mate usually stands the twelve-to-four watch in charge of the navigating bridge; another, the four-to-eight watch; and another, the eight-to-twelve watch.

The *radio officer* performs all duties required for the operation and maintenance or repair of radio and other electronic communications devices; maintains depth recording equipment and electronic navigational aids such as Radar and Loran; and receives and records time signals, weather reports, position reports, and other data.

The *boatswain* or *bosun* is in charge of the deck crew. He or she carries out orders for work details as issued by the chief officer, directs maintenance tasks such as chipping and painting, splices rope and wire for rigging, and handles lifeboats and canvas coverings.

The *quartermaster*, or *helmsman*, handles the wheel and steers the ship and is an able seaman.

Able seamen perform general seamen's duties such as rigging cargo booms, readying gear for cargo loading or discharging operations. They stand watch as lookouts, act as helmsmen under direction of the officer on watch, and must be qualified as lifeboatmen able to take charge of a lifeboat crew. Able seamen stand on each of the twelve-to-four, four-to-eight, and eight-to-twelve watches.

Ordinary seamen learn and assist in performing the duties of an able seaman by cleaning, chipping, painting, and washing down the ship. They also coil and splice rope.

The engine department is made up of the following workers:

The *chief engineer* is in charge of and responsible for all propulsion machinery, auxiliaries, and power-generating equipment; keeps logs on machinery performance and fuel consumption; and is responsible for machinery repairs.

The *first assistant engineer* is responsible for maintenance of lubricating systems, electrical equipment, and engine-room auxiliaries.

The *second assistant engineer* is responsible for fuel and water, supervises tank soundings, and keeps records of fuel and water consumption. He or she may be responsible for operation of ship's boilers, boiler-room equipment, the feed water system, pumps, and condensers.

The *third assistant engineer* supervises operation and maintenance of engine-room auxiliaries and ship's pumps.

The *electrician* repairs and maintains all electric motors and electrical circuits.

Wipers, *oilers*, and *firer-watertenders* complete the engine-room gang. *Wipers* assist in keeping engine rooms clean by wiping down machinery with cotton waste or solvents. *Oilers* lubricate moving parts of mechanical equipment throughout a ship. *Firer-watertenders* tend the boilers to keep the steam pressure constant. They regulate the amount of water in boilers, check gauges, control the flow of fuel, and see to the operation of evaporators and condensers. On newer, automated vessels, the ratings of oilers and firer-watertenders have been combined, and those workers may be known as deck-engine mechanics.

The stewards department is responsible for the operation and maintenance of services for living quarters and food preparation.

The *chief steward* supervises the operation and maintenance of services for living quarters, food preparation, and messrooms. The tasks include establishing and maintaining inventory records of foodstuffs, linens, bedding, and furniture and preparing requisitions for voyage requirements. The chief steward oversees the staff who work in maintenance and food service and preparation.

The *chief cook* prepares all meals and, in conjunction with the chief steward, plans menus. He or she issues stores from the ship's refrigerators and storerooms, and butchers meat.

The *second cook and baker* bakes all bread and pies and prepare desserts, salads, and night lunches. They are responsible for the upkeep and safety in the galley, keeping all spaces and storerooms neat.

The *mess attendants* set tables, serve meals, and wash dishes. They also maintain cleanliness of passages, stairways, and corridors, make berths in officers' and crew quarters, and keep the radio room and various ship's offices clean.

Requirements

To obtain the ratings of master, chief, or second mate, an applicant must be at least twenty-one and hold documentary evidence of being a United States citizen. Third mates must be at least nineteen. They must all pass certain U.S. Public Health Service physical exams and certain Coast Guard regulations regarding years of service and size of vessel on which the applicant served. Deck officers must have full knowledge of navigation, cargo handling, and all deck department operations. The master must be a person of good judgment and must know admiralty law, foreign pilots' rules, and preferably, trends in world trade.

A radio operator must be at least nineteen, must know Morse code, and if the sole radio operator on a cargo vessel, must have at least six months' experience at sea.

Most helpful for all the above-mentioned occupations is graduation from the U.S. Merchant Marine Academy.

Applicants must be at least twenty-one to apply for positions as chief engineer, first and second assistants. Third assistants must be at least nineteen. They must also show evidence of citizenship and pass health inspection. To fulfill experience requirements, an applicant must have graduated from the U.S. Naval Academy, Merchant Marine Academy, or Coast Guard Academy; or must have combined education with experience in very specified areas. Engineers must have full knowledge of marine steam, diesel engines, and marine boilers. Chief engineers usually have college engineer training or its equivalent.

Requirements vary greatly for jobs on board merchant ships because of the great differences in the nature of the jobs themselves. The best way to fulfill the many requirements, and also try the various phases of shipboard work, is to attend the U.S. Merchant Marine Academy or one of the state academies in California, Maine, Massachusetts, Michigan, New York, or Texas. Cadets select either the nautical science or the marine engineering program. Upon graduation each cadet receives a B.S. degree, a license either as third officer or as third assistant engineer, and may be granted a commission as ensign in the U.S. Naval Reserve. Those students wishing appointments must be at least seventeen but not yet twenty-two, in good physical condition, single, U.S. citizens, and graduated from an accredited high school. Applicants must be nominated by members of Congress.

Unlicensed crew in the deck department must show proof of a job to obtain a merchant mariner's document from the U.S. Coast

A father and son team pose on the bridge of USNS Meteor. As first officer, the son shares responsibilities for the navigation of the ship and the ship's safety.

Guard. They may not sail without this document. After a required one-year minimum period of service, an ordinary seaman may apply to the Coast Guard for a license as an able seaman. After three years you may secure unlimited endorsement as an able seaman. An able seaman must be a least nineteen, hold an endorsed merchant mariner document, pass a physical examination, and must pass either oral or written examination of his or her knowledge of shipping and seamanship.

Special requirements

To be eligible to serve as a deck, engine, or radio officer, a seaman must have a license issued by the U.S. Coast Guard. Radio operators, furthermore, must have a first- or second-class radiotelegraph operator's license issued by the Federal Communications Commission. Further, he or she must pass a written exam on such subjects as laws regulating communications at sea, radio and telegraph operating practices, message traffic routing, and radio navigational aids.

The unlicensed members of a crew must hold the merchant mariner document from the U.S. Coast Guard. Crew working in the steward's department must carry a certificate from a medical officer of the U.S. Public Health Service.

Opportunities for experience and exploration

There are very few opportunities to explore this field. An interested person could hire on a ship as an ordinary seaman to see if he or she liked the life at sea. Individuals who already have some training or experience, for instance, as a cook, waiter, electrician, or engineer, might hire on for a voyage to try the experience. If living near a port, an aspiring merchant mariner could try to visit a ship in port by contacting a steamship company.

Related occupations

Other water transportation workers include barge captains, boat loaders, dockhands, ferryboat captains, ferry terminal supervisors, fishing vessel captains and mates, lock operators, riverboat masters, stevedores, tugboat dispatchers, and yacht masters.

Methods of entering

An inexperienced person usually gets a first job at sea by applying at a central hiring hall in a major port. An applicant would be given a shipping card on which is stamped the date you registered. In the hiring hall, dispatchers announce job openings as ordered by shipping companies. The best-qualified worker who is longest out of work gets the job. New applicants may have to wait months to get a job, and may have to keep in daily contact with the employment center.

The best way to become an officer is to attend the U.S. Merchant Marine Academy, or one of the state academies.

Advancement

There are many advancements in the merchant marine, whether from ordinary seaman to able seaman or from third mate to chief mate. But in almost every rank it depends on length of service, experience, and training, either formal or on-the-job. Seamen in the deck department ad-

vance along well-defined lines, thus, after applying for rating they take the required examination. To become a boatswain, you must have the ability to handle people as well as an unlimited AB ticket.

In the engine department, a wiper may advance to any one of many jobs, provided legal qualifications are met. In the steward's department, advancement is from messman, to utility man, to assistant cook, to chief cook, and finally to steward.

The deck officer must start as third mate; after one year an individual is eligible to take second mate examinations. He or she gradually works toward more responsible positions by years of service and experience acquired.

Employment outlook

The employment outlook for merchant marine personnel is not very good, mainly because of foreign competition and changes in federal policy. Cargo rates and wages paid to U.S. merchant mariners are the highest in the world; this keeps the industry small because shippers can send goods on cheaper foreign vessels. In addition, the newer ships with more automated equipment can be operated with smaller crews.

It is anticipated that most of the job openings throughout the rest of the 1990s will be to replace older workers who retire or leave the field for other reasons. Applicants can expect to face sharp competition for these jobs.

Earnings

Wages vary according to the rank and the size of the vessel. In the early 1990s, the average yearly base wage for a master on a typical freighter was about $59,400. A chief mate earned more than $33,000. Second mates were paid more than $29,000; and third mates, more than $19,800. Additional wages for overtime or for extra responsibilities averaged about 50 percent of the base wage. Officers also have generous benefits, including pensions, and vacations of up to 180 days a year.

Radio officers in the early 1990s averaged more than $27,700 a year. Electricians averaged $22,400. Able seamen averaged $14,500. Chief bakers made an average of $16,800, while a mess attendant averaged $11,400 a year.

Chief engineers were paid an average wage of more than $54,000 in the early 1990s. A first assistant engineer averaged nearly $33,000; and a second assistant, more than $23,700.

Conditions of work

Working on board ship is not as glamorous as it first may seem. Although traveling throughout the world, the crew rarely has time to see much of the ports they visit. They are away from their homes and families for extended periods of time. They usually share their living area, possibly with three other people. Their messroom is used both at mealtimes and for recreational purposes during other times.

Workers of the merchant marine are exposed to all kinds of weather, no matter what their rating. While at sea fire, collision, and sinking are all possible. Ships are inspected regularly by federal officers to guarantee cleanliness and proper plumbing.

Social and psychological factors

When signing on for a voyage, an individual chooses a very different form of life. Merchant mariners are not only removed from their family, but are limited to a small area of space and must share it with the same people for the length of the trip.

They also submit to a very rigid command in which the captain is absolute master of the ship, under an authority that ranks downward to each worker.

Many people prefer this way of life to a more sedentary, five-day-a-week shore job. Their experience at sea often qualifies them for shoreside jobs with suppliers or shipping companies.

GOE: 05.04.02; SIC: 441; SOC: 824

◇ **SOURCES OF ADDITIONAL INFORMATION**

U.S. Maritime Administration
400 7th Street, SW
Washington, DC 20590

◇ **RELATED ARTICLES**

Volume 1: Transportation
Volume 2: Engineers; Radio and telegraph operators
Volume 4: Engineering technicians; Marine services technicians

Meteorologists

Definition

The *meteorologist* studies weather conditions and forecasts weather changes; analyzes weather maps covering large geographical areas and related charts including upper-air maps and soundings; predicts the movement of fronts, precipitation, and pressure areas to forecast such data as temperature, winds, precipitation, cloud cover, and flying conditions. To predict future weather patterns and to develop increased accuracy in weather study and forecasting, meteorologists conduct research on such subjects as atmospheric electricity, clouds, precipitation, hurricanes, and data collected from weather satellites. Other areas of research used to forecast weather may include ocean currents and temperature.

History

Meteorology is the science of the atmosphere. Although people have always been concerned with the air around them, only relatively recently has anyone been able to learn much about it. Historians have evidence of attempts made in India in the fourth century B.C. to measure rainfall. The development of the first instruments to study the nature of the atmosphere occurred in the sixteenth and seventeenth centuries when Galileo invented the thermometer (1593) and Torricelli invented the barometer (1643). Not until World War II, however, was great financial support given to the development of the science of meteorology. In the war a very clear-cut relationship was established between the effectiveness of new weap-

A meteorologist uses all sorts of instruments to gather data. In this case, she is checking the air quality.

gions. Other specialists include *climatologists* who study past records to discover weather patterns for a given region. The climatologist compiles, makes statistical analyses of, and interprets data on temperature, sunlight, rainfall, humidity, and wind for a particular area over a long period of time for use in weather forecasting, aviation, agriculture, commerce, and public health.

Other specialists are *dynamic meteorologists,* who study the physical laws related to air currents; *physical meteorologists,* who study the physical nature of the atmosphere including its chemical composition and electrical, acoustical, and optical properties; and *industrial meteorologists,* who work on such problems as smoke control and air pollution.

ons and the atmosphere. More accurate instruments for measuring and observing weather conditions, new systems of communication, and the development of high-speed computers to process and analyze weather data have helped people to understand more about the atmosphere. Our need to understand even more has been increased because of the demands of the space age. The meteorologist enjoys a more important role in our society at present than ever before.

Nature of the work

Although most people think of weather forecasting when they think of meteorology, meteorologists do many other kinds of work also. They do research on subjects ranging from radioactive fallout to the dynamics of hurricanes. They study the ozone levels in the stratisphere. Some teach in colleges and universities.

Many meteorologists are needed in radio and televised weather forecasting programs. Networks usually hire their own staff of meteorologists.

Meteorology is a technical field that is becoming ever more technological. Meteorologists generally specialize in one branch of this rapidly developing science; however, the lines of specialization are not clearly drawn and meteorologists often work in more than one area of specialization. The largest group of specialists are called *synoptic meteorologists,* the technical name for weather forecasters, who interpret current weather information reported by observers in many parts of the world and make short- and long-range forecasts for given re-

Requirements

Meteorology is a science. Students interested in a career in meteorology can best prepare themselves for a college major in meteorology by taking as much high-school coursework as possible in mathematics, physics, and chemistry. To succeed in such a course of study, the interested student must have above-average intelligence and considerable interest and aptitude in mathematics and the physical sciences. A good command of the English is essential, because the meteorologist must be able to describe complex events and patterns both orally and in writing.

Although some beginners in meteorological work have majored in some subject related to meteorology, the normal minimal requirement for work in this field is a bachelor's degree in meteorology from one of the almost one hundred colleges offering a major in this field. The federal government, for example, requires beginners to have had a minimum of twenty semester hours in meteorology, supplemented by work in physics and mathematics. Advanced graduate training in meteorology and related areas is required for research and teaching positions, as well as for other high-level positions in meteorology. Doctorates are quite common among high-level personnel.

Because the armed forces require the services of so many meteorologists, they have programs whereby they send new college graduates who have been recently commissioned to civilian universities for intensive work in meteorology. The armed forces also send a smaller number of personnel on for this advanced training.

Special requirements

Special requirements for work in meteorology are specified by the agency employing meteorologists. Most often these requirements are related to the extent of formal training and nature of previous work experience. This is especially true for individuals seeking civil service positions in meteorology.

Opportunities for experience and exploration

An interested student can explore the possibility of a career in meteorology in several ways. Each year the federal government's National Weather Service accepts a limited number of student volunteers, mostly college students but also a few high-school students. Some universities offer credit for a college student's volunteer work in connection with meteorology courses. The National Oceanographic and Atmospheric Administration has details about the volunteer program. The armed forces can also be a means of gaining experience in meteorology.

Interviews can be held with meteorologists at airports or at colleges and universities offering work in meteorology. Students can also gain more information by getting in touch with the sources listed at the end of this article.

Related occupations

Meteorologists who also hold a degree in another major may establish careers in aerospace engineering, agriculture, astronomy, civil engineering, computer science, environmental engineering, geography, geology, hydrology, or oceanography. Individuals with an aptitude for mathematics and the physical sciences may find something of interest in the occupations of the following workers as well: cartographers, chemists, computer programmers, environmental analysts, geophysicists, mathematicians, physicists, and statisticians.

Methods of entering

Individuals may enter the field of meteorology in a number of ways. Some are assisted in securing positions by placement officials at the colleges and universities where they have stud-

ied. Others, who have volunteered at the National Weather Service, may receive permanent positions as meteorologists upon completing their formal training. Members of the armed forces who have done work in meteorology often assume positions in meteorology when they return to civilian life. In fact, the armed forces give preference in the employment of civilian meteorologists to former military personnel with appropriate experience. Individuals interested in teaching and research careers generally assume these positions upon receiving their doctorates in meteorology and related subjects.

Advancement

The avenues of advancement open to meteorologists are dependent upon the setting in which they are employed. Meteorologists employed by the National Weather Service are advanced according to civil service regulations. After meeting certain experiential and educational requirements, they are advanced to classifications that carry more pay and, often, more responsibility. Opportunities available to meteorologists employed by airlines are more limited. A few of these workers, however, do advance to such positions as flight dispatcher and to administrative and supervisory positions. A few meteorologists go into business for themselves by establishing their own weather consulting services. Meteorologists who are employed in teaching and research in colleges and universities receive advancement by being promoted in academic rank or by assuming administrative positions in the university setting.

Employment outlook

The employment outlook through the end of the 1990s for meteorologists is well above average. The National Weather Service, which employs many meteorologists, is expected to create numerous new positions in their field offices. There will be fewer opportunities for meteorologists in other parts of the federal government, however. In private industry, an increasing number of organizations are recognizing the value of private weather forecasting and will be hiring their own meteorologists. In addition, openings will occur as older, experienced meteorologists die, retire, or transfer to another occupation. As is true for most scientists, those in meteorology will have the best

417

chance of competing for available positions if they obtain advanced degrees.

In the early 1990s, about 5,600 civilians were working as meteorologists in the United States. In addition, meteorological faculties in colleges and universities accounted for another 1,000 or so jobs in this field. The National Oceanic and Atmospheric Administration (NOAA) employed more than 1,800 meteorologists. About half of the NOAA meteorologists worked in the National Weather Service; the rest worked mainly in research. The Department of Defense employed more than 250 civilian meteorologists.

Of civilian meteorologists, most were working for private industry, including weather consulting firms, engineering service firms, commercial airlines, radio and television stations, and companies that design and manufacture meteorological instruments and aircraft and missiles.

In addition to the civilian meteorologists, thousands of members of the armed forces also were engaged in government meteorological work.

Earnings

The beginning salaries of meteorologists are related to the amount of formal training they have received and the setting in which they are employed. Beginning meteorologists employed by the federal government in the early 1990s entered at the following approximate salaries: with a bachelor's degree and no experience, $14,800 or $18,400 a year; with a master's degree, $18,400 or $22,500; with a doctorate, $27,200 or $32,600. The average salary of meteorologists employed by the federal government was about $39,700 a year.

Conditions of work

Weather stations are operated on a twenty-four-hour, seven-day-a-week basis. This means that some meteorologists, often on a rotating basis, work evenings and weekends. Although most of these weather stations are at airports located near cities, a number of weather stations are located in isolated and remote areas. One of the remotest meteorological posts is on the Antarctic. It, however, provides much of the most interesting and relevant data in meteorology. In these latter places, the life of a meteorologist can be quiet and lonely. Meteorologists who work in college and university

settings enjoy the same working conditions as do other professors. The meteorologist spends much time working at a desk with little if any physical stress.

Social and psychological factors

Meteorologists are involved in very important work. The manner in which they interpret and relay weather information influences the lives of many people. They must be accurate and responsible workers. Because the work of the meteorologist is often concerned with gaining new understanding about the atmosphere and making predictions, he or she does have a stimulating and interesting job. However, the meteorologist assigned to a remote station must be prepared to tolerate loneliness and isolation.

Meteorologists generally hold membership in the American Meteorological Society, which is the professional organization in this field.

GOE: 02.01.01; SIC: 8999; SOC: 1846

◇ **SOURCES OF ADDITIONAL INFORMATION**

American Meteorological Society
45 Beacon Street
Boston, MA 02108

National Oceanic and Atmospheric Administration
Personnel Office
Room 706
6010 Executive Boulevard
Rockville, MD 20852

USAF Recruiting Service
Wright-Patterson AFB, OH 45899

◇ **RELATED ARTICLES**

Museum occupations

Definition

Museums preserve and display natural, cultural, and historic objects for viewing by the public. The success of a museum in generating interest in these objects depends greatly on the numerous people who work in the museum, collecting, restoring, and interpreting them in exhibits. Each museum exhibit has come about because of the efforts of a variety of museum employees, whose jobs range from acquiring objects to restoring and displaying them.

History

The first museums in the United States originated before the Revolutionary War, but these museums were privately owned and could be viewed only by a select few. Private collections of art, for example, were often developed by wealthy citizens and displayed for persons with established social status and education.

A public art gallery did open in New York in the 1840s, but was closed because of a lack of interest by the general public. A few years later, in 1853, a wealthy American named Thomas Jefferson Bryan opened a public gallery of artworks he had purchased in Europe. Soon after that, between 1850 and 1900, more museums were established.

This increase in museum interest paralleled the increasing growth of the cities. The educational levels of Americans began to grow; newspapers brought news of art and science and politics to the general public. Sparked by an increasing awareness of the world and the environment, many cities and states opened museums.

Many private citizens donated money and artworks to museums around the country. One individual, an Englishman named John Smithson, donated his half-million dollar fortune to the United States, even though he had never seen this country. His dream of establishing a place for the "increase and diffusion of knowledge among men," became a reality in 1852, with the establishment of the Smithsonian Institution.

The number of museums grew throughout the last years of the nineteenth century. Cities sponsored fairs and exhibits to honor various happenings and occasions, including the U.S. centennial. Many of these fairs and exhibits started museums that are still open today.

Although the number of museums was greatly increasing, museums did little to encourage and entice visitors, and most of the population still had minimal interest in them. Public attitude, however, began to change sometime between the 1940s and 1960s.

Many factors contributed to this change. An increase in population, greater mobility, and higher educational levels all helped generate a greater public interest in museums. In addition, museums were beginning to house displays that interpreted and explained the objects exhibited.

Today, there are thousands of museums around the country, and new ones continue to open. Most are art, history, or science museums, but others are dedicated to such specialties as whaling, woodcarving, and circuses. Museums have become informative and interesting places of learning that can be enjoyed and visited by everyone.

Nature of the work

The activities of workers employed by museums vary greatly because of the vast differences in both the size and type of museums. Basically, however, museum employees all work toward the same goal: to collect and restore objects of lasting value and interpret and display them in exhibits.

Museum curators use their knowledge of art, history, and science to decide which objects to acquire and how to best display them. They are responsible for collecting, restoring, displaying, and interpreting items of interest. Their work may be very specific, very general, or somewhere in-between. For example, an art curator in a large museum may be in charge of Italian paintings only, while an art curator in a smaller museum may be responsible for collecting all types of artworks from many different countries.

Curators have a variety of duties. They may advise people who are making a film about a particular culture. They may be present at archaeological diggings. They may collect animal species for museum. Or, they may study newspapers and legal documents to gain information about historic sites. In larger museums, some of their duties may be taken over by other

419

The curator of prints and drawings in a museum stores the works of art in well-organized flat file cases. Her job requires full knowledge of the museum's collection of prints and drawings.

workers, such as art conservators, exhibit artists, historic sites supervisors, and restorers.

Museum directors administer and oversee the administrative affairs of the museum. *Museum attendants* conduct the operation of the museum and provide information about regulations, facilities, and exhibits to visitors. *Restorers* work on damaged or faded objects. They attempt to restore items to as close to original condition as possible. Restorers may work on paintings, ceramics, textiles, or paper products. *Paintings restorers* preserve paintings and restore damaged or faded paintings. *Lace and textile restorers* restore and prepare ancient textile and lace materials for displays. *Ceramic restorers* clean, preserve, restore, and repair objects made of glass, porcelain, china, and other ceramic materials. *Paper-and-prints restorers* clean, restore, and preserve books, documents, maps, photographs, and other paper objects of value.

Once the items are restored, *fine arts packers* determine the types of packing materials and handling procedures needed to ship or store various museums objects. *Museum registrars* maintain records as to the attainment, location, and condition of objects and oversee the movement, packing, and shipping of objects.

Because museums are places of learning, many employees work in education. *Education directors* plan, develop, and administer the educational programs of the museum. *Educational resource coordinators* direct the educational resource center of the museum. *Teachers* instruct classes, lead workshops, and participate in other activities to further the educational programs of the museum. *Research associates* plan, organize, and conduct research in scientific, cultural, historical, or artistic fields for their own projects or for projects sponsored by the museum.

Historic sites supervisors direct and coordinate the activities of persons who investigate, acquire, and preserve historic sites. *Historic-site administrators* manage the operation of historic sites or structures.

Exhibit artists produce artwork for exhibits in the museum. *Art conservators* coordinate and oversee the activities of employees who examine and repair art objects.

There are all kinds of jobs in museums, one to suit just about every personality type. Currently, more than 6,000 museums exist in the United States.

Requirements

Employment for most museum occupations requires at least a bachelor's degree; some positions require graduate training and substantial work experience. A general liberal arts program is recommended, with special studies in art, history, science, and languages. Some colleges and universities offer specific programs in museology; most lead to advanced degrees, although some lead to bachelor's degrees.

Some workers obtain employment after completing an internship at a museum; internships include full-time work and self-paid courses. Even if a person is not offered a job after the internship is over, the experience is very helpful in securing employment elsewhere.

Continuing education is very important for many museum employees, such as curators. Curators need to keep abreast of developments and improvements in the field. They should attend workshops and conferences sponsored by various museum associations and by large museums, such as the Smithsonian Institution.

For some positions, such as fine arts packers and furniture restorers, work experience and vocational training are more important than a college degree; there are no formal educational requirements for these and other museum jobs.

Special requirements

There are no special licenses or certificates required for museum employees. Museum workers may, however, join a number of professional organizations if they choose. For example, employees of art, history, and science museums may wish to pursue membership in the American Association of Museums. Other professional organizations include the Association of Art Museum Director, the Association of Science-Technology Centers, and the American Association for State and Local History.

Opportunities for experience and exploration

Because museums are open to the public, students have a great opportunity to learn more about occupations in this field by visiting museums and talking with museum employees. In addition, museums often welcome volunteers, and students may decide to donate their time to gain insight into the nature of the work. Information about careers with museums can also be obtained by writing to the associations listed at the end of this article.

High-school students interested in museum occupations should take courses in art, history, science, and foreign languages.

Related occupations

Persons working in museums share a love of learning and the preservation and dissemination of that learning. Other occupations that share these traits include librarians, information scientists, teachers, university and college faculty, and scientists.

Methods of entering

Most museum workers do not attempt to enter this field until all applicable educational and/or work requirements have been met. Curators, for example, must obtain at least a bachelor's degree before seeking employment; those with a master's or a doctorate degree will have a better chance of securing employment. Some individuals may decide to apply for an internship at a museum; the experience is very valuable. Others may decide to work part-time or as a volunteer to gain experience. In addition, many universities have services for placing students.

Advancement

Most promotions for museum workers involve transferring from one museum to another. Curators who have earned advanced degrees and who have published articles in journals will have the best chance of securing a promotion. In large museums, some workers may be promoted to an administrative position, such as museum director.

Employment outlook

Employment for museum occupations is expected to increase more slowly than the average for all occupations through the mid-1990s. In addition, competition for positions such as museum curator will increase over the next decade because of an over-supply of well-educated applicants. Those applicants with the best credentials, both in education and experience, will be offered the best jobs.

Earnings

Earnings of museum workers vary greatly according to the nature of the position and the size ad type of museum. For example, salaries in large, well-funded museums are much higher than in small museums. Natural science museums generally offer higher paying jobs than history museums. And federal salaries are higher than state salaries.

Curators may earn a wide range of salaries, depending on educational background and work experience. For example, in the early 1990s curators employed by the federal government averaged $34,500 a year. Those curators with a bachelor's degree and experience or a master's degree started at $21,800, while those with a doctorate started at $26,440 or $31,600.

Conditions of work

The specific working conditions vary according to the size, type and location of the museum, but employees in all kinds of museums enjoy interesting and comfortable surroundings. Employees may work in offices, exhibit areas, laboratories, or auction halls.

Museum workers are part of an interesting, challenging profession. They share information with the public about cultural, scientific, and historical objects of lasting value, and derive a great feeling of satisfaction from their work. They support professional research and public education.

Social and psychological factors

Museum workers should have an intellectual curiosity and an interest in their chosen field, whether it be art history, archaeology, or natural science. Curators and other museum employees should be able to express themselves well, both in speech and in writing and should be able to think creatively. The ability to analyze and interpret various artifacts and other items of interest is also a plus. It is also important for museum workers to be able to communicate with the public.

GOE: 01.06.02; SIC: 8412; SIC: 252

◇ **SOURCES OF ADDITIONAL INFORMATION**

American Association of Museums
1225 I Street, NW, Suite 200
Washington, DC 20005

American Association of Zoological Parks and Aquariums
Route 88
Oglebay Park
Wheeling, West Virginia 26003

American Institute for Conservation of Historic and Artistic Works
1400 16th Street, NW
Suite 340
Washington, DC 20036

Society of American Archivists
600 South Federal Street
Suite 504
Chicago, IL 60605

National Trust for Historic Preservation
1785 Massachusetts Avenue, NW
Washington, DC 20036

◇ **RELATED ARTICLES**

Volume 1: Design; Education; Library and Information Science
Volume 2: Anthropologists and archaeologists; Display workers; Historians; Librarians; Taxidermists
Volume 4: Exhibit technicians

Musical occupations

Definition

People who teach, write, arrange, direct, or perform music of any kind are employed in musical occupations. Teachers and performers may be either instrumental musicians or singers. They may teach or perform classical music, jazz, folk, blues, opera, or any other form of music. They teach private and group or class lessons or perform before audiences of all sizes.

History

Ancient art shows us that people have made music for many centuries. Early music was probably almost entirely vocal. Early singing took the form of chanting, sometimes accompanied by crude instruments. Musicians are depicted in ancient paintings from Egypt, Greece, and the Orient. Both the instruments and the tonal qualities used in ancient music have changed, and today's music is very much different from the first music notes performed by man.

A great catalyst for both change and preservation in music arrived in the form of Guido d'Arezzo, an eleventh century monk who devised a system for writing music down on paper, so that music might be preserved and later read and played by other musicians. Many monks throughout the Middle Ages devoted their lives to the music of the church, and we owe much of our knowledge of early religious music to their dedication to preserving this form of music.

Through the Middle Ages, singers and musicians roamed Europe, going from town to town to play for new audiences. In the Renaissance, many singers and musicians depended on wealthy patrons for their support. If they did not please their patrons, they did not make a living. What we now call classical music developed during the Renaissance period.

In the seventeenth century, opera was created. An extremely popular form of singing, orchestral music, and theater, opera opened up a whole new range of opportunities for musicians, especially singers. The idea of great fame for singers developed with opera and its demand for singers with voices of high quality and wide range. The image of singers changed—from lackeys of the wealthy to talented, creative artists. Soon opera singers were entertained even by the royal families of Europe.

Operatic, classical, and European nationalistic music came to America with the Europeans who loved it. Time and technology have combined to create American music. In the early nineteenth century American symphony orchestras played solely European compositions. Today, however, they increasingly perform works by American composers.

U.S. popular music has influenced music all over the world. America invented jazz, and from jazz came swing. Blues and rock are also mainly American music forms. With the advent of the mass media, the musical superstar was created, as millions of people at a time could hear or see musical performers. While the mass media brings performers' music into homes all over the world, it has ironically limited the market for singers and musicians. As appearance, personality, and showmanship became as important to the mass media audience as musical ability, it became clear that few people would ever be able to reach these mass audiences. However, regional performers still may make musical livings in this country without benefit of national media exposure.

Nature of the work

Instrumental musicians play one or more musical instruments, usually in a group. Instruments fall into several categories: strings—violins, cellos, basses, and so on; woodwinds—oboes and clarinets, for example; brass—trumpets, French horns, and tubas; and percussion—including drums, rhythm instruments such as tambourines and triangles, and pianos.

These musicians may play in symphony orchestras, dance bands, jazz bands, rock bands, or other groups. Some play in recording studios for music on records. Most musicians specialize in either classical, jazz, or popular music. A few play more than one kind of music professionally. Classical musicians perform in orchestra concerts, opera performances, theater orchestras, and chamber music concerts. The most talented may work as soloists with orchestras. Other musicians accompany singers, choirs, and solo instrumentalists on the piano during rehearsals or performances. Classical musicians also perform in churches and may direct or accompany church choirs.

Musicians who play popular music make heavy use of such rhythm instruments as piano, bass, drums, and guitar. Jazz musicians also play bass and woodwind instruments. Musicians in jazz, blues, country, and rock groups play clubs, festivals, and concert halls, and may perform music for recordings, television, and movie soundtracks. A few appear in movies themselves.

Singers use their knowledge of musical tone, phrasing, harmony, and melody to interpret vocal music. Opera singers tour the country and the world in opera productions. Many singers perform in large or small choral groups, often in churches or synagogues. Other classical singers may be soloists, performing classical and operatic songs with orchestras in a concert setting. Singers are usually designated by the range of their voices—either soprano, contralto, tenor, or bass—or by the type of popular music they perform—rock, folk, jazz, blues, or country.

Many popular vocalists are employed singing with small dance bands in clubs, restaurants, and lounges around the country. These singers need a repertoire of standard numbers, the ability to learn new popular songs, and a variety of costumes.

Singers also work in jazz, rock, and country bands. Those who are extremely successful appear on television and have their music played on the radio. Some work primarily as recording artists and largely depend on record sales for their earnings.

The job of singers and instrumental musicians is to use their vocal or instrumental skills to convey the form and meaning of written music. Instrumentalists and vocalists work to achieve precision, fluency, and clarity of tone; vocalists also work to express emotion through phrasing and characterization.

Many singers and musicians also supplement their incomes through teaching. Some teach full-time. Singing and music teachers work in colleges, high schools, elementary schools, and conservatories, giving lessons and often staging concerts and recitals involving

At its fullest capacity, an orchestra may contain 80 string instruments, 30 wind instruments, several percussionists, and nearly 200 chorus members. These musicians and singers are performing at Orchestra Hall in Chicago, Illinois.

their students. Many professional musicians give private lessons. Teachers help students learn to read music, develop their voices, breathe correctly, and hold their instruments properly. They supervise their students in mastering progressively more difficult pieces of music as the students learn techniques.

Choral directors direct groups of singers in schools and other organizations. Church choirs, community oratorio societies, and professional symphony choruses are among the groups that employ choral directors outside of school settings. Within schools, glee clubs, swing choirs, concert choirs, and choral ensembles all take their cues from the choral director, whose job it is to audition singers, select music, and direct the singers in achieving the tone, variety, intensity, and phrasing he or she desires. Relying on conducting techniques and knowledge of musical theory, choral directors use singers' voices to achieve a musical effect. *Orchestra conductors* do the same with instrumental musicians. Many work in schools and smaller communities. The best conduct symphonies in major cities around the world. Some are resident conductors; others travel constantly, mak-

ing guest appearances throughout the country and the world. They conduct rehearsals and performances and are responsible for the overall sound and competence of the orchestras they direct.

Music teachers and performers, of course, need written music to teach and perform. *Composers, arrangers, orchestrators, copyists, librettists,* and *lyricists* give musicians works to play and songs to sing. Composers create original music—symphonies, songs, operas. They use musical notation to express their ideas through melody, rhythm, and harmony. Arrangers and orchestrators take composers' melodies and transcribe them for other instruments or voices, work them into scores for film, theater, or television, or adapt them to styles different from the one in which the music was written. Copyists help arrangers by writing down arrangements in musical notation. Librettists write words to opera and musical theater scores, and lyricists write words to songs and other short musical pieces. Some writers compose both music and lyrics.

Also in musical occupations are *music directors,* who are in charge of the music and personnel for studio orchestras—orchestras that perform only on records. In addition, *prompters* help stage operas by assuring that singers and musicians enter and perform on cue.

Requirements

Teachers in schools and conservatories must complete formal education programs, but most other musical careers require no formal qualifications. Succeeding in music, however, does have many, many other requirements. Foremost among these is a love of music strong enough to endure the arduous training and working life of the professional musician.

Both singers and instrumental musicians begin learning their musical skills at an early age. From then on, long hours of practice and study are essential. Most musicians train under the supervision of an experienced musician, either in a conservatory or through private lessons. Singers of popular music may never receive formal vocal training and still succeed, but most do benefit from learning from an experienced vocalist. Most successful musicians read music notation.

Singers and instrumentalists also need to gain experience working with other musicians. Those who perform on stage need to learn to communicate with an audience. Singers must be in good physical condition, as well, since their instrument is their entire body. A wide vocal range and strength of voice are essential for opera and concert singers, and for many popular singers as well.

Musicians who choose to study in universities or conservatories usually need to audition for admission. In such institutions, students learn musical theory, music composition, interpretation, conducting, and instrumental or vocal technique. Persons hoping to become conductors, composers, or arrangers also need this type of training. Many schools of higher education offer degrees in music.

Most important of all, musicians must have dedication, self-discipline, and drive. Only if they feel they cannot happily pursue any other career should they enter this difficult and highly competitive field.

Special requirements

Music teachers in elementary and secondary schools must acquire a state certificate to teach in these schools. The requirements for these certificates include a college education gained from an institution of higher education authorized by an accrediting body to offer preparation in music education. About 600 conservatories, universities, and colleges offer bachelor's degrees in music education to qualify students for state certificates.

Music education programs are composed of study in general education, development of various performance skills, music theory, and professional education, including supervised practice teaching. To teach music in colleges and schools of music or in conservatories, one must generally have a graduate degree in music. However, widely recognized performers sometimes obtain positions in higher education without having pursued formal graduate training.

In addition, the ability to play the piano and read music will help any type of musician to succeed. Knowledge of Romance languages, Latin, and German is also important to singers, choir conductors, and music writers.

Opportunities for experience and exploration

Musicians have many opportunities to explore the field. Elementary schools, high schools, and institutes of higher education all afford students opportunities to practice and perform with groups—in choirs, ensembles, bands, and orchestras. Singers can perform in school musicals, as well. Many schools have jazz bands and talent shows, where students can also gain experience in performing. Music students studying privately are usually able to perform in recitals arranged by their teachers. College, university, and conservatory students also appear in recitals.

Many communities sponsor amateur nights or put on amateur productions of operettas and musicals, in which amateur musicians can gain experience and hone their skills. Churches also provide many opportunities for singers, instrumentalists, and directors to perform and learn. Musical summer camps and amateur musical groups give amateurs all over the country thousands of opportunities to perform with others, gain experience on stage, and find out if they have what it takes to become a professional musician.

The student-teaching requirement in the student music teacher's curriculum gives would-be teachers a chance to explore the field. Directing work in churches can give them experience in working with groups of musicians.

Related occupations

There are many music-related occupations other than those that involve performing, composing, or teaching. Some are mentioned elsewhere in this article. Others include artists' agents or personal managers; concert managers; disc jockeys and radio or TV announcers; music critics; music directors for motion pictures, radio, and television; music librarians; music publishers; music store owners or sales workers; and music therapists. Persons interested in the technical aspects of music may consider training for work as instrument repairers and tuners or sound and audio technicians.

Methods of entering

Musicians who want to perform in established groups, such as choirs and symphonic orchestras, enter the field through auditions. Recommendations from teachers and other musicians often help would-be musicians obtain the chance to audition. Concert and opera soloists must also audition. Many begin in choirs and opera choruses before they audition as soloists. Singers and instrumentalists must prepare thoroughly for these demanding and stressful auditions. If they audition before they are ready they may fail badly and then have trouble getting chances to audition in the future.

Popular musicians often begin by performing without pay at community and social functions. Eventually they may find low-paying work at clubs or restaurants. These performers gradually build an audience of people who like their music, and if that audience grows large enough they may be able to get bookings in better clubs and larger halls. Eventually they may be able to get recording contracts.

Music teachers enter the field by applying directly to schools. College and university placement offices often have listings of positions. Professional associations and journals also often list teaching openings, as do newspapers. Newspaper advertisements are also good sources for leads on jobs with performing groups and bands.

In addition, agents and managers help many singers and musicians find performing engagements.

Advancement

Advancement is not as easily defined in the music business as it is in others. Singers feel they have made progress if they advance in any or all of three ways: technical skill, public acceptance, and income. Determination and ability play large parts in determining whether a singer will make such advancement.

Teachers of music in the elementary and secondary schools may, with experience and further training, aspire to careers as supervisors of music for a school system, a school district, or an entire state. With further graduate training, these teachers sometimes secure positions on the professional staffs of music conservatories or in music departments of colleges and universities.

Popular musicians advance by moving up to better-known bands and by leading their own bands. Instrumental musicians advance by becoming the "first chair" (the leading player of a certain instrument) in a symphony orchestra. Once instrumental musicians acquire a reputation as accomplished artists, they may receive engagements that are more desirable in terms of status and/or financial remuneration. As their reputations develop, both classical and popular musicians may receive attractive offers to make lucrative recordings and personal appearances.

Employment outlook

In the early 1990s, an average of about 189,000 musicians were employed at any one time in the United States. Because musicians rarely work full-time all year, the number of professional musicians is probably much higher.

The employment outlook for musicians, singers, and music teachers is influenced by a number of factors, and few general predictions can be made for musical careers as a whole. Overall, the employment of musicians is expected to grow at an average rate through the end of the 1990s. The field is extremely competitive, however, attracting many people with musical ambitions while requiring very little in the way of formal training for many types of jobs. The demand for musicians will be best in theaters, bands, and restaurants as the public continues to spend more money on recreational activities. The outlook is not so favorable in churches and synagogues, though, because of generally slow growth in religious organizations. Popular musicians may receive many short-term engagements in nightclubs, restaurants, and theaters, but these engagements offer little employment stability. The supply of qualified popular musicians for such positions is expected to exceed the demand in the foreseeable future.

The opportunities for careers in teaching music are expected to grow at an average rate in elementary schools and in colleges and universities, and at a slower than average rate in secondary schools. Although increasing numbers of colleges and universities have begun to offer music programs, enrollments in schools at all levels have been depressed and are not expected to increase until toward the end of the 1990s. In addition, some public schools have reduced or eliminated their music programs because of budget problems. The competition for positions as teachers of music, therefore, is expected to be especially keen throughout the decade.

Although music teachers may give private lessons, they will have to compete with the many instrumental musicians who cannot find work and become private music teachers either full- or part-time. This oversupply of private music teachers is expected to prevail in the future because of the ease with which people can set themselves up as music teachers. No formal training or license is required to give individual or private lessons.

Earnings

Because earnings for musicians depend greatly on the performer's skill, reputation, geographic location, type of music, and number of engagements per year, it is difficult to estimate the earnings of the average professional musician.

In the early 1990s, musicians in the thirty major U.S. symphony orchestras earned minimum salaries of between $440 and $840 a week, according to the American Symphony Orchestra League. Some musicians earned much more than the minimum, however. Regional orchestra members earned less, between $162 and $565 per week minimum. The major orchestras perform an average of about forty-eight weeks a year. Regional symphonies' seasons are generally shorter.

Studio recording is well-paying work for musicians, when they can get it. Musicians recording music for motion pictures earned no less than $173 for each three-hour session, and those employed by record companies earned a minimum of $204 for a three-hour session.

Popular instrumentalists performing live may earn anywhere from $30 to $300 per engagement, depending on their talent and the size of the nightclub or other location.

Singers' wages follow similar patterns. Opera chorus and concert singers earned minimums of about $70 per performance. Featured soloists earned a minimum of about $234 per

The annual Newport Jazz Festival features famous jazz musicians from all over the world.

performance. Singers performing in groups on television earned a minimum of between $248 and $265 per singer, per one-hour program. Television soloists or those in duets earned about $536 each, minimum. Recording artists' minimum scale was $110 per record side.

The few famous opera and concert stars and top recording artists of popular music who earn thousands of dollars for a single performance may not have as many performances a year as one might expect. Therefore, although the income for what appears to be only a few hours' work may seem attractive, the annual income may not be so impressive. Perhaps several times as many popular singers as concert or operatic singers earn incomes that reach well into the thousands each year. It must be remembered, however, that their productive years may be few, and that the income they earn during the period of their public acclaim may have to serve them for life.

Church organists, choir directors, and soloists usually supplement income from other jobs with the $40 to $100 they may earn each week working with church music.

The salaries received by music teachers in elementary and secondary schools are the same as for other teachers. In public elementary schools, the average salary received by teachers in the early 1990s was about $24,800 per year. The figure for public secondary school teachers was about $26,100. Music teachers in colleges and universities had widely ranging salaries. Most teachers often supplement their income by providing private instruction and by working in the musical programs of churches and other organizations.

With the exception of musicians and music teachers who are affiliated with schools and colleges, musicians do not, as a rule, work steadily for one employer. They often undergo long periods of unemployment between engagements. Because of these factors, few musicians can qualify for unemployment compensation. Nor do most musicians enjoy such benefits as sick leave and paid vacations. On the other hand, music teachers on the staffs of schools, colleges, and universities receive such fringe benefits as retirement pensions, health programs, and insurance programs.

Conditions of work

The working conditions of musicians and music teachers vary greatly. Performing musicians generally work in the evenings and on weekends. They also spend much time in practice and rehearsing for performances. Performers may be given a star's dressing room or share a mirror in the basement of a school. They may work under the hot camera lights of motion pictures or television, or tour with a troupe in subzero temperatures. They may sing or play in an elegant nightclub or sit on a chair in one corner of a small alcove enclosing a four-piece band. They may work amid the noise and confusion of a large rehearsal of a Broadway show or in the relative peace and quiet of a small recording studio. Seldom are two days in a performer's life just alike.

Many musicians and singers travel a great deal. The chief characteristic of musical employment is its lack of continuity. Few musicians work full-time and most experience periods of unemployment between engagements. Most work day jobs to supplement their musical incomes.

Better-known musicians may travel with staffs to make their arrangements and take care of their wardrobes. Agents and managers often negotiate performers' contracts and help plan their careers.

Music teachers affiliated with institutions work the same hours as do other classroom teachers. Many of these teachers, however, spend time after school and on weekends directing and instructing school vocal and instrumental groups. Teachers may also have wide differences in the conditions of their work. They may teach in a large urban school, conducting five different choruses each day. Or they may work with rural elementary schools and spend much of their time driving from school to school.

College or university teachers may divide their time between group instruction and individual instruction. They may teach several musical subjects. They may also supervise student music teachers when they go out into public schools to do practice teaching.

Private teachers may have their studio in their own home or obtain a studio in a building away from their home. They may teach adults who are primarily concerned with their own enjoyment of music, or adolescents who hope to make music their career. Private teachers may work a full eight-hour day or arrange their work to suit others.

Work for musicians is found all over the country, but is concentrated in larger cities and in those with large recording industries—Chicago, New York, Los Angeles, Nashville, and Miami Beach, for example. In other cities, most musicians may find work in churches, synagogues, clubs, and restaurants, at weddings, in opera and ballet productions, and on television and radio.

Professional musicians generally hold membership in the American Federation of Musicians (AFL-CIO), and concert soloists also hold membership in the American Guild of Musical Artists, Inc. (AFL-CIO). Singers may belong to a branch of Associated Actors and Artistes of America (AFL-CIO). Teachers of music in schools and colleges often hold membership in the Music Educators National Conference, which is a department of the National Education Association, and in appropriate local, state, and regional music groups.

Social and psychological factors

Singers, musicians, and music teachers have the satisfaction that comes from bringing music and music appreciation to people. They have the satisfaction of knowing that they are making the lives of their fellow human beings more pleasant and rewarding. The ability to perform well, however, requires long and trying hours of practice. The musician must be thoroughly committed to the importance of music for self-fulfillment to tolerate the many demands that a career in music places on an individual.

Musicians must also be able to tolerate the anxieties that accompany an insecure financial status. They must be able to live with the threats to their continued existence provided by the technological developments that place the best work of a few accomplished artists within reach of great numbers of people and thereby deprive many less accomplished artists of a means of livelihood.

Teachers of music in schools and colleges, however, enjoy more security. For this reason, many people attempt to combine teaching and performing careers.

GOE: 01.04; SIC: 7929; SOC: 251

◇ SOURCES OF ADDITIONAL INFORMATION

American Federation of Musicians of the United States and Canada
Paramount Building
1501 Broadway, Suite 600
New York, NY 10036

American Guild of Musical Artists
1727 Broadway
New York, NY 10019

American Guild of Organists
475 Riverside Drive, Suite 1260
New York, NY 10115

American Symphony Orchestra League
777 14th Street, NW
Washington, DC 20005

Music Educators National Conference
1902 Association Drive
Reston, VA 22091

Music Teachers National Association
617 Vine Street
Suite 1432
Cincinnati, OH 45202

National Association of Schools of Music
11250 Roger Bacon Drive, Number 21
Reston, VA 22090

◇ RELATED ARTICLES

Volume 1: Broadcasting; Education; Motion Pictures; Performing Arts; Recording
Volume 2: Actors and actresses; Adult and vocational education teachers; College and university faculty; Dancers and choreographers; Literary agents and artists' managers; Teachers, kindergarten and elementary school; Teachers, secondary school

Nuclear medicine technologists

Definition

Nuclear medicine technologists prepare and administer chemicals known as radiopharmaceuticals (radioactive drugs) used in the diagnosis and treatment of certain diseases. These drugs are given to a patient so that radioactive chemicals are absorbed into a specific location in the patient's body. Technologists operate diagnostic equipment to trace the concentration of the radioactive drugs through the patient's body and perform laboratory tests of the patient's blood volume and fat absorption to determine the effect of the radioactive material.

History

Just as the field of radiology had its beginnings in the 1890s when Wilhelm Roentgen discovered the X ray, nuclear medicine had its origins at the turn of the twentieth century when Marie Curie and her fellow scientists discovered radium. Radium, however, had no medical application until after World War II when scientists discovered ways of producing artificial radionuclides.

In nuclear medicine an "image" is transmitted that enables the physician to diagnose diseased tissue and functional disorders. Unlike X

429

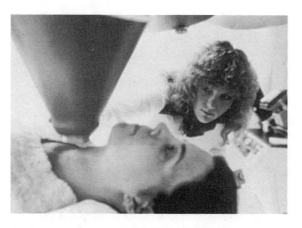

A nuclear medicine technologist uses an X ray viewer to test the absorption of radioactive medicine into a patient's thyroid.

rays, however, where the radiation passes through the body to expose the photographic film, with nuclear medicine the radiation comes from radioactive isotopes inside the body. A compound is made radioactive and then is injected into or swallowed by the patient. The rate of absorption and elimination can be determined by measuring the radiation over a period of time with special cameras, or scanners. This information is then used in the diagnosis and treatment of certain diseases, such as a dysfunctional thyroid gland.

All forms of radiation are potentially harmful, but carefully controlled and precisely directed doses of radiation are frequently used with great success.

Nature of the work

Nuclear medicine technologists work directly with patients, preparing and administering radioactive drugs. All work is supervised by a physician. Because of the potential danger of radioactive material, the preparation of the drugs requires the adherence to strict safety precautions. All safety procedures are overseen by the Nuclear Regulatory Commission.

After administering the drug to the patient, the technologist operates a gamma scintillation camera, or scanner, as a diagnostic imaging unit to take pictures of the radioactive drug as it passes through or accumulates in parts of the patient's body. These images are then put on a computer screen, where the technologist helps the physician examine the images.

A nuclear medicine technologist also has administrative responsibilities. Careful records of treatment and continuing therapy must be maintained and records of the use and mainte-

nance of equipment must also be kept. Laboratory testing of a patient's body specimens, such as blood or urine, is also the responsibility of the technologist.

Chief nuclear medicine technologists generally manage large radiology departments; they might also teach in training programs. *Radiation-therapy technologists* operate X ray equipment and position patients during treatment. They are also responsible for maintaining medical records for review by the attending physician.

Requirements

High-school courses should include biology and chemistry; physics would also be helpful. Professional training is available at some colleges as part of a bachelor's program. Some hospitals and technical schools also offer training programs. All programs should be accredited by the American Medical Association's Committee on Allied Health Education and Accreditation.

Many training programs are designed for people, such as registered nurses, who already have a background in a health- or science-related field. Therefore a good knowledge of anatomy and physiology is helpful. Coursework covered in the program includes radiation biology and protection, radioactivity and instrumentation, radiopharmaceuticals and their use on patients, and radiation therapy.

Special requirements

Some states require technologists to be certified or registered by the American Registry of Radiologic Technologists (ARRT) or the Nuclear Medicine Technology Certification Board (NMTCB).

Opportunities for experience and exploration

A person can not get any hands-on experience without the necessary qualifications. However, it is possible to become familiar with the job responsibilities by talking with practicing nuclear medicine technologists or teachers in the subject.

Related occupations

Many occupations in the health-care industry are similar to the work done by nuclear medicine technologists. Beyond the most familiar, such as physicians, registered nurses, licensed practical nurses, other related occupations include radiologic technologists, ultrasound technologists, respiratory therapists, cardiology technologists, surgical technicians, physical therapists, medical laboratory technicians, pharmacists, and pharmacologists.

Methods of entering

Many nuclear medicine technologist positions, especially those in hospitals, are open only to certified or registered technologists. Information on becoming registered or certified is available from the American Registry of Radiologic Technologists or the Nuclear Medicine Technology Certification Board.

In some cases, a bachelor's degree with the appropriate courses or completion of a specialized training program is sufficient for an entry level position.

Advancement

Growth in the field should lead to advancement opportunities. Advancement usually takes the form of promotion to a supervisory position, with a corresponding increase in pay. With increased competition for positions in the large metropolitan hospitals, it may be necessary to transfer to another hospital or city to secure a promotion. Rural area hospitals have much less competition for positions and therefore are more likely to give promotions.

Promotions are normally to positions of supervisor, chief technologist, or nuclear medicine department administrator. Some may choose to leave laboratory work and teach or work with equipment development and sales.

Employment outlook

Employment is expected to grow about as fast as the average for all occupations through the early 1990s. There are two main factors that will impact employment opportunities. Opportunities are likely to be constrained by competition from imaging techniques, such as magnetic resonance imaging (MRI), in which the physician uses a scanner to see inside the patient's body in a noninvasive way and without the use of radiation. At the same time, advances in medical diagnostic procedures could lead to the increased use of nuclear medicine technology in the diagnosis and treatment of more diseases, including an increased use in cancer treatment and cardiology.

The fact that most of the job opportunities are in hospitals means that opportunities will be better in areas with large hospitals. Jobs will also be available in health clinics, research facilities, and some private laboratories.

Earnings

Starting salary averages about $19,000 per year for entry level positions. Chief technologists can expect to make about $30,000 annually.

Conditions of work

Nuclear medicine technologists can expect to work thirty-five to forty hours a week, although larger hospitals often require overtime. Night and weekend work can also be expected. Because the job usually takes place inside a hospital or other health care facility, the environment is always clean and well-lighted. The placing or positioning of patients on the diagnostic equipment is sometimes required. There is a small chance of low-level contamination from the radioactive material or from the handling of body fluids. Strict safety precautions make contamination a very slight possibility.

Social and psychological factors

A nuclear medicine technologist must sometimes work with patients who are frightened. The technologist must be able to calm these people. Attention to detail is very important, as is the ability to follow instructions. Technologists, like all medical professionals, must treat all patient information with confidentiality. Although there can be some disappointment in working with very sick patients, helping people during a time of need can be very rewarding.

GOE: 10.02.02; SIC: 806; SOC: 365

◇ **SOURCES OF ADDITIONAL INFORMATION**

General information about career opportunities as a nuclear medicine technologist is available from:

The Society of Nuclear Medicine
Technologists Section
136 Madison Avenue, 8th Floor
New York, NY 10016

Information on certification is available from:

The American Registry of Radiologic Technologists
2600 Wayzata Boulevard
Minneapolis, MN 55405

Nuclear Medicine Technology Certification Board
PO Box 806
Tucker, GA 30085

Numerical control tool programmers

Definition

Numerical control tool programmers use their knowledge of machining operations and blueprint reading to write programs that enable machine tools to make metal parts automatically.

History

Although much of the manufacturing industry involves the mass production of products, some items are still made in small batches. Items that are not mass produced include some types of industrial equipment, aircraft, motor vehicles, and other related products; these products are manufactured through a process called "machining," which is the cutting of metal or plastic workpieces into parts for final products.

For many years, machining was performed by skilled workers who used milling machines, lathes, and other tools. As the cost and complexity of parts used for various products increased, however, it became apparent that alternative methods of machining were necessary.

During the late 1940s, in response to the rising costs of aircraft parts, the Air Force sponsored research to develop machine tools that could be programmed to make parts automati-cally. The research was conducted at the Massachusetts Institute of Technology and led to the development, in 1952, of the first numerically controlled machine tool that could be programmed to make parts of different dimensions automatically.

There are two main components to numerical control machine tools: an electronic controller and a machine tool. The controller, which is a type of computer, reads and directs the machine tool to perform various commands that have been written into a computer program. A computer program is prepared for each job required. For example, one program might contain commands that would instruct a drill bit to move to certain spots and drill holes. A workpiece may have to be worked on by several numerical control tools before it is finished.

For the numerical control machine tools to do their job, they must be set up with a proper program. These computer programs are planned and designed by numerical control tool programmers.

Nature of the work

Tool programmers write the programs that direct machine tools to make parts automatically. Programmers must understand how the various machine tools operate and must know the working properties of the metals and plastics that are used in the process. Tool programmers should have an aptitude for mathematics and blueprint reading.

Writing a program for a numerically controlled tool involves several steps. Before tool programmers can begin writing a program, they must first analyze the blueprints of the items to be made. After the blueprints have been analyzed, the programmers determine the steps that must be taken and the cutting tools that will be needed to machine the workpiece into a desired shape. They must determine the size and position of the cuts that must be made, as well as the speed and rate that will be needed.

After all necessary computations have been made, they write a program in the language of the electronic controller and store the program on punch tape, magnetic tape, or disks.

Programmers usually use computers to write the programs. They write a series of simple commands in a computer language; the computer then computes the necessary mathematics, translates the program into the language of the controller, and stores it. Some programmers have computer-aided design (CAD) systems. CAD systems can be used to write the program for the computer. Tool programmers use computers and CAD systems as aids; they do not, however, write the computer software themselves.

To ensure that a program has been properly designed, programmers often perform a trial run. Trial runs help ensure that a machine is functioning properly and that the final product is correct. Some computers will run a simulation to check a specific program.

A tool programmer tests a new program to ensure that it is properly designed before it is used in production.

mathematics, blueprint reading, metalworking, data processing, physics, and drafting.

Special requirements

There are no licenses required or other special requirements. The only requirements are those that may be established by the firms that employ tool programmers.

Opportunities for experience and exploration

Students who are interested in a career as a tool programmer may test their interest and aptitude by taking shop and vocational classes. Most vocational schools offer a variety of classes.

It may also be a good idea for students to visit firms that employ numerical control tool programmers. Talking directly with tool programmers is an excellent way to gain practical information on what the work is like and how to best prepare for it.

Summer jobs at manufacturing firms and machine shops may provide insight into the work, as will part-time work. A person may start out in an entry-level job to gain machining experience before deciding to obtain formal training in machine tool programming.

Requirements

Although tool programmers learn their jobs through both work experience and vocational studies, the growing complexity of the work makes formal training essential. Many vocational schools and junior colleges offer applicable courses; employers may even pay for some classes. There are many brands of numerically controlled tools, and manufacturers often provide training to employees of firms that purchases their machines.

Employers prefer to hire experienced machine workers. An individual who has completed courses in tool programming, however, may be hired in spite of a lack of experience. It is valuable for persons interested in tool programming to have a background knowledge of

Related occupations

Tool programmers are highly skilled workers in the metal machining field. Other such workers include machinists, tool-and-die designers, tool-and-die makers, and tool planners. Persons attracted to tool programming who are willing and able to acquire more extensive education and training, might consider the occupations of mechanical engineers or mechanical engineering technicians.

Methods of entering

Tool programming is not generally considered an entry-level job; most employers prefer to hire people with both job experience and vocational training. Sometimes, however, firms may promote skilled machine workers to programming jobs and then pay for vocational courses for these workers. On the other hand, employees may hire individuals who have no direct job experience if they have completed vocational courses. Thus, there are various ways to enter this field. Some vocational schools help place students with manufacturing firms and machine shops.

Advancement

Employees may advance to better-paying jobs by transferring to larger or more established manufacturing firms or shops. Tool programmers with experience may also be promoted to supervisory positions or may transfer to related jobs, such as tool designers.

Employment outlook

There were about 8,800 tool programmers employed in the early 1990s. Openings for numerical control tool programmers are expected to increase about as fast as the average rate for all occupations through the rest of the decade. Besides openings resulting from a growth in demand for these workers, other openings will arise as programmers transfer to other jobs, retire, or die. Even though the employment outlook is fairly good, this is still a small occupation; the total number of openings will be less than for other machining occupations.

The demand for industrial machinery, aircraft, motor vehicles, and other products that use machined parts is expected to increase as U.S. firms continue to compete with foreign manufacturers. U.S. companies will have to increase their use of numerical control machine tools to curb rising costs; this will increase the demand for tool programmers. Some of the demand for tool programmers may be offset, however, by higher import levels as well as by the standardization of programming languages, which would simplify the tool programmers' work and increase their productivity.

Earnings

In the early 1990s, tool programmers earned approximately $27,000 a year. That figure compares to about $18,200 a year for all production workers, except farmers. Tool programmers generally work a forty-hour week, although overtime is common during peak periods. Overtime may include evening and weekend work during production periods when the tool programs are operating.

Conditions of work

Tool programmers usually work in pleasant, comfortable surroundings. Their work is not as physically demanding as those workers who operate machine tools. In addition, the areas in which they work are separated from the noisier areas in which the machine tools are in use. Most tool programmers work in large metropolitan areas, where the majority of factories and machine shops are located.

Social and psychological factors

Numerical control tool programmers are highly skilled workers who must be able to work both individually and as part of a team. Tool programmers should be logical, analytical, and detail-oriented. They must be accurate and careful because mistakes are costly.

Tool programmers are part of a growing technical profession that is changing and expanding. The variety of the work and the challenges that must be faced bring pride and satisfaction to tool programmers.

GOE: 05.01.06; SIC: 3625; SOC: 3974

Occupational therapists

Definition

Occupational therapists, following physicians' instructions, select and direct educational, vocational, and recreational activities designed to restore maximum function to mentally or physically disabled patients.

History

Through the centuries "curing by doing" had been a form of treatment for persons in need of therapy and rehabilitation.

During the late 1700s, physicians in Germany and France and Benjamin Rush in the United States were using occupational therapy for treating the mentally ill. In the 1790s, the Pennsylvania Hospital for the Insane was teaching patients carpentry, shoe repairing, needle work, and music.

Occupational therapy as we know it today, however, had its beginning in World War I. The need to help disabled veterans of that war, and years later the veterans of World War II, stimulated its growth.

Even though its inception was in the psychiatric field, occupational therapy has developed an equally important role in other medical fields, including rehabilitation of physically disabled patients.

Nature of the work

Occupational therapists use several types of therapy to attain the rehabilitation goals set for patients. These goals include restoring physical, mental, or emotional stability; combating boredom during a long-term illness; aiding in developing maximum self-sufficiency in activities of daily living, such as eating, dressing, writing, and using a telephone; and helping patients, in the latter stages of treatment, to perform jobs in a work situation.

The occupational therapist works as a member of a medical team that can include physicians, nurses, social workers, and any other required specialists.

A patient's recovery frequently quickens from the moment he or she discovers some satisfying occupation for using an artificial limb or crippled fingers. Under the guidance of the physician, occupational therapists use creative, educational, and recreational activities, as well as human ingenuity, in helping men, women, and children get well. Physical and mental recovery are the main objective, but a second goal

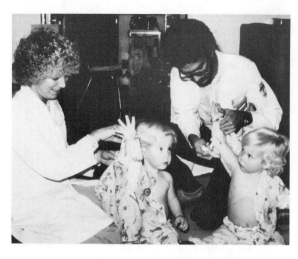

These therapists are working with twins to assess any developmental problems that may have occurred during birth.

is almost equally important that of helping the handicapped acquire job skills.

Working alongside their patients, occupational therapists learn their likes and dislikes, their abilities, their creative, educational, and recreational experiences, their hopes, fears, and ambitions. After talking things over with patients, therapists can recommend what activity would have most appeal and value for them. For example, weaving may be the most beneficial activity for someone with arthritic fingers. Learning to type might help a young person whose legs have been paralyzed as the result of a car accident. The therapist must first catch the patients' interest and then bring them along to develop a practical skill and increase their sense of independence.

Traditionally, occupational therapists have taught manual and creative arts such as weaving, clay modeling, leather work, jewelry making, woodcraft, photography, metalwork, reed and cane work, and bookbinding. All these are used for therapeutic purposes. For the same reason, therapists may sometimes organize educational activities such as the study of languages or creative writing, but in such specialized areas they usually call in others to assist. In some hospitals, they coach dramatics in which groups of patients take part. Though therapists cannot be expert in all these activities, they know enough to set a program in motion.

Today, occupational therapists also teach business and industrial skills such as typing, operation of a CRT terminal, and the use of power tools. In large hospitals with rehabilitation departments, therapists may be responsible for programs that offer extensive prevocational testing and training. Some former patients now earn their living by using the new skills learned through occupational therapy.

Occupational therapists may be required to design and make special equipment or splints to aid some disabled patients in performing their activities. Other duties may include supervision of volunteer workers, student therapists, and occupational therapy assistants who give instruction in a particular skill. A duty of therapists is to prepare reports to keep members of the professional team informed.

Chief occupational therapists in a hospital may teach medical and nursing students the principles of occupational therapy. Many occupational therapists have administrative duties such as directing different kinds of occupational therapy programs, coordinating patient activities, and acting as consultants or advisors to local and state health departments, mental health authorities, and the Division of Vocational Rehabilitation.

Requirements

Preparation for occupational therapy requires four years of college training leading to the degree of bachelor of science in occupational therapy. In some schools, the wording of the degree is different. In the early 1990s, about sixty-six colleges and universities offering training in occupational therapy were accredited by the Council on Medical Education and Hospitals of the American Medical Association and the American Occupational Therapy Association.

About half of the schools with approved programs accept college graduates with training in other fields and allow them to earn a certificate in occupational therapy upon completion of eighteen months of specialized training. This advanced-standing, eighteen-month program includes both academic and clinical work.

In addition to the four years of academic education, a clinical training period of six to nine months is required to qualify for professional registration. Some colleges permit their students to take the clinical practice during the summer or during part of their senior year in college. The armed forces offer programs whereby graduates of approved schools of occupational therapy, who meet the requirements to become commissioned officers, may receive the clinical part of their training while in the service.

In college preparation for occupational therapy, the emphasis is on health sciences and occupational skills. Science courses include anatomy, physiology, neurology, psychology, and sociology. Clinical subjects cover general medical and surgical conditions, tuberculosis and heart diseases, interpretation of the principles and practice of occupational therapy in pediatrics, psychiatry, orthopedics, and general medicine and surgery. Other subjects are creative arts, skills and crafts, educational subjects, and recreational activities.

About thirty-six universities offer programs leading to a master's degree in occupational therapy. This degree is often required for teaching, research, or administrative work.

Programs have been set up in some areas for the training of occupational therapy assistants. These are paid workers whose efforts are directed by a registered therapist. To be eligible for the twelve-week minimum program for assistants, applicants must be at least eighteen years old, have a high-school education, be in good physical condition and emotionally stable, and have the ability to work well with others.

Students interested in this career should be sincerely interested in helping people and sympathetic but objective regarding illness and disability. They should also be manually dexterous, ingenious, and imaginative.

Special requirements

Upon graduation and completion of the clinical practice period, therapists are eligible to take the examination given by the American Occupational Therapy Association. Those who pass this examination may use the initials OTR (Occupational Therapist, Registered) after their names. Many hospitals require that their occupational therapists be registered. A license to practice occupational therapy is required by twenty-eight states and the District of Columbia. Applicants for a license must have a degree or certificate from an accredited educational program and pass the national certification examination.

Opportunities for experience and exploration

One may become acquainted with the field of occupational therapy while in high school by talking with occupational therapists and seeing the facilities and equipment they use. A young person who has a special skill or talent may perform some needed task as a volunteer. Trained volunteers play an important part in

occupational therapy services throughout the country. These unpaid but skilled workers assist the therapist and, in turn, the patients by lending their abilities and talents.

Related occupations

Occupational therapists have a desire to help people overcome disabilities and live a normal, independent life. Other workers with similar goals include audiologists, orthotists, physical therapists, prosthetists, rehabilitation counselors, and speech-language pathologists. Occupations that combine therapy with other interests include art therapists, dance therapists, manual arts therapists, music therapists, and recreational therapists. With less training, interested persons can become occupational therapy assistants or physical therapy assistants.

Methods of entering

High-school graduation without specified unit credit is generally adequate to enter college for a degree in occupational therapy. For the certificate course, a bachelor's degree with credits in another field is acceptable. Individual schools very frequently have other specific requirements as stated by the college or university in which they are organized.

A number of colleges and universities offer scholarships to students interested in becoming occupational therapists, as do private and governmental agencies.

In all cases, the school attended will usually provide assistance in securing the initial employment.

Advancement

Newly graduated occupational therapists usually begin as staff therapists and may qualify as senior therapists after several years on the job. The Army, Navy, Air Force, and the U.S. Public Health Service commission occupational therapists; other branches of the federal service give civil service ratings. Experienced therapists may become directors of occupational therapy programs in large hospitals, clinics, or workshops, or may become teachers. Some positions are available as program coordinators and as consultants with large institutions and agencies.

A few colleges and health agencies offer advanced courses in the treatment of special disabilities, such as those resulting from cerebral palsy, for graduates of approved curriculums. Some institutions provide in-service programs for therapists.

Employment outlook

In the early 1990s, approximately 29,000 occupational therapists worked in hospitals, schools, nursing homes, home health agencies, mental health centers, adult day care programs, outpatient clinics, and residential care facilities. A growing number are self-employed, in either solo or group practice or in consulting firms. Opportunities for occupational therapists are expected to be highly favorable through the end of the decade. Despite the number of persons enrolled in occupational therapy courses, new positions are being created.

The demand for occupational therapists has been increasing because of growing public interest in the rehabilitation of disabled persons and the success of occupational therapy programs in helping restore people to health. There will be numerous opportunities for work with psychiatric patients, children, and aged persons, as well as with persons suffering from disabling diseases. In addition, disabled veterans require prolonged and intensive rehabilitation services. As the health care industry continues to be restructured, there should be many more opportunities for occupational therapists in nontraditional settings. This factor plus recent changes in the law (permitting occupational therapists to bill Medicare directly for their services) should create an excellent climate for therapists wishing to enter private practice. Home health care may experience the greatest growth in the next decade.

Hospitals and other employers prefer to hire registered occupational therapists. The shortage of registered therapists, however, will probably create continuing good employment opportunities for therapists who are not registered but have some of the required training and skills. Opportunities for part-time employment should be excellent in many areas.

The employment of occupational therapists in special education programs in public schools seems to have leveled off, and there may be little growth in new jobs in this area. However, there will still be a demand for occupational therapists to replace those who retire or leave the field for other reasons.

Earnings

In the early 1990s, beginning salaries in hospitals for occupational therapists without experience averaged about $21,000 a year. Experienced therapists averaged about $26,000, and some administrators earned as much as $39,000. Beginning occupational therapists working for the federal government, mostly in the Department of Veterans Affairs, earned starting salaries of about $16,500 a year, while those in supervisory positions earned as much as $40,500. The average for all occupational therapists with the federal government was $25,000.

Occupational therapists employed in public schools earned salaries that varied by school district. In some states, they are classified as teachers and are paid accordingly. In the early 1990s, elementary school teachers earned an average of $24,800 a year and secondary school teachers had average earnings of $26,100.

Conditions of work

Occupational therapists work in attractively decorated occupational therapy workshops or clinics. Generally, they work an eight-hour day, forty-hour week, with some evening work required in a few organizations. Vacation leave usually ranges from two to four weeks a year, and many positions offer health and retirement benefits.

Social and psychological factors

Occupational therapists often have the satisfaction of helping handicapped, discouraged people to find within themselves talents and interests they never knew they had. This in turn may help patients find suitable work after discharge from the hospital. The social worker may also be able to help the patient to resolve personal and family problems that stand in the way of good adjustment outside the hospital. Thus, the timing of needed patient referral to social service by the therapist is important. Therapists can also provide the vocational counselor with much valuable information about the patient's abilities.

GOE: 10.02.02; SIC: 8049; SIC: 3032

◇ **SOURCES OF ADDITIONAL INFORMATION**

American Occupational Therapy Association
1383 Piccard Drive
Suite 301
Rockville, MD 20850

For information about jobs with the federal government, contact the Office of Personnel Management at the Federal Job Information Center nearest you.

◇ **RELATED ARTICLES**

Volume 1: Health Care
Volume 2: Biomedical engineers; Kinesiotherapists; Physical therapists; Physician assistants; Prosthetists and orthotists; Respiratory therapists; Social workers; Therapists, miscellaneous
Volume 3: Nursing and psychiatric aides
Volume 4: Biomedical engineering technicians; Orthotic and prosthetic technicians; Physical therapist assistants

Oceanographers

Definition

The *oceanographer* attempts to obtain information about the ocean through extensive tests, observational programs, and detailed surveys and experiments. This person studies the physical, chemical, and biological composition of the ocean and geological structure of the seabed. He or she studies and analyzes phenomena involving the water itself, the atmosphere above it, the land beneath it, and the coastal borders. He or she also studies such aspects as the acoustical properties of water so that a comprehensive and unified picture of oceanic behavior may be developed. The *limnologist* is a specialist who studies fresh water life.

History

The waters of the earth have always been of considerable importance to humans, who have fought for control of vital seaways. Cities have arisen on strategic locations for water trade and transportation. We have studied and charted the flow of currents and tides not only in an attempt to master the sea but to make more effective use of its resources. In the past, we have been concerned more with what we could observe and study about the surface of the ocean than with the hidden contents of its depths. With such relatively recent inventions as the bathysphere, deep-sea diving gear, and

scuba, or "Self-Contained Underwater Breathing Apparatus," we have been able to begin a more detailed study of underwater life. Today, just as we are busy learning about and exploring outer space, so we are involved in investigating the unknown of the ocean.

Nature of the work

Because more than two-thirds of the earth is covered with water, one might say the world is the oceanographers' laboratory. Oceanographers conduct surveys and experiments and collect and study data about the motions of ocean water (waves, currents, and tides), marine life (sea plants and animals and their habits), ore and petroleum deposits (minerals and oils contained in the nodules and oozes of the ocean floor), and the contour of the ocean floor (ocean mountains, valleys, and depths). Many of their findings are compiled for maps, charts, graphs, and special reports and manuals. Some of the oceanographer's time may be spent on the water each year gathering data and making observations. Additional oceanographic work is done on dry land and by people who infrequently go to sea. Experiments using models or captive organisms may be made in the seaside laboratory. Oceanographic equipment designed and manufactured in specially equipped shops includes devices to measure depths by sound impulses; special thermometers to measure wa-

·An oceanographer studies coral formations on the ocean floor during an exploratory dive off Grand Bahama Island.

ter temperatures; special cameras for underwater photography; and diving gear and machines (such as the bathyscaphe). In addition to some of the commonly used equipment, many strange and new devices have been developed for specific types of underwater work. The oceanographer of the future may be using such tools as a hydraulic miner (a dredge to extract nodules from the ocean floor), an electronic beater (a machine used to drive fish), dye curtains, fish pumps, and instrument buoys; while, above surface level, this scientist may watch underwater action on television. New technologies that are being developed today include satellite sensors and acoustic current measuring devices.

The oceanographer is usually part of a highly skilled team with each member specializing in one of the four main branches of the profession. The biological oceanographer or marine biologist studies all aspects of the ocean's plant and animal life. Physical oceanographers study such physical aspects of the ocean as temperature and density, waves and currents, and the relationship between the sea and the atmosphere. Geological oceanographers study the topographic features and physical composition of the ocean bottom. The chemical oceanographer investigates the chemical composition of the water and ocean floor. However, in actual work, there is a tremendous amount of overlap between the four main branches.

Most oceanographers are employed by institutions of higher education, the federal government, oil companies, corporations supporting the Department of Defense, or environmental groups. Federal agencies employing oceanographers include the Oceanographer of the Navy, Office of Naval Research and the National Oceanic and Atmospheric Administration (NOAA). An increasing number of oceanographers are being employed each year by industrial firms, particularly those in the construction, oceanographic instrument and equipment manufacturing, shipbuilding, and chemical fields. Oceanographers in colleges and universities are involved in teaching, research, writing, and consultant activities.

It is difficult to project, however, what oceanographers of the future may be doing. They may be living and working on the ocean floor. The U.S. Navy Medical Research Laboratory has conducted experiments where people lived in 200 feet of water. Surely many of the duties of the oceanographer will remain the same in years ahead. For some time, however, particularly for those who wish to explore and pioneer in underwater research, the challenge and opportunity will increase.

Oceanography now includes the study of air and sea interaction in weather forecasting; solving sea mining problems and predicting, and preventing pollution; and improving methods of deriving foods from the ocean.

Requirements

Because four years of college are required for beginning positions in oceanography, students in high school should pursue an academic course of study including as many of the basic and advanced courses in mathematics and science as they can obtain. In college, a broad program covering the basic sciences with a major in physics, chemistry, biology, or geology is desirable. In addition, one should include courses in field research or laboratory work in oceanography where available. Graduate work in oceanography is required for most positions in research and teaching. More than one hundred institutions have programs in marine studies, but only nineteen universities have graduate programs leading to the doctorate in oceanography.

Personal traits helpful to a career in oceanography are a strong interest in science, particularly the physical and earth sciences; an interest in situations involving activities of an abstract and creative nature (observing nature, performing experiments, creating objects); an interest in outdoor activities such as hunting, fishing, swimming, boating, or animal care; interest in scholarly activity (reading, researching, writing); interests that cut across the traditional academic boundaries of biology, chemistry, and physics; and, finally, an interest in working in a real "last frontier."

Scholastic ability should include above-average verbal, numerical, and spatial aptitudes. Another important aptitude is the ability to discriminate detail among objects such as shape, size, color, or markings.

The person who is curious, imaginative, adventuresome, persistent, open-minded, and objective will find these traits also helpful in preparing for a career in oceanography, as in any other scientific pursuit.

In preparing for graduate work in oceanography, a student should take mathematics through differential and integral calculus; at least one year each of chemistry and physics; biology or geology; and enough of a modern foreign language to be able to read it well.

Special requirements

Generally, there are no special licensure or certification requirements for employment as an oceanographer.

Before diving into the ocean, an oceanographer adjusts his mask and checks his gear.

Opportunities for experience and exploration

Some work or leisure-time experiences will provide opportunities to explore particular aspects of oceanography. Possible opportunities include work in marine or conservation fisheries, on board seagoing vessels, or field experiences in studying rocks, minerals, or aquatic life. Those people living or traveling near one of the oceanography research centers such as Woods Hole Oceanographic Institution on Cape Cod, the University of Miami's Institute of Marine Science, or the Scripps Institute of Oceanography in California, should plan to spend some time learning about their activities and studying their exhibits.

For college-age (and on occasion high-school-age) students, volunteer work is often available with research teams, non-profit organizations, and public centers such as aquariums.

Related occupations

Oceanographers have much in common with scientists in the geology occupations, including geologists, geophysical prospectors, geophysicists, hydrologists, mineralogists, paleontologists, and soils engineers. Would-be oceanographers may also want to explore the work of environmental researchers, geographers, marine engineers, and meteorologists. Other occupations that may be of interest are cartographers, chemists, divers, and fisheries scientists.

Methods of entering

Most college placement offices are staffed to help students find positions in business and industry upon graduation. Often positions can be located by personal contact with friends, relatives, or college professors or through the col-

441

lege's placement office by application and interview. College and university assistantships, instructorships, and professorships are usually obtained by recommendation of the student's major professor or department chairman. The American Institute of Biological Science maintains an employment service and lists both employers and job seekers.

Advancement

Initial positions in oceanography usually involve activity as laboratory or research assistants with on-the-job training in the application of oceanographic principles to the problems at hand. Some beginning oceanographers with doctorates may qualify for college teaching or research positions. Experienced personnel, particularly those with advanced graduate work or doctorates, assume supervisory or administrative positions. Such positions involve considerable responsibility of planning and policy-making or policy interpretation. They may plan and supervise research projects involving a number of workers, or they may be in charge of an oceanographic laboratory.

Employment outlook

Although oceanography is growing, persons entering the field in the next few years will face competition for the positions that are open. Those with a doctorate will have the best opportunities for employment throughout the 1990s. Persons with less education will have opportunities for employment as assistants or technicians doing more routine work. Oceanographers who also have training in other sciences or in engineering will probably have better opportunities for employment than persons whose training is limited to oceanography. Growth in the field will largely depend on federal spending for research and development. It is anticipated that oil and mining companies will employ more oceanographers to look for oil, and new jobs will be created in industry for oceanographers to do consulting work and environmental studies.

The demand for oceanographers is increasing somewhat as people become determined to learn more about the sea and its resources. Many people feel that it is as important to know about our own planet as it is to learn about and explore others. World affairs, technological achievements, and the nation's econ-

omy will no doubt affect the rapidity with which ocean research progresses.

Earnings

In the early 1990s, beginning oceanographers in civil service positions with the federal government started at about $15,700 or $19,500 per year with a bachelor's degree; those with a master's degree started at about $23,800; those with a doctorate began at about $28,900. The salary for experienced oceanographers in the federal government in the early 1990s averaged about $38,000 a year. College teaching positions, depending on rank and experience, covered the same salary range as other faculty members. In addition to regular salaries, oceanographers may supplement their incomes with fees earned from consulting, lecturing, and writing.

Conditions of work

Oceanographers in shore stations, laboratories, and research centers will work on a five-day, forty-hour-week basis. Occasionally, they will serve a longer shift, particularly when conditions of a research experiment demand around-the-clock surveillance. Such assignments may also involve unusual working hours depending on the nature of the research or the purpose of the trip. Trips at sea necessitate that one be away from home for periods of time extending from a few days to months. Also, sea expeditions may be more demanding physically, and certainly one must be prepared to cope with an entirely different way of life on board ship. Weather conditions may impose some hazards during these assignments. Those who choose to engage in underwater research may, like the astronauts, find a more adventuresome and hazardous way of life than in other occupations.

Social and psychological factors

A career in oceanography offers a variety of opportunities from which one can elect a way of life." The individual who likes the water, who enjoys life aboard ship, and who is willing to be away from home for periods of time will find these satisfactions in certain oceanographic positions. On the other hand, people who do not wish to leave their family or interrupt their community activities have an opportunity to seek positions where travel away from home is not necessary. Adventure, travel, family life, and community service are a few of the goals that one can pursue along with a career in oceanography.

GOE: 02.01.01; SIC: 8221; SOC: 1847

◇ **SOURCES OF ADDITIONAL INFORMATION**

American Institute of Biological Sciences
730 11th Street, NW
Washington, DC 20001

American Society of Limnology and Oceanography
Virginia Institute of Marine Science
College of William and Mary
Gloucester Point, VA 23062

International Oceanographic Foundation
3979 Rickenbacker Causeway
Miami, FL 33149

Marine Technology Society
1825 K Street, NW, Suite 203
Washington, DC 20006

Oceanic Society
1536 16th Street, NW
Washington, DC 20036

Scripps Institution of Oceanography
UCSD, Public Affairs
La Jolla, CA 92093

Woods Hole Oceanographic Institution
Woods Hole, MA 02543

◇ **RELATED ARTICLES**

Volume 1: Biological Sciences
Volume 2: Biologists; Chemists; Geologists
Volume 4: Biological technicians; Chemical technicians; Deep-water diving and life-support technicians; Geological technicians; Hydrological technicians

---

Operations-research analysts

Definition

Operations-research analysts are problem solvers who convert management and operational problems into mathematical terms and then apply logical analysis and mathematical techniques to solve them. They prepare models of business problems in the form of mathematical equations and then apply judgment and statistical tests to find possible cost-effective solutions. Operations-research analysts are often part of a research team consisting of other mathematicians and engineers, and they usually use data-processing equipment as a research tool. They frequently prepare written and oral reports of their findings for upper management officials. There are a variety of business problems that operations-research can evaluate. The problems range from shipping procedures to the physical layout of a factory.

History

Although mathematics may be considered a "pure" science, which one studies for its own sake, this abstract knowledge has often been applied to produce engineering and other scientific achievements. The non–Euclidean geometry developed by Bernard Riemann in 1854, for example, seemed quite impractical at the time, yet some years later Albert Einstein used it as part of his work in the development of the theory of relativity.

In the last several decades, operations-research analysts and other applied mathematicians have begun to apply mathematical formulas to research efforts in such fields as business management.

The techniques they use generally revolve around the use of a set of mathematical equations that explains how things happen within a specified business environment. They develop

of equations that explain how things happen within the represented system.

Models are simplified representations that enable the analyst to break down systems into their component parts, assign numerical values to each component, and examine the mathematical relationships between them. For example, a model for the inventory of coal might include an analysis of the projected level of output, the cost of coal, and storage and transportation costs. These models can be altered to determine what will happen to the system under different sets of circumstances. Different types of models include simulation and linear programming. Because many of these models have been computerized, analysts need to be able to write computer programs or use existing ones.

After analysts define the problem, they learn everything they can about it. They prepare charts, tables, and diagrams to describe the flow of information or products. This involves the use of mathematical methods as analytical tools as well as various other techniques such as cost accounting and sampling. This may also involve talking to other company personnel. Operations-research analysts then construct one or more mathematical models that simulate the problem under study and embody its essential features. Some deal only with problems in accounting and inventory control; others concern themselves with such problems as planning and forecasting sales. For some problems, there may be several techniques that can be used. The analyst would probably try the model using several sets of business assumptions and experiment with several models to ensure that the most efficient model is being used.

At this point, the analyst interprets the results and translates them into terms understandable to management. It is then up to management officials to implement a decision or ask the research analyst to develop other options. After a final decision is made, the analyst works with staff to implement it as successfully as possible.

An operations-research analyst consults computer-generated data while writing a report on his findings.

models that examine the mathematical relationships between different managerial concerns, such as inventory control and distribution systems.

Nature of the work

Operations-research analysts help businesses and other organizations operate in an efficient manner by applying mathematical principles to organizational problems and then developing alternatives that enable managers to choose a cost-effective course of action. Operations-research analysts investigate such issues as personnel schedules, resource allocation, and delivery methods.

The specific job responsibilities of an analyst vary according to the firm that the specialist works for. For example, an analyst for a retail store might use operations-research to design store layouts, select the best store location, and analyze customer characteristics, while an analyst for a hospital might work on analyzing patient flow and forecasting demand for new medical services. Some analysts specialize in one type of application; others are generalists.

Despite differences in specific job duties, all operation researchers process work in the same general way. Company managers begin the process by describing a business problem to the analyst. The problem might be either general or specific. For example, a bank president might want to improve the overall check processing procedure or more specifically want to know which type of personnel should handle specific job responsibilities. The analyst then defines the problem with a mathematical model or set

Requirements

A career as a operations-research analyst demands the ability to think logically as well as the ability to work well with other people. Aspiring analysts should also have a strong background and aptitude for mathematics, science, or engineering. Some employers request that operations-research analysts have a bachelor's degree in mathematics, business administration, operations research, or other quantitative discipline; others demand graduate work in one of these fields. An increasing number of employers look for those with degrees in computer science, information science, or data processing. Course work in statistics, economics, and quantitative mathematics are strongly recommended.

High-school students interested in pursuing a career as an analyst should take college-preparatory courses such as English, history, science, and as many mathematics and statistics courses as possible. Because the computer is an important tool for the research analyst, any computer programming courses that are available should also be taken.

Special requirements

Generally, there are no special licenses or certificates required for employment as a operations-research analyst. Government positions usually require the applicant to pass a civil service examination.

The increasing specialization of the field means that employers will seek out analysts who are trained to handle certain types of problems. For example, someone with a background in business administration might be asked to handle problems dealing with financial data or personnel scheduling. Many employers also have on-the-job training for assistant analysts.

Opportunities for experience and exploration

Because only those with a college degree can work in this field, it is hard to get any hands-on experience. High-school students or others interested in a career as a operations-research analyst should seek part-time work in a setting that develops their mathematical interests and abilities. A temporary job at a bank or insurance company with an in-house operations research department may offer this opportunity. Students should also take advantage of opportunities to enroll in special summer sessions or advanced placement mathematics courses to develop their knowledge of mathematics.

In addition to job and school exploration, interested persons are encouraged to talk with professionals already working in the field to get an accurate picture of the rewards and responsibilities of an operations-research analyst.

Related occupations

Other occupations that use standardized mathematical techniques to solve business and managerial problems include mathematicians, computer-applications engineers, statisticians, and actuaries. Human factors specialists, ergonomists, and time management consultants do evaluative studies.

Methods of entering

College placement counselors usually help place qualified graduates find business and industry opportunities. College graduates can also contact appropriate companies on their own. Major employers include manufacturers of machinery and transportation equipment, telecommunications companies, banks, insurance companies, and private management consulting firms. The federal government, especially the armed forces, also hires operations-research analysts.

New employees usually have several months of on-the-job training in which the individual company's systems are comprehensively explained. Entry level employees work closely with experienced personnel during this period.

Advancement

Numerous opportunities for advancement to higher-level management positions or into related areas of employment are available to operations-research analysts. Skilled analysts may be promoted to the head of a operations research staff or may move to another upper-level management position within a firm. They may also choose to move to a larger company. Some successful analysts with a great deal of experience may choose to open their own consulting company. Those with the proper education and experience may also move into a related field, such as statistics or actuarial work.

Employment outlook

Because of the increasing importance of quantitative analysis in decision making, job opportunities for operations-research analysts are expected to grow much faster than the average through the early 1990s. The success of companies that have used operations research as part of a systematic approach to decision making as well as the availability of smaller, less expensive computers have fueled this growth. There should be a demand for qualified operations-research analysts all over the country, and this demand should be greatest in the manufacturing sector and the trade and service industries. Little growth is expected in opportunities with the federal government

As usual, those with the most training and experience should find the best employment opportunities.

Earnings

Earnings depend on experience, type of job, and the geographic location of the firm. Beginning operations-research analysts should expect to earn between $16,000 and $23,000 per year, depending on specific job responsibilities and the size of the company. Those entering with a master's degree should expect to earn somewhat more to start. Experienced workers should expect to earn between $22,000 and $42,000 per year, with some highly skilled workers in extremely competitive job markets earning even more. Those working for the federal government might experience somewhat lower salaries to start, but salaries should be fairly competitive for experienced workers. Overall, the highest salaries will be found in the private sector.

Employees should also receive health insurance, paid vacation, pension plans, and other standard benefits.

Conditions of work

The work environment is typically a well-lighted office setting, with computers close at hand. Operations-research analysts generally work forty-hour weeks, although they may work overtime if a project is on deadline. The work is sedentary in nature and may require long periods of close concentration on mathematical formulas.

Social and psychological factors

Operations-research analysts must be able to work closely with engineers and other technical personnel and also be able to work closely with management officials. They must be able to spend long hours concentrating on complex mathematical equations and think creatively on

how to apply those equations to specific management concerns. Diligence and attention to detail are extremely important, as is patience. Communications skills are important because all research findings must be fully explained, both in written reports and during meetings with management officials.

Top management officials often consider operations-research analysts to be saviors of a troubled business and expect too much of them and their mathematical "miracles." Nevertheless, the rewards of this profession, both in position and sense of accomplishment, can be great for analysts who significantly improve aspects of their employer's operations.

GOE: 11.01.01; SIC: Any industry; SOC: 1721

◇ **SOURCES OF ADDITIONAL INFORMATION**

General career information is available from:

The Operations Research Society of America
Mount Royal and Guilford Avenues
Baltimore, MD 21202

Society for Industrial and Applied Mathematics
1400 Architects Building
117 South 17th Street
Philadelphia, PA, 19103

For information concerning career opportunities in the armed forces, contact:

Military Operations Research Society
Landmark Towers
101 South Whiting Street, Suite 202
Alexandria, VA 22304

◇ **RELATED ARTICLES**

Volume 1: Computer Software; Mathematics; Personal and Consulting Services
Volume 2: Ergonomists; Human factors specialists; Mathematicians; Statisticians; Systems analysts
Volume 3: Mathematical technicians

Optometrists

Definition

An *optometrist*, or doctor of optometry, examines and determines the condition of one's eyes and prescribes treatment to conserve or improve vision. In some states, optometrists may prescribe drugs to treat eye diseases; they also refer patients to other health care practitioners. Optometrists prescribe the lenses, prisms, or vision therapy that may be necessary for patients and may specialize in a particular phase of optometry, such as prescribing and fitting contact lenses.

History

Modern optometry is derived from the work of a number of Europeans in the nineteenth century who were interested in measuring the eye and in inventing instruments for testing sight. Research in physics, mathematics, and optics helped the early fathers of optometry to make significant discoveries. As more became known in the field, professional organizations were formed to gain legal recognition for optometry and to establish education programs for optometrists.

Two particular landmarks in the development of the profession of optometry are noteworthy. A national association of optometrists was first formed in 1897. In 1901, the state of Minnesota passed the first state law regulating the practice of optometry. Today, every state and the District of Columbia has such a law.

The number of optometrists has continued to grow to meet the demands of our increasing population.

Nature of the work

Optometrists are primarily concerned with examining eyes and performing other services to safeguard and improve vision. To do this work, they employ special tests and instruments to identify and evaluate eye health problems and defects in vision. They prescribe what should be done to correct or improve one's vision. Prescriptions are concerned with eyeglasses, contact lenses, vision therapy, and, in some states, therapeutic drugs. Optometrists do not perform surgery. They do, as a rule, supply their patients with the eyeglasses and contact lenses they prescribe. Some optometrists devote most of their time and energy to working with special kinds of cases, such as providing low-vision aids for individuals who are nearly blind and working with children who have vision-related learning problems. A relatively small number of optometrists spend most of their time in teaching and research.

Optometrists are one of two professional groups involved in treatment of the eyes. Ophthalmologists are medical school graduates with specialized training in working with the medical and surgical care of the eyes. They prescribe drugs, perform surgery, and prescribe lenses and exercises.

Opticians use the prescriptions provided by ophthalmologists and optometrists to grind lenses, make the eyeglasses, and fit and adjust them.

Requirements

As with most professional people, prospective optometrists must be able to get along well with people. Their practices will often depend on how people regard them. The optometrist must also have above-average intelligence, mechanical aptitude, and good vision and coordination. These characteristics are essential to the training required for licensure.

The educational requirements for becoming an optometrist are quite rigid. Two or three years of college plus four years in a school or college of optometry is the minimum requirement for becoming an optometrist. The first two years of college are generally devoted to coursework in mathematics, physics, biology, and chemistry, as well as the other general education subjects studied by students in colleges of liberal arts and sciences. The professional degree program is devoted to laboratory, classroom, and clinical work in the field of optometry. Upon completion of study, graduates receive the doctor of optometry (O.D.) degree. Some optometrists pursue further study leading to a master's degree or doctorate in physiological optics or other fields.

Before individuals can practice as optometrists, they must secure a license in the state in which they wish to practice. To do this, they must pass an examination prepared by the state. An individual cannot take the examina-

447

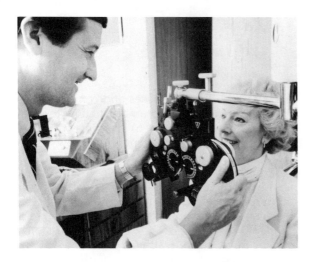

An optometrist's primary responsibility is to correct eyesight by diagnosing the problem and prescribing proper glasses.

tion unless he or she is a graduate of a school or college of optometry recognized by the state in question.

Students interested in a career in optometry should find out what kind of high-school and preoptometry courses schools and colleges of optometry want their applicants to pursue prior to admission. There are many more applicants than places in the eighteen accredited schools, and interested students should plan their preprofessional work so that it will help them to gain admission to an accredited school of optometry.

Special requirements

Each of the fifty states and the District of Columbia requires an individual to have a state license to practice optometry. To be eligible to take the licensing examination, an individual must be a graduate of an accredited school or college of optometry. The examination is administered by a state board of optometry and generally covers the following subjects: ocular anatomy, ocular pathology (disease), optometric methods, theoretical optometry, psychological optics, physical and geometrical optics, physiological optics, physiology, optometrical mechanics, and a clinical examination. In forty-six states, optometrists must earn continuing education credits in optometry to renew their licenses. The most frequently recognized license is given by the National Board of Examiners in Optometry.

Opportunities for experience and exploration

As is the case with many professions, it is difficult for interested students to gain any direct experience on a part-time basis in optometry. The first opportunities afforded students generally come in the clinical phases of their training program. Interested students, however, can explore the desirability of a career in optometry in several ways. They can write the sources listed at the end of this article for reading material on optometry. Perhaps more important, they can visit an optometrist to talk about the work.

Related occupations

The work of the optometrist involves the application of logical thinking and scientific knowledge to the prevention, diagnosis, and treatment of disease, disorders, or injuries. Other professionals with similar aptitudes and training include chiropractors, dentists, physicians, podiatrists, and veterinarians.

Methods of entering

There are several ways of entering the field of optometry once an individual has a license to practice. Most optometrists set up their own practice or purchase an established practice. Other beginners serve as associates to established optometrists until they gain sufficient experience and financial resources to establish their own practices. Some work in health maintenance organizations (HMOs). Still other beginners work in government-supported clinics or in the armed forces. Some students of optometry earn their doctorates and go directly into research and teaching in schools and colleges of optometry.

Advancement

Optometrists may advance in their profession by specializing in one phase of it. Or they may move from employment by or association with a practicing optometrist to having their own practice.

Employment outlook

In the early 1990s, there were approximately 37,000 optometrists practicing in the United States. The vast majority were employed in private practice, but others were to be found in health clinics, industries, the armed forces, and in schools and colleges of optometry. About 35 percent of the total number were employed in five states California, New York, Illinois, Pennsylvania, and Ohio.

The employment outlook for optometrists is expected to be very favorable through the 1990s. Factors upon which this favorable outlook is based include the following: the demand for eye-care services will become greater as people through increased education become more health-conscious; people are more likely to seek such services because they are better able to pay for them as a result of higher income levels, the growing availability of employee vision-care plans, and the change in Medicare law allowing coverage for optometrists' services; the increased use of computers and VDTs by many individuals appears to lead to eyestrain and aggravated vision problems; and there are projected increases in the number of elderly—the group most likely to need eyeglasses. Some of the needed eye care will be provided by physicians who specialize in the treatment of the eyes, but there will be more than ample opportunity for optometrists to supply a substantial amount of service. Additional opportunities will arise as older optometrists retire or leave the profession for other reasons. About one-fourth of all experienced practitioners are now between the ages of fifty and sixty-four; a great many of them are likely to become inactive before the end of the 1990s, leaving openings for younger optometrists.

Earnings

Graduates of schools and colleges of optometry who accept salaried positions with clinics and government agencies generally have higher earnings in the first few years than do private practitioners. This situation, however, often changes after the private practitioners have had an opportunity to establish themselves. In the early 1990s, the net earnings of new optometry graduates averaged about $30,000 a year. The average earnings for experienced optometrists during the same period was about $60,000. Incomes can vary widely, depending on a number of factors. Optometrists in group practice or partnerships often earn substantially higher incomes than optometrists practicing alone.

Conditions of work

Optometrists generally have excellent working conditions, and their work is not strenuous. Optometrists are generally in command of their own offices and are free to set their own office hours and to arrange their vacations and free time. The optometrist usually works in quiet surroundings and is seldom faced with emergencies. Although most optometrists still have solo practices, some have chosen to work in partnerships or teams to alleviate the rising cost of set-up, insurance, and repayment of school loans.

Social and psychological factors

Optometrists must be able to get along well with people. Their success is related to the satisfaction that people express for the services they provide.

Optometrists are afforded the satisfaction of knowing that they play an important role in keeping their community healthy. Their work is important and is viewed as such by the general citizenry.

Optometrists in good standing are eligible for membership in the American Optometric Association, which is the major professional organization for optometrists. A smaller number of optometrists who meet very rigid requirements are also eligible for membership in the American Academy of Optometry. Optometrists also hold membership in state and local optometric societies.

GOE: 02.03.04; SIC: 8042; SOC: 281

◇ SOURCES OF ADDITIONAL INFORMATION

American Optometric Association
243 North Lindbergh Boulevard
St. Louis, MO 63141

National Health Council
350 Fifth Avenue
Suite 1118
New York, NY 10118

For information on licensing procedures in each state, contact the Board of Optometry in the capital.

For information on the entrance exam, the Optemetric Admissions Test (OAT), and accredited schools, contact:

Association of Schools and Colleges of Optometry
6110 Executive Boulevard
Suite 514
Rockville, MD 20852

◇ **RELATED ARTICLES**

Volume 1: Health Care
Volume 2: Dispensing opticians; Physicians
Volume 3: Contact lens manufacturing workers; Opticians and optical mechanics
Volume 4: Ophthalmic laboratory technicians; Optics technicians; Optometric technicians

Packaging engineers

Definition

The *packaging engineer* designs and develops protective containers for all types of goods, such as food, clothing, medicine, toys, electronics, appliances, and computers. Almost everything people buy, send, or use is wrapped, boxed, crated, and bottled by the packaging industry. In creating packaging materials, some of the packaging engineer's activities may include product and cost analysis, management of packaging personnel, development of packing procedures and materials, and negotiations with customers or sales representatives.

History

The need for packaging arose when people first started storing food and trading goods. The first kinds of packaging used in prehistoric times were animal skins, baskets woven from reeds, plant leaves, and earthenware vessels. Later, in the ancient world, clay, glass, and leather were used as packaging materials. The ancient Greeks produced vases, urns, pitchers, and bottles of exquisite beauty. Decorations on them are still perfectly preserved; sometimes their contents are even identifiable. Also, woven materials such as linen or burlap were used to wrap articles of various kinds.

It was not until the Industrial Revolution that the packaging industry became important. Shipping and storage containers were needed for the large numbers of goods that were produced. As shipping distances from producer to consumer expanded, more care had to be put into packaging so that goods would not be damaged in transit. Also storage and perishability factors became important with the increased numbers and longer shelf life of goods produced.

Modern packaging methods have developed since the 1920s with the introduction of cellophane wrappings. Since World War II, traditional packaging materials such as cloth and wood have been largely replaced by cheaper, more durable materials such as steel, aluminum, and plastics. Modern production methods have also allowed for the low-cost mass-production of traditional materials such as glass and paper.

Nature of the work

Packaging engineers plan, design, develop, and produce containers for all types of products. In developing a package, they must first determine the needs of their clients and potential users. Packaging for a product may be needed for a variety of reasons: for shipping, storage, display, or protection. A package for display must be attractive as well as durable and easy to store; labeling and perishability have to be considered, especially for food, medicine, and cosmetics. If the purpose of packaging is for storage and shipping, then ease of handling and durability have to be considered. Safety factors may be involved if the materials to be packaged are hazardous, such as toxic chemicals or explosives. Finally, the costs of producing and implementing the packaging have to be considered.

After determining what purpose the packaging should serve, packaging engineers study the physical properties and handling requirements of the product in order to develop the best kind of packaging for it. They study drawings and descriptions of the product or the actual product itself to learn about its size, shape, weight, and color, materials used in it, and the way it functions. They then decide what kind of packaging material to use. With the help of designers and production people, they make sketches, draw up plans, and make samples of the package. These samples, along with lists of materials and cost estimates, are submitted to management or directly to the customer.

In finalizing plans for packaging a product, packaging engineers contribute additional expertise in other areas. They are concerned with efficient use of raw materials and production facilities as well as conservation of energy and reduction of costs. For instance, they may use materials that can be recycled or they try to cut down on weight and size. They keep up with the latest developments in packaging and often recommend innovative ways to package products. Once all the details for packaging are worked out, packaging engineers may be involved in drawing up contracts with customers or sales representatives.

After a sample is approved, packaging engineers may supervise testing of the package. Testing may involve simulation of all the various conditions a packaged good will undergo. Often the reliability of functioning of a product will depend upon how well the packaging was done. For instance, the physical relationships of packaged electronics components can affect the overall performance of the product.

Once a package has tested out satisfactorily, then production of packaging has to be set up. This can be quite a complex operation involving several steps. Part of the processing or production of the product could be involved at the first step of packaging. For instance, perishable items such as food and beverages have to be packaged to avoid spoilage, or electronics components have to be packaged in such a way as to avoid damage. Whether the items to be packaged are food, chemicals, medicine, electronics, or factory parts, considerable knowledge of the properties of these products is often necessary to make suitable packaging.

Then there are design and marketing factors to consider in creating the actual package that will be seen by the consumer. To design effective packaging that will appeal to consumers, knowledge of marketing and design are essential. Package designers consider color, shape, and convenience as well as labeling and other informative features when designing packages which will be put on display. Very often the consumer is able to evaluate a product

only from the package it is in. Finally, there is the package in which the product will be stored or shipped.

All of these different kinds of packages require different kinds of machinery and skill to implement. For instance, the beverage industry alone produces billions of cans, bottles, and cardboard containers. Often packaging engineers are involved in designing packaging machinery in conjunction with other kinds of engineers and production personnel. Packaging can be manufactured either at the same facility where the goods are produced or at facilities that specialize in producing packaging materials.

The packaging engineer must also consider environmental factors when designing packaging. Disposing of used packages has presented a serious problem for many communities. The United States uses more than 500 billion packages yearly, 50 percent of these are used for food and beverages, and another 40 percent for other consumer goods. To help solve this problem, the packaging engineer looks for solutions such as the use of recyclable, biodegradable, or less bulky packaging.

Safety, health, and legal factors must also be considered by the packaging engineer. Labeling and packaging of products are regulated by various federal agencies such as the Federal Trade Commission and the Food and Drug Administration. The Consumer Product Safety Commission requires that safe packaging materials be used for food and cosmetics. Government agencies along with manufacturers and designers are constantly trying to improve packaging so that it is more convenient, safe, and informative.

Requirements

Several colleges and universities have a major in packaging engineering. Students interested in this field often structure their own program. High-school students should emphasize courses of a scientific or technical nature such as mathematics, chemistry, physics, and mechanical drawing. Speech, writing, and art courses will also prove useful. In college, if no major is offered in packaging engineering, then a related discipline such as mechanical, industrial, electrical, chemical, materials, or systems engineering would be appropriate. It is useful to take courses in graphic design, computer science, marketing, and management.

Students may wish to pursue a packaging engineering career without getting involved in the advanced science or mathematical theory

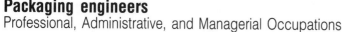
required for a bachelor's or master's degree. Two- and four-year degrees in engineering technology are offered by some junior and community colleges, technical institutes, and universities. Engineering technologists, specializing in such fields as electronics, computer maintenance, or machine design, form an important part of an engineering team.

Other members of a packaging team perform tasks such as marketing, design, research, product development, finance, purchasing, and computer science. Materials handling, materials science, and food technology are other subjects a packaging professional might study. Degrees in any of these fields would be useful for someone wishing to be a packaging professional.

Special requirements

Special licensing is required for engineers whose work affects the public. Much of the work of packaging engineers falls under this category because their work affects such factors as food and drug spoilage, protection from hazardous materials, or protection from damage. A state board of engineering examiners administers the licensing and registration of engineers. Licensing laws vary from state to state, but, in general, states have similar requirements. The engineer must be a graduate of an approved engineering school, have four years of engineering experience, and pass the state licensing examination.

For those interested in working with the specialized field of military packaging technology, the U.S. Army offers courses in this field. Generally, a person would obtain a bachelor of science degree in packaging engineering from another school before taking these specialized courses. The National Institute of Packaging, Handling, and Logistic Engineers will have information about the field of military packaging.

Opportunities for experience and exploration

To get firsthand experience of the packaging industry, call on local manufacturers to see how they handle and package their products. Often factories will allow visitors if you call in advance. If you live in an agricultural in the South, Midwest, or West there will be plenty of opportunity to visit food and beverage manufacturers. A host of other consumer and indus-

trial products as well as specialty food items are produced in more metropolitan areas.

Another way to learn about packaging is in your daily life, because most packaged goods are ordinary consumer products. Study the containers for food, beverages, and household goods at home or in stores to see how products are packaged, stored, or displayed. Study the shape and labeling on the container as well as its ease of use, durability for storage, convenience of opening and closing, disposability, and attractiveness.

Related occupations

In addition to the packaging engineer, many other kinds of engineers are employed in the packaging industry. Chemical and materials engineers are concerned with the materials that make up the product and its package. They study how the chemical properties of product and package interact or how long the product can be stored in the package before deteriorating. Mechanical, electrical, and electronic engineers are involved in designing packaging machinery. Robotics engineers are becoming increasingly involved with making packaging operations more efficient and cost-effective.

Other technical occupations, some of which require less training than engineering, are widely found on packaging engineering teams. Some of these are engineering technicians and technologists; food service technologists, machine and computer technicians; and pollution control technicians. Computer science occupations such as computer programming and data processing are also in demand. Nontechnical but related occupations are merchandise displayers, advertising and marketing personnel, graphic and industrial designers.

Methods of entering

College graduates with a degree in packaging or a related field of engineering will find it easy to get jobs as the packaging industry continues its rapid growth. Many companies send recruiters to college campuses to fill their engineering employment needs. Job leads can also be obtained from trade publications, from teachers, or from the school placement office.

Beginning packaging engineers generally do routine work under the supervision of experienced engineers and may also receive some formal training through their company. As they become more experienced, they are given more difficult tasks and more independence in solving problems, developing designs, or making decisions.

Advancement

Packaging engineers may advance from being a member of a team to a project supervisor or department manager. Qualified packaging engineers may advance through their department to become a manager or vice president of their company. To advance to a management position, the packaging engineer must not only demonstrate good technical and production skills, but must also demonstrate managerial ability. He will have demonstrated the ability to successfully manage projects within his department with such skills as leadership, getting along with co-workers, budgeting, and planning, After years of experience, a packaging engineer might wish to become self-employed as a packaging consultant.

To improve chances for advancement, the packaging engineer may wish to get a master's degree in another branch of engineering or in business administration. Many executives in government and industry began their careers as engineers. Some engineers become patent attorneys by combining a law degree with their technical and scientific knowledge.

Employment outlook

The packaging industry, which employs more than a million people, offers almost unlimited opportunities for packaging engineers. The packaging engineer can find employment in almost any industry because virtually all manufactured products need one or more kinds of packaging. Some of the industries with the fastest growing packaging needs are food, drugs, and cosmetics. In general, the demand for packaging engineers is expected to increase faster than the average for all occupations as newer, faster ways of packaging are continually being sought to meet the needs of economic growth, world trade expansion, and the environment.

Earnings

In the early 1990s the starting salary for a packaging engineer with a bachelor's degree averaged about $30,000 per year. The mean salary for those with experience was about $60,000. Engineers with a master's degree start at higher pay and have higher average earnings. Benefits include health insurance, bonus and retirement plans, and paid vacations. Most packaging engineers have a five-day, forty-hour work week, although sometimes overtime work is necessary.

Conditions of work

The conditions of work for packaging engineers vary with the employer and with the tasks of the engineer. Those who work for companies that make packaging materials or who direct packaging operations might work around noisy machinery. Generally they will have offices near the packaging operations, allowing them to where they consult with or manage others in their department such as technicians and other engineers.

Packaging engineers also work with nontechnical staff such as designers, artists, and marketing and financial people. Depending on the size of the organization and nature of the product, these people might be in the same department or in different departments or even in different companies. For instance, a product could be manufactured in one company, then sent to another for packaging. Sometimes, a firm will hire design or marketing consultants to come in and advise on packaging new products or helping with the design of new kinds of packaging. Packaging engineers must be alert to keeping up with new trends in marketing and technological developments.

Some travel may be involved, especially if the packaging engineer is involved in sales. Also, travel between plants may be necessary to coordinate packaging operations. At various stages of developing packaging, the packaging engineer will be engaged in a lot of hands-on activities. These activities may involve handling objects, working with machinery, carrying light loads, and using tools and instruments.

Social and psychological factors

A packaging engineer should have an analytical mind, capacity for detail, and creativity. Theoretical and practical knowledge of science and engineering will help in the thinking, planning, and research stages. Technical expertise will be needed for developing packaging products and operations. Designing attractive packaging will require artistic and design skills. Human relations skills are necessary for working well with others as part of a team. Good speaking and writing skills are necessary for expressing ideas to team members and writing technical reports.

The work of packaging engineers also involves other, social concerns such as consumer protection, environmental pollution, and conservation of natural resources. Packaging engineers are constantly searching for safer, tamperproof packaging, especially because harmful substances have been found in some food and drugs. They also experiment with new packaging materials and techniques conserve resources and reduce the disposal problem. Many environmentalists are concerned with managing the waste from discarded packages. Efforts are being made to stop littering; to recycle bottles, cans and other containers; and to use more biodegradable substances in packaging materials. The qualified packaging engineer, then, will have a broad awareness of social issues.

Another major social concern of packagers is world hunger. The introduction of packaging techniques to developing nations is helping solve problems of food storage and distribution. With effective packaging of food, much waste and spoilage could be eliminated thus allowing individual countries to be more self- sufficient in fulfilling their food production needs.

GOE: 05.05.05; SIC: 2671, 3565 SOC: 6178

◇ **SOURCES OF ADDITIONAL INFORMATION**

National Institute of Packaging, Handling, and Logistic Engineers
6902 Lyle Street
Lanham, MD 20706

Packaging Institute International
20 Summer Street
Stamford, CT 60901

Packaging Machinery Manufacturers Institute
1343 L Street, NW
Washington, DC 20005

Paperboard Packaging Council
1101 Vermont Avenue, NW
Suite 411
Washington, DC 20005

◇ **RELATED ARTICLES**

Volume 1: Advertising; Chemicals and Drugs; Computer Software; Electronics; Engineering; Food Processing; Foreign Trade; Machining and Machinery; Packaging; Plastics; Pulp and Paper; Retailing
Volume 2: Advertising workers; Chemists; Commercial artists; Computer programmers; Cost estimators; Designers; Engineers; Export-import specialists; Food technologists; Industrial designers; Marketing research personnel; Operations research analysts; Systems analysts
Volume 3: Canning and preserving industry workers; Dairy products manufacturing workers; Industrial machinery mechanics; Macaroni and related products industry workers; Manufacturers' sales workers; Meat packing production workers; Paper processing operations; Plastics products manufacturing workers
Volume 4: Chemical technicians; Drafting and design technicians; Graphic arts technicians; Industrial engineering technicians; Packaging and paper products technicians; Pollution-control technicians

Painters and sculptors

Definition

Painters use watercolors, oils, acrylics, and other substances to paint a variety of sub-

jects, including landscapes, people, and objects. *Sculptors* design and construct three-dimensional artworks from various materials, such as stone, concrete, plaster, and wood.

History

Man has communicated through art for many centuries. Even the earliest cave dwellers drew pictures and sketches in an attempt to convey thoughts and ideas. Although language evolved into a more effective and practical means of communication, art has remained an aesthetic medium for conveying images and feelings.

The importance and value of art has been recognized throughout history. During the Middle Ages, many artists were commissioned by the Church to produce paintings and other works of art. The Sistine Chapel in Rome, for example, is famous for its beautiful frescoes, which were painted by Michelangelo and other artists. Many artists, such as Leonardo da Vinci, Rembrandt, and Rodin, created works of art that continue to touch and inspire each new generation.

Over the past several centuries, many different styles of art have emerged, each with distinct and recognizable characteristics. During the late nineteenth century, for example, a style of art known as impressionism developed; impressionist painters, such as Monet and Renoir, attempted to capture a momentary glimpse of a subject by applying paint to canvas in short strokes of pure color. Abstract expressionism is another style of art, one which emerged after World War II and which emphasizes spontaneous and self-expressive applications of paint by artists.

Each new generation brings artists who contribute original and valued artistic creations. Some of the most cherished and beautiful artworks that have ever been created are now displayed in art museums all over the world. There are literally thousands of museums housing various works of art, museums such as the Louvre in Paris, which is visited by countless art enthusiasts each year. The products of painters and sculptors are a valued and appreciated part of our culture and history.

Nature of the work

Painters and sculptors use their creative abilities to produce original works of art. Painters and sculptors are generally classified as fine artists, rather than commercial artists, because they are responsible for selecting the theme, subject matter, and medium of their artworks. As fine artists, painters and sculptors create works to be viewed and judged for aesthetic content.

Painters use a variety of media to paint portraits, landscapes, still lifes, abstracts, and other subjects. They use brushes, palette knives, and other artist's tools to apply color to canvas or other surfaces. Painters develop line, space, color, and other visual elements to produce the desired effect. They may prefer a particular style of art, such as realism or abstract art, and they may be identified with a certain technique or subject matter.

Sculptors use a combination of media and methods to create three-dimensional works of art. They may carve objects from stone, plaster, concrete, or wood. They may use their fingers to model clay or wax into objects. Some sculptors create forms from metal or stone, using various masonry tools and equipment. Like painters, sculptors may be identified with a particular technique or style. Sculptors usually work under contract or commission.

It is imperative that both painters and sculptors be good at business and sales if they intend to support themselves through their art. As small-business persons, they must be able to market and sell their products to wholesalers, retailers, and the general public.

Because earning a living as a fine artist is very difficult, especially when one is just starting out, many painters and sculptors must work at another job. With the proper training and educational background, many painters and sculptors can hold down another job that is still associated with art, such as art teacher, art director, or graphic designer.

Requirements

The most important requirement for a career as a painter or sculptor is artistic ability. In addition to natural ability, artists should also be creative and imaginative; they must understand how to use color and composition to produce a desired visual effect. Painters and sculptors should also exhibit certain personal traits, such as patience, persistence, determination, independence, and sensitivity.

It is becoming increasingly advantageous, if not essential, that persons interested in careers in fine art receive formal art training and education. There are many art schools around the country that have excellent programs. Most colleges and universities also offer degrees in fine art, applied art, and art history. Specific courses include work in perspective, design, color, and composition. In addition to art courses, students study liberal arts subjects.

455

The American painter Thomas Hart Benton portrayed the simple daily lives of the middle class. He strove to paint in a wholly American style that was free of any European influence.

Special requirements

Although there are no special licenses or certificates needed to enter the fine arts field, artists who sell their works to the public may need special permits from the local or state tax office. In addition, artists should check with the Internal Revenue Service for laws on selling and for tax information on income received from the sale of artwork.

There are also a number of professional organizations that artists may wish to join; these organizations often provide artists with helpful and informative advice and tips.

Opportunities for experience and exploration

Persons may explore the world of art in many ways. Virtually all elementary, junior high, and high schools offer classes in art. Special artistic projects can be undertaken at school or at home; art can be explored in many ways in one's spare time. Many art associations and schools also offer beginning classes in various types of art for the general public.

Related occupations

Fine artists may use their talents as commercial artists, illustrators, and designers or move into related occupations in the advertising industry, such as account executive or creative director. Other workers who use visual art skills include architects, display workers, floral designers, industrial designers, interior designers, landscape architects, and photographers, as well as some workers in printing occupations and teachers of art and design.

Methods of entering

Artists interested in exhibiting or selling their products should investigate potential markets. Reference books, such as *Artist's Market*, may be helpful, as well as library books that offer information on business laws, taxes, and related issues. Local fairs and art shows often let new artists display their work; art councils are a source of information on upcoming fairs in the area.

Some artists sell their work on consignment. When a painter or sculptor sells work this way, a store or gallery displays an item; when the item is sold, the artist gets the price of that item minus a commission that goes to the store or gallery. Artists who sell on consignment should read contracts very carefully.

Many art schools and universities have placement services to help students find jobs. Although fine artists are generally self-employed, many need to work at another job, at least initially, to support themselves while they make a name and establish a reputation.

Advancement

Painters and sculptors are self-employed; thus, the channels for advancement are not as well defined as they are at a company or firm. The success of the fine artist depends on a variety of factors, including talent, drive, and determination. Artists with a great deal of talent and drive may open their own galleries; those with appropriate educational backgrounds may become art teachers, agents, and critics.

Employment outlook

The employment outlook for painters and sculptors is difficult to predict. Because they are usually self-employed, much of their success depends on the amount and type of work created and the drive and determination in selling the work.

Talented artists who are able to predict artistic trends will be the most successful. Although artists should not let their style be completely dictated by market trends, it is important to determine what types of artwork are wanted by the public.

It often takes many, many years for an artist's work and reputation to be established. Many artists have to support themselves through other employment. There are numerous employment opportunities for commercial artists in such fields as publishing, advertising, fashion and design, and teaching. Painters and sculptors should consider employment in these and other fields. They should be prepared, however, to face strong competition from the many others who are attracted to this field.

Earnings

The amount of money earned by painters and sculptors varies greatly. Most are self-employed and set their own hours and prices. Artists often work long hours and earn little, especially when they are first starting out. The price they charge is up to them, but much depends on the value the public places on their work. A particular item may sell for a few dollars, a few hundred, or a few thousand.

Some artists obtain grants that allow them to pursue their artwork; others win prizes and awards in competitions. Most artists, however, have to work on their projects part-time while holding down a regular, full-time job. For many artists, their jobs are teaching in an art school, high school, or out of their studios. Artists who sell their products must deduct social security and other taxes from any money they receive.

Conditions of work

Most painters and sculptors work out of their homes or in studios. Some work in small areas in their apartments; others work in large, well-ventilated lofts. Occasionally, painters and sculptors may work outside. In addition, artists often work at fairs, shops, museums, and other places where their work is being exhibited.

Artists often work long hours, and those who are self-employed do not receive the paid vacations, insurance coverage, or any of the other benefits usually offered by a company or firm. However, artists are able to work at their own pace, set their own prices, and make their own decisions. The energy and creativity that go into an artist's work bring feelings of pride and satisfaction. Most artists genuinely love what they do.

Social and psychological factors

Painters and sculptors must have a natural artistic ability, a strong interest in the profession, and a dedicated commitment to their art to succeed. They should be creative, imaginative, and sensitive. These traits must be balanced, however, with good business and marketing skills.

GOE: 01.02.02; SIC: 8999; SOC: 325

◇ **SOURCES OF ADDITIONAL INFORMATION**

The National Art Education Association
1916 Association Drive
Reston, VA 22091

American Society of Artists
PO Box 1326
Palatine, IL 60078

National Endowment for the Arts
1100 Pennsylvania Avenue, NW
Washington, DC 20506

Sculptors Guild
110 Greene Street
New York, NY 10012

◇ **RELATED ARTICLES**

Volume 1: Design
Volume 2: Commercial artists; Designers
Volume 4: Graphic arts technicians

Perfusionists

Definition

Although *perfusionists* are not well known to the general public, they play a crucial role in the field of cardiovascular surgery by operating what is known as the "heart-lung machine." The perfusionist, formerly known as a *cardiovascular perfusionist*, is responsible for assembling, setting up, and operating the heart-lung machine whenever it becomes necessary to interrupt or replace the functioning of the heart by circulating blood outside of a patient's body, a practice known as "extracorporeal circulation." Without heart-lung machines and the specialists who operate these machines, modern-day heart operations would not be possible.

History

When open heart surgery began in 1953, surgeons found it was virtually impossible to operate on the heart while at the same time expecting the heart to maintain its normal functions. Because of this heart-lung machines were developed to circulate the patients' blood outside the body and to maintain certain body temperatures during surgery. These machines solved the problem of maintaining stable bodily functions during the operation so that the heart can resume its normal functioning following the operation. Those who operated the early heart-lung machines were not specifically trained for this subspeciality but, rather, came from the ranks of respiratory therapists, operating room technologists, biomedical and laboratory technologists, and even nursing. These early heart-lung machine operators were often called *pump technicians, perfusion technicians, extracorporeal technologists,* and *extracorporeal perfusionists.*

From the mid-1950s until 1968, perfusionists gained their training primarily by apprenticing under existing practitioners. In 1968, The American Society of Extracorporeal Technology (AmSECT) instituted a program of perfusionists' certification which the American Medical Association recognized with formal status in the 1970s. Also at this time, the American Board of Cardiovascular Perfusion (ABCP) was established. In 1980, the American Board of Cardiovascular Perfusion established formal requirements for the education and accredita-

tion of perfusionists. Today, the ABCP approves and accredits perfusion training programs in twenty-four schools throughout the United States.

Reflecting the increased sophistication and specialization of open-heart surgery, perfusionism has grown more complex. The job of the perfusionist now encompasses the assemblage and operation of the heart-lung machine, the artificial heart, blood transfusion devices, the intra-aortic balloon pump, and various ventricular-assist devices.

Nature of the work

Perfusionists perform one of the most delicate and crucial services for patients during open-heart surgery, coronary bypass, or any other procedure that involves the heart or the heart and lungs. The perfusionist operates equipment that literally takes over the functioning of the patient's heart and lungs during open-heart surgery. Such equipment may also be used in emergency cases of respiratory failure.

When surgeons pierce the patient's breast bone and the envelope surrounding the heart, which is known as the "pericardial sac," they must transfer the functions of the patient's heart and lungs to the heart-lung machine before any surgery can begin on the heart itself. This process is known as establishing extracorporeal bypass, or outside, heart and lung functions. The heart-lung machine is activated by inserting two tubes into the heart, one of which circulates blood from the heart to the machine, with the other circulating blood from the machine back into the heart. It is necessary during this procedure not only to maintain circulation and pumping action but also to maintain the appropriate oxygen, carbon dioxide, and other blood gas levels. In addition, perfusionists must effectively control the body temperature of patients who are undergoing extracorporeal bypass circulation because the flow of blood through the body greatly influences body temperature. To slow metabolism and reduce the stress on the heart and other bodily systems, perfusionists often reduce the body temperature of patients during open-heart surgery to 70° F or below. Perfusionists use various probes within the body to monitor body temperature, blood gases, kidney functioning, electrolytes, and blood pressure.

Although the ultimate responsibility for open-heart surgery and for decisions concerning blood circulation, temperature, and other matters rests with the surgeon in charge of the operation, surgeons tend to rely heavily upon the judgment of perfusionists who are regarded as specialists in their own right. Although the perfusionist may never have a discussion with the patient, perfusionists almost always have preoperative conferences with the surgeon to discuss the condition and other characteristics of the patient, the nature of the operation, the choice of equipment to be used, and other details.

Because of the nature of their work, perfusionists work in hospitals in cardiac operating rooms. They are called upon to be working members of a cardiac surgery team, and it is not uncommon for perfusionists to work through several successive operations in a row as well as to work in emergency cases. Because open-heart surgery cannot be performed without these specialists, perfusionists are usually on call a great deal of the time. It is not an exaggeration to say that the life of a patient is frequently in the hands of a perfusionist. For this reason, as well as the delicate, fast-paced and high-pressure nature of the work, a perfusionist must have a special temperament.

Requirements

The field of cardiovascular perfusion requires formal training from one of twenty-four schools throughout the United States accredited by the Joint Review Committee on Perfusion Education. As a prerequisite to admission, these schools generally require four years of college and a bachelor of science degree, although in some cases they will accept applicants who have trained at nursing schools and other technical schools, and had experience as nurses or health technicians. The accredited perfusion technology training courses range in length from one and one-half to two years. Several of the accredited schools offer a combined undergraduate degree and a degree in perfusion technology, but it is more often the case that perfusionists are trained following undergraduate training or other training as described above.

Those desiring entry to an accredited perfusion technology program can expect intense competition because only 10 to 20 percent of applicants are accepted in such programs. The accredited schools carefully examine academic record, character, and even personal temperament before accepting new students.

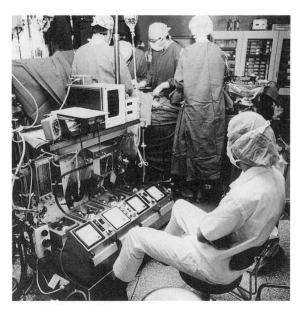

A perfusionist monitors the heart-lung machine for a patient who is undergoing surgery.

The admissions officers at these schools realize that it takes a special individual to function under the kind of pressure and long hours perfusionists frequently confront.

A strong background in biology, mathematics, and other sciences is recommended for applicants to perfusion technology programs, because these programs are designed to convey a great deal of technical information as well as clinical training over a one and one-half to two year period. The perfusion technology program involves courses in physiology, cardiology, respiratory therapy, pharmacology, and heart surgery. Classroom experience is combined with extensive clinical experience where students learn about extracorporeal circulation, respiratory therapy, general surgical procedures, anesthesia, and other operating room procedures. Nearly all of the accredited perfusion technology programs attempt to involve students as early as possible and as much as possible in clinical experience, because the practice of extracorporeal circulation relies so much upon actual operating room experience.

High-school students interested in perfusion technology should prepare themselves for a college curriculum emphasizing basic sciences, mathematics, and health sciences. In addition to normal channels of college financial aid, the American Society of Extracorporeal Technology offers some scholarships, and a number of the schools offer work-study programs as well as their own financial aid programs.

Special requirements

Upon the completion of instruction from an accredited school of perfusion technology, perfusionists may take a written test administered by the American Board of Cardiovascular Perfusion. Perfusionists are then qualified to take the oral examination. The written and the oral examinations are given once per year, and candidates are permitted to take these tests three times, after which if they are not able to pass the test, they become ineligible for further examinations. The written exam must be passed first. Each year the location of the examination varies; the examination fee is $250 plus travel expenses. Once certified by the American Board of Cardiovascular Perfusion, members who are certified perfusionists pay an annual $75 fee to maintain their certification.

Certification is not an absolute requirement for perfusionists at this time, but it is rapidly becoming a practical requirement as more than two thirds of perfusionists nationally are now certified. At the present time, perfusionists do not need separate state licenses to practice their profession. It is to the student's advantage to have graduated from a school accredited by the Joint Review Committee on Perfusion Education.

To maintain their certification in good standing, perfusionists are expected to engage in continuing education programs so that they may remain abreast of the latest techniques. The field of cardiovascular surgery is constantly changing, and open-heart surgery, bypass surgery, heart transplants, and other complicated operations are becoming increasingly commonplace throughout the health care system. Therefore, it can be expected that the field of perfusion technology will become increasingly complicated in the coming years and that the tendency to certify technologists will probably lead to the point in the future where all perfusionists must be certified.

Opportunities for experience and exploration

As is the case with any technical medical field, one of the best ways to learn about the field is to meet an existing practitioner. All hospitals performing open-heart surgery have perfusionists on staff or under contract. These people may be located through the surgical departments of hospitals and, with some advanced notice, would very likely make themselves available for interviews with students. The American Society of Extracorporeal Technology makes available a list of accredited perfusion technology programs, and those interested in such programs can talk to the professors, instructors, and admissions officers in these respective schools.

Related occupations

The health care field is incredibly diverse and will continue to become more so. The same qualities that make for a good perfusionist are the same qualities necessary in other medical occupations. These occupations include physicians, registered nurses, licensed practical nurses, medical technologists, and the many different specialties that technicians work in.

Methods of entering

The most important prerequisite for entering the field of perfusion technology is acceptance at an accredited school that offers such a program. Once students have entered a program they should begin to investigate the field first through their professors and teachers and then through the American Society of Extracorporeal Technology. The AmSECT, which is a professional society of perfusion technologists, has an active student membership division that hosts meetings and conferences and that is a good source of advice and information concerning various job openings in the field. Because the field is highly specialized and employs only 2,500 individuals nationwide, it is not difficult to contact professionals and employers in the field.

Advancement

Because there is a relatively small number of perfusionists nationwide in comparison with the rapidly growing field of extracorporeal technology (open-heart surgery), perfusionists do have advancement opportunities from the standpoint of both high salaries and the opportunity to perform more complicated work over time. At the same time, the field of perfusion technology is so specialized and so small that the concept of advancement is related more to improving one's technical skills over time than to administering large departments or large numbers of people. Perfusionists do have the capacity, however, to advance into perfusion department management, in addition to the technological side of the field. The practicing perfusionist advances through the negotiation of higher pay, better working conditions, and the ability to be involved in more complicated procedures as well as to train younger perfusionists. In addition, perfusionists may enter the field of teaching in one of the accredited schools, and there are opportunities to conduct research funded by educational institutions, foundations, or professional societies.

Employment outlook

There were approximately 2,500 perfusionists employed throughout the United States in the early 1990s, and these professionals worked in approximately 750 hospitals with open-heart surgery departments. The field is expected to grow by about 100 to 150 additional professionals per year through the 1990s.

As with many medical fields, advancing technology that permits more complicated procedures to be performed calls for additional professionals as these procedures are performed on a more regular basis. The field of open-heart surgery and expanded scope of extracorporeal technology grew dramatically during the 1980s and is expected to continue to expand, so that the job opportunities and job stability for perfusionists is expected to be excellent. Open-heart surgery is among the more complex surgical procedures and is usually performed only in medical centers with 300 beds or more. There is not likely to be an explosion in the numbers of perfusionists but, rather, a steady growth throughout the 1990s.

Earnings

Salaries for perfusion technologists compare favorably with those of other health technicians, with the national range of salaries starting at about $30,000 per year for entering perfusionists and rising to an average of $55,000 per year for more experienced professionals. Some perfusionists, however, earn as much as $120,000 per year, but those earning higher salaries are generally employed by a physician directly or are self-employed. Roughly half of all the perfusionists are directly employed by hospitals, and the other half are independent contractors or independent practitioners who make themselves available by contract to one or more hospitals. Those perfusionists who are independent contractors are responsible for their own business affairs including medical health insurance, uniforms, liability insurance, and other items.

Conditions of work

Perfusionists nearly always work in operating rooms of hospitals. They and their equipment are located adjacent to the operating table among the surgical team; it is the responsibility of the perfusionist to see that the equipment is properly assembled and properly maintained at all times.

The two most significant characteristics relating to working conditions are the long hours which perfusionists frequently must spend in operating rooms and the stress under which they must operate. Although the average number of procedures is 125 per perfusionist per year, some of these procedures can be quite lengthy, and they may occur at odd hours as well as under emergency conditions.

Social and psychological factors

Successful perfusionists must have a combination of high technical skill, good reflexes, alertness, calm temperament, and composure under pressure. The perfusionist must be both a skilled technician able to make decisions and recommendations and a team player able to get along with other members of the surgical team and to follow directions.

Functioning in the quiet, sterile, sometimes eerie atmosphere of the operating room for long hours and under intense pressure requires a person who derives his or her job satisfaction from performing a crucial job well rather than from direct interaction with patients, external excitement, and constant interaction with a variety of people. It is important that perfusion technologists be dedicated, mature, dependable individuals, for the lives of patients often depend upon the abilities of the man or woman operating the heart-lung machine. A recognition of the marked responsibilities of this profession and a willingness to conduct one's self accordingly are essential prerequisites for entry into the field, and most of the schools educating profusion technologists look very carefully at a person's character in addition to academic credentials before granting admission.

Perfusion technologists must be able to withstand disappointments that can occur during open-heart surgical operations, including loss of life. On the other hand, the advancements in open-heart surgery and coronary ar-

461

tery bypass have been extensive in recent years, and the dedicated perfusionist is likely to take great satisfaction in contributing significantly to the quality of a patient's life during successful operations. Perfusionists do not have an opportunity to talk with many of the patients who rely on them during the critical hours of open-heart surgery, and few patients or members of the general public even know what a perfusionist is. But for the right individual the opportunity to participate in the frontiers of open-heart surgery and to be an integral part of a surgical team can be greatly rewarding.

GOE: None; SIC: 806; SOC: None

◇ **SOURCES OF ADDITIONAL INFORMATION**

American Medical Association
535 North Dearborn Street
Chicago, IL 60610

American Board of Cardiovascular Perfusion
123 South 25th Avenue
Hattiesburg, MS 39401

American Society of Extracorporeal Technology
Suite 100E
Golf Course Plaza
11480 Sunset Hills Road
Reston, VA 22090

◇ **RELATED ARTICLES**

Volume 1: Health Care
Volume 2: Health services administrators; Nuclear medicine technologists; Respiratory therapists
Volume 3: Dental assistants; Nursing and psychiatric aides
Volume 4: Medical and Health Technician occupations

Personnel and labor relations specialists

Definition

Personnel and labor relations specialists are the link between management and employees. They formulate policy and organize and conduct programs relating to all phases of personnel activity, such as recruitment, selection, training, development, retention, promotion, compensation, benefits, labor relations, and occupational safety.

History

Personnel work developed slowly as small businesses became large ones and there was less and less contact between management and the employees. The success of a company is de-

pendent in large part on attracting good employees, matching them up to jobs they are suited for, and motivating them to do their best. A growing awareness of human psychology, the development of more sophisticated business methods, the rise of labor unions, and the enactment of government laws and regulations concerned with the welfare and rights of employees have created a need for a group of specialists who can balance the needs of both employees and employers for the benefit of all.

Nature of the work

Personnel and labor relations specialists are the liaison between the management of an organization and its employees. They see that management makes effective use of employees' skills, while at the same time improving working conditions for employees and helping them find fulfillment in their jobs. Most positions in this field involve heavy contact with people, both management and non-management level.

Both personnel specialists and labor relations specialists are experts in employer employee relations, although the labor relations specialists concentrate on matters pertaining to union members. Personnel specialists interview job applicants and select or recommend those who seem best suited to the openings. Their choices for hiring and advancement must follow the guidelines for equal employment opportunity and affirmative action established by the federal government. Personnel specialists also plan and maintain programs for wages and salaries, employee benefits, and training and career development. Specialists in labor relations, or union-management relations, usually work for unionized organizations, helping company officials prepare for collective-bargaining sessions, participating in contract negotiations, and handling day-to-day labor relations matters.

The personnel work for a small company is often managed by only one person, because it consists of little more than interviewing and hiring. On the other hand, the personnel department of a large organization may be staffed by many specialists, including recruiters, interviewers, job analysts, and specialists in charge of benefits, training, and labor relations, in addition to the personnel clerks and assistants who issue forms, maintain files, compile statistics, answer inquiries, and do other routine tasks. *Personnel managers* and *employment managers* are concerned with the overall management of the department and may be involved with hiring, orientation of new employees, record keeping, insurance reports, wage surveys, budgets, grievances, and analyzing statistical data and reports. *Industrial relations directors* are employee relations administrators who formulate the policies to be carried out by the various department managers.

Of all the personnel specialists, probably the first one that comes to mind is the *recruiter*. Companies depend on personnel recruiters to find the best employees available. (*See also* the article titled "Employment firm workers" elsewhere in this volume.) The search involves developing sources through contacts within the community and perhaps traveling extensively to other cities or to college campuses. On college campuses, *placement directors* or *managers of college placement services* coordinate recruitment activities and assist students and graduates in-

A labor relations specialist conducts a workshop on employer-employee relations for the management personnel of a company that is experiencing labor problems.

dividually to develop employment plans and contact prospective employers.

Personnel recruiters or *employment interviewers* interview applicants to fill job vacancies, evaluate their qualifications, and recommend hiring the most promising candidates. They sometimes administer tests, check references and background, and arrange for indoctrination and training. Prospective and new employees ask many questions about wages, working conditions, and opportunities for advancement. To discuss these matters satisfactorily, recruiters and interviewers need a thorough knowledge of their company and its personnel policies. They must also be familiar and keep up to date with guidelines for equal employment opportunity (EEO) and affirmative action.

This complex and sensitive area is handled in large organizations by special EEO representatives or affirmative-action coordinators or *job development specialists*, who develop employment opportunities and on-the-job training programs for minority or disadvantaged applicants; devise systems or set up representative committees through which grievances can be investigated and resolved as they come up; and monitor corporate practices to prevent possible EEO violations. Preparing and submitting EEO statistical reports is an important part of their work.

Job analysts are sometimes called *compensation analysts*. They study all of the jobs within an organization to determine job and worker requirements. Through observation and interviews with employees, they gather and analyze detailed information about job duties and the training and skills required. They write summaries describing each job, its specifications, and the possible route to advancement. Job analysts classify new positions as they are introduced and review existing jobs periodically. These job descriptions, or "position classifications," form a structure for hiring, training, evaluating, and promoting employees, as well as for establishing an equitable pay system.

On a broader level, *occupational analysts* do technical research concerned with job relationships, functions, and content; worker characteristics; and occupational trends. The results of their studies enable business, industry, and government to utilize the general work force more effectively.

Developing and administering the pay system is the primary responsibility of the *compensation manager*. With the assistance of other specialists on the staff, compensation managers establish a wage scale designed to attract, retain, and motivate employees. A realistic and fair compensation program takes into consideration company policies, government regulations concerning minimum wages and overtime pay, rates currently being paid by similar firms and industries, and agreements with labor unions.

One of a company's major assets is its employees. The trend toward making more effective use of this asset has given rise to an important new area of specialization in personnel administration   human resource development. Training specialists prepare and conduct a wide variety of education and training activities for employees in business, industry, and government agencies. They work with new employees in orientation sessions or with experienced workers who are learning new procedures, the operation of new equipment, or management skills. Other special areas covered may be apprenticeship programs, sales techniques, health and safety practices, and retraining displaced workers. The methods chosen by training specialists for maximum effectiveness may include individual training, group instruction, lectures, demonstrations, meetings, or workshops, using such teaching aids as handbooks, demonstration models, multimedia visual aids, and reference works. These specialists also confer with management and supervisors to determine the needs for new training programs or revision of existing ones; maintain records of all training activities; and evaluate the success of the various programs and methods. *Training instructors* may work under the direction of an *education and training manager*. (*See also* the article titled "Employment firm workers" elsewhere in this volume.) *Coordinators of auxiliary personnel* specialize in training nonprofessional nursing personnel in medical facilities.

An important aspect of any human resource development program is helping employees prepare for future responsibilities and possible promotion. To accomplish this, training specialists may assist individuals to establish career development goals and set up a timetable in which to strengthen job-related skills and learn new ones. Sometimes this involves outside study paid for by the company or rotation to jobs in different departments of the organization. The extent of the training program and the responsibilities of the training specialists vary considerably, depending on the size of the firm and its organizational objectives.

Benefits programs for employees are handled by *benefits managers* or *employee-welfare managers*. The major part of such programs generally involves insurance and pension plans. Since the enactment of the Employee Retirement Income Security Act (ERISA), reporting requirements have become a primary responsibility for personnel departments in large companies. The retirement program for state and local government employees is handled by *retirement officers*. In addition to regular health insurance and pension coverage, employee benefit packages have often grown to include such things as dental insurance, accidental death and disability insurance, automobile insurance, homeowner's insurance, profit sharing and thrift/savings plans, and stock options. The expertise of benefits analysts and administrators is extremely important in designing and carrying out the complex programs. These specialists also develop and coordinate additional services related to employee welfare, such as car pools, child care, cafeterias and lunchrooms, newsletters, annual physical exams, recreation and physical fitness programs, and counseling. Personal and financial counseling for employees close to retirement age is growing especially important.

Occupational safety and health programs may be the responsibility of the personnel department, especially in small companies, or of the labor relations specialist if the union has a safety representative. The trend, however, is toward establishing a separate safety department under the direction of a safety engineer, industrial hygienist, or other safety and health professional.

Personnel departments may have access to resources outside the organization. These resources include:

Employer relations representatives promote the use of public employment services and programs among local employers. (*See also* the article titled "Employment firm workers" elsewhere in this volume.)

Employee-health maintenance program specialists help set up local government-funded programs among area employers to provide assistance in treating employees with alcoholism or behavioral medical problems.

In companies where employees are covered by union contracts, labor relations specialists form the link between union and management. Prior to negotiation of a collective-bargaining agreement, *labor relations managers* counsel management regarding their negotiating position and provide them with background information about provisions of the current contract and the significance of the proposed changes, furnishing reference materials and statistics pertaining to labor legislation, labor market conditions, prevailing union and management practices, wage and salary surveys, and employee benefit programs. This work requires familiarity with sources of economic and wage data and an extensive knowledge of labor law and collective-bargaining trends. In the actual negotiation, the employer is usually represented by the director of labor relations or another top-level official, but the members of the company's labor relations staff play an important role throughout the negotiations.

A large part of the work of labor relations specialists is analyzing and interpreting the contract for management and monitoring company practices to ensure their adherence to the terms. Of particular importance is the handling of grievance procedures. To investigate and settle grievances, these specialists arrange meetings between workers who raise a complaint, managers and supervisors, and a union representative. A grievance, for example, may concern seniority rights during a layoff. Labor relations disputes are sometimes investigated and resolved by *professional conciliators* or *mediators*. Labor relations work requires keeping up to date on developments in labor law, including arbitration decisions, and maintaining close contact with union officials.

Government personnel specialists do essentially the same work as their counterparts in business, except that they deal with public employees whose jobs are subject to civil service regulations. Much of government personnel work concentrates on job analysis because civil service jobs are strictly classified as to entry requirements, duties, and wages. In response to the growing importance of training and career development in the public sector, however, an entire industry" of educational and training consultants has sprung up to provide similar services for public agencies. The increased union strength among government workers has resulted in a need for more highly trained labor relations specialists to handle negotiations, grievances, and arbitration cases on behalf of federal, state, and local agencies.

Requirements

High-school graduates may start out as personnel clerks and advance to a professional position through experience, but such a situation is becoming rare. More and more employers are demanding a college education even for beginning positions in this field. There is little agreement, however, as to what type of undergraduate training is preferable for personnel and labor relations work. Some employers favor college graduates who have majored in personnel administration or industrial and labor relations, while others prefer individuals with a general business background. Another opinion is that personnel specialists do best with a well-rounded liberal arts education, and many of them have degrees in psychology, sociology, counseling, or education. A master's degree in business administration (MBA) is also considered suitable preparation. Persons interested in personnel work with a government agency may find it an asset to have a degree in personnel administration, political science, or public administration.

Programs leading to a degree in the field of personnel and labor relations are offered by many colleges and universities. Other schools have programs in personnel administration or personnel management, and some colleges and universities offer degree or certificate programs in training and development. In many schools, preparation for a career in human resource development may be obtained in departments of business administration, education, instructional technology, organizational development, human services, communication, or public administration.

There are many phases of personnel work, for which a varied educational background would be useful. For example, a combination of courses in the social sciences, behavioral sciences, business, and economics would be entirely appropriate. Individuals preparing for a career as a personnel specialist would benefit from courses in the principles of management, organization dynamics, and human relations. Other relevant courses might include business administration, public administration, psychology, sociology, political science, economics, and statistics. For prospective labor relations specialists, valuable courses include labor law, collective bargaining, labor economics, labor history, and industrial psychology.

Work in labor relations may require graduate study in industrial or labor relations. While not required for entry-level jobs, a law degree is a must for persons who conduct contract negotiations, and a combination of industrial relations courses and a law degree is especially desirable.

Beginners in personnel work are trained on the job or in formal training programs, where they learn how to classify jobs, interview applicants, or administer employee benefits. Then they are assigned to specialized areas in the personnel department. Some people enter the labor relations field after first gaining experience in general personnel work, but it is becoming more common for qualified individuals to enter that field directly.

A number of other qualifications and characteristics are necessary for workers in this sensitive occupation. Personnel and labor relations specialists must be able to communicate effectively and clearly both in speech and in writing and to deal comfortably and easily with people of different levels of education and experience. They must be persons of unquestioned integrity, able to inspire the trust and confidence of others. Objectivity and fair-mindedness are required to consider matters from both the employee's and the employer's point of view. These workers cooperate as part of a team; at the same time, they must be able to handle responsibility individually. Finally, they need strong supervisory skills and a persuasive, pleasant personality.

Special requirements

There are no other requirements for a career in the personnel and labor relations field.

Opportunities for experience and exploration

Part-time and summer employment in firms that have a personnel department are very good ways to explore the personnel field. Large department stores usually have personnel departments and should not be overlooked by applicants for temporary work.

High-school students who enjoy working with others will find helpful experience in managing school teams, planning banquets or picnics, working in the dean's or counselor's office, or reading books about personnel practices in businesses. They may also interview personnel directors of local businesses or industries, such as banks, insurance companies, and manufacturing plants.

Related occupations

All specialties within the personnel and labor relations field are closely related. Other workers with similar skills in interpersonal relations include employment, rehabilitation, and college career planning and placement counselors; lawyers; psychologists; sociologists; and teachers.

Methods of entering

Colleges and universities have placement counselors who can help graduates find employment. Also, large companies often send recruiters to campuses looking for promising job applicants. Otherwise, interested individuals may apply directly to local companies. High-school graduates may apply for entry-level jobs as personnel clerks and assistants. Private employment agencies and local offices of the state employment service are other possible sources for work. In addition, newspaper want ads often contain listings of many personnel jobs.

Advancement

After trainees have mastered the basic personnel tasks, they are assigned to specific areas in the department to gain specialized experience. In time they may advance to supervisory positions or to manager of a major part of the personnel program, such as training, compensation, or EEO/affirmative action. Advancement may also be achieved by moving into a higher position in a smaller organization. A few experienced employees with exceptional ability ultimately become top executives with titles such as director of personnel or director of labor relations.

Employment outlook

Personnel and labor relations specialists held about 381,000 jobs in the early 1990s. Approximately 85 percent of all salaried jobs were in private businesses of all kinds—manufacturing, construction, transportation, communications, finance, insurance, real estate, trade, and services. Around 15 percent of all salaried personnel and labor relations specialists worked for the federal, state, and local governments handling recruitment, interviewing, job classification, training, and other personnel matters relating to the country's 17 million public employees, such as police officers, fire fighters, sanitation workers, teachers, and hospital workers. Personnel and labor relations specialists also were employed by labor unions or management consulting firms or taught college or university courses in personnel administration, industrial relations, and related subjects.

An average growth is expected in the employment of personnel and labor relations specialists through the end of the 1990s. The demand will be greatest in private industry as employers become more aware of the potential benefits of establishing effective employee relations programs for a work force that is increasing. Fast growth will also be experienced in the management and consulting areas as more companies turn to independent contractors to meet their needs and in health care, residential care, and related industries that provide for an expanding population of elderly persons. Opportunities in government personnel work, however, will result primarily from the need to replace workers rather than to fill new positions. In addition, there will be the normal vacancies created when experienced workers retire, die, or change occupations.

Two major factors may be responsible for an increased demand for personnel workers. The reporting and legal requirements of legislation setting standards of employment practices relating to occupational safety and health, equal employment opportunity, and pensions have resulted in more record keeping and paperwork for employers. As they review and evaluate these programs, there may be an additional need for workers. Additional workers may also be required in the field of human resource development. In an effort to increase productivity, employers, both private industry and government, will be investing billions of dollars for training programs to sharpen employees' skills, heighten their motivation, and improve their performance.

Although opportunities in this field will be more numerous in the next few years, the competition for each job will be greater. The field of labor relations, always difficult to break into, will present the keenest competition. Applicants with a master's degree or a strong undergraduate major in industrial relations, economics, or business will have an advantage, as will those with a law degree.

Earnings

Jobs for personnel and labor relations specialists pay salaries that vary widely depending on the nature of the business and the size and location of the firm, as well as on the individual's qualifications and experience.

In the early 1990s, the median salaries for selected occupations in this field were as follows: job analysts, $24,900; benefits planning analysts, $33,300; and recruiters, $30,600. At the managerial level, the median salary for EEO/affirmative action managers was $42,900; for compensation and benefits managers, $51,800; for training managers, $42,000; and for labor relations supervisors, $46,900. Personnel directors in private industry had average annual salaries that ranged from $30,000 to $125,000, while top personnel and labor relations executives in large corporations earned considerably more.

The federal government paid new graduates with a bachelor's degree starting salaries of about $14,800 a year. With a master's degree, new workers started at about $22,500; with a doctorate in a personnel field, about $27,200. The average salary for all personnel and labor relations specialists and managers employed by the federal government in the early 1990s was approximately $31,900 a year. Managers averaged $49,000, while specialists averaged $31,200.

Conditions of work

Personnel employees almost always work under pleasant conditions. Their offices are generally designed to make a good impression on outside visitors and prospective employees and are modern, attractive, well lighted, temperature controlled, and nicely furnished. Personnel specialists are seldom required to work more than thirty-five or forty hours per week, although they may do so if they are developing a program or special project. On the other hand, labor relations specialists often work longer hours, especially when contract agreements are being prepared and negotiated. The difficult aspects of the work may involve firing people, taking disciplinary actions, or handling employee disputes.

Some personnel specialists travel extensively. Recruiters attend professional meetings regularly and visit college campuses across the country to interview prospective employees, and promote their company.

Social and psychological factors

There is much personal satisfaction in performing the job of personnel or labor relations specialist. The personnel specialist should be calm, level-headed, and diplomatic in all work conditions. Much of the reward is intangible (the gratification that comes from protecting the welfare of the company's employees and helping them broaden their career horizons) but it adds up to a fulfilling professional life.

GOE: 11.05.02; SIC: Any industry; SOC: 123

◇ **SOURCES OF ADDITIONAL INFORMATION**

American Arbitration Association
140 West 51st Street
New York, NY 10020

American Compensation Association
Certification Information
14040 Northsight Boulevard
Scottsdale, AZ 85260

American Society for Healthcare Human Resources Administration
American Hospital Association
840 North Lake Shore Drive
Chicago, IL 60611

American Society for Personnel Administration
ASPA Foundation
606 North Washington Street
Alexandria, VA 22314

American Society for Training and Development
PO Box 1443
1630 Duke Street
Alexandria, VA 22313

Industrial Relations Research Association
7226 Social Science Building
University of Wisconsin
Madison, WI 53706

International Foundation of Employee Benefit Plans
18700 West Bluemound Road
PO Box 69
Brookfield, WI 53008

International Personnel Management Association
1617 Duke Street
Alexandria, VA 22314

National Labor Relations Board
1717 Pennsylvania Avenue, NW
Washington, DC 20570

◇ **RELATED ARTICLES**

Volume 1: Business Administration; Human Resources, Trade Unions
Volume 2: Employment counselors; Employment firm workers; Guidance counselors; Human services workers

Petrologists

Definition

Geologists study the overall formation of the earth and its history, the movements of the earth's crust, and the mineral compositions and other natural resources. *Petrologists* focus specifically upon the analysis of the composition, structure, and history of rocks and rock forma-

tions. Petrologists are also interested in the formation of particular types of rocks that contain economically important materials such as gold, copper, uranium, and so on. In addition, they study the formation and composition of metals, precious stones, minerals, and meteorites. They also analyze a wide variety of substances ranging from diamonds and gold to petroleum deposits that may be locked in rock formations beneath the earth's surface.

History

Because much of the earth's solid crust is made up of rocks and rock formations, the field of petrology began to emerge in the early part of the twentieth century as a subspecialty within geology, and as the industrial age proceeded with the mining of oil, coal, precious metals, uranium, and other substances, the field of petrology has become increasingly important as a geological science. Most petrologists are employed by one segment or another of the mining industry, with the petroleum industry being the largest employer. Petrologists are also utilized in many other areas of mining and mineral extraction, and they are also employed by numerous governmental agencies.

A petrologist extracts residue from air-sensitive catalysts.

Nature of the work

The major goal of petrology is to study the origin, composition, and history of rocks and rock formations. Because petrologists are intimately involved in the mining industry, they may work closely with *geologists,* who study the overall composition and structure of the earth as well as mineral deposits; *geophysicists,* who study the physical movements of the earth including seismic activity and physical properties of the earth and its atmosphere; *hydrologists,* who study the earth's waters and water systems; *mineralogists,* who examine and classify minerals and precious stones; and *paleontologists,* who study the fossilized remains of plants and animals found in geological formations.

Depending upon the type of work, petrologists may work frequently in teams with the many specialists mentioned above. For example, in oil drilling they may work with geologists and geophysicists. Here the petrologist would have the major responsibility for analyzing rocks from bored samples beneath the earth's surface. The objective in this case would be for the petrologist to determine the oil-bearing composition of rock samples as well as to determine whether certain rock formations are likely to have oil or natural gas content. In precious metal mining operations, petrologists may work closely with mineralogists. In such cases, the petrologists would analyze core samples of mineral rock formations, called "mineral ore," and the mineralogists would analyze in detail the specific mineral or minerals contained in such samples.

Because the surface of the earth is composed of thousands of layers of rock formations that have been formed over several billion years, the contents of these layers can be revealing depending upon the rock and mineral composition of each respective layer. Each layer, or "stratum," of rock beneath the earth's surface tells a story of the earth's condition in the past and can reveal characteristics such as weather patterns, temperatures, the flow of water, the movement of glaciers, volcanic activity, and numerous other characteristics. These layers can also reveal the presence of minerals, mineral ores, and extractable fossil fuels such as petroleum and natural gas.

Petrologists spend time both in the field gathering samples and in the laboratory analyzing those samples. They use physical samples, photographs, maps, and diagrams to describe the characteristics of whatever rock formation or formations they are analyzing. They use chemical compounds to break down rocks and rock materials to isolate certain elements, and they use X rays, spectroscopic examination, electron microscopes, and other sophisticated means of testing and analyzing samples to isolate the specific components of various minerals or elements within the samples, so that they may draw conclusions from their analysis.

Because much of the practice of petrology has to do with the extraction of minerals, fossil fuels, metals, or natural resources, petrologists frequently work for or in consultation with

469

mining companies. This includes mining on the earth's surface, beneath the earth's surface, and under the ocean floor (in the case of off-shore oil drilling, for example). In addition, petrologists may work for the U.S. government, for the Department of the Interior, the Department of Energy, the Department of Defense, or other governmental departments that may either be monitoring mining and drilling industries or may be surveying certain parts of the earth to conduct research of one type or another. Hence, the field of petrology affords the opportunity to become involved in a number of activities and subspecialties, and during their careers petrologists normally specialize in one area or another.

Requirements

Most professional positions in the field of petrology require a master's degree or a doctorate. Although individuals without these degrees can technically become petrologists, the advances in the field and the requirements of the profession make it very difficult to enter the field without a graduate degree.

There is no special certification for the field of petrology, several states require the registration of petrologists, and government petrologists may be required to take the civil service examination. The two major professional associations providing information and continuing education to petrologists are the Geological Society of America (GSA) and the American Association of Petroleum Geologists (AAPG). The American Geological Institute (AGI) Directory can provide information concerning educational requirements for petrologists as well as schools offering formal training in this area. The address is at the end of this article.

Students who are interested in petrology should concentrate their high-school studies in the sciences and in mathematics, and college students should concentrate upon the earth sciences, physical sciences, geology, paleontology, mineralogy, and, of course, physics, chemistry, and mathematics. Because petrologists frequently analyze large volumes of data and write reports on such data, courses in computer science and in English composition are advisable. Many students begin their careers in this area by first majoring in geology or paleontology and then, as graduate students, enter formal training in the field of petrology. For more information on the role of the petrologist in petroleum and gas exploration, see Volume 1: Energy.

Special requirements

The requirements of the petrology profession depend in large part upon what segment or subspecialty of the profession one chooses. In some cases, petrologists work within a confined geographic area and spend most of their time in laboratories. In other instances, petrologists are called upon to travel throughout the United States and even overseas. This is especially the case with respect to petrologists working for multinational oil companies or other mining operations where they need to be available on short notice to analyze samples in various localities. Where important mining operations are undertaken, petrologists may be required upon to analyze rocks, ore, core samples, or other materials on short notice and under deadline pressure.

As with other scientific disciplines, teamwork is often essential, and it is important that petrologists be able to understand and relate to geologists, paleontologists, mineralogists, and other scientific experts as well as being able to relate to and communicate their findings to supervisory personnel who may not have as extensive a technical background.

Opportunities for experience and exploration

As with any technical scientific profession, it is advisable that interested students meet members of this profession to find out more about the field. Petrologists may be found in universities and colleges that offer courses in geology and petrology, in certain governmental offices and field offices, and especially throughout the mining, oil, and natural gas industries. The oil industry is the largest single employer of petrologists, although the rate of employment growth has fallen off in recent years in connection with the oil industry slump of the 1980s.

Both geologists and petrologists use assistants in their work, and it is possible to obtain summer jobs and part-time employment in certain parts of the country where mining or oil exploration activities are taking place. For further information about the field and about various conferences held throughout the United States in the geological professions, students may contact the American Geological Institute, the American Association of Petroleum Geologists, or the Geological Society of America. The addresses are at the end of this article.

Related occupations

Petrologists by training and nature have a strong interest in the earth and its beginnings, formations, and secrets. These same qualities are inherent in other occupations such as geologists, biological scientists, chemists, physicists, astronomers, oceanographers, limnographers, and many scientific technicians positions.

Methods of entering

It is virtually essential for those seeking to pursue petrology as a career to receive either a master's degree or a doctorate at a qualified college or university. This is especially true in light of the oil industry's slump in the United States during the 1980s, which has affected the fields of geology, paleontology, mineralogy, and petrology.

Because both the federal government and state governments employ petrologists in various agencies, students undertaking graduate programs in petrology should contact both state civil service agencies in their respective states and the federal Office of Personnel Management (OPM), which is the successor to the Civil Service Commission. Federal agencies generally notify the Office of Personnel Management when they wish to fill vacancies in various positions and when new positions are created. The OPM has job information centers located in major cities throughout the United States. Job information concerning employment with the states can be obtained through the respective state capitols.

Although industrial firms do engage in campus recruiting particularly for master's and doctoral level job applicants, recruiting is not as active as in the past because of the oil industry slump in the United States, and job seekers should not hesitate to contact oil exploration companies, mining companies, and other organizations directly. It is always a good idea to make some direct contacts with geologists and petrologists in various companies.

Part-time employment is available to geologists and petrologists from both private industry and various federal and state agencies. In some cases, agencies utilize volunteer students and scientists and pay only some expenses rather than paying a salary; however, this can still be a good way to gain experience and to meet professionals in the field.

Those wishing to teach petrology should consult college and university employment listings. For graduate students in the field, a limited number of part-time jobs as well as jobs at the instructor level are available.

It should be noted that junior high schools and high schools generally need more instructors in this area than do colleges, because many high schools are now beginning to offer a broader range of science courses. Individuals with a master's or doctoral degree are likely to be qualified to teach any one of a variety of science courses at the high-school level including earth science, physics, chemistry, mathematics, or biology.

Advancement

Even though the level of competition in this field is keen and the oil industry has experienced a serious slump during the 1980s, it is important that those entering the petrology profession think seriously about obtaining the highest level degree possible.

As with other scientific professions, advancement generally involves spending a number of years as a staff scientist and then taking on supervisory and managerial skills. The ability to work on a team, the ability to perform accurate and timely research, and the ability to take charge of projects are all important for advancement in this field.

Because petrology, geology, and mineralogy are all related sciences that overlap, especially in industry, it is possible for petrologists to become mineralogists or geologists under the right circumstances. The fact that the three disciplines are so intimately related can be to one's advantage, particularly in changing economic times.

Employment outlook

Because of the continuing relatively low level of activity in the oil exploration industry (historically the largest employer of geologists, petrologists, and mineralogists) the employment outlook during the 1990s is not as good as it is for other scientific professions. In early 1990s, there were approximately 44,000 geologists, geophysicists, petrologists, and mineralogists combined, and this number is expected to grow to 50,000 by the end of the century, an increase of 6,000 professionals in the earth sciences. This projection could change dramatically if worldwide oil prices markedly increase, thereby causing greater oil and natural gas exploration.

Earnings

The earnings of petrologists vary depending upon the type of employment and upon their education. Petrologists holding a bachelor's degree in the early 1990s who are employed by the federal government can expect starting salaries to be $18,000 to $23,000 per year, whereas those with master's degrees have starting salaries above the $23,000 level and those with doctorates can expect starting salaries above $33,000 per year.

Petrologists employed by oil companies or consulting firms will generally start at somewhat higher salaries, but private industry favors those with master's or doctoral degrees, especially because there is increased competition for good jobs among geologists, petrologists, and mineralogists.

Conditions of work

Because the field of petrology involves a considerable amount of testing of rocks, ores, and other materials at mining sites and other types of geological sites, petrologists can expect to travel a considerable amount. In some cases, petrologists are required to travel back and forth from a field site to a laboratory several times while conducting a series of tests. If the petrologist is working on exploratory investigations of a potential site for fuel, he or she may be at a remote location for weeks or months, until the data collected is sufficient to return to the laboratory. The conditions may be arduous, and the leisure time may provide little to do on site.

The hours and working conditions of petrologists vary, but petrologists working in the field can generally expect long hours. Because many mining operations occur in remote locations, petrologists do not generally stay at fancy hotels and eat at expensive restaurants. At the same time, petrologists who have the chance to travel overseas in their work may have extra time to enjoy sightseeing.

Petrologists, geologists, and mineralogists frequently work in teams, and petrologists may work under the supervision of a head geologist, for example. In private industry, they are also frequently working with mining engineers, mine supervisors, drilling supervisors, and others who all form part of a larger mining or drilling operation.

Social and psychological factors

Petrologists need to be willing to travel a good deal and need to be in good health and have excellent stamina. They need to have the temperament and the ability to work long hours and under pressure.

Petrologists also need to have the ability to communicate effectively with others, the ability to get along well with others, and the ability to exercise leadership as well as creative insight.

GOE: 02.01.01; SIC: 1382; SOC: 1847

◇ **SOURCES OF ADDITIONAL INFORMATION**

American Association of Petroleum Geologists
Box 979
Tulsa, OK 74101

American Geological Institute
4220 King Street
Alexandria, VA 22302

Geological Society of America
PO Box 9140
3300 Penrose Place
Boulder, CO 80301

Society of Petroleum Engineers
PO Box 833863
Richardson, TX 75083

◇ **RELATED ARTICLES**

Volume 1: Energy; Engineering; Metals; Physical Sciences
Volume 2: Chemists; Engineers; Geologists; Groundwater professionals; Physicists
Volume 3: Coal mining operatives; Petroleum refining workers; Soil scientists
Volume 4: Energy-conservation technicians; Petroleum technicians

Pharmacists

Definition

Pharmacists compound and dispense medicines and drugs as directed by prescription orders written by licensed physicians, dentists, and others who prescribe medicines. They also act as pharmaceutical consultants for health practitioners and the general public and keep records on the drugs and medicines dispensed to each person.

History

Although the first pharmacy about which we know was operated in Baghdad in the eighth century, the practice of brewing drugs and potions to help cure human ailments is as old as civilization itself. In many civilizations, the medicine man was both physician and pharmacist. In Western society, however, the two professions were separated by royal edict in A.D. 1240, when Emperor Frederick II of the Holy Roman Empire declared that the two practices should be carried on apart.

The word "pharmacist" itself can be traced to the early Greeks. During the time of Aristotle, those who compounded drugs were called "pharmakons." The word came down the ages in a direct line to our day. It has changed little from its original form and still means approximately the same thing: one who compounds drugs, medicines, or poisons.

Pharmacy as a profession grew slowly in the United States. It is said that one of our earliest pharmacists was Governor Winthrop of Massachusetts Bay Colony. He learned to compound drugs because there were no other sources in the colony for obtaining medicines. The first school established to teach pharmacy in this country was the Philadelphia College of Pharmacy, founded in 1821.

In 1906, the Federal Pure Food and Drug Act was passed. Succeeding years have seen the original act strengthened. In modern times, whenever a drug manufacturer makes extravagant and untrue claims for a product, the company is subject to discipline by the courts. The Food and Drug Administration approves all pharmaceuticals and drugs sold in the United States. The FDA was created in 1931, taking over the Bureau of Chemistry. That section of the Agriculture Department had approved chemicals since 1906.

Nature of the work

The work of the pharmacist has become increasingly important because of the complexity and potential side effects of the thousands of drugs on the market. Pharmacists must have thorough knowledge of chemicals and their properties; how drugs are made and tested for purity and strength; and how drugs affect both normal and sick persons. In addition to dispensing drugs and medicines according to written orders from physicians, dentists, and other health care practitioners, the pharmacist advises prescribers on the selection and use of medications. Pharmacists also inform and caution individuals about medicines and how to use them properly, answer questions from customers or patients about symptoms, and discuss nonprescription items such as headache remedies, vitamins, and cough syrups. Pharmacists also keep records of drugs and medications dispensed to each person so that they will be available in case of adverse reactions or side effects.

Some pharmacists specialize in preparing and dispensing radioactive drugs used for patient diagnosis and therapy. Known as *radiopharmacists* or *nuclear pharmacists*, these professionals combine the practice and principles of pharmacy and radiochemistry in their work.

Pharmacists may have a variety of other duties depending on where they are employed. Most pharmacists practice in community pharmacies, but some practice in hospitals and other health care facilities or in industry. Some pharmacists teach; some do research. The pharmacist may be employed in a laboratory, as a manufacturer's representative, or with the armed forces. Many practice with some branch of government, such as the U.S. Public Health Service.

Community pharmacies differ widely. One pharmacist may work in a store where the prescription counter may occupy only a tiny space. In another pharmacy, however, the pharmacist may be in surroundings that resemble a gleaming laboratory, all glass and tile. There are all shades of difference in pharmacies between the two extremes.

Wherever prescription orders are compounded, the area is as clean and sterile as possible. The pharmacist is acutely aware of the necessity for cleanliness, orderliness, and accuracy. He or she works with a variety of measuring and mixing devices, and with beakers,

473

A pharmacist checks the clarity of a solution that consists of vitamins and other nutrients. This solution will be fed intravenously to malnourished patients in a hospital.

bowls, bottles, and test tubes. However, more and more of the drugs we use are prepared for us by the pharmaceutical manufacturer in finished form. The actual compounding of prescription medications, therefore, is taking a smaller amount of time.

In addition to their pharmaceutical duties, pharmacists in community pharmacies may buy and sell other merchandise not related to health, hire and supervise other workers, and oversee the general operation of the pharmacy.

Pharmacists in hospitals and other health care facilities provide pharmaceutical services to aid physicians, nurses, and other health personnel with the care of patients. They dispense inpatient and outpatient prescription medicines, make sterile solutions or special mixtures, buy medical supplies, and perform administrative duties. They may also educate patients, monitor drug regimens, and review drug use. If the hospital is large, there may be the need for a large staff of pharmacists.

For the person with a degree in pharmacy who enjoys getting out and talking to people,

the job of "detail person" is attractive. A detail person is a representative of a pharmaceutical manufacturing firm, whose duty it is to visit physicians and pharmacists to discuss one's company's products, especially its new products. An analysis of the chemical makeup of new drugs and an explanation of the uses to which they may be put are very helpful to the physicians and pharmacists who will be working with them. Because hundreds of new drugs are introduced each year, the detail person has a busy schedule and an important role to play.

Many pharmacists are employed by large pharmaceutical manufacturers. They may be used in one of several capacities. Some are in research, to help develop new drugs or to improve or find new uses for old ones. Others supervise the preparation of ingredients that go into the capsules, ointments, solutions, or other products of the manufacturer. Still others test or standardize the raw or refined chemicals that eventually will go into the finished drug. Some may assist with advertising the company's products, to make sure that nothing untruthful or misleading is said about a drug in professional literature. Some pharmacists in such companies may write up a report on new products for pharmaceutical or technical journals. Others write material for package inserts.

Those who teach will usually do so in one of the seventy-four colleges of pharmacy presently established in this country. They may, however, also teach in medical schools or in schools of nursing.

Pharmacists employed by government agencies may be in one of a number of different kinds of positions. They may be inspectors, and check through drug manufacturing firms, laboratories, or wholesale, or community pharmacies. They may be a part of the law enforcement machinery, especially that part which is concerned with narcotics. Their position may be with an agency that is charged with the responsibility of maintaining the purity of cosmetics, drugs, and foods.

Some pharmacists write or edit reports for journals or draft technical papers; some work in advertising. Others are staff members in professional groups. A few are patent attorneys or experts in pharmaceutical law.

Requirements

A bachelor's degree in pharmacy is the minimum educational level required of anyone who wishes to practice as a pharmacist. Usually, this degree is obtained after five years of study beyond high school. (Some colleges of pharmacy, however, award a doctor of pharmacy [Pharm.D.] degree after six years of course-work.) One or two of these years may be obtained in a four-year undergraduate college or in a junior college. A prepharmacy course should include mathematics, physics, chemistry, and biology.

High-school students who anticipate entering a college of pharmacy should enroll in college preparatory courses and concentrate in the areas of mathematics and science.

When the prospective pharmacist receives a degree, he or she is then required to take a state board examination to be licensed to practice. Most states require that the pharmacist serve a one-year internship before being admitted to full practice. Part of this internship may be served during summer vacations while the young person is still a student. No state, however, allows more than half of the internship to be obtained in this way. Some states require that the hospital pharmacist must have served a two-year internship in a hospital setting before being admitted to full practice.

A master's degree or doctorate in pharmacy is usually required for research work or college teaching.

Special requirements

Pharmacists need a license to practice in all states, the District of Columbia, and U.S. territories. Applicants for a license must have graduated from an accredited pharmacy program and have passed a state board examination. They must also be over the age of twenty-one, be of good character, and have a specified amount of practical experience or have served an internship.

For students who are interested in becoming community pharmacists, there are several special requirements. First, they must like working with people and must be able to meet and talk with them easily. Second, they must like administrative details and be willing to keep records as required by law. They should be in good health and be able to stand on their feet for long hours. They must have a strongly developed sense of responsibility because the welfare of many people depends on their reliability.

They must be patient and tactful with those who try to obtain medicines without the proper prescription order. Pharmacists must also be able to explain without offending, to those who want medical advice, that they are not physicians and are not authorized to prescribe treatment or drugs.

Opportunities for experience and exploration

Students who are interested in pharmacy should obtain a summer or afternoon job in a pharmacy. They may work behind the scenes as a stock clerk, or be a salesperson or a delivery person. In such positions, students will have the opportunity to observe firsthand the kinds of experiences that pharmacists have, and to decide if this is the sort of career they might enjoy. Orderlies in a hospital also have the opportunity to observe the work of the hospital pharmacist.

Because almost every community has a pharmacy, it is not difficult for the average student to find an opportunity to talk with a neighborhood pharmacist. Most pharmacists are glad to discuss their careers and to give a great deal of helpful information to an interested student.

Related occupations

With similar academic preparation and training, persons interested in working with chemical compounds might become chemists, pharmacologists, pharmacy technicians, toxicologists, or scientists. Pharmaceutical industry workers are engaged in the manufacturing aspect of this field; many of these positions have less stringent requirements than those demanded of a fully qualified pharmacist.

Methods of entering

After having achieved the degree, the internship, and the license, most young pharmacists begin their careers by accepting a salaried position in a community pharmacy or a hospital. Many advance in salary and responsibility, but remain as an employee of someone else for the balance of their careers. Those who practice community pharmacy are more often in independent pharmacies than in corporation-owned pharmacies. Those who are employed by large corporations, however, usually earn more money and enjoy more benefits.

Advancement

Many pharmacists who begin their careers as the salaried employees of someone else eventually are able to purchase a pharmacy of their own. The hospital pharmacist may advance to the position of chief pharmacist or director of pharmacy services after accumulating several years of experience.

Pharmacists who are employed by drug manufacturing firms may anticipate increases in both salary and responsibility as they gain experience and increase their value to their firms.

Employment outlook

There were approximately 151,000 practicing pharmacists in the early 1990s. About 10 percent were self-employed; the others were salaried employees. The majority of all pharmacists work in community pharmacies, the next largest group hold positions in hospitals and other health care facilities, and the rest are employed by pharmaceutical manufacturing firms, wholesaling companies, and government and educational institutions.

The employment outlook in this field is expected to be good throughout the 1990s. The majority of job openings will result from the need to replace pharmacists who retire, and some new jobs will be created to meet changing needs.

The development of increasing numbers of drug products and of new ways of administering medication will raise the demand for pharmacists, as will the expansion of health maintenance organizations (HMOs) and other outpatient facilities. A growing and aging population will also create new jobs.

The strongest demand for pharmacists will be in community pharmacies. Not only will the number of traditional drugstores continue to grow, but there will be a great expansion of pharmacy services into nontraditional settings such as grocery stores and department stores.

Earnings

The earnings of salaried pharmacists are largely determined by the location, size, and type of employer as well as by the duties and responsibilities of the individual pharmacist. Pharmacists who do consulting work in addition to their primary job may have higher incomes, and those who own or manage pharmacies often earn considerably more.

In the early 1990s, full-time, salaried pharmacists earned a median salary of $31,600 per year, with about ten percent receiving $42,000 or more.

The average salary for pharmacists employed by chain drugstores was about $32,200; and for those employed by independent drugstores, $28,200.

Hospitals, medical schools, and medical centers paid average starting salaries of $26,700 for beginning pharmacists and $36,100 for experienced pharmacists.

Pharmacy graduates with a bachelor's degree but no experience started with the federal government at about $22,500 or $27,200, depending on their academic records. Those with additional years of experience received higher starting salaries. The overall average for pharmacists in the federal government in the early 1990s was about $30,100 a year.

Faculty personnel in colleges of pharmacy were paid approximately as follows: deans, $76,400; assistant or associate deans, $57,100; full professors, $57,900; associate professors, $43,700; and assistant professors, $36,000.

Conditions of work

The two most unfavorable conditions of the pharmacist's practice are long hours and the necessity for standing. It is not unusual to be on duty at least forty-eight hours a week. Most state laws covering the practice of pharmacy require that there be a pharmacist on duty at all times when the pharmacy is open. Most pharmacies employ at least two pharmacists because it is customary to remain open at least twelve hours a day. Many pharmacies are also open at least part of the time on Sundays.

A pharmacy, however, is usually a pleasant place to work. It is usually a neighborhood institution and often a health information center. Most pharmacies are well lighted, well ventilated, and kept in a clean and orderly fashion. Many chain-owned pharmacies now provide 18- or 24-hour operations. Night-shift positions may be the starting position of new pharmacists.

Hospital pharmacies are efficient, orderly, and busy with important activity. The physicians, nurses, technicians, and other medical personnel with whom the pharmacist works are usually intelligent and concerned people.

The industrial and government agency pharmacists will have varied and interesting experiences. Many will have opportunities to travel. Most salaried pharmacists receive paid vacations, health insurance, and other benefits.

Social and psychological factors

Pharmacists are likely to be able to find a position in the type of community desired. They are usually respected in their town as important professional persons. They often become leaders in community activities.

Pharmacists who operate their own pharmacies have economic responsibilities. They must hire employees, maintain an adequate inventory, keep records, and submit reports to various governmental agencies. They must make rent or mortgage payments and pay insurance premiums and taxes. Many pharmacies do better than $100,000 each year in business. The pharmacy is, therefore, an important economic factor in the community.

GOE: 02.04.01; SIC: 5912; SOC: 301

◇ **SOURCES OF ADDITIONAL INFORMATION**

American Association of Colleges of Pharmacy
1426 Prince Street
Alexandria, VA 22314

American Council on Pharmaceutical Education
311 West Superior Street, Suite 512
Chicago, IL 60610

American Pharmaceutical Association
2215 Constitution Avenue, NW
Washington, DC 20037

American Society of Hospital Pharmacists
4630 Montgomery Avenue
Bethesda, MD 20814

National Association of Chain Drug Stores
PO Box 1417-D49
Alexandria, VA 22313

NARD—National Association of Retail Druggists
205 Daingerfield Road
Alexandria, VA 22314

◇ **RELATED ARTICLES**

Volume 1: Chemicals and Drugs; Health Care
Volume 2: Biochemists; Chemists; Pharmacologists; Toxicologists
Volume 3: Pharmaceutical industry workers
Volume 4: Biological technicians; Chemical technicians; Pharmaceutical technicians

Pharmacologists

Definition

Pharmacologists play an important role in medicine and in science by studying the effects of drugs, chemicals, and other materials on humans and animals. These highly educated specialists perform research designed to identify the effects of drugs and other substances on living organs and tissues and on the vital life processes of humans and animals. The goals of pharmacological research are to determine how drugs and other chemicals act at the cellular level; to discover how drugs should be most effectively used; to standardize drug dosages; to analyze chemicals, food additives, poisons, insecticides, and other substances to determine their effects; and to identify dangerous substances as well as dangerous levels of chemicals.

History

The field of pharmacology is an outgrowth of the field of chemistry, particularly medical chemistry, which in the 1800s developed ways of isolating various plant ingredients and syn-

477

thesizing those ingredients into medicines. These early chemists saw the need not only to isolate active chemical compounds from plants, but also to study the effects of these compounds to produce them in appropriate dosages for use in medicine. A tradition of testing drugs and other chemicals on animals before testing them on humans emerged out of the obvious necessity to protect human life wherever possible while still attempting to introduce new medicines into general use. The forerunners of modern pharmacology were involved in the development of antibiotics, anesthetics, vaccines, tranquilizers, vitamins, and many other substances in wide use today. Pharmacologists have been instrumental, for example, in the development of ether and other anesthetics that have permitted the modernization of surgical procedures. Pharmacologists were involved in the development of lifesaving substances such as penicillin, the tetanus vaccine, the polio vaccine, anti-malaria drugs, and countless other lifesaving compounds. Pharmacologists were able to make use of black mold from bread to develop the chemical known as penicillin. Other such unlikely forms of life are continually studied for their medical potential.

The field of pharmacology became an independent field of research as it became clear that the work of the early chemists was intimately related to the fields of pharmacy and medicine. The field of pharmacology grew as it became increasingly necessary to have specialized pharmacologists devoted to the detailed study and development of medical drugs and compounds and to the proper medical use of such items.

Pharmacology is not the same as pharmacy. Pharmacology is the basic and clinical science concerned with the interactions between chemicals and biological systems. Pharmacy is the health profession responsible for preparation and dispensing of drugs to patients.

Beginning with the establishment of the early academic institutions, such as the Pennsylvania Medical School in 1765 and the Philadelphia College of Pharmacy in 1821–1822, actions of drugs in healing were academic topics. With the scientific advances of the early twentieth century, especially experimental use of drugs in Europe and the introduction of antibacterial drugs into medicine in the early 1900s, pharmacology gained recognition as a distinct discipline. Also, the Federal Food, Drug, and Cosmetic Act of 1938 required rigorous studies of drugs before they could be marketed. Those regulations continue today with the Food and Drug Administration (FDA).

Nature of the work

In general, the activities of pharmacologists can be divided into two areas: the development and testing of new drugs for use in medicine; and the testing of chemicals, pollutants, poisons, and other materials to determine their effects upon animals and humans. Although in its early stages pharmacology was devoted strictly to development of new drugs, more recently society has turned to pharmacologists to perform a much broader range of activities including the testing of pesticides, the identification of poisons and their effects, the analysis of industrial pollutants, the analysis of food preservatives and food colorings, and the study of other substances and their effects upon the environment as well as upon human beings. Pharmacologists are engaged in a range of research that includes all aspects of modern molecular and cellular biology as well as effects of drugs in animals and humans.

Pharmacologists are highly trained individuals who must have a knowledge of chemistry, biology, physiology, mathematics, computer science, and physics to perform their work effectively. Much of pharmacological research is performed in laboratories using laboratory animals, plants, and human tissues to study the effects of drugs, chemicals, or other substances. In some cases, chemicals or substances are injected into laboratory animals, and, in other cases, they are cultured with live tissue samples from animals or from human donors. In recent years, the field of pharmacology has branched beyond pure medical and drug research and into research involving substances used in the environment, in agricultural, and in industry. Pharmacologists have become active in identifying toxic substances in the work place, in pesticides, in food preservatives and colorings, and even in common household items such as paints, aerosol sprays, and cleaning fluid.

Because the field of pharmacology has expanded into a number of subspecialties, most pharmacologists specialize in a particular type of research. Those specializing in drug research utilize animals and humans to study the effects of drugs and medical compounds upon specific organs or bodily systems as well as to study side effects that may be harmful. Once pharmacologists have identified the positive and negative aspects of a drug, they are better able to predict usefulness in specific diseases and to recommend proper dosages as well as to advise the medical community as to the circumstances in which the drug should be administered.

Some pharmacologists specialize in particular parts of the human body: those focusing on drugs relating to the nervous system are known as *neuropharmacologists*; those specializing upon the effect of drugs relating to the cardiovascular and circulatory systems are called *cardiovascular pharmacologists*; and those specializing upon the effects of drugs relating to the hormonal balance of the body are known as *endocrine pharmacologists*. Within the past twenty years, there has been a widespread use of psychotropic drugs, or drugs that influence mood and behavior patterns, and a subspecialty of pharmacology known as *psychopharmacology* has emerged in response to the need to better identify and develop drugs relating to human and animal behavior.

Some pharmacologists specialize strictly in testing various drugs and compounds on human subjects, and these specialists are known as *clinical pharmacologists*. It is not uncommon for teams of pharmacologists to work together, especially in the development of complex drugs as well as drugs and compounds that are capable of treating numerous diseases.

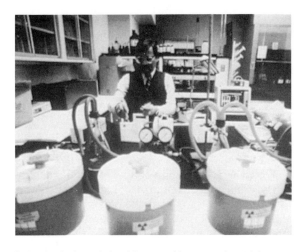

A pharmacologist works in a laboratory with new experimental drugs that are designed for potential medical use.

Requirements

Nearly all pharmacologists earn a doctorate. The doctorate in pharmacology is usually earned at an accredited medical school or at an accredited school of pharmacy. Because pharmacology is so intimately related with the practice of medicine, many pharmacologists are also medical doctors (M.D.s), and some pharmacologists who specialize in animal pharmacology are doctors of veterinary medicine (D.V.M.s). It is not uncommon for the course in pharmacology to resemble closely many aspects of the training for M.D.s, and in some cases pharmacologists become M.D.s, while in other cases M.D.s become pharmacologists. In either case, the best places to study pharmacology are large university medical centers that offer degrees for a variety of medical disciplines. As mentioned above, certain veterinary schools offer degrees in veterinary pharmacology as well. It is important for those aspiring to enter the field of pharmacology to begin preparing for the field in high school because a good science and mathematics background is essential. Both high-school and college students should emphasize the sciences, physical chemistry, biology, organic chemistry, and mathematics. In addition, high-school and college students need to take courses in English so that they may be prepared to write intelligent research reports.

During the last two years of college students should consider what graduate programs in pharmacology they would consider attending and should make certain to apply to accredited institutions. The major professional organization of pharmacologists is the American Society for Pharmacology and Experimental Therapeutics, and this organization, which was founded in 1908, can provide a list of all accredited pharmacology graduate programs as well as other relevant information. Once a student has been accepted to such an institution, the doctoral program requires from four to six years of study. This study involves taking intense courses in biomedical sciences, undertaking independent and supervised research, and successfully completing an original research project as well as writing a doctoral thesis on that project.

Special requirements

Pharmacologists have the advantage of belonging to a profession that is both rigorous and also creative. Pharmacologists must have full command of a great deal of technical information and a thorough knowledge of various types of experimental procedures while, at the same time, possessing the creative drive and abilities to experiment with new ideas and with approaches that could yield results new to the medical community or to society in general.

These specialists need to know when a particular line of inquiry or research is not fruitful and when to give up. It is not uncommon for months of research to be unproductive, and pharmacologists must maintain a positive outlook, realizing that they will not always make the breakthroughs that they desire. Finally, pharmacologists frequently work in teams; therefore, the ability to work with other people

479

as well as to coordinate complex research tasks among a wide group of people are qualities that pharmacologists need to have if they wish to gain advancement in this field.

Opportunities for experience and exploration

The best way for high-school or college students to learn about pharmacology is to become acquainted with pharmacologists and with pharmacology instructors who are usually located at major medical schools. Large medical center hospitals also employ pharmacologists, and these people may provide valuable sources of "real world" information.

Medical and other laboratories frequently employ part-time personnel to assist with various tasks, and it is sometimes possible to secure a part-time job in a pharmacological laboratory, although high-school and college students need to keep in mind that they may be competing with pharmacological graduate students for such positions.

As indicated previously, the major professional society in this field is the American Society for Pharmacology and Experimental Therapeutics (ASPET). ASPET itself has information concerning accredited pharmacology educational programs, information regarding academic institutions and hospitals employing pharmacologists, information relating to laboratories, drug companies, and other branches of the profession who employ pharmacologists, and information concerning the various subspecialties of pharmacology. Some of these subspecialties have organizations and professional societies themselves such as the American Society of Pharmacognosy (the study of natural drugs), the American College of Neuropsychopharmacology, the American Society for Clinical Pharmacology and Therapeutics, the American Association of Pharmaceutical Scientists, the American Society of Veterinary Physiologists and Pharmacologists, and the American Academy of Clinical Toxicology.

Related occupations

The qualities and interests that attract an individual to the field of pharmacology are found in a number of fields. These may include human medicine and the occupations of physicians, osteopaths, registered nurses, licensed practical nurses, orderlies, any number of technicians,

surgeons, veterinarians, pharmacists, dentists, and podiatrists. Or these interests may be focused more toward the research and theoretical professions of university faculty members, chemists, physicists, biological scientists, agricultural scientists, botanists, or a host of industrial or research technician occupations.

Methods of entering

As indicated previously, it is desirable—and for practical purposes required—to earn a doctorate in Pharmacology to enter this profession. The American Society for Pharmacology and Experimental Therapeutics can provide information relating to accredited programs in the field, and college students should be able to obtain information from the job placement offices of their respective college or university.

Drug companies, research organizations, medical schools and universities, and other organizations including the federal and state governments often recruit pharmacologists who are earning their doctorates. Most pharmacologists have a pretty good idea of what subspecialty they would like to pursue by the second year of their doctoral program, and organizations representing and employing members in that subspecialty should be sought out. Because pharmacology has been a growing field in recent years, it is not uncommon for recruiters in their various disciplines from a variety of organizations to seek out qualified candidates from the pharmacology graduate programs.

Advancement

Because the field of pharmacology involves dealing with substances that have wide-reaching implications of life and death, most beginning pharmacologists start out at laboratories at a junior level working for more advanced pharmacologists. They learn the proper laboratory procedures, they learn how to deal with the Food and Drug Administration and various other governmental agencies, and they learn about the testing of drugs and other substances with animal and human subjects. In private industry and in academic laboratories, including drug companies, advancement in the field of pharmacology usually means supervising a number of people in a laboratory setting and heading up major research projects. Government pharmacology workers may obtain similar types of promotions, although the civil service regulations and tenure characteristics do come into play. Some pharmacologists choose to be teachers, in which case they aspire to become department heads, supervise research laboratories at universities, present public papers, and speak at major conferences.

Employment outlook

The field of pharmacology has been growing at a healthy pace and is expected to continue to grow significantly during the 1990s as a result of two factors. First, the health care and health care related industries in general are expected to continue to expand, and this means that the activities of drug companies, hospitals, medical schools, and the government in pharmacological research will continue to be strong. Second, the growing proliferation of pharmacological subspecialties is expected to continue as the pharmacology profession in general is called upon to continue its efforts in evaluating the effects of environmental substances, household products, drugs, atmospheric gases, substances used in the work place, and other substances. In some ways, pharmacologists can be considered to be the chemical, drug, and substance detectives of our society, constantly evaluating the toxicology or therapeutic value of various substances. For these reasons, the field of pharmacology, together with the various subspecialties, is expected to grow significantly in the future.

Earnings

Pharmacologists generally work in laboratories and generally work a regular workweek of approximately forty hours. At times, however, it may be necessary for a professional in this field to work longer hours to complete or supervise specific experiments. Beginning pharmacologists who have earned a doctorate from an accredited institution can expect starting salaries in the range of $30,000 to $45,000 per year. Experienced pharmacologists, including those in supervisory roles, can earn $50,000 or more per year, and pharmacologists who have the Ph.D. and M.D. degree can earn substantially more than $100,000 per year. Normally, the higher-salaried pharmacologists are those who are supervising teams of people in larger laboratory or university settings.

Conditions of work

Most pharmacologists can expect to work in pleasant surroundings, usually in laboratories. While laboratories vary in their condition and quality, most laboratories associated with major research institutions or major hospitals are fairly modern and are equipped with the sophisticated instruments necessary for modern research. Because pharmacologists perform such a vital role with respect to drug and chemical research, their laboratories tend to be fairly up-to-date. This is especially true with respect to pharmacologists who work for large pharmaceutical companies.

Although most pharmacologists work a regular workweek, they are expected to be diligent and to follow through on all experiments. The equipment and the necessary apparatus is sometimes quite costly, and it is not uncommon for experiments to last weeks or months; therefore, perseverance in this field is extremely important, and pharmacologists need to recognize their responsibilities.

Social and psychological factors

As mentioned previously, both diligence and patience are required in field of pharmacology. Results are often not dramatic and are gained in inches rather than yards. In addition, teamwork is an essential ingredient to the successful practice of pharmacology, for one must be able to leverage one's time through a team so that complex experiments can proceed according to an efficient schedule.

There are circumstances in which pharmacologists come under intense time pressure to achieve results especially where loss of life may involve unexplained chemicals or other substances. In some cases, pharmacologists are called upon to work with forensic biologists, coroners, or others involved in attempting to determine causes of death under specific circumstances. The ability to think logically, to function under pressure, and to behave in an even-tempered way are all important ingredients under such circumstances.

Because the major purpose of pharmacology is to find answers to questions that medical science, environmental science, or other aspects of science may not know, it is vitally important that pharmacologists have a creative instinct and the willingness to experiment with new approaches. This creative instinct, combined with the technical background and know-how and with the discipline of proper laboratory methodology, can bring a pharmacologist both financial success and great personal satisfaction as he or she pursues an occupation vital to the livelihood of us all.

GOE: 02.02.01; SIC: 2834; SOC: 1855

American Society for Pharmacology and Experimental Therapeutics
9650 Rockville Pike
Bethesda, Maryland 20814

Photographers and camera operators

Definition

Photographers and *camera operators* take and sometimes develop pictures of people, places, objects, and events, using a variety of cameras and photographic equipment. The work may be ordered by people who want their portraits or by companies that use commercial photographers for various business purposes. Professional photographers are usually specialists. Television and motion picture camera operators film movies, TV programs, and commercials.

History

The word *photograph* means, literally, "to write with light." Although the art of photography goes back only about 150 years, the two Greek words that were chosen and combined to refer to this skill quite accurately describe what it does.

The discoveries that led eventually to photography began early in the eighteenth century when an obscure German scientist, Dr. Johann H. Schultze, made some experiments with the action of light on certain chemicals. He found that when these chemicals were covered by dark paper they did not change color, but when they were exposed to sunlight, they darkened. This observation led eventually to the work of a French painter named Daguerre, who became the first photographer in 1839, when he perfected the process of using silver-iodide-coated plates inside a small box. He then developed the plates by means of mercury vapor. The daguerreotype, as these early photographs came to be known, took minutes to expose and the developing process was directly to the plate. There were no prints made.

Although the daguerreotype was the sensation of its day, it was not until George Eastman invented a simple camera and flexible roll film that photography began to come into widespread use, in 1889. With exposure to the negative, light sensitive paper was used to make positive multiple copies of the image.

Motion pictures were made as early as 1877, using a series of still photographs to create the illusion of motion, but it was Thomas Edison who, in 1889, produced the first single-unit motion picture camera that set the standard for today.

Nature of the work

Photography is both an artistic and a technical occupation because many still photographers produce pictures that not only reveal their own proficiency but also are so beautifully composed that they are works of fine art. In all kinds of photographic work the photographer must be able to use a variety of cameras, lenses, and filters to achieve a desired effect. They also must utilize many kinds of film and must know which to use for each type of picture, lighting condition, camera, and filter. The ability to use different kinds of lighting equipment when necessary is also required knowledge of the photographer. In addition, photographers must understand and be able to use and carry through the processing by which pictures are developed, enlarged, and printed. Although in many large studios photographic technicians are employed to do this technical work, in many small shops and photographic departments the photographers themselves may have to do it.

Many professional *still photographers* specialize, the most common specialties being portrait work, commercial photography, and industrial photography.

Portrait photographers take pictures of individuals or small groups. They try to attain not only a natural-looking and attractive effect, but also one that expresses the personality of the individual. Most portrait photographers work in their own studios, though they also go to people's homes and other places to take pictures.

In commercial photography, a photographer usually takes pictures of merchandise, exteriors and interiors, machinery, and fashions, both indoors and outdoors, to be used in advertising and selling. A great variety of cameras, lights, and props are used in commercial photography, and the photographer must have a full command of all kinds of photographic techniques, including the use of color film.

The industrial photographer does work that is similar to that of the commercial photographer. The main emphasis, however, is on taking pictures for a single company or firm that may lead to the improvement of factory organization and products. To accomplish this end, the industrial photographer takes pictures of workers on the job and of equipment and machinery operating at high speed. The pictures are generally used in company publications or for advertising company products or services.

Some other photographic specialists are described briefly below:

Photojournalists take pictures of newsworthy events, people, places, and things for newspa-

As a member of a news service, this photographer attends a political event where he and other photographers are sectioned off. He is using a powerful zoom lens to take pictures of the event from a distance.

pers and magazines, combining an ability to find and record dramatic action with photographic talent. Some photojournalists specialize in educational photography and prepare slides, film strips, and motion pictures for use in the classroom.

Aerial photographers take photographs from aircraft in flight for news, business, industrial, scientific, or military purposes.

Scientific photographers and *biological photographers* provide photographic illustrations and documentation for scientific publications and research reports. They usually specialize in a field such as engineering, aerodynamics, medicine, biology, or chemistry.

Finish photographers photograph the results of horse races as the horses approach and then cross the finish line.

Nightclub and restaurant photographers circulate among the tables taking pictures of customers who request them.

Motion pictures photographers and *camera operators* film movies, TV programs, and commercials. Some camera operators work for television networks and stations covering news events. In the entertainment field, camera operators are usually supervised by *directors of photography*, who plan and coordinate the filming of motion pictures. Other specialists in this field include *animation camera operators*, who film animated cartoons with special cameras; and *optical-effects-camera operators*, who create illusions for television and movies.

In addition, some photographers write for trade and technical journals, teach photography in schools and colleges, act as representatives of photographic equipment manufacturers, sell photographic equipment and supplies, produce documentary films, or do free-lance work.

483

Requirements

Formal education requirements depend upon the nature of the photographer's specialty. For instance, photographic work in scientific and engineering research generally requires an engineering background with a degree from a recognized college or institute.

A college education is not required to become a photographer, although college training probably offers the most promising assurance of success in fields such as industrial, news, or scientific photography. In the early 1990s, 103 community and junior colleges offered associate degrees in photography, more than 160 colleges and universities offered bachelor's degrees, and 38 offered master's degrees. Many of the same schools offer courses in cinematography, although very few have programs leading to a degree in this specialty. Many men and women, however, become photographers with no formal education beyond high school.

Prospective photographers should have broad technical understanding of photography plus as much practical experience with a camera as possible. They should take many different kinds of pictures with many different kinds of cameras and subjects. They should also learn how to develop pictures and, if possible, should have a darkroom. Experience in picture composition, in cropping prints (cutting to desired size), in enlarging, and in retouching are all valuable.

Students who hope to become a photographer or camera operator should possess manual dexterity, good eyesight and color vision, and artistic ability. They should have an eye for form and line, an appreciation of light and shadow, as well as an ability to use imaginative and creative approaches to photographs or film, especially in commercial work. In addition, they should be patient and accurate and enjoy working with detail.

A pleasing personality and the ability to put people at ease are especially needed by a portrait photographer.

If a student hopes to become a press photographer or photojournalist, he or she should possess good health and stamina, because one may have to work long hours, work during emergencies, and work in all kinds of weather and, possibly, under many varieties of hardship. The press photographer may have to travel, often to distant places.

Beginning photographers and camera operators develop their skills through on-the-job training. This is especially important to camera operators because so few colleges and universities offer full programs in motion picture photography.

Special requirements

There are no special requirements in this field, except where specific technical knowledge might be necessary.

Self-employed (free-lance) photographers, of course, need good business skills. They must be able to manage their own studios, including hiring and managing photographic assistants and other employees, keeping accurate records, and maintaining photographic and business files. Marketing and sales skills are also important to a successful free-lance photography business.

Opportunities for experience and exploration

Photography is a field that almost every young person with a camera may explore. There are high-school camera clubs, photography contests, and community hobby groups. A student may seek a part-time or summer job in a camera shop or work as a developer in a laboratory.

Related occupations

There are many specialties within the field of photography, some of which are mentioned above, under "Nature of the work." Photographers also have talents similar to other visual artists, such as designers, illustrators, painters, and sculptors. Individuals interested in the technical aspect of photography may wish to explore occupations in the photofinishing industry (developing film, making prints and enlargements, and otherwise processing still or motion picture film) or in the manufacture or repair of photographic apparatus, accessories, and materials (including photocopy and microfilm equipment).

Methods of entering

There is no one way in which to become a photographer or camera operator. Some persons choose to enter the field as an apprentice, trainee, or assistant. A trainee may work in a darkroom, a camera shop, or a developing laboratory. He or she may also move lights and arrange backgrounds for a commercial or a portrait photographer or for a motion picture photographer. Trainees may spend many months in learning this kind of job before they move into a job behind a camera. In many large cities there are schools of photography, which may be a good way to start in the field.

A press photographer may work for one of the many newspapers and magazines published in the United States and abroad. Some employers require a probationary period of from thirty to ninety days before a new employee attains full job security. On publications where there is a full Newspaper Guild shop, a photographer will be required to join the Guild.

Some persons go into business for themselves as soon as they have finished their formal education. Setting up a studio may not require a large capital outlay, but beginners will find that success does not come easily.

Advancement

Because photography is such a diversified field, there is no "usual" way in which to get ahead. Those who begin by working with someone else may advance to owning their own businesses. The commercial photographer may gain in prestige as more of his or her pictures are placed in well-known trade journals or popular magazines. The press photographer may advance in salary and in the kinds of important news stories to which he or she is assigned. Camera operators advance as their work circulates and they establish a reputation. A few photographers have become celebrities in their own right. Some have made singular contributions to medical science, engineering science, and to natural or physical science.

Employment outlook

About 109,000 photographers and camera operators were employed in the early 1990s. About half were salaried employees; the rest were self-employed. Most jobs for photographers are provided by photographic or commercial art studios; other employers include newspapers and magazines, radio and TV broadcasting and motion picture companies, government agencies, and manufacturing firms. Colleges, universities, and other educational institutions employ photographers to prepare promotional and educational materials. Camera operators work almost exclusively in TV broadcasting and motion picture studios.

It is predicted that there will be a very favorable employment increase in photography throughout the 1990s as the use of visual images continues grow in many areas, such as communication, education, entertainment, marketing, and research and development. In business and industry, for example, greater use will be made of photographs, videocassettes, training films, and other visual aids in meetings, stockholders' reports, sales campaigns, and public relations programs. Excellent opportunities should exist also for scientific and medical photographers. On the other hand, photojournalism is expected to show slow growth.

The demand for camera operators in the entertainment field will increase rapidly, but there will be strong competition for these much sought after jobs.

More and more, jobs will go to those who are talented and who have had formal post–high-school training in the field, either in college, junior college, or special technical institute.

Earnings

The earnings of photographers and camera operators in private industry varies according to the level of responsibility. In the early 1990s, those who handled routine work were paid an average of about $16,600 per year. At the midlevel, wages averaged from $22,900 to $31,600. Photographers who did difficult work were paid about $35,100. Camera operators usually earn more than photographers.

In the early 1990s, beginning photographers working for newspapers that had contracts with the Newspaper Guild had a median salary of about $19,000 a year. Most earned between $16,500 and $22,500, with the top 10 percent receiving $26,500 or more. Experienced newspaper photographers earned a median of $30,700 a year, with most of them in the $26,300-to-$35,700 range. The top 10 percent of experienced newspaper photographers earned in excess of $38,900.

Photographers in government service earned an average salary of about $23,900 a year. Self-employed photographers often earn more than salaried photographers, but their earnings depend on general business conditions. In addition, self-employed photographers do not have the benefits that a company provides its employees.

Photographers who combine scientific training and camera skill, as do scientific photographers, will usually start at higher salaries than do other photographers. They also usually receive consistently larger advances in salary than do others, so that their income both as beginners and as experienced photographers will place them well above the average in their field. Photographers in salaried jobs usually receive benefits such as paid holidays, vacations, and sick leave.

Conditions of work

Work conditions vary with the job to be done. Many photographers work thirty-five to forty-hour workweek, but freelancers, news photographers, and camera operators often put in long, irregular hours. Commercial and portrait photographers work in comfortable surroundings. Photojournalists can never be assured of physical comfort in their work and may, in fact, face danger when covering stories on natural disasters or military conflicts. Some photographers work in a research laboratory setting, others may work from an aircraft, and still others may work underwater. For some photographers, conditions change from day to day. One day, they may be photographing a hot and dusty rodeo; the next day, they may be taking pictures of a dogsled race in Alaska.

In general, photographers and camera operators work under pressure to meet deadlines and satisfy customers. Free-lance photographers have the added pressure of continually seeking new clients.

Social and psychological factors

Some photographers work a forty-hour week and enjoy approximately the same schedule as do most other working people. Others, however, who work on assignment, may have to spend long periods of time away from home or may find their rest disturbed, their recreation interrupted, and their vacations cancelled because of being called out on a special emergency.

For specialists in fields such as fashion photography, breaking into the field may take years. Working as another photographer's assistant is physically demanding if carrying equipment is required.

For freelance photographers, the cost of equipment can be quite expensive, without any assurance that the money spent will be regained in work assignments. Freelancers in travel-related photography, such as travel and tourism, or photo journalism, have the added cost of transportation. Their accomodations may not be adequate or pre-arranged. Flexibility is a major asset to a photographer.

For those who choose photographic specialties such as press photography, their private life may suffer. The satisfactions to be gained in this profession, however, usually outweigh the disadvantages.

GOE: 01.02.03; SIC: 7221; SOC: 326

◇ **SOURCES OF ADDITIONAL INFORMATION**

American Society of Cinematographers
1728 North Orange Drive
Hollywood, CA 90028

American Society of Magazine Photographers
419 Park Avenue, South
Suite 1407
New York, NY 10016

The Newspaper Guild
8611 Second Avenue
Silver Spring, MD 20910

Professional Photographers of America
1090 Executive Way
Des Plaines, IL 60018

◇ **RELATED ARTICLES**

Volume 1: Advertising; Book Publishing; Broadcasting; Magazine Publishing; Motion Pictures; Newspaper Publishing; Public Relations
Volume 2: Advertising workers
Volume 3: Photographic laboratory occupations
Volume 4: Darkroom technicians; Film laboratory technicians; Photographic equipment technicians; Video technicians

---

Physical therapists

Definition

Physical therapists, formerly called *physiotherapists*, are health care specialists who test and measure the function of the musculoskeletal, neurological, pulmonary, and cardiovascular systems and treat problems in these systems caused by illness, injury, or birth defect. Physical therapists work with preventive, restorative, and rehabilitative treatment for their patients.

History

Physical therapy puts into a formal health care delivery structure some theories and practices that have existed for centuries. The ancient Greeks knew the value of the sun's rays, of exercise in warm water, and of massage. People in the far north countries of Europe have utilized physical therapy principles for centuries to great advantage. In the United States, the fashionable watering places of the very rich have always utilized hot baths, heat applications, and massage for the relief of such ailments as rheumatism, arthritis, the paralysis caused by strokes, and other handicapping ailments. Mental hospitals have used hydrotherapy for many years either to stimulate or to calm patients.

The practice of physical therapy has grown as our knowledge of medicine and our understanding of the functions of the human body have grown. World War I helped to bring about tremendous strides in medical practice, and physical therapy really made its value known during that time. With the organizing of a professional association in 1921, physical therapy began to achieve professional stature. The American Physical Therapy Association (APTA) now serves a membership of more than 45,000 physical therapists, physical therapist assistants, and students and publishes a journal, *Physical Therapy*, which provides information about current developments in the field.

It was during World War II that the real worth of physical therapy was recognized. The experiences of medical teams in the armed forces during that time with rehabilitating seriously injured soldiers by the use of physical therapy contributed toward the medical acceptance of this practice.

Nature of the work

Physical therapy has expanded beyond hospitals, where it has been traditionally practiced. Physical therapists are now working in private practices, nursing homes, sports medicine clinics, home health agencies, public and private schools, academic institutions, hospices, and in industrial wellness programs—a reflection of their versatility of skills and the public's need for comprehensive health care.

To initiate a program of physical therapy, the physical therapist consults the patient's medical history, examines the patient and identifies problems, confers with the physician or other health care professionals involved in the patient's care, establishes objectives and treatment goals that are consistent with the patient's needs, and determines the methods for accomplishing the objectives.

Treatment goals established by the physical therapist include preventing disability, relieving pain, and restoring function. In the presence of illness or injury, the ultimate goal is to assist the patient's physical recovery and reentry into the community, home, and work environment at the highest level of independence and self-sufficiency possible.

To aid and maintain recovery, the physical therapist also provides patient education to involve the patient in his or her own care. The educational program may include exercises, posture reeducation, and relaxation practices. In many instances, the patient's family is involved in the educational program by providing emotional support or physical assistance as needed. These activities evolve into a continuum of self-care when the patient is discharged from the physical therapy program.

The care physical therapists provide for many types of patients of all ages includes working with burn victims to prevent abnormal scarring and loss of movement, with stroke victims to regain movement and independent living, with cancer patients to relieve discomfort, and with cardiac patients to improve endurance and achieve independence. Physical therapists also provide preventive exercise programs, postural improvement, and physical conditioning to individuals who perceive the need to promote their own health and wellness.

Physical therapists should have a creative approach to their work. No two patients respond to exactly the same kind of treatment. The challenge is to find the right way to make

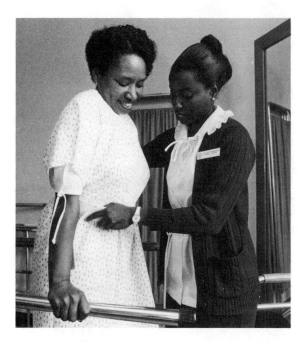

A physical therapist helps a woman learn to walk. Therapists must convey optimism and build confidence in his or her patients before treatment can be truly effective.

the patient want to make progress, to respond to treatment, to feel a sense of achievement, and to refuse to become discouraged if progress is slow.

Sometimes the physical therapist must devise tools or treatments that are uniquely helpful for one patient's problems but that might never be effective with anyone else. The therapist may design a buttonhook that will help one patient learn to dress himself or herself again or may make a combination spoon and fork to help another patient learn to eat unaided. One may have to experiment with new braces or weights and pulleys to help a patient learn to walk upright.

Many physical therapists acquire specialized knowledge through clinical experience and educational preparation in specialty areas of practice, such as cardiopulmonary physical therapy, clinical electrophysiologic physical therapy, neurologic physical therapy, orthopedic physical therapy, pediatric physical therapy, and sports physical therapy.

Requirements

Physical therapists attain their professional skills through extensive educational and clinical training. The educational credentials necessary to practice physical therapy are currently obtained from accredited university or college programs in one of three ways: a bachelor's degree in physical therapy, a certificate in physical therapy if an individual has a bachelor's degree in a related field, or a master's degree if an individual has a bachelor's degree in a related field.

Entry-level training is offered in ninety-seven bachelor's degree programs, six certificate programs, and twenty-five master's degree programs. One way to obtain a master's degree is in the U.S. Army Baylor University Program in Physical Therapy. Applicants must be U.S. citizens under thirty years of age and have a bachelor's degree (or be in the final semester before attaining the degree) with satisfactory completion of courses in the biological, physical, and behavioral sciences and advanced statistics. They must also meet prescribed medical fitness standards. Persons selected for this program are commissioned as second lieutenants in the Army Medical Specialist Corps Reserve.

The curriculum for physical therapy students has been steadily expanding to meet the increasing medical technology. To accommodate this expansion, the minimum professional entry-level requirement is advancing to the postbaccalaureate degree. This change will provide physical therapists with a more comprehensive background in clinical education and research essential for total patient care.

Preparation is the key for potential physical therapy students. Serious competition exists among students for enrollment in physical therapy educational programs; on average, five students apply for every opening. High-school students who plan to become physical therapists should have a strong background in the physical and biological sciences. Additionally, an exhibited desire for helping people—for example, having done some kind of volunteer service—will help ensure a student's successful academic career in physical therapy.

Special requirements

Upon graduating from an accredited physical therapy educational program, physical therapists must secure a license by successfully completing a licensure examination and comply with the legal requirements of the jurisdiction in which they practice. These qualifications are required in all fifty states, the District of Columbia, the Virgin Islands, and the commonwealth of Puerto Rico.

Specialty certification of physical therapists, while not a requirement for employment, is a desirable advanced credential. The American Board of Physical Therapy Specialties, an appointed group of the American Physical Therapy Association, certifies physical therapists who demonstrate specialized knowledge and advanced clinical proficiency in a specialty area of physical therapy practice and who pass a certifying examination. The six areas currently involved in this process are cardiopulmonary, clinical electrophysiologic, neurologic, orthopedic, pediatric, and sports physical therapy.

Opportunities for experience and exploration

The young person interested in exploring the possibility of a career as a physical therapist might work as a counselor in a summer camp for the handicapped or as an orderly or a nurse's aide in a hospital in which there is a physical therapy program. The high-school counselor may invite a physical therapist to talk at Career Day, and students who are interested in the field may then have an opportunity to ask questions or may be invited to visit the therapist at work.

In addition, the American Physical Therapy Association offers a career kit on physical therapy that includes a "Careers in Physical Therapy" brochure listing APTA-accredited physical therapy programs. Students can receive this kit by writing to the American Physical Therapy Association.

Related occupations

Other workers concerned with the treatment and rehabilitation of individuals with physical or mental disabilities or disorders include chiropractors, kinesiotherapists, occupational therapists, orthotists, prosthetists, respiratory therapists, and speech-language pathologists and audiologists. Athletic trainers, too, require similar knowledge and training. Persons interested in the field of physical therapy may also want to examine the occupations of exercise instructors and physical education teachers.

Methods of entering

Physical therapy graduates may obtain jobs through their college placement offices or by answering ads in professional journals. They can apply in person or send letters and resumes to hospitals, medical centers, rehabilitation facilities, and other places that hire physical therapists. Some find jobs through the American Physical Therapy Association. Veterans Administration hospitals and other government agencies offer another source of employment.

Advancement

Advancement made by the therapist is not only in salary scale, but also in responsibility. In a hospital or other type of facility, one may rise from being a staff physical therapist to being the chief physical therapist and then become director of the department.

Administrative responsibilities are usually given to those physical therapists who have had several years of experience, plus the personal qualities that prepare them for undertaking this kind of assignment.

After serving in a hospital or other institution for several years, many physical therapists open up their own practices or go into a group practice.

Employment outlook

Physical therapy is one of the fastest-growing professions in the United States and one of the few professions that enjoy a 100-percent employment rate.

The growth in the number of physical therapy practitioners parallels the progress made in the profession. In 1941 there were approximately 1,200 physical therapists. By the early 1990s, there were about 61,000 licensed physical therapists in the country, and more positions are being created every year.

One reason for this rapid growth is the fact that the population as a whole is getting older and developing problems that cause physical pain and disability. Another reason is the public's growing interest in physical fitness, which has resulted in an increasing number of athletic injuries requiring physical therapy. In industry and fitness centers, a growing interest in pain and injury prevention also has created new opportunities for physical therapists.

Employment prospects for physical therapists should continue to be excellent throughout the 1990s. Hospitals are expected to remain the largest employer, with nursing homes and home health agencies becoming increasingly important sources of jobs. If enrollment in accredited physical therapy programs remains at the current level, there will be more openings for physical therapists than qualified individuals to fill them.

Earnings

In the early 1990s, the average yearly starting salary for a staff physical therapist ranged from about $25,000 to $30,000. Physical therapists in educational settings earned an average of $37,000 per year. Other positions, such as administrators and private practice physical therapists, generally earn more than the pay of a hospital physical therapist.

In the federal government in the early 1990s, beginning physical therapists were paid starting salaries of about $18,400 a year, while supervisory therapists averaged about $38,700. The average for all therapists working in the federal government was about $26,400 per year.

Conditions of work

The average physical therapist works approximately forty to fifty hours each week. Ordinarily, the therapist will work with from five to fifteen patients each day. The sessions may be brief or may last an hour or more. Usually, treatment is on an individual basis, but occasionally therapy may be given in groups when the patients' problems are similar.

Social and psychological factors

Most physical therapists will agree that the most important aspect of their job is the personal satisfaction derived from the patients' return to a normal or nearly normal mode of life. Whether working with paraplegics, amputees, polio victims, or accident victims, the physical therapist's greatest emotional award is to see the attitude of the patient change from "I can't" to "I'll try" to "I can and I will."

Today's physical therapy profession serves a dynamic, comprehensive health care role in improving and maintaining the quality of life for millions of Americans.

GOE: 10.02.02; SIC: 8049; SOC: 3033

◇ **SOURCES OF ADDITIONAL INFORMATION**

American Physical Therapy Association
1111 North Fairfax Street
Alexandria, VA 22314

U.S. Physical Therapy Association
1803 Avon Lane
Arlington Heights, IL 60004

◇ **RELATED ARTICLES**

Volume 1: Health Care
Volume 2: Kinesiotherapists; Occupational therapists; Physician assistants; Prosthetists and orthotists; Recreational therapists; Registered nurses; Rehabilitation counselors; Respiratory therapists; Therapists, miscellaneous
Volume 4: Physical therapist assistants

Physician assistants

Definition

Physician assistants, under the supervision of doctors of medicine or osteopathy, provide various health care services to patients. Much of the work they do was previously in the domain of the physician.

History

Physician assistants are fairly recent additions to the health care profession. The occupation originated in the mid-1960s; many medical corpsmen who were trained during the Vietnam War received additional education that enabled them to help physicians with various medical tasks. Since that time, the work of the physician assistant has grown and expanded; in addition, the number of physician assistants in the United States has greatly increased.

Nature of the work

Physician assistants, or PAs, assist physicians in providing care to patients by performing various medical tasks that had been carried out only by physicians. PAs may be responsible for a variety of tasks; they may take medical histories of patients, do complete, routine physical examinations, order laboratory tests, draw blood samples, give injections, and make tentative diagnoses. Some states allow PAs to prescribe medications. Although PAs may be given many different duties, they always work under the direction and supervision of a licensed physician. The extent of a PA's duties depends on the specific laws of the state and the practices of the employing physician, as well as the experience and abilities of the PA.

PAs work in a variety of health care settings, including hospitals, clinics, and physicians' offices. More than half of all PAs specialize in a particular area of medicine, such as pediatrics, obstetrics, surgery, and emergency medicine. Physician assistants may be known by other occupational titles, such as *child health associates*, *MEDEX*, *physician associates*, and *surgeon's assistants*.

PAs are skilled professionals who assume a high degree of responsibility in their work. By performing various medical tasks for their physician employers, PAs allow physicians more time to diagnose and treat severely ill patients.

Requirements

Most states require that PAs complete an educational program approved by the Committee on Allied Health Education and Accreditation (CAHEA) of the American Medical Association. As of the early 1990s, the CAHEA had approved fifty-two educational programs for PAs and three programs for surgeon's assistants. Admission requirements vary, but two years of college courses in science or health are usually the minimum requirement.

Educational programs generally take two years to complete, although some take only one year and others may take as many as three years. The first six to twenty-four months of a program involve classroom instruction in human anatomy, physiology, microbiology, clinical pharmacology, applied psychology, clinical medicine, and medical ethics. In the last nine to fifteen months, students are engaged in supervised clinical work; the clinical work usually includes assignments, or rotations, in various branches of medicine, such as family practice, obstetrics and gynecology, and emergency medicine.

Graduates of these programs may receive a certificate, an associate's degree, a bachelor's degree, or a master's degree; most programs, however, offer graduates a bachelor's degree.

MEDEX programs, which last only eighteen months, are designed for medical corpsmen, registered nurses, and others who have had extensive patient-care experience. MEDEX students generally obtain most of their clinical experience by working with a physician who will hire them after graduation.

PA programs are offered in a variety of educational and health care settings, including colleges and universities, medical schools, medical centers, hospitals, and the armed forces. State laws and regulations govern the scope of the PA's duties, and, in all but a few states, PAs must be graduates of an approved training program.

Special requirements

Currently, thirty-nine states require that PAs be certified by the National Commission on Certification of Physician Assistants (NCCPA). As of the early 1990s, the NCCPA had certified approximately 18,000 PAs.

To become certified, applicants must be graduates of an approved PA program and must pass a certifying examination. The examination consists of two parts; the first part tests general medical knowledge, while the second section tests the PA's specialty—either primary care or surgery. Once certified, PAs are required to complete one hundred hours of continuing medical education courses every two years; in addition, they must take a recertification examination every six years.

In addition to NCCPA certification, most states also require that PAs register with the state medical board. There is great variation in state rules and regulations governing the work of PAs, and individuals are advised to study the laws of the state in which they plan to practice. It is likely that restructuring of the health care services in the United States in the near future will involve standardized regulations for PAs.

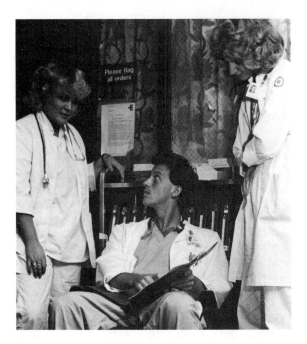

A physician discusses the medical history of a patient with his two assistants.

Opportunities for experience and exploration

High-school students who are interested in exploring the PA profession should talk with school career counselors, practicing PAs, and various health care employees at local hospitals and clinics. Students can also obtain information by writing to one of the associations listed at the end of this article.

While in college, students may be able to obtain summer employment as hospital orderlies, nurse's aides, or medical clerks. Such jobs should help students assess their interest in and aptitude for work as PAs before they formally apply to a PA program.

Related occupations

Physician assistants are frequently classified with such other medicine and health care workers as clinical psychologists, emergency medical technicians, industrial hygienists, licensed practical nurses, medical assistants, nurse midwives, nurse practitioners, occupational therapists, optometric assistants, physical therapists, respiratory care workers, speech and hearing clinicians, and surgical technicians.

Methods of entering

PAs must complete their formal training programs before entering the job market. Once their studies are finished, the placement services of the schools may help them find jobs. PAs may seek employment at hospitals, clinics, medical offices, or other health care settings. In addition, the Office of Personnel Management has information about jobs with the federal government.

Advancement

The PA profession is still quite new, and formal lines of advancement have not yet been established. Hospitals, for example, do not employ head PAs. There are many ways, however, for PAs to advance in their profession.

For example, PAs with experience may be given more responsibility and higher pay, or they may move on to larger hospitals and clinics. In addition, many PAs specialize in a particular branch of medicine, such as pediatrics or emergency medicine.

Employment outlook

The job outlook for PAs is good. The number of job openings for PAs is expected to increase much faster than the average for all occupations through the end of the 1990s. The occupation has already grown dramatically: Fewer than 100 PAs were practicing in 1970; today, there are more than 18,000.

The role of the PA in delivering health care has also expanded over the past decade. PAs have taken on more responsibilities and duties; they now work in a variety of health care settings. Studies have shown that nearly all trained PAs find jobs. Currently, there are seven jobs for every PA graduate.

The long-term outlook for PAs is also excellent. The barrier to reimbursement by third-party payers, which was a constraint for a number of years, has been removed. PA services to hospital and nursing home patients are now covered by Medicare. Physician assistants have become an integral part of the health care team.

Earnings

The salaries of PAs vary according to experience, specialty, and employer. In general, however, starting pay for PAs ranges from $22,000 to $35,000 a year. Those working in hospitals and medical offices earn slightly more than those working in clinics. In the early 1990s, salaries for experienced PAs ranged from $25,000 to $45,000 a year, with the average being $33,880.

Conditions of work

PAs work in a variety of health care environments. Some work for one physician; others work in group practice. PAs work in hospitals, clinics, and medical offices. They also work in nursing homes, long term care institutions, and prisons. Most work settings are comfortable and clean, although, like physicians, PAs spend much of their day standing or walking.

The workweek varies according to the employment setting. Emergency room PAs often work twenty-four-hour shifts, twice a week; others work twelve-hour shifts, three times a week. PAs who work in physicians' offices may have to work some evenings; in addition, they may make early morning hospital rounds to visit patients. PAs employed in clinics usually work five-day, forty-hour weeks.

Social and psychological factors

Individuals who are interested in pursuing work as PAs must be willing to study throughout their careers to keep abreast of medical advances. They must be intelligent, emotionally stable, and patient. They should enjoy working with all kinds of people and have a desire to help the sick and injured.

Most PAs find their work very rewarding and challenging. Although caring for another person can be burdensome, PAs often derive great satisfaction in knowing that they directly help others.

GOE: 10.02.01; SIC: 8049; SOC: 304

◇ **SOURCES OF ADDITIONAL INFORMATION**

American Academy of Physician Assistants
950 North Washington Street
Arlington, VA 22314

Association of Physician Assistant Programs
950 North Washington Street
Alexandria, VA 22314

National Commission on Certification of Physician Assistants
2845 Henderson Mill Road, NE
Atlanta, GA 30341

◇ **RELATED ARTICLES**

Volume 1: Biological Sciences; Health Care
Volume 2: Health services administrators; Kinesiotherapists; Nuclear medicine technologists; Occupational therapists; Perfusionists; Physical therapists; Physicians; Registered nurses; Respiratory therapists; Therapists, miscellaneous
Volume 3: Medical assistants
Volume 4: Medical and Health Technician Occupations

Physicians

Definition

The *physician* is a person of recognized experience, with educational and legal qualifications, who diagnoses, prescribes medicines for, and

otherwise treats diseases and disorders of the human body. A physician may also perform surgery and often specializes in one aspect of medical care and treatment. Physicians hold either a doctor of medicine or osteopathy degree.

A pediatrician performs a medical exam on a young patient. Friendliness and warmth make the exam less frightening for the child.

History

The first great physician was said to be Hippocrates, born on the small Greek island of Cos about 460 B.C. In addition to originating some theories about the practice of medicine and about the anatomy of the human body, Hippocrates developed a set of medical ethics that influences medical practice to this day. The oath that he administered to his disciples is still administered to the physician about to start a practice. His eighty-seven treatises on medicine, known as the "Hippocratic Collection," are believed to be the first authoritative record of early medical theory and practice.

The great civilizations of Egypt, India, and China all developed medical theories of diagnosis and treatment that influenced later cultures of their own countries and those of other countries. The school of medicine at Alexandria, Egypt, for example, incorporated the theories of the ancient Greeks as well as those of the Egyptians. This great medical school flourished and was influential for several hundred years. Research specialists there learned more about human anatomy than had ever been learned before.

The Romans learned the value of a pure water supply, for instance, and the necessity for an adequate sewage system.

The theories and practices of medicine were kept alive almost entirely during the Middle Ages by the monks in the monasteries. Few new theories were developed during this period, but the medical records of most of the great early civilizations were carefully preserved and copied.

The Renaissance saw a renewal of interest in medical research and led to such important discoveries as Harvey's demonstration of the circulation of the blood and Jenner's discovery of an effective vaccine against smallpox.

Many inventions in other fields were to help the progress of medicine. The invention of the microscope, for example, opened the way to research in germ theory. The study of chemistry produced anesthesia and other drugs; Roentgen's discovery of X rays contributed a whole new world of exploration and research to the field of medicine.

In the twentieth century, medical research and practice began to take giant strides toward the relief of human distress and the prolonging of human life. Every day brings new discoveries, and the possibility of major breakthroughs in the areas that have long plagued humans makes every new day an exciting adventure.

Nature of the work

The greatest number of physicians are in private practice. They see patients by appointment in their offices and examining rooms, and visit patients who are confined to the hospital. In the hospital, they may perform operations or give other kinds of medical treatment. Some physicians also make calls on patients at home if the patient is not able to get to the physician's office or if the illness is an emergency.

Approximately 15 percent of physicians in private practice are *general practitioners* or *family practitioners.* They see patients of all ages and both sexes and will diagnose and treat those ailments that are not severe enough or unusual enough to require the services of a specialist. When special problems arise, however, the general practitioner will refer the patient to a specialist.

Although the major portion of this article deals with the doctor of medicine (M.D.), there is another type of physician—the *doctor of osteopathy* (D.O.), or *osteopathic physician.* Despite differences in training and philosophy, osteopaths treat disease and injury just as medical doctors do, but with special emphasis on the musculoskeletal system—ligaments, muscles, nerves, and bones. Osteopathic physicians use all modern diagnostic procedures to determine the extent of a condition, and treatment may include drugs, surgery, or one of the basic treatments of osteopathy manipulative therapy. Most D.O.s are general practitioners, providing primary care; only about 25 percent are specialists.

Not all physicians are engaged in private practice. Some are in academic medicine and teach in medical schools or teaching hospitals. Some are engaged only in research. Some are salaried employees of health maintenance organizations or other prepaid health care plans. Some are salaried hospital employees.

Some physicians, often called *medical officers,* are employed by the federal government, in such positions as public health, or in the service of the Department of Veterans Affairs. State and local governments also employ physicians for public health agency work. A large number of physicians are serving with the armed forces, both in this country and overseas.

More and more physicians are entering industrial medicine. Known as *industrial* or *occupational physicians,* they are employed by large industrial firms for two main reasons: to prevent illnesses that may be caused by the kind of work in which the employees are engaged and to treat accidents or illnesses of employees.

Although most industrial physicians may roughly be classified as general practitioners because of the wide variety of illnesses that they must recognize and treat, their knowledge must also extend to public health techniques and to understanding such relatively new hazards as radiation and the toxic effects of various chemicals, including insecticides.

A specialized type of occupational physician is the *flight surgeon.* Flight surgeons study the effects of high-altitude flying on the physical condition of flight personnel. They place members of the flight staff in special low-pressure and refrigeration chambers that simulate high-altitude conditions and study the reactions on their blood pressure, pulse and respiration rate, and body temperature.

Another growing specialty is the field of nuclear medicine. Some large hospitals have a nuclear research laboratory, which functions under the direction of a *chief of nuclear medicine,* who coordinates the activities of the lab with other hospital departments and medical personnel. These physicians perform tests using nuclear isotopes and use techniques that let physicians see and understand organs deep within the body.

The American Medical Association recognizes about forty different medical specialties, including those described below:

Allergist-immunologists specialize in diseases and conditions caused by allergies or related to the immune system. They treat patients with ailments such as bronchial asthma, skin disorders, diseases of the connective tissues, and impairment of the autoimmune system. They also treat those undergoing surgical transplantation to help prevent rejection of the transplanted organ.

Anesthesiologists administer anesthetics before and during surgery and other medical procedures so the patient will feel no pain. They may induce general anesthesia, rendering the patient unconscious, using drugs, gases, or vapors; or they may use a local or spinal anesthetic, which blocks pain in a specific area while the patient remains awake. Anesthesiologists also work in emergency rooms, where they may help victims of drug overdose, heart attacks, poison, electric shock, drowning, or other accidents that can interfere with breathing. Some of these specialists work in respiratory care units or help plan home care for patients with respiratory illness, and some specialize in the diagnosis and treatment of chronic pain.

Cardiologists concentrate on diseases and functions of the heart. They listen to a patient's heart with a stethoscope, make recordings of its activity with an electrocardiograph, and study X-ray photographs to determine the existence or extent of a heart disorder. They may prescribe medication and recommend special diets and exercise programs and may refer the patient to a surgeon if corrective surgery is indicated.

Dermatologists treat diseases and problems of the human skin, hair, and nails. Their patients may be troubled with something as common as warts or acne or as serious as cancer. Dermatologists may treat boils and abscesses or skin injuries or infections; they may remove lesions, cysts, birthmarks, and other growths. They also treat scars and perform hair transplants.

Gynecologists and *obstetricians* are concerned with the health of the woman's reproductive system. Whereas gynecologists specialize in treating diseases and disorders and obstetricians in providing medical care before, during, and after childbirth, physicians often handle both specialties.

Internists are specialists in internal medicine. In other words, they diagnose and treat diseases and injuries of the internal organs, such as lungs, heart and valves, glands, stomach and intestines, blood, kidneys, tumors, and joints and muscles. Internists are often an adult's primary care physician. They are not to be confused with *interns,* medical school graduates who practice medicine under the supervision of a hospital staff for a specified length of time to gain experience and qualify for a state license.

Neurologists treat disorders of the nervous system. They study the results of tests done on the patient's blood and cerebrospinal fluid and the results of electroencephalograms (brainwave tests) and X rays. They may prescribe medications and drugs or recommend surgery, depending on the diagnosis.

Ophthalmologists are eye specialists. They examine a patient's eyes for poor vision or dis-

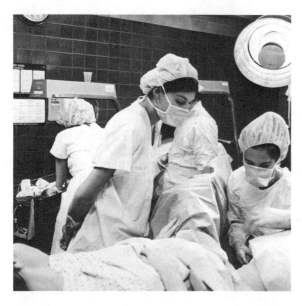

A resident physician observes the work of an obstetrician as a patient gives birth to a baby.

ease, prescribe corrective glasses or medication, and may recommend exercises to strengthen eye muscles. They perform surgery when indicated.

Otolaryngologists are ear, nose, and throat specialists. They treat patients with hearing loss or speech loss from disease or injury, prescribe medications, and may perform surgery. A physician may specialize in only one type of disorder: ear (otologist), nose (rhinologist), or throat (laryngologist).

Pathologists study the nature, cause, progression, and effects of diseases. They perform tests on body tissues, fluids, secretions, and other specimens to see if a disease is present and to determine what stage it is in. They perform autopsies to find out why people died and to study the effects of medical treatment. Pathologists often specialize in areas such as clinical chemistry, microbiology, or blood banking and may supervise the pathology department of a medical school, hospital, clinic, medical examiner's office, or research institution.

Pediatricians give medical care to children from birth through adolescence. They provide a program of preventive health care, including inoculations and vaccinations, and treat illnesses and injuries as they arise.

Physiatrists specialize in the use of physical devices and exercise to rehabilitate patients. They determine the kind of therapy needed; prescribe exercises or treatments using light, heat, cold, or other processes; and instruct the physical therapists who administer these treatments. They also recommend occupational therapy for patients who must remain hospital-

ized for long periods of time or for those who must change their work because of a disability.

Proctologists treat diseases and disorders of the anus, rectum, and colon. They may prescribe medication and recommend changes in the patient's living habits or may perform surgery to remove or repair the affected organ.

Psychiatrists treat persons with mental, emotional, and behavioral disorders. Using psychotherapy and sometimes medication, they help patients to understand and overcome problems that interfere with everyday living. (For a more complete description of this occupation, see the separate article titled "Psychiatrists" elsewhere in this volume.)

Radiologists use X rays and radioactive substances to treat illness. They treat internal and external tumors and growths with radiation and administer radioactive materials to patients to make their internal organs visible on X-ray films or fluoroscopic screens. Radiologists may specialize in diagnostic radiology, radiation therapy, or nuclear medicine. A *director of radiology* plans, organizes, and supervises the activities of a radiology department in cooperation with hospital officials and other department heads.

Surgeons operate to correct deformities, repair injuries, prevent diseases, and improve the health of patients. They examine patients to see whether surgery is necessary, estimate the possible risks, and decide which procedures to use. They take into consideration the patient's general health, medical history, and reaction to drugs. General surgeons perform many kinds of operations, but some surgeons specialize in only one kind of operation. For example: *Neurological surgeons,* or *neurosurgeons,* operate on the brain, spinal cord, and other nerves of the body. *Orthopedic surgeons* treat broken bones and diseases of bones and joints. *Plastic surgeons* correct disfigurements of the face or body, whether present at birth or caused by illness or injury. *Thoracic surgeons* operate on lungs and other organs in the chest cavity.

Urologists treat disorders of the urinary system of both men and women and of the reproductive organs of men. They may prescribe medicines for simple ailments such as bladder infections or perform surgery for more complicated conditions such as kidney stones or enlarged prostate glands.

Requirements

The physician is required to devote many years to study before being admitted to practice. As a high-school student, one should enroll in a college preparatory course. Prospective physicians are encouraged to take courses in English, languages (especially Latin), the humanities, social studies, and mathematics, in addition to courses in biology, chemistry, and physics.

The student who hopes to enter medicine should be admitted first to a liberal arts program in an accredited undergraduate institution. Some colleges offer a "premedical" course, and it is advisable for the student to take such a course where it is offered. A good general education, however, with as many courses as possible in science and perhaps a major in biology, is considered adequate preparation for the study of medicine.

College freshmen who hope to apply to a medical school early in their senior year should have adequate knowledge of the requirements for admission to the 127 accredited schools of medicine or 15 schools of osteopathic medicine in the country. They should consult a librarian for a copy of *Admissions Requirements of American Medical Colleges Including Canada*. If it is not in the college library, a copy may be secured from the Association of American Medical Colleges. If students will read carefully the admissions requirements of the several medical schools to which they hope to apply, they will avoid making mistakes in choosing an undergraduate program.

Students who do not enter a premedical program may find it possible to change to a major in biology or chemistry after they have matriculated. Such majors may make them eligible for consideration to be admitted to many of the medical schools.

Some students may be admitted to medical school after only three years of study in an undergraduate program. There are a few medical schools that will award the bachelor's degree at the end of the first year of medical school study. This practice is becoming less common as more students seek admission to medical schools. Most premedical students plan to spend four years in an undergraduate program and to receive the bachelor's degree before entering the four-year medical school program.

During the undergraduate's second or third year in college, he or she should arrange with an advisor to take the Medical College Admission Test. This test is given each spring and each fall at certain selected sites. The student's advisor should know the date, place, and time. If not, the student may write for this information to the Association of American Medical Colleges. All medical colleges in this country require this test for admission, and the score made on it is one of the factors that is weighed in the decision to take or to reject any applicant. Because the test does not evaluate medical knowledge, most college students who are enrolled in liberal arts programs should not find it to be unduly difficult. The examination covers four areas: verbal facility, quantitative ability, knowledge of the humanities and social sciences, and knowledge of biology, chemistry, and physics.

Students who hope to be admitted to medical school are encouraged to apply to at least three institutions to heighten their chances of being accepted by one of them. Two services are available to medical school applicants to make this step easier. The American Medical College Application Service (AMCAS) and the American Association of Colleges of Osteopathic Medicine Application Service (AACOMAS) will check, copy, and submit applications to medical schools specified by the individual student. More information about this service may be obtained from AMCAS, AACOMAS, premedical advisers, and medical schools.

Approximately one out of every two qualified applicants to medical schools will be admitted each year. The rumors that only one out of six students who apply are admitted to medical school arise from the fact that all students apply to more than one school. For each student, then, at least three applications are made and sometimes more, so the number of applicants seems to be at least three times as great as it actually is.

In addition to the traditional medical schools, there are several schools of basic medical sciences that enroll medical students for the first two years (preclinical experience) of medical school. They offer a preclinical curriculum to students similar to that which is offered by a regular medical school. At the end of the two-year program, the student will then apply to a four-year medical school for the final two years of instruction. Although there are few students who drop out of four-year medical programs, some vacancies do occur during that time. It is therefore feasible to expect that the applications of students who have successfully completed preclinical instruction may be welcomed by admissions officers in medical schools.

Although high scholarship is considered to be a determining factor in the decision about admitting a student who is applying to a medical school, it is actually only one of the criteria upon which such a decision is based. By far the greatest number of successful applicants to medical schools are "B" students. Because admission is also determined by a number of other factors, including a personal interview, one may infer that other qualities in addition to a high scholastic average are considered to be desirable for a prospective physician. High upon the list of desirable qualities are emotional stability, integrity, reliability, resourcefulness, and a sense of service.

The average student enters medical school at age twenty-one or twenty-two. The student then begins another four years of formal schooling. During the first two years of medical school, the student learns human anatomy, physiology, pharmacology, and microbiology. Most instruction in the first two years is given through classroom lectures, laboratories, seminars, independent research, and the reading of textbook material and other types of literature.

During the last two years in medical school, the student becomes actively involved in the treatment process. The student who spends a large proportion of the time in the hospital becomes part of a medical team that is headed by a teaching physician who specializes in a particular area. Others on the team may be interns or residents. Students are closely supervised but learn much firsthand about techniques such as how to take a patient's medical history, how to make a physical examination, how to work in the laboratory, how to make a diagnosis, and how to keep all the necessary records.

Students move from one medical specialty to another, to obtain a broad understanding of each field. Students are assigned to duty in internal medicine, pediatrics, psychiatry, obstetrics and gynecology, and surgery. Students may be assigned to other specialties, too.

In addition to this hospital work, students continue to take coursework. They are expected to be responsible for assigned studies and also for some independent study.

After receiving the M.D. or D.O. degree, the new physician is required to take an examination to be licensed to practice. Every state requires such an examination. It is conducted through the board of medical examiners in each state. Some states have reciprocity agreements with other states so that a physician licensed in one state may be automatically licensed in another without being required to stand another examination. Because this is not true throughout the United States, however, the wise physician will find out about licensing procedures before planning to move.

Most states require all new M.D.s to complete at least one year of postgraduate training, and a few require an internship plus a one-year residency. New D.O.s serve a one-year rotating internship during which they gain experience in surgery, pediatrics, internal medicine, and other specialties.

Physicians wishing to specialize spend from three to five years in advanced residency training plus another two or more years of practice in the specialty. Then they must pass a specialty board examination to become a board-certified M.D. or D.O.

Special requirements

The prospective physician's first special requirement is a strong desire to practice medicine. Unless the individual is sincerely interested for reasons other than the desire for status or the hope to earn a lot of money, he or she is not likely to be able to sustain interest throughout the long training program.

It is also important to have above-average intelligence and have an interest in scholarship and study. The physician must spend a good part of his or her time studying about new developments in medicine. Interested students must also have an aptitude for science, because medicine is one of the most demanding of the sciences.

Prospective physicians must have some plan for financing their long and costly education. They face a period of at least eight years after college when they will not be self-supporting. While still in school, students may be able to work only during summer vacations, because the necessary laboratory courses of the regular school year are so time-consuming that little time is left for any other activities than preparation of daily lessons. Some scholarships and loans are available to qualified students.

Opportunities for experience and exploration

It may be difficult for a high-school student to explore an interest in the medical profession in any way other than through reading, talking with a high-school counselor, attending Career Days at school or perhaps at a nearby hospital, or interviewing physicians.

When students are in college, however, it may be possible to obtain summer jobs as a hospital orderly, nurse's aide, or ward clerk. Such jobs should bring them close enough to medical practice to decide about the strength of their interest. A student may also be able to get a part-time or summer job as receptionist in a physician's office. There are several roles in health care that may provide other opportunities for work in the field. *See* Volume 1: Health care, for an overview.

Related occupations

Many other health-care occupations call for the same kinds of skills and critical judgment required by the physician. Not all of them require the same extensive education and training, however. These other workers include audiologists, chiropractors, dentists, dietitians, medical and dental technologists, optometrists, pharmacists, physical therapists, physician assistants, podiatrists, prosthetists, registered nurses, rehabilitation therapists, speech pathologists, and veterinarians.

Methods of entering

There are no shortcuts to entering the medical profession. Requirements are: an M.D. or D.O. degree; a licensing examination; a one- or two-year internship; and a period of residency that may extend as long as five years.

Upon completing this program, which may take up to fifteen years, physicians are then ready to enter practice. They may choose to open a solo private practice, enter a partnership practice, enter a group practice, or take a salaried job with a prepaid plan. Salaried positions are also available with federal and state agencies, the military, including the Department of Veterans Affairs, and private companies. Teaching and research jobs are usually obtained after other experience is acquired.

Advancement

The average physician in private practice does not advance in the accustomed sense of the word. A physician's progress consists of advancing in skill and understanding, in numbers of patients, and in income. He or she may be made a fellow in a professional specialty or elected to an important office in the American Medical Association or American Osteopathic Association. These kinds of achievements, however, may represent a type of success that is different from the usual definition of advancement.

Employment outlook

There were about 491,000 M.D.s and D.O.s working in patient-care activities in the early 1990s, plus about 44,000 M.D.s involved in research, teaching, administration, and consulting for insurance or pharmaceutical companies. About 60 percent of all physicians practice in offices, 20 percent are on the staff of hospitals, and the rest are situated in a variety of other health care facilities and in schools, prisons, and business firms.

Population growth, particularly among the aging, is expected to accelerate the demand for physicians through the end of the 1990s. Another factor contributing to the predicted increase is the widespread availability of medical insurance, through both private plans and public programs. More physicians will also be needed for medical research, public health, rehabilitation, and industrial medicine.

It is possible, however, that the supply of physicians will exceed the demand. There was a surge in medical school enrollments in the 1970s, when a shortage of physicians appeared imminent, and although the enrollment levels have dropped slightly, it is expected that there will be a continuing oversupply of trained practitioners. In addition to the graduates from domestic medical schools, greater numbers of foreign-trained physicians are expected to enter practice.

The shift in health care delivery from hospitals to outpatient centers and other nontraditional settings, in an effort to contain rising costs, may mean that more and more physicians will become salaried employees. It appears that HMOs and other prepaid arrangements can provide medical services with fewer physicians than a fee-for-service practice can offer. If they continue to grow in popularity, they could possibly cut into the need for physicians.

There will be considerable competition among newly trained physicians entering practice, particularly in large cities. Physicians willing to locate in inner cities and rural areas, where physicians are in short supply, should encounter little difficulty. Opportunities are expected to be best for physicians in family practice, pediatrics, geriatrics, and internal medicine. Other areas in need of physicians include psychiatry, child psychiatry, physical medicine, and rehabilitation.

Earnings

Usually physicians do not begin to earn a good living until their middle 30s. Because they have undergone eight years of education after high school, they may be approximately twenty-six years old before starting postgraduate training. The average resident received a salary of about $20,000 to $24,000 a year in the early 1990s, depending on the type of residency, the size of the hospital, and the geographic area.

Physicians who had completed their residencies but had no other experience began work with the Department of Veterans Affairs at salaries of about $44,400. In addition, those working full-time could receive other cash benefits of up to $13,000.

If the physician enters private practice, earnings during the first year may not be impressive. As the patients increase in number, however, earnings will also increase. The median income, after expenses, for general and family practitioners and pediatricians in the early 1990s was estimated to be about $81,200 per year. For surgeons it was about $170,000.

Physicians have among the highest average earnings of any occupational group. The average income for all physicians in the early 1990s was about $106,300 per year; for those under thirty-six years of age, it was $85,100. The level of income for any individual physician depends on a number of factors, such as region of the country, economic status of the patients, and the physician's skill, experience, professional reputation, and personality. Self-employed physicians generally earn more than those on salary. It is important to consider, however, that the cost of medical malpractice insurance is high. Particularly for physicians in private practice, the cost of operating an office may reduce the salary rate.

Conditions of work

The offices and examining rooms of most physicians are well equipped, attractive, well lighted, and well ventilated. There is usually at least one nurse-receptionist on the physician's staff, and there may be several nurses, a laboratory technician, one or more secretaries, a bookkeeper, receptionist—or any combination of these assistants.

The physician usually sees patients by an appointment that is scheduled according to his or her individual requirements. One may reserve all mornings for hospital visits and surgery. One may see patients in the office only on certain days of the week. If it is necessary to cut down on the workload, one may schedule fewer appointments.

Physicians spend a large part of their time at the hospital, performing surgery, setting fractures, working in the emergency room, or visiting patients. Most hospitals throughout the country are well equipped and have good modern facilities. Physical conditions are usually pleasant.

Physicians in academic medicine or in research have regular hours, work under good physical conditions, and often determine their own workload. Teaching and research physicians alike are usually provided with the best and most modern equipment.

Physicians in private practice have the advantages of working independently, but most put in long hours—an average of fifty-five per week. Also, they may be called from their homes or offices in times of emergency. Telephone calls may come at any hour of the day or night. It is difficult for physicians to plan leisure-time activities, because their plans may have to be changed without notice. One of the advantages of group practice is that members of the group rotate emergency duty.

The areas in most need of physicians are the rural hospitals and medical centers. Because the physician is normally working alone, and covering a broad territory, the work day can be quite long with little opportunity for vacation. Because placement in rural communities has become so difficult, some towns are providing scholarship money to students who pledge to work in the community for a number of years.

Social and psychological factors

Most physicians derive deep satisfaction from the practice of medicine. The burden of carrying a life or death responsibility for others is relieved by the knowledge that they can be of help to others in many ways. They are often physician, confidant, and friend to their patients. For many physicians the most stressful time occurs while in medical school or in internship. The hours are long, the work is quite hard, and financial struggles are common. It is even more difficult for those trying to support a family.

GOE: 02.03.01; SIC: 8011; SOC: 261

◇ SOURCES OF ADDITIONAL INFORMATION

American Medical Association
535 North Dearborn Street
Chicago, IL 60610

American Osteopathic Association
142 East Ontario Street
Chicago, IL 60611

American Association of Colleges of
Osteopathic Medicine
6110 Executive Boulevard
Suite 405
Rockville, MD 20852

Association of American Medical Colleges
One Dupont Circle, NW
Washington, DC 20036

Physicists

Definition

The *physicist* conducts research into phases of physical phenomena. Physicists perform experiments and analyze the products or results of their experiments. They may teach, have charge of scientific projects, or act as consultants in a laboratory. They investigate and attempt to understand the fundamental laws of nature and how these laws may be formulated and put to use.

History

Although humans have been attempting to manipulate the physical environment probably from the time when we discovered that we could cut better with a sharp stone than with teeth or fingernails, it could scarcely be stated that the science of physics began with a cave dweller. All primitive people seem to have attributed natural phenomena, which they did not comprehend, to the presence of good or evil spirits, or to the manipulations of one god or several.

The stars, the sun, and the moon were the greatest wonders for centuries. Our interest in them led to the science of astronomy, which was one of the first offshoots of physics.

One of the monuments to great technological skill is the Great Pyramid in Egypt, which was built about 2600 B.C. These massive structures required a keen knowledge of what we now call mechanics, a branch of physics that calculates the force required to move solid objects, even against opposing forces.

About 330 B.C., Aristotle wrote his great book, *Physics,* in which he laid down some principles that were accepted without question and governed people's thinking about the environment for a thousand years. Aristotle had not tested his theories; he had reached his conclusions by *logic.* So influential were his ideas, however, that when Galileo dared, 1,000 years later, to challenge them, he was discharged from his position as a professor.

Galileo is often called the father of the experimental method. Many persons also call him the first modern physicist. His most famous experiment may be the one in which he is said to have proved that all weights fall at the same speed by dropping a ten-pound weight and a one-pound weight from the Leaning Tower of Pisa. They hit the ground simultaneously.

Galileo's work in astronomy, with the aid of a telescope, proved that the moon was not smooth; by mathematical calculations, he proved that the moon reflects the light of the sun.

Sir Isaac Newton, born the year Galileo died, was one of the discoverers of calculus (with Leibniz); he discovered by experimentation the source of the rainbow.

In the four centuries since Galileo demonstrated the value of conducting experiments to determine whether or not scientific theory may be valid, scholars have made great strides. Faraday conducted experiments that made the modern age of electricity possible. A generation later, Edison took advantage of his studies to produce more than 1,000 inventions, including the incandescent light and the motion picture.

Roentgen conducted experiments that led to the discovery of the X ray; the Curies discovered radioactivity; Sir J. J. Thomson discov-

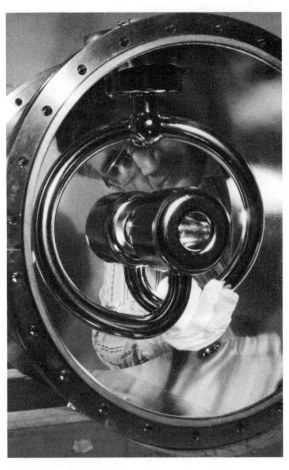

A nuclear physicist works on the "split-ring resonator," the heart of the world's first superconducting linear accelerator for heavy ions.

ered the electron. Niels Bohr proposed a theory of atomic structure; Einstein developed the mathematical theories that have led us into the atomic age.

This progress has been made because people turned their backs on speculation and began to undertake the tedious work of research.

Nature of the work

Physicists have made great progress in recent years in probing the depths of the ocean and research into nuclear energy, communications, and aerospace.

Most physicists are engaged in research. Those who teach in universities usually are also conducting research programs or are supervising the research of graduate students. Because there are many specialties within the field of physics, physicists will often focus their research efforts on one or another of the special fields.

Physics may be differentiated roughly into two fundamental divisions. One, mechanics, has to do with the motion inherent in solids, liquids, and gases. The other, statics, is the study of matter at rest and is closely allied with the study of engineering. Designs of dams and bridges are related to the physical problems in statics. However, physicists are coming to believe more strongly that nothing really is static; matter only seems to be at rest. Matter is defined, briefly, as that of which any physical object is "composed" or whatever occupies "space."

Physicists who are employed by industry devote their attention to the problems of the kind of enterprise represented by their own firm. For example, a physicist may be employed by one of the petroleum industries engaged in conducting experiments that relate to improving methods of obtaining crude oil, or of refining or using it. Aerospace industries employ physicists to conduct research into problems peculiar to their own operations. Communications industries (such as television, radio, or telephone) may employ physicists to work in their laboratories to discover the principles that will improve the technology that underlies the function of their product. *Health physicists* research and develop programs designed to protect those plant and laboratory workers who may risk exposure to radiation hazards.

Physicists work with many other scientists. Sometimes scientific fields overlap. Much of the work of physicists, for example, is done in mathematics and statistics. The physicist must be an expert mathematician and must be skilled in statistical method. In both fields, the physicist must be almost as competent as those who carry the title of the field, mathematician or statistician.

The physicist may also work with engineers. Ascertaining where the field of engineering stops and the field of physics takes over is not always easy. Consider the *electro-optical engineer*, a physicist who researches, designs, and develops lasers, masers, infrared, and other devices that emit light or are sensitive to light. In general, however, engineering is more concerned with technology, and physics is more concerned with the testing of theory. In the constructing of such things as missiles and computers, however, both physicists and engineers contribute.

The fields of geology and physics have worked so closely together that a new science has been born: geophysics. (*See also* the separate article titled "Geophysicists" elsewhere in this volume.

Physics, chemistry, and biology have so often been jointly used in research into the same problem that a new science has developed from the association: biophysics. *Biophysicists* work closely with the field of medical science, because they are concerned with life processes, with the atomic details of organic structure and function, and with the mechanisms of heredity. See the article on biologists in this volume.

Some physicists work with medical research experts. Many gains have been made in both medicine and physics because of the combined efforts of these two kinds of scientists. Medical research experts and *medical physicists* will continue to work even more closely together as the use of computers becomes more widespread.

Physics and chemistry have always enjoyed a close relationship. With the increased interest in the nature of the atom and in molecular physics and chemistry, however, the two fields will join in even closer cooperation. The combined findings of physicists and chemists have contributed to the scientific understanding of dynamic changes in the environment.

As noted above, much of the work of early physicists centered around the study of astronomy. In modern times, astronomy is a separate science from physics, but there is still much interdependence in the two fields. Astronomers use instruments that have been designed by physicists and engineers. Physicists in the study of space phenomena rely on findings by astronomers in such fields as thermonuclear research. Astrophysics may be said to be a combination of the two sciences, although it is generally classified as a field of specialization in astronomy. Although there are relatively few astronomers, their findings are proving to be of increasing importance to the work of the physicist in the space age.

Physicists are concerned with matter and energy. They work on two levels, which are not necessarily exclusive. *Theoretical physicists* work largely on the theoretical level, attempting to formulate laws of physical phenomena and to express these laws in mathematical form. They are not specifically concerned with the practical application of the laws. Other physicists are called experimental physicists and work largely on the practical applications of theory. They make carefully recorded observations of the phenomena under consideration, and perform experiments that measure interactions of matter and energy. They use many and varied instruments. When there is no instrument available to perform the kind of task required for the study which they are conducting, they design the necessary equipment. Sometimes they also build the tools which they need, but equally as often, an engineer or technologist will complete this task for them.

The areas of specialization for most physicists are: mechanics, heat, optics, acoustics, electricity and magnetism, electronics, atomic and molecular physics, nuclear physics, physics of fluids, solid-state physics, or classical theoretical physics. In addition, the studies of cryogenics, plasma physics, and crystallography have developed in recent years.

Requirements

High-school students who are interested in becoming physicists should enroll in a college preparatory course. They should take as much mathematics as is offered in their school, and as many of the sciences as possible. They should not neglect English, however, as communication of ideas is central to the meaning of science.

Physicists may have one, two, or three degrees. The physicist at the doctoral level will probably command the jobs with the greatest responsibility. Those at the master's level will secure good jobs, but with less responsibility, and those at the bachelor's level will compete intensely for positions that hold the least challenge.

Those who plan to teach at the secondary school level may be able to obtain a teaching position with a bachelor's degree if they also meet the certification requirements for teaching that are established by the state department of education in each state. Because different states have different certification requirements, undergraduates are wise to discover the requirements for the state in which they hope to teach and to make sure that they have met them. After starting a teaching career, they may want to begin work toward a master's degree by taking courses during the summer months. A master's degree is usually required for a teaching position in a junior college. Some secondary schools, too, prefer to employ those with a master's degree.

A doctorate is usually required for employment as a college teacher. Physicists with a master's degree may obtain a job as an assistant in a physics department in a university while working toward a doctorate in physics. One will usually be assigned to teaching undergraduates and to supervising students in laboratory work.

Some positions in industry are available for graduates with a bachelor's degree. The firm will often encourage its research employees to obtain advanced training. Sometimes, employers in industry are interested in taking young people who have had a broad background of training and teaching them the specialty in which the firm operates, as, for instance, the manufacture of electrical devices. When the young employees have developed competency in the special field, they may then return to graduate school to concentrate their study in this particular field.

Approximately one-third of all physicists have doctorates. Students who are interested in going to a graduate school that offers the doctor's degree in physics should write to the American Institute of Physics for a list of such graduate institutions. In the early 1990s, there were approximately 250 colleges and universities offering advanced degrees in physics.

Special requirements

Persons who are interested in physics as a career should have above-average intelligence, a good vocabulary, and an ability to express themselves well and easily. They should have interest and ability in mathematics. They should like to build things, but this interest alone is not sufficient to produce a good physicist. It is possible to mistake an interest in mechanical things for an interest in the science of physics.

Physicists should have keen powers of observation and a strong curiosity about the world around them, and they should enjoy working with ideas. They should be able to concentrate on intellectual things, enjoy studying and learning, and be independent thinkers.

Opportunities for experience and exploration

Students interested in a career in physics will find opportunities to gain at least a working acquaintance with various aspects of the subject through talks with their science teachers and through the use of facilities of the school library. Other possibilities are membership in the various organizations that specialize in one aspect of physical science such as science clubs, astronomy clubs, and so forth. Many states sponsor science competitions for high-school and college students. Students living in large cities will find more opportunities to participate in such activities through college and national organizations than will students living in smaller communities.

Related occupations

Other scientific occupations that may appeal to persons interested in physics include astronomy, chemistry, geology, and geophysics. The principles of physics are also employed by engineers and by engineering and science technicians.

Methods of entering

The placement office of the college or university from which the physicist obtained a degree will have listings of jobs available. Many industries send personnel interviewers to the campuses of universities that have programs in physics to seek out and talk to young persons who are about to receive degrees.

Those who are interested in teaching in public schools should apply to several school systems in which they may want to work. There are occasionally some positions available for science teachers. Some of the larger school systems also send personnel interviewers to campuses to talk with students who are about to receive degrees in science and who also have acquired the necessary courses in education.

Teaching jobs in universities are often obtained either through the contacts of the student's own faculty members in the degree program or through the placement office of the university.

Jobs with an agency of the federal government are gained through taking a civil service examination. Notices of such examinations may be obtained through the local post office or by writing to the Office of Personnel Management, Washington DC 20415.

Advancement

The high-school teacher will advance in salary and possibly in degree of responsibility as he or she acquires experience. This advancement is also likely to be facilitated by the attaining of advanced degrees.

The college or university teacher, who should have a doctorate to secure a staff appointment, will advance through regular grades from instructor to full professor, or perhaps to head of department. As one goes up in rank, one is also likely to go up in salary. Higher rank also carries with it additional responsibilities.

The research physicist who is employed by a university may be given greater responsibility for planning and carrying through research programs. The salary level may also be increased as one works in research over a period of years.

Physicists in federal government agencies are advanced in grade and salary as they gain experience. They may also reach positions in which they are asked to make decisions vital to the defense effort or to the safety and welfare of the country.

Scientists employed by industry are usually the highest paid in the profession. They may be advanced to positions in which they are directing the research efforts of the total organization.

Age does not seem to be a factor in the advancement of physicists. Research has tended to show that some of the most dramatic and significant discoveries have been made by relatively young persons. Many physicists have made great contributions to their scientific field before they reached thirty-five years of age.

Employment outlook

There were approximately 36,000 physicists employed in the early 1990s. More than 60 percent held faculty positions in colleges and universities; about 25 percent had jobs in independent research and development laboratories; about 20 percent worked for the federal government, mostly in the Departments of Defense, Energy, and Commerce; and the balance were employed by manufacturers of electrical equipment, noncommercial research labs, engineering service firms, the aircraft and automobile industries, and as nonfaculty researchers in colleges and universities.

The demand for physicists is expected to grow at an average rate throughout the rest of the decade. Employment opportunities should increase as the many physicists who were hired during the 1960s begin to reach retirement age in the late 1990s. In addition, if the decline in graduate school enrollments continues, there will be ample job openings for entrants into this field, particularly in private industry. It is anticipated that increased spending for research and development will result in more jobs becoming available. Also, some physicists with advanced degrees will be needed to teach in colleges and universities.

Opportunities for physicists in defense-related jobs are subject to changes in defense spending. Any cut in these expenditures, especially for research, will have a negative impact on the hiring of physicists in this area.

Graduates with only a bachelor's degree are generally underqualified for most physicist jobs. They may find better employment opportunities as engineers, technicians, or computer specialists. With a suitable background in education, they may teach physics at the high-school level.

Earnings

In industry in the early 1990s, starting salaries for physicists with a master's degree averaged about $31,200 a year, and those with a doctorate averaged about $42,500. Private industry normally provides the highest average wages to physicists.

Starting salaries for college and university teachers of physics averaged $29,500. The salaries of physics teachers in public high schools corresponded to the salaries of secondary teachers in other fields.

Entry salaries for physicists employed by the federal government depend both on the degree and on the individual's college record. Physicists with a bachelor's degree started at about $14,800 or $18,400 in the early 1990s. Those with a master's degree began at about $18,400 or $22,500; with a doctorate, at $27,200 or $32,600. The average salary for physicists working for the federal government in the early 1990s was about $45,600 per year.

Conditions of work

Most physicists work under pleasant circumstances. Laboratories are usually well equipped, clean, well lighted, temperature controlled, and functional. Adequate safety measures are taken when there is any sort of physical hazard involved in the work.

The people with whom the physicist works are usually intelligent companions and stimulating colleagues. Often, a group of scientists will work together as a team. Their association will be a close one and may last over a period of many years.

Sometimes the nature of work in which the physicist is engaged will make it necessary for the greatest possible secrecy measures to be observed. In such cases, the physicist will be required to carry various kinds of identification and may work under guarded conditions, sometimes behind locked doors. This kind of situation requires extreme discretion.

Social and psychological factors

Many physicists exhibit single-purposed devotion to their work. They become so interested in the theories that they are developing or in the experiments that they are conducting that they think of little else.

They may derive personal satisfaction when a theory on which they have done research is proven accurate. They cannot, however, let themselves become discouraged by frustrations and failures. Some physicists devote a lifetime to research on problems in one small area of knowledge.

Whether a physicist works in the laboratory of a university or industrial company, or teaches in a college, that person is taking part in one of humanity's greatest adventures— understanding the world around us.

GOE: 02.01.01; SIC: 8221, 8999; SOC: 1843

◇ **SOURCES OF ADDITIONAL INFORMATION**

American Association of Physics Teachers
5112 Berwyn Road
College Park, MD 20740

American Institute of Physics
335 East 45th Street
New York, NY 10017

American Physical Society
335 East 45th Street
New York, NY 10017

Scientists Institute for Public Information
355 Lexington Avenue
16th Floor
New York, NY 10017

◇ **RELATED ARTICLES**

Volume 1: Engineering; Mathematics; Nuclear Science; Physical Sciences
Volume 2: Astronomers; Chemists; College and university faculty; Engineers; Geologists; Geophysicists; Mathematicians
Volume 4: Geological technicians; Laboratory technicians; Mathematical technicians

Pilots

Definition

The *airplane pilot* may perform any one of several different kinds of flying jobs. In general, however, pilots operate an aircraft for the transportation of passengers, freight, mail, or for other commercial purposes. They are usually designated according to the type of work performed, or by the federal license that they may hold.

History

For more than fifty years before Wilbur and Orville Wright were able to build a machine that could fly, people in various parts of the world had been experimenting with ideas about powered flights. Several were actually built and an attempt was made to fly them. Orville Wright's 120-foot flight on December 17, 1903, at Kitty Hawk, North Carolina, however, is generally considered to be the first actual piloting experience. The history of the job of the pilot is inseparable from that of the development of the plane. In the early days of aviation the pilot's job was startlingly different from that of the pilot of today. As he flew the first plane, for instance, Orville Wright was lying on his stomach in the middle of the bottom wing of the plane. There was a strap across his hips, and to turn the plane, Wright had to tilt his hips from side to side.

Aviation developed fast from its beginnings at Kitty Hawk, North Carolina. By 1911, a pilot had taken a plane across the country in a series of short hops. Twelve years later, the cross-country trip was made nonstop. The first airline in the United States began operating between Tampa and St. Petersburg, Florida, on January 1, 1914. However, this line did not operate on a schedule, nor did it cover a very great distance. The first regularly scheduled airline began operation in 1919, between New York, New York, and Atlantic City, New Jersey. International airmail came into being in the same year, when mail was exchanged between London and Paris.

In the United States, the Army originally flew the mail. Soon after the service was initiated in 1918, the Post Office Department took over the airmail routes, established airports, and flew its own planes. In 1926, airmail service was turned over to private airlines on a contract basis, and this kind of service has been maintained.

Aviation caught the public fancy and for a period of time it was, in one form or another, public amusement. Many aviators earned an uncertain living by taking their planes to local fairs and other outdoor recreation spots. Here they were called "barnstormers" and entertained the crowd by stunting with the plane or taking passengers on short flights around the countryside.

Feats of daring and endurance were greatly admired by the public, and some brave aviators undertook transcontinental, transoceanic, or transpolar flights. In a matter of a few short years, however, flights that were once spectacular became scheduled and routine. No longer could a pilot win fame and fortune by flying from New York to Paris as did Charles Lindbergh in 1927. Flying had passed from the amazing to the mundane in the span of one person's lifetime.

Nature of the work

The best-known pilots are the *commercial airline pilots* who fly for the large airlines. They are responsible, highly-paid professionals who are in complete command of their crew, their plane, and their passengers during the time in which the plane is in motion. Their plane is usually a multimillion-dollar plant, often carrying more than 200 persons. It may be driven by jet engines or by propellers, and may go at speeds approaching that of sound. It is not unusual for jet-powered planes to fly at altitudes higher than 35,000 feet.

Before any flight, the pilot must determine weather and flight conditions, check flight plans, and have them approved by the Federal Aviation Agency (FAA) air traffic control personnel. The *copilot* plots the course to be flown and computes the flying time between various points. On board the plane, the pilot and the copilot test the functioning of the many instruments, controls, and electronic and mechanical systems. The pilot then requests orders from the airline dispatcher, and taxis the plane to the designated runway. If satisfied with the performance, the pilot then requests permission to take off. If not satisfied with the condition of the plane, the pilot may return to the airport for further checking. In either case, it is the pilot's decision.

Flying a large plane is a difficult and responsible job and one that requires great skill and knowledge. Pilots have many people to aid them on the job, but their ability and judgment are the most important factors in maintaining the safety of everyone aboard the plane. Aside from a copilot—and on · some jets, two copilots—the pilot's crew will consist of a flight engineer, and at least one flight attendant, or perhaps several. There may also be a navigator. Airlines refer to the pilot as "captain," because a pilot's functions in many ways parallel those of the captain of a ship.

Much of the time when the plane is in the air, it is being flown by an electronic device known as an automatic pilot. During the flight the pilot and copilot make radio reports to ground control stations about altitude, speed, weather conditions, and other flight details. The captain is always alert for any conditions that might become problems, even when the mechanical device is actually in control of the plane. Before landing, the pilot rechecks landing gear and requests landing clearance from air traffic control personnel. When visibility is poor, the captain may have to rely solely on instruments, such as the altimeter, artificial horizon, gyro compass, and instrument landing systems to land the plane.

When the captain has landed the plane at its destination, there are some final duties to perform. The pilot files a flight report in the office, discharges all responsibilities to the crew, and turns the plane over to the maintenance department. Pilots then are free to rest until they take another plane out.

A number of other kinds of pilots are employed in aviation: *check pilots*, who observe the ability of pilots and copilots over an established air route, observing infringements of company and FAA regulations by airplane and ground crews; *flying instructors*, who instruct students in flying, demonstrate methods of control, and explain methods of operation of various kinds of planes; and *pilot instructors*, who instruct

In preparation for take-off, a pilot checks the flight instruments in the cockpit.

company airline pilots about company regulations and procedures and familiarize the pilots with new equipment. Directing the operation of the flight department of the airline is the *chief pilot*. This individual is in charge of training new pilots, preparing schedules and assigning flight personnel, reviewing their performance, and improving their morale and efficiency. Chief pilots make sure that all legal and governmental regulations affecting flight operations are observed, advise the company during contract negotiations with the pilots' union, and handle a multitude of administrative details.

In addition to airline pilots, there are many business pilots, or *executive pilots*, who fly for large businesses that have their own planes or helicopters. The National Business Aircraft Association estimates that more than 18,000 firms either own or lease planes. These aircraft may be either single-engine planes or multi-engine, either new or bought from the military service as war surplus. They may be used to transport cargo or products or to carry executives of the

firm on various business assignments. In some cases, planes owned by firms fly inspection routes to determine the condition of pipelines or electric power lines or to inspect large company holdings.

Between flights, the business pilot is occupied with the maintenance of the company's planes. Pilots who wish to fly for business firms need to know as much as possible about the mechanics of an aircraft. They may fly to remote areas in which maintenance service would be difficult to secure.

Agricultural pilots are involved in such duties as weed control, insect control, chemical dusting of crops, orchards, soil, forests and swamps, plant disease control, fertilization, and seeding. In addition, the agricultural aircraft pilot may be engaged in such activities as planting small fish in streams or lakes, checking the condition of crops, counting the number of cattle in a herd or the number of animals of a given kind in a particular area, fighting forest fires, feeding either domestic or wild animals by dropping hay in snow-covered areas, and patrolling power lines.

Agricultural aircraft pilots may combine two interests: farming and flying. The pilot who chooses this career should know about farms and farming. This person must be an expert pilot, able to fly at low altitudes carrying a heavy load. This pilot must have a wholesome respect for the chemicals with which the plane may be loaded and must know their potential harm as well as their potential benefits.

Although there are not many *test pilots*, their job is a very important one. Every airplane manufacturer employs several highly skilled people to test new planes. The engineering test pilots combine engineering background with their ability as a pilot. They test new models of planes to ensure that they perform in the manner expected. If they do not, the model is not put into production until corrections are made. Because test pilots understand engineering problems, they are able to make specific suggestions about improvements or corrections in the new model.

Although there are still relatively few *helicopter pilots*, their numbers are expected to increase. Greater use is being made of this kind of aircraft, and pilots for them will be needed more in the future. Because airports that will accommodate jet planes are usually located far from the center of town, helicopters are being used for air-taxi service to take passengers to town or to other airports. They are also being used for transporting mail relatively short distances between the airport and the post office. Helicopters are also being used in sightseeing, in rescue service, in conservation service, and in aerial photography.

Some pilots are employed in the following specialties: *Photogrammetry pilots* fly planes or helicopters over designated areas and photograph the earth's surface for mapping and other purposes. *Facilities-flight-check pilots* fly specially equipped planes to test air navigational aids, air traffic controls, and communications equipment and to evaluate installation sites for such equipment. This testing is directed by a *supervising pilot. Flight-operations instructors* give oral and written exams and flight tests to persons applying for a pilot's license.

Requirements

All prospective pilots should complete high school. More and more, companies that employ pilots are requiring at least two years of college training. The large airline companies are showing preference in their employment to college graduates. Courses in meteorology, physics, algebra, geometry, trigonometry, and mechanical drawing are helpful in preparing for a pilot's career. Flying can be learned in either military or civilian flying schools. As of the early 1990s, the FAA had certified about 1,000 civilian flying schools, including some colleges and universities that offer degree credit for pilot training.

The physical and emotional health of the student who is interested in becoming a pilot are the most important requirements. Emotional stability is essential, because the safety of other people depends upon a pilot remaining calm and level-headed, no matter how trying the situation. Physical health is equally important. Vision and hearing must be perfect; coordination must be excellent; heart and blood pressure must be normal.

To become a pilot, certain rigid training requirements must be met. Although obtaining a private pilot's license is not difficult, it may be quite difficult to obtain a commercial license. Any student who is sixteen or over and who can pass the rigid required physical examination may apply for permission to take flying instruction. When the training is finished, a written examination must be taken. If the prospective pilot passes the examination, he or she may apply for a private pilot's license. To qualify for it, a person must successfully fulfill a solo flying requirement of twenty hours or more and must check out in instrument flying and cross-country flying.

All pilots and copilots must be licensed by the FAA before they can do any type of commercial flying. An applicant who is eighteen years old and has 250 hours of flying time can apply for a commercial airplane pilot's license. In applying for this license, a candidate must pass a rigid physical examination and a written test given by the FAA covering safe flight operations, Federal Aviation Regulations, navigation principles, radio operation, and meteorology. The applicant must also submit proof that the minimum flight-time requirements have been completed and, in a practical test, demonstrate flying skill and technical competence to a check pilot. Before pilots or copilots receive an FAA license, they must also receive a rating for the kind of plane they can fly (single-engine, multi-engine, or seaplane) and for the specific type of plane, such as Boeing 707 or 747.

Most people hired by the scheduled airlines and some larger supplemental airlines begin as flight engineers. For this position, the airlines generally require that the applicant have 500 to 1,000 flying hours of experience. In addition, an instrument rating by the FAA and a restricted radio telephone operator's permit by the Federal Communications Commission (FCC) are required. All airline captains must have an airline transport pilot's license. Applicants for this license must be at least twenty-three years old and have a minimum of 1,500 hours of flight time, including night flying and instrument time.

Special requirements

Pilots who work in special areas must have special training in these areas. The agricultural aircraft pilot, for example, should acquire special training in aerial application of dusts or fluids. Courses in this field are offered at approximately sixteen schools in the West, South, and Midwest, including such institutions as Texas A. & M., Ohio State University, Oklahoma State, and the University of Mississippi, as well as private academies that specialize in this kind of instruction. Both jet pilots and helicopter pilots must have special training in their respective areas.

Opportunities for experience and exploration

High-school students who are interested in flying may join an Air Scouts troop (Boy Scouts of America) or a high-school aviation club. At sixteen, they may start taking flying lessons. One of the most valuable experiences for a high-school student who wants to be a pilot is to learn to be a ham radio operator. By so doing, you will meet one of the qualifications for commercial flying.

Related occupations

Not everyone with a desire to be an aircraft pilot will be able to qualify for that occupation. However, it is not necessary to be in the cockpit to play a significant role in flight operations. Persons interested in aviation work might also consider the work of air traffic controllers and dispatchers, aircraft mechanics, airline flight attendants, and airport managers. They might also explore the occupations of aeronautical engineers, cartographers, meteorologists, and travel agents.

Methods of entering

A large percentage of commercial pilots have received their training in the armed forces. A military pilot who wants to apply for a commercial airplane pilot's license is required to pass only the Federal Aviation Regulations examination if application is made within a year after leaving the service.

Pilots possessing the necessary qualifications and license may apply directly to a commercial airline for a job. If accepted, they will go through a company orientation course, usually including both classroom instruction and practical training in company planes.

Those who are interested in becoming business pilots will do well to start their careers in mechanics. They may also have a history of military flying, but the strongest recommendation for a business pilot's job is an Airframe and Powerplant (A. and P.) rating. They should also have at least 500 hours flying time and have both commercial and instrument ratings on their license. They apply directly to the firm for which they would like to work.

Advancement

The flight engineer with a large commercial airline may spend two to seven years in grade before being promoted to copilot and another five to fifteen years before becoming captain. Seniority is the pilot's most important asset. If a pilot leaves one employer and goes to another,

he or she must start from the bottom again, no matter how much experience was gained with the first employer. The position of captain on a large airline is a high-seniority, high-prestige job, which may take five to ten years longer to attain. Other kinds of advancement may be: to check pilot, testing other pilots for advanced ratings; to chief pilot, supervising the work of other pilots; to administrative or executive positions with a commercial airline (ground operations); to self-employment, opening a flying business, such as a flight instruction, agricultural aviation, air-taxi, or charter service.

Employment outlook

About 76,000 civilian pilots held jobs in the early 1990s. The airlines employed about 60 percent. Many others taught flying at local airports or flew cargo and personnel for large companies that use their own aircraft. Pilots also performed air-taxi services, dusted crops, inspected pipelines, or conducted sightseeing trips. Still other pilots worked for federal, state, or local governments or were self-employed.

There will be faster than average growth in the employment of airline pilots through the end of the 1990s to keep up with the increase in passenger and cargo traffic. The outlook is less favorable, however, for business pilots as more companies choose to fly with smaller and regional airlines rather than buy and operate their own planes and helicopters. Because of computerized flight engineering systems, there may also be a reduced need for flight engineers.

Competition is expected to diminish as the many pilots who were hired during the boom of the 1960s begin to reach mandatory retirement age. In addition, because the military has increased its benefits and incentives, many pilots choose to remain in the service, further reducing the supply of pilots for civilian work. These factors are expected to create a shortage of qualified pilots.

When an economic downswing causes a decline in air travel, airline pilots may be given furlough. Business flying, flight instruction, and testing of new aircraft are also adversely affected by recessions.

Earnings

In the early 1990s, the average earnings of airline pilots were about $80,000 a year. Flight engineers averaged $53,000; copilots, $70,000; and captains, $108,000. Salaries depended on a number of factors, and pilots earned additional pay for night and international flights. Some senior captains on large aircraft earned as much as $165,000. The average starting salary for flight engineers was about $18,000.

Airline pilots are among the highest paid workers in the country. Other pilots generally earn lower salaries. For example, in the early 1990s, chief pilots averaged between $40,000 and $65,000 a year; captains/pilots, between $33,000 and $54,000; and copilots, between $26,000 and $38,000.

Other benefits often include employer-financed life and health insurance, retirement plans, disability payments if the pilots fail the FAA physical exam, and reduced fares for themselves and their families on their own and other airlines. Some pilots also receive an allowance for buying and cleaning their uniforms.

Conditions of work

An airline pilot works with the best possible equipment and under highly favorable circumstances, so far as comfort, staff assistance, and status are concerned. One may work irregular hours, may be away from home a lot, and must recognize the fact that the job carries an element of risk. The work exceeds more than one hundred hours during the month, usually only about sixty hours of which is spent in actual flying, with the remainder spent in ground duties.

The job of the agricultural aircraft pilot is more hazardous than that of the airline pilot. In addition to the normal dangers of flying, one must also work with toxic chemicals and must fly under difficult circumstances. Often, one will not have an airfield from which to work, but will have to take off and land on a relatively smooth piece of farmland.

For other pilots who handle small planes, emergency equipment and supply delivery, or routes to remote and isolated areas, the hazards may be more evident. Dropping medical supplies in Ethiopia or delivering mail to northern Alaska are more difficult tasks than most pilots face.

The business pilot will be responsible both for flying the plane and for maintaining it, as are most private and small plane pilots.

Social and psychological factors

Pilots' careers are completely dependent upon their good health. They must have a physical checkup periodically. If anything is wrong, they are grounded immediately. There is a factor of uncertainty, therefore, connected with every pilot's future.

GOE: 05.04.01; SIC: 451, 452; SOC: 825

◇ **SOURCES OF ADDITIONAL INFORMATION**

Air Force Recruitment Center
Wright-Patterson AFB, OH 45899

Air Line Pilots Association, International
1625 Massachusetts Avenue, NW
Washington, DC 20036

Air Transport Association of America
1709 New York Avenue, NW
Washington, DC 20006

American Helicopter Society
217 North Washington Street
Alexandria, VA 22314

Federal Aviation Administration
Public Inquiry Center, APA-430
800 Independence Avenue, SW
Washington, DC 20591

Future Aviation Professionals of America
4959 Massachusetts Boulevard
Atlanta, GA 30337

◇ **RELATED ARTICLES**

Podiatrists

Definition

Podiatrists, formerly called *chiropodists,* are specialists in the care and treatment of the foot. Treatment may include medical, surgical, and mechanical or physical means.

History

People's foot problems were important enough to be recorded in the writings and pictographs of early times. Gross deformities were recorded by the early Egyptians. Not until the eighteenth century, however, were other foot problems mentioned in literature.

In 1784, a Dr. Low of London wrote a treatise concerning the cause of corns, warts, bunions, and other painful and offensive cutaneous "excrescences," and "chiropody" became the general term for foot care and problems of that nature.

In the 1830s, "corn-doctors" began making the rounds of the larger cities of the United States making a business of "pulling out" corns. Chiropody did not really exist as such in the United States before 1895. Foot problems were handled by barbers, masseurs, or shoemakers before this time.

The first offices devoted exclusively to foot care were established in 1841. The chiropodists at this time had difficulty competing with physicians in the care of ingrown toenails. At this time the law read that a chiropodist had no right to make incisions involving the structures below the true skin. Most of the treatment included removal of corns, warts, calluses, bunions, abnormal nails, and general foot care.

An expert on the history of chiropody, Dr. Felix von Oefele, suggested changing the term to podiatry, because "chir" meant hand and "pod" meant foot, whereas the practice of chiropody actually dealt only with the foot.

Modern operative podiatry did not emerge until the 1920s. In the 1940s came the realization that correct orthopedic taping could help many foot defects and alleviate pain. More recently, surgery has been found to be a necessary part of podiatric care, and biomechanical corrections are often used independently or in conjunction with surgery.

Nature of the work

Podiatrists provide foot care in private offices, sometimes in a professional building with other specialists. They may also serve on the staffs of hospitals and treatment centers or clinics, in the armed forces or government health programs, or on the faculty in health professional schools.

To diagnose a foot problem the podiatrist may take X rays, perform blood tests, or prescribe other diagnostic tests. The most common foot problems treated by podiatrists are bunions, calluses, corns, warts, ingrown toenails, skin diseases such as athlete's foot, deformed toes, flat feet and arch problems.

A main concern of the podiatrist is preventive foot hygiene. The ability to recognize other body disorders is a requirement for a podiatrist, as arthritis or diabetes may first appear in the feet. Circulation problems may also first affect the feet because they are farthest away from the heart's blood supply.

Treatment involves fitting corrective devices, prescribing drugs and medications, physical therapy, performing surgery, and prescribing corrective footgear. Most podiatrists provide all types of foot care; however, some specialize in such areas as orthopedics (bone, muscle and joint disorders), podopediatrics (children's foot ailments), or podogeriatrics (foot disorders of the elderly).

Requirements

A high-school student should take as many courses in biology, zoology, inorganic and organic chemistry, and as much physics and math as possible to determine an interest in this field. The profession requires a scientific aptitude, manual dexterity, a good business sense, and an ability to put patients at ease.

A minimum of three years of prepodiatry education is required for entrance into a college of podiatric medicine. Undergraduate work should include courses in English, chemistry, biology or zoology, physics, and mathematics.

In the early 1990s, there were seven accredited colleges offering the four-year course leading to a Doctor of Podiatric Medicine (D.P.M.). All colleges of podiatric medicine require the Medical College Admissions Test (MCAT) as part of the application procedure. A brochure giving additional information may be obtained from: Medical College Admissions Test, Educational Testing Service, One American Plaza, Evanston, IL 60201.

The first two years in podiatry school are spent in classroom and laboratory work in anatomy, bacteriology, chemistry, pathology, physiology, pharmacology, and other basic sciences. In the final two years, students gain clinical experience in addition to their academic studies. To practice in a specialty, podiatrists need an additional one to three years of postgraduate education, sometimes known as a residency or preceptorship.

Special requirements

Podiatrists must be licensed in all fifty states, the District of Columbia, and Puerto Rico. A state board examination must be passed to qualify for licensing although some states allow the exams given during medical podiatric college, from the National Board of Podiatric Examiners, to substitute for the state boards. Some states also require applicants to serve at least a one-year residency.

Opportunities for experience and exploration

It may be possible for a student to obtain a summer job in a clinic area specializing in podiatrics.

Related occupations

Podiatrists are concerned with the prevention, diagnosis, and treatment of diseases, disorders, and injuries. The skills they employ are similar to those required in such other health-care occupations as chiropractors, dentists, optometrists, physicians, and veterinarians.

Methods of entering

A newly licensed podiatrist might begin working in a clinic, a hospital, or in an established practice with another podiatrist. Most offices will be found in large cities.

After bandaging a patient's right foot, a podiatrist checks the left one for injuries.

Advancement

Podiatrists may begin their careers in a clinic and then, once they become established, may open their own offices. Some podiatrists advance by becoming specialists in an area of podiatry or by becoming foot surgeons.

Employment outlook

There were approximately 13,000 practicing podiatrists in the early 1990s. Podiatrists work mainly in large cities, and the majority set up practices in the seven states where the colleges of podiatry are located California, Florida, Illinois, Iowa, New York, Pennsylvania, and Ohio.

The skills of the podiatrist are in rapidly increasing demand, as the profession gains in recognition as a health-care specialty and as foot disorders become more widespread, in good part because more people are becoming involved in sports and because of an aging population. The demand for podiatric services is expected to grow even more as health insurance coverage for such care becomes widespread. Although routine foot care is not ordinarily covered by health insurance, Medicare and private insurance programs frequently cover acute medical and surgical foot services, as well as diagnostic X rays, fracture casts, and leg braces. Many HMOs and other prepaid plans provide routine foot care as well.

The outlook for podiatrists through the 1990s is favorable throughout the country, but especially in the South and Southwest, where a shortage of practitioners exists.

Competition for residency positions is quite strong. If the state licensing board requires residency, as eleven states currently do, then residency is essential before a podiatrist can begin practicing. With the heavy competition for those posts, it is unlikely that students with average grades will be able to secure employment in those states.

Earnings

Podiatrists in well-established practices have incomes comparable to those earned by other well-paid professionals. The median net income of podiatrists was about $63,000 a year in the early 1990s. The average for newly licensed podiatrists with less than four years of experience was approximately $35,000. The average starting salary for beginning podiatrists hired by the Department of Veterans Affairs hospitals was about $27,200 to $32,600 in the early 1990s.

Conditions of work

Most podiatrists work independently in their own offices or in a group practice. Others are employed in various health-care settings or in colleges. The work week is generally thirty-five to forty hours per week. Podiatrists can usually set their own hours to coordinate office hours with hospital staff time or teaching schedules.

Social and psychological factors

The podiatrist must have a capacity to understand and apply scientific findings, the skill to manipulate delicate instruments and, most important, a liking for all kinds of people and a sincere desire to be of help to those needing care and attention. The same basic personal attributes that make a good medical worker in any field apply to the podiatrist.

GOE: 02.03.01; SIC: 8043; SOC: 283

◇ **SOURCES OF ADDITIONAL INFORMATION**

American Association of Colleges of Podiatric Medicine
6110 Executive Boulevard
Suite 204
Rockville, MD 20852

American Association of Foot Specialists
PO Box 54
Union, NJ 07083

American Podiatric Medical Association
9312 Old Georgetown Road
Bethesda, MD 20814

For information on certification procedures and examinations, contact:

American Board of Podiatric Orthopedics
1377 K Street, NW
PO Box 202
Washington, DC 20005

American Board of Podiatric Surgery
1601 Dolores Street
San Francisco, CA 94110

◇ **RELATED ARTICLES**

Volume 1: Health Care
Volume 2: Chiropractors; Kinesiotherapists; Physical therapists; Physicians; Prosthetists and orthotists
Volume 4: Orthotic and prosthetic technicians; Surgical technicians

Political scientists

Definition

Political scientists study the structure and theory of government. The political scientist attempts to reduce the many facts under study to a number of clear and descriptive principles. He or she attempts to evolve a standard language, because the very basis of scientific finding lies in its capacity for being communicated to others in a precise, clear, and standardized manner. He or she is constantly seeking solutions to political problems on two levels, the theoretical and the practical.

History

Political science is the oldest of the social sciences. It is based upon the premise that there must be some sort of philosophy and standard of human interrelationships wherever more than two people share the same environment. The more people there are, the more complex will be the doctrines that seek to explain the relationship patterns.

The first major work on the subject of political science was Plato's *The Republic*. Essentially, Plato was approaching the study of the relationship of man to government from a philosophical point of view and it was his premise that the state should be organized "to provide the good life" for all citizens.

Modern theories in political science start with the ideas of Machiavelli, the Italian statesman and political philosopher, who lived from 1469 to 1527. His most famous work, *Il Principe*, enunciated his political beliefs, which broke sharply from those of Plato. He believed that politics and morality are two entirely different spheres of human activity and that they should be governed by different standards and different laws.

Thomas Hobbes (1588–1679) is another of the recognized ancestors of current political science theory. He thought of government as a police force, which prevented people from plundering their neighbors. He was also one of the earliest of the status seekers, for he believed that all men were motivated by a desire for power over others. Some of his philosophies have influenced the theories of political science down to the present generation.

Another influential Englishman was John Locke (1632–1704) from whom we get the phi-

losophy of "the greatest good for the greatest number." Some people call him the originator of "beneficent paternalism," which means that the state or ruler acts as a kindly father to citizens, deciding what is best for them, and then seeing to it that the "best" is put into effect, whether the citizens like it or not.

In the world today, there are two different approaches to political science. In Europe and in the Latin American countries, political science is concerned with legal procedures and problems, and the ways in which the law affects human relationships. In the English-speaking countries, on the other hand, political science is concerned with examining political institutions and processes. In recent years, since the techniques and methods of psychology have been developed, political science has tried to take into account the motivation behind various kinds of individual and group behavior in politics. Although human motivation is often difficult to determine, this combined approach is believed to be one of the most productive in the history of political science.

Nature of the work

The greatest number of political scientists are employed as college and university teachers. In addition to teaching, they often write books and articles on the nature of political theory and conduct research projects to determine the adequacy of their theories or to develop new concepts. From time to time, they will serve as consultants to local, state, or national political groups or business firms or industries. They may work for the U.S. Department of State either in this country or in foreign service; they may work for individual congressmen or senators, serving as aides and helping them analyze legislative and administrative issues.

The best-known political scientists are often those who write for nationally distributed publications or who appear as commentators on television or radio. Their philosophies and opinions are well known and influence many people. Others who are influential but who are not so well known as personalities to the public are those who conduct public opinion polls.

Political scientists do not have a standard and inflexible way of work. Individual temperament directs the scientist to work in the way that seems most valid and reliable to that per-

A political scientist elaborates on his recent findings to his colleagues at a university.

son. In all, there seem to be four major ways in which to attack the problems posed by political considerations: (1) some scientists prefer to present careful descriptions of political situations, apparently feeling that to do more than to describe is intellectually dishonest because no one can guess accurately at underlying human motivation; (2) some political scientists feel that the only way to be of service is to analyze the problem presented by any given situation and to classify it according to certain established formulas; (3) some political scientists work by comparisons, attempting to compare one form of government to another, or one method of attempting a solution to one which has been tried in another situation; and (4) some scientists work by using the historical method, tracing each problem to its logical source. There are, of course, political scientists who customarily combine one or more of these methods, and some who occasionally attempt to use all four procedures.

Political scientists must be sure that they do not allow their own prejudices or biases to distort the way in which they see the facts that gather. Then, they must compare their findings and opinions with those of others who have conducted similar investigations. Finally, they must present their data in an objective fashion, even though the findings may not reveal the kinds of facts that they anticipated.

Political scientists work with many tools, all of which may be accessible to the average person. It is the way in which the tools are used that distinguishes the work of political scientists from that of lay people. Political scientists may use the data found in yearbooks and al-

manacs, material from encyclopedias, clippings from periodicals, or bound volumes of magazines or journals. They may refer to law books, to statutes, to records of court cases, to the *Congressional Record,* or to other legislative records. They may consult census records, historical documents, personal documents such as diaries or letters, or statistics from public opinion polls. They use libraries and archives to search out rare or old documents and records.

One of the favorite techniques of the modern-day political scientist is the "participant observer" method. In gathering data, he or she will become part of a group, participate in its proceedings, yet all the while be observing carefully some phase of the interaction that is of particular value to the study being conducted. An example of this kind of study might be the observing of behavior at a polling place. The participant observer might actually be employed at the polls, but may be making a series of systematized observations that will have significant meaning for a research report that he or she will write when this phase of activity is over.

Another technique often used by political scientists is the questionnaire. Questions will be carefully worded to elicit the facts that the researcher will need. Such questionnaires may be administered in a number of ways to a carefully selected sample of persons who are concerned with a given issue. The research, for example, may be directed toward predicting the results of a proposed bond issue which is to be voted upon. It may be decided that the questionnaire will be presented to every fifth person who enters the post office on a certain day. From their responses, the political scientist will make certain statistical calculations and base an estimate of the outcome of the bond issue on these calculations.

In addition to statistical methods for analyzing data, political scientists are also coming to rely on computers to help them organize and analyze facts.

Many political scientists specialize in public administration, in American government, or in international relations. Others specialize in such fields as public law, history of political ideas, political parties, and area studies.

Requirements

A bachelor's degree is the minimum requirement for political scientists. Few positions, however, are open to those who hold only this degree. Most jobs require at least a master's degree; many, including college teaching, require a doctorate.

High-school students who are interested in political science should elect a college preparatory program and seek admission to a college or university that offers a bachelor's degree in political science. Some persons who plan to become political scientists prefer to obtain their master's degree in a specialized subject, such as public administration, city planning, or international relations. Some students who later go to law school have received bachelor's degrees in political science.

People who want to make a career of political science but who are unwilling or unable to go beyond the bachelor's or master's degree may be interested in exploring the possibility of entering high-school teaching. They should determine the certification standards for teaching political science in the state in which they hope to teach and should then be certain to include the necessary courses that will lead to certification in their undergraduate program.

Special requirements

Above-average intelligence, a strong curiosity about government, an interest in its dynamics, and a special persistence in the face of perplexing problems are all needed by the prospective political scientist. This person will look forward to a scholarly life, in which he or she will do a great deal of reading and studying. It is essential that he or she enjoys learning.

If the student is interested in working in the diplomatic service, he or she will need the ability to get along with many different kinds of people.

Knowledge of at least one foreign language is helpful for the diplomat. The person in foreign service also will need good health and endurance because the conditions under which one may have to live and work may be quite unlike those to which he or she is accustomed. Entry to some types of foreign service may be secured only after the successful passing of a rather rigid physical examination.

Opportunities for experience and exploration

The secondary school student who may be interested in exploring the field of political science may consider working as a page with the state legislature or with the Congress of the United States. Such experience may give insights into the workings of government so that those interested may discover the depth of that interest.

In addition, the prospective political scientist may ask the school counselor to include a political scientist as a speaker for Career Day. If possible, one should arrange to interview the political scientist.

The student with a bachelor's degree in political science who hopes to go on for further study but still is not completely sure of the strength of his or her interest in the field may be qualified to accept a position as a trainee in political science research or as an assistant in an independent public opinion research organization. Such a person may work in some of the more routine jobs with agencies or departments of the United States government. Although such positions may offer little opportunity to assume responsibility, they furnish a way for the young person who is still undecided about the future to learn more about the profession before investing time and money in further education.

Related occupations

Political scientists are specialists within the field of social science, which also includes anthropologists, archaeologists, biographers, economists, historians, intelligence specialists (government and military service), scientific linguists, and sociologists. Other workers whose training and personal qualities are similar to those of social scientists include college and university faculty, computer programmers, computer systems analysts, counselors, lawyers, mathematicians, religious workers, reporters and correspondents, social workers, and statisticians.

Methods of entering

Most young graduates with a degree or degrees in political science can secure positions through the placement offices of their own colleges or universities. Entry to some jobs with federal agencies is through civil service examination. Announcements of examinations may be secured through the local post office or by writing to the Office of Personnel Management, Washington, DC 20415.

Advancement

The political scientist who has acquired graduate degrees and gone into college teaching may advance from the rank of instructor through the regular academic grades to full professor. Greatest advancement may be to the position of head of the political science department.

The political scientist who has gone into research work as a career may advance from a position as research assistant to director of research, if qualified to do so and interested in taking on administrative responsibilities. Some persons prefer to continue to conduct the actual research itself, and leave the burden of administrative details to others.

Those who are interested in government service may enter an agency, and may progress as they gain experience to positions of great responsibility. Again, the individual's advancement may depend upon whether he or she is interested in assuming all the administrative responsibilities.

Employment outlook

About 15,000 political scientists were employed in the United States in the early 1990s. Most of them held positions in colleges and universities.

The outlook for those with a bachelor's degree is not considered good because other persons with majors in some of the other social sciences or with majors in business administration may also meet requirements for the same kinds of jobs. The graduate with a bachelor's degree in political science also faces strong competition for teaching positions in secondary schools because fewer vacancies are occurring than in past years.

The employment outlook for graduates with two or more degrees is only slightly better. Because of declining student enrollments, the number of teaching vacancies in colleges and universities is not expected to grow and may actually decrease.

Employment opportunities in public and private organizations are expected to show little change. Professional analysts and administrators will be needed to work in long-range planning, legislation, environmental concerns, urban affairs, risks assessment, or related work. The best opportunities will exist for graduates of public policy schools and institutes, specialists in one particular field (such as public administration or Soviet government), and political scientists with extensive computer training and language skills.

Some openings will be available with federal, state, and local governments in the next decade, as the population expands and expectations of various kinds of government services increase. There will also be some opportunities available with the political parties, with certain industries, and with individuals who have been or who hope to be elected to public office.

Earnings

In the early 1990s, the salaries for all political scientists employed in colleges and universities ranged from less than $18,000 to more than $66,000, depending on rank. Full professors earned from about $25,000 to $66,000 and more; associate professors, from $23,000 to $54,000; and assistant professors, from about $18,000 to $39,000. Lecturers and instructors usually earned considerably less. Teachers at the secondary level earned salaries comparable to teachers in other fields. The average salary of high-school teachers in the early 1990s was about $26,100 a year.

The beginning salary in the federal government for political scientists with a bachelor's degree in the early 1990s was about $14,800 or $18,400, depending on the person's academic record. The starting salary for a person with a master's degree was about $22,500; with a doctorate, $27,200 or $32,600.

The earnings of political scientists working for business organizations on research projects such as public opinion polls depend on the individual's education and experience. In the early 1990s, beginners with a bachelor's degree and little or no experience were paid starting salaries of about $18,400 a year. Doctorates with some experience earned between $34,000 and $36,000. Those with extensive experience and a knowledge of business administration were paid between $40,000 and $80,000 a year to head up research projects.

Conditions of work

Most political scientists work in pleasant surroundings. Those who teach at any level may find associations with students both challenging and refreshing. Those who work in research usually find that they are provided with modern equipment and facilities.

The political scientist in government work usually works in a well-appointed, well-staffed office. It is usually comfortable, well lighted, and temperature controlled. Most political scientists who are employed by government work in large urban centers. Approximately 75 percent of the political scientists who work for the federal government work in or near Washington, D.C.

Political scientists in government service may find that they must travel frequently. Those who enter foreign service will have an opportunity to go to many parts of the world.

Social and psychological factors

Few political scientists find that their jobs are monotonous. From time to time, every political scientist has the experience of making a new discovery, or of seeing personal predictions come true, or of devising a new way of approaching an old problem.

GOE: 11.03.02; SIC: 8221, 8651; SOC: 1914

◇ **SOURCES OF ADDITIONAL INFORMATION**

Academy of Political Science
2852 Broadway
New York, NY 10025

American Academy of Political and Social Science
3937 Chestnut Street
Philadelphia, PA 19104

American Political Science Association
1527 New Hampshire Avenue, NW
Washington, DC 20036

American Society for Public Administration
1120 G Street, NW
Suite 500
Washington, DC 20005

◇ **RELATED ARTICLES**

Volume 1: Civil Service; Personal and Consulting Service; Politics and Public Service; Social Sciences
Volume 2: City managers; College and university faculty; Economists; Foreign-Service officers; Historians; Lawyers and judges; Sociologists; Urban and regional planners

Polygraph examiners

Definition

Polygraph examiners use polygraph equipment and techniques to determine whether individuals have answered questions truthfully or dishonestly. Polygraphs, often called "lie detectors," are instruments that measure and record certain nonvoluntary body responses that are affected by the individual's emotional state. To judge whether the subject has answered all the questions truthfully, the examiner compares the reactions recorded for questions that are not likely to cause stress with the reactions recorded for other questions.

Polygraph examiners work for police departments, the armed forces, business, and industry. They are sometimes called *polygraphers*,

and those who use recording devices to measure stress in their subjects' voices may be called *psychological stress evaluators.*

History

The body carries out such processes as breathing and blood circulation automatically. But the rates of these nonvoluntary processes change in response to stress, and stress is likely to increase when an individual is lying. One of the first attempts to use this knowledge to detect deception or verify truthfulness was made in 1898, when suspected criminals were interrogated while their pulse rates and blood vol-

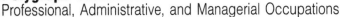

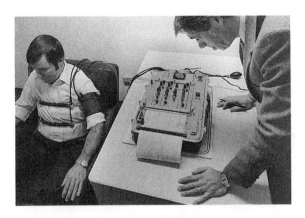

A polygraph examiner studies the readouts from a questioning session. In this particular case, the person questioned is not a suspect.

umes were monitored. Tests conducted in 1914 worked by measuring the volume of the air that test subjects breathed, and tests performed in 1917 showed that changes in blood pressure also could indicate whether the subjects were telling the truth.

The first modern lie detector was invented in 1921 by John A. Larson, a medical student who worked with a member of a local police department. Larson's instrument continuously recorded blood pressure, pulse rate, and respiration, and it was called a polygraph ("many writings") because it recorded all these processes simultaneously. Later polygraphs also recorded the electrical resistance of the skin that results from changes in perspiration.

Polygraphs have been used in police intelligence and security investigations since 1924. Some psychologists, however, still question the validity of polygraph tests, and some courts do not accept the test results as evidence.

Nature of the work

Although polygraph examiners often test suspects and witnesses in criminal cases, the applications of the polygraph are not limited to police work. For example, the armed forces employ polygraph examiners to screen prospective civilian employees, and business and industry may call them in to determine the trustworthiness of new employees or find out who is responsible for pilferage.

Before polygraph examiners meet the subject they will test, they gather information about the individual and the circumstances involved. They try to learn about the subject's childhood, medical history, and any police record; whether the subject has a history of emotional illness or drug or alcohol abuse; and whether the subject is taking any medication. In criminal cases, they may visit the police station, the crime scene, or the morgue for information.

After gathering this information, polygraph examiners spend at least an hour with the test subject to obtain information about his or her background, current health, and knowledge of the circumstances that led to the polygraph examination. They try to calm the subject's fears about the test by showing the person the polygraph instrument, explaining how it works, and explaining the test procedure.

Next, polygraph examiners develop test questions that are easy to understand and not ambiguous. Before they actually give the test, they read the questions to the subject and assure the person there will be no surprise questions. Then the examiners attach the apparatus to the individual to measure changes in certain nonvoluntary body responses.

A tube fastened around the subject's chest measures respiration, and a cuff around the subject's arm measures blood pressure. During the questioning, an electric motor moves the instrument's graph paper while pens record the subject's responses on the paper.

The actual tests are brief; a ten-question test takes about four minutes. The test may consist of control questions, which are not likely to cause stress, and key questions, which are likely to produce a strong reaction if the subject is lying. Another form of the test includes a number of similar questions, with only one question that contains the correct details. Because only the guilty person knows which question has the right details, the subject's reaction to that question can indicate guilt or innocence.

Some people believe they can affect their reactions by taking drugs. But a drug that reduces an individual's reactions to key questions also will reduce the individual's reactions to control questions. Thus the test results will still show a difference between the subject's reactions when answering truthfully and when lying. In the administering of some tests, a written exam is given that lasts at least an hour to allow for drugs to wear off.

After administering the test, polygraph examiners evaluate the subject's recorded responses and then discuss the results with the individual. If it appears that the subject has been untruthful, examiners try to give the individual a chance to explain the reasons for his or her reactions and may even retest the person later.

In addition to administering and evaluating polygraph tests, polygraph examiners keep records and make reports on test results. They may appear in court as witnesses on matters dealing with polygraph examinations, and some also teach classes in polygraph operation and interrogation techniques.

Other uses for polygraph examinations include investigation of clients before hiring, registration for security clearance, and other risk-related positions. The use of polygraph exams is becoming more commonplace.

Requirements

High-school students who are interested in becoming polygraph examiners should take courses that help them understand how the body functions and how it is affected by stress. Courses in psychology, physiology, and biology will be especially useful.

College students should major in science or criminal justice. In addition, classes in English and writing will help prepare them to write reports, and classes in public speaking will help them develop the self-confidence they will need when testifying in court.

Candidates for lie-detector schools usually need four-year college degrees, but applicants with two years of college courses in criminal investigation plus five years of investigative experience may be accepted. Polygraph training in an approved school usually takes from six to eight weeks.

Students must take polygraph tests upon entering a lie-detection school to assure they have the good moral character this field requires. During their training, students learn about the physical responses the polygraph measures, how to operate the polygraph, how to develop and ask questions, how to interpret polygraph charts, and the legal aspects of polygraph testing. They observe polygraph tests administered by others, administer the tests themselves, and hear and see audiotapes and videotapes of their own performances. When they complete lie-detection school, students go on to internships of at least six months.

Polygraph examiners must show good moral character and cannot have police records. They should speak and write well, have self-confidence, be alert, and be able to maintain objectivity and self-control. They also must be comfortable working with strangers and relate well to all kinds of people, and they should not be influenced by such factors as economic status, race, or sex.

In addition, polygraph examiners must be willing to work under pressure and under a variety of conditions and should not be shocked by distressing sights. Finally, they must understand the importance of protecting their subjects' rights and maintaining confidentiality.

Special requirements

Although many states license polygraph examiners, their requirements vary. Typical requirements include a high-school diploma or the equivalent, either a bachelor's degree or five years of experience as a detective, completion of polygraph training at a state-approved school, six months of internship, and successful completion of a state-administered test.

National standards for training, and also for polygraph equipment, are established by the American Polygraph Association (APA), which also conducts research and publishes information.

Opportunities for experience and exploration

Because polygraph examiners must obtain cooperation from their test subjects, activities that involve students in one-to-one contacts can provide valuable experience. Such activities include summer work as a camp counselor and volunteer or part-time work in a hospital or nursing home. And students at some colleges can volunteer for campus security patrols, which provide opportunities to develop their observation and investigative skills.

Students who live near large population centers may be able to visit lie-detection schools and talk with staff members. They also may be able to visit courts and tour police facilities. In addition, students should participate in school career days and should take advantage of any opportunities to talk with people who conduct police or private investigations.

Related occupations

Polygraph examiners must know how to investigate, evaluate information, and obtain cooperation from others. Workers in other occupations who have similar skills include police officers, private investigators, FBI agents, crime laboratory technologists, security consultants and technicians, occupational safety and health workers, health and regulatory inspectors, industrial safety and health technicians, and insurance claims representatives.

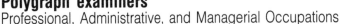

Methods of entering

Lie-detection schools often provide placement assistance for their graduates, and graduates also may learn about job openings from contacts they make during their internships. Professional groups may be a source of job leads, and periodicals that specialize in law enforcement and criminal justice may list job openings. In addition, qualified polygraph examiners can apply to courts and crime laboratories. They also can apply to federal agencies, which may require them to take civil service examinations.

In some cases, people who are already involved in investigative work, such as police and private investigators, criminologists, and particularly for military intelligence staff members, add to their skills by earning polygraph examiner certificates.

Advancement

Polygraph examiners in civil service positions can advance through various job levels and eventually hold management jobs, and examiners who work for private security agencies can advance to such executive positions as director of operations. Polygraph examiners who are employed by business and industry in security positions may become supervisors and eventually head their departments, and those employed in airline security have many opportunities to advance. In addition, some experienced polygraph examiners start their own agencies or work as security consultants or security systems specialists.

Employment outlook

In the early 1990s the American Polygraph Association listed about 30,000 members. Polygraph examiners were needed in large population centers throughout the United States, and the openings in crime laboratories outnumbered the examiners available to fill them.

The growing population and the increasing crime rate were expected to create more openings for polygraph examiners in the future. Courts in at least thirty states had allowed the use of polygraph test results as evidence, and the public's pressure to reduce court backlogs was expected to increase the use of polygraph tests.

Earnings

In the early 1990s polygraph examiners started their internships with earnings of about $16,000, and experienced examiners were earning as much as $52,000. Examiners who were paid employees often received such benefits as sick leave, paid vacations, medical and dental insurance, retirement plans, and bonuses.

Conditions of work

Most polygraph examiners work forty-hour weeks, although some work longer and irregular hours, nights, and weekends. They usually work indoors, in clean and comfortable surroundings, but may travel to their appointments, often carrying their polygraph equipment, which weighs about twenty-five pounds.

Polygraph examiners are employed in many types of organizations, and their surroundings and the type of people they work with are determined by the nature of the organization. Many examiners are involved in law enforcement and may work for criminal or civil courts, police or sheriff departments, the FBI, or the Secret Service. Some work for the armed forces, and many others work for private businesses, such as retail stores, drug firms, companies that have their own security forces, and firms that provide testing services for other business organizations.

Social and psychological factors

Some people have a poor opinion of polygraph examiners. This impression developed, however, at a time when professional standards were not established, and such attitudes should improve as more states adopt strict licensing laws.

There are also people who do not believe test results should be used in court. Some question their accuracy, although studies have rated their validity at 87.2 to 96.2 percent. Others are against the use of polygraph tests because they believe such tests invade the privacy of the test subjects.

Polygraph examiners sometimes encounter hostile subjects who attack them verbally and may even try to attack them physically. Examiners, however, have the satisfaction of contributing to the solution of crimes and clearing individuals who are innocent.

GOE: 02.04.02; SIC: 7381; SOC: 399

◇ **SOURCES OF ADDITIONAL INFORMATION**

American Polygraph Association
PO Box 8037
Chattanooga, TN 37411

American Association of Police Polygraphists
1918 Sleepy Hollow
Pearland, TX 77581

Professional athletes

Definition

Professional athletes compete in athletic events, such as baseball, football, and hockey, for pay.

History

The exact origin of sports is unclear. It is generally assumed, however, that sports began the first time various physical activities, like hunting, fishing, and wrestling, were undertaken for recreation rather than survival. The birth of organized sports, with rules, equipment, and scoring devices, occurred around 776 B.C. when the first recorded Olympic Games were held in ancient Greece. The ancient Romans, although initially scornful of sports, also participated in events of their own, such as chariot racing and gladiatorial battles.

Although the interest in sports diminished during the Middle Ages, sports for entertainment began to reemerge around A.D. 1200 in various European countries. In France, for example, teams played a hockeylike game called *la soule*. Although *la soule* was discouraged by authorities because it was thought to be too rough, the sport generated an interest in games such as tennis, which became very popular in the 1400s.

The popularity of sporting events greatly increased in many countries around the world between the 1400s and the 1800s. In England, especially, competitions were held in various sports, such as track and field, horse racing, and football (the ancestor of soccer).

During the nineteenth century, sports became highly organized. In 1825, for example, the first organized track-and-field meet was held in England. Four years later, Oxford and Cambridge Universities held a rowing match; this represented the first intercollegiate athletic competition.

In the United States, American football evolved from the sport of rugby, and, in 1869, Rutgers and Princeton Universities played the first intercollegiate football game. Many other sports soon followed. Baseball was first played in the United States in 1845, basketball in 1891. Golf and tennis were organized into competitive events soon after, and the first championship boxing match was held in New Orleans in 1892.

The interest and growth of sports has continued to increase. Today, literally tens of millions of sports fans attend various athletic events; sports have become a very popular American pastime.

Nature of the work

Professional athletes are paid to participate in competitive athletic events. To prepare for

Some of the most visible professional athletes are baseball players, who command high salaries to compensate for their short careers and demanding schedules.

these events, professional athletes must practice and exercise for hours and hours each day. *Coaches, instructors,* and *managers* help professional athletes train and condition their bodies. They are responsible for maintaining the athletic strength of the competitor, and assisting in recovery programs for injured athletes. They negotiate fees, salaries, and other compensation.

The specific nature of the work varies according to the specific sport played. Some sports, like tennis and golf, are individual games in which one person competes against one opponent. Other sports, such as football, basketball, and hockey, are team efforts. In some cases, in athletic event may be both an individual and a team event, as in gymnastics and wrestling, where athletes often compete individually toward a total team score.

All sports require physical skills. Some sports may involve greater physical contact with other players than other sports; football, for example, is considered a "rougher" sport than golf. All professional athletes, however, must carefully develop and sharpen physical skills. In addition, all athletes, regardless of the sport, must develop various mental skills as well, such as the ability to concentrate and to play under pressure.

Professional athletes are often well-known by the general public; athletic events are viewed and enjoyed by millions of fans all over the world. In this country, many different types of sports have become popular, including football, baseball, basketball, boxing, tennis, golf, hockey, swimming, skating, skiing, and others.

Requirements

Each sport has its own training and educational requirements. There are no formal requirements in some sports, such as boxing. Other sports, like golf, specify that members meet very strict training and educational requirements. To become a member of the Professional Golfers' Association, for example, an athlete must study various subjects, such as business administration and public relations; the athlete must also pass a written and an oral test and, of course, play a good game of golf.

Most sports have some requirements that are not found in other sports. Professional tennis players, for example, must rank among the top two hundred players in the world to become members of the Association of Tennis Professionals. Professional bowlers, on the other hand, must maintain an average of at least 190 for two years and perform in at least one Professional Bowlers Association tournament each year. Baseball and football players almost always play in college before they are offered contracts by professional teams.

A college education is extremely important for all professional athletes, regardless of the sport. College develops an athlete's physical skills and provides an opportunity for the athlete to be seen by talent scouts. But, more importantly, college prepares athletes for second careers that will have to be pursued when the days of athletic performance are over. The career of a professional athlete is generally very short.

Special requirements

There are no special licenses or certificates needed to become a professional athlete. Individual sports, however, often have specific requirements for potential members. In addition, it is often necessary for a person to begin a sport at a very young age to develop the expertise that is necessary for professional competition.

Opportunities for experience and exploration

Persons who are interested in becoming professional athletes have many opportunities to explore the field. Basically, those individuals interested in a particular athletic area should participate in the sport as much as possible.

Most elementary, junior high, and high schools teach athletics as part of the general curriculum and most have teams in a variety of sports that compete with other teams in the area.

It is usually apparent at an early age whether a person has natural athletic ability. A strong determination and a desire to succeed, however, must also be present if a person is to develop that athletic ability.

Most sports have associations that can provide information to prospective members. Students can also talk with coaches, trainers, and sports figures to determine how to best prepare for a career as a professional athlete.

Related occupations

People who participate in professional sports are usually coordinated and physically fit. The occupations that require an interest in physical fitness include physical therapists, kinesiotherapists, recreational therapists, coaches, sports instructors, and physical therapy technicians.

Methods of entering

Professional sports are organized differently from most other occupations. Professional athletes do not generally go job hunting; instead, talent scouts travel from city to city in search of outstanding athletes. These scouts recommend players to the managers of various professional teams, who may offer the athlete a contract. It is important for amateur athletes to play as much as possible to increase their exposure to scouts. For many sports, college sports programs are the only way for a player to be seen by a scout.

Advancement

Rising to the top of the field and becoming a highly paid and well-known sports figure is the ultimate goal of many athletes. Only a small percentage of athletes, however, become professionals and an even smaller percentage become highly successful professionals. Thus, it is important for athletes to be well-educated so that they can earn a living when they retire from professional sports. After retiring from sports, many players enter the field of broadcasting. Some promote sportswear and other related items, while others become coaches and

Professional bicycling has recently gained popularity, receiving media attention. Many bicyclists identify their town of origin on their shirts.

managers. Others use their name to begin their own businesses.

Employment outlook

Although the number of professional athletes has been steadily increasing over the past several years, the total number of openings in professional sports is still very low when compared to other types of work. In addition, competition for jobs is fierce.

The number of professional athletes varies from one sport to another. The Professional Bowlers Association, for example, has about 2,800 members; the Association of Tennis Professionals ranks about 1,100 players. The Professional Golfers' Association has about 9,000 members. These numbers, however, represent only a small fraction of the number of good players in these three sports.

Becoming a professional baseball, football, basketball, or hockey player has always been, and will continue to be, very difficult. The number of openings, however, in these sports is increasing, and those players with extraordinary talent may find success.

Earnings

Yearly earnings for professional athletes vary according to the skills of the player and the specific sport played. Salaries are higher in some sports, like football, than in others, like boxing.

In the early 1990s, National football League players averaged more than $175,000 a year, while major league baseball players averaged more than $300,000 a year. Professional golfers earn between $12,000 and $100,000, with top players earning more than $200,000. Earnings from a single bowling tournament range from $25,000 to $235,000; bowlers may participate in several tournaments a year. Top-ranking tennis players may earn as much as $1,000,000 in tournaments. In addition, professional athletes in all types of sports earn money from product endorsements and personal deals.

Although professional athletes often receive a great deal of publicity about their extraordinary salaries, it should be remembered that athletes practice and train for many, many hours each day. Actual competitive events account for only a small percentage of total hours worked. In addition, the career of a professional athlete is often very short.

Conditions of work

Regardless of the sport, all professional athletes must travel to compete. Baseball and football players work all over the United States; bowlers have specific circuits to follow; and tennis and golf professionals travel abroad, as well as around this country.

Specific working conditions depend on the sport played. Basketball players and bowlers, for example, play indoors in comfortable temperatures. Baseball players may have to play in very hot weather, although they do not play in rain. Football players, on the other hand, play outdoors in all kinds of weather, including subzero temperatures.

Locker rooms and training facilities also vary greatly, as do the number of behavior of spectators. Football and baseball fans, for example, are often very vocal while watching a game; golf and tennis fans, on the other hand, must be quiet while the athletes are playing. It is essential in all sports that equipment be of the highest quality and that rules be followed to minimize the risk of injuries. Broken bones, torn ligaments, and other injuries do occur, however, regardless of the precautions taken. For professional athletes such as boxers, the injuries sustained may have permanent effects on their physical health. Knee, ankle, elbow, and neck injuries are not uncommon in contact sports. A serious injury may permanently remove a player from competitive life. The professional athlete must keep this possiblity in consideration at all times.

Social and psychological factors

Athletes must have basic athletic ability, especially in terms of strength, stamina, speed, and coordination. Of equal importance, however, are certain personality traits that the successful athlete must exhibit: courage, determination, and concentration. Professional athletes must also have good instincts, think quickly, and be able to play with physical discomfort. And, although they must enjoy competition, athletes should be able to lose graciously.

A professional athlete's career is often very short; the average professional football player's career, for example, lasts less than five years. Thus, the professional athlete should be prepared to embark on another career when the playing days are over.

GOE: 12.01.03; SIC: 7999; SOC: 34

◇ **SOURCES OF ADDITIONAL INFORMATION**

American Alliance for Health, Physical Education, Recreation, and Dance
1900 Association Drive
Reston, VA 22091

Federation of Professional Athletes
2021 L Street, NW
Washington, DC 20036

◇ **RELATED ARTICLES**

Property and real estate managers

Definition

Property and real estate managers plan and supervise the activities that affect land and buildings. Most of them manage rental properties, such as apartment buildings, office buildings, and shopping centers. Others manage the services and commonly owned areas of condominiums and community associations.

Some managers buy and develop real estate for companies that have widespread retail operations, such as franchise restaurants and hotel chains, or for companies that build such projects as shopping malls and industrial parks. And other managers negotiate agreements that allow their companies to lay pipelines and utility lines or drill for oil.

History

Real estate includes land and everything attached to it, such as buildings, fences, and trees. It is a valuable asset that can produce income, and it often increases in value over the years.

For many centuries only a few people could own property, and they usually passed it down from one generation to the next. But changes in society over the last few centuries brought about the development of the business of buying, selling, and renting real estate. More people could afford to own property, a growing and increasingly urban population needed housing, and manufacturers and merchants needed space for their operations. In addition, laws were developed to regulate the transfer of real estate.

Nature of the work

Most property and real estate managers are involved in the day-to-day management of property. Property managers are responsible for residential and commercial real estate and usually manage several properties at one time. Acting as the owners' agents and advisers, they supervise the marketing of space, negotiate lease agreements, direct bookkeeping activities, and report to owners on the status of the property. They also negotiate contracts for trash removal and other services and hire the maintenance and on-site management personnel employed at the properties.

On-site managers are based at the properties they manage, and most of them are responsible for apartment buildings and work under the direction of property managers. They train, supervise, and assign duties to maintenance staffs; inspect the properties to determine what maintenance and repairs are needed; schedule routine service of heating and air conditioning systems; keep records of operating costs; and submit cost reports to the property managers or owners. They deal with residents on a daily basis and are responsible for handling their requests for service and repairs, resolving complaints concerning other tenants, and enforcing rules and lease restrictions.

Apartment house managers work for property owners or property management firms and are usually on-site managers. They show apartments to prospective tenants, negotiate leases, collect rents, handle tenants' requests, and direct the activities of maintenance staffs and outside contractors.

Building superintendents are responsible for operating and maintaining the facilities and equipment of such properties as apartment houses and office buildings. At small properties they may be the only on-site managers and report directly to property managers; at larger properties they may report to on-site managers and also may supervise maintenance staffs.

Housing project managers direct the operation of housing projects provided for such groups as military families, low-income families, and welfare recipients. The housing is usually subsidized by the government and may consist of single-family homes, multi-unit dwellings, or house trailers.

Condominium managers are responsible to unit-owner associations and manage the services and commonly owned areas of condominium properties. They also submit reports to the association members, supervise collection of owner assessments, resolve owners' complaints, and direct the activities of maintenance staffs and outside contractors. In some communities homeowners belong to associations that employ managers to oversee the property and facilities that the homeowners own and use jointly.

Market managers direct the activities of municipal, regional, or state markets where wholesale fruit, vegetables, or meat are sold. They rent space to buyers and sellers and direct the

527

A manager of an apartment building discusses with a prospective renter the advantages of living in the building.

supervisors who are responsible for collecting fees, maintaining and cleaning the buildings and grounds, and enforcing sanitation and security rules. *Public events facilities rental managers* negotiate contracts with organizations that wish to lease arenas, auditoriums, stadiums, or other facilities that are used for public events. They solicit new business and renewals of established contracts, maintain schedules to determine the availability of the facilities for bookings, and oversee operation and maintenance activities.

Real estate firm managers direct the activities of the sales agents who work for real estate firms. They screen and hire sales agents; conduct training sessions; and confer with agents and clients to resolve such problems as adjusting selling prices, determining who is responsible for repairs, and deciding who is responsible for closing costs. *Business opportunity-and-property-investment brokers* buy and sell business enterprises and investment properties on a commission or speculative basis. They investigate such factors as the financial ratings of businesses that are for sale, the desirability of a property's location for various types of businesses, and the condition of investment properties.

Businesses employ real estate managers to find, acquire, and develop the properties they need for their operations and to dispose of properties they no longer need. *Real estate agents* often work for companies that operate retail merchandising chains, such as fast-food restaurants, gasoline stations, and apparel shops. They locate sites that are desirable for their companies' operations and arrange to purchase or lease them. They also review their companies' holdings to identify properties that are no longer desirable and then negotiate to dispose of them. (Real estate sales agents also may be called "real estate agents," but they are not involved in management.) *Land development managers* are responsible for acquiring land for such projects as shopping centers and industrial parks. They also negotiate with local governments, property owners, and public interest groups to eliminate obstacles to their companies' developments, and they arrange for architects to draw up plans and construction firms to build the projects.

Right-of-way agents negotiate with property owners and public officials to obtain access to land that lies in the path of such construction projects as utility lines and pipelines. They may purchase or lease these properties, or they may obtain agreements that grant rights for specific uses of the land. *Right-of-way supervisors* direct the activities of right-of-way agents and are responsible for searches of city and county records to determine the ownership of properties and the status of rights of access along streets, alleys, and highways.

Geophysical prospecting permit agents negotiate with landowners for permits that allow prospecting, surveying, and testing for petroleum and gas deposits. They search local records to determine the ownership of proposed exploration sites, talk with local authorities to determine the regulations that will affect exploration, and draw up agreements that permit their companies to search the land for petroleum and gas deposits. *Leasing managers* direct the land and leasing departments of petroleum companies. Their departments are responsible for negotiating leases, rights-of-way, and other agreements that cover land and mineral rights.

Land leases-and-rentals managers direct the record keeping activities that are concerned with land leases, contracts, and other agreements that give petroleum companies rights to drill wells on public or private lands and produce gas and oil. They insure that files and records are current and their companies comply with the terms of agreements with landowners and local officials. *Lease buyers* work for oil or coal producing firms and negotiate with landowners and other oil or coal companies to obtain leases and other agreements that allow their own companies to carry out exploration, drilling, and producing activities in specified oil or coal fields.

Unlike *real estate sales agents and brokers*, who chiefly negotiate to buy and sell property and usually are paid on a commission basis, most property and real estate managers are salaried employees.

Requirements

Most employers hire college graduates for property and real estate management positions, so high-school students interested in this work should enroll in college preparatory programs. College students should work toward degrees in real estate, business administration, public administration, or finance.

Property and real estate managers must be skilled in both oral and written communication and adept at dealing with people. They also need to be good administrators and negotiators, and those who specialize in land development must be especially resourceful and creative to arrange financing for their projects. Managers for small rental or condominium complexes may be required to have building repair and maintenance skills, as well as business management skills.

Special requirements

Many property and real estate managers attend training programs offered by various professional and trade associations. Employers often send their managers to these programs to improve their management skills and expand their knowledge of such subjects as operation and maintenance of building mechanical systems, insurance and risk management, business and real estate law, and accounting and financial concepts. And many managers attend these programs voluntarily to prepare for advancement to positions with more responsibility.

Managers who have appropriate experience, complete the required training programs, and achieve satisfactory scores on written exams can earn certification and such professional designations as Accredited Resident Manager, Registered Apartment Manager, Professional Community Association Manager, and Master of Corporate Real Estate.

The federal government requires certification for managers of public housing that is subsidized by federal funds. Business opportunity-and-property-investment brokers must hold state licenses, and some states require real estate managers to hold licenses.

Opportunities for experience and exploration

High-school students who are interested in property and real estate management positions should seek activities that help them develop management skills, such as serving as an officer in an organization or participating in Junior Achievement projects. They also should seek part-time or summer jobs in sales or volunteer for work that involves public contact.

In addition, students can participate in school career days and read the career information that is available at school and public libraries. They also may be able to tour apartment complexes, shopping centers, and other real estate developments, and should take advantage of any opportunities to talk with property and real estate managers.

Related occupations

Property and real estate managers plan, organize, staff, and control real estate operations. Workers who perform similar functions in other fields include restaurant and food service managers, hotel and resort managers and their assistants, health services managers, education administrators, and city managers.

Methods of entering

Most employers hire college graduates for property and real estate management positions. They prefer degrees in real estate, business management, and related fields, but they also consider liberal arts graduates.

Advancement

Property and real estate managers often begin as on-site managers for small apartment house complexes, condominiums, or community associations. With experience, they may transfer to larger properties, or they may become assistant property managers, working closely with property managers and acquiring experience in a variety of management tasks. In some cases, inexperienced college graduates with bachelor's or master's degrees enter the field as assistant property managers.

Assistant managers may advance to property manager positions and in this capacity will be responsible for several properties. As they advance in their careers, property managers may be responsible for larger or more complex operations, may specialize in managing specific types of property, or may eventually establish their own companies.

The companies may offer management service to property owners, or the experienced manager may choose to invest in his or her own properties to lease or rent.

Employment outlook

In the early 1990s, about 128,000 people in the United States were employed as property and real estate managers. Most worked for real estate operators and property management firms, but others worked for real estate developers, government agencies that manage public buildings, corporations with large holdings of properties used for their retail operations, real estate investors, and mining and oil companies. Many managers were self-employed developers, apartment building owner managers, property management firm owners, or owners of full-service real estate brokerages.

Employment of property and real estate managers is expected to increase faster than the average for all occupations in the United States through the 1990s. Many job openings are expected to occur as older, experienced managers transfer to other occupations or leave the labor force, and the best opportunities will be for college graduates with degrees in real estate, business administration, and related fields.

In the 1990s, many of the economy's new jobs are expected to be in wholesale and retail trade, finance, insurance, real estate, and various service industries. Growth in these industries will bring a need for more office and retail properties, and for people to manage them. The continued expansion of such merchandising chains as franchise restaurants also should increase the need for real estate managers to acquire and develop more properties for these operations.

In housing, there will be a greater demand for apartments as the high cost of owning a home causes more people to delay leaving rental housing. And new home developments are increasingly organized with community or home owner associations that require managers. In addition, more owners of commercial and multi-unit residential properties are expected to use professional managers to help make their properties more profitable.

Earnings

The earnings of property and real estate managers depend on their levels of responsibility. Annual salaries for on-site apartment managers range from $16,600 to $34,100, and property managers who are responsible for multiple apartment complexes earn from $39,800 to $56,000. Property managers for shopping centers receive from $44,200 to $60,500, and office building managers make from $44,100 to $70,200. Corporate real estate managers for fast-food and restaurant chains earn from $40,400 to $57,000, and real estate directors for retail apparel chains make from $49,200 to $74,000.

Property and real estate managers usually receive such benefits as medical and health insurance. On-site apartment building managers may have rent-free apartments, and many managers have the use of company automobiles. In addition, managers involved in land development may receive a small percentage of ownership in their projects.

Conditions of work

Property and real estate managers usually work in clean, well-lighted offices, but may spend much of their time at the properties they manage. On-site apartment building managers often leave their offices to inspect other areas, check maintenance or repair work, or resolve problems reported by tenants.

Many apartment managers must live in the buildings they manage so they can be available in emergencies, and they may be required to show apartments to prospective tenants at night or on weekends. Property and real estate managers may attend evening meetings with property owners, association boards of directors, or civic groups interested in property planned for development. Real estate managers who work for large companies frequently travel to inspect their companies' property holdings or locate properties their companies might acquire.

Social and psychological factors

Many property and real estate managers make good salaries and enjoy the prestige of management positions. Dealing with tenants can be stressful, however, especially when air conditioning, heating, or water supplies fail. And managers who must attend evening meetings or travel for their companies may have limited time with their families.

GOE: 11.05.01; SIC: 6531; SOC: 1353

◇ **SOURCES OF ADDITIONAL INFORMATION**

Apartment Owners and Managers Association of America
65 Cherry Plaza
Watertown, CT 06795

Building Owners and Managers Association International
1250 I Street, NW, Suite 200
Washington, DC 20005

Community Associations Institute
1423 Powhatan Street, Suite 7
Alexandria, VA 22314

Institute of Real Estate Management
430 North Michigan Avenue
Chicago, IL 60611

NACORE International Executives
471 Spencer Drive, South
Suite 8
West Palm Beach, FL 33409

National Apartment Association
1111 14th Street, NW
Suite 900
Washington, DC 20005

National Association of Home Builders of the U.S.
15th & M Streets, NW
Washington, DC 20005

◇ **RELATED ARTICLES**

Volume 1: Business Administration; Real Estate
Volume 2: City managers; Hotel and motel managers; Urban and regional planners
Volume 3: Real estate agents and brokers

Prosthetists and orthotists

Definition

Prosthetists provide care to patients with total or partial loss of limb by designing and making special devices known as prostheses. *Prosthetics assistants* help provide care to these patients by constructing, fitting, and repairing prostheses.

Orthotists provide care to patients with disabling conditions of limb or spine by designing and making braces and other corrective devices known as orthoses. *Orthotics assistants* help provide care to these patients by constructing, fitting, and repairing orthoses.

History

People have been trying to replace lost limbs and to support weak body parts for many, many centuries. Braces, splints, and other cor-

rective devices have been used since prehistoric times. The ancient Greeks, Romans, and Egyptians were very knowledgeable about various muscular disorders and laid the framework for many later advances in the field.

During the 1500s, a French surgeon named Ambroise Pare made many discoveries that led to the development of special devices to help correct weaknesses of the limb and spine. The types of devices used at that time include metal corsets, splints made out of leather for hips and legs, and special shoes.

In England, during the 1600s, a bill known as the Poor Relief Act of 1601 established many types of government responsibility for the disabled. Many new devices were developed such as leather-covered wooden hands and metal hooks to replace lost limbs.

Some of the most dramatic advances made in the fields of prosthetics and orthotics have occurred during and after major wars. After

531

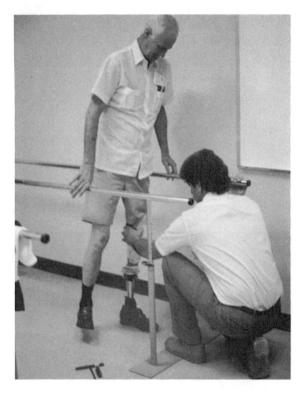

An orthotist adjusts the height of a new left leg for a patient.

The work of a prosthetist or orthotist usually begins with an examination of the patient. It is important that all details of the patient be noted to ensure that the device fits properly. Prosthetists and orthotists use tools, such as rulers, tapes and calipers, to measure limbs or stumps. Each prosthesis or orthosis is individually designed to match a patient's unique needs.

The devices are either made by the prosthetists and orthotists themselves or by their assistants. Using both hand tools and power tools, the individual parts of a device are made and assembled. Prosthetists and orthotists follow a very specific design to make the prosthesis or orthosis. Various materials—such as leather, wood, and plastic—may by used to make the device; all devices should be lightweight, durable and sturdy.

Once the devices are made and fitted on the patients, minor alterations often have to be made. Prosthetists and orthotists work with many other health care practitioners—physicians, therapists, and specialists—to help patients adjust to their prostheses and orthoses. It is essential that all devices be comfortable and properly fitted.

World War II, for example, prosthetists discovered new lightweight plastics that could be used to make artificial arms and hands. In addition, a process known as "cineplasty" was developed in which part of the control mechanism inside a mechanical limb is attached to a patient's biceps muscle for better control over the moving parts of the limb. The Korean War and the Vietnam War also spurred improvements in the design and manufacture of prostheses and orthoses.

Advances in the fields of prosthetics and orthotics continue to be made; specially trained prosthetists and orthotists are always striving to design more comfortable, more useful, and more natural-looking devices.

Nature of the work

Prosthetists and orthotists are highly skilled professionals who use prescriptions from physicians to design and make special devices that help patients who have lost a limb or who have a physical handicap. There is a great need for skilled prosthetists and orthotists: More than half a million people are amputees and thousands of others have some sort of physical handicap.

Requirements

A bachelor's degree, preferably in prosthetics or orthotics, is required for work as a prosthetist or orthotist. Some persons opt to earn their degrees in areas other than prosthetics or orthotics, but they must then study additional courses to meet certification requirements.

To earn a bachelor's degree in prosthetics or orthotics, a person must study a wide range of subjects, including biology, anatomy, physics, and engineering. In addition, students work in laboratories, making and fitting devices. Because advances are always being made in these fields, continuing education is also very important.

High-school students interested in careers in the fields of prosthetics and orthotics should take college prep courses, with an emphasis in science classes. Other courses, like psychology, mechanical drawing, and shop, may also be helpful.

Special requirements

The American Board for Certification in Orthotics and Prosthetics has certified more than 2,000 individuals. To take the exam to qualify for certification, a practitioner must have a bachelor's degree in prosthetics or orthotics from a board-approved college or university and must have at least one year of clinical experience. Practitioners who have a bachelor's degree in another major but who have completed postgraduate work in an approved program and who have one or two years of experience may also qualify to take the exam. A practitioner who passes the exam may become a Certified Prosthetist (C.P.), a Certified Orthotist (C.O.), or a Certified Prosthetist-Orthotist (C.P.O.).

Opportunities for experience and exploration

Without the necessary educational and work requirements, it is very difficult for people to get part-time or summer jobs in the fields of prosthetics or orthotics. There are, however, ways to learn more about the nature of the work in these fields.

Teachers and counselors, for example, may be able to arrange for a visit to a hospital, clinic, or rehabilitation center so students can talk with practitioners. In addition, students can visit departments of prosthetics and orthotics in colleges and universities. High-school and college courses in science and engineering may also give students an opportunity to evaluate their interest and aptitude for work in these fields.

Related occupations

Persons who have an interest in the work of orthotists and prosthetists may also be interested in any of the other careers available in health care, such as physical therapist, physician, osteopathic physician, registered nurse, or kinesiotherapist.

Methods of entering

A person must have a bachelor's degree to enter the fields of prosthetics and orthotics; those individuals with degrees in prosthetics or orthotics from a board-approved college or university will get the best jobs. Most colleges and universities have placement services to help graduates find jobs. Many professional journals and associations also list employment opportu-

nities. Certification should be the goal of all practitioners in these fields; certified prosthetists and orthotists will have better job opportunities available to them.

Advancement

In large departments of prosthetics and orthotics in hospitals, clinics, and rehabilitation centers, certified practitioners may advance to supervisory, training, or other specialized positions. Other certified prosthetists and orthotists may decide to start their own private practice; some decide to go into research or teaching. It is essential, however, that practitioners become certified to advance.

Employment outlook

The job outlook for these practitioners is good; the number of openings for professional prosthetists and orthotists is expected to increase through the 1990s. Many factors are contributing to the growth of this profession, including the increasing elderly population and the greater access to medical and rehabilitation care brought about by private and public insurance companies. In addition, continuing advancements in these fields are enabling more people with different types of disabilities to become candidates for new devices.

Earnings

Salaries of prosthetists and orthotists vary according to education, clinical experience, and certification. In general, their earnings compare favorably with other health care professionals. In the early 1990s, the average starting salary for prosthetists and orthotists was more than $19,000. Those practitioners with experience earned between $24,000 and $29,000; certified practitioners with a great deal of experience can earn much more. Those working in large hospitals, for example, may earn $30,000 to $36,000.

Most practitioners work a thirty-five or forty-hour week. Those in private practice, however, may set their own hours.

Conditions of work

Working conditions for prosthetists and orthotists are usually good. Offices, examination rooms, and fitting rooms are clean, well lit, and well ventilated. Those practitioners who work in labs part of the time may find that they are surrounded by noise and fumes, but working conditions are generally very comfortable.

Most prosthetists and orthotists work five-day weeks. There is very seldom any need for overtime work.

Social and psychological factors

People working in this profession should be inquisitive and inventive; they should also be patient, compassionate, and easy-going. Practitioners must be able to understand the emotional factors that often go along with a physical handicap or disability. Prosthetists and orthotists are highly skilled workers who must be intelligent and have an aptitude for science and engineering. Although the work, at times, can be frustrating and difficult, it also brings practitioners a great sense of pride and satisfaction because they are directly helping people in need.

GOE: 05.05.11; SIC: 3842; SOC: 369

◇ **SOURCES OF ADDITIONAL INFORMATION**

American Board for Certification in Orthotics and Prosthetics
717 Pendleton Street
Alexandria, VA 22314

American Academy of Orthotists and Prosthetists
717 Pendleton Street
Alexandria, VA 22314

International Society for Prosthetics and Orthotics
U.S. National Member Society
317 East 34th Street
New York, NY 10016

◇ **RELATED ARTICLES**

Volume 1: Health Care
Volume 2: Biomedical engineers; Kinesiotherapists; Occupational therapists; Physical therapists
Volume 4: Orthotics and prosthetics technicians; Physical therapy technicians

Protestant ministers

Definition

Protestant ministers provide for the spiritual, educational, and social needs of Protestant congregations and other religious groups. They lead services, perform religious rites, and provide moral and spiritual guidance to their members. Ministers also deliver sermons, help the sick and needy, and supervise the religious educational program of their church. They are involved in community and interfaith activities and also have administrative duties, such as working on congregational committees. They may also be involved in missionary work; this may include establishing or continuing religious education in foreign or remote posts.

History

Protestantism grew out of the Reformation, a religious movement started in 1517 by Martin Luther. Luther, an ordained priest, protested certain concepts of the Roman Catholic Church, such as the primacy of the pope and the doctrine of God's grace. The Protestant movement is made up of many denominations, including Lutherans, Presbyterians, Episcopalians, Methodists, Unitarians, Baptists, and Quakers, but all fall under the domain of Christianity.

Within the Protestant movement the minister has an elevated status in spiritual matters, but most Protestant churches have a relatively democratic form of decision making in which all members participate.

Nature of the work

Ministers are the spiritual leaders of their congregations. Like other clergy, they lead their congregations in worship, officiate at weddings and funerals, supervise religious educational programs, and teach confirmation and adult education courses. Ministers interpret the tenets and doctrines of their faith and instruct persons who seek conversion.

Some Protestant denominations or congregations within a denomination have a traditional order of service, whereas others require that the minister adapt the service to the specific needs of the congregation. Most Protestant services include Bible readings, hymn singing, prayers, and a sermon prepared and delivered by the minister.

Protestant clergy also administer specific church rites, such as baptism, holy communion, and confirmation. They also conduct weddings and funerals. Ministers counsel couples to be married as well as other individuals who seek guidance. They visit the sick, comfort the bereaved, and participate in the administration of their parish or congregation.

In smaller churches, ministers may have close personal contact with all the members of the congregation, while in larger congregations they may have greater administrative duties and therefore less contact with congregants. Administrative duties may include heading or serving on committees that deal with building programs, fundraising, member recruitment, event planning, and religious education. In addition, the minister may be involved in interdenominational and interfaith activities in the wider community. Some ministers have become involved in concerns such as human rights and other nonliturgical issues.

Ministers may share duties with an associate or with an assistant minister as well as other church staff. Some ministers teach in seminaries and other schools. Some write for publications and give speeches within the Protestant community and to those in the community at large. A growing number of ministers are employed only part-time and may serve more than one congregation or have a secular job.

Requirements

Protestant clergy generally must have some higher education before ordination. While some denominations require little more than Bible study, the majority of Protestant groups demand a bachelor's degree plus several years of specialized theological training. The professional study in these theological schools, of which there are about 150 in the United States and Canada, generally lasts about three years and leads to the degree of master of divinity.

An undergraduate degree in the liberal arts is the typical college program for prospective clergy, although persons entering the ministry later in life come from a full range of academic backgrounds. Coursework should include English, foreign languages, philosophy, the natural sciences, psychology, comparative religions, as well as fine arts and music. Many churches are encouraging prospective candidates to the clergy to spend a few years working after college graduation before entering the seminary.

The curriculum in seminaries generally covers four areas: history, theology, the Bible, and practical ministry techniques. Practical ministry techniques include counseling, church administration, and religious education. In addition to classroom study and examinations, the seminary student serves at least one year as an intern to gain practical experience in leading services and other ministerial duties. Some institutions award a doctor of ministry degree to students who complete at least two years of additional study after having served as a minister. Seminary students are eligible for scholarships and loans.

In general, the major Protestant denominations have their own schools of theological training, but many of these schools admit students of other denominations. There are also several interdenominational colleges and theological schools that give training for the ministry. This may be augmented by training in the denomination in which the student will be ordained.

Not all Protestant denominations require seminary training for ordination. Some Evangelical churches, for example, may ordain people with only a high-school diploma.

Special requirements

In addition to the ordination requirements, a primary consideration in choosing a career in the clergy is a strong religious faith coupled with the desire to help others. A minister should also be able to communicate effectively and supervise others. They must have self-confidence and possess initiative and compassion. Protestant ministers only have to meet the requirements of their individual denomination. Both men and women can become ordained as ministers.

Women are welcome to choose a career in the ministry. They are accepted in all Protestant sects as ministers.

Opportunities for experience and exploration

Persons interested in becoming a minister should talk with their own minister and others involved in the work of the church to get a clearer idea of the rewards and responsibilities of this profession. Choosing a career as a minister entails a good deal of thought as to the demands of this profession. There are numerous opportunities for those interested to investigate congregational life. Aspiring ministers would be wise to volunteer some time at a church or other religious institution to get better acquainted with the type of job responsibilities a minister has. Volunteer work can include teaching Sunday school or running guidance sessions. In the final analysis, however, there is no single experience that can adequately prepare a person for the demands of being a minister. Seminary training should offer the best opportunity to explore many of the facets of a career as a minister.

Related occupations

Ministers have many of the same religious leadership and counseling responsibilities as Roman Catholic priests, rabbis, teachers, social workers, and psychologists.

Methods of entry

Only ordained ministers can work in this profession. Students should consult with their minister or contact the appropriate theological seminary to learn how to best meet entrance requirements. Some denominations do not demand seminary training to become ordained.

Advancement

Newly ordained ministers generally begin their careers as pastors of small congregations or as assistant pastors (curates) in larger congregations. From there, advancement depends on individual interests and abilities. Ministers may look forward to heading to a bigger parish, rising to a higher rank within their church, or staying in their original position. Ministers may also become teachers in seminaries and other educational institutions, or chaplains in the armed forces. Ministers may also decide to start a pulpit in a small community in the United States or in another country.

Employment outlook

Most cities and towns in the United States have at least one Protestant church but the increased cost of church operations is expected to limit the demand for ministers through the 1990s. And, although the number of ministry graduates is also declining, ministers should expect competition for some parish jobs, especially the more desirable ones.

The five largest groups of Protestants are Baptists, Episcopalians, Presbyterians, Lutherans, and United Methodists. Demand for ministers will vary on denominational affiliation, with Evangelical churches needing the most ministers. Employment opportunities for other denominations may depend on ministers retiring or otherwise leaving the profession.

Other employment opportunities for clergy include social service work, such as counseling, youth work, family relations guidance, and teaching. Ministers may also find opportunities as chaplains in the armed forces or in a hospital.

Earnings

Salaries vary substantially for Protestant clergy depending on the individual's experience as well as the size of the congregation, its denominational branch, location, and financial status. The estimated income of ministers ranges between $20,000 and $27,000 per year. Additional benefits usually include a housing stipend, a monthly transportation allowance, health insurance, and other fringe benefits. Some ministers may also have part-time secular jobs.

Conditions of work

Ministers spend long hours working under various conditions. There is no such thing as a standard workweek. Like all clergy, ministers are on call at any hour of the day or night. They visit the sick, comfort and counsel families in times of crisis, and help raise funds for the church. Much of the minister's time is also spent reading, studying, writing, and talking to people. They also must prepare sermons and keep up with religious and secular events. Ministers may also have many administrative responsibilities working with staff and various committees. They also participate in community and interfaith events. In some denominations, such as the United Methodist Church, a central governing body may reassign ministers to a new pastorate every few years.

Despite the long hours and sometimes stressful working conditions, many ministers enjoy their work and find helping people in a religious context most satisfying.

Social and psychological factors

A minister is very involved with working with congregants. The career is rewarding in the sense of spiritual values and achievements; one can find much satisfaction in the comfort and leadership offered congregants. There may, however, be social pressure. The public in general and congregations in particular expect ministers (and other clergy members) to set examples of high moral and ethical conduct. There is the added pressure of being 'on call' twenty-four hours a day, and the need to often comfort people in difficult situations. Obviously many people find strength from these commitments and greatly enjoy their work and find it very meaningful. Ministers are generally held in great esteem by their congregants and the community at large.

GOE: 10.01.01; SIC: 8661; SOC: 2042

A Protestant minister delivers a sermon during a Sunday service.

◇ SOURCES OF ADDITIONAL INFORMATION

The minister or church guidance worker of a denomination in which a person is interested can provide information on requirements for the ministry. Seminaries can give a prospective student information on admission and ordination requirements.

Career information about the Protestant ministry is available from:

National Council of the Churches
475 Riverside Drive
New York, NY 10115

For information concerning the work of military chaplains, contact:

National Conference on Ministry to the Armed Forces
4141 North Henderson Road, Suite 13
Arlington, VA 22203

◇ RELATED ARTICLES

Volume 1: Religious Ministries
Volume 2: Clergy and religious workers; Psychiatrists; Psychologists; Social workers

Psychiatrists

Definition

Psychiatrists are physicians who treat patients with mental, emotional, and behavioral symptoms. They have completed all of the training required to become licensed medical doctors (M.D.s) and then have taken additional training specialize in psychiatry.

History

Psychiatry is the branch of medicine that is concerned with mental, emotional, and behavioral disorders. In the eighteenth century B.C. the Code of Hammurabi, a collection of Babylonian laws, recommended opium and olive oil to treat behavior problems, which were believed to result from possession by demons. The Greek physician Hippocrates reasoned that such behavior resulted from natural causes and developed a theory that personality was determined by bodily fluids.

For hundreds of years people believed that witchcraft was responsible for abnormal behavior. One of the first to condemn such superstition was John Weyer, a sixteenth century Belgian physician.

The greatest advances in the treatment of the mentally ill came in the latter part of the nineteenth century. Emil Kraepelin, a German psychiatrist, made an important contribution when he developed a classification system for mental illnesses that is still used for diagnostic purposes. And Sigmund Freud, the famous Viennese psychiatrist, developed techniques for analyzing human behavior that have strongly influenced the practice of modern psychiatry.

Another great change in treatment began in the 1950s with the development of medication that could be used in treating such psychiatric problems as depression and anxiety.

Nature of the work

Psychiatrists treat patients who suffer from mental and emotional illnesses that may make it difficult for them to cope with everyday living or to behave in ways that are socially acceptable. To deal with such problems, psychiatrists are trained in both medicine and psychology.

Some of the patients psychiatrists see may display irritability or have feelings of frustration, while others may be so seriously ill that they have lost touch with reality. Some patients may be involved in such antisocial behavior as alcohol abuse, drug abuse, or criminal activities. Still others may have physical symptoms that are caused by mental or emotional illness. In addition, psychiatrists may specialize in certain types of clients, such as children and adolescents or geriatric patients.

The treatment the psychiatrist employs depends on the patient's needs. In some cases the psychiatrist may refer the patient to another psychiatrist who specializes in the recommended treatment.

Psychotherapy is a widely used technique that is often called the "talking" therapy. The therapist uses persuasion and encouragement to help the patient overcome emotional pain by learning to understand the feelings and ideas that are causing the pain. Psychoanalysis is a form of treatment in which the therapist encourages the patient to talk freely, or "free associate," to uncover troubling subconscious beliefs and their causes.

Psychiatrists may prescribe medication that affects the patient's mood or behavior, such as tranquilizers or antidepressants. The medication may be used alone or combined with other treatment. Depending on the patient's illness medication may be temporary or permanent.

Some psychiatrists have general practices in which they treat patients with a variety of mental disorders, while others specialize in certain types of clients. For example, industrial psychiatrists are employed by industry to deal with problems that affect employee performance, such as alcoholism or absenteeism. And forensic psychiatrists combine their psychiatric skills with a knowledge of the law. They may evaluate defendants and testify on their mental state, or they may help determine whether defendants understand the charges against them and can contribute to their own defense. Others may specialize in the chronically ill.

Psychologists also work with mental or emotionally disturbed clients. They are not physicians, however, and cannot prescribe medication. In some cases disturbed behavior results from disorders of the nervous system. These conditions are diagnosed and treated by *neurologists,* who are physicians specializing in problems of the nervous system.

Requirements

The training required to become a psychiatrist is long, difficult, and costly. Candidates must be licensed physicians before they begin their specialized training.

Students who hope to enter any branch of medicine must have excellent grades in high school and college. High-school students should enroll in college preparatory programs, and their courses should include English, languages, the humanities, social studies, mathematics, biology, chemistry, and physics. College freshman should plan their undergraduate programs to meet the admission requirements explained in the annual publication of the Association of American Medical Colleges, Admission Requirements of American Medical Colleges Including Canada. And during their second or third year in college, students should take the Medical College Admission Test, which most medical schools require.

In medical school, students complete a four-year program of medical studies and supervised clinical work that leads to their M.D. degrees. Finally, the new physicians who plan to specialize in psychiatry begin a four-year resident program. In the first year they work in several specialties, such as internal medicine and pediatrics. Then they work for three years in a psychiatric hospital or a general hospital's psychiatric ward. In addition, psychiatrists who wish to become psychoanalysts spend six years in part-time training, either during or after residency, and also undergo psychoanalysis during this period.

Students need outstanding mental ability to complete all of the required studies. They also need perseverance and good health to survive their long training period. Psychiatrists must be emotionally stable so they can deal with their patients objectively, and they must be good listeners. They also must be tolerant, and they need warm, friendly personalities that help them communicate with their patients.

Special requirements

New M.D.s must be licensed before they can practice medicine. Depending on the requirements of the state in which they plan to practice, they may be required to pass the National Board of Medical Examiners test, the Federal Licensing Examination, or an individual state licensing test. After they complete their resident training in psychiatry, candidates take an intensive examination given by the Board of

In order to keep a patient at ease, most psychiatrists hold their sessions in comfortable surroundings.

Psychiatry and Neurology and, if they pass, they become Diplomates in Psychiatry.

Opportunities for experience and exploration

Students who are interested in becoming psychiatrists should understand that they will spend many years becoming licensed physicians before they can specialize in psychiatry. Therefore, they should learn all they can about the work of licensed physicians.

While they are in high school, students should read about the practice of medicine and the specialty of psychiatry. They also should talk with their high-school counselors, attend Career Days at school or nearby hospitals, and take advantage of any opportunities to interview psychiatrists or other physicians.

It is difficult for high-school students to obtain experience that is directly related to the field of psychiatry. They may, however, find opportunities for contact with physicians and patients in other areas through volunteer, part-time, or summer work at hospitals, clinics, or nursing homes. When students are in college, they may be able to find summer jobs as hospital orderlies, nurse's aides, or ward clerks.

Related occupations

Students who are interested in psychiatry also may wish to consider related occupations. Other professionals in the field of mental health include psychiatric nurses, psychiatric social workers, clinical psychologists, and psychiatric aides and technicians.

Students who are especially interested in becoming physicians may wish to investigate careers in general or family practice and in the many medical specialties, such as internal medicine, pediatrics, gynecology, dermatology, cardiology, and industrial medicine.

Methods of entering

Prospective psychiatrists who are interested in salaried positions should read professional journals and magazines that can give them ideas about where they would like to practice or even offer job leads. It is also helpful to join local and national medical associations. For example, both medical students and psychiatric residents can join the American Psychiatric Association.

Advancement

Most psychiatrists, especially those in private practice, do not advance in the usual sense of the word. Their progress consists of greater skills and understanding, a growing number of patients, and increased earnings. Psychiatrists who work in such facilities as hospitals, clinics, and mental health centers may become administrators, and those who teach or concentrate on research may become heads of their departments.

Employment outlook

Opportunities for both private practice and salaried positions should be excellent in the l990s. There is a serious shortage of psychiatrists, especially in rural areas and in public facilities.

A number of factors contribute to this shortage. The growing population and the increased life span of older adults means there are more people who need psychiatric care. Rising incomes enable more people to afford treatment; higher educational levels make more people aware of the importance of mental health care; and medical insurance, although it usually limits the amount of mental health care, at least provides some coverage.

In addition, there is a need for more research to discover the causes of mental health and develop new ways to treat them. And the need for more psychiatrists creates more openings for psychiatrists to teach them.

Earnings

Psychiatrists' earnings are determined by the kind of practice they have, their experience, the number of patients they treat, and the geographic location in which they practice. Like other physicians, their average income is among the highest of any occupational group. But when physicians graduate from medical school and become hospital residents their annual income is between $20,000 and $24,000. And most physicians, including psychiatrists, do not complete their training and begin earning higher incomes until they are in their middle thirties.

Psychiatrists in private practice have higher incomes than salaried psychiatrists. They may charge between $80 and $100 an hour, and their average income is about $93,000 a year. Those who work in salaried positions at such facilities as clinics, state hospitals, and Department of Veterans Affairs hospitals start at $38,000 to $77,000 a year, and experienced psychiatrists at these institutions earn between $46,000 and $93,000 a year.

Conditions of work

Psychiatrists usually work regular hours. Those in private practice can set their own schedules, although they may work some evenings or on weekends to see patients who cannot take time off during business hours. Some private psychiatrists also work as hospital staff members, consultants, lecturers, or teachers.

Salaried psychiatrists work in such facilities as private hospitals, state hospitals, and community mental health centers. They also work for such government agencies as the U.S. Department of Health and Human Services, the Department of Defense, and the Veterans Administration.

Social and psychological factors

Working with emotionally ill patients can be stressful for the therapist. Some patients may be defensive or hostile. But psychiatrists also have the satisfaction of helping people who are troubled.

Psychiatrists who work in public facilities often have heavy workloads. Changes in treatment have reduced the number of patients in hospitals, but they have increased the number of patients in community health centers. These psychiatrists may feel frustrated because they cannot meet all the demands for their time.

GOE: 02.03.01; SIC: 8011; SOC: 261

◇ **SOURCES OF ADDITIONAL INFORMATION**

Associations and agencies that can provide career and educational information include the following:

American College of Psychiatrists
PO Box 365
Greenbelt, MD 20770

American Medical Association
535 North Dearborn Street
Chicago, IL 60610

American Psychiatric Association
1400 K Street, NW
Washington, DC 20005

Association of American Medical Colleges
One DuPont Circle, NW, Suite 200
Washington, DC 20036

National Association of Private Psychiatric Hospitals
1319 F Street, NW, Suite 1000
Washington, DC 20004

National Institute of Mental Health
5600 Fishers Lane
Rockville, MD 20857

National Mental Health Association
1021 Prince Street
Alexandria, VA 22314-2971

National Science Foundation
1800 G Street, NW
Washington, DC 20550

◇ **RELATED ARTICLES**

Volume 1: Health Care; Social Sciences
Volume 2: Guidance counselors; Health services administrators; Human services workers; Medical technologists; Occupational therapists; Physical therapists; Physicians; Physician assistants; Psychologists; Recreational therapists; Registered nurses; Rehabilitation counselors; Social workers; Therapists, miscellaneous
Volume 3: Nursing and psychiatric aides
Volume 4: Physical therapist assistants; Psychiatric technicians

---

Psychologists

Definition

Psychologists, although their general duties may be in activities as varied as teaching, counseling, research work, or administration, basically attempt to understand people, their capacities, traits, and behavior and to explain their needs. They do this through interviewing and observing individuals, through testing, through the study of personal histories, and through controlled experiments. Psychologists normally hold doctorates in psychology but they are not medical doctors, and cannot prescribe medication.

History

Once considered a part of "philosophy," psychology began to develop its own academic field when it was proved that scientific methods could be applied to the study of human behavior. *Psyche,* from which the first syllable in *psychology* was derived, is a Greek word meaning "soul." The second half of *psychology* contains the same root from which the word *logic* was derived. Thus *psychology* translates as "the science of the soul."

Early philosophers emphasized the differences between the body and the soul. Plato be-

541

lieved that man was composed of two entirely different parts, body and soul. Down through the Middle Ages, the differences between the two were much discussed. One of the great scholars of the Renaissance, Descartes, decided that the soul lived in the pineal gland because there seemed to be no other use for this tiny gland buried deep in the brain. Modern scholars tend to emphasize the unity between mind and body, rather than their dissimilarity. Early scholars who presented theories in what we now call psychology were not primarily philosophers. Many were mathematicians, some were physiologists, some were teachers, some were physicians. The man who is considered the founder of experimental psychology, Wilhelm Wundt, held both an M.D. degree and a Ph.D. degree. Although he was a physician, he served as a teacher at the University of Leipzig, where his title was Professor of Philosophy.

German scholars of the nineteenth century were committed to scientific method, and discovery by experiment was considered to be the only respectable way in which learned thinkers might work. Thus it was not thought strange that in 1879, Dr. Wundt set up an experimental laboratory to conduct research nor that he focused his methods upon human behavior.

Many people who later became famous U.S. psychologists received their training under Dr. Wundt.

At the turn of the twentieth century, a Russian physiologist, Dr. Ivan Pavlov, was studying the processes of digestion. Although he was not a psychologist, his discovery that experimental animals (dogs) began to anticipate the food that they were to receive during the experiment by the involuntary act of salivating led Dr. Pavlov to do some further research into this phenomenon.

It was obvious to Dr. Pavlov that the dogs associated the sound of a bell with the time for presentation of meat. As soon as he was sure that dogs expected to be fed when the bell rang, he started ringing the bell but withholding the food. The dogs' saliva flowed anyway, whether or not they saw or smelled food at the sound of the bell. Dr. Pavlov called this substitute stimulus a "conditioned response." Many psychologists began to incorporate the behaviorist theory of the "conditioned response" into theories of learning.

One of the most famous pioneers in psychology was Dr. Sigmund Freud, whose work has led to many of the modern theories of behavior. Dr. Freud was a physician who lived and practiced in Vienna, Austria, until Hitler's forces caused him to flee to England. His theories on the meaning of dreams, the uncon-

scious, and the nature of various emotional disturbances have had a profound effect upon the profession and practice of psychology for more than sixty years, although many psychologists now disagree with some of his theories.

Many Americans have helped develop the science that seeks to understand human behavior. William James, Robert Woodworth, E. L. Thorndike, Clark Hull, B. F. Skinner and others have contributed greatly to the developing science of psychology.

World War II greatly influenced the growth of psychology. Government and industry discovered that psychologists could help solve many problems of human behavior through various testing procedures. Psychology is a rapidly growing field today, with psychologists working on a great variety of problems.

Nature of the work

Psychology is both a science and a profession. As a science, it is a systematic approach to the understanding of people and their behavior; as a profession, it is the application of that understanding to help solve human problems. The field of learning that is designated as psychology is so vast that no one person can be an expert in all phases of it. The psychologist usually concentrates on one specialty that is of particular interest to him or her. In many of the specialties there is an overlap, both in subject matter and method used to handle it. Graduate preparation in the field of psychology, therefore, is based upon a common core of knowledge from which advanced graduates branch out when they begin to take up their own field of special interest.

Many psychologists work in colleges and universities. The overlap in this occupation, then, is membership on a college faculty. It is also possible that most of the college teachers will be assigned to instruct in some area of basic psychology. The psychologist usually will be given teaching assignments and the supervision of the work of graduate students in his area of special interest, also. It is likely that this person will conduct research in a special field, and direct the research studies of graduates specializing in it.

Clinical psychologists are concerned mainly with people's mental and emotional disorders. The problems they assess and treat range from normal psychological crises such as adolescent rebellion or loss of self-esteem in middle age to extreme conditions such as severe depression and schizophrenia. A clinical psychologist may teach in a college or university. Other clinical psychologists may work with patients in a hospital. In this setting, they may be resonsible both for evaluation (the giving of certain special tests) and therapy.

Some clinical psychologists work almost exclusively with children. They may be members of a staff of a child guidance clinic or may work in a large general hospital in which there is a special treatment center for children. Child psychologists and other clinical psychologists may be engaged in private practice and may have offices to which persons come much as they would come to a physician's office. Clinical psychologists comprise the largest group of specialists.

Developmental psychologists study the development of people from birth through old age. They describe, measure, and explain age-related changes in behavior, the stages of emotional development, universal traits and individual differences, and abnormal changes in development. Many developmental psychologists teach and do research in colleges and universities. Some specialize in programs for children (in day-care centers, preschools, or hospitals and clinics, for example) or programs for the elderly.

Social psychologists are concerned with how people interact with each other and how they are affected by their environment. Social psychologists may teach in a college or university, and they will both lecture and conduct research in the special field of social psychology. They may also work for an agency of the federal or state government, may work in a private research firm, or may work as consultants. In addition, an increasing number of social psychologists work as researchers and personnel managers in such nontraditional settings as advertising agencies, corporations, and architectural and engineering firms. Social psychology has developed from four sources: sociology, cultural anthropology, psychiatry, and psychology. Social psychologists are interested in human behavior, not only in individuals but in groups. They study the ways in which groups influence individuals, and ways in which individuals contribute to group processes. They study many different kinds of groups: ethnic, religious, political, educational, family, and many others. The social psychologist has devised many ways in which to conduct research into the nature, attitudes, leadership patterns, and structure of groups.

Counseling psychologists work with average persons who have problems they find difficult to face alone. These persons are not usually mentally or emotionally ill, but are often emotionally upset, anxious, or struggling with some conflict that may be within themselves or

A parent and a social worker observe the behavior of a child during a session with a psychologist.

in their environment. In helping people solve their problems, make decisions, and cope with everyday stresses, the counseling psychologist actually is working in preventive mental health. The counseling psychologist may work in a college or university counseling center, and may also teach some courses in the department of psychology. He or she may be in private practice or may work in a community health center, with a marriage counseling agency, or with a federal agency, such as the Department of Veterans Affairs.

School psychologists are frequently assigned to diagnostic and remedial work. Their major objective for their own work, though, does not lie in either of these assignments. School psychologists are working toward the day when they may engage primarily in preventive and developmental psychology. Many school psychologists are assigned the duty of giving individual tests to pupils who are suspected of various kinds of exceptionality. Other school psychologists find that their work is almost entirely with children who have proven to be a problem to themselves or to others and have been referred for help by teachers or other members of the school system. Many school psychologists are concerned with pupils who reveal various kinds of learning disability, though they may be of average intelligence or better and thus not eligible for special education. Problems of parent child relationships may also be brought to the school psychologist to solve.

Industrial-organizational psychologists are concerned with the relation between people and work. They deal with organizational structure, worker productivity and job satisfaction, consumer behavior, personnel training and development, and the interaction between humans and machines. Industrial-organizational psychologists may work with the sales department to help salespeople gain insights into their own personalities that may help them become more effective members of the sales force. They may study assembly line procedures and suggest changes to reduce the monotony and increase the responsibility of workers. They may plan various kinds of tests that will help screen applicants for employment with the firm. They may conduct research to determine the kinds of qualities that seem to produce the most efficient employees or help management develop programs to identify staff with management potential. They may be asked to investigate and report on certain differences of opinion between a supervisor and one of the workers. They may design training courses that will help to indoctrinate new employees or counsel older employees on career development or preparation for retirement.

Other industrial psychologists, referred to as *engineering psychologists,* help engineers and technicians to design systems that require people (either workers or consumers) and machines to interact. They may also develop aids for training people to use those systems. The psychologist is asked to lend assistance in the design because certain human factors must be taken into consideration in the designing of any machine that is to be operated by a human being. (*See also* the separate article titled "Ergonomists" elsewhere in this volume.)

Industrial-organizational psychologists, also known as *consumer psychologists,* are interested in consumer reactions to a company's products or services. They may be asked to determine the kind of product the public will buy. For instance, do most people prefer big cars or little cars? They may be asked to make decisions about the most appealing ways to present a product through the medium of television or of magazine advertising. Many of today's most established advertising, promotion, and packaging practices have been influenced by the opinions and advice of consumer psychologists. Consumer psychologists also try to improve the acceptability and safety of products and to help the consumer make better decisions.

Psychometrists work with intelligence, personality, and aptitude tests that are used in clinical, counseling, and school settings, and in business and industry. They administer the tests, score them, and interpret the results as related to standard norms. Psychometrists study the methods and techniques used to acquire and evaluate psychological data and may devise new, more reliable tests. These specialists are usually well trained in mathematics, statistics, and computer programming and technology. They may be employed in colleges and universities, testing companies, private research firms, or government agencies.

The *educational psychologist* is concerned primarily with the ways in which people learn. Large numbers of educational psychologists work on the faculties of colleges or universities, and also conduct research into learning theory. Some, however, are interested in evaluating learning. They may work for test publishing firms and devise and try to standardize tests of ability, aptitude, or personal preferences, attitudes, or characteristics. The whole area of teaching, learning, and the evaluation of learning is of interest.

Experimental psychologists conduct scientific experiments on some particular aspect of behavior, either animal or human. Much experimental study is done in learning, in physiological psychology (the relationship of behavior to physiological processes), or comparative psychology (sometimes called animal psychology). These are not the only areas, however, in which experimental psychologists work. Many experimental psychological studies are carried out with animals, partly because their environments can be carefully controlled.

Many psychologists do a lot of writing. They may write up the results of research efforts for a scholarly journal; they may prepare papers for presentation at meetings of their professional association; they may write books that are directed primarily toward other psychologists; they may write books or articles for the lay public; they may write textbooks. As consultants or industrial psychologists, they may write manuals of instructions for various purposes. As educational psychologists who are working for text publishing companies either on a full-time or part-time basis, they may prepare certain kinds of test manuals.

Some psychologists become administrators. They may accept the responsibility of directing a psychology department in a college or university; they may direct a program of personnel services in a school system or an industry; they may become agency or department directors of research in scientific laboratories. They may be promoted to department head in a state or federal governmental agency. *Chief psychologists* in hospitals or psychiatric centers plan psychological treatment programs, direct the professional and nonprofessional personnel, and have overall responsibility for the psychological services provided by the institution.

Requirements

A doctorate in psychology (Ph.D. or Psy.D.—doctor of Psychology) is recommended for those who hope to make a career in the field. More than 60 percent of all persons who work in psychology hold this degree. Some positions are available to persons who hold a master's degree, but they are never jobs of as great responsibility nor with as high a salary as those open to persons with a doctorate.

In clinical or counseling psychology, the requirements for the Ph.D. or Psy.D. degree usually include one year of internship or supervised experience. The American Board of Examiners in Professional Psychology offers diplomas in clinical, counseling, industrial-organizational, and school psychology to those persons with a doctoral degree with outstanding educational records and experience who can pass the required psychology examinations. Psychologists do not need to attend medical school. Psychiatrists hold medical degrees. (For more information, *see* "Psychiatrists" elsewhere in this volume.)

Many graduate students receive financial help from universities and other sources in the form of fellowships, scholarships, or, sometimes, part-time employment; however, such aid is becoming more difficult to obtain.

Psychologists who wish to enter private practice must meet certification or licensing requirements in all states and in the District of Columbia. State certification is also required for school psychologists employed in the public school system.

The bachelor's degree in psychology does not equip the student to enter into the work of the psychologist any more than the bachelor's degree prepares the prospective lawyer or physician. It may be useful in helping students prepare for later graduate work in psychology or in helping them obtain jobs in related fields.

The high-school student interested in becoming a psychologist should enroll in a college preparatory course. You should concentrate on English courses, for the professional psychologist must make many speeches, write for publication, and be able to talk easily and well with persons who come for help. Mathematics are also valuable for later graduate work in statistics. Students should take all the science courses that can fit into their schedule to prepare for work with scientific method. They should also take modern foreign languages, especially French and German because reading comprehension of these languages is one of the usual requirements for obtaining the doctoral degree.

Special requirements

A real love of learning and an eagerness to spend a lifetime discovering more and more about one special field is a requirement for graduate study in psychology. Psychologists never stop studying. There is no time in their professional life when they may feel that they know all that they need to know about the subject. They must also have a talent for applying the scientific method to problems.

Perseverance and tolerance for frustration are two other special requirements of the prospective psychologist. Research projects do not always go smoothly, nor turn out to be productive, even after many hours of hard work. The psychologist must be able to accept disappointments and not allow them to discourage him or her.

The prospective psychologist must possess the characteristics which are usually called "maturity" and "stability." Only a mature and stable person can help others achieve these qualities.

Opportunities for experience and exploration

There are few opportunities for high-school students to explore the profession of psychology. One may seek an appointment to talk with a psychologist who may work in a nearby community, perhaps as a member of a college faculty or of a hospital staff. It may be difficult, however, for the student to see the psychologist's job firsthand.

Related occupations

Other workers trained to evaluate, counsel, and advise people individually or in groups include clergy, counselors of various types, psychiatrists, social workers, and special education teachers. (*See* Volume 1: Social Sciences.) Persons with an interest in and knowledge of psychology may also wish to consider occupations in anthropology, education, personnel, or social service. For those with a strong desire to help people cope with disabilities and improve their quality of life, there are therapist occupations (such as occupational and recreational) that deal with both physical and emotional needs.

Methods of entering

The placement office of the university from which the psychologist has obtained a degree will be able to help in finding a position. The student's major professor will also know of vacancies in professional positions. The American Psychological Association publishes a monthly employment bulletin for its members, in which job vacancies are listed.

Advancement

The psychologist who is a college or university professor may advance through the academic ranks from instructor. Some college teachers who enjoy administrative work may be advanced to head of the department.

Psychologists who work for state or federal government agencies may, after considerable experience, be promoted to head of the section or department. School psychologists may be made director of pupil personnel services. Industrial psychologists may rise to managerial or administrative positions.

After several years of experience, psychologists may enter private practice or set up their own research or consulting firms.

Employment outlook

Psychologists held about 110,000 jobs in the early 1990s. Around 35 percent of salaried psychologists were employed in educational institutions; 25 percent in hospitals, clinics, rehabilitation centers, and other health care facilities; and 16 percent in federal, state, and local government agencies. Others worked in social service organizations, research organizations, management consulting companies, market research firms, and other businesses. Besides those listed above, another 19,000 psychologists were employed as college and university faculty members. In addition, many psychologists are in private practice or have their own research or consulting businesses. About 40 percent of all psychologists are self-employed.

Employment opportunities for doctoral-level psychologists are expected to be excellent through the end of the 1990s, at least in nonacademic settings. Increased emphasis on health maintenance and the prevention of illness, as well as the growing interest in providing psychological services for special groups (such as children or the elderly), will create a greater demand for psychologists. These areas

are dependent on government funding, however, and could be adversely affected in an economic downswing, when spending is likely to be curtailed. Many openings should be available in business and industry, and the outlook is very good for psychologists in full-time independent practice.

Faculty positions will be less plentiful because of declining college enrollments. Outstanding psychologists with a doctorate from a leading university will have no problem obtaining employment in the top academic institutions, whereas a larger number of Ph.D.s will find teaching positions in smaller, perhaps less prestigious schools or will seek jobs outside the academic field.

Prospects look best for doctorate holders in applied areas such as clinical, counseling, health, and industrial-organizational psychology and for those with extensive technical training in quantitative research methods and computer applications. Competition will be severe for persons with only a master's degree in psychology. The number of jobs for which they qualify are limited, but include counseling in schools and assisting psychologists in community mental health centers. Even fewer opportunities will be available for persons with no more than a bachelor's degree. They may find openings as assistants in rehabilitation centers or, if they meet state certification requirements, as high-school psychology teachers.

Earnings

Median annual salary for all psychologists with doctoral degrees was about $44,000 in the early 1990s. The median for those working in business and industry was $55,000; those in educational institutions earned a median of $42,900 a year. Hospitals and clinics paid those with a doctorate a median of $41,800; state and local governments, $40,700; and in the federal government, $51,700. Doctoral-level psychologists in independent private practice and in applied specialties generally have higher earnings than other psychologists. Many psychologists are able to supplement their basic earnings with fees from consulting, writing, or lecturing.

Salaries for entry-level jobs with the federal government are based on education and experience. In the early 1990s, psychologists with a bachelor's degree received about $14,800 or $18,400 a year, depending on the individual's academic records. Counseling psychologists with a master's degree and one year's experience were paid a starting salary of $22,500. Clinical psychologists with a doctoral degree and one year of internship started at $27,200 or $32,600, depending on other qualifications.

Conditions of work

Psychologists work under many different conditions. Those who work as college or university teachers usually have offices in a building on campus and access to a laboratory in which they may carry out experiments.

The offices of school psychologists may be located in the school system headquarters. They may work both in their own offices and in space set aside for them in several schools in the school district. Their customary pattern of work may be to visit schools on a regular schedule or to remain in the office and see pupils and their parents who come or are sent to see them.

Psychologists in military service may serve either in this country or overseas. They may be stationed in Washington and assigned to an office job, or they may be stationed with other military personnel at a post or, more likely, in a military hospital.

Psychologists employed by federal or state agencies may work in such diverse services as public health agencies, the Department of Veterans Affairs, vocational rehabilitation, the Peace Corps, the U.S. Office of Education, or a state department of education. Their working conditions depend largely on the kind of job they have; they may be required to do a lot of traveling, or may be asked to produce publications. They may work mainly with people, or may be assigned entirely to research.

Psychologists who work with business or industry usually work under highly favorable conditions. Their offices are often attractively decorated. They may have a large clerical or secretarial staff.

Some psychologists are self-employed. Most work as clinical psychologists and have offices to which persons come who need help in adjusting to life. Others work as consultants to business firms. Self-employed psychologists rent or own their office space, and arrange their own work schedules.

Social and psychological factors

Psychologists enjoy high professional status. Their opinions may be sought on many matters, and they are looked to for leadership.

Most psychologists derive deep satisfaction from their professional careers. They feel that they are engaged in work that is of great benefit to humanity. They can see steady progress in the profession toward reaching significant new understanding of behavior, and this is for many an exciting, scholarly, and deeply rewarding experience.

GOE: 11.03.01; SIC: 8049; SOC: 1915

◇ SOURCES OF ADDITIONAL INFORMATION

American Association for Counseling and Development
5999 Stevenson Avenue
Alexandria, VA 22304

American Psychological Association
1200 17th Street, NW
Washington, DC 20036

National Association of School Psychologists
808 17th Street, NW, Suite 200
Washington, DC 20006

National Institute of Mental Health
5600 Fishers Lane, Room 15 C-05
Rockville, MD 20857

National Science Foundation
1800 G Street, NW
Washington, DC 20550

U.S. Department of Veterans Affairs
Department of Medicine and Surgery (10)
Washington, DC 20420

◇ RELATED ARTICLES

Public relations specialists

Definition

Public relations specialists develop and maintain programs that present a favorable public image for the organization represented. This involves providing information about the organization, its goals and accomplishments, and any further plans or projects of public interest. Public relations workers may be paid employees of the organization they represent or they may be part of a P.R. firm that works for organizations on a contract basis. Whether as an in-house staff member or as an outside consultant, the P.R. person prepares news releases, photographs, and other information for the news media and others who may be interested in the organization or individual. Public relations for nonprofit and business organizations, government agencies, and other special interest groups includes promoting goodwill through advertising, speeches, exhibits, films, and panel programs, and may also include research, writing, and designing promotional material. Some public relations persons go before the public to represent the organization. Others may be involved in fund raising or political campaigning. Many serve as members of the board.

History

Although public relations came into being as a formal occupation during this century, it has many historical antecedents. The Foundation for Public Relations Research and Education has made possible grants for a series of lectures that show relations effort employed in 1787 to get the Constitution ratified and the public relations attitudes fostered by both the North and the South during the Civil War. The advance men for circuses and show boats were the forerunners of the press agent who rose to heights during the heyday of movies in the 1920s and the 1930s.

By the end of the 1930s, these pioneers had gained favorable prominence and were joined by several more, usually men from newspapers, who performed the public relations function. The greatest growth of public relations, however, came during and after World War II with the rapid advance of communications techniques. Firms began to realize a need for professional help to make certain their messages were given proper public attention. Manufacturing firms who had turned their productive facilities over to the war effort returned to the manufacture of peacetime products and enlisted the aid of public relations persons to bring these products and the company name forcefully before the buying public.

Large business firms, labor unions, and service organizations, such as the American Red Cross, Boy Scouts of America, and the YMCA, began to recognize the value of establishing positive, healthy relationships with the public that they serve and upon which they depend for support. Often the need for effective public relations was emphasized when circumstances beyond the control of a company or an institution created unfavorable reaction from the public.

In 1944, the first independent public relations weekly, the *Public Relations News*, was started by Denny Griswold. Today it is read by management and public relations executives in ninety countries in the world. The growth of the public relations field since 1945 has been rapid and is testimony to the increased awareness in all circles for the need of professional attention to the proper use of media and the proper public relations approach to the many publics of a firm or an organization—its customers, its employees, its stockholders, its contributors, its competitors, and the large number of people who fall in none of these categories but must be considered in any general public relations program.

Nature of the work

The public relations person seldom works the conventional office hours for many weeks at a time. Time behind the desk may represent only a small part of the total working schedule. Travel is often an important and necessary part of the job.

Public relations may be done for a corporation, retail business, service company, utility, association, nonprofit organization, or educational institution. Public relations specialists may be concerned with one or more, or all, of the eight major job classifications of public relations work: writing reports, news releases, booklet texts, speeches, copy for radio and TV, film sequences and so on; editing employee publications, newsletters, shareholder reports, and other management communications; contacting the press, radio, and TV, as well as magazines on behalf of the employer; handling special events such as press parties, convention exhibits, open houses, new facility or anniversary celebrations; making appearances before groups and selecting appropriate platforms for company officers; using a background knowledge of art and layout for developing brochures, booklets, and photographic communications; programming and determining the public relations needs of the employer, defining the goals of the public relations effort, and recommending steps to carry out the program; and supervising the advertising of a company's or an institution's name and reputation as opposed to advertising a company's wares.

The public relations executive consults with management on company or institutional behavior to ensure that the company or institution conducts itself so as to merit public confidence. Public relations workers are alert to any and all company or institutional events that are newsworthy, prepare the news releases and see that they get to the proper media. For manufacturers and retailers, they are concerned with efforts that will promote sales and create goodwill for the firm's products. They work closely with the marketing and sales departments in announcing new products, preparing displays, and attending occasional dealers' conventions.

A large firm may have a director of public relations who is a vice president of the company and in charge of a staff that includes writers, artists, researchers, and other specialists. Publicity for an individual or a small organization may involve many of the same aspects but these will be carried out by only a few persons, or maybe only one person will handle them all.

Many public relations people work as counsels or consultants rather than as members of the staff of a corporation, college, or a hospital. As staff members of a consulting firm, they have the advantage of being able to operate independently, to state opinions objectively, and to work with more than one type of business or association.

Public relations people are called upon to work with the public opinion aspects of almost every corporate or institutional problem. These can range from a plant opening to a dormitory dedication, merger or sale of a subsidiary, or the condemnation of land for campus expansion. There are press relations, information services, and governmental relations at the local, state, and national levels. Public relations bears family resemblance to journalism and teaching, the objective of all three being to inform. Public relations people are related to the law in that they advise and counsel clients or employers on

Public relations specialists are often energetic people who have an ability to motivate others.

public attitudes and represent them before the bar of public opinion.

As in many other fields, public relations professionals may specialize. For example: *Lobbyists* try to persuade legislators and other office holders to pass laws favoring the interests of the firms or people they represent. *Fundraising directors* develop and direct programs designed to raise funds for social welfare agencies and other nonprofit organizations. (*See also* the separate article titled "Fundraisers" elsewhere in this volume.)

The public relations person may travel a great deal attending meetings, conventions, and conferences with groups and individuals in cities throughout the nation. Social life often revolves around business activities and friends may be limited almost exclusively to business associates.

The working day is often disrupted by sudden changes so that a day intended to be spent writing copy for an informational brochure may have to be devoted to the handling of an unexpected news event. Public relations persons must anticipate a career of anonymity. The speeches they draft will be delivered by company officers, the magazine article they prepare may be credited to the president of the company, and they may be consulted to prepare the message to stockholders from the chairman of the board that appears in the annual report. Early in their career they become accustomed to having others receive credit for their behind-the-scenes work. However, greater recognition is developing for the P.R. executive and his or her contribution to society.

Requirements

Few persons employed in public relations service do not have a college degree. The majors most preferred are public relations, English, or journalism, because public relations is based upon effective communication with others. Some employers feel that majoring in the area in which the public relations person will eventually work, for example, a science degree, is the best training. A knowledge of business administration is most helpful as is a native talent for selling. A graduate degree may be required for administrative and managerial positions while persons with a bachelor's degree in public relations find staff positions with either an organization or a public relations firm.

In the early 1990s, more than 150 colleges and 35 graduate schools offered programs in public relations leading to degree. In addition, about 300 other colleges offer at least one course in the field. Public relations programs are sometimes administered by the journalism or communications department of a school. In addition to courses in theory and techniques of public relations, organization, management and administration, and practical applications are studied. Specialization in areas such as business, government, and nonprofit organizations is possible. Other preparation includes courses in creative writing, psychology, communications, advertising, and journalism.

The student's high-school preparation should consist of courses in English, journalism, public speaking, humanities, and languages.

Special requirements

The successful public relations person should have more than the usual understanding of people and human psychology, be able to analyze unusual situations and make decisions of far-reaching consequence, be persuasively articulate for causes that merit enthusiasm, and enjoy the stimulation of a variety of challenges. Public relations workers should have good verbal skills, extroverted traits, sensitivity to other people, and the qualities necessary for leadership and administrative ability. They must be creative and, to a large extent, self-starters who

can plan and program their own work for the most efficient performance.

The Public Relations Society of America and the International Association of Business Communicators accredit public relations workers who have passed a comprehensive examination. Such accreditation is a sign of competence in this field although it is not a requirement for employment.

Opportunities for experience and exploration

Almost any experience in working successfully with other people may stand young persons in good stead as they seek opportunities in the field of public relations. Summer work on a newspaper or a P.R. trade paper or a job with a radio or television station may give insights into communications media. Work as volunteers on a political campaign may help them understand the ways in which people can be persuaded. Being selected as a page for the U.S. Congress or a state legislature may help them grasp the fundamentals of governmental processes. A selling job will help them understand some of the principles of product presentation; a teaching job will help them organize their presentation in a logical way.

Related occupations

Individuals attracted to the field of public relations can easily transfer their interests and aptitudes to occupations in advertising, marketing, publishing, and radio and television broadcasting. They may also wish to explore the work of Foreign Service officers, political scientists, and sociologists.

Methods of entering

There is no clear-cut formula for getting a job in public relations. Entry is often made after preliminary experience has been gained in another occupation closely allied to the field, usually some segment of communications and frequently in journalism. Coming into public relations from newspaper work is still a recommended route. Another good method, however, is to gain initial employment as a public relations trainee or as a clerk, secretary, or research assistant in a public relations department or a counseling firm.

Most public relations firms are located in large cities that are centers of communications. The main offices of most large industries or associations are also in these same large cities, and it is from these offices that the public relations department functions. New York, Chicago, Los Angeles, and Washington, D.C., are good prospects in which to start a search for a public relations job. Nevertheless, there are a good many opportunities in smaller cities.

Advancement

In some large companies, the young persons who get their first job on a public relations staff may start as trainees in a formal training program for new employees. In others, new employees may expect to be assigned to work that has a minimum of responsibility. They may assemble clippings or do rewrites on material that has already been accepted. They may make posters, or assist in conducting polls or surveys, or compile reports from data that were submitted by others.

As workers acquire experience, they may be given more responsibility. They may be assigned to writing news releases, may be allowed to direct a poll or survey, or may advance to writing speeches for company officials. Progress may seem to be slow, because some skills take a long time to master.

Some persons advance in responsibility and salary in the same firm in which they started. Others, however, find that the path to advancement is to accept a more attractive position in another firm.

The goal of many public relations specialists is to open an independent office or to join an established consulting firm. To start an independent office requires a large outlay of capital and an established reputation in the field. Those who are successful in operating their own consulting firms probably attain the greatest financial success in the public relations field.

Employment outlook

In the early 1990s, an estimated 87,000 public relations specialists were employed in a variety of settings. Many hold jobs in manufacturing, transportation, and insurance companies, public utilities, and trade and professional associations. A large number work for government agencies or for schools, colleges, museums, and other educational, religious, or human service organizations. In addition, P.R. workers are being employed in greater numbers by hospitals, pharmaceutical companies, medical associations, and other organizations in the rapidly expanding health care field. Finally, many P.R., specialists hold positions in public relations consulting firms or work for advertising agencies.

The outlook for employment in public relations through rest of the decade is excellent. The field has expanded rapidly since World War II, and there is every indication this growth will continue.

Most large companies have some sort of public relations resource, either through their own staff or through the use of a firm of consultants. They are expected to expand their public relations activities and create many new jobs. In addition, more and more smaller companies are hiring public relations specialists, adding to the demand for these workers.

Competition will be keen for beginning jobs in public relations, however, because the glamour and excitement of the field appeal to so many job seekers; those persons with both education and experience will have an advantage.

The greatest concentration of public relations firms is found in major cities in the United States, but there is a trend toward establishing small firms in less urban areas throughout the country. Also, opportunities overseas are developing apace.

Earnings

A trainee in public relations for business and industry may begin at about $15,000 a year, but can within a few years work up to $21,000 or more. Public relations specialists in the early 1990s had median annual earnings of about $27,000. Most of them were paid in the range of $21,000 to $43,200, while the top ten percent made $54,200 or more.

Compensation varies from geographic area to area, and with company size and degree of responsibility. For the top-level workers, the median salary in the early 1990s was about $44,100 a year. Median annual earnings ranged from about $33,200 in nonprofit organizations to $62,000 in consumer product companies. Consulting firms tend to pay their public relations workers higher salaries than other business organizations.

A director of public relations for a small to medium-sized company may earn from $28,500 to $40,000 a year, while the range for the larger corporation may easily reach $65,000 or even more. Salaries ranging from $55,000 to more than $200,000 are earned by a number of seasoned public relations executives. These persons, more often than not, carry the title of vice president and their fringe benefits are commensurately higher.

Public relations specialists in the federal government generally start at about $18,400 with a bachelor's degree, $22,500 with a master's. Additional education or experience could qualify applicants for a higher salary. Public information specialists averaged about $32,600 a year in the early 1990s.

Conditions of work

Public relations persons are likely to enjoy the outward signs of prestige—well-appointed offices, adequate secretarial help, regular salary increases, and expense accounts. They will be expected to make a good appearance in tasteful, conservative clothing. They must have social poise, and their conduct in their personal life is important to their firm or their clients. The public relations specialist may have to entertain business associates, which sometimes involves the person's family.

The life of the public relations executive is so greatly determined by the job that many consider this a disadvantage. Because public relations is concerned with public opinion, it is often difficult to measure the results of performance and to sell the worth of a public relations program to an employer or client. Competition in the consulting field is keen, and if a firm loses an account, some of its personnel may be affected. The demands it makes for anonymity will be considered by some as one of the less inviting aspects. Public relations involves much more hard work and a great deal less glamour than is popularly supposed.

There may be a great deal of travel involved in some public relations work. Regular hours may also not be possible; although the workweek may consist of thirty-five to forty hours, these hours may include evenings and even weekends when meetings must be attended and other special events covered.

Social and psychological factors

In the early days of public relations, the job was considered one in which it was only the relationship to "outside others" that was important. As time has passed, it has become increasingly apparent that the stockholders of a firm are equally as important to it as any group of outsiders. The public relations specialist may find that the work often centers around interpreting management's policies to those who actually own the business. This may be a psychologically difficult role, as the public relations person cannot afford to offend either group, but may often find that their views are in conflict.

Another difficult role for the public relations worker to carry out is the job of interpreting company policy to the company's own employees. Again, the worker may be in the untenable position of being unable to offend either group.

Still a third psychological hazard is the public relations worker's mandate to interpret to company officials the moods and attitudes of the company's several publics. It is not easy to report an unfavorable reaction, nor is it always possible for public relations, no matter how efficient, to erase or reverse an unfavorable public view.

As with careers in advertising, a public relations specialist is in a position where he or she may have to promote a product that does not ally with personally held views. It is dilemmas such as this that should be evaluated before accepting a position. If one does not support fur sales, for example, then working for the furrier industry should not be considered. By considering such elements, a prosepctive public relations specialist should be able to maintain a happy and productive career.

GOE: 11.09.03; SIC: 8743; SOC: 332

◇ SOURCES OF ADDITIONAL INFORMATION

International Association of Business Communicators
870 Market Street
Suite 940
San Francisco, CA 94102

PR Reporter
PR Publishing Company, Inc.
Dudley House
PO Box 600
Exeter, NH 03833

Public Relations News
127 East 80th Street
New York, NY 10021

Promotion Marketing Association of America
322 Eighth Avenue
Suite 7201
New York, NY 10001

Public Relations Society of America
Career Information
33 Irving Place
New York, NY 10003

◇ **RELATED ARTICLES**

Volume 1: Advertising; Marketing; Public Relations
Volume 2: Advertising workers; Fundraisers; Marketing, advertising, and public relations managers; Marketing research personnel; Media specialists; Reporters and correspondents; Writers and editors

Purchasing agents

Definition

Purchasing agents buy raw materials, machinery, supplies, and services required by businesses or companies. They must consider cost, quality, quantity, and time needed. Industrial buyers work for large manufacturing companies that have complex requirements in machinery and materials.

History

Careers in the field of purchasing are relatively new and have come into real importance only in the last half of the twentieth century. With the development of production machinery beginning about 200 years ago, manufacturing plants and businesses became greatly enlarged. This necessitated the division of management jobs into various specializations, one of these being that of buying. By the late 1800s buying was considered as a separate job in large businesses. The purchasing of great amounts of supplies was necessary in many industries such as railroads, automobiles, and steel. As business expanded, the trend toward specialized buying grew. In 1915, the purchasing agents in the country established the National Association of Purchasing Agents (now the National Association of Purchasing Management).

The development of the purchasing field was furthered by the necessary expansion of industry and government bureaus during and after World War I. Since World War II the economic importance of centralized buying by trained purchasing agents and specialists has been permanently established.

Nature of the work

When a business annually buys at least $100,000 worth of various goods, the employment of a purchasing agent is economically necessary. The job of purchasing is large and varied. It is important that the most suitable materials be selected in the proper quantity at the best possible price for delivery at the correct time and place. To do this, the agent must consider the exact specifications for the required items, cost, quantity discounts, freight handling or other transportation costs and delivery time. Much of this information can be obtained by comparing listings in catalog and trade journals, interviewing suppliers' representatives, keeping up with current market trends, examining sample goods, and observing demonstrations of equipment. It may be that the agent will find it valuable to visit plants of company suppliers to check the quality of the production of supplies.

The agent is also responsible for following up the order for merchandise, making certain the goods meet the order specifications. In some larger firms it may be necessary for the purchasing staff to consist of several employees assigned to specific jobs usually headed by a director or manager of purchasing who directs the overall buying operation. Most purchasing agents work in firms having fewer than five employees in the purchasing department.

Purchasing agents must keep track of all the supplies and materials they buy. This includes completing purchasing orders, tracking expenses, and filing invoices.

Some large firms may employ as many as 100 or more specialized buyers.

In carrying out their responsibilities, purchasing agents may have access to advice from *purchase-price analysts,* who compile and analyze statistical data about the manufacture and cost of products. Based on this information, they can make recommendations to purchasing personnel regarding the feasibility of producing or buying certain products and suggest ways to reduce costs.

Other purchasing agents may specialize in a particular product or field. For example:

Procurement engineers specialize in aircraft equipment. They establish specifications and requirements for construction, performance, and testing of equipment and are involved in the transactions between buyers and suppliers.

Field contractors negotiate with farmers to grow or purchase fruits, vegetables, or other crops. These experts may advise growers on matters such as methods, acreage, and supplies and may arrange for financing, transportation, or labor recruitment.

Head tobacco buyers are engaged in the purchase of tobacco on the auction warehouse floor. They advise other buyers about grades and quantities of tobacco to buy and the prices to pay.

Grain buyers manage grain elevators, evaluating and buying grain for resale and milling. They are concerned with the quality, market value, shipping, and storing of grain.

Grain broker-and-market operators buy and sell grain for investors through the commodity exchange. They work on a commission basis as other types of brokers do.

Requirements

Employers differ greatly in what they require as to educational background for purchasing agents. With a high-school education and some experience in procurement, it is possible to obtain certain entry-level jobs. But the likelihood of acquiring a supervisory or managerial position will tend to decrease if one does not have a college degree. Some employers require a college degree and prefer applicants with a master's degree in business administration or management. Companies that manufacture machinery or chemicals may require a degree in engineering or science. College work should include courses in general economics, purchasing, accounting, statistics, and business management. A familiarity with computers is also highly desirable.

Among the many personal traits important to a purchasing agent are honesty and integrity. One should be of calm temperament and firm in one's decisions. The position of purchasing agent is partially a public relations assignment, so one should therefore strive to be diplomatic, tactful, and cooperative. One should also possess initiative, good judgment, an inquiring analytical mind, above-average intelligence, and the ability to work on details. A thorough knowledge of business and business practices and understanding of the needs and activities of the employer are essential.

Special requirements

There are no specific licensure or certification requirements imposed by law or official organizations. There are several professional organizations, however, to which purchasing agents frequently belong, including the National Association of Purchasing Management, the National Institute of Governmental Purchasing, and the American Management Association. These organizations confer certification on applicants who meet their educational and experience requirements and who pass the necessary examinations. Although such certification is not essential, it is a recognized mark of professional competence that enhances a purchasing agent's chances for promotion to top management positions.

Opportunities for experience and exploration

There is not much chance for exploring this field, unless through a summer job in the purchasing department of a business or industry. Once employed in a company, purchasing agents might find a program of classroom instruction as well as on-the-job training.

Related occupations

Purchasing agents negotiate and contract to buy equipment, supplies, and other merchandise. Other workers involved in similar activities include procurement services managers, retail and wholesale buyers, and traffic managers.

Methods of entering

Students desiring to enter this field without college can, with suitable business course backgrounds in high school, enter it on a clerical level in business or in the armed forces. For someone interested in military service and in the purchasing field, service in the Quartermaster Corps of the Army or the procurement division of the Navy and Air Force can provide excellent preparation for either a civilian job or a career position in the service.

To enter government purchasing departments, one must take and pass a competitive civil service examination.

Entry into purchasing departments of private businesses is made by direct application to the company where there are openings. Most purchasing personnel start in departments such as accounting, shipping, and receiving and then they can be transferred to purchasing when an opportunity arises. Usually the practice of most large companies is to start a newcomer in the purchasing department on an orientation course of several months. This provides an opportunity to learn the scope of the firm's operations.

College preparation for this field is important. The placement services offered by colleges and universities are very helpful in referring graduates to available jobs.

Advancement

Opportunities for advancement will be available for those trainees or purchasing clerks whose work is good and who demonstrate responsibility. Promotions may be to assistant purchasing agent, purchasing agent, or the head of the purchasing department. Advancement in large departments frequently follows these steps: becoming generally familiar with departmental procedures such as keeping inventory records, filling out forms to initiate new purchase; checking of buying orders, expediting, contacting other departments about purchases, reporting to supervisors, dealing with sellers; purchasing certain products generally under supervision; being responsible for purchasing of one or more classes of important products and becoming a junior buyer of standard catalog items; assistant buyer or purchasing agent—part of the time is spent in administrative duties; and purchasing agent—principally an administrative position with overall responsibility for purchasing, warehousing, traffic, and related functions. At the very top levels, a director or vice-president of purchasing or of materials management will have duties that overlap other management functions, such as production, planning, and marketing.

In addition, there is considerable opportunity for advancement through changing employers. Frequently an assistant purchasing agent for one firm will be hired as a purchasing agent or head of the purchasing department by another company in the same general area.

Employment outlook

The employment of purchasing agents is likely to grow more slowly than average through the 1990s. The principal reasons for this are the computerization of purchasing and the increased reliance on a small number of suppliers, which boost the productivity of purchasing personnel and reduce the number of new job openings. As more and more hospitals, schools, state and local governments, and other service-related organizations turn to professional purchasing agents to help reduce costs, they will become good sources of employment.

555

Nevertheless, most of the job openings will be to replace workers who retire or leave their jobs for other reasons.

Demand will be strongest for holders of a master's degree in business administration with an undergraduate degree in purchasing. Among firms manufacturing complex machinery, chemicals, and other technical products, the demand will be for graduates with a master's degree in engineering, science, or business administration with courses in purchasing. Graduates of two-year programs in purchasing should continue to find good opportunities, especially in smaller companies.

Earnings

The earnings of purchasing agents vary with the size of the employing firm, the experience the employee has had, and the amount of responsibility one must assume. Salaries of college graduates hired as beginning purchasing agents averaged about $21,200 in the early 1990s. Experienced purchasing agents averaged between $26,400 and $33,600 a year, and senior agents averaged about $41,300. The top ten percent of all purchasing agents earned more than $42,400 a year.

Depending on the college record and experience, beginning purchasing agents with the federal government earned about $14,800 or $18,400 in the early 1990s. The average salary for all purchasing agents in the federal government was about $30,500.

Purchasing personnel usually receive the same holidays, vacation, and benefits as do other company employees. Many firms have benefit plans that supplement Social Security. Also, purchasing agents are usually reimbursed for expenses incurred for lodging, transportation, and other travel expenses.

Conditions of work

Working conditions for a purchasing agent are similar to those of other employees. Usually offices are pleasant, well lighted, and clean. Work is year round and generally steady because it is not particularly influenced by seasonal factors. The workweek consists most often of five days and about thirty-five to forty hours. For a purchasing agent, work does not always end when the plant closes. Agents may have to spend time outside regular hours attending meetings, reading, preparing reports, visiting suppliers'

plants, or traveling. While most often the work is done indoors, they may occasionally need to inspect goods outdoors or in warehouses.

Social and psychological factors

It is extremely important for a purchasing agent to be able to develop good working relations with others. He or she must work closely with suppliers as well as personnel in other departments of the company. Frequently it rests on the purchasing agent to get "rush" orders accepted, arrange favorable payment terms, special packaging, and prompt adjustment service. There is also a steady demand made for new ideas needed to meet competition; therefore, one must keep up-to-date to solve the many new problems presented regularly. This may result in a great deal of pressure. Also satisfying is the fact that as a business person, a purchasing agent is usually well respected by the community. However, a purchasing agent on a government level may find it necessary to lead a more isolated social and political life so as not to be accused of undue influence. The loneliness of this position may be an advantage or limitation depending on one's needs and interests.

GOE: 11.05.04; SIC: Any industry; SOC: 1449

◇ **SOURCES OF ADDITIONAL INFORMATION**

American Purchasing Society
11910 Oak Trail Way
Port Richey, FL 34668

National Association of Purchasing Management
2055 East Centennial Circle
PO Box 22160
Tempe, AZ 85282

National Contract Management Association
1912 Woodford Road
Vienna, VA 22180

National Institute of Governmental Purchasing
115 Hillwood Avenue
Falls Church, VA 22046

National Retail Merchants Association
100 West 31st Street
New York, NY 10001

Educational Foundation for the Fashion Industries
Scholarship Information
227 West 27th Street
New York, NY 10001

◇ **RELATED ARTICLES**

Rabbis

Definition

Rabbis are the spiritual leaders of Jewish religious congregations. They interpret Jewish law and tradition and conduct religious services on the Shabbath and holidays. Rabbis perform wedding ceremonies and funeral services, counsel congregants, visit the sick, and are involved in community and interfaith affairs. They also have administrative duties, such as working on congregational committees.

History

The word "rabbi" comes from a Hebrew word meaning "master," and has been used to describe Jewish leaders and scholars for the last 2,000 years. During the Talmudic period (which spans roughly 500 years, from the first to the fifth century A.D.), the term was used to refer to preachers and scholars. Jesus was considered to be a rabbi. Other respected rabbis include Hillel (beginnings of the first century A.D.), Maimonides (1135–1204), and Stephen Wise (1874–1949).

Over the centuries, rabbis became the leading religious authorities in Jewish communities. It has only been in the last 150 years that rabbis have become salaried officials in religious congregations.

Nature of the work

Rabbis serve congregations affiliated with four different divisions of American Judaism: Orthodox, Conservative, Reform, and Recon- structionist. Regardless of their affiliation, all rabbis have similar responsibilities. They conduct religious services, officiate at weddings and funerals, help the sick or needy, supervise religious educational programs, and teach confirmation and adult education courses. They also counsel members of their congregation and visit the sick.

Rabbis are the teachers of their community. They help congregants and other interested individuals interpret Judaism and integrate religious thought and practice into their lives. Rabbis counsel the bereaved or troubled, and instruct persons who seek conversion. They also deliver sermons on political and religious topics. Rabbis may supervise the administration of the congregation, although sometimes this responsibility is shared by an executive director. Rabbis are involved in community activities and often participate in interfaith affairs. They may appear on television or radio programs to give a Jewish perspective on current events. Some rabbis write for publication, and others teach in colleges and theological seminaries.

Within Judaism the rabbi has an elevated status in spiritual matters, but most Jewish synagogues and temples have a relatively democratic form of decision making in which all members participate. Rabbis of large congregations spend much of their time working with their staffs and various committees. They are often aided by an associate or assistant rabbi.

The Jewish traditions differ somewhat in their view of God and of history. These differences also extend to such variations in worship as the wearing of head coverings, the amount of Hebrew used during prayer, the use of mu-

A conservative rabbi teaches a bar mitzvah student how to apply tefillin around his head and forearm. Such knowledge of worship practices is required before he can be bar mitzvahed.

dox seminary have had previous coursework in Jewish practices and concepts. To be ordained, students must have the approval of an authorized rabbi acting either independently or as a representative of a seminary.

Students admitted to the rabbinical program at the Jewish Theological Seminary of America, which is the seminary for Conservative rabbis, or the Hebrew Union College-Jewish Institute of Religion, which is the seminary for Reform rabbis, not only must have received an undergraduate degree but must have received preparatory training in Jewish studies. The program at the Conservative seminary can be completed in four years by a student with a strong background in Jewish studies; otherwise, ordination may take up to six years. Rabbinical studies at the Reform seminary generally require five years. This includes one year of study in Jerusalem at the beginning of the program.

The program at the Reconstructionist Rabbinical College, Judaism's newest branch of worship, generally lasts five years and also requires a bachelor's degree for admission. Each year of study emphasizes a different period of Jewish civilization.

The general curriculum of ordination for all branches of Judaism includes courses in the Bible, the Talmud (post Biblical writings), rabbinic literature, Jewish history, and theology. Students should expect to study Hebrew for both verbal and written skills. Many rabbis are fluent in Hebrew. Courses are also offered in education, public speaking, and pastoral psychology. Training for leadership in community service and religious education is also being stressed as an alternative to the pulpit.

Advanced academic degrees in fields such as biblical and talmudic are offered by some seminaries. All Jewish theological seminaries offer scholarships and loans to qualified students.

sic, the level of congregational participation, and the status of women. Whatever their particular point of view, all Jewish congregations—Orthodox, Conservative, Reform, or Reconstructionist—preserve the substance of Jewish worship in a manner consistent with their beliefs. The rabbi must both lead the congregation and share in the changing traditions as they are wanted or needed.

Requirements

Completion of a course of study in a seminary is a prerequisite for ordination as a rabbi. Entrance requirements, curriculum, and length of the program vary depending on the particular branch of Judaism. Prospective rabbis normally need to complete an undergraduate degree before entering the seminary. There are about thirty-five Orthodox seminaries in the United States. The two largest are the Rabbi Isaac Elchanan Theological Seminary (an affiliate of Yeshiva University) and the Hebrew Theological College. Both offer a formal three-year program and require a bachelor's degree for entry. Other seminaries have no formal requirements but may require more years of study before ordination. Normally students entering an Ortho-

Special requirements

In addition to the ordination requirements, a primary consideration in choosing a career in the clergy is a strong religious faith coupled with the desire to help others. Rabbis should also be able to communicate effectively and supervise others. They must have self-confidence and possess initiative and compassion. Orthodox seminaries only accept men, but all other denominations accept men and women into the rabbinate.

Opportunities for experience and exploration

Those interested in becoming a rabbi should talk with their own rabbi and others involved in the work of the synagogue or temple to get a clearer idea of the rewards and responsibilities of this profession. Choosing a career as a rabbi entails a good deal of thought as to the demands of this profession. There are numerous opportunities for those interested to investigate congregational life. Aspiring rabbis would be wise to volunteer some time at a temple or synagogue in order to get better acquainted with the type of job responsibilities a rabbi has. In the final analysis, however, there is no single experience that can adequately prepare a person for the demands of being a rabbi. Seminary training should offer the best opportunity to explore many of the facets of a rabbinical career.

Related occupations

Rabbis have many of the same religious leadership and counseling responsibilities as Protestant ministers, Roman Catholic priests, teachers, social workers, and psychologists.

Methods of entry

Only ordained rabbis can work in this profession. Students should consult with a rabbi or contact the appropriate theological seminary to learn how to best meet entrance requirements.

Advancement

Newly ordained rabbis generally begin their careers as leaders of small congregations, assistants to experienced rabbis, directors of Hillel foundations on college campuses, teachers in seminaries and other educational institutions, or chaplains in the armed forces. With experience, they may acquire their own or larger congregations or choose to remain in their original position. The pulpits of large, well-established synagogues and temples are usually filled by rabbis of considerable experience. They may also choose to open new synagogues in growing communities that require more religious facilities.

Employment outlook

Job opportunities for rabbis are generally good but the availability of positions varies with the branch of Judaism to which a rabbi belongs.

Orthodox rabbis fill about 1,100 of the approximately 7,000 rabbinical positions in the United States. There are approximately 860 Conservative rabbis, 800 Reform rabbis, and 80 Reconstructionist rabbis. The majority of the rest work in Jewish communal service, teach in Jewish educational institutions, or serve as chaplains in the armed forces. Orthodox rabbis should have fairly good job prospects as older rabbis retire and smaller communities become large enough to hire a rabbi. Conservative and Reform rabbis should also have good employment opportunities, especially because of retirement and new Jewish communities. Reconstructionist rabbis also should find good employment opportunities because this branch of Judaism is growing rapidly.

Opportunities for rabbis exist in Jewish communities throughout the country. Newly ordained rabbis may choose to serve as chaplains in the armed forces, hospitals, or other institutions; work for one of the many Jewish community services; or teach in colleges, universities, or seminaries.

Earnings

Salaries vary according to the size of the congregation, as well as its denominational branch, location, and financial status. Salary information is limited, but in the early 1990s the earnings of rabbis ranged from $25,000 to $75,000, including health insurance and other fringe benefits. Rabbis usually receive gifts or fees for officiating at weddings and other ceremonies, which add to their income.

Conditions of work

Rabbis work long hours. Like all clergy, rabbis are on call at any hour of the day or night. This can make a rabbi's private like difficult at times, particularly if the rabbi is married and has a family. On the other hand, rabbis are generally independent in their positions, responsible only to the board of directors of their congregation rather than to a formal hierarchy in the faith.

There is no such thing as a standard workweek. Rabbis may have a great deal of administrative responsibilities working with staff and various committees. They visit the sick and help comfort families in time of grief. They provide counseling to those in need and also prepare couples for marriage and young boys and girls for bar and bat mitzahs. Much of the rabbi's time is also spent reading, studying, writing, and talking to people. Rabbis also participate in community and interfaith events.

Despite the long hours and sometimes stressful working conditions, many rabbis enjoy their work and find helping people in a religious context most satisfying.

Social and psychological factors

The rabbi is very involved with working with congregants. The career is rewarding in the sense of spiritual values and achievements; one can find much satisfaction in the comfort and leadership offered congregants. There may, however, be social pressure. The public in general and congregations in particular expect rabbis (and other clergy members) to set examples of high moral and ethical conduct. There is the added pressure of being "on call" twenty-four hours a day, and the need to often comfort people in difficult situations. Obviously many people find strength from these commitments and greatly enjoy their work and find it very meaningful. Rabbis are generally held in great esteem by their congregants and the community at large.

GOE: 10.01.01; SIC: 866; SOC: 2042

◇ **SOURCES OF ADDITIONAL INFORMATION**

Rabbinical Council of America
275 Seventh Avenue
New York, NY 10001

American Association of Rabbis
350 Fifth Avenue
Suite 3308
New York, NY 10001

Information about seminary school and career information are available from:

Association of Advanced Rabbinical and Talmudic Schools
175 Fifth Avenue
New York, NY 10010

Association of Hillel
Jewish Campus Professionals
6300 Forsyth Boulevard
Clyton, MD 63105

Rabbi Elchanan Theological Seminary
2540 Amsterdam Avenue
New York, NY 10033

Hebrew Theological College
7135 North Carpenter Road
Skokie, IL 60076

The Jewish Theological Seminary of America
3080 Broadway
New York, NY 10027

Hebrew Union College Jewish Institute of Religion
3101 Clifton Avenue
Cincinnati, OH 45220

Jewish Reconstructionist Foundation
Church Road and Greenwood Avenue
Wyncota, PA 19095

United Orthodox Rabbinate
330 Elmora Avenue
Elizabeth, NJ 07208

United Synagogue of America Commission on Jewish Education
155 Fifth Avenue
New York, NY 10010

For information concerning the work of military chaplains, contact:

National Conference on Ministry to the Armed Forces
4141 North Henderson Road
Suite 13
Arlington, VA 22203

◇ **RELATED ARTICLES**

Volume 1: Religious Ministries; Social Services
Volume 2: Psychiatrists; Psychologists; Social workers; Therapists, miscellaneous

Radio and telegraph operators

Definition

Radio operators and *telegraph operators* operate radiotelephone/radiotelegraph and telegraph equipment, respectively, to transmit and receive messages or signals between, for example, ground stations and aircraft or stations and trains.

History

Man's efforts to expand the field of communication are fairly recent. The days of the ancient Greek runner and the era of the pony express rider, the stagecoach, and the mule train extend across a long period of history. The telegraph and the telephone, in comparison, are very recent discoveries. The twentieth century alone has seen the addition of radio, the motion picture, and television as improved means of communication; and the automobile, airplane, and spacecraft are newer and faster means of transportation.

Our highly complex system of communication and transportation makes it possible to send a message quickly to almost any part of the world in a matter of minutes, or to transport people or goods to any place on the face of the earth in a matter of hours.

The advancements in communication and transport have been mutually dependent to a large extent. Today, the vast transportation industry could not operate without the modern devices of communication. Nor could it function without the personnel to operate them. It is within this complexity and interdependency that we find the roles and contributions of the radio and telegraph operators.

Nature of the work

The majority of radio and telegraph operators are employed in air transportation (divided almost equally between scheduled airlines and the Federal Aviation Administration) and by railroads. The exact nature of their duties depends on the kind of work the employer is engaged in and the particular job the operators are hired to perform.

Airline-radio operators are responsible for transmitting messages between dispatchers, air traffic controllers, or other ground station workers and flight engineers, pilots, or other flight personnel aboard an aircraft. These communications deal with reports on weather or atmospheric conditions and emergency calls. Operators also relay messages relative to flight and ground operation between the air and ground crews, such as number of passengers, the estimated time of arrival, the mechanical condition of the plane, and requests for repairs. The radiotelephone is used to transmit and receive spoken messages, and the radiotelegraph (which has a keyboard similar to that of a typewriter) is used to transmit and receive written messages. Radio operators may be required to make minor repairs on their equipment.

A log of all messages, many of which are sent in code, is maintained. This is required by civil air regulations. Messages are written down, or typed up, as received and posted in the log. The time that the message was sent or received is always noted.

A more narrowly specialized radio operator is the *radio station operator,* located at aircraft factory stations, who maintains contact with pilots during flight testing and delivery of airplanes.

Telegraphers control the movement of railroad trains, using the instructions dispatchers send out to them. They operate a telegraph key or Teletype machine or talk over the telephone to transmit or receive train orders or messages. In smaller stations, a *telegrapher agent* fulfills these duties and may also sell tickets, process baggage and freight, and perform other clerical duties.

Ship-to-shore communications are handled by *radio officers,* who operate and maintain radiotelephone and radiotelegraph equipment aboard ships. In addition to receiving and transmitting messages, these officers maintain a log and monitor the emergency frequency for distress calls from other vessels.

Transportation is not the only industry to employ radio and telegraph operators. Some of the other occupations in this field are described in the paragraphs that follow.

Commercial communications companies employ *radiotelegraph operators* and *radiotelephone operators* to operate and maintain transmitters and receiving equipment. Messages received by radiotelegraph are typed on a form and relayed to the addressee by telephone or Teletype.

Radio communications are important to police and fire departments and other municipal agencies prepared to handle emergencies. *Radio*

561

A telegraph operator controls all telephone traffic for the dispatcher's office at a railroad company.

communications superintendents direct the personnel who install and maintain this equipment, ensuring that government regulations are complied with. These superintendents are also involved in developing and testing communications systems. *Dispatchers* receive messages from fire fighting crews, fire lookout stations, and mobile units and relay the information to officials concerned.

Communications companies have *personnel service representatives* call on agents and customers to demonstrate how to use telegraph equipment, explain operating procedures, discuss rates and services, and make recommendations for meeting the customer's needs.

The federal government employs *radio-intelligence operators* and the military assigns *electronic intelligence operations specialists* to intercept, locate, identify, and record radio transmissions and other electronic emissions generated by suspected enemies.

Requirements

Graduation from high school is essential in this work, and special preparation in programs offered by a number of technical institutes is a plus. The majority of these workers receive extensive training on the job under the supervision of experienced radio and telegraph operators. Those who hope to advance to management levels will find it an advantage to have a college education.

Helpful school courses include speech, typing, algebra, trigonometry, and electronics. Each of these courses can contribute basic knowledge or experience that will be helpful in learning the work of radio or telegraph operation. Speech is useful in learning to express oneself clearly and to speak expressively and

distinctly. Typing is helpful in training the fingers to work machines similar to the Teletype, and algebra and trigonometry provide further knowledge of mathematical processes. Familiarity with electronics will make it easier to grasp the principles of radio and telegraphic communication and the techniques of operating and maintaining the equipment.

Radio operators and telegraphers must be able to type at least forty words a minute and must know standard codes and symbols used in communication. Some of the personal traits that are helpful in this field are memory for detail, alertness, accuracy, mental agility, dependability, and trustworthiness. Emergency situations, the necessity for doing several things at once under certain conditions, the need to recall names, numbers, and times of events, the recording of messages, and the keeping of records all these demand the use of several of these characteristics. Good judgment, particularly when one must decide quickly, is critical.

Good hearing is necessary and also good habits of speech. Radio operators should not have any impediments in speaking because being able to transmit spoken messages clearly and without obvious accents is of utmost importance.

Many railroads require their trainees to pass examinations to qualify for jobs as telegraphers. Those involved in the interpretation or setting of railroad signals must have exceptionally good eyesight and be free from color blindness. The majority of railroad companies also prefer applicants between the ages of twenty-one and thirty.

Special requirements

Ground radio operators are required to have at least a third-class Federal Communications Commission (FCC) license as a radiotelephone or radiotelegraph operator. A second-class operator's permit, however, is preferred. Positions in the Federal Aviation Administration (FAA) are filled as the result of a civil service examination. Applicants for beginning jobs in the FAA should have about three years' experience in air communications, traffic control, or flying. Announcements of federal civil service positions in air transportation can be found in post offices, city and county buildings, libraries, and state and federal agency offices.

Although union membership is not a requirement, most ground radio operators are members of the Communications Workers of America, and the majority of railroad telegraphers belong to the Order of Railroad Telegraphers.

Opportunities for experience and exploration

One of the best ways to learn about radio and telegraph operation is to get some experience related to the field. Part-time and summer jobs at air terminals, air service areas, weather stations, railroad stations, telegraph and telephone companies, and the like, offer an opportunity to see operators at work, to talk with them about jobs, and to see how their tasks relate to the other phases of company operations.

Building a shortwave radio set, becoming an amateur radio operator (a *ham*), repairing radios, and learning about electricity and electronics are but a few of the many exploratory activities in which one can become involved. Many of these activities are represented by groups, clubs, or organizations in one's school and community, and new members are usually most welcome.

Related occupations

Radio and telegraph operators deal with communication and its technical aspects. Other communications workers include air traffic controllers, dispatchers in transportation companies, photoradio operators (who send pictures by radio), radio announcers, and switchboard and telephone operators. On the technical side of communications work are broadcast technicians, communications equipment mechanics, telecommunications technicians, and transmitter technicians. In addition, radio operators are likely to have an interest in a number of related occupations in radio and television broadcasting or in the recording industry.

Methods of entering

Graduates of technical institutes who have received specialized training can receive assistance in locating a position through the placement office of their school.

Direct application can be made to one or more of the companies in which one is interested. A letter of application, personal visit, and telephone call are among the recom-

mended procedures for making the initial contact to secure instructions and application materials.

Professional employment agencies and advertisements in the daily newspapers are other sources for locating certain positions in air transportation.

Information about positions with the FAA can be obtained by writing to the personnel officer at the nearest FAA agency.

Advancement

For radio and telegraph operators there is little opportunity for direct advancement except as one assumes supervisory responsibilities. A number of related occupations exist, however, to which an operator can readily transfer with a little additional training. Some of these positions include dispatcher, assistant dispatcher, airport traffic controller, air-route traffic controller, or railroad station master. For some, depending on their experience and training, opportunities for advancement may exist in one of several aspects of office and sales jobs. Radio and telegraph operators willing to acquire the appropriate experience and education can find many other related areas to move into within the airline, railroad, water transportation, telephone, and broadcasting industries, as well as in a number of small business activities where communication by radio is essential.

Employment outlook

Employment of radio and telegraph operators is expected to remain steady through the 1990s. Opportunities will be better in the air transportation and communications fields than in railroad and water transportation. Automation and expanding technology are factors that have an influence on the demand for radio and telegraph operators. Devices that permit the transmittal of messages over greater distances and improvements in communications equipment permitting direct transmittal between aircraft and air traffic control personnel or between train crew and dispatcher are expected to lessen the need for operators. Most of the openings that arise will be as a result of the need to replace older, experienced workers who retire, change occupations, or leave the field for other reasons.

Earnings

The earnings of radio and telegraph operators vary depending not only on the individual's experience and responsibilities but on the nature and size of the employing company. In the early 1990s, radio operators received average starting salaries ranging from about $15,400 to $18,000 per year. Experienced operators were paid between $24,000 and $33,800. Railroad telegraphers had average earnings of $19,800 to $28,600.

Vacation, health and life insurance, and retirement benefits are available in accordance with the policy of the employer. In general, transportation companies grant employees and their families discounted fares.

Conditions of work

Radio and telegraph operators usually work a forty-hour week. Work schedules are often irregular because transportation companies are in operation twenty-four hours a day. Working hours, therefore, include holidays, weekends, and night shifts when other workers are usually at home. Some companies have established a rotating shift so that the employee will not be working an unusual or late-hour shift regularly.

Operations are usually conducted in quiet, pleasant surroundings, although the work may require long periods of sitting. Despite limited physical movement, the periods of concentration and mental alertness can be mentally exhausting.

Social and psychological factors

Radio and telegraph operation offers young people an opportunity to engage in an interesting occupation. Every message is important and must be transmitted correctly. Some aspects of the job, however, may seem routine and unimportant.

Although the educational qualifications are not unduly high, the personal qualifications demanded are somewhat exacting in the day-to-day conduct of the work. The occupation is of great importance to other workers and to those who use the services of the employer. It is recognized, therefore, as a field of endeavor contributing to the safety and welfare of humanity.

In this regard, a worker can achieve a number of satisfactions: serving and protecting others, contributing in a service that plays an increasingly vital role in American life, and being an active, productive worker.

GOE: 07.04.05; SIC: 4812, 4822, 4899; SOC: 393

◇ SOURCES OF ADDITIONAL INFORMATION

Air Transport Association of America
1709 New York Avenue, NW
Washington, DC 20006

Association of American Railroads
American Railroads Building
50 F Street, NW
Washington, DC 20001

Federal Aviation Administration
Public Inquiry Center
800 Independence Avenue, SW
Washington, DC 20591

Federal Communications Commission
1919 M Street, NW
Washington, DC 20554

Transportation Communications International Union
3 Research Plaza
Rockville, MD 20850

United Telegraph Workers
20525 Center Ridge Road
Suite 420
Cleveland, OH 44116

◇ RELATED ARTICLES

Volume 1: Aviation and Aerospace; Broadcasting; Civil Service; Military Services; Physical Sciences; Telecommunications; Transportation
Volume 2: Air traffic controllers
Volume 3: Telephone operators
Volume 4: Electronics technicians; Telecommunications technicians

Radio and television announcers and newscasters

Definition

Radio and television announcers present news and commercial messages from a script. They may also ad-lib to identify the station, announce station breaks, and introduce and close shows. Interviewing guests, making public service announcements, and conducting panel discussions may be part of the announcer's work. In small stations the local announcer may keep the program log, run the transmitter, and cue the changeover to network broadcasting as well as write scripts or rewrite news releases.

History

Guglielmo Marconi, a young Italian inventor, is usually credited with having invented radio in 1895. His work, however, was based on that of scientists who had been making discoveries about sound waves for as long as a century.

Radio developed rapidly as people began to comprehend the tremendous possibilities in it. KDKA in Pittsburgh and WWJ in Detroit began broadcasting in 1920. Within ten years, there were radio stations in all the major cities in the United States and broadcasting had become big business. The National Broadcasting Company, the first network, was begun in November 1926 and had twenty-five stations on its first hookup. The Columbia Broadcasting System was organized in 1927. In 1934, the Mutual Broadcasting Company was founded. The twenty years between 1930 and 1950 may be considered the zenith years for the radio industry. With the coming of television, radio broadcasting took second place in importance as a recreation facility for the home, but radio's commercial and communications value should not be underestimated.

Credit for the invention of television cannot be given to any one man. Discoveries that led to the development of television can be traced as far back as 1878, when William Crookes invented a tube that produced the cathode ray. Other inventors who contributed to the development of television were Vladimir Zworykin, a Russian-born scientist who came to this country at the age of twenty and is credited with inventing the iconoscope before he was thirty;

Charles F. Jenkins, who invented a scanning disk, using certain vacuum tubes and photoelectric cells; and Philo T. Farnsworth, who invented an image dissector. WNBT and WCBW, the first commercially licensed television stations, went on the air in 1941 in New York. Both suspended operations during World War II but resumed them in 1946 when television sets began to be manufactured on a commercial scale.

As radio broadcasting was fanning out across the country in its early days, the need for announcers grew. They identified the station and brought continuity to broadcast time by linking one program with the next as well as participating in many programs. In the early days, and even today in smaller stations, announcers do a variety of jobs around the station. When television was born many radio announcers and newscasters began to work in the new medium. The need for men and women in radio and television broadcasting has continued to grow. Television news broadcasting requires specialized "on-camera" personnel—anchors, television news reporters, broadcast news analysts, consumer reporters, and sports reporters (sportscasters).

Nature of the work

Some announcers do announcing only; others do a multitude of other jobs depending on the size of the station. But the nature of their work of announcing remains the same.

An announcer is engaged in an exacting career. The necessity for finishing a sentence or a program at the exact second planned makes this a demanding and tension-producing career. It is absolutely essential, however, that announcers be able to keep their audience ignorant of the tension under which they must work.

The announcer whose main job consists of playing recorded music and interspersing the music with a variety of advertising material and informal commentary is usually called a *disc jockey*. This title was bestowed when most music was recorded on conventional flat records. Today much of the recorded music used in commercial radio stations is on magnetic tape

565

A radio announcer reads aloud from a sheet that conveniently hangs behind the microphone. At the same time, she is preparing a cassette that contains an advertisement.

or compact disc. Disc jockeys serve as a bridge between the music itself and the listener. They may also perform such public services as announcing the time, the weather forecast, or important news. It may be a lonely job, for often the disc jockey is the only person in the studio. Because one of their functions is to maintain the good spirits and morale of their listeners, disc jockeys must possess the native ability to be relaxed and cheerful.

Unlike the more conventional radio or television announcer, the disc jockey is not bound by a written script. Except for the commercial announcements, which must be read as written, the disc jockey's statements are usually spontaneous. Usually, disc jockeys are under no mandate to play any musical selection to the end. They may fade out any record should it interfere with a predetermined schedule for commercials, news, time checks, or weather reports.

Announcers who cover sports events for the benefit of the listening or viewing audience are often known familiarly as sportscasters. This is a highly specialized form of announcing because sports announcers must have extensive knowledge of the sports that they are covering, plus an ability to describe quickly and accurately what is going on. They must have a good vocabulary because they cannot risk using any word too many times.

Often, the sportscaster will spend several days with team members, observe practice sessions, interview individuals, and do research on the history of the event or of the teams to be covered. The more information that a sportscaster can acquire about individual team members, the institution they represent, the tradi-

tion of the contest, the ratings of the team, and the community in which the event takes place, the more interesting coverage is to the audience.

The announcer who specializes in reporting the news to the listening or viewing public is called a *newscaster*. This job may be only the reporting of facts, or it may include editorial comments. Newscasters may be called upon to predict certain trends or happenings. They may be given the authority by their employer to criticize certain practices or philosophies that others are adopting. They must make judgments about which news is important and which is not. In some instances, they write their own scripts, based on facts that are, in the main, furnished by international news bureaus. In other instances, they read verbatim what comes in over the teletype machine. They may work only once or twice each day, on a major news program, or they may broadcast news for five minutes once each hour or once each half hour. Their delivery is usually dignified, measured, and impersonal.

The anchorperson generally summarizes and comments on one aspect of the news at the end of the scheduled broadcast. This kind of announcing differs noticeably from the kind practiced by the sportscaster, whose manner may be breezy and interspersed with slang, or from the disc jockey, who may try to be humorous or intimate and confidential.

The newscaster may specialize in certain aspects of the news, such as economics, politics, or military activity. Newscasters also introduce films and interviews prepared by *news reporters* that provide in-depth coverage and information on the event being reported. Radio and television broadcasting news analysts are often called *commentators*, and they interpret specific events and discuss how these may affect us or the nation. They may have a specified daily slot for which material must be written or prepared to be recorded or presented live to meet time requirements. They gather information to be analyzed and interpreted through research, interviews, and public functions such as political conventions, press conferences, and social activities.

Smaller television stations may have an announcer who serves all the functions of reporting, presenting, and commenting on the news as well as introducing network and news service reports.

Many television and radio announcers have become well-known public personalities in broadcasting. They also may participate in community activities as master of ceremonies at banquets and other public events.

Requirements

Although there are no formal educational requirements for entering into the field of radio and television announcing, many large stations are now employing chiefly those who have been to college. The general reason given for this preference is that the broader the cultural background, the more able is the announcer to meet successfully certain unexpected or emergency situations. The greater the knowledge of geography, of history, of literature and the arts, of political science, of music, and of the sound and structure of the English language, the greater the announcer's value. A factual error, a grammatical error, or a mispronounced word can bring many letters of criticism to the station manager. Station managers are very sensitive to criticism.

Poise and a pleasing voice and personality are of great importance to prospective announcers. They must also have a strong sense of responsibility. They must be levelheaded and be able to react calmly even in the face of a major crisis. There is always a possibility that the lives of many persons may depend on their ability to remain calm in the face of some sort of disaster. There are also many unexpected circumstances that demand the skill of thinking easily on one's feet. For example, if guests who are to appear on a program either do not arrive or become too nervous to appear, a quick adjustment must be made by the announcer. An ill-advised phrase, a breakdown in equipment, a technical difficulty all these must be minimized or smoothed over.

Good diction and English usage, thorough knowledge of correct pronunciation, and freedom from regional dialects are very important. In addition, men and women who aspire to a career as a television announcer must present a good appearance. Neatness, cleanliness, and careful attention to the small details of correct dress are important. Television announcers should dress conservatively and becomingly. Nervous mannerisms or annoying behavior habits must be eliminated. The successful television announcer must have the combination of sincerity and showmanship that attracts and captures an audience.

Broadcast announcing is a highly competitive field. While there may not be any specific training program required by prospective employers, station officials pay particular attention to taped auditions of an applicant's delivery, or in the case of television, a videotape of the applicant.

Some vocational schools advertise training for broadcasting. Anyone who might want to prepare in this way should contact local station managers to find out if such training will improve the chances of employment. It is also advisable to contact broadcasting trade organizations and the Better Business Bureau in the area to find out if the school has been successful in training and placing candidates.

Most announcers start in other capacities, such as production secretary, production assistant, researcher, or reporter, in small stations. As the opportunities present themselves, moving from one job to another in broadcasting is a common career route. Work as a disc jockey, sportscaster, or news reporter may become available. Network jobs are few and the competition for them is great. An announcer must have several years of experience as well as a college education to be considered for these positions.

Special requirements

Union membership may be required for employment with large stations in major cities and is a necessity with the networks. The largest talent union is the American Federation of Television and Radio Artists (AFTRA). Most small stations, however, are nonunion.

Although it is not essential, many announcers hold a Federal Communications Commission Radiotelephone Third Class Operator License, which permits the announcers to operate transmitters and control boards. This is particularly useful in the small stations across the country.

Opportunities for experience and exploration

Students who think they may be interested in becoming an announcer might seek a summer job at a radio or television station. Although they will probably not have any opportunity to broadcast, they may be able to judge whether or not that kind of work might appeal to them as a career for life. They might find that the tension or the monotony of the job was not what they had imagined it to be.

Any chance to speak or to perform before an audience should be welcomed by the prospective announcer. Only by appearing as a speaker or a performer can one discover whether or not one has the poise and stage presence necessary to spend one's life before a microphone or camera.

Many colleges and universities have their own radio or television stations and offer courses in radio and television. The student will gain valuable experience working at the college-owned station. Some radio stations, cable systems, and TV stations offer students financial assistance and on-the-job training in the form of internships, apprentice programs, and co-op work programs, as well as scholarships and fellowships.

Related occupations

Radio and television announcers and newscasters depend on their ability to speak effectively to their audiences. Other workers who require similar oral communications skills include actors, interpreters, narrators, public relations specialists, and sales workers.

Methods of entering

One way to enter this field is to apply for a job other than that of announcer. To learn the operation of a station, it may be wise to serve as a technician, clerk, or page for a while and to seek a change in job when a vacancy occurs on the broadcasting staff.

An announcer is employed only after having given an audition. Audition material should be selected carefully to show the prospective employer the range of the applicant's abilities. In addition to presenting prepared materials, applicants may also be asked to read some material that they have not seen previously. This may be a commercial, a news release, a dramatic selection, or even a poem.

A small local station is probably the aspirant's best entry point. If one can acquire some experience while still a student, this can be cited in the application for a first real job after leaving school.

Advancement

Most successful announcers advance from small stations to large ones. The average announcer will have held several jobs before finding one that satisfies ambition. The most successful announcers are probably those who work for the networks. Usually, because of network jobs, they must live in or near the country's largest cities.

Some careers lead from announcing to other phases of radio or television work. Many more persons are employed in sales, promotion, and planning than are employed in performing. These positions are often more highly paid than that of announcer. Because the networks employ relatively few announcers in proportion to the rest of the broadcasting professionals, a candidate must have several years of experience and specific background in several news areas before even being considered for an audition. These top announcers are generally also college graduates.

Employment outlook

In the early 1990s, about 61,000 persons were employed as radio and television announcers and newscasters in the United States. Almost all of them were staff announcers at one of the more than 7,650 radio stations or 730 television stations around the country. Some, however, worked on a free-lance basis on individual assignments for networks, stations, or advertising agencies and other producers of commercials.

Competition for entry employment into announcing during the coming years will be keen because the broadcasting industry always attracts more applicants than are needed to fill the openings available. There is a better chance of working in radio than in television because there are many more small radio stations. Local television stations usually carry a high percentage of network programs and usually need only a very small staff to carry on local operations.

Opportunities for experienced broadcasting personnel are expected to increase about as fast as for other occupations through the 1990s. This is a result of increased licensing of new radio and television stations and cable TV systems. Despite the growing number of radio stations, however, the increased use of automatic programming equipment is likely to weaken the demand for radio announcers. The trend among major networks, and to some extent among many smaller radio and TV stations as well, is toward specialization in such fields as sportscasting or weather forecasting. Newscasters who specialize in such areas as business, consumer, and health news should have an advantage over other job applicants. Some jobs will come available as staff retire or die, but the competition will continue to be very intense for those jobs for announcers and broadcasters. Even in difficult economic times stations tend to cut down on production staff rather than on those persons who are heard or seen by the public. Replacing people who leave, however, may not be done as frequently as was in the past.

Earnings

The range of salaries for announcers is a rather wide one. In general, it may be said that the smaller the community, the smaller the announcer's salary. In the early 1990s, average starting salaries were anywhere from $12,200 to $14,400 a year for radio announcers and from $16,400 to $26,000 for television announcers. Experienced radio announcers were paid an average of between $15,700 and $17,500, while experienced TV announcers had average earnings that ranged from about $22,500 to $44,200.

For both radio and television, salaries are higher in the larger markets. Nationally known announcers and newscasters who appear regularly on network television programs receive salaries that may be quite impressive. Some of them earn upwards of one million dollars per year. For those who have become top television personalities on their own metropolitan-area television stations, salaries also are quite rewarding, though not so impressive as those of network stars. For well-established announcers on large local stations, income may run to $65,000 per year or even higher.

Twenty-four hour broadcasting is usual on most radio or television stations. Although much of the material may be prerecorded, announcing staff must often still be available and as a result may work considerable overtime or split shifts, especially in smaller stations. Evening, night, weekend, and holiday duty all may provide additional compensation.

Conditions of work

Work in radio and television stations is usually very pleasant. Almost all stations are housed in modern facilities and are kept at a comfortable temperature both summer and winter. Temperature and dust control are an important part of the proper maintenance of technical electronic equipment, and people who work around such machinery benefit from the precautions taken to preserve it.

Announcers' jobs will sometimes take them among the great and famous. Being at the nerve center of an important communications medium will make the broadcaster more keenly aware of current issues and of divergent points of view than is the average person.

Announcers and newscasters will usually work a forty-hour week, but they may also work irregular hours. They may have to report for work at a very early hour in the morning. Sometimes they will be free during the regular working hours of others, but will have to work late into the night. Some radio stations operate on a twenty-four-hour basis. The all-night announcers may be alone in the station during their working hours.

Social and psychological factors

The announcer who stays with a station for a period of time becomes a well-known personality in the community. Such celebrities are sought after as participants in community activities; television announcers especially are easily recognized and may be stared at on the street. The relinquishing of anonymity in a crowd is to some persons a real hardship and to others a rewarding or necessary experience.

The irregularity of working hours may make for a difficult family situation at times and may cause interruptions in relationships with friends. In addition, broadcast reporters do not generally stay long at one station. Such moves can create additional stress in those who prefer a more structured career environment.

GOE: 01.03.03; SIC: 483; SOC: 333

◇ **SOURCES OF ADDITIONAL INFORMATION**

American Federation of Television and Radio Artists
260 Madison Avenue
New York, NY 10016

For a list of schools offering degrees in broadcasting, write to:

Broadcast Education Association
1771 N Street, NW
Washington, DC 20036

National Cable Television Association
1724 Massachusetts Avenue, NW
Washington, DC 20036

For information on FCC licensure, write to:

Federal Communications Commission
1919 M Street, NW
Washington, DC 20554

National Association of Broadcasters
1771 N Street, NW
Washington, DC 20036

Radio-Television News Directors Association
1717 K Street, NW, Suite 615
Washington, DC 20006

◇ **RELATED ARTICLES**

Volume 1: Broadcasting
Volume 2: Actors and actresses; Advertising workers; Reporters and correspondents; Writers and editors
Volume 4: See Broadcast Technician Occupations"

Radio and television program directors

Definition

Program directors plan and schedule program material for radio and television stations and networks. They determine the entertainment programs, news broadcasts, and other program material their organizations offer to the public. At a large network the program director may supervise a large programming staff; at a small station one person may manage the station and also handle all programming duties.

History

Radio broadcasting in the United States began after World War I, and the first commercial radio station, KDKA in Pittsburgh, came on the air in 1920 with a broadcast of presidential election returns. About a dozen radio stations were broadcasting by 1921, and in 1926 the first national network linked stations across the country. In the early 1990s there were about 10,600 commercial and public radio stations in the United States.

The first public demonstration of television in the United States came in 1939 at the opening of the New York World's Fair. Further development was limited during World War II, but by 1953 there were about 120 stations. In the early 1990s the United States had about 1,500 commercial and public television stations and more than 3,500 cable television systems.

Nature of the work

Program directors plan and schedule program material for radio and television stations and networks. They work in both commercial and public broadcasting and may be employed by individual radio or television stations, regional or national networks, or cable television systems.

The material program directors work with includes entertainment programs, public service programs, newscasts, sportscasts, and commercial announcements. Program directors decide what material is broadcasted and when it is scheduled, work with other staff members to develop programs, and buy programs from independent producers. They are guided by such factors as the budget available for program material, the audience their station or network wants to attract, their organization's policies on content and other matters, and the kinds of products advertised in the various commercial announcements.

In addition, program directors may have such responsibilities as setting up schedules for the program staff, auditioning and hiring announcers and other on-the-air personnel, and

The program director, master control director, technical director, and support staff broadcast a program on television. The program director must ensure that the broadcast is completed according to his plans.

assisting the sales department in negotiating contracts with sponsors of commercial announcements. The duties of individual program directors are determined by such factors as whether they work for a small or large organization, for one station or a network, in radio or television, or in a commercial or public operation.

At small radio stations the owner or manager may be responsible for programming, but at somewhat larger radio stations and small television stations the staff usually includes a program director. At medium to large radio and television stations the program director usually has a staff that includes such personnel as music librarians, music directors, editors for tape or film segments, and writers. Although program directors at large stations and networks often work forty-hour weeks, many program directors at small to medium stations work from forty-four to forty-eight hours a week and, in addition to working days, often work evenings, late at night, and on weekends.

Some stations and networks employ *public service directors,* who plan and schedule radio or television public service programs and announcements in such fields as education, reli-

gion, and civic and government affairs. Networks often employ *broadcast operations directors,* who coordinate the activities of the personnel who prepare network program schedules, review program schedules, issue daily corrections, and advise affiliated stations on their schedules.

Other managers in radio and television broadcasting include *production managers, operations directors, news directors,* and *sports directors.* The work of program directors usually does not include the duties of *radio directors* or *television directors,* who direct rehearsals and integrate all the elements of a performance.

Requirements

High-school students who are interested in radio and television programming should take courses that develop their communication skills, such as English, literature, writing, and public speaking. They also should take business courses to develop their management skills; current events and history courses to develop their understanding of the news and the trends that affect the public's interests; and such courses as dance, drama, music, and painting to develop their understanding of the creative arts.

College students should work toward four-year degrees in radio and television production and broadcasting, communications, liberal arts, or business administration. Students also may wish to take some technical training that will help them understand the engineering aspects of broadcasting.

Program directors must be creative, alert, and adaptable people who stay up-to-date on the public's interests and attitudes and can recognize the potential in new ideas. They must be able to work under pressure and be willing to work long hours, and they must be able to work with all kinds of people. They also must be good managers who can make decisions, are aware of costs and deadlines, and can handle details.

Special requirements

Small radio stations may prefer hiring program directors who are qualified to operate transmitters. Depending on the work involved, federal law requires employees who work with transmitters to have either Federal Communications Commission (FCC) first-class radio-telephone licenses or FCC restricted permits. To qualify for first-class licenses, applicants must pass a test on such subjects as transmission and receiving equipment and United States and international broadcasting regulations.

Opportunities for experience and exploration

Students whose high schools or colleges have radio or television stations should volunteer to work on their staffs. Students also should look for part-time or summer jobs at nearby stations, and college students should investigate the availability of internships. In addition, students should take advantage of opportunities to visit radio and television stations and talk with their personnel.

Related occupations

People who wish to work in broadcasting also may be interested in jobs as station managers,

writers, reporters, time salespersons, broadcast engineers, or broadcast technicians. They also may be interested in on-the-air jobs as announcers, newscasters, or disc jockeys. For an overview, *see* Volume 1: Broadcasting.

Methods of entering

New graduates should register with their college placement offices and with private and state employment agencies. They also can send resumes to radio and television stations or apply in person.

Beginners should be willing to relocate and are not likely to find employment in large cities. They usually start at small stations that, because they have fewer employees, give them a chance to learn a variety of skills.

Advancement

Most beginners start in entry-level jobs and work several years before they have enough experience to be program directors. Experienced program directors usually advance by moving from small stations to larger stations and networks or by becoming station managers. In some cases, program directors transfer to other departments, such as sales or engineering.

Employment outlook

In the early 1990s more than 20,000 radio and television stations, cable television systems, and regional and national networks employed program directors or had other employees whose duties included programming. Competition for jobs in broadcasting, however, was strong and was expected to remain strong through the mid-1990s. There were more opportunities for beginners in radio than there were in television, and most radio and television stations in large cities were only hiring experienced workers.

New radio and television stations and new cable television systems were expected to create additional openings for program directors, but some radio stations were eliminating program director positions by installing automatic programming equipment.

Earnings

Employees at television stations usually earn more than employees at radio stations, and employees at large stations and at networks usually earn more than employees at small stations. In the early 1990s radio program directors earned about $400 a week and television program directors earned about $575 a week.

Most broadcasting employees have such benefits as health insurance, life insurance, and retirement plans, but station policies vary on such benefits as paid holidays and vacations.

Conditions of work

Program directors at small stations often work forty-four to forty-eight hours a week and frequently work evenings, late at night, and weekends. At larger stations, which have more personnel, they usually work forty-hour weeks.

Program directors usually work in clean, pleasant surroundings, but they frequently work under pressure because of the need to maintain precise timing and meet the needs of sponsors, performers, and other staff members.

Social and psychological factors

Program directors have the satisfaction of working for organizations that inform and entertain the public. Their work is creative and challenging, and they have the opportunity to exercise leadership. Their work, however, is exacting and often stressful, and they have much of the responsibility for building and keeping their organization's audience.

GOE: 11.05.02; SIC: 4832, 4833; SOC: 137

◇ **SOURCES OF ADDITIONAL INFORMATION**

Association of Independent Television Stations
1200 18th Street, NW, Suite 502
Washington, DC 20036

Broadcast Education Association
1711 N Street, NW
Washington, DC 20036

National Association of Farm Broadcasters
Box 119
Topeka, KS 66601

National Cable Television Association
1724 Massachusetts Avenue, NW
Washington, DC, 20036

National Association of Broadcasters
1711 N Street, NW
Washington, DC 20036

◇ **RELATED ARTICLES**

Volume 1: Broadcasting
Volume 2: General managers and top executives; Photographers and camera operators; Radio and television announcers and newscasters
Volume 3: Radio and television sales workers
Volume 4: Audio-control technicians; Sound technicians; Sound effects technicians; Sound-recording technicians; Studio technicians; Transmitter technicians; Video technicians

Recording industry workers

Definition

Recording industry workers produce and market records, tapes, and compact discs. Much of the industry's output is recorded music that features singers, rock groups, dance bands, symphony orchestras, and other musicians. But the industry also produces recordings of such material as children's nursery rhymes and stories, comedy acts, and plays.

A recording industry worker attends a recording session where she adjusts the sound quality in the control room.

In addition to the large, well-known recording companies, many independent producers and small studios make recordings, and they often specialize in such recorded material as soundtracks for films and videos, radio commercials, instructional tapes for foreign languages, and recorded books for visually handicapped people.

History

Thomas Edison invented a machine in 1877 that would record and play back sounds on a cylinder. In 1887, Emile Berliner developed an alternate to the cylinder with his invention of the flat recording disk, to be played on his disc player the "Gramophone." The flat disks were easier to produce and store than the tubes, and soon gained in popularity.

The Gramophone Company eventually expanded into the renamed Victor Talking Machine Company. Victor produced the Victrola, a record player that was unrivalled in popularity and sales for a great number of years after its establishment in 1901. The Gramophone used a crank to wind a spring and then the spring released at a regulated speed to turn the phonograph.

In the 1930s, electrically powered motors were used to turn the phonograph. This allowed for a more even speed on the turntable and longer playing time for the record. The effect of the depression in the 1930s took its toll on record and phonograph sales, though. The ability of radio to fill the void by providing free music (once a radio was purchased) further decreased the sales of phonographs. The combination units of radio and phonographs was the

silver lining for the cloud that radio had brought to the phonograph industry.

In 1948, RCA developed a vinyl disk that could play eight minutes of music. This allowed for an entire classical symphony movement to be recorded on one side on the record. Columbia developed a record that played at 33 1/3 rpm, and carried thirty minutes of music.

The second major development for the record industry came in the method of recording. Magnetic tapes were used to produce the original recording. The quality of sound from the magnetic tape was the finest achieved to date.

The technology for recording boomed with the computer age. Along with the advancement in technology of sound recording, an advancement in the record disk began to chance the shape of the industry once again. Compact discs were invented in Japan in the late 1970s. Compact discs, or CDs for short, are digitally recorded discs that use a laser to read the music instead of a stylus. The change by the record industry to discs has been swift.

Nature of the work

Workers in the recording industry include *artists and repertoire workers,* usually called *A & R people; engineers* and *technicians;* and *promotion* and *business workers.*

Artist and repertoire managers, also called *producers,* choose the music their companies record and the artists who record the music, and often head A & R departments in large companies or serve as chief officers in small companies. Their responsibilities include finding and auditioning performers, negotiating contracts, planning production steps, choosing the studios and equipment used in recording sessions, and approving budgets.

Other A & R workers include *singers, instrumental musicians, arrangers,* and *copyists.* (For more information on A & R workers, see the separate articles titled "Recording" in Volume 1, and "Musical occupations" in Volume 2.)

Engineers and technicians work with the electronic equipment that records music and other sounds. Their titles and duties are determined by their skills and the size of the organizations that employ them.

Setup workers prepare the equipment used in recording sessions, such as microphones, amplifiers, tape recorders, isolation booths, music stands, and musical instruments. They follow written instructions that tell them what equipment is needed and how to arrange it, sometimes using trucks and dollies to move large pieces. After the recording session they dismantle the equipment and return it to storage, making sure they leave the storage areas neat and organized.

Recording engineers, sometimes called *studio engineers,* operate the control console during recording sessions, watching the console dials and using various controls to modulate the volume and intensity of the recorded sound. They also may service and repair the sound equipment, and they sometimes function as directors who tell performers when to start and may ask them to move closer to the microphone, to repeat a passage, or make other changes.

Other engineering workers include *sound mixers,* who blend the sounds of the many tapes or tracks made during the recording session; *tape-transferrers,* who operate the equipment that reproduces recordings from the master; *quality-control inspectors,* who use optical and audio equipment to inspect the metal record produced from the master for defects; and *record testers,* who use optical and audio equipment to test sample recordings.

Promotion and business employees make up the third group of recording industry workers. Promotion workers arrange for recording artists to have radio and television interviews and make personal appearances, and they also visit disc jockeys to ask them to play their companies' records. Salespeople visit record stores to encourage them to display and promote their companies' records. And recording company offices, like those of other businesses, employ secretaries, clerks, accountants, stockroom workers, and other office workers.

Because both A & R workers and promotion and business workers are treated in other articles, the balance of this article will concentrate on engineers and technicians.

Requirements

High-school students who are interested in engineering and technical jobs should take courses in mathematics, electronics, and computer science. They also should be involved in hobbies that deal with sound and video equipment.

High-school graduates who hope to work as engineers will need four to five years of college with majors in electrical or mechanical engineering, and those who wish to be involved in classical music also must learn to read music. High-school graduates who plan to become technicians should attend technical schools, where training programs may take from a few months to two years.

Candidates for engineering and technical positions need an excellent ear for music and should be aware of developments in the recording industry. They must be enthusiastic and able to work under pressure, and they need creativity as well as technical skills.

Special requirements

Engineers and technicians may belong to the Audio Engineering Society and, like other recording industry workers, they also may be members of the National Academy of Recording Arts and Sciences, which presents the annual Grammy awards.

Opportunities for experience and exploration

Students can become familiar with the industry by listening to music on records and radio and by attending concerts. They also can learn by reading record reviews and reading such magazines as *Billboard, Cash Box, Stereo Review,* and *High Fidelity.*

They should make frequent visits to stores that sell records and audio equipment and should try to arrange tours of local recording studios and radio stations. They also should take advantage of any opportunities to talk with A & R people, engineering and technical workers, and those involved in the business aspects of the industry. In addition, students can gain experience from part-time or summer jobs in record stores, local recording studios, or local radio or television stations.

Related occupations

The U.S. Department of Labor classifies recording industry engineers and technicians with others who use electronic equipment to transcribe, reproduce, and regulate the quality of voices, music, and other sounds. Recording industry jobs that are also found in the radio and television industry include sound mixers, recording engineers, and tape transferrers. Other related jobs in the broadcasting industry include video operators, rerecording mixers (also employed in the film industry), and telecine operators.

575

Methods of entering

Schools that train sound engineers and technicians usually maintain placement offices for their graduates. In addition, qualified graduates can apply directly to the recording companies. Freelance and temporary assignments also help build experience and develop a strong resume.

Advancement

Engineers and technicians who do good work are often promoted within the companies that employ them. In addition, some workers advance by moving to competing firms or by joining with producers to form their own companies. Some maintain a good living working independently.

Employment outlook

There are more job seekers than job openings in the recording industry and, although the industry is growing, this situation is expected to continue the early 1990s. Many graduates apply to the major recording companies, which can choose the best, but there is less competition at studios that make recordings for schools, for use as radio commercials, and for similar uses. Most successful candidates, however, have strong educational training in the area of recording they are interested in.

Most well-known companies headquarter in such music centers as New York, Los Angeles, and Nashville and also may have offices in other cities. In addition, there are many small studios in cities throughout the United States. Many smaller companies employ very few people, and several are family-operated businesses.

Earnings

Earnings depend on the company, the duties performed, and the worker's ability. People who hold staff positions usually have paid insurance and pension plans. Many workers, however, in this industry are independent engineers who, in the early 1990s, earned from $30 to $50 an hour and had annual incomes of $25,000 to $75,000 a year. Technicians at the largest studios started at about $11,000 a year, and experienced sound mixers earned about $39,000 a year.

Conditions of work

Recording company offices are much like those of other businesses. Highly successful studios may have beautifully decorated offices, especially if they are open to clients and visitors. Offices for smaller firms may be plain, but they are usually pleasant.

The electronic equipment used in recording is so sensitive that rooms must be kept clean and temperature-controlled, and sound control is essential in recording rooms. A soundproof glass wall divides control rooms from recording rooms, and directors in the control rooms use intercoms to communicate with the performers in the recording rooms.

Recording sessions may need only one or two performers, or they may involve large symphony orchestras. When many performers are involved, it may be necessary to move the recording equipment to auditoriums that are large enough to accommodate everyone. Because costs increase as the number of performers increases, recording sessions involving many people can produce great tension.

Recording even a single work may take hours or days, and performers may need to repeat parts over and over. Everyone involved must have the patience to try for perfection. Engineers and technicians in the recording industry work with all kinds of performers; some are highly experienced and need little direction, while others who have little experience may need more careful guidance.

Most recording companies operate during regular business hours, and their workers usually have forty-hour weeks. Independent engineers work on about three albums a year, and each album takes 300 to 500 hours.

Social and psychological factors

Members of well-known recording companies are usually intelligent, talented, and creative. They strive for perfection and work under pressure. Workers at well-known companies usually experience the greatest stress, because competition is strong. If sales fall or a record is unsuccessful, jobs can be in jeopardy. Despite the stress and uncertainty, most people enjoy the work and are rarely bored.

GOE: 05.10.05; SIC: 7389; SOC: 3719

◇ **SOURCES OF ADDITIONAL INFORMATION**

Audio Engineering Society
60 East 42nd Street, Room 2520
New York, NY 10065

National Academy of Recording Arts and Sciences
303 North Glenoaks Boulevard
Burbank, CA 91502

◇ **RELATED ARTICLES**

Volume 1: Broadcasting; Electronics; Performing Arts; Recording
Volume 2: Engineers
Volume 3: Musical instrument repairers and turners
Volume 4: Audio-control technicians; Electronics technicians; Sound-recording technicians

Recreational therapists

Definition

Recreational therapists plan, organize, and direct medically approved recreation programs for patients in hospitals and other institutions.

History

New horizons in the world of therapy have been discovered in the past few decades. One of the most important was the realization that soldiers suffering from battle fatigue, shock, and emotional trauma respond positively to organized recreation and activity programs. This led the way to the establishment of recreational therapy as a form of medical treatment.

For people in nursing homes, hospitals, mental institutions, and adult-care homes, their time spent in recovery or rehabilitation is no longer limited to physical therapy. Experiments have shown that recovery is aided very much by recreational activities sports, music, art, gardening, dance, drama, field trips, and other pastimes. Elderly people are more healthy and alert when their days are filled with activities, field trips, and social get-togethers. Handicapped persons can gain greater self-confidence and awareness of their unique abilities when they get involved with sports, crafts, and other activities. People recovering from drug or alcohol addiction can reaffirm their self-worth through directed, enjoyable hobbies, clubs, and sports. The recreational therapist is a health professional who organizes these types of activities and helps patients take an active role in their own recovery.

Nature of the work

Recreational therapists work with people who are mentally, physically, or emotionally disabled. They are professionals who employ leisure activities as a form of treatment much as other health practitioners use surgery, drugs, nutrition, exercise or psychotherapy. Recreational therapists strive to minimize patients' symptoms and to improve their physical, mental and emotional well-being. Enhancing the patient's ability to take part in everyday life is the primary goal of recreational therapy; interesting and rewarding activities are the means for working toward that goal.

Recreational therapists work in a number of different settings, including mental hospitals, "psychiatric day hospitals," community mental health centers, nursing homes, adult day care programs, residential facilities for the mentally retarded, school systems, and prisons. They can work as individual staff members, as independent consultants, or as part of a larger therapeutic team. They may get personally involved with patients, or direct the work of assistants and support staff.

Before working directly with an individual patient, the recreational therapist first confers with the doctors, psychiatrists, social workers, physical therapists, and other professionals on staff to coordinate their efforts in treatment. The recreational therapist needs to understand

A recreational therapist helps two mentally handicapped people learn the benefits of exercise.

the nature of the patient's ailment, current physical and mental capacities, emotional state, and prospects for recovery. The patient's family and friends are also consulted, to find out the patient's interests and hobbies. With this information, the recreational therapist then plans an agenda of activities for that person.

To enrich the lives of people in hospitals and other institutions, recreational therapists use imagination and skill in organizing beneficial activities. Sports, games, arts and crafts, movie screenings, field trips, hobby clubs, and dramatics are only a few examples of activities that can enrich the lives of patients. Some therapists specialize in certain areas. Dance therapists plan and conduct dance and body movement exercises to improve patients' physical and mental well-being. Art therapists work with patients in various art methods, such as drawing, painting, and ceramics, as part of their therapeutic and recovery program. Music therapists design programs for patients that can involve solo or group singing, playing in bands, rhythmic and other creative activities, listening to music, or attending concerts. Even flowers and gardening can prove beneficial to patients, as is proved by the work of horticultural therapists. When the treatment team feels

that regular employment would help certain patients, the industrial therapist arranges a productive job for the patient in an actual work environment, one that will have the greatest therapeutic value based on the patient's needs and abilities. Orientation therapists for the blind work with people who have recently lost their sight, helping them to readjust to daily living and independence through training and exercise. All of these professional therapists plan their programs to meet the needs and capabilities of patients. They also carefully monitor and record each patient's progress and report it to the other members of the medical team.

Recreational therapists need to understand their patients and set goals for their progress accordingly. A patient having trouble socializing, for example, may have an interest in playing chess but be overwhelmed by the prospect of actually playing, since that involves interaction with another person. The therapist in this case would proceed slowly, first letting the patient observe a number of games and then assigning a therapeutic assistant to serve as a chess partner for weeks or even months as long as it takes for the patient to gain enough confidence to seek out other patients for chess partners. Of course, the patient might also fail to make progress, or even begin to become more withdrawn or antisocial. Whatever the reaction, the therapist makes a note of the patient's response, modifies the therapy program accordingly, and lets other professionals know of the results. If a patient is responding more enthusiastically to the program, working more cooperatively with others, or is becoming more disruptive, the recreational therapist must note these reactions and periodically reevaluate each patient's activity program.

Responsibilities and elements of the job can vary, depending on the setting in which the recreational therapist works. In nursing homes, the therapist often groups residents according to common or shared interests and ability levels, and then plan field trips, parties, entertainment, and other group activities. The therapists documents residents' responses to the activities and continually searches for ways of heightening residents' enjoyment of recreational and leisure activities, not just in the facility but in the surrounding community as well. Because nursing home residents are likely to remain in the facility for months or even years, the activities program makes a big difference in the quality of their lives. Without the stimulation of interesting events, the daily routine of a nursing home can become monotonous and depressing, and some residents are apt to deteriorate both mentally and physically. In some nursing homes, recreational therapists direct the activities program. In others, activities coordinators plan and carry out the program under the part-time supervision of a consultant who is either a recreational or occupational therapist.

The therapist in a community center might work in a day-care program for the elderly or in a program for mentally retarded adults operated by a county recreation department. No matter what the disability, recreational therapists in community settings face the added logistical challenge of arranging transportation and escort services, if necessary, for prospective participants. Coordinating transportation is less of a problem in hospitals and nursing homes, where the patients all live under one roof. Developing therapeutic recreation programs in community settings accordingly requires a large measure of organizational ability, flexibility, and ingenuity.

Recreational therapy is a relatively new field, but it is already a respected, integral part of the treatment of many elderly and disabled people. These people often need extra encouragement and support to stay active and build on the things they can, rather than can't, do. The activity programs that recreational therapists design and operate can add immeasurable enjoyment to the lives of patients. Beyond this, the activities provide opportunities for exercise and social interaction, and may also help relieve anxiety and loneliness, build confidence, and promote each patient's independence.

Requirements

Currently, a bachelor's degree is required for employment as a recreational therapist. More than 170 academic programs in this field are offered at colleges and universities across the country. Four-year programs include courses in both natural science, such as biology and human anatomy, and social science, such as psychology and sociology. Courses more specific to the profession include programming for special populations; rehabilitative techniques including self-help skills, mobility, signing for the deaf, and orientation for the blind; medical equipment; current treatment approaches; legal issues; and professional ethics. Students also take recreation courses and are required to serve 360 hours of internship under the supervision of a certified therapeutic recreation specialist.

A student who earns a two-year associate's degree in therapeutic recreation will be limited to a job as a therapeutic assistant in hospitals or activities specialist in a nursing home. Increased training is becoming more prevalent among people in this field, however, so jobs at this level are scarce and usually will not lead to promotion. A person with associate's degrees can transfer his or her credits to a four-year college or university and work toward earning a bachelor's degree. The transferability of credits varies from college to college, so students would be advised to look into transferability before enrolling in a two-year program.

Continuing education is increasingly becoming a requirement for professionals in this field. This can be achieved through conferences and seminars, as well as university courses. Many persons with degrees in related fields can enter the profession by earning master's degrees in therapeutic recreation. A doctorate is usually required for those in administrative or teaching positions. These requirements will become more strict as more professionals enter the field.

In high school, a college preparatory program should be followed by students wishing to enter this field. Recommended courses include science, English, speech, mathematics, psychology, physical education, art, music, and drama. Verbal and written communication skills are essential, because of the interaction with people and the report writing that the job requires.

Special requirements

Five states regulate the profession of therapeutic recreation. Licensure is required in Georgia and Utah; professional certification (or eligibility for certification) is required in Maryland's long-term care facilities and California's state hospitals; and titling is regulated in North Carolina.

Certification for recreational therapists is available through the National Council for Therapeutic Recreation Certification, which awards credentials for therapeutic recreation specialists and assistants. Many employers prefer to hire certified recreational therapists, and some insist on this credential.

Several other professional organizations offer continuing education classes and additional benefits to professional members. These include the National Therapeutic Recreation Society; the American Therapeutic Recreation Association; and the American Alliance for Health, Physical Education, Recreation, and Dance. These groups also work to improve the salaries and working conditions of the people in the profession.

Opportunities for experience and exploration

There are many ways to test whether one is suited for a career in recreational therapy. Part-time work as a sports coach or referee, park supervisor, or camp counselor can give persons experience and a taste for the requirements of the job. Volunteer work in a nursing home, hospital, or care facility for disabled adults is also a good way to learn about the daily realities of institutional living. These types of facilities are always looking for volunteers to work with and visit patients.

Related occupations

Recreational therapy is one example of the type of therapeutic work available in the health care field. Other occupations that involve the same kinds of skills include physical therapists, occupational therapists, respiratory therapists, and physical therapy assistants.

Methods of entering

Upon graduation, there are many methods for finding out about available jobs in recreational therapy. A good place to start is the job notices and want ads printed in the local newspapers, bulletins from state park and recreation societies, and publications of the professional associations mentioned above. State employment agencies and human service departments will know of job openings in state hospitals. College placement offices might also be able to put new recreational therapy graduates in touch with prospective employers. Internship programs are sometimes available, which offer good opportunities to find potential full-time jobs.

Recent graduates should also make appointments to meet potential employers personally. Most employers will make themselves available to discuss their programs and the possibility of hiring extra staff. They may also guide new graduates to other institutions currently hiring therapists. Joining professional associations, both state and national, and attending conferences is also a good way to meet potential employers and colleagues.

Advancement

Newly graduated recreational therapists generally begin as staff therapists. Advancement is chiefly to supervisory or administrative positions, usually after some years of experience and continuing education. Some therapists teach, conduct research, or do consulting work on a contract basis; a graduate degree is essential for moving into these areas.

Many therapists continue their education but prefer to continue working with patients. For variety, they may choose to work with new groups of people or get a job in a new setting, such as moving from a retirement home to a facility for the handicapped. Some may also move to a related field such as special education.

Employment outlook

Recreational therapists held more than 29,000 jobs in the early 1990s, according to the U.S. Department of Labor. Three out of five of these people work in nursing homes, while hospitals chiefly psychiatric, rehabilitation, and other specialty hospitals are the second leading employer. Other employers include community mental health centers, adult day care programs, residential facilities for the mentally retarded, and community programs for people with disabilities. A small number of therapists work as independent consultants.

Employment for recreational therapists is expected to grow much faster than the average for other occupations through the end of the century, chiefly because of anticipated expansion of long-term care facilities and services. Reasons for this include the increased life expectancies of elderly persons and persons with developmental disabilities such as Down's syndrome. Significant growth is also projected for the mentally ill, in part because of the large number of young adults who have reached the age of peak risk for schizophrenia and other chronic mental illnesses. The incidence of alcohol and drug dependency problems is also growing.

Most openings for recreational therapists will be in nursing homes because of the increasing numbers and greater longevity of the elderly. There is also greater public pressure to regulate and improve the quality of life in retirement centers, which may mean more jobs and increased scrutiny of recreational therapists. Because many old people live in the South and Southwest, job opportunities are expected to increase in the Sunbelt.

Growth in hospital jobs is not expected to be great. Many of the new jobs created will be in hospital-based adult day care programs or in units offering short-term mental health services. Because of fiscal constraints and other social forces, no growth is expected in public mental hospitals. Many of the programs and services formerly offered there are being shifted to community residential facilities for the disabled. Community programs for special populations are expected to expand significantly by the year 2000; locating a job may require persistence, however, in view of the small scale and embryonic nature of community-based programs.

Earnings

Salaries of recreational therapists vary according to employment setting, educational background, experience, and region of the country. In the early 1990s the average salary of activities directors in nursing homes was $13,800; smaller facilities averaged $11,500, while larger facilities paid an average of $15,500. Another survey found that recreational therapists employed by hospitals had an average starting salary of $19,000, with a top salary of $23,900 for experienced staffers. Starting salaries in institutions and programs funded by state mental health or disabilities agencies ranged from $14,500 to $19,500 a year.

Salaries rise for recreational therapists with experience. After ten years' experience, they might earn more than $30,000 a year. Top salaries in the field average around $50,000 a year for those recreational therapists with twenty years' experience or more. A full benefits package, including health insurance, paid vacations, and sick leave, is usually offered.

Conditions

Working conditions may vary, but generally recreational therapists work in bright, well-ventilated areas. They might work in a ward, a specially equipped activity room, or, at a nursing home, a communal room, or hall. In a community setting, recreational therapists may interview subjects and plan activities in an office, but might be in a gymnasium, swimming pool, playground, or outdoors on a nature walk when leading activities.

The job may be physically tiring because therapists are often on their feet all day and may have to lift and carry equipment. Recreational therapists generally work a standard forty-hour week, although weekend and evening hours may be required. Supervisors may have to work overtime, depending on their workload.

Social and psychological factors

Persons considering a career in recreational therapy must be able to work with people of all ages, temperaments, and personalities. To gain the confidence of patients, a person needs to possess good communication skills and a warm, friendly personality that inspires both trust and respect. Ingenuity and imagination are also very important in adapting activities to individual needs and in keeping the activities program from becoming dull. Some of the people in therapy programs may fail to respond to therapy or even regress. At times like these, a recreational therapist needs compassion and patience.

Recreational therapists can earn a great deal of personal satisfaction in their work, as they help people interact with others, learn more about themselves and their abilities, and develop greater self-confidence. At the same time, the work can be draining, as they work to help people overcome problems day after day; the risk of professional burnout is always present, if the therapist neglects his or her own personal needs. It is a young field, and the many young people entering it bring a vitality and commitment to their work. There are many different groups with special needs with which a therapist can choose to work, and many new fields of therapy that have yet to be developed and explored.

GOE: 10.02.02; SIC: 8049; SOC: 3039

◇ **SOURCES OF ADDITIONAL INFORMATION**

American Association for Leisure and Recreation
1900 Association Drive
Reston, VA 22901

American Dance Therapy Association
2000 Century Plaza, Suite 108
Columbia, MD 21044

American Health Care Association
1201 L Street, NW
Washington, DC 20005

National Council for Therapeutic Recreation Certification
49 South Main Street, Suite 005
Spring Valley, NY 10977

National Institute of Mental Health
Public Inquiries
5600 Fishers Lane
Rockville, MD 20857

National Therapeutic Recreation Society
National Recreation and Park Association
3101 Park Center Drive
Alexandria, VA 22302

◇ **RELATED ARTICLES**

Volume 1: Health Care; Social Services
Volume 2: Human services workers; Kinesiotherapists; Occupational therapists; Physical therapists; Psychiatrists; Recreation workers; Rehabilitation counselors; Sports instructors; Therapists, miscellaneous
Volume 3: Homemaker-home health aides; Nursing and psychiatric aides
Volume 4: Physical therapist assistants; Psychiatric technicians

Recreation workers

Definition

Recreation workers help people, as groups and as individuals, enjoy and use their leisure time constructively. They organize and administer physical, social, and cultural programs; operate recreational facilities; and study recreation needs.

History

Americans are enjoying more leisure time today than at any other period in history. The introduction of new technology, along with other factors such as labor laws, has shrunk the workday and workweek. Workers are receiving increased vacation time, setting their own, flexible hours, and in many cases retiring at an earlier age. The use of laborsaving devices and convenience foods in the home add more free hours to a family's time, while rising incomes provide extra money for recreational activities.

Within only a generation, leisure has leaped to the forefront of national concern. New services and revolutionized old ones have been introduced to help Americans find beneficial ways in which to use their spare time. In addition, the value of organized recreation has been recognized in nursing homes and other extended-care facilities. The occupations in recreation work grew out of the need to provide these services. Today's recreation professionals

are specialists in motivating people. They are trained, responsible leaders who understand and are sensitive to human needs and who are dedicated to helping people help themselves through recreation.

Nature of the work

Recreation workers plan, organize, and direct recreation activities for people of all ages, social and economic levels, and degrees of physical and emotional health. The exact nature of their work varies accordingly and depends on their individual level of responsibility.

Recreation workers employed by local governments and voluntary agencies include recreation supervisors, who direct recreation center directors, who in turn supervise recreation leaders and aides. Together, with the help of volunteer workers, they plan and carry out programs at community centers, neighborhood playgrounds, recreational and rehabilitation centers, correctional institutions, hospitals, and homes for children or the elderly, often working in cooperation with social workers and sponsors of the various centers.

Recreation supervisors plan programs to meet the needs of the people they serve. Well-rounded programs may include arts and crafts, dramatics, music and dancing, swimming, games, camping, nature study, and other pastimes. Special events may include festivals, contests, pet and hobby shows, and various outings. Recreation supervisors also create programs for people with special needs, such as the elderly or those confined in hospitals. Supervisors have overall responsibility for coordinating the work of the recreation workers who carry out the programs and sometimes supervise an entire region.

Recreation center directors run the programs at the recreation buildings, indoor centers, playgrounds, or day camps. In addition to directing the staff of the facility, they oversee the safety of the buildings and equipment, handle financial matters, and prepare reports.

Recreation leaders, with the help of *recreation aides,* work directly with assigned groups and are responsible for the daily operations of a recreation program. In this capacity, they organize and lead activities such as drama, dancing, sports and games, camping trips, and other recreations; give instruction in crafts, games, or sports; and work with other staff on special projects and events. Leaders help train and direct volunteers and carry out other tasks under the guidance of the director.

In industry, recreation leaders plan social and athletic programs for employees and their families. Bowling leagues, softball teams, picnics, dances, and field trips are examples of company-sponsored activities. In addition, an increasing number of employers are providing exercise and fitness programs for their workers.

Camp counselors lead and instruct children and adults in nature-oriented forms of recreation at camps or resorts. Activities usually include swimming, hiking, horseback riding, and other outdoor sports and games, as well as instruction in nature lore. Camp counselors teach skills such as woodcraft, leather working, and basket weaving. Some camps also offer specialized instruction in subjects such as music, drama, gymnastics, or computers. In carrying out the programs, camp counselors are concerned with the safety, health, and comfort of the campers. Counselors are supervised by a *camp director.*

Another type of recreation worker is the *social director,* who plans and organizes recreational activities for guests in hotels and resorts or for passengers aboard a ship. Social directors usually greet new arrivals and introduce them to other guests, explain the recreational facilities, and encourage guests to participate in the planned activities. These activities might include card parties, games, contests, dances, musicals, or field trips and may require setting up equipment, arranging for transportation, or planning decorations, refreshments, or entertainment. In general, social directors try to create a friendly atmosphere, paying particular at-

A National Parks Service employee conducts a nature class at an outdoor education and recreation camp.

tention to lonely guests, so that everyone has a good time.

Requirements

For some recreation positions, a high-school diploma or an associate degree in parks and recreation, social work, or other human service discipline is adequate preparation. However, most full-time career positions require a bachelor's degree, and a graduate degree is often a necessity for high-level administrative posts. Acceptable majors include parks and recreation management, leisure studies, physical education, fitness management, or related disciplines. A degree in any liberal arts field may be sufficient if the person's education included courses relevant to recreation work.

In industrial recreation, employers usually prefer applicants with a bachelor's degree in recreation and a strong background in business administration. Some jobs require specialized training in a particular field, such as art, music, drama, or athletics; others need special certifications a lifesaving certificate to teach swimming, for example. In addition to specialized training, students interested in recreation work should get a broad liberal arts and cultural education and acquire at least a working knowledge of arts and crafts, music, dance, drama, athletics, nature study, and club structure.

In the early 1990s, about 200 community and junior colleges offered associate degrees in parks and recreation programs, and about 300 colleges and universities had similar, but more extensive, programs leading to a bachelor's, master's, or Ph.D. degree. The Council on Accreditation, sponsored by the National Recreation and Park Association and the American Association for Leisure and Recreation, accredits parks and recreation curriculums at the bachelor's-degree level.

Personal qualifications for recreation work include a desire to work with people, an outgoing personality, an even temper, and an ability to lead and influence others. Recreation workers should have good health and stamina, especially to work in athletics, and should be able to stay calm and think clearly and quickly in emergencies.

Special requirements

Neither registration nor certification is required for employment in this field, but many recreation professionals apply for certification as evidence of their professional competence. The National Recreation and Park Association, the American Camping Association, and the National Employee Services and Recreation Association award certificates to individuals who meet their standards. In the early 1990s, more than thirty states had adopted NRPA standards for park/recreation professionals.

The federal government employs many recreation leaders in national parks, the armed forces, the Department of Veterans Affairs, and correctional institutions. It may be necessary to pass a civil service examination to qualify for these jobs.

Opportunities for experience and exploration

Young people interested in the field should obtain related work experience while in high school or college as part-time or summer workers or volunteers in recreation departments, neighborhood centers, camps, and other organizations.

Related occupations

Other occupations that call for leadership ability and a sensitivity in dealing with people and require personal qualities similar to those of recreation workers include clinical and counseling psychologists, human relations counselors, parole officers, recreational therapists, school counselors, social workers, and teachers.

Methods of entering

College placement offices are often useful in helping graduates find employment. Most college graduates begin as either recreation leaders or specialists, and after several years' experience may advance to recreation directors. A few enter trainee programs leading directly to recreation administration within a year or so. Those with graduate training may start as recreation directors.

Advancement

Recreation leaders without graduate training will find advancement limited, but it is possible to obtain better-paying positions through a combination of education and experience. With experience it is possible to become a recreation director. With further experience, directors may become supervisors and eventually head of all recreation departments or divisions in a city. Some recreation professionals become consultants.

Employment outlook

In the early 1990s, there were about 164,000 recreation workers, not counting summer workers or volunteers. More than 50 percent held jobs in government agencies, mostly at the municipal or county level. Nearly 20 percent were employed by civic, social, fraternal, or religious membership organizations (such as the Boy Scouts, YWCA, or Red Cross), and another 12 percent by social service organizations (such as centers for seniors and adult day care) and residential-care facilities (such as halfway houses, institutions for delinquent youths, and group homes). The balance worked in a variety of other settings, including commercial recreation establishments and private industry.

Employment opportunities for recreation workers are expected to increase about as fast as average through the end of the 1990s. The expansion in the recreation field will be come about because of increased leisure time and income for the population as a whole combined with a continuing interest in fitness and health and because of a growing population of the elderly in nursing homes, senior centers, and retirement communities. In addition, there is a demand for recreation workers to conduct activity programs for special groups, such as the emotionally disturbed.

Two areas promising the most favorable opportunities for recreation workers are the commercial recreation and social services industries. Commercial recreation establishments adding to the supply of new jobs include amusement parks, sports and entertainment centers, wilderness and survival enterprises, tourist attractions, vacation excursions, hotels and other resorts, camps, health spas, athletic clubs, and apartment complexes, among others. New employment opportunities will arise also in social service agencies such as senior centers, halfway houses, children's homes, and day-care programs for the mentally retarded and developmentally disabled.

Recreation programs that depend on government funding are most likely to be affected in times of economic downturns, when budgets must be cut. In that event, competition would increase drastically for jobs in the private sector.

In any case, competition is expected to be keen because the field is open to college graduates regardless of major; as a result there are more applicants than there are job openings. Opportunities will be best for individuals who have formal training in recreation and for those with previous experience.

Earnings

Most full-time recreation workers earned between about $8,000 and $18,000 a year in the early 1990s, with the top ten percent receiving $28,000 or more. The median for all recreation workers was about $12,000 a year.

Salaries in industrial recreation are considerably higher. During the same period, newly hired recreation workers in industry had starting salaries of about $18,000 to $24,000 a year.

Camp directors averaged about $1,600 per month in municipally operated camps; in private camps, earnings were higher. Camp counselors employed by the season were paid anywhere from $200 to $800 a month.

Recreation workers in the federal government in the early 1990s started at about $14,800 a year.

Most public and private recreation agencies also provide benefits such as paid vacation, sick leave, and hospital insurance.

Conditions of work

The average workweek of recreation leaders is forty hours. Most agencies provide from two to four weeks' vacation plus fringe benefits. Physical conditions are usually very pleasant, but vary greatly from outdoor parks to nursing homes for the aged.

Social and psychological factors

Because recreation leaders must work while others are enjoying leisure, they usually must work irregular hours, frequently in the evening. A compensating factor is the pleasure of helping people enjoy themselves.

GOE: 07.04.03, 11.07.04; SIC: 7011, 7032, 7997; SOC: 1352, 2033, 5254

◇ SOURCES OF ADDITIONAL INFORMATION

Advisory Council on Camps
174 Sylvan Avenue
Leonia, NJ 07605

American Association for Leisure and Recreation
1900 Association Drive
Reston, VA 22091

American Camping Association
5000 State Road, 67 North
Martinsville, IN 46151

American Health Care Association
1201 L Street, NW
Washington, DC 20005

American Youth Hostels
PO Box 37613
Washington, DC 20013

Future Advancement of Camping
PO Box 8
Hatteras, NC 27943

National Employee Services and Recreation Association
2400 South Downing Avenue
Westchester, IL 60154

For information on placement and accreditation, write:

National Recreation and Park Association
Division of Professional Services
3101 Park Center Drive
12th Floor
Alexandria, VA 22302

◇ **RELATED ARTICLES**

Volume 1: Civil Service; Recreation; Sports
Volume 2: Occupational therapists; Recreational therapists; Sports instructors; Sports occupations; Therapists, miscellaneous

Registered nurses

Definition

Nurses help individuals, families, and groups to achieve health and prevent disease, and they care for the sick and injured, using procedures based on knowledge, skill, and experience. They work in hospitals and other health care facilities, in physicians' offices, in private homes, in public health agencies, schools, camps, and industry, and in their own businesses.

History

Systematic care of the ill and injured is a development of the past century. In primitive times, illness was often believed to be an evil spirit that had entered the body of the afflicted one. The efforts that were made to scourge the spirit often resulted in the death of the patient.

During the Middle Ages, certain religious orders cared for the sick; one such group was the Sisters of Mercy. Their patients were helped more by the sisters' kindness than by their power to heal.

Hospitals were first established by the Romans. These and later institutions bore little resemblance to our modern hospitals. They became the haven of the poor; wealthy people had servants to care for their needs at home. Only the destitute had to go to hospitals. Modern ideas about hospitals and nursing as a profession did not develop until the nineteenth century, and the life and work of Florence Nightingale were a strong influence on these developments.

Miss Nightingale, the daughter of a wealthy, upper-class British family, dedicated her life to improving conditions in hospitals, beginning in an army hospital during the Crimean War.

In this country, many of Miss Nightingale's ideas were put into practice for the care of the wounded during the Civil War. The care, however, was provided by concerned individuals who nursed, rather than by trained nurses. They had not received the kind of training that is required for nurses today. The first school of nursing in the United States was founded in Boston in 1873. Education standards for nurses have been improved constantly since that time. Today's nurse is a highly educated, licensed health care professional.

Nature of the work

Nurses work under the direct supervision of nursing departments and in collaboration with physicians. Many nurses work in hospitals, where they may be assigned to general, operating room, or maternity ward duty. They may also work in caring for sick children, or be assigned to other hospital units, such as emergency rooms, intensive care units, or outpatient clinics.

General duty nurses work in collaboration with other members of the health care team to assess the patient's condition, including the patient's understanding of the problems, and to develop and implement a plan of care to assist the patient in achieving optimum health. The tasks these nurses perform include taking patients' temperatures, pulse, and blood pressure, administering medication and injections, recording the symptoms and progress of patients, changing dressings, assisting patients with personal care, conferring with members of the medical staff, helping prepare a patient for surgery, and completing any number of other duties that require skill and an understanding of patients' needs, such as teaching patients how to care for themselves when they get home and how to lead healthier lives.

Surgical nurses oversee the preparation of the operating room and the sterilization of instruments. They assist the surgeons during operations and coordinate the flow of patient cases in the operating rooms. Maternity nurses help in the delivery room, take care of newborns in the nursery, and teach mothers how to feed and care for their babies.

The activities of staff nurses are directed and coordinated by *head nurses* and *supervisors.* Heading up the entire nursing service in a hospital is the *nursing service director,* who administers the nursing program to maintain standards of patient care; advises the medical staff, department heads, and the hospital administrator in matters pertaining to nursing services; helps prepare the department's budget; performs personnel functions, including in-service training; and participates in community health programs.

Private duty nurses may work in hospitals or in the patient's home. They are employed by the patient they are caring for or by a member of the family. Their service is specifically designed for the individual care of one person and is carried out in collaboration with the patient's physician.

Office nurses usually work in the office of a dentist, physician, or health maintenance organization (HMO). They may be one of several nurses on the staff or the only staff member. If one nurse is the only staff member, this person may have to combine some secretarial duties with those of nursing, such as serving as receptionist, making appointments for the doctor, helping maintain patients' records, sending out monthly statements, and attending to routine correspondence. If the physician's office staff is a large one that includes secretaries and clerks, the office nurse will concentrate on screening patients, assisting with examinations, supervising the examining rooms, sterilizing the equipment, providing patient teaching, and performing other nursing duties.

Occupational health nurses, or *industrial nurses,* have become an important part of many large firms. They maintain a clinic at a plant or factory and are usually engaged in rendering preventive, remedial, and educational nursing services. They work under the direction of an industrial physician, *nursing director,* and/or *nursing supervisor* and may advise on accident prevention, may visit employees on the job to see the conditions under which they are working, and may advise management personnel

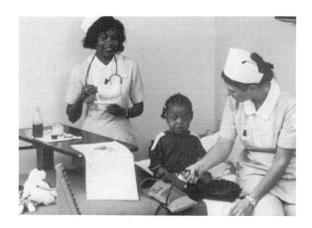

Nurses are responsible for making a patient's hospital visit comfortable. In this case, two registered nurses assist a child, one showing her how to take blood pressure and the other preparing her meal.

about the safety of such conditions. At the plant, they render first-aid treatment in emergencies.

School nurses may work in one school or in several, visiting each for a portion of the day or week. They may supervise the student clinic, treat minor cuts or injuries, or give advice on good health practices. Examining students to detect conditions of the eyes or teeth requiring correction may be part of their job; they may also assist the school physician as that person works with students.

Community health nurses, also called *public health nurses,* require specialized training for their assignments. Their job usually requires them to spend part of the time traveling from one commitment to another. Their duties may be quite different from one case to the next. For instance, in one day they may give instruction to a class of expectant mothers, visit a new mother to help her plan proper care for the baby, visit an aged patient requiring periodic special care, conduct a class in proper nutrition, or work with community leaders to help plan better community health. They usually possess many and varied nursing skills and often are called upon to meet unexpected or unusual situations. Administrators in the community health field include *nursing directors, educational directors,* and *nursing supervisors.*

Some nurses go into nursing education and work with nursing students to teach them the theories and skills that they must have to enter the profession. *Nursing instructors* may give classroom instruction, demonstrations, or supervise nursing students on hospital units. Some instructors eventually become *nursing school directors,* university faculty, or deans of a university degree program. Nurses also have the opportunity to direct staff development and

587

continuing education programs for nursing personnel in hospitals.

There are many specialty practices in the nursing profession. The *nurse anesthetist* specializes in giving anesthesia to patients about to undergo surgery. The nurse anesthetist must be certified and possess great technical skill and theoretical knowledge, for anesthesia requires a delicately balanced procedure, one that carries much responsibility for the well-being of the patient. The nurse anesthetist sometimes works under the supervision of an anesthesiologist, who is a physician, and sometimes is under the supervision of the surgeon performing the operation.

Another special field for nurses is psychiatric nursing. Psychiatric nurses work with patients who are suffering from mental or emotional disorders. They may be employed in a psychiatric hospital, a unit of a general hospital, or in a private home. Some are *psychiatric aide instructors*, teaching attendants psychiatric nursing methods and procedures.

Some nurses enter pediatric nursing and are primarily concerned with the care of babies and children. Pediatric nurses are well educated in growth and development and family interactions.

Throughout history midwives have been helping other women give birth, but nurse-midwifery as a profession was not introduced in the United States until 1925. Today, *nurse-midwives* are well-educated, certified professionals who provide health care and treatment to pregnant and nonpregnant women. Certified nurse-midwives (CNMs) work with other CNMs and obstetricians. They examine pregnant patients and instruct and advise them concerning childbirth, diet, and exercise. They deliver babies and teach new mothers about the care and feeding of newborns. Nurse-midwives examine nonpregnant women, performing tests for pregnancy, Pap tests for cancer, and breast examinations. They counsel patients on family planning and birth control methods, and screen patients for infections and venereal disease. In case of a serious problem, major illness, or difficult labor, the nurse-midwife confers with the team obstetrician.

Another, even more recent entry in the field of nursing is the *nurse practitioner*. Nurse practitioners (NPs) are registered nurses with an advanced education that expands their skills in judgment and decision making. They work in many health care settings, either on their own or as members of a team. In addition to basic nursing responsibilities, they do many tasks formerly handled only by physicians.

Clinical nurse specialists are also nurses with advanced education, usually at the master's degree level. They are specialized in a field of nursing practice, such as cardiovascular nursing, working with cancer patients, or working with high-risk mothers and babies. These nurses work closely with other nursing and health care personnel and facilitate or assist in meeting patient care needs.

Some nurses are *consultants* to hospitals, nursing schools, industrial organizations, and public health groups. They advise their clients on matters such as administrative procedures, organization of staff, nursing techniques, curriculums, and education programs.

Other administrative specialists include educational directors for the state board of nursing, who are concerned with maintaining established educational standards, and executive directors of professional nurses' associations, who administer programs formulated by the board of directors and the members of the association.

Many nurses choose to enter the armed forces. All types of nurses, except private duty nurses, are represented in the military nursing corps. They provide professional nursing care to active-duty and retired members of the armed forces and their family members. In addition to their basic nursing skills, military nurses are trained to provide care in various environments, including field hospitals, on air evacuation flights, and on board ships. Military nurses actively influence the evolution of health care through nursing research. Recent advances influenced by military nurses include the development of the artificial kidney (dialysis unit) and the concept of the intensive care unit.

Requirements

There are three kinds of programs that the prospective nurse may choose. The baccalaureate degree program is offered by a college or university. It requires four (in some institutions, five) years to complete, and the graduate of this program receives a bachelor of science degree in nursing. The associate in arts in nursing is awarded after a two-year study program that is usually offered in a junior or community college. The student usually lives at home and receives hospital training from cooperating hospitals in the general vicinity of the community college.

The diploma program usually lasts three years. Diploma programs are conducted by hospitals and independent schools.

At the conclusion of each of these programs, the student becomes a graduate nurse.

One is not, however, a registered professional nurse until one has taken and passed a licensing examination as is required in all states. After licensing one has the privilege of adding the initials "RN" to one's name, and of seeking employment as a registered nurse.

Whether to choose an associate, diploma, or bachelor's degree program depends on one's career goals. A bachelor's degree in nursing is necessary for most supervisory or administrative positions, for jobs in public health agencies, and for admission to graduate nursing programs. A master's degree is usually required to prepare for a nursing specialty or to teach. For some specialties, such as nursing research, a Ph.D. is essential. In the early 1990s, about 1,473 nursing programs were offered in the United States. In addition, there were 198 master's degree and 33 doctoral degree programs.

Physician assistants are required to have at least two years of medical training. Licensed practical nurses have one year educational programs. These careers have separate articles in this volume.

The high-school student who is interested in becoming a nurse should take as many science and mathematics courses in high school as possible. Biology, chemistry, and physics are basic courses. Mathematics courses are needed because the registered nurse must use the logic and judgment learned in these courses. English and speech courses should not be neglected because the nurse must be able to communicate well with all patients.

Special requirements

All states and the District of Columbia require a license to practice nursing. To obtain a license, graduates from approved schools of nursing must pass a national examination. Nurses may be licensed by more than one state, either by exam or by endorsement of a license from another state. In some states, continuing education is a condition for license renewal.

There is no age limit on students entering the profession, but the prospective nurse will need good health and stamina. He or she must possess a high intelligence and should have an even temperament and the ability to keep calm in emergencies. One must have a real liking and respect for all sorts of persons and must have a real desire to enter this "caring" profession and to devote one's career to the improvement of health care in this country.

Opportunities for experience and exploration

There are several ways in which a student may explore the possibilities of a nursing career. The high-school student may join a Future Nurse's Club. At the age of sixteen one may enroll in an American Red Cross Home Nursing Course. Some hospitals have special programs for teenage volunteers, in which the student observes hospital practices.

Related occupations

Workers with responsibilities and duties similar to those of registered nurses include occupational therapists, paramedics, physical therapists, physician assistants, and respiratory therapists. Prospective registered nurses may find it of value also to explore the work of other health care professionals whose occupations require more extensive education and training. These include physicians and dentists and their many areas of specialization, as well as chiropractors, optometrists, podiatrists, and veterinarians.

Methods of entering

There are no other ways to become a registered nurse than through one of the three types of educational programs, plus the passing of a licensing examination.

Registered nurses may apply for employment directly to hospitals, nursing homes, companies, and government agencies that hire nurses. Jobs may also be obtained through school placement offices or by signing up with a nurse employment service or the state employment office. Other sources for job leads include nurses' associations and professional journals.

Advancement

Most of the administrative and supervisory positions in the nursing profession go to nurses who have earned at least the bachelor of science degree in nursing. Nurses who have accumulated many years of experience but who are graduates of the diploma program may possibly achieve supervisory positions, but requirements for such promotions have become more stringent in recent years.

Nurses with bachelor's degrees are usually those who are employed as public health nurses. Nurses with master's degrees are often those who are employed as clinical nurse specialists, faculty, instructors, supervisors, or administrators.

Some nurses return to school to take courses in special fields. Courses leading to the specialty practice of nurse anesthetist, for example, require eighteen to twenty-four months of graduate education. Once this education is completed, however, the nurse anesthetist may assume a position with a better salary.

Employment outlook

Jobs in most fields of nursing should be plentiful through the 1990s and perhaps beyond. Although there are presently more than 1,900,000 registered professional nurses in the country, there are still unfilled vacancies in many positions. The nursing shortage of recent years still exists today. It exists through the country and affects all specialties and practice settings. Administrative positions are more competitive, however, with an advantage going to those with graduate degrees.

There are always many employment opportunities for hospital nurses, especially in big cities and in rural areas. There are numerous openings in specialties such as geriatrics and in special units for seriously ill patients, such as intensive care and coronary care units.

Employment prospects for nurses are exceptionally good in the home health care field and in nursing homes. In addition, many nurses will be needed to help staff the growing number of outpatient facilities, such as HMOs, group medical practices, and ambulatory surgery centers.

There are many possibilities for part-time employment for nurses who have family responsibilities that prevent them from assuming full-time jobs. Approximately one-fourth to one-third of all nurses work on a part-time basis.

Earnings

In the early 1990s, registered nurses employed in hospitals, medical schools, and medical centers received an average starting salary of $20,400 per year; experienced nurses averaged $27,800. Head nurses were paid about $25,700 to start and $35,000 with experience. Nurse anesthetists averaged $31,000 to start and $42,200 with experience.

Average wages for nurses on the staff of nursing homes and in home health agencies were about $19,900 in the early 1990s.

Entry positions with the Department of Veterans Affairs paid approximately $16,500 for nurses who were graduates of the diploma program or the associate of arts program. Nurses with a bachelor's degree earned about $19,300 in entry positions. The average annual salary for all nurses employed in federal government agencies in the early 1990s was about $26,100.

Registered nurses in hospitals and nursing homes generally earn extra pay for working the evening or night shift and for additional nursing education. Benefits for nurses may include paid vacations and holidays, health care, advanced education, and retirement benefits.

Conditions of work

Most nurses work in clean environments that are well lighted and controlled in temperature, although some work in rundown inner city hospitals under less than ideal conditions. Nurses usually work eight hours each day. Those in hospitals usually work any one of three shifts: 7:00 A.M. to 3:00 P.M., 3:00 P.M. to 11:00 P.M., or 11:00 P.M. to 7:00 A.M.

Nurses spend much of their time on their feet, either walking or standing. Handling patients who are ill or infirm can also be physically strenuous. Nurses who treat patients with infectious diseases must be particularly strict about cleanliness and sterility. Although some nursing duties are routine, many responsibilities (especially in emergency situations) are not so predictable and require thoughtfulness, logic, scientific knowledge, common sense, and sensitivity to the patient's needs. Sick persons often are demanding of service or they may be depressed or irritable. The nurse must preserve a calm manner and must be cheerful to help the patient achieve emotional balance.

Community health nurses may visit homes that are in poor condition or very dirty, or that are different from the nurses' own. They may also encounter social problems such as family violence. Still, the nurse is an important health care provider, if not the sole provider, in many communities.

Both the office nurse and the industrial nurse work during regular business hours; they seldom are required to work overtime. Although both specialties require much walking and standing, there are opportunities to sit at a desk from time to time to perform routine office tasks.

Social and psychological factors

Nurses are in a unique position to help prevent illness and return sick individuals to physical and mental health. Their contributions to those who are ill may lie largely in intangible factors. Although the direct services that they provide in physical care and medication are beneficial to all patients, the nurses' ability to coordinate health care services is even more so. Their obvious skill, their calmness, and their sincere interest in their patients may make the real difference between the will to live and the wish to die on the part of the persons for whom they are caring.

GOE: 10.02.01; SIC: 8049, 805, 806; SOC: 29

◇ **SOURCES OF ADDITIONAL INFORMATION**

American Association of Occupational Health Nurses
50 Lenox Pointe
Atlanta, GA 30324

American College of Nurse-Midwives
1522 K Street, NW, Suite 1120
Washington, DC 20005

American Health Care Association
12001 L Street, NW
Washington, DC 20005

American Hospital Association
840 North Lake Shore Drive
Chicago, IL 60611

American Nurses' Association
2420 Pershing Road
Kansas City, MO 64108

American School Health Association
7263 State Route 43
Kent, OH 44240

National League for Nursing
10 Columbus Circle
New York, NY 10019

U.S. Air Force Nurse Corps
Box 2222
Wright-Patterson AFB, OH 45899

U.S. Department of the Army
Surgeon General
Washington, DC 20310

U.S. Department of the Navy
Chief of Naval Personnel
Washington, DC 20350

U.S. Department of Veterans Affairs
Recruitment and Placement Service
810 Vermont Avenue, NW
Washington, DC 20420

◇ **RELATED ARTICLES**

Volume 1: Health Care
Volume 2: Dental hygienists; Health services administrators; Kinesiotherapists; Licensed practical nurses; Perfusionists; Physical therapists; Physicians; Physician assistants; Respiratory therapists
Volume 3: Medical assistants; Nursing and psychiatric aides
Volume 4: See Medical and Health Technician Occupations

Rehabilitation counselors

Definition

The *rehabilitation counselor* provides counseling and guidance services to persons with disabilities to help them resolve life problems and to train for and locate work that is suitable to their physical and mental abilities, interests, and aptitudes.

A rehabilitation counselor assists a senior citizen with greenhouse activities to stimulate his awareness and promote finger agility.

History

True concern for disabled persons is a development of the past century. In previous times, disabled people were often simply the objects of pity and charity. The modern point of view, however, is that persons with disabilities can and should have the opportunity to become fully independent.

In 1920, Congress passed the first Vocational Rehabilitation Act, which became effective in 1921. The act set in place the Vocational Rehabilitation Program, a federal-state program that provides for the delivery of rehabilitation services, to include counseling, to eligible persons with disabilities.

The profession of rehabilitation counseling has its roots in the Rehabilitation Act, which allowed for funds to train personnel. What was at first a job title developed into a fully recognized profession as it became evident that the delivery of effective rehabilitation services required highly trained specialists.

Nature of the work

The rehabilitation counselor works with persons with disabilities to identify barriers to medical, psychological, personal, social, and vocational adjustment and to develop a plan of action to remove or reduce those barriers.

Persons are referred to rehabilitation programs from many sources. Sometimes they seek help on their own initiative; sometimes their families bring them for help. They may be referred by a physician, hospital, or clinic; they may be referred by social workers or social agencies; they may be sent by employment agencies, schools, or accident commissions. A former employer may seek help for the individual.

The counselor's first step is to determine the nature and extent of the disability and evaluate how that disability interferes with work and other life functions. This determination is made from medical and psychological reports, as well as from family history, educational background, work experience, and other evaluative information.

The next step is to determine a vocational direction and/or plan of services to overcome the handicaps to employment or independent living.

The rehabilitation counselor coordinates a comprehensive evaluation of a client's physical functioning abilities and vocational interests, aptitudes, and skills. This information is used in the counseling relationship to arrive at a vocational or independent living goal and the services necessary to reach that goal. Services that the rehabilitation counselor may coordinate or provide include physical and mental restoration, academic or vocational training, vocational counseling, job analysis, job modification or reasonable accommodation, and job placement. Limited financial assistance in the form of maintenance or transportation assistance may also be provided.

The counselor's relationship with the client may be as brief as a week or as long as several years, depending on the nature of the problem and the needs of the client.

Requirements

A master's degree in rehabilitation counseling is the preferred preparation for a career as a rehabilitation counselor.

The graduate program leading to a master's degree in rehabilitation counseling may cover such courses as medical aspects of disability, psychosocial aspects of disability, testing techniques, statistics, personality theory, personality development, abnormal psychology, techniques of counseling, occupational information, and vocational training and job placement. The master's degree program in rehabilitation counseling is usually a two-year program. There are graduate programs in rehabilitation counseling in many large universities. Federal assistance has been provided for students who are enrolled in these programs in the form of fellowships and scholarships, and these grants are awarded to qualified applicants. In the early 1990s, there were about thirty colleges and universities offering a bachelor's degree in rehabilitation services education, and about seventy-four graduate programs in rehabilitation counseling were accredited by the Council on Rehabilitation Education.

The high-school student who is interested in rehabilitation counseling should enroll in a college preparatory course. Students should be sure to take courses in biology, English, speech, mathematics, psychology, and social studies.

As an undergraduate, the student should include courses in sociology, psychology, biology, anatomy, physiology, testing procedures, and statistics. Students should not neglect English because communication with others is an important part of the job of the rehabilitation counselor. Several universities now offer courses in various aspects of physical therapy and special education training. Students should consider courses in sign language and speech therapy.

The most important personal attribute required for rehabilitation counseling is the ability to get along well with other people. Rehabilitation counselors work with many different kinds of clients and must be able to see situations and problems from the client's point of view. Disabled persons come from all walks of life, and they may not always communicate feelings and ideas as easily as the highly educated counselor. Counselors must have an empathic understanding of the problems with which such persons are faced and be able to communicate to them the fact that they see their situation in a realistic manner.

Second, they work with many professional persons whose assistance is required as steps in the various rehabilitation processes are taken. They must be able to talk with physicians, psychologists, social workers, educators, and other professional people who may be helping the disabled person in the effort to become self-sufficient.

Finally, they must be able to work effectively with the employers who provide jobs for trained disabled workers when they are ready to be employed. The counselor's chief asset in these relationships will be a practical and realistic approach to the problems of the business world.

The rehabilitation counselor must be both patient and persistent. Rehabilitation may be a slow process, with many delays and setbacks. The counselor must maintain a calm, positive manner even when no progress is made. One must give clients feelings of real confidence of success in the efforts they are making in spite of the discouragements of the moment.

Special requirements

Increasingly, state government rehabilitation agencies, which employ about 40 percent of all rehabilitation counselors, require future counselors to meet state civil service and merit system rules. Most states now have these requirements. The applicant must take a written competitive examination and may also have an individual interview and evaluation by a special board.

Many employers now require their rehabilitation counselors to be certified by the Commission on Rehabilitation Counselor Certification (CRCC). The purpose of certification is to provide assurance that professionals engaged in rehabilitation counseling meet acceptable standards and maintain those standards through continuing education. To become certified, counselors must pass an extensive written examination to demonstrate their knowledge of rehabilitation counseling. By 1992, the CRCC will require the master's degree as the minimum educational level for certification.

In about twenty-five states, counselors in private practice must be licensed by the state. Licensing requirements vary by state.

Opportunities for experience and exploration

A student who would like to consider work with disabled persons should seek an opportunity to try out skill in this area. One may volunteer to work as a counselor at a disabled children's camp; also, one may ask a local rehabilitation counselor with the local vocational rehabilitation agency, or a facility such as the Easter Seal Society or Goodwill, to help find persons with disabilities who need such unskilled services as a layman can render. Students may be able to read to blind persons or teach a hobby to someone who has been disabled by accident or illness.

Related occupations

There are many workers in other occupations aimed at helping people deal with physical, personal, social, academic, and career problems. These occupations include college and student personnel workers, equal employment opportunity/affirmative action specialists, members of the clergy, occupational and physical therapists, personnel workers and managers, psychiatrists, psychologists, social workers, teachers, and training and development specialists.

Methods of entering

The National Rehabilitation Counseling Association and the American Rehabilitation Counseling Association (a division of the American Association for Counseling and Development) are excellent sources for employment information, as is the placement service of the university from which the student receives the master's degree in rehabilitation counseling. The prospective counselor should apply directly to the agency for which he or she hopes to work.

Advancement

The rehabilitation counselor will usually receive regular salary increases after gaining experience in the job. If one is interested in administrative or supervisory work, one will probably have an opportunity to advance into such positions after several years of counseling experience. If one wishes to remain a counselor, rather than to become a supervisor, manager, or administrator, one may move from relatively easy cases to increasingly challenging ones. It is also possible to find related counseling and teaching positions, which may represent an advancement in other fields.

Employment outlook

Employment opportunities for rehabilitation counselors are expected to grow at an average rate through the end of the 1990s.

In the early 1990s, there were about 25,000 rehabilitation counselors, and about 10,000 of these were employed by state-local vocational rehabilitation agencies. The Department of Veterans Affairs employed several hundred persons to assist with the rehabilitation of disabled veterans. Many rehabilitation counselors are employed by private for-profit or nonprofit rehabilitation programs and facilities. Others are employed in industry, schools, hospitals, and other settings, while others are self-employed. If legislation for support of the disabled in the workplace is strengthened as expected, rehabilitation counselors will have a broader range of employers.

Earnings

According to limited information, the average beginning salary for rehabilitation counselors was about $22,000 a year in the early 1990s.

Conditions of work

Rehabilitation counselors work approximately forty hours each week and do not usually have to work during evenings or weekends. They are usually given annual vacation and sick leave. Most enjoy the benefits of retirement plans, group insurance, and other related advantages.

Their offices, while not elaborate, are generally comfortable, well lighted and heated, and often air-conditioned during the summer months. They usually have adequate secretarial and clerical assistance.

Rehabilitation counselors work both in the office and in the field. Depending on the type of training required, they may have or use lab space and workout or therapy rooms. They must usually keep detailed accounts of their progress with clients and must write reports. They may spend many hours traveling about the community to visit employed clients, prospective employers, trainees, or training programs.

Social and psychological factors

The rehabilitation counselor should find the work to be both stimulating and challenging. He or she should attain deep satisfaction from being able to help persons to overcome their handicaps and achieve a measure of independence.

Although the people with whom rehabilitation counselors work are often confronted with grave problems, counselors cannot be overwhelmed by them. They must look for positive aspects in the situation, and help the people with whom they are working to find ways in which to dominate their problems, rather than to let problems dominate them. Patience, a positive attitudes, and steadfastness in the counselor's approach to rehabilitation training help develop the best counselor–client relationship.

GOE: 10.01.02; SIC: 8331; SOC: 24

Reporters and correspondents

Definition

Reporters and correspondents gather and analyze information about current events and write stories for publication in newspapers and magazines or for broadcast on radio and television. The term *correspondent* is used to designate reporters who cover the news in outlying areas or foreign countries.

To collect the information, reporters and correspondents may interview people, review available records, observe events, and do research. They may take photographs, may appear on television as interviewers or narrators, and may specialize in a particular news area, such as sports, accidents, politics, court trials, or police activities.

History

Newspapers are primary disseminators of news in the United States. People read newspapers to be informed of things happening to other people; of the activities of their local, state, and federal governments; and of the commercial activities of their communities. Newspapers are also concerned with opinion, criticism, comment, and entertainment.

Newspapers are free to fulfill these functions because of the freedom given to the press. Such was not always the case. The first newspaper published in America (1690) was suppressed four days after it was published. And it was not until 1704 that the first continuous news periodical appeared.

A number of developments in the printing industry made it possible for newspapers to be printed more cheaply. These economic factors, along with an increasing population and such traditional American concepts as the freedom of the press, made it possible for the newspaper industry to enjoy rapid expansion. In 1776, there were only 37 newspapers in the United States. In the early 1990s, there were approximately 1,700 daily and 7,700 weekly newspapers in the country.

As newspapers developed in size and coverage, it became necessary to increase the number of employees and to assign specialized functions to these employees. Reporters, of

A television reporter conducts a live interview for the evening news. With limited air time, the reporter must be prepared to ask pertinent questions.

course, have always been the mainstay of newspaper staffs. In today's complex world, however, with the public avid for news as it occurs, reporters and correspondents are involved in all media—not only newspapers, but magazines, radio, and television as well.

Nature of the work

Reporters and correspondents collect information on newsworthy events and prepare stories for newspaper or magazine publication or for radio or television broadcast. The stories may simply inform us about local, state, or national events, or they may present opposing points of view on issues of current interest. Such attention serves to monitor the actions of public officials and others in positions of power.

The stories may originate as an assignment from an editor or as the result of a lead or news tip. Good reporters are always alert for story ideas and develop sources of information to give them special access to news. To cover a story, they gather and verify facts by interviewing a variety of people, examining documents and public records, observing events as they happen, and performing library and other kinds of research. Reporters generally take notes or use a tape recorder as they are collecting information, then write their stories when they return to their offices. If deadlines are to be met, however, they may have to telephone

the stories to rewriters, who write or transcribe the stories for them. After the facts have been gathered and verified, the reporters transcribe their notes, organize the material, and determine what emphasis (slant) to give the news. The story is then written to meet prescribed standards of editorial style and format.

The basic functions of reporters are to observe events objectively and impartially, to record them accurately, and to explain what the news means. Within this framework, there are several variations.

The most basic is the newspaper reporter. This job involves covering a "beat," such as the police station or the courthouse, to gather news originating in a specific location, or receiving general assignments, such as a story about a school board meeting or an obituary of a community leader. Large daily papers may assign teams of reporters to investigate social, economic, or political conditions.

Many newspaper, wire service, and magazine reporters specialize in one type of story, either because they have a particular interest in or because they have acquired the expertise to analyze and interpret news in a particular subject area. Feature reporters are usually assigned to a departmental staff to cover news for which that department is responsible, such as medicine, politics, foreign affairs, sports, consumer affairs, finance, fashion, art, theater, travel, social events, science, business, education, labor, and religion. Well versed in their special subjects, they will often be asked to write features explaining the history of certain events. Editorial writers and syndicated news columnists present viewpoints that, though based on a thorough knowledge, are opinions on topics of popular interest. The news columnists write under a byline and usually specialize in a particular subject, such as politics or governmental activities. Critics review restaurants, books, works of art, movies, plays, musical performances, and other cultural events.

Specializing permits the reporters to accomplish two things. By focusing all their efforts, talent, and knowledge, they are able to present the news in their area of expertise more effectively. Also, they can more easily develop the contacts and sources necessary to gain access to the news.

Correspondents report events in locations distant from their home offices. They may report news by mail, telephone, or telegraph from rural areas, large cities throughout the United States, or foreign countries. Reporters on small or weekly newspapers not only cover all aspects of the news in their communities, but they also may take photographs, write editorials and headlines, lay out pages, edit wire-service copy, and help out with general office work. Television reporters may have to be photogenic as well as talented and resourceful: they may at times present live reports, filmed by a mobile camera unit, from the scene where the news originates; or they may tape interviews and narration for later broadcast.

Requirements

A college education is essential for people coming into the field at this time, although there is divided opinion as to what kind is best. Most editors prefer graduates with degrees in journalism because their preparation includes studies in liberal arts along with professional training in journalism. Some editors consider it sufficient for a reporter to have a good general education from a liberal arts college. Still others prefer applicants with an undergraduate degree in liberal arts and a master's degree in journalism. The great majority of journalism graduates hired today by newspapers, wire services, and magazines have majored specifically in news-editorial journalism. High-school courses that provide a firm foundation for a career as reporter include English, journalism, social studies, and typing.

More than 300 colleges offer programs in journalism leading to a bachelor's degree. In these schools, around three-fourths of a student's time is devoted to a liberal education and one-fourth to the professional study of journalism, with required courses that include introductory mass media, basic reporting and copyediting, history of journalism, and press law and ethics. Students select other journalism courses according to their specific interests.

Journalism courses and programs are also offered by more than 350 community and junior colleges. Graduates of these programs are prepared to go to work directly as general assignment reporters, but they will encounter difficulty when competing with graduates of four-year programs. Credit earned in community and junior colleges may be transferable to four-year programs in journalism at other colleges and universities. Some journalism training may also be obtained in the armed forces.

A master's degree in journalism may be earned at more than one hundred schools, and a doctorate at about twenty. Graduate degrees may prepare graduates specifically for news careers or for careers as journalism teachers, researchers and theorists, or advertising and public relations workers.

A reporter's liberal arts training should include courses in English (with an emphasis on writing), sociology, political science, economics, history, psychology, business, speech, and computer science. A knowledge of foreign languages would also be useful. To be a reporter in a specialized field, such as science or finance, requires concentrated coursework in that area.

To complete the educational requirements, a journalism career demands typing skill. Reporters type their own stories, and almost all of them now write and edit their material on computerized word-processing equipment. Although not essential, a knowledge of shorthand or speedwriting would make notetaking easier, and an acquaintance with news photography is an asset.

More than 3,000 journalism scholarships, fellowships, and assistantships were awarded in a recent year to college students by universities, newspapers, foundations, and professional organizations. Many newspapers and magazines and the Dow Jones Newspaper Fund make summer internships available to journalism students for the purpose of providing them with practical experience in a variety of basic reporting and editing duties. Students who successfully complete internships are usually placed in jobs more quickly upon graduation.

The more experience a graduate has, the greater will be the advantage in landing a job. Other ways to gain experience are by serving as a writer or editor for school newspapers and church and community newsletters or by working as a "stringer"—a reporter who works part-time covering news in a particular area of the community and is paid on the basis of the stories printed.

Most beginners start out as general assignment reporters or copy editors for small publications. A few outstanding journalism graduates may be hired by large city newspapers or national magazines, but they are the exception because large employers usually require several years' experience. As a rule, novice reporters cover routine assignments, such as reporting on civic and club meetings, writing obituaries, summarizing speeches, interviewing important visitors to the community, and covering police court proceedings. As they become more skilled, they are assigned to more important events or to a regular beat, or they specialize in a particular field.

Besides education and experience, reporters need a number of personal characteristics and attributes. Above all, reporters should have a sense of responsibility and a respect for truth. What they write often influences public opinion; they owe it to their readers—and to their employers—to be objective and impartial in reporting the news and to present the infor-

News reporters gather around a scientist at the Jet Propulsion Laboratory to learn the status of a U.S. space probe. In order to get the scientist's attention, reporters must be aggressive.

mation accurately and clearly. Statements that are untrue or libelous may result in expensive lawsuits. Not only must facts and opinions be presented in a way that is easily understood, but the writing must preclude even the possibility of being misunderstood. An extensive vocabulary is an essential tool for reporters and correspondents.

An avid curiosity, persistence, initiative, resourcefulness, and an accurate memory add up to "a nose for news," which distinguishes successful reporters from the mediocre ones. Also important are a strong constitution and the stability to deal with the physical and emotional demands of pressing deadlines, irregular hours, and sometimes dangerous assignments. Reporters must be able to adapt to unfamiliar surroundings and a variety of people. Finally, their constant contact with the public calls for poise, tact, courtesy, a pleasant manner, and a good appearance.

Special requirements

There are no special requirements for entry into this field of work.

Opportunities for experience and exploration

There are a number of ways in which interested students can explore a career as reporter or correspondent. They can talk to reporters and editors at local newspapers and radio and TV stations. They can also interview the admissions

counselor at the school of journalism closest to their homes.

Besides taking courses in English, journalism, social studies, and typing, high-school students can acquire practical experience by working on school newspapers or church and community newsletters. Part-time and summer jobs on newspapers provide some of the most valuable experience. A small number of students accept jobs as campus correspondents for selected newspapers. People who work as part-time reporters covering news in a particular area of a community are known as stringers and are paid only for those stories that are printed.

College students can develop their reporting skills in the laboratory courses or workshops that are part of the journalism curriculum. Journalism majors may apply for summer internships offered by the Dow Jones Newspaper Fund and individual newspapers and magazines. Those who are accepted will have the opportunity to perform basic reporting or editing duties.

Related occupations

The ability to write clearly and effectively is a requirement not only for reporters and correspondents, but for workers such as advertising copy writers, biographers, editors, educational writers, fiction writers, screen writers, and technical writers.

Methods of entering

Jobs in this field may be obtained through college placement offices or by applying directly to the personnel departments of the individual employers. Applicants with some practical experience will have an advantage; they should be prepared to present a portfolio of material they wrote as volunteer or part-time reporters.

Many graduates of journalism schools accept jobs on small publications as general assignment reporters or copy editors and are promoted to more important, special assignments as they gain some experience and job openings develop. A small number of outstanding journalism graduates are hired immediately by large city newspapers and national magazines that prefer to train them on the job, but large employers generally require several years' experience.

Advancement

There are a number of avenues for advancement open to reporters. The work of beginners usually involves such activities as summarizing speeches, reporting on club meetings, interviewing visitors to the community, preparing obituaries, and covering minor news events. With experience, they are assigned to regular beats or to more important news events or may specialize in a particular field.

Reporters may advance themselves by reporting for larger newspapers or press services, but competition for such positions is unusually keen. Many highly qualified reporters apply for these jobs every year.

A select number of reporters eventually become columnists, correspondents, editorial writers, editors, or top executives. These important and influential positions represent the top of the field, and there is strong competition for them.

Many reporters utilize the contacts and knowledge developed in newspaper reporting in such related fields as public relations or advertising or preparing copy for radio and television news programs.

Employment outlook

Of the approximately 75,000 reporters and correspondents employed in the early 1990s, about 70 percent worked for newspapers of all sizes, from large city dailies to the many daily and weekly papers in suburban communities and small towns across the country. The rest were employed by wire services, magazines, and radio and television broadcasting companies.

The employment outlook for reporters and correspondents through the end of the 1990s varies, but an average increase is expected as compared to the outlook for all occupations.

Because of an increase in the number of small community and suburban daily and weekly newspapers, opportunities will be best for journalism graduates who are willing to relocate and accept relatively low starting salaries. With experience, reporters on these small papers can move up to editorial positions or may choose to transfer to reporting jobs on larger newspapers or magazines.

Openings will be limited on big city dailies. While individual papers may enlarge their reporting staffs, little or no change is expected in the total number of these newspapers. Applicants will face strong competition for jobs on large metropolitan newspapers. Experience is a definite requirement, which rules out most new graduates unless they possess credentials in an area for which the publication has a pressing need. Occasionally, a beginner can use contacts and experience gained through internship programs and summer jobs to obtain a reporting job immediately after graduation.

A significant number of jobs will be provided by magazines and in radio and television broadcasting, but the major news magazines and the larger broadcasting stations generally prefer experienced reporters. For beginning correspondents, small stations with local news broadcasts will continue to replace staff who move on to larger stations or leave the business. Network hiring has been cut drastically in the past few years and will probably plateau or continue to decline.

Overall, the prospects are best for graduates who have majored in news-editorial journalism and completed an internship while in school. The top graduates in an accredited program will have a great advantage, as will talented technical or scientific writers. Small newspapers prefer to hire beginning reporters who are acquainted with the community and are willing to help with photography and other aspects of production. Without at least a bachelor's degree in journalism, applicants will find it increasingly difficult to obtain even an entry-level position.

An indication of the growing competition in this field is the expected rise in enrollments in journalism education programs through the 1990s. This will create a favorable situation, however, for persons qualified to teach journalism. Persons with doctorates and practical reporting experience may find teaching positions at four-year colleges and universities, while highly qualified reporters with master's degrees may obtain employment in journalism departments of community and junior colleges. The bright outlook for journalism educators stands in contrast with the rather bleak prospects for college faculty in other academic disciplines.

Poor economic conditions do not drastically affect the employment of reporters and correspondents. Their numbers are not severely cut back even during a downturn; instead, employers forced to reduce expenditures will suspend new hiring.

Graduates of schools of journalism should also consider the opportunities available in such closely related fields as advertising and public relations. Many jobs in these areas are comparable in level of skill and area of interest to work done by reporters. Some graduates accept sales, management, or other nonmedia positions, while others take additional training for such fields as law, business, public administration, and political science.

Earnings

There are great variations in the earnings of reporters. Salaries are related to experience, the kind of employer for which the reporter works, the geographical location, and whether the reporter is covered by a contract negotiated by the Newspaper Guild. In general, however, reporters earn more than the average for all nonsupervisory workers in private industry, except farming.

In the early 1990s, reporters on daily newspapers having Newspaper Guild contracts were paid starting salaries that ranged from about $9,400 to $50,600 a year, with the majority earning between $18,000 and $25,000.

Reporters with four or five years' experience had an average salary of $32,000. Earnings of more than $25,000 a year are common for experienced reporters. The highest contractual salary paid during the same period was $52,000. Some top reporters on big city dailies earned even more, on the basis of merit.

Newspaper reporters generally work a five-day, thirty-five to forty-hour week. Many of them work overtime, for which they receive extra pay. In addition, they receive benefits such as paid vacations, group insurance, and pension plans. The extent of the benefits depends on length of service and size and location of the newspapers.

Conditions of work

Reporters and correspondents work under a great deal of pressure in settings that differ from the typical business office. Their jobs generally require a five-day, thirty-five to forty-hour week, but overtime and irregular schedules are very common because deadlines have to be met and late-breaking developments often make it necessary to update an earlier report. Reporters employed by morning papers start work in the late afternoon and finish around midnight, while those on afternoon or evening papers start early in the morning and work until early or mid-afternoon. Foreign correspondents often work late at night to send the news to their papers in time to meet printing deadlines.

The day of the smoky, ink-stained newsroom has passed, but newspaper offices are still hectic places. Reporters have to work amid the clatter of typewriters and other machines, loud voices engaged in telephone conversations, and the confusion of people hurrying about. An atmosphere of excitement and bustle prevails especially as press deadlines approach.

Some travel is often required in this occupation, and some assignments may be dangerous, such as covering wars, political uprisings, fires, floods, and other events of a volatile nature.

Social and psychological factors

The job of reporters and correspondents is exceptionally important. The stories they write will often be the only basis upon which many people will develop their opinions of political or other prominent figures in the community or of issues to be voted upon by the electorate. It is essential that reporters be continually aware of the responsibility that accompanies their influence.

Reporters play a role as historians, too. Not only do they observe and record events with accuracy, objectivity, and impartiality, but they often explain the significance of what has occurred by relating it to the past and indicating its possible effect on the future.

Reporters lead exciting lives. They are in on things as they happen. They may get to know many important people on an intimate basis. They are a source of help to many people who have need of their services. These factors help reporters gain considerable prestige in their communities. On the other hand, reporters are sometimes subject to abuse by readers who disagree strongly with the manner in which they have presented certain stories or reported certain events.

GOE: 11.08.02; SIC: 2711, 2721; SOC: 3313

◇ **SOURCES OF ADDITIONAL INFORMATION**

Accrediting Council on Education in Journalism and Mass Communications
School of Journalism
University of Kansas
Lawrence, KS 66045

American Newspaper Publishers Association Foundation
The Newspaper Center
Box 17407
Dulles International Airport
Washington, DC 20041

Association for Education in Journalism and Mass Communication
College of Journalism
University of South Carolina
1621 College Street
Columbia, SC 29208

Dow Jones Newspaper Fund
PO Box 300
Princeton, NJ 08543

National Newspaper Foundation
1627 K Street, NW, Suite 400
Washington, DC 20006

The Newspaper Guild
8611 Second Avenue
Silver Spring, MD 20910

Women in Communications
PO Box 17460
Arlington, VA 22216

Names and addresses of newspapers and a list of journalism schools and departments are published in the *Editor and Publisher International Year Book*, which is available for reference in most public libraries and newspaper offices.

◇ **RELATED ARTICLES**

Volume 1: Broadcasting; Magazine Publishing; Newspaper Publishing
Volume 2: Radio and television announcers and newscasters; Writers and editors

Respiratory therapists

Definition

Respiratory therapists, or *inhalation therapists,* treat patients with deficiencies or abnormalities of the cardiopulmonary (heart/lung) system, either providing temporary relief from chronic ailments or administering emergency care where life is threatened. Working under a physician's direction, these workers set up and operate respirators, mechanical ventilators, and other devices; monitor the functioning of the equipment and the patients' response to the therapy; and maintain the patients' charts. They also assist patients with breathing exercises; inspect, test, and order repairs for respiratory therapy equipment; and may demonstrate procedures to trainees and other health care personnel.

History

In normal respiration, the chest muscles and the diaphragm (a muscular disk that separates the chest and abdominal cavities) draw in air by expanding the chest volume. When this auto-matic response is impaired because of illness or injury, artificial means must be applied to keep the patients breathing and prevent brain damage or death. Respiratory problems can result from many conditions. For example, with bronchial asthma, the bronchial tubes are narrowed by spasmodic contractions, and they produce an excessive amount of mucous. Emphysema is a disease in which the lungs lose their elasticity. Poliomyelitis (a disease that is now extremely rare) is caused by a virus that damages nerve cells that control the breathing muscles. Diseases of the central nervous system and drug poisoning may result in paralysis, which could lead to suffocation. Emergency conditions such as heart failure, stroke, drowning, or shock also interfere with the normal breathing process.

Respirators are mechanical devices that enable patients with cardiorespiratory problems to breathe. The original "iron lung" was designed in 1937 by Philip Drinker and Louise A. Shaw, of the Harvard School of Public Health in Boston, primarily to treat persons stricken with polio. It was a cylindrical machine that enclosed the patient's entire body, except the head. This type of respirator is still in use to-

A respiratory therapy worker assists a patient with breathing exercises that provide temporary relief from chronic problems such as asthma or emphysema.

day. The newer respirators, however, are much smaller, dome-shaped breast plates that wrap around the patient's chest and allow more freedom of motion. Other sophisticated, complex equipment to aid patients with breathing difficulties includes mechanical ventilators, apparatus that administers therapeutic gas, environmental control systems, and aerosol generators.

Respiratory therapists and technicians and their assistants are the workers who operate this equipment and administer care and life support to patients suffering from respiratory problems.

Nature of the work

Respiratory therapists (sometimes called inhalation therapists) treat patients with various cardiorespiratory problems. They may provide care that affords temporary relief from chronic illnesses such as asthma or emphysema, or they may administer life-support treatment to victims of heart failure, stroke, drowning, or shock. These specialists often mean the difference between life and death in cases involving acute respiratory conditions, as may result from head injuries or drug poisoning. Adults who stop breathing for longer than three to five minutes rarely survive without serious brain damage, and an absence of respiratory activity for more than nine minutes almost certainly means death. Respiratory therapists carry out their duties under a physician's direction and supervision. They set up and operate special devices to treat patients who need temporary or emergency relief from breathing difficulties. The equipment may include respirators, positive-

pressure breathing machines, or environmental control systems. Aerosol inhalants are administered to confine medication to the lungs. Patients who have undergone surgery are often treated by these workers because anesthesia depresses normal respiration, and the patients need some support to restore their full breathing capability and to prevent respiratory illnesses.

Respiratory therapists watch the equipment gauges and maintain prescribed volumes of oxygen or other inhalants. Besides monitoring the equipment to be sure it is operating properly, they observe the patients' physiological response to the therapy and consult with physicians in case of any adverse reactions. They also record pertinent identification and therapy information on each patient's chart and keep records of the cost of materials and the charges to the patients.

Therapists instruct patients and their families on how to use respiratory equipment at home, and they may demonstrate respiratory therapy procedures to trainees and other health care personnel. Their responsibilities include inspecting and testing equipment. If it is faulty, they either make minor repairs themselves or order major repairs.

Respiratory therapy workers include therapists, technicians, and assistants. The duties of therapists and technicians are essentially the same, although therapists are expected to have a higher level of expertise, and their responsibilities often include teaching and supervising other workers. Assistants clean, sterilize, store, and generally take care of the equipment but have very little contact with patients. They are usually beginners who are in training to become therapists or technicians.

Requirements

Many respiratory therapists are trained on the job, but the growing complexity of the apparatus they use is fast making formal training essential. Such training is offered in hospitals, medical schools, colleges and universities, trade schools, vocational-technical institutes, and the armed forces. At present approximately 260 of the respiratory therapy programs offered by these institutions are approved by the Committee on Allied Health Education and Accreditation (CAHEA). To be eligible for these programs, applicants must have graduated high school. High-school courses that will best prepare a student for further education in this field include health, biology, mathematics, chemistry, and physics.

The CAHEA-approved programs in respiratory therapy combine both theory and clinical work and last from twenty-one months to four years. A bachelor's degree is awarded to students who successfully complete the four-year program. Students who complete shorter programs may earn an associate degree. The program for technicians runs approximately one year and results in a certificate. The areas of study for both therapists and technicians cover human anatomy and physiology, chemistry, physics, microbiology, and mathematics. Technical courses cover procedures, equipment, and clinical tests.

There are no standard hiring requirements for assistants. The individual department head who is doing the hiring sets the standards and may require only a high-school diploma.

Respiratory therapists must enjoy working with people. They must be sensitive to their patients' physical and psychological needs because they will be dealing with people who may be in pain or who may be frightened. The work of this occupational group is of great significance. Respiratory therapists are often responsible for the life and well-being of persons already in critical conditions. They must pay strict attention to detail, be able to follow instructions and work as part of a team, and remain cool in emergencies. Mechanical ability and manual dexterity are necessary to operate much of the respiratory equipment.

Special requirements

A standard of achievement in this field is to be registered or certified by the National Board for Respiratory Care (NBRC). Application for these credentials is voluntary, but many therapists and technicians choose to apply.

Respiratory therapists and respiratory therapy technicians who have completed a CAHEA–approved educational program may apply for NBRC's Certified Respiratory Therapy Technician (CRTT) credential, a test of entry-level competence in the profession.

CRTTs who have a certificate of completion from a CAHEA–approved training program, sixty-two semester hours of college credit, and one year of experience, or meet certain other educational prerequisites, may apply for registration as an advanced respiratory therapy practitioner. Applicants who pass both a written exam and a clinical simulation test are awarded a Registered Respiratory Therapist (RRT) credential, the highest level of professional achievement in the field.

Opportunities for experience and exploration

High-school students may prepare for a career in respiratory therapy by taking courses in health, biology, mathematics, physics, and bookkeeping. Those considering advanced study may obtain a list of accredited educational programs in respiratory therapy by writing to the Committee for Respiratory Therapy Education at the address listed at the end of this article. Formal training in this field is available in hospitals, vocational-technical institutes, private trade schools, and other noncollegiate settings as well. Local hospitals can provide information on training opportunities. School vocational counselors may be a source of additional information about educational matters and may be able to set up interviews with or lectures by a respiratory therapy expert from a local hospital.

Hospitals are excellent places to obtain part-time and summer employment. They have a continuing need for helpers in many departments. Even though the work may not be directly related to respiratory therapy, the student will gain knowledge of the operation of a hospital and may be in a position to get acquainted with respiratory therapists and observe them as they carry out their duties. If part-time or temporary work is not available, students may wish to volunteer their services.

Related occupations

Many health care occupations deal with the care, treatment, and training of people to improve their physical condition. Workers who require training and skills comparable to those of respiratory therapists include dialysis technicians, emergency medical technicians, occupational therapists, physical therapists, radiation therapy technologists, and registered nurses.

Methods of entering

Graduates of CAHEA-approved respiratory therapy training programs may have the school's placement service to aid them in finding a job. Otherwise, they may apply directly to the individual local hospitals.

High-school graduates may apply directly to local hospitals for jobs as respiratory therapy assistants. If their goals are to become therapists or technicians, however, they would do better to enroll in a formal respiratory therapy educational program. The best programs are those that are accredited by the Committee on Allied Health Education and Accreditation (CAHEA). For a list of accredited programs in respiratory therapy, interested persons may write to the Committee for Respiratory Therapy Education, listed at the end of this article.

Advancement

Many respiratory therapists start out as assistants or technicians. With appropriate training courses and experience, they advance to the therapist level. Respiratory therapists with sufficient experience may be promoted to assistant chief or chief therapist. With graduate education, they may be qualified to teach respiratory therapy at the college level.

Employment outlook

There were approximately 56,000 respiratory therapists in the United States in the early 1990s. Most of them worked in hospitals in the respiratory therapy, anesthesiology, or pulmonary medicine departments. The rest were employed by oxygen equipment rental companies, ambulance services, nursing homes, and home health agencies.

Employment growth for respiratory therapists is expected to be more rapid than the average for all occupations through the rest of the 1990s, even though efforts to control rising health care costs have resulted in a slowing down of job opportunities in hospitals.

The demand for therapists will be greater because of several factors. The population in general, and the proportion of older persons in particular, is increasing and, as people are becoming more health conscious, they are seeking high-quality care more frequently. Also, there is a greater incidence of cardiopulmonary diseases, such as emphysema, coupled with more advanced methods of diagnosing and treating them. More surgery is being performed today, especially among persons sixty-five years of age or older, the group with the most heart and lung problems. Because technological advances have made surgical procedures safer, with the result that the benefits usually outweigh the risks, physicians are more willing to prescribe surgery even for the elderly patient.

A condition that might have a softening affect on the outlook for respiratory therapists,

however, is the trend toward outpatient care, with an accompanying change in the amount and kind of respiratory care provided in hospitals. Because of differences of opinion among medical professionals as to the value of the various forms of respiratory care, there is a strong possibility that hospital administrators and third-party payers (mainly Medicare, Medicaid, and insurance companies) will try to limit the use of respiratory care to cases where it is clearly essential and most likely to be effective. With less need to provide this service, hospitals may decide to reduce labor costs by replacing respiratory therapists with respiratory therapy technicians, registered nurses, or cardiopulmonary technicians.

On the other hand, many hospitals have responded to changes in treatment methods by assigning new duties to their respiratory therapy departments. Respiratory therapists in these hospitals may now perform EKGs or monitor heart functions or handle other duties previously performed by other personnel.

Employment opportunities for therapists should be very favorable in the rapidly growing field of home health care, although this area accounts for only a small number of respiratory therapy jobs. In addition to jobs in home health agencies and hospital-based home health programs, there should be numerous openings for respiratory therapists in equipment rental companies and in firms that provide respiratory care on a contract basis.

Earnings

In the early 1990s, hospitals paid respiratory therapists starting salaries that averaged about $17,800 per year. Experienced therapists employed by hospitals earned an average of approximately $22,300 a year.

Hospital workers receive benefits that include health insurance, paid vacations and sick leave, and pension plans. Some institutions provide additional benefits such as uniforms and parking and offer free courses or tuition reimbursement for job-related courses.

Conditions of work

Respiratory therapists generally work in extremely clean, quiet, well lighted, temperature-controlled surroundings. They usually work forty hours a week, which may include nights and weekends because hospitals are in operation twenty-four hours a day, seven days a week. The work requires long hours of standing and may be very stressful during emergencies.

A possible hazard is that the inhalants these employees work with are highly flammable. The danger of fire is minimized, however, if the workers test equipment regularly and are strict about taking safety precautions.

Social and psychological factors

The role of the respiratory therapist is an extremely important one. People cannot live without oxygen for more than a few minutes. Many lives have been saved by respiratory therapists who acted quickly and calmly in times of emergency. Not only must these specialists be able to tolerate stress themselves, but they should be capable of reassuring sick or injured patients who may be in pain or frightened by what is happening to them. To do this effectively, respiratory therapists need a genuine concern for people. In return, they can experience a feeling of gratification deeper than that provided by many other occupations.

GOE: 10.02.02; SIC: 8049, 806; SOC: 3031

◇ **SOURCES OF ADDITIONAL INFORMATION**

American Association for Respiratory Care
11030 Ables Lane
Dallas, TX 75229

Committee on Allied Health Education and Accreditation
535 North Dearborn Avenue
Chicago, IL 60610

Joint Review Committee for Respiratory Therapy Education
1701 West Euless Boulevard
Suite 200
Euless, TX 76040

National Board for Respiratory Care
11015 West 75th Terrace
Shawnee Mission, KS 66214

◇ **RELATED ARTICLES**

Volume 1: Health Care
Volume 2: Kinesiotherapists; Licensed practical nurses; Medical technologists; Perfusionists; Physical therapists; Physician assistants; Registered nurses
Volume 3: Medical assistants
Volume 4: Radiological (X-ray) technologists. See also Medical and Health Technician Occupations

Restaurant and food service managers

Definition

Restaurant and food service managers are responsible for the overall operation of establishments that serve food. Food service work includes food purchasing, menu selection, food preparation, and maintaining health and sanitation levels. Managers oversee staffing for each of these tasks as well as the business and accounting side of operations.

History

There is no known specific date for the beginning of commercial eating places outside the home, but the first restaurant as we know it dates back to the sixteenth century in England. A midday meal, prepared at a fixed time, was served at a common table. At about the same time, coffeehouses were becoming popular in Constantinople. These coffeehouses spread through Europe during the next century. Usually, the coffeehouses were meeting places for the artistic, literary, and political leaders. Paris became famous for its coffeehouses and cafes and eventually became the world's restaurant capital.

Early American eating places were patterned after the European restaurants and coffeehouses. Delmonico's in New York, Antoine's in New Orleans, and Fred Harvey's in St. Louis were among the elite of the early American eating places.

During the twentieth century in this country many innovations in the restaurant industry developed, including the cafeteria, automat, counter-service restaurant, drive-in, and fast-food chain.

Nature of the work

Restaurant and food service managers may work in restaurants ranging from elegant hotel dining rooms to fast food restaurants and in food service facilities ranging from school cafeterias to hospital food services. Whatever the setting, these managers coordinate and direct the work of the employees whom they usually have hired and trained. Also, they are responsible for buying the foods and equipment necessary for the operation of the restaurant or facility. They may help with menu planning. Periodically they inspect the premises to ensure the maintenance of health and sanitation regulations. They must perform many clerical and financial duties, such as keeping records, directing payroll operations, handling large sums of money, and taking inventories. Their work usually involves much contact with customers and other clients, such as taking suggestions, handling complaints, and creating a friendly atmosphere. In addition, restaurant managers generally supervise any advertising or sales promotion for their operation. In a number of very large restaurants and institutional food service facilities, the manager is assisted by one or more assistant managers and an executive chef or food manager. These specially trained assistants oversee service in the dining room and other areas of the operation and supervise the kitchen staff and preparation of all foods served. To sum up, restaurant and food service managers are responsible for the success of their establishment. They must continually analyze every aspect of its operation and make whatever changes are needed to guarantee its profitability.

These duties are common, in varying degrees, to both owner–managers of relatively small restaurants and to nonowner managers who may be salaried employees in large restaurants and institutional food service facilities. The owner–manager of a restaurant would be more likely to be involved in service functions, sometimes operating the cash register, waiting on tables, and performing a wide variety of tasks.

Requirements

Experience in all areas of restaurant and food service work is an important requirement for successful management. The manager must be familiar with the various operations of the establishment: food preparation, service operations, sanitary regulations, and financial functions.

One of the most important requirements for the restaurant or food service manager is to have good business knowledge. Successful functioning in the job demands that one possess a high degree of technical knowledge in handling business details, such as buying large items of machinery and equipment and large quantities of food.

There are certain personality characteristics, too, that are desirable. Among these are poise, self-confidence, and an ability to get along with people.

The work of the restaurant or food service manager would also require some special physical characteristics. Conditions might demand that the manager be on his or her feet for periods of some duration, and the hours of work might at times be long and irregular. Managers should possess the physical traits necessary to perform these tasks and work long, irregular hours when necessary.

Educational requirements vary greatly. In many cases, no specific requirements exist and managerial positions are filled by promoting experienced food and beverage preparation and service workers. As more colleges, however, offer programs in restaurant and institutional food service management—programs that combine academic work with on-the-job experience—more restaurant and food service chains are seeking individuals with this training. In the early 1990s, more than 130 colleges and universities offered four-year programs leading to a bachelor's degree in restaurant and hotel management or institutional food service management. With an associate degree or other formal award below the baccalaureate from one of the more than 200 community and junior colleges, technical institutes, or other institutions that offer programs in these fields, some individuals can quickly qualify for management training. Others undergo rigorous training programs sponsored by the restaurant chains and food service management companies that hired them as management trainees.

Special requirements

There are no special licenses or memberships required for restaurant or food service management positions.

Opportunities for experience and exploration

Practical restaurant and food service experience is usually easy to get. In colleges with curriculum offerings in these areas, summer jobs in all phases of the work is available and, in some cases, required. Some restaurant and food service chains provide on-the-job training in management.

Related occupations

Managers may direct the activities of a variety of businesses that provide goods and services to the general public. Other occupations that may be of interest to restaurant and food service managers include bank managers, health services administrators, hotel managers and assistants, and retail store managers. Franchises also offer many of the same opportunities.

Methods of entering

Many restaurants and food service facilities provide self-sponsored, on-the-job training for prospective managers.

There are still cases, however, in which people work hard and move up the ladder within the organization's work force, finally arriving at the managerial position. More and more, people with higher educational backgrounds and specialized training move directly into manager-trainee positions and then on to the manager's position.

Advancement

In large restaurants and food service organizations, promotion opportunities are frequent for employees with a knowledge of the overall operation. Experience in all aspects of the work is an important consideration for the food service employee who desires advancement. The employee with a knowledge of kitchen operations may advance first from pantry supervisor to food manager, assistant manager, and finally to restaurant or food service manager. Similar advancement is possible for dining room workers with a knowledge of kitchen operations. Advancement to top executive positions is possible for managers employed by large restaurant and institutional food service chains. A good educational background and some specialized training are increasingly valuable assets to employees who hope to advance.

Employment outlook

In the early 1990s, there were about 470,000 restaurant and food service managers working in the United States. Most of them were employed in eating and drinking establishments. The rest held jobs in educational institutions, hospitals, nursing and personal care facilities, department stores, and civic, social, and fraternal organizations. Nearly half of all managers were self-employed.

The opportunities for well-qualified restaurant and food service managers appear to be excellent throughout the 1990s, especially for those with bachelor's or associate degrees. New restaurants are always appearing in our mobile society, and many more will open to meet an increasing demand from a growing population of consumers with more money to spend for meals away from home. It has been estimated that at least 25 percent of all of the food consumed is eaten in restaurants and hotels.

If the anticipated drop in student enrollments takes place, there will be little increase in the employment of managers in school and college cafeterias. On the other hand, with the growing number of elderly people, there should be many openings for food service managers in nursing homes, residential care facilities, and other health care institutions.

Economic downswings seem to have little effect on employment in eating and drinking establishments; however, competition among restaurants is severe, and many of them do not survive, especially in hard times.

Earnings

The earnings of salaried restaurant and food service managers vary a great deal, depending on the type and size of the establishment. In the early 1990s, manager trainees earned a median base salary of $13,100 a year, with those working in the largest restaurants and food service facilities receiving more than $20,000. In addition, most trainees were given annual bonuses or incentive payments of between $600 and $1,600.

During the same period, experienced managers received a median base salary of about $22,400 a year, although those in charge of the largest restaurants and institutional food service facilities often earned in excess of $40,000. Managers of fast-food restaurants averaged about $15,700 a year; managers of full-menu restaurants with table service, $22,000; and managers of commercial and institutional cafeterias, $25,400. In addition to a base salary, most managers receive bonuses based on profits. In the early 1990s, these payments ranged between $3,000 and $7,500 a year.

Conditions of work

Most restaurants furnish meals to employees during their work hours. This is an attractive feature of restaurant employment. Annual bonuses, group plan pensions, hospitalization, medical, and other benefits are offered in some cases to restaurant managers.

The physical environment in which the restaurant or food service manager performs this work is often a very pleasant one. Usually, the manager has a private office, and the surroundings are clean and attractive. There is usually a great deal of hustle and bustle, however, involved in preparing and serving food to large numbers of people.

The manager will usually work forty to forty-eight hours a week. This may vary, and there may be a certain amount of irregular working hours. This depends largely on the type of establishment in which he or she is employed. In some cafeterias, especially those located within an industry or business establishment, working hours will be regular, and little evening work will be required. Many restau-rants serve late dinners, however, calling for longer, more irregular hours. This may mean that the manager is on duty during a late evening work period.

Social and psychological factors

The restaurant manager should have a certain amount of social awareness. One should be interested in people and be able to get along pleasantly with these people. One must work with and cater to people of all types with many different kinds of backgrounds.

One should be poised, tactful, self-confident, and imaginative. This is necessary to be successful in relationships with both the people who patronize one's establishment and those who work in it.

GOE: 11.11.04; SIC: 5812; SOC: 1351

◇ **SOURCES OF ADDITIONAL INFORMATION**

American Hotel and Motel Association
1201 New York Avenue, NW
Washington DC 20005

Educational Foundation of the National Restaurant Association
250 South Wacker Drive, 14th Floor
Chicago, IL 60606

◇ **RELATED ARTICLES**

Volume 1: Business Administration; Food Service; Travel and Tourism
Volume 2: Caterers; General managers and top executives; Hotel and motel managers; Management trainees
Volume 3: Fast food workers; Food service workers; Hotel and motel industry workers

Retail business owners

Definition

Retail business owners are entrepreneurs who buy their own business or own a franchise operation. They are responsible for all aspects of a business operation, from planning and ordering merchandise to overseeing day-to-day operations. Retail business owners engage in selling items such as clothing, household appliances, groceries, jewelry, and furniture.

History

Retailing is a vital commercial activity, providing customers with an opportunity to purchase goods and services from various types of merchants. Its development parallels the growth of the earliest civilizations, with ancient Greek and Roman planners providing large market places where individual merchants could display and sell their goods.

In the eighteenth century, the mass production techniques of the Industrial Revolution encouraged the development of specialized retail establishments throughout much of Europe.

The first retail outlets in the United States were trading posts and general stores. At trading posts, goods obtained from Indians were exchanged for items imported from Europe or manufactured in other parts of the country. As villages and towns grew, trading posts developed into general stores and began to sell food, farm necessities, and clothing. These stores also often served as the post office and became the social and economic center of their communities.

The last forty years have seen the creation of giant supermarkets and shopping malls, the emergence of discount houses, and the expansion of credit buying. Today, retailing is the second largest industry in the United States. Grocery stores and supermarket chains have the highest annual sales in the retail field, followed by automobile dealers, department stores, restaurants and cafeterias, lumber and building suppliers, drug stores, furniture stores, variety stores, liquor stores, hardware stores, and jewelry stores. Despite the large growth in retailing outlets and the increased competition that has accompanied it, retailing still provides the same basic, important function it did in the earliest of civilizations. Good business people are always needed who can provide customers with the goods and services they need at prices that they can afford.

Nature of the work

Although retail business owners may sell a wide variety of products, from apples to automobiles, the basic job responsibilities remain the same. Simply stated, the retail business owner must do everything necessary to ensure the successful operation of a business.

There are five major categories of job responsibilities within a retail establishment: merchandising and buying, store operations, sales promotion and advertising, bookkeeping and accounting, and personnel supervision. Merchandising and buying determine the type and amount of actual merchandise to be sold. Store operations involve maintaining the building and providing for the movement of goods and personnel within the building. Sales promotion and advertising are the marketing methods used to inform customers and potential customers about the goods and services that are available. Bookkeeping and accounting are the tasks of keeping records of money spent and received, payrolls, taxes, and money due from customers. Personnel involves staffing the store with individuals who are trained and qualified to handle all the work that needs to be done.

The owner must be aware of all aspects of the business operation so that informed decisions can be made. Specific duties of an individual owner depend on the size of the store and the number of employees. In a large store (more than ten employees), many of the operational, promotional, and personnel activities may be supervised by a manager. The owner may plan the overall purpose and function of the store and hire a manager to oversee the day-to-day operations. In a smaller store, the owner may do much of the day-to-day operational activities as well, including sweeping the floor in the morning, greeting the customers throughout the day, and balancing the accounting books in the evening.

In both large and small operations, an owner must keep up-to-date on product information, and economic and technological conditions that might impact business. This entails reading catalogs about product availability, checking current inventories and prices, and re-

Owners of small retail businesses often manage the store and work behind the counter. In this case, the owner of a meat market is the butcher as well.

searching and implementing any technological advances that might make the operation more efficient. For example, an owner might decide to purchase data-processing equipment to help with accounting functions as well as to generate a mailing list to inform customers of special sales.

Because of the risks involved in opening a business and the many economic and managerial demands put on individual owners, a desire to open a retail business should be combined with proper management skills, sufficient economic backing, and a good sense of what the public wants. The large majority of retail businesses fail because of a lack of managerial experience on the part of the owners.

Franchise ownership, whereby an individual owner obtains a license to sell an existing company's goods or services, has grown phenomenally during the 1970s and 1980s. Franchise agreements enable the person who wants to open a business to have expert advice from the sponsoring company about location, hiring and training of employees, arrangement of merchandise, display of good, and record keeping. Some entrepreneurs, however, do not want to be limited to the product lines and other restrictions that accompany marketing a franchised line or running a franchised store. Franchised operations also can fail, but their likelihood of success is greater than that of a totally independent retailer.

Requirements

Retail business owners come from all types of educational and ethnic backgrounds. Successful business people often combined skills in accounting, marketing, and communications. Although there are no specific educational or experiential requirements, those interested in opening their own business are best prepared if, in addition to educational training, they obtain a position in a retail business and learn the rudiments from someone who has been successful. Hard work, study, constant analysis and evaluation, and sufficient capital may then assure the success of a new business venture.

High-school students interested in owning a business should take courses in mathematics, business management, and any of a variety of business-related subjects, such as accounting and typing. In addition, English and other courses enhancing communications skills should also be pursued. Specific skill areas should also be developed. A person who wants to open an electronics repair shop, for example, should study as much about electronics as possible.

As the business environment gets more and more competitive, many people are opting for an academic degree as a way of getting more training. An undergraduate college program emphasizing business communications, marketing, business law, business management, and accounting should be pursued. Some people chose to get a master's of business administration (MBA) or other related graduate degree. There are also special business schools that offer a one- or two-year program in business management. Some correspondence schools also offer courses on how to plan and run a business.

Whatever the experience and training, a retail business owner needs a lot of energy to put into starting a business and patience and fortitude to overcome the slow times that often are part of starting that business.

Special requirements

There are no special licenses or certificates needed to open a business, although individual states or communities may have zoning codes or other regulations specifying what type of business may be located in a particular area. Owners should contact the appropriate city or municipality to determine any relevant regulations.

Opportunities for experience and exploration

Working full- or part-time as a sales clerk or in some other capacity within a retail business is an ideal way to learn about the responsibilities of operating such a business. Discussions with owners of small shops are also helpful in this regard. Most communities have a chamber of commerce, whose members are usually glad to share their insights into the career of a retail business owner. The Small Business Administration, an agency of the U.S. government, is another possible source of information.

Often, high-school clubs offer an opportunity to develop leadership, managerial, and bookkeeping skills.

Related occupations

Business managers, wholesale distributors, freelance professionals, and business executives all have similar job duties and responsibilities. See Volume 1: Franchising for more information on franchise establishment. Retailing, in Volume 1, covers related retail careers.

Methods of entering

Very few individuals start their career as an owner. Many people start as a manager or in some other position within a retail business. While developing managerial skills, and pursuing a college degree or other relevant training, an individual should decide what type of business that he or she would like to own. Many people decide to buy an existing business, because it already has a proven track record and banks or other lending institutions are often more likely to loan money to an existing facility. A retail business owner should anticipate having at least 50 percent of the money needed to start or buy a business. Many people find it helpful to have one or more partners in a business venture.

Owning a franchise is another way of starting a business without such a large capital expense, since franchise agreements often involve some assistance in planning and start-up costs. This fact, however, does not mean that franchise operations are necessarily less expensive than a totally independent business.

Advancement

Because an owner is by definition the boss, there are limited opportunities for advancement. Advancement often takes the form of an expansion of an existing business, leading to increased earnings and prestige. Obviously, expanding a business also entails added risk, as it involves increasing operational costs.

A successful franchise owner may be offered an executive position at corporate headquarters or be offered added franchise rights in a particular location.

A few, very successful, independent retail business owners may chose to franchise their business operations in different areas. Some owners may become part-time consultants or teach a course at a college or university, or as part of an adult education program. This teaching is often not done solely for the financial rewards, but as a way of helping others investigate the option of retail business ownership.

Employment outlook

There are more than 10 million businesses in the United States and the success of each one is largely dependent on the general state of the economy and the individual skills and experiences that each owner brings to bear on the marketplace.

Employment opportunities are often limited by financial considerations and local competition, but there are still many people in all parts of the country who chose to open a business after thoroughly researching an idea.

The major factor that leads to the failure of a retail business is poor management, so only those with some managerial experience or training should consider opening a retail business venture.

Earnings

Earning vary widely and are greatly influenced by the ability of the individual owner, the type of product being sold, and existing economic conditions. Some retail business owners barely make a living, while others make a healthy profit. In general, the majority of retail business owners earn more than $15,000 a year, but the average owner is unlikely to become wealthy.

Conditions of work

Most retail establishments are clean, well lit, well heated in the winter and air-conditioned in the summer. Owners usually have comfortable offices in which to work.

Despite the pleasant surroundings, ownership is a demanding occupation, with owners often working six or seven days a week. A sixty-plus hour workweek is not unusual, especially during the Christmas season and other busy times. An owner of a larger establishment may be able to leave a manager in charge of many of the operational considerations, but the owner still should be on hand to handle the store's receipts as well as solve any pressing concerns. Owners of smaller operations may stay in the store throughout the day, often spending much of the time on their feet.

An owner may occasionally travel out-of-town to attend conferences or solicit new customers or product information.

Social and psychological factors

An owner should be mature, patient, and have good business judgement, as a retail establishment may fail. In addition, an owner should be able to motivate employees and also be able to encourage customers to purchase goods or services. Sometimes an owner, especially that of a smaller establishment, may develop a close relationship with steady customers.

An owner should be able to make decisions after analyzing relevant data and also be able to delegate authority. The owner should be creative in establishing marketing approaches yet disciplined when handling buying and selling decisions.

Despite the pressures of the job, an owner may find providing customers with needed goods and services very rewarding.

GOE: 11.05.04; SIC: Any industry; SOC: 124

◇ **SOURCES OF ADDITIONAL INFORMATION**

General information about careers in retail business ownership is available from:

National Retail Merchants Association
100 West 31st Street
New York, NY 10001

U.S. Small Business Administration
1441 L Street, NW
Washington, DC 20416

National Federation of Independent Business
150 West 20th Avenue
San Mateo, CA 94403

For information on specific training programs, contact:

National Association of Trade and Technical Schools
2251 Wisconsin Avenue, NW
Washington, DC 2000y

◇ **RELATED ARTICLES**

Volume 1: Franchising; Retailing
Volume 2: Buyers; Retail managers; Sales workers in retail trade
Volume 3: Cashiers; Retail clerks; Sales workers in retail trade

Retail managers

Definitions

Retail store managers are responsible for the profitable operation of retail trade establishments. The types of merchandise sold at retail trade establishments include food, clothing, furniture, sporting goods, novelties, and other items. Managers handle staffing, business administration, stock ordering procedures, and other duties.

History

In primitive times, people's only possessions were those items that they could grow, gather, or make themselves. The food supply, for example, was limited to what each individual could produce; if people grew more food than they could eat, the food spoiled and was wasted. The same was true for clothing, tools, and all other goods.

As communication and transportation improved, however, people found that they could barter and trade their surplus items for those of others. Markets were developed, at which people could sell things not needed and buy things that were needed. Gradually, markets grew and expanded.

In the United States, markets have always played an important role in the delivery of food, clothing, and other types of goods. Small, family-owned stores, carrying both products produced locally and products imported from overseas (usually England), have been around for nearly two centuries.

The first large chain store began to operate about a century ago. One of the aims of early chain stores was to prove staples for the pioneers of the newly settled West. Because the chain store corporations were able to buy goods in large quantities and store them in warehouses, they were able to undersell the private merchant.

Retail stores, especially supermarkets, began to grow very rapidly during the 1930s. Stores were often owned and operated by chain corporations, thus benefiting from bulk buying and more sophisticated storage practices. Cheaper transportation also contributed to the growth of retail stores, because goods could be transported and sold more economically.

The retail industry continues to grow and expand. Today, retailing is one of the nation's largest industries, employing more than 5.5 million people.

Nature of the work

Retail managers are responsible for every phase of the stores' operation. They are often one of the first employees to arrive in the morning and the last to leave at night. Their duties include supervising other employees, maintaining the physical facilities, managing stock, accounting for expenditures and receipts, and maintaining good public relations.

Being able to hire, train, and work with qualified employees is an essential skill of the successful manager. It is the manager's respon-

Retail managers must supervise their employees and attend to any customer's problems.

sibility to hire employees, train them and assign duties, promote them when indicated, recommend increases in salaries, and, if necessary, terminate them.

Managers must also be very good at human relations. Differences of opinion and personality clashes among employees are inevitable, and the manager must be able to restore good feelings among staff. In addition, the manager often has to deal with customers' grievances and must attempt to restore each customer's goodwill toward the store if there are negative feelings.

Retail managers should also keep accurate and up-to-date records of store inventory. When new merchandise arrives, the manager should ensure that items are recorded, priced, and displayed or shelved. The manager should be notified when stock is getting low so that new items can be ordered.

Some managers are responsible for advertising and promotions. The manager may confer with advertising agency representatives to decide upon appropriate advertising for the store. The manager may also decide which products to put on sale for advertising purposes.

The duties of store managers vary according to the type of merchandise sold, the size of the store, and the number of employees. In small, owner-operated stores, managers are often involved in a variety of activities, such as accounting, data processing, marketing, research, sales, and shipping. In large retail corporations, however, managers may be involved in one or two specific activities. Regardless of the specific duties, all managers should have good marketing, analytical, and people skills.

Requirements

There are no specified educational requirements for retail managers. A college education, however, is highly recommended, and a high-school diploma is essential. The majority of retailing corporations prefer to hire college graduates; many stores will *only* hire college graduates. In addition a poll of many present retail store managers who do not have a college degree indicated that they feel they would have benefited from courses in business and economics.

To prepare for a career as a retail store manager, the student should take courses in accounting, business, marketing, English, and advertising. Individuals who are interested in retail store management but who are unable to attend college should consider obtaining a job in a store to gain experience and, after starting work, attending college at night.

Special requirements

Good health and stamina are essential requirements for retail store managers. It is not uncommon for managers to spend sixty hours a week on the job; they often work six days a week, from early in the morning until well after dark. In addition, much of their work involves walking and standing.

Retail store managers must also have various personal skills. For example, they must be able to get along well with people, including both employees and customers. Managers must also be attuned to consumer needs, and they must be able to move merchandise.

Opportunities for experience and exploration

Many individuals are able to find part-time, weekend, or summer jobs in clothing stores, supermarkets, and other retail trade establishments. This work experience gives them an excellent opportunity to observe the nature of the retailing industry to determine whether they are interested in pursuing a career in it.

Related occupations

Retailing offers interested persons a wide variety of occupational opportunities at many educational and experiential levels. These include cashiers, clerks, buyers, salespersons, managers, and many others.

Methods of entering

Many new college graduates find managerial jobs in retailing. Most colleges and universities have placement services to help students find jobs. In addition, some of the large retailing chains engage in campus recruiting.

Not all store managers, however, are college graduates. Many store managers have been promoted into their jobs from jobs of less responsibility within the organization. Some have been in the retailing industry for more than a dozen years before being promoted. Those with more education often receive promotions faster.

Regardless of educational background, individuals who are interested in working in the retailing industry should consider working, at least part-time or during the summer, in a retail store. Although there may not be an opening when the application is made, there is often a high turnover of employees and vacancies occur from time to time.

Advancement

Advancement opportunities in retailing vary according to the size of the store, the city in which the store is located, and the type of merchandise sold. Advancement also depends on the individual's work experience and educational background.

A store manager who works for a large, retail chain, for example, might be given responsibility for a number of stores in a given area or region. Or, a manager might be transferred to a larger store in another city. The willingness to relocate to a new city may increase an employee's chances of being promoted.

Some managers may decide to open their own stores after they have acquired enough experience in the retailing industry. After working as a retail manager for a large chain of clothing stores, for example, a person may decide to open a small boutique.

Sometimes, *becoming* a retail manager involves a series of promotions. A person who works in a supermarket, for example, may advance from clerk, checker, or bagger to a regular assignment in one of the several departments in the store. After a certain amount of time, the person might become an assistant manager and then, eventually, a manager.

Employment outlook

Although some retailers have been reducing their management staff to cut costs and make operations more efficient, there are still good opportunities in retailing. Competition for jobs, however, continues to increase. With several department stores closing, consolidating, or being purchased by others, managers are competing for fewer positions.

Those individuals with the best educational backgrounds and work experience will have the best chances of finding jobs. A college degree is becoming very advantageous, if not essential, in securing employment in management. Work experience is also very important.

Although most employers are becoming very selective in their hiring practices, there are still many, many openings in retailing.

Earnings

Salaries for retail managers vary with the size of the store, its ownership, and the number of its customers. Some large retailing chains pay college graduates a starting salary of $16,000 to $21,000. However, the salary range for college graduates may vary by as much as $10,000, and salaries at smaller retailing stores are less. Supermarket managers may earn between $13,000 and $30,000, with the average salary around $17,000.

In addition to yearly salaries, some stores offer special bonuses to managers who have particular success in increasing profits and moving merchandise. Many stores also offer employee discounts on store merchandise.

Conditions of work

Most retail stores are pleasant places in which to work. They are clean, well lit, well heated in winter, and air-conditioned in summer. Man-

agers often have comfortable offices in which to work.

Long hours of work are the main disadvantage to careers as retail managers. Managers often work six days a week and as many as sixty hours a week, especially during certain busy times of year, like the Christmas season. Because peak shopping periods are holiday seasons, it is extremely rare that managers have holidays off, or can schedule vacations around the holiday, even if the store is not open on that day. For managers with family in other states, this can be burdensome. Although managers can usually get away from the store during slack times during the day, they are often present if the store is open at night. It is important that the manager be available to handle the store's daily receipts, which are often put in a safe or taken to the night depository of the bank at the close of business for the day.

Social and psychological factors

The retailing industry can be very interesting, challenging, and stimulating. Retail managers are often involved in a variety of activities; their work is exciting and competitive. Retail managers must be good with people because they must work not only with other employees but also with the public. Hiring and firing people can be difficult for managers who are not comfortable with confrontations situations.

They must also be logical and analytical because much of their work involves the buying and selling of merchandise. In addition, retail managers must be able to work under pressure, especially in the store's busy seasons. Those individuals who possess the right skills and attitudes will find that the retailing industry is a very rewarding one in which to work.

GOE: 11.11.05; SIC: 313; SOC: 403

◇ **SOURCES OF ADDITIONAL INFORMATION**

American Management Association
Management Information Service
135 West 50th Street
New York, NY 10020

National Management Association
2210 Arbor Boulevard
Dayton, OH 45439

For general retail information, contact:

National Retail Merchants Association
100 West 31st Street
New York, NY 10001

◇ RELATED ARTICLES

Volume 1: Franchising; Retailing; Wholesaling
Volume 2: Buyers; Marketing research personnel; Sales workers in retail trade
Volume 3: Cashiers; Retail clerks

Roman Catholic priests

Definition

Roman Catholic priests provide for the spiritual, educational, and social needs of Catholic congregations. They offer mass, administer the sacraments, hear confession, visit the sick, and are involved in community and interfaith affairs. They also perform funeral services and counsel members of their congregations. Priests also have administrative duties, such as working on congregational committees.

History

Priests and other clergy are part of the hierarchical structure of the Roman Catholic Church. The pope is spiritual leader of the worldwide church. The pope appoints bishops who oversee a diocese, a territorial district of the Church. The bishops appoint the priests, who are spiritual leaders of individual parishes.

The role of the clergy within the Roman Catholic faith is to help people become and remain holy by means such as worship and religious education. The central act of the Catholic worship is The Eucharist, or mass, where congregants receive holy communion from the priest.

Nature of the work

Priests are the spiritual leaders of Catholic congregations. Like other clergy, they conduct services, give sermons, and help and counsel those in need. Priests administer the sacraments and perform funeral services. They interpret the tenets and doctrines of the faith and

instruct persons who seek conversion. Priests usually begin the day with meditation and mass and may spend the evening hearing confessions or visiting the sick. Many priests involve themselves in the work of various church committees, civic and charitable organizations, and community projects. Some priests have become involved in concerns such as human rights and other nonliturgical issues.

There are two categories of priests—diocesan (secular) and religious. All priests have the same powers bestowed on them through ordination by a bishop, but their way of life, the type of work they do, and the authority to whom they report depends on whether they are members of a religious order or working in a diocese. Diocesan, or secular, priests generally work in parishes to which they are assigned by their bishop. Religious priests, such as Dominicans, Jesuits, or Franciscans, work as members of a religious community, teaching, doing missionary work, or engaging in other specialized activities as assigned by their superiors. Both categories of priests teach and hold administrative positions in Catholic seminaries and educational institutions. Religious priests, however, make up the largest percentage of the staff at seminaries, colleges and universities, and many high schools, while diocesan priests usually work in parochial schools attached to parish churches and diocesan high schools. Most of the missionary work carried out by the Catholic Church is performed by members of religious orders.

Members of the Catholic clergy do not choose their work assignments; this is done by their superiors in the Church hierarchy. Work assignments, however, are always made with the interests and abilities of the individual priest in mind. Every effort is made to place a priest in the type of ministry he feels comfortable with. Priests may serve in a wide range of ministries, from counseling full-time and working in social services to being chaplains in the armed forces, prisons, or hospitals.

Requirements

The Roman Catholic Church usually requires eight years of study following high-school graduation. There are about 240 seminaries, many of which start the training and education for the priesthood in the first year of high school. Candidates for the priesthood may also choose to enter at the college level or begin their studies in theological seminaries after college graduation.

The seminary high school prepares students for college with emphasis on English, speech, literature, and social studies. Latin is required, and the study of other foreign languages such as Spanish is encouraged. The liberal arts program offered by seminary colleges stresses philosophy, religion, the behavioral sciences, history, the natural sciences, and mathematics.

The additional four years of preparation for ordination include studies in moral and pastoral theology, sacred scriptures, church history, homiletics (the art of preaching), liturgy (the mass), and cannon law. The academic study is balanced by fieldwork in parishes and the general community. Because the work expected of secular and religious priests differs, they are trained in different major seminaries offering slightly varied programs.

Postgraduate work in theology and other fields is available and encouraged for priests, who may study in American Catholic universities or at ecclesiastical universities in Rome or other places around the world. Continuing education for ordained priests in the last several years has stressed sociology, psychology, and the natural sciences.

All Catholic seminaries offer scholarships and grants to qualified students. In seminaries for secular priests, scholarships and loans are available. In religious seminaries, students are financed by contributions from benefactors.

Special requirements

In addition to the ordination requirements, a primary consideration in choosing a career in the priesthood is a strong religious faith coupled with the desire to help others. A priest

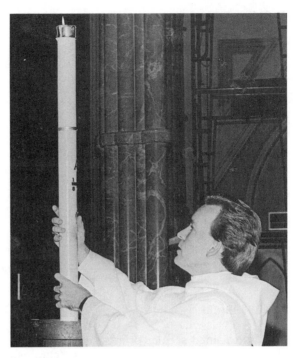

A priest places a candle during the Easter Vigil mass. Lit at every mass, the candle will last for an entire year.

should also be able to communicate effectively and supervise others. Priests must have self-confidence and possess initiative and compassion. In the Roman Catholic Church only men are ordained and marriage is forbidden to the clergy. Many members of a religious order take vows of poverty, chastity, and obedience.

Opportunities for experience and exploration

Persons interested in the priesthood, joining a religious order, or becoming involved in religious work should talk with their parish priest and other involved in the work of the church to get a clearer idea of the rewards and responsibilities of this profession. Choosing a career as a priest entails a good deal of thought as to the demands of this profession. There are numerous opportunities for those interested to investigate congregational life. Aspiring priests would be wise to volunteer some time at a church or other religious institution in order to get better acquainted with the type of job responsibilities a priest has. In the final analysis, however, there is no single experience that can adequately prepare a person for the demands of being a priest. Seminary training should offer the best opportunity to explore many of the facets of a career in the priesthood.

617

Related occupations

Priests have many of the same religious leadership and counseling responsibilities as Protestant ministers, rabbis, teachers, social workers, and psychologists.

Methods of entering

Only ordained priests can work in this profession. Students should consult with a priest or contact the appropriate theological seminary to learn how to best meet entrance requirements.

Advancement

Newly ordained secular priests generally begin their careers as assistant pastors (curates), while new priests of religious orders are assigned to duties for which they are specially trained, such as missionary work. With experience, priests of sufficient talent and with strong interests may advance to positions of increasing responsibility within the church or choose to remain at their original position. They may acquire their own or larger congregations. Priests may also become teachers in seminaries and other educational institutions, or chaplains in the armed forces. The pulpits of large, well-established churches are usually filled by priests of considerable experience.

Employment outlook

There is a growing shortage of priests in the Catholic Church. In the last thirty years the number of priests has decreased by about 25 percent because or retirement and those leaving the profession for other reasons. At the same time, the number of Catholics has increased. Therefore, the opportunities for positions in the priesthood are increasing and will probably continue to do so through the 1990s. Currently, about 58,000 priests serve nearly 50 million Roman Catholics in the United States. About 20,00 of these priests serve congregations as pastors. Priests are needed in all areas of the country, but most opportunities are in metropolitan areas that have a large Catholic population or in communities near Catholic educational institutions.

Earnings

Religious priests, who take a vow of poverty, are supported by their religious order. Secular priests receive small salaries calculated to cover their basic needs. These salaries vary according to the size of the congregation, as well as its location and financial status, and range from approximately $5,000 and $10,000 per year. Additional benefits usually include a monthly travel allowance, free room and board in the parish rectory, health insurance, and retirement benefits. Priests who teach or do special work usually receive a small stipend that is less than that paid to lay persons in similar positions. Occasionally, priests who do special work are compensated at the same level as a lay person.

Conditions of work

Priests spend long hours working under various conditions. There is no such thing as a standard workweek. Like all clergy, priests who function as pastors are on call at any hour of the day or night. They visit the sick, comfort and counsel families in times of crisis, and administer the sacraments. Much of the priest's time is also spent reading, studying, writing, and talking to people. Priests also must prepare sermons and keep up with religious and secular events. Priests may also have a great deal of administrative responsibilities working with staff and various committees. Priests also participate in community and interfaith events. They are responsible to the bishop of the diocese.

Religious priests are responsible to the superior of their order. Like secular priest, they often work long, irregular hours for the church and community. Some religious priest live in monasteries and keep apart from the outside world. Others work as missionaries and may live for many year under difficult conditions in foreign countries.

Despite the long hours and sometimes stressful working conditions, many priests enjoy their work and find helping people in a religious context most satisfying.

Social and psychological factors

A priest is very involved with working with congregants. The career is rewarding in the sense of spiritual values and achievements; one can find much satisfaction in the comfort and leadership offered congregants. There may, however, be social pressure. The public in general and congregations in particular expect priests (and other clergy members) to set examples of high moral and ethical conduct. There is the added pressure of being "on call" twenty-four hours a day, and the need to often comfort people in difficult situations. Obviously many people find strength from these commitments and greatly enjoy their work and find it very meaningful. Priests are generally held in great esteem by their congregants and the community at large.

GOE: 10.01.01; SIC: 8661; SOC: 2042

◇ **SOURCES OF ADDITIONAL INFORMATION**

For information on seminaries and religious orders, contact the diocesan Director of Vocations in your area through the office of the local pastor or bishop.

Career information about the priesthood and related occupations is available from:

National Conference of Diocesan Vocational Directors
1307 South Wabash Avenue, Suite 350
Chicago, IL 60605

National Federation of Priests' Council
1337 West Ohio
Chicago, IL 60626

National Assembly of Religious Brothers
National Assembly of Religious Women
1307 South Wabash
Room 206
Chicago, IL 60605

For information concerning the work of military chaplains, contact:

National Conference on Ministry to the Armed Forces
4141 North Henderson Road
Suite 13
Arlington, VA 22203

◇ **RELATED ARTICLES**

Volume 1: Religious Ministries; Social Services
Volume 2: Clergy and religious workers; Social workers

School administrators

Definition

School administrators are the leaders who keep individual schools and entire school systems running smoothly. They plan and set goals related to the educational, administrative, and counseling programs of the schools; coordinate and evaluate the activities of teachers and other school personnel to ensure that they adhere to deadlines and budget requirements and meet established objectives; negotiate contracts and settle labor disputes; and enlist and maintain the support of the public. Administrators are the levels above the teachers. Their division of management extends to the regional district staff, in positions such as superintendent.

History

The history of school administrators is almost as old as the history of education itself. In ancient Greece and Rome, education was centered in the family, with children learning from their parents. As the societies became more complex, requiring more highly specialized skills and knowledge, the custom of formal schooling was introduced. At first, servants or slaves were assigned to teach or tutors were hired; then teachers set up schoolrooms in their homes; and eventually groups of prosperous parents established separate schools and employed schoolmasters. In these small early schools, the teachers were also the administra-

An elementary school principal discusses a student's report card with one of the teachers.

tors, charged with the operation of the school as well as with the instruction of the pupils.

Centuries later, on the American frontier, schools were run in a similar manner. As the importance of education gained recognition among people from all classes of society and the government became involved in providing schooling without cost to all children, schools grew larger, a more complex system of schools evolved, and there developed a demand for educators specializing in the area of administration.

In the United States, each state has its own school system, headed by a state superintendent or commissioner of education who works in conjunction with the state board of education. The states are divided into local school districts, which may vary in size from New York City to a sparsely populated area containing a single classroom of children. The board of education in each district elects a professionally trained superintendent or supervising principal to administer the local schools, except in one-room school districts employing one teacher, where the chairman or another board member performs the necessary administrative duties under the supervision of a county superintendent or other representative of the state department of education. In most school districts the superintendent has one or more assistants, and in a very large district the superintendent may also be assisted by a business manager or directors of curriculum, personnel, or research and testing. Individual schools within a district are usually headed by a school principal, with perhaps one or more assistant principals. The administrative staff of a very large secondary school

may also include deans, registrars, department heads, counselors, and others.

Nature of the work

The occupation of school administrator includes school district superintendents, assistant superintendents, school principals, and assistant principals. They are the leaders responsible for the smooth, efficient operation of an individual school or an entire school system. Their jobs may vary considerably, depending on the size and type of school or the size of the district; but, in general, school administrators make plans, set goals, and supervise and coordinate the activities of teachers and other school personnel in carrying out those plans within the established time framework and budget allowance. For practical purposes, the general job descriptions that follow refer to administrators in the public school system.

School principals far outnumber the other school administrators and are the most familiar to the students, who often think of them as disciplinarians. Although principals do spend a great deal of their time resolving conflicts that students and teachers may have with one another, with parents, or with school board policies, their authority extends to many other matters. Each principal is responsible for the performance of an individual school, directing and coordinating educational, administrative, and counseling activities according to standards set by the superintendent and the board of education. They hire and assign teachers and other staff, help them improve their skills, and evaluate their performance. They plan and evaluate the instructional programs jointly with teachers. Periodically, they visit classrooms to observe the effectiveness of the teachers and teaching methods, review educational objectives, and examine learning materials—always seeking ways to improve the quality of instruction.

Principals are responsible for the registration, schedules, and attendance of pupils. In cases of severe educational or behavioral problems, they may confer with teachers, students, and parents and recommend remedial measures. They cooperate with community organizations, colleges, and other schools to coordinate educational services. They oversee the day-to-day operations of the school building and requisition and allocate equipment, supplies, and instructional materials.

The numerous duties of a school principal necessitate a great deal of paperwork: filling out forms, preparing administrative reports, and keeping records. Nevertheless, principals spend much of each day meeting with people: teachers and other school personnel, colleagues, students, parents, and other members of the community.

In larger schools, usually secondary schools, principals may have one or more assistants. *Assistant principals,* who may be known as *deans of students,* provide counseling for individuals or student groups related to personal problems, educational or vocational objectives, and social and recreational activities. They often handle discipline, interviewing students, and taking whatever action is necessary in matters such as truancy or delinquency. Assistant principals generally plan and supervise social and recreational programs and coordinate other school activities.

Superintendents are responsible for managing the affairs of an entire school district, which may range in size from a small town with a handful of schools to a city with a population of millions. Superintendents are elected by the board of education to oversee and coordinate the activities of all the schools in the district in accordance with board of education standards. Their responsibilities are many. They select and employ staff, negotiate contracts with union employees, and settle labor disputes. They formulate and implement plans and policies for an educational program and, when necessary, interpret the school-system program and policies for school personnel, individuals and local citizens' groups, and government agencies. Superintendents are responsible for the development and administration of a budget, the acquisition and maintenance of school buildings, and the purchase and distribution of school supplies and equipment. They coordinate related activities with other school districts and agencies; and, in the area of general public relations, they speak before community and civic groups and try to enlist their support. In addition, superintendents collect statistics, prepare reports, enforce compulsory attendance, and oversee the operation of the school transportation system and provision of health services.

School district superintendents usually have one or more assistants or deputies, whose duties vary depending on the size and nature of the school system. Assistant superintendents may have charge of a particular geographic area or may specialize in activities pertaining, say, to budget, personnel, or curriculum development.

Boards of education vary in their level of authority and their method of appointment or election to the post of board member. Normally board members are elected from leaders in the community in business and education. It is not uncommon to have the board selected by the mayor or other city administrator.

Requirements

School administration calls for a high level of education and experience. Principals and assistant principals are generally required to have a master's degree in educational administration in addition to several years' experience as a classroom teacher. Qualified candidates may also come from other administrative jobs, such as curriculum specialist, financial advisor, or director of audio-visual aids, arts, or special education. The important thing is that they be experienced in organizing and supervising school programs and activities.

School superintendents usually must have had graduate training in educational administration, preferably at the doctoral level. Further, some larger districts require a law degree or a business degree in addition to a graduate degree in education. Candidates for the position of school superintendent generally must have had previous experience as an administrator.

Around 250 universities offer graduate programs in educational administration accredited by the National Council for Accreditation of Teacher Education. Programs are designed specifically for elementary-school principals, secondary-school principals, or school district superintendents and include such courses as school management, school law, school finance and budgeting, curriculum development and evaluation, systematic planning, supervision of instruction, research design and data analysis, personnel administration, community relations, politics in education, and leadership. A semester of internship and field experience are extremely valuable.

Ideally, an applicant's academic training will have provided an understanding of the educational process and its goals and a familiarity with educational technology, curriculum development, and strategies for meeting educational needs; and the applicant's past work record and reputation will testify to administrative competence. But the requirements to be a successful school administrator do not end there. Certain personal characteristics are also needed. They include leadership and managerial skills, the ability to communicate and get along with many different types of people, strong self-motivation, self-confidence, and the ability to withstand criticism from groups pursuing their own goals.

Special requirements

Certification of school administrators is mandatory in all fifty states and the District of Columbia. Requirements to become certified may include U.S. citizenship or state residency, graduate training in educational administration, experience, and good health and character. In some states, candidates must pass a qualifying examination. Persons interested in certification may obtain information on specific requirements from the Department of Education in each state.

Opportunities for experience and exploration

Individuals considering a career as school administrator must have experience in education. The way to begin is to prepare for a position as teacher. School counselors can offer vocational guidance, provide occupational materials, and help students plan appropriate programs of study. Teachers themselves are a source of practical advice and would very likely be flattered to be sought out and willing to discuss their field with interested students.

Related occupations

Organizational and leadership skills are necessary to be a successful school administrator. The same qualities are required by other administrators who provide services to individuals. These include health services administrators, library directors, museum directors, professional and membership organization executives, recreation and park managers, and social service agency administrators. In education, college administrators and faculty and guidance counselors handle some of the same tasks.

Methods of entering

Most school administrators enter the field as teachers. College or university placement offices may help place beginning teachers, or graduates may apply directly to the school system in their locality. Teachers, of course, must meet the requirements for state certification.

Advancement

Teachers sometimes are placed directly in principalships, but more often they begin as assistant principals and in time are promoted. Experienced administrators may advance to assistant superintendent and then superintendent. In fact, many school superintendents are former principals who worked their way up the administrative ladder.

Employment outlook

In the early 1990s, there were approximately 148,000 elementary- and secondary-school administrators employed throughout the United States, most of them in public school systems. About 125,000 of them were principals and assistant principals, while about 23,000 were superintendents and their assistants.

The demand for school administrators is expected to show slow growth throughout the 1990s as the decline in enrollments that began in the 1970s begins to reverse itself. It is anticipated that the number of elementary-school students will increase moderately, while enrollments in secondary schools will show only a slight gain. So the need for elementary-school principals will probably be greater than for secondary-school administrators. Nevertheless, most job openings will occur when older, experienced workers retire, die, or change occupations.

The number of school administrators employed is determined to a large extent by state and local expenditures for education. Public opposition to increased spending, with its almost inevitable rise in taxes, could limit funds for public education and prohibit the expansion of staffs. On the other hand, if enough taxpayers are concerned about improving the quality of education, they can exert pressure to increase spending in this area.

Competition for jobs in this field will be strong. Of the many teachers and other school personnel who graduate with advanced degrees in education or educational administration, a large number will compete for promotions to administrative positions. Some will do so to escape "burnout" from years in a difficult classroom environment, and others will seek the challenge of greater responsibilities or be attracted by the more interesting variety of duties or the higher salaries; but the net result will be to limit the opportunities for those with less experience.

Earnings

The income of school administrators depends on their position, the level of responsibility, and the size and geographic location of the school or school district. The highest salaries are paid in the Far Western and Mid-Atlantic States; the lowest, in the Southeast.

In the early 1990s, the average salary for superintendents was about $68,100 per year; for assistant superintendents, $56,900. In senior high schools, principals were paid an average of about $50,500 a year; assistant principals, $41,800. Junior-high/middle-school principals received $47,100; their assistants, $40,100. Elementary-school principals earned an average of $43,700; assistant principals, $36,400.

Conditions of work

The standard workweek for school administrators is forty hours, although they may work longer if there are meetings to attend or urgent matters to handle in the evenings or on weekends. Also, their jobs requires year-round attention, even during school vacations.

School administrators work in a pleasant office environment, usually seated at a desk. At times, however, they attend meetings elsewhere with PTA members, the school board, or civic groups. Principals and their assistants periodically leave their desks to sit in on classes, attend a school assembly or sporting event, or to conduct an inspection of the school's physical facilities.

Social and psychological factors

The problems of school administrators today are much more complex than in the past and require political as well as administrative skills. School leaders are confronted by such volatile issues as desegregation, school closings and reduced enrollments, contract negotiations with teachers, and greatly increased costs coupled with public resistance to higher taxes. In addition, schools and school systems are much larger now as a result of consolidation, and the people affected by these changes have become angry and outspoken about their needs and frustrations.

All of this demands a high degree of professional competence and diplomacy, but the emotional rewards are just as great when considering the importance of a good education to the future of the students and the future of our society.

GOE: 11.07.03; SIC: 8211; SOC: 1282

◇ SOURCES OF ADDITIONAL INFORMATION

American Association of Colleges for Teacher Education
One Dupont Circle, Suite 610
Washington, DC 20036

American Association of School Administrators
1801 North Moore Street
Arlington, VA 22209

National Association of Elementary School Principals
1615 Duke Street
Alexandria, VA 22314

National Association of Secondary School Principals
1904 Association Drive
Reston, VA 22091

National Council for Accreditation of Teacher Education
2029 K Street, NW, Suite 500
Washington, DC 20006

National Education Association
1201 16th Street, NW
Washington, DC 20036

◇ RELATED ARTICLES

Volume 1: Education
Volume 2: College and university faculty; College student personnel workers; Teachers, kindergarten and elementary school; Teachers, secondary school

Security consultants

Definition

Security consultants plan, design, and oversee implementation of security systems that safeguard property from theft or vandalism, or protect individuals from harm. They may work for commercial or governmental organizations, or private individuals. Security consultants study the needs of each client before developing their proposals. They often integrate such components as electronic surveillance, burglar alarms, and security personnel. Although most of their work is in crime prevention, security consultants also investigate actual crimes, including background checks of suspects.

History

People have been concerned with protecting valuable possessions since the time they began accumulating goods. At first, most security plans were rather simple, as several family units might have banded together to watch food, clothing and other valuables.

In the Middle Ages, European royalty and other wealthy individuals took to assigning trusted members of their royal guard to watch their jewels, paintings, and other valuable possessions. Several people were assigned to test the royalty's food and provide other personal security services.

In the United States, as populations grew and guns became more readily available, wealthy cattle ranchers and others began to hire armed guards to protect their property. Comprehensive security services, such as the one started by detective Allan Pinkerton, began to develop in the mid-1800s.

The Secret Service was established by Congress to combat counterfeiting of U.S. currency, in 1865. After the assassination of President McKinley in 1901, they began protecting the President as well.

With today's sophisticated technology, security consultants are needed to safeguard not only property and valuables, but also information. Many consultants are hired to devise plans to protect data processing material. Protecting individuals has also become a booming business, as many rich or famous people want their privacy protected.

Nature of the work

A security consultant is engaged in protective service work. Anywhere there is valuable property or information, or important people, a security consultant may be called in to devise and implement security plans as a means of protection. Security consultants may work for a variety of clients, including large stores, art museums, factories, laboratories, data-processing centers, and political candidates. They are involved in preventing theft, vandalism, fraud, kidnapping, and other crimes. Specific job responsibilities depend on the type and size of the client's company, and the scope of the security system required.

A security consultant always works closely with company officials in the development of a comprehensive security program that will fit the needs of the individual client. After discussing goals and objectives with leading company executives, the consultant will study the physical conditions and internal operations of a client's operation, and then analyze appropriate company documents. Much is also learned by simply observing day-to-day operations.

The size of the security budget also influences the type of equipment ordered and methods used. For example, a large factory that produces military hardware may fence off its property and place electric eyes around the perimeter of the fence. They may also install perimeter alarms and utilize passkeys to allow appropriate access to restricted areas. A smaller company may only utilize entry control mechanisms in specified areas. The consultant may recommend sophisticated technology, such as closed circuit surveillance or ultrasonic motion detectors, and may also utilize guard personnel. Usually, a combination of electronic and human resources are utilized.

Security consultants not only devise plans to protect equipment but also recommend procedures on safeguarding and possibly destroying classified material. Increasingly, consultants are being called on to develop strategies to safeguard data-processing equipment. They may have to safeguard the transmission lines to keep unwanted people from intercepting messages.

A consultant's job does not end when a security plan has been developed. The consultant must oversee the installation of the equipment, ensure that it is working properly, and then check frequently with the client to make sure the client is satisfied. In the case of a crime against the facility, a consultant must investigate the nature of the crime (often in conjunction with police or other investigators) and then modify the security system so that similar problems are not repeated. Many consultants work for security firms that have several types of clients (manufacturing plants, telecommunications facilities, and so on). Sometimes a consultant will handle a variety of clients, while sometimes the firm will assign one security consultant to handle all the work in a particular area. For example, one security consultant will be assigned to handle the protection of nuclear power plants and another will be assigned to handle data processing companies.

Security consultants may be called on to safeguard famous individuals from kidnapping or other type of harm. For example, Allan Pinkerton, one of the first security agents in the United States, protected President-elect Abraham Lincoln on his way to the 1861 inaugural and helped thwart a possible assassination attempt in the process. Now, government officials are protected by the Secret Service, but security consultants are still very involved in providing security services to presidents of large companies, media personalities, and others who want their safety and privacy protected. These consultants plan and review client travel itineraries and usually accompany the client on trips, checking accommodations and appointment locations along the way. They often check the backgrounds of people who interact with the client, especially those who only see the client infrequently.

Security consultants are also sometimes called in for special events, such as sporting events and political rallies, when there is no specific fear of danger, but just a need for overall coordination of a large security operation. Here, the consultants will oversee security preparation, such as the stationing of appropriate personnel, and then direct specific responses to any security problems.

Security officers develop and implement security plans for companies that manufacture or process material for the federal government. They ensure that their client's security policy in areas such as storing and handling classified documents and allowing personnel access to restricted areas comply with federal regulations.

Secret Service agents are employed by the Department of the Treasury. *Special agents* work on financial crimes, such as counterfeiting, illegal wire transfers of money, and insider trading on the stock market. They also handle protection of government officials, including the President and Vice-President, while traveling abroad and in the United States. There are

After examining a warehouse, a security consultant discusses his findings and suggests new methods of security with the owner.

overseas positions for Secret Service special agents after completing ten years of service.

Uniformed Secret Service officers protect the White House grounds, the residents of top government officials, and the embassies of foreign nations in the District of Columbia. They are a police force for the Secret Service.

The Secret Service promotes their officers into administrative and directorial positions. The people who run the Secret Service department are all long-term employees who have worked their way up from the position of agent.

Requirements

Although there are no specific educational or professional requirements, many security consultants have had previous experience with police work or other forms of crime prevention. It is also helpful if a person develops an expertise in a specific area. For example, if a person wants to work devising plans securing data-processing equipment, it is helpful if the consultant has had previous experience working with computers.

The Secret Service requires a college degree for its special agents. They prefer applicants with foreign language skills because of the regular work abroad and work with foreigners in the United States. Applicants are favored who have a background in work with the public—police or security work, nursing, education, and other positions. The applicant will take physical, medical, and polygraph examinations.

For work with the uniformed division of the Secret Service, the applicant must be 21 years old, have a high-school diploma, and be able to pass physical, medical, and polygraph examinations. Both the special agent and the uniformed officer positions are subject to a field check of the applicant's background history.

High-school students interested in pursuing a career as a security consultant should take college-preparatory courses, such as history, mathematics, and science. Good written and verbal skills are important so courses in English and writing should be taken. Because many consulting companies have overseas clients, the ability to speak a foreign language is a real advantage.

Most companies prefer to hire those with a college degree. An undergraduate or associates degree in criminal justice, business administration, or related field is best. Coursework should be broad and include business management, communications, computer courses, sociology, and statistics. As the security consulting field gets more competitive, many consultants chose to get a master's in business administration (MBA) or other graduate degree.

Special requirements

There are currently no special licenses or certificates needed to work in this profession, although this may be changing as the field gets more competitive and sophisticated.

Many security consultants are certified by the Certified Protection Professionals. To be eligible for certification, a consultant must pass a written test and have ten years work and educational experience in security work. Information on certification is available from the American Society for Industrial Security, a professional organization to which many security consultants belong.

Opportunities for experience and exploration

Part-time or summer employment as a clerk with a security firm is an excellent method of gaining insight into the skills and temperament needed to become a consultant. Discussions with professional security consultants are another way of exploring career opportunities in this field. Young people may find it helpful to join a safety patrol at school.

Those interested in a particular area of security consulting, data processing for example, can join a club or association to learn more about the field. This is also a good way to make professional contacts as well.

Related occupations

Other occupations concerned with protecting property and maintaining security include: private detectives, police officers, maintenance personnel, park rangers, and border guards.

Methods of entering

Most entry-level positions are filled by those with a bachelor's or associate's degree in criminal justice, business administration, or a related field. Those with a high-school diploma and some experience in the field may find work with a security consulting firm, although they usually start off as a security guard and, after training, may become a consultant.

Because many consulting firms have their own techniques and procedures, most require entry-level personnel to complete an on-the-job training program, where company policy is introduced.

Advancement

As in other professions, those with the most education and training have the best advancement possibilities. Experienced consultants are often promoted to management positions, with an accompanying increase in salary. A few skilled, well-known, security consultants may start their own private consulting firms.

Employment outlook

As concerns for security continue to rise, employment opportunities for consultants are expected to grow much faster than average through the year 2000. Major factors for this increase include: a rise in crime and vandalism, and an associated increase in the need for security around manufacturing plants and commercial outlets; an increase in terrorism and other threats to personal safety, resulting in an increase in protective services for individuals; an increase in the cost of business equipment, causing business executives to safeguard their investments with heightened security; an increase in the use of computer technology, leading to a rise in the demand for sophisticated security apparatus to prevent the theft of program information and other sensitive data.

Employment opportunities figure to be best in large urban settings, where many large companies are located.

Earnings

Although earnings can vary greatly depending on the consultant's training and experience, most consultants earn fairly substantial salaries. Entry-level consultants with a bachelor's degree can expect to earn $26,000 to $30,000 per year, while those with a graduate degree should earn between $30,000 to $41,000 per year. Experienced consultants can earn upwards of $50,000 per year, and those who own their own company have a potential of earning twice that much, if not more. (Of course, ownership also has its risks, and a slow period could result in lower earnings.)

Many consultants work on a project-by-project basis, and they get paid an hourly rate. Rates will vary with experience, but could easily be in the $75.00 per hour range. Hourly employees usually do not receive medical insurance or other benefits.

Conditions of work

Consultants usually split their time between their own offices and a client's business. Much time is spent analyzing various security apparatus and developing security proposals. The consultant will talk with a variety of employees at a client's company, including the top officials, and also discuss alternatives with other people at his or her own consulting firm. A consultant makes a security proposal presentation to the client and then works with the client on any modifications. A consultant must be sensitive to budget issues and develop a security system that the client can afford.

Consultants may specialize in one type of security work (nuclear power plants, for example), or there may be a variety of large and small clients, such as museums, data-processing companies, and banks.

Although there may be a lot of travel and some of the work may require outdoor activity,

there should be no strenuous work. A consultant may oversee the implementation of a large security system, but is not involved in the actually installation process. A consultant may sometimes have to confront people suspected of a crime, but they are not expected to do the job of a police officer.

Social and psychological factors

A consultant's job can have a great deal of variety, as client needs may vary. The consultant should be able to work with a variety of people, both at the client's place of business and at his or her own consulting firm. A consultant should have a good temperament and be trustworthy.

GOE: 04.02.02; SIC: 7393; SOC: 5144

◇ **SOURCES OF ADDITIONAL INFORMATION**

General information on career opportunities is available from:

International Association of Security Service
PO Box 8202
Deerfield, IL 60093

United States Secret Service
1800 G Street, NW
Washington, DC 20223

Information on certification procedures is available from:

American Society for Industrial Security
1655 North Fort Myer Drive, Suite 1200
Arlington, VA 22209

◇ **RELATED ARTICLES**

Volume 1: Personal and Consulting Services
Volume 2: FBI agents; Police officers; Security guards; State police officers

Social workers

Definition

Social workers attempt to alleviate and prevent social problems and needs caused by such factors as poverty, unemployment, illness, broken homes, family maladjustments, physical, mental, and emotional handicaps, antisocial behavior, limited recreation, and inadequate housing. Employed by a public or private agency, the social worker does this by individual casework, group work, or else through community organizations.

History

Social work is primarily a development of this century. Although persons in fortunate circumstances have always felt that it was necessary to come to the aid of those who were unfortunate, they thought of their aid as being charity or philanthropy. Help for the poor has often been provided by various churches, but usually the help was on an emergency basis and temporary in nature. There seldom was any attempt to follow up with persons who had been helped, and rehabilitation was not considered the central part of the process. It has been said that charity was often given more to ease the consciences of the rich than to help the conditions of the poor.

The opening of Hull House in 1889 is usually marked as the beginning of formal social work. Jane Addams, the daughter of a banker, devoted her life to helping underprivileged persons begin to help themselves to gain a more satisfying existence. Her work and her philosophy inspired others to try similar programs. It was not until after World War I, however, that social work began to be recognized as a true occupation. World War II and its aftermath, when thousands of persons had to be assisted to adjust to changed conditions of life, provided the impetus for a growth in social work.

Nature of the work

Social work is divided into three major categories: casework, group work, and community organization work. Social workers often are employed by agencies that specialize in one of the three approaches to community problems.

Casework is primarily concerned with face-to-face contacts between the *caseworker* and an individual or a family. It may involve conferences in the caseworker's office, home visits, work with individual patients in a hospital setting, or work with children who need assistance, either in schools, institutions, or homes. Any case may entail all of these procedures or any one of them.

Group workers may be involved in either rehabilitation or recreation, or a combination of both. They may be employed in community centers, settlement houses, youth organizations, institutions for children or the aged, hospitals, penal facilities, or housing projects. Group workers may work with groups of children with social adjustment problems in an effort to divert their interests to wholesome activities. They may work with old people, with groups who face similar handicaps (for instance, diabetic children), or groups with similar economic and cultural problems (migrant workers). *Public housing community-relations-and-services advisors* are concerned with the welfare of tenants in public housing developments. *Human relations or drug and alcohol counselors* help social group workers develop and conduct programs to resolve problems related to human relations or substance abuse. (*See also* the separate article titled "Human services workers" elsewhere in this volume.)

The *community organization worker* attempts to analyze the problems of the whole community and to discover ways in which to meet them. Problems inherent in juvenile delinquency, for instance, may require total community cooperation for solution. *Delinquency prevention social workers* try to mobilize the efforts of all agencies to focus on the complex aspects of such a problem. *Community workers* are assigned to particular neighborhoods to seek out and assist persons disadvantaged because of income, age, or other economic or personal handicaps. (*See also* the separate article titled "Human services workers" elsewhere in this volume.)

In addition to the workers in the three basic types of social work, there are some who are in teaching positions in one of the nearly one hundred recognized and accredited graduate schools of social work. There are also a few social workers who devote themselves to research either exclusively or to a large extent.

Caseworkers are employed in many different kinds of activities, but the basic pattern of working with distressed individuals or families characterizes most of their effort. Caseworkers are employed to assist many other kinds of professional occupations, such as the teaching and medical professions, the courts, the penal institutions, and many others.

Child welfare caseworkers monitor the problems of children, visiting their homes and working with their parents and teachers. If necessary, the child welfare caseworker places children in adoptive or foster homes. These caseworkers may work with other agencies in the community, either taking or referring a child to them for further help. They also work with the courts, particularly the juvenile courts, in an attempt to help children and parents work out a satisfactory pattern of relationships and behavior.

School social workers aid and consult with students, teachers, and parents. Their basic function is to provide a bridge of communication between the school and the home, and to help each exert maximum effort to aid the child. They may work with a child who is habitually truant or who exhibits other kinds of "problem" behavior. They attempt to help the child find a happy and productive role at home and in school life and to achieve better relationships with those in the child's environment. School social workers try to help the parent understand the problem and to meet it successfully. They work with school personnel, such as teachers, the principal, and the guidance counselor, to aid them in their efforts to help the child.

Caseworkers also are employed as medical, psychiatric, or clinical social workers. Those who are so employed attempt to help the individual and the family adjust to the facts of illness and the changes that illness may bring to their lives. The caseworker confers with the physician and with other members of the medical team to make plans about the best way in which to be of service to the patient. He or she explains the treatment and its anticipated outcome to both the patient and the family. He or she helps the patient who faces long hospitalization and isolation from the family to adjust to this circumstance and helps the family to make appropriate arrangements to maintain the home and keep the family together even with the temporary loss of one of its key members. When the patient has recovered sufficiently to be released from the hospital, the caseworker helps in the readjustments that must be made, particularly if the homecoming means that the patient will continue to need special care.

Family caseworkers are employed by agencies whose major concern is the welfare of the family. They work with family members to find so-

In cases of rape, social workers comfort the victims and help them through police interrogations and on to the trial. They will see the victims through the trial as well.

lutions to financial, vocational, medical, and other problems. These workers may provide counseling services for married people who are seeking to stay together or to overcome discord. They may provide help with children whom their parents can no longer reach. They may seek to place children in foster or adoptive homes. They may provide direct financial aid to families that are destitute. They may help with problems of inadequate housing. They may help families meet emergencies such as fire, flood, or earthquakes that destroy their homes and completely disrupt their lives. Often, family caseworkers refer families to other agencies or professionals who can provide help needed by a family member.

Rounding out the social work team are administrators and support staff. *Social welfare administrators* are responsible for the overall direction of a social welfare agency or organization. Assisting the professional staff in public social service agencies are *social service aides*. *Casework supervisors* assign casework duties, coordinate the activities of the casework staff and volunteers, help develop and carry out administrative policies, and perform other supervisory duties. *Case aides* assist caseworkers with the less complex aspects of their work.

A specialized administrator in this field is the *alcohol-and-drug-abuse-program administrator,* who coordinates government programs dealing with the prevention and treatment of alcohol and drug abuse problems among employees in the private and public sectors of the work force.

There are caseworkers who are employed by the courts or the police. They may be known as *juvenile court workers* or *parole* or *probation officers.* Those assigned to the juvenile court may work as investigators as often as they work with individuals. They may investigate the conditions of a child's home; they may be asked to give the judge a pretrial report of the circumstances of the misbehavior for which the child is to appear; they may cooperate with other social workers (such as school social workers) in making investigations or reports.

Probation officers work with offenders who have been given a second chance by the courts. These social workers attempt to help people on probation stay out of trouble and make an adequate adjustment to the circumstances of their lives. *Parole officers* work with those who have been in prison and who have been released on the premise that they will make a new start and overcome previous problems. It is the function of both probation and parole officers to give emotional support to persons in trouble, as well as actual assistance with such problems as finding a job, making new friends, or finding a suitable place to live.

Counseling for both juvenile and adult offenders begins even before they are granted probation or parole. *Probation-and-parole officers* explain the legal conditions of their release. *Preparole counseling aides* work with inmates of a correctional facility who are eligible for parole and need help in preparing to return to community life. *Correctional-treatment specialists* provide regular casework services for inmates in penal institutions.

Requirements

A social worker should hold a bachelor's or master's degree in social work. The master's program is a two-year training period, about half of which is spent in fieldwork.

The high-school student who is interested in becoming a social worker should take a college preparatory course and earn a college degree preferably in social work or liberal arts. College courses and possible majors may include English, sociology, psychology, human growth and development, marriage and family relations, criminology, education, economics, political science, biology, and other natural sciences.

Upon receiving a bachelor's degree, some people choose to begin as social workers. Increasingly, however, people interested in social work are applying to a school of social work for graduate study. If students have had a good academic record in their undergraduate program, their chances of being admitted and of being granted financial aid are improved.

It is possible to secure a position as a social worker with only a bachelor's degree. Jobs available for bachelor's degree applicants do not carry the salary or the responsibility of master's degree level jobs. Promotions come more slowly, too, for those with one degree.

There are a few positions open for "junior caseworkers" or "case aides" that do not require a college degree. Case aides work under the supervision of caseworkers and relieve them of the more routine aspects of the job.

Those who are interested in college teaching or research should plan to obtain at least a master's degree in social work. A doctorate is required for some positions.

Special requirements

The prospective social worker must have a genuine liking for other people and an ability to work easily with all kinds of people, from the wealthiest and best educated to the most impoverished and ignorant. This is a quality that cannot be pretended. It must be genuine, for it will be tested every day during a social worker's career.

Emotional maturity is another special requirement for social workers. They must be well balanced enough not to be upset by the sometimes difficult and sordid conditions with which they must work.

Opportunities for experience and exploration

The high-school student who is interested in exploring a career in social work may apply for a summer job as receptionist or file clerk with a local social agency. If there is no opportunity for paid employment, perhaps the student may work as a volunteer in such an agency to get a sample of the kind of work that is done.

Another good experience for a prospective social worker is to act as a counselor in a camp for inner city or handicapped children. Another possibility is to work at the local YMCA in group recreation programs, especially those programs that are designed for the prevention of delinquency.

A student may volunteer to spend an afternoon each week in a retirement home, reading to the people who can no longer see to read, or conducting some small recreation program. Tutorial assistance is normally used in both public and special education schools.

Related occupations

Individuals with an interest in helping people solve a variety of personal problems may also consider the occupations of the clergy, counselors, counseling psychologists, and vocational rehabilitation counselors.

Methods of entering

The placement office of the college from which the student receives a degree will be able to provide the applicant with a list of vacancies in social work positions throughout the United States. An entry position in social work will not present a problem for a qualified holder of a master's degree who is flexible about location.

Graduates holding only bachelor's degrees will have more difficulty in locating exactly the job in which they may be interested.

Advancement

The social worker who has gained experience in a job and who holds a graduate degree may look forward to being promoted to an administrative or supervisory position. Such promotions are open to only a limited number of those who hold a bachelor's degree.

Employment outlook

Of approximately 365,000 social workers employed in the early 1990s, about 40 percent worked in state, county, and municipal government agencies, with relatively few in federal government jobs. Other social workers were employed in voluntary nonprofit agencies; community and religious organizations; hospitals, nursing homes, and home health agencies; and other human service organizations. Some social workers are employed in business and industry, mainly in personnel departments or health units.

The overall employment prospects for social workers are expected to be better than average through the end of the 1990s, mainly because of a growing and aging population. An individual's opportunities will vary, however, depending on academic credentials, experience, field of practice, and geographic location desired.

Although state and local governments will remain the leading employer of social workers, jobs in public agencies will be less plentiful than in the past because of budget cutbacks. Public programs that have a good chance of expansion include child protective services, services for the elderly, and community-based services for the mentally retarded and chronically mentally ill. Programs most likely to be reduced include public assistance, state mental hospitals, and training schools for the mentally retarded.

Despite a projection of slow growth in the hospital industry as a whole, the prospects look bright for social workers in hospitals, particularly for those with a knowledge of community programs. The trend toward early discharge of patients has placed greater emphasis on the need for discharge planning, which will create a demand for social workers experienced in community-based programs for the elderly.

In addition, more social workers will be needed in the home health care field, in outpatient facilities including HMOs, and in rehabilitation programs for victims of alcohol and drug abuse.

The job outlook is excellent in private agencies providing services for abused and neglected children, troubled youths, rape and spouse abuse victims, the elderly and their families, refugees, farm workers, couples with marital problems, and so forth.

Opportunities for social workers in private practice will continue to expand because of increased acceptance on the part of the profession and the public, but success will not come quickly and will depend on the private practitioner's ability to market him- or herself and to deal with competition from psychologists, psychiatric nurses, counselors, and other mental health providers.

Competition for jobs will be heavy in large cities, but there is a growing demand for social workers in the "sunbelt" states and in rural areas. A decline in college enrollments may improve the job market for social workers with master's and bachelor's degrees, but competition will continue for entry-level human service jobs that do not require formal preparation in social work.

Earnings

Social workers employed by public agencies in direct-service positions requiring a bachelor's degree, such as casework or group work, received starting salaries of about $16,700 a year in the early 1990s. At the same time, caseworkers in supervisory positions requiring a master's degree had average salaries of $21,500 or more, depending on experience. Hospitals and medical centers paid social workers with a master's degree an average of $20,700 to start and $27,300 with experience.

Beginning social workers with a master's degree employed by the federal government in the early 1990s earned about $22,900 a year, while those with a doctorate or job experience had higher starting salaries. The average for all social workers in the federal government was about $31,800. Most of these workers were employed by the Department of Veterans Affairs and the Departments of Health and Human Services, Education, Justice, and Interior.

Most social work agencies provide fringe benefits such as paid vacations, sick leave, and retirement plans.

Conditions of work

The offices of most social workers are neat, clean, and functional. Social workers do not always work at a desk. When they do, they may be interviewing clients or writing reports or conferring with other staff members.

Most social workers need to be able to drive and usually need to own a car that they can use in their work. They may often have to drive to remote areas to make a home visit. They may go into inner city neighborhoods on visits. They may go to schools, to courts or jails, or to recreation centers to carry out their jobs.

Social and psychological factors

The social worker often deals with human tragedy. There are many problems that cannot be solved. In such insoluble cases, the social worker's task is to help the individual or family to adjust to the problem.

Social workers often see much that is sordid and discouraging. They must be able to deal with the unfortunate aspects of any situation without becoming upset. Their role is to be of help; they must find emotional satisfaction in being able to provide help that no one else can furnish.

It may be said that a social worker's primary aim is to work him- or herself out of a job—to help clients reach a point where they can get along without assistance.

GOE: 10.01.02; SIC: 8322; SOC: 2032

◇ **SOURCES OF ADDITIONAL INFORMATION**

Council on Social Work Education
1744 R Street, NW
Washington, DC 20009

National Association of Social Workers
7981 Eastern Avenue
Silver Spring, MD 20910

◇ **RELATED ARTICLES**

Volume 1: Health Care; Social Sciences; Social Services
Volume 2: Career counselors; College career planning and placement counselors; Guidance counselors; Human services workers; Psychologists; Rehabilitation counselors; Sociologists

Sociologists

Definition

Sociologists study the origin, behavior, and interaction of the many groups that humans form, such as families, tribes, communities, villages, and states. They also examine and categorize a great variety of social, religious, professional, business, and other organizations that have arisen out of people living together. Their study focuses on human interaction.

History

Considered from the broadest point of view, sociology may be said to have existed since people began to be aware of their lives as members of a group. The great philosophers of the Greco-Roman period formulated ideas about social structure that still have value. The scholars of ancient India and China also formulated philosophies about the nature of society.

The social science that is known today as sociology, however, had its origins in the nineteenth century. Because sociology is a science, it is based on experiment and measurement rather than upon philosophical speculation. Until an experimental basis for the testing of theory and speculation was devised, the study of society remained in the area of philosophy and not in that of science.

Auguste Comte (1798–1857), a French mathematician, is generally credited with being the originator of modern sociology; he coined the term, which is derived from the Latin *socius*, meaning "companion." His idea was that sociology should become the science that would draw knowledge from all sciences to produce fundamental understandings of human society. It was his feeling that once all sciences were blended together, human society could be viewed as a totality. Comte's points of view are not now widely held among scientists; in fact, the development of sociology through the past century has been basically in the opposite direction.

Emile Durkheim (1858–1917), a French sociologist, initiated the use of scientific study and research methods to develop and support sociological theories.

The field has tended to become more and more specialized as it has grown. The study of the nature of human groups has proven to be one which is so all-encompassing that only by specializing in one aspect of this science can scholars hope to make progress toward the formulating of fundamental principles. For example, such areas as criminology and penology, while still technically within the field of sociology, have already become so specialized that those who work in these areas require training that is different in emphasis and content from that which is required in other areas of the professional field.

Sociologists today may study individuals, families, or communities in an attempt to discover the causes of social problems—such as crime, juvenile delinquency, or poverty; the pattern of family relationships; and the differing patterns of living in urban and suburban communities.

A sociologist discusses the value of her findings with a colleague, in the hopes of publishing the results of her research.

Nature of the work

The sociologist investigates the origin, development, and functioning of groups of human beings and the social relationships that have arisen out of group life in society. He or she collects, organizes, and interprets scientific data relating to community organizations, social customs, the family, and other social phenomena for use by administrators, lawmakers, educators, and other officials engaged in solving social problems.

More than two-thirds of the sociologists working in this country teach in colleges and universities. In connection with their teaching jobs, many also do research and direct the research efforts of others.

Some sociologists work for agencies of the federal government. In such agencies, their work lies largely in research, though they may also serve their agencies in an advisory capacity. Some sociologists are employed by private research organizations, and some work in management consultant firms.

A few sociologists who have met state teacher's certification requirements teach in high schools.

Sociologists work closely with many other professionals. One of the closest working relationships is between sociologists and statisticians, to analyze the significance of data.

The sociologist works closely with the psychologist. The two social sciences have been so related that a new specialization which cuts across both fields has been developed: social psychology. Social psychologists also acknowledge the contributions of both cultural anthropology and psychiatry. Psychologists attempt to understand individual human behavior, while sociologists try to discover basic truths about groups. When these two social sciences are combined, the focus then is upon the study of persons as members of groups and the ways in which individual behavior affects group behavior. Conversely, social psychologists attempt to comprehend the ways in which groups influence individual conduct.

Sociologists may work with cultural anthropologists. The anthropologist studies whole societies and tries to discover what cultural factors have produced certain kinds of patterns in given communities. He or she spends much time usually several years in a cultural group while trying to become as well acquainted as possible with practices common to the culture. Such things as attitudes toward and practices in marriage and child rearing, ways in which members of the community earn their living or obtain food to eat and clothing to wear, religious beliefs and practices, all are made significant by the cultural anthropologist. The sociologist is able to use comparison techniques to emphasize the important aspects of his or her own study.

Sociologists may also work with economists because the ways in which people buy and sell, contribute their services in return for recompense, or barter and trade are all basic to understanding the ways in which groups behave.

The work of the political scientist is also important to the sociologist. The systems of government under which men live may be determined by the nature of the group or of the community. The study of the state is one of the special areas of sociology. Every sociologist must understand the theories of political science.

Ethnology and ethnography, social sciences that treat the subdivision of mankind and their description and classification, are other fields with which sociologists work closely. Problems in racial understanding and cooperation, in failures in communication, and in differences in belief and behavior are all concerns of the sociologist who tries to discover underlying reasons for group conduct.

Sociologists also work with various medical groups and with physicians. Public health is in great measure dependent upon the research efforts of sociologists for its effectiveness. Many sociologists work for public health agencies. The National Institute of Mental Health also employs sociologists for consultative work, for research, and for experimentation and investigation. Some foundations give grants to sociologists to work on special problems.

Sociologists and psychiatrists have cooperated to try to discover community patterns of mental illness and mental health. They have attempted to compare such things as socioeconomic status, educational level, residence, and occupation to the incidence and kind of mental ill health to determine in what ways society may be contributing to or preventing emotional disturbances.

Some sociologists choose to work in a specialized field; following is a list of their various title designations and their work:

The *clinical sociologist* is concerned with group dysfunction and works with individuals and groups to identify and alleviate problems related to factors such as group organization, authority relationships, and role conflicts.

The *criminologist* specializes in investigations of causes of crime and methods of prevention.

The *demographer* is a population specialist who collects and analyzes vital statistics related to population changes, such as birth, marriages, and death.

The *industrial sociologist* specializes in the investigation of group relationships of persons employed in an industrial organization.

The *penologist* investigates punishment for crime, management of penal institutions, and rehabilitation of criminal offenders.

The *rural sociologist* investigates customs and institutions of rural communities and the contrasts with urban communities that result from economic, political, and also religious differences.

The *social ecologist* investigates effects of physical environment upon the distribution and activities of individuals or groups.

The *social pathologist* specializes in investigation of group behavior that is considered detrimental to the proper functioning of society.

The *social welfare research worker* conducts research that is used as a tool for planning and carrying out social welfare programs.

The *urban sociologist* investigates origin, growth, structure, composition, and population of cities and the social and economic pattern of living that results from urban environments.

Other specializations, such as the sociology of law, are in the process of development.

Sociologists work with many different kinds of tools. They use census data, consult historical documents, and study the research that has been reported by other scientists. They may utilize such techniques as questionnaires, tests, interviews, observation, and attitude scales. To a lesser extent, they also use case histories, before-and-after experimental design, and clinical records.

634

Many sociologists write books, articles, and reports. These writings may cover such topics as studies of caste and class systems, progress in the achievement of social status, the origin and growth of a culture or of cultural patterns, juvenile delinquency, social disorganization, patterns of crime or of poverty, changes in family relationships, or problems of migrant workers.

Requirements

It is difficult to find a job as a sociologist with only a bachelor's degree. However, one may be able to enter a job with a research organization as an interviewer, or one may assist in other ways with the collection of data. One may meet teaching certification requirements and become a secondary-school teacher.

Master's degree-level persons may find employment as sociologists with the federal government, industrial firms, or research organizations. Those with specific training in research methods have a better chance of weathering the rigors of competition. If they have taken courses beyond a master's degree, they may be able to teach at a college.

Considerably more than half of all sociologists hold doctorates. A large majority of the sociologists at the doctoral level teach in four-year colleges and universities throughout the country. Job candidates fare better if their graduate work includes research and field work. Specialized study is also helpful.

High-school students who are interested in becoming a sociologist should take a college preparatory program. They will need English, mathematics, and foreign language courses, as most graduate schools demand competence in two languages other than English as one of the requirements for a doctorate. They will also need to take courses in science, as knowledge of the scientific method is essential for a career in the social sciences. They will also want to include the social studies, which are closely related to the chosen field.

Prospective sociologists must have an inquiring mind. They should enjoy studying and learning. They should have a deep curiosity about the nature of society and why groups and people seem to believe and act as they do.

Anyone who plans to become a sociologist should be able to relate easily and well to other people because the science of sociology is really the study of people and the institutions and groups that people create.

Special requirements

Those who intend to work in government jobs may be required to pass the civil service examination. A language proficiency test may be administered to those seeking overseas employment.

Some clinical sociologists may need to be certified by the Clinical Sociology Association (CSA). To qualify for certification, the candidate is usually required to have a doctorate from an accredited school and at least one year of experience in clinical sociology and must demonstrate competence at CSA sponsored training workshops or conferences.

Opportunities for experience and exploration

There are only limited opportunities for a high-school student to explore the field of sociology. The student may read books and articles on the subject or may talk with a high-school counselor; he or she may request that a sociologist be invited to speak at the high school Career Day; or the student may make an appointment with a sociologist in a nearby university or government agency and discuss the work.

Related occupations

Sociologists understand social processes and institutions. This kind of expertise is required also of anthropologists, economists, geographers, historians, political scientists, psychologists, urban and regional planners, reporters and correspondents, and social workers. Persons interested in sociology sometimes find suitable careers in advertising, market research, public relations, or recreation.

Methods of entering

Many sociologists obtain initial employment through the placement offices of their own colleges and universities. Some are placed through the professional contacts of faculty members.

Those who wish to enter a research organization, an industrial firm, or a government agency should apply directly to the prospective employer.

Advancement

Sociologists who enter college or university teaching may advance through the academic ranks from instructor to full professor. Those who like administrative work may become a head of a department.

Those who enter research organizations, government agencies, or private business advance to positions of responsibility as they acquire experience. Salary increases usually follow promotions.

Employment outlook

There were approximately 18,600 sociologists employed in the United States in the early 1990s. About 13,000 of them were faculty members or did research at colleges and universities. Approximately 2,240 were employed in federal government agencies dealing with poverty, public assistance, crime, mental health, social rehabilitation, population policy, community development, racial and ethnic relations, environmental impact studies, and similar matters. Most of the balance worked in research or consulting firms, schools, corporations, professional and trade associations, hospitals, and welfare or other nonprofit organizations. Some sociologists are self-employed, providing counseling, research, or consulting services.

Employment opportunities for sociologists are expected to increase more slowly than the average for other occupations throughout the 1990s. Most job openings will be to replace older, experienced workers who retire or leave the field for other reasons, but an increased demand for sociologists should be prompted by research in fields such as demography, criminology, and gerontology and by the need to evaluate and administer programs concerned with social and welfare problems. Competition will be strong in all areas, however, as more sociology graduates continue to enter the job market than there are positions to fill.

Those sociologists with doctorates holders will find few faculty positions open in colleges and universities and will thus seek nonacademic careers in government agencies, research firms, and business establishments. Those with extensive training in quantitative research methods (including survey techniques, advanced statistics, and computer science) will be favored for many jobs, such as evaluating social programs.

There will also be strong demand for doctoral-level sociologists in practice areas, such as clinical, medical, and environmental sociology; criminology; social gerontology; and demography. For example: Demographers will be needed to help businesses plan their marketing and advertising programs or to help countries analyze their population and formulate long-range public planning programs. Gerontologists will be needed to help create programs for an expanding population of the elderly. There will also be managerial and administrative jobs for those trained in other applied disciplines, such as public policy, public administration, and business administration.

Competition will be even more severe for sociologists with a master's degree. They will have difficulty finding teaching positions even in the junior and community colleges. Therefore, many of them will be vying for the few opportunities available in nonacademic settings. There will be some research and administrative jobs for sociologists with a master's degree in research firms, business, and government. Those with a background in business and quantitative research, for example, are good prospects for market research firms.

Graduates with only a bachelor's degree are not likely to find work as sociologists. They may, however, be hired as trainees and assistants in business, industry, and government, where, once again, the outlook is best for those with training in quantitative research methods. Some bachelor's degree-holders may obtain work in social welfare agencies. Others will put their sociology background to use in other careers, such as journalism, law, business, social work, recreation, counseling, and other related fields. With the proper state certification, some may teach sociology in high schools.

Earnings

In the early 1990s, the federal government paid sociologists with a bachelor's degree average starting salaries of about $14,800 or $18,400 a year, depending on individual academic records. Beginning sociologists with a master's degree earned approximately $22,500. Those with a doctorate generally started at about $27,200, although someone with exceptional qualifications could start at $32,600. The average salary for experienced sociologists in the federal government was about $40,400 a year.

The median annual salary for all sociologists in the early 1990s was about $34,000. For those in educational institutions, it was $33,000; and in business and industry, $38,200. In addition, many sociologists supplement their income with earnings from counseling, consulting, and other sources.

Conditions of work

Most sociologists work under stimulating conditions. If they teach, they have an opportunity to watch their students grow in skill and understanding. If they are concerned primarily with research, they will find that there are seldom two days in which the job is exactly the same.

Social and psychological factors

The sociologist is in the very middle of our culture. Those who enjoy analyzing the meaning of current trends should enjoy thoroughly the professional experiences of sociology.

GOE: 11.03.02; SIC: 8221, 8732, 8733; SOC: 1916

◇ **SOURCES OF ADDITIONAL INFORMATION**

American Sociological Association
1722 N Street, NW
Washington, DC 20036

American Society of Criminology
1314 Kinnear Road, Suite 212
Columbus, OH 43212

Population Association of America
1429 Duke Street
Alexandria, VA 22314

Rural Sociology Society
Wilson Hall
Montana State University
Bozeman, MT 59717

Sociological Practice Association
2600 Timber Lane
La Crusse, WI 54601

◇ **RELATED ARTICLES**

Volume 1: Social Sciences
Volume 2: Anthropologists and archaeologists; College and university faculty; Demographers; Economists; Political scientists; Psychologists; Social workers; Urban and regional planners

Speech-language pathologists and audiologists

Definitions

Speech pathologists and *audiologists* aid adults and children with speech and hearing defects by identifying and evaluating their problems and by providing treatment. They may also do research in the speech and hearing area and conduct training programs at colleges and universities.

Speech pathologists specialize in problems with speech disorder; audiologists work with hearing disorders. It is not uncommon for patients to require assistance in both areas so the specialists may work as a team in patient care.

History

The diagnosis and cure of speech and hearing defects is a recent addition to medical science. Because there was usually nothing visibly wrong, physicians had little to work with, and what they did know was often confused by the interrelation of speech and hearing. Until the middle of the nineteenth century, medical researchers could not satisfactorily answer this question: How could one know whether speech defects were caused by lack of hearing, or whether the patient was the victim of two separate ailments? And even if cause-and-effect were determined, how could one communicate

637

An audiologist conducts a hearing test for a child who has problems pronouncing words correctly.

and federal government agencies, industry, and private practice.

The duties performed by speech-language pathologists and audiologists vary with education, experience, and employment setting. In a clinical capacity, they identify and evaluate speech and hearing disorders using prescribed diagnostic procedures. The initial treatment is usually followed by an organized program of therapy, with the cooperation of other specialists in psychology, social work, physical therapy, and the like. In a research environment, speech pathologists and audiologists investigate communicative disorders and their causes and methods of improving clinical services. Finally, those teaching in colleges and universities provide instruction in the principles and bases of communication, communication disorders, and clinical techniques used in speech and hearing.

with the patient? Some of the answers were provided by Alexander Graham Bell, the inventor of the telephone. His grandfather had taught elocution, and Bell grew up interested in the problems of speech and hearing. It became his profession, and by 1871, Bell was lecturing to a class of teachers of deaf-mutes at Boston University. Soon afterward, Bell opened his own school, where he experimented with the idea of making speech visible to his pupils. If he could make them see the movements made by different human tones, they could speak by learning to produce similar vibrations. Bell's efforts greatly aided deaf-mutes and led directly to the invention of the telephone in 1876. Probably the most famous deaf-mute was Helen Keller, whose teacher, Anne Sullivan, applied the discoveries of Bell and others so that her pupil was able to overcome both handicaps.

Nature of the work

The functions of the two specialties, speech-language pathology and audiology, are quite distinct. Speech pathologists are concerned primarily with speech and language disorders; audiologists deal with hearing problems. However, because both speech and hearing are so interrelated, a person competent in one must have a familiarity with the other. Most persons in either specialty work in public school systems. Colleges and universities employ the next largest number in classrooms, clinics, and research centers. The remainder of speech-language pathologists and audiologists are distributed among hospitals, rehabilitation and community speech and hearing centers, state

Requirements

Most states require a master's degree in speech-language pathology or audiology, or its equivalency, for a beginning job in either profession. Undergraduate training in speech-language pathology and audiology should include coursework in anatomy, biology, physiology, physics, and other related areas, such as linguistics, semantics, and phonetics. It is also helpful to have some exposure to child psychology and mental hygiene. The opportunities for graduate work in speech-language pathology and audiology are extensive. About 235 universities and colleges offered this level of education in the early 1990s, involving extensive training in the fundamental areas of speech and hearing, such as acoustics, the psychological aspects of communication, the nature of hearing and speech disorders, and analysis of speech and auditory processes.

Special requirements

Persons who wish to work in public schools must meet not only the standards for a teacher's certificate but often special state requirements for those helping handicapped children.

Licensing is required in thirty-six states to offer speech-language pathology or audiology services in other than a school setting in private practice or in a clinic, for example. Applicants must have a master's degree in speech-language pathology or audiology, with 300 hours or supervised clinical experience, and must pass an examination. Some states may have additional, varying requirements.

Opportunities for experience and exploration

The specialized, sensitive nature of the work makes it difficult for someone interested in speech pathology and audiology to get an informal introduction to either. Training must begin at the college or university level. It is possible, however, to do volunteer work in clinics and hospitals and thus become acquainted with illnesses and their cures. In addition, the prospective speech-language pathologist or audiologist can readily explore some of the basics of speaking and listening through everyday contacts with other people.

Related occupations

Workers in other rehabilitation programs deal with people who have various disabilities, including speech, language, and hearing problems. Prospective speech-language pathologists or audiologists may want to investigate the work of occupational therapists, physical therapists, recreational therapists, and rehabilitation counselors.

Methods of entering

Those seeking employment with the public school systems would find assistance in interviewing in the college placement office. Professors sometimes know of job openings and may have such offerings on a centrally located bulletin board. It may be possible to find employment by contacting a hospital or rehabilitation center. To work in colleges and universities as a specialist in the classroom, clinic, or research center, it is almost mandatory to be working on a graduate degree. Many scholarships, fellowships, and grants for assistants are available in colleges and universities giving courses in speech-language pathology and audiology. Again, most of these and other assistance programs are offered at the graduate level. The U.S. Rehabilitation Services Administration, the Children's Bureau, the U.S. Department of Education, and the National Institutes of Health allocate funds for teaching and training grants to colleges and universities with gradu-

ate study programs. In addition, the Department of Veterans Affairs provides stipends for predoctoral work.

Advancement

Advancement in speech-language pathology and audiology hinges chiefly on education. Individuals who have completed graduate study will have the best opportunities to enter research and administration, supervising other speech-language pathologists or audiologists either in developmental work or in public school systems.

Employment outlook

There were about 45,000 speech-language pathologists and audiologists working in the early 1990s, almost two-thirds of whom were employed in elementary and secondary schools and in colleges and universities. Other employers include speech, language, and hearing centers, hospitals, nursing homes, and physicians' offices. A small but growing number of speech-language pathologists and audiologists are in private practice, generally working with patients referred to them by physicians and other health practitioners.

Population growth, lengthening life spans, and increased public awareness of the problems associated with communicative disorders indicate a highly favorable employment outlook for well-qualified personnel through the end of the 1990s. Much depends, however, on the degree to which the public seeks treatment for speech, language, and hearing disorders; on economic factors, including the price of the speech and hearing services, people's ability to pay for them, and further budget cutbacks by health care providers and third-party payers; and on legal mandates requiring services for the handicapped.

Nearly half of the new jobs arising through the end of the decade are expected to be in speech and hearing clinics, physicians' offices, and outpatient care facilities, where speech-language pathologists and audiologists will be needed, for example, to carry out the increasing number of rehabilitation programs for stroke victims and patients with head injuries.

Substantial job growth has already occurred in elementary and secondary schools because of the Education for All Handicapped Children Act of 1975. Further growth should result from a 1986 amendment to the act extending services

Speech-language pathologists and audiologists
Professional, Administrative, and Managerial Occupations

to handicapped children three to five years of age and from an anticipated upturn in elementary school enrollments.

Many new jobs will be created in hospitals, nursing homes, rehabilitation centers, and home health agencies; but most of these openings will probably be filled by private practitioners employed on a contract basis. Thus, opportunities for speech-language pathologists and audiologists in private practice should be excellent in the years ahead. This may well result in a sharp increase in the number of private practitioners in these fields. In addition, there should be a greater demand for consultant audiologists in the area of industrial and environmental noise as manufacturing companies and others develop and carry out noise control programs.

Enrollments in master's degree programs have remained steady since the late 1970s, while the demand for graduates has grown. If the demand for rehabilitation services continues to increase, the employment picture will become even brighter.

Earnings

In the early 1990s, hospitals and medical centers paid speech-language pathologists and audiologists starting salaries that averaged about $22,500 a year. Experienced workers averaged approximately $28,000.

In the public schools, speech-language pathologists and audiologists are generally classified as teachers or special education teachers and are paid accordingly. In the early 1990s, beginning teachers with a bachelor's degree earned an average of $18,300 a year; those with a master's degree, $19,700.

Conditions of work

Most speech-language pathologists and audiologists work forty hours a week. Personnel engaged in research, however, may work longer hours. Almost all employment situations provide fringe benefits such as paid vacations, sick leave, and retirement programs.

Social and psychological factors

Speech-language pathologists and audiologists should have an interest in and a liking for peo-

ple, and the ability to approach problems with objectivity. To work effectively with people who have speech and hearing disorders, one must be sensitive, patient, and have emotional stability. The rewards can be great; however, much time must be invested before results can be seen.

GOE: 02.03.04; SIC: 8049; SOC: 3034

◇ SOURCES OF ADDITIONAL INFORMATION

American Auditory Society
1966 Inwood Road
Dallas, TX 75235

American Speech-Language-Hearing Association
10801 Rockville Pike
Rockville, MD 20852

Coucil on Professional Standards in Speech-Language Pathology and Audiology
10801 Rockville Pike
Rockville, MD 20852

National Student Speech, Language, and Hearing Association
Cathedral of Learning
11th Floor
University of Pittsburgh
Pittsburgh, PA 15260

◇ RELATED ARTICLES

Volume 1: Education; Health Care
Volume 2: Physical therapists; Psychologists; Social workers
Volume 3: Medical and health technician occupations

Sports instructors

Definition

Sports instructors demonstrate and explain the skills and rules of particular sports, such as golf, swimming, and tennis, to individuals or to groups. They help beginners learn the basic stances, movements, and techniques of a game and also help experienced athletes sharpen and improve their skills. Instructors advise people on equipment and clothing, and teach them basic safety precautions.

History

Physical activities, such as fishing, hunting, and wrestling have been a necessary part of our survival since primitive times. Sports probably began when various physical activities were undertaken for fun rather than survival. The first organized athletic events occurred around 776 B.C. when the Greeks initiated the ancient Olympic Games.

In the United States, the interest in sports greatly expanded during the 1800s. The English sport of rugby led to the development of American football, and, in 1869, Rutgers and Princeton Universities played the first intercollegiate football game. Golf and tennis were organized into competitive events soon after, and the first championship boxing match was held in New Orleans in 1892.

As the popularity of sports grew, so too did employment opportunities for sports-related occupations, such as sports instructor. Now, health clubs, community centers, park and recreational facilities, and private businesses all offer sports activities for young and old alike. This has led to an increased need for qualified, dedicated instructors.

Nature of the work

The specific job requirements of a sports instructor varies according to the type of sport being taught and who they teach. For example, a person teaching advanced skiing at a ski resort will have different duties and responsibilities than a person teaching beginning swimming at a health club. The skills taught will be different, the location will be different, and the teaching method will be somewhat different.

Nevertheless, all sports instructors must combine a knowledge of their sport with an effective teaching method that clearly reinforces correct techniques and procedures. They also must be very knowledgeable in the basic rules and strategies of the game, and they must be open to new procedures and techniques.

Many sports instructors develop their own teaching style through experience. They find individualized ways of demonstrating skills that are clear and effective. Of course, instructors must gear their presentations to their students' level of ability and understanding. What works for a group of advanced golfers may not work with a group of beginners. Also, an instructor should be able to work with students of varying backgrounds. As leisure time has increased in the United States, more and more older adults have become involved in sports that were formerly reserved for younger, more athletic people.

A primary concern of all sports instructors is the safety of their students. They ensure that students have the right clothing and that they know how to use properly any equipment, such as a ski pole or hockey stick. A major component of safety is helping a student feel comfortable and confident with his or her ability. This entails teaching the proper stances, techniques, and movements of a game, instructing students on the basic rules and regulations as well as answering any questions the student may have.

An instructor may work with a large group or tutor students on an individual basis. In each case, an instructor will use lectures and demonstration techniques to show the student or students the proper skills and help them correct any deficiencies. An instructor may incorporate films or illustrations to help explain an activity. The main emphasis in usually on helping students enjoy the sport that they are learning.

Motivation is another factor in sports instruction. Particularly with a sport that requires stamina, preparing a trainee psychologically is as important as physical training.

A sports instructor also has administrative responsibilities. The instructor will evaluate a students progress and give a grade when appropriate. The instructor may also plan and organize contests or events in which athletic proficiency is shown. The instructor is also responsible for maintaining the sports equipment while the class is in progress.

A golf instructor holds a class for avid golfers who wish to improve their game.

Requirements

Training and educational requirements vary as to the specific nature of the job. Most instructors need to combine several years of successful experience in a particular sport with some educational background in teaching.

High-school students should take courses which give them training in sports as well as knowledge of human physiology. Biology, health, and exercise classes are recommended. Courses in English and public speaking are also important to provide necessary communications skills.

Of course, there is no substitute for developing a proficiency in a particular sport. Training in such sports as tennis, skiing, track and field, swimming, or any other sport the student enjoys should be pursued either within school or with a club or association. Cross-training with a variety of sports and skills is also quite helpful.

A college degree, especially one in physical education or a related field, is also be helpful. College is also a good time to continue training in a particular sport.

Special requirements

Some facilities may require sports instructors to be certified. Specific information on certification procedures and requirements is available from the relevant sports association or organization. An academic degree is also becoming more important as a part of an instructors background. Sports physiology and other sports education degrees are highly regarded.

Opportunities for experience and exploration

In general, individuals should gain as much experience as they can in their specific sport. High school and college are ideal times to participate in sporting events, either as a player, manager, or trainer. Most areas also have community sports programs, such as Little League baseball and YMCA and YWCA athletic programs. Discussions with sports instructors already working in the field are also a good way of discovering specific job information and exploring career opportunities.

Related occupations

Physical education instructors, coaches, athletic trainers, and athletic managers all combine a knowledge of a particular sport with an ability to explain necessary movements and techniques to others. Lifeguards and recreation center workers also demonstrate and explain sporting activities.

Methods of entering

People with an expertise in a particular sport should apply directly to an appropriate facility, such as a health club, a ski resort, or tennis club. Sometimes a facility will provide training for instructors, but often the facility will expect the applicant to have some training in teaching a particular sport.

Advancement

Advancement opportunities depend on the individual's skills, abilities, and drive. Sports instructors should continue their education and training to advance quickly; expert instructors often build a good reputation and get more students. A few instructors may become sufficiently well-known to open their own sports school.

Well-known instructors may write articles for local publications and this may lead to publication of a book or series of pamphlets on proper instruction for a particular sport.

Employment outlook

Employment opportunities are expected to grow through the 1990s. A primary reason for this increase is the expanding level of leisure time now enjoyed in our society. More and more people are spending their leisure time pursuing health-related activities, such as running, swimming, golf, and tennis. This has led to an increase in demand for instructors in these particular sports. Other sports, such as skiing, skating, and horseback riding, also figure to draw in beginners who are in need of instruction. The boom in women's sports that

started in the 1970s and 1980s should continue throughout the 1990s, offering employment opportunities in women's athletics.

Job opportunities will be most plentiful in large urban areas, where the number of possible participants is higher. Health clubs, camps, swimming pools, adult education programs, and other organizations will be hiring competent, dedicated instructors. As always, those with the most training and education figure to have the best employment possibilities.

One drawback to employment prospects is the lack of job security. An organization may choose to hire a different instructor on very little notice, or enrollment in a course may drop, forcing cancellation of a class. If injured, an instructor's job may be in jeopardy.

Earnings

Earnings vary greatly depending on the sport being taught and the employer. Much of the work is part-time, so often sports instructors do not get health insurance or other benefits. Hourly wages can range anywhere between $6 and $75, and sometimes more. Many sports instructors work in camps, teaching swimming, golf, and other activities. These instructors usually earn between $700 and $1,000 plus room and board for a summer session. Full-time instructors can expect to earn between $11,500 and $22,000 per year, with some well-known instructors earning even more. As is usually the case, instructors with many years experience and a college degree should have the highest earning potential.

Conditions of work

An instructor may work indoors, such as in a gym or health club, or work outdoors, such as at a tennis court or camp. Often, an instructor may work both indoors and outdoors, using an indoor setting to explain and demonstrate techniques and an outdoor setting for supervising student practice. Much of the work is part-time, and can vary from one or two hours a week to twenty or more hours a week. Full-time sports instructors work between thirty five and forty hours a week.

It is not unusual for a sports instructor to work mainly in the evenings and on weekends, as that is when adult students are most likely to be available. Seasonal work, such as that of an instructor at a ski resort or summer camp, is also fairly common.

Social and psychological factors

Sports instructors should be able to enjoy working with a wide variety of people. They should be able to communicate clearly and possess good leadership skills so as to effectively teach sometimes complex skills. Patience and enthusiasm are vital characteristics of a successful instructor. Instructors must be able to develop their own ideas in directing sports activities and be able to structure courses so as to encourage and teach both beginners and more skilled participants.

A sports instructor must also be able to cope with the realities of having a profession that relies heavily on part-time and seasonal employment. There is little job security for many instructors, especially those who have not developed a reputation or following. If injured, an instructor may lose his or her job.

GOE: 12.01.01; SIC: 7999; SOC: 239

◇ **SOURCES OF ADDITIONAL INFORMATION**

American Alliance for Health, Physical Education, Recreation, and Dance
1900 Association Drive
Reston, VA 22091

American Athletic Trainers Association and Certification Board
660 West Duarte Road
Arcadia, CA 91006

American Sports Education Institute
200 Castlewood Drive
North Palm Beach, FL 33408

National Athletic Trainers Association
1001 East 4th Street
Greenville, NC 27858

◇ **RELATED ARTICLES**

Volume 1: Recreation and Park Services; Sports Careers
Volume 2: Adult and vocational education teachers; Kinesiotherapists; Physical therapists; Professional athletes; Recreation workers; Sports occupations; Teachers, secondary school

---

Sports occupations

Definition

Persons who work in sports-related occupations are concerned with the theoretical and practical aspects of organized athletics. There are many different types of jobs in the field of sports, including coaching, managing, scouting, instructing, and others.

History

No one knows the exact beginnings of sports. Physical activities, such as fishing, hunting and wrestling, have been a necessary part of our survival since primitive times. Sports probably began when various physical activities were undertaken for fun rather than survival. The first organized athletic events occurred around 776 B.C., with the ancient Olympic Games in Greece. The Olympic Games made use of rules, equipment, and scoring devices and laid the framework for many other athletic events. The interest in sports lessened during the Middle Ages, but began to grow again in Europe around A.D. 1200. A hockeylike game known as *la soule*, for example, became very popular in France around this time. Because *la soule* was considered a rough sport, it was discouraged by the authorities. Nevertheless, the sport generated an interest in other games, such as tennis, which became popular in the 1400s.

Between the 1400s and the 1800s, the interest in sports grew, and many countries sponsored competitive events. In England, for example, competitions were held in a variety of sports, including track and field, football, and horse racing.

Beginning in the 1800s and continuing through the early 1900s, sports became very organized. For example, the first organized track and field meet was held in England in 1835. In 1829, the first intercollegiate athletic competition took place, when Oxford and Cambridge Universities held a rowing match.

In the United States, the interest in sports greatly expanded during the 1800s. The English sport of rugby led to the development of American football, and, in 1869, Rutgers and Princeton Universities played the first intercollegiate football game. Many other sports soon followed. Baseball was first played in the United States in 1845, basketball in 1891. Golf and tennis were organized into competitive events soon after, and the first championship boxing match was held in 1892, in New Orleans.

As the popularity of sports grew and expanded, so too did employment opportunities in sports-related occupations. The increasing number and variety of professional sports teams brought a need for coaches, managers, trainers, and scouts. Similarly, high-school and college athletic programs became highly organized and sophisticated, especially during the last several decades, and many new jobs were created. In addition, sports have become one of the most popular pastimes as more and more people are flocking to gyms, health clubs, tennis courts, golf courses, and other recreational settings. These factors and many others have contributed to the growing number of jobs in the sports fields.

Nature of the work

The specific nature of the work in this field varies greatly. Although all workers employed in sports occupations are concerned with the theoretical and practical aspects of athletics, responsibilities range from coaching to managing, from training to instructing, and from scouting to umpiring. Each job has its own requirements; each worker must have the proper training and education for the job.

Athletic coaches, both *head coaches* and *professional athletes coaches*, teach and inspire their players to produce winning teams. They must be very knowledgeable in the basic rules and strategies of the game, and they must be open to new procedures and techniques. Coaches analyze their players' performances by reviewing videotapes and film clips of games; they then identify errors in an attempt to avoid them at future games. Regardless of the sport, athletic coaches are in charge of their teams and are responsible for the teams' win/loss records.

Athletic trainers work with both amateur and professional players, helping them to remain healthy and advising them on how to avoid injuries. Trainers evaluate the physical condition of athletes and recommend certain exercise programs, diets, and equipment. If an injury does occur, the athletic trainer is often responsible for treating it. During a game, trainers may treat cuts and bruises; they may also see that a player with a bad sprain or a broken bone receives proper medical attention. In addition, trainers work with injured players to ensure that they heal and recover properly.

Athlete managers manage the affairs of professional athletes by directing training activities and by negotiating contracts and other business matters.

Umpires and *referees* officiate at various athletic events. They are responsible for enforcing the rules of the game and for calling plays. Their specific duties depend on the sport with which they are associated. Baseball umpires, for example, call balls and strikes, decide whether balls are fair or fowl, determine whether a runner is safe or out, and, in general, ensure that the game is played fairly. Hockey officials, on the other hand, keep track of playing time, call penalties on players, and record the goals that are scored. Each sport has its own rules and regulations that must be enforced if the game is to be played fairly.

Professional sports scouts evaluate the athletic skills of athletes to determine their potential for professional sports.

Sports instructors teach the rules and skills of a particular sport to individuals or to groups. They help beginners learn the basic stances and movements of the game; they also help experienced players sharpen and improve their skills. Instructors advise people on equipment and clothing and teach them basic safety precautions.

Athletes are the participants in a sporting event. Professional athletes receive financial compensation for a competion. Amateur athletes normally do not. (See volume 2: Professional Athletes.)

There are many different types of sports occupations, and new jobs continue to emerge as the popularity of athletics and physical fitness continues to increase.

Members of Wisconsin's football team, the Green Bay Packers, listen attentively to their coach as he reviews a variety of possible plays.

Requirements

Because there are so many different kinds of jobs within the sports field, it would be impossible to write a single set of qualifications applicable to all workers. As far as educational requirements are concerned, there is no one ideal background for a career in sports. Each job has its own requirements.

Athletic trainers, for example, must earn at least a bachelor's degree and should be certified. Umpires and referees must have at least a high-school diploma and should attend a special school for officials in their sport. Coaches and instructors, on the other hand, should have experience as a player in the sport that they coach or teach.

Regardless of the sport, individuals interested in a career in athletics should enjoy and understand the sport they want to work in. They must also be able to handle the mental and physical pressures that are part of competitive athletics.

Special requirements

Some jobs in the sports field require special licenses or permits. Athletic trainers, for example, should earn a certificate from the Athletic Trainers Association (NATA); applicants must pass an extensive exam and must have at least two years of experience under the supervision of a NATA-certified athletic trainer. High-school coaches must be certified teachers; some schools require that they also be certified coaches. Instructors may or may not need special certificates, depending on the sport. Scuba diving instructors, for example, must be trained

and certified by a nationally recognized scuba diving association. Regardless of the specific sport, workers should all possess the physical and mental stamina that is crucial to succeeding in sports occupations.

Opportunities for experience and exploration

Individuals explore careers in sports in many ways. To begin with, high-school and college students should participate in sporting events, either as players, managers, or trainers. Persons interested in a career in sports should learn as much about the sport as possible. Most cities have community sports programs, such as Little League baseball and YMCA athletic programs, and students may opt to volunteer to work with players in these community programs. In general, students should gain as much experience as they can in their specific sport.

Methods of entering

There are various ways to enter the sports field; specific methods of entering depend on the type of position sought and the sport itself. In general, however, participation in the sport is a good way to gain the necessary skills, training, and experience, and it often helps students meet people who can give practical advice on how to prepare for a sports career. Individuals who graduate from college may get assistance from the school placement service.

It is important that students gain as much experience as possible. Volunteering to work with various community sports programs may prove very helpful in helping to secure future employment.

Advancement

Advancement opportunities vary greatly according to the specific job and sport. Coaches, managers, and trainers, for example, may advance from working with an amateur high-school or college team to a professional athletic team. Sports instructors, on the other hand, should actively continue their education and training to advance quickly; well-known instructors may build a larger client base and, ultimately, open their own sports clubs. In general, the advancement opportunities depend on the individual's drive, determination, patience, and abilities.

Many individuals in sports-related occupations add to their earnings by teaching, writing, and endorsing and promoting sports equipment and other products. Some move into management positions; others go into public relations or broadcasting.

Employment outlook

The number of openings in most sports occupations is expected to increase throughout the next decade. The demand for coaches, managers, trainers, umpires, and referees should increase because of the continuing popularity of sports, the population growth, and the rising number of women in sports. Sports instructors should also experience a growing job market, as people continue to pursue physical fitness and recreational activities.

Opportunities in some sports are likely to increase faster than in other sports. Scuba diving, jogging, and gymnastics, for example, have become very popular in recent years. Regardless of the sport, it should be remembered that the total number of openings in sports occupations is lower than in most other industries. In addition, competition for jobs is very strong, especially for jobs with professional sports teams.

Earnings

Salaries vary greatly in the sports world; they depend not only on the experience and education of the employee, but also on the sport and the work environment. Individuals employed by professional teams, for example, earn more than those employed by high schools or colleges. People who work in football or baseball generally earn more than those who work in boxing. And, workers with a college degree may start at a higher salary than workers who do not have one. General salary ranges can, however, be identified for most sports occupations.

In the sports of professional football, basketball, and baseball, head coaches earn between $90,000 and $250,000. College coaches earn around $50,000, although large universities usually pay more; high-school coaches generally earn between $20,000 and $30,000.

Athletic trainers who work for professional baseball, football, basketball, or hockey teams

The manager and the sports physician of a baseball team examine an injured player on the field.

earn from $1,500 to $4,000 per month; some trainers work all year, others only during the playing season. Trainers who work for schools usually earn a teacher's salary plus an additional amount for training; salaries generally range from $12,000 to $30,000.

Major league baseball umpires earn between $22,000 and $50,000, and while traveling receive a small amount of expense money per day; umpires in the rookie leagues earn around $1,000 a month plus expense money; college and high-school umpires earn considerably less. Professional football referees may earn between $300 and $500 for each regular season game; postseason games pay more.

The salaries of sports instructors vary greatly according to the sport and the employer. Sports instructors who have college degrees may earn starting salaries of $10,000 for full-time work, but most instructors do not work full time. Well-known golf instructors may earn very high salaries.

It should be remembered that although professional sports teams generally pay very high salaries, very few people are able to work for pro teams. Most work for schools, amateur teams, or sports clubs.

Conditions of work

Working conditions vary with the sport and the duties of the specific job. People employed in the sports field may work outdoors or indoors, all year long or only during the playing season. In general, however, people who work in sports occupations travel quite extensively, are often under a great deal of pressure, and work

647

long hours. During the playing season, for example, trainers, managers, and coaches usually work seven days a week. In addition, the work is often physically demanding; umpires and referees, for example, often get injured while officiating at games.

On the other hand, people who work in sports occupations usually find their work very interesting and exciting. They also tend to enjoy the challenges and competitiveness that are part of the sports profession.

Social and psychological factors

To be successful in the sports profession, individuals must have the type of temperament and mental outlook that will allow them to handle physical and emotional pressure. Coaches, managers, and umpires must cope with heckling fans, irritated players, and questions from sportswriters and broadcasters. Sports instructors must be patient and understanding to effectively teach their sport to others.

People who work in sports occupations must be intelligent, hardworking, and physically fit. It is important they get proper exercise, rest, and nutrition. A sense of humor and a calm temperament may also prove helpful.

GOE: 12.01.03; SIC: 7999; SOC: 34

◇ **SOURCES OF ADDITIONAL INFORMATION**

The Athletic Institute
200 Castlewood Drive
North Palm Beach, FL 33408

Society of State Directors of Health, Physical Education, and Recreation
9805 Hillridge Drive
Kensington, MD 20895

American Alliance for Health, Physical Education, Recreation, and Dance
1900 Association Drive
Reston, VA 22091

Statisticians

Definition

A *statistician* collects, analyzes, and interprets numerical data in a particular subject-matter field, to provide help to business and governmental officials and professional workers in determining the best way to produce results in their work.

History

One of the first known uses of statistical technique was undertaken in England, in 1854. A disastrous epidemic of cholera broke out in a certain section of London. The usual medical practices of the day were unable to control it. A physician of that time, Dr. John Snow (1813–1858), conducted a survey to discover what sections of the city were affected by the disease. He constructed a map that showed the distribution of the infection, and he was able to interview those who survived the illness to discover some of their accustomed habits. He found that everyone who had contracted the illness had drawn water from a certain pump in the area. When the pump was sealed, the cholera epidemic subsided. This was the first time that it was known definitely that cholera was transmitted through an infected water supply. Once the source was located, cholera could be controlled.

Statistical methods had uncovered a fact that has since saved countless lives.

Statistics as a science was not actually born, however, during Dr. Snow's lifetime. A British scholar, Karl Pearson (1857–1936), is generally conceded to be the father of statistics. He was professor of mathematics at the University of London when, in 1899, he published a book that has proved to be a timeless classic, *The Grammar of Science*. Although his initial interest was in establishing statistical methods, his later interest was in applying those methods to the study of genetics. Thus, it may be said that he was both a mathematical statistician and an applied statistician.

Nature of the work

Statisticians work with numbers and symbols that have a special meaning for them. In many ways, the symbols that they use resemble those of a special language. The symbols serve as a sort of shorthand method to convey rather complex thoughts in a simple manner. When these thoughts must be expressed in everyday English, they take much longer to explain.

Most statisticians work in one of three kinds of jobs: They may teach and do research at a large university, or they may work in a governmental agency (such as the Bureau of Census), or they may work in a business or industry. A few statisticians work in private consulting agencies and sell their services to industrial or governmental organizations. Some statisticians work in well-known public opinion research organizations, to try to discover what most people think about the major issues of the day or even to try to find out which radio or television programs have the largest audiences.

The work of the statistician has been greatly extended by the invention of computers.

There is hardly an endeavor that concerns the welfare of large numbers of people in which the statistician does not work. There are statisticians in the fields of economics, political science, medicine, education, the physical and natural sciences, the space program, communication, agriculture, meteorology, national defense, and transportation.

The statistician works in two major areas of the science. A *mathematical statistician* works primarily with theory, with devising new ways in which statistical method may be applied, and new ways in which the work may be accomplished. Mathematical statisticians use mathematical techniques for designing and improving statistical methods to obtain and interpret numerical information. They are primarily theore-

A statistician and her assistant work together to interpret the data they collected.

ticians, concerned with developing new statistical tools in areas such as probability theory, experimental design, and regression analysis.

The *applied statistician*, on the other hand, works in the present and uses the accepted theories and known formulas to solve pressing present-day problems. He or she uses statistical methods to collect and analyze data in a particular subject-matter field, such as economics, agriculture, psychology, education, public health, demography, physics, or engineering. (*See also* the separate article "Demographers" elsewhere in this volume.) He or she may forecast population growth or economic conditions, estimate crop yield, predict and evaluate the result of a new marketing program, or help engineers and scientists determine the best design for a jet airplane.

In some few cases, the statisticians themselves actually go out and gather the facts. More usually, however, facts are gathered by those who are trained especially in fact-gathering techniques. In the Bureau of Census, for example, statisticians work with material that has been compiled as a result of the efforts of thousands of census takers. When the data is gathered, it is then turned over to the statistician for organization, analysis, and either conclusions or recommendations.

In its simplest form, statistics is a science that organizes many facts into a systematized picture of the data. Numbers are arranged, for instance, from the smallest to the largest; sometimes they are arranged within this system in logical intervals. The statistician may need to determine which number occurs most frequently, what is the average of all of the numbers, which number represents the middle point of all the numbers in the group, or how great is the span from the largest to the smallest number. One may make certain charts, plot the numbers on graph paper, or distribute them along a curve. One may compare one set of numbers to another to discover the similarities and the differences. Each number has a real significance and represents something important to one person or to several people. It is not just an arbitrary figure chosen by whim. Any way in which numbers, sets of numbers, or groups of numbers may be organized to produce new and useful information is the way in which the statistician works to contribute to the store of human knowledge.

Most statisticians work on the basis of a "sampling" technique. This is a method by which the characteristics of the whole population are judged by taking a sample of a part of it.

Requirements

To become a statistician, a student must have achieved at least one college degree. Chances for success are enhanced if he or she has acquired two degrees, or even three. Some positions are open only to those who have a master's degree or a doctorate.

Opinions differ as to the appropriate course of study for the prospective statistician to pursue. Some authorities advise the student to take an undergraduate major in mathematics. Because more than sixty universities offer an undergraduate major in statistics, this is advice that is usually possible to follow. Still other authorities are of the opinion that the wisest course for a student is to major in the subject-matter field in which he or she hopes to work, as in chemistry or psychology. The graduate degrees, then, should be in statistics, so that one will have acquired a deep background of knowledge in both of the professional fields in which one will be working. In the early 1990s, more than one hundred universities offered a master's degree program in statistics, and about eighty had programs leading to a doctorate in statistics.

The high-school student who is interested in entering the field of statistics should elect a college preparatory course that contains as much mathematics and science as possible.

Prospective statisticians should have a strong aptitude and liking for mathematics.

They should be able to think in mathematical concepts, should have above-average intelligence and a strong curiosity that will prompt them to explore any given subject; and should have the ability to be objective and free of preconceived ideas or prejudices.

They should have patience and an ability to tolerate frustration. Also, good eyesight and a good general physical condition are important. They must enjoy detailed work and must like to study and to learn. Interested students should look forward to the prospect of a continuing education and must not feel that seven years of study beyond high school is too great a period of time to devote to learning about their chosen profession. Not every statistician will go the full seven years; an individual may not feel that a doctorate is necessary for his or her particular interests. But all statisticians must consider the possibility of advanced graduate study, whether they decide to pursue it or not.

Special requirements

Some federal or state government jobs may require a civil service examination.

Opportunities for experience and exploration

College students can frequently obtain jobs as student assistants in the offices of faculty members who are engaged in some kind of research. Although these jobs would carry little responsibility for undergraduate students, they would be able to gain some insights into the nature of the research process by observing the professor and the research assistants at work.

A high-school student who is able to secure a part-time or summer job in an industry in which statisticians work will be able to observe how they go about their jobs. If a high-school student can work as a clerk in a business in which there is a data-processing operation, he or she can get some good ideas about the ways in which computers contribute to the functioning of this particular firm and can perhaps draw some inferences about the ways in which statistics contribute to the well-being of the total economy.

High-school students who are enrolled in mathematics courses may ask their teachers to give them some simple statistical problems, perhaps related to grades or student government, and let them practice the kinds of techniques that statisticians use.

A high-school student who is interested in exploring the profession of statistician may visit a local insurance agency, the local office of the Internal Revenue Service, or a nearby college and talk to persons who are either engaged in or have close knowledge of the statistical methods used by their employers.

Related occupations

Statisticians are often classified with others in mathematics occupations. The list of workers who use statistics or mathematics, or both, is extensive and includes the following: actuaries, computer programmers, criminologists, demographers, economists, educators, engineers, environmental scientists, financial analysts, health scientists, information scientists, life scientists, marketing researchers, mathematicians, operations researchers, physical scientists, sociologists, systems analysts, and weight analysts. Persons with an interest in and an aptitude for statistics should be able to establish a career in virtually any field.

Methods of entering

The young person at the bachelor's degree level cannot expect to find as attractive nor as highly paid a job as does the one who has achieved a master's or doctorate. The person with a bachelor's degree will probably find that the job does not carry with it a great deal of responsibility and that the work is largely routine or of a high-clerical nature. One may spend many years in a routine job before one is given greater responsibility, though the salary may be increased at regular intervals.

Most new graduates find positions through their own college placement offices. For those students who are particularly interested in working for a government agency, jobs are listed with the Office of Personnel Management. Some jobs may be obtained only after the successful passing of a civil service examination. Few teaching jobs at the college level may be found unless the young graduate has at least one degree beyond the bachelor's. College teaching jobs are usually obtained by making a direct application to the dean of the school or college in which the statistics department is located.

Advancement

Statisticians who advance most rapidly to positions of responsibility are usually those with advanced degrees. Though it is possible to advance in salary and responsibility with a bachelor's degree, the person who does so must have unusual ability. Most young statisticians enter a job with the rank of junior statistician; if they are in college teaching, they may enter a job with the rank of instructor. After having acquired experience on the job and value to the employer, the statistician may be promoted to a position as high as chief statistician, director of research, or full professor. Advancement usually takes many years, and may be dependent upon the statistician's returning to graduate school or a special technical school in order to achieve a higher level of competency.

Employment outlook

Most of the 18,000 or so statisticians employed in the early 1990s worked in industry (mainly in manufacturing, finance, and insurance companies) and in business service firms (such as consultants' offices). Most of the rest were employed in federal, state, or local government; and some held positions in hospitals, academic institutions, and nonprofit organizations. Jobs for statisticians are concentrated most heavily in large metropolitan areas such as New York, Washington, D.C., Chicago, and Los Angeles but can be found throughout the United States.

Employment in this field is expected to be good through the 1990s, especially for trained statisticians with a background in computer science or with extensive knowledge of a field of application.

There will be a demand for statisticians in many areas. In business, they will be needed to forecast sales, analyze business conditions, modernize accounting procedures, and help solve management problems. In companies that manufacture products such as motor vehicles, food products, and chemicals, they will work on quality control. In pharmaceutical firms, they will assess the effectiveness of a rapidly expanding line of drugs. In research and development, statisticians with a knowledge of engineering and the physical sciences will work with engineers and scientists. In consulting firms, these professionals will provide sophisticated statistical services on a contract basis. And in government agencies, increasing numbers of statisticians will work in fields such as agriculture, consumer and producer surveys, demography, energy conservation, environmental quality control, health, social security, and transportation. The National Institutes of Health and other national medical and science organizations rely on statistical work.

The opportunities for statisticians increase with each level of education. Graduates with a bachelor's degree, especially those with a strong background in mathematics and computer science, will find the best jobs related to their field of study in private industry or government. With the proper certification, they may teach statistics in high schools. Statisticians with a master's degree and a knowledge of computer science will find many openings in private industry in computerized data processing and in research. They are also qualified to teach in junior colleges and small four-year colleges. The employment outlook is exceptionally good for those with doctorates in statistics. These individuals are eagerly sought by large corporations. They are in demand also by colleges and universities, where the trend is to set up separate departments of statistics.

Earnings

In the early 1990s, the federal government paid new graduates with a bachelor's degree starting salaries of about $14,800 to $18,400 a year, depending on their academic records. Beginning statisticians with a master's degree received $22,500 or $27,200; and those with a doctorate received $27,200 or $32,600. The overall average for statisticians in the federal government was about $39,400 a year.

Earnings for statisticians in private industry are generally somewhat higher than those paid by the federal government. In the early 1990s, the average starting salary ranged from $20,000 to $25,000 a year for statisticians with a bachelor's degree and $25,000 for those with graduate degrees. Statisticians in top posts earned from $50,000 to $90,000 a year.

Statisticians who enter college and university teaching can expect to earn salaries comparable to those of other faculty members. The compensation level usually varies depending on faculty rank and the type of institution. In the early 1990s, colleges and universities paid average salaries that ranged from approximately $21,300 a year for instructors to about $45,500 for full professors. In addition, as college and university teachers gain experience, they may earn additional income from extra work as a consultant, an author, or as the director of some outside research project.

Conditions of work

Most statisticians work under pleasant circumstances. The employee of government or industry usually has a desk job in a well-appointed, well-lighted, and temperature-controlled office. Often, the statistician will have some responsibility for the supervision of other statisticians of a lower rank or grade, or clerical personnel. Except under unusual circumstances, one will work a forty-hour week and will have an annual vacation and other benefits, such as sick leave and group insurance.

Those who choose to teach at the college level should enjoy the association of students and the customary stimulating atmosphere of a college campus.

Social and psychological factors

The statistician is a respected professional member of any community who associates with others with similar interests. Most of the work done after hours will consist of reading current professional books and journals to keep abreast of new developments in this rapidly changing field.

GOE: 11.01.02; SIC: Any industry; SOC: 1733

◇ **SOURCES OF ADDITIONAL INFORMATION**

American Statistical Association
1429 Duke Street
Alexandria, VA 22314

Institute of Mathematical Statistics
3401 Investment Boulevard
Suite 7
Hayward, CA 94545

National Council of Teachers of Mathematics
1906 Association Drive
Reston VA 22091

Society for Industrial and Applied Mathematics
1400 Architects Building
117 South 17th Street
Philadelphia, PA 19103

For information on educational and employment opportunities in statistics and related fields, write:

Association for Women in Mathematics
Careers information
Education Department
Box 178
Wellesley College
Wellesley, MA 02181

◇ **RELATED ARTICLES**

Volume 1: Computer Hardware; Computer Software; Mathematics
Volume 2: Actuaries; Demographers; Mathematicians; Operations research analysts
Volume 3: Statistical clerks
Volume 4: Mathematical technicians

Surveyors

Definition

Surveyors make exact measurements and locations of elevations, points, lines, and contours on or near the earth's surface. They measure the distances between points to determine property boundaries and to provide data for mapmaking, construction projects, and other engineering purposes.

History

In early civilizations, people needed to determine their property lines. Although the methods of these tribal organizations were crude, they marked the recognition of individual and group ownership and established a basis for the development of law and order. Landholding became even more important in the Egyptian civilization, and with the development of hieroglyphics, people were then able to keep a record of their holdings. Eventually, nations found it necessary to establish boundaries, and people found it necessary not only to mark property lines and borderlines but also to lay out and record their principal means of commerce and transportation. Records of the Babylonians tell of their canals and irrigation ditches. The Romans surveyed and mapped the principal roads of their empire. As the United States expanded from the Atlantic to the Pacific, and as people poured over the mountains and plains into the uncharted regions of the West, they found it necessary to mark their routes and to establish their new land ownership by surveying and filing claims.

Whether for the location of a trail, highway, or road; the site of a log cabin, frame house, or skyscraper; the right-of-way for water pipes, drainage ditches, or telephone lines; or for the charting of unexplored regions, bodies of water, land, or underground mines,—people have recognized the need for precise and accurate geographical measurements. Through the years we have improved our ability to establish exact locations and to measure points on the surface of the earth, from the deepest point in the ocean to mountain tops. This has been, and will continue to be, the work of the surveyor.

Nature of the work

The *surveyor's party chief* and party are usually the first workers to be involved in any job requiring the precise determination of points, locations, lines, or elevations. Thus, on proposed construction projects superhighways, airstrips, housing developments, bridges it is the surveyor's responsibility to make the necessary measurements by conducting an accurate and detailed survey of the area.

The surveyor usually works with a field party consisting of several persons. *Instrument assistants* handle a variety of surveying instruments including the theodolite, transit, level, surveyor's chain, rod, and different types of electronic equipment used to measure distance or locate a position. In the course of the survey, it is important that all readings be accurately recorded and that field notes be maintained so that the survey can be checked for accuracy by the surveyor.

Working on a construction site, a surveyor determines the property boundaries before breaking ground for the new building.

As is true in many careers, surveyors can specialize. They may become expert in one or more particular types of surveying.

A *land surveyor* establishes township, property, and other tract-of-land boundary lines. Using maps, notes, or actual land title deeds, one surveys the land, checking the accuracy of existing records. This information is used to prepare legal documents such as deeds and leases. *Land surveying managers* coordinate the work of land surveyors and their survey parties with that of legal, engineering, architectural, and other staff involved with the project. In addition, these managers develop policy, prepare budgets, certify work upon completion, and handle numerous other administrative duties.

A highway surveyor establishes points, grades, lines, and other points of reference for highway construction projects. This survey information is essential to the work of the engineers and the construction crews that will actually plan and build the new highway.

A *geodetic surveyor* measures such large masses of land, sea, or space that the measurements must take into account the curvature of the earth and its geophysical characteristics. This person's work is helpful in establishing points of reference for smaller land surveys, for determining national boundaries, and in preparing maps. *Geodetic computers* calculate latitude, longitude, angles, areas, and other information needed for mapmaking. They work from field notes made by an engineering survey party using reference tables and a calculating machine or computer.

A *marine surveyor* makes surveys of harbors, rivers, and other bodies of water. This person determines the depth of the water, usually by taking soundings or sound measurements, in relation to land masses. These surveys are essential in planning navigation projects; in developing plans for and constructing breakwaters, dams, piers, marinas, and bridges; or in constructing nautical charts and maps.

A *mine surveyor* makes surface and underground surveys, preparing maps of mines and mining operations. Such maps are helpful in examining underground passages on and between levels and in assessing the strata and volume of raw material available.

A *geophysical prospecting surveyor* locates and marks sites considered likely to contain petroleum deposits. *Oil-well directional surveyors* use sonic, electronic, or nuclear measuring instruments to gauge the characteristics of earth formations in boreholes from which they evaluate the productivity of oil- or gas-bearing reservoirs. A *pipeline surveyor* determines rights-of-way for oil pipeline construction projects. This surveyor establishes the right-of-way, property lines, and assembles the information essential to the preparation for and laying of the lines.

A *photogrammetric engineer* determines the contour of an area to show elevations and depressions, and indicates such features as mountains, lakes, rivers, forests, roads, farms, buildings, and other landmarks. Aerial, land, or water photographs used in their work are taken with special photographic equipment installed in the airplane or ground station that permits pictures of large areas to be made. From these pictures accurate measurements of the terrain and of surface features can be made. These surveys are helpful in highway and engineering planning and in the preparation of topographical maps. Photogrammetry, as photo surveying is termed, is particularly helpful in charting areas that are inaccessible or difficult to travel.

Requirements

Either graduation from high school or an associate degree is considered a basic requirement for most opportunities in surveying of a professional or technical nature. Mathematics, including as many courses in algebra, geometry, and trigonometry as possible, is most important. In addition, physics, mechanical drawing, and other related science or drafting courses should be taken.

If one is interested in the professional level, a four-year college program is recommended and often required. In college, one should pursue a program leading to a bachelor's degree in surveying or engineering. Civil engineering, with a surveying emphasis, is a common major selected by students wishing to become surveyors because the two fields are so closely allied.

For those who are interested in technical but not professional positions, opportunities for training beyond high school are available in a number of junior colleges, technical institutes, and specialized schools. These programs range from one to three years and usually offer technical courses in engineering and surveying and include learning how to use surveying instruments. A program of this type in surveying would prepare a student for a position as a surveying technician at the end of two years. Some enter the field immediately after high school by securing a position in which on-the-job training is provided. This experience is supplemented by taking courses in surveying.

For persons planning a career in the more specialized branches of surveying, such as geodesy, topography, or photogrammetry, a bachelor's degree in engineering or the physical sciences is required. Included would be courses in the specific branch of surveying in which they are interested. For advancements in the highly technical areas, graduate study is especially desirable.

Personal qualifications that might be considered include one's interests, abilities, personal temperament, and physical capacities.

Because the surveyor spends a great deal of time in field surveys, an interest in working outdoors is necessary. Surveying involves working with other people and often requires directing or supervising the work of others. A surveyor must, therefore, have leadership qualities for supervisory positions.

The ability to work with numbers and to perform mathematical computations accurately and quickly is very important, as is the ability to understand words and ideas and to use them effectively. Other abilities that are helpful in surveying work include the ability to visualize and understand objects in two or three dimensions (spatial relationships) and the ability to discriminate between and compare shapes, sizes, lines, shadings, and other forms (form perception).

As a member of a survey party in the field or as a self-employed surveyor, one should be in good health and be able to negotiate all types of terrain—the rugged, mountainous, densely covered areas as well as the flat, open fields and plains. In their work, surveyors, do a great deal of walking and are on their feet much of the time. They may also have to carry equipment over all types of terrain. Their eyesight needs to be very good because they communicate with their fellow workers a great deal with hand and arm movements. Their hearing likewise should be good as they must also communicate by shouting, sometimes over great distances. In either case, instructions must be given loudly and precisely and must be seen or heard clearly and accurately. Endurance, coordination and the ability to compensate for physical impairment are the more important physical assets to be desired in the surveyor.

Special requirements

All fifty states require that land surveyors making property and boundary surveys be licensed or registered. The requirements for state licensure vary from state to state, but in general they include one of the following: be a college graduate with two to four years of experience; have at least six years' experience and be able to pass an examination in land surveying; or have at least ten years' experience. Information on the specific requirements can be obtained by contacting the appropriate state agency in the capital of the state in which one wishes to work. Those who seek employment in the federal government will have to take a civil service examination and must meet the educational, experience, and other specified requirements for the type and level of position in which they are interested.

Opportunities for experience and exploration

One of the best opportunities for experience is to seek a summer job with a construction outfit or a company that is planning survey work. This may be private or government work. Even if the job does not involve direct contact with survey crews, it will offer an opportunity to observe them at work and to talk informally with them about surveying.

Some colleges have work-study programs that will permit periodic on-the-job experiences. These opportunities, like summer and part-time jobs, can be beneficial to the person who is considering this field as a career.

Related occupations

Occupations closely related to that of surveyors and cartographers (mapmakers) include cartographic drafters, map editors, mapping supervisors, mosaicists, and photogrammetric engineers. Prospective surveyors may also want to consider the work of civil engineers, construction managers, geographers, geologists, forest technicians, land developers, landscape architects, real estate appraisers, soil scientists, and urban planners.

Methods of entering

Some people get jobs as instrument assistants with a surveying firm. The graduate of an engineering school, a technical institute, or a four-year college will find the placement service of their institution to be very helpful in arranging for necessary examinations or interviews. In many cities there are employment agencies that specialize in positions in surveying and related fields.

Advancement

On-the-job training programs over a period of time will provide an instrument assistant with a variety of experiences. As one gains experience, one can advance to positions of greater responsibility and eventually to chief of party or surveyor. The latter is difficult without more formal education beyond high school. Steps are being taken by some of the professional engineering and surveying associations to upgrade the requirements for registration or licensure as a land surveyor. One of the requirements being considered is an engineering school education. If this action is taken, it will be nearly impossible for the young person who enters the field directly after high school to advance to higher level or professional positions.

Graduates of junior college and technical institute programs can enter the field immediately as instrument assistants and secure positions as surveyor aides, instrument operators, computers, observers, recorders, plane-table operators, and a host of other jobs with a surveying crew. These graduates are viewed as the technicians of the field and with experience can move to higher level positions. Graduates of these two- and three-year programs may transfer to degree-granting engineering programs. Some survey workers choose to work for a year or two before going ahead with their formal education; others make the transfer immediately.

There are many who believe that surveying has been too long isolated from engineering, and that land surveying is engineering. With the increasing requirement of an engineering degree for entrance to surveying in several states, it will be easier to transfer to a larger number of related positions. Although a surveying or civil engineering program is recommended for a prospective surveyor, one could major in electrical, mechanical, or chemical engineering. Drafting is another related field to which a surveyor might move.

Employment outlook

In the early 1990s, nearly half of the estimated 50,000 surveyors in the United States were employed in engineering, architectural, and surveying firms. Federal, state, and local government agencies employed about one-fourth, and most of the rest worked for construction companies, oil and gas extraction companies, and public utilities. Approximately 8,000 surveyors were self-employed.

The employment outlook in surveying through the end of the 1990s is expected to be fairly good. In view of the pressure for preparation in engineering as a prerequisite for professional status and licensure, opportunities will favor those who have college degrees or junior college certificates.

Some of the factors that are expected to increase the demand for surveyors are growth in urban and suburban areas, with new streets, homes, shopping centers, schools, gas and water lines requiring property and boundary line surveys; expanding state and federal highway improvement programs; increasing number of urban redevelopment programs; expansion of industrial and business firms and the relocation of some firms in large undeveloped tracts; and increasing demand for land and nautical maps and charts. Many such projects, however, can be canceled or postponed during times of economic stress; openings for surveyors, therefore, are dependent in part on the state of the national and local economy.

Although the new electronic equipment and devices are reducing the time necessary to complete land surveys, it is not expected that they will reduce the number of job opportunities available. The new equipment being introduced in surveying may result in the necessity for additional training, however, particularly at the technician or instrument worker level.

Earnings

The federal government hired high-school graduates as surveyor helpers at about $10,800 per year in the early 1990s, while high-school graduates with one year of related training earned almost a thousand dollars more. Students graduating with an associate degree in surveying were hired as instrument assistants at about $13,300 per year. Surveying technicians averaged $18,300 annually. The federal government hired land surveyors at $14,800 to $18,400 per year, depending on their qualifications. The average salary for all land surveyors in the federal government was $29,900.

In private industry, beginning salaries were comparable to those offered by the federal government, according to the limited information available.

Most positions with the federal, state, and local governments and with private firms provide the usual medical, pension, insurance benefits, and vacation and holiday periods.

Conditions of work

The surveyor works the usual forty-hour week except when overtime is necessary to complete a survey so that a project can be started immediately. The peak work period for the surveyor comes during the summer months when weather conditions are most favorable. It is not uncommon, however, for the surveyor to be exposed to all types of weather conditions.

Some survey projects involve a certain amount of hazard, depending upon the region and the climate as well as the plant and animal life. Field survey crews encounter snakes, poison ivy, and other plant and animal life; they are subject to heat exhaustion, sunburn, and frostbite. Some survey projects, particularly those being conducted near construction projects or busy highways, impose the dangers of injury from heavy traffic, flying objects, and other accidental hazards. Much of the surveying of vast lands and large mountain formations is beginning to be done with satellite technology. So remote area studies may become less frequent. However, small areas of study will be more cost-effective when surveyed by teams on the ground. Unless the surveyor is employed for office assignments, where the working conditions are similar to those of other office workers, the work location quite likely will change from survey to survey. Some assignments may necessitate being away from home for varying periods of time.

Social and psychological factors

Surveying offers a great deal of opportunity for the adventurous type—travel, change, and exploration. One can secure positions that require extensive travel to new places and exposure to varied conditions of living, from field campsites to hotel accommodations. The surveyor, as he or she moves from one location to another, can find a certain uniqueness to each assignment. Each survey represents a break from the routine and offers an opportunity to open new areas for mankind to develop. In this sense, the surveyor becomes explorer.

For people who see themselves as non-office types, this line of work offers the capacity to be outdoors more frequently than most other occupations.

GOE: 05.03.01; SIC: 8713; SOC: 1649

◇ SOURCES OF ADDITIONAL INFORMATION

American Congress on Surveying and Mapping
210 Little Falls Street
Falls Church, VA 22046

American Society of Photogrammetry and Remote Sensing
210 Little Falls Street
Falls Church, VA 22046

◇ RELATED ARTICLES

Volume 1: Construction; Engineering
Volume 2: Cartographers; Engineers; Geographers; Geologists; Geophysicists; Mathematicians
Volume 4: Civil engineering technicians; Geological technicians; Surveying and mapping technicians

Systems analysts

Definition

Systems analysts do the planning, scheduling, and coordination of activities required to develop methods of processing data. They obtain solutions to complex business, scientific, or engineering problems. Although any system can be developed to run manually or mechanically, the definition of *systems analyst* has come to include only those who make use of electronic computers to process data.

History

The computer is an elaborate counting machine, and counting machines have been with us since the Chinese developed the abacus 3,000 years ago. Slide rules and even hourglasses are considered computers in a rudimentary sense.

The first mechanical calculator, and adding machine, was invented by the French mathematician philosopher, Blaise Pascal, around 1642. Later that century in Germany, Gottfried Leibniz devised a machine that was able to multiply and divide as well. But the drawback to these calculators was that every operation had to be performed by someone punching a key or moving a register.

Not until the mid-nineteenth century did Charles Babbage, an English inventor, think of a way of "programming" a machine to do a series of tasks automatically. Babbage's Difference Engine could take a problem, calculate results, store instructions and intermediate results, and print out final answers. Although it was too costly to be manufactured in quantity—only one small model was ever built—the Difference Engine supplied the basis for the Automatic Sequence Controlled Calculator built by Dr. Howard Aiken in 1944. It was a combination of electrical and mechanical parts, and changes in wiring made possible its use on many kinds of problems.

John Mauchley and J. P. Eckert completed work on the first completely electronic computer, called ENIAC, in 1946. Since then, succeeding "generations" of computers have been introduced, each more sophisticated electronically than the last. Volume 1 articles, Computer Hardware and Computer Software, explain the advances.

Nature of the work

Systems analysts are instrumental in business's shift from manual and mechanical methods of doing accounting, payroll, and the like. With the assistance of department managers or specialists in the function, they determine the exact nature of the data-processing problem, and then structure the answer so that the results can be gained more efficiently by a computer. Systems analysts prepare charts, tables, and diagrams to describe the flow of information and the steps necessary to make it flow. This may involve various techniques such as cost accounting, sampling, and mathematical methods as analytical tools.

After the system has been devised, systems analysts often recommend the type of equipment to be used and prepare instructions for the programmers. Finally, they may interpret results and translate them into terms understandable to management. Because of the number and complexity of data-processing assignments, systems analysts tend to specialize. Some deal only with problems in accounting and inventory control; others limit themselves to such problems as determining the flight path of a space vehicle or planning and forecasting sales.

Systems engineers help clients determine the type of equipment needed to provide the data-processing capabilities they require. They may recommend purchasing new computers and related equipment or modifying existing equipment to accomplish the task.

Computer applications engineers prepare mathematical models of scientific and engineering problems, then draw data flow charts of the mathematical steps required to solve them and set up analog or hybrid computer systems to obtain the solutions. *Engineering analysts* develop mathematical models of technical problems to be solved by digital computer.

Information scientists design systems for collecting, organizing, interpreting, classifying, and retrieving information stored in a computer.

Requirements

There is no universally acceptable way of preparing for work in systems analysis. Some employers request that candidates have a bachelor's degree and experience in mathematics, science, engineering, accounting, or business; others stress graduate work in one of these fields. An increasing number of employers look for those with degrees in computer sciences, information sciences, or data processing. Specialization often means that employers will seek out systems analysts who are trained to handle certain types of problems. Thus someone with a background in business administration will likely be asked to work in financial data processing.

Special requirements

Developing new analytical techniques is called "advanced" systems design and usually requires a strong background in science, mathematics, or engineering.

Certification is not a requirement for systems analysts, but it is valued as an indication of experience and professional competence. The Institute for Certification of Computer Professionals confers the designations Certified Data Processor and Certified Systems Professional on candidates who have five years' experience and successfully complete a five-part examination.

Opportunities for experience and exploration

Computer programming is a good introduction to systems analysis. Many secondary schools offer at least a basic course in computer programming, and some work in cooperation with such businesses as banks and insurance companies to involve students more deeply. A young person can also learn to use electronic data-processing equipment through home study courses offered by colleges and computer manufacturers. And summer or part-time clerical jobs may afford the opportunity to gain an introduction to computers.

Related occupations

Systems analysts use logic and reasoning ability to solve problems, as do actuaries, computer programmers, engineers, financial analysts, mathematicians, operations research analysts, scientists, and urban planners.

Methods of entering

Most employers prefer to hire people as systems analysts who have had some experience in computer programming. Once on the job, prospective systems analysts can further their knowledge of computers through courses given by their company or by computer manufacturers. In the government, for example, systems analysts begin their careers as programmers. After gaining some experience, they may become systems analyst trainees.

Advancement

In large electronic data-processing departments, a person who begins as a junior systems analyst may be promoted to the position of field or lead systems analyst. Those with proven managerial abilities may take over administrative duties, making them responsible for overall systems design or for assignment to other analysts to various phases of a project. As electronic data processing has taken on greater importance in recent years, systems analysts have been promoted out of their specialty and into broader managerial duties, where their knowledge helps with corporate decisions.

Employment outlook

Systems analysts are employed by the full gamut of American industry. In the early 1990s, about 331,000 systems analysts were employed by insurance companies, manufacturing concerns, banks, wholesale and retail businesses, and various branches of the federal and state government. In addition, a growing number of systems analysts work for universities and independent service organizations that furnish computer time to businesses on a fee basis.

There should be no shortage of systems analysts' positions throughout the 1990s. Indeed, even though the profession is one of the fastest growing, employers have found it difficult to hire qualified people. What they have found is intense competition for persons with systems analyst backgrounds from the fields of science and mathematics. The demand for systems analysts will be fueled by rapid expansion of electronic data processing in most businesses, telecommunications, scientific research, utilities, and government and by the increasing sophistication and complexity of computers. The upward mobility of systems analysts, many of whom are graduating to management positions, means a number of other openings to be filled.

College graduates with a background in computer programming, systems analysis, and other data-processing subjects who also have some training or experience in an applied field will be most in demand. Job applicants without a degree and college graduates with no data-processing knowledge will have difficulty competing for positions as systems analysts.

Earnings

The median beginning salary of systems analysts in private industry ranged from about $27,000 to $32,000 a year in the early 1990s. Experienced systems analysts earned between $36,000 and $48,000; systems managers and computing systems directors, between $50,000 and $75,000 a year.

Salaries for systems analysts currently are highest in the Northeast and lowest in the Midwest. In addition, they tend to be highest in mining and public utilities and lowest in finance, insurance, and real estate.

In the early 1990s, the federal government paid entry-level salaries of about $18,000 a year for college graduates with a bachelor's degree. The average for all systems analysts in federal government was about $32,700.

Conditions of work

Systems analysts work the forty-hour week of professional and office employees. Unlike many of those involved with the computer, such as console operators, who work one of two or three shifts, systems analysts are on the job only during the day, although an occasional rush project or emergency may call for their presence on weekends or evenings. The environment of computer installations includes quiet, clean, well-maintained surroundings. Systems analysts are bothered by little more than the clutter of paperwork.

Social and psychological factors

Systems analysts are a breed apart from most employees, even those with technical back-

grounds. They have been initiated to the world of computers; the others have not. As a result, systems analysts must be prepared to deal with either awe or distrust on the part of their fellow workers. Neither situation is healthy, and in fact the former usually breeds the latter. Top management often considers systems analysts as saviors of a troubled business and expects too much of them and their "electronic brains." It is thus not unusual for systems analysts to have a heightened sense of "corporate politics." The rewards are great, however, both in position and sense of accomplishment, for systems analysts who can significantly improve aspects of their employer's operations. And this much is within their power.

GOE: 11.01.01; SIC: Any industry; SOC: 1712

◇ **SOURCES OF ADDITIONAL INFORMATION**

American Federation of Information Processing Societies
1899 Preston White Drive
Reston, VA 22091

Association for Systems Management
24587 Bagley Road
Cleveland, OH 44138

Data Processing Management Association
505 Busse Highway
Park Ridge, IL 60068

◇ **RELATED ARTICLES**

Volume 1: Banking and Financial Services; Computer Hardware; Computer Software; Insurance
Volume 2: Computer programmers; Data base managers; Mathematicians
Volume 3: Computer and peripheral equipment operators; Data entry clerks
Volume 4: Data-processing technicians; Semiconductor-development technicians; Scientific and business data-processing technicians; Software technicians

Taxidermists

Definition

Taxidermists preserve animal skins and parts to assemble stuffed replicas of the animal for show. Taxidermists prepare the underpadding and mounting that the skin will be attached to. They model the structure to resemble the animal's body, and then attach the skin, fur, feathers, or other covering to the structure to make a realistic looking model of the original animal. The animals may be for private or public display; museums frequently use creations from taxidermists to display rare, exotic, or extinct animals.

History

Animal tanning and skin preservation has been practiced over the millennia for clothing, decoration, and weapons. The American Indians used tanned hides to make their tents. Trophies from hunts of dangerous animals were often worn to display the bravery of the hunter. Tanning methods included stringing skins up to dry, scraping them, and perhaps soaking them in water with tannins from leaves. The animal skins were preserved for many different purposes, but not specifically from interest in the natural sciences until the eighteenth century.

During the eighteenth century, tanning methods were improved. Displaying the skin on models stuffed with hay or straw became popular for museums and private collections. With improvements in display models and tanning techniques, realistic poses were done with the models. Eventually backgrounds were added to the display areas in museums to show the habitat of the animal.

By the nineteenth century, taxidermy was a recognized discipline for museum workers. In Paris, Maison Verreaux became the chief supplier of exhibit animals. Carl Akeley (1864–1926), working for Ward's Natural Science Establishment in New York, brought the techniques to the taxidermists that are still used today. He mastered taxidermic techniques that allowed for realistic modeling of large animals such as bears, lions, and elephants. His works are still on display in the Chicago Field Museum of Natural History and the New York Natural History Museum.

Nature of the work

Taxidermists use a variety of methods to create realistic, lifelike models of birds and animals. Although specific processes and techniques vary, most taxidermists follow a series of basic steps in their work.

First, they must remove the skin from the carcass of the animal with special knives, scissors, and pliers. The skin must be removed very carefully to preserve the natural state of the fur or feathers. Once the skin is removed, it is preserved with a special solution.

Some taxidermists still make the body foundation, or skeleton, of the animal. These foundations are made with a variety of materials, including clay, plaster, burlap, papier-mache, wire mesh, and glue. In recent years, however, thanks to modern technology, several taxidermy supply companies have developed lifelike mannequins to be used as the foundation for fish, birds, and fur-bearing animals. These are made in various sizes so the taxidermist may simply take measurements of the specimen to be mounted and order the proper size from the supplier. The taxidermist uses special adhesives or modeling clay to attach the skin to the foundation or mannequin. Then artificial eyes, teeth, and tongues are attached. Sometimes taxidermists use special techniques to enhance the final appearance of the specimen.

Many taxidermists work for museums, creating models of animals for exhibits; others work for various private companies that serve hunters and fishers. Some taxidermists are self-employed. Taxidermists may work with a variety of animal types, including one-cell organisms, large game animals, birds, fish, and reptiles. They may make models of extinct species of animals; they may mount animals on trophies for fishers and hunters.

The specific work often depends on where the taxidermist is employed, including the geographic location. In addition, museum work often differs from commercial work. Regardless of the specific employment setting, new techniques in the art and science of taxidermy continue to be developed and used.

Requirements

To be successful taxidermists, students should have good manual dexterity, a general knowl-

Two taxidermists add the final touches to a recently preserved and mounted fox.

edge of animal anatomy, and training in the taxidermy processes. In the United States, there are six schools that offer courses in taxidermy; these schools are located in Anchorage, Alaska; Louisville, Kentucky; Baton Rouge, Louisiana; Canandaigua, New York; Roxboro, North Carolina; and Janesville, Wisconsin. High-school courses in art, biology, shop, and woodworking may also be helpful.

Few museums hire full-time taxidermists; instead, most museums contract the services of commercial taxidermists. Therefore, most taxidermists who work full-time in museums have additional skills and training and have taken special courses in museum-related subjects.

Special requirements

Taxidermists are required to be licensed in most states. Specific licensing requirements vary from state to state. Many taxidermists choose to become members in various professional associations, such as the National Taxidermists Association, the American Association of Museums, the International Guild of Taxidermy, and their home state's taxidermy association.

Opportunities for experience and exploration

Because taxidermy is a very specialized occupation, there are few opportunities for part-time or summer work. Students may learn more about the profession, however, by visiting local museums; museum employees should

be able to provide information on how to prepare for a career as a museum taxidermist. In addition, students can write to the schools, some of which are listed at the end of this article, that offer courses in taxidermy.

Related occupations

Individuals attracted to the field of taxidermy may also be interested in some of the following occupations, depending on which aspect of taxidermy they find most compatible: biologists, dog groomers, funeral directors and embalmers, leather tanning and finishing workers, museum occupations, painters and sculptors, veterinarians, and zoo keepers.

Methods of entering

Taxidermy is a profession that requires expertise. Workers should not attempt to enter the market until they have been adequately trained in methods and techniques. Jobs are difficult to find, because most taxidermists are self-employed and prefer to do the work themselves. Beginning taxidermists usually operate out of their home or garage on a part-time basis until they can develop enough customers to open a professional studio.

Jobs in museums are often difficult to obtain: applicants should have a background in both taxidermy and general museum studies. Taxidermy schools train their students to become self-employed but sometimes are able to offer job placement.

Advancement

Advancement opportunities are good for taxidermists with the proper skills, education, and experience. Taxidermists who can work on a wide range of projects will have the best chances of advancing. Workers employed in museums may advance to positions with greater responsibility and higher pay. Experienced taxidermists may open their own shops.

Employment outlook

The job outlook for taxidermists should be fairly good over the next decade. Although jobs in museums may be scarce, the demand for hunting and fishing trophies continues to provide work for taxidermists. In addition, many educational institutions actively seek models of animal and bird species that are nearing extinction. Talented taxidermists who can take on a variety of projects should be able to find steady employment.

Earnings

The earnings of salaried taxidermists depend on training and experience. Beginning workers often are paid only minimum wage, while experienced taxidermists generally have salaries ranging in the teens. The earnings of self-employed taxidermists vary greatly according to the number of hours worked, the geographic location, and the types of projects undertaken. Experienced taxidermists who are highly skilled in all areas of taxidermy and situated in a good geographic location can earn $25,000 a year or more.

Conditions of work

Most taxidermists work forty hours a week, although overtime is not uncommon during certain times of the year. Taxidermists who have their own shops may have to work long hours, especially when first starting out.

Taxidermy is hard work. Workers must often work with strong-smelling chemicals and sharp tools. In addition, animal carcasses may be diseased. Therefore, taxidermists must be willing to put up with occasional inconveniences in their work.

Social and psychological factors

Taxidermy is an art, and workers should have basic artistic ability. They should also have a basic knowledge of the anatomy of animals; models should be as realistic and lifelike as possible.

Taxidermists are highly skilled artists. They should be creative and imaginative. They pro-

vide an important service to the general public. As more people become aware of the interdependence of all life forms, the work of the taxidermist will continue to be appreciated and valued.

GOE: 01.06.02; SIC: 7699; SOC: 399

◇ **SOURCES OF ADDITIONAL INFORMATION**

American Institute of Taxidermy
3232 McCormick Drive
Janesville, WI 53545

Fin, Feather, Fur School of Taxidermy
515 DuPree Drive
Jacksonville, AR 72076

National Taxidermists Association
18626 St. Clair Avenue
Cleveland, OH 44110

Piedmont Technical College
College Drive
PO Box 1197
Roxboro, NC 27573

Professional-Taxidermist School of Louisville
7715 Dominique
Louisville, KY 40228

Southland School of Taxidermy
2603 Osceola Street
Baton Rouge, LA 70805

◇ **RELATED ARTICLES**

Volume 1: Biological Sciences
Volume 2: Biologists; Commercial artists; Museum occupations; Painters and sculptors
Volume 4: Biological specimen technicians; Museum technicians

Teachers, kindergarten and elementary school

Definition

Kindergarten teachers teach children from four to six years old obedience, cleanliness, punctuality, and cooperation. The teachers help the pupils develop confidence by participation in games. They train the children to use their hands to make simple objects, and they develop natural aptitudes by furnishing the children with music, poetry, various art objects, and material for modeling and drawing. These teachers also introduce their pupils to science, numbers, language, and social studies. They may discuss various problems of the children with their parents.

Elementary school teachers instruct pupils in rural or urban communities. These teachers work up a teaching outline, give lectures relative to the lesson, keep class attendance records, and assign and hear lessons. They usually work with one group of pupils during the entire school day, teaching several subjects and supervising such various activities as lunch and play periods.

History

Friedrich Froebel, a German educator, founded the first kindergarten in 1837. The first kindergarten (a German word that means "child's garden") was opened in Blankenburg, Germany. When it proved successful, Froebel established others throughout the country. He also taught adults how to conduct kindergartens.

One of the students of Froebel, Mrs. Carl Schurz emigrated to the United States. In 1855 she opened the first U.S. kindergarten in a small community at Watertown, Wisconsin, for the children of her fellow German immigrants.

Five years later, an English-speaking kindergarten was established in Boston by Elizabeth Peabody. Both of these kindergartens were private schools. The first public school kindergarten was started in St. Louis in 1873.

The history of elementary education goes much further back. The people of Judah established schools for young children within synagogues about 100 B.C., as part of the children's religious training.

In the early days of elementary education, the teacher had only to have completed elementary school himself to be considered qualified to teach. There was little incentive for an elementary school teacher to seek further education. School terms were generally short (about six months); the school building was often small, poorly heated, and badly lighted. Many elementary schools combined the entire eight grades into one room, and the course of study was the same for everyone. The teacher was not well paid and had little status or recognition in the community.

When it began to be realized that teachers should have had the advantage of education, the normal school was established. The first normal school, opened in Concord, Vermont, in 1823, was a private school. The first state-supported normal school was established in Lexington, Massachusetts, in 1839. By 1900, nearly every state had at least one state-supported normal school.

The forerunner of the present-day college or school of education in large universities was the "Normal Department" that was established at Indiana University in 1852. Today, normal schools have given way to teachers' colleges, and almost every university in the country has a school or college of education.

There is now no qualitative difference between the education of the elementary school teacher and the secondary school teacher. As more has been learned about child growth and development, it has become obvious that no teacher can serve the elementary age group with indifferent training.

Nature of the work

Kindergarten teachers usually work with two groups of students, teaching two classes a day. Some may teach only one group all day, however. After school, hours will usually be spent planning the next day's work, studying and preparing the children's school records, conferring either with parents or professional personnel about individual children, and participating in teachers' in-service activities.

Elementary school teachers usually teach a grade between one and six. In some school systems, however, grades seven and eight are also classified as elementary grades. In such school systems, a teacher placed in one of these two grades would also be considered an elementary school teacher. In some of the smaller schools grades are combined. The teacher may be assigned to grades one and two, or grades four, five, and six. There are still a few one-room, one-teacher elementary schools in remote rural areas.

In the average school system, the elementary teacher instructs approximately twenty to thirty children who are in the same grade. This person will teach all subjects in the prescribed course of study, and may supervise play periods, rest periods, and lunch periods. Not all school programs are standard; there are many variations on the nature of an elementary teacher's job. In some schools, there are art and music teachers, and the regular teacher is not expected to prepare lessons in those areas. There may also be playground supervisors, who relieve the teacher of the necessity of teaching outdoor games.

Recent developments in elementary school curricula have led to experimental programs in such areas as the ungraded primary, where one teacher is responsible for teaching all children the basic skills. Children may stay in one teacher's room for the average time required to master the content of the first three grades. On the other hand, they may master their basic skills in less time and move into the fourth grade program. Some children may need extra time to master the fundamental skills, and may remain with their original teacher for a longer period than three years. A child moves at his or her own rate and is judged on an individual basis. A teacher who works in an ungraded primary program comes to know all of the pupils well, having the opportunity to work with them longer than does the teacher in the traditional program.

There have also been many experiments with departmentalizing the elementary school. In this kind of program, the teachers are not responsible for teaching all subjects at a given grade level. The pupils are assigned to different teachers for different subjects. The supposition of those who are in favor of departmentalizing the elementary school is that teachers have an opportunity to learn more about subject matter if they concentrate on one or two subjects. Thus, the specialized teacher may be in a position to give children more depth in each subject and more individual attention than is the teacher who is prepared to instruct pupils in all subjects at one grade level.

There are other experimental plans for changing the traditional pattern of the elemen-

A kindergarten teacher observes the creative work of one of her students. As she circulates about the classroom, she gives each student a moment of undivided attention.

tary school, and some may offer promise for the future. Elementary schools, however, have not been noted for dramatic changes in plan over the centuries, and whatever change may take place in the future is likely to be gradual.

Elementary school teachers use many teaching devices to instruct pupils. They may use textbooks, workbooks, resource books, magazines, or newspaper clippings. They may use slide films, motion pictures, record players, or television programs. They may use charts, posters, or maps. The teachers may bring to the classroom certain specimens of plant life, or may bring animals such as goldfish, frogs, or turtles. They may keep a terrarium or an aquarium in the room for the children to observe.

Although most teachers spend fewer hours in the classroom with their pupils than the usual worker spends at a job, the teachers' work is not finished when the final bell has rung in the afternoon. They must prepare lesson plans for each of the subjects that they are to teach the next day, gather the instructional materials that they plan to use, complete certain necessary forms and records, and grade papers and enter the grades in their record books.

Elementary school teachers also work with their fellow teachers in the school and with the school principal. They confer with such specialists as the school psychologist and the school social worker to assist certain students with learning or adjustment problems. They also may work with parents to help the children develop in ways that are best for each individual.

All teachers devote many hours to educational meetings. The principal of the school may schedule faculty meetings at regular intervals. The teacher will also be expected to attend the meetings of the Parent Teacher Association. Most teachers are members of some professional educational association and may be members of more than one such association. In addition, most teachers attempt to keep up to date on new educational materials, information, and trends.

Most teachers work for nine or ten months each year. Those who need additional income may seek employment in other fields during the summer months. Many teachers, however, choose the summer to return to the campus of a college and take courses that will help them to do a better job in their present position. Some states require teachers to take courses to renew or upgrade teaching certificates.

School hours are usually 8:00 A.M. until after 3:00 P.M., Monday through Friday. Teachers are usually able to take all school holidays, including the Christmas and spring vacations.

Requirements

Prospective kindergarten or elementary school teachers must have a genuine liking for children and an ability to get along well with them. They must regard children as individuals, with likes and dislikes, strengths and weaknesses of their own. They must be patient and self-disciplined and have a high standard of personal conduct at all times.

Prospective elementary school teachers should have a quiet authority and enough self-respect to command respect from others. They should have a sense of humor and an ability to bend with the situation. They should have a good sense of fair play, for fairness is a quality that pupils respect highly in their teachers.

Teachers should enjoy learning and be able to communicate this enjoyment to the young people being taught. Above all, elementary school teachers establish attitudes toward education in children who are in their formative years. Elementary school teachers have a serious responsibility to inculcate positive attitudes in students.

Practice teaching in an actual school situation is usually required. The student is placed in a public school to work with one of the regular teachers there for a specified number of hours, days, or weeks. During the period of practice teaching, the undergraduate student will observe the ways in which the classroom is managed, will learn to keep records of such details as attendance and grades, and have actual experience in handling the class, both under supervision and alone.

Special requirements

Kindergarten and elementary school teachers who are employed by public schools must be certified under regulations established by the state department of education in the state in which they are teaching. Not all states require certification for teachers in private or parochial schools. Most states require the aspiring teacher to have completed four years of accredited college work and to have achieved the bachelor's degree to be certified to teach. Certification requirements usually state the kinds of courses that must be taken in preparation for the teaching profession. Most states require the elementary education teacher to have majored in elementary education.

When students receive their degrees, they may request that a transcript of their college record be sent to the certification section of the state department of education. If they have met certification requirements, they will receive a certificate and thus be eligible to teach in the public schools of the state. If they move to another state, they will have to submit college transcripts to the state department of education in the new state to be able to teach there.

High-school students who are interested in becoming elementary school teachers should take a college preparatory course. They should take English, mathematics, science, history, and geography. Nor should they neglect such studies as art and music, as these courses may be important preparation both for college work and for later work in the schools.

Opportunities for experience and exploration

High-school students interested in exploring an interest in teaching in kindergarten or elementary school may volunteer to teach elementary classes in Sunday School, may become an assistant in a Scout troop, may act as a counselor in a summer camp, or may assist a local recreation director in a public park or recreation center.

In college, they may be able to work part-time in a college-related kindergarten; may join a chapter of the Future Teachers of America; or may discuss their interest with professors in the field of elementary education.

Related occupations

The skills and aptitudes that go into kindergarten and elementary school teaching may be applied in other occupations as well. Other workers requiring the ability to communicate, motivate, and train others, combined with a talent for organization and administration, creativity, and patience, include childcare attendants, counselors, employment interviewers, librarians, personnel specialists, public relations specialists, social workers, and trainers and employee development specialists.

Methods of entering

Most young graduates from colleges and universities who are prepared to teach in elementary school try to obtain positions through the placement office of their own institution or by direct application to a school principal or county superintendent.

Advancement

Most teachers advance only in the sense that they become more expert in the job that they have chosen. There is usually an increase in salary, also, as teachers acquire experience. Additional training or study usually brings salary increases.

A few teachers with administrative ability and interest in administrative work may advance to the position of principal. Others may work into supervisory positions, and some may become "helping teachers" who are charged with the responsibility of helping other teachers find appropriate instructional materials and develop certain phases of their courses of study. Still others may go into teacher education at a college or university. For most of these positions, additional education is required.

Employment outlook

In the early 1990s, there were about 1,527,000 kindergarten and elementary school teachers employed in public and private elementary schools in the United States. It is predicted that employment opportunities for these teachers will be good through the end of the 1990s. Rising pupil enrollments, the current emphasis on improving the quality of education, and lower pupil teacher ratios are contributing to the growth in this field.

As the federal government continues to emphasize early education, it is likely that school districts will be pushed to continue lowering the pupil teacher ratio in the classroom. If the supply of graduates of teacher education programs continues to increase, however, as it has in recent years, entry requirements for kindergarten and elementary school teachers are likely to rise, making it difficult for less-qualified applicants to compete for jobs.

Prospects look particularly good in the South and West, as more and more families migrate to those areas, adding to the school population and creating teacher shortages. Opportunities should be plentiful, also, in central cities and rural areas, which traditionally have difficulty attracting teachers.

Earnings

The average salary for public elementary school teachers in the United States in the early 1990s was about $24,800 for the school year. Some states paid far above this average, some far below. Salaries were generally higher in the Mid-Atlantic and far western states. Most states recommend higher salaries for those with advanced degrees. Salaries are generally lowest in rural schools and highest in large city school systems. Earnings in private schools are lower, on the average, than in public schools.

Salary is only part of the benefit derived from teaching, however. There are sometimes other benefits, such as retirement programs, group insurance plans, paid sick leave, and some other types of leave with pay.

Collective bargaining in teacher contract negotiations is required in thirty-three states and the District of Columbia and is permitted in nine other states. Where collective bargaining agreements exist, public school systems with 1,000 students or more must bargain with teacher organizations over wages, hours, and the terms and conditions of employment.

Conditions of work

Teachers work under generally pleasant conditions. Modern classrooms are well lighted, temperature controlled, attractively furnished, and comfortable. The teacher is usually provided with materials to make the work as effective as possible.

Although the job of the elementary school teacher and the kindergarten teacher is not usually a strenuous one, a certain amount of fatigue is incurred. The teacher must stand for many hours each day, and must do a lot of talking.

The number of hours in school each day are often fewer for the elementary teacher than for the secondary teacher. The work of elementary teachers is more confining, because they are often with their pupils constantly throughout their day's activities.

Social and psychological factors

The teaching profession is valuable to society. Most teachers are greatly respected in their communities. Teachers may have a satisfying feeling of being engaged in work that is useful.

Teachers with family responsibilities are able to be at home with their children, especially during school vacation periods.

GOE: 11.02.02; SIC: 8211; SOC: 231, 232

◇ **SOURCES OF ADDITIONAL INFORMATION**

American Association of Colleges for Teacher Education
One Dupont Circle, Suite 610
Washington, DC 20036

American Federation of Teachers
555 New Jersey Avenue, NW
Washington, DC 20001

Association for Childhood Education International
11141 Georgia Avenue, Suite 200
Wheaton, MD 20902

International Reading Association
800 Barksdale
PO Box 8139
Newark, DE 19714

National Association for the Education of Young Children
1824 Connecticut Avenue, NW
Washington, DC 20009

National Council for Accreditation of Teacher Education
2029 K Street, NW, Suite 500
Washington, DC 20006

National Education Association
1201 16th Street, NW
Washington, DC 20036

U.S. Department of Education
400 Maryland Avenue, SW
Washington, DC 20202

◇ **RELATED ARTICLES**

Volume 1: Education; Recreation and Park Services; Social Services
Volume 2: Guidance counselors; Recreation workers; School administrators; Teachers, preschool; Teachers, secondary school
Volume 3: Childcare workers; Nannies; Teacher aides

Teachers, preschool

Definition

Preschool teachers instruct and supervise young children (under the age of five) in day-care centers, nursery schools, and other preschool facilities. They plan and lead activities developed in accordance with the specific ages and needs of the children.

History

Preschools were established in Europe in the late 1800s and early 1900s and were introduced in the United States in the 1920s. At that time teachers and other educators were testing different methods of instructing young children, such as utilizing cooperative playtime within an educational framework.

Preschool programs expanded rapidly in the United States during the 1960s, due in large part to the government instituting the Head Start program, designed to help preschool-aged children from low-income families receive educational and socialization opportunities and therefore be better prepared for elementary school. This program also allowed the parents of the children to work during the day.

Today, the increasing number of working mothers and fathers is a primary reason for the growth of preschool programs. Day care provides a safe environment where children can learn and play according to the specific developmental needs of each child. More than six million children currently use preschool facilities, and as these numbers continue to grow so will the job opportunities for well-trained preschool teachers.

A preschool teachers reads from a picture book as her students listen with interest. Reading aloud is one of the many daily tasks that a preschool teacher performs.

Nature of the work

Because of the young age of the children, a preschool teacher's primary responsibility is the social development and health of each child. Preschool teachers design and implement activities that build on the children's native abilities and help them develop skills and characteristics that will help them grow. Attention to the individual needs of each child is vital and therefore the teacher should be aware of individual needs and capabilities and, when possible, adapt activities to the specific needs of the individual child. Teachers should be aware of the developmental stages that children go through and plan activities accordingly. For example, a teacher should plan activities based on the understanding that a three-year-old child has different motor skills and reasoning abilities than a child of four years of age. A teacher should also understand the psychology of a young child.

To accommodate the variety of abilities and temperaments within a preschool program, a teacher should develop a flexible schedule with varying amounts of time for music, playtime, rest periods, and other activities. A preschool teacher should plan activities that encourage children to develop skills that they will need

later in life. To develop a child's reasoning ability, for example, a preschool teacher might introduce a word problem that takes several questions to figure out. A preschool teacher will also help children with such simple, yet important tasks as tying shoelaces and washing hands before snack time. Self-confidence and the development of communications skills are encouraged in such ways as giving children simple art projects (finger painting, for example) and having the children show and explain the finished project to the rest of the class.

For most children, preschool is their first time away from their parents and home environment for an extended period of time and a major portion of a preschool teacher's day is often spent helping children adjust to being on their own and encouraging them to play nicely and quietly together. Preschool teachers should recognize that some children may become frightened or homesick and be able to gently reassure these children. They also must be sensitive to the fact that not all children are alike and use lessons to point out the fact that children from different ethnic groups or otherwise different are all equal and part of the same "family."

A preschool teacher often has an assistant to help with the duties and responsibilities. The assistant helps the teacher manage the classroom throughout the day. For example, the assistant might supervise nap time for the youngest children while the teacher supervises the older children playing with blocks or some similar activity. Preschool teachers also work with the parents of each child. It is not unusual for a parent to come to preschool and observe a child, and preschool teachers often take this opportunity to discuss the progress of each child as well as any specific problems or concerns. Scheduled meetings are available for parents who can not come to preschool during the day. Solutions to fairly serious problems are worked out in tandem with the parents, often with the aid of the director of the preschool.

The preschool teacher adopts many of the parenting responsibilities while the child is in school. The teacher will greet each child in the morning, help the child off with his or her jacket, and then carefully supervise the child throughout the day, always on the lookout for small complaints or the need for a silent hug. Often these responsibilities get quite demanding and complicated. In harsh weather, for example, there are not only boots, hats, coats, and mittens to contend with, but also the inevitable sniffles, colds, and generally cranky behavior that all young children are prone to.

In both full-day and half-day programs, the teacher supervises snack time, helping children learn how to eat properly and clean up after themselves. Proper hygiene, such as the washing of hands before meals, is also a subject stressed. Other activities include storytelling, music, and simple arts and crafts projects. Full-day programs involve a lunch period and several nap times. Programs usually have excitement interspersed with calm. Even though the children have nap time, a preschool teacher must be energetic throughout the deal, ready to face with good cheer the many small challenges that young children continually come up with.

Preschool teachers not only supervise children, they also help prepare them for kindergarten and the other school years that are to follow. And while the atmosphere at a preschool is one that stresses warmth and socialization, and not academic progress, the teacher must also be trained to help children begin to read, understand, see patterns, and above all, enjoy a school environment. Children should be encouraged to think creatively and express feelings and ideas. It is important that children are involved in projects, such as simple art projects, that can be finished. This helps a child see a reward in purposeful action and encourages a child to be confident in his or her own ability.

Because young children look up to adults and learn through example, it is especially important that a preschool teacher be a good role model. An ability to be firm, yet fair is desirable. With more families putting children into daycare, the age range of preschoolers can vary from two or three years old to five. Teachers must be able to work with each group.

Requirements

Specific requirements vary from state to state and also depend on the specific guidelines of the preschool facility. Many schools and day-care centers require preschool teachers to have a bachelor's degree in education or a related field, but others will accept an adult with a high school diploma and experience working with children. Preschool facilities that accept high-school graduates often offer on-the-job training to their teachers until they are sufficiently trained to work in a classroom alone. In all cases, a person interested in teaching in a preschool should be patient, mature, and creative.

There are several groups that offer on-the-job training programs for prospective preschool teachers. The Child Development Associate (CDA) Program provides an on-the-job training program that is structured somewhat differently for each individual and is based on developing the skills of the individual teacher based on the skills of the individual and the needs of the preschool facility. The American Montessori Society also offers a program designed for those wanting a career as a preschool teacher. This program involves a three-month classroom training period followed by one-year of supervised on-the-job training. Contact the two organizations at the addresses shown at the end of this article for further information.

A high-school student interested in pursuing a career as a preschool teacher should take courses in early childhood development and home economics. Coursework in art and music is also important, as these two skills are of great help in the preschool environment. A college degree program should include coursework in nutrition, child development, psychology of the young child, and sociology.

Special requirements

In some states, certification might be required. Many states accept the Child Development Associate (CDA) Credential or an associate or bachelor's degree as sufficient for working in a preschool facility. Contact the state Board of Education for specific certification information.

Opportunities for experience and exploration

A good way of gaining experience in this field in to volunteer at a day-care or other preschool facility. Some high schools provide internships with local preschool facilities for students interested in working as a teacher's aide. Discussions with preschool teachers are another good way of discovering specific job information and exploring career opportunities.

Related occupations

Other occupations that utilize many of the same teaching and supervisory skills include elementary school teachers, teacher's aides, and tutors who work with young people.

Methods of entering

Qualified individuals should contact day-care centers, nursery schools, Head Start programs, and other preschool facilities for specific job opportunities.

Advancement

Many teachers advance only in the sense that they become more expert in the job. Skilled preschool teachers, especially those with additional training, usually receive salary increases as they become more experienced. A few preschool teachers with administrative ability and an interest in administrative work may advance to the position of director. Administrators need to have at least a master's degree in child development or a related field and may have to comply with state or federal licensing regulations. Some may become directors of a Head Start program or another government program. A relatively small number of experienced preschool teachers may open their own facility. This entails not only the ability to be an effective administrator, but also the knowledge of how to operate a business.

Employment outlook

Employment opportunities are expected to grow through the 1990s, as an increase in working mothers coupled with the knowledge of the importance of preschool increases the need for skilled preschool teachers. Specific job opportunities may vary from state to state, depending on demographic considerations and the level of government funding. Jobs should be available at private day-care centers, nursery schools, Head Start facilities, and laboratory schools connected with universities and colleges. In the past, the large majority of preschool teachers were female, and while this will continue to be the case, more and more males are becoming involved in early childhood education.

Because of low pay and often poor working conditions, there is a very high turnover of child care workers, such as preschool teachers. On the one hand, this may lead to dissatisfaction with the career, but on the other hand it means there are usually positions available to those willing to accept the limitations of the job.

Earnings

Although there have been some attempts to correct the discrepancies in salaries between preschool teachers and other teachers, salaries in this profession tend to be lower than teaching positions in public elementary or high schools. Because some preschool programs are only in the morning or afternoon, many preschool teachers work only part-time. As part-time workers, they often do not receive medical insurance or other benefits and may get paid $4 to $5 per hour to start. Full-time preschool teachers, especially those with a college degree, earn larger salaries and average between $10,500 and $16,000 a year. Earnings also depend on the geographic region in which the preschool facility is located.

Conditions of work

Preschool teachers spent much of the day on their feet in a classroom or on a playground. Often they have to sit on the floor or bend down on their knees. There is generally a good deal of noise in a room, even during nap time, although this is usually a sign that young and old are enjoying themselves. Toys and other play things are usually an important part of the scenery.

Facilities vary from a single room to large buildings. Class sizes also vary greatly; some preschools serve only a handful of children, while others serve several hundred. Classrooms may be crowded.

Most children do not go to preschool all day, so work may be part-time. Part-time employees can expect to work between eighteen and thirty hours a week, while full-time employees can expect to work thirty-five to forty hours weekly. Part-time work gives the employee flexibility and this is one of the advantages of the job.

Some preschool teachers may only work nine months of the year (with summers off), but many others work all year round.

Social and psychological factors

A preschool teacher should be able to deal with a large variety of children and parents. Parents may sometimes be more difficult to deal with than the children, as parents may have a lot of concerns about their children and may be frustrated by an inability to share more time with them.

A preschool teacher should be able to handle working long hours on their feet and sometimes stressful working conditions (including low pay). Most of all, a preschool must have an active interest in the welfare of his or her students as well as young children in general. The preschool teacher should be able to understand and appreciate the psychology of young children. A preschool teacher must be mature, firm, and fair. A preschool teacher should have leadership skills to effectively supervise and guide the students, as well as direct a teacher's assistant when available. The preschool teacher should be creative, especially in the use of art and music in the classroom, and be able to plan and implement their own programs.

GOE: 10.02.03; SIC: 8351; SOC: 231

◇ **SOURCES OF ADDITIONAL INFORMATION**

Information on training programs is available from:

American Montessori Society
Child Development Associate Program
150 Fifth Avenue
Suite 203
New York, NY 10011

General information on preschool teaching careers is available from:

National Association for the Education of Young Children
1834 Connecticut Avenue, NW
Washington, DC 20009

U.S. Department of Education
400 Maryland Avenue, SW
Washington, DC 20202

◇ **RELATED ARTICLES**

Volume 1: Education; Recreation and Park Services; Social Services
Volume 2: Teachers, kindergarten and elementary school; Teachers, secondary school; Teachers' aides
Volume 3: Homemaker–home health aides; Nannies

Teachers, secondary school

Definition

The basic duty of the *secondary school teacher* is to instruct junior or senior high-school students, usually in a specific subject, such as English, Spanish, history, mathematics, or biology. The teacher also assumes responsibility for a number of other duties including management of a homeroom, preparation of lesson plans, preparation and correction of tests, maintenance of student records, and consultation with students and parents. The teacher may also be asked to perform extracurricular duties ranging from the supervision of a lunchroom to the performance of routine clerical functions.

History

Credit for the establishment of the first secondary education system is usually given to ancient

Greece, where the privilege of schooling was available to children of wealthy citizens. This idea was incorporated into their way of life by the conquering Romans, in many instances through the use of captured Greek slaves as tutors.

In the Middle Ages, education was limited to those studying for the clergy, and general education was not advanced.

The Boston Public Latin School was established in 1635 for the express purpose of providing a literate clergy and, as might be expected, the main subject was Latin grammar. Similar schools were established throughout New England as rapidly as funds could be found.

A more practical approach to secondary education was inaugurated by Benjamin Franklin. Franklin's school—known as an academy—offered a flexible curriculum, and a wide variety of subjects were taught. After Franklin's success, other academies were founded, all of them private schools catering to the privileged classes.

The first English Classical School, which was to become the model for public high schools throughout the country, was established in 1821, in Boston.

An adjunct to the high school, the junior high school, was conceived by Dr. Charles W. Eliot, president of Harvard. In a speech before the National Education Association in 1888, he recommended that secondary studies be started two years earlier than was then the custom. The first such school was opened in 1908, in Columbus, Ohio. Another opened a year later in Berkeley, California.

Little is known about the first teachers in American secondary schools. In the early years, it is possible the teacher needed only a high-school education to be employed as a secondary school teacher. The first known normal school movement for the training of teachers was started in Concord, Vermont, in 1823. Samual Read Hall, a Congregational minister, established a three-year seminary in that city for the express purpose of training teachers for America's schools. New York State began action in 1834 to establish publicly supported normal schools throughout the state. The first such tax-supported normal school, however, was opened in Massachusetts in 1839.

Nature of the work

Secondary school teachers begin the school day early, usually around 7 or 8 A.M. Before school starts, they must collect whatever mail and messages have accumulated, organize the day's teaching material, and talk with students who may have come to school early for tutoring or guidance.

If, as is usually the case, the teacher is in charge of a homeroom, he or she will begin the day by taking attendance and making any announcements. Once these routine but necessary functions are over, the actual teaching day may begin. The number and style of classes will depend on the grades taught.

Junior high school and middle school teachers (sixth, seventh, eighth, and ninth grades) may have limited or no departmentalization in these grades. Teachers working in such programs are assigned a self-contained classroom. The students remain with the same teacher throughout most of the day while he or she teaches all the subjects they study. A variation of this method is for two teachers to share the same pupils. Teaching duties are divided. One teacher instructs students in science and arithmetic, for example, and the other teaches English and social science.

Senior high school teachers, on the other hand, will more often teach the same subject to several different groups of students throughout the day. The teachers may have in each classroom period as many as thirty or more students; the average secondary school teacher will teach 150 students during the day.

Some senior high schools cover grades nine through twelve; others, grades ten through twelve. Many secondary school teachers are employed in six-year combined junior–senior high schools (grades seven through twelve).

Not all high schools have the same number of course periods in a day nor are the periods of uniform length. The average school day is from approximately 8:30 A.M. to 3:00 P.M. The lunch period and homeroom duties occupy about an hour. Of the six hours available for student instruction, the high-school teacher will probably teach at least five of them. The free hour is usually spent in more routine but necessary functions—grading papers, giving special assistance to students, and/or planning the next day's lessons.

The number of subjects a teacher is required to teach will vary from school to school. Smaller schools prefer teachers capable of preparing lessons in more than one subject. Some school administrators have contended that a teacher who can conduct classes in three separate fields is of great value to the school. Thus teachers who have majored in one subject and minored in another may be licensed to teach both and, in some instances, may return to college to obtain the knowledge necessary to achieve certification in yet a third subject.

A high school science teacher shows great enthusiasm for his subject. His eagerness stimulates the entire classroom, as he rouses student interest and participation in his class.

Other administrators prefer a teacher specializing in one area. Teachers in such a situation will return to college to extend their knowledge and understanding of this special subject. Teachers that almost always specialize include *art teachers, industrial arts teachers,* and *physical education instructors.*

The trend in certification standards seems to be toward limiting the number of subjects in which a teacher may be certified. Many states do not permit teachers to teach subjects for which they are not certified, while an increasing number of states are limiting the number of subjects that a single teacher may teach.

At the end of the day, the teacher begins preparations for the next day. Homework, themes, test papers, and other student assignments must be graded, records updated, and student problems discussed. In addition, the teacher may be involved in student projects, such as student council, the school newspaper, or Future Teachers of America, which require his or her presence, usually after school hours. There are also many educational meetings the teacher must attend such as faculty, departmental, and those away from the community.

Some teachers, in addition to being qualified to teach secondary school subjects, must be trained in special teaching methods designed for handicapped or disabled students. For example: *Teachers of the deaf* communicate with hearing-impaired students using sign language, finger spelling, cued speech, or lip reading. *Teachers of the blind* teach visually impaired stu-

dents using the Braille system of reading and writing. *Educational therapists,* who teach students who are educationally handicapped because of neurological or emotional disorders, must be able to deal with disruptive, violent, or destructive behavior. *Teachers of physically handicapped students* must take into consideration their physical limitations. *Teachers of the mentally handicapped* teach basic academic and living skills using teaching techniques that reinforce learning.

Requirements

High-school students hoping to become secondary school teachers should take a college preparatory course and seek admission to a college or university that has a strong school or college of education.

Prospective teachers must have above-average intelligence, a real liking for study and learning, and a genuine enthusiasm for working with other people, both adults and youngsters. Most teachers will spend their lives learning more about their subject and keeping up with current trends in the field. They must also acquire a broad knowledge of other fields to relate this knowledge to their specialty.

Special requirements

In every state, a certificate is required for public secondary school teaching. A bachelor's degree is necessary to qualify for this certificate. The prescribed course of study for most prospective teachers consists of twenty-four to thirty-six hours in the subject they wish to teach and eighteen to twenty-four hours in teaching techniques or related educational courses. The balance of the college coursework is seventy to eighty-eight hours of electives, including the courses necessary for a minor field of study. Part of the college preparation consists of actual teaching experience under the supervision of a university professor. Almost half the states require a fifth year of study or a master's degree, and many school systems require additional qualifications. In many public school systems, financial compensation in increased wages is offered to teachers who receive graduate degrees.

Some private schools do not require teaching certificates.

Opportunities for experience and exploration

High-school students interested in secondary school teaching will have many opportunities to observe teachers in action. They will usually find their teachers willing to discuss candidly the advantages and disadvantages of the profession. Interested students may also join Future Teachers of America and have the opportunity to attend many educational functions.

Related occupations

Persons interested in teaching at the secondary level may wish to explore the work of others in educational occupations, such as adult education teachers, athletic directors, college deans and faculty members, elementary school teachers, kindergarten teachers, preschool teachers, and school administrators. With appropriate education, prospective secondary school teachers also may direct their aptitudes and interests to work outside the field of education, as counselors, employment interviewers, librarians, public relations representatives, sales representatives, social workers, or trainers and employee development specialists.

Methods of entering

Many colleges and universities maintain placement agencies to aid beginning teachers to obtain employment. Teachers with a preference for a specific locality may apply directly to the school system in that locality, either to the school superintendent or a designated personnel office.

Teachers who meet the requirements for certification will be issued a certificate by the state and may then apply for a teaching position.

Advancement

Usually, the first few years of a teaching career are on a trial basis. When the teacher has demonstrated competence, tenure is granted. Advancement in the teaching profession may then proceed along one of two paths. Those who wish to remain in strictly teaching positions may advance in salary, prestige, and teaching techniques. Such teachers may become in-volved in special aspects of teaching, such as counseling, teaching homebound or handicapped students, or teaching special remedial subjects.

Teachers who are willing to give up the actual teaching of students may take on educational administration duties. Such teachers may return to graduate school to take courses in administration or supervision (or both). They may then seek positions in these fields. Although it is not true in all cases, most teachers who accept such posts no longer actually teach students.

Employment outlook

There were about 1,128,000 teachers employed in U.S. public and private secondary schools in the early 1990s. The general outlook for persons trying to enter secondary school teaching appears fairly good throughout the 1990s, although the demand for such teachers may be softened by the number of new college graduates qualified to teach and the many former teachers trying to reenter the field. The outlook, however, does vary according to subject matter. Competition among teachers of computer programming, mathematics, and science may not be as intense because so many of these teachers have left the field for more highly paid positions in industry and government. The outlook for employment also varies somewhat according to the region of the country, with opportunities being more plentiful in the South and West, where the population is growing as people migrate from other parts of the country. Teaching jobs are easier to obtain, too, in central cities and rural areas, which usually have difficulty attracting qualified applicants.

Earnings

The average annual salary for classroom teachers in public secondary schools in the early 1990s was approximately $26,100. Salaries vary greatly, however, according to the region of the country, the state, and the size of the school. Schools in the Mid-Atlantic and far western states generally paid higher salaries, as did schools in large cities and in suburban areas. Earnings in private schools were lower. Teachers who hold a master's degree qualify for higher-level certification status and increased starting salaries.

Teachers' salaries often depend on collective bargaining agreements, which are required

675

by law in thirty states and the District of Columbia and are permitted in another nine states.

Conditions of work

Teachers working in new schools enjoy many conveniences unavailable to teachers working in older plants. Most new school plants are attractive, well lighted, and comfortably heated, although few as yet have air conditioning.

The working year for teachers is nine to ten months a year. They are not paid for the two or three months in the summer they do not teach, and many teachers, especially those with families, usually find work during the summer to supplement their teaching income. Many teachers return to school in the summer to take additional courses and work toward a higher degree. Other may choose to teach summer school for extra income. Some schools offer distribution of wages over a twelve month period, if desired.

Social and psychological factors

Although a great deal of time is devoted to the job of teaching, most teachers find their work compatible with family responsibilities. They find themselves able to spend a great deal of time with their families during vacations and holidays and during the summer months. Teachers with children of school age are often able to be home when their children are.

Teachers who undertake the education of the young accept a great deal of responsibility. This responsibility may result in a certain number of tension-producing situations. This may include dealing with uninterested, undisciplined, or even emotionally disturbed children. Parents may not be cooperative, and the teacher's role may be limited in bringing about an effective change.

The conscientious teacher is concerned about the need to include certain material in teaching that may be of value to the students. Depending on the subject taught by the teacher, this can include sex education, interpersonal interaction, and various aspects of human development and ethics.

For teachers who work in schools with low graduation rates, limited financial support, or low parent interest, the role of teacher may become frustrating. Once located in a school with poor academic achievement, it may be difficult to transfer to another school. Teacher "burn-out" is often associated with difficult school assignments. Many school districts recognize this and offer counseling, training and placement priorities to teachers who find it difficult to handle pressures.

In spite of this responsibility—or perhaps because of it—most teachers enjoy their work. They consider students interesting as individuals and find it a challenge to bring out the best in them. Students who like people and enjoy an intellectual atmosphere will enjoy a teaching career.

GOE: 11.02.01; SIC: 8211; SOC: 233

◇ **SOURCES OF ADDITIONAL INFORMATION**

American Alliance for Health, Physical Education, Recreation, and Dance
1900 Association Drive
Reston, VA 22091

American Association of Colleges for Teacher Education
One Dupont Circle
Suite 610
Washington, DC 20036

American Federation of Teachers
555 New Jersey Avenue, NW
Washington, DC 20001

International Technology Education Association
1914 Association Drive
Reston, VA 22091

National Council for Accreditation of Teacher Education
2029 K Street, NW
Suite 500
Washington, DC 20006

National Council for the Social Studies
3501 Newark Avenue, NW
Washington, DC 20016

National Council of Teachers of English
1111 Kenyon Road
Urbana, IL 61801

National Council of Teachers of Mathematics
1906 Association Drive
Reston, VA 22091

National Education Association
1201 16th Street, NW
Washington, DC 20036

National Science Teachers Association
1742 Connecticut Avenue, NW
Washington, DC 20009

U.S. Department of Education
400 Maryland Avenue, SW
Washington, DC 20202

◇ **RELATED ARTICLES**

Volume 1: Education; Social Services
Volume 2: Adult and vocational education
teachers; College and university faculty; Guidance counselors; Librarians; Recreation workers;
School administrators; Teachers, kindergarten
and elementary school; Teachers, preschool
Volume 3: Teacher aides

Technical writers

Definition

The *technical writer* understands the language of
the scientist, engineer, or technician and has
the ability to interpret it and convey the meaning clearly and accurately to the public and to
workers in special fields.

History

For many years the technical writer has been
writing the instructions that came with such
equipment as refrigerators or automotive parts.
But recent advances in science and technology
have greatly expanded the subject matter.

Since World War II, business and industrial
firms have increased research, development,
testing, and experimentation. The planning,
designing, testing, producing, and marketing
of new equipment and products require considerable communication. It is necessary to
communicate among departments within a
company, and also to the public. Today, ideas
and information often need to be exchanged
among several companies, particularly if they
are working on different phases of a project.

In the past, this writing was done by the
scientists and technicians who were doing the
work. Today, technical writers are needed who
have the ability to communicate highly technical information in a more common language.
As technology became more advanced, scientists found it difficult to dilute and reduce essential information into laymen terms. Technical writers fill that need.

Nature of the work

The subject matter for technical writers may
vary, but the nature of their work remains the
same. They prepare service manuals or handbooks, instruction or repair booklets, sales literature, research proposals and reports, contract specifications, and research abstracts.
They also write publicity releases, catalogs, brochures, stockholder reports, and articles for
trade journals and daily newspapers. Occasionally they assist in the preparation of speeches
and scientific papers and manuscripts. The
type of document and range of subjects is varied, depending on the emphasis of the firm or
organization in which the writer is employed.
Some writers may arrange for the preparation
of graphs, tables, charts, and other artwork for
the reports they write.

Technical writers must know their subject
before they can prepare the material. They begin by learning as much as they can about the
subject. They study reports, journals, notes,
engineering drawings, and any other material
that is available. They consult with drafters, engineers, scientists, technicians, production supervisors, and other workers who may know
the product or process they are concerned with.
Sometimes, writers will engage in the work for
a short period of time to gain firsthand knowledge. This not only helps them understand the
subject better but often provides them with
ideas about how they can present the material
most effectively and clearly.

After they have gathered and organized the
information they need, they prepare a first
draft. They may ask technicians from the group

A technical writer designs graphs and tables on a computer. He will eventually incorporate the graphics into the text of his report.

for which the document is being written to read this initial draft. The technicians' reactions help the writers to check their understanding of the subject and to find out if they need additional information or need to change the style or content of the manuscript material.

They may prepare or rewrite several drafts of the manuscript, depending upon the complexity of the subject and the audience for whom the material is being prepared.

In general, the process of collecting and organizing the information and then writing and rewriting the manuscript until it is ready for publication is basically the same for all technical writers.

Requirements

Technical writing is a field for which the educational requirements are varying and changing. A bachelor's degree is a desirable minimum requirement. Many firms, in the past, have sought individuals who had writing ability but who also had special knowledge or training in areas directly or indirectly related to their product or processes. As a result many of the technical writers currently in the profession have been selected from among qualified technical and professional employees who displayed an interest in and an ability for writing. Other employers prefer to select their writers from among those who have majored in English or journalism. Most employers would prefer a person who has a background in both writing and in some scientific or technical area. Possible college majors include English, jour-

nalism, science or engineering programs, or a combination of these.

In high school, the student should pursue the regular college preparatory program, including English, social studies, science, and mathematics.

The work of the technical writer involves more than a "flair for writing," because one must often deal with ideas, words, and language courses. If eligible, a student should enroll in advanced placement courses in English or science. If such electives in writing and reporting are available, the student should try to include them in his or her program of study. Any courses of a scientific or technical nature would be helpful in determining an interest and ability in this area.

The writer must also be accurate and logical in reporting and fit his or her style to the type of document being prepared. Conforming to such technical accuracy and precision can stifle creative or imaginative characteristics, but this type of writer must precisely interpret the messages of others. In this regard, the work differs greatly from other, more creative types of communication.

Special requirements

There are no special requirements or licenses for admission to this field. It should be emphasized, however, that the numerous scientific discoveries and the rapidity of technological change in this age of automation and space exploration will necessitate that the technical writer keep up to date on current trends, issues, and events.

The technical writer may want to join the professional organization representing the industry in which one is working; one may also join the Society for Technical Communication (STC).

Opportunities for experience and exploration

A good way to explore qualifications for and interest in this field is to seek experiences where one must engage in writing activities similar to those of a technical writer. The student's school newspaper or yearbook as well as the course of studies are possible areas for initial tryout experiences. In addition to some creative writing, the student may volunteer to contribute some technical reports. Perhaps a church and other community organizations may provide some writing experiences that will help in testing any interests and abilities in real situations. Once in college, students may be able to secure summer or part-time positions working on technical writing projects as a freelancer.

Beginning positions, such as a junior technical writer, usually involve library research, preparation of rough drafts for part or all of a report, cataloging, and other related writing tasks. These are generally carried on under the supervision of a senior technical writer.

Related occupations

There are many similarities between a technical writing and the work of other writers such as advertising copywriters, editorial writers, newscasters and newswriters, playwrights, reporters, and screenwriters. Individuals with technical interests may also wish to explore the occupations of advertising agency workers, archivists, computer programmers, drafters, information scientists, legal assistants, medical records administrators, public relations specialists, title examiners, or translators. Those with artistic aptitudes may even want to consider the work of technical or medical illustrators.

Methods of entering

Most college placement offices help students find positions with business and industrial firms or with government agencies. Private and public employment offices carry out listings of job openings, as do newspaper want ads. Those who wish to enter government positions will have to take a civil service examination and meet certain specified requirements, according to the type and level of position.

Some writers have entered the field by working in advertising and public relations departments and have transferred to technical writing as openings have occurred. Many firms are now hiring writers directly upon application or recommendation of college professors and placement offices. Most firms expect to see a sample of a student's writing ability.

Advancement

A technical writer can be promoted to positions of responsibility by moving from such jobs as cataloger or junior technical writer to senior technical writer and then to technical editor or publications chief. Opportunities in specialized positions are possible. Promotions are also possible through company transfer from one plant location to another or by accepting positions of greater responsibilities with another firm. This may involve moving one's family from one section of the country to another. A technical writer may move to related areas of work in advertising, public relations, radio and television, trade publishing, and college teaching.

With these several avenues to advancement, a technical writer should be able to find positions suitable to his or her interests and capacities. Those with their major preparation in the areas of English and journalism may find that they will advance to positions involving more writing or supervision of writing, whereas those with science and engineering backgrounds may wish to advance to different types of administrative, supervisory, research, or other positions.

Employment outlook

More than half of the estimated 80,000 to 100,000 technical writers who were employed in the early 1990s worked in the computer industry documenting software and hardware. Many were employed by companies that produced other electronic equipment, chemicals, pharmaceuticals, and aircraft. Others were employed in the communications and energy fields. Still others held positions in technical publishing houses, research laboratories, or in government or were self-employed.

Technical writing is one of the newer, more promising professional career fields. It is expected that the present shortage of qualified technical writers will continue at least through the 1990s. Thus, employment opportunities for both men and women are most favorable, particularly for those with exceptional writing abilities.

As in other occupational fields, the demand for workers will vary with national economic conditions. Three developments are considered important in the future demand for technical writers. They are: the increasing volume and complexity of scientific and technical data necessitating the need to convert it into clear, concise language that can be understood by management and by production personnel; the need for companies engaging in the mutual production of products or product components to share process and assembly data; the expansion of joint research efforts among business, industry, and government.

Earnings

In the early 1990s, the salaries of technical writers were comparable with those of other professional writers. In general, the beginning wage for those with a college degree ranged from about $18,400 to $29,300 per year. Salaries for experienced writers depended on experience, the type and size of the firm, and other factors. The salaries of experienced writers ranged from $19,300 to $37,800 per year, with the median for technical writers around $34,000. Earnings of those in administrative and supervisory positions were somewhat higher. Federal government positions paid salaries that averaged about $28,000 per year.

Conditions of work

Technical writers work the usual five-day, forty-hour week in offices that are quiet and conducive to the kind of concentration required. The technical writer works at a desk or typewriter or computer to prepare the copy. Often one must visit other departments in the plant to observe processes, to consult with workers, or to participate in other information-collecting activities. From time to time, the technical writer must work late hours or on weekends to meet project deadlines. Working under such pressure can result in some mental or physical strain. Generally, however, workers are not subject to undue physical strain or health hazards. Their vacations and benefits are the same as those of other employees in their organization. Free-lancers may have irregular work weeks.

Social and psychological factors

For the person who enjoys working with words and ideas of a scientific nature, technical writing is a rewarding and satisfying occupation. Technical writers can see the results of their efforts in the manual, handbook, or report they have that carefully and thoughtfully developed word by word. In addition to their inner satis-

faction and the recognition that they may achieve for themselves, technical writers know that their work will be useful to others. The writers' contribution to progress and to the betterment of society is a tangible type of achievement.

The technical writer has an opportunity to work alone and also with others. The work will depend on communication with others, and much of the job satisfaction may depend on one's willingness to work for and with the "team." Although writing is the focus of their work, many writers find the great variety in the nature of the projects and the type of publications being prepared to be the most satisfying part of their job. Each project is a new challenge and can be attacked with vigor and excitement.

GOE: 11.08.02; SIC: 8999; SOC: 398

◇ SOURCES OF ADDITIONAL INFORMATION

National Association of Science Writers
PO Box 294
Greenlawn, NY 11740

Society for Technical Communication
815 15th Street, NW
Washington, DC 20005

Women in Communications
PO Box 17460
Arlington, VA 22216

◇ RELATED ARTICLES

Volume 1: Automotives; Aviation and Aerospace; Book Publishing; Chemicals and Drugs; Computer Hardware; Computer Software; Electronics; Magazine Publishing; Newspaper Publishing; Telecommunications
Volume 2: Advertising workers; Computer programmers; Engineers; Public relations specialists; Reporters and correspondents; Writers and editors

Therapists, miscellaneous

Definition

Therapists treat and rehabilitate persons with physical and mental disabilities. They usually specialize in one particular type of therapeutic activity.

History

Therapy programs are fairly recent additions to the health care field. Although many theories of physical therapy have existed for centuries, it has been only in the last few decades that health care professionals have realized the healing powers of music, art, and other ordinary activities.

During World War II, the Department of Veterans Affairs (VA) developed and organized various art, music, and recreational activities for patients for VA hospitals. These activities had a dramatic effect on the physical and mental well-being of the World War II veterans, and therapists began to help treat and rehabilitate patients in other health care settings.

The number of therapists has increased greatly over the past thirty years. In addition, the types of therapeutic activities used in the treatment of patients have grown and expanded; today, patients may participate in a variety of activities, including woodworking, photography, dance, and gardening. Colleges and universities offer degree programs in many types of therapies, and national associations for certifying therapists have been established.

Therapists are an important part of the health care profession. Their work is often crucial to the physical and mental health of patients with a variety of disabilities.

Nature of the work

Therapists plan and conduct programs that are designed to improve the physical and mental well-being of patients who have disorders or disabilities. Therapists usually work as members of a health care team that may include physicians, nurses, social workers, and psychologists. Although often employed in hospitals, therapists also work in schools, clinics, rehabilitation centers, and nursing homes; they treat both children and adults.

The therapist's primary goal is to enhance the patient's physical and emotional health. How this goal is accomplished depends on the therapist's area of specialization.

Music therapists develop and conduct various musical exercises and activities aimed at improving the patient's overall health. Specific duties vary according to the employment setting and the age of the patients. They may teach individuals or groups to sing or play an instrument, or they may perform for patients. They may arrange concerts or plan background music for dining areas and treatment rooms. Patients may help take care of musical instruments and equipment.

Art therapists plan and lead art programs for patients who are mentally ill or physically disabled. Art programs are developed according to the specific nature of the patient's illness. Therapists may teach patients a variety of artistic skills, such as drawing, sketching, painting, and sculpting. Patients are encouraged to be creative and expressive in their art.

Dance therapists consult with medical personnel to develop dance therapy programs for patients. They organize and lead dance and body movement activities in accordance with a patient's specific disability. Therapists conduct both individual and group dance sessions.

Horticultural therapists develop, coordinate, and conduct gardening programs to help rehabilitate patients with physical and mental handicaps. Gardening programs are designed around each patient's particular needs. Therapists may teach the basics of gardening to individuals and to groups.

Manual-arts therapists help improve patients' work skills by conducting programs in various manual arts activities. Programs are designed to be consistent with the patient's particular capabilities and disabilities. Therapists may teach patients in either actual or simulated work environments. Manual-arts activities may include metalworking, electrical wiring, and graphic arts.

Industrial therapists help motivate and prepare mentally ill patients for employment outside the institution by arranging for salaried work activities. Work is tailored to each patient's individual needs and disabilities.

Although specific duties vary according to the therapist's area of specialization, all therapists follow the same basic steps in their work. First, therapists work with other health care professionals to evaluate a patient's capabilities

A therapists assists a mentally handicapped person on the sewing machine. Teaching such skills instills confidence in her students.

and limitations. Then, they develop and administer a treatment program for the patient. And, finally, they monitor the success of the treatment program in helping the patient.

Requirements

A bachelor's or a master's degree from an accredited college or university is a requirement for work as a therapist. Students should major in the specific type of therapy they are interested in. Many types of therapist jobs demand certain skills that must be developed and refined before a student even reaches college. Music therapists, for example, must have instrumental and vocal skills that often take years to develop; art therapists, on the other hand, must have natural artistic ability.

In addition, all types of therapists must be able to work well with other people. They must have both the patience and the stamina to teach patients who are often unable to learn skills quickly because of various physical and emotional disorders.

Special requirements

Most therapists must be certified or registered by a nationally recognized association. There are many different certifying associations; requirements vary according to the specific type of therapy. In addition, therapists who work in

public schools must meet the licensing requirements of the department of education in the state in which they are employed.

Related occupations

The range of occupations available to persons interested in helping others or in health care specifically is quite wide. Other similar areas of work include physical therapists, prosthetics and orthotists, physicians, registered nurses, nurse anesthetists, nurse practitioners, nurse and psychiatric aides, dentists, and so on.

Opportunities for experience and exploration

There are many ways to explore the possibility of a career as a therapists. Many hospitals, clinics, and rehabilitation centers offer part-time and summer jobs to students. A summer job as a nurse's aide, for example, may help provide insight into the nature of therapy, including both its rewards and demands. In addition, students may want to work as volunteers in various health care institutions. By volunteering, students will gain practical experience in working with patients and may be better able to determine their interest in and aptitude for therapy work. Students can also write to various professional associations for information on therapy careers, and students can talk with people who are working in the therapy field.

Methods of entering

A person must meet the necessary educational and training requirements before seeking employment as a therapist. Many colleges and universities have placement offices to help graduates find jobs; in addition, many professional associations compile lists of job openings for their members. The National Association for Music Therapy and the American Association for Music Therapy, for example, assist members in finding jobs.

People interested in careers as therapists may volunteer or work part-time at hospitals or clinics that have programs in various types of therapy. By doing so, they can determine whether they have the necessary interest and aptitude for working with disabled persons;

they may also meet people in the profession who can provide job leads.

Advancement

Many of the advancement opportunities for therapists involve increases in pay. A good percentage of therapist jobs in hospitals and clinics are under government sponsorship, and promotions center around higher salaries and rank. Therapists may also be given more responsibility over time; a therapist may advance from being one of several staff therapists to becoming the supervisor of an entire therapy department. Therapists may also go into research or teaching, although additional education may be required.

Some therapists may advance to administrative positions. Usually, however, therapists must have several years of experience and good management skills before they are given administrative responsibilities.

Employment outlook

Therapy professions are growing very rapidly, and many new positions are created each year. Although enrollment in college therapy programs is increasing, new graduates are able to find jobs without difficulty. In addition, job openings in nursing homes should continue to increase as the elderly population grows over the next several decades. The demand for therapists of all types should continue to increase as more people become aware of the need to help disabled patients.

Earnings

Salaries for therapists vary according to educational background and experience. During the early 1990s, starting salaries ranged from $15,000 to $23,000, with $17,000 the average. Those therapists with experience earn approximately $25,000; those with administrative or management responsibilities may earn between $25,000 and $40,000. In general, staff therapists averaged about $21,000 in the early 1990s.

Many therapist jobs are under government sponsorship. Most therapist jobs are at the GS-5, CS-6, and GS-7 levels; salaries range from $14,000 to $25,000.

Conditions of work

Most therapists work a forty-hour, five-day week; at times, however, they may have to work extra hours. Although many therapists work in hospitals, they may also be employed by clinics, rehabilitation centers, children's homes, schools, and nursing homes. The number of patients under a therapist's care depends on the specific employment setting, however, most buildings are pleasant, comfortable, and clean places in which to work.

Social and psychological factors

Therapists must have patience, tact, and understanding; they must also be very strong and healthy. Because their work centers on helping other people, they have to be able to develop a rapport with their patients. The abilities to adapt to changing circumstances, to handle disappointments, and to maintain a sense of humor are also very important qualities. Depending on the type of patient the therapist works with, the emotional commitment and pressure can be quite strong on the part of both therapist and patients.

The therapist's work can be frustrating and disappointing, but it is also very rewarding and exciting. Therapists derive great satisfaction from helping to improve their patient's physical, mental, and emotional outlooks.

GOE: 10.02; SIC: 80; SOC: 303

◇ **SOURCES OF ADDITIONAL INFORMATION**

American Art Therapy Association
505 East Hawley Street
Mundelein, IL 60060

American Dance Therapy Association
2000 Century Plaza
Suite 108
Columbia, MD 21044

National Association for Music Therapy
505 11th Street, SE
Washington, DC 20003

Department of Veterans Affairs
Department of Medicine and Surgery (10)
810 Vermont Avenue, NW
Washington, DC 20420

National Institute of Mental Health
5600 Fishers Lane
Rockville, MD 20857

National Therapeutic Recreation Society
3101 Park Center Drive
Alexandria, VA 22302

American Health Care Association
1201 L Street, NW
Washington, DC 20005

Toxicologists

Definition

Staff toxicologists conduct research to determine the potential toxicity of substances on humans, plants, and animals. They provide information on the hazards of these substances to the federal government, private businesses, and the public. Toxicologists may suggest alternatives to using products that contain dangerous amounts of toxins, often by testifying at official hearings.

History

The study of the effects of poisons (toxins) began in the 1500s when doctors began to document changes in the body tissues of people who died after a long illness. Over the next three hundred years, physicians and scientists continued to collect information on the causes and effects of various diseases, although the research was hampered by the lack of sophisticated research equipment.

As microscopes and other forms of scientific equipment began to improve, scientists were able to study in greater detail the impacts of chemicals on the human body and the causes of disease. In the mid-1800s, Rudolf Virchow, a German scientist who is considered the father of pathology (the study of diseased body tissue), took a huge step in unlocking the mystery of the nature of disease with his suggestion that body cells affected by the disease should be studied. This discovery helped pathologists pinpoint the path of a disease throughout the body.

With the growing use of chemicals, pharmaceutical, and illicit drugs within our society, the study of the impact of these potential toxins on public health and environmental quality has become increasingly important. The toxicologist's role in determining the extent of the toxic problem, as well as suggesting possible alternatives or antidotes, will play an important part in any long-term solution to problems such as air and water pollution, and the dumping of toxic waste into landfills or the recognition of an unusual response to a pharmaceutical.

Nature of the work

As scientists, toxicologists are concerned with the detection of toxins, the effects of toxins, and the treatment of intoxication (poisonings). A primary objective of a toxicologist is to reduce the hazards of accidental exposure to potential toxins and thereby increase consumer protection and industrial safety. This entails investigating the many areas in which our society utilizes chemicals or potential toxins, and then documenting their impact. For example, a toxicologist may chemically analyze a fish to find the level of mercury that has accumulated in it. This information might be used by government or industry officials in lessening the discharge level of mercury that manufacturing companies, such as electronics companies, released following the manufacturing process.

On many projects, a toxicologist may be part of a research team, such as at a poison control center or a research laboratory. *Clinical toxicologists* may work to help save emergency drug overdose victims. *Industrial* and *academic toxicologists* work on solving long-term issues, such as studying the level of toxic effects of cigarettes. They may work on developing research techniques that improve and speed up testing methods without sacrificing safety. They utilize the most modern equipment, such as electron microscopes, atomic absorption spectrometers, and mass spectrameters, are also aware of any new research instrumentation that may help with sophisticated research procedures.

Industrial toxicologists test new products for private companies in order to determine the products' toxicity. For example, before a new cosmetic can be sold, it must be tested according to strict guidelines. Toxicologists oversee this testing, which is often done in laboratory animals. These toxicologists may apply the test article ingredients topically or orally, or they may inject them into the animals. They test the results through observation, blood analysis, and dissection and detailed pathologic examination. Results from the testing are used on labeling and packaging instructions to help physicians and customers to use the product safely. Toxicologists are required to use humane procedures when experimenting with animals, and although animal experimentation has created some controversy, humane procedures are stressed throughout.

Toxicologists carefully document research procedures and then write reports on their findings. They often interact with lawyers and legislators on writing legislation, and they may appear at official hearings designed to discuss or implement policy decisions.

Because toxic materials are often handled during research and experimentation, a toxicologist must pay careful attention to safety procedures.

Requirements

Many years of training are needed in order to become a toxicologist. The successful applicant must have a doctorate degree in pharmacology, chemistry or related discipline, with some post-doctorate work in toxicology also required. The undergraduate degree should be in a scientific field, such as pharmacology or chemistry. Coursework should include mathematics (including courses on mathematical modeling), biology, chemistry, statistics, biochemistry, pathology, anatomy, and research methods. A

This toxicologist is testing a substance for potentially harmful matter.

toxicologist must also have a knowledge of computers.

High-school students can best prepare for a career as a toxicologist by taking courses in both the physical and biological sciences (chemistry and biology for example), algebra and geometry, and physics. English and other courses that improve written and verbal communications skills should also be stressed.

Special requirements

There are two organizations involved with the licensing/certification process. The Academy of Toxicological Sciences certifies a toxicologist after checking the references and work history of applicants. The American Board of Toxicologists certifies a toxicologist after the applicant passes a comprehensive two-day examination and completes the necessary educational requirements. Further information on licensing/certification procedures is available from these organizations at the addresses given at the end of this article.

Along with all the other medical professionals, toxicologists belong to professional organizations in order to facilitate professional training and enrichment. These organizations include the College of American Pathologists, the American College of Toxicology, the Society of Toxicology, and the American Academy of Clinical Toxicology.

Opportunities for experience and exploration

High-school students interested in pursuing a career as a toxicologist should join science clubs, and use classes in biology and chemistry to learn laboratory skills. Discussions with practicing toxicologists are also recommended as a way of exploring career options. Some people may find a part-time job in a research laboratory or at a hospital helpful, although it is impossible to get any hands-on training without the required education and training.

Related occupations

Chemists, geneticists, biologists, and physiologists, all are involved in research projects that are concerned with health-related issues and utilize many of the same research methods and techniques as toxicologists.

Methods of entering

People with the necessary education and experience should contact the appropriate research departments in hospitals, colleges and universities, government agencies, or private businesses. Often the instructors at the school in which the toxicologist did his or her training can provide job leads and recommendations. University placement departments can also be of assistance.

Advancement

Skilled toxicologists will find many advancement opportunities, although specific promotions depend on the size and type of organization with which the toxicologist is employed. Those working for a private company may become head of the research department. Because toxicologists are often involved with developing company policy, a highly skilled and respected toxicologist may become the vice-president or the president of the company. Obviously, this type of promotion would entail a change in job responsibilities, as the administrative tasks of a company executive would take precedence over research activities.

Toxicologists working for educational institutions may become professors, heads of a department, and deans. Toxicologists who want to continue full-time research and teaching find advancement in the way of higher pay and increased job responsibilities. Toxicologists working at universities usually have to write grants, teach courses, and train graduate students. University positions often are not as well paid as industrial positions, but offer more independence in pursuing research interests.

Employment outlook

Employment opportunities are expected to grow throughout the 1990s, as the use of chemicals by our society creates the need for trained professionals to determine and limit the health risks of chemical usage. Job opportunities should be greatest in large urban areas, as most large hospitals, chemical manufacturers, and university research facilities are located in these areas. As always, those with the most training and experience should fare the best in finding employment.

Earnings

As trained professionals, toxicologists have good earning potential. Those with a master's degree can expect to make $24,000 to $29,000 a year to start, while those entering with a doctorate. should earn between $30,000 to $50,000 per year. Experienced toxicologists can earn upwards of $80,000 per year.

Conditions of work

Toxicologists usually work in well lit laboratories or offices, either as part of a team or alone. Research in libraries or in the field is a major part of the job. Some toxicologists work a standard forty hour workweek, although many work longer hours. Overtime should be expected if an important research project is on deadline. Research and experimentation can be both physically and mentally tiring, with much of the laboratory work and analysis done while under certain time restrictions.

Some travel may be required to testify at hearings, collect field samples, or to attend professional conferences.

Social and psychological factors

The toxicologist's work demands patience and an eye for detail. A toxicologist may work on a research project for over a year, with limited results   this requires perseverance and a good deal of self-confidence. The many years of training required to become a toxicologist also demands perseverance and a strong desire to enter this profession. A toxicologist must be able to work well with people, either as a leader of a group or as part of a team. The toxicologist must also be able to work alone, sometimes spending long periods pouring over research material.

Because the work of a toxicologist involves studying the impact of toxic material, a toxicologist should be willing to handle contaminated material and be able to adhere to strict safety precautions that surround these activities.

The toxicologist often work on research that has important health considerations. At a poison control center, a toxicologist may try to find information about the poisonous properties of a product while an overdose victim's life is on the line. Toxicologists may have to testify at official hearings and be able to use live animals as laboratory subjects. A toxicologist must also be comfortable dissecting animals. This may cause some community controversy which may put emotional pressure on the toxicologist.

Despite the pressures of the job, a toxicologist will likely find researching important health and environmental issues rewarding.

◇ **SOURCES OF ADDITIONAL INFORMATION**

General career information is available from:

American College of Toxicology
9650 Rockville Pike
Bethesda, MD 20814

Society of Toxicology
1133 15th Street, NW, Suite 1000
Washington, DC, 20005

Certification and licensing information is available from:

American Board of Toxicologists
PO Box 76422
Washington, DC 20013

National Board of Medical Examiners
3930 Chestnut Street
Philadelphia, PA 19104

◇ **RELATED ARTICLES**

Volume 1: Biological Sciences; Chemical and Drugs; Chemistry
Volume 2: Biologists; Chemists
Volume 4: Chemical technicians; Pharmaceutical technicians; Pharmacy technicians

GOE: 02.02.01; SIC: Any industry; SOC: 1854

Underwriters

Definition

Underwriters review individual applications for insurance to evaluate the degree of risk involved. They decide whether the insurance company should accept an applicant, and, if the applicant is accepted, underwriters determine the premium that the policyholder will be charged.

History

The roots of the modern insurance industry can be traced back to the craft guilds of the Middle Ages; these guilds paid benefits to their members in the event of disability or illness. As the guilds gradually declined, there was no formal insurance protection until the formation of mutual-aids societies in England.

Lloyd's of London is generally considered to be the first insurance underwriter. Formed in the early 1700s, Lloyd's subscribed marine insurance policies for seagoing vessels. Over the years, the principles of insurance were adopted by various fraternal and trade unions.

In the United States, private insurance companies began to furnish insurance protection in the early 1900s. Insurance companies have greatly grown and expanded since World War II. Today, the insurance business has become very complex and sophisticated.

Nature of the work

People buy insurance policies to protect themselves against financial loss resulting from injuries, illnesses, or lost or damaged property; policyholders transfer this risk of loss from themselves to their insurance companies. As a result, insurance companies assume billions of dollars in risks each year. Underwriters are responsible for evaluating the degree of risk posed by each policy application to determine whether the insurance company should issue a policy.

Underwriters base their decisions on a number of factors, including the applicant's health, occupation, and income. They review and analyze information in insurance applications, medical reports, and actuarial studies. If an applicant appears to be at a greater risk level than normal, the underwriter may decide that an extra premium is needed. Underwriters must exercise sound judgment when deciding whether to accept an applicant and in deciding upon the premium; their decisions are crucial to the financial success of the insurance company.

Insurance underwriting is a very competitive business. If the underwriter evaluates risks too conservatively and quotes prices that are too high, the insurance company may lose business to competitors. On the other hand, the company will have to pay more claims, and ultimately lose money, if the underwriters evaluate risks too liberally and accept applications at inadequate prices. It is essential that underwriters evaluate applications very carefully.

Many underwriters specialize in either life, property, or health insurance; many further specialize in individual or group policies. Property or liability underwriters may specialize by the type of risk involved, such as fire or automobile. Some underwriters work exclusively with business insurance. These commercial account underwriters must often evaluate the firm's entire business operation.

Group contracts are becoming increasingly popular. In a group policy, life or health insurance protection is given to all persons in a certain group at uniform rates. Group contracts may also be given to specified groups as individual policies reflecting individual needs. A labor union, for example, may be given individual casualty policies covering automobiles.

Underwriters must assess the acceptability of risk from a variety of policy applications. They must be able to review and analyze complex and technical information.

Requirements

Most insurance companies prefer to hire college graduates for beginning underwriting jobs. A degree in any major is acceptable; a degree in business administration may be particularly helpful. Small insurance companies may hire persons without a college degree for trainee positions, and high-school graduates may be trained for underwriting work after working as underwriting clerks. In general, however, a college education is very advantageous.

Continuing education is extremely important in the underwriting profession. Most insurance companies encourage and pay for underwriting courses for employees. In addition, the following associations offer independent study programs: the American Institute of Property and Liability Underwriters, the American College of Life Underwriters, the Academy of Life Underwriters, the Health Insurance Association of America, the Insurance Institute of America, and the Life Office Management Association.

Special requirements

Underwriters must possess several personal qualifications. First, they must be logical, analytical, and objective. They must be able to make difficult decisions based on technical, complicated information. Underwriters must also be able to communicate well both in speech and in writing. And, they should enjoy assuming responsibility.

Experienced underwriters may try to become a fellow of the Academy of Life Underwriters. Becoming a fellow is considered a great achievement in the underwriting profession. To qualify, applicants must pass a series of exams and also must write a paper on an underwriting issue.

Opportunities for experience and exploration

There are many different ways to explore the underwriting profession. Students may visit insurance companies to talk with underwriters and other insurance employees. Many insurance organizations, such as those listed at the end of this article, will send basic information on underwriting jobs to interested persons. In addition, students may apply for part-time or summer jobs at insurance companies.

High-school graduates may decide to work at insurance companies before going to college to determine their interest in and aptitude for underwriting work. In addition, many insurance companies are willing to train and hire college students during the summer months.

Related occupations

In addition to underwriting, the insurance field offers other opportunities in various phases of the business, from sales to the processing of policies to investigating claims. Persons with an interest in underwriting can also utilize their ability to make decisions based on financial data by working as auditors, credit managers, loan officers, or real estate appraisers.

Methods of entering

The most effective way to enter the underwriting profession is to seek employment after earning a college degree. Most insurance companies prefer to hire college graduates, and college courses in business may be very helpful. University placement offices often assist students in securing employment.

It is possible to enter this field without a college degree. Underwriting clerks who show exceptional promise may be trained for underwriter positions. In addition, some insurance companies will hire persons without a college degree for trainee jobs.

Advancement

Advancement opportunities for underwriters depend on an individual's educational background, on-the-job performance, and leadership abilities. Continuing education is also very important.

Experienced underwriters who have taken continuing education courses may be promoted to chief underwriter or underwriting manager. Underwriting managers may advance to senior management positions.

Employment outlook

In the early 1990s, about 99,000 underwriters were employed, mostly in the home offices of insurance companies located in large cities such as New York, Chicago, San Francisco, Dallas, Philadelphia, and Hartford.

The job outlook for underwriters is very good. The number of underwriting positions is expected to increase at a faster rate than the average for all occupations through the end of the 1990s.

There are many reasons for the expected growth in the profession. First, the insurance business in general is expected to grow in volume and complexity over the next decade. More people will enter the twenty-five to fifty-four age group, which is the group with greatest insurance needs. New businesses will seek protection for new plants and equipment, insurance for workers' compensation, and product liability. The public's growing security consciousness and the increasing importance of employee benefits will result in more opportunities in this field. And, finally, greater competition among insurance companies should increase the demand for underwriters.

Earnings

Specific salaries of underwriters vary according to the size and location of the employer and the education and experience of the individual underwriter. General ranges, however, can be determined.

During the early 1990s, underwriters had median salaries of $23,300 to $25,600 a year. Senior underwriters earned a median income of $31,000; underwriting supervisors had incomes ranging from $33,700 to $35,200; and underwriting managers, in the commercial or personal divisions, averaged salaries of $40,600 to $49,000. In addition, most insurance companies have generous employee benefits, normally including corporate perks such as liberal vacation allowances and employer-financed group life and retirement plans.

Conditions of work

Underwriters generally work at a desk or table in pleasant, quiet, well-ventilated offices; their jobs entail no unusual physical activity, although at times they may have to work under emotional pressure. The normal workweek is thirty-five to forty hours; overtime may be required from time to time. Occasionally, underwriters may travel away from home to attend meetings or continuing education classes. In general, working conditions are very good for underwriters.

Social and psychological factors

Underwriting work requires great concentration and mental alertness. Underwriters must be analytical, logical, and detail-oriented. They must be able to make intelligent decisions based on sound judgment and reason; the decisions they make are often crucial to the financial success of their companies. People with the proper qualifications find that underwriting work is very challenging, interesting, and rewarding.

GOE: 11.06.03; SIC: 63; SOC: 1414

◇ **SOURCES OF ADDITIONAL INFORMATION**

Alliance of American Insurers
1501 Woodfield Road, Suite 400
Schaumburg, IL 60195

American Council of Life Insurance
10001 Pennsylvania Avenue, NW
Washington, DC 20004

Insurance Information Institute
110 William Street
New York, NY 10038

National Association of Independent Insurers
Public Relations Department
2600 River Road
Des Plaines, IL 60618

◇ **RELATED ARTICLES**

Volume 1: Insurance
Volume 2: Accountants and auditors; Actuaries; Financial institution officers and managers; Insurance claims representatives
Volume 3: Insurance agents and brokers, life; Insurance agents and brokers, property and casualty; Insurance policy processing occupations

Urban and regional planners

Definition

Urban and regional planners take charge of or assist in planning the development or redevelopment of a city, metropolitan area, or region. Planning programs involve evaluation of individual buildings, city blocks, or can be as large as entire new subdivisions, neighborhoods, or even towns.

History

For centuries, towns and cities developed and expanded at random. The acceptance of a designed or planned city, or of planned extensions to cities, or of planned rebuilding in areas of older cities is a twentieth-century phenomenon in the United States. Philadelphia and Washington are examples of cities that were planned from the beginning, but these were exceptions. The first zoning laws, giving the city government authority to regulate and otherwise control building, were passed in New York in 1916 and had wide influence on the development of organized city planning and city planning commissions.

Today, nearly every major city is concerned with a plan for its expanding development. Too, nearly every major city is attempting to rebuild and modernize its central or downtown section. Expansion and redevelopment are being carefully planned. The same is true of suburbs and broader regions.

Cities such as New York, Chicago, Philadelphia, Pittsburgh, and Los Angeles have urban planners to design new sections of these cities. They also have unusual demands concerning the revitalization of old residential, business, and industrial areas. The need to balance development pressures with social concerns is an important part of planners' work.

Urban planners discuss the layout of a renovation proposal for an industrial complex. Large schemes such as this one require the participation of many planners.

Nature of the work

A planner assists in the development of well-ordered and attractive communities. This person may be a member or chairman of a commission employed by the mayor or city, or may be a county administrative officer. Each new building, house, or section of new homes must be planned in terms of streets, water facilities, transportation, and safety.

The planner becomes familiar with the existing buildings and roads and their supporting conveniences. Commercial and industrial plants are considered in terms of access to transportation, water and power facilities, and the residential areas. Care must be given to each of these factors to make possible their fullest development.

Schools, churches, recreational areas, and residential tracts are studied to determine how they fit into a plan of usefulness and beauty. As with the other factors, specifications of the nature and kinds of buildings must be considered. The planning of zoning, to regulate the specific use of land and buildings, is one phase of the work of the planner.

In redevelopment areas, the planner directs or assists in the rejuvenation of run-down areas and in rehabilitating or replacing the old buildings. The planner works closely with other experts to encourage business development and job opportunities.

Some urban and regional planners teach in colleges or schools of planning and may do consulting work. Planners today are concerned

not only with city codes, but also with environmental problems of water pollution, solid waste disposal, water treatment plants, and public housing.

Planners are now able to reevaluate model cities such as Columbia, Maryland, and Reston, Virginia, both built in the 1960s as planned communities. Before plans for such communities can be developed, the urban planner must prepare detailed maps and charts showing the proposed use of land for housing, business, and community needs. These studies provide information on types of industry, location, and the problems that can be expected, such as transportation, water, and sewage. After the charts have been analyzed, the urban planner designs the layout in a form that will illustrate his or her ideas to others who will be involved, such as land developers, city officials, housing experts, architects, and construction firms.

Requirements

A college education, with a major in planning, architecture, landscape architecture, civil engineering, or public administration, is the minimum requirement for trainee jobs with most municipal or other governmental boards or agencies. For a career in planning, however, a master's degree in city or regional planning is usually essential; in the early 1990s, about eighty colleges and universities offered a two-year graduate course leading to the degree, with work experience included. The practical experience connected with the last part of the master's program is often called an internship.

This is usually completed by regular paid employment during the summer in a planning office approved by the college.

Special requirements

Persons desiring to enter urban and regional planner positions in federal, state, and local government agencies frequently must pass civil service examinations. This is one basis for becoming eligible for appointment. Notice of these examinations is publicized nationally.

Although certification is not a requirement, it is a valued credential that often leads to more responsible, better-paying positions. The American Institute of Certified Planners, a branch of the American Planning Association, grants certification to urban planners who meet certain academic and professional requirements and successfully complete an examination.

In addition to the educational requirements, planners must know the law relating to land purchase and use. They must have a general knowledge of trends in population of urban areas.

An understanding of spatial relationships is important, as is an ability to solve a variety of problems.

Opportunities for experience and exploration

The high-school and college student may find opportunities in helping with planning school building projects. Training in an architect's office or with an engineering crew is helpful. The student can interview planners and gain details of the job in a particular community.

Related occupations

Persons considering a career as an urban planner are likely to find varying degrees of similarity in the following occupations: architects, cartographers, city managers, city planning aides, civil engineers, drafters, environmental engineers, geographers, landscape architects, park superintendents, political scientists, social workers, sociologists, traffic technicians, and urban designers.

Methods of entering

Experience in an architect's office or with a construction engineering firm, for qualified graduates with the bachelor's degree is useful before applying to city, county, or regional planning boards or agencies. Membership in one of the professional organizations is helpful in locating job opportunities. These include the American Planning Association, American Institute of Architects, American Society of Civil Engineers, International City Managers Association, and the Engineers Council for Professional Development. Federal agencies and an increasing number of municipal departments, however, require the master's degree in planning for beginning jobs, and applicants thus qualified may try for jobs by taking the prescribed civil service examinations of the agency in which they are interested.

Advancement

Advancement takes place as the beginning assistant moves to more inclusive and responsible jobs within the planning board or department and to appointment as planner. The positions of senior planner and planning director are succeeding steps in some agencies. Frequently, the experienced planner obtains advancement by moving to a larger city or county planning board, where he or she can become responsible for larger and more complicated problems and projects.

Employment outlook

There were about 20,000 planners employed in the early 1990s. About two-thirds of them worked in local government agencies. Most of the rest were employed in state agencies for housing, transportation, and environmental protection or in the federal government, primarily in the Departments of Defense and Transportation. The balance held positions in architectural and surveying, consulting, or land development firms.

For graduates with professional city and regional planning training, the opportunities for jobs will be present, but the market is small and highly competitive. The overall demand for city planners is expected to grow at an average rate through the end of the 1990s. More communities will be turning to professional planners for help in determining the most effective way to meet the rising requirements for physical facilities resulting from urbanization and the growth in population. As urban communities continue to spill into neighboring areas or merge with other urban areas, open spaces for recreation disappear, smog and traffic congestion get worse, and the need for more and better-planned facilities becomes more acute. The important role of planners in the large-scale development of land and physical facilities for both public and private use has been recognized by many governmental and private organizations.

At least through the rest of this decade, there will be a demand for urban and regional planners to help fulfill the following needs: to zone and plan land use for undeveloped and non- metropolitan areas; for commercial development in rapidly growing suburban areas; to redevelop the central cities; to replace old public facilities such as bridges, highways, and sewers; and to preserve historic sites and rehabilitate older buildings.

The demand will be particularly strong in rapidly expanding areas such as California and Florida and in smaller cities and towns in older areas of the Northeast and Midwest, for example, that are undergoing preservation and re-development.

Earnings

The median starting salary of employees with a graduate degree in planning was about $25,000 a year in the early 1990s. The median for all urban and regional planners was $36,000. In city, county, and other local governments, the median was about $32,900; in state governments, $35,500; in private consulting firms and in business, $42,500; and in nonprofit foundations, $36,100. Salaries for planning directors were considerably higher, generally as much as $9,000 more per year than staff members with comparable levels of experience. Salaries are higher, also, in larger cities, where planners may earn as much as $10,000 more than those in small jurisdictions. Consultants are generally paid on a fee basis. Their earnings are often high and vary greatly according to their reputations and work experience. Their earnings will depend on the number of consulting jobs they accept.

Because most planners work for government agencies, they usually have sick leave and vacation privileges and are covered by retirement and health plans. Although most planners have a scheduled workweek of forty hours, they may occasionally work in the eve-nings and on weekends to meet with citizen groups, because the support of these groups is often essential to the adoption of proposed plans.

Conditions of work

Conditions of work are good. As in all professions, a job must get done when it is needed. It may require extra work at times to complete a project. Patience is needed in planning and examining the many details for urban development. Work will be mostly indoors with some outdoor duties. The planner often works on an individual time schedule.

Social and psychological factors

The urban and regional planner is one of a number of persons working on development concerns. Therefore, one needs to be alert to demands to complete projects in a hurry. Much of the planner's work is detailed, time-consuming, and done alone, although other aspects of planning involve a high level of cooperation with others. It takes time to show the results of one's ability. The planner may not always be in the spotlight for what he or she has achieved.

Most planners find the work rewarding. They must, at the same time, be able to face the discouragement of seeing carefully designed plans fall through because of opposition or lack of understanding. But this is actually a challenge, and planners have become increasingly attuned to the importance of developing community support for their work.

GOE: 11.03.02; SIC: 8748; SOC: 192

◇ **SOURCES OF ADDITIONAL INFORMATION**

American Planning Association
1776 Massachusetts Avenue, NW
Washington, DC 20036

Association of Collegiate Schools of Planning
PO Box 413
University of Wisconsin—Milwaukee
Milwaukee, WI 53201

Institute of Urban and Regional Development
University of California
Berkeley, CA 94720

National Association of State Development Agencies
444 North Capital Street, NW, Suite 611
Washington, DC 20001

◇ **RELATED ARTICLES**

Volume 1: Civil Service; Construction; Engineering; Real Estate
Volume 2: Architects; City managers; Engineers, civil; Landscape architects; Surveyors

Veterinarians

Definition

The *veterinarian,* or *doctor of veterinary medicine,* diagnoses animal illnesses, treats diseased and injured animals medically and surgically, inoculates animals against diseases, and gives advice on the care and breeding of animals.

History

Some beginnings in the scientific care of animals were made along with the development of scientific medicine. In 1762, the first school of veterinary medicine was established at Lyons, France. Nearly one hundred years later, a Frenchman named Alexandre Franois Liautard emigrated to America and become a leader in the movement to establish veterinary medicine as a science in this country. Through his efforts, an organization was started in 1863 that later became the American Veterinary Medical Association.

At about this time, many small colleges of veterinary medicine began to spring up all around the country. Most of them were privately endowed and small. Because their facilities and resources were limited, most did not survive into this century. In 1879, however, Iowa State College established a school of veterinary medicine that still is in existence.

Veterinary medicine has made tremendous strides since it was introduced into this country a century ago. One dramatic effect of this progress is the reduction of the incidence of human disease that is contracted from animals, such as tuberculosis, which is normally contracted from unpasteurized dairy products. Both farms and zoos have benefited tremendously from veterinary work.

Nature of the work

People generally think of the veterinarian as the doctor who cares for sick pets, and most veterinarians do indeed work with small animals such as cats and dogs. Other veterinarians, however, work with horses or food-producing animals such as cattle, sheep, swine, and poultry. Still others conduct research on the causes and cures of human and animal diseases.

Small-animal veterinarians maintain office hours, as do all health officers. They are also subject to emergency house calls and night calls. Often, they may work forty-eight to sixty hours during a week, especially when an infectious disease is sweeping the community. They spend some time keeping records on sick animals, on telephone calls from owners of sick animals, and on ordering medicines and other supplies. They advise on the care, feeding, and breeding of pets. Small-animal clinics may contain kennels for boarding healthy cats and dogs and sometimes provide an area for bathing and grooming pets.

Some veterinarians practice in small towns or in rural areas. They also may care for pets and other small animals, but their practice will include the care of large farm animals, which the veterinarian must be prepared to travel to in order to treat. This may involve many hours of driving on remote rural roads and traveling in emergencies at all hours of the day or night. The animal to be treated may be in a barn or in an open field, but neither location may be ideally suited for treatment purposes. There may be times when the veterinarian has to struggle with a large animal all alone or with the help of just one other person. One may work with healthy animals to prevent illness or may work with sick ones to try to cure them.

Some veterinarians work entirely with large animals. Some of the large cattle ranches or horse farms have veterinarians on their staffs. The doctor of veterinary medicine who prefers work with large animals may find conditions in such employment almost ideal. Facilities are often modern, well equipped, well lighted, and well ventilated. Large dairies, too, may maintain staff veterinarians. Facilities there may be almost as sanitary as those in a city hospital.

Zoo veterinarians work with a wide variety of animals. Most large zoos employ a full-time veterinarian to direct the health care, feeding, and treatment of the zoo's animal collection.

The armed forces have many veterinarians serving in this country and abroad. Their responsibility is to make sure that the meat that is to be served to armed forces personnel is neither diseased nor contaminated. In addition, they provide care for the animals owned by the government, and they do research related to space travel, diet, food packaging, radiation, and other military matters.

Federal and state veterinarians work with horses and food animals to detect, isolate, and eradicate diseases and pests. Those who provide advice on the care and feeding of food-producing animals as well as on their health problems include *livestock inspectors* and *poultry veterinarians*.

A large number of federal and state veterinarians perform regulatory inspections of food animals, poultry, and their processed products to insure that the food items are wholesome, unadulterated, and truthfully labeled. *Veterinary meat-inspectors* examine animals or fowl before they are slaughtered to make sure that they present no evidence of disease. After the slaughtering and dressing, the veterinarians examine the carcasses to double-check the disease-free condition of the meat. This kind of veterinary practice is of vital importance to the public and is one of the greatest services that a veterinarian can perform. There are also veterinarians who are assigned to inspect meat that has been imported from foreign countries. These are usually government jobs.

Some veterinarians, known as *veterinary virus-serum inspectors*, examine the facilities that manufacture serums, toxins, and other products used to treat animals, to be sure they are adhering to the sanitation, purity, labeling, and storage standards set by government.

A small number of veterinarians work in teaching positions in schools of veterinary medicine. A still smaller number work in research. It has been through their efforts that causes of many diseases that afflict people and animals have been discovered and both cures and preventive measures have been found.

A veterinarian employed by the U.S. Department of Agriculture immunizes a cow against common cattle diseases.

Veterinarians involved in research include the following: *Veterinary anatomists* study the physical structure of animals through direct observation or use of a microscope. *Veterinary bacteriologists* are concerned with bacteria and other microorganisms that cause diseases in animals. *Veterinary epidemiologists* investigate the spread of communicable diseases among animals or between animals and humans. *Veterinary parasitologists* conduct research on methods to control and prevent parasites that attack animals. *Veterinary pathologists* study the cause and development of animal diseases and their effects on the tissues, organs, and other parts of animals' bodies. *Veterinary pharmacologists* specialize in drugs used in the treatment of animals. *Veterinary physiologists* are concerned with the way systems and organs work in healthy and diseased animals. *Veterinary virologists* study viruses that cause diseases in animals, including those that can be transmitted to humans. *Laboratory animal care veterinarians* do research related to diseases and other health-related problems of laboratory animals.

Requirements

The degree of doctor of veterinary medicine (D.V.M.) is required before a veterinarian may be licensed to practice. The degree is achieved, as a rule, seven or eight years after graduation from high school. Most of the twenty-seven accredited schools of veterinary medicine in the United States offer a four-year program leading to the D.V.M. degree. Some, however, require five years to complete the degree course. Before a student may be admitted to a school of veterinary medicine, he or she must have completed at least three years in an undergraduate college program. It is possible to obtain preveterinary training in a junior college. Most preveterinary students, however, enroll in four-year colleges. Most obtain a bachelor's degree before applying for admission to the D.V.M. degree program. Each college of veterinary medicine has its own preveterinary requirements, which typically include basic language arts, social sciences, humanities, mathematics, chemistry, and the biological and physical sciences. Applications for admission to a school of veterinary medicine should be filed well in advance of April 1st of the year in which the prospective student hopes to enroll. Fewer than half of the applicants to schools of veterinary medicine may be admitted, because of limited facilities. High scholarship both in high school and in college is a determining factor in the decision to admit an applicant. The program is a full one, involving many hours of laboratory work, which makes outside employment to handle expenses difficult for students with limited financial resources. There are, however, various scholarship programs offered to qualified students who need financial help.

For the high-school student who is interested in admission to a school of veterinary medicine, a college preparatory course with a strong emphasis on science is a wise choice. It will be helpful, too, if the student is able to determine a liking for or interest in such areas as zoology, anatomy, pathology, and chemistry.

Special requirements

Upon completion of the D.V.M. degree, the prospective veterinarian who wishes to enter private practice must obtain a license by passing an examination conducted by the state in which the license is to be issued. The examination is difficult, and about 15 percent of those who take it fail to pass. There is no limit to the number of times an applicant may take the examination, but the applicant must pay the fee each time. Veterinarian may be employed by a government agency (such as the United States Department of Agriculture) without having been licensed. They may also teach without a license.

Strength and stamina are two of the special requirements for work in veterinary medicine. There are times when the veterinarian must work long hours, especially in an emergency case or when an epidemic is sweeping the community.

The veterinarian also must possess physical courage. Animals in pain may attempt to bite, claw, or strike those who are trying to help them. There is, however, probably greater danger from becoming infected by the disease that the animal is harboring than there is from being bitten or clawed.

Students who contemplate entering the field of veterinary medicine must have a real love for animals and a strong desire to want to help them. They must know animals well, and have no fear of them. And they must overcome early any tendency to flinch or become faint at the sight of blood or injury.

The prospective veterinarian must have a good talent for observation—the sick or injured animal cannot describe its symptoms. Whatever is learned about the animal must be gleaned through observation, touch, hearing, and smell. There are medical aids that supplement the veterinarian's skill, such as thermometers and stethoscopes, X-ray machines and microscopes, but veterinarians basically must rely on themselves.

Opportunities for experience and exploration

The young people who have grown up on a farm will know whether their interest in animals is great enough for them to spend their lives in working with animals. A city person should seek summer farm work to discover whether or not he or she likes work with domestic animals. Other possibilities include part-time or volunteer work in small-animal clinics, pet shops, and animal shelters. Many of the schools of veterinary medicine require extensive experience with animals of all kinds as a criterion for admission to their program.

Related occupations

Many individuals with an interest in veterinary medicine will not be able to enter a veterinary school because the educational facilities are limited. Students should select an alternate career in case their applications are turned down. Other occupations that involve animals include animal technologists, marine biologists, naturalists, and zoologists, as well as many occupations in the fields of animal husbandry, animal welfare, and wildlife conservation. Other workers that require skills similar to those of the veterinarian include audiologists, chiropractors, dentists, optometrists, physicians, podiatrists, and speech pathologists.

Methods of entering

The only way in which to enter the practice of veterinary medicine is through the prescribed degree program. There are internship and residency programs available for those who prefer not to establish their own practices immediately; however, the internship is not a requirement. Veterinarians who wish to enter private practice must have a license, obtained by examination, before opening an office.

Advancement

The veterinarian who is employed by a government agency may advance in grade and salary after accumulating time and experience on the job. For the veterinarian in private practice, advancement usually consists of an expanding practice and the higher income that will result from it.

Those who teach or do research may obtain a doctorate and move from the rank of instructor to that of full professor, or advance to an administrative position.

Employment outlook

About 75 percent of the more than 40,000 veterinarians in the early 1990s were in private practice. The federal government employed about 2,300, mostly in the Department of Agriculture and the Public Health Service. Veterinarians also worked for state and local governments, international health agencies, colleges of veterinary medicine, medical schools, research laboratories, livestock farms, animal food companies, and pharmaceutical companies.

There will continue to be a strong demand for veterinarians through the rest of the 1990s. Many of the number being graduated from accredited schools replace those who are removed from the profession by death or retirement.

Small-animal clinics will have need for additional personnel as the pet population increases along with the trend toward suburban living. Rural large-animal practice will have need for additional doctors of veterinary medicine. The growing emphasis on scientific methods of raising and breeding livestock and poultry, and the expansion of public health and disease control programs, will create additional employment opportunities for veterinarians.

Despite the availability of additional jobs, competition among veterinarians is likely to be stiff. Although freshman enrollments in veterinary schools have declined somewhat, the number of students in graduate-degree and certificate programs has risen dramatically. If enrollments remain at the current levels, there may well be an oversupply of graduates entering the field, particularly in pet practices.

Veterinarians with specialty training will have the brightest prospects, especially in toxicology, laboratory animal medicine, and pathology. They will also be needed in greater numbers as faculty members at colleges of veterinary medicine. Specialty training requires at least two years of formal education beyond the basic degree.

Earnings

Depending on their academic record, newly graduated veterinarians employed by the federal government started at salaries of about $22,500 or $27,200 a year in the early 1990s. The average yearly salary of all veterinarians working for the federal government was about $41,300.

The earnings of veterinarians in private practice varied according to a number of factors. The location, type of practice, and years of experience are among the most important factors. New graduates employed in the established private practices of other veterinarians generally were paid between $20,000 and $22,000 a year, with a significant rise in earnings after two to four years. The average annual income of all veterinarians in private practice in the early 1990s was about $43,000.

Conditions of work

Veterinarians in private practice enjoy favorable working conditions much of the time. They may, however, be subject to emergency and night calls, they may have to work long hours, and they may have to drive great distances on poor roads. Also, they often work under difficult conditions in barns or open fields.

Veterinarians who work in processing plants of the meat and poultry industries typically have a more stable and predictable work schedule of from forty to fifty hours a week, with time-and-a-half overtime pay for additional hours worked above the basic forty. Conditions in the abattoir may subject the veterinarian to noise and temperature extremes.

Herd inspectors are important protectors of the public health. Veterinarians who spend long hours immunizing cattle against disease protect the economy of the country as well as its health, but no one can deny that they have a difficult and sometimes uncomfortable job.

The most comfortable persons in veterinary medicine are probably those who go into teaching or research. Research can be frustrating as well as rewarding, of course, and both teaching and research may be considered confining by those who enjoy working outdoors and away from desks and telephones.

Social and psychological factors

Veterinarians are professional people who are respected members of their communities.

Most veterinarians have feelings of deep satisfaction with their chosen profession. They feel that they are providing a much-needed service both to animals and to human beings.

Although emergency and night calls may sometimes disrupt an orderly family life, this is to be expected when the veterinarian enters the profession, and one does not become distressed when plans must be altered to meet a crisis.

Veterinarians in private practice enjoy the freedom of being their own boss. Those who work with domestic animals may enjoy the freedom of working outdoors.

GOE: 02.02.01; SIC: 0742; SOC: 27

◇ **SOURCES OF ADDITIONAL INFORMATION**

American Veterinary Medical Association
930 North Meacham Road
Schaumburg, IL 60196

U.S. Department of Agriculture
Animal and Plant Health Inspection Service
Veterinary Services
Training/Information Management Staff
Room 853
Federal Building
Hyattsville, MD 20782

U.S. Department of Agriculture
Food Safety and Inspection Service
Personnel Division
Butler Square West
4th Floor
100 North 6th Street
Minneapolis, MN 55403

◇ **RELATED ARTICLES**

Volume 1: Agriculture; Biological Sciences
Volume 2: Biologists; College and university faculty; Health and regulatory inspectors
Volume 3: Agricultural extension service workers; agricultural scientists; Dairy farmers; Dog groomers; Farmers; Farriers (horseshoers)
Volume 4: Animal health technicians; Animal production technicians; Biological technicians

Wood science and technology careers

Definition

Wood scientists and technologists explore the physical, biological, and chemical properties of wood to find better ways to grow, process, and use wood. Wood science is conducted for academics and industrial research. It is carried out in labs and on forest grounds.

History

Wood is one of humanity's oldest and most versatile raw materials, providing shelter, tools, furniture, and fuel from prehistoric times to the present. Since the technological revolution, science has found ways to treat and process wood in more innovative ways, and wood now can be used in many products—everything from plywood to wood plastics—that were unheard of only a few decades ago. Experiments during World War II marked the beginning of modern wood science technology, and the field has advanced remarkably since then. Today, more than 5,000 different products use wood as their major raw material.

Before wood can be used, it has to be processed. This can include drying, finishing, seasoning, gluing, machining, or treatment for preservation. Wood scientists and technologists study these techniques and the chemical and structural properties of wood to discover new ways to modify and make use of wood's strength, endurance, and versatility. Like metallurgy and plastics manufacturing, wood science is concerned with materials engineering. While wood is one of the earth's few renewable resources, society is becoming more aware of the need to conserve forests and their products. Wood science helps to fulfill this goal, as it works toward more economical and efficient ways to satisfy people's need for wood products.

Nature of the work

Wood science and technology is involved in research designed to determine the composition, properties, behavior, utilization, development, treatments, and processing methods of wood and wood products. This type of research can be conducted in the laboratory, the forest, the sawmill, or the wood processing plant. The specialists who work in this field can be grouped in one of three categories: wood scientists; wood technologists or wood products engineers; and wood products technicians.

Wood scientists explore the chemical, biological, and physical properties of different woods. They try to find ways to make wood last longer and work better, and new products using wood as a raw material. For example, they develop and improve ways to season or chemically treat wood to increase resistance to wear, fire, fungi, decay, insects, and marine borers. They also explore new methods of processing wood. All wood needs to be dried before it can be put to any permanent use in construction or furniture.

Wood scientists experiment with methods of drying or curing wood, firing the wood in kilns to determine ways that will save energy and toughen the wood against warping and other defects.

Because of their thorough knowledge of the properties of different types of wood—pliability, strength, resistance to wear, and so on—wood scientists are able to recommend which woods are most appropriate for certain uses. They can tell which hard and soft woods will make useful lumber; which fast-growing trees could be harvested for plywood and particle board; which resilient, attractive wood will make good veneers; how to make use of waste wood or previously unusable trees; and which woods could be harvested to make good paper, wood alcohol, wood plastics, and other products. Wood is a renewable resource, but it must be grown and harvested. Proper cultivation of timberlands is important both to the lumber industry and to the nation's ecology. Because of this, lumber companies have to plan when and what to harvest, and what types of trees to plant now for harvesting in thirty years. The work of wood scientists and new breakthroughs in wood technology can have important ramifications for the business economics of the industry.

While wood scientists can work in academic or research facilities, *wood technologists* work mainly for industry. They are knowledgeable of the scientific properties of wood, but they look at the subject from a business perspective. They are interested in new ways to make wood products, with a minimum of wood, time, and money wasted. They may specialize in and combine work in areas that are usually considered the exclusive domain of either business or science, including materials engineering, research, quality control, production, management, marketing, or sales.

In many ways, wood technologists carry on the work of the wood scientists, by testing the properties of woods and experimenting with new methods of drying, joining, gluing, machining, and finishing lumber. Wood technologists also work closely with their clients, buyers and distributors of wood products, and wood manufacturers. If a sporting goods manufacturer is looking for light, resilient woods for making skis, for example, the wood technologist machines, treats, and supplies this wood. The technologist may even direct scientific research into new methods of improving the quality of wood for making skis. The wood technologist will also know the ways the wood should be tested for the qualities the buyer needs. New tooling machines may have to be designed, new processing techniques may need to be perfected, workers may need to be hired or specially trained. The wood technologist is able to coordinate all of these activities, both for the good of the company and the advancement of wood science.

Wood technicians often oversee the work of *wood products technicians,* who add to the efficiency and profitability of their companies

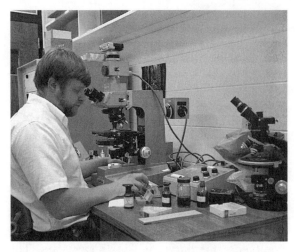

A wood scientist observes slivers of different types of wood under a microscope.

terials for making wood products. Some business courses may also be included. Students may wish to earn a two-year degree and then transfer to another school to earn a bachelor's degree. They should check first, however, to see how many of their academic credits will be accepted by the college or university to which they are transferring.

Many different specialties are contained within the wood science field. Therefore, a broad understanding of many subjects will prove more useful than extensive study of a single discipline. In high school, students who plan to pursue careers in wood science and technology should take courses in biology, chemistry, mathematics, drafting, physics, and English. Students should seek to fulfill the entrance requirements of the school or college they wish to attend.

through their knowledge of wood and its properties. Wood products technicians operate kilns, plywood presses, and other machines, and make sure they are working properly. They may also work in product testing and quality control, helping technologists and engineers overcome problems and expand the horizons of wood science.

Requirements

Because of the variety of work done in wood science, there are several academic paths that can be taken to prepare a person well for a career. Almost all of the jobs in this field, however, require education after high school.

A bachelor's degree is required for employment as a wood scientist or wood technician. Degrees can be earned in wood technology or forest products. Degree programs in chemistry, biology, physics, mechanical engineering, materials science, or business administration can be very useful if combined with courses in wood science. For more advanced work as a researcher, a master's degree or a doctorate is usually required. Advanced studies cover such topics as pulp and paper science, business administration, production management, and forestry-wood sciences.

Apprenticeships used to be the most common method of training for wood products technicians, but today most earn a certificate or associate's degree from a two-year college. Their coursework in wood science includes the identification, composition, and uses of wood. It also covers wood design, manufacturing, seasoning and machining, and methods and ma-

Special requirements

There are several professional associations in the wood science industry that work for the interests and concerns of its members. The Society of Wood Science and Technology is a professional society for wood scientists, and co-publishes the journal, Wood and Fiber Science. The Forest Products Research Society has as its members those people involved in the development, research, production, distribution, and use of wood products. One industry group, the National Forest Products Association, deals with the concerns of forestry companies, such as federal and private land management, markets for wood and wood products, and international trade.

Opportunities for experience and exploration

While in college, students may be able to find volunteer or paying jobs on campus, helping their professors in their wood science experiments and research. These jobs can offer valuable experience and give students a feel for the requirements of the field. Students may also become better acquainted with faculty members, whose advice and connections may be a great help in finding a good job after graduation. Interested individuals in areas with timber production and forestry programs will be at a distinct advantage over others.

Related occupations

The work of persons in wood science necessitates an interest in science, natural resources, and technology. People with these interests might also find enjoyment in working as biological scientists, farmers, agronomists, sawmill workers, range managers, foresters, or chemists.

Methods of entering

College students can often learn about employment opportunities in wood science through their colleges' career placement offices. Many forestry firms recruit new employees straight from campus. Another source of information is professional groups such as those mentioned above. The Society of Wood Science and Technology maintains a job referral service, and trade magazines, such as the Forest Products Research Society's Forest Products Journal, often carry want ads for job openings. Information on jobs with the federal government can be gotten from the Office of Personnel Management in Washington.

Advancement

Moving ahead in the wood science field depends on ingenuity, skills, and the ability to handle important projects. Advancement can come in the form of promotions, pay raises, more important assignments, and the permission to conduct independent research. People with management skills may rise to become division chiefs, directors, administrators, or heads of research operations. Advanced degrees are usually required for these last two positions.

The size of the company can often limit the opportunities for advancement, because larger companies obviously offer more places to go within the organization. Ambitious people may find that education can help them climb the ladder. Wood products technicians may find that earning a bachelor's degree can help them move up to the position of wood technologist.

Employment outlook

Wood technology is a relatively new science, with new breakthroughs in products and technology occurring very frequently. Still, it is a field in which the supply of qualified wood scientists and technologists is far short of the demand. About 2,500 wood scientists and technologists are employed across the country. The employment outlook for these specialists is expected to be very good.

The demand for wood products is projected to double by the year 2000. At the same time, the costs of growing and harvesting timber and processing wood products are rising rapidly. Wood manufacturers need the skills of wood science specialists to keep their operations profitable and efficient and to help them compete with plastics manufacturers and the makers of other wood substitutes. Even as wood becomes more popular as a fuel, concerns about the earth's atmosphere may prompt a backlash against wood burning. With pressures to preserve timberlands and increase the use of a renewable resource, the work of wood scientists and technologists will continue to be important in the future.

Conservation programs will affect wood technologists positively and negatively. Pressure to reduce lumber harvests will continue to increase, particularly in threatened areas such as the rain forest.

Those pressures, however will force increased study of reforestation projects. It should also emphasize better utilization of wood currently being harvested and used. Producing faster maturing trees may be one method of assistance.

Earnings

Salary levels in the wood sciences depend on a person's employer, experience, level of education, and work performed. Starting salaries for wood scientists and technologists with bachelor's degrees ranged from $16,500 to $22,000 in 1985, while starting salaries for those with doctoral degrees could be between $27,500 and $33,000 a year. Wood science specialists who move up into administrative positions with large companies may earn $55,000 to $75,000 a year, or more.

Wages for wood products technicians are usually comparable to those for other types of technicians. The starting pay for those with a two-year college degree might be anywhere from $13,200 to $17,600, while technicians with experience can earn $22,000 or more per year. Usually wood scientists, wood technologists, and wood products technicians all receive fringe benefits, including health insurance, pension plans, and paid vacations.

Government pay for wood scientists and technologists ranges from $17,824 a year for newly hired persons (GS-7) to $52,262 a year for experienced workers (GS-15). Starting salaries for forest product technicians in grades GS-2 to GS-9 ranged from $10,501 to $21,804 a year.

Conditions

Depending on the type of work they perform, wood science specialists operate in a variety of settings, everywhere from the office to the open forest. Wood scientists and researchers work in laboratories and, if they are on university faculty, in classrooms. Their experimental work may take them to tree farms and forests. Wood technologists and technicians may work in offices, manufacturing plants, sawmills, or research facilities. Those technologists who are involved in sales often need to travel.

These types of employees work a normal forty-hour week, but extra hours may be required in certain situations. Technologists who supervise technicians and other production workers may have to work second and third shifts. Administrators may also have to put in extra hours. Workers paid by the hour often get overtime pay, but salaried employees do not get extra monetary compensation for their extra hours.

Social and psychological factors

Wood science and technology specialists have a difficult but rewarding job: applying scientific principles such as chemistry, physics, and mathematics to a commonplace raw material, and finding new ways for society to use wood in more productive, efficient ways. Applying new ideas and techniques to old problems requires intelligence, curiosity, flexibility, analytical thinking, and imagination.

At the same time, the jobs in wood science require the ability to work and communicate with various groups of people, from co-workers to clients and research foundations. Good communication techniques and the ability to work well with others is important. Particularly for people working in areas where tensions may build between wood harvestors and conservationists opposed to such activity, diplomacy and patience may be required.

Many people in wood science gain satisfaction from the idea that their work improves the quality of life in this country. As concerns for the environment grow, products made from synthetic, man-made materials such as plastics are becoming less popular. Wood is one of the few renewable resources. The better we are able to use it, the more beneficial will be our stewardship of the earth.

GOE: 02.02.02; SIC: 24; SOC: 1852

◇ **SOURCES OF ADDITIONAL INFORMATION**

Forest Products Research Society
2801 Marshall Court
Madison, WI 53705

Hardwood Research Council
PO Box 34518
Memphis, TN 38184

Society of American Foresters
5400 Grosvenor Lane
Bethesda, MD 20814

Society of Wood Science and Technology
PO Box 5062
Madison, WI 53705

U.S. Department of Agriculture
Extension Service
Natural Resources and Rural Development
Washington, DC 20250

◇ **RELATED ARTICLES**

Volume 1: Agriculture; Biological Sciences; Chemistry; Furniture; Machining and Machinery; Pulp and Paper; Wood
Volume 2: Biochemists; Biologists; Chemists
Volume 3: Manufacturers' sales workers; Agricultural scientists; Foresters; Paper processing operations; Sawmill workers; Furniture manufacturing occupations; Operating engineers
Volume 4: Forestry technicians

Writers and editors

Definitions

Writers and *editors* are involved with expressing, editing, promoting, and interpreting ideas and facts in written form for books, magazines, trade journals, newspapers, technical studies and reports, company newsletters, radio and television broadcasts, and advertisements.

Writers develop fiction and nonfiction ideas for plays, novels, poems, and other related works; report, analyze, and interpret facts, events, and personalities; review art, music, drama, and other artistic presentations; and persuade the general public to choose or favor certain goods, services, and personalities.

Editors assign, select, and prepare written materials for publication, broadcast, or motion picture production. They arrange, rewrite, verify, compile, and abstract material to conform to standards of consistency, organization, development, or specified viewpoint. They also coordinate the work of authors, designers, production personnel, and printers.

History

Fragments of papyrus left by ancient Egyptians and reports of public readings made by early Greeks mark the first known use of written languages, dating from about 3000 B.C.

A number of technical obstacles had to be overcome before printing and the professions of writer and editor evolved. Books of the Middle Ages were copied by hand on parchment. The ornate style that marked these books helped ensure their rarity. Also, few people were able to read. Religious fervor prohibited, as in the case of art, the reproduction of secular literature.

The development of the printing press by Johannes Gutenberg in the middle of the fifteenth century, the liberalism of the Protestant Reformation, which helped encourage a wider range of publications, greater literacy, and the creation of a number of works of literary merit helped develop a publishing industry. The first authors worked directly with printers. As errors of logic, grammar, or type appeared, the necessity for editors became apparent.

The eighteenth century marks the birth of the modern publishing age. Printing became mechanized, and the novel, magazine, and newspaper began their rise. The first newspaper in the American colonies appeared in the early eighteenth century, but it was Benjamin Franklin who, as editor, made the *Pennsylvania Gazette* one of the most influential in setting a high standard for his fellow American journalists. Likewise, it was Franklin who published the first magazine in the colonies, *The American Magazine,* in 1741.

Advances in the printing trades, photoengraving, retailing, and the availability of capital produced a boom in newspapers and magazines in the nineteenth century. Further mechanization in the printing field, such as the use of the linotype machine, high-speed rotary presses, and special color reproduction processes, set the stage for still further growth in the book, newspaper, and magazine industry.

In addition to the print media, the broadcasting industry has contributed to the occupations of writer and editor. Since the introduction of radio by Marconi in 1895 and the development of television beginning in 1923, the field of broadcasting has grown to have an enormous influence over our lives. It is a source of entertainment, information, and education that provides employment for thousands of people, including writers and editors.

Nature of the work

Writers and editors work in the field of communications. Specifically, they deal with the written word, whether it is destined for the printed page or for broadcast. The nature of their work is as varied as the materials they produce: books, magazines, trade journals, newspapers, technical reports, company newsletters and other publications, advertisements, scripts for motion picture and stage productions, and scripts for radio and television broadcast. To define the occupations broadly, writers develop and write fiction and nonfiction prose for the various media; editors assign work to writers and select and prepare materials for publication or broadcast. A detailed description of the duties of each occupation follows.

Prose writers may select a topic of personal interest or may be assigned one by an editor to suit the needs of a particular publication or broadcast. In either case, they begin by gathering as much information as possible about the subject, through library research, interviews,

Editors must have excellent grammatical and organizational skills in order to prepare a manuscript for publishing.

and personal experience and observation. They keep extensive notes from which they draw material for the story or article. Once the material has been organized and arranged in logical sequence, the writers prepare a written outline. The process of developing a piece of writing is a dynamic one. A writer may start out with a certain purpose or goal in mind only to discover, while researching and outlining the material, that a different perspective or a related topic would be more effective, entertaining, or interesting. Fiction writers have the additional factors of plot, characterization, and story line to develop.

When working on assignment, writers submit their outlines to an editor or other company representative for approval. Then they write a first draft of the manuscript, trying to put the material into words that will have the desired effect on their audience. They often rewrite or polish sections of the material as they go along, always searching for just the right way of imparting information or expressing an idea or opinion. A manuscript may be reviewed, corrected, and revised numerous times before a final copy is submitted. Even after that, an editor may request additional changes.

Writers often specialize in a particular type of writing: novels, biographies, short stories, essays, magazine articles, or *humor*. Those who specialize in descriptive or critical interpretations or analyses for publication or broadcast include *columnist/commentators*, who ana-

lyze news and write columns or commentary about it from the standpoint of their own experience or knowledge; *critics*, who review literary, musical, or artistic works and performances; *editorial writers*, who write on topics of public interest and whose comments, consistent with the viewpoints and policies of their employers, are intended to stimulate or mold public opinion. *Newswriters* work for newspapers or radio and TV news departments, writing news stories from notes supplied by reporters or wire services.

Still other kinds of writers include the following:

Screenwriters prepare scripts for motion pictures or television. They select or are assigned a subject, conduct research, write and submit a plot outline and narrative synopsis (treatment), and confer with the producer and/or director about possible revisions. Screenwriters may adapt books or plays for film and television dramatization. They often collaborate with other screenwriters and may specialize in a particular type of script or writing. *Continuity writers* prepare the material read by radio and TV announcers to introduce or connect various parts of their programs.

Playwrights do similar writing for the stage. They write dialogue and describe action for plays that may be tragedies, comedies, or dramas, with themes sometimes adapted from fictional, historical, or narrative sources. Playwrights combine the elements of action, conflict, purpose, and resolution to depict events from real or imaginary life. They often make revisions even while the play is in rehearsal.

Copywriters write copy designed to sell goods and services. Their work appears as advertisements in newspapers, magazines, and other publications or as commercials on radio and television broadcasts. Sales and marketing representatives provide information on the product and help determine the style and length of the copy. The copywriters conduct additional research and interviews; to formulate an effective approach, they study advertising trends and review surveys of consumer preferences. Armed with this information they write a draft that is submitted to the account executive and the client for approval. The copy is often returned for correction and revision until everyone involved is satisfied. Copywriters may also write articles, bulletins, news releases, sales letters, speeches, and other related informative and promotional material. Many copywriters are employed in advertising agencies, but they may also work for public relations firms or in communications departments of large companies.

Poets make up a small group of writers who create narrative, dramatic, or lyric poetry for books, magazines, and other publications. Some poets write doggerel or other types of verse.

The occupations of technical writers and reporters and correspondents are specialized enough to be discussed separately in other sections of this encyclopedia.

Editors also do some original writing, but most often they do rewriting. Their basic role, however, is to plan the contents of a publication and to supervise its preparation. This role varies with the field of publication, type of written material, and resources available within the organization.

Editors who work for book publishing companies combine literary talents with the financial know-how of the entrepreneur. Each book represents a new financial investment. The editors must study book manuscripts to make sure they are suitable both financially and from the standpoint of their contribution to the professional reputation of the publisher.

Book editors spend much of the time evaluating manuscripts for publication. While the company may receive as many as a hundred manuscripts a week, they will publish only one or two percent of them. Editors review most of the potential books themselves, while others of a specialized nature may be sent outside for evaluation by experts in the fields. Some manuscripts are submitted by literary agents, who represent established authors. Or, sensing a market for a book, the editor may seek out a potential author, particularly in the textbook field.

Before a contract to publish a book is signed, the editors are usually asked to describe the book before an editorial committee composed of colleagues within the organization. This committee evaluates the literary and financial merits of the book and must approve its publication. If the committee approves, the editors then proceed to negotiate a contract granting the author a royalty (a percentage of the cover price) on each copy sold in exchange for specified publishing rights. Editors must also arrange for copyright to ensure that both the publisher's and the author's rights are protected.

After the contract is signed, the editors confer with the author regarding the completion or revision of the book. When the manuscript is completed, the editors review it for final revisions, often polishing and rewriting portions of the copy themselves. Then they or their assistants edit the manuscript for spelling, punctuation, grammar, consistency, and style. Editors may confer with the production department to choose the best typeface and printing style; interface with the art department to plan an appropriate dust jacket or cover; and coordinate the activities of the advertising, promotion, and sales departments to make sure the book receives the public reviews necessary to maximize its exposure and its sales.

Editors often specialize in technical books, art books, or children's books, or in a particular type of fiction or nonfiction, such as mysteries or business books. Two editorial positions that require unusual expertise are those of *dictionary editor* and *index editor*.

Newspaper editors lead much different lives. Whereas a book may take six to thirty-six months to prepare for publication, a newspaper is assembled for publication on a daily or weekly basis. To do this effectively, newspaper editors must know local, national, and international issues and with this background evaluate the merits of individual stories. Actual newspaper content comes from several sources: Reporters and correspondents are assigned to cover "regular beats," such as city hall, police headquarters, and other local places where news is likely to occur. *Bureau chiefs* gather news in foreign countries and other remote locations and transmit it to the home office. Syndicated columns of national interest are sold to newspapers throughout the country for simultaneous publication. Extensive materials are made available by the various wire services, such as the Associated Press. *Wire editors* select and edit news items received by wire from these press associations. In the case of a chain of newspapers, materials may be especially developed for use in the entire group of newspapers.

On newspapers, the *editors-in-chief* or the *managing editors* are the direct representatives of the owner and the overall executives of the editorial department. These editors are responsible for the paper's editorial and reportorial policies and procedures. They appoint an editorial board and write leading or policy editorials, and they directly supervise editors in charge of various departments or functions.

City editors broadly interpret the policy set down by the managing editors in the direction of the collecting and handling of local news. They are assisted by reporters, photographers, rewriters, and special writers.

The *news editors*, working closely with the advertising department to learn what space (after ads are sold) is available for news and features, plan the actual layout, or makeup, of the paper. The number of pages in the paper will vary depending upon the volume of news and the income from advertising.

Newspaper reporters work on tight deadlines, often completing their articles minutes before they are due.

Department editors on newspapers are those who cover specific fields. In addition to being skilled writers, they are authorities on specialized subjects, including sports, fashion, food, finance, science, business, society, drama, music, films, radio, television, politics, art, books, travel, and education.

On small weekly newspapers, one person or one family may perform virtually all duties. This may include selling advertisements, collecting news, planning layouts, setting headlines, and arranging for distribution of the paper. In this case, the editor is often the owner of the paper.

Magazines tend to be more specialized and may be classified according to their specialized readership. They include news magazines, juveniles, fashion and health magazines, fiction magazines (divided in turn into mystery, detective, true story, and so on), women's or men's magazines, technical journals, and house and garden magazines.

General-circulation magazines face extreme competition for newsstand sales, regular subscriptions, and advertising and thus are produced to encourage maximum readership. A general-circulation magazine will attempt to balance its stories to include articles on business, fashion, recreation, travel, Hollywood, international affairs, homemaking, education, art, and humor.

Although there are obvious dissimilarities between newspapers and magazines, the nature of the magazine editors' work is quite similar to that of the newspaper editor, although not quite as hectic. Magazine editors determine what will appeal to their readers, assign topics to writers, and supervise the production of the publication. They work with a great variety of people, such as authors, free-lance writers, reporters, printers, artists, photographers, layout specialists, and advertising people. Their administrative duties may include hiring and firing personnel and free-lance contributors, negotiating contracts for editorial material, and planning budgets.

Key assistants to the *editorial director* or the managing editor of a magazine are the *fiction editor* who develops short stories and serials, and the *articles editor* who plans the nonfiction content. These editors, together with a staff of assistants, critically review submitted manuscripts in their area, as well as commission interesting material from known authors. *Editors of technical and scientific publications* are specialists with some depth of knowledge in the fields they work with.

In broadcasting, program directors have responsibilities similar to those of an editorial director or managing editor. They plan the overall content of a program and supervise the specialized editors, such as *story editors*, who select written material or assign topics to writers for dramatic scripts; *assignment editors*, who supervise and coordinate the activities of the news-gathering staff; and *continuity editors*, who assign duties to and supervise the writers of continuity material (read by announcers to introduce or connect various parts of a program) and edit the material in accordance with company policy, broadcasting regulations, and laws.

An editor who does not fit into any of the usual categories is the *greeting card editor*, who selects and edits the messages printed on greeting cards.

Editors, whether employed by book or magazine publishers or by broadcasting companies, are usually helped by *editorial assistants*. These assistants generally hold entry-level jobs, but with a little experience may be designated assistant editors, associate editors, copy editors, or production assistants. Their duties are many and may include evaluating and reporting on manuscript submissions; correcting copy for spelling, grammar, syntax, punctuation, and consistency; rewriting copy for clarity or conformity to style; verifying facts and performing research; proofreading printers' galleys and page proofs; selecting photographs; preparing layouts of pages; writing or rewriting headlines, captions, and other copy; and answering letters about published or broadcast material. Production assistants clip stories that come over wire-service printers, answer phones, and make copies of material for newswriters, editors, and program directors.

Large publishing houses, magazines, and newspapers usually hire full-time *proofreaders* rather than depend on entry-level editorial assistants to handle proofreading duties. Also, major retail outlets or their advertising agencies may have a *production proofreader* on staff to compare proofs of store ads with the original copy.

Requirements

Competition for writing and editorial jobs almost always demands the background of a college education. Many employers prefer graduates with a broad liberal arts background or majors in English, literature, history, philosophy, or one of the social sciences. Other employers desire communications or journalism training in college. Occasionally a master's degree in a specialized writing field may be required. A number of schools offer courses in journalism, and some of them offer courses or majors in book publishing, publication management, newspaper editing, and magazine editing.

High-school courses that are helpful include English, literature, foreign languages, general science, social studies, and typing. The ability to type is almost a requisite for all positions in the communications field. Some editors also recommend studying shorthand.

In addition to formal coursework, most employers look for practical writing experience. Persons who have served on high-school or college newspapers, yearbooks, or literary magazines make better candidates, as do those who have worked for small community newspapers or radio stations, even if in unpaid positions. Many book publishers, magazines, newspapers, and radio and television stations have summer internship programs that provide valuable training for students who want to learn about the publishing and broadcasting business. Interns do many simple tasks such as running errands and answering phones, but some employers also allow them to perform research, conduct interviews, or even write some minor pieces.

Writers and editors should be creative and able to express ideas clearly, have a broad general knowledge, and be skilled in research techniques. Other assets include curiosity, persistence, initiative, resourcefulness, an accurate memory, and physical stamina for an active, fast-paced life. For some jobs, on a newspaper, for example, where the activity is hectic and deadlines short, the ability to concentrate and produce under pressure is essential. Editors must be able to exercise good judgment in evaluating and selecting material for publication and must use tact in dealing with writers and others who need their guidance and encouragement in completing assignments on deadline.

Special requirements

There are no special requirements for employment as writers and editors, except as established by individual employers. However, writers and editors who specialize in technical fields may need degrees, concentrated coursework, or experience in specific subject areas. This applies frequently to engineering, business, or one of the sciences.

Opportunities for experience and exploration

High-school and college students may test their interest and aptitude by serving as reporters, writers, and editors of school newspapers, yearbooks, and literary magazines. Various writing courses and workshops offer the opportunity to sharpen writing skills.

Small community newspapers and local radio stations often welcome contributions from outside sources, although they may not have the resources to pay for them. Jobs in bookstores, magazine shops, and even newsstands offer a chance to become familiar with the various publications.

Information on writing or editing as a career may also be obtained by visiting local newspapers, publishers, or radio and TV stations and interviewing some of the writers and editors who work there. Career conferences and other guidance programs frequently include speakers on the entire field of communications from local or national organizations.

Related occupations

The ability to communicate ideas and information is essential to all occupations in the communications field. Workers in these occupations include advertising and public relations workers, newspaper reporters and correspondents, radio and television announcers, and teachers of journalism and English. Not all writing jobs are in the communications field per se. Large corporations and other establishments, institutions, and organizations often hire writers for their corporate communications, internal communications, or publications departments.

Methods of entering

To acquire a fully responsible position in this field requires much experience. Most writers and editors start out in entry-level positions, such as editorial assistants or production assistants. These jobs may be listed with college placement offices, or they may be obtained by applying directly to the employment departments of the individual publishers or broadcasting companies. Graduates who previously served internships with these companies often have the advantage of knowing someone there who can give them a personal recommendation. Want ads in newspapers and trade journals are another source for jobs. Because of the competition for positions, however, few vacancies are listed with public or private employment agencies.

Employers in the communications field usually are interested in samples of published writing. These are often assembled in an organized portfolio or scrapbook. Bylined or signed articles are more impressive than stories whose source is not identified.

Advancement

Prior to reaching their present position, most writers and editors served as editorial or production assistants. Advancement may be more rapid in small companies, where beginners learn by doing a little bit of everything and may be given writing and editing tasks immediately. In large firms, duties are usually more compartmentalized. Assistants in entry-level positions are assigned such tasks as research, fact checking, and copy editing, but it generally takes much longer to advance to full-scale writing and editing duties.

Promotion into more responsible positions may come with the assignment of more important articles and stories to write or edit, or it may be the result of moving to another company. Mobility among employees in this field is common. An assistant editor in one publishing house may switch to an executive editor's position in another. A senior editor with one publisher may become a vice president in charge of a new or revamped department at another firm. Or a writer or editor may switch to a related

field as a type of advancement: from publishing, for example, to teaching, public relations, advertising, radio, or television.

Free-lance, or self-employed, writers earn advancement in the form of larger fees as they gain exposure and establish a following, but very few ever achieve best-seller status.

Employment outlook

Total employment of writers and editors in the early 1990s was an estimated 214,000. Of that number, nearly 40 percent worked for newspapers, magazines, and book publishers. Business and nonprofit organizations, such as professional associations, labor unions, and religious organizations, employed a large number to work on journals, newsletters, and other publications. Other writers and editors were employed in various ways: producing advertising and public relations materials for advertising and public relations agencies and large corporations; writing and editing broadcast materials for radio and television broadcasting companies; and developing publications for federal, state, and local governments. A few earned their living as independent, or self-employed, writers and editors, but most free-lancers depended on income from other sources as their primary support.

Compared with all occupations, the employment of writers and editors is expected to increase at a faster than average rate through the end of the 1990s. Newspapers, periodicals, book publishers, and nonprofit organizations, such as research agencies and religious, business, professional, and civic associations, will hire more salaried writers and editors to meet the growing demand for their publications. In addition, the expansion of the advertising and public relations fields will create new jobs.

The outlook for writers and editors in radio and television broadcasting is even brighter. Employment there is expected to rise faster than the average, as a result of the rapidly growing number of FM radio and educational TV stations, as well as the increased use of cable TV and television sets that receive news directly from servicing companies.

The major book and magazine publishers, broadcasting companies, advertising agencies, and public relations firms, and the federal government account for the concentration of writers and editors in large cities such as New York, Chicago, Los Angeles, Boston, Philadelphia, San Francisco, and Washington, D.C. Opportunities for writers and editors, however, exist throughout the country in the many newspapers, corporations, and professional, religious, business, technical, and trade union magazines or journals.

Persons entering this field should realize that the competition for jobs is extremely keen. Beginners, especially, may have difficulty finding employment. Of the thousands who graduate each year with degrees in English, journalism, communications, and the liberal arts, intending to establish a career as writer or editor, many turn to other occupations when they find that applicants far outnumber the job openings available. College students would do well to keep this in mind and prepare for an unrelated alternate career in the event they are unable to obtain a position as writer or editor; another benefit of this approach is that, at the same time, they will become qualified as writers in a specialized field. The practicality of preparing for alternate careers is borne out by the fact that opportunities are best in firms that prepare business and trade publications and in technical writing.

Potential writers who end up working in a different field may be able to earn some income as free-lancers, selling articles, stories, books, and possibly TV and movie scripts; but it is usually difficult for anyone to support him- or herself entirely from independent writing.

Earnings

In the early 1990s, beginning writers and editorial assistants received starting salaries ranging from $18,400 to $29,300 a year. Experienced writers and researchers were paid between $20,500 and $36,500, depending on their qualifications and the size of the publication they worked on. Annual salaries for experienced editors generally were between $20,900 and $39,000; and for supervisory editors, between $28,600 and $42,600. In book publishing, some divisions pay better than others. Normally fiction divisions pay the lowest wages.

On daily papers in towns with a population of less than 20,000, copy editors started at about $9,700 in the early 1990s; in cities of 500,000 or more, they earned an average of $13,000. Senior editors on newspapers and magazines with large circulations, however, were able to command in excess of $60,000 a year.

Writers and editors working for the federal government averaged $28,000 a year.

In addition to their salaries, many writers and editors earned some income from free-lance work.

Conditions of work

Working conditions vary for writers and editors, but their jobs are generally characterized by their pressures. Although the workweek usually runs thirty-five to forty hours, many work overtime. A publication that is issued frequently has more deadlines closer together, creating greater pressures to meet them. The work is especially hectic on newspapers and at broadcasting companies, which operate seven days a week. Writers and editors often work nights and weekends to meet deadlines or to cover a late-developing story. Deadlines for book editors are longer, but these editors must bear the responsibility created by their company's investment in each publication, which may range from several thousand dollars to develop a general book to the more than $750,000 needed to develop a new dictionary with scholarly standing.

Most writers and editors work independently, but they often must cooperate with artists, photographers, rewriters, and advertising people who may have widely differing ideas of how the materials should be prepared and presented.

Physical surroundings range from comfortable private offices to noisy, crowded newsrooms filled with other workers typing and talking on the telephone. Some writers and editors must confine their research to the library or telephone interviews, but others may travel to other cities or countries or to local sites, such as the theater, the ballpark, the airport, factories, or other offices.

Social and psychological factors

The work is arduous, but writers and editors are seldom bored. Each day brings new and interesting problems. There is often contact with famous or notorious figures. The jobs occasionally require travel. The most difficult element is the continual pressure of deadlines. People who are the most content as editors and writers enjoy and work well with deadline pressure.

Writers and editors can sense their key role in a society that depends very heavily on mass communications. They help inform, entertain, persuade, and inspire the public. Their occupations may command a great deal of respect.

GOE: 01.01.02; SIC: 27; SOC: 3312

◇ **SOURCES OF ADDITIONAL INFORMATION**

Information on writing and editing careers in the field of communications is available from:

Women in Communications
PO Box 17460
Arlington, VA 22216

A journalism career and scholarship guide may be obtained from:

The Dow Jones Newspaper Fund
PO Box 300
Princeton, NJ 08540

For information on college internships in magazine or newspaper editing, write to:

American Society of Magazine Editors
575 Lexington Avenue
New York, NY 10022

American Society of Newspaper Editors
PO Box 17004
Washington, DC 20041

Information on careers in business communications may be obtained by contacting:

Association for Business Communications
100 English Building
608 South Wright Street
Urbana, IL 61801

◇ **RELATED ARTICLES**

Volume 1: Advertising; Book Publishing; Broadcasting; Magazine Publishing; Motion Pictures; Newspaper Publishing
Volume 2: Advertising workers; Public relations specialists; Radio and television announcers and newscasters; Reporters and correspondents; Technical writers

Photographic Credits

Index

718

729